UNDERSTANDING

HUMAN SEXUALITY

UNDERSTANDING
HUMAN
SEXUALITY

Fourteenth Edition

Janet Shibley Hyde
University of Wisconsin—Madison

John D. DeLamater
University of Wisconsin—Madison

McGraw
Hill

UNDERSTANDING HUMAN SEXUALITY, FOURTEENTH EDITION

2 3 4 5 6 7 8 9 LWI 21 20

ISBN 978-1-260-50023-3 (bound edition)
MHID 1-260-50023-3 (bound edition)
ISBN 978-1-260-04176-7 (loose-leaf edition)
MHID 1-260-04176-X (loose-leaf edition)
ISBN 978-1-260-39463-4 (instructor edition)
MHID 1-260-39463-8 (instructor edition)

Senior Portfolio Manager: *Nancy Welcher*
Product Development Manager: *Dawn Groundwater*
Executive Marketing Manager: *AJ Laferrera*
Marketing Manager: *Olivia Kaiser*
Content Project Managers: *Ryan Warczynski, Katie Reuter, Sandra Schnee*
Senior Buyer: *Laura Fuller*
Design: *Egzon Shaqiri*
Content Licensing Specialists: *Jacob Sullivan*
Cover Image: *©Science Photo Library/Getty Images*
Compositor: *Cenveo® Publisher Services*

Library of Congress Cataloging-in-Publication Data

Names: Hyde, Janet Shibley, author. | DeLamater, John D., author.
Title: Understanding human sexuality / Janet Shibley Hyde, University of
    Wisconsin, Madison, John D. DeLamater, University of Wisconsin, Madison.
Description: Fourteenth Edition. | Dubuque : McGraw-Hill Education, [2019] |
    Revised edition of the authors' Understanding human sexuality, [2017]
Identifiers: LCCN 2019001234 | ISBN 9781260500233 (alk. paper)
Subjects: LCSH: Sex. | Sex customs. | Sexual health. | Sex (Psychology)
Classification: LCC HQ12 .H82 2019 | DDC 306.7–dc23
LC record available at https://lccn.loc.gov/2019001234

mheducation.com/highered

In Memoriam

John D. DeLamater (1940–2017)

In 2017 I lost my coauthor and husband, John DeLamater, to a fatal heart attack. A professor of sociology at the University of Wisconsin–Madison, John dedicated his career to the field of sexuality. He taught an undergraduate human sexuality course every year beginning in 1975. John worked hard at that course, always seeking new ideas and training dozens of graduate students as teaching assistants. Especially worthy of note is John's outstanding service to the field as editor of the *Journal of Sex Research* for two terms totaling 10 years. He was deeply committed to the journal and mentored many authors in ways to improve their papers.

John's contributions to sexuality research began with an early study in the 1970s of patterns of what was then called premarital sex among college students, resulting in a book coauthored with Patricia MacCorquodale. Over the last decade, John devoted himself to developing a life cycle approach to sexuality, resulting in multiple journal articles and a coedited book, *Sex for Life: From Virginity to Viagra.*

John earned his PhD at the University of Michigan in 1969 in social psychology at a time when Michigan had a remarkable joint PhD program between sociology and psychology. John continued to be committed to social psychology throughout his career, teaching the undergraduate course annually. He was the author of the textbook *Social Psychology,* framed for an audience of sociologists.

His contributions to the field of sex research are undeniable and were recognized by awards such as the Kinsey Award from the Society for the Scientific Study of Sexuality. He will be sorely missed.

Author Biographies

Janet Shibley Hyde, the Helen Thompson Woolley Professor of Psychology and Gender & Women's Studies at the University of Wisconsin–Madison, received her education at Oberlin College and the University of California, Berkeley. She has taught a course in human sexuality since 1974, first at Bowling Green State University, then at Denison University, and now at the University of Wisconsin. Her research interests are in gender differences and gender development in adolescence. Author of the textbook *The Psychology of Women and Gender: Half the Human Experience +,* she is a past president of the Society for the Scientific Study of Sexuality and is a Fellow of the American Psychological Association and the American Association for the Advancement of Science. She has received many other honors, including an award for excellence in teaching at Bowling Green State University, the Chancellor's Award for teaching at the University of Wisconsin, and the Kinsey Award from the Society for the Scientific Study of Sexuality for her contributions to sex research. In 2000–01 she served as one of the three scientific editors for U.S. Surgeon General David Satcher's report *Promoting Sexual Health and Responsible Sexual Behavior.* In 2019, Dr. Hyde was the inaugural recipient of the Alfred C. Kinsey Award from the Kinsey Institute at Indiana University.

John D. DeLamater passed away in December 2017. He was the Conway-Bascom Professor of Sociology at the University of Wisconsin–Madison, having received his education at the University of California, Santa Barbara, and the University of Michigan. He created the human sexuality course at the University of Wisconsin in 1975 and taught it regularly. He published papers on the influence of marital duration, attitudes about sex for elders, and illness and medications on sexual expression. He coedited the *Handbook of the Sociology of Sexualities.* He was the coauthor of the textbook *Social Psychology.* He was a Fellow of the Society for the Scientific Study of Sexuality and the 2002 recipient of the Kinsey Award from the Society for the Scientific Study of Sexuality. He received awards for excellence in teaching from the Department of Sociology and the University of Wisconsin and was a Fellow and past Chair of the Teaching Academy at the University of Wisconsin. He regularly taught a seminar for graduate students on teaching undergraduate courses.

Contents in Brief

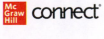

McGraw-Hill Education Psychology APA Documentation Style Guide

Contents

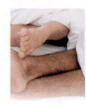

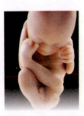

Preface

Hyde and DeLamater—Continuing a research-based tradition in sexuality

Since its conception, *Understanding Human Sexuality* has achieved distinction and success by following the science of human sexuality. The first of the modern sexuality textbooks, *Understanding Human Sexuality* introduced this topic to students through the science that has uncovered what we know about the field. Groundbreaking when it first appeared, this research-based tradition continues to result in a contemporary, balanced introduction to human sexuality in an integrated system that engages students in learning the content of the course, about others, and about themselves.

A Personalized Experience that Leads to Improved Learning

SMARTBOOK™ How many students think they know everything about human sexuality but struggle on the first exam? Students study more effectively with Connect and SmartBook.

SmartBook helps students study more efficiently by highlighting what to focus on in the chapter, asking review questions, and directing them to resources until they understand. Connect's assignments help students contextualize what they've learned through application, so they can better understand the material and think critically.

New to this edition, SmartBook is now optimized for mobile and tablet and is accessible for students with disabilities. Content-wise, it has been enhanced with improved learning objectives that are measurable and observable to improve student outcomes. SmartBook personalizes learning to individual student needs, continually adapting to pinpoint knowledge gaps and focus learning on topics that need the most attention. Study time is more productive and, as a result, students are better prepared for class and coursework.

For instructors, SmartBook tracks student progress and provides insights that can help guide teaching strategies.

Better Data, Smarter Revision, Improved Results

For this edition, data were analyzed to identify the concepts students found the most difficult, allowing for expansion upon the discussion, practice, and assessment of challenging topics. The revision process for a new edition used to begin with gathering information from instructors about what they would change and what they would keep. Experts in the field were asked to provide comments that pointed out new material to add and dated material to review. Using all these reviews, authors would revise the material. But now, a tool has revolutionized that model.

McGraw-Hill Education authors have access to student performance data to analyze and to inform their revisions. This data is anonymously collected from the many students who use SmartBook, the adaptive learning system that provides students with individualized assessment of their own progress. Because virtually every text paragraph is tied to several questions that students answer while using the SmartBook, the specific concepts with which students are having the most difficulty are easily pinpointed through empirical data in the form of a "heat map" report.

STEP 1. Over the course of three years, data points showing concepts that caused students the most difficulty were anonymously collected from SmartBook for *Understanding Human Sexuality.*

STEP 2. The data was provided to the author in the form of a *Heat Map,* which graphically illustrated "hot spots" in the text that impacted student learning.

STEP 3. The author used the *Heat Map* data to refine the content and reinforce student comprehension in the new edition. Additional quiz questions and assignable activities were created for use in Connect for Human Sexuality to further support student success.

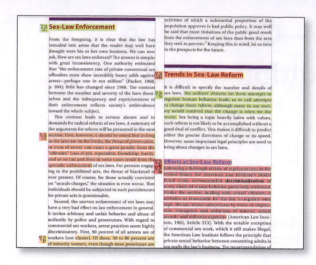

Powerful Reporting

Whether a class is face-to-face, hybrid, or entirely online, McGraw-Hill Connect provides the tools needed to reduce the amount of time and energy instructors spend administering their courses. Easy-to-use course management tools allow instructors to spend less time administering and more time teaching, while reports allow students to monitor their progress and optimize their study time.

- The **At-Risk Student Report** provides instructors with one-click access to a dashboard that identifies students who are at risk of dropping out of the course due to low engagement levels.

- The **Category Analysis Report** details student performance relative to specific learning objectives and goals, including APA learning goals and outcomes and levels of Bloom's taxonomy.

- **Connect Insight** is a one-of-a-kind visual analytics dashboard—now available for both instructors and students—that provides at-a-glance information regarding student performance.

- The **SmartBook Reports** allow instructors and students to easily monitor progress and pinpoint areas of weakness, giving each student a personalized study plan to achieve success.

Preparing Students for Higher-Level Thinking

New to the Fourteenth Edition, **Power of Process,** now available in McGraw-Hill Connect™, guides students through the process of critical reading, analysis, and writing. Faculty can select or upload their own content, such as journal articles, and assign analysis strategies to gain insight into students' application of the scientific method. For students, Power of Process offers a guided visual approach to exercising critical thinking strategies to apply before, during, and after reading published research. Additionally, utilizing the relevant and engaging research articles built into Power of Process, students are supported in becoming critical consumers of research.

Concept Clips help students comprehend some of the most difficult ideas in human sexuality. Colorful graphics and stimulating animations describe core concepts in a step-by-step manner, engaging students and aiding in retention. Concept Clips can be used as a presentation tool in the classroom or for student assessment.

New in the Fourteenth Edition, Concept Clips are embedded in the ebook to offer an alternative presentation of these challenging topics. New clips cover topics such as attraction, mate selection, and learning gender roles. Concept Clips help students comprehend some of the most difficult concepts in human sexuality.

Interactivities, assignable through Connect, engage students with content through experiential activities. Topics include first impressions and attraction.

Through the connection of human sexuality to students' own lives, concepts become more relevant and understandable. **Newsflash** exercises tie current news stories to key principles and learning objectives. After interacting with a contemporary news story, students are assessed on their ability to make the link between real life and research findings.

At the Apply and Analyze level of Bloom's Taxonomy, Scientific Reasoning Exercises offer in-depth arguments to sharpen students' critical thinking skills and prepare them to be more discerning consumers regarding information in their everyday lives. For each chapter, there are multiple sets of arguments related to topics in the Human Sexuality course, accompanied by autograded assignments that ask students to think critically about claims presented as facts. These exercises can also be used as group activities or for discussion.

Following the Science to Understand Human Sexuality

Understanding Human Sexuality is grounded in science and the research that informs science. This foundation, drawn from several perspectives, is reflected by the authors. Janet's background is in psychology and biology. John's was in sociology. We bring these different perspectives to this introduction to human sexuality. The importance we place on science and evidence-based reasoning comes from the desire to provide students with an understanding of human sexuality based on the best available research and also on what we see and do as researchers ourselves. Janet's research has explored psychological gender differences and similarities, focusing on gender and sexuality as well as topics such as sexuality in dual-earner couples. John's research investigated the influences of the person's history and current relationships on sexual expression, and the relative importance of illnesses and medications on sexuality in later life.

The quality of sex research is highly variable, to put it mildly. Some journalists think they are sex researchers if they have interviewed 10 people and written a book about it! Too often we see equal weight given to an article from the local newspaper and a refereed journal article from the *New England Journal of Medicine* or the *Journal of Sex Research*—and those few readers who are motivated enough have to do a lot of detective work to find the real source for a statement. It is the responsibility of authors to sift through available studies and present only those of the best quality and the greatest relevance to this course. It is a thrill to observe that the quality of sex research improves every decade.

Following the Science to Understand Oneself and Others

Studying human sexuality requires more than simply progressing through the material. To genuinely learn the concepts, students must look at their own sexual health, relationships, and consider how sex impacts their lives. For that reason, it is important that everyone who reads *Understanding Human Sexuality* feels connected to the content and finds it useful. The author has used a research-proven approach to ensure this book is diverse and practical. Here are some of the major themes found throughout:

- Chapters are as "trans-friendly" as possible, both in language used and content covered.
- The Supreme Court ruled and established nationwide same-sex marriage just as the last edition was

going to print, so it was covered only briefly. Now this ground-breaking decision and the social trends it reflects is integrated into multiple chapters.

- Inclusion of practical information such as finding sexual satisfaction, how cohabitation can impact relationships, and the benefits of mindfulness-based sex therapy.
- A multi-ethnic and multi-cultural perspective is presented throughout on topics such as same-gender relationships and contraception.
- Appreciation of the diversity of human sexuality along many dimensions including age, marital status, special needs, and gender preferences.

Understanding Human Sexuality aims to help students feel confident in what they are learning and show them how to apply it.

Additional Resources

 The **Instructor Resources** have been updated to reflect changes to the new edition; these can be accessed by faculty through Connect for Human Sexuality. Resources include the test bank, instructor's manual, PowerPoint presentation, and image gallery.

Easily rearrange chapters, combine material, and quickly upload content you have written, such as your course syllabus or teaching notes, using **McGraw-Hill Education Create.** Find the content you need by searching through thousands of leading

McGraw-Hill Education textbooks. Arrange your book to fit your teaching style. Create even allows you to personalize your book's appearance by selecting the cover and adding your name, school, and course information. Order a Create book, and you will receive a complimentary print review copy in three to five business days or a complimentary electronic review copy via e-mail in about an hour. Experience how McGraw-Hill Education empowers you to teach your students your way: http://create.mheducation.com

 Capture lessons and lectures in a searchable format for use in traditional, hybrid, "flipped classes" and online courses by using **Tegrity** (http://www.tegrity.com). Its personalized learning features make study time efficient, and its affordability brings this benefit to every student on campus. Patented search technology and real-time Learning Management System (LMS) integrations make Tegrity the market-leading solution and service.

 **McGraw-Hill Education Campus** ("http://www.mhcampus.com" www.mhcampus.com) provides faculty with true single sign-on access to all of McGraw-Hill Education's course content, digital tools, and other high-quality learning resources from any LMS. This innovative offering allows for secure and deep integration, enabling seamless access for faculty and students to any of McGraw-Hill Education's course solutions, such as McGraw-Hill Education Connect® (all-digital teaching and learning platform), McGraw-Hill Education Create (state-of-the-art custom-publishing platform), McGraw-Hill Education LearnSmart (online adaptive study tool), and Tegrity (fully searchable lecture-capture service).

McGraw-Hill Education Campus includes access to McGraw-Hill Education's entire content library, including ebooks, assessment tools, presentation slides, multimedia content, and other resources. McGraw-Hill Education Campus provides instructors with open, unlimited access to prepare for class, create tests/quizzes, develop lecture material, integrate interactive content, and more.

Annual Editions: Human Sexualities

This volume offers diverse topics on sex and sexuality with regard to the human experience. Learning Outcomes, Critical Thinking questions, and *Internet References* accompany each article to further enhance learning. Customize this title via **McGraw-Hill Create** at http://create.mheducation.com.

Taking Sides: Clashing Views in Human Sexuality

This debate-style reader both reinforces and challenges students' viewpoints on the most crucial issues in human sexuality today. Each topic offers current and lively pro and con essays that represent the arguments of leading scholars and commentators in their fields. *Learning Outcomes*, an *Issue Summary*, and an *Issue Introduction* set the stage for each debate topic. Following each issue is the *Exploring the Issue* section with *Critical Thinking and Reflection* questions, *Is There Common Ground?* commentary, *Additional Resources*, and *Internet References* all designed to stimulate and challenge the student's thinking and to further explore the topic. Customize this title via **McGraw-Hill Create** at http://create.mheducation.com.

Chapter Changes in the Fourteenth Edition

Human sexuality is one of the most exciting courses to take or teach. Part of the reason is that things are constantly changing across science, social attitudes, and even the law. Sex impacts all of our lives in countless ways and that's why watching the field progress is enlightening and encouraging. Each year there are advances in contraception and a better understanding about how outside variables, such as drugs, impact those options. We are still learning how the adolescent brain manages sex, especially while negotiating social networking. Each year, advances are made in the prevention and treatment of AIDS. There is even a deeper understanding of love and attraction.

A major goal of the previous edition was to make the book "trans friendly." This revision has taken an even bigger step towards ensuring a book that is comfortable for transgender individuals to read and study. It includes a strong section in the chapter "Gender and Sexuality" on the transgender experience, those who have a nonbinary identity, and those who seek gender reassignment.

Much has changed in the new edition of this textbook. A list of chapter-by-chapter changes follows:

Chapter 1. Sexuality in Perspective

- Section on media effects and media theories rewritten to reflect the latest thinking
- Concepts of individualistic, collectivistic, and honor cultures added

- New data challenging the universality of romantic-sexual kissing
- Updated Table 1 on social class variations in sexuality
- Updated Table 2 on ethnic group variations in sexuality
- The term *Latinx* added
- Biracial and multiracial added to discussion of ethnicity
- New data on LGBTs in China

Chapter 2. Theoretical Perspectives on Sexuality
- Gender-neutral evolutionary theory (Gowaty) added to section on evolutionary theories
- Sexual fields theory deleted to streamline chapter
- Performativity (e.g., performing gender) added to section on critical theories

Chapter 3. Sex Research
- More information on ethnicity in research
- Updated material on studies of special populations, including recruitment through websites
- "Prevalence" added in statistical concepts
- Section on web-based research updated

Chapter 4. Sexual Anatomy
- New data on pubic hair removal and its consequences
- Updated material on female genital cutting and labiaplasty
- Updates on cancer statistics and treatments
- Updates on the male circumcision controversy and the data

Chapter 5. Sex Hormones, Sexual Differentiation, and the Menstrual Cycle
- Surprising new findings that estradiol and progesterone levels do not differ between men and women; only testosterone levels do
- Evidence on endocrine disrupters updated
- New data on fluctuations in performance, or lack thereof, across the menstrual cycle
- New information on the Nepalese Hindu custom of chhaupadi, in which a menstruating woman may not live in her home and sometimes resorts to living in an animal shed

Chapter 6. Pregnancy and Childbirth
- Chapter streamlined and shortened substantially
- New evaluation of the accuracy of websites and cell phone apps in predicting the fertile window
- Updated material on fetal alcohol spectrum disorder
- Section on assisted reproductive technology (ART) updated

Chapter 7. Contraception and Abortion
- Table 1 on contraceptive practices around the world updated
- Added information on drugs that may interact with emergency contraception drugs
- Reasons the U.S. abortion rate is down 25 percent from 2008
- Updated information on FDA approval of use of mifepristone for medical abortion
- Table with abortion rates around the world updated
- Nestorone-testosterone contraceptive gel for men added in New Advances
- Sperm-binding beads added in New Advances

Chapter 8. Sexual Arousal
- Chapter streamlined and shortened
- New data on reasons people pretend orgasm
- New material in Mapping the Sexual Brain: research on brain regions activated when deciding on risky sexual behavior
- New section on sexual satisfaction

Chapter 9. Sexuality and the Life Cycle: Childhood and Adolescence
- New study on nudity and doctor games in Danish preschools
- Section on the media and adolescent sexuality updated
- Updates on teen pregnancy and sharp declines in rates
- New section on Risky Sex and the Adolescent Brain
- Thorough updating of material on adolescents' use of social networking sites and sexting

Chapter 10. Sexuality and the Life Cycle: Adulthood
- Figure 2 on sexual frequency as a function of relationship status, gender, and age, converted to an easier-to-read table
- Updated discussion of the cohabitation effect and serial cohabitation
- New feature: Are Americans Having Sex More Frequently?

- Statistics on extramarital sex updated and streamlined
- New material on open nonmonogamy

Chapter 11. Attraction, Love, and Communication

- Chapter streamlined and shortened
- Table 1 on homophily in marriage updated and racial homophily in online dating added
- Section on online and app-based attraction, meeting, and dating revised and updated
- New material in section on Attachment Theory of Love
- New section on Love Styles replaces section on love as a story
- Table 2 on cross-cultural views of love improved
- New Critical Thinking box

Chapter 12. Gender and Sexuality

- New conceptualizations of parents' gendered socialization
- New material on gender differences in impulsivity
- Replaced the classic Heiman (1975) psychophysiology study of gender and arousal to erotic materials with a contemporary study (Suschinsky et al., 2009)
- Section on Transgender Issues and Experience reorganized, updated, and expanded
- New section on Affirmative Therapy with TGNC people

Chapter 13. Sexual Orientation: Gay, Straight, or Bi?

- Updated statistics in Table 1 show continuing trend toward more favorable attitudes
- New material on implicit attitudes toward LGBs
- Updated statistics in Table 2 on percentages of people with same-gender sexual behavior, identity, and attractions
- A positive psychology approach to same-gender couple relationships introduced
- New table on attitudes toward homosexuality in nations around the world
- The term *pansexual* introduced

Chapter 14. Variations in Sexual Behavior

- Chapter streamlined and updated throughout
- Section on sexual addictions/compulsions rewritten and updated

- New research on asexuality
- New material on cybersex use and abuse

Chapter 15. Sexual Coercion

- New material on what friends and family can do to support a rape survivor
- Phenomenon of sextortion introduced
- Section on Sexual Harassment updated, including the #MeToo movement and the new National Academy of Sciences report

Chapter 16. Sex for Sale

- Chapter streamlined throughout
- New material on the Internet and sex work, including camgirls
- New data from pornhub.com
- New technology of virtual reality pornography
- Section on Effects of Porn Exposure rewritten, framed by the differential susceptibility to media effects model

Chapter 17. Sexual Disorders and Sex Therapy

- New section on Mindfulness-Based Sex Therapy
- New section on Testosterone Treatments for Testosterone Deficiency (hypogonadism) in men
- Added coverage of new combination drugs for women's sexual desire problems

Chapter 18. Sexually Transmitted Infections

- Statistics updated throughout

Chapter 19. Ethics, Religion, and Sexuality

- Pro-life and pro-choice statements of religious groups updated

Chapter 20. Sex and the Law

- Chapter rewritten to reflect the *Obergefell v. Hodges* Supreme Court decision legalizing same-sex marriage
- New box, *Legal Issues for Transgender Persons*
- New Critical Thinking box on transgender rights and the distinction between legal evidence and scientific evidence

- New section on crisis pregnancy centers and the Supreme Court ruling on them
- Updated with new Supreme Court cases, e.g., *Whole Woman's Health v. Hellerstedt* on abortion

Looking to the Future: Sexuality Education

- Updates on federal spending on abstinence-only programs, and rebranding them as "sexual risk avoidance"
- New evaluations of condom availability programs

Acknowledgments

We are grateful to the many professionals associated with McGraw-Hill Education who have supported the development of this new edition: Nancy Welcher, Senior Portfolio Manager; Dawn Groundwater, Product Development Manager; Nicole Bridge, Product Developer; AJ Laferrera and Olivia Kaiser, Marketing Managers; and Ryan Warczynski, Content Project Manager. We would also like to thank our two expert reviewers: Dr. Stephanie Budge, University of Wisconsin–Madison, and Dr. Jennifer Higgins, University of Wisconsin–Madison.

Over the course of the first 13 editions, numerous reviewers contributed to the development of *Understanding Human Sexuality.* Space limitations prevent me from listing all of them, but their contributions endure, as does my gratitude to them. I am especially grateful to the reviewers who helped shape this edition:

Judi Addelston, *Valencia College*

David de Jong, *Western Carolina University*

Celeste Favela, *El Paso Community College*

Robert Gallagher, *Broward Community College*

Jeri Lloyd, *Piedmont Virginia Community College*

Ken Locke, *University of Idaho*

John McDaniel, *San Mateo Community College District*

Heidi Pierce, *Kirkwood Community College*

Paulina Ruf, *Seminole State University*

Margaret Staton, *Valencia College*

Bradley Thurmond, *Ivy Technical Community College*

Jovana Vukovic, *Broward Community College*

Amy Yeates, *Illinois Wesleyan University*

©Corbis/VCG/Getty Images

CHAPTER

1

Sexuality in Perspective

CHAPTER HIGHLIGHTS

"**Y**ou're so beautiful," he whispered. "I want a picture of you like this with your face flushed and your lips wet and shiny." . . . He tore open a foil packet he'd retrieved from his pocket. Mesmerized, she watched him sheath himself, amazed at how hard he was. She reached out to touch him, but he moved back, made sure she was ready, and then slid neatly inside her, so deeply she gasped. She contracted her muscles around him, and he closed his eyes and groaned, the sound so primal, it made her skin tingle.*

Human sexual behavior is a diverse phenomenon. It occurs in different physical locations and social contexts, consists of a wide range of specific activities, and is perceived differently by different people. An individual engages in sexual activity on the basis of a complex set of motivations and organizes that activity on the basis of numerous external factors and influences. Thus, it is unlikely that the tools and concepts from any single scientific discipline will suffice to answer all or even most of the questions one might ask about sexual behavior.†

*Debbi Rawlins. (2003). *Anything goes*. New York: Harlequin Blaze. Used by permission.
†Laumann et al. (1994).

Strikingly different though they may seem, both of the above quotations are talking about the same thing—sex. The first quotation is from a romance novel. It is intended to stimulate the reader's fantasies and arousal. The second is from a scholarly book about sex. It aims to stimulate the brain but not the genitals. From reading these two brief excerpts we can quickly see that the topic of sexuality is diverse, complex, and fascinating.

Why study sex? Most people are curious about sex, particularly because exchanging sexual information is somewhat taboo in our culture, so curiosity motivates us to study sex. Sex is an important force in many people's lives, so there are practical reasons for wanting to learn about it. Finally, most of us at various times experience problems with our sexual functioning or wish that we could function better, and we hope that learning more about sex will help us. This book is designed to address all of these needs. So let's consider various perspectives on sexuality—the effects of religion, science, and culture on our understanding of sexuality, as well as the sexual health perspective. These perspectives will give you a glimpse of the forest before you study the trees: sexual anatomy and physiology (the "plumbing" part) and sexual behavior (the "people" part), which are discussed in later chapters. But first we must draw an important distinction between sex and gender.

Sex and Gender

Gender: Being male, female, or some other gender such as trans.
Gender binary: Conceptualizing gender as having only two categories, male and female.

Sometimes the word *sex* is used ambiguously. In some cases it refers to being male or female, and sometimes it refers to sexual behavior or reproduction. In most cases, of course, the meaning is clear from the context. If you are filling out a job application form and one item says, "Sex:," you don't write, "I like it" or "As often as possible." It is clear that your prospective employer wants to know whether you are a male or a female. In other cases, though, the meaning may be ambiguous. For example, when a book has the title *Sex and Temperament in Three Primitive Societies,* what is it about? Is it about the sexual practices of primitive people and whether having sex frequently gives them pleasant temperaments? Or is it about the kinds of personalities that males and females are expected to have in those societies? Not only does this use of *sex* create ambiguities, but it also clouds our thinking about some important issues.

To remove—or at least reduce—this ambiguity, the term *sex* will be used in this book in contexts referring to sexual anatomy and sexual behavior, and the term **gender** will be used to refer to being male or female or some other gender such as trans.

Almost all the research that we discuss in this book has been based on scientists' assuming the **gender binary,** the idea that there are only two genders, male and female. In the chapter "Gender and Sexuality," we consider some of the contemporary research on people who are outside the gender binary.

This is a book about sex, not gender; it is about sexual behavior and the biological, psychological, and social forces that influence it. Of course, although we are arguing that sex and gender are conceptually different, we would not try to argue that they are totally independent of each other. Certainly gender roles—the ways in which males and females are expected to behave—exert a powerful influence on the way people behave sexually, and one chapter is devoted to gender and its connections to sexuality.

How should we define *sex,* aside from saying that it is different from *gender?* Many Americans count only penis-in-vagina intercourse as sex (Peterson & Muehlenhard, 2007; Sewell & Strassberg, 2015). Nearly everyone agrees that penis-in-vagina intercourse counts as sex, but there is less agreement about whether oral-genital sex counts as "having sex." Some people think it does and others think it doesn't (Horowitz & Spicer, 2013). Our definition in this textbook includes much more than that, though.

A biologist might define sexual behavior as "any behavior that increases the likelihood of gametic union [union of sperm and egg]" (Bermant & Davidson, 1974). This definition emphasizes the reproductive function of sex. However, medical advances such as the birth control pill allow us to separate reproduction from sex. Most Americans now use sex not only for procreation but also for recreation.[1]

These definitions assume that sex is heterosexual. What about same-gender sexuality? A study of sexual minority people indicated that, for men, anal intercourse was the behavior most likely to count as "sex" (Sewell et al., 2017). For women, it was oral-genital sex.

The noted sex researcher Alfred Kinsey defined *sex* as behavior that leads to orgasm. Although this definition has some merits (it does not imply that sex must be associated with reproduction), it also presents some problems. If a woman has intercourse with a man but does not have an orgasm, was that not sexual behavior for her?

To try to avoid some of these problems, **sexual behavior** will be defined in this book as *behavior that produces arousal and increases the chance of orgasm.*[2]

The History of Understanding Sexuality: Religion and Science

Religion
Throughout most of recorded history, at least until about 100 years ago, religion (and rumor) provided most of the information that people had about sexuality. The ancient Greeks openly acknowledged both heterosexuality and homosexuality in their society and explained the existence of the two in a myth in which the original humans were double creatures with twice the normal number of limbs and organs; some were double males, some were double females, and some were half male and half female (LeVay, 1996). The gods, fearing the power of these creatures, split them in half, and forever after each one continued to search for its missing half. Heterosexuals were thought to have resulted from the splitting of the half male, half female; male homosexuals, from the splitting of the double male; and female homosexuals, from the splitting of the double female. It was through this mythology that the ancient Greeks understood sexual orientation and sexual desire.

Fifteenth-century Christians believed that "wet dreams" (nocturnal emissions) resulted from intercourse with tiny spiritual creatures called *incubi* and *succubi,* a notion put forth in a papal bull of 1484 and a companion book, the *Malleus Maleficarum* ("witch's hammer"); the person who had wet dreams was considered guilty of sodomy (see the chapter "Ethics, Religion, and Sexuality") as well as witchcraft.

Over the centuries, Muslims have believed that sexual intercourse is one of the finest pleasures of life, reflecting the teachings of the great prophet Muhammad. However, the way that the laws of the Koran are carried out varies greatly from country to country (Boonstra, 2001; Ilkkaracan, 2001).

People of different religions hold different understandings of human sexuality, and these religious views often have a profound impact. A detailed discussion of religion and sexuality is provided in the chapter "Ethics, Religion, and Sexuality."

Science
It was against this background of religious understandings of sexuality that the scientific study of sex began in the 19th century, although, of course, religious notions continue to influence our ideas about sexuality. In addition, the groundwork for an understanding of the biological aspects of sexuality had already been laid by the research of physicians and biologists. The Dutch microscopist Anton van Leeuwenhoek (1632–1723) had discovered sperm swimming in human semen. In 1875 Oskar Hertwig (1849–1922) first observed the actual fertilization of the egg by the sperm in sea urchins, although the ovum in humans was not directly observed until the 20th century.

A major advance in the scientific understanding of the psychological aspects of human sexuality came with the work of the Viennese physician Sigmund Freud (1856–1939), founder of psychiatry and psychoanalysis (Figure 1a). His ideas are discussed in detail in the chapter "Theoretical Perspectives on Sexuality."

It is important to recognize the cultural context in which Freud and the other early sex researchers

[1]Actually, even in former times sex was not always associated with reproduction. For example, a man in 1850 might have fathered 10 children; using a very conservative estimate that he engaged in sexual intercourse 1,500 times during his adult life (once a week for the 30 years from age 20 to age 50), one concludes that only 10 in 1,500 of those acts, or less than 1 percent, resulted in reproduction.
[2]This definition, though an improvement over some, still has its problems. For example, consider a woman who feels no arousal at all during intercourse. According to the definition, intercourse would not be sexual behavior for her. However, intercourse would generally be something we would want to classify as sexual behavior. It should be clear that defining *sexual behavior* is difficult.

Sexual behavior: Behavior that produces arousal and increases the chance of orgasm.

(a)

(b)

Figure 1   Two important early sex researchers. (*a*) Sigmund Freud. (*b*) Henry Havelock Ellis.

(a) ©AP Images; (b) ©Hulton-Deutsch Collection/Corbis/Getty Images

crafted their research and writing. They began their work in the Victorian era, the late 1800s, both in the United States and in Europe. Norms about sexuality were extraordinarily rigid and oppressive (Figure 2). Historian Peter Gay characterized this repressive aspect of Victorian cultural norms as

> a devious and insincere world in which middle-class husbands slaked their lust by keeping mistresses, frequenting prostitutes, or molesting children, while their wives, timid, dutiful, obedient, were sexually anesthetic and poured all their capacity for love into their housekeeping and their child-rearing. (Gay, 1984, p. 6)

Certainly traces of these Victorian attitudes remain with us today. Yet, at the same time, the actual sexual behavior of Victorians sometimes violated societal norms. In his history of sexuality in the Victorian era, Gay documented the story of Mabel Loomis Todd, who, though married, carried on a lengthy affair with Austin Dickinson, a community leader in Amherst, Massachusetts. Many people actually knew about the "secret" affair, yet Mrs. Loomis did not become an outcast (Gay, 1984). Doubtless, this wide discrepancy between Victorian sexual norms and actual behavior created a great deal of personal tension. That tension probably propelled a good many people into Dr. Freud's office, providing data for his theory, which emphasizes sexual tensions and conflict.

An equally great—though not so well known—early contributor to the scientific study of sex was Henry Havelock

Ellis (1859–1939; Figure 1b). A physician in Victorian England, he compiled a vast collection of information on sexuality—including medical and anthropological findings, as well as case histories—which was published in a series of volumes titled *Studies in the Psychology of Sex* beginning in 1896. Havelock Ellis was a remarkably objective and tolerant scholar, particularly for his era. He believed that women, like men, are sexual creatures. A sexual reformer, he believed that sexual deviations from the norm are often harmless, and he urged society to accept them. In his desire to collect information about human sexuality rather than to make judgments about it, he can be considered the forerunner of modern sex research.

Another important figure in 19th-century sex research was the psychiatrist Richard von Krafft-Ebing (1840–1902). His special interest was "pathological" sexuality. He managed to collect more than 200 case histories of pathological individuals, which appeared in his book titled *Psychopathia Sexualis*. His work tended to be neither objective nor tolerant. Nonetheless, it has had a lasting impact. He coined the concepts of sadism, masochism, and pedophilia, and the terms *heterosexuality* and *homosexuality* entered the English language in the 1892 translation of his book (Oosterhuis, 2000). One of his case histories is presented in the chapter "Variations in Sexual Behavior."

One other early contributor to the scientific understanding of sexuality deserves mention, the German Magnus Hirschfeld (1868–1935). He founded the first sex research institute and administered the first large-scale

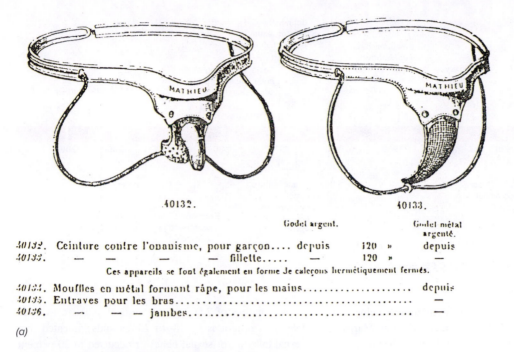

40132.

40133.

Godet argent.

Godet métal argenté.

40132. Ceinture contre l'onanisme, pour garçon.... depuis   120 »   depuis
40133.   —   —   —   — fillette.....   —   120 »   —
Ces appareils se font également en forme de caleçons hermétiquement fermés.

40134. Moufles en métal formant râpe, pour les mains..................... depuis
40135. Entraves pour les bras..   —
40136.   —   —   — jambes...   —

(a)

(b)

Figure 2 Devices designed to prevent masturbation. (*a*) The Victorian era, from which Freud and Ellis emerged, was characterized by extreme sexual repression. Here are some apparatuses that were sold to prevent onanism (masturbation). (*b*) Are things so different today? Here are current devices for sale on the Internet, for the same purpose.

(a) ©Granger/Granger—All rights reserved; (b) Courtesy of A.L. Enterprises

sex survey, obtaining data from 10,000 people on a 130-item questionnaire. (Unfortunately, most of the information he amassed was destroyed by the Nazis.) Hirschfeld also established the first journal devoted to the study of sex, established a marriage counseling service, worked for legal reforms, and gave advice on contraception and sex problems. His special interest, however, was homosexuality. Doubtless some of his avant-garde approaches resulted from the fact that he was himself both homosexual and a transvestite and, in fact, he introduced the term *transvestite*. His contributions as a pioneer sex researcher cannot be denied (Bullough, 1994).

In the 20th century, major breakthroughs in the scientific understanding of sex came with the massive surveys of human sexual behavior in the United States conducted by Alfred Kinsey and his colleagues in the 1940s and with Masters and Johnson's investigations of sexual disorders and the physiology of sexual response. At about

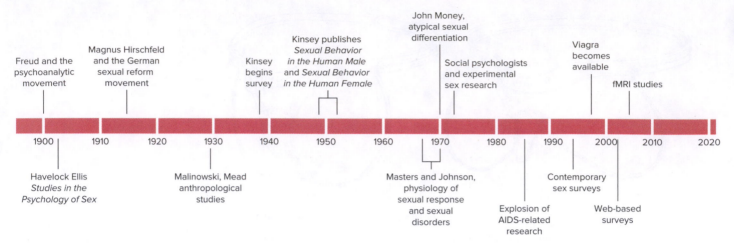

Figure 3   Milestones in the history of scientific research on sex.

the same time that the Kinsey research was being conducted, some anthropologists—most notably Margaret Mead and Bronislaw Malinowski—were beginning to collect data on sexual behavior in other cultures. Other, smaller investigations also provided important information. By the 1990s we had a rich array of sex research, including major national surveys (e.g., Laumann et al., 1994), detailed investigations of sexual disorders and sexual orientation, and studies of the biological processes underlying sexual response.

The scientific study of sex has not emerged as a separate, unified academic discipline like biology or psychology or sociology. Rather, it tends to be interdisciplinary—a joint effort by biologists, psychologists, sociologists, anthropologists, and physicians (see Figure 3). This approach to understanding sexuality gives us a better view of humans in all their sexual complexity.

The Media

In terms of potency of influence, the mass media in America today may play the same role that religion did in previous centuries. In U.S. homes with children, 99 percent have a television and 86 percent have a computer (Lauricella et al., 2015). American adolescents spend 11 hours per day with some form of mass media (Rideout et al., 2010). According to the American Time Use Survey, television viewing occupies the most time of all leisure activities, at an average of 2.7 hours per day for those aged 15 and older (Bureau of Labor Statistics, 2017).

Cultivation theory: In communications theory, the view that exposure to the mass media makes people think that what they see there represents the mainstream of what really occurs.
Framing theory: The theory that the media draw attention to certain topics and not to others, suggesting how we should think about or frame the issues.
Social cognitive theory: In communications theory, the idea that the media provide role models whom we imitate.

An analysis of 2,600 scenes from the 30 most-viewed television programs by 18- to 25-year-olds indicated that sexual talk and/or sexual behavior occurred in 20 percent of scenes (Carpentier et al., 2017). Twenty-five percent of scenes contained jokes about sexual organs. Only 7 percent of scenes mentioned any health consequences of sex, and most of those were about emotional heartache; only 1 of the 2,600 scenes mentioned sexually transmitted infections. And only 12 scenes (less than 1 percent) mentioned condoms or contraceptives. In short, the average American's views about sexuality are likely to be much more influenced by the mass media than by scientific findings. Communications theorists have formulated several theories about how the media can influence us (Valkenburg et al., 2016).

Cultivation theory focuses on the notion that people begin to think that what they see on television and in other media really represents the mainstream of what happens in real life in our culture (Gerbner et al., 2002). For example, an analysis of *Jersey Shore* indicated that on average one sexual instance occurred every minute; college students' reports of how often they viewed the show were positively correlated with permissive sexual attitudes, exactly as cultivation theory would predict (Bond & Drogos, 2014). In addition, the students' permissive sexual attitudes were correlated with their own sexual activity.

According to **framing theory,** the media draw attention to certain topics and not to others, suggesting how we should think about or frame the issues (Scheufele, 1999). For example, in 1998 the media chose to highlight the sexual dalliances of President Bill Clinton, suggesting to the public that these matters were important. In contrast, the illicit sexual activities of President John F. Kennedy were not revealed during his presidency. The media tell us what is important and what is not.

Social cognitive theory is a broad theory in psychology, and it is discussed in detail in the chapter "Theoretical Perspectives on Sexuality." Social cognitive theory applied to the media analyzes how the media influence our behavior, thoughts, and affect (emotions) through processes such as modeling, imitation, and identification (Bandura, 2009). The example of *Jersey Shore* and how frequency of viewing correlated with permissive sexual attitudes is also consistent with social cognitive theory, which might say that viewers imitated the attitudes and behaviors they saw in the show.

Another important process in media theories is **selectivity,** which refers to the principle that people select and pay attention only to certain media and their messages, and not to others (Knobloch-Westerwick, 2015). Nick gets all of his TV news from Fox News and Olivia gets all of hers from CBS News. They get different information. Brandon watches Internet porn, and Lorewell does not. People can be affected only by media to which they are exposed. Moreover, people do not select media randomly. Generally, we select media content according to our own needs, and we seek information that is consistent with our own views.

According to **reinforcing spiral theory,** one's social identities and ideologies predict one's media use (consistent with selectivity) and, in turn, media use affects our identity and beliefs (Slater, 2015). It therefore recognizes the dynamic interplay, the back and forth, between individuals and the media they consume. For example, if I am Black and that identity is important to me, I will be likelier to watch a television network such as BET, which will in turn reinforce my Black identity and beliefs, which will keep me watching BET, and so the spiral goes.

According to the **differential susceptibility model,** not everyone reacts the same to the same media exposure (Valkenburg et al., 2016). For example, people high on the trait of aggressiveness are more susceptible to—more influenced by—violent media than are other people.

The Internet is a powerful mass media influence. Computer and Internet use is spreading more rapidly than any previous technology, and today 89 percent of U.S. adults use the Internet (98 percent for those between 18 and 29 years of age; Pew Research Center, 2018). Exposure to sex on the Internet is also growing rapidly. In one study, 28 percent of male adolescents reported looking at pictures of people having sex at least once a week, compared with 3 percent for female adolescents (Peter & Valkenburg, 2008). As we discuss in later chapters, the Internet has the potential for both positive and negative effects on sexual health. A number of sites, such as that for the American Sexual Health Association (www.iwannaknow.org), provide excellent information about sexuality and promote sexual health. At the same time, a repeated, well-sampled study of youth between the ages of 10 and 17 indicated that in 2000 19 percent had been sexually solicited on the Internet, but by 2010 the number had fallen to only 9 percent (Mitchell et al., 2013a). Most youth who received a solicitation responded

by removing themselves from the situation (blocking the solicitor, leaving the site) or by telling the solicitor to stop. Experts believe that there is greater online safety for youth today than in the past, for a number of reasons. One is that they receive more talks about online safety from teachers and police (Mitchell et al., 2013a).

In the chapters that follow, we examine the content of the media on numerous sexual issues, and we consider what the effects of exposure to this media content might have on viewers.

Let us now consider the perspectives on sexuality that are provided by scientific observations of humans in a wide variety of societies.

Cross-Cultural Perspectives on Sexuality

Humans are a cultural species (Heine & Norenzayan, 2006). Although some other species are capable of learning from others, humans are unique in the way that cultural learning accumulates over time. Cultural psychologists define **culture** as the part of the environment created by humans, including the set of meanings that a group adopts; these meanings facilitate social coordination, clarify where boundaries between groups lie, and make life seem predictable (Oyserman, 2017).

Cultural psychologists have documented that cultures tend to have one of three main themes: individualism, collectivism, or honor (Oyserman, 2017). **Individualistic cultures** stress independence and autonomy and the individual rights of people. **Collectivistic cultures** emphasize interdependence and connections among people. In these cultures, the group is more important than the individual. The United States and Canada are highly individualistic cultures, whereas east Asian cultures such as Japan tend to be collectivistic. **Honor cultures** stress "face," that is, individuals' reputation and the respect or honor that people show toward others. In an

Do they have sex in other cultures the same way we do in the United States?

Selectivity: In media theories, the principle that people select and pay attention only to certain media and ignore others.
Reinforcing spiral theory: A theory that one's social identities and ideologies predict one's media use and, in turn, media use affects our identity and beliefs.
Differential susceptibility model: Some people are more susceptible than others to certain types of media (e.g., violent media).
Culture: The part of the environment created by humans, including the set of meanings that a group adopts; these meanings facilitate social coordination and clarify where boundaries between groups lie.
Individualistic cultures: Those that stress independence and autonomy and the individual rights of people.
Collectivistic cultures: Those that emphasize interdependence and connections among people; the group is more important than the individual.
Honor cultures: Those that stress "face," that is, individuals' reputation and the respect or honor that people show toward others.

Figure 4   Margaret Mead, an anthropologist who contributed much to the early cross-cultural study of sexuality.

©AP Images

honor culture, for example, it might seem reasonable to stone to death a woman who committed adultery, because of her profound violation of the honor valued in that culture. Honor cultures tend to be found in the Middle East, but also in the southern part of the United States.

Ethnocentrism tends to influence our understanding of human sexual behavior. Most of us have had experience with sexuality in only one culture—the United States, for example—and we tend to view our sexual behavior as the only pattern in existence, and certainly as the only "natural" pattern. But anthropologists have discovered that there are wide variations in sexual behavior and attitudes from one culture to the next (Figure 4). Considering these variations should help us to put our own sexual behavior in perspective.

The major generalization that emerges from cross-cultural studies is that all societies regulate sexual behavior in some way, though the exact regulations vary greatly from one culture to the next (DeLamater, 1987). Apparently no society has seen fit to leave sexuality totally unregulated, perhaps fearful that social disruption would result. As an example, **incest taboos** are nearly universal: Sex is regulated in that intercourse between blood

> **Ethnocentrism:** The tendency to regard one's own ethnic group and culture as superior to others and to believe that its customs and way of life are the standards by which other cultures should be judged.
> **Incest taboo:** A societal regulation prohibiting sexual interaction between blood relatives, such as brother and sister or father and daughter.

relatives is prohibited (Gregersen, 1996). Most societies also condemn forced sexual relations such as rape.

Beyond this generalization, though, regulations vary greatly from one society to the next, and sexual behavior and attitudes vary correspondingly (see A Sexually Diverse World: Sexuality in Two Societies). Let's look at the ways in which various societies treat some key areas of human sexual behavior.

Variations in Sexual Techniques

Romantic sexual kissing might seem to be the most basic of sexual behaviors, but it is not found in all societies. Researchers surveyed anthropologists' records from 168 cultures around the world and discovered that the romantic sexual kiss was *not* present in 54 percent of them (Jankowiak et al., 2015). Romantic sexual kissing was absent in 87 percent of African cultures, but it was present in 100 percent of Middle Eastern cultures. When the Thonga of Africa first saw Europeans kissing, they laughed and said, "Look at them; they eat each other's saliva and dirt." There is also some variation in techniques of kissing. For example, among the Kwakiutl of Canada and the Trobriand Islanders, kissing consists of sucking the lips and tongue of the partner, permitting saliva to flow from one mouth to the other. Many Americans might find such a practice somewhat repulsive, but other peoples find it sexually arousing.

Cunnilingus (mouth stimulation of the female genitals) is fairly common in our society, and it occurs in a few other societies as well, especially in the South Pacific. A particularly interesting variation is reported on the island of Ponape; the man places a fish in the woman's vulva and then gradually licks it out prior to coitus.

Inflicting pain on the partner is also a part of the sexual technique in some societies. The Apinaye woman of the Brazilian highlands may bite off bits of her partner's eyebrows, noisily spitting them aside. Ponapean men usually tug at the woman's eyebrows, occasionally yanking out tufts of hair. People of various societies bite their partners to the point of drawing blood and leaving scars; most commonly, men and women mutually inflict pain on each other (Frayser, 1985).

The frequency of intercourse for married couples varies considerably from one culture to the next. The lowest frequency seems to be among the Irish natives of Inis Beag (discussed in A Sexually Diverse World: Sexuality in Two Societies), who engage in intercourse perhaps only once or twice a month; however, the anthropologists who studied them were unable to determine exactly how often couples did have sex because so much secrecy surrounds the act. At the opposite extreme, the Mangaians (also described in A Sexually Diverse World: Sexuality in Two Societies) have intercourse several times a night, at least among the young. The Santals of southern Asia copulate as often as five times per day every day early in

A Sexually Diverse World

Sexuality in Two Societies

Inis Beag

Inis Beag is a small island off the coast of Ireland. It is probably one of the most naive and sexually repressive societies in the world.

The people of Inis Beag seem to have no knowledge of a number of sexual activities such as French kissing, mouth stimulation of the breast, or hand stimulation of the partner's penis, much less oral sex or homosexuality. Sex education is virtually nonexistent; parents do not seem to be able to bring themselves to discuss such embarrassing matters with their children, and they simply trust that, after marriage, nature will take its course.

Menstruation and menopause are sources of fear for the island women because they have no idea of their physiological significance. It is commonly believed that menopause can produce insanity; in order to ward off this condition, some women have retired from life in their mid-forties, and a few have confined themselves to bed until death years later.

The men believe that intercourse is hard on one's health. They will desist from sex the night before they are to do a job that takes great energy. They do not approach women sexually during menstruation or for months after childbirth; a woman is considered dangerous to the man at these times.

The islanders abhor nudity. Only babies are allowed to bathe while nude. Adults wash only the parts of their bodies that extend beyond their clothing—face, neck, lower arms, hands, lower legs, and feet. The fear of nudity has even cost lives. Sailors who never learned to swim because it involved wearing scanty clothing drowned when their ships sank.

Premarital sex is essentially unknown. In marital sex, foreplay is generally limited to kissing and rough fondling of the buttocks. The husband invariably initiates the activity. The male-on-top is the only position used, and both partners keep their underwear on during the activity. The man has an orgasm quickly and falls asleep immediately. Female orgasm either is believed not to exist or is considered deviant.

Mangaia

In distinct contrast to Inis Beag is Mangaia, an island in the South Pacific. For the Mangaians, sex—for pleasure and for procreation—is a principal interest.

The Mangaian boy first hears of masturbation when he is about 7, and he may begin to masturbate at age 8 or 9. At around age 13 he undergoes the superincision ritual (in which a slit is made on the top of the penis, along its entire length). This ritual initiates him into manhood; more important, however, the expert who performs the superincision gives him sexual instruction. He shows the boy how to perform oral sex, how to kiss and suck breasts, and how to bring his partner to orgasm several times before he has his own. About two weeks after the operation, the boy has intercourse with an experienced woman, which removes the superincision's scab. She provides him with practice in various acts and positions and trains him to hold back until he can have simultaneous orgasms with his partner.

After this, the Mangaian boy actively seeks out girls, or they seek him out; soon he has coitus every night. The girl, who has received sexual instruction from an older woman, expects demonstration of the boy's virility as proof of his desire for her. What is valued is the ability of the male to continue vigorously the in-and-out action of coitus over long periods of time while the female moves her hips "like a washing machine." Nothing is despised more than a "dead" partner who does not move. A good man is expected to continue his actions for 15 to 30 minutes or more.

The average "nice" girl will have three or four successive boyfriends between the ages of 13 and 20; the average boy may have 10 or more girlfriends. Mangaian parents encourage their daughters to have sexual experiences with several men. They want them to find marriage partners who are congenial.

At around age 18, the Mangaians typically have sex most nights of the week, with about three orgasms per night. By about age 48, they have sex two or three times per week, with one orgasm each time.

All women in Mangaia apparently learn to have orgasms. Bringing his partner to orgasm is one of the man's chief sources of sexual pleasure.

Sources: Marshall (1971); Messenger (1993).

marriage (Gregersen, 1996). Recent surveys of U.S. sexuality indicate that our frequency of intercourse is about in the middle compared with other societies (e.g., Herbenick et al., 2010a).

Very few societies encourage people to engage in sexual intercourse at particular times (Frayser, 1985). Instead, most groups have restrictions that forbid intercourse at certain times or in certain situations. For example, almost every society has a postpartum sex taboo—that is, a prohibition on sexual intercourse for a period of time after a woman has given birth, with the taboo lasting from a few days to more than a year (Gregersen, 1996).

Masturbation

Attitudes toward **masturbation,** or sexual self-stimulation of the genitals, vary widely across cultures. Some societies tolerate or even encourage masturbation during childhood and adolescence, whereas others condemn the practice at any age. Almost all human societies express some disapproval of adult masturbation, ranging from mild ridicule to severe punishment (Gregersen, 1996). However, at least some adults in all societies appear to practice it.

Female masturbation certainly occurs in other societies. The African Azande woman uses a phallus made of a wooden root; however, if her husband catches her masturbating, he may beat her severely. The following is a description of the Lesu of the South Pacific, one of the few societies that express no disapproval of adult female masturbation:

> A woman will masturbate if she is sexually excited and there is no man to satisfy her. A couple may be having intercourse in the same house, or near enough for her to see them, and she may thus become aroused. She then sits down and bends her right leg so that her heel presses against her genitalia. Even young girls of about six years may do this quite casually as they sit on the ground. The women and men talk about it freely, and there is no shame attached to it. It is a customary position for women to take, and they learn it in childhood. They never use their hands for manipulation. (Powdermaker, 1933, pp. 276–277)

Premarital and Extramarital Sex

Societies differ considerably in their rules regarding premarital sex (Frayser, 1985). At one extreme are the Marquesans of eastern Polynesia. Both boys and girls in that culture have participated in a wide range of sexual experiences before puberty. Their first experience with intercourse occurs with a heterosexual partner who is 30 to 40 years old. Mothers are proud if their daughters have many lovers. Only later does marriage occur. In contrast are the Siwans of Egypt. In this culture a girl's clitoris is removed at age 7 or

Masturbation: Self-stimulation of the genitals to produce sexual arousal.

8 in order to decrease her potential for sexual excitement and intercourse. Premarital intercourse is believed to bring shame on the family (note the honor culture theme). Marriage usually occurs around the age of 12 or 13, shortening the premarital period and any temptations it might contain.

These two cultures are fairly typical of their regions. According to one study, 90 percent of Pacific Island societies permit premarital sex, as do 88 percent of African and 82 percent of Eurasian societies; however, 73 percent of Mediterranean societies prohibit premarital sex (Frayser, 1985).

Extramarital sex is complex and conflicted for most cultures. Extramarital sex ranks second only to incest as the most strictly prohibited type of sexual contact. One study found that it was forbidden for one or both partners in 74 percent of the cultures surveyed (Frayser, 1985). Even when extramarital sex is permitted, it is subjected to regulations; the most common pattern of restriction is to allow extramarital sex for husbands but not wives.

Sex with Same-Gender Partners

A wide range of attitudes toward same-gender sexual expression—what many in the United States call *homosexuality*—exists in various cultures (Murray, 2000). At one extreme are societies that strongly disapprove of same-gender sexual behavior for people of any age. In contrast, some societies tolerate the behavior for children but disapprove of it in adults. Still other societies actively encourage all their male members to engage in some same-gender sexual behavior, usually in conjunction with puberty rites (Herdt, 1984). A few societies have a formalized role for the adult gay man that gives him status and dignity.

Even across European nations, attitudes about homosexuality vary considerably (Lottes & Alkula, 2011). For example, people in Denmark, the Netherlands, and Sweden have the most positive attitudes. Positive attitudes are also found in a large group of countries including Austria, Belgium, France, Germany, Great Britain, Greece, Italy, and Spain. Attitudes are more negative in Belarus, Bulgaria, Estonia, and Russia; and the cluster of countries with the most negative attitudes includes Croatia, Lithuania, Poland, Portugal, Romania, and Ukraine.

There is wide variation in attitudes toward homosexuality and in same-gender sexual behavior, but two general rules do seem to emerge (Ford & Beach, 1951; Murray, 2000; Whitam, 1983): (1) No matter how a particular society treats homosexuality, the behavior always occurs in at least some individuals—that is, same-gender sexuality is found universally in all societies; and (2) same-gender sexual behavior is never the predominant form of sexual behavior for adults in any of the societies studied.

The first point, that same-gender sexual behavior is found universally in all cultures, is so well established that there was quite a stir in 2010 when a team of anthropologists reported on a group of people, the Aka foragers of the Central African Republic (Hewlett & Hewlett, 2010). The Aka were not aware of such practices and had no term for them. In fact, it was difficult for the anthropologists to convey what they meant. We may need to amend the earlier statement, to say that same-gender sexual behavior is *nearly* universal across societies.

In the United States and other Western nations, we hold an unquestioned assumption that people have a sexual identity, whether gay, lesbian, bisexual, or heterosexual. Yet sexual identity as an unvarying, lifelong characteristic of the self is unknown or rare in some cultures, such as Indonesia (Stevenson, 1995). In those cultures the self and individualism, so prominent in American culture, are downplayed. Instead, a person is defined in relation to others and behavior is seen as much more the product of the situation than of lifelong personality traits. In such a culture, having a "gay identity" just doesn't compute.

Sex with same-gender partners is discussed in detail in the chapter "Sexual Orientation: Gay, Straight, or Bi?"

Standards of Attractiveness

In all human societies physical characteristics are important in determining whom one chooses as a sex partner. What is considered attractive varies considerably, though (Figure 5). For example, the region of the body that is judged for attractiveness varies from one culture to the next. For some peoples, the shape and color of the eyes are especially significant. For others, the shape of the ears is most important. Some societies go directly to the heart of the matter and judge attractiveness by the appearance of the external genitals. In a few societies, elongated labia majora (the pads of fat on either side of the vaginal opening) are considered sexually attractive, and it is common practice for a woman to pull on hers to make them longer. Among the Nawa women of Africa, elongated labia majora are considered a mark of beauty and are quite prominent.

Our society's standards are in the minority in one way: In most cultures, a plump woman is considered more attractive than a thin one.

One standard does seem to be a general rule: A poor complexion is considered unattractive in the majority of human societies.

Research on sexual attraction is discussed in detail in the chapter "Attraction, Love, and Communication."

Social-Class and Ethnic-Group Variations in the United States

The discussion so far may seem to imply that there is one uniform standard of sexual behavior in the United States and that all Americans behave alike sexually. In fact, though, there are large variations in sexual behavior

(a)

(b)

Figure 5 Cross-cultural differences, cross-cultural similarities. (*a*) Woman of West Africa. (*b*) North American beauty queen. The custom of female adornment is found in most cultures, although the exact definition of beauty varies from culture to culture.

(a) ©Nigel Pavitt/Getty Images; (b) ©Getty Images

within our culture. Some of these subcultural variations can be classified as social-class differences and some as ethnic differences.

Social Class and Sex

Table 1 shows data on some social-class variations in sexuality. Education is used as an indicator of social class. The more educated women are, the more likely they are to use the pill for contraception. The differences are dramatic, with college graduates (22 percent) being more than twice as likely as high school graduates (9 percent) to use the pill.

Is sexual behavior similar in all social classes in the United States?

These findings raise the possibility that, especially for women, social class and sexuality exert a mutual influence on each other. That is, thus far we have assumed that one's social class affects one's sexual behaviors. But it may also be true that a person's sexuality influences their social class. In this case, choosing to use an effective method of contraception, the pill, may allow women to continue their education and graduate from college.

In the third line in the table, we can see that the percentage of first premarital cohabitations that transition to marriage is substantially higher for college graduates (53 percent) than it is for those who did not go beyond high school (39 percent). By first premarital cohabitation, we mean the first time a person lived together with a romantic partner, and then whether those two people went on to marry. College graduates have a better than 50 percent chance of that occurring. Those who only graduated from high school have a lower chance, which may mean that they do not go on to marry but continue to cohabit, or perhaps that they cohabit with a second or third partner before marrying.

Finally, there are some social-class similarities in Table 1. The percentage of first marriages for men that are still intact after 20 years hovers around 50 percent for those with less than high school, high school, and some college (although it is somewhat higher for college graduates).

In summary, some social-class variations in sexuality have been found. For example, the percentage of women who use the pill rises steadily with the level of education. At the same time, there are some social-class similarities.

Ethnicity and Sexuality in the United States

The U.S. population is composed of many ethnic groups, and there are some variations among these groups in sexual behavior. These variations are a result of having different cultural heritages, as well as of current economic and social conditions. Here we discuss the cultural heritages and their influence on sexuality of five groups: African Americans, Latinos, Asian Americans, American Indians, and Whites. A summary of some ethnic-group variations in sexuality is shown in Table 2.

In examining these data on ethnic-group variations in sexuality, it is important to keep in mind two points: (1) There are ethnic-group variations, but there are also ethnic-group similarities. The sexuality of these groups is not totally different. (2) Cultural context is the key. The sexuality of any particular group can be understood only by understanding the cultural heritage of that group as well as its current social and economic conditions (Figure 6). The sexuality of white Euro-Americans, for example, is influenced by the heritage of European cultures, such as the Victorian era in England. In the following sections, we briefly discuss the cultural contexts for African Americans, Latinos, Asian Americans, and American Indians and examine how these cultural contexts are reflected in their sexuality.

African Americans. The sexuality of African Americans is influenced by many of the same factors influencing the sexuality of Euro-Americans, such as the legacies of the Victorian era and the influence of the Judeo-Christian tradition. In addition, at least three other factors act to make the sexuality of Blacks somewhat different from that of Whites (Kelly & Shelton, 2013): (1) the African heritage (Staples, 2006), (2) the forces that acted upon Blacks during slavery, and (3) current economic and social conditions. Compared with Whites, Black Americans are

Table 1 Social-Class Variations in Sexuality in the United States (education is used as an indicator of social class).

	Less than High School	High School Graduates	Some College	College Graduates
Women aged 15–44 using the pill	4%	9%	16%	22%
Women whose first union was cohabitation	70%	62%	59%	47%
First premarital cohabitations that transition to marriage	30%	39%	40%	53%
Percent of first marriages for men that are intact at 20 years	54%	47%	54%	65%

Sources: Daniels et al. (2014); Copen et al. (2013); Copen et al. (2012a).

Table 2 Comparison of the Sexuality of Whites, African Americans, Latinos, and Asian Americans

	Whites	African Americans	Latinos/ Latinas	Asian Americans
Gender ratio (number of males per 100 females), 30- to 34-year-olds	100	84	104	101
Percentage of women 15–44 using the pill	19%	10%	11%	NA
Oral sex experience with the opposite sex among females 15–24 years old	69%	63%	59%	NA
Oral sex occurred before first vaginal intercourse, females	49%	27%	37%	NA
Percent who masturbated in the last year, 18- to 24-year-olds				
Women		50%	56%	
Men		54%	89%	
Percent of first marriages intact after 10 years	68%	56%	73%	83%
Abortion rate*	7.6	25.3	16.1	NA

*Abortion rate is the number of abortions per year per 1,000 women in the group (Pazol et al., 2014).

NA means not available.

Sources: U.S. Bureau of the Census (2000a, 2000b); Daniels et al. (2014); Copen et al. (2012a, 2012b); Dodge et al. (2010).

significantly more likely to live in neighborhoods characterized by racial segregation, poverty, and unemployment (Bowleg et al., 2017).

Like other U.S. ethnic groups, Black Americans, who constitute 15 percent of the U.S. population (Rastogi et al., 2011), are not homogeneous. They vary in whether they are of Caribbean origin (Afro-Caribbeans) or are descendants of people brought to the United States as slaves (African Americans); in whether they are rural and southern or urban; and in social class. These variations

are reflected in sexual attitudes. Afro-Caribbeans emphasize sexual propriety and teach girls to be modest; this group tends to view African Americans as morally suspect and sexually undisciplined (Lewis & Kertzner, 2003; Reid & Bing, 2000).

Table 2 shows some data comparing the sexuality of African Americans with Whites, Latinos, and Asian Americans. In some cases, differences between Blacks and Whites are striking. For example, compared with Whites, Blacks are considerably less likely to engage in

(a)

(b)

Figure 6 The sexuality of members of different ethnic groups is profoundly shaped by their cultures. (*a*) Roman Catholicism has a powerful impact on Latinos. (*b*) There is strong emphasis on the family among American Indians.

(a) ©Digital Vision/Getty Images; (b) ©Hill Street Studios/Blend Images LLC

oral sex before the first time they engage in vaginal intercourse. The differences, though, must be balanced against the similarities. For example, Black women are about as likely as White women to engage in oral sex.

The marriage rate is lower for African Americans than for other groups. This is due to a number of factors. First, there is not an equal gender ratio among Blacks. As shown in Table 2, the gender ratio is nearly equal among Whites, Asian Americans, and Latinos; that is, there are about 100 men for every 100 women. Among African Americans, however, there are only about 84 men for every 100 women. This creates lower marriage rates among African American women because there are simply not enough Black men to go around (in the United States, 87 percent of marriages are between two people of the same race [Goodwin et al., 2010]). Second, lower marriage rates among African American men are also due to the obstacles that they have encountered in seeking and maintaining the jobs necessary to support a family. Since World War II, the number of manufacturing jobs, which once were a major source of employment for working-class Black men, has declined dramatically. The result has been a decline in the Black working class and an expansion of the Black underclass.

In later chapters, we discuss other issues having to do with race/ethnicity and sexuality, always bearing in mind the cultural context that shapes and gives meaning to different sexual patterns.

Latinos. **Latinos,** who constitute 16 percent of the U.S. population (Humes et al., 2011), are people of Latin American heritage; therefore, the category includes many different cultural groups, such as Mexican Americans, Puerto Ricans, and Cuban Americans. *Latinos* can refer to the entire group or specifically to men; the term *Latinas* refers exclusively to women of Latin American origin. Some now prefer the term **Latinx,** to get away from the gender designations, while also including people outside the gender binary.

Latinx have a cultural heritage distinct from that of both African Americans and Anglos, although forces such as the Judeo-Christian religious tradition affect all three groups. In traditional Latin American cultures, gender roles are sharply defined (Melendez et al., 2013; Rafaelli & Ontai, 2004). Such roles are emphasized early in the socialization process for children. Boys are given greater freedom and are encouraged in sexual exploits. Girls are expected to be passive, obedient, and weak. Latinx in the United States today have a cultural heritage that blends these traditional cultural values with the contemporary values of the dominant Anglo culture.

The gender roles of traditional Latinx culture are epitomized in the concepts of *machismo* and *marianismo* (Melendez et al., 2013). The term *machismo,* or *macho,* has come to be used loosely in American culture today. Literally, *machismo* means "maleness" or "virility." More generally, it refers to the "mystique of manliness" (Ruth, 1990). The cultural code of *machismo* among Latin Americans mandates that the man must be responsible for the well-being and honor of his family, but in extreme forms it also means tolerating men's sexual infidelities. *Marianismo,* the female counterpart of *machismo,* derives from Roman Catholic worship of Mary, the virgin mother of Jesus. Thus, motherhood is highly valued, whereas virginity until marriage is closely guarded.

Familismo is another important aspect of Latinx culture. This cultural value emphasizes the importance of family—nuclear and extended—in matters such as support, loyalty, solidarity, and family honor (Becker et al., 2014).

Asian Americans. The broad category of Asian Americans includes many different cultural groups, such as Japanese Americans, Chinese Americans, and Indian Americans, as well as the relative newcomer groups such as Vietnamese Americans and the Hmong. Asians constitute 6 percent of the U.S. population (Hoeffel et al., 2012). As discussed in A Sexually Diverse World: Sex in China, traditional Asian cultures, such as the Chinese, have been repressive about sexuality. Traditional Cambodian society, for instance, believed that a lack of information about sexuality would prevent the premarital sex that would tarnish a family's honor (Okazaki, 2002).

Several core Asian values persist in the United States and doubtless affect sexual expression. Among the core values that are relevant to sexuality are the following (Kim et al., 2005):

1. *Collectivism.* Others' needs, especially those of the family, should be considered before one's own. Open expression of some forms of sexuality would represent a threat to the highly interdependent social structure as well as to the family (Okazaki, 2002).

2. *Conformity to norms.* The individual should conform to the expectations of the family and society. Shame and the threat of loss of face, which can apply both to the individual and to their family, are powerful forces shaping good behavior.

3. *Emotional control.* Emotions should not be openly expressed. Emotions such as love or passion should be muted and controlled.

Given all these forces, it is not surprising that Asian Americans today tend to be the sexual conservatives of the various ethnic groups (Meston & Ahrold, 2010). For example, they have the lowest incidence of multiple sexual partners (Laumann et al., 1994; Meston & Ahrold, 2010).

Latinos: People of Latin American heritage.
Latinx: A term for Latinos that gets around the gender designations of Latino and Latina and includes people outside the gender binary.
Familismo: Among Latinx, a strong cultural valuing of one's nuclear and extended family.

American Indians. American Indians, like other U.S. ethnic groups, are diverse among themselves, as a result of the different heritages of more than 500 tribes, such as the Navajo, Hurons, Mohicans, and Cheyenne. In addition, there are distinctions between those who are city dwellers and those who live on reservations (Sarche et al., 2017; Weaver, 1999).

The popular media over the last century have portrayed American Indian men as noble savages who are both exotic and erotic (Bird, 1999). They have been shown nearly naked, emphasizing well-developed masculine bodies. In romance novels of the 1990s, American Indian males became cultural icons for vanishing standards of masculinity. They are handsome and virile, yet tender and vulnerable, and magnificent lovers for White women (Van Lent, 1996).

American Indian women have been less visible in the popular media. When present, they are stereotyped as princesses or squaws (Acoose, 2015; Bird, 1999). The princess is noble, beautiful, and erotic. The Disney animated film *Pocahontas* features such a voluptuous princess. The stereotypical squaw, in contrast, is unattractive, uninteresting, and ignored.

Although traditional American Indian cultures had strict courtship rules that regulated premarital sex, today there is great pressure in the youth culture to have sex (Hellerstedt et al., 2006). In one study of youth in a Northern Plains tribe, 9 percent had first intercourse before age 13, compared with national statistics of 5 percent (Kaufman et al., 2007).

Unfortunately, the major national sex surveys such as those from which Table 2 was drawn have had such small samples of American Indians that they have not been able to report reliable statistics for this group.

Biracial and Multiracial People. Although it is common to think of people falling into one of the four ethnic groups discussed here, there is increasing recognition that many people do not fit into these neat categories. Instead, they are biracial or multiracial, with ancestors from two or more races (Figure 7). Former president Barack Obama is a good example, having had a White American mother and a Black Kenyan father. Recognizing the fact that many people are multiracial, beginning in 2000 the U.S. Census allowed respondents to indicate more than one race for themselves. According to that census, roughly 2 percent of Americans are multiracial.

Racial Microaggressions. Old-fashioned, obvious, overt racism has become rare in the United States. It has been replaced by more subtle forms of prejudiced attitudes and behaviors. **Racial microaggressions** are subtle insults directed at people of color, often done nonconsciously (Sue et al., 2007; Sue, 2010). Members of ethnic minorities in the United States experience them frequently, and they can be a source of stress. Consider the following example.

Figure 7 Although most people like to think of individuals as falling into distinct race categories, there is increasing recognition that many Americans are biracial or multiracial. Meghan Markle, who married Britain's Prince Harry, has an African American mother and a White father.

©*WPA Pool/Getty Images*

Neil Henning, a White professor, had just finished a lecture on Greco-Roman contributions to the history of psychology. He asked for questions. An African American student raised his hand. The student seemed frustrated and said that the history of psychology was ethnocentric and Eurocentric, and that it left out contributions from African, Asian, and Latin American cultures and psychologies.

The professor responded, "Aidan, please calm down. We are studying American psychology. We will eventually address how it has influenced and been adapted to Asian and other societies." (adapted from Sue, 2010, p. 3)

Can you spot the microaggressions? Telling a person to calm down is often an expression of dominance that invalidates the legitimacy of the person's feelings. Then, the professor implied that American psychology was the norm and that it influenced other societies, with no consideration of the possibility that other societies might have developed psychological concepts and principles on their own. All of this was very subtle, though. Aidan undoubtedly felt dissatisfied with the interaction, but it would be difficult for him to say that the professor said something horrible. The subtlety and ambiguity of microaggressions make them even more difficult to deal with.

As we will see in later chapters, the concept of microaggressions also extends to *gender microaggressions, sexual orientation microaggressions,* and *microaggressions against transgender persons.*

> **Racial microaggressions:** Subtle insults directed at people of color and often done nonconsciously.

A Sexually Diverse World

Sex in China

The first 4,000 years of recorded Chinese history were characterized by open, positive attitudes about human sexuality, including a rich erotic literature. Indeed, the oldest sex manuals in the world come from China, dating from approximately 200 B.C.E. The most recent 1,000 years, however, have been just the opposite, characterized by repression of sexuality and censorship.

A major philosophical concept in Chinese culture, yin and yang, originated around 300 B.C.E. and is found in important writings on Confucianism and Taoism. According to the yin-yang philosophy, all objects and events are the products of two elements: yin, which is negative, passive, weak, and destructive; and yang, which is positive, active, strong, and constructive. Yin is associated with the female, yang with the male. For several thousand years, the Chinese have used yin and yang in words dealing with sexuality. For example, *yin fu* (the door of yin) means "vulva," and *yang ju* (the organ of yang) means "penis." *Huo yin yang* (the union of yin and yang) is the term used for sexual intercourse. This philosophy holds that the harmonious interaction between the male and female principles is vital, creating positive cultural attitudes toward sexuality.

Of the three major religions of China—Confucianism, Taoism, and Buddhism—Taoism is the only truly indigenous one, dating from the writings of Chang Ling around 143 C.E. Taoism is one of the few religions to advocate the cultivation of sexual techniques for the benefit of the individual. To quote from a classic Taoist work, *The Canon of the Immaculate Girl,*

> Said P'eng, "One achieves longevity by loving the essence, cultivating the spiritual, and partaking of many kinds of medicines. If you don't know the ways of intercourse, taking herbs is of no benefit. The producing of man and woman is like the begetting of Heaven and Earth. Heaven and Earth have attained the method of intercourse and, therefore, they lack the limitation of finality. Man loses the method of intercourse and therefore suffers the mortification of early death. If you can avoid mortification and injury and attain the arts of sex, you will have found the way of nondeath." (Ruan, 1991, p. 56)

The tradition of erotic literature and openness about sexuality began to change about 1,000 years ago, led by several famous neo-Confucianists, so that negative and repressive attitudes became dominant. In 1422 there was a ban on erotic literature, and a second major ban occurred in 1664. A commoner involved in printing a banned book could be beaten and exiled.

When the communist government founded the People's Republic of China in 1949, it imposed a strict ban on all sexually explicit materials. The policy was quite effective in the 1950s and 1960s. By the late 1960s, however, erotica was being produced much more in Western nations, and in China there was increased openness to the West. By the late 1970s, X-rated videotapes were being smuggled into China from Hong Kong and other countries, and they quickly became a fad. Small parties were organized around the viewing of these tapes. The government reacted harshly, promulgating a new antipornography law in 1985. According to the law, "Pornography is very harmful, poisoning people's minds, inducing crimes . . . and must be banned" (Ruan, 1991, p. 100). Publishing houses that issued pornography were given stiff fines, and by 1986, 217 illegal publishers had been arrested and 42 forced to close. In one incident, a Shanghai railway station employee was sentenced to death for having organized sex parties on nine different occasions, during which pornographic videotapes were viewed and he engaged in sexual activity with women.

Male homosexuality is recognized in historical writings in China as early as 2,000 years ago. Homosexuality was then so widespread among the upper classes that the period is known as the Golden Age of Homosexuality in China. One historical book on the Han dynasty contained a special section describing the emperors' male sexual partners. There were also tolerant attitudes toward lesbianism. But with the founding of the People's Republic in 1949, homosexuality, like all other sexuality, was severely repressed. Most Chinese in the 1980s claimed that they had never known a homosexual and argued that there must be very few in Chinese society.

In the early 1980s, China was characterized by a puritanism that probably far exceeded that observed by the original Puritans. It was considered scandalous for a married couple to hold hands in public. Prostitution, premarital sex, homosexuality, and variant sexual behaviors were all illegal, and the laws were enforced. Even sexuality in marriage was given little encouragement.

A moderate sexual liberation began in the 1980s and continues today, sparked in part by increased access to sexual media and in part by government policies demanding contraception, which open the door to premarital sex without the worry of pregnancy. Open displays of affection, such as holding hands in public, are now no longer treated as signs of promiscuity. High schools now include sex education in the curriculum. The rationale is that a scientific understanding of sexual development is essential to the healthy development of young people and to the maintenance of high moral standards and well-controlled social order. Yet the Chinese international students in our classes tell us that sex education in reality is nearly nonexistent in China.

Noted American sex researcher Edward Laumann has extended his surveys to China (Laumann & Parish, 2004; Parish et al., 2007; Table 3). The results indicate that the liberalizing trends are occurring mainly in the larger cities, whereas the majority of Chinese live in more rural areas that are still extremely conservative. In regard to premarital sex, only 16 percent of men and 5 percent of women from the older generation say that they engaged in it, compared with 31 percent of men and 14 percent of women today. These rates are still low compared with Western nations such as the United States. For extramarital sex, 4.5 percent of women engaged in it in the past 12 months, as had 11 percent of men in noncommercial and 5.5 percent of men in commercial sex (Zhang et al., 2012). These rates are similar to those reported in many other nations. It will be interesting to see whether liberalization continues or an eventual swing back to repression occurs.

A 2016 report, in cooperation with the United Nations, tells a less optimistic tale about the status of LGBT people in China ("Being LGBTI in China," 2016). The report documents repression and discrimination: "Sexual and gender minority people in China still live in the shadows, with only 5% of them willing to live their diversity openly." They continue to face marked discrimination, especially within the family, where they may be forced into heterosexual relationships. Yet, at the same time,

Table 3	Contemporary Data on Sex in China: A Liberalizing Trend	
	Older Cohort*	Current Cohort*
Percent who masturbated by age 23		
Men	31%	52%
Women	3	8
Percent who engaged in premarital sex		
Men	16	31
Women	5	14
Percent who viewed pornographic materials in the last year		
Men	13	74
Women	6	37

* "Older cohort" refers to those who turned 20 before 1980 and therefore grew up in the conservative culture of the time. "Current cohort" refers to those who turned 20 after 1980 and therefore grew up in the era of liberalization.

Source: Parish et al. (2007).

the general population is beginning to show attitudes that are less negative, but most are uninformed about LGBT people.

Sources: Evans (1995); Jeffreys (2006); Parish et al. (2007); Ruan (1991); Ruan & Lau (1998); Zhang et al. (2012); "Being LGBTI in China" (2016).

The Significance of Cross-Cultural Studies

What relevance do cross-cultural data have to an understanding of human sexuality? They are important for two basic reasons. First, they give us a notion of the enormous variation that exists in human sexual behavior, and they help us put our own standards and behavior in perspective. Second, these studies provide impressive evidence concerning the importance of culture and learning in the shaping of our sexual behavior; they show us that human sexual behavior is not completely determined by biology or drives or instincts. For example, a woman of Inis Beag and a woman of Mangaia presumably have vaginas that

are similarly constructed and clitorises that are approximately the same size and have the same nerve supply. But the woman of Inis Beag never has an orgasm, and all Mangaian women orgasm.[3] Why? Their cultures are different, and they and their partners learned different things about sex as they were growing up. Culture is a major determinant of human sexual behavior.

[3]We like to use the word *orgasm* not only as a noun but also as a verb. The reason is that alternative expressions, such as "to *achieve* orgasm" and "to *reach* orgasm," reflect the tendency of Americans to make sex an achievement situation (an idea to be discussed further in the chapter "Sexual Arousal"). To avoid this, we use "to have an orgasm" or "to orgasm."

The point of studying sexuality in different cultures is *not* to teach that there are a lot of exotic people out there doing exotic things. Rather, the point is to remind ourselves that each group has its own culture, and this culture has a profound influence on the sexual expression of the people who grow up in it. We offer more examples in many of the chapters that follow.

Cross-Species Perspectives on Sexuality

Humans are just one of many animal species, and all of them display sexual behavior. To put our own sexual behavior in evolutionary perspective, it is helpful to explore the similarities and differences between our own sexuality and that of other species.

There is one other reason for this particular discussion. Some people classify sexual behaviors as "natural" or "unnatural," depending on whether other species do or do not exhibit those behaviors. Sometimes, though, the data are twisted to suit the purposes of the person making the argument, so there is a need for a less biased view. Let's see exactly what some other species do.

Is homosexuality found in other species?

Masturbation

Humans are definitely not the only species that masturbates. Masturbation is found among many species of mammals, particularly among the primates (monkeys and apes). Male monkeys and apes in zoos can be observed masturbating, often to the horror of the proper folk who have come to see them. At one time it was thought that this behavior might be the result of the unnatural living conditions of zoos. However, observations of free-living primates indicate that they, too, masturbate. Techniques include hand stimulation of the genitals or rubbing the genitals against an object. In terms of technique, monkeys and nonhuman apes have one advantage over humans: Their bodies are so flexible that they can perform mouth–genital sex on themselves.

Female masturbation is also found among many species beside our own. The prize for the most inventive technique probably should go to the female porcupine. She holds one end of a stick in her paws and walks around while straddling the stick; as the stick bumps against the ground, it vibrates against her genitals (Ford & Beach, 1951). Human females are apparently not the only ones to enjoy vibrators.

Same-Gender Sexual Behavior

Same-gender behavior is found in many species beside our own (Bagemihl, 1999; Leca et al., 2014; Vasey, 2002; Figure 8a). Indeed, observations of other species indicate that our basic mammalian heritage is bisexual, composed of both heterosexual and homosexual elements (Bagemihl, 1999).

Males of many species will mount other males, and anal intercourse has been observed in some male primates (Wallen & Parsons, 1997). Among domestic sheep, 9 percent of adult males strongly prefer other males as sex partners (Ellis, 1996; Roselli et al., 2002). In a number of primate species, including bonobos and Japanese macaques, females mount other females (Leca et al., 2015; Vasey & Jiskoot, 2010).

Sexual Signaling

Female primates engage in sexual signaling to males, in effect, flirting (Dixson, 1990; Figure 8b). For example, females in one species of macaque engage in parading in front of males to signal their interest. Among baboons, spider monkeys, and orangutans, the female makes eye contact with the male. The female patas monkey puffs out her cheeks and drools. The parading and eye contact sound very familiar—they could easily be observed among women at a singles bar. The puffing and drooling probably wouldn't play as well, though.

Human Uniqueness

Are humans in any ways unique in their sexual behavior? The general trend, as we move from lower species such as fish or rodents to higher ones such as primates, is for sexual behavior to be more hormonally (instinctively) controlled among the lower species and to be controlled more by the brain (and therefore by learning and social context) in the higher species (Beach, 1947; Wallen, 2001). Thus, environmental influences are much more important in shaping primate—especially human—sexual behavior than they are in shaping the sexual behavior of other species.

An illustration of this fact is provided by studies of the adult sexual behavior of animals raised in deprived environments. If mice are reared in isolation, their adult sexual behavior will nonetheless be normal (Scott, 1964). But if rhesus monkeys are reared in isolation, their adult sexual behavior is severely disturbed, to the point where they may be incapable of reproducing (Harlow et al., 1963). Thus, environmental experiences are crucial in shaping the sexual behavior of higher species, particularly humans; for us, sexual behavior is a lot more than just "doin' what comes naturally."

Female sexuality provides a particularly good illustration of the shift in hormonal control from lower to higher species. Throughout most of the animal kingdom, female sexual behavior is strongly controlled by hormones. In

(a)   (b)

Figure 8   (*a*) Same-gender sexuality in animals: Two male giraffes "necking." They rub necks and become aroused. (*b*) The sexual behavior of primates: Females have various ways of expressing choice. Here a female Barbary macaque presents her sexual swelling to a male. He seems to be interested.

(a) ©Thomas Michael Corcoran/PhotoEdit; (b) ©Meredith F. Small

virtually all mammals, females do not engage in sexual behavior at all except when they are in "heat" (estrus), which is a particular hormonal state. In contrast, human females are capable of engaging in sexual behavior—and actually do engage in it—during any phase of their hormonal (menstrual) cycle. Thus, the sexual behavior of human females is not nearly as much under hormonal control as that of females of other species.

Traditionally it was thought that female orgasm is unique to humans and does not exist in other species. Then some studies found evidence of orgasm in rhesus macaques (monkeys), as indicated by the same physiological responses indicative of orgasm in human females—specifically, increased heart rate and uterine contractions (Burton, 1970; Goldfoot et al., 1980; Zumpe & Michael, 1968). Humans can no longer claim to have a corner on the female orgasm market. This fact has interesting implications for understanding the evolution of sexuality. Perhaps the higher species, in which the females are not driven to sexual activity by their hormones, have the pleasure of orgasm as an incentive.

In summary, there is little in human sexuality that is completely unique to humans, except for elaborate, complex cultural influences. In other respects, we are on a continuum with other species.

The Nonsexual Uses of Sexual Behavior

Two male baboons are locked in combat. One begins to emerge as the victor. The other "presents" (the "female"

sexual posture, in which the rump is directed toward the other and is elevated).

Two male monkeys are members of the same troop. Long ago they established which one is dominant and which subordinate. The dominant one mounts (the "male" sexual behavior) the subordinate one.

These are examples of animals sometimes using sexual behavior for nonsexual purposes (Small, 1993; Wallen & Zehr, 2004). Commonly such behavior signals the end of a fight, as in the first example. The loser indicates his surrender by presenting, and the winner signals victory by mounting. Sexual behaviors can also symbolize an animal's rank in a dominance hierarchy. Dominant animals mount subordinate ones. As another example, male squirrel monkeys sometimes use an exhibitionist display of their erect penis as part of an aggressive display against another male in a phenomenon called *phallic aggression* (Wickler, 1973).

All this is perfectly obvious when we observe it in monkeys. But do humans ever use sexual behavior for nonsexual purposes? Consider the rapist, who uses sex as an expression of aggression against and power over a woman (Zurbriggen, 2010), or over another man in the case of same-gender rape. Another example is the exhibitionist, who uses the display of his erect penis to shock and frighten women, much as the male squirrel monkey uses such a display to shock and frighten his opponent. Humans also use sex for economic purposes; the best examples are male and female prostitutes.

There are also less extreme examples. Consider the couple who have a fight and then make love to signal an end to the hostilities.[4] Or consider the woman who goes to bed with an influential—though unattractive—politician because this gives her a vicarious sense of power.

You can probably think of other examples of the nonsexual use of sexual behavior. Humans, just like members of other species, can use sex for a variety of nonsexual purposes.

The Sexual Health Perspective

The important new concepts of sexual health and sexual rights provide yet another broad and thought-provoking perspective on sexuality. **Sexual health** is a social and political movement that is gaining momentum worldwide. Although many discussions of sexual health are about sexual disease, such as HIV infection, sexual health is a much broader concept that involves a vision of positive sexual health (Edwards & Coleman, 2004; Parker et al., 2004). The World Health Organization (WHO) definition is as follows:

> Sexual health is a state of physical, emotional, mental and social well-being in relation to sexuality; it is not merely the absence of disease, dysfunction or infirmity. Sexual health requires a positive and respectful approach to sexuality and sexual relationships, as well as the possibility of having pleasurable and safe sexual experiences, free of coercion, discrimination and violence. For sexual health to be attained and maintained, the sexual rights of all persons must be respected, protected and fulfilled. (World Health Organization, 2006)

Notice that this definition includes not only sexual physical health but also sexual mental health and positive sexual relationships. Therefore, public health efforts to prevent HIV or chlamydia infection, programs to enhance romantic relationships, and activism to end discrimination and violence against gays and lesbians all fall under the umbrella of sexual health. Notice also that the definition includes both negative and positive rights. Negative rights are freedoms *from*—for example, freedom from sexual violence. Positive rights are freedoms *to*—for example, freedom to experience sexual pleasure or to express one's sexuality with same-gender partners.

With the growth of the sexual health movement, the concept of **sexual rights** has also come to center stage; in fact, the term is used in the WHO definition. The idea here is that all human beings have certain basic, inalienable rights regarding sexuality, just as in America's Declaration of Independence the writers asserted that all people have the right to life, liberty, and the pursuit of happiness (that last one is interesting in the context of sexuality, wouldn't you say?). The question then is, What are humans' basic sexual rights? The principles are new and evolving, but they generally include elements such as a right to reproductive self-determination and freedom from sexual abuse and sexual violence, as well as the right to sexual self-expression (provided, of course, that it doesn't interfere with someone else's sexual rights) (Sandfort & Ehrhardt, 2004). Some would argue that same-sex marriage, in this context, is a basic sexual right, and these arguments are gaining momentum worldwide. Argentina, Australia, Belgium, Canada, France, the Netherlands, Spain, and now the United States are among the nations offering a legally recognized relationship for both heterosexual and same-gender couples. And South Africa's constitution of 1996 bars discrimination on the basis of sexual orientation (Parker et al., 2004).

Sexual health: A state of physical, emotional, mental, and social well-being in relation to sexuality.

Sexual rights: Basic, inalienable rights regarding sexuality, both positive and negative, such as rights to reproductive self-determination and sexual self-expression and freedom from sexual abuse and violence.

---

[4]It has been our observation that this practice may not always mean the same thing to the man and the woman. To the man it can mean that everything is fine again, but the woman can be left feeling dissatisfied and not at all convinced that the issues are resolved. Thus, this situation can be a source of miscommunication between the two.

An introduction to critical thinking

In this and all other chapters in this textbook, you will find boxes labeled CRITICAL THINKING SKILL. Each of these boxes is designed to improve your critical thinking skills as applied to sexuality, but the skills you learn will be useful in many other areas of life.

According to Diane Halpern, an expert in critical thinking,

> *Critical thinking* is the use of those cognitive skills or strategies that increases the probability of a desirable outcome. It is purposeful, reasoned, and goal directed. It is the kind of thinking involved in solving problems, formulating inferences, calculating likelihoods, and making decisions. . . . Critical thinking also involves evaluating the thinking process—the reasoning that went into the conclusion we have arrived at or the kinds of factors considered in making a decision. (Halpern, 2002, p. 93)

Critical thinking is logical, rational, and free of self-deception. Critical thinking is also an attitude that people carry with them into situations, a belief that can and should be used to make better decisions. Over time, those with excellent critical thinking skills should experience better outcomes (e.g., making a good career choice or making a good decision about where to live) compared with those who have poor critical thinking skills (Halpern, 1998).

For these reasons, colleges and universities believe that it is important for students to improve their critical thinking skills. Those skills are also increasingly important in the world of work, as our industrial, manufacturing economy has been replaced by a knowledge-based economy, and the ability to evaluate information carefully is a major asset.

In each chapter of this textbook, you will find boxes called CRITICAL THINKING SKILL. Each teaches a particular critical thinking skill with an application in sexuality, but each skill will have applications throughout your life. Here's to better critical thinking by all of us!

Understanding that other cultures think differently about some issues

One way to improve critical thinking skills is to understand that some cultures have different ideas about certain issues than we have in our culture. This cross-cultural view widens our perspective and helps us to think more rationally about unspoken assumptions in our culture. For example, in the Netherlands, the schools are expected to provide comprehensive sexuality education to children. One of their programs is Long Live Love, developed for 13- to 15-year-olds (Schutte et al., 2014). Moreover, the Netherlands has a low rate of teen pregnancy, much lower than in the United States. Many factors are involved in the low teen pregnancy rate in the Netherlands, and experts believe that an important one is the excellent sexuality education provided by the schools.

How does knowing about these practices apply to how we do things in the United States? For example, some religious groups and some parents object to sexuality education in the schools. How would that debate change if we looked at how things are done in the Netherlands?

SUMMARY

Sex and Gender

Sexual behavior is activity that produces arousal and increases the chance of orgasm. Sex (sexual behavior and anatomy) is distinct from gender (being male or female or some other gender such as genderqueer).

The History of Understanding Sexuality: Religion and Science

Historically, the main sources of sexual information were religion and, beginning in the late 1800s, science. Important early sex researchers were Sigmund Freud, Havelock Ellis, Richard von Krafft-Ebing, and Magnus Hirschfeld, all emerging from the rigid Victorian era. By the 1990s, major, well-conducted sex surveys were available.

The Media

Today, the mass media—whether television, magazines, or the Internet—carry extensive portrayals of sexuality and are a powerful influence on most people's understanding of sexuality. The mass media may have an influence through cultivation, framing, social learning, and reinforcing spirals.

Cross-Cultural Perspectives on Sexuality

Studies of various human cultures around the world provide evidence of enormous variations in human sexual behavior. Frequency of intercourse may vary from once a week in some cultures to three or four times a night in others. Attitudes regarding premarital and extramarital sex, masturbation, same-gender sexual behavior, and gender roles vary considerably across cultures. Within the United States, sexual behavior varies with social class and ethnic group. These great variations provide evidence of the importance of learning and culture in shaping sexual behavior. Yet all societies regulate sexual behavior in some way.

Cross-Species Perspectives on Sexuality

Studies of sexual behavior in various animal species show that masturbation, mouth–genital stimulation, and same-gender sexual behavior are by no means limited to humans. In many species, sexual behavior may be used for nonsexual purposes, such as expressing dominance.

The Sexual Health Perspective

A new international movement focuses on sexual health and the principles of sexual rights.

SUGGESTIONS FOR FURTHER READING

Bagemihl, Bruce. (1999). *Biological exuberance: Animal homosexuality and natural diversity.* New York: St. Martin's. The author documents the blindness of scientists to the same-gender sexual behavior they observed and at the same time catalogs the extensiveness of same-gender behaviors in hundreds of species.

Gregersen, Edgar. (1996). *The world of human sexuality.* New York: Irvington. Gregersen, an anthropologist, has compiled a vast amount of information about sexuality in cultures around the world. The book also includes a treasure trove of fascinating illustrations.

Lutz, Deborah. (2011). *Pleasure bound: Victorian sex rebels and the new eroticism.* New York: Norton. Historian Lutz documents Victorian antisex norms, as well as those who rebelled against them.

Staples, Robert. (2006). *Exploring Black sexuality.* New York: Rowman & Littlefield. Staples, considered the dean of Black family studies, writes authoritatively about topics such as the myth of Black sexual superiority.

Zuk, Marlene. (2002). *Sexual selections: What we can and can't learn about sex from animals.* Berkeley: University of California Press. Zuk, a biologist, carefully analyzes what can be inferred from studies of the sexual behavior of animals.

Are YOU Curious?

1. Is the heterosexual male preference for the "hourglass" female figure universal?

2. What theory accounts for how the smell of perfume or cologne becomes sexually arousing?

3. Why do most sexual interactions in our society follow the same patterns?

Read this chapter to find out.

CHAPTER **2**

Theoretical Perspectives on Sexuality

CHAPTER HIGHLIGHTS

Evolutionary Theories
Sociobiology
Evolutionary Psychology
Gender-Neutral Evolutionary Theory

Psychological Theories
Psychoanalytic Theory
Learning Theory
Social Exchange Theory
Cognitive Theories

Critical Theories
Feminist Theory
Queer Theory

Sociological Perspectives
Symbolic Interaction Theory
Sexual Scripts
Social Institutions

One of the discoveries of psychoanalysis consists in the assertion that impulses, which can only be described as sexual in both the narrower and the wider sense, play a peculiarly large part, never before sufficiently appreciated, in the causation of nervous and mental disorders. Nay, more, that these sexual impulses have contributed invaluably to the highest cultural, artistic, and social achievements of the human mind.*

From an evolutionary perspective, no single decision is more important than the choice of a mate. That single fork in the road determines one's ultimate reproductive fate.†

*Sigmund Freud. (1924). *A General Introduction to Psychoanalysis.* New York: Permabooks, 1953. (Boni & Liveright edition, 1924). pp. 26–27.
†Buss (2000), p. 10.

Imagine, for a moment, that you are sitting in a bedroom, watching two people making love. Imagine, too, that sitting with you in the room, thinking your same thoughts, are Sigmund Freud (creator of psychoanalytic theory), E. O. Wilson (a leading sociobiologist), Albert Bandura (a prominent social learning theorist), and John Gagnon (a proponent of script theory). The scene you are imagining may evoke arousal and nothing more in you, but your imaginary companions would have a rich set of additional thoughts as they viewed the scene through the specially colored lenses of their own theoretical perspectives. Freud might be marveling at how the biological sex drive, the *libido,* expresses itself so strongly and directly in this couple. Wilson, the sociobiologist, would be thinking how mating behavior in humans is similar to such behavior in other species of animals and how it is clearly the product of evolutionary selection for behaviors that lead to successful reproduction. Bandura might be thinking how sexual arousal and orgasm act as powerful positive reinforcers that will lead the couple to repeat the act frequently and how they are imitating a technique of neck nibbling that they saw in a film last week. Finally, Gagnon's thoughts might be about the social scripting of sexuality; this couple begins with kissing, moves on to petting, and finishes up with intercourse, following a script written by society.

Some of the major theories in the social sciences have had many—and different—things to say about sexuality, and it is these theories that we consider in this chapter. Theories provide us with answers to the question "why?" We often wonder why others do or do not engage in particular sexual behaviors and relationships. We sometimes ask the "why" question about our own sexuality. Given the diversity in human sexuality, we need a range of theories to understand it.

Evolutionary Theories

Sociobiology

Sociobiology is defined as the application of evolutionary biology to understanding the social behavior of animals, including humans (Barash, 1982). Sexual behavior is, of course, a form of social behavior, and so the sociobiologists try, often through observations of other species, to understand why certain patterns of sexual behavior have evolved in humans.

In terms of **evolution,** what counts is producing lots of healthy, viable offspring who will carry on one's genes. Evolution occurs via **natural selection,** the process by which the animals that are best adapted to their environment are more likely to survive, reproduce, and pass on their genes to the next generation.

How do humans choose mates? One major criterion is the physical attractiveness of the person (see the chapter "Attraction, Love, and Communication"). The sociobiologist argues that many of the characteristics we evaluate in judging attractiveness—for example, physique and complexion—are indicative of the health and vigor of the individual. These in turn are probably related to the person's reproductive potential; the unhealthy are less likely to produce many vigorous offspring. Natural selection would favor individuals preferring mates who would have maximum reproductive success. Thus, perhaps our concern with physical attractiveness is a product of evolution and natural selection. (See Barash, 1982, for an extended discussion of this point and the ones that follow.) We choose an attractive, healthy mate who will help us produce many offspring. Can you guess why it is that the

Sociobiology: The application of evolutionary biology to understanding the social behavior of animals, including humans.
Evolution: A theory that all living things have acquired their present forms through gradual changes in their genetic endowment over successive generations.
Natural selection: A process in nature resulting in greater rates of survival of those plants and animals that are best adapted to their environment.

sociobiologist thinks most men are attracted to women with large breasts?

If attractiveness is an indicator of health, it should be more important in mate selection in societies where more people are unhealthy. An online survey obtained ratings of the attractiveness of images of male faces from women ages 21 to 40 from 30 countries. Facial masculinity, manipulated by computer, had more impact on attractiveness ratings in countries with poorer health, as measured by mortality, life expectancy, and communicable disease (DeBruine et al., 2010).

From this viewpoint, dating, playing sports, getting engaged, and similar customs are much like the courtship rituals of other species (see Figure 1). For example, many falcons and eagles have a flying courtship in which objects are exchanged between the pair in midair. The sociobiologist views this courtship as an opportunity for each member of the prospective couple to assess the other's fitness. For example, any lack of speed or coordination would be apparent during the airborne acrobatics. Evolution would favor courtship patterns that permitted individuals to choose mates who would increase their reproductive success. Perhaps that is exactly what we are doing in our human courtship rituals. The expenditure of money by men on dates indicates their ability to support a family. Dancing permits the assessment of physical prowess, and so on.

Sociobiologists have an explanation for why the family structure of a man, a woman, and their offspring is found in every society. Once a man and a woman mate, there are several obstacles to reproductive success, two being infant vulnerability and maternal death. Infant vulnerability is greatly reduced if the mother provides continuing physical care, including breast-feeding. It is further reduced if the father provides resources and security from attack for mother and infant. Two mechanisms that facilitate these conditions are a *pair-bond* between mother and father and *attachment* between infant and parent (Miller & Fishkin, 1997). Thus, an offspring's chances of survival are greatly increased if the parents bond emotionally, that is, love each other, and if the parents have a propensity for attachment. Further, an emotional bond might lead to more frequent sexual interaction; the pleasure of sex in turn will reinforce the bond. Research with small mammals, including mice and moles, demonstrates the advantages of biparental care of offspring and the critical role of bonding (Morell, 1998).

(a)   *(b)*

Figure 1   *(a)* The courtship rituals of great egrets. *(b)* Dancing is a human dating custom. According to sociobiologists, human customs of dating and becoming engaged are biologically produced and serve the same functions as courtship rituals in other species: They allow potential mates to assess each other's fitness.

According to this theory, parents are most interested in the survival and reproductive success of their genetic offspring. **Parental investment** refers to behaviors or other resources invested in the offspring by the parent that increase the offspring's chance of survival. Because of the high rates of divorce and remarriage in the United States, many men have both biological children and stepchildren. This situation leads to the prediction that men will tend to invest more in their genetic children than in their stepchildren. Research indicates that fathers invest the most money on the genetic children of their current union and the least money on stepchildren from a past relationship. However, they spend an equal amount on their genetic children and the stepchildren of their current relationship, perhaps to cement the pair-bond with their current partner (Anderson et al., 2001).

In addition to natural selection, Darwin also proposed a mechanism that is not as much a household word, sexual selection (Buss, 2009; Gangestad & Thornhill, 1997). **Sexual selection** is selection that creates differences between males and females. It consists of two processes: (1) competition among members of one gender (usually males) for mating access to members of the other gender, and (2) preferential choice by members of one gender (usually females) for certain members of the other gender. In other words, in many—though not all (Clutton-Brock, 2007)—species, males compete among themselves for the right to mate with females; and females, for their part, prefer certain males and mate with them while refusing to mate with other males. Researchers have tested with humans some of the predictions that come from the theory of sexual selection. For example, the theory predicts that men should compete with each other in ways that involve displaying material resources that should be attractive to women, and men should engage in these displays more than women do (Buss, 1988). Examples might be giving impressive gifts to potential mates, flashy showing of possessions (e.g., cars), or displaying personality characteristics that are likely to lead to the acquisition of resources (e.g., ambition). Research shows that men engage in these behaviors significantly more than women do, and that both men and women believe these tactics are effective (Buss, 1988).

Many criticisms of sociobiology have been made. Some critics object to the biological determinism that it implies. Also, sociobiology has been criticized for resting on an outmoded version of evolutionary theory that modern biologists consider naive (Gould, 1987). For example, sociobiology has focused mainly on the individual's struggle for survival and efforts to reproduce; modern biologists focus on more complex issues such as the survival of the group and the

species. Furthermore, sociobiologists assume that the central function of sex is reproduction; this may have been true historically but is not true today (Meston & Buss, 2007). Recent research does not support some of the evidence that is widely cited in support of the theory. One sociobiologist reported that the winners of the Miss America contest and *Playboy*'s centerfold models have consistently had a waist-to-hip ratio of .7, arguing that this reflects a universal standard related to reproductive fitness (Singh, 1993). A closer look at the data shows that the average for Miss America winners has steadily declined since 1921, from .78 to .64 in 1986, contradicting the claim that a preference for .70 was hardwired by evolution thousands of years ago (Freese & Meland, 2002). Research analyzing waist-to-hip ratios across a large number of cultures, Western and non-Western, finds that the .7 ratio is most common in societies where women are economically dependent on men (not all cultures, as the theory asserts) (Cashdan, 2008).

Is the heterosexual male preference for the "hourglass" female figure universal?

Evolutionary Psychology

A somewhat different approach is taken by **evolutionary psychology,** which focuses on psychological mechanisms that have been shaped by evolution (Buss, 1991). If behaviors evolved in response to selection pressures, it is plausible to argue that cognitive or emotional structures evolved in the same way. Thus, a man who accurately judged whether a woman was healthy and fertile would be more successful in reproducing. If his offspring exhibited the same ability to judge accurately, they in turn would have a competitive advantage.

One line of research has concentrated on *sexual strategies* (Buss & Schmitt, 1993). According to this theory, women and men face different adaptive problems in short-term, or casual, mating and in long-term mating and reproduction. These differences lead to different strategies, or behaviors, designed to solve these problems. In short-term mating, a woman may choose a partner who offers her immediate resources, such as food or money. In long-term mating, a woman may choose a partner who appears able and willing to provide resources for the indefinite future. A man may choose a sexually available woman for a short-term liaison but avoid such women when looking for a long-term mate.

According to the theory, females engage in intrasexual competition for access to males. Women pursuing a long-term strategy should respond negatively to women who make sex easily available to men (a "slut"?). An experimental study found that undergraduate women reacted negatively to a female confederate dressed sexily (cleavage, very short skirt), but not to the same person

---

Parental investment: In evolutionary theories, behaviors or other investments in the offspring by the parent that increase the offspring's chance of survival.
Sexual selection: A specific type of selection that creates differences between males and females.
Evolutionary psychology: The study of psychological mechanisms that have been shaped by evolution.

engaging in the same behavior dressed in a loose shirt and jeans (Vaillancourt & Aanchai, 2011). On the other hand, females pursuing a short-term strategy want to appear sexy. Women at ovulation chose sexier and more revealing clothing from an online catalog than they did 3 or more days before or 7 days after ovulation (Durante et al., 2011).

Buss (1994) and others have reported data that support a number of specific predictions based on this theory. However, other research using the same measures with both men and women, and controlling for confounding effects, finds that men and women are very similar in their stated mating preferences. Both prefer long-term strategies and few or no short-term partners (Pedersen et al., 2002). Another criticism of evolutionary psychology is that it assumes that every characteristic that we observe must have some adaptive significance, but in fact some human traits may be simply "design flaws" (de Waal, 2002).

Evolutionary psychology is based on assumptions about what the ancestral environment was like. Although we can't study it directly, we can study very traditional societies such as the Ache and Mayan. Research on male sexual strategies in these two societies finds that male strategies are not constant but change in response to personal characteristics and environmental contingencies (Waynforth et al., 1998).

Critics also question the data used to support much of the research. These theories claim that the processes and behaviors are the result of human evolution, and therefore universal, but most of the data testing them comes from WEIRD (Western, Educated, Industrialized, Rich, Democratic) societies (Henrich et al., 2010). We don't know whether these results can be applied to people in other societies. Further, tests of sexual strategies theory rely heavily on data from undergraduates at four-year colleges and universities; note this criticism applies to research testing other theories as well.

Gender-Neutral Evolutionary Theory

Evolutionary biologist Patricia Gowaty of UCLA has proposed a gender-neutral evolutionary theory that offers an alternative to sociobiology and evolutionary psychology (Gowaty, 2018; Gowaty & Hubbell, 2009). Gowaty is critical of sociobiology's and evolutionary psychology's argument that biology is destiny—that evolution over millions of years has determined our behavior and, in particular, has determined gender differences in behavior. Gowaty notes that the environments in which humans—and other species—find themselves vary enormously, both across geographical spaces and across an individual's lifetime. It is therefore not in the least adaptive for humans to display fixed behaviors determined by evolution. Neither should there be fixed gender differences in behavior.

Instead, it is most adaptive for individuals to be flexible in their behaviors, and that is exactly what evolution has

selected for—flexibility and adaptability. An individual may behave in ways that are more male-typical in some situations and more female-typical in others because different behaviors are adaptive in those different situations. Likewise, a fixed mating strategy for females (or males) would not be adaptive across numerous environments. Instead, a flexible mating strategy would be most successful.

The evidence for this theory, at least so far, is based on mathematical modeling and proofs that show that individuals who can and do change their mating behaviors in adaptive ways depending on the environment have the best reproductive fitness—are the most likely to mate successfully. Beyond that, the theory is too new to be able to evaluate it thoroughly. Notice, though, that it is a theory that can accommodate transgender individuals because the theory does not insist on fixed male and female behaviors.

Psychological Theories

Four of the major theories in psychology are relevant to sexuality: psychoanalytic theory, learning theory, social exchange theory, and cognitive theory.

Psychoanalytic Theory

Sigmund Freud's **psychoanalytic theory** has been one of the most influential of all psychological theories. Because Freud saw sex as one of the key forces in human life, his theory has much to say about human sexuality.

Freud termed the sex drive or sex energy **libido,** which he saw as one of the two major forces motivating human behavior (the other being *thanatos,* or the death instinct).

Id, Ego, and Superego

Freud described the human personality as being divided into three major parts: the id, the ego, and the superego. The **id** is the basic part of personality and is present at birth. It is the reservoir of psychic energy (including libido), and it operates on the *pleasure principle*.

Whereas the id operates only on the pleasure principle and can thus be pretty irrational, the **ego** operates on the *reality principle* and tries to keep the id in line. The ego functions to make the person have realistic, rational interactions with others.

Finally, the **superego** is the conscience. It contains the values and ideals of society that we learn, and it operates on *idealism*. Thus, its

Psychoanalytic theory: A psychological theory originated by Sigmund Freud; it contains a basic assumption that part of human personality is unconscious.
Libido (lih-BEE-doh): In psychoanalytic theory, the term for the sex energy or sex drive.
Id: According to Freud, the part of the personality containing the libido.
Ego: According to Freud, the part of the personality that helps the person have realistic, rational interactions.
Superego: According to Freud, the part of the personality containing the conscience.

aim is to inhibit the impulses of the id and to persuade the ego to strive for moral goals rather than just realistic ones.

To illustrate the operation of these three components of the personality in a sexual situation, consider the case of the CEO of a corporation who is at a meeting of the board of directors; the meeting is also attended by her handsome, buff colleague, Mr. Hunk. She looks at Mr. Hunk, and her id says, "I want to throw him on the table and make love to him immediately. Let's do it!" The ego intervenes and says, "We can't do it now because the other members of the board are also here. Let's wait until 5 P.M., when they're all gone, and then do it." The superego says, "I shouldn't make love to Mr. Hunk at all because I'm a married woman." What actually happens? It depends on the relative strengths of this woman's id, ego, and superego.

The id, ego, and superego develop sequentially. The id contains the set of instincts present at birth. The ego develops later, as the child learns how to interact realistically with their environment and the people in it. The superego develops last, as the child learns moral values.

Erogenous Zones

Freud saw the libido as being focused in various regions of the body known as **erogenous zones.** An erogenous zone is a part of the skin or mucous membrane that is extremely sensitive to stimulation; touching it in certain ways produces feelings of pleasure. The lips and mouth are one such erogenous zone, the genitals a second, and the rectum and anus a third.

Stages of Psychosexual Development

Freud believed that the child passes through a series of stages of development. In each of these stages a different erogenous zone is the focus.

The first stage, lasting from birth to about 1 year of age, is the *oral stage.* The child's chief pleasure is derived from sucking and otherwise stimulating the lips and mouth. Anyone who has observed children of this age knows how they delight in putting anything they can into their mouths. The second stage, which occurs during approximately the second year of life, is the *anal stage.* During this stage, the child's interest is focused on elimination.

The third stage of development, lasting from age 3 to perhaps age 5 or 6, is the *phallic stage.* The boy's interest is focused on his phallus (penis), and he derives great pleasure from masturbating.[1] Perhaps the most important occurrence in this stage is the development of the **Oedipus complex,** which derives its name from the Greek story of Oedipus, who unknowingly killed his father and married his mother. In the Oedipus complex, the boy loves his mother and desires her sexually. He hates his father, whom he sees as a rival for the mother's affection. The boy's hostility toward his father grows, but eventually he comes to fear that his father will retaliate by castrating him—cutting off his prized penis. Thus, the boy feels *castration anxiety.* Eventually the castration anxiety becomes so great that he stops desiring his mother and shifts to identifying with his father, taking on the father's gender role and acquiring the characteristics expected of males by society. Freud considered the Oedipus complex and its resolution to be one of the key factors in human personality development.

As might be expected from the name of this stage, the girl will have a considerably different, and much more difficult, time passing through it. For a girl, the phallic stage begins with her traumatic realization that she has no penis, perhaps after observing that of her father or a brother. She feels envious and cheated, and she suffers from *penis envy,* wishing that she too had a wonderful wand. (Presumably she thinks her own clitoris is totally inadequate, or she is not even aware that she has it.) She begins to desire her father, forming her version of the Oedipus complex, sometimes called the **Electra complex.** In part, her incestuous desires for her father result from a desire to be impregnated by him, to substitute for the unobtainable penis. Unlike the boy, the girl does not have a strong motive of castration anxiety for resolving the Oedipus complex; she has already lost her penis. Thus, the girl's resolution of the Electra complex is not so complete as the boy's resolution of the Oedipus complex, and for the rest of her life she remains somewhat immature compared with men.

Freud said that following the resolution of the Oedipus or Electra complex, children pass into a prolonged stage known as *latency,* which lasts until adolescence. During this stage, the sexual impulses are repressed or are in a quiescent state, and so nothing much happens sexually. The postulation of this stage is one of the weaker parts of Freudian theory, because it is clear from the data of modern sex researchers that children do continue to engage in behavior with sexual components during this period.

With puberty, sexual urges reawaken, and the child moves into the *genital stage.* During this stage, sexual urges become more specifically genital, and the oral, anal, and genital urges all fuse together to promote the biological function of reproduction.

According to Freud, people do not always mature from one stage to the next as they should. A person might remain permanently fixated, for example, at the oral stage; symptoms of such a situation would include incessant cigarette smoking and fingernail biting, which gratify oral urges. Most adults have at least traces of earlier stages remaining in their personalities.

> **Erogenous (eh-RAH-jen-us) zones:** Areas of the body that are particularly sensitive to sexual stimulation.
> **Oedipus (EH-di-pus) complex:** According to Freud, the sexual attraction of a little boy for his mother.
> **Electra (eh-LEK-tra) complex:** According to Freud, the sexual attraction of a little girl for her father.

---

[1]Masturbation to orgasm is physiologically possible at this age, although males are not capable of ejaculation until they reach puberty (see the chapter, "Sex Hormones, Sexual Differentiation, and the Menstrual Cycle").

Figure 2 What does magnetic resonance imaging have to do with psychoanalytic theory? The answer is that by studying patterns of brain activity, we can test some of Freud's ideas about the unconscious.

©Cultura/Image Source

Evaluation of Psychoanalytic Theory

From a scientific point of view, one of the major problems with psychoanalytic theory is that most of its concepts cannot be evaluated scientifically to see whether they are accurate. Freud postulated that many of the most important forces in personality are unconscious, and thus they could not be studied using the scientific techniques common to the 20th century.

Recent advances in our ability to image brain activity, for example, using fMRI technology (described in the chapter "Sex Research"), have opened the possibility of testing some of Freud's ideas (Figure 2). Research in the developing area of neuropsychoanalysis suggests, for example, that what Freud termed the unconscious is represented by widespread neural networks in the brain that are humming in the background while the conscious mind is busy with other things (Ginot, 2017).

Another criticism is that Freud derived his data almost exclusively from his work with patients who sought therapy from him. Thus, his theory may provide a view not so much of the human personality as of *disturbances* in the human personality.

Feminists have also been critical of Freudian theory as a male-centered theory that may cause harm to women (Lerman, 1986). They object to Freud's assumption that because women do not have a penis they are biologically inferior to men. One could just as easily argue that men have a powerful envy of women's reproductive capacity, which is just what psychoanalyst Karen Horney (1926/1973) did when she coined the concept *womb envy,* although this notion is equally open to criticism.

Feminists also criticize the distinction Freud made between *vaginal orgasm* (obtained through heterosexual intercourse with the penis stimulating the vagina) and *clitoral orgasm* (obtained through clitoral stimulation) in women. Research by Masters and Johnson has shown there is no physiological difference between orgasms resulting from clitoral stimulation and those resulting from heterosexual intercourse. Further, Freud's assertion that vaginal orgasm is more mature is not supported by findings that most adult women experience orgasms as a result of clitoral stimulation.

Finally, many modern psychologists feel that Freud overemphasized the biological determinants of behavior and instincts and that he gave insufficient recognition to the importance of the environment and learning.

Nonetheless, Freud did make some important contributions to our understanding of human behavior. He managed to rise above the sexually repressive Victorian era of which he was a member and teach that the libido is an important part of personality (although he may have overestimated its importance). Perhaps most important from the perspective of this text, Freud took sex out of the closet, brought it to the attention of the general public, and suggested that we could talk about it and that it was an appropriate topic for scientific research.

Learning Theory

While psychoanalytic and sociobiological theories are based on the notion that much of human sexual behavior is biologically controlled, it is also quite apparent that much of it is learned. Some of the best evidence for this point comes from studies of sexual behavior across different human societies, which are considered in the chapter "Sexuality in Perspective." Here the various principles of modern learning theory will be reviewed, because they can help us understand our own sexuality (for more detailed discussions, see Hoffman, 2017; Hogben & Byrne, 1998).

Classical Conditioning

Classical conditioning is a concept usually associated with the work of the Russian scientist Ivan Pavlov (1849–1936). Think of the following situations: You salivate in response to the sight or smell of food, you blink in response to someone poking a finger in your eye, or you experience sexual arousal in response to stroking the inner part of your thigh. In all these cases, an unconditioned stimulus (US; for example, appealing food) automatically, reflexively elicits an unconditioned response (UR; for example, salivation). The process of learning that occurs in classical conditioning takes place when a new stimulus,

> **Classical conditioning:** The learning process in which a previously neutral stimulus (conditioned stimulus) is repeatedly paired with an unconditioned stimulus that reflexively elicits an unconditioned response. Eventually the conditioned stimulus itself will evoke the response.

the conditioned stimulus (CS; for example, the sound of a bell) repeatedly occurs paired with the original unconditioned stimulus (food). After this happens many times, the conditioned stimulus (the ringing bell) can eventually be presented without the unconditioned stimulus (food) and will evoke the original response, now called the conditioned response (CR, salivation).

As an example, suppose that Nadia's first serious boyfriend in high school always wears Erotik cologne when they go out. As they advance in their sexual intimacy,

> **What theory accounts for how the smell of perfume or cologne becomes sexually arousing?**

they have many pleasant times, where he strokes her thighs and other sexually responsive parts of her body and she feels highly aroused, always with the aroma of Erotik in her nostrils. One day she enters an elevator full of strangers in her office building and someone is wearing Erotik. Nadia instantly feels sexually aroused, although she is not engaged in any sexual activity. From the point of view of classical conditioning, this makes perfect sense, although Nadia may wonder why she is feeling so aroused in the elevator. The thigh-stroking and sexy touching were the US. Her arousal was the UR. The aroma of the cologne, the CS, was repeatedly paired with the US. Eventually, the aroma occurred by itself, evoking arousal, the CR.

Classical conditioning of sexual arousal has been demonstrated in an experiment with men (Lalumiere & Quinsey, 1998). Participants in the conditioning group were exposed to multiple pairings of a photo of a moderately attractive, partially nude woman (the CS) paired with a highly erotic video of heterosexual sexual interactions (the US). Participants in the control group were shown the photo multiple times but not with the erotic video. Arousal was measured with a penile strain gauge, which measures erection of the penis (both the UR and CR). When the men in the conditioning group were then shown just the photo of the woman (with no video), they showed an increase in arousal compared with their response to her photo before conditioning. This finding demonstrates classical conditioning of sexual arousal. Men in the control group actually showed a decrease in arousal, probably due to the process known as *habituation*. We return to the issue of habituation in the chapter "Sexuality and the Life Cycle: Adulthood," in a discussion of sex in long-term marriages. Subsequent research demonstrated classical conditioning of sexual arousal in women (Hoffmann et al., 2004; Hoffman, 2017).

Classical conditioning is useful in explaining a number of phenomena in sexuality. One example is fetishes, the attachment of great erotic significance to some object other than a human being (see the chapter "Variations in Sexual Behavior").

Operant Conditioning

Operant conditioning, a concept that is often associated with the psychologist B. F. Skinner, refers to the following process. A person performs a particular behavior (the operant). That behavior may be followed by either a reward (positive reinforcement) or a punishment. If a reward follows, the person will be likely to repeat the behavior again in the future; if a punishment follows, the person will be less likely to repeat the behavior. Thus, if a behavior is repeatedly rewarded, it may become very frequent, and if it is repeatedly punished, it may become very infrequent or even be eliminated.

Some rewards are considered to be primary reinforcers; that is, there is something intrinsically rewarding about them. Food is one such primary reinforcer; sex another. Rats, for example, can be trained to learn a maze if they find a willing sex partner at the end of it. Thus, sexual behavior plays dual roles in learning theory: It can itself be a positive reinforcer, but it can also be the behavior that is rewarded or punished.

Simple principles of operant conditioning can help explain some aspects of sex (McGuire et al., 1965). For example, if a woman repeatedly experiences pain when she has intercourse (perhaps because she has a vaginal infection), she will probably want to have sex infrequently or not at all. In operant conditioning terms, sexual intercourse has repeatedly been associated with a punishment (pain), and so the behavior becomes less frequent.

Another principle of operant conditioning that is useful in understanding sexual behavior holds that consequences, whether reinforcement or punishment, are most effective in shaping behavior when they occur immediately after the behavior. The longer they are delayed after the behavior has occurred, the less effective they become. As an example, consider a young man who has had gonorrhea three times yet continues to have unprotected sexual intercourse. The pain associated with gonorrhea is certainly punishing, so why does he persist in having sex without a condom? The delay principle suggests the following explanation: Each time he engages in intercourse, he finds it highly rewarding; this immediate reward maintains the behavior; the punishment, the pain of gonorrhea, does not occur until several days later and so is not effective in eliminating that behavior.

A third principle that has emerged in operant conditioning studies is that, compared with rewards, punishments are not as effective in shaping behavior. Often, as in the case of the child who is punished for taking an illicit cookie, punishments do not eliminate a behavior but rather teach the person to be sneaky and engage in

---

Operant (OP-ur-unt) conditioning: The process of changing the frequency of a behavior (the operant) by following it with positive reinforcement (which will make the behavior more frequent in the future) or punishment (which should make the behavior less frequent in the future).

it without being caught. As an example, some parents, as many commonly did in earlier times in our culture, punish children for masturbating; yet most of those children continue to masturbate, perhaps learning instead to do it under circumstances (such as in a bathroom with the door locked) in which they are not likely to be caught.

One important difference between psychoanalytic theory and learning theory should be noticed. Psychoanalytic theorists believe that the determinants of human sexual behavior occur in early childhood, particularly during the Oedipal complex period. Learning theorists, in contrast, believe that sexual behavior can be learned and changed at any time in one's life span—in childhood, in adolescence, in young adulthood, or later. When we try to understand what causes certain sexual behaviors and how to treat people with sex problems, this distinction between the theories will have important implications.

Behavior Modification

Behavior modification involves a set of techniques, based on principles of classical or operant conditioning, that are used to change (or modify) human behavior. These techniques have been used to modify everything from problem behaviors of children in the classroom to the behavior of schizophrenics. In particular, these methods can be used to modify problematic sexual behaviors—that is, sexual disorders such as orgasm problems or problematic sexual behavior such as child molesting. Behavior modification methods differ from more traditional methods of psychotherapy such as psychoanalysis in that the behavioral therapist considers only the problem behavior and how to modify it using learning-theory principles; the therapist does not worry about detailed analysis of the person's personality to see, for example, what unconscious forces might be motivating the behavior.

One example of a technique used in modifying sexual behavior is *olfactory aversion therapy* (Abel et al., 1992). In aversion therapy, the problematic behavior is punished using an aversive stimulus. Repeated pairing of the behavior and the aversive stimulus should produce a decline in the frequency of the behavior. In olfactory aversion therapy, the problematic sexual behavior is punished using an unpleasant odor, such as the odor of spirits of ammonia, as the aversive stimulus. With the help of a therapist, the patient first identifies the behavior chain or sequence that leads up to the problem behavior. Then the patient imagines one event in the chain and is simultaneously exposed to the odor. The odor can be administered by the patient, using a breakable inhaler. This form of therapy not only punishes the behavior but also creates the perception in the patient that the behavior is under their control.

Social Learning

Social learning theory (Bandura, 1977; Bandura & Walters, 1963) is a somewhat more complex form of learning

Figure 3 According to social learning theory, children learn about sex and gender in part by imitation. These children may be imitating their parents or a scene they have watched on TV.

©Girl Ray/Getty Images

theory. It is based on principles of operant conditioning, but it also recognizes other processes at work: imitation and observational learning (Figure 3). Imitation is useful in explaining how children acquire gender-stereotyped behavior. For example, a little girl may get into a dress and her mother's high heels after observing her mother getting ready to go to a party. Also, various forms of sexuality may be learned through imitation. In high school, for example, the sexiest girl in the senior class may find that other girls are imitating her behaviors and the way she dresses. Or a boy might see a movie in which the hero's technique seems to "turn women on"; then he tries to use this technique with his own dates. The latter example points to the importance of mass media as a source of images of sexuality that young people imitate (in the chapter "Sexuality and the Life Cycle: Childhood and Adolescence," see Milestones in Sex Research: The Impact of Media on Adolescent Sexuality).

Once a behavior is learned, the likelihood of its being performed depends on its consequences. The young man who imitates actor Brad Pitt's romantic technique may not succeed in arousing his companion. If the behavior is not reinforced, he will stop performing it. If it is reinforced, he will repeat it.

A later version of social learning is cognitive social learning theory or social cognitive theory (Bandura, 1986). It keeps social learning theory and adds cognitive processes, such as self-efficacy, to it. Successful experiences with an activity

Behavior modification: A set of operant conditioning techniques used to modify human behavior.

over time create a sense of competence, or **self-efficacy** (Bandura, 1982), at performing the activity. If a woman feels efficacious at using the female condom, she will expend more effort (going to the drugstore to buy one) and will show greater persistence in the face of difficulty (continuing to adjust it until it fits properly) than she did before. The concept of self-efficacy has been widely used in designing health intervention programs such as those that encourage individuals to use condoms to prevent transmission of sexually transmitted diseases and HIV infection (e.g., DeLamater et al., 2000). These programs provide opportunities for participants to practice the behaviors that are being promoted and be successful.

Social Exchange Theory

An important process based on the principle of reinforcement is social exchange. **Social exchange theory** (Cook et al., 2013) uses the concept of reinforcement to explain stability and change in relationships between people. The theory assumes that we have freedom of choice and often face choices among alternative actions. Every action provides some rewards and entails certain costs. There are many kinds of rewards—money, goods, services, sexual gratification, approval by others—and costs—time, effort, money, embarrassment. The theory states that we are *hedonistic,* that we try to maximize rewards and minimize costs when we act. Thus, we choose actions that produce profits (profits equaling rewards minus costs) and avoid actions that produce losses.

As its name indicates, social exchange theory views social relationships primarily as exchanges of goods and services among persons. People participate in relationships only if they find that the relationships provide profitable outcomes. An individual judges the attractiveness of a relationship by comparing the profits it provides against the profits available in alternative relationships. The level of outcomes in the best alternative relationship is called the *comparison level for alternatives* (Thibaut & Kelley, 1959). These ideas have been applied to personal relationships. Studies of heterosexual couples in long-term dating relationships have found that the concepts of rewards and costs can explain whether people stay in or exit from such relationships (Rusbult, 1983; Rusbult et al., 1986). Individuals are more likely to stay in when the partner is physically and personally attractive, when the relationship does not entail undue costs (such as high monetary commitments, broken promises, or arguments), and when romantic relationships with others are not available. In other words, they are more likely to stay in a relationship when its rewards are high, its costs are low, and the comparison level for alternatives is low.

Self-efficacy: A sense of competence at performing an activity.
Social exchange theory: A theory, based on the principle of reinforcement, that assumes that people will choose actions that maximize rewards and minimize costs.

Social exchange theory also predicts the conditions under which people try to change their relationships. A central concept is *equity* (Walster [Hatfield] et al., 1978). A state of equity exists when participants in a relationship believe that the rewards they receive from it are proportional to the costs they bear. If a participant feels that the allocation of rewards and costs is inequitable, then the relationship is unstable. People find inequity unpleasant and may feel cheated or angry. As we will see in the chapter "Sexuality and the Life Cycle: Adulthood," a married person experiencing inequity may cheat on the spouse as a result.

This perspective leads to the *matching hypothesis* (see the chapter "Attraction, Love, and Communication"), which predicts that men and women will choose as mates people who match them on physical and social characteristics. People who match will provide each other with similar rewards on dimensions such as attractiveness, social status, and wealth. We noted earlier that sociobiologists predict that we will choose attractive mates—if true, men would fight for the most attractive woman in the area and unattractive women would not have partners. In fact, people at all levels of attractiveness find partners, reflecting the operation of matching.

Social exchange theories have been criticized for applying ideas of rewards and costs to romantic relationships. Some people believe that love is not and should not be about what one can get out of a relationship (i.e., its rewards). A related criticism is that social exchange theories downplay other motivations. Because of the emphasis on rewards and costs, such theories cannot explain, for example, selfless behaviors such as altruism.

Cognitive Theories

In the 1980s and 1990s, a "cognitive revolution" swept through psychology. In contrast to the older behaviorist tradition (which insisted that psychologists should study only behaviors that could be directly observed), cognitive psychologists believe that it is very important to study people's thoughts—that is, the way people perceive and think.

Cognition and Sexuality

Cognitive psychology can readily explain some aspects of human sexuality (Walen & Roth, 1987). A basic assumption is that what we think influences what we feel. If we think happy, positive thoughts, we will tend to feel better than if we think negative ones. Therapists using a cognitive approach believe that psychological distress is often a result of unpleasant thoughts that are usually not tuned to reality and include misconceptions, distortions, exaggerations of problems, and unreasonably negative evaluations of events.

To the cognitive psychologist, how we perceive and evaluate a sexual event makes all the difference in the

A Sexually Diverse World

Learning Theory and Sexual Orientation in a Non-Western Society

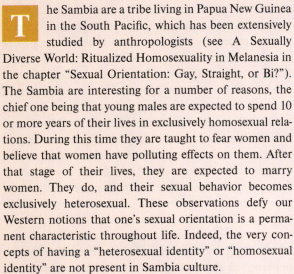

The Sambia are a tribe living in Papua New Guinea in the South Pacific, which has been extensively studied by anthropologists (see A Sexually Diverse World: Ritualized Homosexuality in Melanesia in the chapter "Sexual Orientation: Gay, Straight, or Bi?"). The Sambia are interesting for a number of reasons, the chief one being that young males are expected to spend 10 or more years of their lives in exclusively homosexual relations. During this time they are taught to fear women and believe that women have polluting effects on them. After that stage of their lives, they are expected to marry women. They do, and their sexual behavior becomes exclusively heterosexual. These observations defy our Western notions that one's sexual orientation is a permanent characteristic throughout life. Indeed, the very concepts of having a "heterosexual identity" or "homosexual identity" are not present in Sambia culture.

Can social learning theory explain these patterns of sexual behavior? It can, according to the analysis of John and Janice Baldwin. The thing that is puzzling is how the Sambia male, who has had years of erotic conditioning to same-gender sexual behavior just at puberty when he is most easily aroused and sensitive to conditioning, would then switch to heterosexual behavior and do so happily.

According to the Baldwins' analysis, several factors in social learning theory explain this switch. First, positive conditioning in the direction of heterosexuality occurs early in life. The boy spends the first 7 to 10 years of his life with his family. He has a close, warm relationship with his mother. In essence, he has been conditioned to positive feelings about women.

Second, observational learning occurs. In those same first 7 to 10 years, the boy observes closely the heterosexual relationship between two adults, his mother and father. This observational learning can be used a decade later when it is time for him to marry and form a heterosexual relationship.

Third, the boy is provided with much cognitive structuring, a notion present in cognitive social learning theory as well as cognitive psychology. He is instructed that a boy must pass through a series of stages to become a strong, masculine man. This includes first becoming the receptive partner to fellatio, then being the inserting partner to fellatio, marrying, defending himself from his wife's first menstruation (girls are usually married before puberty and undergo no homosexual stage of development), and then fathering a child by her. Essentially he is given all the cognitive structures necessary to convince him that it is perfectly natural, indeed desirable, to engage in sex with men for 10 years and then switch to women. Finally, there is some aversive conditioning to the same-gender sexual behavior that leads it to be not particularly erotic. The boy performs fellatio for the first time after several days of initiation, when he is exhausted. The activities are staged so that the boy feels fearful about it. He must do it in darkness with an older boy who may be an enemy, and he is required to do it with many males in succession. In essence, unpleasantness or punishment is associated with same-gender sexual behavior.

In summary, then, social learning theory provides a sensible explanation of the seemingly puzzling shift that Sambia males make from exclusively same-gender sexual behavior to exclusively heterosexual behavior.

Sources: Baldwin & Baldwin (1989); Herdt (1984).

world (Walen & Roth, 1987). For example, suppose that a man engaged in sexual activity does not get an erection. Starting from that basic event, his thoughts might take one of two directions. In the first, he thinks that it is quite common for men in his age group (fifties) not to get an erection every time they have sex; this has happened to him a few times before, once every two or three months, and it's nothing to worry about. At any rate, the oral sex was fun, and his partner had an orgasm from that, so all in all it was a nice enough encounter. In the second possibility, he began the activity thinking that he had to have an erection, had to have intercourse, and had to have an orgasm. When he didn't get an erection, he mentally labeled it *impotence* and imagined that he would never again have an erection. He thought of the whole episode as a frustrating disaster because he never had an orgasm.

As cognitive psychologists point out, our perception, labeling, and evaluating of events are crucial. In one case, the man perceived a slight problem, labeled it a temporary erection problem, and evaluated his sexual experience as pretty good. In the other case, the man perceived a serious problem, labeled it impotence, and evaluated the experience as horrible.

We shall see cognitive psychology several times again in this book, as theorists use it to understand the cycle of sexual arousal, the causes of some sexual variations such as fetishes, and the causes and treatment of sexual disorders. Before we leave cognitive psychology, however, we will look at one cognitive theory, schema theory, that has been used especially to understand issues of sex and gender.

Gender Schema Theory

Psychologist Sandra Bem (1981) proposed a schema theory to explain gender-role development and the impact of gender on people's daily lives and thinking. *Schema* is a term taken from cognitive psychology. A **schema** is a general knowledge framework that a person has about a particular topic. A schema organizes and guides perception; it helps us remember, but it sometimes also distorts our memory, especially if the information is inconsistent with our schema. Thus, for example, you might have

> **Schema (SKEE-muh):** A general knowledge framework that a person has about a particular topic.

a "football game schema," the set of ideas you have about what elements should be present at the game (two teams, spectators, bleachers, and so on) and what kinds of activities should occur (opening kickoff, occasional touchdown, band playing at half-time, and so on).

Bem proposed that all of us possess a *gender schema*—a cognitive structure comprising the set of attributes (behaviors, personality, appearance) that we associate with males and females. Our gender schema, according to Bem, predisposes us to process information on the basis of gender. That is, we tend to think of things as gender-related and to dichotomize them on the basis of gender. A good example is the case of the infant whose gender isn't clear when we meet them. We eagerly seek out the information or feel awkward if we don't, because we seem to need to know the baby's gender in order to continue to process information about it.

Bem (1981) conducted a number of experiments that provide evidence for her theory, and there are confirming experiments by other researchers as well, although the evidence is not always completely consistent (Ruble & Stangor, 1986). In one of the most interesting of these experiments, 5- and 6-year-old children were shown pictures like those in Figure 4, showing boys or girls performing either stereotype-consistent activities (such as a girl baking cookies) or stereotype-inconsistent activities (such as girls boxing) (Martin & Halverson, 1983). One week later the children were tested for their recall of the pictures. The results indicated that the children

(a)   *(b)*

Figure 4   Pictures like these were used in the Martin and Halverson research on gender schemas and children's memory. (*a*) A girl engaged in a stereotype-consistent activity. (*b*) Girls engaged in a stereotype-inconsistent activity. In a test of recall a week later, children tended to distort the stereotype-inconsistent pictures to make them stereotype consistent; for example, they remembered that they had seen boys boxing.

distorted information by changing the gender of people in the stereotype-inconsistent pictures but did not make such changes for the stereotype-consistent pictures. That is, children tended to remember a picture of girls boxing as having been a picture of boys boxing. These results are just what would be predicted by gender schema theory. The schema helps us remember schema-consistent (stereotype-consistent) information well, but it distorts our memory of information that is inconsistent with the schema (stereotype-inconsistent).

Our gender schema influences many everyday behaviors, for example, what we look at in magazines. Male and female undergraduates completed a measure of masculinity/femininity of self-concept. They were later allowed to select from three male-typed (*Men's Health, Game Informer, Sports Illustrated*), three female-typed (*Shape, Us Weekly, Glamour*), and three gender-neutral news magazines. Their selection and reading behavior were videotaped. Biological sex influenced choice of magazine. Gender schema (masculinity/femininity) predicted what they read in the selected magazine(s) (Knobloch-Westerwick & Hoplamazian, 2012).

One of the interesting implications of gender schema theory is that stereotypes—whether they are about males and females, or gay people, or other groups—may be very slow to change. The reason is that our schemas tend to filter out stereotype-inconsistent (that is, schema-inconsistent) information so that we don't even remember it.

Critical Theories

The theories we have considered so far focus on understanding the nature of various behaviors and types of persons. Since 1990, a new perspective has emerged, the *social constructionist* viewpoint. It calls our attention to the fact that these behaviors and types of people are social constructions, categories that are developed by groups and subcultures and then applied to objects in the world around them. Theories that use this perspective are more interested in understanding how these categories are created and their consequences for individuals and groups. Two theories are especially relevant to a broad understanding of sexuality: feminist theory and queer theory.

Feminist Theory

Feminist theory was not proposed by a single theorist but rather by many independent scholars (for an overview, see Enns, 2004). Here we crystallize four of the essential assertions of feminist theory.

Gender as Status and Inequality

According to the theory, gender signals status in a culture, with men having greater status and power (Ridgeway, 2011;

Ridgeway & Bourg, 2004). As such, gender is a dimension of inequality, just as race and social class are. Evidence of this inequality can be seen at many levels, from the low representation of women in the powerful U.S. Congress and Supreme Court, to discrimination against women in promotions in the workplace. A closely related concept is the *inequality of power* between women and men, with women having less power (Pratto & Walker, 2004). Feminist analysis extends the power principle to other areas, for example, to viewing rape not as a sexual act but as an expression of men's power over women.

Sexuality

Sexuality is a central issue in feminist theory (MacKinnon, 1982). Sexuality in the theory includes many specific issues, including rape, abortion, birth control, sexual harassment on the job, and pornography. According to feminist analysis, women's sexuality has been repressed and depressed, but rarely expressed. These problems are the result of men's control of women's sexuality; for example, men dominate the legislatures that pass laws limiting access to abortion. We will revisit feminist analysis of some of these issues in later chapters.

Gender Roles and Socialization

Feminist theory highlights the importance of gender roles and gender socialization. Our culture has well-defined roles for males and for females. From their earliest years, children are socialized to conform to these roles. On these points, feminist theory is in agreement with social learning theory. The problem is that gender roles tell individuals that they may not do certain things. A boy, for example, cannot grow up to be a nurse or—horrors—a ballet dancer. A girl cannot grow up to be a physicist. Because gender roles restrict people in these ways, feminist theorists argue that we would be better off without gender roles, or at least that they need to be modified and made much more flexible.

Intersectionality

The experiences of women, for example, are not all the same, nor are the experiences of men all the same. They vary by the person's race/ethnicity, sexual orientation, social class, and so on. **Intersectionality** is an approach that says that we should simultaneously consider a person's multiple group memberships and identities, including gender, race, social class, and sexual orientation (Cole, 2009). For example, to understand a person's sexuality, it matters not only that the person is a woman, but also that she is African American and a lesbian. She has multiple identities, as an African American, as a woman, and as a lesbian. All of these identities intersect and are part of her, and in different situations, one may be more important than another.

> **Intersectionality:** An approach that simultaneously considers the consequences of multiple group memberships, e.g., the intersection of gender and ethnicity.

Performativity

A concept that comes out of feminist theory and queer theory, **performativity** refers to ways in which we perform gender or sexuality based on society's norms, much as actors perform in a play (Butler, 1988; Fahs, 2011). Women often perform gender by wearing dresses and jewelry. As a second example, suppose that we see two women kissing in a college bar. What is the meaning of their behavior? On one hand, they might be kissing because they are attracted to each other. On the other hand, they might be doing it to attract the attention of men. In the first case, the behavior reflects their authentic feelings. In the second, the performance of same-gender sexuality is just that—a performance.

Queer Theory

Over the years, "queer" has been used as a derogatory term referring to homosexuals. Why is it now a theory? Contemporary gays have reappropriated the term and given it a positive meaning. A gay person may self-label as queer, and the major contemporary theorizing about sexual orientation is termed queer theory (for overviews, see Sullivan, 2003; Tolman & Diamond, 2014). Queer theory is broader than just the topic of sexual orientation, though, and includes other topics that have been considered "deviant," such as intersex and transgender.

Queer theory questions the social categorization of sexuality and gender. It challenges binaries (the idea that people fall into one of just two categories), especially the sexual orientation binary, that is, the assumption that people are either homosexual or heterosexual and there are no other possibilities or spaces in between. Similarly, it questions the *gender binary* that separates people into male and female, as if they were opposites, with no recognition of similarities or other gender possibilities. It also argues that sexual identities are not fixed for the individual. That is, sexual identities may display fluidity and vary depending on the situation or time in one's life. We will return to this idea in the chapters "Gender and Sexuality" and "Sexual Orientation: Gay, Straight, or Bi?"

The use of "queer" in the theory has a second meaning, though. Another definition of queer is peculiar or odd, that is, different from the norm. In this sense, queer theory questions what is categorized as peculiar and what is not. It questions norms. It uses this approach to challenge **heteronormativity,** the belief that heterosexuality is the only pattern of sexuality that is normal and natural. Queer theory argues that social norms privilege heterosexuality and marginalize other sexual orientations.

Performativity: Ways in which we perform gender or sexuality based on society's norms, much as actors perform in a play.

Heteronormativity: The belief that heterosexuality is the only pattern that is normal and natural.

Symbolic interaction theory: A theory based on the premise that human behavior and the social order are products of communication among people. Also called symbolic interactionism.

Sociological Perspectives

Sociologists are especially interested in the ways in which social interaction and the larger society shape human sexuality. (For a detailed articulation of the sociological perspective, see DeLamater, 1987.)

Symbolic Interaction Theory

An important sociological theory is **symbolic interaction theory** or symbolic interactionism (Charon, 1995; Stryker, 1987). Its basic premise is that human behavior and the social order are products of symbolic communication among people. A person's behavior is constructed through their interaction with others. People can communicate successfully with one another only to the extent that they ascribe similar meanings to objects and people. An object's meaning for a person depends not on the properties of the object but on what a person might do with it; an object takes on meaning only in relation to a person's plans. Thus, the theory views people as proactive and goal seeking. Achieving most goals requires the cooperation of others.

This is especially true of many forms of sexual expression. For example, suppose a woman invites a person she is dating to her apartment; what meaning does this invitation have? Does she want to prolong the conversation, or engage in sexual activity? The two people will have to achieve an agreement about the purpose of the visit before joint activity is possible. In terms of the theory, they have to develop a *definition of the situation*. Thus, to fit their actions together and achieve agreement, people interacting with each other must continually reaffirm old meanings or negotiate new ones.

Can a woman go to a strip club and get a lap dance? It depends on whether she can, in interaction with one of the dancers, create a definition of herself as a "patron." Many strippers are oriented toward male customers and pass over women because they perceive them as unlikely to pay for a dance. A few perceive the situation as different and negotiate with women; the result may be more intimate contact than in the typical male lap dance (Wosick-Correa & Joseph, 2008).

Central to social interaction is the process of *role taking,* in which an individual imagines how they look from the other person's viewpoint. By viewing the self and potential actions from the perspective of the other person, we are often able to anticipate what behavior will enable us to achieve our goal. One consequence of role taking is self-control; we see ourselves from the viewpoint of others and so strive to meet their standards, in the process exercising control over our behavior.

This perspective emphasizes the importance of symbolic communication (see the chapter "Attraction, Love, and Communication"). It also alerts us to the mutual effort required to arrive at a definition of the situation. Criticisms of this theory include the fact that it emphasizes rational, conscious thought, whereas in the realm of sexuality, emotions may be very important in many interactions. Also, this perspective portrays humans as *other-directed individuals,* concerned primarily with meeting others' standards. A third criticism is that we don't always consciously role take and communicate in an effort to achieve agreement. Sometimes we rely on past experience and habit. Situations such as these are the province of script theory.

Sexual Scripts

The outcome of social influences is that each of us learns a set of *sexual scripts* (Gagnon, 1977, 1990; Gagnon & Simon, 1973). The idea is that sexual behavior (and virtually all human behavior, for that matter) is scripted much as a play in a theater is. That is, sexual behavior is a result of elaborate prior learning that teaches us an etiquette of sexual behavior (see Figure 5). According to this concept, little in human sexual behavior is spontaneous. Instead, we have learned an elaborate script that tells us who, what, when, where, and why we do what we do sexually. For example, the "who" part of the script tells us that sex should occur with someone of the other gender, of approximately our own age, of our own race, and so on. Even the sequence of sexual activity is scripted.

Scripts, then, are plans that people carry around in their heads for what they are doing and what they are going to do; they are also devices for helping people remember what they have done in the past (Gagnon, 1977, p. 6).

Why do most sexual interactions in our society follow the same patterns?

How could we study these scripts? How could we find out if there are widely shared beliefs about how one should behave in a specific situation? One way is to ask people to describe what one should do in such a situation. Researchers asked male and female college students to describe a typical "hookup" (Holman & Sillars, 2012). The hypothetical script written by many participants included a basic sequence: attending a party, friends present, drinking alcohol, flirting, hanging out/talking, dancing, and a sexual encounter. Reflecting the ambiguity of a hookup, the sexual encounter might include oral, anal, or vaginal intercourse, just "fooling around" (not intercourse), or "only hugging and kissing." The results also reflect contemporary gender roles; males were more likely to provide a script than females. The widely shared nature of this script enables relative strangers to interact smoothly.

One study attempted to identify the sequence of sexual behaviors that is scripted for males and females in a heterosexual relationship in our culture (Jemail & Geer, 1977). People were given 25 sentences, each describing an event in a heterosexual interaction. They were asked to

Figure 5   According to some people's sexual scripts, a man taking a woman to dinner is one scene of the first act in a sexual script that features intercourse as Act V.

©Steve Mason/Getty Images

rearrange the sentences in a sequence that was "the most likely to occur." There was a high degree of agreement among the participants about what the sequence should be. There was also high agreement between males and females. The standard sequence was kissing, hand stimulation of the breasts, hand stimulation of the genitals, mouth–genital stimulation, intercourse, and orgasm. Does this sound familiar? Interestingly, not only is this the sequence in a sexual encounter, it is also the sequence that occurs as a couple progresses in a relationship. These results suggest that there are culturally defined sequences of behaviors that we all have learned, much as the notion of a "script" suggests.

Researchers collected data from several hundred young adults in 2010 using both focus groups and questionnaires (Sakaluk et al., 2014). The participants endorsed most elements of the traditional heterosexual script identified by past research, suggesting little change.

While the hookup script provides guidelines, each couple will enact that script in a unique way. What they talk about, what they eat or drink, and whether they dance will reflect the desires and expectations of each, and the course of their interaction. Whether they only kiss, fool around, or engage in intercourse will depend on each person's past experience, current desire and arousal, and how much each has had to drink.

Scripts also tell us the meaning we should attach to a particular sexual event (Gagnon, 1990). Television programs and films frequently suggest but do not show sexual activity between people. How do we make sense out of these implicit portrayals? A study of how women interpret such scenes in films found that they utilize scripts. If the film showed a couple engaging in two actions that are part of the accepted script for sexual intercourse (e.g., kissing and undressing each other) and then faded out, viewers inferred that intercourse had occurred (Meischke, 1995).

Social Institutions

Sociologists approach the study of sexuality with three basic assumptions: (1) Every society regulates the sexuality of its members. (For discussion of the reasons why, see Horrocks, 1997; Reiss, 1986.) (2) The appropriateness or inappropriateness of a particular sexual behavior depends upon the institutional context within which it occurs. (3) Basic institutions of society (religion, economy, family, medicine, and law) affect the rules governing sexuality in that society. Each of these institutions supports a sexual ideology, or discourse, about sexual activity. The ideology affects the beliefs and behaviors of those affiliated with the institution.

Religion

In our culture, the Judeo-Christian religious tradition has been a powerful shaper of sexual norms. A detailed discussion of that religious tradition and its teachings on sexuality is provided in the chapter "Ethics, Religion, and Sexuality." Suffice it to say here that the Christian religion has contained within it a tradition of asceticism, in which abstinence from sexual pleasures—especially by certain people such as monks and priests—is seen as virtuous. The tradition, at least until recently, has also been oriented toward procreation—that is, a belief that sexuality is legitimate only within traditional heterosexual marriage and only with the goal of having children, a *procreational ideology*. This view has created within our culture a set of norms, or standards for behavior, that say, for example, that premarital sex, extramarital sex, and same-gender sex are wrong. The procreational ideology is the basis for asserting that marriage is exclusively for a man and a woman because only a heterosexual couple can procreate.

The Economy

The nature and structure of the economy is another macro-level influence on sexuality. Before the Industrial Revolution, most work was done in the family unit in the home or farm. This kind of togetherness permitted rather strict surveillance of family members' sexuality and thus strict norms could be enforced. However, with the Industrial Revolution, people—most frequently men—spent many hours per day at work away from the home. Thus, they were under less surveillance, and scripts such as extramarital affairs and same-gender sex could be acted out more often.

Today we see much evidence of the extent to which economic conditions, and especially the unemployment rate, can affect the structure of the family and thus sexuality (see Figure 6). For example, when a group of men—such as lower-class Black men—have less access to jobs and thus have a high unemployment rate, they are reluctant to marry because they cannot support a family. The result is many female-headed households, with sexuality occurring outside marriage and children born without a legal father, although the father may be present in the household, providing care for the children. The point is that a culture's economy may have a profound effect on patterns of sexuality, marriage, and childbearing (Teachman et al., 2000).

In a capitalist economy such as the United States, goods and services become commodities that can be sold for a price (an exchange). Not surprisingly, this includes sexual images and sexual gratification, giving rise to the sale of sexually explicit materials, in stores and on the Internet, and commercial sex work. The increasing globalization of the economy has led to the development of sex tourism, in which well-to-do men and women travel to other cultures, such as Thailand, to purchase sexual gratification from "exotic" (e.g., Asian) sex workers (see the chapter "Sex for Sale").

Figure 6   According to sociologists, a culture's economy may have a profound effect on patterns of sexuality, marriage, and childbearing. High rates of male unemployment may lead to an increase in the number of female-headed households.

©Image Source/Blend Images

The Family

The family is a third institution influencing sexuality. As we noted earlier, before the Industrial Revolution the family was an important economic unit, producing the goods necessary for survival. As that function waned after the Industrial Revolution, there was increased emphasis on the quality of interpersonal relationships in the family. At the same time, love was increasingly seen as an important reason for marriage. By 1850, popular American magazines sang the praises of marriage based on romantic love (Lantz et al., 1975). Thus, a triple linkage between love, marriage, and sex was formed. Ironically, the linkage eventually became a direct one between love and sex (removing marriage as the middleman) so that, by the 1970s, some people were arguing that sex outside of marriage, if in the context of a loving relationship, was permissible, as was same-gender sex, again if the relationship was a loving one. This is the *relational ideology.*

The family exerts a particularly important force on sexuality through its *socialization* of children. That is, parents socialize their children—teach them appropriate norms for behavior—in many areas, including sexuality. Others, of course, such as the peer group, also have important socializing influences.

Medicine

The institution of medicine has become a major influence on our sexuality over the last 150 years. Physicians tell us what is healthy and what is unhealthy. In the late 1800s, physicians warned that masturbation could cause various pathologies. Today sex therapists tell us that sexual expression is natural and healthy and sometimes even "prescribe" masturbation as a treatment.

Another example is provided by childbirth; until after the Civil War, most babies were born at home, with an experienced woman (a midwife) providing assistance to the laboring woman and her partner. Today the vast majority of births occur in hospitals or birthing facilities, with medical personnel in charge.

We tend to have great confidence in medical advice, so the pronouncements of the medical establishment, based on a *therapeutic ideology,* have an enormous impact on sexuality. According to this ideology, a wide range of individual and social problems require medical treatment.

The increasing influence of medicine on sexuality has not been taken lying down. The domination of contemporary theory and research by the biomedical model is referred to as the **medicalization of sexuality** (Tiefer, 2004; Cacchioni, 2015). Medicalization has two components: Certain behaviors or conditions are defined in terms of health and illness, and problematic experiences or practices are given medical treatment. The medicalization of male sexuality is being hastened by the development of drugs to

> **Medicalization of sexuality:** The process by which certain sexual behaviors or conditions are defined in terms of health and illness, and problematic experiences or practices are given medical treatment.

treat erectile disorders, and many physicians and pharmaceutical companies are seeking to medicalize female orgasmic disorders by finding a pill that will "cure" it. Although referred to as the "female viagra," the recently approved drug flibanserin, trade name Addyi, is actually a treatment for low sexual desire, not orgasmic dysfunction (see the chapter "Sexual Disorders and Sex Therapy").

The Law

The legal system is another institution influencing sexuality at the macro level. A detailed discussion of laws relating to sexuality is provided in the chapter "Sex and the Law." The point to be made here is that from a sociological perspective, the law influences people's sexual behaviors in a number of ways. First, laws determine norms. Generally we think that what is legal is right and what is illegal is wrong. Thus, a society in which prostitution is illegal will have much different views of it than a society in which it is legal.

Second, laws are the basis for the mechanisms of social control. They may specify punishments for certain acts and thus discourage people from engaging in them. An example is public sexual acts such as exhibitionism or nudity on beaches. One wonders how many people would prefer to be nude at the beach if they did not fear arrest because the behavior is generally illegal and if they did not fear possible embarrassing publicity such as having their names in the news as the result of an arrest.

Third, the law reflects the interests of the powerful, dominant groups within a society. In part, the law functions to confirm the superiority of the ideologies of these dominant groups. Consider the Mormons in the United States. In the past, their religion approved of polygyny (a man having several wives). Mormons did not become the dominant group in American society. Rather, the Judeo-Christian tradition was the ideology of the dominant group, and that tradition takes a very dim view of polygyny. Accordingly, polygyny is illegal in the United States, and Mormons have been arrested for their practice. Also, one wonders what kinds of laws we would have on prostitution or sexual harassment if the compositions of the state legislatures were 90 percent women rather than 90 percent men. Would prostitution, for example, be legal? Or would it still be illegal, but would the male customer be held as guilty as or guiltier than the female prostitute?

In summary, then, the sociological perspective focuses on how society or culture shapes and controls our sexual expression, at levels from institutions such as religion and the law to the interpersonal level of socialization by family and peers.

Critical THINKing Skill

Understanding the difference between truth and scientific validity

In this chapter, we presented several theories about human sexuality. A common reaction by students is to ask, "So which one is right?" That question reflects the belief that a theory is correct or incorrect, true or false. Truth can be defined as consistent with facts or reality. The belief that some things are true and others are not is one that most of us rely on as we navigate the world, so we often try to sort out truth from falsity.

However, this belief will not serve us well if we apply it to evaluating theory. A theory is an abstraction, a simplification, an intentional focus on one or a few elements of a complex situation in order to make sense of that situation. We noted at the beginning of the chapter that our four theorists, Freud, Wilson, Bandura, and Gagnon, are all watching the same couple make love, but each views that scene through the lens of his particular theory. Freud may focus on the strength of the sex drive and the vigor of the bodily movements. Wilson may be focused on the potential (or lack thereof) for reproduction inherent in their activities. Bandura is reflecting on where they learned a special technique of nibbling each other's necks. Gagnon is marveling at how this couple is repeating the same sequence of behavior he has observed many times before. Each theorist's observations are consistent with some of the reality they are observing, so in this sense each theory is "true." So asking "Which one is true?" doesn't help us evaluate the different theories.

Instead, we evaluate theories in terms of their scientific validity. We look for *evidence*. We use the theory to generate testable questions or hypotheses, collect observations (data) that are relevant to the hypotheses, and evaluate the consistency between the observations and the hypotheses. To the extent that evidence is consistent with the theory each time the theory is tested, we develop confidence that the theory is valid. Evidence that is not consistent, or evidence reported by one researcher that cannot be confirmed by subsequent research, gives us less confidence in the validity of the theory. We provided several examples in this chapter of claims by various theories that were not verified by evidence. So the next time you meet a new theory, what question will *you* ask?

SUMMARY

Theories provide explanations for sexual phenomena.

Evolutionary Theories

Sociobiologists view human sexual behaviors as the product of natural selection in evolution and thus view these behavioral patterns as being genetically controlled. Gender-neutral evolutionary theory argues against fixed behaviors and gender differences and instead argues that natural selection favored flexible behaviors that could adapt to changing environmental conditions.

Psychological Theories

Among the psychological theories, Freud's psychoanalytic theory views the sex energy, or libido, as a major influence on personality and behavior. Freud introduced the concepts of erogenous zones and psychosexual stages of development. Learning theory emphasizes how sexual behavior is learned and modified through reinforcements and punishments according to principles of operant conditioning. Behavior modification techniques—therapies based on learning theory—are used in treating sexual variations and sexual disorders. Cognitive social learning theory adds the concepts of imitation and self-efficacy to learning theory. Social exchange theory highlights the role of rewards and costs in relationships. Cognitive psychologists focus on people's thoughts and perceptions—whether positive or negative—and how these influence sexuality. One example of a cognitive theory is gender schema theory.

Critical Theories

Critical theories focus our attention on the social construction of categories, the ways they are applied to people, and the consequences for individuals and society. Feminist theory systematically analyzes the meaning of gender in contemporary society. Gender is a status characteristic, and men have greater status than women. Their higher status has generally allowed men to control women's sexual expression. Gender roles perpetuate status inequality by virtue of the restrictions they place on men's and women's behavior. Queer theory challenges the gender binary and the sexual orientation binary, arguing that gender expression and sexual orientation are both dimensions along which individuals vary.

Sociological Perspectives

Sociologists study the ways in which society influences our sexual expression. Symbolic interaction theory calls attention to the processes of communication and interaction that influence behavior. Sexual scripts provide us with concrete guidelines for romantic and sexual interactions. At the macro level, sociologists investigate the ways in which institutions such as religion, the economy, the family, medicine, and the law influence sexuality.

SUGGESTIONS FOR FURTHER READING

Buss, David M. (2016). *The evolution of desire: Strategies of human mating* (Rev. updated ed.). New York: Basic Books. Buss is perhaps the most prominent evolutionary psychologist, and this book articulates that view of human sexuality.

Fahs, Breanne. (2011). *Performing sex: The making and unmaking of women's erotic lives.* Albany, NY: State University of New York Press. Fahs delves deeply into the concept of performativity and how it applies to women's sexuality in acts such as faking orgasm.

Freud, Sigmund. (1943). *A general introduction to psychoanalysis.* Garden City, NY: Garden City Publishing. (Original in German, 1917.) Good for the reader who wants a basic introduction to Freud. For a one-chapter summary, see Hall, C. S., and Lindzey, G. (1970). *Theories of personality* (2nd ed.). New York: Wiley.

Ridgeway, Cecilia L. (2011). *Framed by gender: How gender inequality persists in the modern world.* New York: Oxford University Press. Ridgeway, a sociologist, uses feminist theory and data to propose new ideas about the puzzling question of why gender inequality persists in contemporary U.S. society despite so many efforts to establish gender equality.

Wiederman, Michael. (2015). Sexual scripts theory. In John DeLamater and Rebecca Plante (Eds.), *Handbook of the Sociology of Sexualities.* Dordrecht, NL: Springer. A good, concise description of script theory.

©Pixtal/age fotostock

Are **YOU** Curious?

1. How would you conduct an effective sex survey?
2. Is the Kinsey report still the best available sex survey?
3. Is it possible to study sexuality scientifically with methods other than questionnaires?

Read this chapter to find out.

CHAPTER

Sex Research

CHAPTER HIGHLIGHTS

What is research, but a blind date with knowledge.
                                        —**William Henry**

Over the last several decades, sex research has made great advances, and the names of Kinsey and Masters and Johnson have become household words. How do sex researchers do it? How valid are their conclusions?

There are many different types of sex research, but basically the techniques vary in terms of the following: (1) how sexuality is measured, whether from people's self-reports, through observations of behavior, or using biological measures; (2) whether large numbers of people are studied in surveys, or whether a smaller number of people are studied (in laboratory studies and qualitative studies); (3) whether the studies are conducted in the laboratory or in the field; and (4) whether sexual behavior is studied as it occurs naturally or whether some attempt is made to manipulate it in an experiment. Examples of studies using all of these techniques are described and evaluated later in this chapter.

It is important to understand the techniques of sex research and their strengths as well as their limitations. This knowledge will help you evaluate the studies that are cited as evidence for various conclusions in later chapters and will also help you decide how willing you are to accept these conclusions. Perhaps more important, this knowledge will help you evaluate future sex research. Much sex research has been conducted already, but much more will be done in the future. The information in this chapter should help you understand and evaluate sex research that appears 10 or 20 years from now. Moreover, the media often report poor-quality research as enthusiastically as high-quality research. You should be equipped to tell the difference.

Measuring Sex

The first thing that researchers have to decide is how to measure the particular aspect of sexuality that they want to study. Multiple methods are available, including self-reports, behavioral measures, implicit measures, and biological measures, each of which is discussed in the sections that follow.

Self-Reports

The most common method for measuring sexuality is self-reports, in which the participants are asked questions about their sexual behavior—for example,

1. At what age did you begin masturbating?
2. Did you use a condom the last time you had sex?

Self-reports are also used to measure attitudes about sexuality—for example,

3. Regarding gay marriage, I (circle the number that applies)

Strongly disapprove	Moderately disapprove	Neither approve nor disapprove	Moderately approve	Strongly approve
1	2	3	4	5

Self-reports can be collected in a number of ways: with paper questionnaires, in interviews, and online. The strengths and weaknesses of self-reports are discussed in a later section of this chapter, Issues in Sex Research.

Behavioral Measures

Several alternatives are available for behavioral measures of sexuality. One is **direct observation,** in which the scientist directly observes the behavior and records it. As one example, sex researcher Charles Moser observed S/M (sadomasochistic) interactions in semipublic settings, attending more than 200 S/M parties (Moser, 1998). Masters and Johnson (1966), in research discussed later in this chapter, collected direct observations of sexual behavior in laboratory studies of sexual intercourse and masturbation.

Psychologists have devised other clever behavioral measures. One of these is **eye-tracking,** in which participants, in the laboratory, wear an eye-tracking device that measures their point of gaze over time, as they are shown pictures on a computer (Wenzlaff et al., 2016). For example, in one study researchers tracked the eye movements of adult men as they were shown photos of a front-posed naked woman, with multiple photos created through Photoshop to show different sized breasts and different waist-to-hip ratios (e.g., small waist relative to hips) (Dixson et al., 2011). With this method, they could answer questions such as, "Where do men look first?" As it turns out, the first thing that men look at is the breasts or the waist, not the genitals.

Another possible behavioral measure, for those studying illegal sexual behaviors, is to use police reports. For example, to study sexual assault or rape, a researcher could look at statistics reported by the FBI in their *Uniform Crime Reports.* The problem with this sort of measure, though, is that it detects

Direct observation: A behavioral measure in which the scientist directly observes the behavior being studied.
Eye-tracking: A behavioral measure in which a device measures the participant's point of gaze over time.

only cases that are reported to the police. In the case of rape, for example, we know that only a small proportion of cases are reported and the great majority go unreported.

Implicit Measures

Most researchers who measure attitudes about sexuality use self-reports. However, newer measures are available. For example, a method used to measure implicit stereotypes is the Implicit Association Test (IAT), which measures an individual's relative strength of association between different pairs of concepts (Nosek et al., 2002). The key to measuring these associations is reaction time, measured on a computer in milliseconds. We react quickly to two concepts that we associate strongly, and more slowly to two concepts that we do not associate strongly. One of the great features of this measure is that people can't fake their reaction times. For example, they cannot hide their socially unacceptable stereotyped ideas.

In one important experiment, researchers measured the association between math and gender (Nosek et al., 2002). In the practice phase, participants placed one finger on the left key of a keypad and another finger on the right key. They were instructed to press the left key if the word they saw on the screen in front of them was in the category *math* (e.g., algebra, equation) or if it was in the category *pleasant* (e.g., peace, love). They were to press the right key for topics in the *arts* (e.g., drama, poetry) or words that were *unpleasant* (e.g., hatred). After following this pattern for many trials, the instructions changed and they had to press the left key for math words and unpleasant words, and the right key for arts and pleasant words. All of this was practice for the real task. In the first phase of it, participants pressed the left key if the words were in the *math* category or the *male* category (e.g., male, boy) and the right key if the words were in the *arts* category or the *female* category (e.g., female, girl). Then in the second phase the pairings were reversed, so that participants pressed the left key for the math category or the female category and the right key for the arts category and the male category. Implicit stereotyping is indicated if people respond faster to the male and math pairing than they do to the female and math pairing, and that is exactly what participants do! That is, people have an implicit association between math and males but not math and females.

In another study, researchers developed an IAT to measure attitudes about condom use (Czopp et al., 2004). In one phase, participants pressed the left key if the word on the screen was related to condoms (e.g., condom, Trojan, latex) or pleasant, and the right key if the word was a type of tree (e.g., oak, maple, pine) or unpleasant. Then in a second phase, the pairings were reversed,

Is it possible to study sexuality scientifically with methods other than questionnaires?

so that they pressed the left key for condom words or unpleasant words and the right key for trees or pleasant words. This allowed the researchers to determine if participants had a stronger association between condoms and pleasant or between condoms and unpleasant.

If you want to try the IAT yourself, you can do it online at www.implicit.harvard.edu.

Biological Measures

Masters and Johnson (1966) pioneered the biological measurement of sexual response (see Milestones in Sex Research: Masters and Johnson). Today, many biological measures are available.

Genital measures of sexual response assess arousal by using devices that measure erection in males and vaginal changes in females (Chivers et al., 2014). In males, penile plethysmography is used, in which a flexible loop is placed around the penis that measures changes in circumference. Penile plethysmography can be used, for example, to measure a man's sexual response to pictures in different categories, such as one gender versus another, or adults versus children. In females, a vaginal photoplethysmograph is used to optically measure blood flow to the vagina.

MRI (magnetic resonance imaging) and fMRI (functional magnetic resonance imaging) are being used increasingly in sex research (Chivers et al., 2014). MRI looks at *anatomy,* such as the size or shape of specific brain regions or the genitals, by using magnets to send and receive signals that give information while participants lie in the center of the magnet (scanner). For example, an MRI scan that shows the internal structure of the clitoris is shown in the chapter "Sexual Anatomy." One strength of MRI is that it provides good contrast between different soft tissues of the body. Another strength is that it is noninvasive—that is, in the old days, to get at brain structure, anatomists had to dissect the brain of a dead person. Today, researchers can look inside the brain of a living person without disturbing it! fMRI looks at brain *activity* by measuring relative levels of blood flow. In this way, scientists can measure the difference in activity across regions of the brain when the person is looking at, for example, a sexual picture versus a boring picture. An example of fMRI research is given in the "Sexual Arousal" chapter in Milestones in Sex Research: Mapping the Sexual Brain. Some regions of the brain are very active, with large changes in blood flow when the person looks at a sexual stimulus, whereas other regions have less blood flow or no change in blood flow. Because fMRI does not measure neural activity directly but rather measures blood flow, fMRI is an indirect measure of neural activity. In addition, there is a lot of "noise" in fMRI data, and complex statistical analyses are required to get at the important patterns. Two limitations that affect its use in sex research are (1) participants must be lying very still to get good images; and (2) fMRI depends on contrasting the difference between two stimuli (for example, blood flow while looking at sexual stimuli versus other stimuli).

PEARLS BEFORE SWINE   BY STEPHAN PASTIS

Figure 1 Sex research can be more difficult than other kinds of behavioral research.

Credit: PEARLS BEFORE SWINE ©Stephen Pastis/Dist. by United Feature Syndicate, Inc. Reprinted with permission.

Therefore, the results depend very much on the choice of each set of stimuli.

Other biological measures include measures of pupil dilation (Attard-Johnson et al., 2017). Devices are available that measure the amount of dilation of the pupils. Our pupils dilate when we look at something that is especially interesting or arousing, or that puts a big load on our brain. Pupil dilation is sometimes used with sex offenders, for example, to determine if they are especially interested in children (Flak et al., 2007). If we asked the sex offender about his interest in children using a self-report measure, he might very well lie about his illegal and taboo behavior. Experts hope that pupil dilation measures get around this problem, although they are not perfect.

[1]A detailed discussion of probability sampling is beyond the scope of this book. For a good description of this method as applied to sex research, see Cochran et al. (1953). In brief, with a random sample, each individual in the population has an equal probability of being chosen. With a probability sample, the researchers can set a higher probability of inclusion for certain groups, a technique called *oversampling*. For example, if we had funds to interview 1,000 people in the United States, a random sample would yield only about 150 Blacks and 160 Latinx because these groups constitute about 15 percent and 16 percent of the population, respectively. We might not feel confident reaching conclusions about Blacks or Latinx based on only 150 or 160 people, so we could decide to use probability sampling and give Blacks and Latinx a double probability of inclusion compared with Whites. The resulting sample of 1,000 would include 300 Blacks, 320 Latinx, and 380 Euro-Americans, and we would feel more confident about making conclusions about each group. We could do even more oversampling of Asian Americans and American Indians, who constitute even smaller percentages of the U.S. population.

Issues in Sex Research

Sampling

An important step in conducting sex research is to identify the appropriate **population** of people to be studied. Does the population in question consist of all adult human beings, all adolescents in the United States, all people guilty of sex crimes, or all married couples who engage in swinging? Generally, of course, the scientist is unable to get data for all the people in the population, and so a **sample** is taken.

At this point, things begin to get sticky. If the sample is a **random sample** or representative sample of the population in question and if it is a reasonably large sample, then results obtained from it can safely be generalized to the population that was originally identified. That is, if a researcher has really randomly selected 1 out of every 50 adolescents in the United States, then the results obtained from that sample are probably true of all adolescents in the United States. One technique that is sometimes used to get such a sample is **probability sampling.**[1] But if the sample consists only of

How would you conduct an effective sex survey?

Population: A group of people a researcher wants to study and make inferences about.
Sample: A part of a population.
Random sample: An excellent method of sampling in research in which each member of the population has an equal chance of being included in the sample.
Probability sampling: An excellent method of sampling in research in which each member of the population has a known probability of being included in the sample.

Table 1 The Percentage of People Reporting Having Sex at Least Once a Week: Comparing a Convenience Sample with a Probability Sample

	Men		Women	
Age	Convenience Sample (Janus Report)	Probability Sample (General Social Survey)	Convenience Sample (Janus Report)	Probability Sample (General Social Survey)
18–26	72%	57%	68%	58%
27–38	83	69	78	61
39–50	83	56	68	49
51–64	81	43	65	25
Over 65	69	17	74	6

Source: Review of the Janus Report on Sexual Behavior by Samuel S. Janus & Cynthia L. Janus in *Contemporary Sociology,* Vol. 23, No. 2 (March 1994), p. 222, table 1.

adolescents with certain characteristics—for example, only those whose parents agree to let them participate in sex research—then the results obtained from that sample may not be true of all adolescents. Sampling has been a challenge in sex research.

Typically, sampling proceeds in three phases: the population is identified, a method for obtaining a sample is adopted, and the people in the sample are contacted and asked to participate. What is perhaps the thorniest problem occurs in the last phase: getting the people identified for the sample to participate. If any of the people refuse to participate, then the great probability sample is ruined. This is called the **problem of refusal or nonresponse.** As a result, the researcher is essentially studying volunteers, that is, people who agree to be in the research. The outcomes of the research may therefore contain **volunteer bias.** The problem of refusal in sex research is difficult because there is no ethical way of forcing people to participate when they do not want to do so.

The problem of volunteer bias would not be so great if those who refused to participate were identical in their sexual behavior to those who participated. But it seems likely that those who refuse to participate differ in some ways from those who agree to, and that means the sample is biased. Evidence suggests that volunteers who participate in sex research hold more permissive attitudes about sexuality and are more sexually experienced than those who don't; for example, they

masturbate more frequently and have had more sexual partners (Boynton, 2003; Dunne et al., 1997; Strassberg & Lowe, 1995; Wiederman et al., 1994). In addition, women are less likely to volunteer for sex research than men are (Boynton, 2003; Gaither et al., 2003), so that female samples are even more highly selected than male samples. In sum, volunteer bias is potentially a serious problem when we try to reach conclusions based on sex research.

Table 1 shows how different the results of sex surveys can be, depending on how carefully the sampling is done (Greeley, 1994). The table shows results from the Janus report (Janus & Janus, 1993), which used sampling methods so haphazard that the researchers ended up with what some call a **convenience sample.** It included volunteers who came to sex therapists' offices and friends recruited by the original volunteers. This report contrasts with the probability sample obtained in the General Social Survey conducted in 1993 by the University of Chicago. Notice that a considerably higher level of sexual activity is reported by the convenience sample in the Janus report, compared with the probability sample. This difference is especially pronounced among the elderly. Convenience samples simply do not give us a very good picture of what is going on in the general population. New sampling issues are raised in web-based surveys, which are discussed in a later section of this chapter.

Accuracy of Measurement

Earlier we described various methods for measuring sexuality. How accurate are those measures? We focus mainly on self-reports because they are used so frequently in sex research (Figure 2).

Problem of refusal or nonresponse: The problem that some people will refuse to participate in a sex survey, thus making it difficult to study a random sample.
Volunteer bias: A bias in the results of sex surveys that arises when some people refuse to participate, so that those who are in the sample are volunteers who may in some ways differ from those who refuse to participate.
Convenience sample: A sample chosen in a haphazard manner relative to the population of interest. Not a random or probability sample.

Figure 2   The reliability of self-reports of sexual behavior. If you were interviewing this man in a sex survey and he said that he had never masturbated, would you believe him, or would you think that he was concealing a taboo behavior?

©Digital Vision

Purposeful Distortion

If you were an interviewer in a sex research project and a 90-year-old man said that he and his wife made love twice a day, would you believe him, or would you suspect that he might be exaggerating slightly? If a 35-year-old woman told you that she had never masturbated, would you believe her, or would you suspect that she had masturbated but was unwilling to admit it?

Respondents in sex research may, for one reason or another, engage in **purposeful distortion,** intentionally giving self-reports that are distortions of reality. These distortions may be in either of two directions. People may exaggerate their sexual activity (a tendency toward *enlargement*), or they may minimize their sexual activity or hide the fact that they have done certain things (*concealment*).

Distortion is a basic problem when using self-reports (McCallum & Peterson, 2012). To minimize distortion, participants must be impressed with the fact that because the study will be used for scientific purposes, their reports must be as accurate as possible. They must also be assured that their responses will be completely anonymous; this is necessary, for example, so that a politician would not be tempted to hide an extramarital affair or a history of sex with animals for fear that

the information could be used to defeat him in the next election.

But even if all respondents were very truthful and tried to give information as accurately as possible, two factors might still cause their self-reports to be inaccurate: memory and difficulties with estimates.

Memory

Some of the questions asked in sex surveys require respondents to recall what their sexual behavior was like many years before. For example, some of the data we have on sexual behavior in childhood come from the Kinsey study, in which adults were asked about their childhood sex behavior. This might involve asking a 50-year-old man to remember at what age he began masturbating and how frequently he masturbated when he was 16 years old. It might be difficult to remember such facts accurately (Brener et al., 2003). The alternative is to ask people about their current sexual behavior, although getting data like this from children raises serious ethical and practical problems. Another alternative to avoid memory problems is the use of *daily diaries,* in which

> **Purposeful distortion:** Purposely giving false information in a survey.

people report their behavior each day, for just the last 24 hours (Gilmore et al., 2010).

Difficulties with Estimates

One of the questions sex researchers have asked is, "How long, on the average, do you spend in foreplay?" If you were asked this question, how accurate a response do you think you could give? It is rather difficult to estimate time to begin with, and it is even more difficult to do so when engaged in an absorbing activity. The point is that in some sex surveys people are asked to give estimates of things that they probably cannot estimate very accurately. This may be another source of inaccuracy in self-report data.

Evidence on the Reliability of Self-Reports

Scientists have developed several methods for assessing how reliable or accurate people's self-reports are. One is the method of **test-retest reliability,** in which the respondent is asked a series of questions and then is asked the same set of questions after a period of time has passed, for example, a week or a month (Njitray et al., 2010). The correlation[2] between answers at the two times (test and retest) measures the reliability of responses. If people answer identically both times, the correlation would be 1.0, meaning perfect reliability. If there were absolutely no relationship between what they said the first time and what they said the second time, the correlation would be 0, meaning that the responses are not at all reliable.

In one study, urban African American and Latinx girls between the ages of 12 and 14 were interviewed about their sexual experiences and then were reinterviewed three weeks later (Hearn et al., 2003). The test-retest reliability was .84 for their age when they had their first crush and .95 for the age at which they first touched a penis, which indicates excellent reliability. Other research generally indicates that respondents give their best estimates about short, recent time intervals (Catania et al., 1990).

Yet another study examined people's reports of their age at first heterosexual intercourse at age 21, and then 17 years later, at age 38 (Dickson et al., 2016). Overall, 85 percent of people reported the same age or within one year the second time as they did the first time, a remarkable degree of reliability over a very long time span. Sexual events such as first intercourse tend to be memorable, which should increase the accuracy of reporting.

Another method for assessing reliability involves obtaining independent reports from two different people who share sexual activity, such as husbands and wives. We used this method of checking for agreement between spouses (Hyde et al., 1996). On a simple item such as whether they had engaged in intercourse in the last month, there was 93 percent agreement. When reporting on something that requires somewhat more difficult estimation, the number of times they had intercourse in the past month, the correlation was .80, which still indicates good reliability.

One useful method is the **computer-assisted self-interview (CASI)** method, which can be combined with an audio component so that the respondent not only reads but also hears the questions. This method offers the privacy of the written questionnaire while accommodating poor readers. The computer can be programmed to follow varying sequences of questions depending on respondents' answers, just as a human interviewer does. In one survey, among 15-year-old boys, 16 percent reported in a personal interview that they had engaged in vaginal intercourse, but 25 percent said they had when CASI was used (Mosher et al., 2005). These findings indicate that CASI gives more honest responses. (For similar results with adults, see Lau et al., 2003.)

Accuracy of Behavioral Observations

As we noted earlier, two techniques of measurement in sex research involve whether the scientist relied on people's self-reports of their behavior or observed the sexual behavior directly.

The problems of self-reports have just been discussed. In a word, self-reports may be inaccurate, although the evidence indicates that they are generally accurate. Direct observations have a major advantage over self-reports in that they are accurate. No purposeful distortion or inaccurate memory can intervene. On the other hand, direct observations have their own set of problems. They are expensive and time consuming, with the result that generally only a rather small sample is studied. Furthermore, obtaining a random or probability sample of the population is even more difficult than in survey research. Some people are reticent about completing a questionnaire concerning their sexual behavior, but even more would be unwilling to come to a laboratory where their sexual behavior would be observed by a scientist or where they would be hooked up to recording instruments while they engaged in sex. Thus, results obtained from the unusual group of volunteers who would be willing to do this might not be generalizable to the rest of the population. One study showed that volunteers for a laboratory study of sexual arousal felt less guilty and were more sexually experienced than nonvolunteers (Plaud et al., 1999). Moreover, only 27 percent of males and 7 percent of females volunteered, showing how selective the sample was.

Extraneous Factors

Various extraneous factors may also influence the outcomes of sex research. Extraneous factors such as the

---

Test-retest reliability: A method for testing whether self-reports are reliable or accurate; participants are interviewed (or given a questionnaire) and then interviewed a second time sometime later to determine whether their answers are the same both times.
Computer-assisted self-interview (CASI): A method of data collection in which the respondent fills out questionnaires on a computer. Headphones and a soundtrack reading the questions can be added for young children or poor readers.

---

[2]The statistical concept of correlation is discussed in the last section of this chapter.

gender, race, or age of the interviewer or experimenter may influence respondents' answers. Even the mode of administering a questionnaire—whether responding on a paper questionnaire or a computer—can influence people's self-reports (McCallum & Peterson, 2015). With questionnaires, even such simple factors as the wording of a question may influence the results. In one study, respondents were given either standard or supportive wording of some items (Catania et al., 1995). For the question about extramarital sex, the standard wording was as follows:

At any time while you were married during the past 10 years, did you have sex with someone other than your (husband/wife)?

The supportive wording was as follows:

Many people feel that being sexually faithful to a spouse is important, and some do not. However, even those who think being faithful is important have found themselves in situations where they ended up having sex with someone other than their (husband/wife). At any time while you were married during the past 10 years, did you have sex with someone other than your (husband/wife)?

The supportive wording significantly increased reports of extramarital sex from 12 percent with the standard wording to 16 percent with the supportive wording, if the interviewer was of the same gender as the respondent; the wording made no difference when the interviewer and respondent were of different genders. Sex researchers must be careful to control these extraneous factors so that they influence the results as little as possible.

Ethical Issues

There is always a possibility of ethical problems involved in doing research. Ethical problems are particularly difficult in sex research, because people are more likely to feel that their privacy has been invaded when you ask them about sex than when you ask them to name their favorite presidential candidate or memorize a list of words. The ethical standards specified by the U.S. government and university regulations involve three basic principles: informed consent, protection from harm, and justice (see, for example, U.S. National Commission, 1978).

Informed Consent

According to the principle of **informed consent,** participants have a right to be told, before they participate, what the purpose of the research is and what they will be asked to do. They may not be forced to participate or be forced to continue. An investigator may not coerce people to be in a study, and it is the scientist's responsibility to see to it that all participants understand exactly what they are agreeing to do. In the case of children who may be too young to give truly informed consent, it is usually given by the parents.

The principle of informed consent was adopted by scientific organizations in the 1970s. It was violated in some of the older sex studies, as discussed in later chapters.

Protection from Harm

Investigators should minimize the amount of physical and psychological stress to people in their research. Thus, for example, if an investigator must shock participants during a study, there should be a good reason for doing this. Questioning people about their sexual behavior may be psychologically stressful to them and might conceivably harm them in some way, so sex researchers must be careful to minimize the stress involved in their procedure. Research actually shows, though, that respondents are no more distressed by participating in questionnaire research about sexuality than they are by participating in common research such as vocabulary testing (Rinehart et al., 2017). The principle of anonymity of response is important to ensure that participants will not suffer afterward for their participation in research if, for example, they report an illegal sexual behavior to researchers.

Justice

The **justice principle** in research ethics holds that the risks of participating in research and the benefits of the results of the research should be distributed fairly across groups in society. For example, early testing of the birth control pill was done on poor women in Puerto Rico, not on wealthy women in Manhattan. The risks were not distributed fairly, and a particular group bore a disproportionate burden. As a second example, research on the potential benefits of taking aspirin for preventing heart attacks was conducted with an all-male sample. Whether this effect works for women as well remains unknown. Thus, the benefits of the research did not extend fairly to everyone. Researchers have an obligation to make sure that they conduct their work in a way that benefits as wide a range of people as possible.

A Cost–Benefit Approach

Considering the possible risks involved in sex research, is it ethical to do such research? Officials in universities and government agencies sponsoring sex research must answer this question for every proposed sex research study. Typically they use a **cost–benefit approach.** That is, the stress to the research participants should be minimized as much as possible, but some stresses will remain; they are the cost. The question then becomes, Will the benefits that result from the research be greater than the cost? That is, will

Informed consent: An ethical principle in research in which people have a right to be informed, before participating, of what they will be asked to do in the research.
Justice principle: An ethical principle in research that holds that the risks of participation should be distributed fairly across groups in society, as should the benefits.
Cost–benefit approach: An approach to analyzing the ethics of a research study, based on weighing the costs of the research (the participants' time, stress to participants, and so on) against the benefits of the research (gaining knowledge about human sexuality).

the participants benefit in some way from being in the study, and will science and society in general benefit from the knowledge resulting from the study? Do these benefits outweigh the costs? If they do, the research is justifiable; otherwise, it is not.

As an example, Masters and Johnson considered these issues carefully and concluded that their research participants benefited from being in their research; they collected data from former participants that confirmed this belief. Thus, a cost–benefit analysis would suggest that their research was ethical, even though their participants might have been temporarily stressed by it.

In another study, 15- to 25-year-olds completed a questionnaire about sex; later they rated how distressing and how positive the experience had been for them (Kuyper et al., 2012). Little distress was reported and positive feelings predominated; overall, 89 percent agreed that surveys like this should be carried out. Research actually shows that, compared with people who complete innocuous cognitive measures, people who complete surveys about sex and trauma feel more positive and perceive more benefits in the research (Yeater et al., 2012).

Even in a study as ethically questionable as Laud Humphreys's study of the tearoom trade (discussed in the chapter "Sexual Orientation: Gay, Straight, or Bi?"), the potential cost to the participants should be weighed against the benefits that accrue to society from being informed about this aspect of sexual behavior.

The Major Sex Surveys

In the major sex surveys, the data were collected from a large sample of people by means of questionnaires or interviews. The best known of these studies is the one done by Alfred C. Kinsey, so we consider it first. His data were collected in the late 1930s and 1940s, and thus the results are now largely of historical interest. However, Kinsey documented his methods with extraordinary care, so his research is a good example to study for both the good and the bad points of surveys.

The Kinsey Report

The Sample

Kinsey (see Milestones in Sex Research: Alfred C. Kinsey) and his colleagues interviewed a total of 5,300 males, and their responses were reported in *Sexual Behavior in the Human Male* (1948); 5,940 females contributed to *Sexual Behavior in the Human Female* (1953). Though some Blacks were interviewed, only interviews with Whites were included in the publications. The interviews were conducted between 1938 and 1949.

Initially, Kinsey was not much concerned with sampling issues. His goal was simply to collect sex histories from as wide a variety of people as possible. He began conducting interviews on the Indiana University campus and then moved on to large cities such as Chicago.

In the 1953 volume on females, Kinsey said that he and his colleagues had deliberately chosen not to use probability sampling methods because of the problems of nonresponse. This is a legitimate point. But as a result, we have almost no information on how adequate the sample was. One might say that the sampling was haphazard but not random. For example, there were more respondents from Indiana than from any other state. Generally, the following kinds of people were overrepresented in the sample: college students, young people, well-educated people, Protestants, people living in cities, and people living in Indiana and the Northeast. Underrepresented groups included manual laborers, less well-educated people, older people, Roman Catholics, Jews, members of racial minorities, and people living in rural areas.

The Interviews

Although scientists generally regard Kinsey's sampling methods with some dismay, his face-to-face interviewing techniques are highly regarded. More than 50 percent of the interviews were done by Kinsey himself and the rest by his associates, whom he trained carefully. The interviewers made every attempt to establish rapport with the people they spoke to, and they treated all reports matter-of-factly. They were also skillful at phrasing questions in language that was easily understood. Questions were worded so as to encourage people to report anything they had done. For example, rather than asking, "Have you ever masturbated?" the interviewers asked, "At what age did you begin masturbating?" They also developed a number of methods for cross-checking a person's report so that false information would be detected. Wardell Pomeroy recounted an example:

> Kinsey illustrated this point with the case of an older Negro male who at first was wary and evasive in his answers. From the fact that he listed a number of minor jobs when asked about his occupation and seemed reluctant to go into any of them [Kinsey] deduced that he might have been active in the underworld, so he began to follow up by asking the man whether he had ever been married. He denied it, at which Kinsey resorted to the vernacular and inquired if he had ever "lived common law." The man admitted he had, and that it had first happened when he was 14.
> "How old was the woman?" [Kinsey] asked.
> "Thirty-five," he admitted, smiling.
> Kinsey showed no surprise. "She was a hustler, wasn't she?" he said flatly.
> At this the subject's eyes opened wide. Then he smiled in a friendly way for the first time, and said, "Well, sir, since you appear to know something about these things, I'll tell you straight."
> After that, [Kinsey] got an extraordinary record of this man's history as a pimp. (Pomeroy, 1972, pp. 115–116)

Milestones in Sex Research

Alfred C. Kinsey

Alfred C. Kinsey (Figure 3) was born in 1894 in New Jersey. In high school he did not date, and a classmate recalled that he was "the shyest guy around girls you could think of."

His father was determined that Kinsey become a mechanical engineer. From 1912 to 1914 he tried studying engineering at Stevens Institute, but he showed little talent for it. At one point he was close to failing physics, but a compromise was reached with the professor, who agreed to pass him if he would not attempt any advanced work in the field! In 1914 Kinsey made his break and enrolled at Bowdoin College in Maine to pursue his real love: biology. Because this went against his father's wishes, Kinsey was put on his own financially.

In 1916 he began graduate work at Harvard. There he developed an interest in insects, specializing in gall wasps. While still a graduate student he wrote a definitive book on the edible plants of eastern North America.

In 1920 he went to Bloomington, Indiana, to take a job as assistant professor of zoology at Indiana University. That fall he met Clara McMillen, whom he married six months later. They had four children.

With his intense curiosity and driving ambition, Kinsey quickly gained academic success. He published a high school biology text in 1926, which received enthusiastic reviews. By 1936 he had published two major books on gall wasps; they established his reputation as a leading authority in the field.

Kinsey came to the study of human sexual behavior as a biologist. His shift to the study of sex began in 1938, when Indiana University began a "marriage" course; Kinsey chaired the faculty committee teaching it. When confronted with teaching the course, he became aware of the appalling lack of information on human sexual behavior. Thus, his research resulted in part from his realization of the need of people, especially young people, for sex information. In 1939 he made his first field trip to collect sex histories in Chicago. His lifetime goal was to collect 100,000 sex histories.

His work culminated with the publication of the Kinsey reports in 1948 (*Sexual Behavior in the Human Male*) and 1953 (*Sexual Behavior in the Human Female*). While the scientific community generally received them as a landmark contribution, they also provoked hate mail.

In 1947 Kinsey founded the Institute for Sex Research (known popularly as the Kinsey Institute) at Indiana University. It was financed by a grant from the Rockefeller Foundation and, later, by book royalties. But in the 1950s Senator Joseph McCarthy, the communist baiter, was in power. He made a particularly vicious attack on the institute and its research, claiming that its effect was to weaken

Figure 3 Alfred C. Kinsey (on the left), with colleagues Martin, Gebhard, and Pomeroy.

©Hulton Archive/Getty Images

American morality and thus make the nation more susceptible to a communist takeover. Under his pressure, the Rockefeller Foundation terminated its support.

Kinsey's health began to fail, partly as a result of the heavy workload he set for himself, and partly because he saw the financial support for the research collapsing. He died in 1956 at the age of 62 of heart failure while honoring a lecture engagement when his doctor had ordered him to convalesce.

By 1957 McCarthy had been discredited and the grant funds returned. The institute was then headed by Paul Gebhard, an anthropologist who had been a member of the staff for many years. The institute continues to do research today; it also houses a large library on sex and an archival collection including countless works of sexual art.

In a highly publicized, tell-all biography of Kinsey, James Jones (1997) argued that, although Kinsey's public self was a stable, married man, he was in fact homosexual (more accurately, bisexual) and practiced masochism. According to Jones, this discredits Kinsey's research. Jones's logic is poor, though, because one can evaluate the quality of the research methods independently of Kinsey's personal sex life. Moreover, Kinsey's sexual experimenting may have contributed importantly to the innovativeness of his research.

Sources: Bancroft (2004); Christensen (1971); Drucker (2014); Gathorne-Hardy (2000); Gebhard (1976); Jones (1997).

Put simply, the interviewing techniques were probably very successful in minimizing purposeful distortion.

Kinsey took strict precautions to ensure that responses were anonymous and remained anonymous. The data were stored on IBM cards, but using a code that was never written down and had been memorized by only a few people directly involved in the project. The research team had even made contingency plans for destroying the data in the event that the police tried to demand access to the records for prosecuting people.

How Accurate Were the Kinsey Statistics?

When all is said and done, how accurate were the statistics presented by Kinsey? The American Statistical Association appointed a blue-ribbon panel to evaluate the Kinsey reports (Cochran et al., 1953; for other evaluations see Terman, 1948; Wallin, 1949). While the panel members generally felt that the interview techniques had been excellent, they were dismayed by Kinsey's failure to use probability sampling and concluded, somewhat pessimistically,

> In the absence of a probability-sample benchmark, the present results must be regarded as subject to systematic errors of unknown magnitude due to selective sampling (via volunteering and the like). (Cochran et al., 1953, p. 711)

However, they also felt that this was a nearly insoluble problem for sex research in that even if a probability sample were used, refusals would still create serious problems.

The statisticians who evaluated Kinsey's methods felt that one aspect of his findings might have been particularly subject to error: the generally high levels of sexual activity, and particularly the high prevalence of homosexual behavior. These conclusions might, they felt, have been seriously influenced by sampling problems, particularly Kinsey's tendency to seek out people with unusual sexual practices.

Is the Kinsey report still the best available sex survey?

Kinsey's associates felt that the most questionable statistic was the prevalence of male homosexuality. Wardell Pomeroy commented, "The magic 37 percent of males who had one or more homosexual experiences was, no doubt, overestimated" (1972, p. 466).

In sum, it is impossible to say how accurate the Kinsey statistics are; some may be very accurate and some may contain serious errors. Probably the single most doubtful figure is the high prevalence of homosexuality. Also, at this point the Kinsey survey is roughly 70 years old; for accurate information about sexuality today, we need to look to more recent research.

The NHSLS

After the Kinsey report, many sex surveys were conducted, most using slipshod sampling methods. What was needed was a large-scale, national survey of sexuality using probability sampling methods to tell us what Americans' patterns of sexual behavior are. Such a study appeared in 1994. The research team was headed by Edward Laumann, a distinguished sociologist at the University of Chicago, and was conducted by the National Opinion Research Center (NORC), one of the best-respected survey organizations in the country. The survey was called the National Health and Social Life Survey; to keep things simple, we will call this study the NHSLS (Laumann et al., 1994; Michael et al., 1994).

The research method involved a probability sampling of households in the United States. This excluded less than 3 percent of Americans but did exclude people living in institutions (e.g., prisons, college dormitories) and the homeless. People were eligible if they were adults between the ages of 18 and 59.

The researchers obtained an impressive 79 percent response rate. Apparently, the great majority of people are willing to respond to a carefully conducted sex survey. The response rate is particularly impressive in view of the fact that today even surveys of more neutral topics such as political opinions generally have a response rate of only about 75 percent.

The researchers had originally planned to poll a sample of 20,000 people. However, federal funding for the project was blocked by some politicians. The researchers were able to obtain funding from private foundations, but only enough to interview a sample of 3,432 people.

The data were obtained in face-to-face interviews supplemented by brief written questionnaires, which were handed to the respondents for particularly sensitive topics (such as masturbation) and sealed in a "privacy envelope" when they had been completed. The researchers chose the face-to-face interview because they felt that it would yield a higher response rate than a written questionnaire alone, and it allowed the researchers to ask more complex, detailed sequences of questions than would have been possible with just a written questionnaire.

The NHSLS is one of the best sex surveys of the general population of the United States that we have today, and its findings are referred to in many chapters in this book. The researchers made outstanding efforts to use the best sampling methods and interview techniques.

Nonetheless, the study has some limitations. It sampled only people between ages 18 and 59, giving us no information about the sexuality of older adults. The sample did not include enough people from some statistically small minority groups—in particular, American Indians—to compute reliable statistics for them. This problem would probably not have occurred if there had been funding for the full sample of 20,000. On the other hand, for other ethnic minority groups—African Americans, Latinx, and Asian Americans—there are lots of interesting findings. No doubt some respondents engaged in concealment, and perhaps also in enlargement, because self-reports were used. The skill of the interviewers and their ability to build rapport are crucial in overcoming such problems.

The NSSHB

The most recent major national U.S. sex survey is the National Survey of Sexual Health and Behavior (NSSHB), with data collected in 2009 for people between the ages of 14 and 94 (Herbenick et al., 2010b; Reece et al., 2010a). A probability sample was identified based on a combination of random-digit dialing of telephone numbers and sampling of residential addresses from the U.S. Postal Service's list of deliverable addresses in the United States. For the adolescent part of the sample, parents were contacted first to provide consent and 62 percent agreed, and then 62 percent of the eligible adolescents participated, for a sample of 820 adolescents. In addition, 9,600 potential adult participants were contacted and 53 percent provided data. The overall sample size, then, combining adults and adolescents, was 5,865. Participants completed the survey on the Internet and those without computers were provided them for completing the questionnaire. Overall, 69 percent of the sample was White, 14 percent were Hispanic, 11 percent were Black, and 7 percent were from other groups, a distribution that is close to that of the U.S. population. Results from the survey will be presented in many chapters that follow.

How good is the NSSHB? The methods for identifying the initial probability sample—random-digit dialing of phone numbers and sampling of residential addresses—were excellent. The response rate was 50 percent, which is considerably lower than what the NHSLS obtained, but it is probably getting more difficult to recruit participants because Americans are increasingly oversaturated with solicitations from fund-raising organizations, telemarketers, and so on. Statistically, with a 50 percent response rate, we cannot be sure that the results generalize to the whole population, but volunteer bias is always a problem with sex research. Certainly the size of the sample is a strength, as is the ethnic diversity; and generally administering sex questionnaires online is a good idea because respondents feel more anonymous and therefore presumably answer more truthfully.

Sexual Behavior in Britain and Australia

Stimulated by a need for better information about sexual behavior to improve sexual and reproductive health, Britain conducts a major sex survey once every 10 years. Called the National Survey of Sexual Attitudes and Lifestyles (Natsal), the most recent one is Natsal-3, based on data collected between 2010 and 2012 (Erens et al., 2014). The survey used excellent sampling methods by conducting probability sampling of addresses within postal codes (equivalent to American zip codes) and achieved a response rate of 58 percent. Funding from the British government

allowed researchers to collect a very large sample, with 15,162 completed interviews. Although the data collection method was called interviewing, in fact interviewers went to homes and respondents completed the questionnaires on computers to ensure anonymity. In addition, with a subsample of about 4,000 people, researchers collected urine samples to test for sexually transmitted infections (STIs) and saliva samples to test for testosterone. Space limitations do not allow us to report all of the extensive findings here, so we will give just one example. Among participants between the ages of 16 and 44, the percentage of women who reported a sexual experience involving genital contact with another woman went from 1.8 percent in Natsal-1 (1990) to 4.9 percent in Natsal-2 (2000) to 7.9 percent in Natsal-3 (2010) (Mercer et al., 2013). Natsal-3 is one of the largest well-conducted sex surveys to date, along with the Australian survey described next.

Another team of researchers conducted a major sex survey in Australia (Rissel et al., 2003a, 2003b; Smith et al., 2003). The study is called the Australian Study of Health and Relationships (ASHR), and there is now a second ASHR with data collected in 2013 (Richters et al., 2014). Using computer-assisted telephone interviews, the ASHR-2 researchers recruited a sample of 20,000 men and women aged 16 to 69. Their response rate was 66 percent.

Their findings indicate that the age of first intercourse has declined over the last several decades, consistent with trends in the United States (Rissel et al., 2014). In respondents aged 16 to 19, the youngest cohort, 26 percent of the men and 26 percent of the women reported that they had engaged in intercourse before age 16. Fully 29 percent of the men and 21 percent of the women reported that they used no contraception the first time they had intercourse, a pattern that is also similar to the United States and is of great concern.

Ethnicity in Research

Much research in psychology has been conducted with college students, and these samples are predominantly White and middle class. Yet ethnicity—ethnic heritage, their skin color, their experiences of microaggressions—has a profound impact on people and their interactions with others. When we consider ethnicity in research, several approaches can be taken (Hall et al., 2016): (1) For the sexual behavior being studied, are there similarities across ethnic groups, or are there differences between ethnic groups? (2) If there are differences, what aspects of culture account for those differences? (3) What can we learn from an in-depth study of a single ethnic minority group? As an example of research using the first two approaches, researchers investigated sexual aggression among Asian Americans and European Americans (Hall et al., 2016). Men from both groups had similar rates of reported sexual aggression. Yet for Asian American men, loss of face was a strong deterrent against committing sexual aggression, whereas it was not for European American men. Loss of face is a powerful cultural value for Asian Americans, but less of a value for European Americans. As an example of a study using the third approach, Carlos Cuevas and his colleagues (2010) conducted a survey of Latinx in the United States to assess patterns of interpersonal victimization, including sexual assault and partner violence. The study is called SALAS, for Sexual Assault among Latinx. The researchers used a random-digit dialing method, which generates random lists of telephone numbers across the United States. Among the phone numbers that had an eligible person (a woman over the age of 18 who identified as Latinx), the researchers obtained interviews with 2,000 women, for a 31 percent response rate. Interviews were conducted by phone in either English or Spanish, whichever the respondent preferred. The sample represented the great diversity among Latinx today. For example, 29 percent were U.S.-born citizens, 33 percent were naturalized citizens, 28 percent had permanent resident status, and 5 percent had another status such as undocumented. For language, 19 percent preferred English and 76 percent preferred Spanish.

The results indicated that 17 percent of the women had been sexually assaulted, which is in line with figures from national surveys of women of all ethnicities (see the chapter "Sexual Coercion"). Physical assault had been experienced by 22 percent, and 18 percent had experienced stalking. Many had experienced polyvictimization, that is, more than one kind of victimization.

The researchers used many of the methods that are recommended for research with ethnic minority populations. All interviewers were women, to match the gender of the interviewer to that of the respondent. Bilingual interviewers were available for those who preferred to be interviewed in Spanish.

Conducting sex research with ethnic minorities in the United States requires more than just administering the same old surveys to samples of minorities (Matsumoto, 2000). It also dictates revisions to methods so that they are culturally sensitive on issues such as the ethnicity of the interviewer, the language used in the questions, and the special sensitivity of some groups regarding certain topics.

Magazine Surveys

Many large-scale sex surveys have been conducted through magazines. Often the survey is printed in one issue of the magazine and readers are asked to respond. The result can be a huge sample—perhaps 20,000 people—which sounds impressive. But are these magazine surveys really all they claim to be?

Sampling is just plain out of control with magazine surveys. The survey is distributed only to readers of the magazine, and different magazines have different clienteles. No one magazine reaches a random sample of Americans. If the survey appeared in *Redbook,* it would

Figure 4   Research conducted among racial and ethnic minority groups in the United States must be culturally sensitive. Ideally, for example, interviewers should be of the same cultural background as research participants.

©*Thinkstock/Getty Images*

go to certain kinds of women; if it were in *Ladies' Home Journal,* it would go to others. It would be risky to assume that women who read *Redbook* have the same sexual patterns as those who read *Cosmo.* To make matters worse, the response rate is unknown. We can't know how many people saw the survey and did not fill it out, compared with the number who did. The response rate could be something like 3 percent. One does not, therefore, even have a random sample of readers of that magazine.

As an example, let's consider a survey that was reported in the August 2009 issue of *Cosmopolitan.* The headline on the cover announces "Guys Rate 125 Sex Moves." The description of the methods in the article says that *Cosmo* "paired up with AskMen.com and got thousands of guys between the ages of 18 and 35 to confess what they want in bed." A subtitle clarifies that "thousands" actually means "6,000 horny guys." That sample is twice the size of the NHSLS, but, in sex surveys as in some other aspects of sexuality, bigger is not always better. What we can't tell from the article is who these 6,000 horny guys are. Are they representative of all American men between the ages of

18 and 35? That's highly unlikely, because only men who go to AskMen.com saw the survey. How can we know the response rate? Among the respondents, how many were married? Single? What about their ethnic backgrounds? Of course, these details are not the sort of thing that *Cosmo* probably thinks will entertain its readers. Nonetheless, they could have printed the information in a small box at the end of the article. More important, these details are crucial in evaluating whether one can take their claims seriously.

One question in the survey asked what is the absolute sexiest sight she can treat you to. Of the men who were polled, the most frequent choice (34 percent of those polled) was "touching herself in front of me." From this, can we conclude that 34 percent of U.S. men are most turned on by the sight of their partner touching herself? Or that this is the favorite choice of U.S. men, even if it isn't exactly 34 percent? That conclusion would require a leap of logic that is too big for safety. *Cosmo* wasn't even close to having a random sample in this survey.

For all these reasons, it would not be legitimate to infer that these statistics characterize U.S. men in general. We could continue with more examples of magazine surveys, but the general conclusion should be clear by now. Although they may appear impressive because of their large number of respondents, magazine sex surveys are poor in quality because the sample is generally seriously biased.

Studies of Special Populations

In addition to the large-scale studies of the U.S. population discussed earlier, many studies of special populations have been done, often focusing on populations defined by their sexual behavior. One example is the Grov study of highly sexually active gay and bisexual men in New York City (Grov et al., 2016). The study is called Pillow Talk and is headed by the prominent sex researcher Jeffrey Parsons. Grov and his New York colleagues wanted to better understand the sexual behavior of gay and bisexual men given that HIV continues to be a public health crisis in this population. Methodologically, the researchers took on the issue of the accuracy of self-reports as well as sampling. In regard to sampling, how does a researcher obtain a random sample of such a population when no one has a convenient list of all the members of the population? In response, the researchers used a combination of four recruitment strategies: (1) Internet advertisements on social and sexual networking websites; (2) e-mails to New York City gay sex party listservs; (3) active recruitment in city venues such as gay bars, gay neighborhoods, and gay community events; and (4) **snowball sampling** or respondent-driven sampling. This last technique involves asking people who are already enrolled in the study to nominate others who would be eligible to participate.

To overcome some of the difficulties with self-reports, discussed earlier in this chapter, and to maximize accuracy in reporting, Grov used the daily diary method. Every day, participants completed a report online of their sexual behaviors that day. Each day they were asked whether they had engaged in any sexual activity with another person and, if so, they received a series of questions for each partner they reported that day. They responded to questions about the particular sexual behavior with that person (e.g., anal sex, receptive or insertive) and whether a condom was used. They reported the HIV status of the partner as well as the perceived ethnicity of the partner. As noted earlier, the daily diary method overcomes problems with relying on memory in self-reports (McAuliffe et al., 2007). It also allows a much richer, contextualized description of people's sexual encounters. In this case, the researchers were interested in whether high-risk sexual behaviors (condomless anal sex) occurred primarily between men of the same race, which could account for the persistence of higher rates of HIV infection among gay and bisexual men of color. They found some evidence in favor of this hypothesis, but also some evidence contradicting it. When doing research with sexual minorities, it is important to show the same kind of cultural sensitivity as in research with ethnic minorities (Bauer & Wayne, 2005). For example, if interviews are conducted, the interviewers should themselves be sexual minorities.

Web-Based Surveys

Web-based surveys include two methodological components: (1) recruiting participants using the Internet; and (2) having participants complete questionnaires online rather than in a paper questionnaire or interview. Compared with other methods, web-based surveys have many advantages but also some disadvantages (Bowen, 2005; Catania et al., 2015; Gosling et al., 2004; Kraut et al., 2004; Schick et al., 2014). Online completion of questionnaires, because it increases anonymity, should lead to more honest responding, and the evidence indicates that it does (Robertson et al., 2018). Here we focus on the use of the Internet for recruiting participants.

Web-based sex surveys can recruit much larger samples than can traditional interview or questionnaire studies. For example, one Internet survey of men who have sex with men yielded 1,052 completed surveys in less than two months (Matthews et al., 2012). And online surveys can potentially produce broader samples than can traditional survey

> **Snowball sampling:** A method for acquiring a sample of people in which existing participants suggest names of future participants to be recruited. Also called respondent-driven sampling.

methods. For example, if you were conducting a survey on college students' sexuality using traditional methods, you would probably sample students at your own college or university. If, instead, you administered the questionnaire on the Internet, you could sample students from colleges and universities across the nation and, indeed, around the world. In what is perhaps the most spectacular example to date, the *BBC Internet Study* obtained data from 255,000 people on questions about gender and sexuality (Reimers, 2007). These methods open up exciting possibilities for cross-cultural research.

Web-based surveys have particular advantages for studying special populations defined by their sexual behavior, particularly if the behavior is taboo. For example, traditional studies of gays and lesbians have used methods such as recruiting the sample through gay activist organizations and gay bars. These methods have been criticized because they omit from the sample closeted gays and those who do not actively participate in organizations or go to bars. Closeted gays have equal access to web-based surveys and can answer them in a highly anonymous way, respecting their own decisions to remain closeted. Therefore, online methods can access this population that had previously been studied very little and can yield a much wider sample of gays and lesbians. Online methods can also locate stigmatized sexual minorities, such as those involved in sadomasochism, bondage, and discipline, by recruiting participants through virtual communities and websites designed for that particular sexual group.

Web-based surveys, then, have substantial strengths on the issue of sampling. Nonetheless, they still rely on self-reports, which, as we saw earlier, can be inaccurate to some degree.

Web-based surveys have the ability to eliminate extraneous influences on responding. For example, the gender or ethnicity of the interviewer may influence an individual's responses, but these factors are eliminated in a questionnaire administrated online.

Do all these substantial advantages come with any disadvantages? Some bias is introduced because not everyone has Internet access. Access grows every day, but Internet users still, on average, have incomes above the national average. Internet samples are nonetheless considerably more diverse than the college-student samples used in much research. The researcher lacks control of the environment in which the respondent completes the survey—something that can be controlled in personal interviews but cannot in mailed-out questionnaires. One can imagine, for example, a group of fraternity brothers filling out an online sex survey together and having fun faking the answers. Individuals might respond multiple times or might try to sabotage or skew the results to show a particular outcome. Internal checks can be built into the sequence of questions that can detect faked patterns of answers, and methods have been devised to detect repeat responders. Nonetheless, these issues continue to be a concern.

On balance, then, web-based surveys offer substantial advantages over traditional survey methods and offer researchers access to special populations that previously were difficult to recruit.

Media Content Analysis

To this point we have focused on methods used to analyze people's sexuality. Yet we have also recognized the profound impact of the mass media on Americans' sexuality. To be able to understand this impact, we need to be able to analyze the media; the standard technique for this is called **content analysis** (Krippendorff, 2004).

Content analysis refers to a set of procedures used to make valid inferences about text. The "text" might be romance novels, advice columns in *Cosmopolitan* magazine, lyrics from rap music, or prime-time television programs. As it turns out, many of the same methodological issues discussed earlier also come into play with content analysis.

Sampling is one such issue. Suppose that you want to do a content analysis of advice columns in *Cosmo*. First, you need to define the population. Do you want to sample only from *Cosmo,* or do you want to sample from all sex-oriented magazines? If you want to focus only on *Cosmo,* then you will surely want to collect your sample of columns from more than one issue. You will have to define the span of years of magazine issues in order to define the population. Finally, you will have to decide whether you will analyze all advice columns from those years, sample from only certain years, or sample some columns in some issues.

The next step is to create a coding protocol. First, you must define the recording unit—is it the word, the sentence, the entire text, or perhaps themes that run across several sentences? Then, perhaps most important, you need to define the coding categories. Creating the coding scheme involves defining the basic content categories, the presence or absence of which will be recorded, for example, in the advice columns. These coding categories will depend on the question you want to ask. For example, suppose your question about prime-time television shows is, "What is the frequency on these shows of nonmarital compared with marital sex?" In creating a coding scheme, you would have to define carefully what observable behaviors on television count as "sex." Suppose you include kissing, fondling of the breasts or genitals, sexual intercourse actually shown, and implied sexual intercourse. You could then code each of these behaviors as they occurred on a sample of prime-time shows and indicate, for each act, whether it was between married or unmarried people.

Content analysis: A set of procedures used to make valid inferences about text.

Figure 5   Precise methods have been developed for analyzing the content of the media.

©Janet Hyde

The reliability of the coding must be demonstrated in content analysis just as it must in research with human participants. Reliability establishes that the methods are objective. Without a demonstration of reliability, a critic might accuse you of bias, for example, seeing far more acts of sex on the programs than actually occurred. Usually a measure called **intercoder reliability** is used (Manganello & Blake, 2010). The researcher trains another person in the exact use of the coding scheme. Then the researcher and the trained coder each independently code a sample of the texts in the study—for example, 20 of the advice columns or 20 of the prime-time shows. The researcher then computes a correlation or percent of agreement between the two coders' results, which gives the measure of intercoder reliability. If the two coders agree exactly, the correlation will be 1.0.

Content analysis is a powerful scientific technique that allows us to know how the media portray sexuality. As an example, let's suppose that your friend Rachel says that it is deeply disturbing that women are shown in nothing but traditional roles on prime-time TV, and this situation hasn't improved a bit over the years. Your other friend Tanisha disagrees, saying that there may still be some traditional images of women, but there are many examples of women in nontraditional roles such as doctors, and that the media's portrayals of women have changed a lot

over the years. How can you decide who is right? Arguing won't settle the debate. What is needed is a content analysis of current prime-time shows, counting instances of women in traditional and nontraditional roles, together with an analysis of archived prime-time shows from 10 and 20 years ago. We will see examples of content analyses such as these in the chapter "Sexuality and the Life Cycle: Childhood and Adolescence."

Qualitative Methods

Most of the research methods discussed so far are *quantitative methods,* that is, people's responses are quantified or given numerical values. For example, respondents rate their attitudes about gay marriage on a scale from (1) strongly disapprove to (7) strongly approve; or participants report their number of sexual partners in the past year.

An alternative to quantitative methods is **qualitative research,** in which the results are conveyed not

> **Intercoder reliability:** In content analysis, the correlation or percent of agreement between two coders independently rating the same texts.
> **Qualitative research:** A collection of naturalistic, holistic methods, including participant observation and in-depth interviewing, in which the results are conveyed not in numbers but in words.

Milestones in Sex Research

Masters and Johnson: The Physiology of Sexual Response

William Masters began his research on the physiology of sexual response in 1954. No one had ever studied human sexual behavior in the laboratory before, so he had to develop all the necessary research techniques from scratch. He began by interviewing 188 female prostitutes, as well as 27 male prostitutes working for a gay clientele. They gave him important preliminary data in which they "described many methods for elevating and controlling sexual tensions and demonstrated innumerable variations in stimulative techniques," some of which were useful in the later program of therapy for sexual disorders.

Meanwhile, Masters began setting up his laboratory and equipping it with the necessary instruments: an electrocardiograph to measure changes in heart rate over the sexual cycle, an electromyograph to measure muscular contractions in the body during sexual response, and a pH meter to measure the acidity of the vagina during the various stages of sexual response.

Sampling

Masters made a major breakthrough when he decided that it should be possible to recruit normal participants from the general population and have them engage in sexual behavior in the laboratory, where their behavior and physiological responses could be carefully observed and measured. This approach had never been used before, as even the daring Kinsey had settled for people's verbal reports of their behavior.

Masters let it be known in the medical school and university community that he needed volunteers for laboratory studies of human sexual response. Some people volunteered because of their belief in the importance of the research. Some, of course, came out of curiosity or because they were exhibitionists; they were weeded out in the initial interviews. Participants were paid for their hours in the laboratory, as is typical in medical research, so many medical students and graduate students participated because it was a way to earn money.

Initially, all prospective participants were given detailed interviews by Masters and his colleague Virginia Johnson. People who had histories of emotional problems or who seemed uncomfortable with the topic of sex either failed to come back after this interview or were eliminated even if they were willing to proceed. Participants were also assured that the anonymity and confidentiality of their participation would be protected carefully. In all, 694 people participated in the laboratory studies reported in *Human Sexual Response*. The men ranged in age from 21 to 89, and the women ranged from 18 to 78.

Certainly the group of people Masters and Johnson studied were not a random sample of the population of the United States. In fact, one might imagine that people who would agree to participate in such research would be rather unusual. The data indicate that they were more educated than the general population and the sample was mostly White, with only a few ethnic minority persons participating. Paying the participants probably helped broaden the sample because it attracted some people who simply needed the money. The sample omitted two notable types of people: those who were not sexually experienced or did not respond to sexual stimulation and those who were unwilling to have their sexual behavior studied in the laboratory. Therefore, the results Masters and Johnson obtained might not generalize to such people.

In defense of their sampling techniques, even if they had identified an initial probability sample, they would still almost surely have had a very high refusal rate, higher than in survey research, and the probability sample would have been ruined. At present, this seems to be an unsolvable problem in this type of research.

Data Collection Techniques

After they were accepted for the project, participants then proceeded to the laboratory phase of the study. First, they had a "practice session," in which they engaged in sexual activity in the laboratory in complete privacy, with no data being recorded and no researchers present. The purpose of this was to allow the participants to become comfortable with engaging in sexual behavior in a laboratory setting.

The physical responses of the participants were then recorded during sexual intercourse, masturbation, and "artificial coition." Masters and Johnson made an important technical advance with the development of the artificial coition technique. In it, a female participant stimulates herself with an artificial penis constructed of clear plastic; it is powered by an electric motor, and the woman can adjust the depth and frequency of the thrust. There is a light and a recording apparatus inside the artificial penis, so the changes occurring inside the vagina can be photographed.

Measures such as these avoid the problems of distortion that are possible with self-reports. They also answer much different questions. That is, it would be impossible from such measures to tell whether the person had had any same-gender sexual experiences or how frequently they masturbated. Instead, they ascertain how the body responds to sexual stimulation, with a kind of accuracy and detail that would be impossible to obtain through self-reports.

One final potential problem also deserves mention. It has to do with the problems of laboratory studies: Do people respond the same sexually in the laboratory as they do in the privacy of their own homes?

Ethical Considerations

Masters and Johnson were attentive to ethical principles. They were careful to use informed consent. Potential participants were given detailed explanations of the kinds of

things they would be required to do in the research and were given ample opportunity at all stages to withdraw from the research if they so desired. Furthermore, Masters and Johnson eliminated people who appeared too anxious or distressed during the preliminary interviews.

It is also possible that participating in the research itself might have been harmful in some way to some people. Masters and Johnson were particularly concerned with the long-term effects of participating in the research. Accordingly, they made follow-up contacts with the participants at 5-year intervals. In no case did a participant report developing a sexual disorder. In fact, many of the couples reported specific ways in which participating in the research enriched their marriages. Thus, the available data seem to indicate that such research does not harm the participants and may in some ways benefit them, not to mention the benefit to society that results from gaining information in such an important area.

in numbers, but in words—what is sometimes called thick description (Berg, 2001; Denzin & Lincoln, 2011). Qualitative research encompasses a collection of methods that may involve the researcher's participation in a setting; direct observation; or in-depth, open-ended interviews. This method is naturalistic and holistic. It seeks to understand people in their natural environment, not in a lab or an experiment; and it seeks a complete picture of the participants and their context, not focusing on just one or two variables.

Alexa Albert's book *Brothel: Mustang Ranch and Its Women* (2001) is an example of qualitative research. Albert's goal was to study brothel prostitution in the context of legalized, regulated prostitution in Nevada. She collected data in a variety of ways—for example, in-depth interviews with the women who worked in the brothel, and observations inside the brothel, including the "line-up," in which the women line up, dressed in their best seductive clothing, for the clients to view and pick whom they want. This type of research would be called an **ethnography,** a method used widely in anthropology and sociology. An ethnography is a research method that aims to provide a complete, probing description of a human society—whether a preliterate group on a remote island or a brothel in Nevada. Ethnography is one of the qualitative methods.

Qualitative research generally differs from quantitative research in several ways. Qualitative researchers typically do not use random or probability samples, and they typically have small samples, perhaps only 20

people. Compared with quantitative research, qualitative research is more likely to be exploratory and to focus on generating hypotheses rather than testing hypotheses. Qualitative methods and quantitative methods can therefore be used together.

Another type of qualitative research, used by anthropologists and sociologists, is the **participant-observer technique.** In this type of research, the scientist actually becomes a part of the community to be studied, and makes observations from inside the community. In the study of sexual behavior, the researcher may thus be able to get direct observations of sexual behavior combined with interview data.

Examples of this type of research are studies of sexual behavior in other cultures, such as those done in Mangaia, and Inis Beag, which are discussed in the chapter "Sexuality in Perspective." One other example is Charles Moser's study of S/M (sadomasochistic) parties.

Sex researcher Charles Moser observed S/M interactions in semipublic settings, attending more than 200 S/M parties (Moser, 1998). Such parties are typically highly scripted. The person who gives the party may advertise it widely (e.g., on the Internet) or may issue personal invitations to only a very select list. The parties may have a particular theme, such as female

Ethnography: A research method used to provide a description of a human group, a social setting, or a society.
Participant-observer technique: A research method in which the scientist becomes part of the community to be studied and makes observations from inside the community.

dominant/male submissive only or women only. The party might be held at a person's home or in a rented space; some cities have spaces dedicated for S/M party rental.

Each party has a particular set of rules—which vary from one party to another—and guests may be required to sign a written agreement to them. Issues covered in these rules include who may talk to whom (can a submissive be spoken to?), who may play with whom, who may have sex with whom, prohibited S/M or sexual behaviors, what constitutes safer sex, not blocking equipment by sitting on it, and so on. Drunkenness is never acceptable; some parties allow wine or beer, but others ban all alcohol.

Some individuals plan to have a first "date" at a party. Parties clearly have the function of ensuring safety for participants because others are always present if an interaction goes too far. Potential partners negotiate what kind of interaction they desire—for example, pain versus humiliation.

Perhaps most interesting is the fact that coitus or genitally focused activity designed to produce orgasm is very rare at these parties. The participants describe the S/M experiences as highly sexual, but orgasm typically is not the goal.

Moser did not report that he obtained informed consent from the people he observed. However, their behavior was public, leading to a relaxation of human subjects regulations. In his report he was careful not to divulge any identifying information about individuals.

Experiments

All the studies discussed so far have had one thing in common: They were all studies of people's sexual behavior as it occurs naturally, conducted by means such as self-reports or direct observations. Such research is **correlational;** that is, the data obtained can tell us that certain factors are related. They cannot, however, tell us what *causes* various aspects of sexual behavior.

For instance, suppose we conduct a survey and find that women who masturbated to orgasm in adolescence are more likely to have a high consistency of orgasm in heterosexual sex than women who did not. From this it would be tempting to conclude that practice in masturbating causes women to have more orgasms in heterosexual sex. Unfortunately, this is not a legitimate conclusion

to draw from the data because many other factors might also explain the results. For example, it could be that some women have a higher sex drive than others, which causes them to masturbate and also have orgasms in heterosexual sex. Therefore, the most we can conclude is that masturbation experience is related to (or correlated with) orgasm consistency in heterosexual sex.

An alternative method that does allow researchers to determine the causes of various aspects of behavior is the **experiment.** According to its technical definition, in an experiment one factor must be manipulated while all other factors are held constant. Thus, any differences among the groups of people who received different treatments on that one factor can be said to be caused by that factor. For obvious reasons, most experimental research is conducted in the laboratory.

As an example of an experiment, let us consider a study that investigated whether being interviewed face to face causes children to underreport their sexual experiences (Romer et al., 1997). The participants were approximately 400 low-income children between the ages of 9 and 15. Some were assigned to a face-to-face interview with an experienced adult interviewer of their own gender. Others were assigned to be interviewed by a "talking computer," which had the same questions programmed into it (Figure 6). The questions appeared on the screen and, simultaneously, came through headphones, for those who were not good readers. Presumably in the talking computer condition, the child feels more of a sense of privacy and anonymity and therefore responds more truthfully.

Correlational study: A study in which the researcher does not manipulate variables but rather studies naturally occurring relationships (correlations) among variables.

Experiment: A type of research study in which one variable (the independent variable) is manipulated by the experimenter while all other factors are held constant; the researcher can then study the effects of the independent variable on some measured variable (the dependent variable); the researcher is permitted to make causal inferences about the effects of the independent variable on the dependent variable.

Figure 6 An innovation in surveys of children is the use of "talking computers" to ask questions, with the children entering their answers using the mouse or the keyboard.

©JGI/Jamie Grill/Getty Images

Among 13-year-old boys interviewed by the talking computer, 76 percent said they had "had sex," compared with only 50 percent of the boys in the face-to-face interview. Forty-eight percent of 13-year-old girls interviewed by computer said they had had sex, compared with 25 percent of those interviewed by a human. The children clearly reported more sexual activity to the computer than to a human interviewer.

In the language of experimental design, the *independent variable* (manipulated variable) was the type of interview (computer or human interviewer). The *dependent variable* (the measured variable) was whether they had had sex (there were a number of other dependent variables as well, but a discussion of them would take us too far afield).

The results indicated that those interviewed by humans reported significantly less sexual activity than those interviewed by computer. Because the research design was experimental, we can make causal inferences. We can say confidently that the type of interview had an effect on children's answers. We might also say that a face-to-face interview causes children to underreport their activity. That statement is a bit shakier than the previous one because it assumes that the answers given to the talking computer were "true." It is possible that children overreported or exaggerated in responding to the computer and that their answers to the human interviewer were accurate, although this interpretation seems rather far-fetched.

Experimental sex research permits us to make much more powerful statements about the causes of various kinds of sexual phenomena. That is, it allows us to make **causal inferences**—inferring that the independent variable actually influences the dependent variable. As for disadvantages, much of the experimental sex research, including the study described here, still relies on self-reports. Experimental sex research is time consuming and costly, and it can generally be done only on small samples of participants. Sometimes in their efforts to control all variables except the independent variable, researchers control too much. Finally, experiments cannot address some of the most interesting—but most complex—questions in the field of sexual behavior, such as what factors cause people to develop different sexual orientations.

Meta-Analysis

At this point in the field of sex research, there can be dozens or even hundreds of studies investigating a particular question. Let's say our question is whether there are differences between males and females in attitudes about homosexuality (Petersen & Hyde, 2010). Studies can contradict each other. With this example, some might show that women are more approving of homosexuality than

men are and others might show that there is no gender difference. What is a scientist or a student to conclude?

Meta-analysis is a technique that allows researchers to bring order out of the seeming chaos of contradictory studies (Lipsey & Wilson, 2001). Meta-analysis has become the gold standard for research conclusions in many fields, including medicine, education, and psychology. Meta-analysis is a statistical technique. Using it, a researcher can statistically combine the results from all previous studies of the question of interest to determine what, taken together, the studies say. In conducting a meta-analysis, the researcher goes through three steps:

1. The researcher locates all previous studies on the question being investigated (e.g., gender differences in attitudes toward homosexuality). This step is typically done using searches of databases such as PsycINFO or Web of Science.

2. For each study, the researcher computes a statistic that measures how big the difference between males and females was, and what the direction of the difference was (males scored higher or females scored higher). This statistic is called d. The formula for it is

$$d = \frac{M_M - M_F}{s}$$

where M_M is the mean or average score for males, M_F is the mean or average score for females, and s is the average standard deviation of the male scores and the female scores. If you've studied statistics, you know what a standard deviation is. If you haven't, the standard deviation is a measure of how much variability there is in a set of scores. For example, if the average score for students on Quiz 1 is 20 and all scores fall between 19 and 21, then there is little variability and the standard deviation will be small. If, in contrast, the average score for students is 20 and scores range from 0 to 40, then there is great variability and the standard deviation will be large. The d statistic, then, tells us, for a particular study, how big the difference between the male and female means was, relative to the variability in scores. If d is a positive number, then males scored higher; if d is negative, females scored higher; and if d is zero, there was no difference.

3. The researcher averages all the values of d over all the studies that were located. This average d value tells us, when all studies are combined, what the direction of the gender difference is (whether males score higher or females score higher) and how large the difference is. Although there is some disagreement among experts, a general guide is that a d of 0.20 is a small difference, a d of 0.50 is a moderate

> **Causal inference:** Reaching the conclusion that one factor actually causes or influences an outcome.
> **Meta-analysis:** A statistical method that allows the researcher to combine the results of all prior studies on a particular question to see what, taken together, they say.

difference, and a *d* of 0.80 or more is a large difference (Cohen, 1988).

Many meta-analyses of gender differences are now available. In addition, meta-analysis can be used to synthesize the results of any group of studies that all used a two-group design to investigate the same question. For example, meta-analysis could be used for all studies on the effectiveness of Viagra compared with a placebo pill. Whenever possible in the chapters that follow, we present evidence based on meta-analyses.

Statistical Concepts

Before you can understand reports of sex research, you need to understand some basic statistical concepts.

Average

Suppose we get data from a sample of married heterosexual couples on how many times per week they have sexual intercourse. How can we summarize the data? One way to do this is to compute some average value; this will tell us how often, on the average, these people have intercourse. In sex research, the number that is usually calculated is either the mean or the median; both of these give us an indication of approximately where the average value for that group of people is. The **mean** is simply the average of the scores of all the people. The **median** is the score that splits the sample in half, with half the respondents scoring below that number and half scoring above it.

> **Mean:** The average of respondents' scores.
> **Median:** The middle score.

Variability

In addition to having an indication of the average for the sample of respondents, it is also important to know how much variability there is from one respondent to the next in the numbers reported. That is, it is one thing to say that the average couple in a sample had intercourse three times per week, with a range in the sample from two to four times per week, and it is quite another thing to say that the average was three times per week, with a range from zero to fifteen times per week. In both cases the mean is the same, but in the first there is little variability, and in the second there is a great deal of variability. These two alternatives are shown graphically in Figure 7. There is great variability in virtually all sexual behavior.

Average versus Normal

It is interesting and informative to report the average frequency of a particular sexual behavior, but this also introduces the danger that people will confuse "average" with "normal." That is, there is a tendency, when reading a statistic like "the average person has sex twice per week," to think of one's own sexual behavior, compare it with that average, and then conclude that one is abnormal if one differs much from the average. If you read that statistic and your frequency of sex is only once a week, you may begin to worry that you are undersexed or that you are not getting as much as you should. If you are having sex seven times per week, you might begin worrying that you are oversexed. Such conclusions are a mistake, first because they can make you miserable and second because there is so much variability in sexual behavior that any behavior (or frequency or length of time) within a wide range is perfectly normal. Don't confuse average with normal.

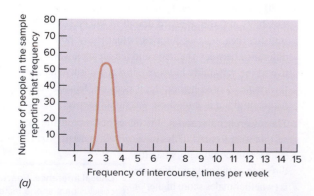

(a)

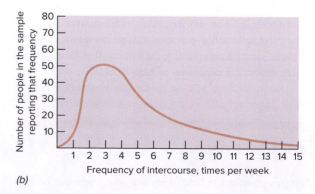

(b)

Figure 7 Two hypothetical graphs of the frequency of intercourse for heterosexual couples in a sample. In both, the average frequency is about three times per week, but in (*a*) there is little variability (almost everyone has a frequency between two and four times per week), whereas in (*b*) there is great variability (the frequency ranges from 0 to 15 or more times per week). The graph for most sexual behavior looks like (*b*), with great variability.

Incidence, Prevalence, and Frequency

In sex statistics, the terms prevalence and frequency are often used. **Prevalence** is the percentage of people in a population who have engaged in a certain behavior (e.g., masturbation) or have a certain condition (e.g., gonorrhea infection) at a specific time point. **Frequency** refers to how often people do something. Thus, we might say that the prevalence of genital herpes in the adult U.S. population is 20 percent. And we might say that the frequency of masturbation among 18- to 22-year-old men in the United States is, on average, 2 times per week. Prevalence and incidence are terms that come from public health, so they most often refer to diseases, but they can also refer to behaviors. **Incidence** refers to the number of new cases in a time period, e.g., a year. So, for example, we might say that the prevalence of herpes is 20 percent and the incidence in the last 12 months is 3 percent of the population.

A closely related concept is that of cumulative incidence. If we consider a sexual behavior according to the age at which each person in the sample first engaged in it, the *cumulative incidence* refers to the percentage of people who have engaged in that behavior before a certain age. Thus, the cumulative incidence of masturbation in males might be 10 percent by age 11, 25 percent by age 12, 82 percent by age 15, and 95 percent by age 20. Graphs of cumulative incidence always begin in the lower left-hand corner and move toward the upper right-hand corner. An example of a cumulative-incidence curve is shown in Figure 8.

Correlation

In this chapter the concept of correlation has already been mentioned several times—for example, test-retest reliability is measured by the correlation between people's answer to a question with their answer to the same question a week or two later—and the concept of correlation reappears in later chapters.

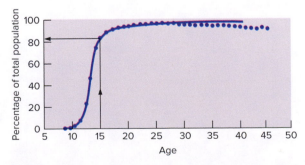

Figure 8 A cumulative-incidence curve for masturbation in males. From the graph, you can read off the percentage of males who report having masturbated by a given age. For example, about 82 percent have masturbated to orgasm by age 15.

The term *correlation* is used by laypeople in contexts such as the following: "There seems to be a correlation here between how warm the days are and how fast the corn is growing." But what do statisticians mean by the term *correlation?* A **correlation** is a number that measures the relationship between two variables. A correlation can be positive or negative. A positive correlation occurs when there is a positive relationship between the two variables; that is, people who have high scores on one variable tend to have high scores on the other variable; low scores go with low scores. A negative correlation occurs when there is an opposite relationship between the two variables; that is, people with high scores on one variable tend to have low scores on the other variable. We might want to know, for example, whether there is a correlation between the number of years a couple has been together and the frequency with which they have sexual intercourse. In this case we might expect that there would be a negative correlation, and that is just what researchers have found. That is, the *greater* the number of years in the relationship, the *lower* the frequency of intercourse.

Correlations range between $+1.0$ and -1.0. A correlation of $+1.0$ indicates a perfect positive relationship between two variables, meaning that the person in the sample who scores highest on one variable also has the highest score on the other variable, the person with the second highest score on the first variable also has the second highest score on the other variable, and so on. A correlation of 0 indicates no relationship between the two variables. Knowing a person's score on one variable tells us nothing about whether the person will have a high or a low score on the other variable. Positive correlations between 0 and $+1.0$, for example, $+.62$, say that the relationship is positive but not a perfect relationship.

Returning to the example of test-retest reliability discussed earlier in this chapter, suppose we administer a questionnaire to a sample of adults. One of the questions asks, "How many times did you masturbate to orgasm during the month of September?" We ask this question of the sample on October 1 and again on October 8. If each person in the sample gives us the same answer on October 1 and on October 8, the correlation between the two variables (the number given on October 1 and the number given on October 8) would be $+1.0$ and the test-retest reliability would be a perfect $+1.0$. In fact, test-retest reliabilities for questions about sex typically range between $+.60$ and $+.90$, indicating that people's answers on the two occasions are not identical but are very similar.

> **Incidence:** The number of new cases within a specified time period.
> **Prevalence:** The percentage of people in a population who have engaged in a certain behavior or have a certain condition at a specific point in time.
> **Frequency:** How often a person does something.
> **Correlation:** A number that measures the relationship between two variables.

Critical THINKing Skill

Understanding the importance of sampling

As we have explained in this chapter, recruiting a random or probability sample is an important aspect of high-quality sex research. The quality of the sampling has an enormous impact on the conclusions that we can reach from a particular study. Consider the following example.

Researchers were interested in learning about the motivations for extramarital sex among individuals actively involved in extramarital relationships (Omarzu et al., 2012). The researchers recruited their sample by posting a message on a website aimed at adults who engage in extramarital infidelity. A sample of 22 men and 55 women agreed to participate. According to the results, for both women and men, sexual needs, emotional needs, and falling in love were the top reasons for beginning affairs.

The population of interest here is all adults who have engaged in extramarital relationships. Did the researchers recruit a random sample of that population? If not, who did they miss?

What can we conclude from this study? Given that 22 men and 55 women participated, could we conclude that women are more than twice as likely as men to engage in extramarital relationships? Could we conclude that sexual needs, emotional needs, and falling in love are the top reasons for beginning affairs among the population of people who engage in extramarital sex? After you have answered these questions for yourself, read on to the next paragraph, which provides some answers.

The researchers did not recruit a random sample of the population of those who engage in extramarital sex. Instead, they recruited a sample of people who participate on a website aimed at this topic. Therefore, we can't reach any statistical conclusions, such as that women are more than twice as likely to engage in extramarital affairs. We only know about the people who spend time on that website. It is likely that certain categories of people are missing from the sample, such as the person who had an extramarital fling once while away from home and drunk at a convention, who feels terribly guilty about it, and never wants to think about it again, much less go to a website to discuss it. Therefore, the motives that the researchers found in their sample might not characterize the whole population, including all the people who were missed.

A random, or representative, or probability sample is crucial if we are to make valid conclusions from research.

Critical THINKing Skill
Understanding the importance of experiments

In this chapter, you learned how it is crucial to have a true experiment—with an independent variable that is manipulated, and with random assignment of participants to experimental groups—to be able to make *causal inferences* from a study. By *causal inference* we mean a conclusion that one variable causes or influences another variable.

Suppose we want to determine whether substantial exposure to pornography as an adolescent leads men to commit sex crimes. Notice here that the word "leads" is a causal term. It is equivalent to saying that exposure causes or influences men to commit sex crimes.

To find an answer to the question, we recruit two samples from a prison. One is a group of sex offenders who are in prison because they committed a sex crime. The second group is composed of offenders who are in prison for some other offense (for example, murder or robbery) but have not committed a sex crime. Both groups fill out a questionnaire that asks about their use of pornography while they were adolescents and, sure enough, the sex offenders had twice as much exposure to pornography as the other offenders. From this, can we conclude that exposure to pornography in adolescence makes men commit sex crimes? Was this a true experiment?

The answer to both questions is no. It is tempting to conclude that this was a true experiment because there were two groups, sex offenders and non–sex offenders. The problem, though, is that men were not randomly assigned to be in one group or the other. Moreover, here the hypothesized independent variable, the causal variable, is pornography exposure, not sex offending, and the men were also not randomly assigned to pornography exposure or not. Therefore, this is actually a correlational study, and all we can conclude is that there is an association between pornography exposure and sex offending, not that pornography causes sex offending.

To clarify why a causal conclusion is not warranted with a correlational study like this, it is often helpful to think of another explanation for the findings. Often this is a *third-variable* explanation; that is, there might be some third variable that influences both of the variables that were studied. In this case, the third variable may be genetics or experiences of child sexual abuse that influence men to commit sex offenses and increase their desire to use pornography. This explanation makes it even clearer why we cannot conclude that substantial exposure to pornography makes men commit sex crimes.

The effects of pornography are discussed in detail in the chapter "Sex for Sale."

SUMMARY

Measuring Sex
Researchers measure various aspects of human sexuality using (1) self-reports, (2) behavioral measures (e.g., direct observation, eye-tracking), (3) implicit measures (e.g., the IAT), and (4) biological measures (e.g., plethysmography, fMRI, pupil dilation).

Issues in Sex Research
Three crucial methodological issues in sex research are (1) sampling: Random samples or probability samples are best but are difficult to obtain because some people refuse to participate. (2) The accuracy of measurement: Much sex research relies on people's reports of their own sexual behavior. Research shows that these self-reports are generally accurate, but they can also be distorted in several ways. (3) Ethical issues: Sex researchers, like all researchers, are bound by the rules of informed consent, protection from harm, and justice.

The Major Sex Surveys
One major sex survey is the Kinsey report: Based on data collected in the 1940s, it was a large-scale interview study of the sexual behavior of Americans. The interviewing techniques were excellent, but the sampling was not. The NHSLS, published in 1994, is a large-scale survey, based on probability sampling. The more recent NSSHB used online methods. Surveys comparable to the NHSLS have been conducted in Britain and Australia.

Studies of Special Populations

Studies of special populations involve studies of populations defined by their sexual behavior, such as gays or those interested in sadism and masochism.

Web-Based Surveys

In web-based surveys, sex researchers recruit the sample and collect data online, which is especially useful in tapping hidden populations.

Media Content Analysis

Media content analysis involves a set of scientific procedures used to make valid inferences about some aspect of the media, such as sexuality in prime-time television programs or the content of advice columns in *Cosmopolitan*.

Qualitative Methods

Qualitative methods yield results that are conveyed not in numbers but in words and aim at an in-depth description of people in their natural environment. Participant-observer studies are one kind of qualitative method, in which the scientist becomes part of the community to be studied and makes observations from inside the community.

Experiments

Experiments are defined technically as a type of research in which one variable (the independent variable) is manipulated so that the researcher can study the effects of it on the dependent variable.

Meta-Analysis

Meta-analysis is a statistical method for combining all of the studies that have been done on a particular question, such as gender differences in attitudes about casual sex.

Statistical Concepts

Statistical concepts that are important for understanding reports of sex research include average, variability, prevalence versus frequency, and correlation.

SUGGESTIONS FOR FURTHER READING

Matsumoto, David, & Juang, Linda. (2017). *Culture and psychology* (6th ed.). Boston, MA: Cengage Learning. This is an authoritative textbook on cultural psychology; it includes an excellent chapter on cross-cultural research methods.

Wiederman, Michael W. (2001). *Understanding sexuality research.* Belmont, CA: Wadsworth. This slim volume, written for undergraduates, takes up where the present chapter leaves off and offers an excellent analysis of methodological issues in sex research, with interesting examples.

Are **YOU** Curious?

1. Do women ejaculate?
2. Are there any medical advantages to circumcising baby boys?
3. Are there any cancers of the sex organs that affect young men?

Read this chapter to find out.

©Anton Vengo/Purestock/SuperStock

CHAPTER

4

Sexual Anatomy

CHAPTER HIGHLIGHTS

It is a well-documented fact that guys will not ask for directions. This is a biological thing. This is why it takes several million sperm cells... to locate a female egg, despite the fact that the egg is, relative to them, the size of Wisconsin.*

*"Dave Barry's Complete Guide to Guys" by Dave Barry, 1995, Random House.

Everyone needs more information about their own body. The purpose of this chapter is to provide basic information about the structure and functions of the parts of the body that are involved in sexuality and reproduction. Some readers may anticipate that this will be a boring exercise. Everyone, after all, knows what a penis is and what a vagina is. But even today, we find some bright college students who think a woman's urine passes out through her vagina. And how many know what the epididymis and the seminiferous tubules are? If you don't know, keep reading. You may even find out a few interesting things about the penis and the vagina that you were not aware of.

Female Sexual Organs

The female sexual organs can be classified into two categories: the external organs and the internal organs.

External Organs

The external genitals of females consist of the clitoris, the mons pubis, the inner lips, the outer lips, and the vaginal opening (see Figure 1 [Ginger & Yang, 2011]). Collectively, they are known as the **vulva** ("crotch"; other terms such as "cunt" and "pussy" may refer either to the vulva or to the vagina, and some ethnic groups use "cock" for the vulva—slang, alas, is not so precise as scientific language).[1] *Vulva* is a wonderful term, but, unfortunately, it tends to be underused—the term, that is. The appearance of the vulva varies greatly from one woman to another (see Figure 2).

Vulva (VULL-vuh): The collective term for the external genitals of the female.
Clitoris (KLIT-or-is): A highly sensitive sexual organ; the glans is in front of the vaginal entrance, and the rest of the clitoris extends deeper into the body.

The Clitoris

The **clitoris** is a sensitive organ that is exceptionally important in female sexual response (Figure 3). It consists of the tip (glans), a knob of tissue situated externally in front of the vaginal opening and the urethral opening; a shaft consisting of two corpora

[1]For a discussion of slang terms for female and male genitals, see Braun and Kitzinger (2001).

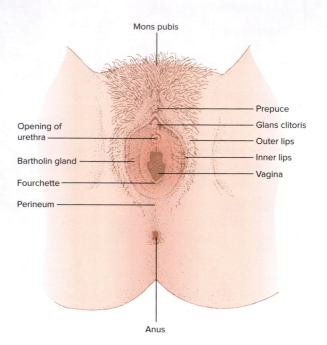

Figure 1 The vulva: The external genitals of the female.

cavernosa (spongy bodies similar to those in the penis) that extends perhaps an inch into the body; and two crura (singular "crus"), longer spongy bodies that lie deep in the body and run from the tip of the clitoris to either side of the vagina, under the major lips (Clemente, 1987). Some refer to the entire structure as having a "wishbone" shape. Close to the crura are the vestibular bulbs, which are discussed in the section on internal organs.

As we will see in the chapter "Sex Hormones, Sexual Differentiation, and the Menstrual Cycle," female sexual organs and male sexual organs develop from similar tissue before birth; thus we can speak of the organs of one gender as being *homologous* (in the sense of developing from the same source) to the organs of the other gender. The clitoris is homologous to the penis; that is, both develop from the same embryonic tissue. The clitoris has a structure similar to that of the penis in that both have corpora cavernosa. The clitoris varies in size from one woman to the next, much as the penis varies in size from man to man. Also, the clitoris, like the penis, is erectile. Its erection is possible because its internal structure contains corpora cavernosa that fill

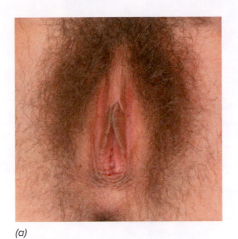
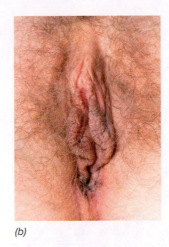

(a)   *(b)*   *(c)*

Figure 2   Genital diversity: The shape of the vulva varies widely from one woman to the next.

(a) ©Daniel Sambraus/Science Source; (b) ©H.S. Photos/Alamy; (c) ©Daniel Sambraus/Science Source

with blood, as the similar structures in the penis do. The corpora cavernosa and the mechanism of erection will be considered in more detail in the discussion of the male sexual organs. Like the penis, the clitoris has a rich supply of nerve endings, making it very sensitive to stroking. Most women find it to be more sensitive to erotic stimulation than any other part of the body.

The clitoris is unique in that it is the only part of the sexual anatomy with no known reproductive function. All the other sexual organs serve sexual and reproductive functions. For example, not only is the vagina used for sexual intercourse, but it also receives the sperm and serves as the passageway through which the baby travels during childbirth. The penis not only produces sexual arousal and pleasure but also is responsible for ejaculation and impregnation. The clitoris clearly has an important function in producing sexual arousal. Unlike the other sexual organs, however, it appears to have no direct function in reproduction.

The Mons

Other parts of the vulva are the mons pubis, the inner lips, and the outer lips. The **mons pubis** (also called the *mons* or the *mons veneris,* for "mountain of Venus") is the rounded, fatty pad of tissue, covered with pubic hair, at the front of the body. It lies on top of the pubic bones.

The Labia

The **outer lips** (or *labia majora,* for "major lips") are rounded pads of fatty tissue lying along both sides of the vaginal opening; they are covered with pubic hair. The **inner lips** (or *labia minora,* for "minor lips") are two hairless folds of skin lying between the outer lips and running right along the edge of the vaginal opening. Sometimes they are folded over, concealing the vaginal opening until they are spread apart. The inner lips extend forward and come together in front, forming the clitoral hood. The inner and outer lips

are well supplied with nerve endings and thus are also important in sexual stimulation and arousal.

Speaking of pubic hair, people are giving it a lot of attention these days. Some women trim theirs and others remove some or all of it, using methods ranging from shaving to waxing. In one study, 60 percent of Australian undergraduate women reported that they removed some of their pubic hair, and 48 percent said they removed most or all of it (Tiggemann & Hodgson, 2008). The women gave a number of reasons for removing pubic hair, including feeling cleaner, feeling attractive, feeling sexy, and making the sexual experience better. Some experts attribute increases in pubic hair removal to increased access to pornography on the Internet (Ramsey et al., 2009). Female porn stars invariably have some form of pubic hair removal, and they therefore show women what they should look like, in addition to teaching men what to expect from women. Men, too, both gay and straight, are increasingly likely to remove pubic hair (Martins et al., 2008).

In a recent U.S. national sample, 67 percent of men and 85 percent of women reported a history of pubic hair "grooming" (Truesdale et al., 2017). Unfortunately, there seems to be a downside to all this fussing over fur. In the same U.S. study, 26 percent of those who groomed suffered injuries (Truesdale et al., 2017). Most common were lacerations, followed by burns and rashes. As if that weren't enough, the research showed a correlation between pubic hair grooming and STIs (Osterberg et al., 2017). Those with a history of grooming had roughly twice the chance of having had an STI, such as herpes, HPV, or chlamydia, compared with those who had never groomed. "Extreme" groomers (complete removal of all pubic hair more than 11 times per year) had 4 times the chance of

---

Mons pubis (PYOO-bis): The fatty pad of tissue under the pubic hair.
Outer lips: Rounded pads of fatty tissue lying on either side of the vaginal entrance.
Inner lips: Thin folds of skin lying on either side of the vaginal entrance.

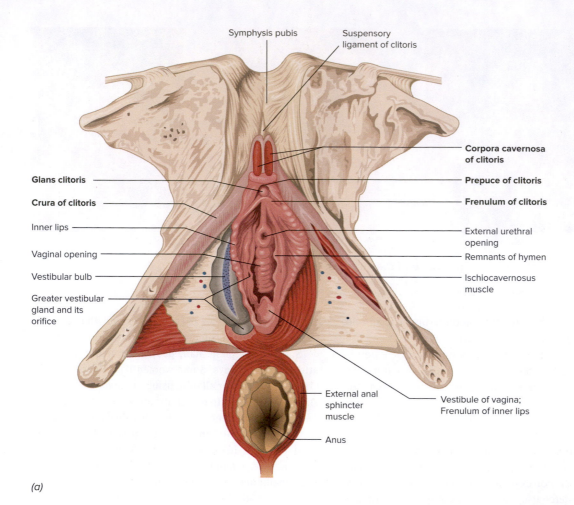

Symphysis pubis

Suspensory ligament of clitoris

Corpora cavernosa of clitoris

Glans clitoris

Prepuce of clitoris

Crura of clitoris

Frenulum of clitoris

Inner lips

External urethral opening

Vaginal opening

Remnants of hymen

Vestibular bulb

Ischiocavernosus muscle

Greater vestibular gland and its orifice

External anal sphincter muscle

Vestibule of vagina; Frenulum of inner lips

Anus

(a)

having had an STI. This makes sense because even small lacerations around the genitals are a great way for STI microbes to enter the body.

A pair of small glands, the **Bartholin glands,** lie just inside the inner lips (Figure 1). They seem to have no significant function, and they are of interest only because they sometimes become infected.[2]

A few more landmarks should be noted (Figure 1). The place where the inner lips come together behind the vaginal opening is called the *fourchette.* The area of skin between the vaginal opening and the anus is called the **perineum.** The vaginal opening

Bartholin glands: Two tiny glands located on either side of the vaginal entrance.
Perineum (pair-ih-NEE-um): The skin between the vaginal entrance and the anus.

[2]And there is a limerick about them:

There was a young man from Calcutta
Who was heard in his beard to mutter,
"If her Bartholin glands
Don't respond to my hands,
I'm afraid I shall have to use butter."

Actually, there is a biological fallacy in the limerick. Can you spot it? If not, see the chapter "Sexual Arousal."

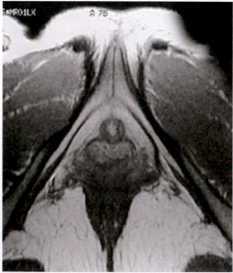

(b)

Figure 3   (*a*) Structure of the clitoris; (*b*) MRI scan of the same region.

(b) From "The use of magnetic resonance imaging for studying female sexual function: A review," Christine M. Vaccaro, ©2015 Clinical Anatomy. Reproduced with permission of John C. Wiley and Sons, Ltd.

itself is sometimes called the **introitus.** Notice also that the urinary opening lies about midway between the clitoris and the vaginal opening. Thus urine does not pass out through the clitoris (as might be expected from analogy with males) or through the vagina, but instead through a separate pathway, the **urethra,** with a separate opening.

Self-Knowledge

One important difference between the male sex organs and the female sex organs—and a difference that has some important psychological consequences—is that females' external genitals are much less visible than males'. A male can view his external genitals directly either by looking down at them or by looking into a mirror while naked. Either of these two strategies for females, however, will result at best in a view of the mons. The clitoris, the inner and outer lips, and the vaginal opening remain hidden. Indeed, many adult women have never taken a direct look at their own vulva. This obstacle can be overcome by simply using a mirror. The genitals can be viewed either by putting a mirror on the floor and sitting in front of it or by standing up and putting one foot on the edge of a chair, bed, or something similar and holding the mirror up near the genitals (see Figure 4). We recommend that all women use a mirror to identify on their own bodies all the parts shown in Figure 1.

The Hymen

The **hymen** ("cherry," "maidenhead") is a thin membrane which, if present, partially covers the vaginal opening. The hymen may be one of a number of different types (see Figure 5), although it generally has some openings in it; otherwise, the menstrual flow would not be able to pass out.[3] At the time of first intercourse, the hymen

Figure 4   Body education: The mirror exercise lets women see their own genitals.

©*Thomas Michael Corcoran/PhotoEdit*

may be broken or stretched as the penis moves into the vagina. This may cause bleeding and possibly some pain. Typically, though, it is an untraumatic occurrence and goes unnoticed in the excitement of the moment. For a woman who is very concerned about her hymen and what will happen to it at first coitus, there are two possible approaches. A physician can cut the hymen neatly so that it will not tear at the time of first intercourse, or the woman herself can stretch it by repeatedly inserting a finger into the vagina and pressing on it.

The hymen, and its destruction at first intercourse, has captured the interest of people in many cultures. In Europe during the Middle Ages, the lord might claim the right to deflower a peasant bride on her wedding night before passing her on to her husband

> **Introitus:** The vaginal entrance.
> **Urethra:** The tube through which urine passes from the bladder out of the body.
> **Hymen (HYE-men):** A thin membrane that may partially cover the vaginal entrance.

[3]The rare condition in which the hymen is a tough tissue with no opening is called *imperforate hymen* and can be corrected with fairly simple surgery.

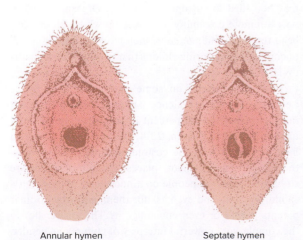

Annular hymen   Septate hymen   Cribriform hymen   Imperforate hymen

Figure 5   There are several types of hymens.

A Sexually Diverse World

Female Genital Cutting

Today a worldwide sexual health controversy rages over **female genital cutting** (FGC, also known as female genital mutilation, or FGM). According to UNICEF, 200 million girls and women have been subjected to FGC in 30 countries, 27 of them in Africa, together with Yemen, Iraq, and Indonesia (Andro & Lesclingand, 2017). Half of the genitally mutilated girls and women live in just three countries: Indonesia, Ethiopia, and Egypt. Typically FGC is performed on girls between infancy and age 15. Often it is performed by a native woman without anesthetic and under unsanitary conditions.

FGC is practiced in several forms, depending on the customs of the particular culture. The simplest is *clitoridectomy,* the partial or total removal of the glans of the clitoris, and sometimes just the prepuce. The World Health Organization (WHO) classifies this as Type 1. *Excision* (Type 2) involves the partial or total removal of the clitoris and the inner lips. The most extreme form is *infibulation* (Type 3), in which the clitoris and all of the inner lips are removed, part of the outer lips are removed, and the raw edges of the outer lips are stitched together to cover the urethral opening and the vaginal entrance, with only a small opening left for the passage of urine and menstrual fluid. WHO Type 4 refers to all other female genital procedures for nonmedical purposes, including nicking or piercing the prepuce, which is favored by some as preserving the tradition but injuring the body the least. The term *female circumcision* is also used, although its definition is less clear; generally it means the Type 1 procedure.

All of these procedures pose health risks and infibulation creates especially severe problems. Hemorrhaging may occur, leading to shock and even death. Because of unsanitary conditions present during the procedure, tetanus and other infections are risks. The same instrument may be used in turn on multiple girls, so HIV and hepatitis B can be transmitted. A common problem is that the pain of the wound is so severe and the stitching so tight that the girl avoids urinating or cannot urinate properly, leading to urinary infections. A tightly infibulated woman can only urinate drop by drop, and her menstrual period may take 10 days and be extremely painful. Women who have

Figure 6   Twenty-seven African nations practice some form of ritualized genital cutting of young girls. Clitoridectomy is also practiced in Muslim countries outside Africa and was practiced in the United States during the Victorian era. Today there is a grassroots movement in Africa to end the practice. The sign says, "let's stop excision!"

©Jamie Carstairs/Alamy

undergone FGC are at higher risk of infections such as herpes and bacterial vaginosis.

The sexual and reproductive health consequences are no less severe. Infibulation is an effective method for ensuring virginity until marriage, but on the wedding night the man must force an opening through stitching and scar tissue. It is painful and may take days; a midwife may be called to cut open the tissue. Orgasm would be only a remote possibility for a woman whose clitoris has been removed. Infibulated women have a substantial risk of complications during childbirth and of newborn deaths (WHO, 2012).

FGC has declined in some nations such as Sierra Leone, where the prevalence has gone from 96 percent in older cohorts to 70 percent in younger cohorts (Population Reference Bureau, 2014). Villages across Senegal have pledged to end the custom (Dugger, 2011). Nonetheless, it persists in many places. If the procedures are so harmful, why do people continue them? Why do girls submit to them, and even ask for them, and why do their parents permit or even encourage it? The answer lies in the complex and powerful interplay of culture and gender. Infibulation indicates not only virginity but also a woman's loyalty to her culture and its traditions, a particularly

Female genital cutting: Cutting or removing parts of the clitoris or inner and outer lips. Also called *female genital mutilation.*

sensitive issue for people long dominated by European colonizers. A woman who is not infibulated is not marriageable in these cultures, in which marriage is the only acceptable way of life for an adult woman. When those are the rules of the game, it is less surprising that girls submit or even want to be circumcised and that their parents require them to do it. Some communities may also hold certain beliefs that make these procedures seem necessary. Some Muslims mistakenly believe that it is required by their faith, although it is not mentioned in the Koran. Research also shows that the more empowered women are, the less they favor FGC (Afifi, 2009).

FGC raises a number of dilemmas for North Americans. In universities, we generally encourage the approach of *cultural relativism,* an openness to and appreciation of the customs of other cultures. If we apply standards of cultural relativism, we should say, "Great, if that's what those people want." But should there be limits to cultural relativism? Can one oppose certain practices that pose well-documented, serious health risks, even though they are popular in the culture? Medical personnel in North America face difficult dilemmas. Immigrant women whose daughters are born in North America may request that a physician perform an excision, knowing that the procedure will be far safer if done by a physician in a hospital. Should the physician comply, knowing that the realistic alternative is that the procedure will be performed by an untrained person from that culture under unsanitary conditions?

On a more hopeful note, a grassroots movement of women that is dedicated to eliminating these practices has sprung up in a number of African nations, including Kenya, Gambia, Senegal, Sudan, Somalia, and Nigeria.

And some surgeons in Western nations are developing reconstructive surgeries to restore anatomy and function to women who experienced FGC; scar tissue is removed and the clitoris is uncovered. These procedures seem to be effective in reducing pain and restoring pleasure (Foldès et al., 2012).

Several points help to put matters into perspective. First, only about 15 percent of cultures that practice FGC do the severe form, infibulation. The remaining cultures practice the milder forms ranging from a slit in the prepuce to clitoridectomy. Second, far more cultures practice male genital modifications than female genital modifications. An example is the United States, where male circumcision is widespread but FGC is extremely rare.

Third, currently there is a cult in the United States that advocates genital surgeries such as removal of the inner or outer lips, because they believe that the vulva is more beautiful and erotic that way (Miklos & Moore, 2008). More broadly, genital plastic surgery has become widely available and is raising controversies in the medical community (Liao et al., 2010). For example, some women want to have their inner lips trimmed (labiaplasty), saying that they don't like the appearance of their natural ones and that surgery will improve their self-confidence (Ozer et al., 2018). How should a surgeon respond? Would education and psychotherapy achieve a better result? And, why are these genital plastic surgeries legal in Western nations where FGC is prohibited (Johnsdotter & Essén, 2010)?

Additional sources: Almroth et al. (2001); Morrison et al. (2001); Shell-Duncan (2008); Yoder et al. (2004).

(the practice is called *droit du seigneur* for "right of the lord" in French and *jus primae noctis* for "law of the first night" in Latin). The hymen has been taken as evidence of virginity. Thus, bleeding on the wedding night was proof that the bride had been delivered intact to the groom; the parading of the bloody bedsheets on the wedding night, a custom of the Kurds of the Middle East, is one ritual based on this belief.

Such practices rest on the assumption that a woman without a hymen is not a virgin. However, we now know that this is not true. Some girls are simply born without a hymen, and others may tear it in active sports such as horseback riding. Unfortunately, this means that some women have been humiliated unjustly for their lack of a hymen.

Internal Organs

The internal sex organs of the female consist of the vagina, the vestibular bulbs, the Skene's glands, the uterus, a pair of ovaries, and a pair of fallopian tubes (see Figure 7).

The Vagina

The **vagina** is the tube-shaped organ into which the penis is inserted during coitus; it also receives the ejaculate. Because it is the passageway through which a baby travels during birth, it is sometimes also called the *birth canal.* In the resting or unaroused state, the vagina is about 8 to 10 centimeters (3 to 4 inches) long and tilts slightly backward from the bottom to the

> **Vagina (vuh-JINE-uh):** The tube-shaped organ in the female into which the penis is inserted during coitus and through which a baby passes during birth.

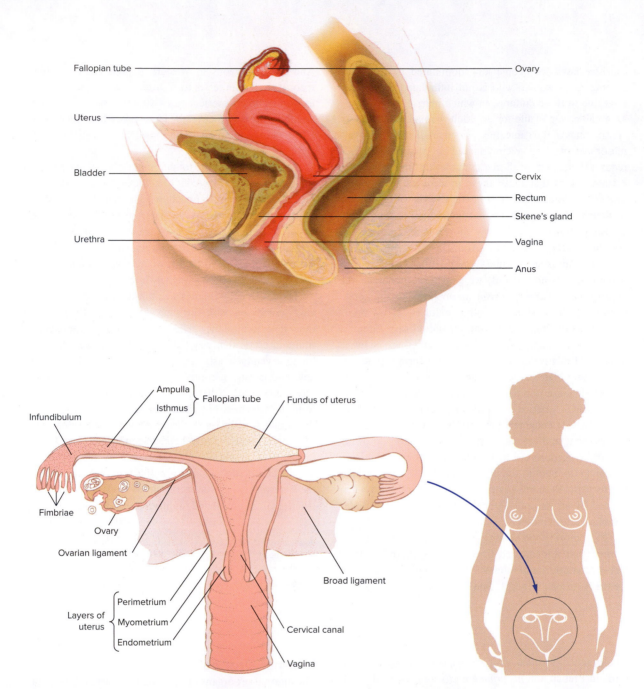

Fallopian tube

Uterus

Bladder

Urethra

Ovary

Cervix

Rectum

Skene's gland

Vagina

Anus

Ampulla

Isthmus

Fallopian tube

Fundus of uterus

Infundibulum

Fimbriae

Ovary

Ovarian ligament

Broad ligament

Layers of uterus

Perimetrium

Myometrium

Endometrium

Cervical canal

Vagina

Figure 7   Internal sexual and reproductive organs from a side view (top) and a front view.

top. At the bottom it ends in the vaginal opening, or *introitus.* At the top it connects with the cervix (the lower part of the uterus). It is a very flexible organ that works somewhat like a balloon. In the resting state its walls lie against each other like the sides of an uninflated balloon; during arousal it expands like an inflated balloon, allowing space to accommodate the penis.

The walls of the vagina have three layers. The inner layer, the *vaginal mucosa,* is a mucous membrane similar to the inner lining of the mouth. The middle layer is muscular, and the outer layer forms a covering. The walls of the vagina are extremely elastic and are capable of expanding to the extent necessary during intercourse and childbirth, although with age they become thinner and less flexible.

The nerve supply of the vagina is mostly to the lower one-third, near the introitus. That part is sensitive to erotic stimulation. The inner two-thirds of the vagina contains almost no nerve endings and is therefore relatively insensitive except to feelings of deep pressure. Some women have a spot on the front wall of the vagina that is more sensitive than the rest of the vagina, but even it is not nearly so sensitive as the inner lips, outer lips, or clitoris (Schultz et al., 1989). This spot is referred to by some as the G spot (see discussion of Skene's gland).

The number of slang terms for the vagina (for example, "beaver," "cunt") and the frequency of their usage testify to its power of fascination across the ages. One concern has been with size: whether some vaginas are too small or too large. As noted earlier, though, the vagina is highly elastic and expandable. Thus, at least in principle, any penis can fit into any vagina. The penis is, after all, not nearly so large as a baby's head, which manages to fit through the vagina. The part of the vagina that is most responsible for a man's sensation that it is "tight," "too tight," or "too loose" is the introitus. One of the things that can stretch the introitus is childbirth; indeed, there is a considerable difference in the appearance of the vulva of a woman who has never had a baby *(nulliparous)* and the vulva of a woman who has *(parous)* (see Figure 8).

Surrounding the vagina, the urethra, and the anus is a set of muscles called the *pelvic floor muscles.* One of these muscles, the **pubococcygeus muscle,** is particularly important. It may be stretched during childbirth, or it may simply be weak. However, it can be strengthened through exercise, which is recommended by sex therapists (see the chapter "Sexual Disorders and Sex Therapy") as well as by many popular sex manuals.

Do women ejaculate?

The Vestibular Bulbs

The **vestibular bulbs** (or clitoral bulbs) are two organs about the size and shape of a pea pod. They lie on either side of the vaginal wall, near the entrance, under the inner lips (O'Connell & DeLancey, 2005). They are erectile tissue and lie close to the crura of the clitoris.

The Skene's Gland or Female Prostate

The **Skene's gland,** or female prostate (also called the *paraurethral gland*), lies between the wall of the urethra and the wall of the vagina (Zaviačič et al., 2000b). Its ducts empty into the urethra, but it can be felt on the front wall of the vagina. The evidence indicates that, in some women, it secretes fluid that is biochemically similar to male prostate fluid. Many women find it to be a region of special erotic sensitivity on the wall of the vagina. The size of the female prostate varies considerably from one woman to the next, as does the amount of its secretions. Some women experience no secretion, whereas others have an actual ejaculation when they orgasm. This is the organ, dubbed the G spot, that is responsible for female ejaculation, discussed in the chapter "Sexual Arousal."

The Uterus

The **uterus** (womb) is about the size and shape of an upside-down pear. It is usually tilted forward and is held in place by ligaments.

> **Pubococcygeus muscle (pyoo-bo-cox-ih-GEE-us):** A muscle around the vaginal entrance.
> **Vestibular bulbs:** Erectile tissue running under the inner lips.
> **Skene's gland:** Female prostate located on the front wall of the vagina.
> **Uterus (YOO-tur-us):** The organ in which the fetus develops.

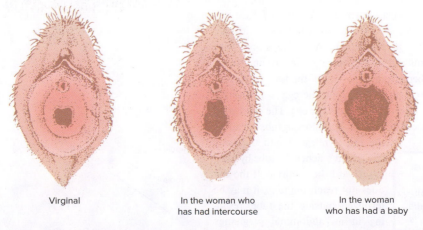

Virginal

In the woman who has had intercourse

In the woman who has had a baby

Figure 8   Appearance of the vulva of a woman who is a virgin; a woman who has had intercourse but has not had a baby (nulliparous); and a woman who has had a baby (parous).

The narrow lower third, called the **cervix,** opens into the vagina. The top is the *fundus,* the main part, the *body.* The entrance to the uterus through the cervix is very narrow, about the diameter of a drinking straw, and is called the *os* (or cervical canal). The major function of the uterus is to hold and nourish a developing fetus.

The uterus, like the vagina, consists of three layers. The inner layer, or *endometrium,* is richly supplied with glands and blood vessels. Its state varies according to the age of the woman and the phase of the menstrual cycle. It is the endometrium that is sloughed off at menstruation and creates the menstrual discharge. The middle layer, the *myometrium,* is muscular. The muscles are very strong, creating the powerful contractions of labor and orgasm, and also highly elastic, capable of stretching to accommodate a 9-month-old fetus. The outer layer—the *perimetrium*—forms the external cover of the uterus.

The Fallopian Tubes

Extending out from the sides of the upper end of the uterus are the **fallopian tubes,** also called the *oviducts* ("egg ducts"). The fallopian tubes are extremely narrow and are lined with hairlike projections called *cilia.* The fallopian tubes are the pathway by which the egg travels toward the uterus and the sperm reach the egg. Fertilization of the egg typically occurs in the infundibulum, the section of the tube closest to the ovary; the fertilized egg then travels the rest of the way through the tube to the uterus. The infundibulum curves around toward the ovary; at its end are numerous fingerlike projections called *fimbriae* that extend toward the ovary.

The Ovaries

The **ovaries** are two organs about the size and shape of unshelled almonds; they lie on either side of the uterus. The ovaries have two important functions: they produce eggs (ova), and they manufacture the sex hormones *estrogen* and *progesterone.*

Each ovary contains numerous follicles. A *follicle* is a capsule that surrounds an egg (not to be confused with hair follicles, which are quite different). A female is born with an estimated 1 million immature eggs (Federman, 2006). Beginning at puberty, one or several of the follicles mature during each menstrual cycle. When the egg has matured, the follicle bursts open and releases the egg. The ovaries do not actually connect directly to the fallopian tubes. Rather, the egg is released into the body cavity and reaches the tube by moving toward the fimbriae. If the egg does not reach the tube, it may be fertilized outside the tube, resulting in an abdominal pregnancy (see the section on ectopic pregnancy in the chapter "Pregnancy and Childbirth"). Cases have been recorded of women who, although they were missing one ovary and the opposite fallopian tube, nonetheless became pregnant. Apparently, in such cases the egg migrates to the tube on the opposite side.

The Breasts

Although they are not actually sex organs, the *breasts* deserve discussion here because of their erotic and reproductive significance. The breast consists of about 15 or 20 clusters of *mammary glands,* each with a separate opening to the nipple, and of fatty and fibrous tissues that surround the clusters of glands (see Figure 9). The nipple, into which the milk ducts open, is at the tip of the breast. It is richly supplied with nerve endings and therefore very important in erotic stimulation for many women. The nipple consists of smooth muscle fibers; when they contract, the nipple becomes erect. The darker area surrounding the nipple is called the *areola.*

There is wide variation among women in the size and shape of breasts (Figure 10). One thing is fairly consistent, though: Few women are satisfied with the size of their breasts. Most women think they are either too small, too large, or too droopy; few women think theirs are just right (Frederick et al., 2008). It is well to remember that there are the same number of nerve endings in small breasts as in large breasts. It follows that small breasts are actually more erotically sensitive per square inch than are large ones.

Breasts may take on enormous psychological meaning; they can be a symbol of femininity or a means of attracting men. Ours is a very breast-oriented culture. Many American men develop a powerful interest in, and

Cervix: The lower part of the uterus, which opens to the vagina.
Fallopian tubes (fuh-LOW-pee-un): The tubes extending from the uterus to the ovary; also called the *oviducts.*
Ovaries: Two organs on either side of the uterus that produce eggs and sex hormones.

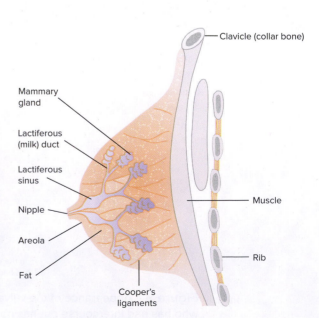

Clavicle (collar bone)

Mammary gland

Lactiferous (milk) duct

Lactiferous sinus

Nipple

Areola

Fat

Cooper's ligaments

Muscle

Rib

Figure 9   The internal structure of the breast.

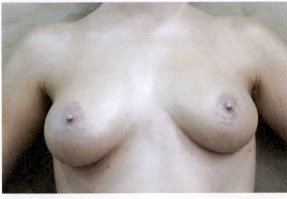

(a)

(b)

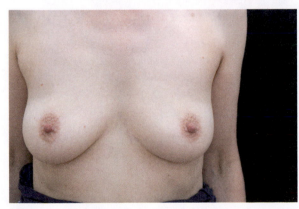

(c)

Figure 10   Breasts come in many sizes and shapes.

*(a) ©Jessica Abad de Gail/age fotostock; (b) ©Chris Rout/Alamy;
(c) ©Dr. P. Marazzi/Science Source*

attraction to, women's breasts. The social definition of beauty is a compelling force; many women strive to meet the ideal and a few overadapt, going too far in their striving (Sansone & Sansone, 2007). Breast augmentation surgery has increased steadily, while other women have undergone breast reduction surgery, in both cases to meet a socially defined standard of beauty.

Male Sexual Organs

Externally, the most noticeable parts of the male sexual anatomy are the penis and the scrotum, or scrotal sac, which contains the testes (see Figure 11).

External Organs

The Penis

The **penis** (phallus, "prick," "cock," "johnson," and many other slang terms too numerous to list) serves important functions in sexual pleasure, reproduction, and elimination of body wastes by urination. It is a tubular organ with an end or tip called the *glans.* The opening at the end of the glans is the *meatus,* or *urethral opening,* through which urine and semen pass. The main part of the penis is called the *shaft.* The raised ridge at the edge of the glans is called the *corona* ("crown"). While the entire penis is sensitive to sexual stimulation, the corona and the rest of the glans are the most sexually excitable region of the male anatomy.

Internally, the penis contains three long cylinders of spongy tissue running parallel to the *urethra,* which is the pathway through which semen and urine pass (see Figure 12). The two spongy bodies lying on top are called the **corpora cavernosa,** and the single one lying on the bottom of the penis is called the **corpus spongiosum** (the urethra runs through the middle of it). During erection, the corpus spongiosum can be seen as a raised column on the lower side of the penis. As the names suggest, these bodies are tissues filled with many spaces and cavities, much like a sponge. They are richly supplied with blood vessels and nerves. In the flaccid (unaroused, not erect) state, they contain little blood. *Erection,* or *tumescence,* occurs when they become filled with blood (engorged) and expand, making the penis stiff.

Erection is purely a vascular phenomenon; that is, it results entirely from blood flow. Some people believe that the penis in humans contains a bone. This is not true, although in some other species—for example, dogs—the penis does contain a bone, which aids in intromission (insertion of the penis into the vagina). In human males, however, there is none.

The skin of the penis usually is hairless and is arranged in loose folds, permitting expansion during erection. The **foreskin,** or *prepuce,* is an additional layer of skin that forms a sheathlike covering over the glans; it may be present or absent in adult males, depending on whether they have been circumcised (see Figure 13).

Penis: The male external sexual organ, which functions both in sexual activity and in urination.

Corpora cavernosa: Two spongy bodies running the length of the top of the penis.

Corpus spongiosum: A spongy body running the length of the underside of the penis.

Foreskin: A layer of skin covering the glans or tip of the penis in an uncircumcised male; also called the *prepuce.*

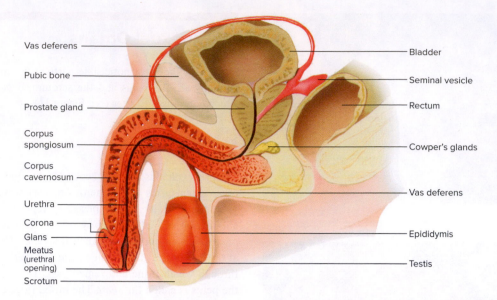

Vas deferens

Pubic bone

Prostate gland

Corpus spongiosum

Corpus cavernosum

Urethra

Corona

Glans

Meatus (urethral opening)

Scrotum

Bladder

Seminal vesicle

Rectum

Cowper's glands

Vas deferens

Epididymis

Testis

Figure 11   The male sexual and reproductive organs from a side view.

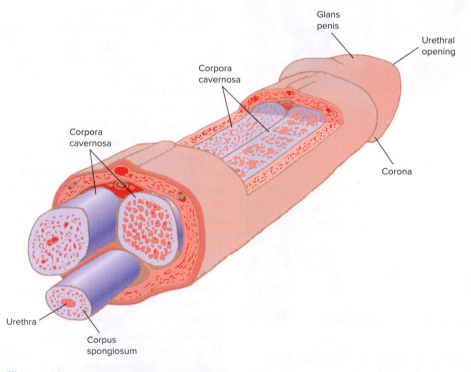

Glans penis

Urethral opening

Corpora cavernosa

Corpora cavernosa

Corona

Urethra

Corpus spongiosum

Figure 12   The internal structure of the penis.

Under the foreskin are small glands (Tyson's glands) that produce a substance called *smegma,* which is cheesy in texture. The foreskin is easily retractable,[4] this being extremely important for proper hygiene. If the foreskin is not pulled back and

---

| **Circumcision:** Surgical removal of the foreskin of the penis. |

---

[4]In a rare condition, the foreskin is so tight that it cannot be pulled back; this condition, called *phimosis*, requires correction by circumcision.

the glans washed thoroughly, the smegma may accumulate, producing an unpleasant smell.

Circumcision refers to the surgical cutting away or removal of the foreskin. Circumcision is practiced in many parts of the world and, when parents so choose, is done to boys in the United States within a few days after birth.

Circumcision may be done for cultural and religious reasons. Circumcision has been a part of Jewish religious practice for thousands of years. It symbolizes the covenant

(a)

(b)

Figure 13 (*a*) A circumcised penis and (*b*) an uncircumcised penis, showing the foreskin.

(a) ©Medicshots/Alamy (b) ©Dr. P. Marazzi/Science Source

between God and the Jewish people and is done on the eighth day after birth, according to scriptural teaching (Genesis 17: 9–27). Circumcision is also common in Muslim cultures. In some cultures circumcision is done at puberty as an initiation ritual, or *rite de passage*. The ability of the young boy to stand the pain may be seen as a proof of manhood.

Today 80 percent of American men and boys between the ages of 14 and 59 are circumcised (Introcaso et al., 2013). Yet circumcision is controversial in the United States and in many other nations. Both the American Academy of Pediatrics (2012) and the Centers for Disease Control and Prevention (2015c) recommend circumcision, stating that there are medical benefits and advantages to circumcisions that outweigh potential risks. The evidence indicates, for example, that uncircumcised male babies are 11 times more likely to get urinary tract infections than are circumcised babies (Wiswell et al., 1987). There is also evidence that uncircumcised men have a higher risk of infection with HIV, the AIDS virus. It is thought that the foreskin can harbor HIV and other viruses. In a five-nation study, including Spain, Colombia, Brazil, Thailand, and the Philippines, circumcised men showed lower rates of HPV infection (Castellsagué et al., 2002). HPV is the virus that causes genital warts and predisposes women to cervical cancer (see

Are there any medical advantages to circumcising baby boys?

the chapter "Sexually Transmitted Infections"). In this same study, the monogamous women partners of the circumcised men had lower rates of cervical cancer. Circumcision also reduces the risk of prostate cancer (Wright et al., 2012). In a randomized controlled trial in Kenya and Uganda, adult men who wanted to be circumcised were circumcised (or not in the control group) (Bailey et al., 2007; Roehr, 2007). Over the next two years, the circumcised men had half the rate of HIV infection of the uncircumcised men. The trial was actually halted over ethical concerns about withholding circumcision from those who wanted it.

Opponents of male circumcision cite biomedical ethics concerns about surgical interventions with minors performed prior to the age of consent (Svoboda & Van Howe, 2013). They argue that the foreskin is an erotic, functional piece of human tissue that should not be removed without good reason (Earp, 2015). They criticize the cost–benefit analysis of the AAP and the CDC (Frisch & Earp, 2016). One concern is whether trials of the effectiveness of circumcision conducted in Africa, where HIV is highly prevalent, are relevant to the United States, where HIV is less prevalent. And yet in some urban centers in the United States, in some sexual networks, the prevalence of HIV is high.

Other arguments have focused on whether the circumcised or the uncircumcised man receives more pleasure from sexual intercourse. In fact, Masters and Johnson (1966) found that there is no difference in excitability between the circumcised and the uncircumcised penis.

Other forms of male genital cutting are done throughout the world. In fact, male genital cutting is done in more cultures than is female genital cutting (Gregersen, 1996). A common form, across most of Polynesia, is **supercision** (also known as *superincision*), which involves making a slit the length of the foreskin on the top, with the foreskin otherwise remaining intact (Gregersen, 1996). With **subincision,** which is common in some tribes in central Australia, a slit is made on the lower side of the penis along its entire length and to the depth of the urethra. Urine is then excreted at the base rather than at the tip of the penis.

To say the least, the penis has been the focus of quite a lot of attention throughout history. Not surprisingly, the male genitals were often seen as symbols of fertility and thus were worshipped for their powers of procreativity. In ancient Greece, phallic worship centered on Priapus, the son of Aphrodite (the goddess of love) and Dionysus (the god of fertility and wine). Priapus is usually represented as a grinning man with a huge penis.

In contemporary American society, phallic concern often focuses on the size of the penis. E-mail spam leers at us with products that ostensibly increase penis size. While there is variation in the length of the penis from one man to the next—the average penis is generally somewhere between 7 centimeters (3 inches) and 10 centimeters (4 inches) in length when flaccid (not erect; Veale et al., 2015)—there is a tendency for the small penis to grow more in erection than one that starts out large. As a result, there is little correlation between the length of the penis when flaccid and its length when erect. As the saying has it, "Erection is the great equalizer." The average erect penis is about 13 centimeters (5 inches) long and 11–12 cm (4.5 inches) in circumference.

Phallic concern has also included an interest in the variations in the shape of the penis when flaccid and when erect, as reflected in this limerick:

There was a young man of Kent
Whose kirp in the middle was bent.
To save himself trouble
He put it in double,
And instead of coming, he went.

The Scrotum

The other major external genital structure in males is the **scrotum;** this is a loose pouch of skin, lightly covered with hair, that contains the testes ("balls" or "nuts" in slang).[5]

> **Supercision (superincision):** A form of male genital cutting in which a slit is made the length of the foreskin on top.
> **Subincision:** A form of male genital cutting in which a slit is made on the lower side of the penis along its entire length.
> **Scrotum (SKROH-tum):** The pouch of skin that contains the testes in the male.
> **Testes:** The pair of glands in the scrotum that manufacture sperm and sex hormones.
> **Seminiferous tubules (sem-ih-NIFF-ur-us):** Tubes in the testes that manufacture sperm.
> **Interstitial cells (int-er-STIH-shul):** Cells in the testes that manufacture testosterone.

---

[5]This brings to mind another limerick:

There once was a pirate named Gates
Who thought he could rhumba on skates.
He slipped on his cutlass
And now he is nutless
And practically useless on dates.

Internal Organs

The **testes** are the *gonads,* or reproductive glands, of the male, which are analogous to the female's ovaries. Like the ovaries, they serve two major functions: to manufacture germ cells (sperm) and sex hormones, in particular *testosterone.* Both testes are about the same size, although the left one usually hangs lower than the right one.

In the internal structure of the testes, two parts are important: the seminiferous tubules and the interstitial cells (see Figure 14). The **seminiferous tubules** carry out the important function of manufacturing and storing sperm, a process called *spermatogenesis.* They are a long series of threadlike tubes curled and packed densely into the testes. There are about 1,000 of these tubules, which if they were stretched out end to end would be several hundred feet in length.

The **interstitial cells** carry out the second important function of the testes, the production of testosterone. These cells are found in the connective tissue lying between the seminiferous tubules. The cells lie close to the blood vessels in the testes and pour the hormones they manufacture directly into the blood vessels. Thus, the testes are endocrine (hormone-secreting) glands.

One of the clever tricks that the scrotum and testes can perform, as any man will testify, is to move up close to the body or down away from it. These changes are brought about mainly by changes in temperature (although emotional factors may also produce them). If a man plunges into a cold lake, the scrotum will shrivel and move close to the body. If the man is working in an extremely hot place, the scrotum will hang down

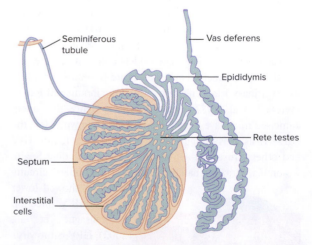

Figure 14   Schematic cross-section of the internal structure of the testis.

and away from the body. This mechanism is important because the testes should remain at a fairly constant temperature, slightly lower than normal body temperature. This constancy of temperature is necessary to protect the sperm, which may be injured by extremes of temperature. Thus, if the air is cold, the testes move closer to the body to maintain warmth, but if the air is too hot, they move away from it to keep cool. The mechanics of this movement are made possible by the *cremasteric reflex,* named for the cremaster muscle connecting the scrotum to the body wall. Reflex contraction of this muscle pulls the testes up.

Many people believe that taking hot baths, wearing tight athletic supporters, or having a high fever can cause infertility. Indeed, in some countries the men take long, hot baths as a method of contraception. Such a practice has some basis in biological fact because sperm can be damaged by heat (Paul et al., 2008). As a method of contraception, this practice has not been particularly effective; however, men with problems of infertility can sometimes cure them by getting out of their tight jockstraps and jockey shorts.

Following initial cell division in the seminiferous tubules, the male germ cells go through several stages of maturation. At the earliest stage, the cell is called a *spermatogonium.* Then it becomes a *spermatocyte* (first primary and then secondary) and then a *spermatid.* Finally, when fully mature it is a *spermatozoan,* or **sperm.** *Spermatogenesis,* the manufacture of sperm, occurs continuously in adult men. An average ejaculate contains about 200 million sperm (Bang et al., 2005). This number is down, in Western nations, by roughly 50 percent compared with data from the 1970s (Levine et al., 2017).

A mature sperm is very tiny—about 60 micrometers, or 60/10,000 millimeter (0.0024 inch), long. A normal human sperm carries 23 chromosomes in the head. These 23 are half the normal number in the other cells of the human body. When the sperm unites with the egg, which also carries 23 chromosomes, the full complement of 46 for the offspring is produced.

After the sperm are manufactured in the seminiferous tubules, they proceed into the *rete testes,* a converging network of tubes on the surface of the testis toward the top. The sperm then pass out of the testis and into a single tube, the epididymis. The **epididymis** is a long tube (about 6 meters, or 20 feet, in length) coiled into a small crescent-shaped region on the top and side of the testis. The sperm are stored in the epididymis, in which they mature, possibly for as long as six weeks.

Upon ejaculation, the sperm pass from the epididymis into the **vas deferens** (it is the vas that is cut in a vasectomy). The vas passes up and out of the scrotum and then follows a peculiar circular path as it loops over the pubic bone, crosses beside the urinary bladder, and then turns downward toward the prostate. As the tube passes through the prostate, it narrows and at this point is called the *ejaculatory duct.* The ejaculatory duct opens into the *urethra,* which has the dual function of conveying sperm and transporting urine; sperm are ejaculated out through the penis via the urethra.

Sperm have little motility (capability of movement) of their own while in the epididymis and vas. Not until they mix with the secretions of the prostate are they capable of movement on their own (Breton et al., 1996). Up to this point, they are conveyed by the cilia and by contractions of the epididymis and vas.

The **seminal vesicles** are two saclike structures that lie above the prostate, behind the bladder, and in front of the rectum (see Figure 11). They produce about 60 percent of the seminal fluid, or ejaculate. The remaining 40 percent is produced by the prostate (Ndovi et al., 2007). They empty their fluid into the ejaculatory duct to combine with the sperm.

The **prostate** lies below the bladder and is about the size and shape of a chestnut. It is composed of both muscle and glandular tissue. The prostate secretes a milky alkaline fluid that is part of the ejaculate. The alkalinity of the secretion provides a favorable environment for the sperm and helps prevent their destruction by the acidity of the vagina. The prostate is fairly small at birth, enlarges at puberty, and typically shrinks in old age. It may become enlarged enough so that it interferes with urination, in which case surgery or drug therapy is required. Its size can be determined by rectal examination.

Cowper's glands, or the *bulbo-urethral glands,* are located just below the prostate and empty into the urethra. During sexual arousal these glands secrete a small amount of a clear alkaline fluid, which appears as droplets at the tip of the penis before ejaculation occurs. It is thought that the function of this secretion is to neutralize the acidic urethra, allowing safe passage of the sperm. Generally it is not produced in sufficient quantity to serve as a lubricant in intercourse. The fluid often contains some stray sperm. Thus, it is possible (though not likely) for a woman to become pregnant from the sperm in this fluid even though the man has not ejaculated.

Sperm: The mature male reproductive cell, capable of fertilizing an egg.

Epididymis (ep-ih-DIH-dih-mus): A highly coiled tube located on the edge of the testis, where sperm mature.

Vas deferens: The tube through which sperm pass on their way from the testes and epididymis, out of the scrotum, and to the urethra.

Seminal vesicles: Saclike structures that lie above the prostate and produce about 60 percent of the seminal fluid.

Prostate: The gland in the male, located below the bladder, that secretes some of the fluid in semen.

Cowper's glands: Glands that secrete a clear alkaline fluid into the male's urethra.

First Person

The Pelvic Exam

All adult women should have a checkup every year that includes a thorough pelvic exam. Among other things, such an exam is extremely important in the detection of cervical cancer, and early detection is the key to cure. Some women neglect to have the exam because they feel anxious or embarrassed about it or because they think they are too young or too old; however, having regular pelvic exams can be a matter of life and death. Actually, the exam is quite simple and need not cause any discomfort. The following is a description of the procedures in a pelvic exam (Boston Women's Health Book Collective, 2011).

First, the health care provider inspects the vulva, checking for irritations, discolorations, bumps, lice, skin lesions, and unusual vaginal discharge. Then there is an internal check for *cystoceles* (bulges of the bladder into the vagina) and *rectoceles* (bulges of the rectum into the vagina), for pus in the Skene glands, for cysts in the Bartholin glands, and for the strength of the pelvic floor muscles and abdominal muscles. There is also a test for stress incontinence; the physician asks the patient to cough and checks to see whether urine flows involuntarily.

Next comes the speculum exam. The *speculum* is a plastic or metal instrument that is inserted into the vagina to hold the vaginal walls apart to permit examination (Figure 15). Once the speculum is in place (it should be prewarmed to body temperature if it is metal), the health care provider looks for any unusual signs, such as lesions, inflammation, or unusual discharge from the vaginal walls, and for any signs of infection or damage to the cervix. The health care provider then uses a small metal spatula to scrape a tiny bit of tissue from the cervix for the Pap test for cervical cancer. If this is done properly, it should be painless. A battery of tests for sexually transmitted diseases can also be run.

If the woman is interested in seeing her own cervix, she can ask the provider to hold up a mirror so that she can view it through the speculum. Indeed, some women's groups advocate that women learn to use a speculum and give themselves regular exams with it; early detection of diseases would thus be much more likely. (For a more detailed description, see the Boston Women's Health Book Collective, 2011.)

Next, the health care provider does a bimanual vaginal exam. They slide the index and middle fingers of one hand into the vagina and then, with the other hand, press down from the outside on the abdominal wall. The health care provider then feels for the position of the uterus, tubes, and ovaries and for any signs of growths, pain, or inflammation.

Cancer of the Sex Organs

Breast Cancer

Cancer of the breast is the most common form of cancer in women. About 12 percent of American women have breast cancer at some time in their lives. Every year, 40,000 women in the United States die of breast cancer (Siegel et al., 2018). The risk is higher for the woman whose mother, sister, or grandmother has had breast cancer.

Causes

Approximately 5 to 10 percent of the cases of breast cancer in women are due to genetic factors (American Cancer Society, 2014). Other risk factors include long-term use of menopausal hormone therapy (MHT) and obesity (American Cancer Society, 2014). The evidence indicates that abortion does not increase risk.

There have been great breakthroughs in research into the genetics of breast cancer. Scientists have identified two breast cancer genes: BRCA1 (for BReast CAncer 1) on chromosome 17 and BRCA2 on chromosome 13 (Ezzell, 1994; Miki et al., 1994; Shattuck-Eidens et al., 1995). Mutations of these genes create a high risk of breast cancer. BRCA1 and BRCA2 mutations also increase susceptibility to ovarian cancer. In one study, of women having a mutation in BRCA1 or BRCA2, 82 percent eventually developed breast cancer and 54 percent developed ovarian cancer (King et al., 2003). In fact, among men carrying mutations of these genes, 16 percent develop prostate cancer. Genetic screening tests are available that detect BRCA mutations in women who have a family history of breast cancer. If a BRCA mutation is found, the woman

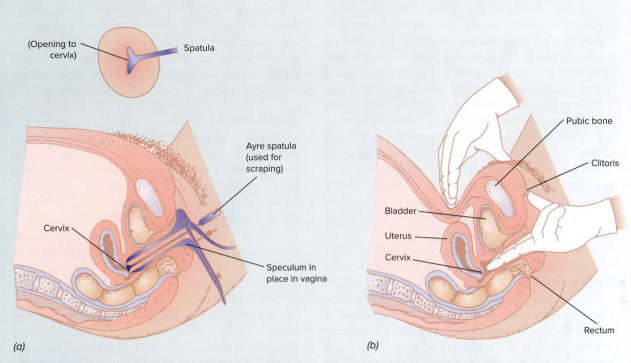

(a)

(b)

Figure 15 (*a*) The speculum in place for a pelvic exam. The Ayre spatula is used to get a sample of cells for the Pap test. (*b*) The bimanual pelvic exam.

Finally, the health care provider may do a recto-vaginal exam by inserting one finger into the vagina and one into the rectum; this provides further information on the positioning of the pelvic organs and can include a test for colon cancer.

Once again, it is important to emphasize that these are not painful procedures and that having them performed regularly is extremely important to a woman's health.

can be monitored closely, and if it is not found, she can feel relieved!

Some women carrying the BRCA mutation choose to have a mastectomy before they develop cancer, as a preventive measure. Research indicates that this approach is highly effective (Domchek et al., 2010). Other research indicates that some of the drugs used to treat breast cancer, such as tamoxifen, can also be used to prevent it in high-risk individuals (Cuzick et al., 2011).

Researchers are currently exploring gene therapy (Choudhury et al., 2016). This research is based on the finding that cancer is more likely to occur when tumor-suppressor genes are not functioning properly.

Diagnosis

Women can do breast self-exams, and it is good for all women to know how their breasts feel normally so that

they can detect any changes. The website of the American Cancer Society has instructions. However, self-exams are no substitute for mammograms and exams by clinicians.

There are three kinds of breast lumps: *cysts* (fluid-filled sacs, also called *fibrocystic* or *cystic mastitis*), *fibroadenomas,* and *malignant tumors.* The important thing to realize is that 80 percent of breast lumps are cysts or fibroadenomas and are benign—that is, not dangerous. Therefore, if a lump is found in your breast, the chances are fairly good that it is not malignant; of course, you cannot be sure of this until a doctor has performed a biopsy.

The main technique available for early detection of breast cancer is mammography. Basically, *mammography* involves taking an X ray of the breast. This technique is highly accurate, although some errors are still made. The major advantage, though, is that it is capable of detecting tumors that are so small that they cannot yet be felt; thus it can detect cancer in very early stages, making complete recovery more likely. Nonetheless, mammography involves some exposure to radiation, which itself may increase the risk of cancer. Therefore, the benefits of early detection need to be weighed against the risks of radiation. Moreover, mammograms sometimes give false positives, looking like a tumor is there when there isn't one. The result can be overdiagnosis and overtreatment. Taking all of this into account, the American Cancer Society recommends that women between the ages of 45 and 54 should receive annual screening mammograms, and women ages 40 to 44 should receive it if they choose to do so (Oeffinger et al., 2015). Beginning at age 55, women should receive screening mammograms every two years. These recommendations are for women who are at average risk. Women who have close relatives who have had breast cancer, or who know they are carrying the BRCA gene, are treated in a different way.

Recently, MRI scans have been developed to detect breast tumors. They are generally recommended only for high-risk cases.

Once a lump is discovered, one of several diagnostic procedures may be carried out. One is *needle aspiration,* in which a fine needle is inserted into the breast; if the lump is a cyst, the fluid in the cyst will be drained out. If the lump disappears after this procedure, then it was a cyst; the cyst is gone, and there is no need for further concern. If the lump remains, it must be either a fibroadenoma or a malignant tumor.

Most physicians feel that the only definitive way to differentiate between a fibroadenoma and a malignant tumor is to do a *biopsy.* A small slit is made in the breast and the lump is removed. A pathologist then examines it to determine whether it is cancerous. If it is simply a fibroadenoma, it has been removed and there is no further need for concern.

Treatment

Several forms of surgery may be performed when a breast lump is found to be malignant. If the lump is small and has not spread, the surgery may involve only a **lumpectomy,** in which the lump and a small bit of surrounding tissues are removed. The breast is thus preserved. Research indicates that in cases of early breast cancer when the cancer has not spread beyond the breast (e.g., to the lymph nodes), lumpectomy followed by radiation therapy is highly effective (American Cancer Society, 2014). In *simple mastectomy,* the breast and possibly a few lymph nodes are removed. In *modified radical mastectomy,* the breast and the underarm lymph nodes are removed; this procedure is used when there is evidence that the cancer has spread to the lymph nodes. If the cancer has spread more, the surgery is **radical mastectomy,** in which the entire breast, the underlying pectoral muscle, and the underarm lymph nodes are removed.

Following surgery, radiation therapy and/or chemotherapy are used. These may be followed by drug therapy such as tamoxifen.

Treatments generally are highly effective. If the cancer is localized, the survival rate is more than 98 percent five years after treatment (American Cancer Society, 2014).

Psychological Aspects

A lot more is at stake with breast cancer than technical details about diagnosis and surgery. The psychological impact of breast cancer and mastectomy can be enormous. There seem to be two sources of the trauma: Finding out that one has cancer of any kind is traumatic, and the surgery and possibly amputation of the breast is additionally stressful.

The typical emotional response of breast cancer patients is depression, often associated with anxiety (Compas & Luecken, 2002; Montazeri, 2008). These responses are so common that they can be considered normal. The woman who has had a mastectomy must make a number of physical and psychological adaptations, including different positions for sleeping and lovemaking and, for many women, a change to less revealing clothing. Reconstruction surgery is available, though (Figure 16). Scientists are exploring the possibility of using stem cells so that breast tissue can be regrown in the body (Findlay et al., 2011).

It is common for women to have difficulty showing their incisions to their sexual partners. Relationship tensions and sexual problems may increase.

Long-term studies, however, indicate that most women gradually adapt to the stresses they have experienced. One study found that breast cancer survivors did not differ from controls on measures of depression (Cordova et al., 2001). Many women manage to find meaning in the cancer experience and some show *posttraumatic growth,* such as finding new meaning in relationships and appreciating life more.

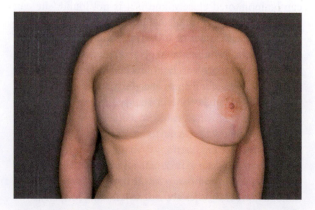

Figure 16 Appearance of a breast reconstructed after a mastectomy.

©*David J. Green - lifestyle themes/Alamy*

Lumpectomy: A surgical treatment for breast cancer in which only the lump and a small bit of surrounding tissue are removed.
Radical mastectomy (mast-ECT-uh-mee): A surgical treatment for breast cancer in which the entire breast, as well as underlying muscles and lymph nodes, is removed.

Educational classes providing relevant information can be very helpful. However, peer support groups, though popular, have not fared well in tests of their effectiveness in improving mental health (Helgeson et al., 2001). For women who are more severely distressed, cognitive behavioral therapy with a trained therapist can be very effective (Antoni et al., 2001).

Cancer of the Cervix, Endometrium, and Ovaries

Cancers of the cervix, endometrium, and ovaries are the most common cancers in women after breast cancer, accounting for about 11 percent of all new cancers in women. Each year about 30,000 U.S. women die of these cancers (Siegel et al., 2018). Other cancers of the female sexual-reproductive organs include cancer of the vulva, vagina, and fallopian tubes; these are all relatively rare.

Approximately 95 percent of cases of cervical cancer are caused by the human papillomavirus, HPV (Janicek & Averette, 2001). Early initiation of heterosexual intercourse during the teenage years is a known risk factor for cervical cancer, as is intercourse with multiple partners. Both early intercourse *and* multiple partners, of course, increase the risk of HPV infection. Research shows that tumor suppressor genes are active in normal cells, preventing them from becoming cancerous. HPV interferes with the activity of those tumor suppressor genes (Janicek & Averette, 2001).

It is encouraging to note that the death rate from cervical cancer has decreased sharply since the mid-1960s, mainly as a result of the *Pap test* (invented by G. N. Papanicolaou) and more regular checkups (American Cancer Society, 2015a). The Pap test is performed during a pelvic examination (described in First Person: The Pelvic Exam). Because this highly accurate test can detect cancer long before the person has any symptoms, all women between the ages of 21 and 29 should have one once every three years. Those between 30 and 65 should have a Pap test and an HPV test once every five years.

The best news is that a vaccine is available that prevents the most common HPV infections that cause cervical cancer. It is approved for use in females between the ages of 9 and 26, and all girls and women in this group should receive the vaccine, ideally at age 11 or 12.

Cancers of the ovaries and the uterine corpus (most of which is endometrial cancer) have multiple symptoms, making diagnosis difficult. Endometrial cancer may be suspected when a woman has vaginal bleeding during times in the menstrual cycle other than her period, or after menopause. Ovarian cancer symptoms—abdominal bloating and cramping, vomiting and diarrhea—can be, and usually are, indicative of much less serious conditions like a stomach virus or irritable bowel syndrome. Imaging techniques such as pelvic sonogram and MRI,

and minimally invasive surgical techniques such as hysteroscopy, can help diagnose these cancers.

Treatment for cervical cancer varies according to how advanced it is when diagnosed. If it is detected very early, it is quite curable with methods such as cryotherapy, a nonsurgical technique that uses extreme cold to destroy just the abnormal cells. Another common treatment is cone biopsy, in which a segment of the cervix is surgically removed, leaving the cervix largely intact. For women with advanced cervical cancer that has spread beyond a small, localized spot, **hysterectomy** (surgical removal of the uterus) is the usual treatment, although radiation therapy may be an alternative.

For women with endometrial cancer, hysterectomy is the standard treatment. Ovarian cancer is treated by *oophorectomy* (surgical removal of the ovaries), often accompanied by hysterectomy. These surgeries are typically followed by radiation treatments or chemotherapy.

It is important to note some facts about hysterectomy. Although it carries risks similar to those of any major surgery, hysterectomy does not leave a woman "masculinized," with a beard and deep voice. Beard growth is influenced by testosterone, not estrogen or progesterone. And it is the ovaries that manufacture estrogen and progesterone. They are not removed in a hysterectomy except in rare cases when the cancer has spread to them. Women who have their ovaries removed before age 50 usually take hormone replacement therapy (HRT) to avoid the effects of premature menopause. Another fallacy about hysterectomy is that it prevents a woman from enjoying, or even having, sex. In fact, though, the vagina is left intact, so intercourse is quite possible (for more detail, see the chapter "Sexuality and the Life Cycle: Adulthood").

Cancer of the Prostate

Cancer of the prostate is the most common cancer in men and is the second leading cause of cancer death in men, the most common being lung cancer. Most cases are not lethal, however, and survival rates are high because most of the tumors are small and spread (metastasize) only very slowly. On the other hand, a certain percentage of prostate tumors do spread and are lethal. Prostate cancer causes 29,000 deaths a year (Siegel et al., 2018). A number of genes contribute to prostate cancer and how aggressive it is (Alvarez-Cubero et al., 2015).

Early symptoms of prostate cancer are frequent urination (especially at night), difficulty in urination, and difficulty emptying the bladder. These are also symptoms of benign prostate enlargement, which itself may require treatment by surgery or drugs. These symptoms result from the pressure of the prostate tumor on the urethra. In the early stages there may be frequent erections and an increase in sex drive; however, as the disease progresses, there are often problems with sexual functioning.

Hysterectomy (his-tuh-REK-tuh-mee): Surgical removal of the uterus.

First Person

Testicular Examination

D octors agree that examination of a man's testicles is an important part of a general physical examination. The American Cancer Society includes the examination in its recommendations for routine cancer-related checkups. The issue of regular testicular self-examination is more controversial. The ACS does not feel that there is any medical evidence to suggest that, for men with average testicular cancer risk, monthly examination is any more effective than simple awareness and prompt medical evaluation. However, the choice of whether or not to perform this examination should be made by each man, so instructions for testicular examination are provided here.

The best time to perform the self-exam is during or after a bath or shower, when the skin of the scrotum is relaxed (Figure 17). Stand in front of a mirror and hold the penis out of the way. Examine each testicle separately. Hold the testicle between the thumbs and fingers with both hands and roll it gently between the fingers. Look and feel for any hard lumps or *nodules* (smooth rounded masses) or any change in the size, shape, or consistency of the testes. Contact your doctor if you detect any troublesome signs. Be aware that the testicles contain blood vessels, supporting tissues, and the epididymis and that some men may confuse these with a cancer. If you have any doubts, ask your doctor.

These are warning signs of testicular cancer:

1. A painless or an uncomfortable lump on a testicle
2. A testicular enlargement or swelling
3. A sensation of heaviness or aching in the lower abdomen or scrotum
4. In rare cases, men with germ cell cancer notice breast tenderness or breast growth

Figure 17 The technique used in the testicular self-exam.

©*Teri L. Stratford/Science Source*

See a physician promptly if you have any of these symptoms.

Preliminary diagnosis of prostate cancer is by a rectal examination, which is simple and causes no more than minimal discomfort. The physician (wearing a lubricated glove) inserts one finger into the rectum and palpates (feels) the prostate. All men over 50 should have a rectal exam at least once a year. If the rectal exam provides evidence of a tumor, further laboratory tests can be conducted as confirmation. The rectal exam has its disadvantages, though. Some men

dislike the discomfort it causes, and it is not 100 percent accurate. A blood test for PSA (prostate-specific antigen) is also available and should be done as well.

Treatment often involves surgical removal of some or all of the prostate, plus some type of hormone therapy, radiation therapy, or anticancer drugs. Because prostate cancer is often a slow-growing cancer, it may be left untreated, particularly if the man is elderly. Surgery may result in erection problems (Perez et al., 2002). Just as research has found that a greater number of sexual partners increases women's risk of cervical cancer, research indicates that men with a greater number of female sex partners have an increased risk of prostate cancer (Rosenblatt et al., 2001).

Cancer of the penis is another cancer of the male sexual-reproductive system, but it is rare compared with prostate cancer. It seems to be much more common among uncircumcised men than among circumcised men, suggesting that the accumulation of smegma under the foreskin may be related to its cause. Treatment may consist of surgery or radiation therapy.

Are there any cancers of the sex organs that affect young men?

Cancer of the Testes

Cancer of the testes is not a particularly common form of cancer. About 9,000 new cases are diagnosed each year (Siegel et al., 2018). However, it tends to be a disease of young men, and it is the most common form of cancer in men between the ages of 29 and 35.

The first sign is usually a painless lump in the testes, or a slight enlargement or change in consistency of the testes. There may be pain in the lower abdomen or groin. Unfortunately, many men do not discover the tumor, or if they do they do not see a physician soon, so that in most cases the cancer has spread to other organs by the time a physician is consulted. When a lump is reported to a physician early and is localized, the five-year survival rate is 99 percent. However, if the lump is not discovered or the man waits to see a physician and the cancer has progressed to Stage III, the survival rate is 70 percent (American Cancer Society, 2015b).

It is also true that not every lump in the testes is cancerous. Some lumps are varicoceles, that is, varicose veins.

Diagnosis is made by a physician's examination of the testes (see First Person: Testicular Examination) and by ultrasound. Final diagnosis involves surgical removal of the entire testis. This is also the first step in treatment. Fortunately, the other testicle remains, so that hormone production and sexual functioning can continue unimpaired. An artificial, gel-filled testicle can be implanted to restore a normal appearance.

The cause of testicular cancer is not known for certain. An undescended testis has a much greater risk of developing cancer.

Critical *THINK*ing Skill

Understanding the difference between anecdotal evidence and scientific evidence

Maria is 50 years old. According to the American Cancer Society, she should have a mammogram every year to screen for breast cancer. Maria's doctor has told her that she needs to start having mammograms. Maria's best friend, Dashni, is 52 and had a small, cancerous lump in her breast a year ago. The lump was not detected on a mammogram, but Dashni found it herself, received prompt treatment, and is healthy. Dashni says that mammograms are worthless because they did not detect her lump, and she tells Maria not to bother with them. What should Maria do?

In this case, Dashni's experience, although real, represents a single case or an anecdote. The sample size is 1. Dashni's evidence, then, is anecdotal evidence, which stands in contrast to scientific evidence, based on carefully conducted research with large samples. Maria needs to find out what the scientific evidence is on the effectiveness of mammograms. One approach would be trust an expert, such as her doctor, or trust a well-respected organization such as the American Cancer Society. She could also ask her doctor about the scientific information. How accurate are mammograms? What is their rate of false positives (saying you have a tumor when you don't)? What is their rate of false negatives (saying you have no tumor when you actually do)?

With access to the Internet, Maria could also dig out the scientific evidence herself. One strategy would be to visit the website of the National Institutes of Health (www.nih.gov), the major health research agency of the United States. We did that just now, and quickly found an article that examined the accuracy of a large sample of mammograms (Paliwal et al., 2006). Among 69,012 mammograms that the radiologist said were "negative" (no cancer), 68,933 were accurate and in 79 cases there was a cancer that was missed. That represents a false negative rate of less than 1 percent (0.1 percent, to be exact). Cases such as Dashni's false negative do occur, but they are very, very rare, occurring less than 1 percent of the time.

If Maria goes with the anecdotal evidence from her friend, she will conclude that mammograms are inaccurate and worthless. If Maria goes with the scientific evidence, she will conclude that they are highly accurate. Good critical thinking involves going with the scientific evidence.

SUMMARY

Female Sexual Organs

The external female sexual organs are the clitoris, mons, inner lips, outer lips, and vaginal opening. Collectively these are referred to as the vulva. The clitoris is highly sensitive and is very important in female sexual response. Clitoridectomy and infibulation are rituals that involve cutting of the clitoris and inner and outer lips and are widely practiced in some African nations and elsewhere. The important internal structures are the vagina, which receives the penis during coitus; the uterus, which houses the developing fetus; the ovaries, which produce eggs and manufacture sex hormones; and the fallopian tubes, which convey the egg to the uterus. The breasts also function in sexual arousal.

Male Sexual Organs

The external male sexual organs are the penis and the scrotum. The penis contains the corpora cavernosa and corpus spongiosum, which when filled with blood produce an erection. Circumcision, or surgical removal of the foreskin of the penis, is a practice debated in the United States but has some health advantages. The scrotum contains the testes, which are responsible for the manufacture of sperm (in the seminiferous tubules) and sex hormones (in the interstitial cells). Sperm pass out of the testes during ejaculation via the vas deferens, the ejaculatory duct, and the urethra. The seminal vesicles and prostate manufacture the fluid that mixes with sperm to form semen.

Cancer of the Sex Organs

Breast cancer is the most common form of cancer in women. Women should do a monthly self-exam, but it is no substitute for annual exams by a clinician and, beginning at age 45, annual mammograms. The Pap test is used to detect cervical cancer. Prostate cancer is the most common form of cancer in men, but it generally affects older men. Cancer of the testes, although rare, is the most common cancer in men between the ages of 29 and 35. Men can do a monthly testicular self-exam.

SUGGESTION FOR FURTHER READING

Boston Women's Health Book Collective. (2011). *Our bodies, ourselves.* New York: Simon & Schuster.
A good, easy-to-read source on female biology and sexuality.

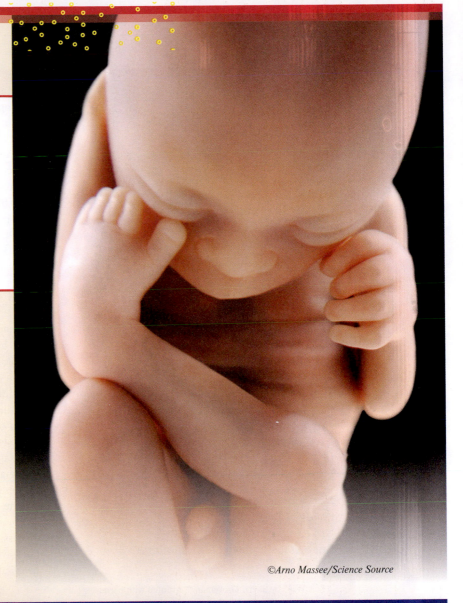

Are YOU Curious?

1. Can chemicals in our environment affect sexual development?
2. What is an "intersex" condition, and what does it mean if you have it?
3. How does the body regulate sex hormone levels over the menstrual cycle?

Read this chapter to find out.

CHAPTER

5

Sex Hormones, Sexual Differentiation, and the Menstrual Cycle

CHAPTER HIGHLIGHTS

This Way

I have AIS, I guess,
because there is a god,
and he or she or both,
peered deep into my heart
to see
that all that I can be
is best expressed
in female form.

The alternative for me
would be XY, and I
would be virilized;
so all that's soft and tender
would instead surrender
to a strand of DNA.
In the lie of X and Y
I came to challenge the
immutability
of "he" and the certainty
of "she." Blended and infused,
a ruse of gender
that upends
a different fate.

Non-functioning receptors
have rescued me
Not a failed mess
But a smashing success of nature!*

*"This Way" by Sherri Groveman. Reprinted with permission of the author. Sherri Groveman is an intersex individual who has complete androgen insensitivity syndrome (AIS). In *Hermaphrodites with attitude,* 1995, p. 2.

Prenatal period (pree-NAY-tul): The time from conception to birth.
Hormones: Chemical substances secreted by the endocrine glands into the bloodstream.
Testosterone: A hormone secreted by the testes in males (and also present at lower levels in females).
Androgens: A group of sex hormones, one of which is testosterone.
Estrogens (ESS-troh-jens): A group of sex hormones, one of which is estradiol.
Progesterone (pro-JES-tur-ohn): A sex hormone secreted by the ovaries as well as the testes.
Pituitary gland (pih-TOO-ih-tair-ee): A small endocrine gland located on the lower side of the brain below the hypothalamus; the pituitary is important in regulating levels of sex hormones.

One of the marvels of human biology is that the complex and different male and female anatomies—males with a penis and scrotum, and females with a vagina, uterus, and breasts—arise from a single cell, the fertilized egg, which varies only in whether it carries two X chromosomes (XX) or one X and one Y (XY). Many of the structural differences between males and females arise before birth, during the **prenatal period,** in a complex and delicate process called *prenatal sexual differentiation.* Further differences develop during puberty.

Yet as the chapter opening poem suggests, gender is not always a simple matter. Sex and gender and their development are complex and variable. Further variety in the human condition results.

In this chapter, we examine the process of sexual differentiation—both prenatally and during puberty. We also consider the biological and psychological aspects of the menstrual cycle. Let's start, however, with a basic biological system, the endocrine or hormonal system, paying particular attention to the sex hormones. They play a major role in the differentiation process.

Sex Hormones

Hormones are powerful chemical substances manufactured by the *endocrine glands* and secreted directly into the bloodstream. Because they go into the blood, their effects are felt fairly rapidly and at places in the body quite distant from where they were manufactured. The most important sex hormones are **testosterone** (one of a group of hormones called **androgens**) and **estrogens** and **progesterone.** The thyroid, the adrenals, and the pituitary are examples of endocrine glands. We are interested here in the gonads, or sex glands: the testes in males and the ovaries in females.

The **pituitary gland** and a closely related region of the brain, the **hypothalamus,** are also important to our discussion because the hypothalamus regulates the pituitary, which regulates the other glands, in particular the testes and ovaries. Because of its role, the pituitary has been called the *master gland* of the endocrine system. The pituitary is a small gland, about the size of a pea, that projects down from the lower side of the brain. It is divided into two lobes: the anterior and the posterior. The anterior lobe interacts with the gonads. The hypothalamus is a region at the base of the brain just above the pituitary (see Figure 1). It plays a part in regulating many vital behaviors, such as eating, drinking, and sexual behavior.[1] It is important in regulating the pituitary.

These three structures—the hypothalamus, the pituitary, and gonads (testes or ovaries)—function together. They influence such important sexual functions as the menstrual cycle, pregnancy, the changes of puberty, and sexual behavior.

Sex Hormone Systems in Males
The pituitary and the testes both produce hormones. The important hormone produced by testes is *testosterone.* A masculinizing sex hormone, testosterone has important

[1]One psychologist summarized the functions of the hypothalamus as being the four F's: fighting, feeding, fleeing, and, ahem, sexual behavior.

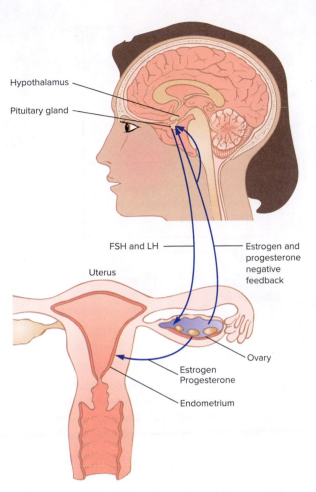

Figure 1   The hypothalamus-pituitary-gonad feed-back loop in women regulates production of sex hormones.

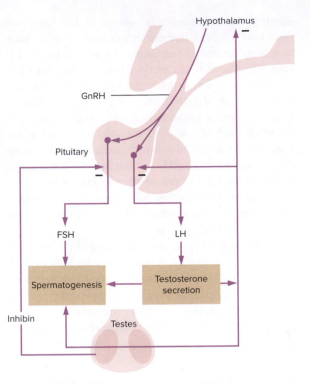

Figure 2   Schematic diagram of hormonal control of testosterone secretion and sperm production by the testes. The negative signs indicate that testosterone inhibits LH production, in both the pituitary and the hypothalamus.

functions in stimulating and maintaining the secondary sex characteristics (such as beard growth), maintaining the genitals and their sperm-producing capability, and stimulating the growth of bone and muscle.

The pituitary produces several hormones, two of which are important in this discussion: **follicle-stimulating hormone (FSH)** and **luteinizing hormone (LH).** These hormones affect the functioning of the testes. FSH controls sperm production, and LH controls testosterone production.

Testosterone levels in males are relatively constant. The hypothalamus, pituitary, and testes operate in a negative feedback loop that maintains these constant levels (Figure 2). The levels of LH are regulated by a substance called **GnRH (gonadotropin-releasing hormone),** which is secreted by the hypothalamus. (FSH levels are similarly regulated by GnRH.) The system comes full circle because the hypothalamus monitors the levels of testosterone present, and in this way testosterone influences the output of GnRH. This feedback loop is sometimes called the **HPG axis,** for *hypothalamus-pituitary-gonad* axis.

This negative feedback loop operates much like a thermostat-controlled heating system. When a room cools down, certain changes occur in the thermostat, which then signals the furnace to turn on. The action of the furnace warms the air in the room. Eventually the air becomes so warm that another change is produced in the thermostat, which sends a signal to the furnace to turn off. The temperature in the room then gradually falls until it triggers another change in the thermostat, which turns on the furnace, and the cycle is repeated. This cycle is a *negative* feedback loop because *increases* in temperature turn *off* the furnace, and *decreases* in temperature turn *on* the furnace.

The hypothalamus, pituitary, and testes work together in a similar negative feedback loop,

Hypothalamus (hy-poh-THAL-ah-mus): A small region of the brain that is important in regulating many body functions, including the functioning of the sex hormones.
Follicle-stimulating hormone (FSH): A hormone secreted by the pituitary; it stimulates follicle development in females and sperm production in males.
Luteinizing hormone (LH): A hormone secreted by the pituitary; it regulates estrogen secretion and ovum development in females and testosterone production in males.
GnRH (gonadotropin-releasing hormone): A hormone secreted by the hypothalamus that regulates the pituitary's secretion of gonad-stimulating hormones.
HPG axis: Hypothalamus-pituitary-gonad axis, the negative feedback loop that regulates sex-hormone production.

ensuring that testosterone is maintained at a fairly constant level, just as a thermostat can keep room temperature fairly constant. The pituitary's production of LH stimulates the testes to produce testosterone. But when testosterone levels get high, the hypothalamus reduces its production of GnRH, in turn causing the pituitary to reduce production of LH, and consequently decreasing production of testosterone by the testes. When testosterone levels fall, the hypothalamus again increases the production of GnRH, and the process starts again. Although the level of testosterone in men is fairly constant, there is some cycling, with variations according to the time of day, and possibly to the time of month, as we discuss later in this chapter.

Inhibin is another hormone produced in the testes (by cells called Sertoli cells). It acts to regulate FSH levels in a negative feedback loop, just as testosterone does with LH. Interest in inhibin has been intense because the hormone shows great promise, at least theoretically, as a male contraceptive. In other words, because inhibin suppresses FSH production, sperm production in turn is inhibited.

Sex Hormone Systems in Females

The ovaries produce two important hormones, *estrogen*[2] and *progesterone*. Estrogen brings about many of the changes of puberty (stimulating the growth of the uterus and vagina, enlarging the pelvis, and stimulating breast growth). Estrogen is also responsible for maintaining the mucous membranes of the vagina and stopping the growth of bone and muscle, which accounts for females being generally smaller than males.

In adult women the levels of estrogen and progesterone fluctuate according to the phases of the menstrual cycle and during various other stages such as pregnancy and menopause. The two pituitary hormones, FSH and LH, regulate the levels of estrogen and progesterone. In this way the levels of estrogen and progesterone are controlled by a negative feedback loop of the hypothalamus, pituitary, and ovaries that is similar to the negative feedback loop in males (see Figures 1 and 3). For example, as shown on the right side of Figure 3, increases in the level of GnRH increase the level of LH, and the increases in LH produce increases in the output of estrogen. Finally, the increases in the level of estrogen inhibit (decrease) the production of GnRH and LH.

Inhibin is produced by the ovaries, just as it is by the testes. It inhibits FSH production and

Inhibin: A hormone secreted by the testes and ovaries that regulates FSH levels.

Prolactin: A pituitary hormone that stimulates milk production by the mammary glands.

Oxytocin: A pituitary hormone that stimulates milk ejection from the nipples and contractions of the uterus during childbirth.

[2]We really should say *estrogens* because they are a group of hormones like the androgens. Estradiol is one of the estrogens. To keep things simple, we will just use the term *estrogen*.

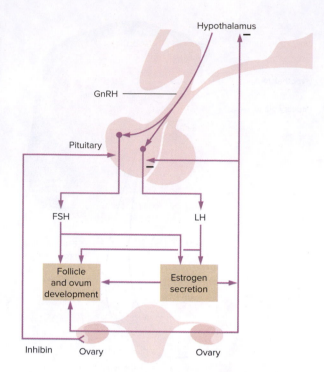

Figure 3   Schematic diagram of hormonal control of estrogen secretion and ovum production by the ovaries (during the follicular phase of the menstrual cycle). Note how similar the feedback loop is to the one in males.

participates in the feedback loop that controls the menstrual cycle.

The pituitary produces two other hormones, **prolactin** and **oxytocin.** Prolactin stimulates secretion of milk by the mammary glands after a woman has given birth to a child. Oxytocin stimulates ejection of that milk from the nipples. Oxytocin also stimulates contractions of the uterus during childbirth. In addition, oxytocin has gained a popular reputation as the "snuggle chemical," because it seems to promote affectionate bonding, for example, with one's newborn baby (Feldman et al., 2007). Oxytocin is produced in both males and females. In fact, in cotton-top tamarins, a species of monogamous monkeys, males and females have similar oxytocin levels, and oxytocin secretion is stimulated by touching, grooming, and sex (Snowdon et al., 2010).

The female sex hormone system functions much like the male sex hormone system. The ovaries and testes produce many of the same hormones. In fact, contrary to stereotypes, levels of estradiol and progesterone do not differ between adult men and women (Liening et al., 2010; van Anders, 2010). Only testosterone levels differ between men and women, with men having more. We consider the functioning of the female sex hormone system and the menstrual cycle in more detail later in this chapter.

Prenatal Sexual Differentiation

Sex Chromosomes

At the time of conception the future human being consists of only a single cell, the fertilized egg. The specific sex chromosomes carried in that fertilized egg are the deciding factor in whether it will become a male or a female. If there are two X chromosomes, the result will typically be a female, but if there are one X and one Y, the result will typically be a male. Although incredibly tiny, the sex chromosomes carry a wealth of information that they transmit to various organs throughout the body, giving instructions on how to differentiate in the course of development. Because the Y chromosome is smaller, it has fewer genes and carries less information than the X. The Y chromosome has about 80 genes, compared with 1,090 on the X (Federman, 2006).

Occasionally, individuals receive at conception a sex chromosome combination other than XX or XY. Such atypical sex chromosome complements may lead to a variety of clinical syndromes, such as *Klinefelter's syndrome*. In this syndrome, a genetic male has an extra X chromosome (XXY). As a result, the testes are small, no sperm are produced, and testosterone levels are low (Pacenza et al., 2012).

During development, the single cell divides repeatedly, becoming a two-celled organism, then a four-celled organism, then an eight-celled organism, and so on. By 28 days after conception, the embryo is about 1 centimeter (less than a half inch) long, but male and female embryos are still identical, except for the sex chromosomes. In other words, the embryo is still in the undifferentiated state. However, by the 7th week after conception, some basic structures have been formed that will eventually become either a male or a female reproductive system. At this point, the embryo has a pair of gonads (and each gonad has two parts—an outer cortex and an inner medulla), two sets of ducts (the *Müllerian ducts* and the *Wolffian ducts*), and rudimentary external genitals (the genital tubercle, the urethral folds, and the genital swelling) (see Figure 4, top).

Gonads

In the 7th week after conception, the sex chromosomes direct the gonads to begin differentiation. In males, the undifferentiated gonads develop into testes at about 7 weeks. In females, the process occurs somewhat later, with the ovaries developing at around 13 or 14 weeks.

An important gene that directs the differentiation of the gonads, located on the Y chromosome, is called **SRY,** for *sex-determining region, Y chromosome* (Skaletsky et al., 2003). The SRY gene causes the manufacture of a substance called *testis-determining factor* (TDF), which makes the gonads differentiate into testes, and male development occurs. (See Figure 6 for a summary of all the genes that regulate sexual differentiation.) The X chromosome carries genes that control normal functioning of the ovaries (Winter & Couch, 1995). Surprisingly, a number of genes on the X chromosome also affect cells in the testes that manufacture sperm (Wang et al., 2001).

Prenatal Hormones and the Genitals

Once the ovaries and testes have differentiated, they begin to produce sex hormones, which then direct the differentiation of the rest of the internal and external genital system (see Figure 4, middle).

In the female the Wolffian ducts degenerate, and the **Müllerian ducts** turn into the fallopian tubes, the uterus, and the upper part of the vagina. The tubercle becomes the clitoris, the folds become the inner lips, and the swelling develops into the outer lips.

The testes secrete Müllerian inhibiting substance (MIS) (Vilain, 2000). MIS causes the Müllerian ducts to degenerate, and the **Wolffian ducts,** supported by testosterone, turn into the epididymis, the vas deferens, and the ejaculatory duct. The tubercle becomes the glans penis, the folds form the shaft of the penis, and the swelling develops into the scrotum.

The process by which the internal and external genitals differentiate is the subject of much exciting new research. At least six different genes are involved in prenatal sexual differentiation (Figure 6), and a mutation in any one of them can cause atypical development (Vilain, 2000).

By 12 weeks after conception, the gender of the fetus is clear from the appearance of the external genitals (Figure 4, bottom).

Descent of the Testes and Ovaries

As these developmental changes are taking place, the ovaries and testes are changing in shape and position. At first, the ovaries and testes lie near the top of the abdominal cavity. By the 10th week they have grown and have moved down to the level of the upper edge of the pelvis. The ovaries remain there until after birth, and later they shift to their adult position in the pelvis.

The testes must make a much longer journey, down into the scrotum via a passageway called the *inguinal canal*. Normally this movement occurs around the 7th month after conception. The inguinal canal closes off after the testes descend.

Two problems may occur in this process. First, one or both testes may fail to descend into the scrotum by the time of birth, a condition known as *undescended testes,* or **cryptorchidism.** This condition

SRY: Stands for sex-determining region, Y chromosome.

Müllerian ducts: Ducts found in both male and female fetuses; in males they degenerate, and in females they develop into the fallopian tubes, the uterus, and the upper part of the vagina.

Wolffian ducts: Ducts found in both male and female fetuses; in females they degenerate, and in males they develop into the epididymis, the vas deferens, and the ejaculatory duct.

Cryptorchidism: Undescended testes; the condition in which the testes do not descend to the scrotum as they should during prenatal development.

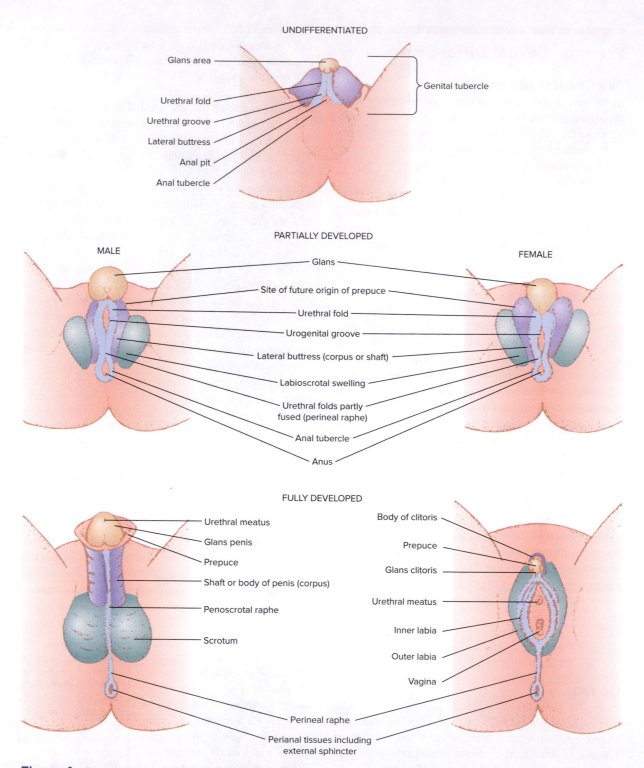

UNDIFFERENTIATED

- Glans area
- Genital tubercle
- Urethral fold
- Urethral groove
- Lateral buttress
- Anal pit
- Anal tubercle

PARTIALLY DEVELOPED

MALE   FEMALE

- Glans
- Site of future origin of prepuce
- Urethral fold
- Urogenital groove
- Lateral buttress (corpus or shaft)
- Labioscrotal swelling
- Urethral folds partly fused (perineal raphe)
- Anal tubercle
- Anus

FULLY DEVELOPED

- Urethral meatus
- Glans penis
- Prepuce
- Shaft or body of penis (corpus)
- Penoscrotal raphe
- Scrotum

- Body of clitoris
- Prepuce
- Glans clitoris
- Urethral meatus
- Inner labia
- Outer labia
- Vagina

- Perineal raphe
- Perianal tissues including external sphincter

Figure 4   Development of the male and female external genitals from the undifferentiated stage during prenatal development. Note homologous organs in the female and male.

occurs in about 3 percent of all males. Most frequently, only one testis is undescended, and the other is in the normal position. In most of these cases, the testes do descend by the first birthday. If the testes do not descend spontaneously, however, the condition is usually corrected by surgery. The optimum time for doing this is soon after the first birthday. Otherwise, if both testes fail to descend, the man will be sterile, because, as we discussed in the chapter "Sexual Anatomy," the high temperature of the testes inside the body inhibits the production of sperm. Undescended

Milestones in Sex Research

Endocrine Disrupters

Male Florida panthers have low sperm counts. Frogs are born hermaphroditic, with mixed male and female organs. Male turtledoves display reduced courtship and nesting behaviors. A preschool girl begins growing pubic hair. These cases and dozens of others have appeared in the news in the last decade. Are they unrelated bizarre occurrences, or is there a common link?

Scientists believe that underlying all these troubling cases is the phenomenon of **endocrine disrupters** (sometimes called endocrine-disrupting chemicals or EDCs), which are chemicals found in the environment that affect the endocrine system and cause adverse effects on animals, including humans. Evidence of the effects of endocrine disrupters comes both from studies of animals in the wild and from carefully controlled laboratory experiments.

Can chemicals in our environment affect sexual development?

What chemicals are the culprits? Some are pesticides such as atrazine and DDT, used by farmers and others to kill unwanted insects and weeds. Bisphenol A (BPA) is used in making plastics such as baby bottles. More BPA is produced every year than any other chemical—15 billion pounds in 2013 (Gore et al., 2015). PCBs, which were banned from production in the United States in 1976, were used in making products such as paints, plastics, and printing ink. Some have a half-life of over 1,000 years and thus are still abundant in the environment despite being banned.

Fracking (hydraulic fracturing to extract oil from the earth) involves the use of fracking chemicals, 35 percent of which are endocrine disrupters (Alcid & Miller, 2014). These chemicals have been linked to infertility, miscarriage, birth defects, and cancers of the reproductive organs.

How do these chemicals exert their effects on sexual biology and behavior? All of them affect the endocrine system and, specifically, the sex hormone system. Many have multiple effects. Atrazine, for example, affects both estrogen and testosterone and inhibits their binding to estrogen receptors and androgen receptors. It also depresses the LH surge that causes ovulation, described later in this chapter in the discussion of the menstrual cycle. The insecticide DDT affects estrogen, progesterone, and testosterone by mimicking estrogen and binding to estrogen receptors, as well as by altering the metabolism of both progesterone and testosterone. PCBs are both anti-estrogens and anti-androgens. Endocrine disrupters can cause epigenetic changes that result in effects later in the individual's life and can be passed down to their offspring. These chemicals are in the food we eat and the water and milk that we drink.

Why should we care about a few hermaphroditic frogs or preschoolers with pubic hair? Scientists see these cases as examples of the proverbial canary in the mine shaft—that is, they are small signs that something terribly dangerous is happening. The European Union is taking steps to regulate these chemicals, but we have seen little action on the issue in the United States.

Meanwhile, a carefully controlled study shows that pregnant women with high exposure to phthalates (found in plastics) are more likely to give birth to baby boys with undescended testes, hydroceles, and hypospadias, a condition in which the urethral opening is not at the tip of the penis, but somewhere else along it (see Figure 5) (Sathyanarayana et al., 2016). Studies in both the United States and Denmark show that breast development in girls is occurring one year earlier now than it did a few decades ago (Aksglaede et al., 2009). The pesticide residues in fruits and vegetables have been linked to lower sperm counts in men (Chiu et al., 2015). And on a Chippewa Indian reservation in a part of Ontario that is heavily populated with chemical manufacturing plants, only 35 percent of the babies born today are boys. According to an official statement by the Endocrine Society, "The [research] identifies EDCs as contributing to outcomes related to impaired reproduction, neurodevelopment, thyroid function, and metabolism and increased propensity for hormone-sensitive cancers" (Gore et al., 2015).

Endocrine disrupters: Chemicals in the environment that affect the endocrine system and cause adverse effects on animals, including humans.

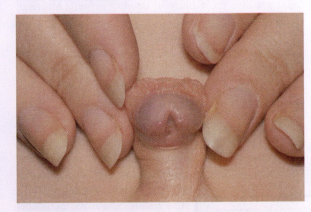

Figure 5   An example of hypospadia, in which the urethral opening is not at the tip of the penis.

©Allan Harris/Diomedia

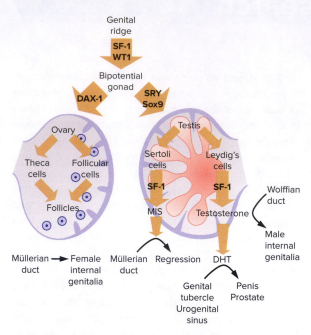

Figure 6 The functions of the genes linked to sexual differentiation in mammals: SRY, Sox9, WT1, SF-1, and DAX-1 (MacLaughlin & Donahoe, 2004; Marx, 1995). **WT1** stands for Wilms tumor gene 1, and is required for expression of the Sox9 gene (Gao et al., 2006). **DAX-1** stands for *D*osage-sensitive sex reversal–*A*drenal hypoplasia congenital gene on the *X* chromosome, gene 1 (also called NrOb1; Hoyle et al., 2002; McCabe, 1996; Meeks et al., 2003). **Sox9** is the SRY-box containing gene 9 (on chromosome 17 in humans). SF-1 is steroidogenic factor 1 (Gummow et al., 2006; Hammer & Ingraham, 1999), MIS is Müllerian inhibiting substance, and DHT is dihydrotestosterone, a potent androgen.

testes are also more likely to develop cancer (American Cancer Society, 2012).

The second possible problem occurs when the inguinal canal does not close off completely. It may then reopen later in life, creating a passageway through which loops of the intestine can enter the scrotum. This condition, called *inguinal hernia,* can be remedied by simple surgery.

Brain Differentiation

During the prenatal period, when sex hormones are having a big impact on genital anatomy, they are also acting on the brain (Arnold, 2003). The results of many experiments with animals indicate that in certain regions there are differences between male and female brains. The primary sex-differentiated structure is the hypothalamus, in particular a region of it called the

Epigenetics: A functional change to DNA that does not alter the genetic code itself but leads to changes in gene expression. Often an epigenetic change involves methylation, that is, a methyl group is attached to the base cytosine in the DNA.

preoptic area. The hypothalamus is gender-differentiated in humans as well (Campbell & Herbison, 2014).

One of the most important effects of this early sexual differentiation is the determination of the estrogen sensitivity of certain cells in the hypothalamus, cells that have *estrogen receptors* (Choi et al., 2001; McEwen, 2001). If testosterone is present during fetal development, these specialized cells in the hypothalamus become insensitive to estrogen. If estrogen is present, these cells become highly sensitive to levels of estrogen in the bloodstream. This sensitivity is crucial to the hypothalamic-pituitary-gonad feedback loop discussed earlier. Male hypothalamic cells are relatively insensitive to estrogen levels, but female hypothalamic cells are highly sensitive to them. Male hypothalamic cells have more androgen receptors (Donahue et al., 2000).

A major new study in 2015 reported evidence of epigenetic changes during prenatal sexual differentiation of the brain (Spiers et al., 2015). **Epigenetics** refers to a functional change to DNA that does not alter the genetic code itself but leads to changes in gene expression. Often an epigenetic change involves methylation, that is, a methyl group is attached to the base cytosine in the DNA. Differences between male and female brains in DNA methylation were found for a number of genes. These results suggest that prenatal sexual differentiation of the brain may involve more than anatomical differences in structures and androgen receptors; it may also involve epigenetic factors that can lead genes to be expressed or silenced. The researchers hope that this research will eventually help to explain why, for example, autism affects so many more males than females.

The brains of men and women are actually quite similar in most regions, but a few brain structures show gender differentiation (Eliot, 2009; Joel, 2011). These structures include the hypothalamus, which we have already discussed, and the amygdala, which is important in emotion (Cahill, 2005; Ngun et al., 2011). Modern neuroscientists, however, reject the notion that these represent "hardwired" differences present from birth (Eliot, 2009). Instead, neuroscientists emphasize the *plasticity* of the brain, which is constantly changing in response to experiences that the person has. For example, an 8-year-old boy has a father who practices tossing footballs with him every day, whereas the father of the 8-year-old girl next door doesn't toss footballs with her. Within weeks, the neural circuits in the boy's brain involved in catching and throwing will have strengthened, whereas the same circuits in the girl's brain will not. Their brains will now be different in that region, but as a result of their different experiences, not hardwiring present from birth.

Homologous Organs

Our discussion of sexual differentiation highlights the fact that the reproductive organs of men and women have

Table 1 Homologous and Analogous Organs of the Male and Female Reproductive Systems

Embryonic Source	Homologous Organs		Analogous Organs	
	In the Adult Male	In the Adult Female	In the Adult Male	In the Adult Female
Gonad (medulla plus cortex)	Testes (from medulla)	Ovaries (from cortex)	Testes	Ovaries
Genital tubercle	Glans penis	Clitoris	Glans penis	Clitoris
Genital swelling	Scrotum	Outer lips		
Müllerian duct	Degenerates, leaving only remnants	Fallopian tubes, uterus, part of vagina		
Wolffian duct	Epididymis, vas deferens, seminal vesicles	Degenerates, leaving only remnants		
Urethral primordia	Prostate, Cowper's glands	Skene's glands, Bartholin glands	Prostate, Cowper's glands	Skene's glands, Bartholin glands

similar origins, even though adult men and women appear to have very different reproductive anatomies. When an organ in males and an organ in females both develop from the same embryonic tissue, the organs are said to be **homologous**. When the two organs have similar functions, they are said to be **analogous**. Table 1 summarizes the major homologies (similar origins) and analogies (similar functions) of the male and female reproductive systems. For example, ovaries and testes are homologous (because they develop from an undifferentiated gonad) and analogous (because they produce gametes and sex hormones).

Atypical Prenatal Gender Differentiation

Gender is not a simple matter, as you may have noticed from the preceding discussion. Most people, however, assume that it is. In other words, people typically assume that if a person is female, she will be feminine; will think of herself as a woman; will be sexually attracted to men; will have a clitoris, vagina, uterus, and ovaries; and will have sex chromosomes XX. They also assume that all males are masculine; think of themselves as male; are sexually attracted to women; have a penis, testes, and scrotum; and have sex chromosomes XY.

A great deal of research over the last several decades challenges these assumptions and provides much information about sexuality and gender and their development. Before we consider the results of this research, however, some background information is helpful.

We can distinguish among the following eight variables of gender (adapted from Money, 1987)[3]:

1. *Chromosomal gender.* XX in females; XY in males.
2. *Gonadal gender.* Ovaries in females; testes in males.

[3]The distinction between the terms *gender* and *sex,* discussed in the chapter "Sexuality in Perspective," is being maintained here.

3a. *Prenatal hormonal gender.* Testosterone and MIS in males but not females before birth.

3b. *Prenatal and neonatal brain differentiation.* Testosterone present for masculinization, absent for feminization.

4. *Internal organs.* Fallopian tubes, uterus, and upper vagina in females; prostate, vas, and seminal vesicles in males.

5. *External genital appearance.* Clitoris, inner and outer lips, and vaginal opening in females; penis and scrotum in males.

6. *Pubertal hormonal gender.* At puberty, estrogen and progesterone in females; testosterone in males.

7. *Assigned gender.* The announcement at birth, "It's a girl" or "It's a boy," based on the appearance of the external genitals; the gender the parents and the rest of society believe the child to be; the gender in which the child is reared.

8. *Gender identity.* The person's private, internal sense of maleness or femaleness or something else, such as nonbinary.

These variables might be subdivided into biological variables (the first six) and psychological variables (the last two).

In most cases, of course, all the variables are in agreement in an individual. In other words, the person is a "consistent" female or male. If the person is a female, she has XX chromosomes, ovaries, a uterus and vagina, and a clitoris; she is reared as a female; and she thinks of herself as a female.

However, as a result of any one of a number of factors during the course of prenatal sexual development, the gender indicated by one or more of these variables may disagree with the gender indicated

Homologous organs (huh-MOLL-uh-gus): Organs in the male and female that develop from the same embryonic tissue.
Analogous organs (an-AL-uh-gus): Organs in the male and female that have similar functions.

Figure 7   Diversity in prenatal sexual differentiation. The female spotted hyena has a clitoris as large as a penis and no vaginal opening because the labia fuse together like a scrotum. Urine passes out through the clitoris and she gives birth through the clitoris. Pregnant female hyenas produce high levels of an androgen (A_4), and the hyena placenta produces an enzyme that converts the A_4 to testosterone, leading to the masculinized genitals of daughters (Drea, 2009).

©Ingram Publishing

by others. When the contradictions occur among several of the biological variables (1 through 6), the person is said to have an **intersex** condition. The medical term is **disorder of sex development (DSD)** (Berenbaum, 2006; Hughes et al., 2006; Reis, 2007). Biologically, the gender of such a person is ambiguous. The reproductive structures may be partly male and partly female, or they may be incompletely male or female. Approximately 2 percent of births have an intersex condition (Blackless et al., 2000).

A number of syndromes can cause an intersex condition. Two of the most common are congenital adrenal hyperplasia and the androgen-insensitivity syndrome. In **congenital adrenal hyperplasia (CAH),** a genetic female develops ovaries normally as a fetus, but later in the course of prenatal development, the adrenal gland begins to function abnormally (as a result of a recessive genetic condition unconnected with the sex chromosomes) and produces an excess amount of androgens. Prenatal sexual differentiation then does not follow the typical female course. As a result, the external genitals are partly or completely male in appearance. The labia are partly or totally

Intersex: A condition in which the individual has a mixture of male and female reproductive structures, so that it is not clear at birth whether the individual is a male or a female. Formerly called a *pseudohermaphrodite.*
Disorders of sex development (DSD): Another term for intersex conditions.
Congenital adrenal hyperplasia (CAH): A condition in which a genetic female produces excess levels of androgens prenatally and therefore has male-appearing genitals at birth.
Androgen-insensitivity syndrome (AIS): A genetic condition in which the body is unresponsive to androgens so that a genetic male may be born with a female-appearing body.

fused (so there is no vaginal opening), and the clitoris is enlarged to the size of a small penis or even a full-sized one. For this reason, at birth these genetic females are sometimes identified as males. Long-term follow-ups indicate that CAH girls have a female gender identity, tend toward male-stereotyped interests and activities, and generally function well as girls and women (Berenbaum, 2018).

The reverse case occurs in **androgen-insensitivity syndrome (AIS)** (Wisniewski et al., 2000). In this syndrome a genetic male produces typical levels of testosterone, but as a result of a genetic condition, the body tissues are insensitive to the testosterone, and prenatal development is feminized. For this reason, the individual is born with the external appearance of a female: a small vagina (but no uterus) and undescended testes. The individual whose poem appeared at the beginning of this chapter has AIS.

> What is an "intersex" condition, and what does it mean if you have it?

Intersex persons provide good evidence of the great complexity of sex and gender and their development. Many variables are involved in gender and sex, and there are many steps in gender differentiation, even before birth. Because the process is complex, it is vulnerable to disturbances, creating conditions such as intersex.

Indeed, the research serves to question our basic notions of what it means to be male or female. In CAH, is the genetic female who is born with male external genitals a male or a female? What makes a person male or female—chromosomal gender? External genital appearance? Gender identity?

A related phenomenon was first studied in a small community in the Dominican Republic (Imperato-McGinley et al., 1974). Due to a genetic-endocrine problem, a large number of genetic males there appeared to be females at birth. The syndrome is called *5-alpha reductase deficiency syndrome.* These infants had a vaginal pouch instead of a scrotum and a clitoris-sized penis. The uneducated parents, according to the researchers, were unaware that there were any problems, and these genetic males were treated as typical females. At puberty, a spontaneous biological change caused a penis to develop. Significantly, the psychological identity of these individuals also changed. Despite their rearing as females, their gender identity switched to male, and they developed heterosexual interests. In their culture, these people are called Guevodoces ("penis at 12").

Anthropologist Gilbert Herdt (1990) is critical of the research and interpretations about the Guevodoces. The major criticism is that the Western researchers assumed that this culture is a two-gender society, like the United States, and that people have to fall into one of only two categories, either male or female.

Anthropologists, however, have documented the existence of three-gender societies—that is, societies in which there are three, not two, gender categories—and the society in which the Guevodoces grow up is a three-gender society. The third gender is the Guevodoces. Their gender identity is not male or female but Guevodoce. The 5-alpha reductase deficiency syndrome has also been found among the Sambia of New Guinea, who also have a three-gender culture. Again we see the profound effect of culture on our most basic ideas about sex and gender.

Sexual Differentiation during Puberty

Puberty is not a point in time but rather a process during which there is further sexual differentiation. It is the stage in life during which the body changes from that of a child into that of an adult, with secondary sexual characteristics (such as breasts or a beard) and the ability to reproduce sexually.

Puberty can be scientifically defined as the time during which there is sudden enlargement and maturation of the gonads, other genitalia, and secondary sex characteristics, leading to reproductive capacity (Tanner, 1967). It is the second important period—the first being the prenatal period—during which sexual differentiation takes place. Perhaps the most memorable single event in the process is the first ejaculation for boys and the first menstruation for girls. First menstruation is not necessarily a sign of reproductive capability because girls typically do not produce mature eggs until a year or two after the first menstruation.

The physiological process that underlies puberty in both genders is a marked increase in levels of sex hormones. For this reason, the hypothalamus, pituitary, and gonads control the changes.

Adolescence is a socially defined period of development that bears some relationship to puberty. Adolescence represents a psychological transition from the behavior and attitudes of a child to the behavior, attitudes, and responsibilities of an adult. In the United States it corresponds roughly to the years from age 10 to age 20. Modern American culture has an unusually long period of adolescence (Steinberg, 2018). A century ago, adolescence was much shorter. The lengthening of the educational process has served to prolong adolescence. In some cultures, in fact, adolescence does not exist. Instead, the child shifts to being an adult directly, with only a *rite of passage* in between.

Before describing the changes that take place during puberty, we should note two points. First, the timing of the pubertal process differs considerably for males and females. Girls begin the change around 8 to 12 years of age, and boys do so about 2 years later. Girls reach their full height by about age 16, whereas boys continue growing until about age 18 or later. The phenomenon of males and females being out of step with each other at this stage creates no small number of crises. Girls are interested in boys long before boys are aware that girls exist. A girl may be stuck with a date who barely reaches her armpits, and a boy may have to cope with someone who is better qualified to be on his basketball team than he is.

Second, there are large individual differences (differences from one person to the next) in the age at which the processes of puberty take place. For this reason there is no one "normal" time to begin menstruating or growing a beard. Instead, we give age ranges in describing the timing of the process.

Changes in Girls

A summary of the physical changes of puberty in males and females is provided in Table 2. The first sign of puberty in girls is the beginning of breast development, on average around 8 to 9 years of age. The ducts in the nipple area swell, and there is growth of fatty and connective tissue, causing the small, conical buds to increase in size. These changes are produced by increases in the levels of the sex hormones by a process that is described in the following pages.

As the growth of fatty and supporting tissue increases in the breasts, a similar increase takes place at the hips and buttocks, leading to the rounded contours that distinguish adult female bodies from adult male bodies. Individual females have unique patterns of fat deposits, so there are also considerable individual differences in the resulting female shapes.

Another visible sign of puberty is the growth of pubic hair, which occurs shortly after breast development begins. About two years later, axillary (underarm) hair appears.

Body growth increases sharply during puberty, during the approximate age range of 9.5 to 14.5 years. The growth spurt for girls occurs about two years before the growth spurt for boys (Figure 9). This timing is consistent with girls' general pattern of maturing earlier than boys. Even prenatally, girls show an earlier hardening of the structures that become bones.

Estrogen eventually stops the growth spurt in girls. The presence of estrogen also causes the growth period to end sooner in girls than in boys, in this way accounting for the lesser average height of adult women as compared with adult men.

> **Puberty:** The time during which there is sudden enlargement and maturation of the gonads, other genitalia, and secondary sex characteristics, so that the individual becomes capable of reproduction.

A Sexually Diverse World

The Debate over the Treatment of Intersex Individuals

When Chris was born, her clitoris was 1.7 cm long. That's about halfway between the length of the average newborn clitoris and the average newborn penis. She had a scrotum but no testes in it, and the physician was unsure whether she was a girl or a boy. A blood test revealed that her sex chromosomes were XY. After 24 hours of consultations, during which her parents were in agony, the physician decided that Chris should be a girl because it would be impossible for her to function as a boy with such strange genitals. While a baby, she had several surgeries, one to remove her testes, which were still in her abdomen. Her clitoris was surgically reduced in size when she was age 5, old enough to remember it. Today she is 27 and angry about what she considers the mutilations of her body. She now knows that she has androgen-insensitivity syndrome. So much of her clitoris was removed that she is not able to orgasm.

Chris (a composite of several case histories in the scientific literature) is an intersex individual; that is, her genitals have combined male, female, or ambiguous elements. She was treated according to a protocol that became standard beginning in the 1960s. This protocol was based on the pioneering research of Dr. John Money and others. According to him, individuals such as Chris, whom he called "pseudohermaphrodites," could successfully be assigned to either gender, provided that it was done before 18 months of age and that the necessary surgeries and follow-up medical treatments (such as hormone treatment) occurred. Money's research indicated that individuals treated with the standard protocol grew up to be healthy and well adjusted.

More recently, however, intersex individuals have come out of the closet and formed an activist organization, the Intersex Society of North America (ISNA). That organization ended in 2008 and was replaced by Accord Alliance, which promotes integrated care for those with disorders of sex development and their families.* Intersex activists argue that they have cases of genital *variability,* not genital abnormality. The medical standard is that an infant's organ that is 0.9 cm or less is

*For information about Accord Alliance and other sexuality organizations, including the Accord Alliance website, see the Directory of Resources.

a clitoris and 2.5 cm or more is a penis. Activists argue that these cutoffs are arbitrary. What is wrong with a clitoris that is 1.7 cm long? Perhaps the only thing wrong with it is that it makes doctors, and perhaps parents, embarrassed. Issues of medical ethics are raised: Should essentially cosmetic surgery be performed on a baby who cannot give informed consent? Should parents be encouraged to lie to their child?

Sex researcher Milton Diamond conducted long-term follow-ups on several individuals treated using Money's standard protocol. He found that, contrary to the glowing picture of perfect adjustment painted by Money and others, these individuals had serious adjustment problems that they traced directly to the medical "management" of their condition. Diamond's research sparked a debate over the proper treatment of disorders of sex development (DSD), which activists say should be called differences in sexual development. Diamond proposed a protocol in which he urges physicians, in cases of infants with these disorders, (1) to make their most informed judgment about the child's eventual gender identity (CAH girls, for example, almost invariably have a female identity) and counsel the parents to rear the child in that gender; (2) not to perform surgeries that might later need to be reversed; and (3) to provide honest counseling and education to the parents and child as they grow up so that the child can eventually make an informed decision regarding treatment.

Diamond's research was quickly followed by more systematic studies. Micropenis is a condition in which a genetic XY male is born with a very small penis. One study followed up 18 of these individuals in adulthood; 13 had been reared as boys and 5 as girls (Wisniewski et al., 2001). All of the individuals raised as men reported good or fair erections, but 50 percent were dissatisfied with their genitals. In contrast, 80 percent of the individuals raised as women were dissatisfied with their genitals, and 40 percent had no sexual interest or experience. In this case, it seems that rearing as a male worked better.

Another study examined the success of "feminizing" genital surgery—that is, performing surgery to reduce the size of an overlarge clitoris or to create or enlarge a vagina, as might happen with CAH girls (Creighton et al.,

2001). Of the surgeries done in childhood, 41 percent were judged as having a poor outcome, supporting Diamond's recommendations against these early surgeries. Another study of women with DSD—many of them with CAH—who had had clitoral surgery in childhood indicated approximately twice as many of them (39 percent) being unable to orgasm, compared with a control group (20 percent) of women with DSD who had not had clitoral surgery (Minto et al., 2003).

Recognizing these new developments, the American Academy of Pediatrics (2000; Lee et al., 2006) issued guidelines for primary care pediatricians on how to care for newborns with ambiguous genitals. They include what tests to run to determine the cause of the ambiguous genitals, when the baby should be referred to a center specializing in DSD, and what factors should be used to decide the sex of rearing. These factors include fertility potential (for example, a CAH girl is potentially fertile and should be raised as a girl) and capacity for normal sexual functioning. Only with long-term studies will we learn whether these new treatments will yield better results for individuals with intersex conditions.

Sources: American Academy of Pediatrics (2000); Meyer-Bahlburg (2013); Creighton et al. (2001); Creighton & Minto (2001); Diamond (1996, 1999); Diamond & Beh (2008); Diamond & Sigmundson (1997); Kessler (1998); Lee et al. (2006); Meyer-Bahlburg et al. (2004); Money & Ehrhardt (1972); Wisniewski et al. (2000, 2001).

Figure 8 Cheryl Chase, an activist for those with disorders of sex development.

©Catherine Opie

At about 12 years of age, the **menarche** (first menstruation) occurs. The girl, however, is not capable of becoming pregnant until ovulation begins, typically about two years after the menarche. The first menstruation is not only an important biological event but also a significant psychological one. Various cultures have ceremonies recognizing its importance. In some families, it is a piece of news that spreads quickly to the relatives. Girls themselves display a wide range of reactions to the event, ranging from negative ones, such as fear, shame, or disgust, to positive ones, such as pride and a sense of maturity and womanliness.

Some of the most negative reactions occur when the girl has not been prepared for the menarche, which is still the case surprisingly often. Parents who are concerned about preparing their daughters for the first menstruation should remember that there is a wide range in the age at which it occurs. It is not unusual for a girl to start menstruating in the fifth grade, and instances of the menarche during the fourth grade, while rare, do occur.

What determines the age at which a girl first menstruates? One explanation is the *percent body fat hypothesis* (Frisch & McArthur, 1974; Hopwood et al., 1990; Lassek & Gaulin, 2007). During puberty, deposits of body fat increase in girls. According to the percent body fat hypothesis, the percentage of body weight that is fat must rise to a certain level for menstruation to occur for the first time and for it to be maintained. For this reason, very skinny adolescent girls would tend to be late in the timing of first menstruation. **Leptin,** a hormone, is related to the onset of puberty in both girls and boys (Israel et al., 2012; Terasawa

Menarche (MEN-ar-key): First menstruation.
Leptin: A hormone related to the onset of puberty.

Table 2   Summary of the Changes of Puberty and Their Sequence

Girls			Boys		
Characteristic	Average Age of First Appearance (Years)	Major Hormonal Influence	Characteristic	Average Age of First Appearance (Years)	Major Hormonal Influence
1. Growth of breasts	8–9	Pituitary growth hormone, estrogens, progesterone, thyroxine	1. Growth of testes, scrotal sac	9–10	Pituitary growth hormone, testosterone
2. Growth of pubic hair	9–10	Adrenal androgens	2. Growth of pubic hair	10–11	Testosterone
3. Body growth	9.5–14.5	Pituitary growth hormone, adrenal androgens, estrogens	3. Body growth	10.5–16	Pituitary growth hormone, testosterone
4. Menarche	12–12.5	GnRH, FSH, LH, estrogens, progesterone	4. Growth of penis	11–14.5	Testosterone
5. Underarm hair	10–11	Adrenal androgens	5. Change in voice (growth of larynx)	About the same time as penis growth	Testosterone
6. Oil- and sweat-producing glands (acne occurs when glands are clogged)	About the same time as underarm hair	Adrenal androgens	6. Facial and underarm hair	About 2 years after pubic hair	Testosterone
			7. Oil- and sweat-producing glands, acne	About the same time as underarm hair	Testosterone

Sources: Tanner (1967), updated with Biro et al. (2013); Herman-Giddens et al. (1997, 2012).

et al., 2012). In prepubertal girls and boys, leptin levels rise as body fat increases. Leptin stimulates the growth of skeletal bone and the release of LH. And leptin stimulates the secretion of kisspeptin.

The hot new hormone that has been discovered to be involved in the initiation of puberty is **kisspeptin** (Ojeda & Lomniczi, 2014). It is encoded by a gene called KISS1. Don't you just love the way these biologists name things! Other genes control when the KISS1 gene starts to be expressed so that it produces kisspeptin. Kisspeptin then stimulates the hypothalamus to produce more GnRH and to produce it in a "pulsatile" fashion—that is, in pulses. This initiates a cascade of secretion of hormones, including LH and FSH, which stimulates the ovaries to produce estrogen, and the pubertal race is on!

The percent body fat hypothesis also helps to make sense

of two related phenomena: the cessation of menstruation in anorexics and the cessation of menstruation in women distance runners. *Anorexia nervosa* is a condition in which the person—most commonly an adolescent girl—engages in compulsive, extreme dieting, perhaps to the point of starving herself to death. As anorexia progresses, the percentage of body fat declines and menstruation ceases. It is also fairly common for women who are runners, and all women who exercise seriously to the point where their body fat is substantially reduced, to cease menstruating. For both anorexics and female runners, it seems that when the percentage of body fat falls below a critical value, the biological processes that control the menstrual cycle shut down menstruation.[4]

Kisspeptin: A hormone involved in the initiation of pubertal development.

[4]On the other hand, moderate exercise has been associated with reduced menstrual problems such as cramps (Hightower, 1997).

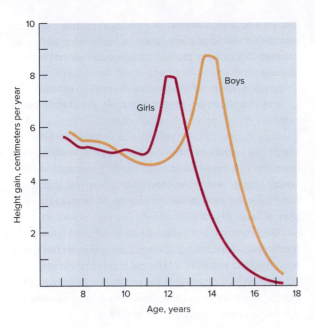

Figure 9 The adolescent spurt of growth for boys and girls. Note that girls experience their growth spurt earlier than boys do.

Before leaving the topic of running, we should note that there is some evidence that serious exercise also affects the male reproductive system. One study of male distance runners found that their testosterone levels were only about 68 percent as high, on average, as a control group's testosterone levels, and other studies have found similar effects (Hackney, 2008; Wheeler et al., 1984). There are some reports of male long-distance runners complaining of a loss of sex drive, but it is unclear whether this results from reduced testosterone levels or from the perpetual feelings of fatigue that such runners have from their intensive training.

Other body changes in girls during puberty include a development of the blood supply to the clitoris, a thickening of the walls of the vagina, and a rapid growth of the uterus, which doubles in size between ages 10 and 18. The pelvic bone structure grows and widens, contributing to the rounded shape of females and creating a passageway large enough for an infant to move through during birth.

The dramatic changes that occur during puberty are produced, basically, by the endocrine system and its upsurge in sex hormone production during puberty. The process begins with the hypothalamus releasing pulses of GnRH, which triggers an increase in secretion of FSH by the pituitary gland. FSH in turn stimulates the ovaries to produce estrogen. Estrogen is responsible for many of the changes that occur. It stimulates breast growth and the growth of the uterus and vagina.

Also involved in puberty are the paired **adrenal glands,** which are located just above the kidneys. In females, the adrenal glands are a major producer of androgens. Adrenal androgens stimulate the growth of pubic and axillary hair and are related to the female sex drive. **Adrenarche**— the time of increasing secretion of adrenal androgens— generally begins slightly before age 8 (Styne & Grumbach, 2008).

Changes in Boys

As noted earlier, puberty begins at about 10 or 11 years of age in boys, a year or two later than it does in girls. The physical causes of puberty in boys parallel those in girls. They are initiated by increased production of FSH and LH by the pituitary. At the beginning of puberty, the increase in LH stimulates the testes to produce testosterone, which is responsible for most of the changes of puberty in males.

The first noticeable pubertal change in boys is the growth of the testes and scrotal sac, which begins on average at around 9 to 10 years of age as a result of testosterone stimulation. The growth of pubic hair begins at about the same time. About a year later the penis begins to enlarge, first thickening and then lengthening. This change also results from testosterone stimulation. As the testes enlarge, their production of testosterone increases even more, leading to rapid growth of the penis, testes, and pubic hair at ages 13 and 14.

The growth of facial and axillary hair begins about two years after the beginning of pubic hair growth. The growth of facial hair begins with the appearance of fuzz on the upper lip, but adult beards do not appear until two or three years later. Indeed, by age 17, 50 percent of American males have not yet shaved. These changes also result from testosterone stimulation, which continues to produce growth of facial and chest hair beyond 20 years of age.

Erections increase in frequency. The organs that produce the fluid of semen, particularly the prostate, enlarge considerably at about the same time the other organs are growing. By age 13 or 14, the boy is capable of ejaculation.[5] By about age 15, the ejaculate contains mature sperm and the boy is now fertile. The pituitary hormone FSH is responsible for initiating and maintaining the production of mature sperm.

Beginning about a year after the first ejaculation, many boys begin having nocturnal emissions, or "wet dreams." For the boy who has never masturbated, a wet dream may be his first ejaculation.

At about the same time penis growth occurs, the larynx

> **Adrenal glands (uh-DREE-nul):** Endocrine glands located just above the kidneys; in females they are major producers of androgens.
> **Adrenarche (AD-ren-ar-key):** In childhood, the maturation of the adrenal glands, resulting in increased secretion of androgens.

---

[5]Note that orgasm and ejaculation are two separate processes, even though they generally occur together, at least in males after puberty. But orgasm may occur without ejaculation, and ejaculation may occur without orgasm.

(a)

(b)

Figure 10 There is great variability in the onset of puberty and its growth spurt. Both girls (*a*) are the same age. Both boys (*b*) are the same age.

(a) ©Simone van den Berg/Shutterstock; (b) ©Skjold Photographs/ The Image Works

("voice box") also begins to grow in response to testosterone. As the larynx enlarges, the boy's voice drops, or "changes." Typically the transition occurs at around age 13 or 14.

A great spurt of body growth begins in males at around 11 to 16 years of age (Figure 9). Height increases rapidly. Body contours also change. Although the changes in girls involve mainly the increase in fatty tissue in the breasts and hips, the changes in boys involve mainly an increase in muscle mass. Eventually testosterone brings the growth process to an end, although it permits the growth period in boys to continue longer than it does in girls.

Puberty brings both changes and problems. One problem is *acne*, a distressing skin condition that is stimulated by androgens and affects boys more frequently than girls. It is caused by a clogging of the sebaceous (oil-producing) glands, resulting in pustules, blackheads, and redness on the face and possibly the chest and back.

Gynecomastia (breast enlargement) may occur temporarily and embarrassingly in boys. About 80 percent of boys in puberty experience this growth, which is probably caused by small amounts of feminizing sex hormones being produced by the testes. Obesity may also be a temporary problem, although it is more frequent in girls than boys.

In various cultures around the world, puberty rites are performed to signify the adolescent's passage to adulthood (Figure 11). In the United States the only remaining vestiges of such ceremonies are the Jewish bar mitzvah for boys and bat mitzvah for girls. In a sense, it is unfortunate that we do not give more formal recognition to puberty. Puberty rites probably serve an important psychological function in that they are a formal, public announcement of the fact that the boy or girl is passing through an important and difficult period of change. In the absence of such rituals, the young person may think that their body is doing strange things. The lack of recognition may be particularly problematic for boys, who lack an obvious sign of puberty like the first menstruation (the first ejaculation is probably the closest analogy) to help them identify the stage they are in.

Changes in Behavior

Puberty brings not only changes in the body but changes in behavior as well (Forbes & Dahl, 2010). To use terminology introduced earlier in the chapter, puberty has both organizing effects and activating effects. Pubertal development results in changes in the brain and genitals (organizing effects) and also activates certain behaviors. The research evidence indicates that puberty increases sensation-seeking behaviors—that is, wanting high-intensity, exciting experiences—and sex is one sensation that might be sought. Puberty also reorients social

(a) (b)

Figure 11 Most cultures celebrate puberty, but cultures vary widely in the nature of the celebration. (*a*) American Jewish youth celebrate a bar mitzvah (for boys) or bat mitzvah (for girls). (*b*) Boys wear ceremonial skirts for their circumcision ceremonies, Democratic Republic of Congo. During their grueling initiation into manhood, boys about 9 to 12 years old are circumcised and then marched into the forest, where they spend several months hunting and fishing. Each morning the boys are whipped by their elders to instill toughness.

(a) ©Nancy Louie/Getty Images; (b) ©Randy Olson/Getty Images

behavior, so that adolescents are motivated to seek social experiences with their peers and with potential romantic partners.

The Menstrual Cycle

Women's sexual and reproductive lives have a rhythm of changes. One notable sign that marks the changes is menstruation. The events surrounding it are not only biological but psychological as well.

Biology of the Menstrual Cycle
The menstrual cycle is regulated by fluctuating levels of sex hormones, which produce certain changes in the ovaries and uterus. The hormone cycles are regulated by the HPG axis and by means of the negative feedback loop discussed earlier in this chapter.

Humans are nearly unique among species in having a menstrual cycle. Only a few other species of apes and monkeys also have menstrual cycles. All other species of mammals (for example, horses and dogs) have *estrous* cycles. There are several differences between estrous cycles and menstrual cycles, and it is important to note them because some people mistakenly believe that women's cycles are like those of a dog or a cat, when in fact the cycles are quite different.

First, in animals that have estrous cycles there is no menstruation. There is either no bleeding or only a slight spotting of blood, which is not a real menstruation. Second, the timing of ovulation in relation to bleeding is different in the two cycles. For estrous animals, ovulation occurs while the animal is in "heat," or estrus, which is also the time of slight spotting. In the menstrual cycle, however, ovulation

How does the body regulate sex hormone levels over the menstrual cycle?

occurs about midway between the periods of menstruation. A third difference is that female animals with estrous cycles engage in sexual behavior only when they are in heat, that is, during the estrus phase of the cycle. In contrast, females with menstrual cycles are capable of engaging in sexual behavior throughout the cycle.

The Phases of the Menstrual Cycle

The menstrual cycle has four phases, each characterized by a set of hormonal, ovarian, and uterine changes (see Figure 12). Because menstruation is the easiest phase to identify, it is tempting to call it the first phase, but biologically, it is actually the last phase. (Note, however, that in numbering the days of the menstrual cycle, the first day of menstruation is counted as day 1 because it is the most identifiable day of the cycle.)

The first phase of the menstrual cycle is called the **follicular phase** (also called the *proliferative phase*). At the beginning of this phase, the pituitary secretes relatively high levels of FSH (follicle-stimulating hormone). As the name of this hormone implies, its function is to stimulate follicles in the ovaries. At the beginning of the follicular phase, it signals one follicle (occasionally more than one) to begin to bring an egg to the final stage of maturity. At the same time, the follicle secretes estrogen.

The second phase of the cycle is **ovulation,** which is the phase during which the follicle ruptures open, releasing the mature egg (see Figure 13). By this time, estrogen has risen to a high level, which inhibits FSH production, and so FSH has fallen back to a low level. The high levels of estrogen also stimulate the hypothalamus to produce GnRH, which causes the pituitary to begin production of LH (luteinizing hormone).[6] A surge of LH triggers ovulation.

The third phase of the cycle is called the **luteal phase** (also called the *secretory phase*). After releasing an egg, the follicle, under stimulation of LH, turns into a glandular mass of cells called the **corpus luteum**[7] (hence the names *luteal phase* and *luteinizing hormone*). The corpus luteum manufactures progesterone, so

> **Follicular phase (fuh-LIK-you-lur):** The first phase of the menstrual cycle, beginning just after menstruation, during which an egg matures in preparation for ovulation.
> **Ovulation:** Release of an egg from the ovaries; the second phase of the menstrual cycle.
> **Luteal phase (LOO-tee-uhl):** The third phase of the menstrual cycle, following ovulation.
> **Corpus luteum:** The mass of cells of the follicle remaining after ovulation; it secretes progesterone.
> **Menstruation:** The fourth phase of the menstrual cycle, during which the endometrium of the uterus is sloughed off in the menstrual discharge.

progesterone levels rise during the luteal phase. But high levels of progesterone also inhibit the pituitary's secretion of LH, and as LH levels decline, the corpus luteum degenerates. With this degeneration comes a sharp decline in estrogen and progesterone levels at the end of the luteal phase. The falling levels of estrogen stimulate the pituitary to begin production of FSH, and the whole cycle begins again.

The fourth and final phase of the cycle is **menstruation.** Physiologically, menstruation is a shedding of the inner lining of the uterus (the endometrium), which then passes out through the cervix and the vagina. During this phase, estrogen and progesterone levels are low and FSH levels are rising. Menstruation is triggered by the sharp decline in estrogen and progesterone levels at the end of the luteal phase.

What has been happening in the uterus while the ovaries and endocrine system were going through the four phases that we just described? During the first, or follicular, phase, the high levels of estrogen stimulate the endometrium of the uterus to grow, thicken, and form glands that will eventually secrete substances to nourish the embryo. In other words, the endometrium proliferates (giving us the alternative name for this first phase, the *proliferative phase*). Then, during the luteal phase, the progesterone secreted by the corpus luteum stimulates the glands of the endometrium to start secreting the nourishing substances (giving us the name *secretory phase*). If the egg is fertilized and the timing goes properly, about 6 days after ovulation the fertilized egg arrives in a uterus that is well prepared to cradle and nourish it.

The corpus luteum continues to produce estrogen and progesterone for about 10 to 12 days. If pregnancy has not occurred, its hormone output declines sharply at the end of this period. The uterine lining cannot be maintained and is shed, resulting in menstruation. Immediately afterward, a new lining starts forming in the next proliferative phase.

The menstrual fluid itself is a combination of blood (from the endometrium), degenerated cells, and mucus from the cervix and vagina. Normally the discharge for an entire period is only about 2 to 4 tablespoons. Common practice is to use sanitary napkins, which are worn externally, or tampons, which are worn inside the vagina, to absorb the fluid.

Length and Timing of the Cycle

How long is a normal menstrual cycle? Generally, anywhere from 21 to 36 days is considered within the normal range. The average is about 28 days, but somehow this number has taken on more significance than it deserves. There is enormous variation from one woman to the next in the average length of the cycle, and for a given woman there can be considerable variation in length from one cycle to the next.

---

[6]This statement may seem to contradict the earlier statement that high estrogen levels cause a decline in LH. Both of these effects occur, but at different times in the menstrual cycle (Molitch, 1995). There are two centers in the hypothalamus: One produces a negative feedback loop between estrogen and LH; the other produces a positive feedback loop between the two.

[7]*Corpus luteum* is Latin for "yellow body." The corpus luteum is so named because the mass of cells is yellowish in appearance.

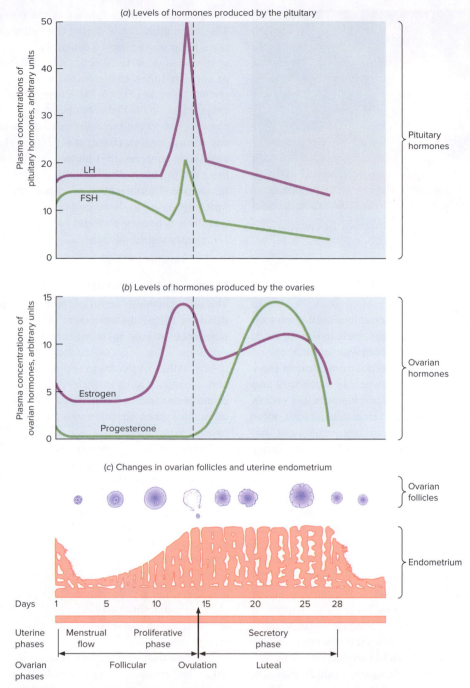

Figure 12 The biological events of the menstrual cycle. Changes in the levels of hormones produced by the pituitary (*a*) and the ovaries (*b*) bring about changes (*c*) in the ovarian follicles and the endometrium of the uterus.

What is the timing of the four phases of the cycle? In a perfectly regular 28-day cycle, menstruation begins on day 1 and continues until about day 4 or 5. The follicular phase extends from about day 5 to about day 13. Ovulation occurs on day 14, and the luteal phase extends from day 15 to the end of the cycle, day 28 (see Figure 12c).

But what if the cycle is not a perfect 28-day one? In cycles that are shorter or longer than 28 days, the principle is that the length of the *luteal* phase is relatively constant. In other words, the time from ovulation to menstruation is always 14 days, give or take only a day or two. It is the follicular phase that varies in length. For this reason, if a woman has a 44-day cycle, for example, she ovulates on about day 30. If she has a 22-day cycle, she ovulates on about day 8.

Some women report that they can actually feel themselves ovulate, a phenomenon called *Mittelschmerz*

Figure 13   Ovulation, showing the egg bursting forth from the wall of the ovary.

©C. Edelmann/Science Source

("middle pain"). The sensation described is a cramping on one or both sides of the lower abdomen, lasting for about a day, which is sometimes confused with appendicitis.

It is also true that ovulation does not occur in every menstrual cycle. In other words, menstruation may take place without ovulation. When this happens, the woman is said to have an *anovulatory cycle*. Such cycles occur once or twice a year in women in their twenties and thirties and are fairly common among girls during puberty and among women in their forties.

Other Cyclic Changes

Two other biological processes fluctuate with the menstrual cycle: the cervical mucus cycle and the basal body temperature cycle.

The cervical mucus cycle involves glands in the cervix that secrete mucus throughout the menstrual cycle. One function of the mucus is to protect the entrance to the cervix, helping to keep bacteria out. These glands respond to the changing levels of estrogen during the cycle. As estrogen increases at the start of a new cycle, the mucus is alkaline, thick, and viscous. When LH production begins, just before ovulation, the cervical mucus changes markedly. It becomes even more alkaline, thin, and watery. These changes make the environment for sperm passage most hospitable just at ovulation. After ovulation, the mucus returns to its former viscous, less alkaline state.

If a sample of mucus is taken just before ovulation and allowed to dry, the dried mucus takes on a fern-shaped pattern. After ovulation, during the luteal phase, the fernlike patterning will not occur. For this reason, the "fern test" is one method for detecting ovulation.

A woman's *basal body temperature,* taken with a thermometer,

> **Dysmenorrhea (dis-men-oh-REE-uh):** Painful menstruation.
> **Prostaglandins:** Chemicals secreted by the uterus that cause the uterine muscles to contract; they are the cause of painful menstruation.

also fluctuates with the phases of the menstrual cycle. The temperature is low during the follicular phase and takes a dip on the day of ovulation. Then, on the day after ovulation, it rises noticeably, generally by 0.4°F or more, and then continues at the higher level for the rest of the cycle (Figure 14). Progesterone raises body temperature, so the higher temperature during the luteal phase is due to the increased production of progesterone during that time (Baker et al., 2002). This change in basal body temperature is important when a couple are using the rhythm method of birth control (discussed in the chapter "Contraception and Abortion") and when a woman is trying to determine the time of ovulation so that she may become pregnant (discussed in the chapter "Pregnancy and Childbirth").

Menstrual Problems

The most common menstrual problem is painful menstruation, called **dysmenorrhea.** Almost every woman experiences at least some menstrual discomfort at various times in her life, but the frequency and severity of the discomfort vary considerably from one woman to the next. Cramping pains in the pelvic region are the most common discomfort. Other symptoms may include headaches, backaches, nausea, and a feeling of pressure and bloating in the pelvis.

Dysmenorrhea is caused by **prostaglandins,** hormonelike substances produced by many tissues of the body, including the lining of the uterus (Deligeoroglou, 2000). Prostaglandins can cause smooth muscle to contract and can affect the size of blood vessels. Women with severe menstrual pain have unusually high levels of prostaglandins. The high levels cause intense uterine contractions, which in turn choke off some of the supply of oxygen-carrying blood to the uterus. Prostaglandins may also cause greater sensitivity in nerve endings. The combination of the uterine contractions, lack of oxygen, and heightened nerve sensitivity produces menstrual cramps.

The best treatment for menstrual cramps is nonsteroidal anti-inflammatory drugs (NSAIDs), such as ibuprofen (Motrin) or naproxen (Aleve) (Hatcher et al., 2007). These drugs are antiprostaglandins, so they interrupt the basic cause of cramps.

A more provocative remedy suggested by, among others, Masters and Johnson is masturbation. This makes good physiological sense because part of the discomfort of menstruation—the pressure and bloating—results from pelvic edema. During sexual arousal and orgasm, pelvic edema increases, but after orgasm, the edema dissipates. For this reason, orgasm, whether produced by masturbation or some other means, should help to relieve the pelvic edema causing menstrual discomfort. And it's a lot more fun than taking medicine!

Figure 14 A basal body temperature graph. Note the dip in temperature, indicating ovulation on day 14.

A menstrual problem that may be mistaken for dysmenorrhea is **endometriosis.** The endometrium, or the lining of the uterus, grows during each menstrual cycle and is sloughed off in menstruation. Endometriosis occurs when the endometrium grows in a place other than the uterus—for example, the ovaries, fallopian tubes, rectum, bladder, vagina, vulva, cervix, or lymph glands. The symptoms vary, depending on the location of the growth, but very painful periods that last an unusually long time are the most common symptom. Endometriosis is fairly serious and should be treated by a physician. If left untreated, it can lead to sterility. Hormones are generally used in treatment, but if the problem is severe, surgery may be required. Laser surgery is one treatment option.

Another menstrual problem is **amenorrhea,** or the absence of menstruation. It is called *primary amenorrhea* in girls who have not yet menstruated by about age 18. It is called *secondary amenorrhea* in girls who have had at least one period. Some of the causes of amenorrhea include pregnancy, hormonal imbalance, cysts or tumors, disease, and stress. As we discussed earlier in the chapter, amenorrhea can also result from programs of strenuous exercise and from anorexia.

Psychological Aspects of the Menstrual Cycle

It is part of the folk wisdom of our culture that women experience fluctuations in mood over the phases of the menstrual cycle. In particular, women are supposed to be especially cranky and depressed just before and during their periods. An analysis of tweets indicated that both women and men complained about women's negative emotions during "that time of the month" (Thornton, 2013).

What is the scientific evidence concerning the occurrence of such fluctuations in mood, and, if they do occur, what causes them?

Fluctuations in Mood:
Do Women Become Extra Emotional?

The term **premenstrual syndrome (PMS)** refers to cases in which the woman has a particularly severe combination of physical and psychological symptoms that occur premenstrually. These symptoms may include depression, irritability, breast pain, and water retention (Stanton et al., 2002). To be clear, PMS is not a medical term; it is a term used by laypeople. In the last several decades much research has been done on moods during the premenstrual period and on whether moods fluctuate during the cycle (Taylor, 2006).

Of the numerous studies that have been conducted, many offer contradictory results, and many have used weak methods. We focus on one study that used the best design of any to date. The researchers collected data from a random sample of Canadian women daily for 6 months (Romans et al., 2013). Notice that by collecting data every day, the researchers overcame problems of memory distortion in self-report. Each participant received a handheld Palm device loaded with mental health telemetry software. *Telemetry* refers to a method in which data are collected at remote locations and transmitted to a central computer for data storage and analysis. This method allows researchers to verify that each woman actually completed the questionnaire each day, and it allows the women to go about their usual daily routines without having to go to a lab. The questionnaire—which had to be kept short so participants would cooperate and complete it daily—included 4 negative mood items, 4 positive mood items, 9 items assessing physical activity, health, social

> **Endometriosis:** A condition in which the endometrium grows abnormally outside the uterus; the symptom is unusually painful periods with excessive bleeding.
> **Amenorrhea:** The absence of menstruation.
> **Premenstrual syndrome (PMS):** A combination of severe physical and psychological symptoms, such as depression and irritability, occurring just before menstruation.

support, and stress, and one item about whether they had their menstrual period that day. The diverse items were used to disguise the fact that the study was about mood and the menstrual cycle; had participants known the point of the study, it might have activated their stereotypes about menstrual cycle fluctuations in mood, leading them to respond in a stereotyped way.

The results were surprising. No positive mood items showed cycle fluctuations. Only 2 negative mood items, sadness and irritability, showed significant variations across the cycle. Irritability was greater both premenstrually and during menses, compared with midcycle. Notice that greater irritability was not just *premenstrual*, challenging the basic concept of *P*MS. Overall, mood was more strongly associated with stress, physical health, and social support than it was with cycle phase.

According to this study, there is no scientific evidence of PMS, although there are plenty of stereotypes about it. That said, it may be that a small percentage of women do experience PMS. Averaging across data from a random sample of women, there are too few with PMS to produce average mood fluctuations. The best conclusion seems to be that the great majority of women do not experience menstrual cycle fluctuations in mood, but a small percentage may.

Despite this study and other similar ones, the American Psychiatric Association has formalized PMS with the diagnosis **premenstrual dysphoric disorder (PMDD)** in the DSM-5 (American Psychiatric Association, 2013). Symptoms must occur during the last week of the luteal phase and include feeling sad or hopeless, tense or anxious, tearfulness, irritability, difficulty concentrating, and changes in appetite. The symptoms have to have occurred most months for the past year. This diagnostic category is very controversial, however (Caplan, 1995). Some argue that it represents nothing but a medicalizing of women's experience. Others point out that the scientific basis for PMDD is nonexistent and that many studies, including the one described earlier, fail to confirm it (Romans et al., 2013).

Fluctuations in Performance

So far our discussion has concentrated on fluctuations in psychological characteristics such as depression, anxiety, and irritability. However, in some situations performance is of more practical importance than mood. For example, is a woman's work as an accountant less accurate premenstrually and menstrually? Is a female athlete's coordination or speed impaired during the premenstrual–menstrual period?

Research on performance—such as performance on cognitive tests—produces contradictory results but, overall, mainly evidence of no cycle fluctuations in performance (Poromaa & Gingnell, 2014).

One study of elite and nonelite women athletes showed that, for the elite athletes, competitiveness was associated not with estrogen and progesterone levels over the cycle but with fluctuations in testosterone levels (Brewther & Cook, 2018). The elite athletes had higher testosterone levels at the time of ovulation than at other times in the cycle, and that is when they reported the strongest feelings of competitiveness. The elite athletes had higher testosterone levels than the nonelite athletes, but we can't know which is cause and which is effect. That is, do women with higher testosterone levels have an advantage, making them more likely to become extraordinary athletes? Or do the experiences of being an elite athlete—such as many victories—raise their testosterone levels?

Fluctuations in Sex Drive

Another psychological characteristic that has been investigated for fluctuations over the cycle is women's sex drive or arousability. Studies have yielded contradictory results. Some have found a peak frequency of intercourse around ovulation, which would be biologically functional. But others have found peaks just before and just after menstruation.

Moreover, we should be cautious about using frequency of intercourse as a measure of a woman's sex drive. Intercourse requires some agreement between partners, and for this reason reflects not only a woman's desires but her partner's as well. One study assessed both sexual activity with a partner and self-rated sexual desire (Bullivant et al., 2004). The results indicated that sexual activity initiated by the woman—but not by the man—peaked during the three days before and three days after ovulation. Sexual desire showed the same pattern.

In a sophisticated study, women kept daily electronic diaries on a website, reporting their sexual fantasies each day (Dawson et al., 2012). They also completed self-administered urine tests for LH to determine the day of ovulation. The fantasies were then content analyzed, using methods like those described in the chapter "Sex Research." The results indicated that both the frequency and the arousability of sexual fantasies were highest at ovulation. There was even an increase in the number of males in the fantasies at the time of ovulation. These results seem to indicate that maximum sexual arousability does occur at the time of peak fertility. Interestingly, testosterone levels also peak at ovulation (Van Goozen et al., 1997).

If there is a link between phase of the menstrual cycle and sexual interest, it most likely reflects an association between testosterone levels and sexuality with a peak in sexual interest around the time of ovulation. But with humans, psychological and social factors—such as some couples' dislike of intercourse when the woman is menstruating—play a strong role as well (Allen & Goldberg, 2009).

Premenstrual dysphoric disorder (PMDD): A diagnostic category in the DSM, characterized by symptoms such as sadness, anxiety, and irritability in the week before menstruation.

Why Do We Believe in PMS?

Researchers note the widespread cultural expectations and taboos surrounding menstruation (Johnston-Robledo & Chrisler, 2013; Stubbs, 2008). In some nonindustrialized cultures, women who are menstruating are isolated from the community and may have to stay in a menstrual hut at the edge of town during their period. Often the menstrual blood itself is thought to have supernatural, dangerous powers, and the woman's isolation is considered necessary for the safety of the community.

In rural Nepal, for example, religious Hindus consider a menstruating woman to be toxic; if she handles her family's food, everyone would become sick, and if she enters a temple, she pollutes it (Sharma & Gettleman, 2018). The custom is called *chhaupadi*, and women are not allowed to sleep in the family home during their periods. They therefore often go to crude animal sheds, where they are exposed to harsh weather. In recent years, dozens of women have died from the practice. The Nepalese government outlawed it in 2017, but it is still widely practiced.

Such practices do not occur only among non-Western people. Note that there is a history of similar practices in our own culture as well. For example, the following passage is from the book of Leviticus in the Bible:

> When a woman has a discharge of blood which is her regular discharge from her body, she shall be in her impurity for seven days, and whoever touches her shall be unclean until the evening. . . . And whoever touches her bed shall wash his clothes, and bathe himself in water, and be unclean until the evening; whether it is the bed or anything upon which she sits, when he touches it he shall be unclean until the evening. (Leviticus 15:19–23)

Among the most common menstrual taboos are those prohibiting sexual intercourse with a menstruating woman. For example, the passage from Leviticus quoted above continues,

> And if any man lies with her, and her impurity is on him, he shall be unclean seven days; and every bed on which he lies shall be unclean. (Leviticus 15:24)

To this day, Orthodox Jews abstain from sex during the woman's period and for seven days afterward. At the end of this time the woman goes to the *mikvah* (ritual bath) to be cleansed, and only after this cleansing may she resume sexual relations (Guterman, 2008).

The argument, then, is that we believe in PMS because of a long tradition of many cultural forces, such as menstrual taboos, that create negative attitudes toward menstruation. In addition, women's expectations may play a role (Stanton et al., 2002). Our culture is filled with teachings that women are supposed to behave strangely just before and during their periods. According to this line of reasoning, women are taught that they should be depressed around the time of menstruation, and because they expect

Figure 15 Does advertising for menstrual drugs contribute to negative stereotypes about women and PMS?

©Amy Etra/PhotoEdit

to become depressed, they interpret any small mood disturbance as meaning that they have PMS (Figure 15). In addition, women who experience painful cramps and other uncomfortable symptoms might quite reasonably feel irritable (Kiesner, 2009).

Surely such forces do exist in our culture. But is there any evidence that they really have an effect on women's moods and behavior? Psychologist Diane Ruble did a clever experiment to determine whether women's culturally induced expectations influence their reporting of premenstrual symptoms (1977; see also Klebanov & Jemmott, 1992; Kues et al., 2018). College students were tested on the sixth or seventh day before the onset of their next menstrual period. They were told that they would participate in a study on a new technique for predicting the expected date of menstruation using an electroencephalogram (EEG), a method that had already been successfully tested with older women. After the EEG had been run (it actually wasn't), each woman was informed of when her next period was to occur, depending on which of three experimental groups she had randomly been assigned to: (1) the woman was told she was "premenstrual" and her period was due in 1 or 2 days; (2) the woman was told she was "intermenstrual" or "midcycle" and her period was not expected for at least a week to 10 days; or (3) she was given no information at all about the predicted date of menstruation (control group). The women then completed a self-report menstrual distress questionnaire.

The results indicated that women who had been led to believe they were in the premenstrual phase reported significantly more water retention, pain, and changes in eating habits than did women who had been led to believe they were around midcycle. (In fact, women in these groups did not differ significantly in when their periods actually arrived.) There were no significant differences between the groups in ratings of negative moods, however. This study indicates that, probably because of learned beliefs, women overstate the changes in body experiences that occur over the menstrual cycle. When they think they are in the premenstrual phase, they report more problems than when they think they are at midcycle.

Cycles in Men

The traditional assumption, of both laypeople and scientists, has been that monthly biological and psychological cycles are for women only and that men experience no monthly cycles. These assumptions are made, at least in part, because men have no obvious signs like menstruation to call attention to the fact that some kind of periodic change is occurring. One study, in fact, found no differences between men and women in day-to-day mood changes. Men were neither more nor less changeable than women (McFarlane et al., 1988; see also McFarlane & Williams, 1994).

Another study found that men's testosterone levels displayed weekly fluctuations, peaking on weekends (Hirschenhauser et al., 2002). Men who had a female partner and wished to have a child with her displayed a 28-day cycle of testosterone levels, leading the researchers to hypothesize that the men's hormone cycles might have synchronized with their partner's. Strikingly, men's testosterone levels also respond to sexual activity. In this same study, men who had sex with an unfamiliar partner showed a 100 percent increase in their testosterone levels the following morning!

Critical THINKing Skill

Understanding how scientific research can be applied to making policy decisions

Environmental activists want to do much to clean up the environment, including banning the use of certain substances in manufacturing. Manufacturers often oppose these efforts, arguing that they are too costly, that they will handicap American business, and that the risks are minimal or nonexistent anyway. How should the average person, or a government official, decide?

The best way to make a good decision is to use the best available scientific evidence and think clearly about it. The evidence might come from field studies as well as laboratory experiments. Suppose that the substance that is causing concern is the pesticide atrazine and the worry is that it inhibits sperm production. In a field study, scientists might recruit a sample of men who live in different locations, both urban and rural. The scientists would take a sample of soil from each man's location and also get a sperm count from each one. The researchers would then see if there is a correlation between atrazine levels and sperm count. Suppose that the correlation is negative and significant—that is, the higher the atrazine level, the lower the sperm count. That result is consistent with the hypothesis, but the problem is that it is a correlational study.

Another way to get at the question would be with a laboratory experiment. Scientists would expose the experimental group of rats to atrazine in a concentration equivalent to what is found in the natural environment, while the control group of rats does not receive atrazine. After two months of exposure (or not, for the control group), the sperm counts of the rats are measured. Suppose that the rats in the experimental group have significantly lower average sperm counts than those in the control group. From that result, we can make a causal inference, that atrazine decreases sperm count. The problem here is that it is a laboratory experiment with rats. Perhaps it does not apply to humans in a natural environment.

We can be most confident of a conclusion if there is *converging evidence* from multiple studies, both field studies and laboratory experiments. Putting these two hypothetical studies together gives us more confidence in the conclusion that atrazine has real negative effects. Each study addresses some of the limitations of the other.

How can these studies inform a policy decision? The manufacturers and farmers are still saying that it would be way too expensive to eliminate atrazine. Without it, the pests will gobble up the crops. At this point, a good policy decision would involve a cost–benefit analysis. The costs of eliminating atrazine have already been calculated. We would also want to calculate the costs of the lower sperm counts. How many cases of infertility do they cause? What is the cost of the infertility treatments? We might also want to compute the benefit, over many years, of the elimination of atrazine.

In general, when making policy decisions where scientific evidence is available, we should evaluate the quality of that evidence and then weigh the costs and benefits of implementing policies based on the evidence.

SUMMARY

Sex Hormones

The major sex hormones are testosterone, estrogen, and progesterone, all of which are manufactured by both testes and ovaries. Levels of the sex hormones are regulated by two hormones secreted by the pituitary: FSH (follicle-stimulating hormone) and LH (luteinizing hormone), which in turn are regulated by GnRH (gonadotropin-releasing hormone) secreted by the hypothalamus. The gonads, pituitary, and hypothalamus regulate one another's output through a negative feedback loop.

Prenatal Sexual Differentiation

At conception males and females differ only in the sex chromosomes (XX in females and XY in males). As the male fetus grows, the SRY gene on the Y chromosome directs the gonads to differentiate into testes. In the absence of the SRY gene, ovaries develop. The ovaries and testes then secrete different hormones in females and males, respectively, and these hormones stimulate further differentiation of the internal and external reproductive structures. A male organ and a female organ that derive from the same embryonic tissue are said to be homologous to each other. Epigenetic changes are also involved.

Intersex conditions (disorders of sex development or differences in sex development) are generally the result of various syndromes (such as CAH) that alter the course of prenatal sexual differentiation. Currently there is a debate over the best medical treatment of these individuals.

Sexual Differentiation during Puberty

Puberty is characterized by a great increase in the production of sex hormones. Pubertal changes in both males and females include body growth, the development of pubic and axillary hair, and increased output from the oil-producing glands. Changes in females include breast development and menarche (the beginning of menstruation). Changes in males include growth of the penis and testes, the beginning of ejaculation, and a deepening of the voice. The hormones leptin and kisspeptin are involved.

The Menstrual Cycle

Biologically, the menstrual cycle is divided into four phases: the follicular phase, ovulation, the luteal phase, and menstruation. Corresponding to these phases, there are changes in the levels of pituitary hormones (FSH and LH) and in the levels of ovarian hormones (estrogen and progesterone), as well as changes in the ovaries and the uterus. A fairly common menstrual problem is dysmenorrhea (painful menstruation).

Research questions whether PMS is a real phenomenon. Averaged across a sample of women, there are no mood fluctuations, although individual women might experience them. Research indicates that there are no fluctuations in performance over the cycle. Research attempting to document whether men experience monthly biological and/or psychological cycles is limited.

SUGGESTIONS FOR FURTHER READING

Fine, Cordelia. (2017). *Testosterone Rex: Myths of sex, science, and society*. New York: Norton. This book is loaded with fascinating, surprising facts about testosterone. Fine, a psychology professor, has a wonderfully engaging writing style.

Melmed, Shlomo, et al. (2016). *Williams textbook of endocrinology,* 13th ed. Philadelphia: Elsevier. An outstanding endocrinology textbook.

Steinberg, Laurence. (2018). *Adolescence,* 11th ed. New York: McGraw-Hill. This is the definitive textbook on adolescence, written by a leading researcher.

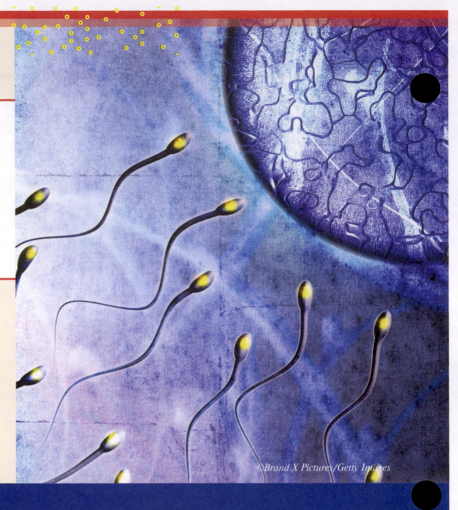

Are YOU Curious?

1. What substances, if taken during pregnancy, threaten the fetus?
2. How does sexual activity change in the months following childbirth?
3. What reproductive problem can result from untreated STIs?

Read this chapter to find out.

CHAPTER

6

Pregnancy and Childbirth

CHAPTER HIGHLIGHTS

was very sexy during pregnancy and enjoyed looking at myself and felt I was looking good in spite of becoming heavier. . . .

Then you are . . . big and fat, just like a whale, and you do not feel very sexy.[*]

*Bender, Sóley S. et al. (2018). "You stop thinking about yourself as a woman." An interpretive phenomenological study of the meaning of sexuality for Icelandic women during pregnancy and after birth. *Midwifery, 62,* 14–19.

The chapter "Sex Hormones, Sexual Differentiation, and the Menstrual Cycle" describes the remarkable biological process by which a single fertilized egg develops into a male or a female human being. This chapter is about some equally remarkable processes involved in creating human beings: conception, pregnancy, and childbirth.

Conception

Sperm Meets Egg: The Incredible Journey

On about day 14 of an average menstrual cycle the woman ovulates. The egg is released from the ovary into the body cavity. Typically it is then picked up by the fimbriae (long, fingerlike structures at the end of the fallopian tube—see Figure 1) and enters the fallopian tube. It then begins a leisurely trip down the tube toward the uterus, reaching it in about five days if it has been fertilized. Otherwise, it disintegrates in about 48 hours. The egg, unlike the sperm, has no means of moving itself and is propelled by the cilia (hairlike structures) lining the fallopian tube. The egg has begun its part of the journey toward conception.

Meanwhile, the couple have been having intercourse. The woman's cervix secretes mucus that flushes the passageways to prepare for the arrival of the sperm. The man has an orgasm and ejaculates inside the woman's vagina. The sperm are deposited in the vagina, there to begin their journey toward the egg. Actually, they have made an incredible trip even before reaching the vagina. Initially they were manufactured in the seminiferous tubules of the testes (see the chapter "Sexual Anatomy"). They then collected and were stored in the epididymis. During ejaculation they moved up and over the top of the bladder in the vas deferens; then they traveled down through the ejaculatory duct, mixed with seminal fluid, and went out through the urethra.

The sperm is one of the tiniest cells in the human body. It is composed of a *head,* a *midpiece,* and a *tail* (see Figure 2). The head is about 5 micrometers long, and the total length, from the tip of the head to the tip of the tail, is about 60 micrometers (about 2/1,000 inch, or 0.06 millimeter). The DNA, which is the sperm's most

important contribution when it unites with the egg, is contained in the nucleus, which is in the head of the sperm. Sperm also contain RNA, carrying the instructions for early embryonic development, and a large number of proteins (Ainsworth, 2005). The *acrosome,* a chemical reservoir, is in the head of the sperm. The midpiece contains mitochondria, tiny structures that generate energy. This energy is used when the sperm lashes its tail back and forth. The lashing action (called *flagellation*) propels the sperm forward.

A typical ejaculate has a volume of about 3 milliliters, or about a teaspoonful, and contains about 200 million sperm. Although this might seem to be a wasteful amount of sperm if only one is needed for fertilization, the great majority of the sperm never even get close to the egg. Some of the ejaculate, including one-half of the sperm, will flow out of the vagina as a result of gravity. Other sperm may be killed by the acidity of the vagina, to which they are very sensitive. Of those that make it safely into the uterus, half swim up the wrong fallopian tube (the one containing no egg).

But here we are, several hours later, with a hearty band of sperm swimming up the fallopian tube toward the egg, against the currents that are bringing the egg down. Sperm are capable of swimming 1 to 3 centimeters (about 1 inch) per hour, although it has been documented that sperm may arrive at the egg within 1½ hours after ejaculation. By the time a sperm reaches the egg, it has swum approximately 3,000 times its own length. This would be comparable to a swim of more than 3 miles for a human being.

Contrary to the popular belief that conception occurs in the uterus, typically it occurs in the outer third (the part near the ovary) of the fallopian tube. Of the original 200 million sperm, only about 2,000 reach the tube containing the egg. As they approach, a chemical secreted by the egg attracts the sperm to the egg. Chemical receptors on the surface of the sperm respond to the attractant, and the sperm swims toward the egg (Spehr et al., 2003). The egg is surrounded by a thin, gelatinous layer called the *zona pellucida.* Sperm swarm around the egg and secrete an enzyme called **hyaluronidase** (produced by the acrosome located in the head of the sperm—see Figure 2); this enzyme dissolves

> **Hyaluronidase:** An enzyme secreted by the sperm that allows one sperm to penetrate the egg.

First Person

Planning a Pregnancy?

R esearch has identified a number of things that can cause harm to mother or fetus during pregnancy. Some of these are preventable. Here is a preconception checklist.

1. Folic acid can prevent birth defects. Take a multivitamin containing 400 micrograms of folic acid every day.

2. Get your vaccinations up-to-date. Get catch-up vaccines for rubella and varicella at least one month before trying to get pregnant. Tdap, which protects infants against whooping cough, and flu vaccines can be taken in early pregnancy.

3. Women with a family history of sickle cell anemia, thalassemia, Tay-Sachs disease, and cystic fibrosis should consider genetic screening.

4. Healthy moms have healthy babies; aim for a healthy weight before you get pregnant. Obese pregnant women are at greater risk for preeclampsia, stillbirth, preterm delivery, and C-sections.

5. Women with diabetes need to maintain tight control of blood sugar.

6. No drinking and no smoking; stop before you get pregnant. (Your partner should stop too.)

Source: Fryhofer, Sandra. (2012). Preconception checklist for women planning pregnancy. Medscape Internal Medicine. www.medscape.com/viewarticle/762801.

---

the zona pellucida, permitting one sperm to penetrate the egg.[1] Conception has occurred (see Figure 3).

The fertilized egg, called the **zygote,** continues to travel down the fallopian tube. About 36 hours after conception, it begins the process of cell division, by which the original one cell becomes a mass of two cells, then four cells, then eight cells, and so on. About five to seven days after conception, the mass of cells implants itself in the lining of the uterus, there to be nourished and grow. For the first eight weeks of gestation the *conceptus* (product of conception) is called an *embryo;* from then until birth it is called a *fetus.*

Improving the Chances of Conception: Making a Baby

While this topic may seem rather remote to a 20-year-old college student, whose principal concern is probably *avoiding* conception, some couples do want to have a baby. The following are points for them to keep in mind.

> **Zygote:** A fertilized egg.

[1]Although only one sperm is necessary to accomplish fertilization, it is important for it to have a lot of buddies along to help it get into the egg. Sperm of some rodent species form trains, with several dozen sperm attaching to one another while they swim; trains swim 50 percent faster than individual sperm (Whitfield, 2010). Therefore, maintaining a high sperm count is important for conception.

The whole trick, of course, is to time intercourse so that it occurs around the time of ovulation. To do this, it is necessary to determine when the woman ovulates. If she is that idealized woman with the perfectly regular 28-day cycle, then she ovulates on day 14. But for the vast majority of women, the time of ovulation can best be determined by keeping a *basal body temperature chart* (see the chapter, "Sex Hormones, Sexual Differentiation, and the Menstrual Cycle"). To do this, the woman takes her temperature every morning immediately upon waking (that means before getting up and moving around or drinking a cup of coffee). She then keeps a graph of her temperature. During the preovulatory phase, temperature will be relatively constant (the temperature is below 98.6°F because temperature is low in the early morning). On the day of ovulation the temperature drops, and on the day following ovulation it rises sharply, by 0.4° to 1.0°F above the preovulatory level. The temperature should then stay at that high level until just before menstruation. The most reliable indicator of ovulation is the rise in temperature the day after it occurs. From this, the woman can determine the day of ovulation, and that determination should be consistent with menstruation occurring about 14 days later. After doing this for a couple of cycles, the woman should have a fairly good idea of the day in her cycle on

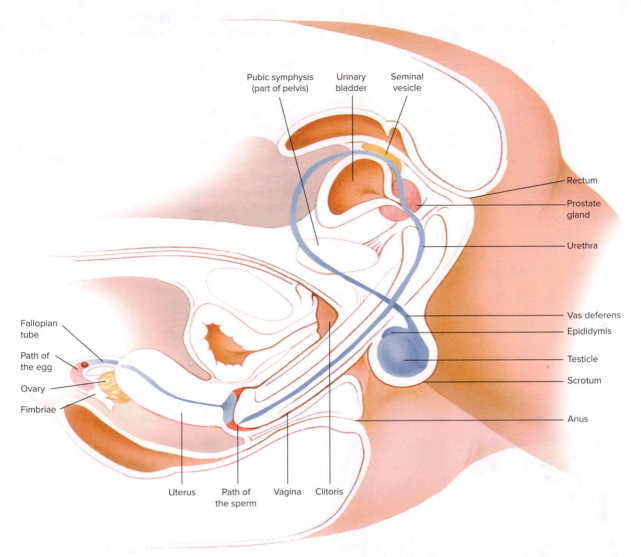

Figure 1   Sexual intercourse in the man-on-top position, showing the pathway of sperm and egg from manufacture in the testes and ovary to conception, which typically occurs in the fallopian tube.

which she ovulates. Two other methods for determining when a woman is ovulating are the cervical mucus and sympto-thermal methods, described in the chapter "Contraception and Abortion."

Sperm live inside the woman's body for up to five days (Wilcox et al., 1995). The egg is capable of being fertilized for about the first 12 to 24 hours after ovulation. Allowing the sperm some swimming time, this means that intercourse should be timed right at ovulation or within the five days before ovulation (Wilcox et al., 1995).

Fertility websites and apps are available that tell the user the best time to have sex if the goal is to achieve pregnancy. A scientific evaluation of their accuracy showed, sadly, that most of them are inaccurate relative to the scientifically determined standard of the five days before ovulation plus the day of ovulation (Setton et al., 2016).

Of the 40 apps tested, only 3 correctly identified the window of fertility.

Assuming you have some idea of the time of ovulation, how frequent should intercourse be? Although more may be merrier, more is not necessarily more effective. The reason for this is that it is important for the man's sperm count to be maintained. It takes a while to manufacture 200 million sperm—at least 24 hours. For purposes of conceiving, then, it is probably best to have intercourse about every 24 to 48 hours, or two to three times during the six days of maximum fertility. Abstaining for more than 48 hours may lead to a low sperm count (Mayo Clinic, 2012b).

It is also important to take some steps to ensure that, once deposited in the vagina, the sperm get a decent chance to survive and to find their way into the fallopian tubes.

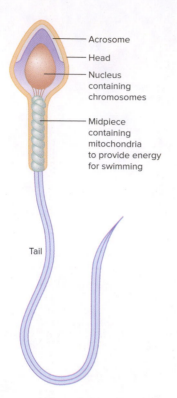

Figure 2   The structure of a mature human sperm.

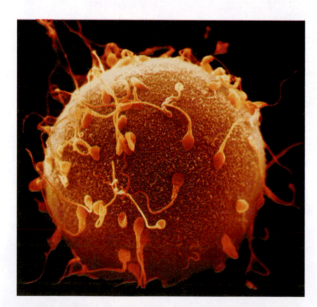

Figure 3   The egg is fertilized by one sperm as many sperm cluster about.

©*David M. Phillips/Science Source*

For purposes of conceiving, the best position for intercourse is with the woman on her back (man-on-top, or "missionary," position—see the chapter "Sexual Arousal"). If the woman is on top, much of the ejaculate may run out of the vagina because of the pull of gravity. After intercourse, she should remain on her back, possibly with her legs pulled up and a pillow under her hips, preferably for about a half hour to an hour. This allows the semen to remain in a pool in the vagina, which gives the sperm a good chance to swim up into the uterus. Because sperm are very sensitive to the pH (acidity-alkalinity) of the vagina, this factor also requires some consideration. Acidity kills sperm. Douching with commercial preparations or with acidic solutions (such as vinegar) should be avoided. Finally, lubricants and/or suppositories should not be used; they may kill sperm or block their entrance into the uterus, or significantly impair motility (Mayo Clinic, 2012a). If lubricants are necessary to make sex comfortable, use canola oil or baby oil (Sandhu et al., 2014).

Development of the Conceptus

For the nine months of pregnancy, two organisms—the conceptus and the pregnant woman—coexist and undergo parallel, dramatic changes. The changes that occur in the developing conceptus are discussed in this section; a later section discusses the changes that take place in the pregnant woman.

Typically the nine months of pregnancy are divided into three equal periods of three months, called *trimesters.* Thus the first trimester is months 1 to 3, the second trimester is months 4 to 6, and the third (or last) trimester is months 7 to 9.

The Embryo and Its Support Systems

We left the conceptus, which began as a single fertilized egg cell, dividing into many cells as it passed down the fallopian tube, finally arriving in the uterus and implanting itself in the uterine wall.

During the embryonic period of development (the first eight weeks), most of the fetus's major organ systems are formed with amazing speed (see Figure 4a and b). The inner part of the ball of cells, implanted in the uterus now, differentiates into two layers, the endoderm and the ectoderm. Later a third layer, the mesoderm, forms between them. The various organs of the body differentiate themselves out of these layers. The *ectoderm* will form the entire nervous system and the skin. The *endoderm* differentiates into the digestive system—from the pharynx to the stomach and intestines to the rectum—and the respiratory system. The muscles, skeleton, connective tissues, and reproductive and circulatory systems derive from the *mesoderm.* Fetal development generally proceeds in a cephalocaudal order—that is, the head develops first, the lower body last. For this reason the head of a fetus is enormous compared with the rest of the body.

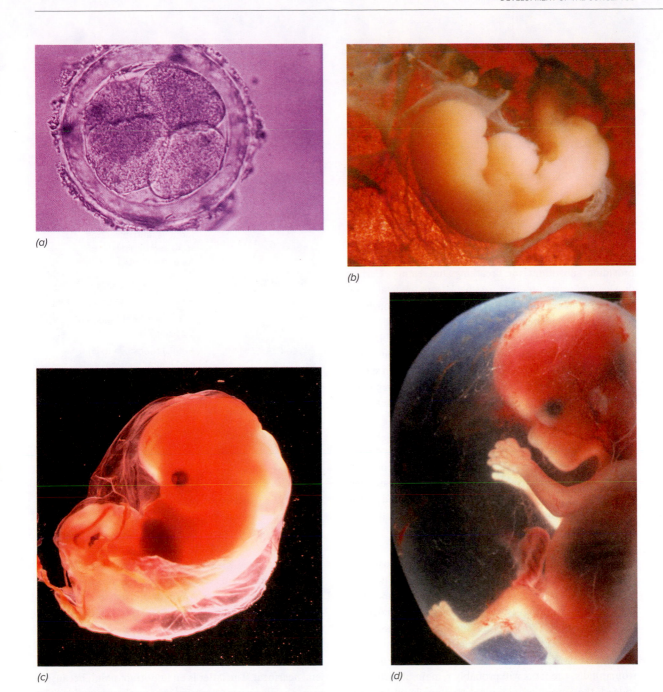

Figure 4 (*a*) This embryo has divided into four cells and would still be traveling down the fallopian tube. (*b*) The embryo after 4 weeks of development. The major organs are forming; the bright red, blood-filled heart is just below the lower jaw. (*c*) At 9 weeks the human fetus is recognizable as a primate. Limbs have formed and ears are clearly visible. (*d*) By about 3 months the fetus is approximately 10 centimeters long and weighs about 19 grams. Muscles have formed, which move the limbs and body.

(a) ©Claude Edelmann/Science Source; (b) ©Petit Format/Science Source; (c) ©Science Pictures Ltd./Science Source; (d) ©Claude Edelmann/Science Source

Meanwhile, another group of cells has differentiated into the *trophoblast,* which will eventually become the placenta. The **placenta** is the mass of tissues that surrounds the conceptus early in development and nurtures its growth. Later it moves to the side of the fetus. The placenta has a number of important functions, perhaps the most important being that it serves as a site for the exchange of substances between the woman's blood and

Placenta (plah-SEN-tuh): An organ formed on the wall of the uterus through which the fetus receives oxygen and nutrients and gets rid of waste products.

the fetus's blood. It is important to note that the woman's circulatory system and the fetus's circulatory system are completely separate. That is, with only rare exceptions, the woman's blood never circulates inside the fetus, nor does the fetus's blood circulate in the woman's blood vessels. Instead, the fetus's blood passes out of its body through the **umbilical cord** to the placenta. There it circulates in the numerous *villi* (tiny fingerlike projections in the placenta). The woman's blood circulates around the outside of these villi. Thus there is a membrane barrier between the two blood systems. Some substances are capable of passing through this barrier, whereas others are not. Oxygen and nutrients can pass through the barrier, and thus the woman's blood supplies oxygen and nutrients to the fetus, providing substitutes for breathing and eating. Carbon dioxide and waste products pass back from the fetal blood to the woman's blood. Some viruses can pass through the barrier. But some other organisms cannot pass through the barrier; for instance, the woman may have a terrible cold, but the fetus will remain completely healthy. Various drugs can also cross the placental barrier, and the woman should therefore be careful about drugs taken during pregnancy (see Effects of Substances Taken during Pregnancy, later in this chapter).

Another major function of the placenta is that it secretes hormones. The placenta produces large quantities of estrogen and progesterone. Many of the physical symptoms of pregnancy are caused by these elevated levels of hormones. Another hormone manufactured by the placenta is **human chorionic gonadotropin (hCG),** the hormone that is detected in pregnancy tests.

Two membranes surround the fetus, the *chorion* and the *amnion,* the amnion being the innermost. The amnion is filled with a watery liquid called **amniotic fluid,** in which the fetus floats and can easily move. It is the amniotic fluid that is sampled when an amniocentesis is performed. The amniotic fluid maintains the fetus at a constant temperature and, most important, cushions the fetus against possible injury. Thus, even if the woman falls, the fetus will probably remain undisturbed. Indeed, the amniotic fluid might be considered the original waterbed.

Fetal Development

Table 1 lists the major milestones of fetal development. The development of the fetus during the first trimester is more remarkable than its development during the second and third trimesters. That's because during the first trimester the small mass of cells implanted in the uterus develops into a fetus

Table 1	Milestones of Fetal Development	
First Trimester	
Weeks 3 and 4	Development of the head
	Nervous system begins to form
	Backbone is constructed
Week 5	Formation of the umbilical cord
Weeks 4 to 8	External body parts develop—eyes, ears, arms, hands, fingers, legs, feet, and toes Liver, lungs, pancreas, kidneys, and intestines form and begin limited functioning
Second Trimester	
Week 14	Fetal movement, or *quickening*
Week 18	Fetal heartbeat detected by examiner
Week 24	Fetus is sensitive to light and sound in utero
Third Trimester	
Week 28	Fat deposits form—gains chubby baby appearance
Weeks 29 to birth	Rapid growth

with most of the major organ systems present and with recognizable human features.

At the end of week 12 (end of the first trimester), the fetus is unmistakably human and looks like a small infant (see Figure 4d). It is about 10 centimeters (4 inches) long and weighs about 19 grams (⅔ ounce). From this point on, development consists mainly of the enlargement and differentiation of structures that are already present.

By week 18, the woman has been able to feel movement for two to four weeks, and the physician can detect the fetal heartbeat. The latter is an important point, because it helps the physician determine the length of gestation. The baby should be born about 20 weeks later.

During month 7 the fetus turns in the uterus to assume a head-down position. If this turning does not occur by the time of delivery, there will be a *breech presentation.* Women can try assuming various positions to aid the turning (Boston Women's Health Book Collective, 2011). Physicians and midwives can also perform certain procedures to turn the fetus.

The fetus's growth during the last two months is rapid. At the end of month 8 it weighs an average of 2,500 grams (5 pounds 4 ounces). The average full-term baby weighs 3,300 grams (7.5 pounds) and is 50 centimeters (20 inches) long.

Umbilical cord: The tube that connects the fetus to the placenta.
Human chorionic gonadotropin (hCG): A hormone secreted by the placenta; it is the hormone detected in pregnancy tests.
Amniotic fluid: The watery fluid surrounding a developing fetus in the uterus.

Pregnancy

The Stages of Pregnancy

The First Trimester (The First 12 Weeks)

Symptoms of Pregnancy.   For most women, the first symptom of pregnancy is a missed menstrual period. Of course, there may be a wide variety of reactions to this event. For the teenager who is not married or for the married woman who feels that she already has enough children, the reaction may be depression, anger, and fear. For the woman who has been trying to conceive for several months, the reaction may be joy and eager anticipation.

In fact, there are many other reasons besides pregnancy for a woman to have a late period or miss a period. Illness or emotional stress may delay a period, and women occasionally skip a period for no apparent reason.

It is also true that a woman may continue to experience some cyclic bleeding or spotting during pregnancy. This is not particularly a danger sign, except that in a few cases it is a symptom of a miscarriage.

If the woman has been keeping a basal body temperature chart, it can provide a very early sign that she is pregnant. If her temperature rises abruptly at about the time ovulation would normally occur and then stays up for more than two weeks—say, about three weeks—the chances are fairly good that she is pregnant. The increased temperature results from the high level of progesterone manufactured by the corpus luteum and, later, the placenta.

Other early symptoms of pregnancy are tenderness of the breasts—a tingling sensation and special sensitivity of the nipples—and nausea and vomiting (called *morning sickness,* although these symptoms may happen anytime during the day). More frequent urination, feelings of fatigue, and a need for more sleep are other early signs of pregnancy.

Pregnancy Tests.   It is important that women make use of early, accurate pregnancy tests, for several reasons. A woman needs to know that she is pregnant as early as possible so that she can see a physician or midwife and begin getting good prenatal care. She also needs to know so that she can get the nutrition she requires during pregnancy (see Nutrition during Pregnancy). And if she does not want to carry the baby to term, she needs to know as soon as possible, because abortions are much safer and simpler when performed in the first trimester than in the second.

A pregnancy test may be done at a doctor's office, at a Planned Parenthood or family planning clinic, or at a medical laboratory. The most common pregnancy test is an immunologic test based on detecting the presence of hCG (human chorionic gonadotropin, secreted by the placenta) in the woman's urine. It can be done in a matter of minutes and is very accurate.

The laboratory tests for pregnancy are 98 to 99 percent accurate. A laboratory test may produce a false negative (tell the woman she is not pregnant when she really is) if it is done too early or if errors are made in processing. Also, some women simply do not show positive signs in the tests or do not do so until the second or third test. The modern urine tests are 98 percent accurate seven days after implantation (just when a period is missed).

A different type of test, called the *beta-hCG radioimmunoassay,* assesses the presence of beta-hCG in a blood sample. It can detect hCG at very low levels, so it can reliably detect pregnancy seven days after fertilization. It is much more expensive than the urine tests and is available only in laboratories associated with hospitals or large clinics.

Home (over-the-counter) pregnancy tests are widely available in drug stores and on the Internet. They are sold under such names as Answer, Clearblue, Easy, e.p.t., and First Response; all are urine tests designed to measure the presence of hCG. They cost from $5 to $20, depending upon the number of tests in the package. There are also hCG test strips sold under a variety of names. The charm lies in their convenience and the privacy of getting the results. Manufacturers claim their tests will accurately detect a pregnancy on the first day of the missed period. A comparison of eight home pregnancy tests found that two of them were more than 95 percent accurate (Clearblue PLUS and Clearblue DIGITAL) and all the others were less than 75 percent accurate (Johnson et al., 2015). A high rate of false negatives is very serious because it leads a pregnant woman to think she is not pregnant; as a result she might take substances or medicines that would harm the fetus, and would not seek prenatal care. Rare but dangerous conditions such as an ectopic pregnancy (discussed later in this chapter) could go undetected. Complicating matters is the fact that levels of hCG in early pregnancy vary from one woman to the next. Accuracy also depends on following directions *exactly.* All in all, relying on such tests is not a good idea.

Once the pregnancy has been confirmed, the woman generally is very interested in determining her expected delivery date (called EDC for a rather antiquated expression, "expected date of confinement"). The EDC is calculated using *Nägele's rule.* The rule says to take the date of the first day of the last menstrual period, subtract three months, add seven days, and then add one year. Thus, if the first day of the last menstrual period was September 10, 2019, the expected delivery date would be June 17, 2020: subtracting three months from September 10 gives June 10, adding seven days yields June 17, and adding one year gives June 17, 2020. In cases where the date the last menstrual period began is not known, an ultrasound procedure may be used to determine gestational age.

Physical Changes. A major change that takes place in the woman's body during the first trimester is a large increase in the levels of hormones, especially estrogen and progesterone, that are produced by the placenta. Many of the other physical symptoms of the first trimester arise from these endocrine changes.

The breasts swell and tingle. This results from the development of the mammary glands, which is stimulated by hormones. The nipples and the area around them (areola) may darken and broaden.

There is often a need to urinate more frequently. This is related to changes in the pituitary hormones that affect the adrenals, which in turn change the water balance in the body so that more water is retained. The growing uterus also contributes by pressing against the bladder.

Some women experience morning sickness—feelings of nausea, perhaps to the point of vomiting, and of revulsion toward food or its odor. The nausea and vomiting may occur on waking or at other times during the day. Their exact cause is not known. One theory is that nausea and vomiting cause pregnant women to expel and subsequently avoid foods containing toxic chemicals (Flaxman & Sherman, 2000). Supporting evidence includes a lower rate of miscarriage among women who experience morning sickness. While these symptoms are quite common, about 33 percent of pregnant women experience no vomiting at all.

Vaginal discharges may also increase at this time, partly because the increased hormone levels change the pH of the vagina and partly because the vaginal secretions are changing in their chemical composition and quantity.

The feelings of fatigue and sleepiness are related to the high levels of progesterone, which is known to have a sedative effect.

Psychological Changes. Our culture is full of stereotypes about the psychological characteristics of pregnant women. According to one view, pregnancy is supposed to be a time of happiness and calm. Radiant contentment, the "pregnant glow," is said to emanate from the woman's face, making this a good time for her to be photographed. According to another view, pregnancy is a time of emotional ups and downs. The pregnant woman swings from very happy to depressed and crying, and back again. She is irrational, sending her partner out in a blizzard for kosher dill spears.

Research indicates that the situation is more complex than these stereotypes suggest. A woman's emotional state during pregnancy, often assessed with measures of depression, varies according to several factors. First, her attitude toward the pregnancy makes a difference; women who desire the pregnancy are less anxious than women who do not

(Kalil et al., 1993). A second factor is social class. Several studies have found that low income is associated with depression during pregnancy (Hobfoll et al., 1995). This may be due to the economic situation these women face; also, there may be more unwanted pregnancies among low-income women. A third influence is the availability of social support. Women with a supportive partner are less likely to be depressed, perhaps because the partner serves as a buffer against stressful events (Chapman et al., 1997).

Depression is not uncommon during this time. Women who led very active lives prior to becoming pregnant may find fatigue and lack of energy especially distressing. Depression during the first trimester is more likely among women experiencing other stressful life events, such as moving, changes in their jobs, changes in relationships, or illnesses (Kalil et al., 1993). In this trimester, women's anxieties often center on concerns about miscarriage.

Research also shows that a woman's emotional state during pregnancy may have an effect on the developing fetus. This may occur because the stress hormone cortisol crosses the placenta (Talge et al., 2007). Chronic stress, anxiety, and depression during pregnancy have been linked to low birth weight for the baby (Schetter, 2011).

The Second Trimester (Weeks 13 to 26)

Physical Changes. During month 4, the woman becomes aware of the fetus's movements (quickening). Many women find this to be a very exciting experience.

Most of the physical symptoms of the first trimester, such as morning sickness, disappear, and discomforts are at a minimum. Physical problems at this time include constipation and nosebleeds (caused by increased blood volume). **Edema**—water retention and swelling—may be a problem in the face, hands, wrists, ankles, and feet; it results from increased water retention throughout the body.

By about midpregnancy, the breasts, under hormonal stimulation, have essentially completed their development in preparation for nursing. Beginning about week 19, a thin amber or yellow fluid called **colostrum** may come out of the nipple, although there is no milk yet.

Psychological Changes. While the first trimester can be relatively tempestuous, particularly with morning sickness, the second is usually a period of relative calm and well-being. The discomforts of the first trimester are past; the tensions associated with labor and delivery are not yet present. Fear of miscarriage diminishes as the woman feels fetal movement.

Depression is less likely during the second trimester if the pregnant woman has a cohabiting partner or spouse (Hobfoll et al., 1995). Furthermore, women who report more effective partner support report less anxiety in the second trimester (Rini et al., 2006). Interestingly, women who have had a previous pregnancy are more distressed

Edema (eh-DEE-muh): Excessive fluid retention and swelling.
Colostrum: A watery substance that is secreted from the breasts at the end of pregnancy and during the first few days after delivery.

during this time than women who have not (Wilkinson, 1995). This may reflect the impact of the demands associated with the care of other children when one is pregnant. Research also indicates that feelings of nurturance, or maternal responsiveness to the infant, increase steadily from the prepregnant to the postpartum period (Fleming et al., 1997).

The Third Trimester (Weeks 27 to 38)

Physical Changes.   The uterus is very large and hard by the third trimester. The woman is increasingly aware of her size and of the fetus, which is becoming more and more active. In fact, some women are kept awake at night by its somersaults and hiccups.

The extreme size of the uterus puts pressure on a number of other organs. There is pressure on the lungs, which may cause shortness of breath. The stomach is also being squeezed, and indigestion is common. The navel is pushed out. The heart is being strained because of the large increase in blood volume. At this stage most women feel low in energy.

The weight gain of the second trimester continues. The Mayo Clinic (2012b) recommends that the amount of weight gained should range from 11 to 40 pounds, depending on the woman's weight prior to pregnancy. Women who are underweight (BMI less than 18.5) should gain relatively more, 28 to 40 pounds, whereas women who are obese (BMI 30 or more) should gain less, 11 to 20 pounds. The average infant at birth weighs 7.5 pounds; the rest of the weight gain is accounted for by the placenta (1–2 pounds), the amniotic fluid (about 2 pounds), enlargement of the uterus (about 2 pounds), enlargement of the breasts (1–3 pounds), and the additional fat and water retained by the woman (8 or more pounds). Physicians restrict the amount of weight gain because the incidence of complications such as high blood pressure and strain on the heart is much higher in women who gain an excessive amount of weight. Also, excessive weight gained during pregnancy can be very hard to lose afterward.

The uterus tightens occasionally in painless contractions called **Braxton-Hicks contractions.** These are not part of labor. It is thought that they help to strengthen the uterine muscles, preparing them for labor.

In a first pregnancy, around two to four weeks before delivery, the baby turns and the head drops into the pelvis. This is called *lightening, dropping,* or *engagement.* Engagement usually occurs during labor in women who have had babies before.

Some women are concerned about the appropriate amount of activity during pregnancy—whether some things constitute "overdoing it." Current thinking holds that for a healthy pregnant woman, moderate activity is not dangerous and is actually psychologically and physically beneficial. Modern methods of childbirth encourage

sensible exercise for the pregnant woman so that she will be in shape for labor (see Childbirth Options later in this chapter). The matter, of course, is highly individual.

Psychological Changes.   The patterns noted earlier continue into the third trimester. Psychological well-being is greater among women who have social support (often in the form of a cohabiting partner or husband), have higher incomes, are middle class, and experience fewer concurrent stressful life events.

The Father's Experience in Pregnancy

Physical Changes.   Some men experience pregnancy symptoms, including indigestion, gastritis, nausea, change in appetite, and headaches (Kiselica & Scheckel, 1995), referred to as *couvade syndrome.* These may be caused by hormonal changes in the male. A longitudinal study of 34 couples collected blood samples from both before and after the birth of the infant (Storey et al., 2000). Men and women displayed stage-specific hormone changes including high levels of prolactin prenatally and low levels of testosterone postnatally. Men with more pregnancy symptoms had higher levels of prolactin prenatally.

In some cultures this phenomenon takes a more dramatic form, known as *couvade ritual.* In this ritual, the husband retires to bed while his wife is in labor. He suffers all the pains of delivery, moaning and groaning as she does. Couvade is still practiced in parts of Asia, South America, and Oceania (Gregersen, 1996).

Psychological Changes.   In 21st-century American culture, many men expect to be actively involved in fathering. The study of hormonal changes during pregnancy presented videotapes with auditory and visual cues from newborns after the blood sample was drawn. Men who showed higher levels of responsiveness had higher levels of prolactin prenatally and lower levels of testosterone postnatally (Storey et al., 2000). Lower levels of testosterone may facilitate paternal behavior.

A review of 25 articles about fathers' experiences during pregnancy identified several patterns (Poh et al., 2014). Early in the pregnancy fathers wanted to connect with the fetus. Feeling fetal movements and viewing an ultrasound examination gives fathers a sense of the reality of the pregnancy. As pregnancy progresses, many fathers interact with the fetus by talking to them, and feeling and responding to their movement. Fathers may be worried about the challenges that the child will create. As the due date approaches, first-time fathers worry about how to help during delivery; experienced fathers worry about the pain their partners may experience. Fathers—especially first-time ones—want information about pregnancy and childbirth;

> **Braxton-Hicks contractions:** Contractions of the uterus during pregnancy that are not part of labor.

Figure 5   Dads change diapers at a "Bootee Camp." Such classes help new fathers adjust to their new role.

©*The Free Lance-Star, Scott Neville/AP Images*

many of them spend hours searching the media. Late in the pregnancy, many fathers express an increased sense of maturity as they reflect on how they are meeting their increasing responsibilities.

Preparing for the Baby.   Fathers or other partners play an important role in preparing for a baby. The birth or arrival of a first child may require finding a larger home or making physical changes to the present one. There will be visits to medical personnel, tests to be taken, and arrangements to be made. More than 90 percent of fathers in the United States participate in prenatal activities (Poh et al., 2014). Fathers or partners who participate in these activities provide support to their partner and become more involved themselves. Many couples take some form of classes in preparation for childbirth. These joint activities contribute to the bond between the partners, which in turn provides a better foundation for the arrival of the new member of the family.

Diversity in the Contexts of Pregnancy
There are lots of family contexts in which women have babies besides the traditional one of being married to the baby's father. These include living in a stable relationship with the baby's father but not being married; not being married to or living with the baby's father but seeing him regularly; being a single mother-to-be who has no contact with the baby's father; being a single mother-to-be who is pregnant as a result of artificial insemination or other reproductive technologies; and being a woman in a stable relationship with another woman, who is pregnant as a result of artificial insemination or other technologies. Because it is too complicated to mention these alternatives constantly, in the sections that follow, our language is based on a situation in which the woman is married to the baby's father, which is still statistically the most common context in which babies are born in the United States. Readers should, however, keep in mind all these other possible family scenarios.

Sex during Pregnancy
Many women and men are concerned about whether it is safe or advisable for a pregnant woman to have sexual intercourse, particularly during the latter stages of pregnancy. Medical opinion is that—given a normal, healthy pregnancy—intercourse can continue safely (Jones et al., 2011). There is no evidence that intercourse or orgasm is associated with preterm labor (Sayle et al., 2001;

Schaffir, 2006). The only exception is a case where a miscarriage or preterm labor is threatened.

Most pregnant women continue to have intercourse throughout the pregnancy (Reamy & White, 1987). The most common pattern is a decline in the frequency of intercourse during the first trimester, variation in the second trimester, and an even greater decline in the third trimester (Fox et al., 2008).

During the latter stages of pregnancy, the woman's shape makes intercourse increasingly awkward. The man-on-top position is probably best abandoned at this time. The side-to-side position (see the chapter "Sexual Arousal") is probably the most suitable one for intercourse during the late stages of pregnancy. Couples should also remember that there are many ways of experiencing sexual pleasure and orgasm besides having intercourse; hand–genital stimulation or oral–genital sex may be good alternatives.[2] The best guide in this matter is the woman's feelings. If intercourse becomes uncomfortable for her, alternatives should be explored.

Nutrition during Pregnancy

During pregnancy, another living being is growing inside the woman, and she needs lots of energy, protein, vitamins, and minerals at this time. Therefore, diet during pregnancy is extremely important. If the woman's diet is good, she has a much better chance of remaining healthy during pregnancy and of bearing a healthy baby; if her diet is inadequate, she stands more of a chance of developing one of a number of diseases during pregnancy herself and of bearing a child whose weight is low at birth. Babies with low birth weights do not have as good a chance of survival as ones with normal birth weights.

Part of a good diet is maintaining a healthy weight, as overweight and obese women are at increased risk of negative outcomes for both themselves and the fetus. Risks to the mother include hypertension, gestational diabetes, and cesarean delivery (Practice Committee, 2008). Risks to the fetus include congenital abnormalities such as spina bifida, cleft palate, and hydrocephaly (Stothard et al., 2009).

It is particularly important that a pregnant woman get enough protein, folic acid, calcium, magnesium, and vitamin A (Luke, 1994). Protein is important for building new tissues. Folic acid is also important for growth. A pregnant woman needs much more iron than usual because the fetus draws off iron for itself from the blood that circulates to the placenta. Muscle cramps, nerve pains, sleeplessness, and irritability may all be symptoms of a calcium deficiency. Severe calcium deficiency during pregnancy is associated with increased blood pressure, which may lead to a serious condition called eclampsia, discussed later in this chapter (Repke, 1994). Deficiencies of calcium and magnesium are associated with premature birth. Sometimes even an excellent diet does not provide enough iron, calcium, or folic acid, in which case the pregnant woman should take supplements.

Daily consumption of artificially sweetened soft drinks is linked to increased likelihood of preterm birth (Halldorsson et al., 2010). Drinking four per day was associated with greater odds of preterm delivery than drinking one per day. There was no effect of drinking sugar-sweetened sodas.

Effects of Substances Taken during Pregnancy

We are such a pill-popping culture that we seldom stop to think about whether we should take a certain drug. The pregnant woman, however, needs to know that when she takes a drug, not only does it circulate through her body, but it may also circulate through the fetus. Because the fetus develops so rapidly during pregnancy, drugs may produce severe consequences, including serious malformations. Drugs that produce such defects are called **teratogens.** Of course, not all drugs can cross the placental barrier, but many can. The drugs that pregnant women should be cautious in using are discussed below.

> **What substances, if taken during pregnancy, threaten the fetus?**

Antibiotics

Long-term use of antibiotics by the woman may cause damage to the fetus. Tetracycline may cause stained teeth and bone deformities. Gentamycin, kanamycin, neomycin, streptomycin, and vancomycin may cause deafness. Nitrofurantoin may cause jaundice. Accutane (isotretinoin), used to treat acne, can cause severe birth defects if taken by a pregnant woman. Some drugs taken by diabetics may cause various fetal anomalies.

Alcohol

WARNING: ACCORDING TO THE SURGEON GENERAL, WOMEN SHOULD NOT DRINK ALCOHOLIC BEVERAGES DURING PREGNANCY BECAUSE OF THE RISK OF BIRTH DEFECTS.

A substantial amount of research has documented the risks to a child of maternal drinking during pregnancy. Alcohol consumed by the woman circulates through the fetus, so it can have pervasive effects on fetal growth and development (Jones, 2006). In turn, these can cause behavioral and neurological impairments extending into adulthood (Dorrie et al., 2014).

> **Teratogen:** A substance that produces defects in a fetus.

[2]There is, however, some risk associated with cunnilingus for the pregnant woman, as discussed in the chapter "Sexual Arousal."

Fetal alcohol spectrum disorder is an umbrella term referring to the range of outcomes of *any* amount of alcohol exposure in utero (Sokol et al., 2007). Children with fetal alcohol spectrum disorder (FASD) tend to have characteristic facial features: a small opening between the eyelids, the groove between the nose and upper lip is flattened, and the upper lip is thin (Cook et al., 2015). A diagnosis of FASD is made when there are symptoms of widespread impairment of brain functioning as evidenced by problems in areas such as motor skills, cognition, language, attention, impulse control, and emotion regulation (Cook et al., 2015).

The abuse of alcohol during pregnancy may result in an offspring who displays a pattern of malformations termed **fetal alcohol syndrome (FAS)** (Figure 6a). Among the characteristics of the syndrome are both prenatal and postnatal growth deficiencies, a small brain, small eye openings, and joint, limb, and heart malformations. Perhaps the most serious effect is intellectual disability. About 85 percent of children with FAS score 2 or more standard deviations below the mean on intelligence tests—that would be an IQ of 70 or below. Indeed, FAS is the leading preventable cause of intellectual disability (Dorrie et al., 2014).

"Risk drinking," seven or more drinks per week, or five or more drinks per occasion, pose a serious health risk to the fetus (Centers for Disease Control, 2002). A study of 655,979 births in Missouri found that women who drank during pregnancy were 40 percent more likely to experience a stillbirth (Aliyu et al., 2008). A meta-analysis of empirical studies found a relationship between binge drinking (four to five drinks per occasion) and diverse aspects of cognitive functioning in children aged 6 months to 14 years (Flak et al., 2014).

"Safe" limits for alcohol consumption have not been established and probably don't exist, so the best advice about drinking for women who are, or may be, or want to be pregnant is Don't. Men should stop drinking before attempting to conceive. Alcohol damages sperm count, concentration, and quality, and the degree of damage is dose-dependent (Jensen et al., 2014).

Cocaine

Cocaine use during pregnancy is associated with an increased risk of premature birth (Handler et al., 1991) and low birth weight (Phibbs et al., 1991) (see Figure 6b). The only regularly noted physical abnormality is smaller head circumference (Cherukuri et al., 1988); cocaine-exposed children are more likely to be microcephalic, which is in turn associated with poorer growth and lower intelligence-test scores in school-age children. A carefully done longitudinal study measuring infant development at 6, 12, and 24 months compared 218 cocaine-exposed and 197 unexposed infants on cognitive

> **Fetal alcohol syndrome (FAS):** Serious growth deficiency and malformations in the child of a mother who abuses alcohol during pregnancy.

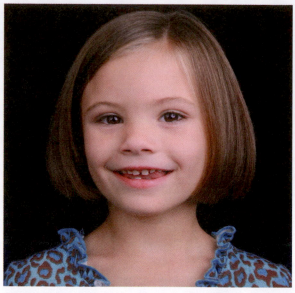

(a)

(b)

Figure 6 The effects of prenatal exposure to alcohol and other drugs. (*a*) A child born with fetal alcohol syndrome. (*b*) A preterm baby whose mother used crack cocaine during pregnancy.

(a) ©Rick's Photography/Shutterstock; (b) ©Chuck Nacke/Alamy

outcomes (Singer et al., 2002). Cocaine exposure was associated with a 6-point deficit in scores on a cognitive measure at 2 years of age.

Marijuana

Marijuana is a psychoactive substance derived from dried flowers of cannabis plants. In 2011–2012, marijuana was reportedly used in the preceding month by 5.2 percent of pregnant women in the United States (SAMHSA, 2012). The legalization of marijuana in several states is making the drug more widely available, and its use by pregnant women is increasing (Foeller & Lyell, 2017). The psychoactive chemicals in marijuana, varieties of THC, cross the placental barrier (Harbison & Mantilla-Plata, 1972). Research on the effects of use during pregnancy in the 1970s and 1980s used strains available at that time. By 2012, the potency of the strains in use had increased sixfold (Warner et al., 2014), markedly increasing its potential effects.

The best evidence comes from three prospective, longitudinal studies (Huizink, 2014). The results indicate varied effects on fetal development and birth outcomes. The effects varied by study, and included preterm birth, reduced fetal growth, and reduced fetal birth weight. As with alcohol, the effects on the fetus and child are dose-dependent. Children who were heavily exposed to cannabis prenatally scored lower on verbal skills and memory functioning at 48 months. In the behavioral realm, prenatal cannabis exposure was related to more symptoms of externalizing behavior—impulsivity, hyperactivity—at 6 years and 10 years.

THC also has been found in the breast milk of users (Foeller & Lyell, 2017). Because of accumulating evidence, several professional societies, including the American College of Obstetrics and Gynecology and the American Pediatric Association, have issued statements discouraging the use of marijuana during pregnancy and the period of breast-feeding.

Marijuana use is also implicated in infertility (Warner et al., 2014). Use in men is associated with reduced production of reproductive hormones, including luteinizing hormone and testosterone, and reduced sperm motility. Chronic use in women is associated with reduced hormone production and suppressed ovulation.

Steroids

Synthetic hormones such as progestin can cause masculinization of a female fetus, as discussed in the chapter "Sex Hormones, Sexual Differentiation, and the Menstrual Cycle." Corticosteroids are linked with low birth weight, cleft palate, and stillbirth in some studies but not in others (Ostensten, 1994). Excessive amounts of vitamin A are associated with cleft palate. Excesses of vitamins D, B_6, and K have also been associated with fetal defects. A potent estrogen, diethylstilbestrol (DES), has been shown to cause cancer of the vagina in girls whose mothers took the drug while pregnant (Herbst, 1972).

Other Substances

According to the U.S. Public Health Service, maternal smoking during pregnancy slows fetal growth, indicated by decreased infant birth weight and increased incidence of prematurity. A study of 18,000 live births assessed infants for evidence of 22 types of congenital defects; infants whose mothers smoked were more likely to be born with cardiovascular anomalies, conditions involving arteries, veins, or the heart (Woods & Raju, 2001). A study in Finland replicated the finding that infants of smokers were more likely to be preterm and low birth weight. A seven-year follow-up found that these children were more likely to have developed asthma; the risk was greater for children whose mothers smoked from 1 to 10 cigarettes per day, and greater still for those whose mothers smoked more than 10 per day during pregnancy (Jaakkola & Gissler, 2004). A study comparing the risk due to smoking, drinking, and limited prenatal care found that the largest and most consistent effect on children of white women was associated with smoking (Li & Poirier, 2001).

Selective serotonin reuptake inhibitors such as fluoxetine (Prozac) are frequently used to treat depression. A meta-analysis of prospective cohort studies found that newborns exposed to SSRIs are more likely to be low birth weight and to be admitted to special or intensive care nurseries at birth (Lattimore et al., 2005). They were also more likely to show signs of poor neonatal adaptation, including respiratory distress and jaundice. A retrospective cohort study of 600,000 births found that fluoxetine and paroxetine use during pregnancy were associated with isolated heart defects (Malm et al., 2011). Fluoxetine use is also associated with spontaneous abortion (Nakhai-Pour et al., 2010) and pregnancy-induced hypertension (De Vera & Berard, 2012).

Because the risks of psychiatric medications to mother and baby vary, management of pregnancy in women with psychiatric disorders should involve the woman, her obstetrical services provider, and a psychiatrist. It should include an individualized assessment of risks and benefits of various treatment options (Kent, 2008).

Chemical solvents are used in the manufacture of and found in many commercial products, including paint, glues, dyes, cosmetics, and cleaning agents. The neurotoxicity of these to adults is well-established (Pele et al., 2013). A large-scale longitudinal study in France recruited women at the beginning of pregnancy and followed them until the child was two years old. One-fifth of the mothers reported occasional exposure on the job to these solvents, and 31 percent reported regular exposure at work. Children who were exposed prenatally were given higher scores at age 2 by their caregivers on attention deficit/hyperactivity and aggression (fighting, hitting, kicking others). Again, greater exposure was associated with more pronounced effects.

Although not classified as a drug, X rays deserve mention here because they can damage the fetus, particularly during the first 42 days after conception.

Dads and Drugs

Most research has focused on the effects of drugs taken by the pregnant woman. However, other research suggests that drugs taken by men before a conception may also cause birth defects, probably because the drugs damage the sperm and their genetic contents (Narod et al., 1988). In addition, one study found evidence that a mother's smoking during the first trimester of pregnancy increased her offspring's risk of cancer in childhood; but a father's smoking during the pregnancy in the absence of the mother's smoking also increased the risk of childhood cancer (John et al., 1991).

Birth

The Beginning of Labor

The signs that labor is about to begin vary from one woman to the next. There may be a discharge of a small amount of bloody mucus (the "bloody show"). This is the mucus plug that was in the cervical opening during pregnancy, its purpose being to prevent germs from passing from the vagina up into the uterus. In about 10 percent of all women the membranes containing the amniotic fluid rupture (the bag of waters bursts), and there is a gush of warm fluid down the woman's legs. Labor usually begins within 24 hours after this occurs. More commonly, the amniotic sac does not rupture until the end of the first stage of labor. The Braxton-Hicks contractions may increase before labor and may be mistaken for labor. Typically, they are distinct from the contractions of labor in that they are very irregular.

The Stages of Labor

Labor is typically divided into three stages. The whole process of childbirth is sometimes referred to as *parturition.*

First-Stage Labor

First-stage labor begins with the regular contractions of the muscles of the uterus. These contractions are responsible for producing two changes in the cervix, both of which must occur before the baby can be delivered. These changes are called **effacement** (thinning out) and **dilation** (opening up). The cervix must dilate until it has an opening 10 centimeters (4 inches) in diameter before the baby can be born.

First-stage labor itself is divided into three stages: early, late, and transition. In *early first-stage labor,* contractions are spaced far apart, with perhaps 15 to 20 minutes between them. A contraction typically lasts 45 seconds to a minute. This stage of labor is fairly easy, and the woman is comfortable between contractions. Meanwhile, the cervix is effacing and dilating.

Late first-stage labor is marked by the dilation of the cervix from 5 to 8 centimeters (2 to 3 inches). It is generally shorter than the early stage, and the contractions are more frequent and more intense.

The final dilation of the cervix from 8 to 10 centimeters (3 to 4 inches) occurs during the **transition** phase, which is both short and difficult. The contractions are very strong, and it is during this stage that women report pain and exhaustion.

The first stage of labor can last anywhere from 2 to 24 hours. It averages about 12 to 15 hours for a first pregnancy and about 8 hours for later pregnancies. (In most respects, first labors are the hardest, later ones easier.) The woman is usually told to go to the hospital when the contractions are 4 to 5 minutes apart. Once there, she is put in the labor room or birthing room for the rest of first-stage labor.

Second-Stage Labor: Delivery

Second-stage labor (Figure 7) begins when the cervix is fully dilated and the baby's head (or whichever

(a)

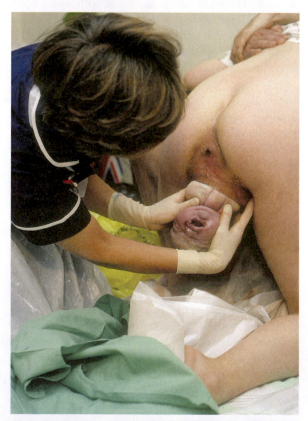

(b)

Figure 7   Second-stage labor. (*a*) Baby's head crowning and then (*b*) moving out.

(a) ©Petit Format/Science Source; (b) ©Eddie Lawrence/ Science Source

---

Effacement: A thinning out of the cervix during labor.
Dilation: An opening up of the cervix during labor; also called *dilatation.*
First-stage labor: The beginning of labor, during which there are regular contractions of the uterus; the stage lasts until the cervix is dilated 8 centimeters (3 inches).
Transition: The difficult part of labor at the end of the first stage, during which the cervix dilates from 8 to 10 centimeters (3 to 4 inches).
Second-stage labor: The stage during which the baby moves out through the vagina and is delivered.

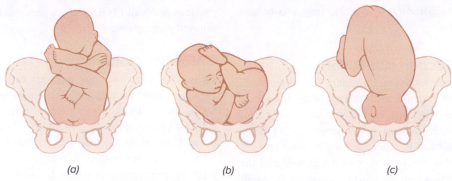

(a)   (b)   (c)

Figure 8 Possible positions of the fetus during birth. (*a*) A breech presentation (4 percent of births). (*b*) A transverse presentation (less than 1 percent). (*c*) A normal, headfirst or cephalic presentation (96 percent of births).

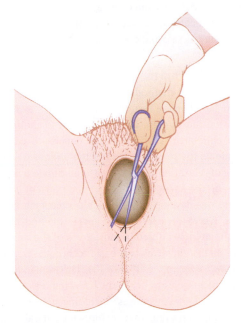

Figure 9 Episiotomy. A mediolateral or median cut may be performed.

part comes first, depending on the baby's position; see Figure 8) begins to move into the vagina, or birth canal. It lasts from a few minutes to a few hours and is generally much shorter than the first stage.

During this stage, many women feel an urge to push or bear down, which is effective in pushing the baby out. With each contraction the baby is pushed farther along.

When the baby's head has traversed the entire length of the vagina, the top of it becomes visible at the vaginal entrance; this is called *crowning.* It is at this point that some physicians perform an **episiotomy** (see Figure 9), in which an incision or slit is made in the perineum, the skin just behind the vagina. Most women do not feel the episiotomy being performed because the pressure of the baby against the pelvic floor provides a natural anesthetic.

The incision is stitched closed after the baby is born. The reasons physicians give for performing an episiotomy are that it will prevent impaired sexual functioning later, reduce the severity of perineal lacerations, and reduce postdelivery pain and medication use. However, a review of research conducted between 1950 and 2004 found no evidence that any of these benefits result from episiotomies (Hartmann et al., 2005). Critics claim that it is unnecessary and is done merely for the doctor's convenience, while causing the woman discomfort later as it is healing. They note that episiotomies are usually not performed in western European countries, where delivery still takes place quite nicely.

The baby is finally eased completely out of the mother's body. At this point, the baby is still connected to the mother by the umbilical cord, which runs from the baby's navel to the placenta, and the placenta is still inside the mother's uterus. As the baby takes its first breath of air, the functioning of its body changes dramatically. Blood begins to flow to the lungs, there to take on oxygen, and a flap closes between the two atria (chambers) in the heart. This process generally takes a few minutes, during which time the baby changes from a somewhat bluish color to a healthy, pink hue. At this point, the baby no longer needs the umbilical cord, which is clamped and cut off about 7 centimeters (3 inches) from the body. The stub gradually dries up and falls off.

To avoid the possibility of transmitting gonorrhea or other eye infections from the mother to the baby, drops of silver nitrate or a similar drug are placed in the baby's eyes.

Third-Stage Labor

During **third-stage labor,** the placenta detaches from the walls of the uterus, and the afterbirth (placenta and fetal membranes) is expelled. This stage may take from a few minutes to an hour. Several contractions may accompany the

> **Episiotomy (ih-pee-see-AH-tuh-mee):** An incision made in the skin just behind the vagina, allowing the baby to be delivered more easily.
> **Third-stage labor:** The stage during which the afterbirth is expelled.

expulsion of the placenta. The episiotomy and/or any tears are sewn up.

Cesarean Section (C-Section)

Cesarean section is a surgical procedure for delivery; it is used when normal vaginal birth is impossible or undesirable. Cesarean section may be required for a number of different reasons: if the baby is too large or if the mother's pelvis is too small to allow the baby to move into the vagina; if the labor has been very long and hard and the cervix is not dilating or if the mother is nearing the point of total exhaustion; if the umbilical cord *prolapses* (moves into a position such that it is coming out through the cervix ahead of the baby); if there is an Rh incompatibility; or if there is excessive bleeding or the mother's or the infant's condition takes a sudden turn for the worse.

In the cesarean section, an incision is made first through the abdomen and then through the wall of the uterus. The physician lifts out the baby and then sews up the uterine wall and the abdominal wall.

Cesarean delivery rates in the United States have been increasing steadily since 1996, reaching 33 percent of all births in 2009. This is the highest rate in U.S. history, and higher than most Western countries. The rate declined slightly in 2013, to 32.7 (Martin et al., 2014). Cesarean deliveries are associated with higher rates of complications requiring hospitalization of mother or infant (Stranges et al., 2011) than vaginal deliveries. Thus, they should be performed only when medically necessary. A comparison of births in 1959–1966 with births in 2002–2008 found that mothers were older and weighed more in the later period, and that obstetrical interventions, including C-sections, were more frequent (Laughon et al., 2012). Rates among an American Indian population in New Mexico are one-third the overall rate in the United States (Leeman & Leeman, 2003).

There is concern about the high U.S. cesarean rates. An analysis of nearly a million primary C-sections and repeat cesarean births in 2001 classified 11 percent of the former and 55 percent of the latter as potentially unnecessary (Kabir et al., 2005).

Contrary to popular opinion, it is not true that once a woman has had one delivery by cesarean, she must have all subsequent deliveries by the same method. Up to 60 percent of women with a prior cesarean delivery attempt a subsequent vaginal birth (vaginal birth after cesarean or VBAC).

The American College of Obstetricians and Gynecologists (2017) has issued a Practice Bulletin regarding VBAC. It is based on an extensive review of data and expert opinion. The Bulletin states that trial of labor after a previous cesarean (TOLAC) is a reasonable approach in selected pregnancies.

Childbirth Options

Pregnant women and their partners can choose from a variety of childbirth options. Foremost among these is taking childbirth classes to prepare mentally and physically for labor and delivery. In addition, there are several options regarding the use of anesthesia during childbirth. Third, women can often choose to give birth in a birthing or maternity center, in a hospital delivery suite, or at home.

In many communities, pregnant women can select a midwife, instead of a physician, to provide prenatal care and deliver the infant. Midwives are specially trained and often affiliated with a medical practice or birth facility. Research indicates that care by a midwife, compared to standard care, is safe and cost effective (Tracy et al., 2013).

Prepared Childbirth

There are several methods of preparation for childbirth. Most are based on the assumption that fear causes tension and tension causes pain. Thus, to attempt to eliminate the pain of childbirth, such programs consist of education (to eliminate the woman's fears of the unknown) and the learning of relaxation techniques (to eliminate tension).

One of the most widely used methods of *prepared childbirth* was developed by French obstetrician Fernand Lamaze. Classes teaching the Lamaze method or variations of it are now offered in most areas of the world. The **Lamaze method** involves two basic techniques, *relaxation* and *controlled breathing* (Figure 10). The woman learns to relax all the muscles in her body. Knowing how to do this has a number of advantages, including conservation of energy during an event that requires considerable endurance and, more important, avoidance of the tension that increases the perception of pain. The woman also learns a series of controlled breathing exercises, which she will use to help her during each contraction.

Finally, because of the assumption that fear and the pain it causes are best eliminated through education, the woman learns a great deal about the processes involved in pregnancy and childbirth.

One other important component of several methods is the requirement that the woman be accompanied during the training and during childbirth itself by her partner or some other person, who serves as coach. The coach plays an integral role in the woman's learning of the techniques. He (let's assume that it is the baby's father) is present during labor and delivery. He times contractions, checks on the woman's state of relaxation and gives her feedback, suggests breathing patterns, helps elevate her back as she pushes the baby out, and generally provides encouragement and moral support. Aside from the obvious benefits to the

---

Cesarean section (C-section): A method of delivering a baby surgically by an incision in the abdomen.
Lamaze method: A method of "prepared" childbirth involving relaxation and controlled breathing.

Figure 10 Practice in relaxation and breathing techniques is essential in preparing for childbirth.

©Spencer Grant/PhotoEdit

woman, this allows the partner to play an active role in the birth of the child and to experience more fully one of the most basic and moving of all human experiences. The presence of a companion of a woman's choice during labor and delivery has a positive influence on satisfaction with the birth process and does not interfere with other events (Bruggemann et al., 2007).

Instead of or in addition to a partner, a mother-to-be may engage a *doula* to provide supportive care before and during labor and delivery. A doula can provide education and emotional and physical support. Six hundred women giving birth for the first time were randomly assigned to receive either care from a doula of the woman's choice or standard care. Women supported during labor by a doula experienced significantly shorter labors, and their infants received higher Apgar scores (overall health rating) at 1 and 5 minutes after birth (Campbell et al., 2006).

One common misunderstanding about prepared childbirth is that the use of anesthetics is prohibited. In fact, the goal is to teach each woman the techniques she needs to control her reactions to labor so that she will not need

an anesthetic; however, her right to have an anesthetic if she wants one is affirmed.

The Use of Anesthetics in Childbirth

Throughout most of human history, childbirth has been "natural"; that is, it has taken place without anesthetics and in the woman's home or other familiar surroundings. A major change came around the middle of the 19th century, with the development of anesthetics for use in surgery. When their use in childbirth was suggested, there was initially opposition from physicians. Opposition to the use of anesthetics virtually ceased, however, when Queen Victoria gave birth under chloroform anesthesia in 1853. Since then, the use of anesthetics has become routine (too routine, according to some) and effective. Before discussing the arguments for and against the use of anesthetics, let us briefly review some of the common techniques of anesthesia used in childbirth.

The medications most commonly used during labor are regional and local anesthetics, which numb only a specific region of the body. A *spinal* block is a regional anesthetic used to provide pain relief late in the first stage of labor. The medication is injected in the back into a sac of fluid below the spinal cord. It provides complete pain relief for one to two hours, and is usually only given once. The *epidural* block numbs the body from the waist down. It is administered via an injection in a small area near the spinal cord (the epidural space). It may be given during labor, or before a cesarean section. A *pudendal* block (named for the pudendum or vulva) involves an injection into the vaginal wall which relieves pain in the lower vagina and perineum for up to one hour. It may be given shortly before delivery. A local anesthetic injection does not relieve labor pain but is used to numb an area if an incision or repair is necessary. Tranquilizers are rarely used during labor; they may be used if the woman is extremely anxious, or needs some rest due to the length of the labor. (For further information, see Mayo Clinic, 2014.)

The routine use of anesthetics has been questioned by some. Proponents of the use of anesthetics argue that, with modern technology, women no longer need to experience pain during childbirth and that it is therefore silly for them to suffer unnecessarily. Opponents argue that anesthetics have a number of well-documented dangerous effects on both mother and infant. Anesthetics in the mother's bloodstream pass through the placenta to the infant. Thus, while they have the desired effect of depressing the mother's central nervous system, they also depress the infant's nervous system. Anesthetics may prevent the mother from using her body as effectively as she might to help push the baby out. If administered early in labor, anesthetics may inhibit uterine contractions, slow cervical dilation, and prolong labor. They also numb a woman to one of the most fundamental experiences of her life.

Research shows that the negative effects of epidural anesthesia, such as the increased likelihood of the use of instruments during delivery, and longer second stage of labor, can be reduced by using low dosages and techniques that allow the woman to move around (COMET, 2001).

Perhaps the best resolution of this controversy is to say that a pregnant woman should participate in prepared childbirth classes and should use those techniques during labor. If, when she is in labor, she discovers that she cannot control the pain and wants an anesthetic, she should feel free to request it and to do so without guilt; the anesthetic should then be administered with great caution at a low dose.

Home Birth versus Hospital Birth

In the chapter "Theoretical Perspectives on Sexuality" we discuss the process of *medicalization,* in which various life conditions and events are defined in medical terms, as requiring medical treatment. Childbirth was one of the first processes to be medicalized in the United States, resulting in the shift of almost all births from homes to hospitals. The study described previously comparing deliveries in 1960–1969 with those in 2002–2008 found that various interventions, including induction of labor, use of anesthesia, and C-sections, have become much more common in the past 50 years (Laughon et al., 2012). Bucking this trend are advocates of home birth, who argue that the atmosphere in a hospital—with its forbidding machines, rules and regulations, and general lack of comfort and "homeyness"—is stressful to the woman and her family and detracts from what should be a joyous, natural human experience (Figure 11). Furthermore, hospitals are meant to deal with illness, and the delivery of a baby should not be viewed as illness. As we have seen, hospital births encourage the use of interventions that are themselves dangerous. Birth at home is likely to be more relaxed and less stressful; friends and other children are allowed to be present. Recent research indicates

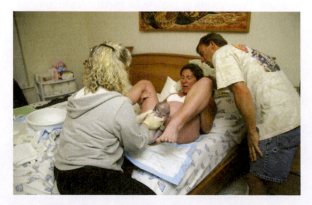

Figure 11   A home birth (Meyvis et al., 2012).

©*Inga Spence/Getty Images*

that there are "no significant differences in maternal and fetal outcomes between planned home births and planned hospital births in women who have been identified as low risk, have qualified birth attendants, and have timely access to specialized care when necessary" (Vedam et al., 2010).

On the other side of the argument, if unforeseen emergency medical procedures are necessary, home birth may be downright dangerous for the mother, the baby, or both. Furthermore, hospital practices in labor and delivery have changed radically, particularly with the increased popularity of prepared childbirth; thus hospitals are not the forbidding, alien environments they once were. Most hospitals, for example, allow fathers to be present for the entire labor and delivery, and many allow the father to be present in the operating room during cesarean deliveries. Many hospitals have created birthing centers that contain a set of homelike rooms, with comfortable beds and armchairs, that permit labor and delivery to occur in a relaxed atmosphere, while being only a minute away from emergency equipment if it is required.

Home births account for about 1 percent of births in the United States (MacDorman et al., 2014). In preparation for a home birth, a qualified home-birth provider should be consulted in advance and should be present at the delivery. Such providers include some M.D.s, certified nurse midwives (CNM, an RN with midwifery training), certified midwives (CM), and certified professional midwives (CPM) (Vedam et al., 2010). There should be access to a hospital in case of an emergency.

After the Baby Is Born: The Postpartum Period

Physical Changes

With the birth of the baby, the woman's body undergoes a drastic physiological change. During pregnancy the placenta produces high levels of both estrogen and progesterone. When the placenta is expelled, the levels of these hormones drop sharply, and thus the postpartum period is characterized by low levels of both estrogen and progesterone. The levels of these hormones gradually return to normal over a period of a few weeks to a few months. Other endocrine changes include an increase in hormones associated with breast-feeding.

In addition, the body undergoes considerable stress during labor and delivery, and the woman may feel exhausted. Discomfort from an episiotomy or lacerations is common in the first postpartum weeks.

Psychological Changes

For a day or two after parturition, the woman typically remains in the hospital, although many women leave the hospital less than 24 hours after delivery. For the first two days, women often feel elated; the long pregnancy is over, they have been successful competitors in a demanding athletic event and are pleased with their efforts, and the baby is finally there, to be cuddled and loved.

Following childbirth, many women experience some degree of depression. The depressed mood and other experiences range from mild to severe. In the mildest, *postpartum blues,* or "baby blues," women experience mood swings, with periods of feeling depressed, being irritable, and crying alternating with positive moods. The symptoms usually begin a few days after delivery, are most intense at one-week postpartum, and lessen or disappear by two weeks postpartum. Between 50 and 80 percent of women experience these mild baby blues (Kennedy & Suttenfield, 2001). **Postpartum depression** is more severe, characterized by depressed mood, insomnia, tearfulness, feelings of inadequacy, and fatigue. It usually begins two to three weeks postpartum but may occur any time after delivery. Between 8 and 15 percent of women will experience it, with symptoms lasting six to eight weeks (Morris-Rush & Bernstein, 2002; O'Hara & Swain, 1996). The most severe disturbance is *postpartum psychosis,* for which early symptoms include restlessness, irritability, and sleep disturbance; later ones include disorganized behavior, mood swings, delusions, and hallucinations. Its onset can be dramatic, within 72 hours of delivery, or four to six weeks postpartum. It is very rare, affecting only 1 or 2 women out of 1,000 (Kennedy & Suttenfield, 2001).

It appears that many factors contribute to this depression. Being in a hospital in and of itself is stressful, as noted earlier. Once the woman returns home, another set of stresses faces her. She has probably not yet returned to her normal level of energy, yet she must perform the exhausting task of caring for a newborn infant. For the first several weeks or months she may not get enough sleep, rising several times during the night to tend to a baby that is crying because it is hungry or sick, and she may become exhausted. Clearly she needs help and support from her partner and friends at this time. Some stresses vary depending on whether this is a first child or a later one. The first child is stressful because of the woman's inexperience. In the case of later-born children, and some firstborns, the mother may become depressed because she did not really want the baby. Women experiencing multiple births have elevated depressive symptom scores nine months postpartum compared to mothers of singletons (Choi et al., 2009).

Physical stresses are also present during the postpartum period; hormone levels have declined sharply, and the body has been under stress. Thus it appears that postpartum depression is caused by a combination of physical and social factors.

Risk factors for postpartum depression include genetic vulnerability (some genes predispose people to depression), severe negative life events or stressors, and a poor-quality relationship with her partner or her own mother (Yim et al., 2015).

Postpartum depression and psychosis should be treated; depression improves in response to antidepressant drugs, individual psychotherapy, partner and peer support, and nurse home visits (Gjerdingen, 2003; Mehta & Sheth, 2006). A review of the research using randomized controlled trials to assess psychological interventions reported that the most promising is intensive professional postpartum support (Dennis, 2005).

Fathers, too, sometimes experience depression after the birth of a baby. A study in Great Britain assessed depression in both mothers and fathers eight weeks after delivery. Ten percent of the mothers and 4 percent of the fathers had high scores (Ramchandani et al., 2005).

Attachment to the Baby

While much of the traditional psychological research has focused on the baby's developing attachment to the mother, more recent interest has been about the development of the mother's attachment (bond) to the infant (see the chapters "Theoretical Perspectives on Sexuality" and "Sexuality and the Life Cycle: Childhood and Adolescence"). Research clearly shows that this process begins even before the baby is born. Two studies of women expecting their first child found that feelings of nurturance grew during pregnancy and increased further at birth (Fleming et al., 1997). In this sense, pregnancy is, in part, a psychological preparation for motherhood.

Sex Postpartum

The birth of a child has a substantial effect on a couple's sexual relationship. Following the birth, the mother is at some risk of infection or hemorrhage, so the couple should wait at least two weeks before resuming intercourse. When coitus is resumed, it may be uncomfortable or even painful for the woman. If she had an episiotomy or laceration, she may experience vaginal discomfort; if she had a cesarean birth, she may experience abdominal discomfort. Fatigue of both the woman and her partner also may influence when they resume sexual activity.

> **How does sexual activity change in the months following childbirth?**

A longitudinal study of the adjustment of couples to the birth of a child collected data from 570 women (and 550 partners) four times: during the second trimester of pregnancy, and at one, four, and twelve months postpartum (Hyde et al., 1996). Data on the sexual relationship are displayed in Table 2. In the month following

> **Postpartum depression:** Mild to moderate depression in women following the birth of a baby.

Table 2 Sexual Behaviors within the Previous Month, Reported by Mothers during Pregnancy and the Year Postpartum

Behavior	Pregnancy 2nd Trimester	Postpartum 1 month	4 months	12 months
Intercourse	89%	17%	89%	92%
Mean frequency of intercourse/month	4.97	0.42	5.27	5.1
Fellatio	43%	34%	48%	47%
Cunnilingus	30%	8%	44%	49%
Satisfaction with sexual relationship*	3.76	3.31	3.36	3.53

*Satisfaction with the relationship was rated on a scale from 1 (very dissatisfied) to 5 (very satisfied).

Source: Hyde et al., 1996, pp. 143–151.

birth, only 17 percent resumed intercourse; by the fourth month, nine out of ten couples had, the same percentage as reported intercourse during the second trimester. Reports of cunnilingus showed a similar pattern, while reports of fellatio did not indicate a marked decline. Note that although sexual behavior was much less frequent in the month following birth, satisfaction with the sexual relationship remained about the same. A major influence on when the couple resumed intercourse was whether the mother was breast-feeding. At both one month and four months after birth, breast-feeding women reported significantly less sexual activity and lower sexual satisfaction. One reason is that lactation suppresses estrogen production, which in turn results in decreased vaginal lubrication; this makes intercourse uncomfortable. This problem can be resolved by the use of vaginal lubricants.

Breast-Feeding

Biological Mechanisms

Two hormones, both secreted by the pituitary, are involved in lactation (milk production). One, *prolactin,* stimulates the breasts to produce milk. Prolactin is produced fairly constantly for whatever length of time the woman breast-feeds. The other hormone, *oxytocin,* stimulates the breasts to eject milk. Oxytocin is produced reflexively by the pituitary in response to the infant's sucking of the breast. Thus sucking stimulates nerve cells in the nipple; this nerve signal is transmitted to the brain, which then relays the message to the pituitary, which sends out the messenger oxytocin, which stimulates the breasts to eject milk. Research with animal models indicates that oxytocin promotes "fearless mothering" (Cohen et al., 2018). That is, oxytocin promotes maternal behavior and reduces anxiety, so, if necessary, a mother will be fearless in defending her young.

Actual milk is not produced for several days after delivery. For the first few days, the breast secretes colostrum, discussed earlier, which is high in protein and gives the baby a temporary immunity to infectious diseases. Two or three days after delivery, true lactation begins; this may be accompanied by discomfort for a day or so because the breasts are swollen and congested.

It is also important to note that, much as in pregnancy, substances ingested by the mother may be transmitted through the milk to the infant. The nursing mother thus needs to be cautious about using alcohol and other substances.

Physical and Mental Health

The National Institutes of Health strongly encourages mothers to breast-feed, because breast milk is the ideal food for a baby and has even been termed the "ultimate health food." It provides the baby with the right mixture of nutrients, it contains antibodies that protect the infant from some infections (Fewtrell et al., 2011), and it contains good microbes that stimulate a healthy microbiome in the baby's gut (Toscano et al., 2017). Breast-feeding is associated with a reduced risk of obesity at ages 5 and 6 (von Kries et al., 1999). Thus there is little question that it is superior to cow's milk and commercial formulas. The American Academy of Pediatrics (2012) agrees. It recommends exclusive breast-feeding for the first six months, followed by breast-feeding plus the introduction of food in the next six months (Figure 12). It is also true that, for a variety of reasons, some women are unable to breast-feed, and their babies can thrive too.

In 2011, 81 percent of non-Hispanic White babies and 61 percent of non-Hispanic Black babies were ever breast-fed. Among those, 52 percent of White mothers and 35 percent of Black mothers continued breast-feeding until at least six months (CDC, 2014d). A systematic review of programs designed to promote breast-feeding concluded

Figure 12   Breast-feeding has a number of psychological and physical health benefits.

©Nancy Ney/Getty Images

that educational sessions that review benefits, lactation, common problems and solutions, and provide skills training as well as in-person or telephone support programs improve rates of the initiation and maintenance of breast-feeding at six months (Guise et al., 2003). A CDC analysis found that practices such as these that support breast-feeding were less available in maternity facilities in areas where more than 12 percent of the population is Black (CDC, 2014c).

From the mother's point of view, breast-feeding has several advantages. These include a quicker shrinking of the uterus to its normal size and a faster loss of the weight gained during pregnancy. Breast-feeding reduces the likelihood of pregnancy by inhibiting ovulation. Full breast-feeding, short intervals between feedings, night feeds, and the absence of supplemental feeding are all associated with greater delay in ovulation (Hatcher et al., 2011). However, it is important to note that a woman can become pregnant again before she has a period; recall from the chapter "Sex Hormones, Sexual Differentiation, and the Menstrual Cycle" that ovulation precedes menstruation. Research indicates that breast-feeding reduces negative moods, and breast-feeding mothers report having less perceived stress (Mezzacappa & Katkin, 2002). Breast-feeding is also associated with reduced risk of breast cancer; the relative risk decreases by 4.3 percent for every 12 months of breast-feeding (Collaborative Group, 2002).

Some women report sexual arousal during breast-feeding, and a few even report having orgasms. Unfortunately, this sometimes produces anxiety in the mother, leading her to discontinue breast-feeding. However, there is nothing "wrong" with this arousal, which appears to stem from activation of hormonal mechanisms. Clearly, from an adaptive point of view, if breast-feeding is important to the infant's survival, it would be wise for nature to design the process so that it is rewarding to the mother.

A few women are physically unable to breast-feed, and some others feel psychologically uncomfortable with the idea. And breast-feeding can be very inconvenient for the woman who works outside the home.

Problem Pregnancies

Ectopic Pregnancy

An **ectopic pregnancy** (misplaced pregnancy) occurs when the fertilized egg implants somewhere other than the uterus. Most commonly, ectopic pregnancies occur when the egg implants in the fallopian tube (tubal pregnancy). In rare cases, implantation may also occur in the abdominal cavity, the ovary, or the cervix.

A tubal pregnancy may occur if, for one reason or another, the egg is prevented from moving down the tube to the uterus, as when the tubes are obstructed as a result of a sexually transmitted infection. Early in a tubal pregnancy, the fertilized egg implants in the tube and begins development, forming a placenta and producing the normal hormones

> **Ectopic pregnancy:** A pregnancy in which the fertilized egg implants somewhere other than the uterus.

of pregnancy. The woman may experience the early symptoms of pregnancy, such as nausea and amenorrhea, and think she is pregnant; or she may experience some bleeding, which she mistakes for a period, and think that she is not pregnant. It is therefore quite difficult to diagnose a tubal pregnancy early.

A tubal pregnancy may end in one of two ways. The embryo may spontaneously abort and be released into the abdominal cavity, or the embryo and placenta may continue to expand, stretching the tube until it ruptures. Symptoms of a rupture include sharp abdominal pain or cramping, dull abdominal pain and possibly pain in the shoulder, and vaginal bleeding. Meanwhile, hemorrhaging is occurring, and the woman may go into shock and, possibly, die. It is extremely important for a woman displaying these symptoms to see a doctor quickly.

The rate of ectopic pregnancy increased 600 percent in the United States from 1980 to 2004, to a rate of approximately 2 percent of all pregnancies (Dialani & Levine, 2004). Part of the increase is due to improved diagnostic techniques, but most of the increase is real. Similar increases have been observed in a number of western European nations. It is thought that these changes are due to (1) increased rates of sexually transmitted infections (STIs), some of which lead to blocking of the fallopian tubes; and (2) increased use of contraceptives such as the IUD and progestin-only methods that prevent implantation in the uterus but do not necessarily prevent conception. A comparison of women whose first pregnancies were ectopic, miscarried, or aborted found that women whose first pregnancy is ectopic are much more likely to have repeat ectopic pregnancies and less likely to later deliver a baby at term (Karhus et al., 2013). These women should seek specialized reproductive health care after the first experience.

Pseudocyesis (False Pregnancy)

In **pseudocyesis,** or *false pregnancy,* the woman believes that she is pregnant and shows the signs and symptoms of pregnancy without really being pregnant. She may stop menstruating and may have morning sickness. She may begin gaining weight, and her abdomen may bulge. The condition may persist for several months before it goes away, either spontaneously or as a result of psychotherapy. In rare cases it persists until the woman goes into labor and delivers nothing but air and fluid.

Pregnancy-Induced Hypertension

Pseudocyesis: False pregnancy, in which the woman displays the signs of pregnancy but is not pregnant.
Preeclampsia: A serious disease of pregnancy, marked by high blood pressure, severe edema, and proteinuria.

Pregnancy may cause a woman's blood pressure to rise to an abnormal level. *Pregnancy-induced hypertension* includes three increasingly serious conditions: (1) hypertension, (2) preeclampsia, and (3) eclampsia. Hypertension refers to elevated blood pressure alone. **Preeclampsia** refers to elevated blood pressure accompanied by generalized edema (fluid retention and swelling) and proteinuria (protein in the urine). The combination of hypertension and proteinuria is associated with an increased risk of fetal death. In *eclampsia,* the woman has convulsions, may go into a coma, and may die (Cunningham et al., 1993).

Preeclampsia usually does not appear until after week 20 of pregnancy. It is especially common among teenagers. The risk of preeclampsia rises steadily as prepregnancy body mass index increases. For overweight women, a reduction in prepregnancy weight may reduce their risk (Bodnar et al., 2004). The possibility of preeclampsia emphasizes the need for proper medical care before and during pregnancy. Hypertension and preeclampsia can be managed well during their early stages. Most maternal deaths occur among women who do not receive prenatal medical care.

Viral Infection during Pregnancy

Certain viruses may cross the placental barrier from the woman to the fetus and cause harm, particularly if the illness occurs during the first trimester of pregnancy. The best-known example is rubella, or German measles. If a woman gets German measles during the first month of pregnancy, there is a 50 percent chance that the infant will be born deaf or with an intellectual disability or with cataracts or congenital heart defects. The risk declines after the first month, so that by the third month of pregnancy the chance of abnormalities is only about 10 percent. While most women have an immunity to rubella because they had it when they were children, a woman who suspects that she is not immune can receive a vaccination that will give her immunity; she should do this well before she becomes pregnant.

Herpes simplex is also teratogenic. Symptoms of herpes simplex are usually mild: cold sores or fever blisters around the mouth. Genital herpes (see the chapter "Sexually Transmitted Infections") is a form of herpes simplex in which sores may appear in the genital region. Usually the infant contracts the disease by direct contact with the sore; delivery by cesarean section can prevent this. Women with genital herpes also have a higher risk of aborting spontaneously.

Birth Defects

As has been noted, a number of factors, such as substances taken during pregnancy and illness during pregnancy, may cause defects in the fetus. Other causes include genetic defects (e.g., phenylketonuria, PKU, which causes intellectual disability) and chromosomal defects (e.g., Down syndrome, which causes intellectual disability).

Of all babies born in the United States, 2 to 3 percent have a significant birth defect. About one-fourth of miscarried fetuses are malformed. The cause of more than half of these defects is unknown (O'Shea, 1995).

In most cases, families have simply had to learn, as best they could, to live with a child who had a birth defect. Now, however, amniocentesis, chorionic villus sampling (explained below), and genetic counseling are available to help prevent some of the sorrow, provided that abortion is ethically acceptable to the parents.

Amniocentesis involves inserting a fine tube through the pregnant woman's abdomen and removing some amniotic fluid, including cells sloughed off by the fetus, for analysis. The technique is capable of providing an early diagnosis of most chromosomal abnormalities, some genetically produced biochemical disorders, and sex-linked diseases carried by females but affecting males (hemophilia and muscular dystrophy), although it cannot detect all defects. If a defect is discovered, the woman may then decide to terminate the pregnancy with an abortion.

Amniocentesis should be performed between weeks 13 and 16 of pregnancy. This timing is important for two reasons. First, if a defect is discovered and an abortion is to be performed, it should be done as early as possible (see the chapter "Contraception and Abortion"). Second, there is a 1 percent chance that the amniocentesis itself will cause the woman to miscarry (Enzensberger et al., 2012), and the risk becomes greater as the pregnancy progresses.

Because amniocentesis itself involves some risk, it is generally thought (although the matter is controversial) that it should be performed only on women who have a high risk of bearing a child with a birth defect. A woman is in this category if (1) she has already had one child with a genetic defect; (2) she believes that she is a carrier of a genetic defect, which can usually be established through genetic counseling; and (3) she is over 35, in which case she has an increased chance of bearing a child with a chromosomal abnormality.

Chorionic villus sampling (CVS) is an alternative to amniocentesis for prenatal diagnosis of genetic defects. A major problem with amniocentesis is that it cannot be done until the second trimester of pregnancy; if genetic defects are discovered, there may have to be a late abortion. Chorionic villus sampling, in contrast, can be done in the first trimester of pregnancy, usually around 9 to 11 weeks' postconception. Chorionic villus sampling can be performed in one of two ways: transcervically, in which a catheter is inserted into the uterus through the cervix as shown in Figure 13, and transabdominally, in which a needle (guided by ultrasound) is inserted through the abdomen. In either case a sample of cells is taken from the chorionic villi (the chorion is the outermost membrane surrounding the fetus, the amnion, and the amniotic fluid), and these cells are analyzed for evidence of genetic defects. Studies indicate that CVS is as accurate as amniocentesis. Like amniocentesis, it carries with it a

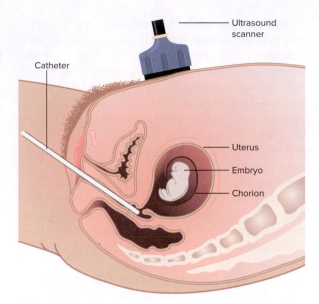

Figure 13 Chorionic villus sampling (CVS) and amniocentesis are both available for prenatal diagnosis of genetic defects. CVS (shown here) detects chromosomal abnormalities and sex-linked diseases.

slight risk of fetal loss (due, for example, to miscarriage). For amniocentesis, the fetal loss rate is around 1 percent; for transcervical CVS it is higher, while for transabdominal the risk is about the same as amniocentesis (Alfirevic, et al., 2009).

Rh Incompatibility

The Rh factor is a substance in the blood; if it is present, the person is said to be Rh positive (Rh+); if it is absent, the person is said to be Rh negative (Rh−). The Rh factor is genetically transmitted, with Rh+ being dominant over Rh−.

The presence or absence of the Rh factor does not constitute a health problem except when an Rh− person receives a blood transfusion or when an Rh− woman is pregnant with an Rh+ fetus (which can happen only if the father is Rh+). A blood test is done routinely early in pregnancy to determine whether a woman is Rh−. Fortunately, about 85 percent of Whites and 93 percent of Blacks are Rh+; thus the problems associated with being Rh− are not very common.

If some Rh+ blood gets into Rh− blood, the Rh− blood forms antibodies as a reaction against the Rh factor in the invading blood. Typically, as has been noted, there is little interchange between the woman's blood and

Amniocentesis (am-nee-oh-sen-TEE-sus): A test done to determine whether a fetus has birth defects; done by inserting a fine tube into the woman's abdomen in order to obtain a sample of amniotic fluid.
Chorionic villus sampling (CVS): A technique for prenatal diagnosis of birth defects, involving taking a sample of cells from the chorionic villus and analyzing them.

the fetus's blood; the placenta keeps them separate. However, during childbirth there can be mixing of the two. Thus during birth, the blood of an Rh+ baby causes the formation of antibodies in an Rh– woman's blood. During the next pregnancy, some of the woman's blood enters the fetus and the antibodies attack the fetus's red cells. The baby may be stillborn, severely anemic, or have an intellectual disability. Thus there is little risk for an Rh– woman with the first pregnancy because antibodies have not yet formed; however, later pregnancies can be dangerous.

Fortunately, techniques for dealing with this situation have been developed. An injection of a substance called *Rhogam* prevents the woman's blood from producing antibodies. If necessary, the fetus or newborn infant may get a transfusion.

Miscarriage (Spontaneous Abortion)

Miscarriage, or *spontaneous abortion,* occurs when a pregnancy terminates through natural causes, before the conceptus is viable (capable of surviving on its own). It is not to be confused with *induced abortion,* in which a pregnancy is terminated by mechanical or medicinal means (what is commonly called *abortion*—see the chapter "Contraception and Abortion"), or with *prematurity,* in which the pregnancy terminates early, but after the infant is viable.

Many people assume that most conceptions lead to a live birth. But, in fact, only a minority do. About 50 percent of preclinical (not medically diagnosed) pregnancies are terminated by an early miscarriage. Very early spontaneous abortions are usually not detected. The woman may not know she is pregnant, and she may mistake the products of the miscarriage for a menstrual period. Twenty to 25 percent of clinically diagnosed pregnancies are lost (Kwak-kim et al., 2013). Most spontaneous abortions—80 percent—occur during the first trimester of pregnancy.

Most spontaneous abortions occur because the conceptus is defective. Studies of spontaneously aborted fetuses indicate that 61 percent showed abnormalities that were incompatible with life; for example, many had gross chromosomal abnormalities (Ljunger et al., 2005). Thus, contrary to popular belief, psychological and physical traumas are not common causes of miscarriage. In fact, spontaneous abortions seem to be functional in that they naturally eliminate many defective fetuses. However, research indicates that maternal obesity, BMI greater than 30, is associated with spontaneous abortion, and with infant death in the year following birth (Tennant et al., 2011).

Preterm Birth

A major complication during the third trimester of pregnancy is premature labor and delivery of the fetus. When delivery occurs prior to 37 weeks' gestation, it is considered *preterm.* Because the date of conception cannot always be accurately determined, preterm birth (prematurity) may be defined in terms of the birth weight of the infant; an infant weighing less than 2,500 grams (5½ pounds) is considered to be in the low-birth-weight category. The National Center for Health Statistics reports that 11.4 percent of all births in the United States in 2013 were preterm (Martin et al., 2014).

Preterm birth is a cause for concern because a premature infant is much less likely to survive than a full-term infant. It is estimated that more than half of the deaths of newborn babies in the United States are due to preterm birth. Preterm infants are particularly susceptible to respiratory infections and must receive expert care. Advances in medical techniques have considerably improved survival rates for preterm infants. Currently, 99 percent of infants weighing 2,500 grams at birth survive, as do 64 percent of those weighing 1,000 grams (Cunningham et al., 1993). However, prematurity may cause damage to an infant who survives. Disability occurs in 60 percent of survivors born at 26 weeks and 30 percent of those born at 31 weeks (Swamy et al., 2008).

Maternal physical factors such as poor health, poor nutrition, obesity, heavy smoking, cocaine use, and genital or systemic infections are associated with prematurity. Pregnancy-induced hypertension can also lead to preterm birth. Young teenage mothers, whose bodies are not yet ready to bear children, are also very susceptible to premature labor and delivery. Maternal stress during pregnancy contributes to prematurity (Coussons-Read, 2012). Stress affects endocrine, immune, and inflammatory processes, and these can affect the developing fetus. Stress due to major life changes—in relationships, job status, or housing—or to anxiety related to the pregnancy—over fetal health, the ability to be a good parent, or an abusive relationship—can all adversely affect fetal development.

Infertility

Infertility refers to a woman's inability to conceive and give birth to a living child, or a man's inability to impregnate a woman. At least 12 percent of women 15 to 44 years old in the United States have received infertility services at least once (Chandra et al., 2005). When fertile couples are purposely attempting to conceive a child, about 20 percent succeed within the first menstrual cycle, and about 70 percent succeed within the first six cycles (Hatcher et al., 2004). A couple is considered infertile if they have not conceived after one year of frequent, unprotected intercourse, or after six months if the woman is over 35. The term *sterile* refers to an individual who has an absolute factor preventing conception.

Miscarriage: The termination of a pregnancy before the fetus is viable, as a result of natural causes (not medical intervention; also called *spontaneous abortion*).

Infertility: A woman's inability to conceive and give birth to a living child, or a man's inability to impregnate a woman.

Causes of Infertility

Among couples with an identifiable cause, in about 35 percent, male factors are responsible; female factors are responsible in an additional 35 percent. In the remaining 30 percent, both have problems (Hammoud et al., 2012).

Causes in Women

The most common cause of infertility in women is pelvic inflammatory disease (PID) caused by a sexually transmitted infection, especially gonorrhea or chlamydia. Problems with ovulation may cause 18 to 30 percent of cases. Ovulatory disorders are associated with poor diet, large BMI, and low activity levels (Chavarro et al., 2007). Other causes include blockage of the fallopian tubes, and "hostile mucus," meaning cervical mucus that blocks the passage of sperm. Less common causes include, eating disorders, exposure to toxic chemicals such as lead or pesticides, smoking, and use of alcohol, narcotics, or barbiturates. Age may also be a factor; fertility declines in women after 35 years of age, the decline being especially sharp after age 40.

Causes in Men

The most common cause of infertility in men is infections in the reproductive system caused by sexually transmitted diseases. Another cause is low sperm count (often due to varicoceles—varicose veins in the testes). Couples concerned about low sperm count may decide to abstain from vaginal intercourse in the hope of increasing the count, but research indicates this does not work. In men with low sperm counts, the sperm become less mobile and begin to show signs of becoming stale after only 24 hours of abstinence (Levitas et al., 2003). Another cause is low motility of the sperm, which means the sperm are not good swimmers.

What reproductive problem can result from untreated STIs?

Cigarette smoking has been linked to reduced motility, decreased sperm concentration, and levels of DNA damage in sperm (Pasqualotto et al., 2008). Less common causes include exposure to toxic agents such as lead, alcohol and marijuana use, and use of some prescription drugs. Obesity in men is associated with abnormalities in the sperm (Practice Committee, 2008). Research has shown that exposure to environmental estrogens (endocrine disrupters) causes sperm to mature too fast, reducing their fertilizing capacity (Adeoya-Osiguwa et al., 2003). Exposure to environmental estrogens comes through contact with substances such as beer and pesticides. Exposure to bisphenol A (BPA) and phthalates, chemicals found in most everyday products containing plastics, is associated with a 20 percent decline in male fertility (Buck Louis et al., 2014).

Research also reports that the quality of male semen declines with age. As men age, the volume of the semen and the number and motility of the sperm decline (Eskenazi et al., 2003). Also, the rate of sperm with various genomic abnormalities increases with age (Wyrobek et al., 2006).

Combined Factors

In some situations a combination of factors in both the man and the woman causes the infertility. One such factor is an immunologic response. The woman may have an allergic reaction to the man's sperm, causing her to produce antibodies that destroy or damage the sperm. Immune reactions occur in response to novel cells entering the body; if the body has been exposed to the cells frequently in the past, the reaction is less likely. Frequent prior exposure of a woman to a specific man's semen would reduce the likelihood of rejecting his sperm, so frequent vaginal intercourse prior to the attempt to get pregnant may increase the chances of a successful pregnancy (Robertson & Sharkey, 2001).

Sperm have a chemical sensor that causes them to swim toward the egg, attracted by a chemical on the surface of the egg (Spehr et al., 2003). Researchers have already identified one chemical that disrupts this process by shutting down the receptor. This chemical, or chemicals, that influence the surface of the egg can cause infertility. Finally, a couple may also simply lack knowledge; for instance, they may not know how to time intercourse correctly so that conception may take place. A survey of 1,000 women ages 18 to 44 found that 40 percent did not understand the ovulatory cycle (Lundsberg et al., 2014).

Psychological Aspects of Infertility

It is important to recognize the psychological stress to which an infertile couple may be subjected. Because the male role is defined partly in our society by the ability to father children, the man may feel that his masculinity or virility is in question. Similarly, the female role is defined largely by the ability to bear children and be a mother, so the woman may feel inadequate. Historically, in most cultures fertility has been encouraged and, indeed, demanded; hence, pressures on infertile couples may be high, leading to more psychological stress. As emphasis on population control increases in our society, and as childlessness[3] becomes an acceptable and more recognized option, the stress on infertile couples may lessen.

At the same time, people need social support in coping with these stresses. A study of couples entering treatment for infertility found that 11.6 percent of the women

---

[3]Semantics can make a big difference here. Many couples who choose not to have children prefer to call themselves *child-free* rather than *childless*.

and 4.3 percent of the men reported severe depressive symptoms (Peterson et al., 2014).

Infertility does not significantly reduce marital satisfaction, but it does cause conflict (Abbey et al., 1992). It does affect the couple's sexual relationship; it reduces spontaneity (especially for couples in treatment programs that include scheduled intercourse) and is associated with lower sexual satisfaction (Zoldbrod, 1993).

Treatment of Infertility

There are physicians and clinics that specialize in the evaluation and treatment of infertility. An infertility evaluation should include an assessment of the couple's knowledge of sexual behavior and conception, and lifestyle factors such as regular drug use. Infertility caused by such factors can be easily treated.

If the infertility problem stems from the woman not ovulating, the treatment may involve the so-called fertility drugs. The drug of first choice is clomiphene (Clomid). It stimulates the pituitary to produce LH and FSH, thus inducing ovulation. The treatment produces a pregnancy in about half the women who are given it. Multiple births occur about 8 percent of the time with Clomid, compared with 1.2 percent with natural pregnancies. If treatment with Clomid is not successful, a second possibility is injections with HMG (human menopausal gonadotropin).

If the infertility is caused by blocked fallopian tubes, delicate microsurgery can sometimes be effective in removing the blockage. Endometriosis and endometrial adhesions can also be successfully treated surgically.

If the infertility is caused by varicoceles in the testes, the condition can usually be treated successfully by a surgical procedure known as varicocelectomy.

Finally, a number of assisted reproductive technologies, such as in vitro fertilization, are now available for those with fertility problems, as discussed in the next section.

A Canadian study is helpful in putting issues of the treatment of infertility into perspective. Among infertile couples seeking treatment, 65 percent subsequently achieved a pregnancy with *no treatment* (Rousseau et al., 1983). For some couples, conception just takes a bit longer. Thus the risks associated with treatments need to be weighed against the possibility that a pregnancy can be achieved without treatment.

Assisted Reproductive Technologies

Artificial insemination: A procedure in which sperm are placed into the female reproductive system by means other than sexual intercourse.

Reproductive technologies offer many ways to conceive and birth babies besides sexual intercourse and pregnancy. These are collectively referred to as assisted reproductive technologies (ART). Overall, ART accounts for 2 percent of births in the United States, including 10 percent of births to women between the ages of 40 and 44 (Levine et al., 2017).

Artificial Insemination

Artificial insemination involves artificially placing semen in the vagina or uterus or fallopian tubes to produce a pregnancy; thus it is a means of accomplishing reproduction without having sexual intercourse. Artificial insemination in animals was first done in 1776. In 1949, when British scientists successfully froze sperm without any apparent damage to them, a new era of reproductive technology for animals began. Today cattle are routinely bred by artificial insemination.

In humans there are two kinds of artificial insemination: artificial insemination by the husband (AIH) and artificial insemination by a donor (AID). AIH can be used when the husband has a low sperm count. Several samples of his semen are collected and pooled to make one sample with a higher count. This sample is then placed in the woman's vagina or fallopian tube at the time of ovulation. AID is used when the husband is sterile, or when a male partner is not available. A donor provides semen to impregnate the woman. Estimates are that between 4,000 and 5,000 babies are born each year in the United States as a result of AID.

Sperm Banks

Because it is possible to freeze sperm, it is possible to store it, which is just what some people are doing: using frozen human *sperm banks.* The sperm banks open up many new reproductive choices. For example, suppose that a couple decide, after having had two children, that they want a permanent method of contraception. The husband then has a vasectomy. Two years after he has the vasectomy, however, one of their children dies, and they very much want to have another baby. If the man has stored semen in a sperm bank, they can.

Young men can use sperm banks to store sperm before they undergo radiation therapy for cancer. They can later father children without fearing that they will transmit damaged chromosomes (as a result of the radiation) to their offspring.

Since the mid-1990s, sperm banks have gone online, making their services available to millions of people around the world (Springen & Noonan, 2002). There are an estimated 40 sperm banks in the United States, and the larger ones have developed websites. These sites allow prospective parents to browse through information about each potential donor, enabling them to select not only on the basis of height, weight, and eye and hair color but also education and family medical history. As recipients demand more information about prospective donors, it becomes harder to maintain the donor's anonymity. Some

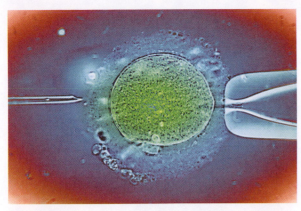

(a)

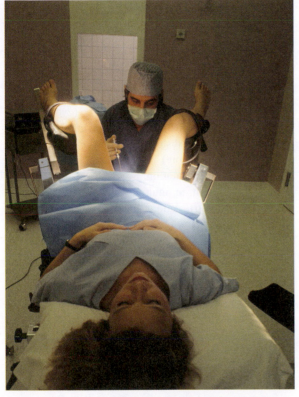

(b)

Figure 14   New reproductive technologies. (*a*) Intra-cytoplasmic sperm injection, or ICSI. (*b*) Vicken Sahakian, MD, medical director of a fertility center, collects eggs from Deborah, 38. She and her husband, Eric, came in for in vitro fertilization. Out of 13 eggs produced by her, 5 became fertilized and were reintroduced into Deborah.

(a) ©ISM/Phototake; (b) ©Eric Préau/Sygma via Getty Images

donors of eggs or sperm advertise directly on the Internet; while the cost may be lower than the costs associated with clinic services, as is often true on the Internet, there is no guarantee that the donor has given accurate information.

Test-Tube Babies

It is possible for scientists to make sperm and egg unite outside the human body (in a "test tube"). The scientific term for this procedure is **in vitro fertilization,** or **IVF** (*in vitro* is Latin for "in glass"). The fertilized egg or embryo can then be implanted in the uterus of a woman and carried to term (see Figure 14). This technique can be of great benefit to couples who are infertile because the woman's fallopian tubes are blocked.

A milestone was reached with the birth of Louise Brown, the first test-tube baby, in England on July 25, 1978. Obstetrician Patrick Steptoe and physiologist Robert Edwards had fertilized the mother's egg with her husband's sperm in a laboratory dish and implanted the embryo in the mother's uterus. The pregnancy went smoothly, and Louise was born healthy and normal. Edwards was awarded the 2010 Nobel Prize in Physiology for Medicine for developing the technique (Abbott, 2010).

According to data collected by the Centers for Disease Control and Prevention, 60 percent of the ART procedures performed in the United States in 2010 were IVF using freshly fertilized embryos from the patients' eggs (CDC, 2011a). The CDC (2011a) reports that in 2010, 56 percent of transfer of fresh embryos and 35 percent of the transfer of frozen embryos resulted in a live birth. The procedure is expensive, around $12,400 per attempt, not counting preliminary procedures. It is estimated that the average IVF baby costs between $10,000 and $18,000 to produce.

There is evidence that babies born as a result of IVF are more likely to be low in birth weight and have congenital abnormalities. In one study, mothers were interviewed by telephone six weeks to two years after giving birth. Among singleton births, babies conceived by ART were two to four times more likely to have heart defects, cleft lip, and esophageal and anorectal defects (Reefhuis et al., 2009). Using Australian data, researchers assessed the occurrence of nine specific birth defects for five years following 308,974 births. The rate of defects was 8.3 for babies conceived via ART, versus 5.8 for unassisted conceptions (Davies et al., 2012). It is not clear whether the increased risk is due to the procedure, or to related factors—for example, mothers are typically older (Kovacs, 2002a).

Intra-cytoplasmic sperm injection (ICSI) is an improved kind of in vitro fertilization in which a single sperm is injected directly into the cytoplasm of the egg (Figure 16). This procedure improves the chances of successful fertilization.

It is also possible to freeze eggs that have been fertilized in vitro, resulting in frozen embryos. Research finds that babies born after procedures using thawed embryos were less likely to be low birth weight but more likely

> **In vitro fertilization (IVF):** A procedure in which an egg is fertilized by sperm in a laboratory dish.
> **ICSI (Intra-cytoplasmic sperm injection):** A type of assisted reproductive technology in which one sperm is injected directly into the cytoplasm of the egg to accomplish a fertilization outside the body.

Figure 15   The latest medical technique in assisted reproduction is uterus transplants. The child shown here was born in 2016 in Sweden, to his mother, who had received a uterus transplant. Women may lack a uterus for any of several reasons. In rare cases, girls are born without one. In other cases, women have had to have their uterus removed for reasons such as cancer.

©Niklas Larsson/AP Images

Figure 16   Multiple births, such as these triplets, are a common consequence of ART, resulting from implanting multiple fertilized eggs. Many specialists now agree that no more than two embryos should be implanted.

©Photos by Jeremy Tan/Getty Images

to be preterm (Wright et al., 2007). The legal and moral status of the frozen embryo is a difficult question, and some worry about *embryo wastage*, that is, embryos that are never used and therefore are disposed of.

Embryo Transfer

With **embryo transfer,** a fertilized, developing egg (embryo) is transferred from the uterus of one woman to the uterus of another woman. This technique may enable a woman who can conceive but who always miscarries early in the pregnancy to transfer her embryo to another woman who serves as the *surrogate mother*—that is, the person who provides the uterus in which the fetus grows (and whom the media, somewhat callously, have called a "rent-a-womb"). The embryo transfer procedure also essentially can serve as the opposite of artificial insemination. That is, if a woman produces no viable eggs, her husband's sperm can be used to artificially inseminate another woman (who donates her egg), and the fertilized egg is then transferred from the donor to the mother.

GIFT

With **GIFT** (gamete intrafallopian transfer), sperm and eggs (gametes) are collected and then inserted together into the fallopian tube, where natural fertilization can take place, followed by natural implantation.

> **Embryo transfer:** A procedure in which an embryo is transferred from the uterus of one woman into the uterus of another.
> **GIFT:** Gamete intrafallopian transfer, a procedure in which sperm and eggs are collected and then inserted together into the fallopian tube.
> **ZIFT:** Zygote intrafallopian transfer, an assisted reproductive technology in which the egg is fertilized by sperm in the laboratory, and then the developing fertilized egg (zygote) is placed in the fallopian tube.

Yet another improvement is **ZIFT** (zygote intrafallopian transfer), which involves fertilizing the egg with sperm in a laboratory dish and then placing the developing fertilized egg (zygote) into the fallopian tube, again allowing natural implantation.

ART may result in multiple births: twins, triplets, or more (Figure 16). Among infants conceived through ART, 35 percent are multiple births, compared with 3 percent among all infants (Sunderam et al., 2018). Multiple-birth infants resulting from ART are more likely to be preterm and low birth weight, which involve substantial health risks. Scandalous cases have occurred, such as the birth of octuplets to Nadya Suleman (the Octomom) in 2008. In the wake of these cases, some professional societies have issued guidelines for the number of embryos to transfer. The number depends on the age of the mother and other factors. One recommendation is to transfer only one embryo in women under 35 and no more than four in women over 39 (Joint SOGC-CFAS Guidelines, 2008, 2010).

There is controversy over whether ART should be available to single men and women, unmarried couples, and same-gender couples. The Ethics Committee of the American Society for Reproductive Medicine has issued a statement, concluding "we find no sound ethical basis for licensed professionals to deny reproductive services to unmarried or gay and lesbian persons" (2013, p. 1526). In 2015, the statement was expanded to include provision of services to transgender persons.

Gender Selection

Some couples want to choose whether to have a boy or a girl. Such a technology would be useful to parents who have six girls and really want a boy, or for people who would like to have two children, one of each gender. Problems might arise, though. Some scientists fear that the result of being able to choose gender would be a great imbalance in our population, with many more males than females, because many couples prefer their first child to be a boy.

There is a good deal of "conventional wisdom" about various home methods of increasing the likelihood that a fetus will be male or female. One technique is timing intercourse in relation to ovulation, based on the belief that sperm carrying a Y chromosome swim faster; thus intercourse at the time of ovulation should increase the chances of a male, whereas intercourse at a time before and remote from ovulation should favor the slow but hardy sperm carrying X chromosomes, resulting in a female. Several studies have tried to test these ideas, relying on indirect measures of time of ovulation (cervical mucus changes, BBT); they suggest that a female is more likely when intercourse coincides with ovulation. Thus conventional wisdom is wrong. Studies have also investigated the effect of douching; conventional wisdom has it that douching with vinegar will change the vaginal pH, increasing the chances of a boy. Neither of these, or other, "natural" methods will reliably affect the offspring's gender (Kovacs, 2002b).

As usual, entrepreneurs are taking advantage of people's desire to pick the baby's sex and selling kits that promise results. Some of the kits capitalize on the natural methods, providing the purchaser with thermometers, douching solutions, and other paraphernalia. At least one company is selling kits via the Internet. Again, there is no evidence that these kits will produce the expected result. *Caveat emptor* (buyer beware)!

Several scientific laboratory procedures can be used to separate sperm containing X vs. Y chromosomes. Older techniques involved separation based on swimming speed or immunologic characteristics; these work with 70 to 80 percent accuracy. The latest sorting technique, the Micro-Sort method, uses the fluorescence-activated sorter, which can select sperm with an X chromosome with 90 percent accuracy; this technique greatly reduces sperm count and requires ART. There is little data on the long-term outcomes of using this procedure (Kovacs, 2002b). Numerous infertility clinics advertise Micro-Sort; combined with IVF, success rates of up to 99 percent are claimed.

The most reliable method of gender selection is preimplantation genetic diagnosis (PGD). This technique involves the removal of eggs from the woman and

fertilizing them via IVF. After three days, a cell is taken from each embryo, and its chromosomal makeup is determined. An embryo of the preferred type would then be implanted via ART. This method is very invasive of the woman's body and very expensive. The likelihood that the implanted egg would result in the live birth of a healthy infant is the same as for other ART pregnancies. PGD is banned in Britain and Canada and is controversial in the United States (Check, 2005).

The technologies discussed here, especially GIFT and ZIFT, require expert practitioners and appropriate facilities. Consequently, they are very expensive. For these and other reasons, these procedures raise complex legal questions (discussed in the chapter "Sex and the Law") and ethical concerns (discussed in the chapter "Ethics, Religion, and Sexuality").

Prenatal Genetic Diagnosis

Prenatal genetic diagnosis, determining a fetus's genotype at a specific locus, has been done on a small scale for decades. In the past, amniocentesis and CVS, discussed earlier, have been the primary procedures. Both are invasive, carry a slight risk of harm, and allow only limited analysis of the cells retrieved. As a result, less than 2 percent of pregnant women undergo these tests, primarily to detect a marker for Down syndrome. In the near future, noninvasive prenatal diagnosis (NIPD) may become a reality, allowing a sample of maternal blood to be tested for hundreds of fetal traits.

During pregnancy, some fetal cells pass through the placenta into the mother's bloodstream (Greely, 2011), including cells containing fetal DNA. If samples of fetal DNA can be isolated in the mother's blood, cheap and sensitive genetic sequencing techniques can be used to analyze the fetal genome. This type of analysis is currently used to determine the Rh type of the fetus (see earlier discussion). Tests are now feasible for many single-gene diseases, such as cystic fibrosis, sickle cell anemia, and Tay-Sachs disease. The same techniques could be used to identify fetal sex, not to mention hair and eye color.

Two factors will determine how quickly NIPD becomes readily available—its accuracy as an indicator of the specific disease or trait, and its cost. When and if it becomes available, NIPD will be controversial, raising serious religious, social, and political issues. One fundamental issue will be whether it should be used to determine which fetuses to abort.

Critical THINK *ing Skill*
Evaluating alternatives in making a health care decision

One of our goals in writing this book is to enable you to make the best decisions about your health care. To do that, you need to (1) know the alternatives, (2) collect valid information about the pros and cons of each alternative, and (3) weigh the alternatives with respect to your circumstances.

A very important decision facing a pregnant woman is where to have her baby. In this chapter we discussed two alternatives: hospital birth and home birth. Let's collect information about them. The major benefit of hospital birth is proximity to sophisticated equipment and medical treatment. A secondary benefit is the ability to rely on (one hopes) knowledgeable professionals to direct the birth process and make decisions following the birth—that is, peace of mind. What are the cons? A big one is cost, a significant one for those without insurance coverage. According to the Agency for Healthcare Research and Quality Healthcare Cost and Utilization Project, on average, U.S. hospital deliveries cost $3,500. We noted research suggesting that various interventions have become more common in hospital deliveries, interventions that sometimes are themselves dangerous. The pros of home birth include the comfort and reduced stress of giving birth at home, and proximity to friends and family. The major con is distance from sophisticated equipment and medical treatment, if needed. We cited the research conclusion that home birth is not more risky than hospital birth for women who are "low risk, have qualified birth attendants, and have timely access to specialized care."

Now it is up to you to evaluate these alternatives. Do you have health care insurance? Are you a worrier? Are you at some risk for difficulty during birth? Do you live 20 miles or more from a labor and delivery facility? All of these support a hospital-birth decision.

On the other hand, do you have limited or no insurance coverage? Do you dislike hospitals? Does the peace and quiet of home appeal to you as a birth setting? Has a medical professional determined that you are at "low risk"? Do you live 3 miles from a maternity hospital? All of these support a home-birth decision with a qualified home-birth provider. If you or your partner were pregnant, what decision seems the best for you?

SUMMARY

Conception

Sperm are manufactured in the testes and ejaculated through the vas deferens and urethra into the vagina. Then they begin their swim through the cervix and uterus and up a fallopian tube to meet the egg, which has already been released from the ovary. When the sperm and egg unite in the fallopian tube, conception occurs. The single fertilized egg cell then begins dividing as it travels down the tube, and finally it implants in the uterus. Various techniques for improving the chances of conception are available.

Development of the Conceptus

The placenta, which is important in transmitting substances between the woman and the fetus, develops early in pregnancy. The most remarkable development of the fetus occurs during the first trimester (first three months), when most of the major organ systems are formed and human features develop.

Pregnancy

For the woman, early signs of pregnancy include amenorrhea, tenderness of the breasts, and nausea. The most common pregnancy tests are designed to detect hCG in the urine or blood. Physical changes during the first trimester are mainly the result of the increasing levels of estrogen and progesterone produced by the placenta. Despite cultural myths about the radiant contentment of the pregnant woman, some women do have negative moods during the first trimester. During the second trimester the woman generally feels better, both physically and psychologically.

Despite people's concerns, sexual intercourse is generally quite safe during pregnancy. Nutrition is exceptionally important during pregnancy because the woman's body has to supply the materials to create another human being. Pregnant women must also be very careful about ingesting drugs because some can penetrate the placental barrier and enter the fetus, possibly causing damage.

Birth

Labor is typically divided into three stages. During the first stage, the cervix undergoes effacement (thinning) and dilation. During the second stage, the baby moves out through the vagina. The placenta is delivered during the third stage. Cesarean section is a surgical method of delivering a baby.

Prepared childbirth has become very popular; it emphasizes the use of relaxation and controlled breathing to minimize the woman's discomfort. Anesthetics may not be necessary, which seems desirable because they are potentially dangerous.

After the Baby Is Born: The Postpartum Period

During the postpartum period, estrogen and progesterone levels are very low. Postpartum depression may arise from a combination of this hormonal state and the many environmental stresses on the woman at this time.

Breast-Feeding

Two hormones are involved in lactation: prolactin and oxytocin. Breast-feeding has a number of psychological as well as health advantages.

Problem Pregnancies

Problems of pregnancy include ectopic (misplaced) pregnancy, pseudocyesis (false pregnancy), preeclampsia and eclampsia, illness (such as German measles), a defective conceptus, Rh incompatibility, spontaneous abortion, and preterm birth.

Infertility

The most common cause of infertility in men and women is sexually transmitted infections. The causes of infertility are about evenly divided between women and men.

Assisted Reproductive Technologies

Assisted reproductive technologies include artificial insemination, frozen sperm banks, in vitro fertilization (test-tube babies), embryo transfer, and GIFT (gamete intrafallopian transfer), all of which are now a reality. These procedures are costly. In addition, the practice of transferring multiple embryos often results in multiple births, which are riskier for both mother and infants.

On the horizon is widespread use of NIPD to determine fetal genotype. If the technique is used to determine whether a fetus will be aborted, it will create a host of social and ethical debates.

SUGGESTIONS FOR FURTHER READING

Almeling, Rene. (2011). *Sex cells: The medical market for eggs and sperm*. Berkeley, CA: University of California Press. A fascinating look at how egg agencies and sperm banks recruit donors and market their gametes.

Markens, Susan. (2007). *Surrogate motherhood and the politics of reproduction*. Berkeley, CA: University of California Press. A good discussion of issues raised by surrogacy, including legal and ethical ones. Considers media "frames" of the issue and some of the diverse legislative responses.

Nova: The miracle of life. PBS Video: NOVA402 (DVD). Renowned Swedish photographer Lennart Nilsson presents the incredible voyage of a new life with his stunning look at the microscopic world of the human body.

Potter, Daniel, & Hanin, Jennifer. (2013). *What to do when you can't get pregnant: The complete guide to all the technologies for couples facing fertility issues*. Boston: Da Capo Press. Just what the subtitle says.

Are YOU Curious?

1. I'd like to use the birth control pill, but I'm terrible at remembering to take a pill every day. What are my other options?
2. Can a man still ejaculate after a vasectomy?
3. How does mifepristone work for an abortion?
4. Are there any male hormonal contraception methods?

Read this chapter to find out.

©Doug Menuez/Getty Images

Contraception and Abortion

CHAPTER HIGHLIGHTS

I f every woman who's had an abortion took tomorrow off in protest, America would grind to a halt. And that would be symbolic: because women grind to a halt if they are not in control of their fertility.*

*"How To Be A Woman" by Caitlin Moran, 2011, Harper Collins.

The average student of today grew up in the pill era and takes for granted that highly effective methods of contraception are available. We tend to forget that contraception was once a hit-or-miss affair at best. Contraception is less controversial than it once was, and yet the use of contraceptives was illegal in Connecticut until 1965 (the Supreme Court decision in the case of *Griswold v. Connecticut,* 1965, is discussed in the chapter "Sex and the Law").

Today, individuals use contraceptives for a variety of reasons. Both babies and mothers are healthier if pregnancies are spaced three to five years apart (Setty-Venugopal & Upadhyay, 2002). Most couples want to limit the size of their family—usually to one or two children. Individuals not in a committed relationship typically wish to avoid pregnancy. In some cases a couple know, through genetic counseling, that they have a high risk of bearing a child with a birth defect, and they therefore wish to prevent pregnancy. And in this era of successful career women, many women feel that it is essential to be able to control when and whether they have children.

At the level of society as a whole, there are also important reasons for encouraging the use of contraceptives. There are approximately 450,000 adolescent pregnancies annually in the United States (Kost et al., 2017), which constitute a major social problem. In the United States, rates of unintended pregnancy remain persistently high, at 51 percent of all pregnancies (Finer & Zolna, 2014). On the global level, overpopulation is a serious problem. In 1900 the world population was 1.6 billion—and it had taken millions of years to reach that level. By 1950 it had increased to 2.5 billion. In 2014 it hit 7.2 billion, an alarming increase, and experts estimate that it will reach 9.6 billion in 2050 and 10.9 billion in 2100 (Gerland et al., 2014). With the resulting destruction of the environment and increased consumption of natural resources, grave concerns arise about the ability of the planet to sustain such a large population, even in the near future (Weisman, 2013). Most experts believe that we must limit the size of the U.S. population as well as assist other countries in limiting theirs. For a summary of contraceptive practices around the world, see Table 1.

Contraception is also economical! California instituted a program to provide contraceptives and related medical services at no cost to low-income women. An analysis of the data indicated that, in one year, 205,000 unwanted pregnancies were averted (Foster et al., 2006). The researchers estimated that those 205,000 pregnancies would have resulted in 79,000 abortions and 94,000 births (as well as many miscarriages), and 21,400 of those births would have been to adolescent mothers. The births would have cost government agencies an estimated $1.1 billion over two years, in health care, social services, and education. According to the researchers' calculations, for every $1 California spent on these contraceptive services, it saved $2.76—a great investment.

As noted earlier, roughly 50 percent of pregnancies each year in the United States are unintended. Another economic analysis indicated that the direct medical cost of those unintended pregnancies is $5 billion per year (Trussell, 2007). Contraceptive use results in $19 billion per year in medical cost savings.

While we are on the topic of finances, it is important to note that the Affordable Care Act ("Obamacare") requires that insurance plans in the Health Insurance Marketplace must cover contraceptive methods prescribed by a health care provider, with no copay. Therefore, anyone enrolled in one of those plans should have access to the highly effective methods described in this chapter at no out-of-pocket cost. The Affordable Care Act is under attack, however, so it is unclear whether the coverage for contraception will continue. Most college students have access to free or low-cost contraceptives through their university health service.

In this chapter we discuss various methods of birth control, how each works, how effective each is, what side effects it has, and its relative advantages and disadvantages. We also discuss abortion and advances in contraceptive technology.

Hormonal Methods

Hormonal methods of contraception are highly effective and come in a number of forms: the pill, the patch, the vaginal ring, and injections.

Table 1 Contraception around the World, Reported by Women Aged 15–49 (the great variations reflect differences among cultures in such factors as availability of medical services, people's education about contraception, and gender roles)

| | | | Percentage Using Method | | | | | |
Country	Voluntary Sterilization, Men	Voluntary Sterilization, Women	Pill	IUD	Male Condom	Injectables*	Rhythm	All Methods
Bangladesh	1	5	27	1	6	12	6	62
Colombia	3	35	8	8	7	9	2	79
Egypt	0	1	16	30	1	9	1	59
France	NA	4	41	22	7	NA	NA	83
India	1	36	4	2	6	NA	NA	54
Kenya	0	3	7	5	1	29	2	66
Morocco	NA	NA	48	4	NA	NA	4	67
Netherlands	6	3	NA	15	10	NA	NA	73
United States	12	21	13	9	9	1	<1	74

NA: information not available.

*Includes injections such as Depo-Provera.

Source: United Nations Population Division (2017).

The Combination Pill

With **combination birth control pills** (sometimes called *oral contraceptives*) such as Loestrin, the woman[1] takes a pill that contains estrogen and progestin (a synthetic progesterone), both at doses higher than natural levels, for 21 days. Then she takes no pill or a placebo for 7 days, after which she repeats the cycle.

The traditional 21-on, 7-off pattern is still very common, but variations have been introduced. One is Loestrin 24, which has 24 active pills and 4 inactive pills. Another is Seasonale, which provides 84 days of combined hormones and 7 days of placebo. This pattern means that the woman has a period only once in three months.

The preferred method for a woman starting on the pill is QuickStart. That is, she starts taking the pill the first day she gets the prescription, regardless of the day of the menstrual cycle.

How It Works

The pill works mainly by preventing ovulation. Recall from the chapter "Sex Hormones, Sexual Differentiation, and the Menstrual Cycle" that in a natural menstrual cycle the low levels of estrogen during and just after the menstrual period trigger the pituitary to produce FSH, which stimulates the process of ovulation. When a woman starts taking birth control pills, estrogen levels are high. This high level of estrogen inhibits FSH production, and the message to ovulate is never sent out. The high level of progesterone inhibits LH production, further preventing ovulation.

The progestin provides additional backup effects. It keeps the cervical mucus very thick, making it difficult for sperm to get through, and it changes the lining of the uterus in such a way that even if a fertilized egg were to arrive, implantation would be unlikely.

When the estrogen and progestin are withdrawn (after day 21 in the traditional pill), the lining of the uterus disintegrates, and withdrawal bleeding or menstruation occurs. The flow is typically reduced because the progestin has inhibited development of the endometrium.

Effectiveness

Before we discuss the effectiveness of the pill, let's define several technical terms that are used in communicating data on the effectiveness of contraceptives in general. If 100 women use a contraceptive method for one year, the number of them who become pregnant during that first year of use is called the **failure rate** or *pregnancy rate*. In other words, if 5 women out of 100 become pregnant during a year of using contraceptive A, then A's failure rate is 5 percent. *Effectiveness* is 100 minus the failure rate; thus contraceptive A would be said to be 95 percent effective.

There are two kinds of failure rate: the *failure rate for perfect users* and the *failure rate for typical users*. The perfect-user failure rate refers to studies of the best possible use of the method—for example, when the user has been well taught about the method, uses it with perfect consistency,

---

Combination birth control pills: Birth control pills that contain a combination of estrogen and progestin (progesterone).
Failure rate: The pregnancy rate occurring using a particular contraceptive method; the percentage of women who will be pregnant after a year of use of the method.

---

[1] Mindful of the transgender population, we realize that not all female-bodied people identify as women. To keep the language simple, we will refer to "women" in this chapter, with the understanding that we are using that as shorthand for people with female bodies. We also focus on heterosexual sex in this chapter because that is the context in which contraception is most likely to be needed.

and so on. The failure rate for typical users is just that—the failure rate when people actually use the method, perhaps imperfectly when they forget to take a pill or do not use a condom every time. The good news is that if you are very responsible about contraception, you can anticipate close to the perfect-user failure rate for yourself.

Combination pills are one of the most effective methods of birth control. The perfect-user failure rate is 0.3 percent (i.e., the method is essentially 100 percent effective), and the typical-user failure rate is 9 percent (Hatcher et al., 2011). Failures occur primarily as a result of forgetting to take a pill for 2 or more days. If a woman forgets to take a pill, she should take it as soon as she remembers and take the next one at the regular time. This does not appear to increase the pregnancy risk appreciably. If she forgets for 2 days, she should do the same thing—take one as soon as possible and then continue taking one a day. If she forgets for 3 or more days, she should follow the same instructions, taking one pill as soon as possible and then one pill a day, but in addition she should use condoms or abstain from sex until she has taken hormonal pills for 7 days in a row, at which point she will again be well protected (Salem, 2005).

Side Effects

You may have seen reports in the media on the dangerous side effects of birth control pills. Some of these reports are no more than scare stories with little or no evidence behind them. However, some well-documented risks are associated with the use of the pill, and women who are using it or who are contemplating using it should be aware of them.

Among the serious side effects associated with use of the pill are slight but significant increases in certain diseases of the circulatory system. One of these is problems of blood clots (thromboembolic disorders or venous thrombosis). Women who use the pill have a higher chance than nonusers of developing blood clots (thrombi) (Lidegaard et al., 2012). Often these form in the legs, and they may then move to the lungs. A stroke may occur if the clot goes to the brain. The clots may lead to pain, hospitalization, and (in rare cases) death. Symptoms of blood clots are severe headaches, severe leg or chest pains, and shortness of breath. Most cases of clots occur in women over 35 who smoke. For some women, the pill can cause high blood pressure. For this reason it is important to have regular checkups so that this side effect can be detected if it occurs.

There have been many reports in the media of the pill causing cancer. However, the scientific data do not provide evidence that the pill causes cancer of the cervix, uterus, or breast. The good news is that the pill actually protects women from endometrial cancer and ovarian cancer (Iversen et al., 2017). However, the pill may aggravate already existing cancer such as breast cancer.

For women who have taken the pill for more than five years, the risk of benign liver tumors increases (Hatcher et al., 2011). Although these problems are relatively rare,

they underline the importance of the health care professional giving a thorough examination before prescribing birth control pills and of the woman having regular checkups while using them.

The pill increases the amount of vaginal discharge and the susceptibility to vaginitis (vaginal inflammations such as monilia—see the chapter "Sexually Transmitted Infections") because it alters the chemical balance of the lining of the vagina. Women on the pill have an increased susceptibility to chlamydia. Although the matter is controversial, some good evidence indicates that use of the pill—or any of the hormonal contraceptives—increases the rise of HIV infection (Heffron et al., 2012).

The pill may cause some nausea, although this almost always goes away after the first month or two of use. Some brands of pills can also cause weight gain, by increasing appetite or water retention, but this side effect can often be reversed by switching to another brand.

Finally, there may be some psychological effects. About 20 percent of women on the pill report increased irritability and depression, which become worse with the length of time they use the pill. These side effects are probably related to the progesterone in the pill; switching to a different brand may be helpful. There may also be changes in sexual desire. Some women report an increase in sexual interest, but others report a decrease in sexual desire as well as a decrease in vaginal lubrication. Once again, switching brands may be helpful.

Because of the side effects discussed previously, women in the following groups should *not* use the pill (Hatcher et al., 2011): those with poor blood circulation or blood-clot problems; those who have had a heart attack or who have coronary artery disease; those with liver tumors; those with breast cancer; those with uncontrolled high blood pressure; and pregnant women. Women over 35 who are cigarette smokers should use the pill only with caution, because the risk of heart attack is considerably higher in this group.

After all this discussion, just how dangerous is the pill? The answer to this question depends on who you are and how you look at it. If you have blood-clot problems, the pill is dangerous to you; if you have none of the contraindications listed above, it is very safe (Hatcher et al., 2011). One's point of view and standard of comparison also matter. While a death rate of 1.6 per 100,000 sounds high, it is important to consider that one alternative to the pill is intercourse with no contraceptive, which can mean pregnancy, with its own set of side effects and a death rate all its own. For example, the death rate for the pill is 1.6 per 100,000, but the death rate for pregnancy and delivery is 12 per 100,000 (Cheng et al., 2003). From this perspective, in many ways the pill is no more dangerous than the alternative, pregnancy, and actually may be safer. Another possible standard of comparison is drugs that are commonly taken for less serious reasons. Aspirin, for example, is routinely used for headaches. Recent reports indicate that aspirin has side effects, and the birth

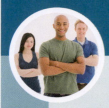

First Person

Margaret Sanger—Birth Control Pioneer

Margaret Higgins Sanger (1879–1966) was a crusader for birth control in the United States; to reach her goals, she had to take on a variety of opponents, including the U.S. government, and she served one jail term.

Sanger was born in Corning, New York, the daughter of a tubercular mother who died young after bearing 11 children. Her father was a free spirit who fought for women's suffrage. After caring for her dying mother, Sanger embarked on a career in nursing. She married William Sanger in 1902.

She became interested in women's health and began writing articles on the subject. Later these were published as books entitled *What Every Girl Should Know* (1916) and *What Every Mother Should Know* (1917).

Perhaps Sanger's strongest motivation came from her work as a nurse. Her patients were poor maternity cases on New York's Lower East Side. Among these women, pregnancy was a "chronic condition." Margaret Sanger saw them, weary and old at 35, resorting to self-induced abortions, which killed many of them. Frustrated at her inability to help them, she renounced nursing:

> I came to a sudden realization that my work as a nurse and my activities in social service were entirely palliative and consequently futile and useless to relieve the misery I saw all about me.

She determined, instead, to "seek out the root of the evil." Though she was often accused of wanting to lower the birthrate, she instead envisioned families, rich and poor alike, in which children were wanted and given every advantage.

Impeding her work was the Comstock Act of 1873, which classified contraceptive information as obscene and made it illegal to send it through the mail. In 1914 she founded the National Birth Control League, launching the birth control movement in the United States. Though her magazine, *Woman Rebel,* obeyed the letter of the law and did not give contraceptive information, she was nonetheless indicted on nine counts and made liable to a prison term of 45 years.

Margaret Sanger left the United States on the eve of the trial. Touring Europe, in Holland she visited the first birth control clinics to be established anywhere. There she got the idea of opening such clinics in the United States. Meanwhile, the charges against her had been dropped.

She returned to the United States and, in 1916, opened the first U.S. birth control clinic, in Brooklyn. The office was closed by the police after 9 days of operation, and Margaret Sanger was put in jail for 30 days. On appeal, however, her

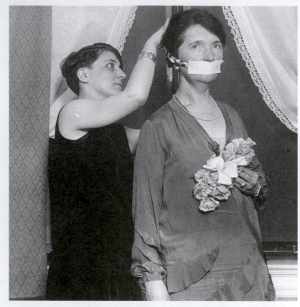

Figure 1   Margaret Sanger, a pioneer of the birth control movement, shown here in 1929. She was forbidden by Boston authorities to speak on birth control, so she taped her mouth in protest and wrote on a chalkboard.

©Bettmann/Getty Images

side was upheld by the courts, and in 1918 a decision was handed down allowing doctors to give contraceptive information to women for the "cure and prevention of disease."

The birth control movement was gaining followers, and the first National Birth Control Conference was held in 1921 in New York, attended by doctors, scientists, and lay supporters. In 1931 the Pope approved the rhythm method for use by Roman Catholics.

In 1923, Sanger incorporated the American Birth Control League, which became Planned Parenthood Federation of America. This organization is still alive and strong nearly 100 years later.

Margaret Sanger's role in getting birth control information to American women and in making it legal for them to use the information is unquestioned (see Figure 1). When Heywood Broun once remarked that Margaret Sanger had no sense of humor, she replied, "I am the protagonist of women who have nothing to laugh at."

Sources: Chesler (1992); Current Biography (1944); Van Preagh (1982).

control pill may be no more dangerous than drugs we take without worrying much.

In short, the pill does have some serious potential side effects, particularly for high-risk individuals, but for most women it is an extremely effective means of contraception that poses little or no danger.

Advantages and Disadvantages

The pill has a number of advantages. It is highly effective if used properly. It does not interfere with intercourse, as do some other methods—the condom and foam. It is not messy. Some of its side effects are also advantages. For example, it reduces the amount of menstrual flow and thus reduces cramps. Indeed, it is sometimes prescribed for the noncontraceptive purpose of regulating menstruation and eliminating cramps. Iron-deficiency anemia is less likely to occur among pill users. The pill can clear up acne, and it has a protective effect against some rather serious things, including endometriosis and ovarian and endometrial cancer (Hatcher et al., 2011).

The side effects of birth control pills, discussed earlier, are of course major disadvantages. Another disadvantage is the cost, which is about $50 a month (or much less through a Planned Parenthood clinic) for as long as they are used. They also place the entire burden of contraception on the woman. In addition, taking them correctly is a little complicated; the woman must understand when they are to be taken, and she must remember when to take them and when not to take them. This effort would not be too taxing for today's college student, but for an illiterate peasant woman in a developing nation who thinks the pills are to be worn like an amulet on a chain around the neck, or for individuals with intellectual disabilities (who need contraceptives too), currently available birth control pills may be too complicated. The Planned Parenthood website has a link to an app that will give reminders.

One other criticism of the pill is that for a woman who has intercourse only infrequently (say, once or twice a month or less), it represents contraceptive overkill. In other words, the pill makes her infertile every day of the month, and yet she needs it only a few days each month. Women in this situation might consider a method, such as the condom or diaphragm, that is used only when needed.

Finally, it is important to recognize that, although it is an excellent contraceptive, the pill provides absolutely no protection against sexually transmitted infections.

Reversibility

When a woman wants to become pregnant, she simply stops taking pills after the end of one cycle. Some women experience a brief delay (two or three months) in becoming pregnant, but pregnancy rates are about the same as for women who never took the pill.

Drug Interactions

If you are taking birth control pills, you are taking a prescription drug that may interact with other prescription drugs you take (Hatcher et al., 2011). Some anticonvulsant drugs, for example, decrease the effectiveness of the pill, as do some of the antiretroviral drugs used to treat HIV infection.

The pill may also increase the metabolism of some drugs, making them more potent (Hatcher et al., 2011). Examples include some antianxiety drugs, corticosteroids used for inflammations, and theophylline (a drug used for asthma and an ingredient in, for example, Primatene). For this reason, women using the pill may require lower doses of these drugs.

Some over-the-counter drugs may also interact with the pill. St. John's wort, for instance, can substantially decrease the effectiveness of the pill.

Other Kinds of Pills

To this point, our discussion has centered chiefly on the *combination pill,* so named because it contains both estrogen and progestin. This variety of pill is the most widely used, but there are many kinds of combination pills and several kinds of pills other than combination ones.

Combination pills vary from one brand to the next in the dosages of estrogen and progestin. The dose of estrogen is important because higher doses are more likely to induce blood-clot problems. Most women do well on pills containing no more than 20 to 35 micrograms of estrogen. Because of concerns about side effects due to the estrogen in the pill, current pills have considerably lower levels of estrogen than early pills; for example, Ortho-Novum 1/35 has one-third the amount of estrogen of the early pill Enovid 10. High-progestin brands are related to symptoms such as vaginitis and depression. Depending on what side effects the woman wants to avoid, she can choose a brand for its high or low estrogen or progestin level. (See Hatcher et al., 2011, page 312, for a list of symptoms related to dosages of estrogen and progestin.)

Progestin-only pills have also been developed. They are sometimes called *minipills.* The pills contain only a low dose of progestin and no estrogen and were designed to avoid the estrogen-related side effects of combination pills. The woman takes one beginning on the first day of her period and one every day thereafter, at the same time each day. Progestin-only pills work by changing the cervical mucus such that sperm cannot get through, inhibiting implantation and inhibiting ovulation (although while taking minipills, about 40 percent of women ovulate consistently).

Progestin-only pills have a typical-user failure rate that is higher than that of combination pills. Their major side effect is that they produce very irregular menstrual cycles. The minipill is probably most useful for women who cannot take combination pills—for example, women over 35 who smoke, or women with a history of high blood pressure or blood-clot problems.

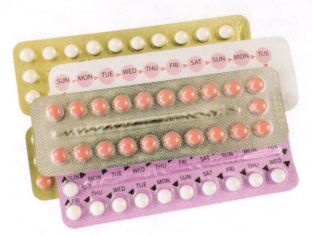

Figure 2   Birth control pills.

©Areeya Yodplob/Alamy

Progestin-only pills are also useful for women who are breast-feeding and cannot use combination pills because they reduce milk production. Neither kind of pill should be used in the first six weeks after birth when breast-feeding, because trace amounts of the hormones can reach the infant through the breast milk. After that time, though, progestin-only pills can be used.

The Patch

The patch (Ortho Evra) contains the same hormones as combination birth control pills but is administered transdermally—that is, through the skin. The patch itself is thin, beige, and about the size of a double Band-Aid. It consists of an outer, protective layer of polyester, an adhesive layer that contains the hormones, and a polyester liner that is removed before applying.

The patch lasts for seven days, so the woman places a new one on once a week for three weeks and then has a patch-free week. The first time it is used it takes a couple of days for the hormones to reach effective levels, so a backup method such as a condom should be used for a while. One advantage is that women using it do not have to remember to take a pill every day, only to replace the patch every week. In addition, with the patch, the hormones enter the body through the skin rather than going to the stomach and needing to be digested.

Because the hormones are the same as in the pill, the benefits and side effects should be quite similar to those of the pill (Hatcher et al., 2011). Compared with the pill, the patch has a slightly higher rate of thromboembolic disorders (Lidegaard et al., 2012). It is somewhat less effective in women weighing more than 200 pounds. There is also concern that a woman gets more estrogen from the patch than she would with a combination pill.

The Vaginal Ring

It's not the latest in body piercing. Rather, the vaginal ring (NuvaRing) is a flexible, transparent ring made of

plastic and filled with the same hormones as those in the combination pill, at slightly lower doses (Figure 3). The ring is placed high up in the vagina and remains in place for 21 days. It is removed and the woman goes ring-free for—you guessed it—7 days. She then inserts a new ring. This method requires even less remembering than the patch does.

Because the hormones in it are the same as those in the combination pill, the side effects should be the same. Like the patch, it has a somewhat higher risk of thromboembolic disorders than the pill does (Lidegaard et al., 2012). It acts mainly by stopping ovulation. Although it was hoped that its typical-user failure rate would be lower than that of the pill (because of less need to remember to use it), in fact it is about the same as the pill (Hatcher et al., 2011).

Depo-Provera Injections ("The Shot")

Depo-Provera (DMPA) is a progestin administered by injection. The injections must be repeated every 3 months for maximum effectiveness.

How It Works

Depo-Provera works like the other progestin-only methods, by inhibiting ovulation, thickening the cervical mucus, and inhibiting the growth of the endometrium.

Effectiveness

Depo-Provera is highly effective, with a typical-user failure rate of 6 percent, making it somewhat more effective than the pill.

Side Effects

No lethal side effects of Depo-Provera have been found, although long-term studies have not yet been done.

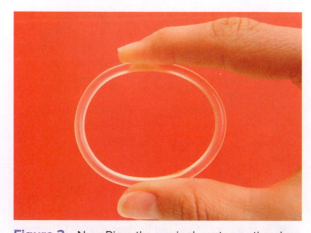

Figure 3   NuvaRing, the vaginal contraceptive ring.

©vario images GmbH & Co.KG/Alamy

Advantages and Disadvantages

Depo-Provera has many advantages. It does not interfere with lovemaking. It requires far less reliance on memory than birth control pills do, although the woman must remember to have a new injection every 3 months. It is available for women who cannot use the combination pill, such as those over 35 who smoke and those with blood pressure problems.

Most users experience amenorrhea (no menstrual periods). Sometimes there is just some spotting. However, this may be an advantage. It can relieve anemia due to heavy menstrual periods, and Depo-Provera can be used in the treatment of endometriosis.

Reversibility

The method is reversible simply by not getting another injection. Many women are infertile for 6 to 12 months after stopping its use, but then are able to become pregnant at normal rates (Hatcher et al., 2011).

Emergency Contraception

Emergency contraception is available in pill form for situations such as rape or a condom breaking (Hatcher et al., 2011). The treatment is most effective if begun within 24 hours and cannot be delayed longer than 120 hours (5 days). Regular birth control pills containing levonorgestrel (a progestin) are taken at higher doses. Plan B and Next Choice, products specifically for emergency contraception, contain the same important hormone. Nausea is a common side effect, but a drug can be taken to prevent it. In 2006 the FDA approved Plan B for sale in the United States over the counter, without prescription. Women can keep a supply on hand for . . . emergencies.

Ella, which contains a different drug, ulipristal acetate, is another type of pill for emergency contraception. Yet another alternative is to take multiple combination birth control pills. The exact number depends on the brand of pill; for a listing, see http://ec.princeton.edu.

Emergency contraception may work in any of several ways, depending on when in the cycle it is taken. It may stop ovulation, inhibit the functioning of sperm, prevent fertilization, or inhibit the development of a nourishing endometrium. Its action is almost always to prevent pregnancy, not to cause abortion.

Emergency contraception is between 75 and 89 percent effective (Hatcher et al., 2007). These statistics underestimate its actual effectiveness, though, because they refer to the effectiveness during the most fertile part of the cycle. Actual pregnancy rates are between 0.5 and 2.0 percent (von Hertzen et al., 2002). Emergency contraception, then, is highly effective. Emergency contraception (EC) drugs may interact with other drugs, making EC less effective. Examples of these drugs include those used in the treatment of epilepsy, tuberculosis, HIV, and certain fungal infections.

Opponents of Plan B had argued that it would lead women, and especially teenagers, to become irresponsible about contraception and their sexual behavior if emergency contraception were widely available. Research, however, indicates that making Plan B available to teenagers has no effect on whether they had unprotected intercourse or on their number of sexual partners (Harper et al., 2005).

The American Academy of Pediatrics is solidly behind making emergency contraception available to adolescents, including providing a prescription so that the adolescent can have it on hand (American Academy of Pediatrics, 2012).

An IUD can also be used for emergency contraception for a woman who wants continuing protection (Cleland et al., 2012). The failure rate is less than 1 percent if inserted within 5 days of unprotected intercourse.

LARC

LARC stands for Long-Acting, Reversible Contraceptives. That is, the methods last for more than a year, and they can also be reversed, unlike sterilization. The LARC methods include implants and IUDs. LARC is rapidly growing in popularity in the United States, and it is recommended by family planning experts because these methods are even more effective than the pill. The LARC methods are safe for adolescents and are used by 7 percent of teenagers seeking contraception (Romero et al., 2015).

Implants

Implants are thin rods or tubes containing progestin. They are inserted under the skin in a woman's arm and are effective for 4 years. The only implant currently available in the United States is Nexplanon, which uses a single rod 4 cm long and 2 mm wide (Hatcher et al., 2011).

> I'd like to use the birth control pill, but I'm terrible at remembering to take a pill every day. What are my other options?

How It Works

Implants work like the other progestin-only methods, by suppressing ovulation, thickening the cervical mucus, and inhibiting the growth of the endometrium.

Effectiveness

Nexplanon is highly effective, with a typical-user failure rate of 0.05. The typical-user failure rate is the same as the perfect-user rate because there is no need to remember to take a pill, replace a patch, and so on. It is therefore more effective than the pill.

Side Effects

No lethal side effects of Nexplanon have been detected in research to date.

LARC: Long-Acting, Reversible Contraceptives; implants and IUDs

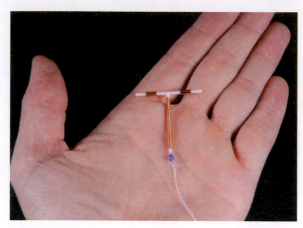

Figure 4   The copper T IUD.

©McGraw-Hill Education/Jill Braaten, photographer

Advantages and Disadvantages

Nexplanon has many advantages. It requires no reliance on memory for 4 years, and it does not interfere with love-making. It contains no estrogen, for those who experience estrogen-related side effects.

A large proportion of women on Nexplanon experience changes in their menstrual bleeding patterns. The changes are unpredictable and may include unusually long bleeding, frequent bleeding, and amenorrhea.

Reversibility

If the woman wishes to become pregnant, she can have the implant removed, which must be done by a clinician. In most cases, the menstrual cycle returns to normal within 3 months, and the woman can become pregnant.

IUDs

The **intrauterine device (IUD,** also called intrauterine contraceptives or IUCs) is a small piece of plastic (Figure 4). Metal or a hormone may also be part of the device. An IUD is inserted into the uterus by a doctor or nurse practitioner and then remains in place until the woman wants to have it removed. One or two plastic strings hang down from the IUD through the cervix, enabling the woman to check to see whether it is in place.

The basic idea for the IUD has been around for some time. In the 1920s the German physician Ernst Gräfenberg reported data on 2,000 insertions of silk or silver wire rings. In spite of the high effectiveness of these devices (98.4 percent), his work was poorly received. Not until the 1950s, with the development of plastic and stainless-steel devices, did the method gain much popularity. In the 1970s and 1980s the use of the IUD in the United States was sharply reduced by lawsuits against manufacturers by persons

Intrauterine device (IUD): A plastic device sometimes containing metal or a hormone that is inserted into the uterus for contraceptive purposes; also called *intrauterine contraceptive (IUC)*.

claiming to have been damaged by the device, specifically by the IUD known as the Dalkon Shield, which was taken off the market in 1975 (Hubacher, 2002).

Five IUDs are available in the United States today. All are T-shaped; one contains copper (the copper T, or ParaGard), the other four progestin (Mirena, Kyleena, Liletta, and Skyla).

How It Works

The foreign body in the uterus creates an environment that is toxic to both sperm and eggs (Hatcher et al., 2011). In the rare event of a fertilization, the IUD prevents implantation.

The progestin-containing ones release progestin directly into the uterus. One effect is to reduce the endometrium. This results in reduced menstrual flow and reduced risk of anemia, overcoming two undesirable side effects of other IUDs. The progesterone also disrupts ovulation and thickens cervical mucus.

The small amount of copper that is added to the copper T is thought to have an additional contraceptive effect. It seems to alter the functioning of the enzymes involved in implantation.

Effectiveness

The IUD is extremely effective. The pregnancy rate for the copper T is 0.7 percent for the first year of use, and after that, the failure rate is even lower (Hatcher et al., 2011). The copper T is effective for 12 years, Mirena is effective for 6 years, and Skyla is effective for 3 years.

Most failures occur during the first 3 months of use, either because the IUD is expelled or for other, unknown reasons. The expulsion rate is about 2 to 10 percent in the first year (Hatcher et al., 2011).

Side Effects

The most common side effects of the copper T are increased menstrual cramps, irregular bleeding, and increased menstrual flow. These symptoms occur in 10 to 20 percent of women using it and are most likely immediately after insertion. Mirena, in contrast, reduces menstrual flow and about 20 percent of users stop bleeding altogether.

There is no evidence that the IUD causes cancer.

Advantages and Disadvantages

One disadvantage of the IUD is its initial cost, which is about $300 for a full-paying client at Planned Parenthood, for the IUD plus insertion. Even at that rate, though, the IUD is a cheap means of contraception over a long period of use. The cost is incurred only once and the copper T, for example, lasts 12 years.

The effectiveness of the IUD is a major advantage. The typical-user failure rate is only 0.8 percent, making it more effective than combination birth control pills and Depo-Provera.

Once inserted, the IUD is perfectly simple to use. The woman has only to check periodically to see that the strings are in place. It has an advantage over methods like the condom in that it does not interrupt intercourse in any way. It has an advantage over the pill in that the woman does not have to remember to use it. The IUD can be used safely by women after having a baby and while breast-feeding.

Contrary to what some people think, the IUD does not interfere with the use of a tampon during menstruation, nor does it have any effect on intercourse.

Reversibility

When a woman who is using an IUD wants to become pregnant, she simply has a health care provider remove the device. She can become pregnant immediately.

Condoms

The Male Condom

The **male condom** ("rubber," "jimmies," "safe") is a thin sheath that fits over the penis (Figure 5). It comes rolled up in a little packet and must be unrolled onto the penis before use. It may be made of latex ("rubber"),

polyurethane, or the intestinal tissue of lambs ("skin"). The polyurethane condom (Avanti, Trojan Supra) is a recent innovation that is helpful to people who are allergic to latex.

The widespread use of the modern condom, both for contraception and for protection against diseases, dates from about 1843, when vulcanized rubber was developed, but the use of a sheath to cover the penis has been known throughout most of recorded history.[2] The legendary Italian adventurer and lover Casanova (1725–1798) was one of the first to popularize it for its contraceptive ability as well as its protective value. Condoms have become increasingly popular because they help protect against sexually transmitted infections (STIs), including HIV.

To be effective, the condom must be used properly (Figure 6). It must be unrolled onto the erect penis before the penis ever enters the vagina—*not* just before ejaculation, because

> **Male condom:** A contraceptive sheath that is placed over the penis.

[2]Condoms have also been the stimulus for humor throughout history, an example being this limerick:

There was a young man of Cape Horn
Who wished he had never been born
And he wouldn't have been
If his father had seen
That the end of the rubber was torn.

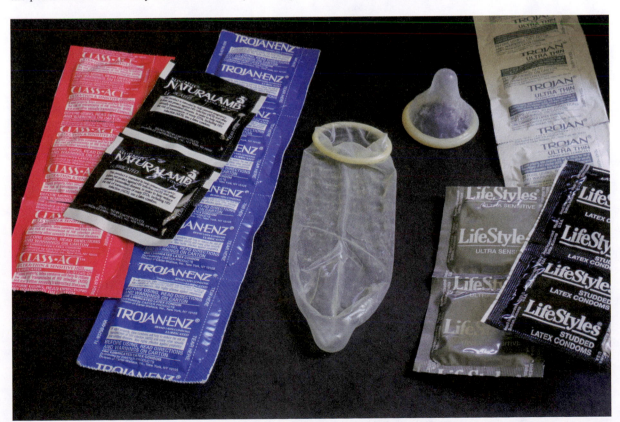

Figure 5 A variety of male condoms.

(a)   (b)

Figure 6   Putting on a condom correctly. (*a*) The tip is pinched to keep air out. (*b*) The condom is then rolled down over the erect penis.

(a) ©H.S. Photos/Science Source; (b) ©H.S. Photos/Science Source

long before then some drops containing a few thousand sperm may have been produced. To be effective in preventing STIs, too, it must be put on before the penis enters the vagina.

Condoms come in two shapes: those with plain ends and those with a protruding tip that catches the semen. If a plain-ended one is used, about ½ inch of air-free space should be left at the tip to catch the ejaculate. Care should be taken that the condom does not slip during intercourse. After the man has ejaculated, he must hold the rim of the condom against the base of the penis as he withdraws. It is best to withdraw soon after ejaculation, while the man still has an erection, in order to minimize the chances of leakage. A new condom must be used with each act of intercourse.

Condoms may be either lubricated or unlubricated. Some further lubrication for intercourse may be necessary. A sterile lubricant such as K-Y Jelly may be used.

How It Works

The condom catches the semen, preventing it from entering the vagina. For condoms coated with a spermicide, the spermicide kills sperm and in theory provides extra protection. Spermicide-coated condoms are no longer recommended, though. They may create allergies to the spermicide for the man or his partner, and the amount of spermicide is probably not sufficient to be very effective. For couples who want to improve on the effectiveness of the condom, it is probably wiser for the woman to use a contraceptive foam or, better yet, a diaphragm.

Effectiveness

Condoms are much more effective as a contraceptive than most people think. The perfect-user failure rate is about 2 percent. The typical-user failure rate is about 18 percent, but many failures result from improper or inconsistent use. The FDA controls the quality of condoms carefully, so the chances of a failure due to a defect in the condom itself are small. Combined with a contraceptive foam or cream or a diaphragm, the condom is close to 100 percent effective.

Side Effects

The condom has no side effects, except that some users are allergic to latex. For them, nonlatex condoms made of polyurethane or other plastics are available.

Advantages and Disadvantages

One disadvantage of the condom is that it must be put on just before intercourse, raising the spontaneity problem again. If the couple can make an enjoyable, erotic ritual of putting it on together, they can minimize this problem.

Some men complain that the condom reduces their sensation, lessening their pleasure in intercourse ("It's like taking a shower with a raincoat on"). The reduction in sensation, however, may be an advantage for some. For example, it may help men who tend to ejaculate prematurely. Polyurethane condoms are thinner and should provide more sensation.

There are several advantages to condoms. They are the only contraceptive currently available for men except sterilization. They are cheap (around $1 each), readily available without prescription at any drugstore and some convenience stores, and fairly easy to use. The man (or woman) must plan ahead, however, so they will have one available when it is needed.

Finally, a major advantage of condoms is that they provide protection against many sexually transmitted infections (Hatcher et al., 2011). Over the past several years, far-right political groups have mounted a campaign to convince the public that condoms are completely ineffective at STI prevention. However, the scientific data say otherwise. Condoms are highly effective protection against STIs that are transmitted mainly through genital secretions (semen, cervical and vaginal secretions) because they keep the secretions away from the other person. STIs in this category include chlamydia, gonorrhea, trichomoniasis, hepatitis B, and HIV (Hatcher et al., 2011). Condoms can and should be used during anal intercourse for protection against STIs.

Condoms also provide some, although not perfect, protection against STIs that are transmitted mainly by skin-to-skin contact, such as herpes, syphilis, and human papillomavirus. They won't protect against these diseases, of course, if the area producing the microbe is not covered by the condom—for example, if herpes blisters are on the scrotum. Latex and polyurethane condoms are the effective ones. Animal-skin condoms are much less effective because they have larger pores that allow some viruses, such as HIV, to pass through them. For a more complete discussion, see the chapter "Sexually Transmitted Infections."

Reversibility

The method is easily and completely reversible. The man simply stops using condoms if conception is desired.

The Female Condom

The female condom, FC2, is sometimes called the internal condom (compared with the male or external condom). It is made of polyurethane and resembles a clear balloon (Figure 7). There are two rings in it, one at either end. One ring is inserted into the vagina much like a diaphragm, while the other is spread over the vaginal entrance. The inside is prelubricated, but additional lubrication may be applied. The penis must be guided into the female condom so that the penis does not slip in between the condom and the vaginal wall. The condom is removed immediately after intercourse, before the woman stands up. The outer ring is squeezed together and twisted to keep the semen inside. A new female condom must be used with each act of intercourse.

How It Works

The female condom works by preventing sperm from entering the vagina and by blocking the entrance to the uterus.

Effectiveness

The typical-user failure rate is 21 percent (Hatcher et al., 2011), which is unacceptably high for many women. The perfect-user failure rate is 5 percent.

Figure 7   The female condom. One ring fits over the cervix, and the other goes outside the body, over the vulva, so that the condom lines the vagina and partly covers the vulva.

©Keith Brofsky/Getty Images

Side Effects

There are few if any side effects with the female condom. A few women experience vaginal irritation and a few men experience irritation of the penis as a result of using it.

Advantages and Disadvantages

The female condom is made of polyurethane, not the latex used in most male condoms. Polyurethane is less susceptible to tearing and does not deteriorate with exposure to oil-based substances in the way that latex does. It does not create the allergic reactions that some people have to latex.

One major advantage is that the female condom is a method that a woman can use herself to reduce her risk of contracting an STI. The polyurethane is impermeable to HIV and to the viruses and bacteria that cause other STIs.

In regard to disadvantages, the spontaneity problem presents itself again. The female condom, at least in the original form, is awkward and makes rustling noises while in use, although additional lubricant reduces this problem. It makes

> **Diaphragm:** A cap-shaped rubber contraceptive device that fits inside a woman's vagina over the cervix.

the male condom seem sophisticated and unobtrusive by comparison. Also, it is the least effective of the methods discussed so far in this chapter.

Reversibility

The method is easily and completely reversible. The woman simply stops using the condom.

Diaphragms, FemCap, and the Sponge

The Diaphragm

The **diaphragm** is a circular, dome-shaped piece of thin rubber with a rubber-covered rim of flexible metal (Figure 8). It is inserted into the vagina and, when properly in place, fits snugly over the cervix. In order for it to be used effectively, a contraceptive cream or jelly (such as Delfen) must be applied to the diaphragm. The cream is spread on the rim and the inside surface (the surface that fits against the cervix). The diaphragm may be inserted up

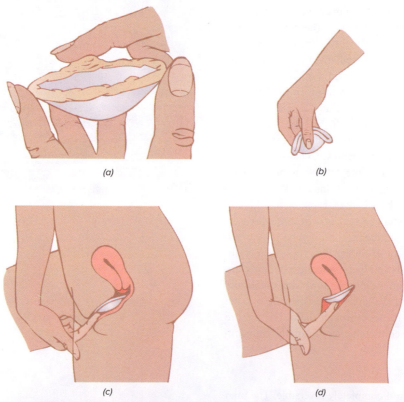

(a)   (b)   (c)   (d)

Figure 8   The proper use of a diaphragm. (*a*) Spermicide is applied (about 1 tablespoon in center and around the rim). (*b*) The edges are held together to permit easier insertion. (*c*) The folded diaphragm is inserted up through the vagina. (*d*) The diaphragm is placed properly, covering the cervix. To check for proper placement, feel the cervix to be sure that it is completely covered by the diaphragm.

to 6 hours before intercourse, and it must be left in place for at least 6 hours afterward and may be left in for as long as 24 hours. Wearing it longer than that is thought to increase the risk of toxic shock syndrome.

The diaphragm was the earliest of the highly effective methods of contraception for women. In 1925 Margaret Sanger's husband funded the first U.S. company to manufacture diaphragms, and they were the mainstay of contraception until about 1960.

How It Works

The primary action of the diaphragm itself is mechanical. It blocks the entrance to the uterus so that sperm cannot swim up into it. The contraceptive cream kills any sperm that manage to get past the barrier. Any sperm remaining in the vagina die after about 6 hours (this is why the diaphragm should not be removed until at least 6 hours after intercourse).

Effectiveness

The typical-user failure rate of the diaphragm has been estimated to be 12 percent. Most failures are due to improper use—for example, it is not used every time, it is not left in long enough, or contraceptive cream is not used. Even with perfect use, there is still a failure rate. For example, Masters and Johnson found that expansion of the vagina during sexual arousal may cause the diaphragm to slip. To get closer to 100 percent effectiveness, the diaphragm can be combined with a condom around the time of ovulation or throughout the cycle.

Failure rates for the diaphragm and FemCap (which we discuss later) are often stated as ranges, for example, 17 to 25 percent, because failure rates for these methods depend so much on the fertility characteristics of the user. For example, a woman under 30 who has intercourse four or more times weekly has twice the average failure rate of a woman over 30 who has intercourse less than four times a week.

Diaphragms come in different sizes. Because proper fit of the diaphragm is essential to its effectiveness, it is important for the woman to be individually fitted for one by her health care provider. She must be refitted after the birth of a child, extreme weight gain or loss, or any similar occurrence that would alter the shape and size of the vagina.

Side Effects

The diaphragm has few side effects. One is the possible irritation of the vagina or the penis. This irritation is caused by the spermicidal cream or jelly and can be relieved by switching to another brand. Another side effect is the rare occurrence of toxic shock syndrome that has been reported in women who left the diaphragm in place for more than 24 hours. For this reason, users should be careful not to leave the diaphragm in place for much more than the necessary 6 to 8 hours, especially during menstruation.

Advantages and Disadvantages

Some people think that the diaphragm is undesirable because it must be inserted before intercourse and therefore ruins the spontaneity of sex. People with this attitude, of course, should not use the diaphragm as a means of birth control because they probably will not use it all the time, in which case it will not work. However, a student told us that she and her partner made the preparation and insertion of the diaphragm a ritual part of their foreplay; he inserts it, and they both have a good time! Couples who maintain this kind of attitude are much more likely to use the diaphragm effectively. In addition, the diaphragm can be inserted an hour or more before sex.

The diaphragm requires some thought on the woman's part. She must remember to have it with her when she needs it and to have a supply of cream or jelly. She also needs to avoid becoming so carried away with passion that she forgets about it or decides not to use it.

A disadvantage is that the spermicide may leak out after intercourse.

The cost of a diaphragm is about $75 plus the cost of the office visit and the cost of the contraceptive cream. With proper care, a diaphragm should last about two years, so it is not expensive.

The major advantages of the diaphragm are that it has few side effects and, when used properly, is very effective. For this reason, women who are worried about the side effects of the pill should seriously consider the diaphragm as an alternative. There is also evidence of a reduction in the rate of cervical cancer among longtime users of the diaphragm. And the diaphragm provides some protection against sexually transmitted infections such as chlamydia because it covers and protects the cervix.

Reversibility

If a woman wishes to become pregnant, she simply stops using the diaphragm. Its use has no effect on her later chances of conceiving.

FemCap

FemCap is a vaginal barrier device similar to the diaphragm. FemCap is shaped like a sailor's cap (see Figure 9), is made of silicone, and comes in three sizes. It should be used with a spermicide or one of the new microbicides. The FemCap must be obtained through a health care provider.

The Sponge

The contraceptive sponge is another vaginal barrier method like the diaphragm and FemCap. Made of polyurethane, the sponge is small and shaped like a pillow

Figure 9 FemCap is a silicone rubber barrier contraceptive shaped like a sailor's hat, with a dome that covers the cervix and a brim that conforms to the vaginal walls.

©McGraw-Hill Education/Jill Braaten

with a concave dimple on one side. The other side has a woven loop to aid in removal. The sponge contains a spermicide and is inserted much like a diaphragm, with the concave side over the cervix. The sponge is effective for 24 hours, even with multiple acts of intercourse, but, overall, it is not a very effective method. It should not be left in place for more than 24 hours, though, because of a risk of toxic shock syndrome. It comes in one size and is available without prescription.

Spermicides

Contraceptive foams (Delfen, Emko), creams, and jellies are all classified as **spermicides,** that is, sperm killers (Figure 10). Most contain nonoxynol-9 (N-9). They come in a tube or a can, along with a plastic

> **Spermicide (SPERM-ih-side):** A substance that kills sperm.

applicator. The applicator is filled and inserted into the vagina. The applicator's plunger is then used to push the spermicide into the vagina near the cervix, so the spermicide is inserted much as a tampon is. It must be left in for 6 to 8 hours after intercourse. One application provides protection for only one act of intercourse.

Spermicides are not to be confused with the various feminine hygiene products (vaginal deodorants) on the market. Hygiene products are not effective as contraceptives.

How They Work
Spermicides consist of a spermicidal chemical in an inert base. They work in two ways: chemical and mechanical. The chemicals in them kill sperm, while the inert base itself mechanically blocks the entrance to the cervix so that sperm cannot swim into it.

Effectiveness
Failure rates for spermicides can be as high as 28 percent. Put simply, they are not very effective. Foams tend to be more effective, creams and jellies less so. Spermicidal

Figure 10 Contraceptive foams, creams, and gels are all spermicides.

©McGraw-Hill Education/Christopher Kerrigan, photographer

| **Table 2**   Summary of Information on Methods of Contraception and Abortion |

Method	Failure Rate, Perfect Use, %	Failure Rate, Typical Use, %	Death Rate (per 100,000 Women)	Yearly Costs, $*	Advantages	Disadvantages
IUD, Copper T	0.6	0.8	1.0	250[†]	Requires no memory or motivation	May be expelled
IUD, Progesterone T	0.2	0.2		250		
Implant	.05	.05		250[†]		
Depo-Provera	0.2	6		200	Requires less memory	
Combination birth control pills	0.3	9	1.6	600	Highly effective; not used at time of coitus; improved menstrual cycles	Cost; possible side effects; must take daily
Patch	0.3	9		600	Requires less memory than pill	
Vaginal Ring	0.3	9	—	600		
Condom, male	2	18	1.7	150	Easy to use; protection from STIs	Used at time of coitus, continual expense
Condom, female	5	21	2.0	600	Protection from STIs	Awkward
Diaphragm with spermicide	6	12	2.0[‡]	100	No side effects, inexpensive	Aesthetic objections
FemCap with spermicide				100	No side effects, inexpensive	—
Parous women	26	32	2.0[‡]			
Nulliparous women	9	16	2.0[†]			
Vaginal foam, cream	18	28	2.0[‡]	150	Easy to use; availability	Messy, continual expense
Sponge	9–20	12–24		750		
Withdrawal	4	22	2.0	None	No cost	Requires high motivation
Rhythm	3–5	24	2.0	None	No cost, accepted by Roman Catholic Church	Requires high motivation, prolonged abstinence; not all women can use
Unprotected intercourse	85	85	9[†]	None[§]		
Legal abortion, first trimester	0	0	0.5	350–700	Available when other methods fail	Expensive; moral unacceptability
Sterilization, male	0.10	0.15	0.3	1,000**	Permanent; highly effective	Permanence; expense
Sterilization, female	0.5	0.5	1.5	1,500–6,000**	Permanent; highly effective	Permanence; expense

*Based on 150 acts of intercourse. Prices are provided by Planned Parenthood, 2009, for full-paying clients (http://www.plannedparenthood.org/health-topics /birth-control-4211.htm). Prices are reduced for those with low incomes. Prices are higher for private physicians.

[†]Based on a cost of $500 for the IUD or implant including insertion by a physician, and the assumption that the IUD will be used for two years. The cost per year is much less if the IUD is used for more than two years.

[‡]Based on the death rate for pregnancies resulting from the method. Of every 100,000 live births in the United States, 12 women die (Cheng et al., 2003).

[§]But having a baby is expensive.

**These are one-time-only costs.

Source: Adapted from Robert A. Hatcher et al., *Contraceptive Technology,* 2011.

tablets and suppositories are also available, but they are the least effective. Spermicides are highly effective only when used with a diaphragm or a condom.

Side Effects

Some people experience an allergic reaction—irritation of the vagina or penis—to spermicides. Because we couldn't find any scientific studies on the incidence of these allergies, we surveyed our sexuality classes. We found that, of the students who had used spermicides, about 2 percent of the men and 26 percent of the women reported an allergic reaction.

Advantages and Disadvantages

The major advantage of spermicides is that they are readily available, without a prescription, in any drugstore. For this reason, they can be used as a stopgap method until the woman can see a health care provider and get a more effective contraceptive. Their failure rate is so high, though, that we cannot recommend using them by themselves. Always combine them with a second method such as a condom.

> **Withdrawal:** A method of birth control in which the man withdraws his penis from his partner's vagina before he has an orgasm and ejaculates.

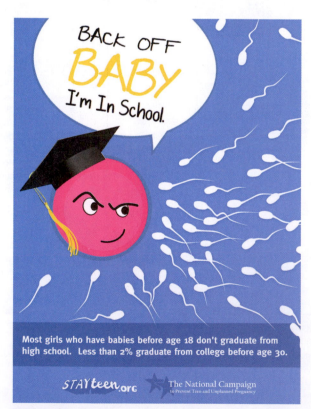

Figure 11 The National Campaign to Prevent Teen and Unplanned Pregnancy works to reduce teen pregnancy with media campaigns like this. Do you think the message is effective?

Source: National Campaign to Prevent Teen Pregnancy

Spermicides provide no protection against bacterial STIs such as chlamydia and gonorrhea. Neither do they protect against HIV, and there is some evidence that their frequent use increases susceptibility to HIV (Hatcher et al., 2011).

Their major disadvantage is that by themselves they are not very effective. They also interrupt the spontaneity of sex, although only briefly. Some women dislike the sensation of the spermicide leaking out after intercourse, and some are irritated by the chemicals. Finally, some people find that they taste terrible, and so their use interferes with oral sex.

Withdrawal

Withdrawal (*coitus interruptus,* "pulling out") is probably the most ancient form of birth control. (A reference to it is even found in Genesis 38:8–9, in the story of Onan. For this reason it is sometimes called *onanism,* although this term is also used for masturbation.) Withdrawal is still widely used throughout the world. The man withdraws his penis from his partner's vagina before he has an orgasm and ejaculates outside the vagina. For this method to be effective as contraception, the ejaculation must occur completely away from the woman's vulva. Reliance on withdrawal highlights the key issue of male responsibility in birth control.

Effectiveness

Withdrawal is not very effective as a method of birth control. The failure rate is around 22 percent. Failures occur for several reasons: The few drops of fluid that come out of the penis during arousal may carry enough sperm for conception to occur. If ejaculation occurs outside the vagina but near or on the vulva, sperm may still get into the vagina and continue up into the uterus. And sometimes the man simply does not withdraw in time.

Side Effects

Withdrawal produces no direct physical side effects.

Advantages and Disadvantages

The major advantage of withdrawal is that it is the only last-minute method. It can be used when nothing else is available, although if the situation is that desperate, the couple might consider abstinence or some other form of sexual expression, such as mouth–genital sex, as alternatives. Obviously, withdrawal requires no prescription and is free.

One major disadvantage is that withdrawal is not very effective. In addition, it requires exceptional motivation on the part of the man, and it may be psychologically stressful to him. The woman may worry about whether he really will withdraw in time, and the situation is certainly less than ideal for her to orgasm. Nonetheless, withdrawal may be useful as part of a dual method approach, in which it is used together with another method such as rhythm.

Fertility Awareness (Rhythm) Methods

Rhythm (fertility awareness) methods are the only form of "natural" birth control and are the only methods officially approved by the Roman Catholic Church. They require abstaining from intercourse during the woman's fertile period (around ovulation). There are several rhythm methods, in each of which the woman's fertile period is determined in a different way (Hatcher et al., 2011).

The **calendar method** is the basic rhythm method. It is based on the assumption that ovulation occurs about 14 days before the onset of menstruation. It works best for the woman with the perfectly regular 28-day cycle. She should ovulate on day 14, and almost surely on one of days 13 to 15. Three days are added in front of that period (because previously deposited sperm may result in conception), and 2 days are added after it (to allow for long-lasting eggs), so the couple must abstain from sexual intercourse from day 10 to day 17. For these reasons, even for the woman with perfectly regular cycles, 8 days of abstinence are required

> **How does the rhythm method work, and how effective is it?**

in the middle of each cycle. Research shows that sperm can live up to 5 days inside the female reproductive tract, and eggs live less than a day (Hatcher et al., 2011).

The woman who is not perfectly regular must keep a record of her cycles for at least 6 months, and preferably for a year. From this she determines the length of her shortest cycle and the length of her longest cycle. The preovulatory safe period is then calculated by subtracting 18 from the number of days in the shortest cycle, and the postovulatory safe period is calculated by subtracting 11 from the number of days in the longest cycle (see Table 3). For a woman who is somewhat irregular—say, with cycles varying from 26 to 33 days in length—a period of abstinence from day 8 to day 22 (a total of 15 days) would be required.

The standard days method (SDM) is a variation on the calendar method, designed to make it simpler (Hatcher et al., 2011). Proponents of this method say that 80 percent of women have cycle lengths between 26 and 32 days. For those women the fertile period is very likely to fall between days 8 and 19. For this reason, if a woman knows that she is regular and that her cycle length is between 26 and 32 days, all she needs to do is keep track of the day of the cycle and abstain from days 8 to 19. Of course, abstaining for 12 days each month would not be an enticing prospect for many women or their partners. In trials, the perfect-user failure rate was 5 percent and the typical-user failure rate was 12 percent (Arévalo et al., 2002).

> **Rhythm (fertility awareness) method:** A method of birth control that involves abstaining from intercourse around the time the woman ovulates.
>
> **Calendar method:** A type of rhythm method of birth control in which the woman determines when she ovulates by keeping a calendar record of the length of her menstrual cycles.

Table 3	Determining the Fertile Period Using the Calendar Method		

Shortest Cycle (Days)	Day Fertile Period Begins	Longest Cycle (Days)	Day Fertile Period Ends
22	4	23	12
23	5	24	13
24	6	25	14
25	7 (Minus 18)	26	15
26	⑧	27	16
27	9	28	17
28	10	29	18
29	11	30	19
30	12	31	20
31	13	32 (Minus 11)	21
32	14	33	㉒
		34	23
		35	24

Example: If a woman's cycles vary in length from 26 days to 33 days, she can be fertile any time between days 8 and 22 of the cycle. To avoid getting pregnant, she must abstain from sexual intercourse from day 8 to day 22.

A somewhat more accurate method for determining ovulation is the **basal body temperature (BBT) method.** We discussed the principle behind this method in the chapter "Sex Hormones, Sexual Differentiation, and the Menstrual Cycle." The woman takes her temperature every day immediately upon waking. During the preovulatory phase her temperature will be at a fairly constant low level. On the day of ovulation it drops (although this does not always occur), and on the day after ovulation it rises sharply and then stays at that high level for the rest of the cycle. Intercourse would be safe beginning about three days after ovulation.

As a form of contraception, the BBT method has a major disadvantage in that it determines safe days only *after* ovulation, and theoretically, according to the method, there are no safe days before ovulation. For this reason the BBT method is best used in combination with the calendar method or the cervical mucus method, which determine the preovulatory safe period, while the BBT method determines the postovulatory safe period.

Another rhythm method is based on variations over the cycle in the mucus produced by the cervix. The **cervical mucus method** works in the following way.

There are generally a few days just after menstruation during which no mucus is produced and there is a general sensation of vaginal dryness. This period is relatively safe. Then there are a number of days of mucus discharge around the middle of the cycle. On the first days, the mucus is white or cloudy and tacky. The amount increases, and the mucus becomes clearer, until there are one or two *peak days,* when the mucus is like raw egg white—clear, slippery, and stringy. There is also a sensation of vaginal lubrication. Ovulation occurs within 24 hours after the last peak day. Abstinence is required from the first day of mucus discharge until 4 days after the peak days. After that, the mucus, if present, is cloudy or white, and intercourse is safe.

The **sympto-thermal method** combines two rhythm methods to produce better effectiveness. The woman records changes in her cervical mucus (symptoms) as well as her basal body temperature (thermal). The combination of the two should give a more accurate determination for the time of ovulation.

Recently, home tests for the detection of ovulation have been developed. Most such tests have been designed for use by couples wanting to conceive, but a few are now available for contraception (Hatcher et al., 2011). One kind (PG53, PC 2000, and Maybe Baby) involves minimicroscopes to examine saliva or cervical mucus. Others involve temperature computers that work on the BBT method. Hormone computers (for example, Persona) assess hormone levels in urine. Costs range between $50 and $500. The effectiveness of these tests is not yet well enough researched for them to be recommended as reliable.

Effectiveness

The effectiveness of the rhythm method varies considerably, depending on a number of factors, but basically it is not very effective with typical users (giving rise to its nickname, "Vatican roulette," and a number of old jokes like, "What do they call people who use the rhythm method?" Answer: "Parents"). Although the typical-user failure rate is around 25 percent for all methods, ideal-user failure rates vary considerably. They are 5 percent for the calendar method, 2 percent for BBT, 2 percent for the sympto-thermal method, and 3 percent for the cervical mucus method (Hatcher et al., 2011).

Failure rates are lower when the woman's cycle is very regular and when the couple are highly motivated and have been well instructed in the methods. The effectiveness of the rhythm method also depends partly on one's purpose in using it: whether for preventing pregnancy absolutely or for spacing pregnancies. If absolute pregnancy prevention is the goal (as it probably would be, for example, for an unmarried teenager), the method is just not effective enough. But if the couple simply wish to space pregnancies further apart than would occur naturally, the method will probably accomplish this. Knowing when the woman's fertile times occur can also improve the effectiveness of other methods of contraception. Combining the sympto-thermal method with use of a condom during fertile days can lead to better effectiveness with no need for abstinence.

Advantages and Disadvantages

For many users of the rhythm method, its main advantage is that the Roman Catholic Church considers it an acceptable method of birth control.

The method has no side effects except possible psychological stress, and it is cheap. It is easily reversible. It also helps the woman become more aware of her body's functioning. The method requires cooperation from both partners, which may be considered either an advantage or a disadvantage.

Its main disadvantages are its high failure rate and the psychological stress it may cause. Periods of abstinence of at least 8 days, and possibly as long as 2 or 3 weeks, are necessary, which is an unacceptable requirement for many couples.

A certain amount of time, usually several months, is required to collect the data needed to make the method work. Thus one cannot simply begin using it on the spur of the moment.

Basal body temperature (BBT) method: A type of rhythm method of birth control in which the woman determines when she ovulates by keeping track of her temperature.
Cervical mucus method: A type of rhythm method of birth control in which the woman determines when she ovulates by checking her cervical mucus.
Sympto-thermal method: A type of rhythm method of birth control combining the basal body temperature method and the cervical mucus method.

Sterilization

Sterilization, or voluntary surgical contraception (VSC), is a surgical procedure whereby an individual is made permanently sterile, that is, unable to reproduce. Sterilization can be an emotion-laden topic, for a number of reasons. Some people confuse sterilization with castration, though the two are quite different. This is also an emotional topic because sterilization means the end of one's capacity to reproduce. The ability to impregnate and the ability to bear a child are very important in cultural definitions of manhood and womanhood. We hope that as gender roles become more flexible in our society and as concern about reproduction is replaced by a concern for limiting population size, the word *sterilization* will no longer carry such emotional overtones.

Most physicians are conservative about performing sterilizations; they want to make sure that the patient has made a firm decision on their own and will not be back a few months later wanting to have the procedure reversed. The physician has an obligation to follow the principle of informed consent. This means explaining the procedures involved, telling the patient about the possible risks and advantages, discussing alternative methods, and answering any questions the patient has.

Despite this conservatism, both male sterilization and female sterilization have become increasingly popular as methods of birth control. Female sterilization is the most common method of birth control for women, used by 31 percent of U.S. women between the ages of 35 and 44 (Daniels et al., 2014).

Male Sterilization

The male sterilization operation is called a **vasectomy,** so named for the vas deferens, which is tied or cut. It can be done in a physician's office under local anesthesia and requires only about 20 minutes to perform. In the traditional procedure, the physician makes a small incision on one side of the upper part of the scrotum. The vas is then separated from the surrounding tissues, tied off, and cut. The procedure is then repeated on the other side, and the incisions are sewn up. For a day or two the man may have to refrain from strenuous activity and be careful not to pull the incision apart.

Now a *no-scalpel vasectomy* procedure has been developed (Hatcher et al., 2011). It involves making just a tiny pierce in the scrotum (Figure 12). This procedure has an even lower rate of complications than a standard vasectomy.

Typically, the man can return to having intercourse within a few days. It should not be assumed that he is sterile yet, however. Some stray sperm may still be lurking in his ducts beyond the point of the incision. Men should not rely completely on the vasectomy until 3 months after it was performed (Hatcher et al., 2011). Until then, an additional method of birth control should be used. Ideally, the man should have a semen analysis after 3 months to confirm that his ejaculate is sperm free.

Misunderstandings about the vasectomy abound. In fact, a vasectomy creates no physical changes that interfere with erection. Neither does it interfere in any way with

> **Sterilization:** A surgical procedure by which an individual is made sterile, that is, incapable of reproducing.
> **Vasectomy (va-SEK-tuh-mee):** A surgical procedure for male sterilization involving severing of the vas deferens.

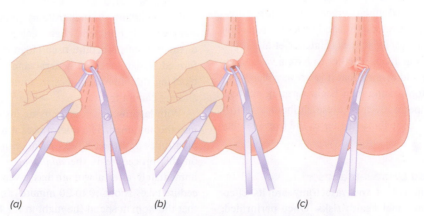

(a)   (b)   (c)

Figure 12   The no-scalpel vasectomy. (*a*) The vas (dotted line) is grasped by special ring forceps and the scrotum is pierced by sharp-tipped forceps. (*b*) The forceps stretch the opening slightly, and (*c*) the vas is lifted out and then tied off. The other vas is then lifted out through the same small hole and the procedure is repeated.

sex hormone production; the testes continue to manufacture testosterone and secrete it into the bloodstream. Nor does a vasectomy interfere with the process or sensation of ejaculation. As we noted earlier, virtually all the fluid of the ejaculate is produced by the seminal vesicles and prostate, and the incision is made long before that point in the duct system. Thus the ejaculate is completely normal, except that it does not contain any sperm.

How It Works

The vasectomy makes it impossible for sperm to move beyond the cut in the vas. Thus the vasectomy prevents sperm from being in the ejaculate.

Effectiveness

The vasectomy is essentially 100 percent effective; it has a failure rate of 0.1 percent. Failures occur because stray sperm are still present during the first few months after surgery, because the physician did not completely sever the vas, or because the ends of the vas have grown back together.

Side Effects

The physical side effects of the vasectomy are minimal. In rare cases there is a minor complication from the surgery, such as infection of the vas (Hatcher et al., 2011).

Some psychologically based problems may arise. Thus the man's attitude toward having a vasectomy is extremely important. Only about 5 percent regret having had a vasectomy (Hatcher et al., 2011).

Reversibility

Quite a bit of effort has been devoted to developing techniques for reversing vasectomies (the surgical procedure for reversal is termed *vasovasostomy*) and to developing vasectomy techniques that are more reversible. At present, with sophisticated microsurgery techniques, pregnancy rates following reversal range between 38 percent and 89 percent in various studies (Hatcher et al., 2011). In making a decision about whether to have a vasectomy, though, a man should assume that it is irreversible.

After a vasectomy some men begin forming antibodies to their own sperm. Because these antibodies destroy sperm, they might contribute further to the irreversibility of the vasectomy.

Advantages and Disadvantages

The major advantages of the vasectomy are its effectiveness and its minimal health risks. Once performed, it requires no further thought or planning on the man's part. As a permanent, long-term method of contraception, it is very cheap.

Laparoscopy: A method of female sterilization.

The operation itself is simple—simpler than the female sterilization procedures—and requires no hospitalization or absence from work. Finally, it is one of the few methods that allow the man to assume contraceptive responsibility.

The permanency of the vasectomy may be either an advantage or a disadvantage. If permanent contraception is desired, the method is certainly much better than something like birth control pills, which must be used repeatedly. But if the couple change their minds and decide that they want to have a child, the permanence is a distinct disadvantage. Some men put several samples of their sperm into a frozen sperm bank so that artificial insemination can be performed if they do decide to have a child after a vasectomy.

Another disadvantage of the vasectomy is the various psychological problems that might result if the man sees sterilization as a threat to his masculinity or virility. However, in studies done around the world, the majority of vasectomized men say that they have no regrets about having had the sterilization performed, that they would recommend it to others, and that there has been no change or else an improvement in their happiness and sexual satisfaction in marriage. Fewer than 5 percent of vasectomized men regret having the vasectomy.

Can a man still ejaculate after a vasectomy?

Finally, if a married couple use the vasectomy as a permanent method of birth control, the woman is not protected if she has intercourse with someone other than her husband.

Female Sterilization

Several surgical techniques are used to sterilize a woman (sometimes called tubal ligation or "having the tubes tied"), including minilaparotomy, laparoscopy, and the transcervical approach. These techniques differ in terms of the type of procedure used (Figure 13). They are performed under local or general anesthesia, and involve blocking the fallopian tubes in some way so that sperm and egg cannot meet.

With **laparoscopy,** a magnifying instrument is inserted into the abdomen. The doctor uses it to identify the fallopian tubes and then blocks them with clips. A variation on this procedure is the *minilaparotomy,* which is used immediately after a woman has given birth. Either procedure takes about 10 to 20 minutes and does not require that the woman spend the night in the hospital.

Another procedure is the *transcervical approach,* which does not require an incision. Instead, the instruments enter through the cervix and uterus, and a blockage device called Essure is placed in each fallopian tube. Scar tissue

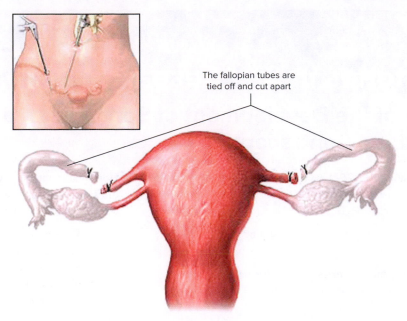

The fallopian tubes are
tied off and cut apart

Figure 13 Tubal ligation using the laparoscopic method.

Source: http://www.nlm.nih.gov/medlineplus/ency/images/ency/fullsize

forms around it, blocking the fallopian tube. In 2018, the FDA raised concerns about adverse events with Essure, such as pain and uterine perforation, and issued restrictions on its use.

The female sterilization procedures do not interfere with the ovaries. For this reason, the production of sex hormones continues normally, so female sterilization does not bring on premature menopause. Some misunderstandings arise from confusing female sterilization procedures with hysterectomy (surgical removal of the uterus) or oophorectomy (surgical removal of the ovaries, which does impair hormonal functioning). These two operations do produce sterility, but they are generally performed for purposes other than sterilization, such as treatment of cancer.

How It Works
Female sterilization procedures make it impossible for the egg to move down the fallopian tube toward the uterus. They also prevent sperm from reaching the egg.

Effectiveness
These procedures are essentially 100 percent effective. The failure rate of 0.5 percent is due to an occasional rejoining of the ends of the fallopian tubes, and rare cases in which the woman was pregnant before the sterilization procedure was performed.

Side Effects
Occasionally there are side effects arising from the surgery, such as infections, hemorrhaging, and problems related to the anesthetic. Generally, only 1 percent of women undergoing the surgery experience complications.

Reversibility
Highly refined microsurgery techniques make it possible to reverse female sterilization in some cases. The success rate varies considerably, depending on the method that was used to perform the sterilization. Pregnancy rates range between 50 percent and 75 percent, depending on the woman's age and other factors (Gordts et al., 2009). However, in deciding whether to have sterilization surgery, a woman should assume that it is irreversible. Five years after sterilization, only 7 percent of women regret having had the procedure (Jamieson et al., 2002).

Advantages and Disadvantages
Female sterilization has some of the same advantages as male sterilization in terms of effectiveness, permanence, and cheapness when used for long-term contraception. One disadvantage is that it offers no protection from sexually transmitted infections.

Milestones in Sex Research

History of the Development of Sophisticated Methods of Contraception

Late 1700s	Casanova (1725–1798) popularizes and publicizes use of the sheath, or "English riding coat."
1798	Malthus urges "moral restraint" or abstinence.
1840s	Goodyear vulcanizes rubber. Production of rubber condoms soon follows.
1883	Mensinga invents the diaphragm.
1893	Harrison performs the first vasectomy.
1909	Richter uses the intrauterine silkworm gut.
1910–1920	Sanger pioneers in New York City; the term *birth control* is coined.
1930	Gräfenberg publishes information documenting his 21 years of experience with the ring (silver and copper) and catgut as IUDs.
1930–1931	Knaus and Ogino elucidate "safe and unsafe" periods of the woman's menstrual cycle: the rhythm method.
1934	Corner and Beard isolate progesterone.
1937	Makepeace demonstrates that progesterone inhibits ovulation.
1950s	Abortions are used extensively in Japan.
1950–1960	Hormonal contraceptive research results in FDA approval of the use of the pill as a contraceptive in 1960.
1960s	Many Western nations liberalize abortion laws. Modern IUDs become available. Contraceptive sterilization becomes more acceptable. The laparoscopic tubal ligation technique is developed.
1973	The U.S. Supreme Court rules on abortion.
1970s	Depo-Provera contraceptive injections become available in more than 50 nations (though not in the United States until 1992).
1990	Norplant implant becomes available.
1994	Female condom becomes available over the counter.
2001	NuvaRing and Ortho Evra patch approved by FDA.
2003	Seasonale approved by FDA.
2006	Plan B emergency contraception approved by FDA for sale over the counter.

Sources: Hatcher et al. (1976); Institute of Medicine (2004).

Psychological Aspects: Attitudes toward Contraception

It is a favorite old saying that contraceptives are only as effective as the people who use them. In other words, no contraceptive method is effective if it is not used or if it is used improperly. For this reason the user is at least as important as all the technology of contraception.

Each year in the United States, 450,000 teenagers become pregnant (Kost et al., 2017). It is not an overstatement to say that teenage pregnancy is at epidemic proportions. Approximately 29 percent of these unwanted pregnancies are terminated by abortion, 57 percent result in live births (to single teenagers or to couples joined in "shotgun" matrimony), and the rest end in miscarriage (Guttmacher Institute, 2006).

The great majority of these unwanted pregnancies occur because sexually active persons fail to use contraceptives responsibly. Among sexually active teenage girls, 10 percent used no method of contraception the last time they had sex (Abma & Martinez, 2017). In a study of U.S. women having abortions, 49 percent had used no method of contraception in the month when the conception occurred (Jones, 2018).

If we are to understand this problem and take effective steps to solve it, we must understand the psychology of contraceptive use and nonuse. Many researchers have been investigating this issue.

When adolescents are asked why they do not use contraceptives, they tend to give reasons such as the following (Boyce et al., 2006): They didn't expect to have sex and therefore didn't have contraception available; they believed that they (or their partner) couldn't get pregnant; they had problems obtaining contraceptives, such as not knowing where to get them or believing that they would be too expensive; they did not like to use a method such as a condom; and they were too drunk or high to make a smart decision. And some think that pregnancy would not be such a bad thing and might even be a good thing.

We can also approach this question from the opposite direction: What are the characteristics of teens who are conscientious about contraception? One study examined the sexual and contraceptive knowledge, beliefs, and motivations of a well-sampled group of American teenagers between the ages of 15 and 19, focusing only on those who were sexually active (Ryan et al., 2007). Compared with girls who were inconsistent users of contraception or nonusers, consistent users of contraception were more likely to think that they had access to contraceptives, had a strong sense of self-effectiveness at using birth control, were more strongly motivated to use birth control, and had stronger motivations to avoid pregnancy. Boys who consistently used contraceptives, compared with their inconsistent peers, felt that they knew more about condom use. Interestingly, the groups did not differ on measures such as IQ.

These results highlight factors that experts believe are crucial for teens to be consistent users of contraception: access to contraceptives and a belief that one has access; knowledge about sexual and reproductive health and contraception; and strong motivation to use contraception, rather than having a lot of excuses such as "it's too much of a hassle" or "it interferes with sexual enjoyment." Fortunately, all of these factors can be addressed in educational programs for teens.

Although it is generally recognized that *fantasy* is an important part of sexual expression, fantasy may also play an important role in contraceptive behavior. Most of us have fantasies about sexual encounters, and we often try to make our real-life sexual encounters turn out like the scripts of our fantasies. An important shaper of our fantasies is the mass media. Through movies, television, the Internet, and romance novels we learn idealized techniques for kissing, holding, and lovemaking. But the media's idealized versions of sex almost never include a portrayal of the use of contraceptives (American Academy of Pediatrics, 2010). In the popular series *Grey's Anatomy,* intern Cristina has sex with resident Burke with

no contraception in sight—and they're doctors! One content analysis of media (television, magazines, music, and movies) that are popular with adolescents found that on the rare occasions when contraception was presented, it was portrayed as embarrassing or humiliating (Hust et al., 2008).

Positive examples come from the series *Sex and the City.* In one sequence, Miranda had "mercy sex" with her ex-boyfriend Steve, who had just undergone treatment for testicular cancer. They didn't use a condom, and Miranda got pregnant. After that, she frequently reminded her friends to use a condom, using herself as an example of the consequences if one didn't. These episodes were excellent in showing that negative consequences do occur when contraception is not used, and they provide examples of honest discussions of contraception. Nonetheless, this show was on HBO, and it remains to be seen whether the major networks would air such open and truthful approaches. If teenagers saw lots of instances of their heroes and heroines behaving responsibly about contraception, it would probably influence their behavior. But right now that is not what the media gives them.

What are the solutions? Can this research and theorizing on the psychology of contraceptive use be applied to reducing the teenage pregnancy problem? The most direct solution would be to have better programs of sex education in the schools. Many districts have no sex education programs, and those that do often skip the important issue of contraception, fearing that it is too controversial. Sex education programs would need to include a number of components that are typically missing. These include legitimizing presex communication about sex and contraception; legitimizing the purchase and carrying of contraceptives; discussing how one weighs the costs and benefits of pregnancy, contraception, and abortion; legitimizing noncoital kinds of sexual pleasure, such as masturbation and oral–genital sex; and encouraging males to accept equal responsibility for contraception. For further information on sexuality education, see Looking to the Future: Sexuality Education, at the end of this book.

Abortion

Abortion (the termination of a pregnancy) is highly controversial in the United States. Pro-choice groups talk of the woman's right to control her own body, whereas members of right-to-life groups speak of the fetus's rights. In 1973 the U.S. Supreme Court made two landmark decisions (*Roe v. Wade* and *Doe v. Bolton*) that essentially decriminalized abortion by

> **Abortion:** The termination of pregnancy.

Table 4	Abortion Rates around the World	
Region	Abortion Rate*	% of Pregnancies Ending in Abortion
Southern Africa	35	24%
East Asia	36	34%
South America	47	34%
North America	17	17%
Western Europe	18	21%

*"Abortion rate" is the number of abortions per 1,000 women aged 15–44.

Source: Sedgh et al. (2016).

denying the states the right to regulate early abortions. The conservative Supreme Court of the 1990s made some rulings that partly reversed these decisions (see the chapter "Sex and the Law"). Nevertheless, 926,000 legal abortions are performed each year in the United States (Jones & Jerman, 2017). That rate is down 25 percent from 2008. This decline in the number of abortions may be due to several factors, including increased use of highly effective LARC methods and the increase in state laws restricting access to abortion.

In other countries, policies on abortion vary widely. It is legal and widely practiced in Russia and Japan, parts of eastern and central Europe, and South America. The use of abortion in the developing nations of Africa and Asia is limited because of the scarcity of medical facilities. Table 4 gives rates of abortion in various regions.

In this section we discuss methods of abortion and the psychological aspects of abortion. We explore the ethical and legal aspects in the chapters "Ethics, Religion, and Sexuality" and "Sex and the Law."

Abortion Procedures

Several methods of abortion are available, which can be categorized as surgical or medication abortion. Which one is used depends in part on how far the pregnancy has progressed.

Surgical Abortion

The **vacuum aspiration method** (also called *suction curettage*) can be performed during the first trimester of pregnancy and up to 14 weeks' gestation. It is done on an outpatient basis with a local anesthetic. The procedure itself takes only about 10 minutes, and the woman stays in the clinic for a few hours.

The woman is prepared as she would be for a pelvic exam, and an instrument is inserted into the

> **Vacuum aspiration:** A method of abortion that is performed during the first trimester and involves suctioning out the contents of the uterus; also called *suction curettage*.

vagina; the instrument dilates (stretches open) the opening of the cervix. A tube is then inserted into this opening until one end is in the uterus (see Figure 14). The other end is attached to a suction-producing apparatus and the contents of the uterus, including the fetal tissue, are sucked out.

Vacuum aspiration is the most common method of early (first trimester) abortion because it is simple and entails little risk. There are rare risks of uterine perforation, infection, hemorrhaging, and failure to remove all the fetal material. In the United States today, 67 percent of abortions are surgical abortions performed in the first trimester (first 13 weeks of gestation) and 23 percent are medical abortions (discussed in the next section) performed in the first 8 weeks (Jatlaoui et al., 2017).

Dilation and evacuation (D&E) is used especially for later, second trimester abortions (Hatcher et al., 2011). It is somewhat similar to vacuum aspiration, but it is more complicated because the fetus is relatively large by the second trimester.

A summary of statistics on death rates associated with abortion, compared with childbirth, is shown in Table 5.

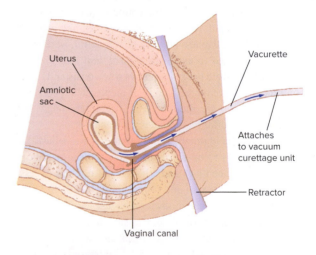
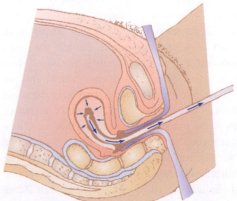

Figure 14 A vacuum aspiration abortion.

Table 5 Summary of Death Rates Associated with Legal Abortion and with Normal Childbirth

Deaths per 100,000 legal abortions*	
Curettage	0.1
Deaths per 100,000 normal childbirths	13
Blacks	30.0
Whites	8.1
Others	9.8

*Centers for Disease Control (2006).

Sources: Cheng et al. (2003); Hatcher et al. (2004).

Medication Abortions

The drug **mifepristone** (brand name Mifeprex, formerly called RU-486) is used for a medication or medical abortion, so called because it involves only the administration of a drug. It can induce a very early abortion. It has a powerful antiprogesterone effect, causing the endometrium of the uterus to be sloughed off and thus bringing about an abortion. It is administered as a tablet followed 24 to 48 hours later by a small dose of prostaglandin (misoprostol), which increases contractions of the uterus, helping to expel the embryo (Figure 15). It can be used during the first 70 days (10 weeks) of pregnancy. Research shows that it is effective in 92 percent of cases when combined with prostaglandin (Hatcher et al., 2007). Early research has found little evidence of side effects, although the woman experiences some cramping as the uterine contents are expelled.

How does mifepristone work?

Until 1994 the drug was blocked from use in the United States by pressure from antiabortion groups. Because the drug can be easily administered in any doctor's office and reduces the use of abortion clinics, these groups fear that it will become more difficult to protest abortions. The drug was finally approved in 2000 and is now widely available. Today, medication abortions account for 23 percent of all abortions in the United States (Jatlaoui et al., 2017).

Another alternative in drug-induced early abortion involves the use of a combination of the drug *methotrexate,* which is toxic to the embryo, with misoprostol, which causes uterine contractions that expel the embryo (Hatcher et al., 2011). Both of these drugs are already widely used for other purposes, methotrexate for the treatment of cancer and misoprostol for ulcers. Like mifepristone, they permit the early induction of abortion in a physician's office rather than an abortion

clinic, allowing women to avoid sidewalk picketers and potential violence by protestors at abortion clinics. Methotrexate is also used to treat ectopic pregnancy, which is a life-threatening condition.

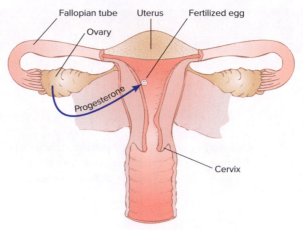

Progesterone, a hormone produced by the ovaries, is necessary for the implantation and development of a fertilized egg.

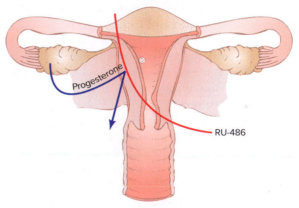

Taken early in pregnancy, mifepristone blocks the action of progesterone so that the endometrium is sloughed off.

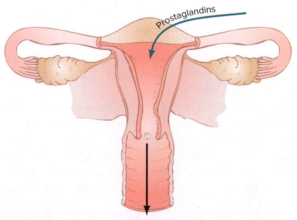

Prostaglandins, taken 24 to 48 hours later, cause the uterus to contract and the cervix to soften and dilate. As a result, the embryo is expelled in 97 percent of the cases.

Figure 15 How mifepristone works.

Mifepristone (RU-486): The "abortion pill."

A Sexually Diverse World

Abortion in Cross-Cultural Perspective

Beliefs about abortion show dramatic variations in different cultures around the world. The following is a sampling from two very different cultures.

Ekiti Yoruba

The Ekiti Yoruba, many of whom have a high school or college education, live in southwest Nigeria. For them, abortion is not a distinct category from contraception but rather is on a continuum with it (Renne, 1996).

Traditionally in the Ekiti Yoruba culture the ideal was for a woman to have as many children as possible, spaced at two- to three-year intervals. The spacing of children is made possible by a period of sexual abstinence for two years postpartum. The Ekiti Yoruba believe that sexual intercourse while a woman is still breast-feeding a baby causes illness or death to the child; men whose children have died in infancy have been blamed for breaking the postpartum sex taboo and causing the death. Because of the high value placed on fertility, use of contraceptives and abortion must be kept secret. Even though condoms, foam, and birth control pills are available at a local clinic, few people take advantage of the service because they would not want others to know that they engaged in such practices. Abortion then becomes the chief method of birth control. Estimates are that between 200,000 and 500,000 pregnancies are aborted each year in Nigeria and that about 10,000 women die each year from botched abortions.

If a woman has an unwanted pregnancy, she generally will consult a local divine healer or herbalist first, in order to "keep the pregnancy from staying." They generally provide pills or substances to insert in the vagina. If the treatment does not work, the woman then goes to a clinic and has a dilation and curettage (D&C; a procedure similar to D&E).

Women who abort generally fall into two categories: unmarried high school or college students who want to finish their education, and married women who are pregnant because of an affair. Here is one woman's story:

In 1991, when awaiting entrance into university, I became pregnant by one boyfriend whom I later decided not to marry in favor of another. Since I did not want my chosen fiancé to know of the pregnancy, I decided to abort it. I first used 3 Bee-codeine tablets, Andrew's Liver Salt, and Sprite, mixing them together and then drinking them.

When this did not work, I went to a clinic in a neighboring town for D&C. The abortion cost N80 and was paid for by my boyfriend. There were no after-effects. (Renne, 1996, p. 487)

The ease with which Ekiti Yoruba people rely on abortion is related in part to their understanding of prenatal development. Many believe that the "real child" is not formed until after the fourth month of pregnancy, and before that the being is lizardlike.

Greece

Birth control for women was legalized in Greece only in 1980, and abortion was not legalized until 1986. Yet Greece has had a sharply declining birthrate since World War II, accounted for, in large part, by abortion (Georges, 1996). Among European nations, Greece is unique in its combination of very little use of medical contraception, a low fertility rate, and the highest abortion rate in Europe.

Three powerful institutions—the government, the Greek Orthodox Church, and the medical profession—have exerted a strong pronatalist (in favor of having babies) influence. The Greek Orthodox Church equates abortion with murder and prohibits all methods of birth control except rhythm and abstinence. The government, for its part, encourages large families by a variety of measures, including paying a monthly subsidy to families with more than three children, making day care centers widely available, and keeping female methods of contraception illegal (until 1980). Despite all this, Greek women achieved a low fertility rate, which is regarded by the government as a threat to the Greek "race," Greek Orthodoxy, and the military strength of Greece in relation to hostile neighbors such as the extremely fertile Turks.

Despite the illegality of abortion in Greece until 1986, abortion was widespread and a very open secret. Abortions were not back-alley affairs but rather were performed by gynecologists in private offices. Physicians, as members of a powerful and prestigious profession, were successful at legal evasion. As a result, Greek women did not have to face the life-threatening risks that occur with illegal abortion in other countries. They had access to safe, illegal abortion.

Why is there so much reliance on abortion and so little access to contraception in this modern European nation? As noted earlier, the Greek Orthodox Church opposes all medical contraception and the Greek government kept contraception illegal until 1980. But even then, contraception did not become widespread. In 1990 only 2 percent of women of reproductive age were using the pill. Some blame this on the medical profession, which is thought to block access to contraception in order to continue a thriving abortion practice that is more lucrative. Greek women, too, resist contraception. They distinguish between "contraception" (such as birth control pills) and "being careful" (withdrawal and condoms). They reject contraception, but being careful—especially the use of withdrawal—is widespread. Rhythm is not widely used and would not be very successful if it were, since Greek women commonly believe that they are most fertile for the four to seven days just before and after the menstrual period. The mass media have spread scare messages about the pill, and many women believe that it causes cancer.

How do Greek women, the great majority of whom are Orthodox, deal with the contradiction between their church's teaching—that abortion is murder and that a woman who has had an abortion may not receive Communion—and their actual practice of having abortions? First, the Greek Orthodox Church is not as absolutist in its application of doctrines regarding abortion as the Roman Catholic Church is. Some attribute this to the fact that Orthodox priests can be married and are therefore more in touch with the realities of life. In some cases, women do abstain from receiving Communion following

an abortion but then later make a confession to the priest. Priests typically are forgiving.

In Greece, motherhood is highly esteemed and idealized, yet abortion is not considered contradictory to the high value placed on motherhood. Good motherhood today is thought to require an intense investment of time and energy in one's children; by definition, then, the good mother limits family size, and abortion is a means to achieve that goal.

Cross-Cultural Patterns

Several patterns emerge from the study of abortion in these quite distinct cultures and other cultures (e.g., Gursoy, 1996; Johnson et al., 1996; Rigdon, 1996; Rylko-Bauer, 1996). First, no matter how strict the prohibitions against abortion, some women in all cultures choose and manage to obtain abortion. Second, the meaning of abortion is constructed in any particular culture based on factors such as beliefs about prenatal development, when life starts, and how much large families are valued. Third, the legality and morality of abortion in any culture is determined in part by political forces, such as the Greek government's desire to expand the size of the Greek population.

Sources: Georges (1996); Gursoy (1996); Johnson et al. (1996); Renne (1996); Rigdon (1996); Rylko-Bauer (1996).

Psychological Aspects

The discovery of an unwanted pregnancy triggers a complicated set of emotions, as well as a complex decision-making process. Initially women tend to feel anger and some anxiety. They then embark on the decision-making process studied by psychologist Carol Gilligan (1982). In this process women essentially weigh the need to think of themselves and protect their own welfare against the need to think of the welfare of the fetus. Even focusing only on the welfare of the fetus can lead to conflicting conclusions: Should I complete the pregnancy, because the fetus has a right to life; or should I have an abortion, because the fetus has a right to be born into a stable family with married parents who have completed their education and can provide good financial support? Some women consider whether to give birth to the baby and then give it up for adoption. By the time women seek an abortion, research

shows that they display a high level of certainty about the decision (Ralph et al., 2017). In fact, the level of certainty is higher than found in patients undergoing other medical procedures, such as reconstructive knee surgery.

Is there a "postabortion syndrome"? Antiabortion activists claim that women are psychologically traumatized by having an abortion (Bazelon, 2007). What do the scientific data say? The best scientific evidence indicates that most women do not experience severe negative psychological responses to abortion (Gomez, 2018; Major et al., 2009; Munk-Olsen et al., 2011). When women are interviewed a year or so after their abortion, most show good adjustment. Typically they do not feel guilt or sorrow over the decision. Instead, they report feeling relieved, satisfied, and relatively happy and say that if they had the decision to make over again they would do the same thing. Nonetheless, some women benefit from talking about their experience, and it is important that postabortion support groups be available.

Research in this area raises many interesting questions. Women generally show good adjustment after having an abortion, but good adjustment compared with what? That is, what is the appropriate control or comparison group? One comparison group that could be studied is women who requested an abortion but were denied it.

The Turnaway Study is a well-designed U.S. study of exactly these issues (Harris et al., 2014; Roberts et al., 2014). The background is that all abortion facilities have a gestational age limit on the abortions they perform; perhaps it's 12 weeks or 15 weeks or 20 weeks. In the Turnaway Study, researchers recruited nearly 1,000 women from multiple clinics across the country who fell into one of three groups: (1) Near Limit Abortion Group (they were within 2 weeks of the clinic's limit and received their abortion); (2) Turnaway Group (they were slightly over the clinic's limit, by no more than 3 weeks, and therefore did not receive an abortion, i.e., they were turned away and later gave birth); and (3) First Trimester Abortion Group. The clever aspect of the design is that the Near Limit Abortion Group and the Turnaway Group do not differ by much. They are within a few weeks of each other in gestational age, and all the psychological and social factors that go with it. Yet women in one group received an abortion and women in the other did not and subsequently carried the pregnancy to term. Data were then collected from the women months and even years later.

Several interesting findings have emerged so far from the study. When data were collected 5 years later, the three groups did not differ in depression (Biggs et al., 2017). That is, women who had abortions felt no more depressed than women who had not, again confirming the generally good adjustment of women following an abortion. In other data from the study, it turns out that one reason women seek an abortion is that they have a partner who is violent toward them (Roberts et al., 2014). Intimate partner violence decreased following abortion for women in the two groups who had abortions, but intimate partner violence persisted at the same level for women in the Turnaway Group. Therefore, denial of abortion may keep women in contact with violent partners, putting both them and their children at risk.

Another group that has been studied is children who were born because an abortion request was denied. In some countries access to abortion depends on obtaining official approval. One such country was the former Czechoslovakia. Researchers followed up 220 children born to women denied abortion (the study group) and 220 children born to women who had not requested abortion; the children were studied when they were 9 years old and again when they were 14 to 16 years old, 21–23, 30, and 35 (David et al., 2003). By age 14, compared with the control group, more children from the study group had been referred for counseling. Although there were no differences between the groups in tested intelligence, children in the study group did less well in school and were more likely to drop out. At age 16, the boys (but not the girls) in the study group more frequently rated themselves as feeling neglected or rejected by their mothers and felt that their mothers were less satisfied with them. By their early 20s, the study group reported less job satisfaction, more conflicts with coworkers and supervisors, and fewer and less satisfying friendships. Several other studies have found results similar to the Czech one (David et al., 2003). These results point to the serious long-term consequences for children whose mothers would have preferred to have an abortion. In fact, one analysis has shown that legalized abortion in the United States has lowered crime rates because it reduces the number of unwanted children (Donohue & Levitt, 2004).

Men and Abortion

Only women become pregnant, and only women have abortions, but where do men enter the picture? Do they have a right to contribute to the decision to have an abortion? What are their feelings about abortion?

A large survey of women who had abortions indicated that 82 percent of the male partners knew they were having an abortion, although the percentage was lower for women in abusive relationships (Jones et al., 2011). Among the men who knew, 80 percent were supportive of the decision.

Although counseling for women undergoing abortion is a standard procedure, counseling is rarely available for the men who are involved. On a political level, some men's activists argue that, just as women should not be forced to carry a pregnancy to term, so men should not be subjected to forced fatherhood and an 18-year financial commitment (Marsiglio & Diekow, 1998).

New Advances in Contraception

According to some, a really good method of contraception is not yet available. The highly effective methods either are permanent (sterilization) or have associated health risks (the pill). Other, safer methods (such as the condom and the diaphragm) have failure rates that cannot be ignored. Most of the methods are for women, not men. With the exception of the condom, none of the methods provide protection from sexually transmitted infections. Because of the limitations of the currently available methods, contraception research continues. Next we discuss some of the more promising possibilities for the future.

Male Methods

Several possibilities for new or improved male contraception are being explored.

New Condoms

Several new models of condoms are being tested. To deal with the problem of allergies to latex, polyurethane condoms have been developed, as noted earlier. They are thinner than latex, so they should provide more sensation. Another model is one that could be put on before erection.

Male Hormonal Methods

The basic idea underlying the development of male hormonal methods is to suppress the production of LH and FSH by the pituitary, so that sperm would not be produced or would not develop properly (Kogan & Wald, 2014). Unfortunately, many of the hormone preparations that have been tried shut down sperm production but also shut down the user's sex drive, making them unacceptable to most men. The most promising of the male hormonal methods is a gel called Nestorone-Testosterone, which is applied to the arms and shoulders every day (Roth et al., 2014; Zitzmann et al., 2017). It contains both progestin (Nestorone) and testosterone. The progestin works on the hypothalamus-pituitary-gonad feedback loop, inhibiting sperm production, and the testosterone is added to maintain sex drive. It is currently in clinical trials with humans.

> **Are there any male hormonal contraception methods?**

Slow progress is also being made on a "male pill." A promising possibility involves the drug DMAU, which is a molecule that has properties like both androgens and progesterone (Ayoub et al., 2017).

RISUG

RISUG is the name for Reversible Inhibition of Sperm Under Guidance, a method that has been developed mainly in India and is billed as a nonsurgical vasectomy (Kogan & Wald, 2014; Lohiya et al., 2014). It involves injection of a porous polymer into the vas through a small incision. Sperm can pass through the polymer, but the polymer disrupts the membranes of the sperm cells as they pass through, so that they are not viable. RISUG, then, is somewhat like a vasectomy except that it is easily reversible. Test results with monkeys look promising. RISUG is being evaluated in preclinical trials in the United States under the trade name Vasalgel.

Female Methods

Microbicides

Microbicides are substances that kill microbes (bacteria and viruses) and, preferably, sperm. Experts had hoped that current contraceptive foams and gels, which contain nonoxynol-9 (N-9), would be effective microbicides, but it turns out that N-9 is ineffective and may actually make women more vulnerable to infection by irritating the vagina. What we need is a microbicide that is highly effective at killing the viruses and bacteria that cause STIs *and* is also effective at killing sperm *and* does not irritate the vagina.

Several microbicides, with trade names such as Buffer-Gel and PRO 2000, are in clinical trials now. To this point, though, they have proven ineffective against HIV, chlamydia, and gonorrhea (Guffey et al., 2014; Obiero et al., 2012).

A Better Pill

The combination birth control pill tends to lower women's testosterone levels, which may explain why some women experience a loss of sexual desire while they are on it. A new pill is being developed that adds an androgen to the combination pill (Zimmerman et al., 2015).

Vaginal Rings

The NuvaRing, discussed earlier, is already available and contains a combination of estrogen and progestin. A new ring, NES/EE, is being developed and would last 12 months (Stifani et al. 2018). The NES stands for Nesterone, a progestin, and EE stands for ethinyl estradiol. Why do we need a new ring when we have LARCs? The answer is that LARCs require trained medical personnel for insertion, and in many countries there aren't many of them around. A vaginal ring can fairly easily be inserted and removed by the woman herself.

One company is developing a ring that contains both contraceptive hormones and tenofovir, an antiretroviral that protects against HIV (Clark et al., 2014). The idea is to produce multipurpose technologies that work as contraceptives and protect from STIs.

Sperm-Binding Beads

This may sound a bit weird, but here's the idea. Scientists have developed tiny beads containing the protein ZP2 (Avella et al., 2016; Figure 16). Sperm like these

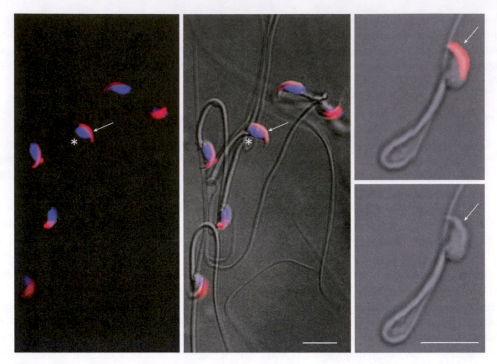

Figure 16   Sperm-binding beads are being explored as a contraceptive. In these photos, the beads have bound to sperm and the sperm do not head to the fallopian tubes.

Source: Science Translational Medicine

beads and bind to them. Once bound to the beads, they won't go after eggs. The idea is to place the beads in the uterus. This process has been tested in mice and seems to work.

Reversible, Nonsurgical Sterilization
This method involves injecting liquid silicone into the fallopian tubes. The silicone hardens and forms a plug. The plugs could later be removed if the woman wished to become pregnant. This method has not yet been approved by the FDA but is being studied in the Netherlands. It might also be used to plug the vas in men.

Critical THINKing Skill

Understanding the concept of probability

Concepts of probability are often misunderstood and misused, yet they are crucial for good decision making. For example, we are grateful to the Weather Service and the forecasts it provides, especially if a tornado is approaching. However, a pet peeve is a weather forecast of a 70 percent chance of rain today when it is currently raining outside. If it is currently raining, then the probability of rain today is 100 percent! It is definitely going to rain and, in fact, it already is.

Understanding concepts of probability is crucial in understanding the effectiveness of contraceptives and in deciding which one you should use. Probability refers to the chance that an event will occur. Probabilities can range between 0 (no chance) and 1.0 (definitely will occur). Often probabilities are stated as percentages ranging between 0 percent and 100 percent. For example, if we toss a fair coin, the probability that it will come up heads is 0.5, or 50 percent. Statisticians tend to talk a lot about tossing coins and rolling dice. Here we will think about rolling the pregnancy dice.

As explained earlier in the chapter, contraception experts define the failure rate of a contraceptive method as follows: If 100 people use the method for one year, the number of them who become pregnant is the failure rate. If 100 women use the vaginal ring for a year and 8 of them become pregnant during that time, then the ring has a failure rate of 8, or 8 percent. That 8 percent is really a probability. It means that if Samantha uses that method for a year (and is of reproductive age and engages in sexual intercourse regularly), her probability of pregnancy at some time during that year is 8 percent. The effectiveness of a method is 100 minus the failure rate. If the ring has an 8 percent failure rate, then it is 92 percent effective, which means that Samantha has a 92 percent probability of not getting pregnant during that year.

Suppose that your friend Eunjung comes to you, knowing that you are taking a human sexuality course and wanting advice. She is considering using the vaginal ring. She is an unmarried college student and her parents would be furious if she got pregnant. Her boyfriend attends a college 500 miles away, so they get together only once a month. So far, they have abstained from sex, but both of them really want to do it next month. Eunjung, who has a good understanding of probability and statistics but not contraception, asks you the probability that she will get pregnant this one time she has sex if she is using the vaginal ring. What would you tell her?

It is tempting to say that the answer would be 8 percent, but the 8 percent probability of pregnancy while using the ring is over a whole year, assuming intercourse 2–3 times per week, or perhaps 100–150 times over the year. The probability of pregnancy from a single act of intercourse is therefore much less than 8 percent, but we can't know exactly what it is from the information we have. You could explain all of that to Eunjung. She could then weigh the likelihood of pregnancy (which might be 1 percent or less) against the seriousness of the costs of pregnancy.

The other complication in thinking about the probability of pregnancy is that it depends not only on the contraceptive method but also on some other factors. Mathematicians call this *conditional probability,* which is the probability of an event occurring given some other event. If Eunjung has one act of intercourse while using the ring and the act of intercourse occurs one day before she ovulates, that carries a higher probability of pregnancy than if the intercourse occurred the day before her period, long after she ovulated.

People engage in the best decision making if they understand and use concepts of probability.

SUMMARY

Table 2 earlier in the chapter provides a comparative summary of the various methods of birth control discussed in this chapter.

SUGGESTIONS FOR FURTHER READING

Eig, Jonathan. (2014). *The birth of the pill: Four crusaders reinvented sex and launched a revolution*. New York: Norton. This book recounts the stories of the four most crucial people in the creation of the birth control pill: Margaret Sanger; lead scientist Gregory Goodwin Pincus; John Rock, a Roman Catholic physician; and Katharine McCormick, who provided the finances.

Hatcher, Robert A., et al. (2011). *Contraceptive technology*. 20th ed. New York: Ardent Media. This authoritative book provides the most recent information on all methods of contraception.

©Stockbyte/Getty Images

CHAPTER **8**

Sexual Arousal

CHAPTER HIGHLIGHTS

Here are some colors of different people's orgasms: champagne, all colors and white and gray afterward, red and blue, green, beige and blue, red, blue and gold. Some people never make it because they are trying for plaid.*

* Eric Berne. (1970). *Sex in Human Loving.* New York: Simon & Schuster, p. 238.

In this chapter, we focus on the ways the body becomes sexually aroused, responds during arousal and orgasm, and the physiological, hormonal, neural, and social processes involved in these responses. This information is important in developing good techniques of lovemaking and in analyzing and treating sexual disorders such as premature ejaculation (see the chapter "Sexual Disorders and Sex Therapy").

First, we examine how the body responds physiologically during arousal and orgasm. Our basic knowledge of these processes comes from the classic research of Masters and Johnson. Their research was later criticized, though, which led to the development of alternative, expanded models, considered in the next section. Then we focus on how hormones, the brain, and the spinal cord contribute to sexual behavior and response. We also consider research on pheromones and their influence on sexual behavior in animals and humans. Finally, we discuss sexual techniques.

What happens, biologically, when a man has an erection? When a woman's vagina lubricates?

The Sexual Response Cycle

Sex researchers William Masters and Virginia Johnson provided one of the first models of the physiology of human sexual response. Their research culminated in 1966 with the publication of *Human Sexual Response,* which reported data on 382 women and 312 men observed in more than 10,000 sexual cycles of arousal and orgasm. Recent biological research has confirmed many of their findings, while questioning a few and augmenting some. All of this research is the basis for the sections that follow.

Sexual response typically progresses in three stages: *excitement, orgasm,* and *resolution.* The two basic physiological processes that occur during these stages are vasocongestion and myotonia. **Vasocongestion** occurs when a great deal of blood flows into the blood vessels in a region, in this case the genitals, as a result of dilation of the blood vessels in the region. **Myotonia** occurs when muscles contract, not only in the genitals but also throughout the body. Let us now consider in detail what occurs in each of the stages.

Excitement

The **excitement** phase is the beginning of erotic arousal. The basic physiological process that occurs during excitement is vasocongestion. This produces the obvious arousal response in males—erection. Erection results when the corpora cavernosa and the corpus spongiosum fill (becoming engorged) with blood (see Figure 1). Erection may be produced by direct physical stimulation of the genitals, by stimulation of other parts of the body, or by erotic thoughts or sensory images. It occurs rapidly, within a few seconds of the stimulation, although it may take place more slowly as a result of a number of factors including age, intake of alcohol, and fatigue. As the man gets closer to orgasm, a few drops of fluid (for some men, quite a few), secreted by the Cowper's gland, appear at the tip of the penis. Although they are not the ejaculate, they may contain active sperm.

More recent research—stimulated, in part, by the search for drugs to treat erectile disorder—has given us much more detailed information about the physiological processes involved in erection (Adams et al., 1997; Heaton, 2000). Several arteries supply the corpora cavernosa and spongiosum (see Figure 11 in the chapter "Sexual Anatomy"). For an erection to occur, these arteries must dilate (vasodilation), allowing a strong flow of blood into the corpora. At the same time, the veins carrying blood away from the penis are compressed, restricting outgoing blood flow. The arteries dilate because the smooth muscle surrounding the arteries relaxes. Multiple neurotransmitters are involved in this process, including, especially, nitric oxide (NO). Dopamine is involved as well. The drug Viagra acts on the NO system.

Nice as they are, erections would become a pain if they lasted forever, so there is a reverse process, vasoconstriction, that makes an erection go away, for example, following orgasm. The neurotransmitters epinephrine and norepinephrine are involved. These processes occur in the resolution phase, which we discuss below.

An important response of females in the excitement phase is lubrication of the vagina (Figure 2). Although

Vasocongestion (vay-so-con-JES-tyun): An accumulation of blood in the blood vessels of a region of the body, especially the genitals; a swelling or erection results.
Myotonia (my-oh-TONE-ee-ah): Muscle contraction.
Excitement: The first stage of sexual response, during which erection and vaginal lubrication occur.

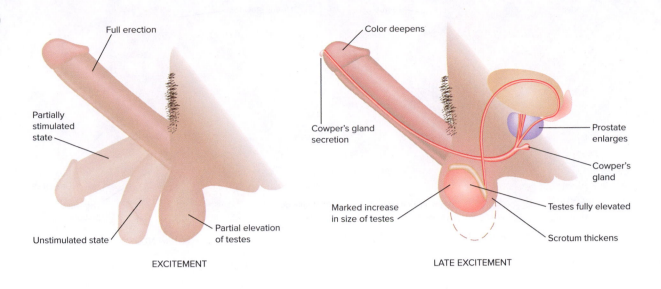

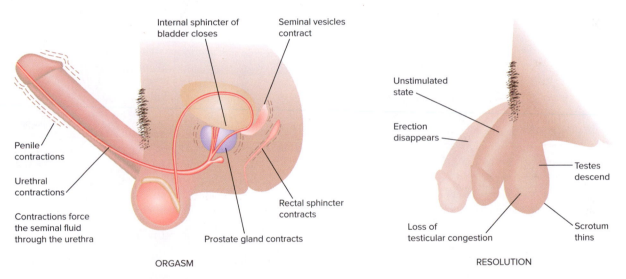

Figure 1   Changes during the sexual response cycle in the male.

this response might seem much different from the male's, actually they both result from the same physiological process: vasocongestion. During excitement, the capillaries in the walls of the vagina dilate and blood flow through them increases (Levin, 2005). Vaginal lubrication results when fluids seep through the semipermeable membranes of the vaginal walls, producing lubrication as a result of vasocongestion in the tissues surrounding the vagina. This response to arousal is also rapid, though not quite so fast as the male's; lubrication begins 10 to 30 seconds after the onset of arousing stimuli.[1] Like the male sexual response,

female responding can be affected by factors such as age, intake of alcohol, and fatigue.

During the excitement phase, the glans of the clitoris (the tip) swells. This swelling results from engorgement of its corpora cavernosa and is similar to erection in the male. The clitoris can be felt as larger and harder than usual. The crura of the clitoris, lying deeper in the body (see Figure 3 in the chapter "Sexual Anatomy"), also swell as a result of vasocongestion. The vestibular bulbs, which lie along the wall of the vagina, are also erectile and swell during the excitement phase. Late in the excitement phase, elevation of the clitoris may occur. The clitoris essentially retracts or draws up into the body.

Vasocongestion in females results from the same underlying physiological processes as those in males. That is, relaxation of the smooth muscle surrounding the

[1]Before the Masters and Johnson research, it was thought that the lubrication was due to secretions of the Bartholin glands, but it is now known that these glands contribute little if anything. At this point, you might want to go back to the limerick about the Bartholin glands in the chapter "Sexual Anatomy" and see whether you can spot the error in it.

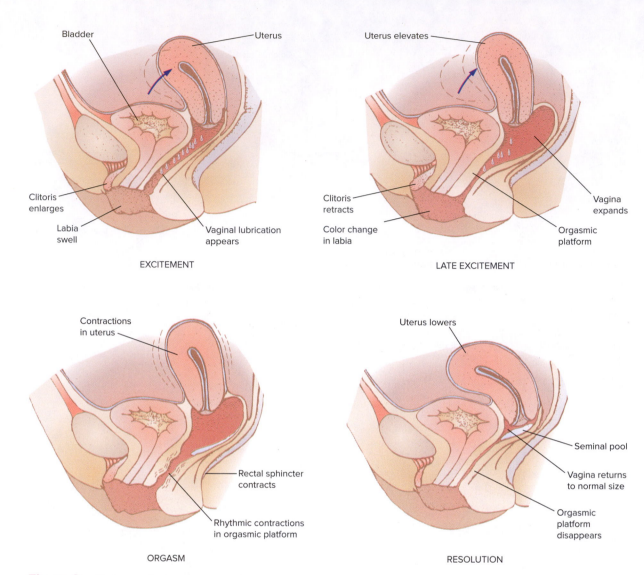

Figure 2   Changes during the sexual response cycle in the female.

arteries supplying the glans and crura of the clitoris and the vestibular bulbs occurs, allowing a great deal of blood flow to the region (Berman et al., 2000). As in males, nitric oxide is a key neurotransmitter involved in the process (Traish et al., 2002). Estrogen helps the vasodilation.

During excitement the nipples become erect. This response results from contractions of the muscle fibers (myotonia) surrounding the nipple. The breasts themselves swell and enlarge somewhat in the late part of the excitement phase (a vasocongestion response). The nipples may not actually look erect but may appear somewhat flatter against the breast because the breast has swollen. Many males also have nipple erection during the excitement phase.

In the unaroused state the inner lips are generally folded over, covering the entrance to the vagina, and the outer lips lie close to each other. During excitement the inner lips swell and open up (a vasocongestion response).

The vagina shows an important change during excitement. Think of the vagina as being divided into two parts, an upper (or inner) two-thirds and a lower (or outer) one-third. In the unaroused state the walls of the vagina lie against each other, much like the sides of an uninflated balloon. During the excitement phase, the upper two-thirds of the vagina expands dramatically in what is often called a "ballooning" response. In other words, it becomes more like an inflated balloon (Figure 2). This ballooning helps accommodate the entrance of the penis. As part of the ballooning, the cervix and uterus also pull up.

As the woman becomes more aroused and gets closer to orgasm, the **orgasmic platform** forms. This response is a tightening of the bulbospongiosus muscle around the entrance of the vagina (Figure 2). As a result, the size of

Orgasmic platform: A tightening of the entrance to the vagina caused by contractions of the bulbospongiosus muscle (which covers the vestibular bulbs) that occur during the excitement stage of sexual response.

the vaginal entrance actually becomes smaller, and there may be a noticeable increase in gripping of the penis.

Pulse rate, breathing rate, and blood pressure also increase in both men and women.

In men, the skin of the scrotum thickens. The scrotal sac tenses, and the scrotum is pulled up and closer to the body (see Figure 1). The spermatic cords shorten, pulling the testes closer to the body.

Late in the excitement phase, the processes of vaso-congestion and myotonia continue to build until there is sufficient tension for orgasm.

Orgasm

In males, **orgasm** consists of a series of rhythmic contractions of the pelvic organs at 0.8-second intervals. Male orgasm occurs in two stages. In the preliminary stage, the vas, seminal vesicles, and prostate contract, forcing the ejaculate into a bulb at the base of the urethra (see Figure 1). Masters and Johnson call the sensation in this stage one of *ejaculatory inevitability* ("coming"). In other words, there is a sensation that ejaculation is just about to happen and cannot be stopped. And, indeed, it cannot be stopped once the man has reached this point. In the second stage, the urethral bulb and the penis itself contract rhythmically, forcing the semen through the urethra and out the opening at the tip of the penis.

In both males and females, pulse rate, blood pressure, and breathing rate increase sharply during orgasm.[2] Muscles contract throughout the body. The face may be contorted in a grimace; the muscles of the arms, legs, thighs, back, and buttocks may contract; and the muscles of the feet and hands may contract in *carpopedal spasms*. Generally, in the passion of the moment, a person is not really aware of these occurrences, but an aching back or buttocks may serve as a reminder the next day.

The process of orgasm in females is basically similar to that in males. It is a series of rhythmic muscular contractions of the orgasmic platform. The contractions generally occur at about 0.8-second intervals; there may be three or four in a mild orgasm or as many as a dozen in a very intense, prolonged orgasm. The uterus also contracts rhythmically. Other muscles, such as those around the anus, may also contract.

Female orgasm is a funny thing. As with love, you can almost never get anyone to give you a solid definition of what it is. Instead, people usually fall back on, "You'll know what it is when you have one." This evasiveness is probably related to several factors, most notably that female orgasm leaves no tangible evidence of its occurrence like ejaculation—except for those women who do ejaculate. Also, women often do not reach orgasm as

© Original Artist
Reproduction rights obtainable from
www.CartoonStock.com

"Did the Earth move for you."

Figure 3

www.cartoonstock.com. Used by permission.

quickly as men do, a point to be discussed in more detail in the chapter "Gender and Sexuality." In fact, some women, particularly young women, may think they are having an orgasm when they are not. If they have never had an orgasm, they mistake intense arousal for orgasm.

Just what does orgasm in females feel like? The main feeling is a spreading sensation that begins around the clitoris and then spreads outward through the whole pelvis. There may also be sensations of falling or opening up. The woman may be able to feel the contraction of the muscles around the vaginal entrance. The sensation is more intense than just a warm glow or a pleasant tingling. In one study, college men and women gave written descriptions of what an orgasm felt like to them (Vance & Wagner, 1976). Interestingly, a panel of experts (medical students, obstetrician–gynecologists, and clinical psychologists) could not reliably figure out which of the descriptions were written by women and which by men. This result suggests that the sensations are quite similar for males and females.

Some of the men in our classes have asked how they can tell whether a woman has really had an orgasm (see Figure 3). Their question in itself is interesting. In part it reflects a cultural skepticism about female orgasm. There is usually obvious proof of male orgasm: ejaculation. But there is no consistent proof of female orgasm—except that some women do ejaculate.

The question also reflects the fact that men know that women sometimes fake orgasm (see Figure 4). So do men. A survey of college students reported that 25 percent of the men and 51 percent of the women had faked an orgasm during heterosexual activity (Muehlenhard & Skippee,

> **Orgasm:** The second stage of sexual response; an intense sensation that occurs at the peak of sexual arousal and is followed by release of sexual tensions.

[2]With all the current attention to aerobics and exercising the heart, we have yet to hear anyone suggest orgasm aerobics. It seems to us that it should work. Kickboxing, watch out. Here comes sexercise!

Figure 4 How do the behaviors of these people relate to the concept of performativity from the critical theories discussed in the chapter "Theoretical Perspectives"?

J.C. Duffy/The New Yorker Collection/The Cartoon Bank

2010). Most had pretended (scientists prefer this term over "fake") during penile–vaginal intercourse. Analyses of their reports of the situation in which they pretended suggests that pretending reflects a shared *sexual script* (see the chapter "Theoretical Perspectives on Sexuality") in which women should orgasm first, and men are responsible for the orgasms. Other research shows that women (and some men) pretend orgasm for a variety of reasons: it can feel good to do it; to please the partner; to bring an end to the sexual encounter; to feel powerful or gain power over the partner to get something the person wants; because the person feels insecure (e.g., fears the partner may reject her); and to feel close to the partner (Goodman et al., 2017). Pretending is a complex issue. In some ways it is not a good practice, because it prevents the partner from getting valid feedback about sexual technique. On the other hand, we can appreciate that people do it because of the pressures created by the script.[3]

But back to the question: How can a woman's partner tell? There really is not any very good way. From a scientific point of view, a good method would be to have the woman hooked up to an instrument that registers pulse rate. There is a sudden sharp increase in the pulse rate at orgasm, and that would be a good indicator. We doubt, though, that most men have such equipment available, and we are even more doubtful about whether most women would agree to be wired up. Rather than trying to check up on each other, it would be better for partners to establish good, honest communication and avoid setting performance goals in sex, points that we discuss further in later chapters.

Resolution

Following orgasm is the **resolution** phase, during which the body returns physiologically to the unaroused state. Orgasm triggers a massive release of muscular tension and of blood from the engorged blood vessels. Resolution represents a reversal of the processes that build up during the excitement stage.

In the 5 to 10 seconds after the end of the orgasm, the clitoris returns to its normal position, although it takes longer for it to shrink to its normal size. The orgasmic platform relaxes and begins to shrink, and the ballooning of the vagina diminishes. The resolution phase generally takes 15 to 30 minutes, but it may take much longer—as much as an hour—in women who have not had an orgasm.

In both males and females, resolution brings a gradual return of pulse rate, blood pressure, and breathing rate to the unaroused levels.

In men, the most obvious occurrence in the resolution phase is detumescence, the loss of erection in the penis. Detumescence happens in two stages. The first occurs rapidly but leaves the penis still enlarged. This first loss of erection results from an emptying of the corpora cavernosa. The second stage occurs more slowly, as a result of the slower emptying of the corpus spongiosum and the glans.

During the resolution phase, men enter a **refractory period,** during which they are refractory to further arousal. In other words, they are incapable of being aroused again, having an erection, or having an orgasm. The length of this refractory period varies considerably from one man to the next. In some it may last only a few minutes, and in others it may go on for 24 hours. The refractory period tends to become longer as men grow older.

Women do not have a refractory period, making possible the phenomenon of multiple orgasm in women, which we discuss in the next section.

More on Women's Orgasms

Some people believe that women can have two kinds of orgasm: **clitoral orgasm** and **vaginal orgasm.** The words *clitoral* and *vaginal* refer to the region of stimulation: an orgasm resulting from clitoral stimulation versus an orgasm resulting from vaginal stimulation. The distinction originated with Sigmund Freud. Freud believed that

---

Resolution: The third stage of sexual response, in which the body returns to the unaroused state.
Refractory period (ree-FRAK-toh-ree): The period following orgasm during which a male cannot be sexually aroused.
Clitoral orgasm: Freud's term for orgasm in females resulting from stimulation of the clitoris.
Vaginal orgasm: Freud's term for orgasm in females resulting from stimulation of the vagina in heterosexual intercourse; Freud considered vaginal orgasm to be more mature than clitoral orgasm.

---

[3]Indeed, many of the old sex manuals, as well as physicians' textbooks, counseled women to fake orgasm. For example: "It is good advice to recommend to the women the advantage of innocent simulation of sex responsiveness, and as a matter of fact many women in their desire to please their husbands learned the advantage of such innocent deception" (Novak & Novak, 1952, p. 572).

in childhood little girls masturbate and for this reason have orgasms by means of clitoral stimulation, or clitoral orgasms. He thought that as women grow older and mature, they ought to shift from having orgasms as a result of masturbation to having them as a result of heterosexual intercourse, in other words, by means of vaginal stimulation. For this reason the vaginal orgasm was considered "mature" and the clitoral orgasm "immature" or "infantile." Not only were there two kinds of orgasm, but one was regarded as "better" (that is, more mature) than the other.

According to the results of Masters and Johnson's research, though, there is no difference between clitoral and vaginal orgasms. This conclusion is based on two findings. First, their results indicate that all female orgasms are physiologically the same, regardless of the site of stimulation. An orgasm always consists of contractions of the orgasmic platform, whether the stimulation is clitoral or vaginal. Indeed, they found a few women who could orgasm purely through breast stimulation, and that orgasm was the same as the other two, consisting of contractions of the orgasmic platform and the muscles around the vagina. Physiologically there is only one kind of orgasm.

Second, clitoral stimulation is almost always involved in producing orgasm, even during vaginal intercourse. Most women report that clitoral stimulation is an integral part of their orgasm (Prause et al., 2016). The deep structure of the clitoris (see Figure 3 in the chapter "Sexual Anatomy") ensures that the crura of the clitoris are stimulated as the penis moves through the vaginal entrance. For this reason even the purely vaginal orgasm results from quite a bit of clitoral stimulation. Clitoral stimulation is usually the trigger to orgasm, and the orgasm itself occurs in the vagina and surrounding tissues.

Masters and Johnson also discovered that women do not enter a refractory period, and they can have **multiple orgasms** within a short period of time. Actually, women's capacity for multiple orgasms was originally discovered by Kinsey in his interviews with women (Kinsey et al., 1953; see also Terman et al., 1938). The scientific establishment, however, dismissed these reports as another instance of Kinsey's supposed unreliability.

The term *multiple orgasm,* then, refers to a series of orgasms occurring within a short period of time. Multiple orgasms do not differ physiologically from single orgasms. Each is a "real" orgasm, and they are not minor experiences.

How does multiple orgasm work physiologically? Immediately following an orgasm, both males and females move into the resolution phase. In this phase, males typically enter into a refractory period, during which they cannot be aroused again. But females do not enter into a refractory period. That is, if a woman is stimulated again, she can immediately be aroused and move back into the excitement phase and have another orgasm.

Multiple orgasm is more likely to result from hand-genital or mouth-genital stimulation than from intercourse because most men do not have the endurance to continue thrusting for such long periods of time. Regarding capacity, Masters and Johnson found that women in masturbation might have 5 to 20 orgasms. In some cases, they quit only when physically exhausted. When a vibrator is used, less effort is required, and some women were capable of having 50 orgasms in a row.

We should note that some women who are capable of multiple orgasms are completely satisfied with one, particularly in intercourse, and do not wish to continue. We should be careful not to set multiple orgasm as another of the many goals in sexual performance.

Some men are capable of having multiple orgasms (e.g., Hartman & Fithian, 1984; Zilbergeld, 1992). In one study, 21 men were interviewed, all of whom had volunteered for research on multiply orgasmic men (Dunn & Trost, 1989). Some of the men reported having been multiply orgasmic since their sexual debut, whereas others had developed the pattern later in life, and still others had worked actively to develop the capacity after reading about the possibility. The respondents reported that multiple orgasm did not occur every time they engaged in sexual activity. For these men, detumescence did not always follow an orgasm, allowing for continued stimulation and an additional orgasm. Some men reported that some of the orgasms included ejaculation and others in the sequence did not. This study cannot tell us the incidence of multiply orgasmic men in the general population, but it does provide evidence that multiply orgasmic men exist.

Other Models of Sexual Response

Some experts on human sexuality are critical of Masters and Johnson's model. One important criticism is that the Masters and Johnson model ignores the cognitive and subjective aspects of sexual response (Zilbergeld & Ellison, 1980). Masters and Johnson focused almost entirely on the physiological aspects of sexual response, ignoring what the person is thinking and feeling emotionally. Desire and passion are not part of the model.

A second important criticism concerns how research participants were selected and how this process may have created a self-fulfilling prophecy for the outcome (Tiefer, 1991). To participate in the research, participants were required to have a history of orgasm both through masturbation and through coitus. Essentially, anyone whose pattern of sexual response did not include orgasm—and therefore did not fit Masters and Johnson's model— was excluded from the research. For this reason, the model cannot

Multiple orgasm: A series of orgasms occurring within a short period of time.

be generalized to the entire population. Masters and Johnson themselves commented that every one of their participants was characterized by high and consistent levels of sexual desire. Yet sexual desire is certainly missing among some members of the general population, or it is present sometimes and absent at others. The research, in short, claims to be universal when it is not (Tiefer, 1991).

Once these difficulties with the Masters and Johnson research and model of sexual response were recognized, alternative models were proposed. We examine two of them in the following sections.

Kaplan's Triphasic Model

On the basis of her work on sex therapy (discussed in the chapter "Sexual Disorders and Sex Therapy"), Helen Singer Kaplan (1974, 1979) proposed a **triphasic model** of sexual response. Rather than thinking of the sexual response as having successive stages, she conceptualized it as having three relatively independent phases, or components: *sexual desire, vasocongestion* of the genitals, and the reflex *muscular contractions* of the orgasm phase. Notice that two of the components (vasocongestion and muscular contractions) are physiological, whereas the other (sexual desire) is psychological. Kaplan's model adds the cognitive component, desire, that is missing in Masters and Johnson's model. Desire can occur either spontaneously, motivating the person toward sexual activity and excitement, or excitement can come first, activating desire (Levin, 2005). The latter is called *responsive desire*.

There are a number of strengths in Kaplan's approach. First, the two physiological components are controlled by different parts of the nervous system. Vasocongestion—producing erection in males and lubrication in females—is controlled by the parasympathetic division of the autonomic nervous system. In contrast, ejaculation and orgasm are controlled by the sympathetic division.

Second, the two components involve different anatomical structures—blood vessels for vasocongestion and muscles for the contractions of orgasm.

Third, vasocongestion and orgasm differ in their susceptibility to being disturbed by injury, drugs, or age. For example, the refractory period following orgasm in males lengthens with age. Accordingly, orgasm decreases in frequency with age. In contrast, for many men the capacity for erection is relatively unimpaired with age, although the erection may be slower to make its appearance. An elderly man may have nonorgasmic sex several times a week, with a firm erection, although he may have an orgasm only once a week.

Fourth, the reflex of ejaculation in the male can be brought under voluntary control by most men, but the erection reflex generally cannot.

Finally, impairment of the vasocongestion response or the orgasm response produces different disturbances (sexual disorders). Erection problems in men are caused by an impairment of the vasocongestion response, whereas premature ejaculation and delayed ejaculation are disturbances of the orgasm response. Similarly, many women show a strong arousal and vasocongestion response, yet have trouble with orgasm.

Kaplan's triphasic model is useful both for understanding the nature of sexual response and for understanding and treating disturbances in it. Her writing on the desire phase is particularly useful in understanding disorders of sexual desire, which we discuss in the chapter "Sexual Disorders and Sex Therapy."

The Sexual Excitation-Inhibition Model

Researchers at the Kinsey Institute, including John Bancroft and Erick Janssen, have introduced a **dual control model** of sexual response (Bancroft et al., 2009). The model proposes that two basic processes underlie human sexual response: excitation (responding with arousal to sexual stimuli) and inhibition (inhibiting sexual arousal). The researchers argue that almost all sex research has focused on the excitation component, and certainly the Masters and Johnson research falls in that category. They believe that the inhibition component is equally important to understand. They observe that inhibition of sexual response is adaptive across species; sexual arousal can be a powerful distraction that could become disadvantageous or even dangerous in certain situations.

According to the dual control model, propensities toward sexual excitation and sexual inhibition vary widely from one person to the next. Most people fall in the moderate range on both and function well. At the extremes, however, problems can occur. People who are very high on the excitation component and low on the inhibition component may engage in high-risk sexual behaviors. People who are very high on inhibition and low on excitation may be more likely to develop sexual disorders such as erectile dysfunction or problems with sexual desire.

Bancroft and Janssen have developed scales to measure individuals' tendencies toward sexual excitation and sexual inhibition (Janssen et al., 2002). Examples of *excitation* items are these:

When I think of a very attractive person, I easily become sexually aroused.

When I am taking a shower or a bath, I easily become sexually aroused.

When a sexually attractive stranger accidentally touches me, I easily become aroused.

Triphasic model: Kaplan's model of sexual response in which there are three components: vasocongestion, muscular contractions, and sexual desire.
Dual control model: A model that holds that sexual response is controlled both by sexual excitation and by sexual inhibition.

First Person

William Masters and Virginia Johnson

William Howell Masters was born in 1915. He attended Hamilton College in Clinton, New York, graduating with a BS in 1938. At Hamilton he specialized in science courses and yet managed to play on the varsity football, baseball, basketball, and track teams and participate in the Debate Club. The college yearbook called him "a strange, dark man with a future. . . . Has an easy time carrying three lab courses but a hard time catching up on lost sleep. . . . Bill is a boy with purpose and is bound to get what he is working for." His devotion to athletics persisted, and in 1966 a science writer described him as "a dapper, athletically trim gynecologist who starts his day at 5:30 with a two-mile jog."

He entered the University of Rochester School of Medicine in 1939, planning to train himself to be a researcher rather than a practicing physician. In his first year there he worked in the laboratory of the famous anatomist Dr. George Washington Corner. Corner was engaged in research on the reproductive system in animals and humans, which eventually led to important discoveries about hormones and the reproductive cycle. He had also published *Attaining Manhood: A Doctor Talks to Boys About Sex* and the companion volume, *Attaining Womanhood*.

The first-year research project that Corner assigned to Masters was a study of the changes in the lining of the uterus of the rabbit during the reproductive cycle. In this way his interest was focused early on the reproductive system.

Masters was married in 1942 and received his MD in 1943. He and his wife had two children.

After Masters received his degree, he had to make an important decision: To what research area should he devote his life? Apparently his decision to investigate the physiology of sex was based on his shrewd observation that almost no prior research had been done in the area and that he thus would have a good opportunity to make some important scientific discoveries. In arriving at this decision he consulted with Dr. Corner, who was aware of Kinsey's progress and also of the persecution he had suffered (see the chapter "Sex Research"). For this reason Corner advised Masters not to begin the study of sex until he had established himself as a respected researcher in some other area, was somewhat older, and could conduct the research at a major university or medical school.

Masters followed the advice. He established himself on the faculty of the Washington University School of Medicine in St. Louis. From 1948 to 1954 he published 25 papers on various medical topics, especially

Figure 5   Virginia Johnson and William Masters.

©Bettmann/Getty Images

on hormone-replacement therapy for postmenopausal women and on infertility treatment.

In 1954 he began his research on sexual response at Washington University, supported by grants from the U.S. Public Health Service. The first paper based on that research was published in 1959, but the research received little attention until the publication, in 1966, of *Human Sexual Response* and, in 1970, of *Human Sexual Inadequacy* (a topic discussed in the chapter "Sexual Disorders and Sex Therapy"), both of which received international acclaim.

Virginia Johnson was born Virginia Eshelman in 1925 in the Missouri Ozarks. She was raised with the realistic attitude toward sex that rural children often have, as well as many of the superstitions found in that area. She began studying music at Drury College but transferred to the University of Missouri, where she studied psychology and sociology. She married and had two children, one in 1952 and the other in 1955. Shortly after that, she and her husband separated, and she went to the Washington University placement office to find a job. Just at that time, Masters had put in a request for a woman to assist him in research interviewing, preferably a married woman with children who was interested in people. Johnson was referred to him and became a member of the research and therapy team in 1957.

In 1971, following the divorce of Masters and his first wife, he and Virginia Johnson were married. They divorced in 1993. In 1994, at the age of 79, Masters retired and closed his research institute. He died in 2001 and Johnson died in 2013.

Sources: Brecher & Brecher (1966); Maier (2009).

Figure 6   Can the dual control model of sexual arousal explain our response to this? Here a man touches a woman's breast, but it is not sexual. Why not? The context (the medical exam) leads us not to perceive this touch as sexual and excitation processes are not stimulated.

©Owen Franken/Getty Images

Examples of *inhibition* items are (male version/female version) as follows:

I need my penis to be touched to maintain an erection/I need my clitoris to be stimulated to continue feeling aroused.

Putting on a condom can cause me to lose my erection/ Using condoms or other safe-sex products can cause me to lose my arousal.

If I am masturbating on my own and I realize that someone is likely to come into the room at any moment, I will lose my erection/my sexual arousal.

Data collected from large samples using these scales support the model's assumption that individuals do vary widely in their tendencies toward excitation and inhibition. Sexual excitation tends to be at its highest levels between the ages of 26 and 40 and lower at younger ages and older ages (Pinxten & Lievens, 2015).

The dual control model also recognizes that, although both excitation and inhibition have biological bases, early learning and culture are critical factors because they determine which stimuli the individual will find to be sexually exciting or will set off sexual inhibition. Most men in our culture, for example, have learned that children are not appropriate sexual stimuli, so any sexual response to them is inhibited.

Wouldn't evolution have selected purely for sexual excitation? It is the engine that drives reproduction and the passing of one's genes to the next generation. Would inhibition therefore be dysfunctional in an evolutionary sense? Not according to the dual control model. First, sexual activity in some situations could be downright dangerous. Imagine, for example, that the King and Queen are locked in lusty embrace while the castle is being stormed by enemies eager to kill them both. Sexual inhibition would be very adaptive at that point, so that the King and Queen could engage in nonsexual behaviors that would save their lives. Second, sometimes the environment is not conducive to reproduction, and it is better to wait for a better day or a better season. For example, in conditions of drought and famine, women's fertility is usually sharply reduced because any baby born would likely die, and the mother might die as well in the attempt to provide food. Inhibiting sexual response and waiting until conditions improve would be the best strategy. Third, excessive sexual behavior in men, perhaps with ejaculations several times a day, would reduce fertility. The body could not produce sperm quickly enough to have a high sperm count in each of those ejaculations, so the high rate of sexual behavior would not be adaptive in an evolutionary sense.

Data support many aspects of this model. We review some of these data in the next section, then return to it in the chapter on sexual disorders because it is helpful in understanding them.

Emotion and Arousal

A major criticism of Masters and Johnson's model of sexual response is that it is all physiological, ignoring the psychological aspects of sexual responding. The two alternative models that we have reviewed—Kaplan's three-component model and the excitation-inhibition model—make major strides in filling in some of the psychological missing pieces. Cognitive processes are added with Kaplan's component of sexual desire and the emphasis of the excitation-inhibition model on the importance of culture and early learning shaping the way the individual processes and evaluates sexual stimuli.

What is still missing, though, is recognition of the importance of emotion in sexual arousal. No one has proposed a formal model of emotion and arousal; so here we review one study that provides a preview of what these effects might look like. Researchers recruited 81 heterosexual couples and 106 same-gender couples (Ridley et al., 2008). A daily diary method was used, in which each participant logged onto a website at the same time each day for 14 days. The questionnaire each day contained questions about emotions as well as sexual behaviors. Members of the couple were asked to fill it out separately and independently. The results indicated that, over time, positive emotions (e.g., happiness) showed a strong positive association with reports of sexual arousal. That is, when people were happier, they also had more thoughts of sexual arousal. The surprising result was that negative emotions (e.g., anger, anxiety, sadness) were also positively correlated with reports of sexual arousal. When people experienced stronger negative emotions, they also had more thoughts of arousal. The researchers believe that this is because emotions such as anxiety and anger involve generalized arousal, which intensifies arousal responses to sexual stimuli. (For other studies investigating the relationship between emotion and sexual expression, see Burleson et al., 2007, and Fortenberry et al., 2005.)

Disgust is a powerful emotion that seems antierotic. If your partner has some quality that disgusts you, it's a turn-off. Research shows that women who are high in the tendency to experience disgust tend to have worse sexual functioning (Grauvogl et al., 2015). This relationship does not seem to be present in men.

Not only do emotions affect sexual responding, but sex also affects our mood and emotions. Another study using the daily diary method found that, systematically, people were in a more positive mood the day after sexual activity

(Kashdan et al., 2018). This was especially true when the person had a good, close relationship with their partner.

Clearly there is much intriguing research to be done about the role of emotions in sexual responding.

Neural and Hormonal Bases of Arousal

Up to this point we have focused on the genital and psychological responses that occur during sexual activity. But what about the underlying neural and hormonal processes that make the sexual response cycle possible?

The Brain, the Spinal Cord, and Sex

The brain and the spinal cord both have important interacting functions in sexual response. First, we discuss the relatively simple reflexes involved in sexual response, and then we consider the more complex brain processes.

Spinal Reflexes

Several important components of sexual behavior, including erection and ejaculation, are controlled by fairly simple spinal cord reflexes (see the lower part of Figure 7).

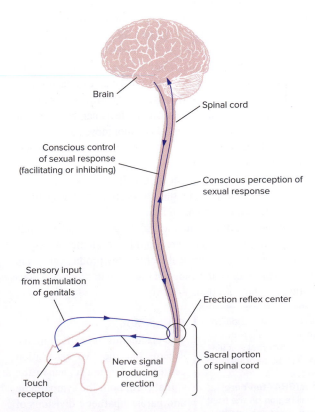

Figure 7 Nervous system control of erection. Note both the reflex center in the spinal cord and brain control.

A reflex has three basic components. The *receptors* are sensory neurons that detect stimuli and transmit the message to the spinal cord (or brain). The *transmitters* are centers in the spinal cord (or brain) that receive the message, interpret it, and send out a message to produce the appropriate response. The *effectors* are neurons or muscles that respond to the stimulation. The jerking away of the hand when it touches a hot object is a good example of a spinal reflex.

Erection

Erection is produced by a spinal reflex that works in a similar way (McKenna, 2000). The penis has lots of receptor neurons, and tactile stimulation (stroking or rubbing) of the penis or nearby regions such as the scrotum or thighs produces a neural signal that is transmitted to an *erection center* in the sacral, or lowest, part of the spinal cord. (There is also another erection center higher in the cord.) This center then sends out a message via the parasympathetic division of the autonomic nervous system to the muscles (the effectors) around the walls of the arteries in the penis. In response to the message, the muscles relax, permitting a large volume of blood to flow into the arteries. Erection results. In addition, the valves in the veins and the compression of the veins caused by the swelling in the tissue around them reduce the blood flow out of the penis (Adams et al., 1997).

The existence of this reflex is confirmed by the responses of men who have had their spinal cords completely severed, as a result of accidents, at a level above that of the reflex center (see A Sexually Diverse World: Sexuality and Disability). They are capable of having erections and ejaculations produced by rubbing their genitals, although it is clear that no brain effects can be operating because signals from the brain cannot move past the point at which the spinal cord was severed. (In fact, these men cannot "feel" anything because neural signals cannot be transmitted up the spinal cord either.) Erection can be produced simply by tactile stimulation of the genitals, which triggers the spinal reflex.

Besides tactile stimulation of the genitals, other conditions may also produce erection. For example, fantasy or other purely psychological factors may produce erection. We explore the importance of the brain in producing erection in a later section.

Retrograde ejaculation: A condition in which orgasm in the male is not accompanied by an external ejaculation; instead, the ejaculate goes into the urinary bladder.
Gräfenberg spot (GRAY-fen-berg) or G-spot: A small region on the front wall of the vagina, emptying into the urethra, and responsible for female ejaculation.

Ejaculation

The ejaculation reflex is similar—except that the two ejaculation centers are located higher in the spinal cord, both the sympathetic and parasympathetic divisions of the nervous system are involved, and the response is myotonia, not vasocongestion (Giuliano &

Clement, 2005; Rowland & Slob, 1997). In the ejaculation reflex, the penis responds to stimulation by sending a message to the *ejaculation center,* which is located in the lumbar portion of the spinal cord. This center then sends out a message via the nerves in the sympathetic nervous system, and this message triggers muscle contractions in the internal organs that are involved in ejaculation.

Ejaculation can often be controlled voluntarily. This fact highlights the importance of brain influences on the ejaculation reflex (Truitt & Coolen, 2002).

The three main problems of ejaculation are premature ejaculation, male orgasmic disorder (delayed ejaculation), and retrograde ejaculation. We discuss premature ejaculation and male orgasmic disorder in the chapter "Sexual Disorders and Sex Therapy." **Retrograde ejaculation** occurs when the ejaculate empties into the bladder rather than going out through the tip of the penis (Kothari, 1984). A *dry orgasm* results, as no ejaculate is emitted. This problem can be caused by some illnesses, by tranquilizers and drugs used in the treatment of psychoses, and by prostate surgery. It happens in the following way (Figure 8): Two sphincters are involved in ejaculation: an internal one, which closes off the entrance to the bladder during a normal ejaculation, and an external one, which opens during a normal ejaculation, allowing the semen to flow out through the penis. In retrograde ejaculation, the action of these two sphincters is reversed. The external one closes, and thus the ejaculate cannot flow out through the penis, and the internal one opens, permitting the ejaculate to go into the bladder. The condition itself is quite harmless, although some men are disturbed by the lack of sensation of emitting semen.

Reflexes in Women

Unfortunately, there is far less research on similar reflexes in women. We know that sensory input—such as touch—to the clitoris travels along the dorsal nerve of the clitoris and continues within the pudendal nerve to a reflex center in the sacral portion of the spinal cord (Berman et al., 2000). Research with nonhumans—mainly male and female rats—has investigated the urethrogenital reflex, which results in muscle contractions similar to orgasm in humans (Meston et al., 2004). This research suggests that the neural circuits for orgasm in women are very similar to those for orgasm and ejaculation in men. The clitoris receives both sympathetic and parasympathetic nerve fibers. The vagina, too, is supplied by both sympathetic and parasympathetic nerves. The limbic system of the brain, which we discuss shortly, is crucial to female sexual arousal just as it is to male sexual arousal.

Research indicates that *female ejaculation* occurs in some women (Addiego et al., 1981; Belzer, 1981; Perry & Whipple, 1981). The region responsible is the **Gräfenberg spot** (or **G-spot**), also called the *female prostate* or the

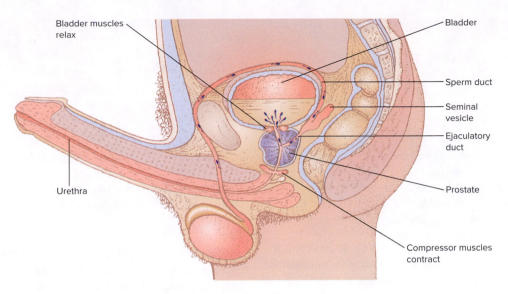

Figure 8   How a retrograde ejaculation occurs.

Skene's glands (Schubach, 2002). It is located on the top side of the vagina (with the woman lying on her back, which is the best position for finding it), about halfway between the pubic bone and the cervix (see Figure 9). Its ducts open into the urethra. Stroking it produces an urge to urinate, but if the stroking continues for a few seconds more, it begins to produce sexual pleasure. The original researchers, Perry and Whipple, argued that continued stimulation of it produces a *uterine orgasm,* characterized by deeper sensations of uterine contractions than the clitorally induced vulvar orgasm investigated in the Masters and Johnson research.

In one survey of adult women, 40 percent reported having experienced ejaculation at the time of orgasm at least once, and 66 percent reported having an especially sensitive area on the front wall of the vagina (Darling et al., 1990). Biochemical analyses indicate that the

female prostate produces prostate-specific antigen (PSA) just as the male prostate does (Zaviačič et al., 2000a). In one study, MRI scans identified a female prostate in 6 of the 7 women studied (Wimpissinger et al., 2009).

Brain Control of Sexual Response

Sexual responses are controlled by more than simple spinal reflexes. Sexual responses may be brought under voluntary control and may be initiated by purely psychological forces, such as fantasy. Environmental factors, such as having been taught as a child that sex is dirty and sinful, may also affect a person's sexual response. All these phenomena point to the critical influence of the brain and its interaction with the spinal reflexes in producing sexual response (see Figure 7). As one scientist commented, the most important sexual organ is the brain.

Research using sophisticated imaging techniques is revealing a great deal about brain control of sexual response (see Milestones in Sex Research: Mapping the Sexual Brain). The results indicate that distinct brain regions and networks are associated with desire/interest, arousal, orgasm, and the refractory period (Georgiadis & Kringelbach, 2012; Pfaus et al., 2014; Poeppl et al., 2014). Interestingly, these neural networks are quite similar to other pleasure networks in the brain such as those involved in the pleasure of eating food.

Still photos presented to heterosexual men create neural activity in the *sexual interest network*, which includes the nucleus accumbens (NAcc, which is in the center of the brain very close to the hypothalamus), amygdala, anterior cingulate cortex (pACC), and hypothalamus

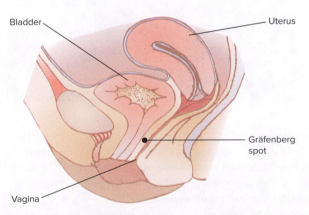

Figure 9   G-spot: Hypothesized to produce ejaculation in some women.

A Sexually Diverse World

Sexuality and Disability

I t is commonly believed that a person in a wheelchair is sexless. People with physical disabilities are thought not to be interested in sex, much less to be capable of engaging in sexual activity. Contrast those stereotypes with the following ideas from one woman with a spinal-cord injury:

> Don't think paralysis takes away your womanhood because you don't feel sex anymore; it doesn't. First of all, you're a woman, you're pretty, and you're able. The point is to have the self-confidence to realize that you haven't changed so much, other than your paralysis (Fritz et al., 2015, p. 3).

Ableism refers to discrimination or oppression of disabled people, which may include denial of rights and the perpetuation of stigma (Gill, 2015). About 10 percent of adults in the United States have a physical disability that imposes a substantial limitation on their activities. Given a chance to express themselves, these people emphasize the importance of their sexuality and sex drive, which are not necessarily altered by their disability. Yet they must face *sexual ableism,* which assumes that there are qualifications that one must meet to be sexual, based on criteria such as ability, intellect, appearance, and age.

Space does not permit a complete discussion of all types of disabilities and their consequences for sexuality. Instead, we concentrate on two illustrative examples: spinal-cord injury and intellectual disability.

Spinal-Cord Injury

Paraplegia (paralysis of the lower half of the body on both sides) and tetraplegia (also known as quadriplegia, paralysis of the body from the neck down) are both caused by injuries to the spinal cord. Many able-bodied people find it difficult to understand what it feels like to be paralyzed. Imagine that your genitals and the region around them

(a)

(b)

Figure 10   In the last 20 years we have become aware of the capacity of people with disabilities for sexual expression. (*a*) There is a need for sex education for children with disabilities. (*b*) Ellen Stohl, the first woman with disabilities to appear in *Playboy* (July, 1987). She has quadriplegia, having suffered several broken bones in her neck in an automobile accident. She was completely paralyzed initially, but her injury was incomplete. She gradually recovered use of her arms and hands. Although she has no movement below the waist, she has some sensitivity in her legs and is hypersensitive in the genitals. She enjoys sex very much and is orgasmic.

have lost all sensation. You would not know they were being touched unless you saw it happen. Furthermore, there could be a loss of bladder and bowel control, which may produce embarrassing problems if sexual activity is attempted (Fritz et al., 2015).

The capacity of a man with a spinal-cord injury to have an erection depends on the level of the spinal cord at which the injury occurred and whether the spinal cord was completely or only partially severed (Overgood et al., 2014; Phelps et al., 2001; Sabharwal, 2014). According to most studies, a majority of men with a spinal-cord injury are able to have erections. In some cases only reflex erections are possible. In other words, erections are produced by direct stimulation of the genitals, even though the man may not be able to feel the sensation. Injuries in the lower, sacral portion of the spinal cord can have especially serious effects if they injure the erection reflex center. Physicians are experimenting with surgeries that would restore sensation to the glans penis in these cases (Overgood et al., 2014). In a few cases, particularly if the injury was not severe, the man can produce an erection by erotic thoughts, but more typically this capacity is lost with spinal-cord injury. When the injury is severe, the man cannot ejaculate, although ejaculation may be possible if the cord was only partially severed.

Women with a spinal-cord injury experience many of the same sexual responses as other women, including engorgement of the clitoris and labia, erection of the nipples, and increases in heart rate. Approximately 50 percent of women with spinal-cord injuries can have orgasms from stimulation of the genitals. Some women with a spinal-cord injury develop a capacity for orgasm from stimulation of the breasts or lips. Nonetheless, many other women with spinal-cord injuries experience problems with desire, arousal, and orgasm (Sipski et al., 2001, 2004).

Because sexuality in our culture is so orgasm-oriented, orgasm problems among people with spinal-cord injury may appear to be devastating. But many of them report that they have been able to cultivate a kind of "psychological orgasm" that is as satisfying as the physical one. Fantasy is one form of sexual expression that their injury does not stop.

For women with spinal-cord injuries whose menstrual cycling returns, their ability to conceive a baby is normal. Therefore, they need access to contraception if they wish not to have a baby. Most pregnancies proceed normally, although there is a higher risk of some complications. Vaginal deliveries are usually possible and can be done without anesthetic.

It is important that sex therapy be available to people with physical disabilities (Mona et al., 2014). (See the chapter "Sexual Disorders and Sex Therapy" for a complete discussion of sex therapy.) When working with people with physical disabilities, the therapist must assess factors such as the individual's mobility and level of pain when engaging in sex. Disability-affirmative therapy is being developed and holds much promise for the future.

Intellectual Disability

The *DSM-5* uses the term *intellectual disability* (or intellectual developmental disorder) for what was formerly called mental retardation (American Psychiatric Association, 2013). To be diagnosed as having an intellectual disability, the individual must display: (1) difficulties in intellectual functions such as reasoning, judgment, and academic learning (this is determined in part by intelligence testing); (2) difficulties in activities of daily living, with deficits such as communication, social participation, and independent living; (3) the onset of these difficulties in childhood. Intellectual disabilities vary considerably, from mild to moderate to severe to profound. This variation is reflected in the spectrum of functioning of those with intellectual disabilities, from those who require institutionalization to others who function well in the community, who can read and write and hold simple jobs.

Four issues are especially important when considering the sexuality of people with intellectual disabilities: their opportunity for sexual expression, the need for sexuality education, the importance of contraception, and the possibility of sexual abuse.

People with intellectual disabilities have sexual desires and seek to express them, despite the fact that they are often viewed by others as asexual (Sinclair et al., 2015). Because children with intellectual disabilities are often slower to learn the norms of society, they may express themselves sexually in ways that offend other people, such as masturbating in public. For this reason and others, better sexuality education for people with intellectual disabilities is essential (Finlay et al., 2015; Schaafsma et al., 2015), education that respects the sexual agency and desires of the students and understands that they may already be engaging in sexual activity (Gill, 2015).

It is important that people with intellectual disabilities be educated about contraception and that contraceptives be made available to them. Because they have typical sexual desires, they may engage in sexual intercourse. In one study, 24 percent of boys and 8 percent of girls with intellectual disabilities had engaged in intercourse by age 16 (Cheng & Udry, 2003). If these youth lack sexuality education, they may not realize that pregnancy can result. An unwanted pregnancy for a woman or couple with intellectual disabilities may be a difficult situation. They may be able to function well when taking care of themselves, but not with the added burden of a baby. On the other hand, some people with intellectual disabilities do function sufficiently well to care for a child. The important thing is that they make as educated a decision as possible. Many experts recommend the IUD for women with intellectual disabilities because it does not require memory and forethought for effective use.

The topic of contraception and individuals with intellectual disabilities raises the ugly issue of involuntary sterilization. Until the mid-1950s, people with mental retardation, as they were called then, who lived in institutions were routinely sterilized, although certainly not with their informed consent. We now view this as a terrible violation of the rights of these individuals. It is now very difficult to gain legal permission to sterilize a person with an intellectual disability.

A final concern is that people with intellectual disabilities may be particularly vulnerable to sexual abuse. Because there is such a spectrum of ability among these people, it raises the question of what level of intellectual ability is required for consent (Gill, 2015).

In summary, there are three general points to be made about sexuality and people with physical or intellectual disabilities: (1) They generally do have sexual needs and desires; (2) they are often capable of a sexual response quite similar to that of able-bodied people of average intelligence; and (3) there is a real need for more information and communication about what people with various disabilities can and cannot do sexually.

(see Figure 11). These are part of the **limbic system.** Interestingly, erection is not associated with activity in these regions, suggesting that the role of the interest network is to recognize sexual opportunity in the environment.

> **Limbic system:** A set of structures in the interior of the brain, including the amygdala, hippocampus, and fornix; believed to be important for sexual behavior in both animals and humans.

Neurochemical Influences on Sexual Response

Distinctive neurochemicals are involved in sexual excitation and sexual inhibition. During excitement and arousal, dopamine, melanocortins, oxytocin, and norepinephrine are involved (Pfaus, 2009). Dopamine and melanocortin stimulate attention to sexual stimuli and sexual desire within the limbic system. Norepinephrine and oxytocin stimulate sexual arousal and erection. In part, the activation of these neurochemicals also blocks the action of inhibitory processes.

Neurochemicals involved in inhibitory processes include opioids, which are released in the cortex, limbic system, hypothalamus, and midbrain in response to sexual pleasure and orgasm/ejaculation. They also include endocannabinoids, which induce sedation (and

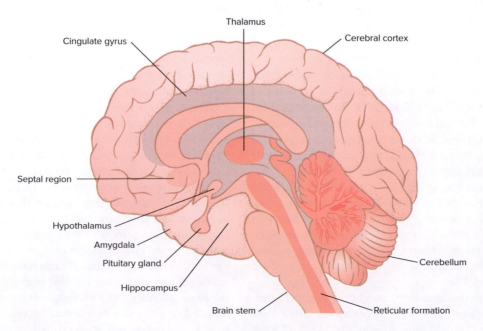

Figure 11   The limbic system of the brain, which is important in sexuality.

Milestones in Sex Research

Mapping the Sexual Brain

Exciting advances in the technology of neuroimaging are giving us inside views of the human brain during various phases of sexual response. Methods such as PET (positron emission tomography) and fMRI (functional magnetic resonance imaging) show which regions of the brain "light up" (have neurons most actively firing) while the individual is solving a math problem or thinking about something sad (Figure 12).

Sex researchers have adopted these techniques with the goal of learning which regions of the brain are most involved in various aspects of sexuality. One of the challenges they have faced is that the participant cannot move while in an MRI scanner, making it difficult to achieve sexual arousal using most of the normal methods. Researchers have solved the problem by showing erotic videos to the person inside the scanner.

In one experiment, heterosexual men viewed erotic video clips, relaxing clips, and sports clips, in random order

(Arnow et al., 2002). Meanwhile, their brains were being scanned in an MRI machine and the erection of the penis was measured. One has to admire these men for being able to become aroused while in an MRI scanner! When the men were exposed to erotic clips and were sexually aroused, as indicated by erection, intense brain activity was found in the right insula and claustrum, striatum (left caudate nucleus and putamen), cingulate gyrus, and—you guessed it—the hypothalamus! The insula is known to be involved in sensory processing, particularly of touch sensations. The cingulate cortex has been demonstrated in other studies to be involved in attentional processes and in guiding responsiveness to new environmental stimuli. Doubtless it was activated because of the men's attention to the erotic film.

Another study used fMRI to assess brain activation in both men and women while viewing erotic video segments (Karama et al., 2002). This study found brain activation in roughly the same regions as the study discussed

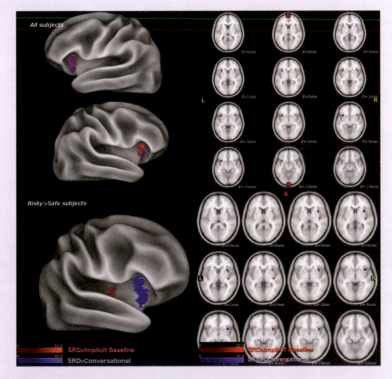

Figure 12   An fMRI study of brain activity associated with risky sexual behavior among men who have sex with men (MSM). (See text for explanation.)

Source: Smith, Benjamin J, et al. "Virtually 'in the Heat of the Moment': Insula Activation in Safe Sex Negotiation among Risky Men." *Social Cognitive and Affective Neuroscience,* vol. 13, no. 1, 2017, pp. 80–91, doi:10.1093/scan/nsx137.

previously. Almost all regions responded similarly in women and men. This study also found evidence of activation of the amygdala during sexual arousal. The amygdala is part of the limbic system, and, as noted earlier in this chapter, plays a role in sexual responding. The amygdala is known to be involved in emotion, and its activation speaks to the strong emotions—sometimes positive, sometimes negative—that are evoked by sexual stimuli.

Social psychologist Stephen Read uses fMRI to study brain activity associated with risky sexual behavior among men who have sex with men (MSM) (Barkley-Levenson et al., 2018; Smith et al., 2018; Xue et al., 2018). Risky sex for MSM refers to anal sex without using a condom, a practice that can spread HIV and other STDs. One study compared a Safe group, who had not engaged in condomless anal sex in the past 90 days, to a Risky group who had (Smith et al., 2018). While in an fMRI scanner, each participant played a virtual sexual hook-up game, in which they had the opportunity to meet an attractive male computer character and have sex with him on a virtual date. Through their avatar, participants had opportunities to make choices about practicing safe sex. In this situation, the Risky group had more activity in the right insula than did the Safe group. The insula is a part of the cortex buried deep in the brain (see Figure 12). These findings suggest that there are group differences in neural processing in the moment of risky versus safe sex decision making.

These studies are fascinating in themselves, as they allow us to view the workings of the brain during sexual responding. As research advances, future studies will help us understand the brain regions and associated neurotransmitters involved in sexual dysfunction, which will lead to more effective treatments for these problems. They will also allow us to better understand and treat arousal problems such as those suffered by individuals with pedophilia, who are aroused by completely inappropriate stimuli—children.

counteract stress!), and serotonin, which induces satiety and the refractory period. (For more detail and diagrams, see Pfaus, 2009; Pfaus et al., 2014.)

Androgens, estrogen, and progestin facilitate or prime the brain to respond to sexual incentives by binding to specific hormone receptor complexes, which in turn lead to the synthesis of these neurochemicals.

Hormones and Sex

The sex hormones are another important physiological force that interacts with the nervous system to influence sexual response.

Organizing versus Activating Effects

Endocrinologists generally make a distinction between the organizing effects of hormones and the activating effects of hormones. As we discuss in the chapter "Sex Hormones, Sexual Differentiation, and the Menstrual Cycle," hormones present during prenatal development have important influences on genital anatomy, creating male or female genitals. Hormone effects such as these are called **organizing effects** because they cause a relatively permanent change in the organization of some structures, whether in the nervous system or in the reproductive system. Typically there are critical periods during which these hormone effects may occur.

> **Organizing effects of hormones:** Effects of sex hormones early in development, resulting in a permanent change in the brain or reproductive system.
>
> **Activating effects of hormones:** Effects of sex hormones in adulthood, resulting in the activation of behaviors, especially sexual behaviors and aggressive behaviors.

It has also been known for some time that if an adult male mouse or rat is castrated (has the testes removed, which removes the source of testosterone), it will cease engaging in sexual behavior (and will be less aggressive). If that animal is then given injections of testosterone, it will start engaging in sex again. Hormone effects such as these are called **activating effects** because they activate (or deactivate) certain behaviors.

The organizing effects of hormones on sexual behavior have been well documented (Keefe, 2002). In a classic experiment, testosterone was administered to pregnant female guinea pigs. The female offspring that had been exposed to testosterone prenatally[4] were, in adulthood, incapable of displaying female sexual behavior—in particular, lordosis, which is a sexual posturing involving arching of the back and raising of the hindquarters so that intromission of the male's penis is possible (Phoenix et al., 1959). It is thought that this result occurred because the testosterone "organized" the brain tissue (particularly the hypothalamus) in a male fashion. These female offspring were also born with masculinized genitals—evidence that their reproductive systems had also been organized in the male direction. But the important point here is that the prenatal doses of testosterone had masculinized their sexual behavior. Experiments with many other species have obtained similar results.

[4]Note the similarity of these experiments to John Money's observations of human intersex individuals in the chapter "Sex Hormones, Sexual Differentiation, and the Menstrual Cycle."

These hormonally masculinized females in adulthood displayed mounting behavior, a male[5] sexual behavior. When they were given testosterone in adulthood, they showed about as much mounting behavior as males did. In this way, the testosterone administered in adulthood *activated* male patterns of sexual behavior.

The analogous experiment on males would be castration at birth, followed by administration of ovarian hormones in adulthood. When this experiment was done with rats, female sexual behavior resulted. These males responded to mating attempts by other males essentially in the same way females do (Harris & Levine, 1965). Their brain tissue had been organized in a female direction during an early, critical period when testosterone was absent, and the female behavior patterns were activated in adulthood by administration of ovarian hormones.

> **What hormone is most important to sexual desire in men? In women?**

It seems, then, that males and females initially have capacities for both male and female sexual behaviors. If testosterone is present early in development, the capacity for exhibiting female behaviors is suppressed. Sex hormones in adulthood then activate the behavior patterns that were differentiated early in development.

How relevant is this research to humans? Generally the trend is for the behavior of lower species to be more under hormonal control and for the behavior of higher species to be more under brain (neural) control (Pfaus et al., 2014). Accordingly, human sexual behavior is less under hormonal control than is rat sexual behavior, and human sexual behavior is controlled more by the brain. For these reasons, learning from past experiences and cultural conventions, which are stored in the brain, is more likely to have a profound effect (Wallen, 2001).

Let us now consider in more detail the known activating effects of sex hormones on the sexual behavior of adult humans.

Testosterone and Sexual Desire

Testosterone has well-documented effects on libido, or sexual desire, in humans (Bancroft & Graham, 2011; van Anders, 2012). In men deprived of their main source of testosterone by castration or by illness, there is a dramatic decrease in sexual behavior in some, but not all, cases. Sexual desire declines if a man is given an antiandrogen drug. Thus testosterone seems to have an activating effect in maintaining sexual desire in men. However, in cases of castration, sexual behavior may decline very slowly and may be present for several years after the source of

[5]The term *male sexual behavior* is being used here to refer to a sexual behavior that is displayed by typical males of the species and either is absent in females of that species or is present at a much lower frequency. Typical females do mount, but they do so less frequently than males do. *Female sexual behavior* is defined similarly.

testosterone is gone. Such cases point to the importance of experience and brain control of sexual behavior in humans.

Research has also demonstrated that levels of testosterone are correlated with sexual behavior in boys around the time of puberty (Udry et al., 1985). Boys in the eighth, ninth, and tenth grades filled out a questionnaire about their sexual behavior and gave blood samples from which their level of testosterone could be measured. Among the boys whose testosterone level was in the highest quartile (top 25 percent of the sample), 69 percent had engaged in sexual intercourse, whereas only 16 percent of the boys whose testosterone level was in the lowest quartile had done so. Similarly, of the boys with testosterone levels in the highest quartile, 62 percent had masturbated, compared with 12 percent for the boys in the lowest quartile. These effects were uncorrelated with age, so it wasn't simply a matter of the older boys having more testosterone and more sexual experience. The authors concluded that at puberty testosterone affects sexual motivation directly.

Research indicates that androgens are related to sexual desire in women also (Bancroft & Graham, 2011). If all sources of androgens (the adrenals and the ovaries) are removed, women lose sexual desire. Women who have undergone oophorectomy (surgical removal of the ovaries, typically because of cancer) report marked decreases in sexual desire. If they are treated with testosterone, their sexual desire increases (Shifren et al., 1998, 2000). Moreover, androgens are used successfully in the treatment of women who have low sexual desire (Kaplan & Owett, 1993). Androgen levels decline with age in women, and research shows that administration of DHEA (a pretestosterone hormone) to women over 60 results in their having increased sexual desire (Baulieu et al., 2000; Spark, 2002).

But it's not a one-way street. Not only does testosterone have an effect on sexual desire and behavior, but sexual behavior also affects testosterone levels (van Anders, 2012). Masturbation, for example, increases testosterone levels. The effects are bidirectional—testosterone influences sex and sex influences testosterone.

Sex Offenders—Castration or Incarceration?

In 2004, James Jenkins, imprisoned for sexually molesting three young girls, asked a guard for a razor, saying that he wanted to be clean-shaven for a court appearance the next day. He then got the blade out of the holder, castrated himself, and flushed his testes down the toilet. Today he is happy with the outcome, saying that he is now free of sexual urges and deviant sexual fantasies (Rondeaux, 2006). In 2018, an Oklahoma legislator proposed a bill that would authorize chemical castration at the time of release of a sex offender from prison (Ducharme, 2018).

Physical castration refers to surgical removal of the testes, technically known as *bilateral orchiectomy. Chemical castration* refers to injections of a drug such as Depo-Provera, an antiandrogen drug that sharply reduces the levels of testosterone in the body.

Cases such as these raise a host of questions, some of them legal and ethical, others within the province of the sciences (Gooren, 2011; Weinberger et al., 2005). Legally, a castration sentence could be challenged on the grounds that it is cruel and unusual punishment, which is forbidden by the U.S. Constitution. And what is the goal of such a punishment? Was the legislator simply being punitive and letting the punishment fit the crime? Or is castration intended to ensure that the man would never commit the crime again? The scientific data become pertinent in addressing this last point.

With either physical castration or chemical castration, the man is left with little natural testosterone in his body. Numerous experiments with other species have demonstrated that the effect of this low level of testosterone is a sharply reduced sex drive and the virtual elimination of sexual behavior. However, the effects in humans are not so clear because we are not as hormone dependent as other species. There are documented cases of castrated men continuing to engage in sexual intercourse for years after the castration. Castration may reduce sexual behavior in humans, but its effects are not completely predictable.

Furthermore, testosterone is available artificially, either by pill or by injection, so a physically castrated criminal might secretly obtain replacement testosterone.

In cases of rape, more than sexual behavior is involved. Many experts believe that rape is better conceptualized as an aggressive or violent crime that happens to be expressed sexually than seen as a sex crime per se. For this reason, the scientific question may be restated from "Does castration eliminate sexual behavior?" to "Does castration eliminate aggressive behavior?" Here, too, there are numerous experiments documenting—in other species—that castration greatly reduces aggressive behavior by lowering testosterone levels. But once again, the hormone effects are not as clear or consistent in humans. So castration might be effective in reducing sexual or aggressive behaviors and for this reason might reduce the chances of the man committing rape again, but such effects cannot be guaranteed.

It seems clear that physical or chemical castration should be only part of the treatment, which should also include intensive psychotherapy (Saleh et al., 2010; Figure 13).

> **What does the scientific evidence say about whether sex offenders should be castrated to prevent them from committing more crimes?**

Figure 13   Sex offenders in a therapy group. Research shows that treatment of sex offenders, whether with the drug Depo-Provera or not, should always include psychotherapy.

©Jon Bradley/Getty Images

Pheromones

Scientists and laypeople alike are intrigued by the role that pheromones play in sexual behavior (Cutler, 1999; McClintock, 2000). Pheromones are somewhat like hormones. Recall that hormones are biochemicals manufactured in the body and secreted into the bloodstream to be carried to the organs they affect. **Pheromones,** in contrast, are biochemicals secreted outside the body. Through the sense of smell, they are an important means of communication between animals. An animal's urine often contains pheromones. The dog that does scent marking by urinating on a tree is actually depositing pheromones. Some pheromones appear to be important in sexual communication, and some have even been called *sex attractants* (Figure 14).

Much of the research on pheromones has been done with animals and demonstrates the importance of pheromones in sexual and reproductive functioning. For example, pheromones present in female urine influence male sexual behavior. If urine from an ovulating monkey is in the cage of a pregnant (and thus not ovulating) female and her mate, the male shows more frequent erections and more mounting (Snowdon et al., 2006). Males also show an increase in testosterone levels following exposure to the urine of the ovulating female.

The sense of smell, olfaction, is essential for pheromone effects to occur. Removal of the olfactory bulbs, and specifically a region called the *vomeronasal organ* (VNO), dramatically reduces the sexual behavior of males from species such as mice and guinea pigs (Thorne & Amrein, 2003). The VNO, located inside the nose, is a chemoreceptor—that is, it is activated by chemicals such as pheromones. Neuroscientists have even recorded the activity of single neurons in the VNO of male mice and found that certain neurons fire when the animal comes into contact with another male, but different neurons fire when he comes into contact with a female (Luo et al., 2003). Activation of the VNO then activates cells in the hypothalamus (Keverne, 1999), and as discussed earlier, the hypothalamus is crucial to sexuality. The VNO is a kind of second olfactory pathway. Sometimes called the *accessory olfactory bulb,* the VNO functions in addition to the main sense of smell.

What relevance does all this have for humans? Humans are not, by and large, "smell animals." Olfaction is much less important for us than for most other species. We tend to rely mostly on vision and, secondarily, hearing. Compare this with a dog's ability to gain a wealth of information about who and what has been in a park simply by sniffing around for a few minutes. Does this mean that pheromones have no influence on our sexual behavior?

It is now clear that human pheromones exist and may play an important role in sexuality (Wyatt, 2003, 2015). Indeed, pheromones may be exactly the "body chemistry" that attracts people to each other. Perfumes with musky scents are popular and presumably increase sexual attractiveness, perhaps because they smell like pheromones.

What scientific evidence is there regarding the existence and effects of pheromones in humans? First, the vomeronasal organ—which, as

> **Pheromones (FARE-oh-mones):** Biochemicals secreted outside the body that are important in communication between animals and that may serve as sex attractants.

(a)

Figure 14 Pheromones. (*a*) Pheromones are a major means of communication between animals. (*b*) Are there human pheromones that are sex attractants?

(a) ©Spiky and I/Shutterstock; (b) ©Brooke Fasani Auchincloss/ Corbis/Getty Images

(b)

noted earlier, is related to olfaction and sexual behavior in other species and essentially seems to function as a pheromone sensor—consists of just a few neurons in humans and seems to be nonfunctional (Georgiadis & Kringelbach, 2012). That said, there is evidence that, when humans smell pheromones, a region of the hypothalamus is activated, as is the amygdala. That is, our brains do respond to pheromones. Even though humans do not have a functional vomeronasal organ, they have cells in the lining of the nose that contain pheromone receptors. Scientists have recently identified several genes in humans that code for these receptors in the lining of the nose (Wallrabenstein et al., 2015).

It is clear that humans do secrete pheromones. Androstenol, an odorous steroid that is well documented as a pheromone in pigs, has been isolated in the underarm sweat of humans (Gower & Ruparelia, 1993). Molecules known to be sex-attractant pheromones to male rhesus monkeys have been isolated in human vaginal secretions (Cowley & Brooksbank, 1991).

Research provides important indications that pheromones may play a role in human sexuality. In one experiment, for example, a synthesized female pheromone was added to women's perfume, and a placebo was added to perfume for women in the control group (McCoy & Pitino, 2002; Rako & Friebely, 2004). The women recorded their sexual behaviors over the next three months. Compared with the control group, pheromone-treated women showed a significantly greater frequency of intercourse, dates, and petting and kissing. They did not differ in frequency of masturbation. The researchers concluded that the pheromone had increased the women's attractiveness to men. In an imaging study, eight heterosexual men were exposed to a woman's perfume (Huh et al., 2008). Two reported "strong" arousal and three reported "moderate" arousal. All eight experienced brain activity in the insula, the gyrus, and the hypothalamus, areas we noted earlier are involved in arousal.

The classic research of Martha McClintock (1971) documented the existence of a phenomenon known as **menstrual synchrony:** the convergence, over several months, of the dates of onset of menstrual periods among women who are in close contact with each other (McClintock, 1998; Weller et al., 1995). This phenomenon is now thought to be due to pheromones produced by the women.

In perhaps the most dramatic experiment to date in humans, the results indicated that the timing of ovulation could be experimentally manipulated with human pheromones (Stern & McClintock, 1998). Odorless secretions from women's armpits were collected in the late follicular phase, just before ovulation. Other women exposed to these secretions showed an accelerated appearance of the LH surge that triggers ovulation. Underarm secretions from

> **Menstrual synchrony:** The convergence, over several months, of the dates of onset of menstrual periods among women who are in close contact with each other.

the same donors collected later in the menstrual cycle had the opposite effect: They delayed the LH surge in other women and lengthened the time to menstruation. In another study, men smelled T-shirts worn by (1) women near ovulation, (2) women far from ovulation, or (3) no one. Men exposed to the scent of an ovulating woman subsequently had elevated levels of testosterone (Miller & Maner, 2010).

Other pheromone research has found that people's preference for human body odors and their brain responses to pheromones differ according to sexual orientation (Berglund et al., 2006; Martins et al., 2005). In one study, armpit secretions were collected from heterosexual men, heterosexual women, gay men, and lesbians (Martins et al., 2005). Odor evaluators then rated the pleasantness of these odors without knowing the source of them. Heterosexual men gave the lowest pleasantness ratings to the pheromones from gay men. Gay men gave low ratings to the pheromones of heterosexual men. The researchers concluded that human "odor prints" may help us identify groups of people who are potential sex partners.

The smell of pheromones does not necessarily have to be consciously perceived in order to have an effect (McClintock, 2000). The olfactory system can respond to odors even when they are not consciously perceived. For this reason, pheromones that we are not even aware of may have important influences.

If these indications about the effects of pheromones on human sexual behavior are correct, our hyperclean society may be destroying the scents that attract people to each other. The normal genital secretions (assuming reasonable cleanliness to eliminate bacteria) may contain sex attractants. Ironically, "feminine hygiene" deodorants may destroy precisely the odors that turn men on.

Sexual Techniques

Earlier in this chapter, we discussed some of the wonderful things that happen to the body during sexual arousal and orgasm. How do we get to these marvelous states, for both ourselves and our partners?

We live in the era of sex manuals. Books like *Electrify Your Sex Life* and *The Illustrated Guide to Extended Massive Orgasm,* as well as feature articles and advice columns in many magazines, give us information on how to produce bigger and longer orgasms in ourselves and our partners. The sex manuals may also set up impossible standards of sexual performance that none of us can meet.

On the other hand, we live in a society that has a history of leaving the learning of sexual techniques to nature or to chance, in contrast to some other societies in which adolescents are given explicit instruction in methods for producing sexual pleasure. For humans, sexual behavior is a lot more than "doin' what comes naturally." We all need some means for learning about sexual techniques, and the sex manuals may help to fill that need, but they may also raise unrealistic expectations. In the sections that follow, we consider sexual techniques.

Erogenous Zones

Although the notion of **erogenous zones** originated in Freud's work, the term is now part of our general vocabulary. It refers to parts of the body that are sexually sensitive. Stroking them or otherwise stimulating them produces sexual arousal. The genitals and the breasts are good examples. The lips, neck, and thighs are generally also erogenous zones. But even some rather unlikely regions—such as the back, the ears, the stomach, and the feet—can also be erogenous. One person's erogenous zones can be quite different from another's. For this reason it is impossible to give a list of sure "turn-ons." The best way to find out is to communicate with your partner, verbally or nonverbally.

One-Person Sex

It does not necessarily take two to have sex. Individuals can produce their own sexual stimulation. Sexual self-stimulation is called **autoeroticism.**[6] The best examples are masturbation and fantasy.

Masturbation

Here we reserve the term *hand–genital stimulation* for stimulation of another's genitals and the term **masturbation** for self-stimulation, either with the hand or with some object, such as a vibrator. Masturbation is a very common sexual behavior. Almost all men and the majority of women in the United States masturbate to orgasm at least a few times during their lives. In the National Survey of Sexual Health and Behavior, 72 to 84 percent of men (depending on age and other factors) ages 18 to 60 reported they had masturbated in the preceding year, as did 54 to 65 percent of the women (Herbenick et al., 2010a,b, Tables 2 and 3). Fifty-six to 66 percent of men and 26 to 52 percent of women had masturbated in the preceding month.

The techniques used by males and females in masturbation are interesting in part because they provide information to their partners concerning the best techniques to use in lovemaking. Most commonly, women masturbate by manipulating the clitoris and the inner lips and outer lips. Some prefer to rub at the side of the clitoris, and a few stimulate the glans of the clitoris directly.

Other techniques used by women in masturbation include breast stimulation and pressing the genitals

[6]For those of you who are interested in the roots of words, *autoeroticism* does not refer to sex in the backseat of a car. The prefix *auto* means "self" (as in *autobiography*); hence self-stimulation is autoeroticism.

(a)

(b)

Figure 15   (*a*) Male masturbation using hand stimulation of the penis. (*b*) Female masturbation using clitoral stimulation.

(a) ©H.S. Photos/Alamy; (b) ©Westend61 GmbH/Alamy

against some object, such as a pillow, or massaging them with a stream of water while in the shower. A few women are capable of using fantasy alone to produce orgasm; fantasy-induced orgasms are accompanied by the same physiological changes as orgasms produced by masturbation (Whipple et al., 1992).

Almost all males report masturbating by hand stimulation of the penis. Those interested in speed can reach an orgasm in only a minute or two. Most men use the technique of circling the hand around the shaft of the penis and using an up-and-down movement to stimulate the shaft and glans. Because the penis produces no natural lubrication of its own, some men like to use lubrication, such as soapsuds while showering. The tightness of the grip, the speed of movement, and the amount of glans stimulation vary from one man to the next. Most increase the speed of stimulation as they approach orgasm, slowing or

---

Erogenous zones (eh-RAH-jen-us): Areas of the body that are particularly sensitive to sexual stimulation.
Autoeroticism: Sexual self-stimulation; for example, masturbation.
Masturbation: Stimulation of one's own genitals with the hand or with some object, such as a pillow or vibrator.

stopping the stimulation at orgasm because further stimulation would be uncomfortable (Masters & Johnson, 1966). Immediately after orgasm, the glans and corona are hypersensitive, and the man generally avoids further stimulation of the penis at that time.

Fantasy

Sexual fantasy refers to any conscious mental imagery or daydream that includes sexual activity or is sexually arousing (Bivona & Critelli, 2009). Almost all men and women report that they have experienced sexual fantasies, often frequently (Kahr, 2008; Leitenberg & Henning, 1995).

The themes of sexual fantasies reported by men and women are similar. Some of the most popular ones for women and men are fantasizing about taking part in fellatio or cunnilingus; having sex in an unusual place (e.g., in the office, public toilets); sex in a romantic place (e.g., on a deserted beach); being masturbated by my partner; and having sex with someone I know who is not my spouse (Joyal et al., 2015).

Gays and lesbians tend to fantasize about sexual partners of the same gender (Price et al., 1985). Heterosexuals may fantasize about sexual activities with someone of the other gender or the same gender.

Sexual fantasy can have a variety of functions for the person doing the fantasizing (Maltz & Boss, 1997). These include enhancing self-esteem and attractiveness, increasing the person's own sexual arousal (e.g., during masturbation or partnered sex), and facilitating orgasm. While many people use fantasy as part of sexual interactions, others may have no sexual contact with another person, relying exclusively on sexual fantasy and masturbation for their erotic pleasure (Kahr, 2008).

Vibrators and Other Sex Toys

Various sexual devices, such as vibrators and dildos, are used by some people in masturbation or by couples as they have sex together (Figure 16).

Both male and female artificial genitals can be purchased. A **dildo** is a rubber or plastic cylinder, often shaped like a penis. It can be inserted into the vagina or the anus. Dildos are used by some women in masturbation, by men, by lesbians, by gays, and by heterosexual couples. Artificial vaginas, and even inflatable replicas of the entire body, male or female, can also be purchased.

Some *vibrators* are shaped like a penis, but others are not. Some models have a cord that plugs into an electric outlet; others are cordless and use batteries. Women may use vibrators to masturbate, stimulating the clitoral and mons area or inserting them into the vagina (Herbenick et al., 2009). Men may also use them during masturbation or during sex with a partner (Reece et al., 2009). They can be purchased in

Sexual fantasy: Sexual thoughts or images that alter the person's emotions or physiological state.
Dildo: A rubber or plastic cylinder, often shaped like a penis.

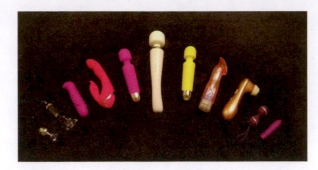

Figure 16 Vibrators and dildos, used for sexual stimulation.

©*Thornova Photography/Shutterstock*

"respectable" stores (where they are sometimes euphemistically called "face massagers"), in sex stores, and by mail.

Vibrators designed for women are not recent. They were invented in the 1880s and sold as a medical device (Maines, 1999). Physicians prescribed their use for the treatment of various female "maladies," especially hysteria.

Body oils are also popular. In fact, their use has been encouraged by experts in the field. For example, sex therapists recommend them for the touching or sensate focus exercises that they prescribe for their patients in sex therapy (see the chapter "Sexual Disorders and Sex Therapy"). Oils have a sensuous quality that heightens erotic feelings. Furthermore, if you are being stroked or massaged for any extended period of time, the oil helps ensure that the part of your body that is being stimulated will not end up feeling like it has been sandpapered. The sex stores sell oils in a variety of exotic scents, but plain baby oil will also do nicely. Be aware that Vaseline and some other lubricants cause condoms to break.

Two-Person Sex

When many of us think of techniques of two-person sex, the image that flashes across our mind generally reflects several assumptions. One assumption is that one of the people is a male and the other a female—that is, that the sex is heterosexual. This image reflects heteronormativity, a belief that heterosexual sex is normative. We also tend to assume that the man is supposed to do certain things during the act and the woman is to do certain other things, reflecting the sexual scripts of our culture. He, for example, is supposed to take the initiative in deciding what techniques are to be used, and she is to follow his lead. Although there is nothing particularly evil in these assumptions, they do tend to impose limitations on our own sexual expression and to make some think that their own sexual behavior is "not quite right." For these reasons we will attempt to avoid these assumptions in the sections that follow.

Kissing

Kissing (or what we might call, technically, "mouth-to-mouth stimulation") is an activity that virtually everyone in our culture has engaged in. In simple kissing, the partners keep their mouths closed and touch each other's lips. In deep kissing ("French kissing"), both people part their lips slightly and insert their tongues into each other's mouths (somehow these clinical descriptions do not make it sound like as much fun as it is). There are endless variations on these two basic approaches, such as nibbling at the partner's lips or tongue or sucking at the lips. There are also plenty of other regions of the body to kiss: the nose, the forehead, the eyelids, the earlobes, the neck, the breasts, the genitals, and the feet, to give a few examples.

Touching

Enjoying touching and being touched is essential to sexual pleasure. Caresses or massages, applied to virtually any area of the body, can be exciting. The regions that are exciting vary a great deal from one person to the next and depend on how the person is feeling at the moment. For this reason, it is important to communicate what sort of touching is most pleasurable to you. (For specific exercises on touching and being touched, see the chapter "Sexual Disorders and Sex Therapy").

As we noted earlier, one of the best ways to find out how to use your hands in stimulating the genitals of another person is to find out how that person masturbates.

When stimulating a woman, generally it is best, particularly if the woman is not already aroused, to begin with gentle, light stroking of the inside of the thighs and the inner and outer lips, moving to light stroking of the clitoris. As she becomes more aroused, the stimulation of the clitoris can become firmer. The clitoris is very sensitive, and this sensitivity can be either exquisite or painful.

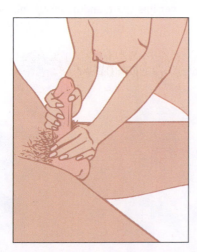

Figure 17   Technique of hand stimulation of the penis.

If the woman is already somewhat aroused, lubrication can be provided by touching the fingers to the vaginal entrance and then spreading the lubrication on the clitoris. If she is not aroused or does not produce much vaginal lubrication, saliva works well too. Moisture makes the stimulation not only more comfortable but also more sensuous. Some women find direct stimulation of the clitoral glans to be painful in some states of arousal. These women generally prefer stimulation on either side of the clitoris instead.

The Other Senses

So far in this section, we have focused on tactile (touch) sensations in sexual arousal. However, the other senses—vision, smell, and hearing—can also make contributions.

What you see can contribute to your arousal. Men seem, in general, to be turned on by a variety of visual stimuli, such as an attractive person or partially dressed or nude bodies. As we discussed earlier, both men and women respond with physiological, neural, and neurochemical arousal to portrayals of partnered sexual activity. Just as erotica may be used during autoerotic activity, viewing sexual activity on a video or on the Internet may contribute to partnered sexual activities. Some men, and a few women, have mild fetishes (see the chapter "Variations in Sexual Behavior" for more detail) and like to see their partner wearing certain types of clothing, such as leather or rubber clothing or schoolgirl dresses. A good rule here, as elsewhere, is to communicate with your partner to find out what they would find arousing.

Perhaps the biggest visual turn-on comes simply from looking at your own body and your partner's. According to the NHSLS, watching a partner undress is one of the most appealing sexual activities (Michael et al., 1994, Table 12).

Odors can be turn-ons or turn-offs. The scent of a body that is clean, having been washed with soap and water, is a natural turn-on. It does not need to be covered up with an "intimate deodorant."[7] In a sense, the scent of your skin, armpits, or genitals is your "aroma signature" and can be quite arousing. Research shows that people who are more sensitive to olfactory stimuli (odors) rate their sexual activities as more pleasant (Bendas et al., 2018). This may occur because reward centers in the brain are stimulated more for these people.

Many people respond with arousal to specific musical stimuli, probably reflecting classical conditioning (see the chapter "Theoretical Perspectives on Sexuality").

---

[7]With the popularity of oral sex, some women worry that the scent of their genitals might be offensive. The advertisements for feminine hygiene deodorant sprays prey upon these fears. These sprays should not be used because they may irritate the vagina. Besides, there is nothing offensive about the scent of a vulva that has been washed; some people, in fact, find it arousing.

Fantasy during Two-Person Sex

Fantasies can be done solo or can heighten the experience of sex with another person. Particularly in a long-term, monogamous relationship, sexual monotony can become a problem. Fantasies are one way to introduce some variety and excitement without violating an agreement to be faithful to the other person. It is important to view such fantasies in this way, rather than as a sign of disloyalty to, or dissatisfaction with, one's sexual partner. Fantasies during two-person sex are generally quite similar to the ones people have while masturbating.

Genital–Genital Stimulation: Positions of Intercourse

One of the most common heterosexual techniques involves the insertion of the penis into the vagina. This technique is called **coitus** or *sexual intercourse.* Ancient love manuals and other sources illustrate many positions of intercourse (Figure 18).

Some authorities state that there are only four positions of intercourse. Personally, we prefer to believe that there are an infinite number. Consider how many different angles your arms, legs, and torso may be in, in relation to those of your partner, and all the various ways in which you can intertwine your limbs—that's a lot of positions. We trust that given sufficient creativity and time, you can discover them all for yourself.

We would agree, though, that there are a few basic positions. One basic variation depends on whether the couple face each other (face-to-face position) or whether one partner faces the other's back (rear-entry position). If you try the other obvious variation, a back-to-back position, you will quickly find that you cannot accomplish much that way. The other basic variation depends on whether one partner is on top of the other or whether the couple are side by side. Let us consider four basic positions that illustrate these variations.

> **Coitus:** Sexual intercourse; insertion of the penis into the vagina.

Figure 18   Erotic sculptures at the Temple of Kandariya Mahadevo, India, built in A.D. 1000.

©Elena Odareeva/123RF

In the face-to-face, *man-on-top position* ("missionary" position—see Figure 19) the man and woman stimulate each other until they are aroused, he has an erection, and she is producing vaginal lubrication. Then he moves on top of her as she spreads her legs apart, either he or she spreads the inner lips apart, and he inserts his penis into

Figure 19   The man-on-top position of intercourse.

her vagina. He supports himself on his knees and hands or elbows and moves his penis in and out of the vagina in what is sometimes called pelvic thrusting.

The woman can have her legs in a number of positions that create variations. She may have them straight out horizontally, a position that produces a tight rub on the penis but does not permit it to go deeply into the vagina. She may bend her legs and elevate them to varying degrees, or she may hook them over the man's back or over his shoulders. The last approach permits the penis to move deeply into the vagina. The woman can also move her pelvis, either up and down or side to side, to produce further stimulation.

The man-on-top position has some advantages and some disadvantages. It is the best position for ensuring conception, if that is what you want. This position, however, does not work well if the woman is in the advanced stages of pregnancy or if either she or the man is extremely obese. Sex therapists have also found that it is not a very good position if the man wants to control his ejaculation; the woman-on-top position is better for this purpose.

For the *woman-on-top position* (Figure 20), the woman kneels over the man, with one knee on either side of his hips. Then his hand or hers guides the erect penis into the vagina as she lowers herself onto it. She then moves her hips to produce the stimulation. Beyond that, there are

numerous variations, depending on where she puts her legs. She can remain on her knees, or she can straighten out her legs behind her, putting them outside his legs or between them. Or she can turn around and face toward his feet.

This position has a number of advantages. It provides a lot of clitoral stimulation, and the woman can control the kind of stimulation she gets. For this reason, many women find it the best position for having an orgasm. It is also a good position for the man who wants to delay his ejaculation, and for this reason it is used in sex therapy.

In the *rear-entry position,* the man faces the woman's back. One way to do this is for the woman to kneel with her head down. The man kneels behind her and inserts his penis into her vagina (Figure 21). (This is sometimes called the "doggie position," because it is the way in which dogs and most other animals copulate.) Rear entry can also be accomplished when the couple are in the side-to-side position. A small amount of air may enter the vagina when this position is used, producing interesting noises when it comes out.

In the *side-to-side position,* the man and woman lie beside each other, either face-to-face or in a rear-entry position (Figure 22). The side-to-side position is good for leisurely or prolonged intercourse or if one or both of the partners are tired. It is also good for the pregnant and the obese.

Figure 20   The woman-on-top position of intercourse.

Figure 21   The rear-entry position of intercourse.

Figure 22   The side-to-side position of intercourse.

Mouth–Genital Stimulation (Oral Sex)

There are two kinds of mouth–genital stimulation (oral sex or "going down on" one's partner): cunnilingus and fellatio.

In **cunnilingus,** or "eating" (from the Latin words *cunnus,* meaning "vulva," and *lingere,* meaning "to lick"), the woman's genitals are stimulated by her partner's mouth. Cunnilingus can be performed by either heterosexuals or lesbian couples. Generally the focus of stimulation is the clitoris. The tongue stimulates it and the surrounding area with quick darting or thrusting movements, or the mouth can suck at the clitoris. The mouth can also suck at the inner lips, or the tongue can stimulate the vaginal entrance or be inserted into the vagina. During cunnilingus, some women also enjoy having a finger inserted into the vagina for added stimulation. The best way to know what she wants is through communication between partners, either verbal or nonverbal.

Many women are enthusiastic about cunnilingus and say that it is the best way—perhaps the only way—for them to orgasm. In one large, well-sampled study of Australians, respondents reported the specific sexual practices that were used in their most recent heterosexual encounter (Richters et al., 2006). If women had intercourse only, 50 percent had an orgasm, but when they had cunnilingus plus intercourse, 73 percent had an orgasm. In contrast, among men who engaged only in intercourse, 95 percent had an orgasm. It just isn't fair.

Cunnilingus, like fellatio, discussed next, can transmit some sexually transmitted infections such as gonorrhea. Oral sex can also result in transmission of HPV (human papillomavirus) from the genitals of an infected person to the mouth of the partner or vice versa. For these reasons, you need to be as careful about whom you engage in mouth–genital sex with as about whom you would engage in intercourse with. A small sheet of latex, called a *dental dam* (or *sex dam),* can be placed over the vulva for those wanting to practice safer sex.

One other possible problem should be noted as well. Some women enjoy having their partner blow air forcefully into the vagina. Although this technique is not dangerous under normal circumstances, when used on a pregnant woman it has been known to cause death (apparently as the result of air getting into the uterine veins), damage to the placenta, and embolism. For these reasons, it should not be used on a pregnant woman.

In **fellatio** ("sucking," "a blow job") the man's penis is stimulated by his partner's mouth. Fellatio can be performed by either heterosexuals or gay male couples. The partner licks the glans of the penis, its shaft, and perhaps the testes. The penis is gently taken into the mouth. If it is not fully erect, an erection can generally be produced by stronger sucking combined with hand stimulation along the penis. After that, the partner can produce an in-and-out motion by moving the lips down toward the base of the penis and then back up, always being careful not to scrape the penis with the teeth. Or the tongue can be flicked back and forth around the tip of the penis or along the corona.

When a couple are engaged in fellatio, the big question in their minds may concern ejaculation. The man may, of course, simply withdraw his penis from his partner's mouth and ejaculate outside it. Or he may ejaculate into it, and his partner may even enjoy swallowing the ejaculate. The ejaculate resembles partially cooked egg white in texture. It does not have a very distinctive flavor but often leaves a salty aftertaste. Because some people have mixed feelings about having the semen in their mouths, it is probably a good idea for the couple to discuss ahead of time (or during the activity) what they plan to do, particularly because ejaculation into the mouth is an unsafe practice in the AIDS era (see the chapter "Sexually Transmitted Infections").

Most men find fellatio to be a highly stimulating experience, which no doubt accounts for the high frequency with which prostitutes are asked to do it.

Fellatio and cunnilingus can be performed simultaneously by both partners. This is often called **sixty-nining**[8] because the numerals "69" suggest the position of the two bodies during simultaneous mouth–genital sex. Sixty-nining may be done either side to side or with one person on top of the other, each with the mouth on the other's genitals (Figure 23).

Anal Intercourse

In **anal intercourse** the man inserts his penis into his partner's rectum. In legal terminology it is sometimes called *sodomy* (although this term may also refer to other sexual practices such as intercourse with animals), and it is sometimes referred to as having sex "Greek style." It may be done by either heterosexual couples or gay male couples.

Anal intercourse is somewhat more difficult than penis-in-vagina intercourse because the rectum has no natural lubrication and because it is surrounded by fairly tight muscles. The man should therefore begin by moistening the partner's anus, either with saliva or with a sterile surgical lubricant such as K-Y Jelly (*not* Vaseline). He should also lubricate his penis. He then inserts it gently into the rectum and begins controlled pelvic thrusting. It is typically done in the rear-entry position or in the man-on-top position. The more the partner can relax, the less uncomfortable it is. Discomfort can also be reduced by allowing the receiving partner to be in control. While some heterosexual couples find the idea repulsive,

> **Cunnilingus (cun-ih-LING-us):** Mouth stimulation of the vulva.
> **Fellatio (feh-LAY-shoh):** Mouth stimulation of the penis.
> **Sixty-nining:** Simultaneous mouth–genital stimulation; also called *soixante-neuf.*
> **Anal intercourse:** Insertion of the penis into the partner's rectum.

---

[8]If you want to be elegant and impress your friends, you can call it *soixante-neuf,* which is "sixty-nine" in French.

Figure 23   Simultaneous mouth–genital stimulation in the sixty-nine position.

others delight in it. Some women report orgasm during anal intercourse, particularly when it is accompanied by hand stimulation of the clitoris. Men also report orgasms from receiving anal intercourse, primarily due to stimulation of the prostate.

Some health risks are associated with anal intercourse. It can cause damage or injury to the tissue of the rectal lining and anal sphincter. It can lead to infections with various organisms. Of greatest concern, HIV can be transmitted through anal intercourse. For these reasons, safer sex consists of either refraining from engaging in anal intercourse or using a condom (or doing it only in a monogamous relationship with an uninfected partner). Furthermore, for heterosexuals the penis should never be inserted into the vagina after anal intercourse unless it has been washed thoroughly. The reason for this is that the rectum contains bacteria that do not belong in the vagina and that can cause a dandy case of vaginitis if they happen to get there. Also, sex toys or other objects inserted in the anus should be thoroughly washed following removal from the anus.

Another variation is **anilingus** (*feuille de rose* in French, "rimming" in slang), in which the tongue and mouth stimulate the anus. The anus may also be stimulated by the hand, and some people report that having a finger inserted into the rectum near the time of orgasm provides a heightened sexual sensation. Anilingus carries with it the risk of AIDS, hepatitis, or *E. coli* infections.

> **Anilingus (ay-nih-LING-us):** Mouth stimulation of the partner's anus.
> **Interfemoral intercourse:** A sexual technique used by gay men in which one man moves his penis between the thighs of the other.
> **Tribadism (TRY-bad-izm):** A sexual technique used by lesbians in which one woman lies on top of another and moves rhythmically in order to produce sexual pleasure, particularly clitoral stimulation.

Techniques of Lesbians and Gays

Some people have difficulty imagining exactly what gays and lesbians do in bed—after all, the important ingredients for sex are one penis and one vagina, aren't they?

The preliminaries consist, as they do for heterosexuals, of kissing, hugging, and petting. Gay men engage in mutual masturbation, oral–genital sex (fellatio), and, less frequently, anal intercourse. Gay men sometimes also engage in **interfemoral intercourse,** in which a man's penis moves between the thighs of the partner. Lesbians engage in mutual masturbation, oral–genital sex (cunnilingus), and a practice called **tribadism** ("dry hump"), which is similar to heterosexual intercourse, with one partner lying on top of the other and making thrusting movements so that both receive genital stimulation (Figure 24).

An important point to note about these practices is that they are all behaviors in which heterosexuals also engage. In other words, gays and lesbians do the same things sexually that heterosexuals do. The only thing that is distinctive about same-gender lovemaking is that the partners are of the same gender.

Masters and Johnson (1979), in their laboratory studies, made direct observations of the lovemaking techniques of gays and lesbians and compared them with those of straights. They found that, in masturbation techniques, there were no differences. However, in couple interactions there were some substantial differences. The major one was that gays and lesbians "took their time"—in other words, they seemed to have less of a goal orientation. Heterosexual couples, in contrast, seemed to be performance oriented—they seemed to strive toward a goal of orgasm for each partner. In the initial approach to stimulating the woman, heterosexuals and lesbians began with holding and kissing, but this lasted only about 30 seconds for the heterosexuals, who quickly moved on to genital stimulation. Lesbians, on the other hand, spent more time in holding and kissing and then went on to a long period of breast stimulation, which sometimes resulted in orgasm in the absence of genital stimulation. Lesbians also appeared to communicate more with each other. In the initial approach to stimulating the man, gays did extensive stimulation of

Figure 24   Female-female sexual expression.

the nipples, generally producing erection, but such a technique was rare among heterosexuals. Gay men were much more likely to stimulate the frenulum (the area of the penis on the lower side, just below the corona). They also used a "teasing technique" in which the man brings his partner near orgasm, then relaxes the stimulation, then increases the stimulation again, and so on, essentially prolonging the pleasure (Figure 25). Among heterosexuals, the man's most frequent complaint was that the woman did not grasp the shaft of the penis tightly enough. Masters and Johnson argued that heterosexuals can learn from gays and lesbians; the technique of gays and lesbians benefits from stimulating another body like their own.

Two-Person Cybersex

The Internet provides not only visual sexual images for people wanting to masturbate, it also creates the opportunity for two-person cybersex. People report forming relationships on the Internet that they consider to be sexually intimate, even though they have never actually met the person face-to-face (Ross, 2005). It has also created a new sexual space that is somewhere between fantasy and action. Essentially, a person can type sexual acts without actually doing them (Ross, 2005). In the chapter "Sexuality and the Life Cycle: Adulthood," we discuss data from a survey of people who used the Internet to meet partners, and the activities that they engaged in. These Internet activities challenge us to think more clearly about our definitions of sexual activity. For example, a wife accuses her husband of having a cybersex affair with another woman and he replies that he was only typing. Who is right?

Aphrodisiacs

Is There a Good Aphrodisiac?

An **aphrodisiac** is a substance—such as a food, a drug, or a perfume—that excites sexual desire. Throughout history people have searched for the surefire aphrodisiac. Before arousing your hopes, we should say that the search has been unsuccessful. There is no known substance that works well as an aphrodisiac.

One popular idea is that oysters are an aphrodisiac. This notion appears to reflect the myth that foods that resemble sexual

Figure 25   Male-male sexual expression.

> **Aphrodisiac (ah-froh-DIZ-ih-ak):**
> A substance that increases sexual desire.

First Person

The Protestant Ethic: Sex as Work

Couples sex therapist Esther Perel (2006) believes that in matters of love and sex the old Protestant ethic—work hard and become successful—is alive and well in modern America. This cultural tendency is represented by books like Rachel Greenwald's *Find a Husband After 35 Using What I Learned at Harvard Business School.* The problem, though, says Perel, is that this work ethic kills eroticism.

Discussions of sex tend to focus on the physical aspects of sex, especially orgasm, while ignoring our feelings about sex. Orgasm is the observable product, and we are concerned with how many orgasms we can produce or have, much as a plant manager is concerned with how many cans of soup are produced on the assembly line each day. Similar beliefs are reflected in a commonly used phrase, *achieving orgasm,* as if orgasm were something to be achieved like a promotion on the job.* Viagra has only

made this situation worse because it encourages people to reduce sexuality to an erection.

The emphasis on simultaneous orgasm expresses how clock-oriented we are. It is important for us to have things running on schedule and happening at exactly the right time, and so orgasms must be timed perfectly.

We tend to set standards of sexual performance, much as we would set standards of work performance on the job. Once we set standards for sexual performance, the possibility of failure looms large, and sexual dysfunction is created.

As Perel puts it,

We are indeed a nation that prides itself on efficiency. But here's the catch: eroticism is inefficient. It loves to squander time and resources. . . . We glorify efficiency and fail to recognize that the erotic space is a radiant interlude in which we luxuriate, indifferent to demands of productivity; pleasure is the only goal. (p. 75)

---

*To avoid this whole notion, we never use the phrase *to achieve orgasm* in this book. Instead, we prefer *to have an orgasm* or simply *to orgasm.* Why not turn it into a verb so that we will not feel we have to work at achieving it?

Source: Perel (2006).

---

organs have sexual powers. For example, bananas and asparagus resemble the penis and have been thought to be aphrodisiacs. Another example is the Asian belief that powdered rhinoceros horn is an aphrodisiac (perhaps this is also the origin of the term *horny*) (Taberner, 1985). Perhaps oysters are thought to have such powers because of their resemblance to the testes. Oysters, however, contain no substances that can in any way influence sexual functioning.

Doubtless some substances gain a continued reputation as aphrodisiacs because simply believing that something will be arousing can itself be arousing. For example, the belief that a bull's testicles ("prairie oysters") or peanuts or clams have special powers may produce a temporary improvement of sexual functioning, not because of the chemicals contained in them but because of a belief in them.

Alcohol also has a reputation as an aphrodisiac. Briefly, drinking small quantities of alcohol may, for some people, decrease psychological inhibitions and for this reason increase sexual desire. Moderate to large quantities, however, rapidly lead to an inability to function

sexually. We discuss the effects of alcohol on sexual functioning in more detail in the chapter "Sexual Disorders and Sex Therapy."

Users of marijuana report that it acts as a sexual stimulant. Probably this effect is due, in part, to the fact that marijuana produces the sensation that time is being stretched out, thus prolonging and intensifying sensations, including sexual sensations. There is no scientific documentation of the aphrodisiac effects of marijuana except for the reports of users. We consider possible negative effects of marijuana on sexual functioning in the chapter "Sexual Disorders and Sex Therapy."

The current interest in nutrition, and in natural and organic foods and supplements, has created a market for "natural" aphrodisiacs. According to one industry source, the popular herbs purchased for this purpose include yohimbe, ginseng, arginine, aventa sativa, and prohormones (testosterone "boosters"). Some companies sell herbal combinations and edible syrups and "brews" that are claimed to increase sexual desire, sexual performance, sexual stamina, or all three. Again, there is no evidence that any of these

First Person

A Personal Growth Exercise—Getting to Know Your Own Body

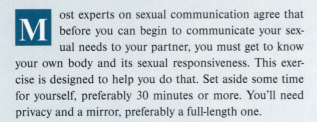

Most experts on sexual communication agree that before you can begin to communicate your sexual needs to your partner, you must get to know your own body and its sexual responsiveness. This exercise is designed to help you do that. Set aside some time for yourself, preferably 30 minutes or more. You'll need privacy and a mirror, preferably a full-length one.

1. Undress and stand in front of the mirror. Relax your body completely.

2. Take a good look at your body, top to bottom. Look at the colors, the curves, the textures. Take your time doing this. Try to discover things you haven't noticed before. What pleases you about your body? What don't you like about your body? Can you say these things aloud?

3. Look at your body. What parts of it influence how you feel about yourself sexually?

4. Run your fingers slowly over your body, from head to toe. How does it feel to you? Are some parts soft? Are some sensitive? Are you hurrying over some places? Why? How do you feel about doing this?

5. Explore your genitals. *If you're a man,* look at them. Do you like the way they look? Now explore your genitals with your fingers. Gently stroke your penis, scrotum, and the area behind the scrotum. Pay close attention to the various sensations you're producing. Which areas feel particularly good when they're stroked? Try different kinds of touching—light, hard, fast, slow. Which kind feels best? If you get an erection, that's okay. Just take your time and learn as much as you can. Are there differences in sensitivities between the aroused state and the unaroused state? *If you're a woman,* take a hand mirror and look at your genitals. Do you like the way they look? Now explore your genitals with your fingers. Touch your outer lips, inner lips, clitoris, vaginal entrance. Which areas feel particularly good? Try different kinds of touching—light, hard, fast, slow. Which kind feels best? If you get aroused, that's okay. Are there differences in sensitivities between the aroused state and the unaroused state? Just take your time and learn as much as you can.

6. Now you're ready to communicate some new information to your partner!

For more exercises like this, see Zilbergeld's *The New Male Sexuality* (1992) and Heiman, LoPiccolo, and LoPiccolo's *Becoming Orgasmic: A Sexual Growth Program for Women* (1976).

---

affect sexual desire (UC Berkeley, 2012), though the belief that they do may enhance sexual functioning.

Unfortunately, some of the substances that are thought to enhance sexual functioning are quite dangerous. For example, cantharides (Spanish fly) has a reputation as an aphrodisiac, but it is poisonous.

Amyl nitrite ("poppers") is popular among some people. Because it relaxes the sphincter muscle of the anus, it is used by those engaging in anal intercourse (Krilis et al., 2013; Romanelli et al., 2004). Users report that it produces heightened sensations during orgasms. Amyl nitrite is a potent source of nitric oxide and has its sexual effects by dilating the blood vessels in the genitals. It may, however, have side effects, including dizziness, headaches, fainting, and, in rare cases, death, so it can be dangerous.

Sexual Satisfaction

Ultimately, what most of us want from our sexual interactions is to feel sexually satisfied. But what does it mean, to feel sexually satisfied? Both laypeople and researchers have tended to assume that everyone knows what it means and that everyone agrees on the meaning. New research is probing the meaning of sexual satisfaction. As it turns out, it means different things to different people (McClelland, 2014). For some people, it means feeling emotionally close and letting your guard down. For others, sex is satisfying if it makes them feel more masculine or more feminine. Some people feel sexually satisfied from their partner feeling satisfied. And for some people, sexual satisfaction is equated with orgasm. What does it mean to you to feel sexually satisfied?

Critical THINKing Skill
Defending against everyday persuasive techniques

Sexual functioning is important throughout life. We often become concerned if our performance doesn't live up to our (or others') expectations. Imagine that the last couple of times you attempted a sexual interaction, you weren't able to enjoy it. One day, your best friend casually inquires about your "love life." Because you have a trusting relationship and like him, you reply, "Well, it's not great these days." He says, "Well, I think you're just too tense. Next time, you should have a couple of beers before you try to get it on."

This is an example of everyday persuasion. A well-meaning friend or coworker or roommate is trying to persuade you to solve a problem in the way they think will work. In this situation, many of us are tempted to follow the suggestion. They mean well; you like them; you don't want to be critical or start an argument. But is it a good idea? Your friend is suggesting that alcohol is an aphrodisiac. Is it? There is a lot of good evidence on this point. We noted in this chapter that alcohol may reduce inhibitions, but it does not improve performance. In fact, two beers may inhibit sexual functioning. There is more information on alcohol and its effect on sexual functioning in the chapter "Sexual Disorders and Sex Therapy."

As we suggest in the chapter "Attraction, Love, and Communication," direct, honest communication is always preferred. If you aren't sure you want to try your friend's advice, you could say, "I appreciate your suggestion. I'll check it out." Then you can gather information about alcohol's effect on sexual functioning. If you conclude it isn't a good idea, you can ignore the advice. If the friend asks later on, you can say that you learned that alcohol isn't an aphrodisiac. That might lead to an interesting conversation!

You should, of course, also gather evidence about sexual dysfunctions if you want to address your concern. A good place to start is the chapter "Sexual Disorders and Sex Therapy."

SUMMARY

The Sexual Response Cycle

William Masters and Virginia Johnson conducted an important program of research on the physiology of human sexual response. They found that two basic physiological processes occur during arousal and orgasm: vasocongestion and myotonia. The sexual response cycle occurs in three stages: excitement, orgasm, and resolution.

Their research indicates that there is no physiological distinction between clitoral and vaginal orgasms in women, which refutes an early idea of Freud's. They also provided convincing evidence of the existence of multiple orgasm in women.

Criticisms of Masters and Johnson's model are that (1) they ignored cognitive and other psychological factors, and (2) their selective sample of research participants may have biased the results.

Other Models of Sexual Response

According to Kaplan's cognitive-physiological model, three components are involved in sexual response: desire, vasocongestion, and muscle contractions. The dual control model holds that two basic processes—excitation and inhibition—are involved in sexual response, and that our

responses to sexual stimuli are shaped by culture and early learning. Emotion is another important psychological aspect of sexual response.

Neural and Hormonal Bases of Arousal

The nervous system functions in sexual response by a combination of spinal reflexes (best documented for erection and ejaculation) and brain influences (particularly from the limbic system). There is evidence that some women ejaculate. Hormones are important to sexual behavior, both in their influences on prenatal development (organizing effects) and in their stimulating influence on adult sexual behavior (activating effects). For both men and women, testosterone is the crucial hormone for maintaining sexual desire.

Sexuality and Disability

Research about sexuality and persons with physical or intellectual disabilities indicates that: (1) persons with disabilities generally do have sexual needs and desires; and (2) they are often capable of a sexual response quite similar to that of able-bodied people of average intelligence. The sexual functioning of people with spinal-cord injuries is particularly interesting for what it reveals about spinal cord and brain control of sexual responding.

Pheromones

Pheromones are biochemicals secreted outside the body that play an important role in sexual communication and attraction. Much of the evidence is based on research with animals, but evidence in humans is accumulating rapidly.

Sexual Techniques

Sexual pleasure is produced by stimulation of various areas of the body called erogenous zones.

Sexual self-stimulation, or autoeroticism, includes masturbation and sexual fantasies. Many people have fantasies while masturbating, as well as during sex with a partner.

Although there are infinite varieties in the positions for heterosexual intercourse, there are four basic positions: man on top (missionary position), woman on top, rear entry, and side to side. The two kinds of oral sex are cunnilingus (mouth stimulation of the vulva) and fellatio (mouth stimulation of the penis). Anal intercourse involves inserting the penis into the partner's rectum.

An aphrodisiac is a substance that arouses sexual desire. There is no known reliable aphrodisiac, and some substances that are popularly thought to act as aphrodisiacs can be dangerous to a person's health.

We have a tendency in our culture, perhaps a legacy of the Protestant ethic, to view sex as work and to turn sex into an achievement situation, as witnessed by expressions such as *achieving orgasm*. Such attitudes make sex less pleasurable and may set the stage for sexual problems.

SUGGESTIONS FOR FURTHER READING

Gill, Michael. (2015). *Already doing it: Intellectual disability and sexual agency.* Minneapolis: University of Minnesota Press. This book traces the history of efforts to limit the sexuality of people with disabilities, and surveys these issues today.

Kahr, Brett. (2008). *Who's been sleeping in your head? The secret world of sexual fantasies.* New York: Basic Books. Psychotherapist Kahr reports the results of his large study of people's sexual fantasies.

Maier, Thomas. (2009). *Masters of sex.* New York: Basic Books. An intimate biography of William Masters and Virginia Johnson and their research by a prize-winning journalist.

Nagoski, Emily. (2015). *Come as you are.* New York: Simon & Schuster. This is a wonderful book on sexual techniques, informed by science.

Are YOU Curious?

1. What is the "sexualization of children" and why is it a problem?
2. Do media portrayals of sex really affect my sexual attitudes and behaviors?
3. How many U.S. teens engage in sexual intercourse early, by the age of 15?
4. What should I consider before I send a Sext?

Read this chapter to find out.

©Digital Vision/Getty Images

CHAPTER **9**

Sexuality and the Life Cycle: Childhood and Adolescence

CHAPTER HIGHLIGHTS

My son Jeremy . . . naively decided to wear barrettes to nursery school. Several times that day, another little boy insisted that Jeremy must be a girl because "only girls wear barrettes." After repeatedly asserting that "wearing barrettes doesn't matter; being a boy means having a penis and testicles," Jeremy finally pulled down his pants as a way of making his point more convincingly. The boy was not impressed. He simply said, "Everybody has a penis; only girls wear barrettes."*

*From Sandra L. Bem, 1989, "Genital knowledge and gender consistency in preschool children." *Child Development, 60*, 649–662. Blackwell Publishing Ltd.

Stop for a moment and think of the first sexual experience you ever had. Some of you will think of the first time you had sexual intercourse; others will remember much earlier episodes, like "playing doctor" with the neighborhood kids. Now think of the kind of sex life you had, or expect to have, in your early twenties. Finally, imagine yourself at 65 and imagine the kinds of sexual behavior you will be engaging in then.

Scientists think about human development, including sexual development, as a process that occurs throughout the lifespan. This process is influenced by biological, psychological, social, and cultural factors. This thinking represents a departure from the Freudian heritage, in which the crucial aspects of development were all thought to occur in childhood. This chapter and the chapter "Sexuality and the Life Cycle: Adulthood" are based on the contemporary approach to **lifespan development,** the study of our sexuality throughout the course of our lives. The things you were asked to remember and imagine about your own sexuality in the preceding paragraph will give you an idea of the sweep of this approach to development.

Data Sources

What kinds of scientific data are available on the sexual behavior of children and adolescents? One source is the Kinsey report (Kinsey et al., 1948, 1953), and more recent studies include the NHSLS (Laumann et al., 1994). The scientific techniques used in these studies are discussed and evaluated in the chapter "Sex Research." Other more recent surveys of adults also provide relevant data.

In these surveys, adults are questioned about their childhood sexual behavior, and their responses form some of the data to be discussed in this chapter. These responses may be problematic, though. For example, a 50- or 60-year-old man is asked to report on his sexual behavior at age 10. How accurately will he remember things that happened 40 or 50 years ago? Thus the data on childhood sexual behavior may be subject to errors that result from adults being asked to recall things that happened a very long time ago.

An alternative would be to interview children about their sexual behavior or perhaps even to observe their sexual behavior. Few researchers have done either. At least in the United States, such a study would arouse tremendous opposition from parents and politicians, who might argue that the research is unnecessary or that it would harm the children who were studied. These reactions reflect in part the widespread belief that children are not yet sexual beings and should not be exposed to questions about sex. Such research also raises ethical issues: At what age can a child give truly informed consent to participate in such a study?

In a few studies children have been questioned directly about their sexual behavior. Kinsey interviewed 432 children, aged 4 to 14, and the results of the study were published after his death (Elias & Gebhard, 1969). One innovation is the use of a "talking computer" to interview children. The computer is programmed to present the questions through headphones, and the child enters his or her answers using the keyboard. This process preserves confidentiality even when others are present because only the child knows the question. In one study, this procedure was used to gather data from samples of high-risk youth ages 9 to 15 (Romer et al., 1997). More children reported sexual experience to the computer than did children in face-to-face interviews.

Many studies of adolescent sexual behavior have been done. Particularly notable are several U.S. surveys using nationally representative samples, including the National Longitudinal Study of Youth (NLSY), the National Survey of Family Growth (NSFG), and the National Longitudinal Study of Adolescent Health (Add Health). All of these studies asked about multiple aspects of adolescents' lives, with a subset of questions about sexuality. These are well-sampled studies and we can have confidence in their results.

The studies of child and adolescent sexual behavior have mostly involved surveys, which have used either questionnaires or interviews. Virtually no researchers have made systematic, direct observations of children's sexual behavior (we know of only one), although some have asked parents to report on their children's sexual behavior (de Graaf & Rademakers, 2011). Once children have learned that sexual behavior

> **Lifespan development:** Development from birth through old age.

has to be kept private or hidden, though, parents may not be able to report their children's behavior very accurately.

Infancy and the Preschool Years (Birth to 4 Years)

Before 1890, it was thought that sexuality was something that magically appeared at puberty. Sigmund Freud first expressed the notion that children—in fact, infants—have sexual urges and engage in sexual behavior.

The capacity of the human body to show a sexual response is present from birth. Male infants, for example, get erections. In fact, boy babies are sometimes born with erections. Ultrasound studies indicate that reflex erections occur in the male fetus for several months before birth (Masters et al., 1982); and vaginal lubrication has been found in baby girls in the 24 hours after birth (Masters et al., 1982).

The first intimate relationship that most children experience is with their mothers, and perhaps their fathers in families in which fathers participate equally in child rearing.[1] The mother–infant relationship involves a good deal of physical contact and engages the infant's tactile, olfactory, visual, and auditory senses (Frayser, 1994). Breast-feeding especially involves close physical contact, but other activities involved in caring for infants, such as diaper changing or bathing, involve intimate contact that can produce a sensuous response in the infant (Martinson, 1994).

> **Attachment:** A psychological bond that forms between an infant and the mother, the father, or other caregiver.

Attachment

The quality of the relationship with the parents in infancy can be very important to the child's capacity for later sexual and emotional relationships. In psychological terms, an **attachment** (or bond) forms between the infant and the mother, the father, or other caregiver. The bond begins in the hours immediately following birth and continues throughout the period of infancy (Coustan & Angelini, 1995). It is facilitated by cuddling and other forms of physical contact. Later, attachments form to other familiar people. These are the individual's earliest experiences with love and emotional attachment. The quality of these attachments—whether they are stable, secure, and satisfying or unstable, insecure, and frustrating—affects the person's capacity for emotional attachments in adulthood. Research (discussed in the chapter "Attraction, Love, and Communication") indicates that adults' styles of romantic attachment are similar to the kinds of attachment they remember having with their parents in childhood.

Figure 1 Some activities associated with nurturing an infant are potentially sensuous, because they involve pleasant physical contact.

©Amy C. Etra/PhotoEdit

[1]According to U.S. Census data (2015a), in 2014, about 73 percent of children from birth to 5 years of age lived with both parents. An additional 22 percent lived with the mother, and small percentages lived with the father (about 3 percent) or some other caregiver (about 2 percent).

Self-Stimulation

Infants have been observed fondling their own genitals. Generally the progression is that, between 6 and 12 months of age, infants discover their genitals by unintentionally touching them (de Graaf & Rademakers, 2006). They learn to walk, their coordination improves, and by 15 to 19 months, some boys and girls increase in genital touching. A survey of Swedish parents of 3- to 5-year-olds found that 71 percent of boys and 43 percent of girls touched their sex parts at home and 28 percent of boys and 18 percent of girls masturbated with their hands (de Graaf & Rademakers, 2006). The comparable data for U.S. parents of 2- to 5-year-olds showed that 60 percent of boys and 44 percent of girls touched their sex parts at home and 17 percent of boys and 16 percent of girls masturbated with their hands. These behaviors, then, are quite normal and do not indicate pathology.

Orgasms from self-stimulation are possible even at this early age, although before puberty boys are not capable of ejaculation.

Child–Child Encounters

Infants and young children are very self-centered or egocentric. Even when they seem to be playing with another

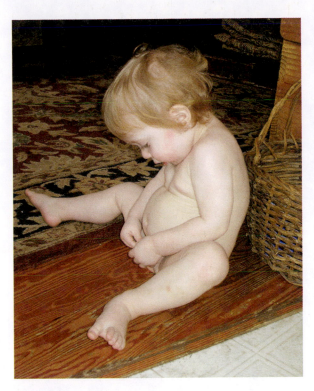

Figure 2   Infant self-stimulation.

©Maya Barnes/The Image Works

Figure 3   Between the ages of 3 and 7 there is a marked increase in sexual interest.

©Cassy Cohen/PhotoEdit

child, they may simply be playing alongside the other child, actually in a world all their own.

By the age of 4 or 5, though, children have become more social and some sexual play occurs. Boys and girls may hug each other or hold hands in imitation of adults. "Playing doctor" can be a popular game at this age. Research indicates that roughly 25 to 50 percent of children engage in this type of play (de Graaf & Rademakers, 2006). It generally involves no more than exhibiting one's own genitals, looking at those of others, and perhaps engaging in a little fondling or touching. One woman recalled,

> It was at the age of 5 that I, along with my three friends who were sisters and lived next door, first viewed the genitals of a boy. They had a male cousin who came to visit and we all ended up behind the furnace playing doctor. No matter what he would say his symptoms were, we were so fascinated with his penis that it was always the center of our examinations. I remember giggling as I punched it and dunking it in some red food-colored water that we were using for medicine. This seemed to give him great enjoyment. One girl put hand lotion and a bandage on his penis and in the process he had an erection. We asked him to do it again, but their [sic] was no such luck. (Martinson, 1994, p. 37)

Some children first learn about heterosexual behavior by seeing or hearing their parents engaging in sexual intercourse, that is, witnessing the *primal scene*. Freud believed that this experience could inhibit the child's subsequent psychosexual development. What little data we have, though, suggest that the experience is not damaging. In surveys, about 20 percent of middle-class parents report that their child observed them when the child was 4 to 6 years of age, typically as a result of accidentally entering the parents' room. Parents report reactions such as curiosity ("Why are you bobbing up and down?"), amusement and giggling, or embarrassment and closing the door (Okami, 1995).

Sexual Knowledge and Interests

In the preschool years, children become interested in sexuality and begin to develop a simple understanding of some aspects of sexuality, although their knowledge is typically vague. For example, preschoolers are often interested in viewing people nude, and they may touch their mother's or other women's breasts (de Graaf & Rademakers, 2011; Kenny & Wurtele, 2013). They become interested in different postures for urinating, and girls attempt to urinate while standing, just like boys. Children at this age are very affectionate and enjoy hugging and kissing their parents. They may even propose marriage to the parent of the other gender.

In one study in Germany, the researcher interviewed children between the ages of 2 and 6 about their sexual knowledge (Volbert, 2000). When the children were shown a drawing of an unclothed child or adult, all 3- and 4-year-olds correctly identified whether it was male or female, but when asked to explain why, they generally gave answers based on characteristics such as hair. The 5- and 6-year-olds provided explanations based on the genitals. By age 4, 80 percent of the children knew some term for the genitals.

By about the age of 5, children have formed a concept of marriage—or at least of its nongenital aspects. They know that a member of the other gender is the appropriate marriage partner, and they are committed to marrying when they get older. They practice marriage roles as they "play house."

A study at Danish preschools indicated that, in previous decades, attitudes were tolerant toward nudity—such as swimming in the nude—and doctor games (Leander et al., 2018). More recently, though, in the wake of concerns about child sexual abuse, children's behavior has been more restricted. For example, they must wear swimsuits for swimming. As one center director commented,

> When adults make rules for children's natural curiosity about examining each other's bodies, we send the message that something is wrong about that. That doesn't make the curiosity disappear, but it connects it to shame. It sometimes seems as though children are more affected by shame owing to our rules, than by any transgression of each other's boundaries. (pp. 870–871)

It is important to remember that children's sex play at this age is motivated largely by curiosity and is part of the general learning experiences of childhood.

Knowledge about Gender

By age 2½ or 3, children know what gender they are—the first step in developing a gender identity. Awareness of being male or female motivates them to be like other members of that group (Martin & Ruble, 2004). They know that they are like the parent of the same gender and different from both the parent of the other gender and other children of the other gender. At ages 4 to 6, ideas about gender are very rigid, as reflected in the opening vignette. As children gain experience, these gender beliefs become more flexible (Martin & Ruble, 2004). As noted, 3- and 4-year-olds typically do not understand the genital differences between males and females, but they acquire this knowledge by 5 or 6.

Some children, perhaps 1 percent, do not identify with the gender assigned to them at birth. These children begin to exhibit cross-gender behavior (Minter, 2012), wanting to dress, play, and be referred to or named in gender-atypical ways. These behaviors may be evident

Adrenarche: In childhood, the maturation of the adrenal glands, resulting in increased secretion of androgens.

as early as age 2. The child's behavior may range from tentative and playful to habitual and insistent, both inside and outside the home. Depending on the circumstances, some children socially transition to the other gender (Fast & Olson, 2018). Children who are adamant about their gender-atypical identification may be taken or referred to a clinician and be identified as experiencing *gender dysphoria* (see the chapter "Gender and Sexuality").

Childhood (5 to 11 Years)

Freud used the term *latency* to refer to the period of childhood following the resolution of the Oedipus complex. He believed that the sexual urges go "underground" during latency and are not expressed. The evidence indicates, however, that Freud was wrong and that children's interest in and expression of sexuality remain lively throughout this period. For many, sexual awakening does not occur until adolescence, but for others it is a very real and poignant part of childhood.

Adrenarche, the maturation of the adrenal glands, occurs around 8 to 10 years of age (as early as 6 for some) and leads to increased levels of androgens in both boys and girls (Del Giudice et al., 2009). In short, some sex hormone action occurs in childhood, well before adolescence. Across several studies of adolescents and adults, the average age at which participants recalled first experiencing sexual attraction to another person was at age 10, probably linked to adrenarche and the rise in androgens (Lamb & Plocha, 2014; McClintock & Herdt, 1996).

Masturbation

During childhood, more and more children gain experience with masturbation. About 40 percent of college students recall masturbating before puberty (Bancroft et al., 2003). Generally boys start masturbating earlier than girls, a trend that is even more pronounced in adolescence. About 40 percent of boys and 20 percent of girls report orgasms from masturbation by age 12 (Larsson & Svedin, 2002).

Boys and girls tend to learn about masturbation in different ways. Typically boys are told about it by their male peers, they see their peers doing it, or they read about it; girls most frequently learn about masturbation through accidental self-discovery (Langfeldt, 1981).

Heterosexual Behavior

There is generally little heterosexual behavior during childhood, mainly because boys and girls divide themselves into groups rigidly by gender. However, children commonly hear about heterosexual intercourse for the first time during this period. For example, in a sample of adult women, 61 percent recalled having learned about intercourse by age 12 (Wyatt et al., 1988). Children's reactions to this new information are an amusing combination of shock and disbelief—particularly disbelief that their parents would do such a thing. A college woman recalled,

> One of my girlfriends told me about sexual intercourse. It was one of the biggest shocks of my life. She took me aside one day, and I could tell she was in great distress. I thought that she was going to tell me about menstruation, so I said that I already knew, and she said, "No, this is *worse!*" Her description went like this: "A guy puts his thing up a girl's hole, and she has a baby." The hole was, to us, the anus, because we did not even know about the vagina and we knew that the urethra was too small. I pictured the act as a single, violent and painful stabbing at the anus by the penis. Somehow, the idea of a baby was forgotten by me. I was horrified and repulsed, and I thought of that awful penis I had seen years ago. At first I insisted that it wasn't true, and my friend said she didn't know for sure, but that's what her cousin told her. But we looked at each other, and we knew it was true. We held each other and cried. We insisted that "my parents would never do that," and "I'll never let anyone do it to me." We were frightened, sickened, and threatened by the idea of some lusty male jabbing at us with his horrid penis. (From a student essay)

And there is some boy–girl contact. A study of Swedish high school seniors asked them to recall consensual childhood sexual experiences with another child (Larsson & Svedin, 2002). Eighty percent of them recalled such an experience between the ages of 6 and 12, but most of this occurred between 11 and 12, the beginning of adolescence. Nonetheless, a substantial number (17 to 44 percent, depending on the behavior) reported kissing and hugging, showing their genitals, or another child touching their genitals, between ages 6 and 10.

For some children, heterosexual activity occurs in a coercive, incestuous relationship, whether with a sibling, parent, stepparent, or other relative. This topic is discussed in detail in the chapter "Sexual Coercion."

Same-Gender Sexual Behavior

It is important to understand same-gender sexual activity as a normal part of the sexual development of children. In childhood, children have a **gender-segregated social organization.** That is, boys play separately from girls, and thus children spend most of their time with members of their own gender. Some of this social separation is actually comical; boys, for example, may be convinced that girls have "cooties" and that they must be very careful to stay away from them.

Given that children are spending time mainly with members of their own gender, sexual exploring at this age is likely to be with partners of the same gender. These activities generally involve masturbation, showing the genitals, and fondling others' genitals. Boys, for example, may engage in a "circle jerk," in which they masturbate as a team. Girls are less likely to engage in such group activities, perhaps because the spectacle of them masturbating is not as impressive or perhaps because they already sense greater cultural restrictions on their sexuality. Nonetheless, girls have their own behaviors, as reported by one team of interviewers:

> Fiona (first grade) said, "Chloe keeps kissing me in school! She kissed me on the back of the neck in line today." Chloe said, "I did, like this," and she crawled over to Fiona and kissed her on the back of her neck. Fiona said, "See!" Fiona was exasperated by these kisses, but she was also amused. Chloe was her best friend. And the kissing clearly entertained the whole group. (Myers & Raymond, 2010, p. 183)

A study of lesbian, gay, and bisexual youth found that the participants reported their first experience of same-gender sexual attraction at age 10 or 11 on average (Rosario et al., 1996). This age is comparable to that of first experiences of heterosexual attraction.

Sex Knowledge and Interests

Children learn very early that male–female pairings are the norm. That is, they learn **heteronormativity,** the belief that heterosexuality is the only pattern that is normal and natural. Intertwined with this view are beliefs that boys and girls are very different from each other, that boys should be attracted to girls, and that girls should be attracted to boys. A study of girls in kindergarten through fifth grade used group interviews, which seem to be good for understanding children's experiences at these ages (Myers & Raymond, 2010). The girls' responses revealed well-learned heteronormativity. Even though they were initially embarrassed to talk about the topic, the girls revealed crushes on boys and then had excited discussions of their crushes. They used the term *hottie* for celebrity adolescent boys, such as *American Idol* contestants, and were excited about them as well. Yet, despite all this talk, the girls thought that actual behaviors, such as kissing, were inappropriate—"Kissing is gross!"

The Sexualization of Children

A major concern of some parents, educators, and researchers is the sexualization of girls and boys in U.S. society. **Sexualization,** as defined in an authoritative report

---

Gender-segregated social organization: A form of social organization in which boys play and associate with other boys, and girls play and associate with other girls; that is, the genders are separate from each other.

Heteronormativity: The belief that heterosexuality is the only pattern that is normal and natural.

Sexualization: A process in which a person is valued only for sex appeal or behavior; is held to a standard that equates physical attractiveness with being sexy; is sexually objectified; or sexuality is inappropriately imposed on the person.

from the American Psychological Association (2007), occurs when

- A person's value comes only from their sexual appeal or behavior.
- A person is held to a standard that equates physical attractiveness with being sexy.
- A person is sexually objectified.
- Sexuality is inappropriately imposed on a child.

One example is beauty pageants for girls, in which girls as young as 4 are thrust into elaborate dresses and "dolled up" with sexy makeup and pouffy hairdos as they compete in a beauty pageant. Another example is sexual harassment by peers, which is discussed in more detail in the chapter "Sexual Coercion." Sexualized products are involved as well, such as Bratz or Barbie dolls, books, and sexy clothing.

Boys are exposed to TV shows, video games, and movies that often teach messages that they should have "buff" bodies, they should be physically powerful and always ready to fight, and that sex for men involves aggressive domination of beautiful women for the pleasure of the man (Levin, 2009, p. 79).

Figure 4   The sexualization of children occurs in part through cultural messages in sexy clothing and sexy dolls. The Bratz dolls are a good example.

©McGraw-Hill Education/Jill Braaten, photographer

One study analyzed the content of the 10 most popular TV shows for Latina and White girls ages 6 to 11 (McDade-Montez et al., 2017). A coding of 32 episodes indicated instances of sexualization in every single episode. Female characters were more likely to be sexualized than male characters, with female characters accounting for 72 percent of the instances of sexualization. Sexualized clothing was the most common form of sexualization; other forms included sexualizing comments and body exposure.

Sexualization also results when girls are treated like sexual objects by peers, family, teachers, or other adults. As a result of learning to view themselves as sexual objects, many girls and women engage in self-sexualization, leading them to purchase clothing because it is sexy and undergoing cosmetic surgery at a young age (American Psychological Association, 2007).

Experts are concerned that sexualization may lead to reduced self-esteem and body dissatisfaction because one does not meet the cultural standard of sexy appearance (Ward, 2016). Cognitive performance, such as math performance, can be impaired as well because of distracting thoughts resulting from sexualization (Gervais et al., 2011). Educational and career aspirations may be reduced. In adolescence, viewing oneself as a sexual object may lead young people to initiate sexual activity, to engage in unwanted sexual activity and relationships, and to engage in risky sexual behavior such as unprotected vaginal intercourse.

Experts suggest many ways to counteract sexualization (APA, 2007; McDade-Montez et al., 2017). Within the schools, we can provide media literacy programs, a broader range of athletic opportunities, and comprehensive sexuality education (see the Epilogue at the end of this book). Within the family, parents can watch TV and movies and navigate the Internet with their children, sharing their values about appropriate and inappropriate content. Youth can create alternative media including "zines," blogs, and alternative magazines and books. Finally, parents, educators, and boys and girls can engage in activism and resistance, such as campaigning against companies that use sexualized images to sell products.

Adolescence (12 to 18 Years)

Researchers today define adolescence as more than the teenage years. Today it begins at age 11 or 12 and extends through the college years, to age 21 or 22 (Steinberg, 2011). Here we use the category of adolescence for ages 12 to 18, through the end of high school. Then we devote a section to sex during the college years.

A tension exists in thinking about adolescent sexuality. On the one hand, sexuality is a normative part of adolescent development and it plays an important positive role in growth and development (Halpern, 2010; Tolman & McClelland, 2011). The last section of this chapter is devoted to the ways in which sexuality aids in psychological development. On the other hand, not all adolescent sex is good sex. Sometimes the person is too young, or the sex is coerced, or the sex is risky and unprotected. Quite frankly, researchers have focused much more of their energy on the second, negative aspect of adolescent sexuality than they have on the first, positive aspect. They have done so because of the enormous potential for negative consequences for the individual, the family, and the broader society when adolescent sex goes awry. (For an exception, see Smiler et al., 2005.) In this chapter, though, we focus mainly on the normative aspects of sexual development.

A surge of sexual interest occurs around puberty and continues throughout adolescence. This heightened sexuality may be caused by a number of factors, including bodily changes and an awareness of them, rises in levels of sex hormones, and increased cultural emphasis on sex. We can see evidence of this heightened sexuality particularly in the data on masturbation. But before examining those data, let's consider some theoretical ideas about how hormones and social forces might interact as influences on adolescent sexuality.

Udry (1988) proposed a theoretical model that recognizes that both social factors and biological factors are potent in adolescent sexuality. He studied eighth-, ninth-, and tenth-graders (13 to 16 years old), measuring their hormone levels (testosterone, estrogen, and progesterone) and a number of sociological factors (e.g., whether they were in an intact family, their parents' educational level, the teenager's response to a scale measuring sexually permissive attitudes, and the teenager's attachment to conventional institutions such as involvement in school sports and church attendance). Overall, 35 percent of the boys and 14 percent of the girls had engaged in sexual intercourse.

For boys, testosterone levels had a strong relationship to sexual activity (including intercourse, masturbation, and feeling "turned on"). But sexually permissive attitudes, a social-psychological variable, were also related to sexuality among boys, although they had a smaller effect than testosterone did. For girls, there was also a relationship between testosterone levels and sexual activity, although it was not as strong as the relationship for boys—and it was testosterone that was related to sexual activity for girls, not estrogen or progesterone. For girls, pubertal development (developing a "curvy" figure) had an effect, probably by increasing boys' attention; and the effects of testosterone were accentuated among girls in father-absent families. Permissive attitudes and church attendance played a role as well.

The bottom line in this study is it shows that testosterone level has an impact on the sexuality of adolescent boys and girls. Social psychological variables (permissive attitudes, father absence for girls, and church attendance) then interact with the biological effects, in some cases magnifying them (father absence for girls) and in some cases suppressing them (church attendance).

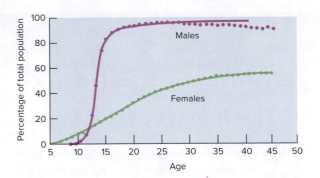

Figure 5 Cumulative incidence of males and females who have masturbated to orgasm, according to Kinsey's data.

Masturbation

According to the Kinsey data, there is a sharp increase in the incidence of masturbation for boys between the ages of 13 and 15, as illustrated in Figure 5. Note that the curve is steepest between the ages of 13 and 15, indicating that most boys begin masturbating to orgasm during that period. By age 15, 82 percent of the boys in Kinsey's study had masturbated. Many girls also begin masturbating in adolescence, but note that the curve on the graph is flatter for them, indicating that many other girls do not begin masturbating until later. The increase in girls' masturbation behavior is much more gradual than for boys and continues past adolescence.

More recent studies show similar results (Robbins et al., 2010). By age 14, 63 percent of the boys and 43 percent of the girls had masturbated at least once. By age 17, the cumulative incidence was 80 and 58, respectively.

Attitudes toward Masturbation

Attitudes toward masturbation underwent a dramatic change across the 20th century. As a result, adolescents today are given much different information about masturbation than were earlier adolescents, which may affect both their behavior and their feelings about masturbation. For example, a popular handbook, *What a Boy Should Know,* written in 1913 by two doctors, advised its readers,

> Whenever unnatural emissions are produced . . . the body becomes "slack." A boy will not feel so vigorous and springy; he will be more easily tired. . . . He will probably look pale and pasty, and he is lucky if he escapes indigestion and getting his bowels confined, both of which will probably give him spots and pimples on his face. . . .

> The results on the mind are the more severe and more easily recognized. . . . A boy who practices this habit can never be the best that Nature intended him to be. His wits are not so sharp. His memory is not so good. His power of fixing his attention on whatever he is doing is lessened. . . . A boy like this is a poor thing to look at. . . .

Milestones in Sex Research

The Impact of the Media on Adolescent Sexuality

A major developmental task of adolescence is learning how to manage physical and emotional intimacy in relationships with others. It is not surprising, therefore, that adolescents are curious about sex and seek information about it. An increasingly important source of information is the mass media. In a survey of youth ages 14 to 16, the most frequently named sources of information about sex were friends (75 percent), teachers (62 percent), mothers (61 percent), and media (57 percent) (Bleakley et al., 2009). *Law & Order: SVU* provides information on rape and the sexual abuse of children. *The Jersey Shore* features plenty of sexual images. How much sexual content is there in the mass media? How much are adolescents exposed to it? What is the impact of this exposure on their sexuality?

Media are a major part of adolescents' lives. On average, they have more than 11 hours of exposure per day, including TV, music, computers, video games, print media, and movies; TV leads that list at 4.5 hours a day (Rideout et al., 2010). Among 13- to 17-year-olds, 95 percent have access to a smartphone, through which they can easily connect to the Internet (Anderson & Jiang, 2018). Even among 11- to 12-year-olds, 33 percent go online one to two hours a day (Blackwell et al., 2014). More than 99 percent of adolescents live in a home with a TV, 97 percent have a DVD or VCR player, 84 percent have Internet access in the home, and 80 percent have their own iPod/MP3 player. On average, there are 3.8 TVs per home, and 71 percent of youth have a TV in their bedroom.

In analyzing how much sexual content there is in the mass media in the United States, *sexual material* is defined to include talk about sex, sexually suggestive behavior, and explicit portrayals of sex. Using the methods of media content analysis (described in the chapter "Sex Research"), a major project analyzed sexual material on television in 2004–2005 (Kunkel et al., 2005). The sample included more than 1,000 programs on the four commercial networks, public television, four cable networks (including HBO), and one independent broadcaster. The sample included all types of programs broadcast between 6:00 A.M. and 10:00 P.M. Sexual material was carefully defined and these definitions were used by trained coders to analyze the content of each program. On prime-time television, 70 percent of the programs included sexual material; 4.6 scenes per hour included talk about sex, and 2 scenes per hour included sexual behavior. These numbers represent substantial increases since the 1990s, when a similar project was carried out. Portrayals of risks or responsibilities associated with sex were notably absent; only 4 percent of scenes carried such material.

Cable movie networks have the largest proportion of programs with sexual content (Fisher et al., 2004). The most frequent portrayals are of unmarried heterosexual intercourse, often in a context of alcohol and drug use. There are no safer sex messages here!

A content analysis of the 40 best-selling books targeting youth ages 9 to 14+ found that they contain a great deal of sex-related information (Callister et al., 2012). One-third of the references were to behavior, one-third to sexual talk and descriptions, and one-third to displays of sexual affection. Portrayals of sexual intercourse involved unmarried couples in uncommitted relationships. Health risks and safe sex practices were rarely mentioned.

To what extent are adolescents exposed to this sexual material? In one study, adolescents (eighth- to tenth-graders) completed questionnaires about their media "diets" (Schooler et al., 2009). The 25 most frequently viewed TV programs were then content-analyzed for sexual material. The results indicated that, in a typical hour of television viewing, these adolescents were exposed to an average of 17 references to sexual talk or behavior.

The newer media, especially the Internet, also contain plenty of sexual content. In one study of U.S. adolescents (12 to 14 years old), 66 percent of boys and 39 percent of girls had seen at least one form of sexually explicit media (Internet sites, X-rated movies, adult magazines) in the past year (Brown & L'Engle, 2009). It would be a mistake, though, to think of adolescents as passive victims of an onslaught of media sex; research indicates that teens actively seek sexual content in their media choices (Bleakley et al., 2011).

What effect do sexual portrayals have on adolescents? Experts say that these portrayals represent *sexual socialization* by the media (Wright, 2009). The images, dialogue, plots, and characters provide insight and instruction into the initiation, nourishment, maintenance, and termination of sexual relationships (Ward et al., 2014). Youth may learn scripts that influence their later sexual decision making and behavior. For example, one team of researchers developed measures of a "heterosexual script" that includes guidelines for men's and women's behaviors (Kim et al., 2007). In this script, masculinity is defined, in part, by sexual conquest and experience, by taking the initiative in relationships and aggressively seeking sex, and by limiting emotional commitment. The script defines femininity as being chaste yet seductive, setting sexual limits, attaining power and status by sexually objectifying oneself, and by seeking commitment. The researchers' analysis of prime-time network TV programs indicated that there were 15.5 portrayals of elements of this heterosexual script per hour.

One college student, recalling his first intercourse, described it in relation to media portrayals:

Interviewer: What were you thinking at the time?

Michael: When I had sex with her? "Let's see if this is really as good as everyone says." And it wasn't. It was pretty bad actually. Just because there was like, no love, no passion, she wasn't like I thought she'd be. You know, you always have these sexual fantasy ideas—the movies, the magazines—you see all this stuff and you're like "Oh yeah! This is the way it is!" And then in real life it's like . . . It was just not a good experience. (Albanesi, 2010, p. 124)

Many studies demonstrate correlations between the amount of sexual media consumption and adolescents' sexual attitudes and behaviors (Seabrook et al., 2017; Ward et al., 2014). In one study, college students' use of sexually explicit materials was correlated with number of intercourse partners, but higher use of sexually explicit materials was also associated with less sexual and relationship satisfaction (Morgan, 2011). In another study, the amount of adolescents' viewing of TV shows and movies portraying the combination of alcohol and sex correlated positively with the adolescents' ratings of their intention to drink alcohol and have sex in the next 6 months (Bleakley et al., 2017). Of course, as we noted in

the chapter "Sex Research," we should not make causal inferences from correlational data. We cannot conclude, for example, that use of sexually explicit materials caused less sexual satisfaction. Therefore, researchers have turned to other designs to test the effects of the media on sexuality—in particular, longitudinal designs and experimental designs.

Several longitudinal studies have assessed adolescents' TV viewing or viewing of sexually explicit Internet material at one time (baseline), and then followed them a year or more later to measure changes in their sexual behavior (Ashby et al., 2006; Bleakley et al., 2008; Brown et al., 2006; Collins et al., 2004; O'Hara et al., 2012; Vandenbosch & van Oosten, 2018). Youth who view more sexual content at baseline are more likely to progress to more advanced sexual activities and to engage in first intercourse in the following year. Researchers believe that this occurs for two reasons (Brown & Bobkowski, 2011). First, exposure to the media content may increase viewers' sense of self-efficacy for engaging in sexual behavior—that is, it helps them figure out what to do and feel confident about doing it. Second, the media portrayals may arouse viewers sexually so that they want to engage in sexual behavior.

Experiments, too, indicate that the media have an impact on sexual attitudes and behavior. For example, in one study youth exposed to four music videos with stereotypic male and female characters expressed more traditional views of gender and sexual relationships, compared with the control group (Ward et al., 2005).

The evidence is strong that media portrayals have an important impact on adolescents' sexual knowledge, attitudes, and behavior (Wright, 2011). Adolescents report that the media are an important source of their knowledge. The problem lies in the fact that these portrayals are not realistic. For example, in sharp contrast to the high rates of nonmarital sex portrayed in the media, most sexual activity involves people who are married or in long-term, committed relationships (see the chapter "Sexuality and the Life Cycle: Adulthood"). Many couples in real life, whether married or not, are responsible users of birth control. Many adolescents and adults use condoms to prevent STIs. It is unfortunate that these realities are invisible in media portrayals of sexual behavior. It is also unfortunate that the media have generally not taken advantage of their opportunity to provide positive sexuality education.

The effect of self-abuse on a boy's character always tends to weaken it, and in fact, to make him untrustworthy, unreliable, untruthful, and probably even dishonest. (Schofield & Vaughan-Jackson, 1913, pp. 30–42)

Masturbation, in short, was once believed to cause everything from warts to insanity.[2]

Attitudes toward masturbation are now considerably more positive, and today few people would subscribe to notions like those expressed earlier. Indeed, masturbation is now recommended as a remedy in sex therapy. As psychiatrist Thomas Szasz said, the shift in attitudes toward masturbation has been so great that in a generation it has changed from a disease to a form of therapy.

Same-Gender Sexual Behavior

According to the National Survey of Family Growth (NSFG), a large, nationally representative U.S. survey, 7 percent of girls and 2 percent of boys between the ages of 15 and 19 report having engaged in oral sex with a same-gender partner (Chandra et al., 2011). It seems that girls are more willing to engage in these behaviors than boys are.

Experts believe that adolescence is the period during which one's identities develop and become stabilized. As noted earlier, sexual minority youth report awareness of attraction to persons of the same gender as early as age 10. The process of self-identification as a sexual minority person typically occurs between 14 and 21 (O'Sullivan & Thompson, 2014) and occurs at somewhat younger ages for boys.

---

[2]In case you're wondering why boys' advice books were saying such awful things, there is an interesting history that produced these pronouncements (Money, 1987). Swiss physician Simon André Tissot (1728–1797) wrote an influential book, *Treatise on the Diseases Produced by Onanism,* taking the term from the biblical story of Onan (Genesis 38:9). In this work he articulated a degeneracy theory, in which loss of semen was believed to weaken a man's body; Tissot had some very inventive physiological explanations for his idea. Benjamin Rush, a famous U.S. physician of the 1800s, was influenced by Tissot and spread degeneracy theory in the United States. The theory became popularized by Sylvester Graham (1794–1851), a religious zealot and health reformer, who was a vegetarian and whose passion for health foods gave us the names for Graham flour and Graham crackers. To be healthy, according to Graham, one needed to follow the Graham diet and practice sexual abstinence. Then John Harvey Kellogg (1852–1943) of—you guessed it—cornflakes fame entered the story. He was an ardent follower of Graham and his doctrines of health food and sexual abstinence. While experimenting with healthful foods, he invented cornflakes. His younger brother, Will Keith Kellogg, thought to add sugar and made a fortune. John Harvey Kellogg contributed further to public fears about masturbation by writing (during his honeymoon, no less) *Plain Facts for Old and Young: Embracing the Natural History and Hygiene of Organic Life,* which provided detailed descriptions of the horrible diseases supposedly caused by masturbation. These ideas then found their way into the advice books for boys of the early 1900s.

Many sexual minority adolescents experience prejudice and rejection within their families or their school (Saewyc, 2011). Calling someone gay is a common form of peer harassment in middle school and high school. Nonetheless, most sexual minority youth successfully navigate these difficulties and emerge at the end of adolescence with well-being comparable to their heterosexual peers (Saewyc, 2011). Research does show that, in school districts that have antibullying policies that specifically prohibit bullying on the basis of sexual orientation, gender identity, and gender expression (SOGIE), LGBT students report less victimization (Kull et al., 2016). These policies, then, seem to be helpful.

Adolescence is also the period during which gender identity, one's sense of being male, female, or in some other gender category, undergoes substantial development (Steensma et al., 2013). Several experiences in late childhood/early adolescence may intensify concerns about one's gender, including the maturation of the sexual parts of the body associated with puberty, intensified cultural and peer pressure to conform to gender-role norms, and increased time spent in gendered social contexts. These may encourage the adolescent to explore the possibility that they are trans people or nonbinary, two identities that are much more available today than they were even a decade ago.

Heterosexual Behavior

In middle and late adolescence, more and more young people engage in heterosexual sex, with more and more frequency. Thus heterosexual behavior gains prominence and becomes the major sexual outlet.

Generally there is a progression beginning with kissing, then petting, moving on to oral sex, and then to penis-in-vagina intercourse (de Graaf et al., 2009). To use terminology introduced in the chapter "Theoretical Perspectives on Sexuality," these behaviors tend to follow a sexual script. Variations on the normative sequence can occur based on factors such as social class and ethnicity. Initially there were claims that most of the oral sex involved girls "servicing" boys; however, research indicates a general pattern of gender equality in giving and receiving oral sex (Tolman & McClelland, 2011).

Data on the percentage of high school students between the ages of 15 and 19 who have engaged in sexual intercourse are shown in Table 1. Overall, a bit less than half have done so, and the percentages are essentially the same for boys and girls. The percentages are also down slightly from the 1990s, as part of a trend for more adolescents to delay intercourse.

When high school students who have never engaged in intercourse are asked the main reason why, the top answers for both girls and boys are: against my religion or morals, don't want to get pregnant, and haven't found the right person yet (Abma et al., 2017). Not wanting to get

Table 1	Percentage of High School Students Who Have Engaged in Intercourse (National Survey of Family Growth)	
Year	**Females 15–19**	**Males 15–19**
1995	49%	55%
2002	46	46
2015	42	44

Sources: CDC (2008, 2009); Abma et al., 2017.

an STD comes in a distant fourth, revealing a poor understanding of the actual risks.

Adolescents also have a variety of reasons for engaging in intercourse. These include relationship goals such as increased intimacy, sexual pleasure (let's not forget that one!), and increased social status (Ott et al., 2006).

First intercourse is a momentous experience for many people. In many cultures, it is a symbol of having reached (reproductive) adulthood. In U.S. culture, it may also be a symbol of the young person's attractiveness and popularity. Generally men report more pleasure and anxiety about first intercourse than women, and women report more guilt than men (Sprecher, 2014). Over the last three decades, men and women have converged somewhat in their reactions, with anxiety decreasing for men and pleasure increasing and guilt decreasing for women.

Using data from undergraduates, researchers found that an experience that was intentional (not spontaneous), involving people who were less committed to "traditional" gender roles (more committed to mutual pleasure?), and more satisfied with their bodies produced more positive emotions (Smiler et al., 2005). Other research using an undergraduate sample found that people who reported a more positive first experience were more emotionally and physically satisfied with their current sexual relationships, up to 7 years later (Smith & Shaffer, 2013). These data suggest that carefully selecting the partner and setting for one's first experience will have more favorable long-term outcomes.

Patterns of adolescent sexuality differ substantially in different cultures around the world, as the data in Table 2 indicate. Most of the data were collected by the Demographic and Health Surveys Program, which administers the same questions to people in different nations (Wellings et al., 2006). Two interesting points emerge. First, the percentage of girls who report intercourse is lower in Latin American countries than in African nations, due partly to the greater influence of the Catholic Church in Latin America. Second, there is variation across nations in the average age of first

Figure 6 Group dating, heterosexual parties, and hanging out emerge during early adolescence, and may include making out.

©*Greg Ceo/Getty Images*

Figure 7 In South American nations, the percentage of unmarried young women who engage in premarital intercourse is lower than in the United States, owing to the strong influence of the Catholic Church.

©*Paul Vozdic/Getty Images*

Table 2   A Global Perspective on Intercourse for Girls in Adolescence

Country	Percent Having Sexual Intercourse before Age 15 Years*	Median Age of First Coitus (Years)*
Africa		
Cameroon	30.7	15.5
Kenya	19	17.5
Nigeria	39.4	15.5
Tanzania	15.6	16.5
Zambia	22.9	16.5
Central America		
Haiti	10.9	18.5
Nicaragua	17	17.5
South America		
Bolivia	9.2	18.5
Brazil	8.8	18.5
United States	12.6	17.5

*These data are for women born between 1964 and 1968 (in each country). These data are for all women, so some of the women were married when they first engaged in coitus.

Source: Wellings et al., 2006.

intercourse; it ranges from 15.5 to 18.5 across the countries listed.

In many countries around the world, the incidence of sexual intercourse in adolescence has risen in the last several decades. Around the globe, especially where modernization has been rapid, adolescents are less and less under the influence of family, community, and religion, and more and more responsive to peers and the mass media.

Too Early Sex

Although sex is a normative part of adolescent development, sometimes sex occurs too early. In fact, in the United States, 6 percent of adolescents have sex before age 13 (Eaton et al., 2012). Experts agree that sex at age 15 or earlier is "early" sex and that it carries a number of risks (Price & Hyde, 2009). Those who engage in intercourse early are more likely not to use a condom and to have sex with more than one partner. The result is increased risk for teen pregnancies (see Milestones in Sex Research: Teen Pregnancy and Parenthood) and sexually transmitted infections.

Factors that predict engaging in early sex include the following: (1) living with other than both biological parents, (2) less parental monitoring, (3) parents with less education, (4) poor relationship with parents, (5) more advanced physical development, (6) more involvement in dating, (7) more television viewing, and (8) more

permissive attitudes about sexual intercourse (Price & Hyde, 2009; Ream & Savin-Williams, 2005; Zimmer-Gembeck & Helfand, 2008). These same factors also tend to predict a higher number of sexual partners (Lansford et al., 2010).

One college woman, reflecting on her decision to have sex at age 14, said this:

> Interviewer: And in junior high? What did you think about sex before you had sex?
>
> Shari: I didn't like it much. It was more about feeling grown up and stuff. Plus everyone was doing it. Plus if I did it early maybe it would be better.
>
> Interviewer: Why would it be better?
>
> Shari: Because of all of my friends I would be the *first* one, so it would be kinda cool. That's what I thought.
>
> Interviewer: So did you decide beforehand . . . or was it just something that happened?
>
> Shari: I decided beforehand. (Albanesi, 2010, p. 23)

Research using the Add Health longitudinal data compared people whose first intercourse experience occurred early (age 14 or younger) with people who were on time (15 to 19) or later (20 or older) (Harden, 2012). Both males and females who had early sex were more likely to cohabit and reported an increased number of premarital partners (considered a measure of "risky sex"). Females who reported early sex were less likely to be married 10 to 12 years later.

Romantic Relationships

Adolescent sexual activity often occurs within the context of a romantic relationship (Giordano et al., 2010; Vasilenko et al., 2016). More than half of U.S. teens say that they have had a special romantic relationship in the past 18 months (Carver et al., 2003).

Experts believe that these relationships can contribute to psychological development, but they can also have negative outcomes such as dating violence (Collins et al., 2009). Low-quality relationships are characterized by antagonism, high levels of conflict, and controlling behavior; they have been linked to lower academic performance and poor emotional health. High-quality relationships are marked by qualities such as supportiveness and emotional intimacy, and relationships such as these can contribute to an adolescent's feelings of self-worth.

Adolescent relationships provide the context in which the individual develops the skills and learns the scripts needed to sustain long-term intimate relationships (O'Sullivan & Meyer-Bahlburg, 2003). Relationships with romantic partners provide opportunities to explore identity, develop future goals, learn communication and conflict resolution skills, and learn how to enhance intimacy and sexuality. On the negative side, these relationships increase the likelihood of experiencing negative emotions—anxiety, jealousy, and depression, perhaps increasing the risk of suicide (Kerpelman, 2014). Research indicates that the process begins, around ages 9 to 12, with a first boyfriend or girlfriend; often there is little direct interaction between the two, but the relationship does provide an opportunity to play an "adult" role. Later comes group dating and perhaps mixed-gender social events at school. These situations provide an opportunity for conversation and for peers to observe and instruct the person in sexual scripts. In mid to late adolescence, youth begin to spend time in mixed-gender, unsupervised interaction, which provides an opportunity for more sexual expression.

We can apply symbolic interaction theory, explained in the chapter "Theoretical Perspectives on Sexuality," to understanding adolescents' romantic relationships (Giordano et al., 2010). The meaning of an adolescent romantic relationship to the individuals depends very much on the communication between them. Intimate self-disclosure (see the chapter "Attraction, Love, and Communication") heightens feelings of emotional intimacy, for example. Power dynamics can be involved as well, as the romantic partner becomes an important influence on behavior and attitudes.

Internet Use, Risk, and Sexting

As we noted above, adolescence is the time when most young people are learning about their bodies and sexuality and developing their gender and sexual identities (Smahel & Subrahmanyam, 2014). New technologies have had a major impact on the ways in which these developments occur. A study by the Pew Research Center of teens and social media revealed the following findings (Anderson & Jiang, 2018):

1. Forty-five percent report that they are online "almost constantly."

2. The most popular online platforms among teens are YouTube (85 percent use it), Instagram (72 percent), Snapchat (69 percent), and Facebook (51 percent).

3. Teens report positive effects of social media; the main advantage to them is making it easy to keep in touch with others.

4. Teens report negative effects, especially online bullying. Some also feel that social media harm relationships and create less meaningful human interactions.

Some researchers note that social networking sites primarily display visual images, leading users to focus on their own and others' physical appearance (Trekels et al., 2018). There is also a trend toward posting increasingly sexualized photos. One study found that 52 percent of teens' profile pictures displayed seductive behavior (Kapidzic & Herring, 2015).

Figure 8   Sexting: Think carefully about the potential consequences.

©*Paul Viant/Getty Images*

Sexting, the sending of sexually charged messages or images by cell phone or other electronic media, has gained national attention. A study of a probability sample of Los Angeles high school students found that 17 percent had both sent and received sexts, and an additional 24 percent had only received sexts (Rice et al., 2018). Thus sexting is common, but the majority of adolescents do not engage in it. In this study, having engaged in sexual intercourse and in unprotected sex were associated with texting overuse, defined as 300 or more texts sent per day.

The consequences can be serious for those who do engage in sexting. Federal law defines nude photos and videos of persons under 18 as child pornography. A person who produces such images or transmits them is manufacturing and distributing child pornography, which is generally a felony. The person who receives such images is guilty of possessing child pornography, which is also a crime. For example, in 2018 a 14-year-old Minnesota girl was charged with felony distribution of child pornography for sending an explicit Snapchat of herself to a boy she liked (Nelson, 2018). If convicted, it could kill her chances for college and some careers, even though the relevant Minnesota law is intended to protect minors.

A study of youth Internet victimization found that, in 2010, 23 percent of adolescents reported unwanted exposure to pornography and 9 percent of adolescents had received an unwanted sexual solicitation via the Internet (Jones et al., 2012). These rates represent a decline from the year 2000, suggesting that various protective measures for the online environment (e.g., Internet education programs, spam filters for e-mail) have been at least partially successful.

Based on concerns about negative consequences for both

Sexting: The sending of sexually charged messages or images by cell phone or other electronic media.

Milestones in Sex Research

Teen Pregnancy and Parenthood

Each year in the United States, roughly 450,000 girls under the age of 20, or about 4 percent of all teenage girls, become pregnant (Kost et al., 2017). Of those teen pregnancies, 61 percent result in live births, 24 percent are terminated by abortion, and 15 percent end with miscarriage or stillbirth. The good news is, this is the lowest teen birth rate since the government started keeping these records around 1950. The bad news is, teen pregnancy and birth are still a terribly difficult situation for the girl and her family.

Experts believe that the decline in teen pregnancy rates is due to two factors: increases in teens' use of highly effective contraceptives, especially LARC (see the chapter "Contraception and Abortion"), and increases in teen pregnancy prevention programs (Hamilton & Matthew, 2016). Despite these positive trends, the U.S. teen pregnancy rate is one of the highest among developed nations (Mollborn, 2017).

Why is teenage pregnancy a major social problem? First, if a birth results, it is likely that the child will be raised for at least a few years by a single mother who is too young for the responsibility. Second, teen childbearing is associated with adverse economic conditions; teenagers who give birth are much more likely to live in a low-income family (National Campaign to Prevent Teen Pregnancy, 2007). Poverty and high rates of unemployment in poor neighborhoods lower young people's educational and occupational aspirations. Girls growing up in these circumstances perceive a greater likelihood that they will have a nonmarital birth while they are young. Third, the pregnancy and birth often interfere with the mother's schooling so that she may not complete high school, or does not go on to get the training necessary for a good job so that she can support herself and her child.

Sociologist Frank Furstenberg and his colleagues (1987) conducted the classic study of teenage childbearing which gave essential information on its effects on the mother and her child. The study is particularly impressive because it followed up the women and their children 17 years after the women were initially interviewed while pregnant. There were approximately 400 respondents, all of them initially residing in Baltimore, and most of them Black.

Furstenberg concluded that although there are many negative consequences to teenage childbearing, they have been exaggerated, and insufficient attention has been paid to the women who, despite the odds against them, manage to cope with adversity and to succeed.

The study shows clearly that there is great diversity in the outcomes for adolescent mothers. Some remain locked in poverty for the rest of their lives, whereas others manage to succeed despite their circumstances. The most important factor is differential resources. Girls with better-educated parents who have more income tend to do better because they have more resources on which to draw. The second most important factor is competence and motivation. The girls who were doing well in school at the time of their pregnancy and had high educational aspirations were more likely to do well following the birth. A third factor is intervention programs such as special schools for pregnant teenagers and hospital intervention programs. When those programs are successful, they help the girls complete high school and postpone other

those who send and those who receive sexual messages or images, the National Campaign to Prevent Teen Pregnancy developed a list of five things to think about before pressing "Send" (see Table 3).

When stories about incidents of sexting became public, the phenomenon quickly became the subject of a media circus. Here are a few of the headlines/story lines:

- Sexting and Sex Go Hand in Hand for Middle Schoolers (*US News and World Report*, 2014)
- Sexting is the new "first base" for teens (CBS News, 2014)
- 2 middle school students charged in 'sexting,' child porn scandal (Chicago Tribune, 2014)
- Sexting, Shame and Suicide (*Rolling Stone*, 2013).

Most major media outlets publish or broadcast sensationalized stories based on one or two incidents, sometimes citing questionable survey results to enhance the apparent magnitude of the problem (Best & Bogle, 2014). Note some of the red flag terms used in the headlines: "sex," "child porn," "suicide." The result is increasing public concern, leading to school administrators, law enforcement officials, and politicians weighing in on the latest threat to children

Figure 9 An important factor in life success for a pregnant teenager is the existence of special programs that allow her to complete high school.

©Purestock/PunchStock

teen pregnancy has negative effects on whether the student graduates from high school (Diaz & Fiel, 2016). Surprisingly, though, teen pregnancy has little effect on college attendance. Perhaps highly motivated teen mothers get a GED and move on to college despite the less than ideal circumstances.

The data from the NLSY indicate that there is great variability in outcomes for different groups of women (Diaz & Fiel, 2016). Here the results are surprising too. Teen pregnancy has the most negative effects on college completion for girls from more advantaged families whose parents have more education. This may be because these girls have more to lose (they almost certainly would have gone to college) and because teen pregnancy is more stigmatized in those families. Girls from lower-income families may benefit from more social support in families and neighborhoods where teen pregnancy is more common.

That said, teen motherhood and poverty are closely linked. For example, 56 percent of infants who live in poverty have teen mothers (Mollborn, 2017). Teen motherhood has consequences not only for the mother but for her child as well.

Nonetheless, teen pregnancy and childbearing will continue. What are the best strategies for addressing the problems it creates? Two factors critical to success are finishing high school (and preferably going on to even more education) and postponing other births. Social programs need to be set up to assist adolescent mothers in finishing high school (including special schools for pregnant teenagers and child care for mothers while attending school). Information on and access to contraception is essential. Programs such as Head Start that help prepare the children of teen mothers for school are critical, because those children are at higher risk for academic difficulties. Others argue that the real problem is poverty in the United States, and that the best strategy would be to work toward eradicating poverty.

births—two factors that are crucial to recovering from the adverse circumstances of a teenage pregnancy. If there are additional births soon after the first, the girl essentially becomes locked out of the job market.

Research based on the well-sampled National Longitudinal Survey of Youth (NLSY) indicates that, indeed, and youth. The result is a **moral panic,** an extreme social response to the belief that the moral condition of society is deteriorating at a rapid pace (Crossman, 2015). Moral panics lead to all sorts of new regulations and laws, often duplicating or fine-tuning ones that already exist. They may also result in cash-strapped school boards and legislatures authorizing millions of dollars for new and often untested "prevention" programs.

Risky Sex and the Adolescent Brain

Why do adolescents engage in risky sexual behaviors, such as sex without a condom or sex when they're too young? Brain researchers believe that it has a lot to do with the uneven pace of brain maturation across adolescence (Casey et al., 2011; Crone & Dahl, 2012).

Here's the issue. In adolescence, areas of the brain that have to do with emotion (the amygdala) and seeking feel-good rewards (the ventral striatum) develop earlier than areas of the brain that have to do with impulse control (the prefrontal cortex). This pattern of brain development leads to a period when teens are more driven by emotion and reward-seeking, with less effective

> **Moral panic:** An extreme social response to the belief that the moral condition of society is deteriorating at a rapid pace.

Table 3	Five Things to Think about Before Pressing "Send"

Don't assume anything you send or post is going to remain private.
Your messages and images will get passed around, even if you think they won't: 40% of teens and young adults say they have had a sexually suggestive message (originally meant to be private) shown to them and 20% say they have shared such a message with someone other than the person for whom it was originally meant.

There is no changing your mind in cyberspace—anything you send or post will never truly go away.
Something that seems fun and flirty and is done on a whim will never really die. Potential employers, college recruiters, teachers, coaches, parents, friends, enemies, strangers and others may all be able to find your past posts, even after you delete them. And it is nearly impossible to control what other people are posting about you. Think about it: Even if you have second thoughts and delete a racy photo, there is no telling who has already copied that photo and posted it elsewhere.

Don't give in to the pressure to do something that makes you uncomfortable, even in cyberspace.
More than 40% of teens and young adults (42% total, 47% of teens, 38% of young adults) say "pressure from guys" is a reason girls and women send and post sexually suggestive messages and images. More than 20% of teens and young adults (22% total, 24% teens, 20% young adults) say "pressure from friends" is a reason guys send and post sexually suggestive messages and images.

Consider the recipient's reaction.
Just because a message is meant to be fun doesn't mean the person who gets it will see it that way. Four in 10 teen girls who have sent sexually suggestive content did so "as a joke," but many teen boys (29%) agree that girls who send such content are "expected to date or hook up in real life." It's easier to be more provocative or outgoing online, but whatever you write, post, or send does contribute to the real-life impression you're making.

Nothing is truly anonymous.
Nearly 1 in 5 young people who send sexually suggestive messages and images, do so to people they only know online (18% total, 15% teens, 19% young adults). It is important to remember that even if someone only knows you by screen name, online profile, phone number or e-mail address, that they can probably find you if they try hard enough.

Source: National Campaign to Prevent Teen and Unplanned Pregnancy. (2009). *Sex and Tech: Results from a Survey of Teens and Young Adults.* http://www.thenationalcampaign.org /sextech/PDF/SexTech_Summary.pdf.

control over these impulses. This pattern of brain development has its good points, because it probably leads teens to be more open to new experiences and may help them to find new strategies in life, but it can also lead them to engage in risky behaviors that have negative consequences.

The College Years

As noted earlier, adolescence researchers now classify traditional-age college students (ages 19 to 22) as adolescents, although some refer to them as emerging adults. Whatever the terminology, the college years are now seen by students as a time for sexual experimenting with little or no responsibility (Bogle, 2008). Adult commitments are seen as being a long way away in the future. Almost all of the research on the sexual behavior of people in this age range has been conducted with college students, so we know little about the non-college population.

Masturbation

Typically about 98 percent of the men and 80 percent of the women in our undergraduate human sexuality classes report that they masturbate. These numbers may be a bit higher than one would see in the general college population because students who choose to take a sex course tend to be somewhat more sexually liberal than average. Nonetheless, it seems likely that almost all college men and the great majority of college women do masturbate.

College students report that they have learned that masturbation is somewhat taboo, yet at the same time it is a source of great pleasure (Kaestle & Allen, 2011). Most men resolve this contradiction in favor of pleasure, whereas women are more likely to struggle with the contradiction.

Patterns of Heterosexual Behavior

One study of entering college students found that, the summer before starting college, 44 percent had already engaged in intercourse (Patrick & Lee, 2010). An additional 11 percent began engaging in intercourse over the next six months, and 48 percent still had not engaged in intercourse six months into college. Another study showed that, by ages 20 to 24 (a sample a bit older than those in the first study), 85 percent have engaged in sexual intercourse (Chandra et al., 2011).

Research shows that there is more than one pattern of sexuality among college students. One study aimed at characterizing these different patterns in a sample of 20- to 21-year-olds, 69 percent of whom were attending college and the remainder of whom were not (McGuire & Barber, 2010). At that point, 8 percent were married and an additional 8 percent were engaged or cohabiting; 12 percent had children. Eighty-six percent had engaged in sexual intercourse. Those who were sexually active fell into several distinct clusters. One group was called Active Unprotected—they had a relatively high frequency of sex and were moderately satisfied with their sex lives, but they did not practice safe sex. The Satisfied group was very satisfied with their sex life, while placing low importance on having regular sex; they also scored high in risk reduction, both in terms of contraceptive use and limiting their number of partners. Those in the Inactive group had a low frequency of sex and gave low ratings to the importance of a sexual relationship, but their satisfaction was also low. The Pressured group reported more frequently being pressured or coerced into sex, and their satisfaction was low. The stories we hear in the mass media tend to characterize all college students as alike in their sex lives—as happy hooker-uppers. Certainly there is a hookup culture at most colleges today, but this study shows how very diverse the patterns of sexuality can be for people of this age.

Casual Sex

Young adults have engaged in casual sex for decades. In recent years, many single men and women, particularly on college campuses, have begun to use the term "hooking up" to refer to it, a term rapidly picked up by the mass media. **Hooking up** is a broad term referring to a sexual encounter that involves people who are strangers or brief acquaintances, without an expectation of forming a committed relationship. Research asking students what happens when they "hook up" finds that their behavior may range from making out to oral sex or intercourse (Bogle, 2008; Heldman & Wade, 2010). In one study, 60 percent of White college students reported hooking up in the past year, compared to only 30 to 40 percent of students of color (Owen et al., 2010).

An unfortunate reality is that much hookup sex is bad sex, whether because it is not pleasurable or because it is coercive (Heldman & Wade, 2010). In one study of college students, 78 percent of coerced sex occurred while hooking up (Flak et al., 2007). Another factor contributing to the bad sex is that there is an "orgasm gap," with women being much less likely to orgasm in such encounters than men are. Happily, though, women of the same age are much more likely to have orgasms when the sex occurs in the context of a committed relationship (Armstrong et al., 2012). In addition, women often appreciate receiving a bit of cunnilingus, but it is not part of the hookup script—although it is part of the script in committed relationships (Backstrom et al., 2012).

Hookups typically occur in the context of college parties, whether Greek, residence-hall, or off-campus (Bersamin et al., 2012). Alcohol use is frequently associated with hooking up. A survey of over 800 college students found that women who were drinking prior to their most recent hookup and who met the partner while drinking were more likely to be unhappy about the decision to hook up. About 30 percent of the men and women who hooked up while drinking reported they would not have hooked up with the partner had they not been drinking. Finally, a greater number of drinks was associated with engaging in vaginal or anal sex (LaBrie et al., 2014).

Some students are enthusiastic about their experiences with hooking up, but others report emotional distress (Heldman & Wade, 2010; Owen & Fincham, 2011b). Often there is a discrepancy between what students want

Figure 10 Friends with benefits relationships have become common on college campuses.

©*Jules Frazier/Getty Images*

and what they get in such encounters, and the lack of emotional connection can leave some feeling lonely. One study found that hookups that involved oral, vaginal, or anal sex increased psychological distress for female students but not for males (Fielder & Carey, 2010).

A double standard exists in hookup culture. Men can gain status by acquiring a large number of partners. On the surface, hooking up is equally acceptable for women and men, but in reality, if a woman has too many partners, she can come to be labeled a slut (Bogle, 2008).

Beyond hookups, there are other kinds of casual sex. Researchers identified four: the one-night stand (or hookup), friends with benefits (FWB), fuck buddy, and booty call (Wentland & Reissing, 2014). **Friends with benefits (FWB)** refers to a situation in which two people who are friends (not romantic partners) occasionally have sex with each other. In one study of college students, 54 percent of the men and 43 percent of the women reported at least one FWB relationship (Owen & Fincham, 2011a). Unlike hookups, FWB relationships involve just that—a relationship, which involves support, companionship,

Hooking up: A sexual encounter that involves people who are strangers or brief acquaintances, without an expectation of forming a committed relationship; the behavior itself may range from making out to oral sex or intercourse.
Friends with benefits: A situation in which two people who are friends (not romantic partners) occasionally have sex with each other.

and common activities. Yet the sex occurs without the expectation that the relationship will become romantic. As one person explained,

> "Being in a real relationship just complicates everything," says Brian, a 16-year-old from New England. "When you're friends with *benefits,* you go over, then play video games or something. It rocks." (Denizet-Lewis, 2004, p. 33, emphasis in original)

A **fuck buddy** refers to a partner with whom one regularly engages in sexual activity but not other types of activity and is not a friend. Thus, there is ongoing interaction over time but not the support and companionship associated with a friendship with benefits. Some refer to such a relationship as "just sex." One study found that men are more likely to use FWB and fuck buddy interchangeably, which may send confusing signals to their female partners (Wentland & Reissing, 2014).

Yet another variation is the **booty call,** which refers to a communication to a person who is not a relationship partner but one knows, conveying an urgent request for sexual activity, perhaps including intercourse (Jonason et al., 2009, 2011). Most often the message is delivered by phone (thus booty *call*), but it also may be delivered by texting or online chatting. In contrast to hooking up, the people are not in the same room with each other, at least not initially. Men are more likely to initiate booty calls and women are more likely to receive them. Reasons for agreeing to the request include the physical attractiveness of the other person and having time for it. Two people can have a booty-call relationship, in which they engage in booty calls repeatedly over time; therefore, this kind of relationship is different from a one-night stand. Behaviors in a booty-call relationship show some signs of intimacy, such as kissing, but they also are characterized by behaviors, such as leaving immediately after sex, that keep the relationship from evolving into a long-term romantic relationship.

Casual sex is associated with negative mental health outcomes. Researchers surveyed more than 3,900 college students at 30 institutions across the United States. Participants reported whether they had had casual sex (sex with someone they had known for less than 7 days) in the last month, and they completed several measures of mental health. Engaging in casual sex was associated with reduced psychological well-being and increased psychological distress among both men and women (Bersamin et al., 2014). However, the aftereffects of engaging in casual sex may depend on the circumstances in which it occurs. A longitudinal study of 528 undergraduates surveyed them at the beginning and end of the academic year (Vrangalova, 2015). Among students who reported hookups involving genital sex during the year, men and women

who reported they engaged in it due to pressure from self or others, alcohol, or unintentionally ("I didn't want to") experienced lower self-esteem, and more depression and anxiety, and more physical symptoms. Men and women who reported autonomous motivations/agency—I wanted to, I believe it is an important experience—did not experience negative outcomes.

Same-Gender Sexual Behavior

Well-sampled research in the United States shows that, among 20- to 24-year-olds, 16 percent of women have engaged in same-gender sexual behavior and 6 percent of men have (Chandra et al., 2011). At these ages, people can show distinct changes in their sexual identity, attractions, and behavior over time, a point discussed in more detail in the chapter "Sexual Orientation: Gay, Straight, or Bi?"

How Sexuality Aids in Development

Erik Erikson postulated a model of psychosocial development according to which we experience crises at each of eight life stages (Erikson, 1950, 1968). Each one of these crises may be resolved in one of two directions. Erikson emphasized the idea that social influences are particularly important in determining the outcomes of these crises.

The stages postulated by Erikson are listed in Table 4. Notice that the outcomes of several of them may be closely linked to sexuality. For example, in early childhood there is a crisis between autonomy and shame, and later between initiative and guilt. The child who masturbates at age 5 is showing autonomy and initiative. But if the parents react to this activity by severely punishing the child, their actions may produce shame and guilt. Thus they may be encouraging the child to feel ashamed and consequently to suffer a loss of self-esteem.

In adolescence, the crisis is between identity and role confusion. One aspect of identity is sexual identity, and

---

Fuck buddy: Refers to a partner with whom one regularly engages in sexual activity but not other types of activity and is not a friend.
Booty call: A communication to a person who is not a relationship partner, conveying an urgent request for sexual activity, perhaps including intercourse.

Table 4	Erikson's Stages of Psychosocial Development

Approximate Stage in the Life Cycle	Crisis
Infancy	Basic trust vs. mistrust
Ages 1½ to 3 years	Autonomy vs. shame and doubt
Ages 3 to 5½ years	Initiative vs. guilt
Ages 5½ to 12 years	Industry vs. inferiority
Adolescence	Identity vs. role confusion
Young adulthood	Intimacy vs. isolation
Adulthood	Generativity vs. stagnation
Maturity	Ego integrity vs. despair

a sexual identity emerges—for example, heterosexual, gay, lesbian, or bisexual. Erikson's concept of role confusion sounds old-fashioned today because we value flexibility in things like gender roles.

In young adulthood, the crisis is between intimacy and isolation. Sexuality, of course, can function in an important way as people develop their capacity for intimacy.

Wyndol Furman (2002), a developmental psychologist, proposed that this behavioral sequence from adolescence through young adulthood parallels a developmental one. Early relationships reflect simple interest. Subsequent ones fulfill affiliative and sexual needs as young people explore their sexual feelings. As the person moves into late adolescence and early adulthood, longer-term relationships fulfill needs for attachments and mutual caring. One important consequence of this process is the development of a sexual identity with regard to both sexual orientation and the sense of one's own sexual attractiveness. The timing of this process varies from one person to another, one influence being culture, with some cultures insisting on more parental control over adolescents. Furman pointed out that many social and cultural arrangements facilitate the emergence of heterosexual relationships and at the same time deter gay and lesbian relationships.

Clearly, sexuality is an integral part of our psychological development.

Critical THINKing Skill
Decision making and problem solving

In making good decisions, it helps to (1) identify your goal(s) in the situation; (2) list at least two possible solutions to the problem; and (3) evaluate the quality of each solution (Does it help you meet your goal? Does it have any negative aspects?) and decide on the best one. Consider the following scenario.

Britney, a student at State U., has been seeing Craig for a month. At a party in a campus house, she sees Kayla flirting with Craig and starts to worry that Kayla will steal him from her. Back at her own apartment the next day, she tries to decide what to do to keep Craig. They have not had intercourse yet but have done just about everything else sexually. She thinks maybe the thing to do is sext him a nude picture of herself to get his interest and make herself seem hot to him.

What should Britney do? Apply the techniques listed above to consider what her best decision is. (1) What is her goal? (2) What are at least two possible solutions? (3) Evaluate each solution in terms of whether it helps her meet her goal and whether it has any negative aspects. Do this before you read the next paragraph.

Britney's goal is to keep Craig. One solution is to send him the nude photo. Another is to do nothing. Did you think of a third or fourth solution? A third solution would be to text him a positive, enthusiastic message without a nude photo. A fourth solution would be to make sure that she bumps into him before class that day so that she can be friendly and flirt. If Britney is feeling emotional and desperate, it would be best to take out a piece of paper and write down her goal and the possible solutions.

Here are evaluations of each solution:

1. Send Craig the nude photo: If her goal is to keep Craig, it might help her achieve her goal but it might not, for example, if the result is that Craig forms a negative impression of her because of the photo (this is an application of the point "consider the recipient's reaction" in Table 3). As for negative aspects, as explained in Table 3, Britney cannot assume that Craig will keep the photo private. He might decide to send it to everyone in his fraternity, with the result that she is highly embarrassed.

2. Do nothing: This strategy does nothing to help Britney achieve her goal of keeping Craig; however, it also carries no risks.

3. and 4. Send a positive text or be sure to see him in person: Both of these solutions are similar; they differ only in whether it's electronic contact or in-person contact. Both of them make use of social psychological research findings discussed in the chapter "Attraction, Love, and Communication," which point to the importance of frequent contact with another person to promote attraction, as well as the importance of positive contact (in contrast to negative contact, such as sending him a nasty message about what a jerk he was to flirt with Kayla). Either one of them could help her achieve the goal. And best of all, neither one of them seems to have a negative aspect.

Overall, then, in making good decisions, it's important to think first! Be clear about the goal. Think of multiple solutions and don't stop with the obvious ones. Then carefully evaluate each possible solution to identify the one that seems likeliest to help you achieve your goal and has few or no negative aspects.

SUMMARY

Data Sources

Data on sexuality in childhood are often based on surveys of adults, asking them to recall their childhood behavior. In addition, parents are sometimes asked about their children's sexual behavior. Much more data are available on adolescents' sexual behavior based on direct information from adolescents.

Infancy and the Preschool Years (Birth to 4 Years)

A capacity for physical sexual response is present from infancy. Attachment processes are important in infancy and may have an impact on the person's capacity for adult romantic relationships. U.S. parents of 2- to 5-year-olds report that about 17 percent of boys and girls masturbate with their hands. Children also engage in some heterosexual play, with games of doctor. Preschoolers are interested in learning about sexuality, although they often have misunderstandings. A small number of children may display cross-gender behavior as early as age 2.

Childhood (5 to 11 Years)

Adrenarche causes increased levels of androgens and occurs around 8 to 10 years of age. More children begin to masturbate in this age range. Children have a gender-segregated social organization, so their sex play tends to occur with same-gender peers. Children also quickly learn heteronormativity. Many experts are concerned about the sexualization of children.

Adolescence (12 to 18 Years)

A tension exists between thinking about adolescent sexuality as a normative, growth-promoting part of development and thinking that much of adolescent sexuality is risky. According to one theory, the increase in sexual activity in adolescence is influenced by the interaction of biological factors (increasing testosterone levels) and social and psychological factors (e.g., sexually permissive attitudes). By age 15, most boys have masturbated, but girls tend to begin masturbating somewhat later than boys and fewer of them do masturbate. The research evidence indicates that the media have an impact on adolescent sexuality. Some girls and boys engage in same-gender sexual behavior in adolescence, and about 43 percent of high school students have engaged in heterosexual intercourse. Heterosexual sex that occurs too early (age 15 or before) is more likely to be risky sex and is a cause for concern. Social networking, through sites such as Facebook, is a popular way for adolescents to communicate. Sexting is not as common as media reports suggest, but it can be serious for those involved. Brain research suggests that adolescents' risky sexual behavior may be a result of brain regions associated with emotion and rewards maturing faster than regions that foster control of impulses.

The College Years

Patterns of heterosexual behavior for college students can be quite varied. Casual sex, involving hookups, friends with benefits, fuck buddies, and booty calls, is one pattern. Other students engage in same-gender sexual behavior or bisexual behavior.

How Sexuality Aids in Development

Following Erikson's theory, experiences with sexuality can serve important functions in a person's psychological development. They may be important, for example, in the process of developing an identity and in developing a capacity for intimacy.

SUGGESTIONS FOR FURTHER READING

Bogle, Kathleen. (2008). *Hooking up.* New York: New York University Press. Bogle, a sociologist, reports on her fascinating qualitative study of hooking up on two college campuses.

Olfman, Sharna (Ed.). (2009). *The sexualization of childhood.* Westport, CT: Praeger. A book of thought-provoking essays on the topic of sexualization of children in the United States.

Orenstein, Peggy. (2016). *Girls & sex: Navigating the complicated new landscape.* New York: Harper Collins. Orenstein, an excellent science writer, reports on scientific research and her own interviews, revealing the contradictions of sexuality for adolescent girls.

Wade, Lisa. (2017). *American hookup: The new culture of sex on campus.* New York: Norton. Wade, a sociologist, reports her research indicating that hookups are now a dominant part of college culture on almost all campuses.

Ward, L. Monique, & Aubrey, Jennifer S. (2017). *Watching gender: How stereotypes in movies and on TV impact kids' development.* San Francisco, CA: Common Sense. https://www.commonsensemedia.org/research/watching-gender. This is the latest authoritative report on the impact of media on kids, focusing especially on gender stereotyping.

Design Elements: A Sexually Diverse World icon (hands): ©Shutterstock/Dragon Images; First Person icon (people with arms crossed): ©Image Source/Getty Images; Milestones in Sex Research icon (survey): ©Ravi Tahilramani/Getty Images

©Darren Greenwood/Design Pics

CHAPTER

Sexuality and the Life Cycle: Adulthood

CHAPTER HIGHLIGHTS

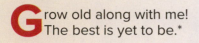

Grow old along with me!
The best is yet to be.*

*Robert Browning. (1864). *Rabbi Ben Ezra*.

This chapter continues to trace the development of sexuality across the lifespan. We look at various aspects of sexuality in adulthood: sex and the single person, cohabitation, marital sexuality, nonmonogamous sexuality, postmarital sexuality, and sex among the elderly. We consider relationships involving same-gender partners in the chapter "Sexual Orientation: Gay, Straight, or Bi?"

Each of these lifestyles is an option in the United States in the 21st century. This represents a huge social change since 1960, when, on any given day, 72 percent of all adults were married. In a major report, the Pew Research Center (2010) summarized this change as "the decline of marriage and the rise of new families." The decline in marriage is class-based: College graduates continue to marry at least once in their lives (64 percent), whereas those with high school diplomas or less are less likely to ever marry (48 percent). Survey data indicate that men and women in the latter group want to marry but fear they won't have the requisite financial stability. Several new relationship and family forms have emerged, as we will see.

Sex and the Single Person

Sexual Unfolding

The process of sexual development discussed in the chapter "Sexuality and the Life Cycle: Childhood and Adolescence" continues into adulthood. In early adulthood, there is a need to solidify one's sexual identity and orientation. Heterosexuality is the norm in our society and many people slip into it easily. Others sense that they are different. Some sense that their orientation is gay or lesbian, and they may struggle with negative messages about these groups. Some are attracted to both males and females and may experience sexual fluidity (see the chapter "Sexual Orientation: Gay, Straight, or Bi?") for years. These struggles over orientation seem to be more difficult for men than women because heterosexuality is such an important cornerstone of the male role in many societies, including ours (see the chapter "Gender and Sexuality").

Another step toward maturity is identifying our sexual likes and dislikes and learning to communicate them to a partner. Learning what one likes and dislikes may occur naturally as the individual experiences various behaviors over time. Alternatively, some people intentionally seek opportunities to engage in novel behaviors or in sexual activity with novel partners.

Two more issues are important in achieving sexual maturity: becoming responsible about sex and developing a capacity for intimacy. Taking responsibility includes being careful about contraception and sexually transmitted infections, being responsible for yourself and for your partner. Intimacy (see the chapter "Attraction, Love, and Communication") involves a deep emotional sharing between two people that goes beyond casual sex or manipulative sex.

The Never Married

The term *never married* refers to adults who have never been married. This group includes those who intend to marry someday and those who have decided to remain single. In one study, among people ages 30 to 35, 39 percent of the men and 30 percent of the women were never married. By age 40 to 45, the percentages were 17 and 13, respectively (Lewis & Kreider, 2015).

Most adults in U.S. society marry. The median age of first marriage in 2012 was 29 for men and 27 for women, so the typical person who marries spends several years of early adulthood in the never-married category. Some of these men and women spend this entire time in one relationship that eventually leads to marriage. According to the NHSLS, among married people 20 to 29 years old, 46 percent of the men and 65 percent of the women are in this category (Laumann et al., 1994). Other young adults continue the pattern of *serial monogamy;* they are involved in two or more sexual relationships prior to marriage. According to the NHSLS, among married people 20 to 29, 40 percent of the men and 28 percent of the women had two or more sexual partners before they married.

The attitudes of never-married people about their status vary widely. Some young men and women decide to live both celibate (unmarried) and chaste (abstaining from sexual intercourse). Little research has been done on celibacy, and published studies often do not distinguish voluntary from involuntary celibates. Research using a questionnaire posted on the Internet identified three types of involuntary celibates (Donnelly et al., 2001). *Virgins* had never had intercourse, had rarely ever dated, and often had not engaged in any partnered sexual activity; the data suggest that they failed to make the developmental transitions discussed earlier. *Singles* had had sexual experience but often reported that it was not satisfying; they were unable to find and maintain relationships. Both their residential and work arrangements made it difficult for people in either group to meet potential partners. Other research suggests that one's competence in romantic relationships in adulthood—being close to and getting along with a partner—is predicted by one's competence in the social and academic domains in late adolescence (Roisman et al., 2004). The third type are *partnered,* people in sexless relationships. Typically, the relationship had included sex in the past, but the frequency gradually declined over time.

What predicts remaining a virgin at age 28? The Add Health longitudinal research began collecting data on 20,000 teenagers in 1994–1995. Four waves of data collection have followed them into adulthood. At Wave 1, in adolescence, there were about 2,800 boys and girls who had not engaged in oral, anal, or vaginal sexual activity. At Wave 4 (average age 28), 269 were still inexperienced (about 3 percent of the original sample). Virginity of both men and women at age 28 was predicted by reports of no sexual attraction at Waves 1 and 3 (Haydon et al., 2014). These people may be asexuals, a pattern discussed in the chapter "Variations in Sexual Behavior." Male virginity was more likely among Asians, men who reported late pubertal development, and men who were rated as unattractive by the interviewer. Female virginity was predicted by being overweight, achieving low scores on a test of cognitive function, and attending religious services more frequently at Wave 1.

Some young people plan to be celibate but not chaste, that is, single but sexually active. They find the single lifestyle exciting and enjoy their freedom. Census data suggest that about 9 percent of the population will never marry; this, of course, includes involuntary celibates and people who are not heterosexual. The next U.S. census, in 2020, will show different patterns now that same-sex marriage is legal and recognized. Other men and women are searching for a spouse. An online survey of Swiss adults found that two-thirds of the single respondents wanted to be in a relationship (Schiftan, 2006). The search reflects increasing desperation as the years go by. According to one researcher, their desperation is fueled by **singleism,** the stigmatizing and stereotyping of people who are not in a socially recognized couple relationship (DePaulo, 2006). She argues that singles can and do live "happily ever after."

Being Single

The person who passes age 25 without getting married gradually enters a new world. The social structures that supported dating—such as college—are gone, and more people of the same age are married. At one extreme, there is the *singles scene.* It is institutionalized in such forms as singles apartment complexes and singles bars. Fitness centers, church groups, school, and parties also provide opportunities for meeting others (Figure 1). A survey of a cross section of Chicago area residents found that 24 percent of men and 20 percent of women met their most recent sex partner at school, 19 percent of men and 23 percent of women met them at work, and 13 percent of

Figure 1 School is one place where people look for Mr. or Ms. Right.

©Tim Pannell/Corbis/Getty Images

men and 18 percent of women met the partner at bars or clubs (Laumann et al., 2004). The singles group, of course, is composed of the divorced and the widowed as well as the never married.

The urban nightclub provides a visible display of the singles scene (Grazian, 2008). Young men and women, most of them single, engage in *sporting rituals,* game-oriented cultural scripts for nightlife participation. These rituals involve elaborate preparations for all genders: careful attention to grooming, to clothing choice and to adornment; young women want to be "alluring," to display (not too much) skin, and stiletto heels are required. There is usually drinking in advance at home, both to jump-start the alcohol and to save money. The number and type of companions are also often chosen to reflect the night's purpose; a group of five or six often goes out to flirt, be seen, and perhaps collect some phone numbers. If the purpose is to find a sexual partner, a pair usually works better. Public behavior in the clubs is intended to display traditional masculinity and femininity. The "pick up" is usually not the purpose according to Grazian; most participants know it is unlikely, but when it is the purpose, it has its own elaborate rituals.

Many singles, however, do not go to singles bars. Some are turned off by the idea; some feel that they cannot compete, that

Do single young adults go out to nightclubs in order to "hook up"?

Singleism: The stigmatizing and stereotyping of people who are not in a socially recognized couple relationship.

they are too old, or that they are not attractive enough; and some live in rural areas where they have no access to such places.

Technology has expanded the ways in which singles can meet. *Tinder, Grindr,* and a number of similar apps enable men and women to find potential partners using their cell phones in a process that takes seconds. For many singles in major metropolitan areas like New York, Chicago, and Los Angeles, these apps have replaced cruising the bars and clubs.

> . . . that's New York's technologized dating scene. Except for ordering their drinks, none of the people I was with that night spoke to any other actual human beings. Their erotic energy was focused on the touchscreens of their smartphones. (Feuer, 2015)

For more information on dating websites, see the chapter "Attraction, Love, and Communication."

Cell phones not only play a key role in meeting and screening potential partners, but they are a major means by which relationships are maintained and terminated (Bergdall et al., 2012). Researchers collected data for five weeks on the sexual and relationship behaviors of a sample of 18- to 25-year-old African American and Puerto Rican men and women. Use of cell phones to maintain relationships included making plans, assessing partner's interest by frequency and type of contact, discussion of difficult topics, and checking partner's phone and e-mail for evidence of other partners. Participants reported concealing multiple partners by deleting data. Use to terminate relationships included reducing frequency of contacts, ending the relationship with a call, and restoring data from other partners.

The visibility of singles ads, singles bars, cruises, and other activities geared toward single adults suggests a fun-loving lifestyle with frequent sexual activity. Undoubtedly some single people live such a life. As Table 1 indicates, among 18- to 24-year-olds, 10 percent of the men and 13 percent of the women in the NSSHB survey reported having vaginal intercourse two or more times per week. Among singles ages 30 to 39, 41 percent of the men but only 17 percent of the women reported vaginal intercourse that often. The reality is different for other singles; among 18- to 24-year-olds, 57 percent of the men and 51 percent of the women did not have vaginal intercourse at all in the preceding year. Among those 30 to 39, single men were much more likely to experience intercourse than their younger counterparts, but three-fourths of the single women had not had intercourse in the past year. Compare these percentages to the percentages for married people in Table 1. Married women are more likely to have frequent

Do single people have sex more frequently than married people?

| Table 1 | Frequency of Sexual Activity Is Closely Related to Marital Status, with Substantial Variability within Each Category |

	Relationship Status	Not at All	2–3/Week or More
Women			
18–24	Single	51%	13%
	Partnered	13	40
	Married	NA	NA
30–39	Single	72	17
	Partnered	15	28
	Married	7	27
50–59	Single	85	9
	Partnered	21	24
	Married	22	18
Men			
18–24	Single	57	10
	Partnered	26	36
	Married	NA	NA
30–39	Single	15	41
	Partnered	16	46
	Married	24	27
50–59	Single	22	33
	Partnered	34	24
	Married	33	17

NA: Not available because sample size in this category was too small. Only selected frequencies and ages are shown.

Sources: Herbenick et al., 2010b; Reece et al., 2010b.

sex (two or more times per week) than single women. The same is not true for men; single men are more likely than married men to be having frequent sex.

As we noted in the chapter "Sexuality in Perspective," Black men and women are more likely to remain single than are their White counterparts (Kreider, 2006b). In 2014, 53 percent of Black households were headed by a single woman, compared with 14 percent of White, 38 percent of Hispanic, and 12.5 percent of Asian households (U.S. Census Bureau, 2015b). In part, these family arrangements reflect choice. And, they reflect the fact that there are more adult Black women than men (Kiecolt et al., 1995). But they also reflect the structural circumstances of Blacks in U.S. society. It is difficult for many Black men to find a job that provides the wages and benefits needed to support a family (Anderson, 1989). As a consequence, some Black women are unable to find a suitable Black man (Chapman, 1997). When they do, they are more likely than White or Hispanic women to report that they are the ones who decide whether sex will occur and that they control what behaviors the couple engages in (Quadagno et al., 1998).

A qualitative study of heterosexually active single men provides insight into their motives and the importance of scripts in their interactions with women (Seal & Ehrhardt, 2003). The men were ethnically diverse and were recruited from inner-city neighborhoods in New York City. Desire for sex was a major motivation for their involvement in courtship rituals. Desire for sex was associated with playing the courtship game via the traditional script of male initiates and female controls. If romance—for example, professions of love—was involved, the goal was actually sex. On other occasions, men were motivated by a desire for intimate relationships; in these interactions, men moved from superficial to in-depth mutual disclosure. These interactions were governed by a script characterized by mutual initiation and control; sex was a secondary goal. A third motive was a desire for sexual passion, for immersion in the partner and the experience of high levels of arousal and lust. These interactions were usually spontaneous and could not be planned. The narratives of courtship told by the men suggested that their selection and pursuit of partners varied according to their motive. A man motivated by a desire for sex sought a physically attractive, sexually available woman; a man motivated by a desire for intimacy sought Ms. Right, a woman who was not easily available.

Single adults engage in a variety of relationships, including "booty calls," "friends with benefits" (see the chapter "Sexuality and the Life Cycle: Childhood and Adolescence"), and casual dating, or in relationships reflecting serious involvement, "seriously dating," or engaged. Do these vary in their quality and the satisfaction the person experiences? An analysis of data from a sample of urban adults ages 18 to 59 addressed this question. It compared the satisfaction and rewards experienced from nonromantic relationships versus serious ones (Paik, 2010a). Sexual activity in nonromantic relationships was associated with lower relationship quality. The results indicate that these differences are due to selection; men and women with more prior sex partners, and who move from meeting to sex quickly, are more likely to be involved in nonromantic relationships—and they report investing less in those relationships. Reduced investment limits the likelihood that the relationships will become more intimate or romantic.

On the border between single and cohabiting is LAT—*living apart together*—intimate relationships involving unmarried people who live in separate residences but consider themselves a couple (Strohm et al., 2009). In the United States, about 7 percent of men and women are in this type of relationship; their average age is mid-30s. Some of these couples involve two men or two women. They are less likely than cohabiters to expect to marry the partner. A study in the UK found that two-thirds of the LAT couples lived within 10 miles of each other (Duncan et al., 2013). Asked why they were living apart, one-third said it was "too early" to live together, one-third preferred to live alone (in some cases to prioritize their children), and the remainder felt constrained by lack (potential loss) of income, or work or living arrangements.

Cohabitation

In early adulthood, it is common for couples to experiment with various levels of commitment, such as an exclusive dating relationship or living together. Even when living together, there are different levels of commitment, from LAT to "some days and nights" to "all the time." Living together is an important turning point not only because it represents commitment but also because it is a public declaration of a sexual relationship. It is rare for a man and woman to live together just because it will save on rent. Cohabiting is an opportunity to try out a committed residential relationship.

The National Survey of Family Growth interviewed women ages 15 to 44 (Copen et al., 2013). The first union reported by 48 percent of them was cohabitation, an increase of 14 percent compared to 1995. Women with a bachelor's degree or higher were less likely to cohabit (47 percent) than women with less than a high school education (70 percent). Forty percent of first cohabitations transitioned to marriage within the first 3 years, 32 percent remained cohabitation, and 27 percent ended.

Among heterosexuals, cohabitation has become an increasingly common alternative to marriage. In 2006–2010, 12 percent of all men and 11 percent of women ages 15 to 44 were cohabiting (Copen et al., 2013). In the UK, in 2010–2012, 12.5 percent of men and 11.4 percent of women were cohabiting with a same or other-sex partner (Mercer et al., 2013). Twenty-five percent of people aged 19 to 24 and 42 percent of people aged 25 to 29 have cohabited at least once. Almost three-fourths of the men and women who are cohabiting have plans to marry or think they will marry their partner. In fact, 60 percent of these couples do marry.

Contrary to what many people think, marriages preceded by cohabitation are more likely to end in divorce than are marriages not preceded by cohabitation (Rhoades et al., 2009; Smith, 2003). In one study, those who had cohabited were more than twice as likely to divorce as those who had not (Dush et al., 2003). Cohabitation is also associated with poorer marital quality and satisfaction (Rhoades et al., 2009). These findings are known as the *cohabitation effect;* they have been replicated a number of times, so they seem to be solid. What are we to make of them? The research is not based on experimental designs. People were not randomly assigned to cohabit or not. So, we shouldn't infer causality, that cohabitation causes troubled marriages and divorce. Cohabitation after engagement does not seem to have these risks (Rhoades et al., 2009). Why might cohabitation before marriage predict negative outcomes in marriage? One possibility is that, once couples are living together, they have a shared apartment or house and shared possessions. They go on to marry in part because separating would be difficult. Another possibility is that the experience of cohabitation itself has negative effects on the people and the relationship. For example, in cohabitation, the commitment to each other is uncertain compared with the commitment that people make in marriage. Perhaps the uncertain commitment makes the partners feel more negative toward each other, and perhaps it makes them less likely to truly commit to the marriage, which, in turn, raises the odds of divorce. The bottom line is not that people should not cohabit but that they should be aware of the risks and possible negative dynamics so they can guard against them. There is also some indication that these trends are diminishing in the current decade (Brown et al., 2017).

The popular image of cohabitation is that it involves young, never-married couples without children. In 2014, 30 percent of cohabiting couples under 35 did not have children, but 40 percent of all cohabiting couples have at least one biologically related child under 18 (U.S. Census Bureau, 2014). Among all stepfamilies, 39 percent are cohabiting, not married (Guzzo, 2015). Some formerly married people choose to live with someone instead of remarrying.

With regard to sexual behavior, the NSSHB found that partnered men reported more frequent vaginal intercourse than did married men (see Table 1). However, notice the wide variation; some partnered men and women report not having sexual intercourse at all. It is interesting that on average cohabiting couples have sex more often than married couples.

A newly emerging trend is serial cohabitation, that is, cohabiting with a sequence of people and not marrying any of them (Vespa, 2014). In addition, more and more women who are cohabitors do not have intentions to marry.

Marital Relationships

Marriage is a sexual turning point (Sarrel & Sarrel, 1984) for a number of reasons (Figure 2). The decision to get married is a real decision these days, in contrast to earlier decades when everyone assumed that they would marry and the only question was to whom. Today, many couples have had a full sexual relationship, sometimes for years, before they marry. Some psychological pressures seem to intensify with marriage, and these pressures may result in problems where there were none previously. Marriage is a tangible statement that one has left the family of origin (the family in which you grew up) and shifted to the family of procreation (in which you become the parents rearing children); for some, this separation from parents is difficult. The pressure for sexual performance may become more intense once married; when just living together, a couple can always say to themselves that if things don't work out in bed, they can simply switch to another partner. And finally, marriage still carries with it an assumption of fidelity or faithfulness, a promise that is hard for some to keep.

In marriage, there is a need to work out issues of gender roles. Who does what? Some of the decisions are as tame as who cooks supper. But who initiates sex is a far more sensitive issue, and who has the right to say no to sex is even more so.

According to the 2010 U.S. Census, there were 131,000 same-sex married couple households, and 514,000 same-sex unmarried partner households (cohabiting couples).

(a)

(b)

Figure 2   Sexual turning points. (*a*) Marriage and the commitment it represents is a major turning point. (*b*) The birth of a baby is a turning point that can have a negative impact on sexual aspects of the relationship, but couples who are aware of this possibility can work to overcome these problems and keep the romance going.

(a) ©Hill Street Studios/Stockbyte/Getty Images; (b) ©Ingram Publishing

These couples face many of the same issues as heterosexual married and cohabiting couples.

As a relationship progresses, it can't stay forever as blushingly beautiful as it seemed on the day of the wedding. The nature of love changes (see the chapter "Attraction, Love, and Communication"), and for some couples there is a gradual disenchantment with sex. Couples need to take steps to avoid boredom in the bedroom. Sexual disorders (see the chapter "Sexual Disorders and Sex Therapy") occur in many relationships, and couples need to find ways to resolve them.

Marital Sexuality

About 94 percent of all people aged 54 or younger are or have been married (U.S. Bureau of the Census, 2010). Of those who divorce, most remarry, one-half within 5 years of divorce (Kreider, 2006a). In our society, marriage is also the context in which sexual expression has the most legitimacy. Therefore, sex in marriage is one of the commonest forms of sexual expression for adults.

The average American married couple have coitus two to three times per week when they are in their twenties, with the frequency gradually declining as they get older. The data on this point from three studies are shown in Table 2. Several things can be noted from the table. Specifically, the frequency of marital sex remained about the same from the 1940s to the 2000s. In each survey, people in their twenties reported having intercourse about 2 to 3 times per week, on average. Also, the frequency of intercourse declines with age; however, in 2003, among couples in their fifties, the frequency was still once per week. Similar results were reported in a survey of Australians in 2001–2002 (Rissel et al., 2003c). Social characteristics such as race, social status, and religion are generally not related to marital sexual frequency (Christopher & Sprecher, 2000).

What happens to sex in long-term relationships over time?

Two general explanations have been suggested for the age-related decline in frequency: biological aging, and habituation to sex with the partner (Call et al., 1995). With regard to aging, there may be physical factors associated with age that affect sexual frequency, such as a decrease in vaginal lubrication in women, or increased likelihood of poor health. These factors are discussed in the section on Sex in Later Life later in this chapter. The habituation explanation states that we lose interest in sex as the partner becomes more and more familiar. Recent data indicate a sharp decline in frequency after the first year and a slow, steady decline thereafter. The decline after the first year may reflect habituation (Call et al., 1995). It is often assumed that this decline in frequency reflects a loss of interest in sex, meaning a decline in quality. However, there is an alternative possibility: that learning about your partner's sexual desires, preferences, and habits results in increased marital sexual quality, if not frequency (Liu, 2003). But analysis of the data on satisfaction with the marital sexual relationship from the NHSLS found a significant decline with length of marriage, controlling for age, consistent with the habituation hypothesis. A third factor is the arrival of children, discussed later.

It is important to note that there is wide variability in these frequencies. For example, as shown in Table 1, 7 percent of married women in their 30s and 24 percent of married men in their 30s are not having sex at all. Research on a large sample of married couples found that sexual inactivity was associated with unhappiness with the marriage, lack of shared activity, the presence of children, increased age, and poor health (Donnelly, 1993).

Techniques in Marital Sex

What do couples do when they have sex? More than 8,600 Australians ages 16 to 64 answered a series of questions about their last heterosexual encounter (Smith et al., 2012). Analysis identified four clusters of activities: (mostly) vaginal intercourse, "basic" (kissing, cuddling, stroking, intercourse), basic and oral sex, and basic plus

Table 2 Marital Coitus: Frequency per Week (male and female estimates combined), 1938–1949, 1970, and 2003

1938–1949 (Kinsey)		1970 (Westoff)		2003 (Smith)	
Age	Mean Frequency per Week	Age	Mean Frequency per Week	Age	Mean Frequency per Week
16–25	2.45	20–24	2.5	18–29	2.1
26–35	1.95	25–34	2.1	30–39	1.7
36–45	1.40	35–44	1.6	40–49	1.4
46–55	0.85			50–59	1.0
56–60	0.55			60–69	0.6
				70+	0.3

oral plus masturbation. This suggests there are a few basic scripts that many couples enact. The NHSLS (Laumann et al., 1994) included a number of questions about specific aspects of sexual interactions. For example, it asked respondents to estimate the duration of their last sexual interaction. Sixteen percent of the married people reported that it lasted 1 hour or more.

Mouth–genital techniques are very common in marital sex. In the NHSLS data, 74 percent of women reported that their partners had stimulated their genitals orally, and 70 percent of them had stimulated their partners orally. Women who have attended college are twice as likely to report both techniques as women who did not complete high school.

Much larger percentages of women under age 50 as compared to those over 50 have given or received oral sex in their lifetime. And those in the oldest age group were less than half as likely to have had or received oral sex the last time they had sex. This is suggestive evidence that oral sex came into vogue in the 1960s (Michael et al., 1994).

According to the NHSLS data, 27 percent of the married men and 21 percent of the married women reported having engaged in anal intercourse (Laumann et al., 1994).

The hot new thing for married couples? Sexting! One study found that 29 percent of married people sext with their spouse (McDaniel & Drouin, 2015). Sending sexy photos was rare. Instead, most of the messages involved sexy talk; 16 percent of wives and 19 percent of husbands sent sexy messages once a week or more often.

Negotiating Sex

Before any of these techniques are executed, there is typically a "mating dance" between the partners. Sexual scripts are played out in established as well as new relationships. Some scripts involve direct verbal statements. How do married people talk about sex? Researchers created a list of 44 diverse words/phrases that refer to various sexual activities, and male and female body parts related to sexual activity (Hess & Coffelt, 2012). A sample of married men and women ages 20 to 73 rated how often they used each word/phrase in interactions with their spouses. A cluster analysis assessing which words were likely to be used together identified three different vocabularies: clinical (coitus, cunnilingus, fellatio), erotic (intercourse, have sex, oral sex), and slang (fuck, blow job). Participants were least likely to report using clinical language; both men and women reported more frequent use of words in the other categories. Participants also rated their satisfaction with their sexual communication with their spouse, their relational satisfaction, and their closeness. The more often they reported using sexual language, the greater their satisfaction on both measures and their reported closeness.

For other couples, deciding to have intercourse involves preliminary negotiations, which are phrased in indirect or euphemistic language, in part so that the person's feelings can be salvaged if their partner is not interested. For example, the man may say, "I think I'll go take a shower" or "I think I'll go take a nap" (that means "I want to, do you?"). His partner might respond with, "I think I'll take one too" (that means yes) or "The kids will be home any moment" or "I have a headache" (that means no). Or conversely, she may put on a lot of his favorite perfume and parade around in front of him (that is *her* offer). He may respond with, "I had an exhausting day at work" (his no) or "I'll meet you upstairs" (his yes). To avoid some of the risk of rejection inherent in such negotiations, some couples ritualize sex so they both understand when it will and when it will not occur—Thursday night may be their time, or perhaps Sunday afternoon.

Masturbation in Marriage

Many adults continue to masturbate even though they are married and have ready access to heterosexual sex. The NSSHB found that 41 to 61 percent of married men and 44 to 52 percent of married women ages 18 to 49 reported solo masturbation in the preceding 90 days (Herbenick et al., 2010b; Reece et al., 2010b). This behavior is perfectly normal, although it often evokes feelings of guilt and may be done secretly. According to the NHSLS, married people were more likely to report that they masturbated than were single people (Michael et al., 1994). Masturbation can serve very legitimate sexual needs in marriage. It can provide sexual gratification while allowing the partner to remain faithful to a spouse when husband and wife are separated or cannot have sex for some reason such as illness.[1]

Research shows that there isn't much difference in masturbation rates between partnered people and those who do not have partners. In one study, 45 percent of partnered people had masturbated in the past two weeks compared with 54 percent for those without partners (Regnerus et al., 2017). In that study, about 50 percent of men masturbated, regardless of the frequency of partnered sex. In contrast, women were more likely to masturbate if they were having more frequent partnered sex. The real factor, though, was whether the person was content with the frequency of partnered sex or not contented (i.e., they wanted more sex). As you might imagine, for both women and men, masturbation was more likely when the person was not content with the frequency of partnered sex.

Satisfaction with Marital Sex

Satisfaction with sex has two components: satisfaction with the sexual activity, and emotional satisfaction. In the NHSLS, 51 percent of the married men and 40 percent of the married women said they were "extremely" or "very" physically satisfied by their sexual relationship. Similarly,

[1]An old navy saying has it, "If your wife can't be at your right hand, let your right hand be your wife."

Milestones in Sex Research

Are Americans Having Sex More Frequently?

Some argue that American culture has become increasingly sexualized, with ready access to Internet porn, increasingly explicit sex portrayed on network TV, and open discussions of politicians' affairs. Contraception is becoming increasingly reliable and erection drugs are available. Are Americans engaging in more sexual behavior as a result of all these trends? Yet there are opposing forces, such as the "addiction" of some adolescents and young adults to playing Internet games, leaving them isolated from actual human social contact for long periods of time. Americans now work more hours.

Jean Twenge used data from the well-sampled General Social Survey, across the period from 1989 to 2014, to address these questions (Twenge et al., 2017a, b). She found that, in fact, Americans are having sex less frequently. Averaged over all adults age 18 and older, the average was 54 times per year in 2010–2014, compared with 62 times per year back in the 1990s. The decline was largest among those in their 50s, but otherwise the trends were similar across gender, race, and educational level. The researchers concluded that the trend toward having sex less frequently is driven by two factors: an increase in the number of individuals who have no steady partner (married or otherwise), and a decline in frequency even among those with partners.

In another study, Twenge found that Millennials (born in the 1980s and 1990s) are more likely to be sexually inactive and to have no sex partners, compared with Gen X'ers (born in the 1960s and 1970s). Specifically, 15 percent of Millennials had had no sexual partners since age 18, compared with 6 percent for Gen X'ers. This trend was stronger among women, and yet the trend was not found for Black Americans.

48 percent of the husbands and 42 percent of the wives said they were "extremely satisfied" emotionally (Laumann et al., 1994). Analyses of the data indicate that married men and women are significantly more satisfied than are cohabiting or single men and women in a continuing relationship (Waite & Joyner, 2000). The results indicate that this greater satisfaction reflects the stronger emotional commitment and sexual exclusivity associated with marriage.

Sexual satisfaction is an important contributor to marital quality. Longitudinal data from married couples found that sexual satisfaction predicted marital quality for both men and women (Yeh et al., 2006). Sexual satisfaction and marital quality both predicted marital stability. Another longitudinal study of several thousand couples found that low frequency of sexual activity was related to the dissolution of both marriages and cohabiting relationships. The relationship was stronger for cohabiting couples (Yabiku & Gager, 2009). Thus, sexuality and relationship education programs that increase sexual satisfaction have the potential to lower the divorce rate.

Sexual satisfaction and frequency are correlated with marital satisfaction, but how important are they relative to other factors? One study examined predictors of marital satisfaction in a longitudinal study (Schoenfeld et al., 2017). The predictors of marital satisfaction turned out to be the quality of partners' behavior toward each other and sexual satisfaction, but not frequency of sex. For wives, sexual satisfaction did not matter; the significant predictors of satisfaction with the marriage were the husband's positive behaviors and negative behaviors toward them. Overall, then, while sexual satisfaction is important, how partners treat each other is as important or more important.

Sexual Patterns in Marriage

Sexual patterns in marriage are influenced by the level of sexual desire experienced by each person. A study of 24 couples obtained daily ratings of relationship affect (positive or negative), relationship status (closeness, equality of power), and lust from each partner (Ridley et al., 2006). On days when positive affect toward the spouse was high, lust was high; when negative affect was high, lust was low. Interestingly, on days when people reported high closeness to spouse, the link between positive affect and lust was stronger. Finally, there was a significant positive association between own lust and partner's lust each day.

Sexual patterns can change during the course of a marriage. After 10 years of marriage they may be quite different from what they were during the first year. One stereotype is that sex becomes duller as marriage wears on, and certainly there are some marriages in which that happens. In a survey of a national sample of adults, 23 percent of the sexually active men and women reported that their sexual relationship was often or always "routine." In contrast, 38 percent

Table 3 Frequency of Activities to Enhance Sexual Interactions Reported by Adults*

	Very Often	Often	Sometimes	Hardly Ever	Never	DK
Do romantic things like eat by candlelight	8%	18%	35%	30%	6%	3%
Act out your fantasies together	4	10	28	39	12	7
Wear sexy lingerie (women†)	9	10	28	35	12	6
Try different sexual positions	11	19	35	23	4	8
Read books or watch videos about improving your sex life	2	3	14	52	26	3
Go out on special evenings or dates or go away on weekends alone	11	22	37	22	5	3

*Number of respondents = 1,109.

†Number of female respondents = 564.

Source: Kaiser Family Foundation (1998).

said it was never or hardly ever routine (Kaiser Family Foundation, 1998) (Table 3). As we noted in the chapter "Sexual Arousal," a boring sexual relationship can be spiced up by telling each other what you really want to do and then doing it, or by consulting a sex manual. One such book changed one 23-year-old married woman's sexual relationship:

> To say that our sex life had been going through the doldrums would be putting it mildly. Sometimes a whole month would go past and I would have another period and realize that during that whole month we hadn't made love once, not even *once,* whereas when we first dated we used to make love six or seven times a week. [I read] *Sex Secrets of the Other Woman,* how "the other woman" takes the trouble to have her hair done well and to look extra good. I went downtown and had my hair highlighted and cut. I bought some really sexy lingerie. When David came home from work that evening, I had a martini ready for him, like I always do. But I wasn't dressed in my usual jeans and sweater. I was wearing my new negligee, and when he sat down I opened it up for him and did a twirl. I was frightened. But he smiled and shook his head and said "Heyyy, that's pretty!" (Masterton, 1993, pp. 86–88)

There are also relationships in which the sex remains very exciting. A 36-year-old engineer said,

> [Though my wife's career] is tremendously important to her, she manages to look attractive, and to dress chicly, and though she is not what many would call a beautiful woman, she is, to me, a handsome woman. In bed, she is the hottest, most exciting woman I have ever known. We have been married seven years. . . . When we get to bed, and she lets herself go, we get wild together. (Janus & Janus, 1993, p. 191)

Having a baby—what researchers call the transition to parenthood—has an impact on a marriage and on the sexual relationship of the couple. Trying to get pregnant and the threat of infertility, which are so much publicized, can be potent forces on one's identity as a sexual being. Pregnancy itself can influence a couple's sexual interactions,

particularly in the last few months (see the chapter "Pregnancy and Childbirth").

A study of parents 6 months and 4 years after the birth of their first child found that sexual frequency did not change significantly during that time; it remained low (Ahlborg et al., 2008).

For the first few weeks after the baby is born, intercourse is typically uncomfortable for the woman. While estrogen levels are low—which lasts longer when breast-feeding—the vagina does not lubricate well. Then, too, the mother and sometimes the father feel exhausted with 2:00 A.M. feedings. The first few months after a baby is born are usually not the peak times in a sexual relationship, so that, too, must be negotiated between partners.

Not all couples have children. Based on data collected in 2012, the Census Bureau reported that there were 31 million childless women between the ages of 15 and 50 (Monte & Ellis, 2014). There were 24.3 million childless women between 15 and 44 in 1990. Some of these women are delaying childbearing while they complete their education and establish their careers. There is some risk in this strategy; fertility declines with age, so some of these women may be unable to have a child when they want to. Other women in this group have made a decision to remain child-free. A third group of women are those who chose to adopt; adopting an infant probably has effects on one's relationships and sexual activities similar to those of having a baby.

Some people will experience fundamental changes in their sexual experience at least once over the course of the marriage. The change may result from developing a capacity to give as well as receive sexual pleasure. A man may outgrow performance anxiety and enlarge his focus to include his partner. A woman may learn that she can take care of her own sexual needs as well as her partner's. Aging may produce change in sexual experience, a topic we consider later in this chapter. There are changes due to illness, such as breast cancer or testicular cancer, which can lead to disaster or triumph depending on how the couple copes with it.

Sex and the Two-Career Family

In our busy, achievement-oriented society, it is possible that work commitments—particularly with the increased incidence of both partners holding jobs—may interfere with a couple's sex life. One couple, both of whom are professionals, commented to us that they actually have to make an appointment with each other to make love.

Research shows that there is little cause for concern. A longitudinal study followed 570 women and 550 of their husbands for one year following the birth of a baby (Hyde et al., 1998). The women were categorized according to the number of hours worked per week: homemakers, employed part-time (6 to 31 hours/week), full-time (32 to 44 hours), and high full-time (45 or more hours). There were no significant differences among the four groups in frequency of sexual intercourse, sexual satisfaction, or sexual desire. It was not the number of hours of work, but rather the quality of work that was associated with sexual outcomes. Women and men who had satisfying jobs reported that sex was better, compared with people who expressed dissatisfaction with their jobs. For women, fatigue was associated with decreased sexual satisfaction, but that was true for both homemakers and employed women; and homemakers reported the same level of fatigue as employed women.

Data from a national survey indicated that there was a positive correlation between hours of work per week (paid work plus housework) and the frequency of sexual activity (Gager & Yabiku, 2010). That is, people who worked more actually had sex more, not less. Clearly, there is not a trade-off between career and sexual frequency (Figure 3).

Keeping Your Mate

Most couples who establish a long-term relationship intend to stay together and be monogamous. However, we all know that not all couples succeed. What makes men and women susceptible to infidelity? A study of 107 couples married less than one year asked each partner how likely they were to be unfaithful in the next year (Buss & Shackelford, 1997b). Each was asked the likelihood that they would flirt, kiss passionately, and have a romantic date, a one-night stand, a brief affair, or a serious affair with someone of the opposite sex. Thirty-seven percent of the men and 38 percent of the women predicted they would flirt, while 5 percent of the men and 7 percent of the women said they would kiss. Two percent (of both men and women) predicted a one-night stand, and less than 1 percent (of both men and women) thought they would have a serious affair. People who scored high on narcissism and impulsiveness gave a higher probability of infidelity. Greater likelihood of infidelity was also associated with reports of conflict, engaging in sexual withholding, and alcohol abuse. Finally, among both men and women, dissatisfaction with the marriage and with marital sex was associated with susceptibility to infidelity.

(a)

(b)

Figure 3 Sex and the two-career family. (a) Research indicates that marital/sexual relationships do not suffer if the woman works outside the home. (b) However, for those working 60 or more hours per week, some experts are concerned because these workaholics literally take their work to bed with them.

(a) ©Ryan McVay/Getty Images; (b) ©Hero Images/Getty Images

Our awareness of the possibility of infidelity sometimes leads us to engage in behaviors designed to preserve the relationship, or *mate retention tactics* (Buss & Shackelford, 1997a). Such tactics may be elicited by our own fear that the partner is losing interest or is dissatisfied, or because we observe some cues to infidelity. Members of the sample of 107 married couples described earlier were given a list of 104 mate-retention behaviors and asked how often they had performed each in the past year. There were marked gender differences in the reported actions. Men reported greater use of resources display (giving her money) and more frequent submission to the partner. Women reported more frequent use of enhancing their appearance or attractiveness and use of possessive verbal statements.

Nonmonogamous Relationships

People who marry in U.S. society usually make a public vow to be (sexually) faithful to the partner—that is, to be monogamous. In the past, those who found it impossible to keep the vow engaged in **extramarital sex** (adultery), sex with someone other than the spouse, and usually tried to hide the activity, sometimes going to great lengths to do so. Similarly, people entering into cohabiting, or even committed ("exclusively dating"), relationships expected themselves and the partner to be faithful. But as we noted at the beginning of the chapter, there has been a decline in marriage and the rise of alternative relationship forms in the recent past. Accompanying this change, there has been a decline in fidelity across the board, with as many as one-third of people dating, cohabiting, and in marriages reporting one or more instances of having sex with someone other than the partner while in the relationship.

Within committed or marital relationships, several new relationship forms have developed. One is Internet infidelity, which, like adultery, is often kept secret. Two others, swinging and polyamory, however, are done with the knowledge and often participation of the long-term partner. These are quite different, reflecting a process of negotiation involving not only the partners but others as well. We need a new term to incorporate all of these, and *nonmonogamous relationships* seems appropriate. We will distinguish between *nonconsensual nonmonogamy,* sexual activity involving a person in a committed relationship with a third person without the knowledge of the partner, and *consensual nonmonogamy,* sexual activity involving a person in a committed relationship with a third (or multiple) person(s) with the consent of the partner (Levine et al., 2018). Most of the research in this area has focused on extramarital sex, and has assumed that it is kept secret from the partner, so extramarital sex and Internet infidelity will be treated as nonconsensual. Negotiated nonmonogamy (e.g., every other Friday from 7:00 P.M. to midnight), swinging, and polyamory will be discussed as consensual nonmonogamy.

How Many People Engage in Extramarital Sex?

First an insider note about methodology and statistics. Some surveys have asked people whether they have had sex with someone other than their spouse in the past year. Other surveys have asked people whether they have *ever* had sex with someone other

> **Extramarital sex:** Sex between a married person and someone other than the spouse. Adultery.

than their spouse. The second question assesses lifetime prevalence and gives higher percentages than the first.

According to the well-sampled General Social Survey, lifetime prevalence of extramarital sex is 21 percent for men and 13 percent for women (Labrecque & Whisman, 2017). Men are about 1.7 times more likely to engage in it than are women. People most commonly reported engaging in extramarital sex with a close personal friend (54 percent) or neighbor, coworker, or long-term acquaintance (29 percent). An additional 8 percent engaged in extramarital sex for pay.

A study of concurrent partnerships among women ages 18 to 44 used data from NSFG 1995. The percentage was 21 percent among Blacks, 11 percent among Whites, 8 percent among Hispanics, and 6 percent among Asians (Adimora et al., 2002). Extramarital sex is more common among people with low incomes, and those who rarely or never attend religious services (Smith, 2003).

Influences on Extramarital Sex

Factors contributing to extramarital sex and nonmonogamy include personal characteristics (sexual excitation and inhibition), dissatisfaction with the relationship, and a person's perception of how powerful they are.

One survey, including both married people and others in relationships (e.g., cohabiting), found that men and women who reported cheating had higher scores on the sexual excitation scale and lower scores on the sexual inhibition scale compared with those who hadn't cheated (Mark et al., 2011). (For an explanation of the sexual inhibition and sexual excitation scales, see the chapter "Sexual Arousal.") Being high on sexual excitation and low on sexual inhibition can contribute to cheating.

Dissatisfaction with the relationship is another factor. A longitudinal study found that dissatisfaction with the relationship measured at Time 1 predicted cheating within the next 20 months (Shaw et al., 2013). Negative communication patterns were also a significant predictor.

Another contributing factor seems to be the person's perception of how powerful they are. In a survey of professionals, respondents rated their power within their organization, and also reported on infidelity (Lammers et al., 2011). Overall, 26 percent reported at least one incident of infidelity. The person's sense of their power was correlated with infidelity, as well as their belief that they could seduce someone. Perhaps surprisingly, the results were the same for the men and the women in the sample. You can see how easily these findings apply to prominent cases of infidelity among politicians and powerful business executives.

Equity theory, discussed in a later section of this chapter, addresses another set of factors that contribute to infidelity: the rewards the person perceives they are getting from the relationship compared with their inputs to it.

Attitudes toward Extramarital Sex

Most people in the United States disapprove of extramarital sex. According to the General Social Survey, 76 percent of adult Americans believe it is always wrong for a married person to have sexual relations with someone other than the marriage partner (Labrecque & Whisman, 2017). Some people view unfaithfulness to a partner in any type of committed relationship as the equivalent of adultery.

Attitudes toward extramarital sex are not very good predictors of extramarital sexual behavior (Thompson, 1983). That is, the person who approves of extramarital sex is not more likely to actually engage in extramarital sex than the person who disapproves of it. Several other factors are related to attitudes toward sex outside one's relationship, including gender (men are more tolerant of it), education (those with more education are more accepting of it), and social class (upper-middle-class people are more tolerant about it) (Willetts et al., 2004).

Because our society condemns extramarital sex, the individual who engages in it typically has confused, ambivalent feelings. A young married woman described her feelings:

> I don't like the illicit part of the affair. Mostly, it's a nuisance, because it's very difficult to find time, and I don't like lying to Freddie and sneaking around. If he wouldn't mind, I'd tell him. I don't think he would go for that. He'd show up with a gun. (Maurer, 1994, p. 393)

Internet Infidelity

The proliferation of websites designed to connect people looking for romantic or sexual partners and chat rooms and other forms of digital communication has created new opportunities for people in committed relationships to be unfaithful. A **cyberaffair** is a romantic or sexual relationship initiated by online contact and maintained primarily via online communication (Young et al., 2000). Once a relationship is established, the online contacts can turn into mutual erotic dialogue, which may be accompanied by masturbation. In some cases, the participants arrange to meet face-to-face and may then engage in sex.

An online survey collected data on online sex-seeking from a large sample of men and women. The results provide a statistical snapshot of the phenomenon (Albright, 2008). By marital status, 69 percent of the never married, 42 percent of the married, and 81 percent of the divorced had accessed online personals; of those who had, 80 percent of the never married, 61 percent of the married, and 83 percent of the divorced reported creating a profile. Asked how many people they had communicated with by e-mail, some said none; an additional one-third of each group reported contacting only 1 person. Among the married, 8 percent went on a date, 12 percent had sex, 8 percent had an affair, and 5 percent developed a committed relationship. The author used equity theory (discussed in the next section) to suggest that married people who go online seeking sex may be dissatisfied, that is, perceive their marriages as inequitable; the Internet provides literally tens of thousands of potential alternative partners.

There has been little empirical study of the outcomes of cyberaffairs. Professionals engaged in relationship and sexual counseling report working with couples whose problems include loss of trust by one person over another's online relationships. Some partners define such a relationship as infidelity even if it did not involve sexual conversation or activity. Note that these can be heterosexual or same-sex couples, who are married, cohabiting, or "committed" to each other. The range and possibilities in technologies today create interesting questions about what counts as cheating, betrayal, or adultery (Utley, 2015). For example, if you reconnect with an ex on Facebook when you are in a relationship, does that count as cheating? Is there a difference between private infidelity and infidelity that goes public on social media? Is it okay for a betrayed partner to follow (or stalk) the "other woman" (other person) using social media? Scientific data cannot answer these questions, but people will doubtless begin to form their own opinions, and perhaps even some kind of societal consensus will emerge about what is acceptable and what is not.

Equity and Extramarital Sex

Equity theory is a social–psychological theory designed to predict and explain many kinds of human relations. In particular, it has been applied to predicting patterns of extramarital sex (Hatfield, 1978).

The basic idea in equity theory is that in a relationship people mentally tabulate their inputs to it and what they get out of it (benefits or rewards); then they calculate whether these are equitable or not. In an equitable relationship between person A and person B, it would be true that

$$\text{Rewards}_A - \text{Inputs}_A = \text{Rewards}_B - \text{Inputs}_B$$

In a traditional marriage, the wife's inputs might include her beauty, keeping an attractive residence, cooking good meals, and so on. The husband's inputs might include his income and his pleasant temperament. His rewards from the relationship might include feeling proud when he is accompanied by his beautiful wife, enjoying her cooking, and so on. Notice that this is not an egalitarian relationship in the modern sense; however, it is an equitable relationship (as defined by equity theory) because both partners derive equal benefits from it.

According to equity theory, if individuals perceive a relationship as inequitable (if they feel

---

Cyberaffair: A romantic or sexual relationship initiated by online contact and maintained primarily via online communication, involving a person who is married or in a committed relationship.

Equity theory: A theory that states that people mentally calculate the benefits and costs for them in a relationship; their behavior is then affected by whether they feel there is equity or inequity, and they will act to restore equity if there is inequity.

Figure 4   Equitable sharing of household tasks in a marriage. According to equity theory, if a person perceives that the marital relationship is inequitable and feels underbenefited, they are more likely to engage in extramarital sex.

©*Ariel Skelley/Blend Images LLC*

they are not getting what they deserve), they become distressed. The more inequitable the relationship, the more distressed they feel. In order to relieve the distress, they make attempts to restore equity in the relationship. For example, people who feel they are putting too much into a relationship and not getting enough out of it might let their appearance go, or not work as hard to earn money, or refuse sexual access, or refuse to contribute to conversations. The idea is that such actions will restore equity.

If these equity processes do occur, they might help to explain patterns of extramarital sex. That is, engaging in extramarital sex would be a way of restoring equity in an inequitable relationship (Figure 4). Social psychologist Elaine Hatfield (1978) tested this notion. Her prediction was that people who felt underbenefited in their marriages (that is, they felt that there was an inequity and that they were not getting as much as they deserved) would be the ones to engage in extramarital sex. Confirming this notion, people who felt they were underbenefited began engaging in extramarital sex earlier in their marriages and had more extramarital partners than did people who felt equitably treated or overbenefited. Apparently, feeling that one is not getting all one deserves in a marriage is related to engaging in extramarital sex. (As an aside, equitable marriages were rated as happier than inequitable ones.) Note that these results are consistent with the research summarized earlier indicating that problems in and dissatisfaction with one's relationship lead to extramarital sex.

Equity theory includes rewards and costs of all kinds, as indicated by our examples. The *interpersonal exchange model* focuses on the rewards and costs associated with the sexual relationship (Lawrence & Byers, 1995). Research based on this model

Swinging: A form of extramarital sex in which couples exchange partners with others.

assesses the perceived rewards and costs, the perceived rewards and costs relative to what one expects, and the perceived rewards and costs relative to one's partner. In a longitudinal study of adults in heterosexual relationships, all six of these measures were related to the participants' reported sexual satisfaction with their relationships three months later. A study of married Chinese men and women living in Beijing and Shanghai yielded similar results (Renaud & Byers, 1997).

Clearly, our assessments of the rewards and costs in our intimate relationships are associated with both our satisfaction with those relationships and the likelihood that we will become involved in extramarital sexuality.

Open Nonmonogamous Relationships

There are several types of open or consensually nonmonogamous relationships, in which all partners explicitly agree that the partner(s) may have other partners (Rubel & Bogaert, 2014). One type are agreements that partners can have other relationships within clearly defined limits, e.g., every other Friday night, or "while I am traveling." There may also be rules limiting behaviors that can occur, or locations ("not in our bed").

Research with representative samples in the United States indicates that about 21 percent of people have engaged in consensual nonmonogamy at some time in their lives (Haupert et al., 2017). Men are more likely to have done so than women, and LGB's are more likely to than heterosexuals. Other than that, though, rates are quite similar across factors such as social class and religious affiliation.

Swinging

One form of open nonmonogamy is **swinging,** in which couples exchange partners with other couples, or engage in sexual activity with a third person, with the knowledge and consent of all involved.[2]

Swingers may find their partners in several ways. Often they advertise, in tabloid newspapers, in swingers' magazines such as the *Swing Times,* or on specialized bulletin boards and websites on the Internet. The following is an example:

> We are engaged bicouple lookin to meet bim, bif and bicouples for friendship and fun . . . we are into nudism, motorcycling, fishin, volleyball, pool and campin . . . she is 22 5′ 5 180# 38-d blond blue . . . he is 24 5′10 145# blond green 7″ and very thick. email: (www. . ./~gnkfoxx /nefriend.htm)

Swingers may also meet potential partners at swingers' clubs, parties, or resorts. Many of these places advertise in swingers' magazines and newsletters and are listed on specialized websites.

[2]Swinging was originally called *wife swapping.* However, because of the sexist connotations of that term and the fact that women were often as eager to swap husbands as men were to swap wives, the more equitable *mate swapping* or *swinging* was substituted.

Several organizations and many local groups or couples sponsor parties. The date and general location of the party is publicized in magazines and on the Internet. Interested persons call or e-mail a contact person who screens them. If they pass, they are told the exact location of the party, often a private home or a hotel. A fee per couple may be charged for membership or entry to the party. The Lifestyle Organization in Southern California sponsors parties and dances at hotels and motels, and it publicizes the exact location in advance. It merely hosts the gathering. Couples who want to swing must connect with others on their own. They are free to rent a room in the hotel or motel or travel to some other location to engage in sexual activity.

A man who frequently hosts parties described what happens:

> A lot of people have the idea that swinger parties are big orgies, where everybody jumps on everybody else. It isn't that way. People are selective, like they are anyplace else. [It starts with the eyes.] So if the interest continues from eye contact to talking, and to desire, there's touching. You just go with it. So you go from talking to touching, and at a swinging party you can go from touching to bed. (Maurer, 1994, p. 120)

Swinging may be closed or open. In *closed swinging,* the couples meet and exchange partners, and each pair goes off separately to a private place to have intercourse, returning to the meeting place at an agreed-upon time. In *open swinging,* the pairs get back together for sex in the same room for at least part of the time. In 75 percent of the cases, this includes the women having sex with each other, although male homosexual sex almost never occurs (Bartell, 1970; Gilmartin, 1975).

How do people get involved in swinging in the first place? One study interviewed married couples who engaged in swinging, recruited through online swingers' communities and a swingers' convention (Kimberly & Hans, 2017). These couples had been married, on average, for 18 years and had been swinging for 7 years. First, fantasies about having sex with another person or couple were verbalized to the partner. For example, one person might read a book such as *The Lifestyle* (Gould, 1999) and then share it with their spouse, opening up a conversation. They then experiment with swinging. They find that their sexual desires are fulfilled, so they continue. This lifestyle works best for couples that establish clear and explicit rules for what is acceptable and what is not. Emotional attachment to other couples, for example, is forbidden. Swinging is just about sex. Many participants said that the swinging lifestyle had increased the trust in their marriage. One person explained, "The fear of cheating isn't there; we always do everything together" (Kimberly & Hans, 2017, p. 794).

Now, of course, we shouldn't infer from this study that all swinging leads to marital bliss. In particular, the sampling method recruited people who were actively involved in swinging because they were part of an online swingers' community or attended a swingers' convention. What this sampling strategy missed are the couples who tried swinging, hated it, and abandoned it, or those who tried it and found that it broke up their marriage. What we can infer from this study is that at least some married couples who try swinging find that it works for them.

Polyamory

Polyamory is "the nonpossessive, honest, responsible, and ethical philosophy and practice of loving multiple people simultaneously" (Ve Ard & Veaux, 2003). Notice that the emphasis is on love, not sex. There are several forms of such relationships, including the *intentional family,* involving three or more persons; the *group relationship,* with committed, loving relationships involving three or more partners; and *group marriage,* involving three or more people. One specific type of group relationship is a triad involving a married couple and an additional man or woman who all love each other and share sexual activity; the third person and one or both members of the couple may be bisexual. Other arrangements involve two or more men and two or more women. Unlike secret nonmonogamous relationships, there is (ideally) full disclosure of the network of relationships among all participants. There is a strong emphasis on honesty and openness, as well as on egalitarian relationships. Unlike swinging, the emphasis is on long-term intimate relationships.

Research involving in-depth interviews with 20 men and 20 women provided information about participants in one geographic area (Sheff, 2005). Those interviewed were in their mid-thirties to late fifties, usually college educated, and employed in professional occupations; they were overwhelmingly White. Their high social status and access to resources may be a prerequisite for participating in the polyamory lifestyle. The interviewees noted that people outside the polyamorous community, including members of their family of origin (parents, siblings), often react negatively and with hostility toward community members. Their social status insulates them against some potential sanctions.

Women involved in polyamory report expanding their family, gender, and sexual roles. For example, some of these women rejected monogamy in favor of a network of intimate partner relationships. With respect to gender, the women adopted a much more assertive style in their relationships with men. In the realm of sexuality, the women often recognized their high sex drive, the emotional and sexual value of intimacy with other women, and their bisexual interests or identities. Moving away from traditional roles was reported to be both liberating and frightening; creating new roles was often difficult.

Research with polyamorists indicates that they often have a primary partner and a secondary partner (Balzarini et al., 2017). Typically the relationship with the

> **Polyamory:** The nonpossessive, honest, responsible, and ethical philosophy and practice of loving multiple people simultaneously.

primary partner has been longer—an average of 8 years in this sample—compared with the secondary partner (average of 2 years). Participants were much more likely to live with the primary partner rather than with the secondary partner. Participants also tended to have a more satisfying relationship with the primary partner but had more sex with the secondary partner.

In multiethnic settings such as Hong Kong, polyamorous relationships may cross ethnic, racial, and social class boundaries (Sik Ying Ho, 2006). For example, a 37-year-old woman described concurrent sexual relationships with both men and women of different races and social classes. Such relationships provide novel experiences that may both be anxiety provoking and expand one's understanding of sexual diversity.

Scholars of polyamory refer to "mononormativity," that is, the normativeness of monogamy in our culture (Schippers, 2016). They believe that people should open themselves up to possibilities other than monogamy.

Consequences of Nonmonogamous Relationships

What are the consequences of nonmonogamy for the primary relationship? A review of the limited published research looked at the consequences for psychological well-being, using measures of anxiety and depression (Rubel & Bogaert, 2014). In most comparisons, monogamists and consensual nonmonogamists did not differ significantly. Turning to measures of relationship quality—adjustment, satisfaction, sexual frequency, jealousy—the authors conclude "there is an absence of evidence that consensual nonmonogamists differ from monogamists in these domains" (p. 19). There is also little evidence that consensual nonmonogamy leads to higher rates of separation and divorce. Of course, these alternative relationship forms are relatively new. As more research is carried out on more diverse samples and over longer time periods, the results may differ.

What about the effects of secret, nonconsensual nonmonogamy on the primary relationship? In a sample of women students, 36 percent reported sexual or romantic infidelity in the preceding two months (Negash et al., 2014). Both emotional and sexual cheating was related to the termination of the primary relationship. Especially interesting is the finding that women who reported cheating on a high-quality relationship were more likely to report that the relationship ended. Research using data from the representative samples of the General Social Survey examined the association between reports of extramarital sex and being divorced (Allen & Atkins, 2014). Relative to married respondents, people who reported extramarital sex were 2 to 5 times more likely to report being separated or divorced. The question remains, who leaves in response to an affair? Researchers studied ex-spouses' reports of who (if either) was having an affair, and who wanted the

divorce more (England et al., 2014). The results indicated that the spouse having the affair was more likely to want the divorce more. There was no gender difference in who had the affair. The results may reflect either the fact that the person who has decided to get divorced initiates an affair, or that an affair leads to the decision to divorce.

Postmarital Sex

From the point of view of developmental psychologists, the sexual relationship in a second union, perhaps following a divorce or the death of one's partner, is especially interesting. In what ways is it the same, and how does it differ from the sexual relationship in the first marriage? It represents the blending of things that are unique and consistent about the person with things that are unique to the new situation and new partner. As we develop sexually throughout the lifespan, these two strands continue to be intertwined—the developmental continuities (the things that are us and always will be) and the developmental changes (things that differ at various times in our lives, either because we are older or have experienced more, or because our partner or the situation is different).

Divorced and widowed people are in a somewhat unusual situation in that they are used to regular sexual expression and suddenly find themselves in a situation in which the socially acceptable outlet for that expression—marital sex—is no longer available. Partly recognizing this dilemma, our society places few restrictions on postmarital sexual activity, although it is not as approved as marital sex.

Table 4 presents data on the number of sexual partners in the past year by a person's current marital status (Fryar et al., 2007). Among women, 26 percent of the widowed, divorced, or separated report two or more (male) partners; 36 percent of the men in this status report more than two (female) partners. It is interesting that cohabiting women and men are more than twice as likely as married women and men to report two or more partners. We noted earlier that the greater extra-relationship sexual activity of cohabiters is thought to reflect their lower commitment, compared to married people. Finally, note that in every category men report a larger number of partners.

Most divorced women, but fewer widowed women, return to having an active sex life. In one study, 77 percent of the widowed had been sexually abstinent in the last year, compared with 29 percent of the divorced (Smith, 2003).

The lower incidence of postmarital sex among widows, compared with divorced women, is due in part to the fact that widows are, on the average, older than divorced women; but even when matched for age, widows are still less likely than divorcees to engage in postmarital sex. There are probably several reasons for this. Widows are

Table 4 Number of Heterosexual Partners in the Past Year, Adults 20–59, United States

	Number of Sexual Partners		
	None	One	Two or More
Women			
Married	6%	91%	3%
Widowed, divorced, or separated	32	42	26
Never married	47	36	17
Cohabiting	11	81	8
Men			
Married	7%	86%	7%
Widowed, divorced, or separated	25	39	36
Never married	41	30	30
Cohabiting	5	80	15

Source: Fryar et al., 2007, Tables 8 and 10.

more likely to be financially secure than divorced women and therefore have less motivation for engaging in sex as a prelude to remarriage. They have the continuing social support system of in-laws and friends, and so they are less motivated to seek new friendships.

Widowed and divorced women who have postmarital sex often begin a relationship within 1 year of the end of the marriage. The evidence suggests that these are long-term relationships. The average frequency of intercourse reported was twice a month (Stack & Gundlach, 1992).

Divorced women face complex problems of adjustment (Lichtenstein, 2012). These problems may include reduced income, a lower perceived standard of living, and reduced availability of social support. Some divorced men face similar problems. These problems may increase the motivation to establish a new long-term relationship. Single parents face a trade-off between parenting their children and devoting resources to establishing a new relationship (Gray et al., 2015). The conflicts may be more intense for mothers because they are more likely to have custody of children. Analyses of data from a survey of 5,481 single persons found that, among single mothers, as number of children under age 2 increased, number of persons dated in the past 3 months increased (Gray et al., 2015). The researchers suggest this may reflect a more intensive search for a new partner to share the workload of caring for young children. Compared to parents of children over 5, parents of children under 5 reported greater frequencies of sexual activity and first dates.

Earlier in this chapter we noted that substantial numbers of men and women cohabit. Like marriages, these relationships can break up. What are the similarities and differences between formerly married and formerly cohabiting

men and women? To answer this question, researchers used the NHSLS data to analyze the rate of acquisition of new partners following the dissolution of a relationship (Wade & DeLamater, 2002). The results indicate that these newly single men and women do not acquire new sexual partners at a high rate, and there were no significant differences between formerly married and formerly cohabiting men and women. Newly single people acquire new partners at a significantly higher rate than single, never-married people in the year following a breakup. Men with custody of children and men and women with low incomes have higher rates of new partner acquisition, perhaps reflecting a search for someone to share child care and expenses. The results suggest that the postdissolution experience is similar across various demographic groups; given the high rates of breaking up in U.S. society, dissolution may be considered a significant life stage with its own specific characteristics.

Researchers interviewed 45 people age 60 or older who were experiencing or had recently experienced a romantic relationship that began late in life (Malta & Farquharson, 2014). Respondents' ages ranged from 60 to 92. All reported that they were seeking a long-term relationship. Twenty reported they experienced a casual relationship that lasted less than 12 months; reasons included that the partner was not who they were looking for, or was not willing to be flexible. Twenty-five developed a long-term relationship; six married or cohabited and the other 19 established LAT relationships. These men and women desired romantic and sexual equality, and generally valued their independence.

As more men and women leave long-term relationships and initiate new ones in later life, a new problem has emerged: increasing rates of STIs, including HIV infection and AIDS, among older people (see the chapter "Sexually Transmitted Infections"). In 2010, 5 percent of the new cases of HIV infection in the United States were among men and women 55 and older (CDC, 2015a). Among men, 23 percent, and among women, 82 percent were transmitted through heterosexual contact. Newly single older people grew up at a time when there was less concern and publicity about STIs. An important tool in preventing STIs in this population is sex education geared toward them. Programs serving senior citizens in major cities are offering classes for "sexy seniors," often in senior centers and residential facilities.

Sex in Later Life

When Freud suggested that young children, even infants, have sexual thoughts and feelings, his ideas met with considerable resistance. When, 50 years later, researchers began to suggest that older men and women also have sexual thoughts and feelings, there was similar resistance (Pfeiffer et al., 1968). This section deals with the sexual behavior of older men and women, the physical changes they undergo, and the attitudes that influence them.

Physical Changes in Women

Biological Changes

The *climacteric* is a period lasting about 15 or 20 years (from about ages 45 to 60) during which a woman's body makes the transition from being able to reproduce to not being able to reproduce; the climacteric is marked particularly by a decline in the functioning of the ovaries. But climacteric changes occur in many other body tissues and systems as well. **Menopause** (the "change of life," the "change") refers to one specific event in this process, the cessation of menstruation; this occurs, on average, over a 2-year period beginning at around age 50 (with a normal menopause occurring anywhere between the ages of 40 and 60).

Biologically, as a woman grows older, the pituitary continues a normal output of FSH and LH; however, as the ovaries age, they become less able to respond to the pituitary hormones. In addition, the brain—including the hypothalamus–pituitary unit–ages (Lamberts et al., 1997). With the aging of the ovaries, there is an accompanying decline in the output of their two major products: eggs and the sex hormones estrogen and progesterone (Figure 5).

There are a number of physical symptoms that may accompany menopause. Research has identified two broad groups: vasomotor symptoms, especially hot flashes and night sweats, and psychosomatic symptoms, including feeling tense, irritable, and depressed (Richard-Davis & Wellons, 2013). The hot flash is probably the best known of the symptoms. Typically it is described as a sudden wave of heat from the waist up. The woman may get red and perspire a lot; when the flush goes away, she may feel chilled and sometimes shiver. The flashes may last from a few seconds to half an hour and occur several or many times a day. They may also occur at night, causing insomnia; the resulting perspiration can actually soak the sheets. Two other possible effects of the decline in estrogen levels are vaginal dryness and *osteoporosis* (porous and brittle bones).

How many women experience symptoms? It depends on the woman's sociocultural environment. Diet, smoking, exercise, attitude, marital status, and socioeconomic status are all potential influences (Richard-Davis & Wellons, 2013). Controlling for a number of these variables, Caucasian women report significantly more psychosomatic symptoms (40 to 56 percent), and African American women are more likely to report vasomotor symptoms (32 to 40 percent). Japanese and Chinese women are less likely than other groups to report any symptoms. This

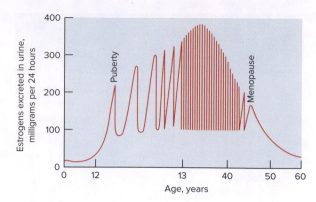

Figure 5 Levels of estrogen production in women across the lifespan.

variation is evidence against the idea that there is a universal menopausal experience. Furthermore, many women who experience symptoms such as hot flashes and night sweats report that they are not bothered by them (Avis & McKinlay, 1995; McKinlay et al., 1992). A study of midlife women assessed their daily stress levels and several potential causes (Woods et al., 2009). The experience of menopausal symptoms by itself was not associated with increases in stress.

There are four approaches to the treatment of symptoms of menopause: hormone therapy, medications to relieve specific symptoms, complementary or alternative treatments, and seeking advice from friends and family. The current guidelines for the use of hormone therapy (HT) were drawn up by the International Menopause Society in collaboration with other medical societies (Baber et al., 2016). HT using estrogen or estrogen combined with progesterone is recommended to treat moderate to severe vasomotor symptoms; it is best to start it in early menopause. HT is also recommended to prevent osteoporosis in high-risk women, including those with low bone mineral density. If the only bothersome symptoms are genitourinary or vaginal dryness, this should be treated with vaginal estrogen or a lubricant, not a systemic medication. Current recommendations are to use the lowest dose of HT for the shortest period that allows successful treatment.

A major health concern is the use of "bioidentical" compounded menopausal hormone therapy products. The Endocrine Society has issued an official statement against their use. These products are compounds of various hormones that are described as "customized" for the patient, and prescribed by various types of physicians. None of these have been approved by the FDA, and they have not been tested for safety or effectiveness. These products are estimated to make up 40 percent of all menopausal hormone treatments used in the United States, and 86 percent of the women taking them have no idea what they are taking (Tucker, 2014).

Menopause: The cessation of menstruation.

A variety of medications can be used to treat specific symptoms, such as headaches, depression, and muscular soreness (Richard-Davis & Wellons, 2013). Some require a prescription and some are sold over the counter. There are many complementary and alternative (CAM) treatments for menopause; it is estimated that 40 percent of the menopausal women in the United States use some form of CAM each year. Treatments include acupuncture, herbal remedies, various spices, and other compounds. Caucasian and Japanese women have the highest rates of use of CAM, while Hispanic women have the lowest. Finally, some ethnic minority women seek advice from elders and close friends as the primary means of managing menopause. Most White women prefer to consult a physician. Japanese women believe menopause is part of normal aging and do not seek advice.

Sexuality and Menopause

During the climacteric, physical changes occur in the vagina. The lack of estrogen causes the vagina to become less acidic, which leaves it more vulnerable to infections. Estrogen is also responsible for maintaining the mucous membranes of the vaginal walls. With a decline in estrogen, there is a decline in vaginal lubrication during arousal, and the vaginal walls become less elastic. Either or both of these may make intercourse painful for the woman. Several remedies are available, including the use of artificial lubricants, and estrogen creams for the vagina by prescription. On the other hand, some women report that intercourse is even better after menopause, when the fear of pregnancy no longer inhibits them.

Experts reviewing the research on women's sexuality during and after menopause have reached the following conclusions (Dennerstein et al., 2003; McCoy, 1996, 1997): (1) The majority of women continue to engage in sexual activity and many enjoy it both during and after menopause. (2) There is some decline in sexual functioning, on average, during menopause and particularly after the last period. (3) Estrogen is related to the decline in sexual functioning, in part because low estrogen levels cause vaginal dryness. There is some evidence that higher estrogen levels are associated with better sexual functioning. (4) Testosterone is also important; a woman's sexual desire may decline as her levels of ovarian testosterone decline. Testosterone therapy is recommended only in cases where the woman is diagnosed with hypoactive sexual desire disorder that she finds distressing (see the chapter "Sexual Disorders and Sex Therapy") (Busko, 2014).

One study analyzed the data from an AARP survey of people age 45 and older (DeLamater & Moorman, 2007). The AARP survey included questions about various factors that might affect the frequency of sexual behavior, including diagnosed physical and emotional illnesses, use of medications, attitudes toward sexuality, and the presence of a sexual partner. Physical limitations such as prior stroke and arthritis, emotional problems such as depression, and use of various medications can interfere with sexual activity. Although both men and women reported these conditions, they were relatively uncommon and were not significantly related to the frequency of oral sexual activity or vaginal intercourse. The factors that were significantly related were high scores on an index of sexual desire (frequent sexual thoughts, desire), positive attitudes toward sex for oneself, and the presence of a partner with no limitations related to sexuality. Men and women who reported that their partner had limitations that interfered with sexual expression were significantly more likely to report masturbating.

Some people believe that having a **hysterectomy** means the end of a woman's sex life. In fact, sex hormone production is not affected as long as the ovaries are not removed (surgical removal of the ovaries is called **oophorectomy** or ovariectomy). On average, there are no changes in frequency of sexual activity or orgasm after hysterectomy (Dragisic & Milad, 2004). If problems do occur, there are two possible physiological causes. If the ovaries have been removed, hormonal changes may be responsible; specifically, the ovaries produce androgens, and they may play a role in sexual response. The other possibility is that the removal of the cervix, and possibly the rest of the uterus, is an anatomical problem if the cervix serves as a trigger for orgasm. Androgen therapy has been shown to improve sexual functioning and sexual well-being in women who have had a bilateral oophorectomy and are experiencing Androgen Insufficiency Syndrome (Chu & Lobo, 2004).

Physical Changes in Men

Testosterone production declines gradually over the years (see Figure 6). Drug manufacturers discovered this a few years ago and started massive advertising campaigns to persuade men to use prescription androgen/testosterone supplements. A combined FDA advisory panel concluded that the only clear indicator of need for such supplements is in men with congenital or acquired primary hypogonadism, a condition requiring medical diagnosis (Tucker, 2014). Men who do not have low levels of testosterone confirmed by hormonal assay should not take these drugs.

Vascular diseases such as hardening of the arteries are increasingly common with age in men, but good circulation is essential to erection (Riportella-Muller, 1989). A major change is that erections occur more slowly. It is important for men to know that this is a perfectly natural slowdown so that they will not jump to the conclusion that they are developing an erection problem. It is also important for partners to know about this so that they will use effective techniques of stimulating the man and not mistake slowness for lack of interest.

> **Hysterectomy (hiss-tur-EK-tuh-mee):** Surgical removal of the uterus.
> **Oophorectomy (OH-uh-fuh-REKtuh-mee):** Surgical removal of the ovaries.

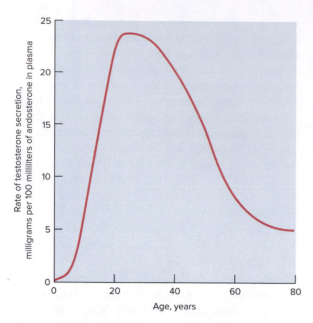

Figure 6 Levels of testosterone production in men across the lifespan.

The refractory period lengthens with age; thus for an elderly man there may be a period of 24 hours after an orgasm during which he cannot get an erection. (Note that women do not undergo a similar change; most women do not enter into a refractory period and are still capable of multiple orgasm at age 80.) Other signs of sexual excitement—the sex flush and muscle tension—diminish with age.

The volume of the ejaculate gradually decreases, and the force of ejaculation lessens. The testes become somewhat smaller, but viable sperm are produced by even very old men. Ninety-year-old men have been known to father children.

One advantage is that middle-aged and older men may have better control over orgasm than young men; thus they can prolong coitus and may be better sexual partners.

A study of healthy men ages 45 to 74, all married, assessed their biological, psychological, and behavioral functioning (Schiavi et al., 1994). Satisfaction with sexual functioning was significantly related to whether the man had erectile difficulties. Men who reported erectile difficulties were less satisfied with their sexual functioning. General satisfaction was related negatively to erectile problems, and positively to sexual information and marital adjustment. Accurate information is important, because it may result in more realistic expectations for sexual performance.

Prostatectomy (pros-tuh-TEK-tuh-mee): Surgical removal of the prostate.

Some people believe that prostate surgery or removal of the prostate, **prostatectomy,** means the end of a man's sex life. It is

true that the volume of the ejaculate will decrease. Prostatectomy can cause damage to the nerves supplying the penis, creating erectile problems. In other cases, retrograde ejaculation may result. Whether there are such problems depends on which of several available methods of surgery is used.

In sum, the evidence suggests that there need be no time limit on sexual expression for either men or women.

A 73-year-old man reported,

> I can't begin to tell you how happy I am. I am married to a wonderful woman who loves me as much as I love her. My children gave me a hard time of it at first, especially because she is a bit younger than me. [My son] was telling me that marrying again and *trying* to have a lot of sex—imagine that, saying to me *trying* to have sex—could be dangerous to the marriage. So, I said to him with a straight face, "Do you think she'll survive it?" He was so shocked, he laughed. (Janus & Janus, 1993, p. 8)

Attitudes about Sex and the Elderly

Our society has a negative attitude toward sexual expression among the elderly.[3] Somehow it seems indecent for two 70-year-old people to have sex with each other, and even more indecent for a 70-year-old to masturbate. Somehow what is "virility" at 25 becomes "lechery" at 75.

Cross-cultural research indicates that the sexual behavior of the elderly is related to these cultural expectations (Winn & Newton, 1982). The elderly continue to be sexually active in 70 percent of societies and in precisely those societies where they are expected to be sexually active. Indeed, in 22 percent of societies, women are expected to become more uninhibited about sexuality when they become old.

Why does our society have such negative attitudes toward sex among the elderly? In part, these attitudes are due to the fact that ours is a youth-oriented culture. We value youth, and the physical characteristics that are considered "sexy" are youthful ones, such as a trim, firm body and smooth skin. It is therefore hard to believe that someone with old, wrinkled skin could be sexually active.

A study of heterosexual, midlife women assessed menopause status, self-rated attractiveness, sexual desire, and frequency of sexual intercourse (Koch et al., 2005). Regardless of menopause status, women who perceived themselves as less attractive than 10 years earlier reported a decline in both sexual desire and sexual behavior. Women who perceived themselves as more attractive reported an increase in sexual desire, frequency of sex, and frequency of orgasm.

[3]These attitudes are reflected in jokes such as "Once you're 80, your sex life is less like the Fourth of July and more like Thanksgiving."

Figure 7 Affection, romance, and sex are not just for the young.

©ejwhite/Getty Images

Our negative attitudes may be a holdover from the belief that sex was for reproductive purposes only—and those past the age of reproduction should therefore not engage in it (Pfeiffer, 1975). The incest taboo may also be involved in our negative attitudes. We tend to identify old people with our parents or grandparents and find it hard to think of them as sexual beings. This attitude is encouraged by the fact that many parents take great pains to hide their sexual activity from their children.

These attitudes affect the way elderly people are treated, and the elderly may even hold such attitudes themselves. One remedy that has been proposed for these negative attitudes is a "coming out of the closet." As one 67-year-old commented,

> The common view that the aging and aged are nonsexual, I believe, can only be corrected by a dramatic and courageous process—the *coming-out-of-the-closet* of sexually active older women and men, so that people can see for themselves what the later years are really like. (Brecher, 1984, p. 21)

Various specific misunderstandings may influence sexuality. For example, a man might believe that sex will precipitate a heart attack or, if he has already had a heart attack, that it will bring on another one. Although Masters and Johnson found that the heart rate accelerates during sexual intercourse, another study showed that the mean heart rate during orgasm was only 117 beats per minute, which is about that attained during many common forms of daily exercise (Hellerstein & Friedman, 1969). This rate is about the equivalent of climbing two flights of stairs at a moderate pace. Thus the demands of sex on the heart are not unreasonable (Jackson, 2009). A study of patients who had had a heart attack questioned them about their activities immediately prior to the attack

and in the year prior to the attack (Muller et al., 1996). The results indicate that the increase in risk caused by sexual activity is one chance in one million for a healthy individual. Furthermore, the relative risk is no greater in patients with a history of cardiac disease.

Ideas such as this, as well as factors such as illness or hospitalization, may lead to a period of sexual inactivity. But being sexually inactive is one of the most effective ways of diminishing sexuality. Masters and Johnson emphasized that two factors are critical in maintaining sexual capacity in old age:

1. *Good physical and mental health.* An excellent study confirms this notion (Persson, 1980). A representative sample of 70-year-olds in one town in Sweden was selected. For both men and women, those who continued to have sexual intercourse had better mental health as rated by a psychiatrist and more positive attitudes toward sexual activity among the aged.

2. *Regularity of sexual expression.* A longitudinal study suggests that, for men, frequency of orgasm is positively associated with longevity. The study involved men aged 45 to 59. At the beginning of the study, the men completed a standard medical history and a questionnaire that assessed sexual behavior. Ten years later, the researchers found out who had died, and compared their questionnaire answers with those of the survivors. Men who reported less than one orgasm per month at the beginning of the study were more than twice as likely to die as the men who reported two or more orgasms per month (Smith et al., 1997).

Apparently some elderly people have caught on to this fact. As one 80-year-old husband said of his relationship with his 75-year-old wife,

> My wife and I both believe that keeping active sexually delays the aging process . . . if we are troubled with an erection or lubrication, we turn to oral methods or masturbation of each other. We keep our interest alive by a great deal of caressing and fondling of each other's genitals. We feel it is much better to wear out than to rust out. (Brecher, 1984, p. 33)

Reformers urge us to change our attitudes about sex and the senior citizen. Nursing homes particularly need to revise their practices (Figure 8); even such simple changes as knocking before entering a resident's room would help (people masturbate, you know). Other reforms would include making provisions for spouses to stay overnight and allowing couples—married or unmarried—to share a bedroom.

The introduction of Viagra© in 1998 ushered in a "new era" that some refer to as the *biomedicalization* of sex in later life (Marshall, 2012). The marketing of Viagra and

Figure 8 Romance is important even for nursing-home residents.

©Purestock/Getty Images

related medicines conveys the message that declining sexual function is a medical problem, not an aspect of normal aging to be accepted. This is leading to changing attitudes about sex in later life, perhaps creating the belief that everyone should be sexually active until they die and there is something wrong with you if you aren't. That is as false as the belief that everyone loses sexual desire and function sometime between age 50 and ? Clearly each person/couple needs to determine the amount and kind of sexual expression that best fits their health, relationship status, living situation, and desires.

Sexual Behavior

While sexual desire and sexual behavior do decline somewhat with age, there are substantial numbers of older men and women who have active sex lives. The National Social Life, Health and Aging Project (NSHAP) interviewed 3,000 women and men ages 57 to 85 (Lindau et al., 2007). Among men 75 to 80, more than 40 percent had frequent sexual thoughts, 30 percent had masturbated in the preceding year, and 45 percent had had sexual intercourse. Among women 75 to 80, the percentages were about 10, 18, and 20, respectively (Das et al., 2012). There does not seem to be any age beyond which all people are sexually inactive.

Some older people do, for various reasons, stop having intercourse after a certain age. Analyses of the data from NSHAP (an extension of the NHSLS to men and women age 57 to 72) and NHSLS (men and women age 44 to 59) found that, for both men and women, frequency of intercourse declines with age (Karraker et al., 2011). Among men, declining frequency is also associated with declining happiness in the past year, and declining physical health. Among women, declining frequency was associated with happiness, and especially with widowhood. Subsequent analyses of NSHAP data indicate that, among men and women 57 to 85 who are married, overall two-thirds remain sexually active; when sexual activity within a marriage stops, it is primarily due to declining health (Karraker & DeLamater, 2013).

One of the most important influences on sexuality in the elderly is that there are far more elderly women than elderly men. Because of both men's earlier mortality and their preference for younger women, elderly women are more likely to be living alone and to have less access to sexual partners. For example, in 2013, among those 65 and over, 74 percent of the men were married and living with their spouses, compared with only 44 percent of the women (U.S. Bureau of the Census, 2014). Some innovative solutions have been proposed, such as elderly women forming lesbian relationships.

We see, then, that among older people who are healthy and have regular opportunities for sexual expression, sexual activity continues well past 70 years of age.

Critical **THINK** *ing Skill*

Thinking as hypothesis testing

In many of our everyday interactions, we function like intuitive scientists. Events occur and we want to explain and then perhaps control them. To do so, we use the same skills as a scientist testing a hypothesis: (1) We accumulate observations; (2) We formulate hypotheses or explanations; and (3) We use the information to see if it confirms or disconfirms the hypothesis.

A common event in a long-term relationship is a decline in the frequency of sexual activity. It can be upsetting because (1) you enjoy sex, (2) it symbolizes the bond between you, (3) it asserts your power, and (4) _____. So one morning, you think, "We haven't had sex for a week; we're having sex a lot less than we did at first." You get upset. You search for a reason and think that your partner is having an affair and is therefore less interested in sex with you. Before you leap to the conclusion that your partner is having an affair, use critical thinking skills. Accumulate observations and track frequency for some period of time. It may be that your initial observation was just about one week and coincided with a string of 12-hour days at work, a visit by the parents, or some other unusual occurrence. If, indeed, over time sex is infrequent, then try to recall accurately how often you did have sex "at first."

If your observations are consistent with the hypothesis of decline, consider possible explanations. An affair is one possibility, but this chapter has suggested several others. Some are job-related; one of you switched to a more demanding job six months ago. You had or adopted a baby eight months ago. You are getting older (look at the data in Table 2). Now you have four plausible hypotheses. You can make observations about work, the baby, fatigue and problems related to age, and odd absences by the partner, and assess the evidence for each of these.

This process will take some time. At some point, you will want to involve your partner by discussing your concerns, your observations, and perhaps your hypotheses. When you do, use the principles of good communication discussed in the chapter "Attraction, Love, and Communication." With good communication skills, the odds are higher that the result will be that both of you become positively engaged in the process.

SUMMARY

Sexuality continues to develop throughout the lifespan. It may be expressed in singlehood, cohabitation, marriage, nonmonogamous relationships, postmarital relationships, or in a variety of contexts as the individual ages.

Sex and the Single Person

Young adults grow toward sexual maturity. Many do so in the context of a single relationship that results in a long-term committed relationship. Others are involved in two or more relationships before they begin to live with or marry someone. Never-married people over 25 may find themselves part of the "singles scene."

Cohabitation

Cohabitation is a stage that close to 50 percent of people experience. The time couples spend living together varies from a few months to several years. Sixty percent of cohabiting couples go on to marry. Some cohabiting couples have children, either together or with previous partners. Men and women who are living together engage in sexual activity more often, on average, than those who are married or single. The cohabitation effect refers to the finding that couples who cohabited before marriage are more likely to divorce and are less satisfied with their marriages than couples who did not cohabit.

Marital Relationships

Marriage represents a major turning point as couples face new responsibilities and problems and try to find time for each other. Married couples in their twenties engage in sexual intercourse two or three times per week on average, with the frequency declining to two or three times per month among couples over 60. Many people continue to masturbate even though they are married. Most people today—both women and men—express general satisfaction with their marital sex life. Sexual patterns in marriage, however, show great variability.

Nonmonogamous Relationships

About 21 percent of all married men and 13 percent of all married women engage in extramarital sex at some time. Extramarital sex is disapproved of in our society and is generally carried on in secrecy. In consensual nonmonogamy, it is agreed that both partners can have extra-relationship sex, as in swinging and polyamory. The Internet has created new kinds of infidelity. Equity theory may be helpful in understanding patterns of extra-relationship sex.

Postmarital Sex

Virtually all widowed and divorced men return to an active sex life, as do most divorced women and about half of widowed women.

Sex in Later Life

Although sexual activity declines somewhat with age, it is perfectly possible to remain sexually active into one's eighties or nineties. Problems with sex or the cessation of intercourse may be related to physical factors. In women, declining estrogen levels result in less lubrication; in men, there is lowered testosterone production and increased vascular disease, combined with slower erections and longer refractory periods. Psychological factors can also be involved, such as the belief that the elderly should not have sex. Masters and Johnson emphasized that two factors are critical to maintaining sexual capacity in old age: good physical and mental health and regularity of sexual expression. The NSHAP survey indicates that all sexual behaviors—including heterosexual intercourse and masturbation—continue past age 70.

SUGGESTIONS FOR FURTHER READING

Carpenter, Laura M., and DeLamater, John (Eds). (2012). *Sex for life: From virginity to Viagra, how sexuality changes throughout our lives.* New York: New York University Press. A collection of articles reporting original research on sexuality from early childhood to old age.

Frank, Katherine. (2013). *Plays well in groups: A journey through the world of group sex.* Lanham, MD: Rowman and Littlefield. From tribal religious rituals to the Playboy mansion, and from ancient Rome to Burning Man, *Plays Well in Groups* explores the phenomenon of group sex. Author Katherine Frank draws on surveys, ethnographic research, participant interviews, and more to provide explanations for both participation in group sex and our complex reactions to it.

Grazian, D. (2008). *On the make: The hustle of urban nightlife.* Chicago: University of Chicago Press. A fascinating ethnography of the urban nightclub scene and the people involved in it. Considers the players (single, married, gay, and lesbian), the servers, and the marketing of the clubs.

Montemurro, Beth. (2014). *Deserving desire: Women's stories of sexual evolution.* New Brunswick, NJ: Rutgers University Press. This is a fascinating book. As a result of thoughtful interviewing, it is full of insights into the dynamics of women's sexual lives and relationships. Montemurro uses her original, developmental model to bring some order to the material and to highlight enduring themes.

Are YOU Curious?

1. Do opposites really attract?
2. How do Internet dating sites match people?
3. How important is intimacy (as opposed to sex) in relationships?
4. Why do people get jealous?

Read this chapter to find out.

©Digital Vision/Photodisc/Getty Images

CHAPTER

11

Attraction, Love, and Communication

CHAPTER HIGHLIGHTS

We made love, Your Honor. He didn't have any and neither did I. So we made some. It was good.*

*Julie in Lois Gould (1988). *Such good friends*. New York: Farrar, Straus, Giroux, p. 161.

Many people believe that there is, or should be, a close connection between love and sex. The sexual standard for many is that sex is appropriate if one loves the other person, and sex seems to be the logical outcome of a loving relationship. For this reason, it is important in a text on sexuality to spend some time considering the emotion we link so closely to sex: love.

This chapter is organized in terms of the way relationships usually progress—if they progress. We begin by talking about attraction, what brings people together in the first place. Then we consider intimacy, which develops as relationships develop. Next, we look at theories and research on love. Finally, we conclude with one of the requirements for fulfilling, long-term relationships: good communication.

Attraction

What causes you to be attracted to another person? Social psychologists have done extensive research on interpersonal attraction. We consider the major results of this research in this section.

The Girl Next Door

Our opportunities to meet people are limited by geography and time. You may meet that attractive person sitting two rows in front of you in the sex class, as the course is referred to at the University of Wisconsin, but you will never meet the wealthy, brilliant engineering student who sits in your seat two classes later. You are much more likely to meet and be attracted to the boy or girl next door than the one who lives across town. In a longitudinal survey, adults were asked where they met their partner (Rosenfeld & Thomas, 2012). Of the heterosexual couples who met between 2005 and 2010, 30 percent met through friends, 20 percent in (primary or secondary) school, 20 percent online, 10 percent in college, and about 5 percent each through family, at work, in church, and in bars. In pre-Internet days (1980–1990), more couples met through family and in school. Of the same-sex couples who met in 2005–2010, almost 70 percent met online, 20 percent in bars, and 10 percent through friends.

Earlier, in 1980–1990, same-sex couples were more likely to meet through friends and in bars.

Among those who work in the same place or take the same class, we tend to be more attracted to people with whom we have had contact several times than we are to people with whom we have had little contact (Finkel et al., 2015; Harrison, 1977; Reis et al., 2011). This tendency has been demonstrated in laboratory studies in which the amount of contact between participants was systematically varied. At the end of the session, people gave higher "liking" ratings to those with whom they had had much contact and lower ratings to those with whom they had had little contact (Saegert et al., 1973). This is the **mere-exposure effect:** Repeated exposure to a person leads to greater liking for that stimulus. In short, familiarity does not breed contempt, it breeds attraction.

Birds of a Feather

We like people who are similar to us. We are attracted to people who are approximately the same as we are in age, race or ethnicity, and economic and social status. **Homophily** refers to the tendency to have contact with people equal in social status. Table 1 presents data on homophily in the United States (Rosenfeld, 2008). Race is the most common type of homophily in marriages, followed by education, and then religion. We can expect

> **Mere-exposure effect:** The tendency to like a person more if we have been exposed to them repeatedly.
> **Homophily:** The tendency to have contact with people who are equal in social status.

Table 1 Percentage of U.S. Marriages That Are Homophilous

	Women	Men
Race		
Whites	96%	97%
Blacks	90	82
Latinx	61	65
Asian	42	48
Education		
Some college	73	85
College degree	63	74
Religion		
Protestant	75	74
Catholic	54	56
Jewish	NA	NA
No religious preference	22	17

NA: not available because sample size was too small.

Source: Rosenfeld (2008, table 1)

these statistics to go down in the next 10 years, at least for race and religion, because of increases in interracial marriage and a decline in the number of people having a religious affiliation. Notice, too, that homophily varies by race, with Asian Americans being the least likely to marry someone of their own race. Educational homophily seems to be on the increase (Schwartz, 2013); that is, people are increasingly likely to marry someone of their own educational level.

Racial homophily is strong on dating websites (Lin & Lundquist, 2013). People are most likely to send messages to people of their own race. Racial homophily and racial hierarchies are so strong that they trump education. White women and White men who are college graduates are more likely to respond to a White dater without a college degree than to a Black dater with a college degree.

Research indicates not only homophily by educational attainment, but homophily in characteristics of institutions attended. Women who attended more elite institutions married/cohabited with men with higher annual incomes. Men who attended elite colleges married/cohabited with women from a more privileged background (Arum et al., 2008). There is even research indicating that spouses share more genetic similarities than people randomly paired from the same population (Domingue et al., 2014).

Social psychologists have done numerous experiments demonstrating that we are attracted to people whose attitudes and opinions are similar to ours (Byrne, 1971). In these experiments, the researcher typically has people fill out an opinion questionnaire. They are then shown a questionnaire that was supposedly filled out by another person and are asked to rate how much they think they would like that person. In fact, the questionnaire was filled out to show either high or low agreement with the participant's responses. Participants report more liking for a person whose attitudes are similar to theirs than for one whose responses are quite different.

Do opposites really attract?

Why are we attracted to a person who is similar to us in, say, attitude? There are a number of reasons (Huston & Levinger, 1978). We get positive reinforcement from that person agreeing with us. The other person's agreement bolsters our sense of rightness. And we anticipate positive interactions with that person.

Folk sayings are sometimes wise and sometimes foolish. The interpersonal-attraction research indicates that the saying "Birds of a feather flock together" contains some truth.

Physical Attractiveness

Given a choice of more than one potential partner, a great deal of evidence shows that individuals will prefer the one who is more physically attractive (Hendrick & Hendrick, 1992). For example, in a classic study, photos were taken of college men and women (Berscheid et al., 1971). A dating history of each person was also obtained. Judges then rated the attractiveness of the men and women in the photographs. For the women there was a fairly strong relationship between attractiveness and popularity. The women judged attractive had had more dates in the last year than the women judged less attractive. There was some relationship between appearance and popularity for men, too, but it was not as marked as it was for women. This phenomenon has even been found in children as young as 3 to 6 years of age, who are more attracted to children with attractive faces (Dion, 1973, 1977).

Physical attractiveness is one aspect of sex appeal, and in fact, young men and women typically rate physical appearance as the most important (Regan, 2004). Other aspects include general body size (measured in various ways) and certain facial features. Much of the research on attractiveness uses data from samples of White people. One exception is research on the impact of lightness of skin on ratings of attractiveness among African Americans. The National Survey of Black Americans involved interviews conducted by Blacks. At the end of the interview, the interviewer rated the respondent's skin color on a five-category scale from "very dark brown" to "very light brown" and rated the respondent's attractiveness. Skin tone was strongly associated with the attractiveness ratings given female respondents by both male and female interviewers (Hill, 2002). Light skin was rated as more attractive, perhaps reflecting the use of white skin as the standard.

In general, then, we are most attracted to good-looking people. However, this effect depends on gender to some extent. Physical attractiveness is more important to males evaluating females than it is to females evaluating males (Feingold, 1990). Also, our perception of attractiveness or beauty of another person is influenced by our evaluation of their intelligence, liking, and respect (Kniffin & Wilson, 2004), and by our own objective attractiveness (Montoya, 2008). And this phenomenon is somewhat modified by our own feelings of personal worth, as we show in the next section.

The Interpersonal Marketplace

Although this may sound somewhat callous, whom we are attracted to and pair off with depends a lot on how much we think we have to offer and how much we think we can "buy" with it. This tendency for men and women to choose as partners people whose social "worth" matches their own is called the **matching phenomenon** (Feingold, 1988). Generally, the

> **Matching phenomenon:** The tendency for people to choose as partners people who match them, that is, who are similar in attitudes, intelligence, and attractiveness.

principle—at least in previous decades—seemed to be that women's worth was based on their physical beauty, whereas men's worth was based on their success. There was a tendency, then, for beautiful women to be paired with wealthy, successful men.

Data from many studies documented this phenomenon. In one study, high school yearbook pictures were rated for attractiveness (Udry & Eckland, 1984). These people were followed up 15 years after graduation, and measures of education, occupational status, and income were obtained. Women who were rated the most attractive in high school were significantly more likely to have husbands who had high incomes and were highly educated (see also Elder, 1969).

The research showing that attractive women marry successful men began in the 1970s when many women did not work, and did not have an occupation or income, and so it seemed as if they were exchanging beauty for money and status. Also, researchers rarely assessed the man's attractiveness. Homophily, of course, would predict that physically attractive people marry each other. By 2010, many men and women each possessed physical attractiveness, educational achievement, occupational status, and income. A study of a probability sample of young heterosexual couples (average age 22 to 23), 500 dating, 500 cohabiting, 500 married, used Add Health data (McClintock, 2014). In fact, for both men and women, the person's physical attractiveness is highly correlated with their education, income, and a measure of social status. In couples, individuals' attractiveness and success are highly correlated with their partner's attractiveness and success. Sophisticated analyses of the data provide little support for the idea that either gender exchanges beauty for status these days. Instead, the results are consistent with the hypothesis that people select mates who match them on these characteristics.

The question becomes, why is there such a high correlation between a person's physical attractiveness and their educational achievement and socioeconomic success? One research project combined analysis of the Add Health data on 7th to 12th graders with observations, interviews, and school records from a large high school in Texas (Gordon et al., 2013). The results show that attractiveness in high school is associated with greater social integration and favorable treatment by teachers and classmates. This, in turn, predicts education, work, and mental health outcomes as the person becomes an adult.

Attraction Online

Technology has created more ways to meet potential partners online and through apps. Popular dating sites vary considerably in the clientele they serve (Meltzer, 2017). eHarmony is designed for people who want to go slowly and get to know each other, and Match.com appeals to

singles age 30 and older who want to settle down. In contrast, SeniorPeopleMeet is for singles 55 and older, and JDate is for Jewish singles. Tinder and Grindr apps are based on location—they match you with someone who is within a certain distance from where you are. These apps can work well if the goal is casual sex or a casual relationship.

How do Internet dating sites match people?

In a survey of online daters, the most common reason for trying online dating was that they were looking for a serious relationship (47 percent of men and 41 percent of women) (Meltzer, 2017). In that survey, when asked where they met their current spouse or partner, the most common site was Match.com, followed by eHarmony, followed, distantly, by PlentyOfFish and OkCupid.

These websites and apps seem to be at least moderately effective. In the same survey of online daters, 44 percent said they have had a serious long-term relationship or have married as a result of online dating. Another study found that couples who met online transitioned to marriage sooner than those meeting offline (Rosenfeld, 2017).

Users say that one advantage of meeting on the Internet is that the technology forces you to focus on the person's interests and values. This focus facilitates finding a person with whom you have a lot in common and getting to know the person before you actually meet.

How do dating websites match people? Different sites use different algorithms (Meltzer, 2017). In general, the sites keep their algorithms secret because if they have a good one, they don't want their competitors to know it. eHarmony uses an extensive questionnaire measuring attitudes, values, and personality, and it matches people based on similarity—a good strategy given the research

(top): ©Darren Greenwood/Design Pics; (top left): ©Jupiterimages/ Getty Images; (top right): ©Glow Images; (bottom left): ©Purestock/ SuperStock; (bottom right): ©conrado/Shutterstock

described in this chapter. Match.com seems to use a similar strategy. OkCupid has its own set of questions, some of which are quirky (e.g., "Do you often find yourself wanting to chuck it all and go live on a sailboat?"), and matches people who should be compatible based on answers to their questions.

Explaining Our Preferences

The research data are quite consistent in showing that we select as potential partners people who are similar to us in social characteristics—age, race, education—and who share our attitudes and beliefs. Moreover, both men and women prefer physically attractive people. The obvious question is, Why? Two answers are suggested, one drawing on reinforcement theory and one on sociobiology (see the chapter "Theoretical Perspectives on Sexuality" for discussions of these theories).

Reinforcement Theory: Byrne's Law of Attraction

A rather commonsense idea—and one that psychologists agree with—is that we tend to like people who give us rewards and to dislike people who give us punishments. Social psychologist Donn Byrne (1997) has formulated the law of attraction. It says that our attraction to another person is proportionate to the number of reinforcements that person gives us relative to the total number of reinforcements plus punishments the person gives us. Or, simplified even more, we like people who are frequently nice to us and seldom nasty (Figure 1).

According to this explanation, we prefer people who are similar because interaction with them is rewarding. People who are similar in race and education are likely to

Figure 1 According to Byrne's law of attraction, our liking for a person is influenced by the reinforcements we receive from interacting with them. Shared activities provide the basis for smooth and rewarding interactions.

©Fuse/Getty Images

have similar outlooks on life, prefer similar activities, and like the same kinds of people. These shared values and beliefs provide the basis for smooth and rewarding interactions. It will be easy to agree about such things as how important schoolwork is, what TV programs to watch, and what to do on Friday night. Disagreement about such things would cause conflict and hostility, which are definitely not rewards (for most people, anyway).

These findings have some practical implications (Hatfield & Walster, 1978). If you are trying to get a new relationship going well, make sure you give the other person some positive reinforcement. Also, make sure you have some good times together, so you *associate* each other with rewards. Do not spend all your time stripping paint off old furniture or cleaning out the garage. And do not forget to keep the positive reinforcements (or "strokes," if you like that jargon better) going in an old, stable relationship.

A variation of the reinforcement view comes from the implicit egotism perspective (Jones et al., 2004). It states that we are attracted to people who are similar because they activate our positive views of ourselves. For example, research found that men and women are more likely to marry people whose names resemble their own.

Sociobiology: Sexual Strategies Theory

Sociobiologists view sexual behavior within an evolutionary perspective. Historically, the function of mating has been reproduction. People who selected mates according to some preferences were more successful than those who chose them based on other preferences (Allgeier & Wiederman, 1994). The successful ones produced more offspring, who in turn produced more offspring, carrying their mating preferences to the present.

Men and women face different adaptive problems in their efforts to reproduce (Buss & Schmitt, 1993). Because women bear the offspring, men need to identify reproductively valuable women. Other things being equal, younger women are more likely to be fertile than older women, leading to a preference for youth, which results in young men choosing young women (homophily). Also, sociobiologists assert that men want to be certain about the paternity of offspring, and for this reason they want a woman who will be sexually faithful.

Other things being equal, a physically attractive person is more likely to be healthy and fertile than someone who isn't, which explains the preference for good-looking partners. If attractiveness is an indicator of health, we would expect it to be more important in societies where chronic diseases are more prevalent. Gangestad and Buss (1993) measured the prevalence of seven pathogens, including those that cause malaria and leprosy, in 29 cultures, and also obtained ratings of the importance of 18 attributes of mates. They found that physical attractiveness was considered more important by residents in societies that had a greater prevalence of pathogens. However, one study found that there was no relationship between rated facial attractiveness (based on a photograph) and a clinical assessment of health in a sample of adolescents. At the same time, the raters ranked more attractive people as being healthier (Kalick et al., 1998).

Some evolutionary analysts have argued that the critical feature of an attractive face is symmetry, having features on one side of the nose that are mirror images of features on the other side. **Fluctuating asymmetry,** asymmetry of bilateral features that are on average symmetrical in the population, are said to reflect developmental instability (DI), the inability of the developing body to buffer itself against random perturbations (Van Dongen & Gangestad, 2011). Visible asymmetry in the face would reflect DI, which could have caused other anomalies that could impair reproductive success. Thus attractiveness might be an important indicator of fertility, fetal survival, and normal growth. There have been dozens of studies of the relationship between symmetry and numerous features, including measures of health, fetal outcomes, hormonal functioning, facial attractiveness, and reproduction (number of sexual partners). They indicate that the correlation between symmetry and health or fitness is small (Van Dongen, 2011; Van Dongen & Gangestad, 2011).

Women must make a much greater investment than men in order to reproduce. They will be pregnant for 9 months, and after the birth they must care for the infant and young child for many years. For these reasons, women want to select as mates men who are reproductively valuable, leading to the preference for good-looking mates. They also want mates who are able and willing to invest resources in them and their children. Obviously, men must have resources in order to invest them, so women, according to the theory, prefer men with higher incomes and status. Among young people, women will prefer men with greater earning potential and, for this reason, prefer men with greater education and higher occupational aspirations. This matter of resources is more important than the problem of identifying a reproductively valuable male, so women rate income and earning potential as more important than good looks.

Note that these arguments assume limited female access to resources, forcing reliance on males. But in contemporary society, more and more women work, and many control their earnings. These women may place less emphasis on a man's resources in selecting a mate. Analysis of survey data from women 18 to 35 (44 percent in a relationship) found that wealthier women prefer older men, and resource control predicted a preference for physical attractiveness over financial prospects (Moore et al., 2006). In effect, wealthier women have more to offer in the relationship marketplace.

Sexual strategies theory asserts that gender differences in mate preferences reflect genetic predispositions based on universal biological functions of men and women in reproduction. An alternative view is that preferences reflect current gender roles in specific cultures. In cultures where women are forced to rely on men for resources and protection, the roles and therefore preferences will be differentiated. In cultures where there is equal access to resources and gender equity, the gender role perspective suggests that gender differences in preferences will be weakened or disappear. To test this hypothesis, an online questionnaire assessed the preferences of more than 2,000 women and 1,000 men from 10 nations for eight characteristics used in prior research that found differences. The 10 countries included 3 with low gender parity, 3 with medium parity, and 4 with high parity. The results indicated that gender differences in mate preferences declined as gender parity increased (Zentner & Mitura, 2012). This indicates that cultural gender roles, rather than biological evolution, better explain gender differences in mate preference.

Intimacy

Intimacy is a major component of any close or romantic relationship. Thus, in this section, we explore intimacy in more detail to try to gain a better understanding of it.

People seek intimate relationships for two reasons. The first is the desire to someday have children and the awareness that raising a child is a lot easier if there are two people. The other is to obtain the benefits of mutual trust and reciprocal recognition by another person. This benefit is increasingly important in an impersonal and sometimes cruel world that is very stressful for some people. Indeed, stress researchers have long recognized the need for interpersonal support to cope successfully with stress.

Defining Intimacy

What is **intimacy**? Psychologists have offered a number of definitions, including the following (Perlman & Fehr, 1987, p. 17):

1. Intimacy's defining features include "openness, honesty, mutual self-disclosure; caring, warmth, protecting, helping; being devoted to each other, mutually attentive, mutually committed; surrendering control, dropping defenses; becoming emotional, feeling distressed when separation occurs."
2. "Emotional intimacy is defined in behavioral terms as mutual self-disclosure and other kinds of verbal sharing, as declarations of liking and loving the other, and as demonstrations of affection."

Fluctuating asymmetry: Asymmetry of bilateral features that are on average symmetrical in the population.
Intimacy: A quality of relationships characterized by commitment, feelings of closeness and trust, and self-disclosure.

Notice that the first definition focuses on intimacy as a characteristic of a person and the second as a characteristic of a relationship. One way to think about intimacy is that certain people have more of a capacity for intimacy or engage in more intimacy-promoting behaviors than others. But we can also think of some relationships as being more intimate than others.

How important is intimacy (as opposed to sex) in relationships?

In one study, college students were asked to respond to an open-ended question asking what they thought made a relationship one of intimacy (Roscoe et al., 1987). The qualities that emerged, with great agreement, were sharing, sexual interaction, trust in the partner, and openness. Notice that these qualities are quite similar to the ones listed in the definitions given above.

Figure 2   Intimacy occurs in a relationship when there is warmth and mutual self-disclosure.

©amelaxa/Shutterstock

Intimacy and Self-Disclosure

One of the key characteristics of intimacy, appearing in psychologists' and college students' definitions, is self-disclosure (Derlega, 1984). **Self-disclosure** involves telling your partner some personal things about yourself. It may range from telling your partner about something embarrassing that happened to you at work today, to disclosing a very meaningful event that happened between you and your parents 15 years ago.

Research consistently shows that self-disclosure leads to reciprocity (Berg & Derlega, 1987; Hendrick & Hendrick, 1992). In other words, if one member of the couple self-discloses, this act seems to prompt the other partner to self-disclose also. Self-disclosure by one member of the couple can essentially get the ball rolling.

Why does this occur? Psychologists have proposed a number of reasons (Hendrick & Hendrick, 1992). First, disclosure by our partner may make us like and trust that person more. Second, as social learning theorists would argue, simple modeling and imitation may occur. That is, one partner's self-disclosing serves as a model for the other partner. Norms of equity may also be involved (see the chapter "Sexuality and the Life Cycle: Adulthood" for a discussion of equity theory). After one partner has self-disclosed, the other person may follow suit in order to maintain a sense of balance or equity in the relationship.

Research shows that there is a positive correlation between the extent of a couple's self-disclosure and their satisfaction with the relationship. In other words, couples that practice more self-disclosure are more satisfied (Hendrick, 1981; Lambert et al., 2013). Self-disclosure of sexual likes and dislikes is associated with sexual satisfaction (Byers & Demmons, 1999; Purnine & Carey, 1997). Sexual self-disclosure leads to a better understanding by your partner of your likes and dislikes, and it can lead to a sexual script that is more rewarding and less costly. Greater rewards and less cost lead to greater sexual satisfaction (MacNeil & Byers, 2009).

Patterns of self-disclosure can predict whether a couple stays together or breaks up. Research in which couples are followed for periods ranging from 2 months to 4 years shows that the greater the self-disclosure, the greater the likelihood that the relationship will continue, and the less the self-disclosure, the greater the likelihood of breakup (Hendrick et al., 1988; Sprecher, 1987).

Self-disclosure promotes intimacy in a relationship and makes us feel close to the other person (Figure 2). It also indicates how important it is for the partner to be accepting in response to self-disclosure. If the acceptance is missing, we can feel betrayed or threatened, and we certainly will not feel on more intimate terms with the partner.

A study of naturally occurring interactions examined the relationships between self-disclosure, perceived partner disclosure, and the degree of intimacy experienced (Laurenceau et al., 1998). Young people recorded data about every interaction lasting more than 10 minutes, for 7 or 14 days. Data were analyzed for more than 4,000 two-person interactions recorded by 158 participants. Both self-disclosure and partner disclosure were associated with the participants' rating of the intimacy of the interaction. In addition, self-disclosure of emotion was more closely related to intimacy than was self-disclosure of facts.

Self-disclosure and intimacy, then, mutually build on each other. Self-disclosure promotes our feeling that the relationship is intimate, and when we feel that it is, we feel comfortable engaging in further self-disclosure. However, self-disclosure and intimacy don't necessarily increase consistently over time. In some relationships, the pattern may be that

Self-disclosure: Telling personal things about yourself.

an increase in intimacy is followed by a plateau or even a pulling back (Collins & Miller, 1994).

Self-disclosure of personal attitudes, experiences, and motives increases one's vulnerability. There is a risk that the partner will evaluate you negatively for disclosing some information or past behaviors. People who are anxious about how others evaluate them may engage in less self-disclosure or avoid it altogether. According to the ideas we have laid out, this should reduce intimacy. Other research finds that greater intimacy is associated with greater relationship and sexual satisfaction.

Measuring Intimacy

Psychologists have developed some scales for measuring intimacy, which can give us further insights. One such scale is the Personal Assessment of Intimacy in Relationships (PAIR) Inventory (Schaefer & Olson, 1981). It measures emotional intimacy in a relationship with items such as the following:

1. My partner listens to me when I need someone to talk to.
2. My partner really understands my hurts and joys.

Another scale measuring intimacy in a relationship includes items such as these (Miller & Lefcourt, 1982):

1. How often do you confide very personal information to him or her?
2. How often are you able to understand his or her feelings?
3. How often do you feel close to him or her?
4. How important is your relationship with him or her in your life?

If you are currently in a relationship, answer these questions for yourself and consider what the quality of the intimacy is in your relationship.

In summary, an intimate relationship is characterized by commitment, feelings of closeness and trust, and self-disclosure. We can promote intimacy in our relationships by engaging in self-disclosure (provided, of course, that we trust the person, but it is quite difficult to develop intimacy when there is a lack of trust) and being accepting of the other person's self-disclosures.

Love

In the following sections, we consider four theories of love: the triangular theory, the attachment theory, the love style theory, and the theory of passionate love. We then consider research on love from multiple perspectives.

Triangular Theory of Love

Robert Sternberg (1986) has formulated a triangular theory of the nature of love. According to his theory, love has three fundamental components: intimacy, passion, and decision or commitment.

Three Components of Love

Intimacy.   Intimacy is the emotional component of love. It includes our feelings of closeness or bondedness to the other person. As discussed in the previous section, the feeling of intimacy usually involves a sense of mutual understanding with the loved one; a sense of sharing one's self; intimate communication with the loved one, involving a sense of having the loved one hear and accept what is shared; and giving and receiving emotional support to and from the loved one.

Intimacy, of course, is present in many relationships besides romantic ones. Intimacy here is definitely *not* a euphemism for sex (as when someone asks, "Have you been intimate with him?"). The kind of emotional closeness involved in intimacy may be found between best friends and between parents and children, just as it is between lovers.

Passion.   Passion is the motivational component of love. It includes physical attraction and the drive for sexual expression. Physiological arousal is an important part of passion. Passion is the component that differentiates romantic love from other kinds of love, such as the love of best friends or the love between parents and children. Passion is generally the component of love that is faster to arouse, but in the course of a long-term relationship it is also the component that fades most quickly.

Intimacy and passion are often closely intertwined. In some cases passion comes first, when a couple experience an initial, powerful physical attraction to each other, and emotional intimacy may then follow. In other cases, people know each other only casually, but as emotional intimacy develops, passion follows. Of course, there are also cases where intimacy and passion are completely separate. For example, in cases of casual sex, passion is present but intimacy is not.

Decision or Commitment.   The third component is the cognitive component, decision or commitment. This component has two aspects. The short-term aspect is the decision that one loves the other person. The long-term aspect is the commitment to maintain that relationship. Commitment is what makes relationships last. Passion comes and goes. All relationships have their better times and their worse times, their ups and their downs. When the words of the traditional marriage service ask whether you promise to love your spouse "for better or for worse," the answer "I do" is the promise of commitment.

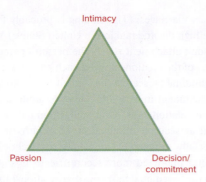

Figure 3   The triangle in Sternberg's triangular theory of love.

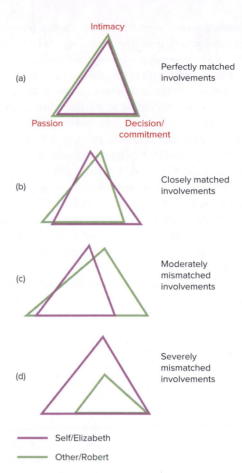

Figure 4   Partners can be well matched or mismatched, depending on whether their levels of intimacy, passion, and decision/commitment match.

The Triangular Theory

Sternberg (1986) calls his theory a *triangular theory of love.* Figure 3 shows Sternberg's love triangle.[1] The top point of the triangle is intimacy, the left point is passion, and the right point is decision or commitment.

This triangle metaphor allows us to show how the two people in a couple can be well matched or mismatched in the love they feel toward each other. In Figure 4(a), Elizabeth feels as much intimacy toward Robert as he does toward her, they both feel equal levels of passion, and they both have the same level of commitment. According to the theory, that is a perfect match. Figure 4(b) shows a situation in which the couple are slightly but not seriously mismatched, and Figure 4(c) shows a moderate mismatch. Figure 4(d) shows a situation in which there is a severe mismatch. Both partners are equally committed, but Elizabeth feels significantly more intimacy and passion than Robert.

Sternberg's research indicates that when there is a good match between the two partners' love, as shown in Figure 4(a) or (b), the partners tend to feel satisfaction with the relationship. When there is a mismatch in the triangles, they feel dissatisfied with the relationship.

Thinking about practical applications of the theory, if a relationship seems to be in trouble, it may be because there is a mismatch of the triangles. We could analyze the love in the relationship in terms of the three components (intimacy, passion, and commitment) to see where the partners are mismatched. It could be that they are well matched for passion, but that one feels and wants more intimacy or commitment than the other does.

Love in Action

Sternberg also argues that each of the three components of love must be translated into action. The intimacy component is expressed in actions such as communicating personal feelings and information (self-disclosure), offering emotional (and perhaps financial) support, and expressing empathy for the other. The passion component is expressed in actions such as kissing, touching, and making love. The decision or commitment component is demonstrated by actions such as saying "I love you," getting married, and sticking with a relationship through times when it isn't particularly convenient.

Evidence for Sternberg's Triangular Theory of Love

What kind of support is there for Sternberg's theory? Sternberg has developed a questionnaire, the Sternberg Triangular Love Scale (STLS), to measure the three components in his theory. Several studies have been done on the characteristics of the scale itself (e.g., Sternberg, 1987, 1997; Whitley, 1993). The scale provides good measures of the components, especially of passion and commitment. Scores for the same relationship are stable for up to 2 months.

---

[1]This terminology should not be confused with the popular use of the term *love triangle,* which refers to a situation in which three people are involved in love, but the love is not reciprocated and so things don't work out quite right. For example, A loves B, B loves C, and C loves A, but A doesn't love C and B doesn't love A. Alas.

Sternberg makes several predictions about how scores ought to change over time. One study recruited 204 adults, ages 18 to 68; 65 percent were married (Acker & Davis, 1992). The average length of the relationship was 9.5 years. As predicted, commitment scores increased as relationships progressed from dating to marriage. Sternberg also expects intimacy to decrease over time as familiarity with the partner increases, and sure enough, behavioral intimacy (sharing inner feelings, trying to understand the partner) decreased as predicted. Similar results were reported in a study of people who were casually dating, exclusively dating, engaged, or married (Lemieux & Hale, 2002).

A study of a sample of German adults assessed the relationship between the three components and sexual activity and satisfaction (Grau & Kimpf, 1993). The theory predicts that the amount of passion should be most closely related to sexual activity, but the results indicated that intimacy was most closely related to sexual behavior and sexual satisfaction.

Attachment Theory of Love

In the chapter "Sexuality and the Life Cycle: Childhood and Adolescence," we discussed the earliest attachment that humans experience, that between infant and parent. One hypothesis is that the quality of this early attachment—whether secure and pleasant or insecure and unpleasant—profoundly affects us for the rest of our lives, and particularly affects our capacity to form loving attachments to others when we are adults.

The *attachment theory of love* is based on these ideas (Hazan & Shaver, 1987; Karantzas et al., 2014; Simpson, 1990). According to the attachment theory, adults are characterized, in their romantic relationships, by one of three styles. *Secure lovers* are people who find it easy to get close to others and are comfortable having others feel close to them. Mutual dependency in a relationship (depending on the partner and having the partner depend on you) feels right to them. Secure lovers do not fear abandonment.

In contrast, *fearful or avoidant lovers* are uncomfortable feeling close to another person or having that person feel close to them. It is difficult for them to trust or depend on a partner.

The third style, *preoccupied or anxious-ambivalent lovers,* want desperately to get close to a partner but often find the partner does not reciprocate the feeling, perhaps because anxious-ambivalent lovers scare away others. They are insecure in the relationship, worrying that the partner does not really love them.

Research shows that about 53 percent of adults are secure, 26 percent are avoidant, and 20 percent are anxious-ambivalent (Hazan & Shaver, 1987). This research also shows that separation from a parent in childhood—perhaps because of divorce or death—is not related to adult attachment styles. In other words, children of divorced parents are no more or less likely to be secure lovers than are children from intact marriages. (This finding is probably fortunate, given the high divorce rate in the United States.) What did predict adult attachment style? The person's perception of the *quality* of the relationship with each parent was key.

Longitudinal research has identified pathways by which attachment in early life relates to adult attachment styles and relationships. One study found that children identified as securely attached at 12 months were rated more socially competent in elementary school. Social competence predicted more secure friendships at age 16, which in turn predicted more positive relationships at ages 20 to 23 (as reported by self and partner) (Simpson et al., 2007). Research also shows that the relationship problems of people with insecure attachments grow worse the longer the relationship lasts (Hadden et al., 2014). Moreover, compared with people who have a secure attachment style, those with anxious or avoidant attachment styles have less satisfying sexual relationships and are more likely to have a sexual dysfunction (Stefanu & McCabe, 2012).

This research has important implications. First, it helps us understand that adults bring to any particular romantic relationship their own personal history of love and attachment. The forces of that personal history can be strong, and one good and loving partner may not be able to change an avoidant lover into a secure lover. Second, it helps us understand that conflict in some relationships may be caused by a mismatch of attachment styles. A secure lover, who wants a close, intimate relationship, is likely to feel frustrated and dissatisfied with an avoidant lover, who is uncomfortable with feeling close. Finally, this theory provides some explanation for jealousy, which is most common among anxious-ambivalent lovers (although present among the others) because of their early experience of feeling anxious about their attachment to their parents.

A study of heterosexual couples in serious dating relationships looked at the dynamics of adult attachment styles (Kirkpatrick & Davis, 1994). In over half the couples, both partners had a secure attachment style. About 10 percent consisted of one person with a secure style and one with an avoidant style, and 10 percent consisted of a secure-anxious pairing. As we might expect, there was not a single anxious-anxious or avoidant-avoidant couple. Such couples would be very incompatible.

How does attachment style have an effect on adult romantic relationships? Research shows that those with anxious and avoidant styles have less trust in their partner, which leads to less intimacy in the relationship, which is associated with less relationship satisfaction (Karantzas et al., 2014). In addition, those with anxious or avoidant styles provide less support for their partners, and conflict becomes destructive (see the section Fighting Fair later in this chapter).

On the basis of his research, sociologist John Alan Lee (1977, 1988) proposed three basic types of love, and he uses Greek and Latin words to distinguish them: eros, storge, and ludus.

Love Styles

Eros, according to this theory, is a powerful attraction to the physical appearance of the loved person. The erotic lover often has an ideal partner in mind, and it may be "love at first sight" when they meet that person. Erotic lovers cultivate a variety of sexual techniques so that they will continually delight in each other's bodies.

Ludus refers to playful love. For ludic lovers, love is a pleasant pastime; however, they refuse to get too involved, to become dependent on the beloved, or to let the beloved become too attached to them. Because of their low commitment, ludic lovers may have more than one lover at a time. They also show little interest in improving sexual techniques, finding it easier to get a new partner than to work out problems in an old relationship.

Storge in this theory is "love without fever, tumult, or folly, a peaceful and enchanting affection." It is the kind of love that sneaks up unnoticed in a relationship; storgic lovers remember no special point in the relationship when they "fell" in love. Because the relationship develops gradually, sex typically does not occur for some time. Storge also tends to be a very stable love that can last through crises in the relationship and even through long separations.

Lee sees these three basic types of love as being analogous to the three primary colors: red, yellow, and blue. Just as new colors are produced by combining primary colors—orange is a mixture of red and yellow, for example—so other types of love result from blendings of the three basic types. For example, in *mania,* which may be viewed as a combination of eros and ludus, love is an obsession (this use of the term "mania" has nothing to do with its use as a diagnosis in psychology and psychiatry). In mania, the person is consumed with thoughts of the beloved and may feel furious jealousy. The manic lover alternates between feelings of ecstasy and despair. Manic lovers have the passion of eros but play the games of ludus. This is the sort of stuff that makes for great novels and movies.

Pragma is a kind of practical love; it combines the compatibility of storge with the game playing of ludus. The pragmatic lover consciously tries to find a lover who has a certain set of characteristics that are thought to be desirable. Once a good match is found, pragmatic love may grow over the years. It is the kind of love that existed for centuries when marriages were arranged by people other than the lovers themselves, and these arrangements still exist in some cultures around the world.

Agape, the classic Christian view of love, is altruistic, undemanding, never jealous, and always kind and patient. It represents a combination of storge and eros.

Research shows that love styles are associated with relationship satisfaction (Vedes et al., 2016). Specifically, eros and agape love styles are associated with greater relationship satisfaction, whereas ludus is associated with lower relationship satisfaction. This pattern has been found across multiple cultures (Rohmann et al., 2016).

What is the practical significance of these ideas? According to Lee, two lovers of the same type are most compatible. Lee believes that many conflicts arise when two different types of lovers are paired with each other. People often think the quantity of love is the problem—the old complaint is "you don't love me enough"—but instead there may be a mismatch of the types of lovers. For example, suppose we have a ludic man and a storgic woman. He feels that she is trying to trap him into a commitment when he just wants to have fun. She wants to develop a slow, lasting relationship and accuses him of playing games just to get sex. The result is conflict, and it may be difficult to identify the source of the conflict—unless you know about love styles!

Passionate and Companionate Love

Another perspective on love differentiates between two kinds of love: passionate love and companionate love (Berscheid & Hatfield, 1978). **Passionate love** is a state of intense longing for union with the other person and of intense physiological arousal. It has three components: cognitive, emotional, and behavioral (Hatfield & Sprecher, 1986). The cognitive component includes preoccupation with the loved one and idealization of the person or of the relationship. The emotional component includes physiological arousal, sexual attraction, and desire for union. Behavioral elements include taking care of the other and maintaining physical closeness. Passionate love can be overwhelming, obsessive, all-consuming.

By contrast, **companionate love** is a feeling of deep attachment and commitment to a person with whom one has an intimate relationship (Hatfield & Rapson, 1993b). Passionate love is hot, and companionate love is warm.

Passionate love is often the first stage of a romantic relationship. Two people meet, fall wildly in love, and make a commitment to each other. But as the relationship progresses, a gradual shift to companionate love takes place. The transformation tends to occur when the relationship is between 6 and 30 months old (Hatfield & Walster, 1978).

Some may find this perspective a rather pessimistic commentary on romantic love. But it may describe a good way for a relationship to develop. Passionate love may be necessary to hold a relationship together in the early

Eros: According to love styles theory, a powerful physical attraction to the loved person.

Ludus: According to love styles theory, a playful type of love.

Storge: In love styles theory, a very stable, reliable type of love.

Passionate love: A state of intense longing for union with the other person and of intense physiological arousal.

Companionate love: A feeling of deep attachment and commitment to a person with whom one has an intimate relationship.

Milestones in Sex Research

Jealousy

Jealousy—the green-eyed monster—is an unpleasant emotion often associated with romantic and sexual relationships. Intense cases of jealousy may result in violence, including partner abuse, assault, and homicide. As a result, it has been the focus of considerable scholarly work. Several perspectives contribute to our understanding of this emotion.

Jealousy is a cognitive, emotional, and behavioral response to a threat to an interpersonal relationship (Guerrero et al., 2004). The cognitive appraisal perspective suggests that emotions are the result of a cognitive appraisal of a stimulus. In this view, jealousy occurs when an individual *interprets* some stimulus as representing a threat to a valued relationship (Figure 5). In reality, there may or may not be a threat to the relationship. A variety of behaviors by the partner may be interpreted as a threat. In one study, individuals in dating relationships said that just having their partner spend time with another person was one of the top three acts of betrayal (Roscoe et al., 1988). In the 21st century, interaction with someone via the Internet can elicit a jealous reaction from the partner. Heterosexual women, but not lesbians, are more likely to react with jealousy to a partner's online activities (Dijkstra et al., 2013). Also, behavior or remarks by third parties may elicit jealousy, or circumstances such as coming home late may arouse suspicion.

Why do people get jealous?

Two situations can activate jealousy (White & Mullen, 1989). One is a situation in which there is a threat to our self-esteem. For example, in a good relationship our romantic partner helps us feel good about ourselves—makes us feel attractive or fun to be with, for example. If a rival appears and our partner shows interest, we may think things like "He finds her more attractive than me" or "She finds him more fun to be with than me." We then feel less attractive or less fun to be with. In other words, our self-esteem is threatened. Two experiments report evidence that supports the hypothesis that it is threats to the self that cause jealousy (DeSteno et al., 2006).

The second situation that activates jealousy is a threat to the relationship. If a rival appears on the scene, we may fear that our partner will separate from us and form a new relationship with the rival. Jealousy is activated because of our negative thoughts and feelings about the loss of a relationship that has been good for us and the loss of all the pleasant things that go along with that relationship, such as companionship and sex.

We go through several stages in the jealousy response, sometimes very quickly (White & Mullen, 1989). The first is cognitive, in which we make an initial appraisal of the situation and find that there is a threat to our self-esteem or to the relationship. Next, we experience an emotional reaction, which has two phases. The first is a rapid stress response, the *jealous flash*. To use the terminology of the two-component theory of love discussed in this chapter, this stress response is the physiological component of the jealous emotion. The second phase of emotional response occurs as we reappraise the situation and decide how to cope with it. In the reappraisal stage, we may shift from seeing the situation as a threat to seeing it as a challenge, for example. The intense initial emotions quiet down and may be replaced by feelings of moodiness.

Attempts to cope with jealousy lead to a variety of behaviors. Some of these behaviors are constructive, such as effective communication with the partner (see the section on Communication later in this chapter for a discussion of techniques of effective communicators). Such communication may lead to an evaluation of the relationship and attempts to change some of the problematic aspects of it. If the problems seem sufficiently serious, a couple may seek advice from a mediator or therapist.

Other behavioral responses to jealousy are destructive. The threat to a person's self-esteem may lead to depression, substance abuse, or suicide. Aggression may be directed at the partner, the third person, or both, and may result in physical or sexual abuse or even murder.

There are two types of jealousy: emotional and sexual. *Emotional jealousy* occurs when one person believes or knows that the partner is emotionally attached to or in love with another. *Sexual jealousy* occurs when the person believes or knows that the partner wants to engage in or has actually engaged in sexual behavior with another. The two may occur together or separately.

The evolutionary perspective has hypothesized that there is a gender difference in jealousy. According to this view, men are more upset by a (heterosexual) partner's sexual infidelity, whereas women are more upset by a (heterosexual) partner's emotional infidelity. This hypothesis is based on the argument that the male adaptive problem (or concern) in reproduction is uncertainty

Figure 5 One situation that activates jealousy is a perceived threat to the relationship.

©Digital Vision/Getty Images

about paternity. For this reason, the male, motivated to pass on his genes to the next generation, wants to be sure the children he cares for are his own, so he is highly vigilant about female sexual fidelity. The female adaptive

stages, while conflicts are being resolved. But past that point, most of us find that what we really need is a friend—someone who shares our interests, who is happy when we succeed, and who sympathizes when we fail—and that is just what we get with companionate love.

Sexual desire and romantic love may often be independent processes (Diamond, 2003). Sexual desire is a motivational state leading to a search for opportunities for sexual activity. It motivates proximity seeking and contact and leads to feelings of passion (passionate love). Romantic love is a motivational state leading to attachment and commitment. It promotes self-disclosure and intimacy leading to long-term relationships (companionate love).

problem is to obtain enough resources to care for herself and her children, so she is highly vigilant about male romantic fidelity. If her partner fell in love with someone else, he might leave her and she would lose the resources he provides.

Several studies have reported results that support this hypothesis, including a study reporting cross-cultural support using data from the United States, Germany, and the Netherlands (Buunk et al., 1996). However, all of the results supporting the hypothesis are based on a single question that forces men and women to say which would upset them more, emotional or sexual infidelity. Studies asking men and women how upset they would be by each separately report just small or insignificant differences. A careful review of five types of evidence finds little support for this hypothesis (Harris, 2003). A study of both heterosexual and homosexual adults found that men and women were more concerned about emotional infidelity of a partner (Harris, 2002). However, a study that included victims of cheating by a heterosexual partner found that both men and women were more likely to report being more upset by sexual infidelity (Berman & Frazier, 2005).

Research suggests that a person's attachment style may be an important influence on how that person responds to jealousy (Sharpstein & Kirkpatrick, 1997). Undergraduates were asked how they had reacted in the past to jealousy. Those with a secure attachment style reported that they had expressed their anger to the partner and maintained the relationship. Those with an anxious style reported the most intense anger, but they were most likely to say they did not express their anger. People with an avoidant style were more likely to direct their anger toward the third person.

The Biology of Love

What causes the complex phenomena of passionate and companionate love? Where does the rush of passionate love come from? Research suggests that bodily chemistry and neural activity in the brain are the causes (see also the chapter "Sexual Arousal"). Studies of the prairie vole, a small rodent, have identified specific patterns of neurochemical activity that are associated with mating and pair-bonding (preference for a specific partner) (Curtis & Wang, 2003). In female prairie voles, the neurotransmitter dopamine is released during mating, and in both male and female voles, the dopamine appears to enhance the likelihood of pair-bonding. Dopamine is associated with euphoria and craving. A surge of dopamine in the human body can produce increased energy, focused attention, and reduced need for food and sleep, and these are common experiences of people in the passionate stage of love.

The frequent presence of the loved one, produced initially by passionate love, triggers the production of two hormones, prolactin and oxytocin. The levels of prolactin rise following orgasm in humans and are also related to pair-bonding in voles.

Oxytocin may contribute to long-term relationships. It has been shown to play an important role in pair-bonding in some animals (McEwen, 1997). In humans it is stimulated by touch, including sexual touching and orgasm, and it produces feelings of pleasure and satisfaction. Research indicates that levels of interpersonal trust correlate positively with oxytocin as well (Zak et al., 2003). In an experiment, researchers administered either oxytocin or a placebo through the nose to young men. The men who received the oxytocin displayed increased trust in others, and trust is a crucial basis for relationships (Kosfeld et al., 2005).

Other research with humans involves the use of magnetic resonance imaging (MRI) to study brain activity related to love. Researchers recruited young men and women who were in love (Bartels & Zeki, 2004). While their brain activity was being measured, each participant was shown photos of the romantic partner and of a close friend. The picture of the partner activated specific areas of the brain. Which ones? The areas rich in dopamine pathways were excited, lending weight to the findings that suggest dopamine is important in the experience of love.

Visual stimuli associated with the lover stimulate subcortical activity in the ventral tegmental area, caudate nucleus, and putamen (Cacioppo et al., 2012b). This area is rich in dopamine pathways. More generally, these are the areas associated with motivation, reward, and euphoria. Activity also occurs in areas associated with complex cognitive processing, including segments of the gyrus and the occipital cortex, such as memory and self-representation.

Little work has been done with humans to identify neural correlates of companionate love. Animal research suggests that it is associated with oxytocin and vasopressin, and neural activity in the nucleus accumbens and ventral pallidum (Cacioppo et al., 2012b).

Is there a difference between passionate love and sexual desire in the brain? (Is love just sex?) Both passionate love and sexual desire activate the same reward-related and cortical areas in the brain. However, love is associated with *reduced* activity in the hypothalamus, amygdala, and somatosensory cortex, compared to sexual desire. These differences are consistent with the view that sexual desire is a motivation with a specific goal, whereas love is an abstract, behaviorally complex phenomenon not dependent on the physical presence of the object (Cacioppo et al., 2012a). The answer? Love is more than sex (neurally speaking).

Measuring Love

We introduced the concept of *passionate love* earlier. Hatfield and Sprecher (1986) developed a self-report measure of this concept. For their Passionate Love Scale, they wrote statements intended to measure the cognitive, emotional, and behavioral components of passionate love. The respondent rates each statement on a scale from 1 (not true at all) to 9 (definitely true of me).

For example, if you feel that you are in love with someone, think about whether you would agree with each of the following statements, keeping that person in mind.

1. *Cognitive component:*
   Sometimes I feel I can't control my thoughts; they are obsessively on _____.
   For me, _____ is the perfect romantic partner.

2. *Emotional component:*
   I possess a powerful attraction for _____.
   I will love _____ forever.

3. *Behavioral component:*
   I eagerly look for signs indicating _____'s desire for me.
   I feel happy when I am doing things to make _____ happy.

Hatfield and Sprecher administered their questionnaire to students at the University of Wisconsin who were in relationships ranging from casually dating to engaged and living together. The results indicated that scores on the Passionate Love Scale (PLS) were correlated positively with other measures of love and with measures of commitment to and satisfaction with the relationship. These correlations give evidence that the PLS is *valid*—in other words, that it measures what it is supposed to measure. The findings confirm that the scale measures passion. For example, students who got high scores on the PLS reported a stronger desire to be with, held by, and kissed by the partner, and said that they were sexually excited just thinking about their partner. Finally, the passionate love scores increased as the nature of the relationship moved from dating to dating exclusively. Hatfield and Sprecher's research is a good example of how to study an important but complex topic—such as love—scientifically.

Two-Component Theory of Love

Social psychologists Ellen Berscheid and Elaine Walster (1974) proposed a **two-component theory of love.**

Two-component theory of love: The theory that two conditions must exist simultaneously for passionate love to occur: physiological arousal and attaching a cognitive label ("love") to the feeling.

According to their theory, passionate love occurs when two conditions exist simultaneously: (1) the person is in a state of intense *physiological arousal,* and (2) the situation is such that the person applies a particular *label*—"love"—to the sensations being experienced. Their theory is derived from an important theory developed by Stanley Schachter (1964).

Suppose that your heart is pounding, your palms are sweating, and your body is tense. What emotion are you experiencing? Is it love—has reading about passionate love led to obsessive thoughts of another person? Is it fear—are you frantically reading this text because you have an exam tomorrow morning? Is it sexual arousal—are you thinking about having sex later tonight?

It could be any of these, or even anger or embarrassment. A wide variety of emotions are accompanied by the same physiological states: increased blood pressure, a higher heart rate, increased muscular tension, and sweating palms. What differentiates these emotions? The key is the way we interpret or label what we are experiencing.

Schachter's (1964) two-component theory of emotion says just this: An emotion consists of a physiological arousal state plus the label the person assigns to it (for a critical evaluation of this theory, see Reisenzein, 1983). Berscheid and Walster have applied this to the emotion of "love." They suggest that we feel passionate love when we are physiologically aroused and when conditions are such that we identify what we are feeling as love.

Several experiments provide evidence for Berscheid and Walster's two-component theory of love. In one study, male research participants exercised vigorously by running in place, and this activity produced the physiological arousal response of pounding heart and sweaty palms (White et al., 1981). Afterward they rated their liking for an attractive woman, who was a confederate of the experimenters. Men in the running group said they liked the woman significantly more than did men who were in a control condition and had not exercised.

This result is consistent with Berscheid and Walster's theory. The effect is called the **misattribution of arousal.** In other words, in a situation like this one, the men misattribute their arousal—which is due to exercise—to their liking for the attractive woman (Figure 6). An analysis of 33 experiments found that arousal affects attraction even when the source of the arousal is unambiguous (Foster et al., 1998).

Another study suggests that even fear can increase a man's attraction to a woman (Dutton & Aron, 1974; see also Brehm et al., cited in Berscheid & Walster, 1974). An attractive female interviewer approached male passersby either on a fear-arousing suspension bridge or on a non-fear-arousing bridge. The fear-arousing bridge was constructed of boards, attached to cables, and had a tendency to tilt, sway, and wobble. The handrails were low, and there was a 230-foot drop to rocks and shallow rapids

Figure 6   The misattribution of arousal. If people are physically aroused (e.g., by jogging), they may misattribute this arousal to love or sexual attraction, provided the situation suggests such an interpretation (e.g., an attractive person in close proximity).

©Bill Aron/PhotoEdit

below. The control bridge was made of solid cedar. It was firm, and there was only a 10-foot drop to a shallow rivulet below. The interviewer asked subjects to fill out questionnaires that included projective test items. These items were then scored for sexual imagery.

There was more sexual imagery in the questionnaires filled out by the men in the suspension-bridge group, and these men made more attempts to contact the attractive interviewer after the experiment than the men on the control bridge. Intuitively, this result might seem to be peculiar: that men who are in a state of fear are more attracted to a woman than men who are relaxed. But in terms of the Berscheid and Walster two-component theory, it makes perfect sense. The fearful men were physiologically aroused, and the men in the control group were not. And according to this theory, arousal is an important component of love or attraction.[2]

Now, of course, if the men (most of them heterosexuals) had been approached by an elderly man or a child, their responses would probably have been different. In fact, when the interviewer in the experiment was male, the effects discussed above did not occur. Society tells us what the appropriate objects of our love, attraction, or liking are.

> **Misattribution of arousal:** When a person in a state of physiological arousal (e.g., from exercising or being in a frightening situation) attributes these feelings to love or attraction to the person present.

[2]According to the terminology of the chapter "Sex Research," note that the Dutton and Aron study is an example of *experimental* research.

In other words, we know for what kinds of people it is appropriate to have feelings of love or liking. For these men, feelings toward an attractive woman could reasonably be labeled "love" or "attraction." Such labels would probably not be attached to feelings for an elderly man.

The physical arousal that is important for love need not always be produced by unpleasant or frightening situations. Pleasant stimuli, such as sexual arousal or praise from the other person, may produce arousal and feelings of love. Indeed, Berscheid and Walster's theory does an excellent job of explaining why we seem to have such a strong tendency to associate love and sex. Sexual arousal is one method of producing a state of physiological arousal, and it is one that our culture has taught us to label as "love." Accordingly, both components necessary to feel love are present: arousal and a label. On the other hand, this phenomenon may lead us to confuse love with lust, an all-too-common error.

Cross-Cultural Research

In the past three decades, researchers have studied people from various ethnic or cultural groups to see whether attraction, intimacy, and love are experienced in the same way outside the United States. Three topics that have been studied are the impact of culture on how people view love, on whom people fall in love with, and on the importance of love in decisions to marry.

Cultural Values and the Meaning of Love

Cross-cultural psychologists have identified two dimensions on which cultures vary (Hatfield & Rapson, 1993a). The first is individualism–collectivism. *Individualistic cultures,* like those of the United States, Canada, and the western European countries, tend to emphasize individual goals over group and societal goals and interests. *Collectivist cultures,* like those of China, Africa, and the east Asian countries, emphasize group and collective goals over personal ones.

Several specific traits have been identified that differentiate these two types of societies (Triandis et al., 1990). In individualistic cultures, behavior is regulated by individual attitudes and cost–benefit considerations, and emotional detachment from the group is accepted. In collectivist cultures, the self is defined by its group membership, behavior is regulated by group norms, and attachment to and harmony within the group are valued.

The two types of cultures have different conceptions of love. American society, for example, emphasizes passionate love as the basis for marriage (Dion & Dion, 1993b). Individuals select mates on the basis of such characteristics as physical attractiveness, similarity (compatibility), and wealth or resources. We look for intimacy in the relationship with our mate. In Chinese society, by contrast, marriages are arranged, and the primary criterion is that

Figure 7 Whether a culture is individualistic or collectivist determines its views on love and marriage. In the United States, an individualistic culture, individuals choose each other and marry for love. In India, a collectivist culture, marriages are traditionally arranged by family members. There is a website, www.shaadi.com, available for parents seeking suitable mates for their offspring.

©Erica Simone Leeds

the two families be of similar status. The person finds intimacy in relationships with other family members.

The second dimension on which cultures differ is independence–interdependence. Many Western cultures view each person as independent and value individuality and uniqueness. Many other cultures view the person as interdependent with those around them. The self is defined in relation to others. Americans value standing up for one's beliefs. The people of India value conformity and harmony within the group.

In a study of university students in Toronto representing four ethnocultural groups, students from Asian backgrounds were more likely to view love as companionate, as friendship, in contrast to those from English and Irish backgrounds (Dion & Dion, 1993a). This tendency is consistent with the collectivist orientation of Asian cultures (Figure 7).

In another study, Mexican American students were found to be similar to American students of European background in the emphasis they placed on trust and communication/sharing as components of romantic love, but they placed greater emphasis on mutual respect (Castaneda, 1993). One student wrote, "[In a love relationship] we must respect each other's feelings as we would expect them to show us respect" (p. 265). Such respect allows each partner to express his or her needs to the other.

Love and Marriage

Individualistic cultures place a high value on romantic love, whereas collectivist cultures emphasize the group.

Table 2 "Would You Marry Someone You Didn't Love?"

Cultural Group	Responses (Percent)		
	Yes	Undecided	No
Australia	5%	15%	80%
Brazil	4	10	86
England	7	9	84
Hong Kong	6	17	78
India	49	27	24
Japan	2	36	62
Mexico	10	9	81
Pakistan	50	10	39
Philippines	11	25	64
Thailand	19	48	34
United States	4	11	86

Source: Levine et al. (1995).

The importance of romantic love is highlighted by responses to the question "If a man (woman) had all the other qualities you desired, would you marry this person if you were not in love with him (her)?" Over time, increasing percentages of American men and women answer no.

Researchers asked this question of men and women in 11 different cultures (Levine et al., 1995). We would predict that members of individualistic cultures would answer no, whereas those in collectivist cultures would answer yes. The results are displayed in Table 2. Note that, as predicted, many Indians and Pakistanis would marry even though they didn't love the person. In the individualistic cultures of Australia, England, and the United States, few would marry someone they did not love.

The Pattern of the Cross-Cultural Findings

When we look at the findings of the cross-cultural research on love, attraction, and marriage, the pattern that emerges is one of *cross-cultural similarities and cross-cultural differences,* a theme we introduced in the chapter "Sexuality in Perspective." In other words, some phenomena are similar across cultures, for example, valuing intelligence, kindness, and understanding in a mate. Other phenomena differ substantially across cultures, for example, whether love is a prerequisite for marriage.

Communication

Consider the following situation:

Josh and Samantha have been married for about three years. Samantha had had intercourse with only one other person before Josh, and she had never masturbated. Since

they have been married, she has had orgasms only twice during intercourse, despite the fact that they make love three or four times per week. She has been reading some magazine articles about female sexuality and is beginning to think that she should be experiencing more sexual satisfaction. As far as she knows, Josh is unaware that there is any problem. Samantha feels lonely and a bit sad.

What should Samantha do? She needs to communicate with Josh. They apparently have not communicated much about sex in the last three years, and they need to begin. In the following sections, we discuss the relationship between sex, communication, and relationships and provide some suggestions on how to communicate effectively.

Communication and Relationships

A good deal of research has looked at differences in communication patterns between nondistressed (happy) married couples and distressed (unhappy, seeking marital counseling) married couples. This research shows, in general, that distressed couples tend to have communication deficits (Gottman, 1994; Markman & Floyd, 1980; Noller, 1984). Research also shows that couples seeking therapy for sex problems have poor communication patterns compared with nondistressed couples (Zimmer, 1983).

An elegant longitudinal study provides evidence that unrewarding, ineffective communication precedes and predicts later relationship problems (Markman et al., 2010). Couples who were planning to marry were recruited for the research. Each person completed a baseline questionnaire, including a rating of the negativity (e.g., she or he criticizes, belittles me) of their communication. Each couple participated in a videotaped interaction, discussing the top problem in their relationship. Trained coders rated each person's communication during the discussion on 10 dimensions, including positive (e.g., problem solving skills, support, validation) and negative (e.g., denial, dominance, withdrawal). Some 200 of the couples married and were assessed near their fifth anniversary. Couples who divorced prior to the fifth year had, at baseline, rated their communication as being significantly more negative. Among those who remained married, both observed and self-reported negative communication at baseline predicted lower marital adjustment 5 years later.

On the basis of this notion that communication deficits cause relationship problems, marriage counselors and therapists often work on teaching couples communication skills.

Other research suggests that it is not just lack of communication skills but also negative communication that can create problems. What are the characteristics of negative, destructive communication? John Gottman (1994) used audiotape, videotape, and monitoring of physiological arousal to answer this question. He identified

Figure 8 Effective communication involves picking the right time and place for an open and honest discussion.

©Lumina Images/Getty Images

four destructive patterns of interaction: criticism, contempt, defensiveness, and withdrawal. *Criticism* refers to attacking a partner's personality or character: "You are so selfish; you never think of anyone else." *Contempt* is intentionally insulting or verbally abusing the other person: "How did I get hooked up with such a loser?" *Defensiveness* refers to denying responsibility, making excuses, replying with a complaint of one's own, and making other self-protective responses instead of addressing the problem. *Withdrawal* involves such actions as responding to the partner's complaint with silence, turning on the TV, or walking out of the room in anger. You can probably see that these types of communication are likely to lead to an escalation of the hostility rather than a solution to the problem.

Positive communication is important in developing and maintaining intimate relationships. Let's look at some of the skills involved in positive communication.

Techniques of Good Communication

Back to Samantha and Josh. One of the first things to do in a situation like Samantha's is to decide to talk to your partner, admitting that there is a problem. Then the issue is to resolve to communicate and, particularly, to be an *effective* communicator. Suppose Samantha begins by saying,

You're not giving me any orgasms when we have sex. (Message 1)

Josh gets angry and walks away. Samantha meant to communicate

> **Intent:** What the speaker means.
> **Impact:** What someone else understands the speaker to mean.
> **Effective communicator:** A communicator whose impact matches their intent.

that she wasn't having any orgasms, but Josh thought she meant that he was a lousy lover.

It is important to recognize the distinction between intent and impact in communicating (Gottman et al., 1976; Purnine & Carey, 1997). **Intent** is what you mean. **Impact** is what the other person thinks you mean. A good communicator is one whose impact matches their intent. Samantha wasn't an **effective communicator** in this example because the impact on Josh was considerably different from her intent.

Many people value spontaneity in sex, and this attitude may extend to communicating about sex. It is best to recognize that to be an effective communicator you may need to plan your strategy. It often takes some thinking to figure out how to make sure your impact will match your intent (Figure 8). Planning also allows you to make sure that the timing is good—that you are not speaking out of anger, or that your partner is not tired or preoccupied with other things.

In the last few decades public communication about sex has become relatively open, but private communication remains difficult (Crawford et al., 1994). This doesn't mean that Samantha can't communicate. But she shouldn't feel guilty or stupid if it is difficult for her. And she will be better off if she uses some specific communication skills and has some belief that they will work. In the following sections, we suggest some skills that are useful in being an effective communicator and how to apply these to sexual relationships.

Good Messages

Every couple has problems. The best way to voice them is to complain rather than to criticize (Gottman, 1994).

Complaining involves the use of **"I" language.** In other words, speak for yourself, not your partner. By doing this, you focus on what you know best—your own thoughts and feelings. "I" language is less likely to make your partner defensive. If Samantha were to use this technique, she might say,

> I feel a bit unhappy because I don't have orgasms very often when we make love. (Message 2)

Notice that she focuses specifically on herself. There is less cause for Josh to get angry than there was in message 1.

One of the best things about "I" language is that it avoids mind reading (Gottman et al., 1976). Suppose Samantha says,

> I know you think women aren't much interested in sex, but I really wish I had more orgasms. (Message 3)

She is engaging in **mind reading.** In other words, she is making certain assumptions about what Josh is thinking. She assumes that Josh believes women aren't interested in sex or having orgasms. Research shows that mind reading is more common among distressed couples than among nondistressed couples (Gottman et al., 1977). Worse, Samantha doesn't *check out* her assumptions with Josh. The problem is that she may be wrong, and Josh may not think that at all. "I" language helps Samantha avoid mind reading by focusing on herself and what she feels rather than on what Josh is doing or failing to do. Another important way to avoid mind reading is by giving and receiving feedback, a technique we discuss in a later section.

Documenting is another important component of giving good messages (Brenton, 1972). In documenting, you give specific examples of the issue. Documenting is not quite so relevant in Samantha's case, because she is talking about a general problem, but even here, specific examples can be helpful. Once Samantha has broached the subject, she might say,

> Last night when we made love, I enjoyed it and felt very aroused, but then I didn't have an orgasm, and I felt disappointed. (Message 4)

Now she has gotten her general complaint down to a specific situation that Josh can remember.

Suppose further that Samantha has some idea of what Josh would need to do to bring her to orgasm: he would have to do more hand stimulation of her clitoris. Then she might do specific documenting, as follows:

> Last night when we made love, I enjoyed it, but I didn't have an orgasm, and then I felt disappointed. I think what I needed was for you to stimulate my clitoris with your hand a bit more. You did it for a while, but it seemed so brief. I think if you had kept doing it for two or three minutes more, I would have had an orgasm. (Message 5)

Now she has not only documented to Josh exactly what the problem was, but she has given a specific

suggestion about what could have been done about it, and therefore what could be done in the future. A study of heterosexual dating couples found that open communication about sex ("I tell my partner when I am especially sexually satisfied") was positively associated with satisfaction with sex and with the relationship (Montesi et al., 2010).

Another technique in giving good messages is to offer *limited choices* (Langer & Dweck, 1973). Suppose Samantha begins by saying,

> I've been having trouble with orgasms. Could we discuss it? (Message 6)

The trouble with this approach is that a "no" from Josh is not really an acceptable answer to her because she definitely wants to discuss the problem. Yet she set up the question so that he could answer by saying no. To use the technique of limited choices she might say,

> I've been having trouble with orgasms when we make love. Would you like to discuss it now, or would you rather wait until tomorrow night? (Message 7)

Now, either answer he gives will be acceptable to her; she has offered a set of acceptable limited choices.[3] She has also shown some consideration for him by recognizing that he might not be in the mood for such a discussion now and would rather wait.

Leveling and Editing

Leveling means telling your partner what you are feeling by stating your thoughts clearly, simply, and honestly (Gottman et al., 1976). This is often the hardest step in communication, especially when the topic is sex. In leveling, keep in mind that the purposes are to

1. Make communication clear.
2. Clear up what partners expect of each other.
3. Clear up what is pleasant and what is unpleasant.
4. Clear up what is relevant and what is irrelevant.
5. Notice things that draw you closer or push you apart. (Gottman et al., 1976)

---

[3]The technique of limited choices is useful in a number of other situations, including dealing with children. For example, when my (author Janet Hyde) daughter was a 2-year-old and she had finished watching *Sesame Street* and I wanted the TV turned off, I didn't say, "Would you turn the TV off?" (she might say no) but, rather, "Do you want to turn off the TV, or would you like me to?" Of course, sometimes she evaded my efforts and said no anyway, but most of the time it worked.

> **"I" language:** Speaking for yourself, using the word "I"; not mind reading.
> **Mind reading:** Making assumptions about what your partner thinks or feels.
> **Documenting:** Giving specific examples of the issue being discussed.
> **Leveling:** Telling your partner what you are feeling by stating your thoughts clearly, simply, and honestly.

A Sexually Diverse World

Gender Differences in Communication

L inguist Deborah Tannen (1991), author of best-selling books such as *You Just Don't Understand: Women and Men in Conversation,* believes that women and men have radically different verbal communication styles, so different that they essentially belong to different linguistic communities. According to this point of view, communication between women and men is as difficult as cross-cultural communication. These arguments have captured the imagination of the general public and worked their way into corporate training programs. Does the scientific evidence support Tannen's claims? Are there substantial gender differences in communication styles, and if so, what are the implications for sexual interactions?

Research has found a number of gender differences in communication. Women are more skilled at reading nonverbal cues than men are. Women are more likely than men to inquire about upsetting situations that another person is in, and to use comforting messages that acknowledge and legitimize the feelings of others. In same-gender pairs, men are more likely to discuss sports, careers, and politics, whereas women are more likely to talk about feelings and relationships. Men interrupt more than women do.

One research finding is that, in conversation, women are more self-disclosing than men are. In other words, women reveal more personal, intimate information about themselves. Yet this pattern is found only with same-gender conversational pairs—men talking with men, and women talking with women. When talking with a woman, men disclose far more than when they talk with a man. Gender differences in self-disclosure, then, are far from universal, and men are capable of being as self-disclosing as women are, depending on the context.

One claim is that women and men have different goals when they speak. Women use speech to establish and maintain relationships, whereas men use speech to exert control, preserve independence, and enhance their status (Wood, 1994). This pattern is consistent with research findings that indicate that women are more concerned than men are with the quality of the relationship in which sex occurs (see the chapter "Gender and Sexuality").

Reviews of dozens of studies of gender differences in communication indicate, however, that the differences, overall, are small (Dindia & Canary, 2006; Leaper & Ayres, 2007). Research simply does not support the contention that gender differences in communication are so large that it is as if women and men are from different cultures. Another problem with the "two cultures" approach is that it assumes that patterns of gender differences are the same for all ethnic groups and social classes, when almost all the research has been done with middle-class Whites.

What are the implications for sexuality? We should not be led astray by flashy claims that men and women have totally different communication styles, making it difficult at best, and impossible at worst, to communicate. Gender differences in communication are small. That is a happy result for sexuality, and particularly for heterosexual interactions.

Good communication is essential for satisfying, mutually pleasurable sex. If men and women could not communicate, it would be a serious problem. Fortunately, the gender differences are small, and, with a little effort, couples should be able to engage in clear, accurate sexual communication.

Sources: Aries (1996); Dindia & Canary (2006); Tannen (1991).

When you begin to level with your partner, you also need to do some editing. **Editing** involves censoring (not saying) things that would be deliberately hurtful to your partner or that would be irrelevant. You must take responsibility for making your communication polite and considerate. Leveling, then, does not mean a "no holds barred" approach. Ironically, research indicates that married people are ruder to each other than they are to strangers (Gottman et al., 1976).

Samantha may be so disgruntled about her lack of orgasms that she's thinking of having an affair to jolt Josh into recognizing her problem, or perhaps in order to see if another man would stimulate her to orgasm. Samantha is probably best advised to edit out this line of thought and concentrate on the specific problem: her lack of orgasms. If she and Josh can solve that problem, she won't need to have an affair.

The trick is to balance leveling and editing. If you edit too much, you may not level at all, and there will be no communication. If you level too much and don't edit, the communication will fail because your partner will respond negatively, and things may get worse rather than better.

Listening

Up to this point, we have concentrated on techniques for you to use in sending messages about sexual relationships. But, of course, communication is a two-way street, and you and your partner will exchange responses. For this reason, it is important for you and your partner to gain some skills in listening and responding constructively to messages.

One of the most important things is that you must really *listen*. Listening means more than just removing the headphones from your ears. It means actively trying to understand what the other person is saying. Often people are so busy trying to think of their next response that they hardly hear what the other person is saying.

Good listening involves positive nonverbal behaviors, such as maintaining eye contact with the speaker and nodding your head when appropriate. Be a *nondefensive listener*: Focus on what your partner is saying and feeling, and don't immediately become defensive or counterattack with complaints of your own.

The next step, after you have listened carefully and nondefensively, is to give *feedback*. Feedback often involves brief vocalizations "Uh-huh," "Okay"—nodding your head, or facial movements that indicate you are listening (Gottman et al., 1998). It may involve the technique of **paraphrasing,** that is, repeating in your own words what you think your partner meant. Suppose, in response to Samantha's initial statement, "You're not giving me any orgasms when we have sex," Josh hadn't walked away angrily. Instead, he tried to listen and then gave her feedback by paraphrasing. He might have responded,

> I hear you saying that I'm not very skillful at making love to you, and therefore you're not having orgasms. (Message 8)

At that point, Samantha would have had a chance to clear up the confusion she had created with her initial message, because Josh had given her feedback by paraphrasing his understanding of what she said. At that point she could have said, "No, I think you're a good lover, but I'm not having any orgasms, and I don't know why. I thought maybe we could figure it out together." Or perhaps she could have said, "No, I think you're a good lover. I just wish you'd do more of some of the things you do, like rubbing my clitoris."

It's also a good idea to *ask for feedback* from your partner, particularly if you're not sure whether you're communicating clearly.

Body Talk: Nonverbal Communication

Just as it is important to be a good listener to your partner's verbal messages, so too is it important to be good at "reading" your partner's nonverbal messages. Often the precise words we use are not as important as our **nonverbal communication**—the way we say them. Tone of voice, expression on the face, position of the body, whether you touch the other person—all are important in conveying the message (see Figure 9).

For example, take the sentence "So you're here." If it is delivered, "So *you're* here" in a hostile tone

> **Editing:** Censoring or not saying things that would be deliberately hurtful to your partner or that are irrelevant.
> **Paraphrasing:** Saying, in your own words, what you thought your partner meant.
> **Nonverbal communication:** Communication not through words, but through the body, e.g., eye contact, tone of voice, touching.

(a)

(b)

Figure 9 (*a*) A couple with good body language (good eye contact and body position); (*b*) a couple with poor body language (poor eye contact and body position).

of voice, the message is that the speaker is very unhappy that you're here. If it is delivered, "So you're *here*" in a pleased voice, the meaning may be that the speaker is glad and surprised to see you here in Wisconsin, having thought you were in Europe. "So you're here" with a smile and arms outstretched for a hug might mean that the speaker has been waiting for you and is delighted to see you.

Suppose that in Samantha and Josh's case, the reason Samantha doesn't have more orgasms is that Josh simply doesn't stimulate her vigorously enough. During sex, Samantha has adopted a very passive, nearly rigid posture for her body. Josh doesn't stimulate her more vigorously because he is afraid that he might hurt her, and he is sure that no lady like his wife would want such a vigorous approach. The response (or rather nonresponse) of her body confirms his assumptions. Her body is saying, "I don't enjoy this. Let's get it over with." And that's exactly what she's getting.

To correct this situation, she might adopt a more active, encouraging approach. She might take his hand and guide it to her clitoris, showing him how firmly she likes to have it rubbed. She might place her hands on his hips and press to indicate how deep and forceful she would like the thrusting of his penis in her vagina to be. She might even take the daring approach of using some verbal communication, perhaps saying "That's good" when he becomes more vigorous.

The point is that in communicating about sex we need to be sure that our nonverbal signals help to create the impact we intend rather than one we don't intend. It is also possible that nonverbal signals are confusing communication and need to be straightened out. *Checking out* is a technique for doing this, which we discuss in a later section.

Interestingly, research shows that distressed couples differ from nondistressed couples more in their nonverbal communication than in their verbal communication (Gottman et al., 1977; Vincent et al., 1979). For example, even when a person from a distressed couple is expressing agreement with their spouse, that person is more likely to accompany the verbal expressions of agreement with negative nonverbal behavior. Distressed couples are also more likely to be negative listeners—while listening, the individuals are more likely to display frowning, angry, or disgusted facial expressions, or tense or inattentive body postures. Contempt is often expressed nonverbally, by sneering or rolling the eyes, for example. In contrast, harmonious marriages are characterized by closer physical distances and more relaxed postures than are found in distressed couples (Beier & Sternberg, 1977). Once again, it is not only what we say verbally but how we say it, and how we listen, that makes the difference.

> **Validation:** Telling your partner that, given their point of view, you can see why they think a certain way.

Validating

Another good technique in communication is **validation** (Gottman et al., 1976), which means telling your partner that, given their point of view, you can see why they think a certain way. It doesn't mean that you agree with your partner or that you're giving in. It simply means that you recognize your partner's point of view as legitimate, given their set of assumptions, which may be different from yours.

All couples will have disagreements. What is important is how you handle these disagreements. If they lead to fights because one partner thinks the other is "wrong," these will likely damage the relationship. It is much better to try to understand the other's viewpoint. In a study of 76 couples, an understanding of the partner's preferences for such things as foreplay, use of erotica, and use of contraception (not agreement with them) was associated with satisfaction with the sexual aspects of the relationship (Purnine & Carey, 1997).

Suppose that Samantha and Josh have gotten into an argument about cunnilingus. She wants him to do it and thinks it would bring her to orgasm. He doesn't want to do it because he finds the idea repulsive and because he believes no real man would do such a thing. If Samantha tried to validate Josh's feelings, she might say,

> I can understand the way you feel about cunnilingus, especially given the way you were brought up to think about sex. (Message 9)

Josh might validate Samantha's feelings by saying,

> I understand how important it is for you to have an orgasm. (Message 10)

Validating hasn't solved their disagreement, but it has left the door open so that they can now make some progress.

Drawing Your Partner Out

Suppose it is Josh who initiates the conversation rather than Samantha. Josh has noticed that Samantha doesn't seem to get a lot of pleasure out of sex, and he would like to find out why and see what they can do about it. He needs to draw her out. He might begin by saying,

> I've noticed lately that you don't seem to be enjoying sex as much as you used to. Am I right about that? (Message 11)

That much is good because he's checking out his assumption. Unfortunately, he's asked a question that leads to a "yes" or "no" answer, and that can stop the communication. So if Samantha replies "yes," Josh had better follow it up with an *open-ended* question like

> Why do you think you aren't enjoying it more? (Message 12)

If she can give a reasonable answer, good communication should be on the way. One of the standard—and best—questions to ask in a situation like this is,

> What can we do to make things better? (Message 13)

Accentuate the Positive

We have been concentrating on negative communications, in other words, communications in which some problem or complaint needs to be voiced. It is also important to communicate positive things about sex (Miller et al., 1975). If that was a great episode of lovemaking, or the best kiss you've ever experienced, say so. A learning theorist would say that you're giving your partner some positive reinforcement. As we noted earlier, research shows that we tend to like people better who give us positive reinforcements. Recognition of the strengths in a relationship offers the potential for enriching it (e.g., Miller et al., 1975). And if you make a habit of positive communications about sex, it will be easier to initiate the negative ones, and they will be better received.

Most communication during sex is limited to muffled groans, or "Mm-m's," or an occasional "Higher, José" or "Did you, Latisha?" It might help your partner greatly if you gave frequent verbal and nonverbal feedback, such as "That was great" or "Let's do that again." This would make the positive communications and the negative ones far easier.

Research shows that nondistressed couples make more positive and fewer negative communications than distressed couples (Billings, 1979; Birchler et al., 1975). In fact, Gottman's (1994) research found that there is a *magic ratio* of positive to negative communication. In stable marriages, there is five times as much positive interaction—verbal and nonverbal, including hugs and kisses—as there is negative. Not only do happy couples make more positive communications, but they are also more likely to respond to a negative communication with something positive (Billings, 1979). Distressed couples, on the other hand, are more likely to respond to negative communication with more negative communication, escalating into conflict. We might all take a cue from the happy couples and make efforts not only to increase our positive communications but even to make them in response to negative comments from our partner.

Fighting Fair

Even if you use all the techniques described above, you may still get into arguments with your partner. Arguments are a natural part of a relationship and are not necessarily bad. Given that there will be arguments in a relationship, it is useful if you and your partner have agreed to a set of rules called **fighting fair** (Bach & Wyden, 1969) so that the arguments may help and won't hurt (Figure 10).

Here are some of the basic rules for fighting fair that may be useful to you (Brenton, 1972; Creighton, 1992):

1. Don't make sarcastic or insulting remarks about your partner's sexual adequacy. This generates resentment,

Figure 10 Arguments are not necessarily bad for a relationship, but it is important to observe the rules for fighting fair.

©Jamie Grill/Getty Images

opens you to counterattack, and is just a dirty way to fight.

2. Don't bring up the names of former spouses, lovers, boyfriends, or girlfriends to illustrate how all these problems didn't happen with them. Stick to the issue: your relationship with your partner.

3. Don't play amateur psychologist. Don't say things like "The problem is that you're a compulsive personality" or "You acted that way because you never resolved your Oedipus complex." You really don't have the qualifications (even after reading this book) to do that kind of psychologizing. Even if you did, your partner would not be apt to recognize your expertise in the middle of an argument, thinking, quite rightly, that you're probably biased at the moment.

4. Don't threaten to tell your parents or run home. This involves ganging up on your partner or retreating like a child.

5. If you have children, don't bring them into the argument. It is too stressful emotionally to force them to take sides between you and your partner.

6. Don't engage in dumping. Don't store up gripes for 6 months and then dump them on your partner all at one time.

7. Don't hit and run. Don't bring up a serious negative issue when there is no opportunity to continue the discussion, such as when you're on the way out the door going to work or when guests are coming for dinner in 5 minutes.

8. Don't focus on who's to blame. Focus on looking for solutions, not on who's at fault. If you avoid blaming, it lets both you and your partner save face, which helps both of you feel better about the relationship.

Fighting fair: A set of rules designed to make arguments constructive rather than destructive.

First Person

How Solid Is Your Relationship?

Good communication enhances a relationship, and a good relationship facilitates good communication. There are several components of a good relationship. Two of these are love and respect. The following self-test assesses the degree of love and respect in a relationship. If you are in an intimate relationship, answer yes or no to each of the following statements. If you agree or mostly agree, answer yes. If you disagree or mostly disagree, answer no. You can either ask your partner to take the test too or take it a second time yourself, answering the way you think your partner would answer.

1. My partner seeks out my opinion.
   YOU: Yes No YOUR PARTNER: Yes No
2. My partner cares about my feelings.
   YOU: Yes No YOUR PARTNER: Yes No
3. I don't feel ignored very often.
   YOU: Yes No YOUR PARTNER: Yes No
4. We touch each other a lot.
   YOU: Yes No YOUR PARTNER: Yes No
5. We listen to each other.
   YOU: Yes No YOUR PARTNER: Yes No
6. We respect each other's ideas.
   YOU: Yes No YOUR PARTNER: Yes No
7. We are affectionate toward one another.
   YOU: Yes No YOUR PARTNER: Yes No
8. I feel my partner takes good care of me.
   YOU: Yes No YOUR PARTNER: Yes No
9. What I say counts.
   YOU: Yes No YOUR PARTNER: Yes No
10. I am important in our decisions.
    YOU: Yes No YOUR PARTNER: Yes No
11. There's lots of love in our relationship.
    YOU: Yes No YOUR PARTNER: Yes No
12. We are genuinely interested in one another.
    YOU: Yes No YOUR PARTNER: Yes No
13. I love spending time with my partner.
    YOU: Yes No YOUR PARTNER: Yes No
14. We are very good friends.
    YOU: Yes No YOUR PARTNER: Yes No
15. Even during rough times, we can be empathetic.
    YOU: Yes No YOUR PARTNER: Yes No
16. My partner is considerate of my viewpoint.
    YOU: Yes No YOUR PARTNER: Yes No
17. My partner finds me physically attractive.
    YOU: Yes No YOUR PARTNER: Yes No
18. My partner expresses warmth toward me.
    YOU: Yes No YOUR PARTNER: Yes No
19. I feel included in my partner's life.
    YOU: Yes No YOUR PARTNER: Yes No
20. My partner admires me.
    YOU: Yes No YOUR PARTNER: Yes No

Scoring: If you answered yes to fewer than seven items, it is likely that you are not feeling loved and respected in this relationship. You and your partner need to be more active and creative in adding affection to your relationship.

Source: Gottman, John M. (1994). *Why Marriages Succeed or Fail.* New York: Simon & Schuster.

Checking Out Sexy Signals

One of the problems with verbal and nonverbal sexual communications is that they are often ambiguous. This problem may occur more often with couples who don't know each other well, but it can cause uncertainty and misunderstanding in long-term couples as well.

Some messages are very direct. Statements like "I want to have sex with you" are not ambiguous at all.

Unfortunately, such directness is not common in our society. In a series of studies of tactics people used to promote sexual encounters, college students reported good hygiene, good grooming, and dressing nicely as the actions they most frequently used (Greer & Buss, 1994). These are *very* indirect signals of sexual interest. Consider Tyler, who stands up, stretches, and says, "It's time for bed." Does he mean he wants to engage in sexual activity or go to sleep?

Ambiguous messages can lead to feelings of hurt and rejection, or to unnecessary anger and perhaps complaints to third parties. If Tyler wants to have sex but his partner interprets his behavior as meaning that Tyler is tired, Tyler may go to bed feeling hurt, unattractive, and unloved. A woman who casually puts her arm around the shoulders of a coworker and gives him a hug may find herself explaining to her supervisor that it was a gesture of friendship, not a sexual proposition.

Ideally, each of us should be an effective communicator, making sure our message clearly matches our intent. As recipients of ambiguous messages, we need to make an effort to clear them up. In response to an invitation to a woman's apartment for coffee, a man might reply, "I would like some coffee, but I'm not interested in sex this time." Or he might draw her out with a question: "I'd like some coffee; is that all you have in mind?" Check out sexy signals. Don't make any assumptions about the meaning of ambiguous messages.

Relationship Education

Recognizing the importance of good communication to reducing conflict, and with an eye toward the high divorce rate in the United States, relationship or marital education programs were developed in the 1980s. There are a substantial number of these programs today; many now have websites and some can be taken entirely online. The best known include Better Marriages, Couple Communication, Marriage Encounter, and PAIRS (Practical Application of Intimate Relationship Skills). Although there is variation in content and curriculum, most of these programs are psychoeducational (not therapeutic). Most focus primarily on developing better communication and problem solving skills, and include much of the material covered in this section, with classroom sessions and many activities designed to encourage practice. A secondary focus may be on information and skills to improve a couple's ability to manage finances, raise children, and cope with stress.

A meta-analysis of evaluations of these programs found that on average they are somewhat effective, with larger effects for communication skills than marital quality. Programs lasting 9 to 20 hours were associated with larger effect sizes than shorter programs (Hawkins et al., 2008). Another meta-analysis found that program effects lasted longer for initially well-functioning couples than distressed ones (Blanchard et al., 2009)—not surprising because these programs are not intended to be therapeutic and usually are not led by therapists. Most participants in these evaluations were White, middle class, primarily married couples. A separate meta-analysis identified 15 evaluation studies of programs targeting low-income couples. The curricula used were adapted to the needs and circumstances of lower-income couples. The programs had small to moderate positive effects on both communication skills and relationship quality (Hawkins & Fackrell, 2010). Other relationship education programs have been aimed at adolescents before they become involved in long-term relationships; these programs, too, show evidence of effectiveness (Simpson et al., 2018).

Military life can be very stressful, especially for married couples. The PREP (Prevention and Relationship Enhancement Program) was delivered to a total of 662 married couples with a spouse in the U.S. Army during the Iraq War (Stanley et al., 2014). About 70 percent of the men and women were White, and 10 percent were Hispanic, 10 percent African American, and 10 percent other minorities. The program provided 14 hours of education over a 2-week period. Couples were followed up for 2 years, and the outcomes measured included communication skills, marital quality, and whether the couple divorced. The couples receiving the education showed an initial improvement in communication skills, but it did not persist. They were less likely to divorce in the next 2 years, and the impact was strongest for the ethnic minority couples.

Thus, relationship education does work for some couples. The next steps are to find out for which couples, and to identify the specific aspects of these programs that produce changes in communication skills and relationship quality (Wadsworth & Markman, 2012).

Critical THINKing Skill

Thinking critically about attraction and relationships

Suppose that a friend tells you about her exciting new relationship. She comes to you for advice, knowing that you are taking a human sexuality course. She wants to know whether this relationship has good prospects for succeeding long term, or whether she would be better off to move on. Your friend is a White, heterosexual, cis woman and will graduate from college this year. She plans a career in nursing. She is a very liberal Democrat who favors strict gun control and has participated in marches on this issue. She describes her sweetie as a White, heterosexual, cis man who is a high school graduate of her age and works as a highly skilled electrician. He is a rock-solid Republican who loves hunting and believes there should be no infringement on Second Amendment rights for anyone and everyone to own a gun. Your friend describes him as kind and fun. The main thing that attracts her to him is that the sex is beyond amazing—it's the best she's ever experienced, and she feels like she's falling passionately in love with him. Thoughts of him fill her mind.

You know that, for good critical thinking, you should use the best available scientific evidence. Look back over this chapter; what elements of it do you think would apply in a situation like this? What advice would you give your friend? Write an answer to this question before you continue reading.

Several sets of scientific findings and theories are relevant here. One is the distinction between passionate and companionate love. You could explain this to your friend and ask her whether, when the relationship gets beyond the hot and bothered stage, her sweetie would make a good long-term companion and friend.

A second relevant area is the research on people generally being attracted to others who have similar attitudes. Reinforcement theory says that this occurs because we feel positively reinforced when our partner agrees with us on issues. Your friend and her sweetie have strikingly different attitudes on a hot button issue—gun control. You could explain this research to your friend. You could ask her whether she and her sweetie agree on a lot of other issues and gun control is the only point of disagreement, or whether they disagree on lots of issues.

The material on communication is also relevant. Do your friend and her sweetie argue a lot about gun control? How does the argument go? Do they end up shouting disrespectfully at each other (displaying contempt, not fighting fair)? These kinds of interactions can be lethal to a relationship.

Above all, be sure to convey to your friend that the scientific research you are describing is about average trends and doesn't perfectly apply to all people and every relationship. The research evidence tells us about *probabilities* (see the Critical Thinking box in the chapter on "Contraception"). The probabilities are better for a couple having a happy long-term relationship if they agree on important issues, but some couples find ways to overcome their points of disagreement.

SUMMARY

Attraction

Research indicates that mere repeated exposure to another person facilitates attraction. We tend to be attracted to people who are similar to us socially (age, race or ethnicity, economic status) and psychologically (attitudes, interests). In first impressions, we are most attracted to people who are physically attractive. We also tend to be attracted to people we believe to be "within reach" of us, depending on our sense of our own attractiveness or desirability. Websites and apps are now popular ways to meet potential new partners, and research shows that these strategies are at least moderately effective.

According to reinforcement theory, we are attracted to those who give us many reinforcements. Interaction with people who are similar to us is smooth and rewarding; they have similar outlooks and like the same things we do. According to sexual strategies theory, we prefer young, attractive people because they are likely to be healthy and fertile. Men prefer women who are sexually faithful, and women prefer men with resources who will invest in them and their children.

Intimacy

Intimacy is a major component of a romantic relationship. It is defined as a quality of a relationship characterized by commitment, feelings of closeness and trust, and self-disclosure. Disclosure by one person generally leads to disclosure by the other. Self-disclosure is positively associated with relationship satisfaction, and with the longevity of the relationship.

Love

According to the triangular theory, there are three components to love: intimacy, passion, and decision or commitment. Love is a triangle, with each of these components as one of the points. Partners whose love triangles are substantially different are mismatched and are likely to be dissatisfied with their relationship.

According to the attachment theory of love, adults vary in their capacity for love as a result of their love or attachment experiences in infancy. This theory says that there are three types of lovers: secure lovers, avoidant lovers, and anxious–ambivalent lovers.

According to the theory of love styles, there are three basic types of love: eros (powerful physical attraction), ludus (playful love), and storge (stable, reliable love).

Love may have a neurochemical component. Passionate love, a state of intense longing and arousal, is associated with dopamine. Like all chemically induced highs, passionate love eventually comes to an end. It may be replaced by companionate love, a feeling of deep attachment and commitment to the partner. This type of love may be accompanied by elevated levels of prolactin and oxytocin, which may be produced by physical closeness and touch.

Passionate love is associated with brain activity in areas associated with reward and complex cognitive processing. Long-term love relationships are associated with brain areas related to attachment.

Hatfield and Sprecher have constructed a scale to measure passionate love. Such scales make it possible to do scientific research on complex phenomena like love. Scores on this scale were correlated with measures of commitment to and satisfaction with romantic relationships.

According to the two-component theory, there are two basic components of romantic love: being in a state of physiological arousal and attaching the label "love" to the feeling.

Cross-cultural research indicates that individualistic cultures like that of the United States emphasize love as the basis for marriage and encourage intimacy between partners. Collectivist cultures emphasize the importance of the group over the individual, and may even practice arranged marriage. Culture affects our standards of beauty and the likelihood that we would marry someone we don't love.

Communication

Research reveals clear differences in communication patterns between happy, nondistressed couples and couples who are unhappy, seeking counseling, or headed for divorce. Destructive patterns of interaction include criticism, contempt, defensiveness, and withdrawal. The key to building a good relationship is reciprocal self-disclosure. The key to maintaining a good relationship is being a good communicator.

Specific principles for being a good communicator include the following: use "I" language; avoid mind reading; document your points with specific examples; use limited-choice questions; level and edit; be a nondefensive listener; give feedback by paraphrasing; be aware of your nonverbal messages; validate the other's viewpoint; draw your partner out; and engage in positive verbal and nonverbal communication. When you do argue, fight fair. Finally, it is important to check out ambiguous sexy signals to find out what they really mean. Communication training and relationship education programs are available and are at least moderately effective.

SUGGESTIONS FOR FURTHER READING

Gottman, John, & Silver, Nan. (2015). *The seven principles for making marriage work: A practical guide from the country's foremost relationship expert*. New York: Harmony Books (Paperback). The latest book by John Gottman, applying what he has learned from 40 years of research on couples and communication. Presents seven principles for making relationships work.

Johnson, Sue. (2013). *Love sense: The revolutionary new science of romantic relationships*. New York: Little Brown. Johnson synthesizes research on love, including attachment theory, with recommendations based on her experience as a therapist.

Mikulincer, Mario, and Goodman, Gail (Eds). (2006). *Dynamics of romantic love*. New York: Guilford Press. A collection of essays exploring the role of attachment in a variety of relationship dynamics, and in sexuality.

CHAPTER

12

©Yao Yongqiang/VCG/Getty Images

Gender and Sexuality

CHAPTER HIGHLIGHTS

The majority of women (happily for them) are not very much troubled with sexual feelings of any kind. What men are habitually, women are only exceptionally.*

The root of all men's desire is to have sex. When you brush your teeth, it's to have sex. When you eat, it's, well, I gotta have energy to have sex. When you get dressed, you think, oh, maybe if I wear these jeans I'll be more likely to have sex.†

*Dr. William Acton. (1857). *The functions and disorders of the reproductive organs.*
†Seth Rogen. (2008, July 20). Quoted in the *New York Times Sunday Magazine*, p. 49.

When a baby is born, what is the first statement made about it? "It's a boy" or "It's a girl," of course. Sociologists tell us that gender is one of the most basic of status characteristics. That is, in terms of both our individual interactions with people and the position we hold in society, gender is exceptionally important. People experience consternation when they are uncertain of a person's gender. They do not know how to interact with such a person, and they feel flustered, not to mention curious, until they can ferret out some clue as to whether the person is a man or a woman. In this chapter we explore gender roles and the impact they may have on sexuality, as well as the phenomenon of transgender, which includes several variations on typical gender.

The consternation that people experience when they are uncertain of another person's gender is rooted in the **gender binary,** which is the classification of people into one of two categories: male or female. Today we know that there are more possibilities. For example, some people see themselves as genderqueer and outside the gender binary. The psychological research on gender stereotypes and gender differences has all been based on the assumption of a gender binary. In the last section of this chapter, we consider transgender individuals, who go beyond the gender binary.

Gender Roles and Stereotypes

One of the basic ways in which societies codify this emphasis on gender is through gender roles.[1] A **gender role** is a set of norms, or culturally defined expectations, that define how people of one gender ought to behave. A closely related phenomenon is a **stereotype,** which is a generalization about a group of people (e.g., men) that distinguishes those people from others (e.g., women). Research shows that in modern U.S. society, and among college students, there is a belief that males and females do differ psychologically in many ways, and these stereotypes have not changed much since 1972 (Bergen & Williams,

[1]The distinction between sex and gender is maintained in this chapter. Male–female roles–and thus gender roles–are discussed here.

1991; DeArmond et al., 2006). Yet gender stereotypes vary by ethnic group in the United States (Ghavami & Peplau, 2013). For example, Asian American women are stereotyped as quiet, whereas African American women are stereotyped as loud.

Heterosexuality is an important part of gender roles (Hyde & Jaffee, 2000). The "feminine" woman is expected to be sexually attractive to men and in turn to be attracted to them. Women who violate any part of this role–for example, lesbians–are viewed as violators of gender roles and are considered masculine. Heterosexuality is even more important in the male role (Pascoe, 2011).

Gender Roles and Ethnicity

As we consider variations in gender roles across various ethnic groups, it is crucial to understand how these gender roles are a product of *culture.* In the sections that follow, we consider some aspects of the cultures of four ethnic groups and their relevance to gender roles and sex.

First, though, we consider a key concept, **intersectionality,** which can be defined as an approach that simultaneously considers the meaning and consequences of multiple categories of identity, difference, and disadvantage (Cole, 2009). That is, according to this approach, we should not consider the effects of gender in isolation. Instead, we should consider the effects of gender, race, social class, and sexual orientation simultaneously. When we talk about the category "women," for example, we are talking about a complex group that differs by ethnicity, social class, sexual orientation, and many other identities, such as religion.

Within this framework, it becomes clear that some groups experience multiple disadvantages, such as poor Black women or lesbian women of color. Others may be part of a disadvantaged group but also part of a privileged group, such as middle-class Blacks. In the sections that follow, we look at the intersection of gender and

> **Gender binary:** Conceptualizing gender as having only two categories, male and female.
> **Gender role:** A set of norms, or culturally defined expectations, that define how people of one gender ought to behave.
> **Stereotype:** A generalization about a group of people (e.g., men) that distinguishes them from others (e.g., women).
> **Intersectionality:** An approach that simultaneously considers the consequences of multiple group memberships, e.g., the intersection of gender and ethnicity.

ethnicity. In the chapter "Sexual Orientation: Gay, Straight, or Bi?" we also examine the intersection of gender, ethnicity, and sexual orientation.

African Americans

Two factors are especially significant in the cultural heritage of African Americans: the heritage of African culture and the experience in America of slavery and subsequent racial oppression (Staples, 2006). African American culture today, like that of some other ethnic groups, emphasizes the collective over the individual (Fairchild et al., 2003), in contrast to the "me generation" of contemporary White culture. Mother–child bonds continue to be extremely important in the structure of African American society, and status and honor are accorded to motherhood (Reid & Bing, 2000).

Stereotyped images of Black women's sexuality abound. Traditional images include the Jezebel, who is promiscuous and immoral; and the Mammy, who is fat and asexual (Stephens & Few, 2007). Contemporary hip-hop culture has added numerous stereotyped images: the Gold Digger, who uses sex to gain economic rewards from men; Gangster Bitches, who live in poverty-stricken, violent environments, focus on survival, and use sex to feel good for the moment; and the Sister Savior, who is strongly tied to African American religious traditions, is virtuous, and avoids sex (Stephens & Few, 2007). Stereotypes about Black women are thus complex and contradictory.

Black men's sexuality, too, has been stereotyped (Fasula et al., 2014). Black men are believed to be hypersexual and to have great sexual prowess. Some experts argue that Black men experience even more discrimination than Black women do, according to several indicators including education and criminal justice (Pieterse & Carter, 2007). There is great concern that few young Black men go to college. Half of all prison inmates are Black, when Blacks are just 13 percent of the U.S. population. Stereotypes about Black men tend to be negative, including a belief that all Black men are dangerous. These stereotypes and the discrimination that results from them can be a source of severe stress for Black men.

The unemployment rate for Black men is double that for White men. The high unemployment rate for Black men creates a gender-role problem because the role of breadwinner or good provider is such an important part of the male role in the United States. In turn, many Black men are less willing to commit to marriage or other long-term romantic relationships, which affects the structure of the Black family.

Latinx

Hispanic Americans are now the nation's largest minority, constituting 16 percent of the population (Humes et al., 2011). When we speak of the cultural heritage of Latinx, we must first understand the concept of **acculturation**, which is the process

Acculturation: The process of incorporating the beliefs and customs of a new culture.

Figure 1 Fathers and sons at the Millions More Movement March in Washington, D.C., in 2005. Leaders of the march wanted to encourage African American men to take more responsibility for their families and community, and some 1 million men seemed to agree.

©Johnny Nunez/Getty Images

of incorporating the beliefs and customs of a new culture. The culture of Mexican Americans (Americans of Mexican heritage) is different from both the culture of Mexico and the dominant Anglo culture of the United States. Mexican American culture is based on the Mexican heritage, modified through acculturation to incorporate Anglo components.

The family is the central focus of Hispanic life. Traditional Latinx place a high value on family loyalty and on warm, mutually supportive relationships, and family and community are highly valued.

As noted in the chapter "Sexuality in Perspective," in traditional Latin American cultures, gender roles are sharply defined (Raffaelli & Ontai, 2004). Such roles are emphasized early in the socialization process for children (Raffaelli & Ontai, 2004). Boys are given greater freedom, are encouraged in sexual exploits, and are not expected to share in household work. Girls are expected to be passive, obedient, virginal, and to stay in the home. One woman described how she and her brother, who was one year older than she, were treated by their mother:

> He had a very much later curfew than I did. He got a car, got to drive a car and then he also got his own car and I never did. . . . I could only go to school-related activities and he could do about anything, he could go any place he wanted. (Raffaelli & Ontai, 2004, p. 290)

These roles are epitomized in the concepts of *machismo* and *marianismo,* discussed in the chapter "Sexuality in Perspective." Young Latinas may feel that they have to choose between being a "good girl" and being a "flirt girl" (Faulkner, 2003).

Figure 2 Asian American women have often been stereotyped as exotic sex toys. In the film *The World of Suzie Wong,* Nancy Kwan portrayed an alluring prostitute.

©AF archive/Alamy

Asian Americans

Chinese—almost all of them men—were recruited first in the 1840s to come to the United States as laborers in the West and later in the 1860s to work on the transcontinental railroad (for excellent summaries of the cultural heritage of Asian Americans, see Root, 1995, and Chan, 2003). Racist sentiment against the Chinese grew, however, and there was a shift to recruiting first Japanese and Koreans and then Filipinos. Then, in the late 1960s and the 1970s, there was a mass exodus to the United States of refugees from war-torn Southeast Asia. Today, Asian Americans make up nearly 5 percent of the U.S. population (Humes et al., 2011).

The cultural values of Asian Americans are in some ways consistent with White middle-class American values but in other ways contradict them. Asian Americans share with the White middle class an emphasis on academic achievement and the importance of education. For example, Asian American women have a higher level of education, on average, than White American women (U.S. Census Bureau, 2010). On the other hand, Asian Americans place far more value on family and group interdependence (Kim et al., 2005), compared with the White American emphasis on individualism and self-sufficiency. For Asian Americans, the family is a great source of emotional nurturance. One has an obligation to the family, and the needs of the family must take precedence over the needs of the individual. For Asian American women, there can be a conflict in cultural values between the

traditional gender roles of Asian culture and those of modern Anglo culture, which increasingly prizes independence and assertiveness in women.

Just as the sexuality of African Americans has been stereotyped, so too has that of Asian Americans. The Asian American man has been stereotyped as asexual (lacking in sexuality), whereas the Asian American woman has been stereotyped as an exotic sex toy (Koo et al., 2015).

Compared with European Americans, Asian Americans tend to hold more conservative sexual attitudes and to experience more anxiety about sex (Brotto et al., 2005). The more acculturated that Asian American women are, the closer their sexual attitudes are to those of European American women (Brotto et al., 2005).

American Indians

At least some Indian tribes, including the Cherokee, Navajo, Iroquois, Hopi, and Zuñi, traditionally had relatively egalitarian gender roles (LaFromboise et al., 1990). That is, their roles were more egalitarian than those of White culture of the same period. The process of acculturation and adaptation to Anglo society seems to have resulted in increased male dominance among American Indians.

Among the more than 200 Native languages spoken in North America, at least two-thirds have a term that refers to a third (or more) gender beyond male and female (Tafoya & Wirth, 1996). Anglo anthropologists labeled this additional category *berdache,* a term rejected by Native peoples,

Figure 3 Some American Indian tribes have three gender categories, the third being known as a two-spirit, "manly hearted woman," or "warrior woman." Chiricahua Tah-des-te was a messenger and warrior in Geronimo's band. She participated in negotiations with several U.S. military leaders and surrendered with Geronimo in 1886.

©*F.A. Rinehart for B.A.E./Smithsonian Institute*

who prefer the term *two-spirit* (Jacobs et al., 1997). These same anthropologists concluded that these people were homosexuals, transsexuals, or transvestites, none of which are accurate from a Native point of view. A man might be married to a two-spirit male, but the marriage would not be considered homosexual because the two were of different genders (Tafoya & Wirth, 1996).

There was also a role of the "manly hearted woman," a role that a woman who was exceptionally independent and aggressive could take on. There was a "warrior woman" role among the Apache, Crow, Cheyenne, Blackfoot, Pawnee, and Navajo tribes (e.g., Buchanan, 1986; House, 1997). In both cases, women could express masculine traits or participate in male-stereotyped activities while continuing to live and dress as women (Figure 3).

In summary, research indicates that gender roles in the United States are not uniform. Different ethnic groups define gender roles differently. Let us turn now to some of the processes that create gender stereotypes.

Socialization: The ways in which society conveys to the individual its norms or expectations for their behavior.

Socialization

Many adult women and men often behave as gender roles say they should. Why does this happen?

Psychologists and sociologists believe that it is a result of gender-role socialization. **Socialization** refers to the ways in which society conveys to the individual its norms or expectations for their behavior. Socialization occurs especially in childhood, as children are taught to behave as they will be expected to in adulthood. Socialization continues in adulthood, as society conveys its norms of appropriate behavior for adult women and men. These norms extend from appropriate jobs to who initiates sexual activity.

Gender socialization comes from multiple sources, including parents, peers, and the media (Leaper & Friedman, 2007; Ward & Aubrey, 2017). Certainly parents have an early, important influence. At least in societies that value gender equality, gendered parenting is not found in broad parenting styles such as warmth toward the child (Mesman & Groeneveld, 2018). In these ways, parents treat boys and girls similarly. Explicit messages from parents—such as "Nice young ladies don't do that"—have pretty much disappeared in such societies too. The place where gendered parenting occurs today is in implicit gendered messages (Mesman & Groeneveld, 2018). These implicit messages covertly convey different expectations for girls and boys without stating them explicitly. For example, especially in early childhood, parents select their children's books and toys. They may choose dolls for girls and action figures for boys. Content analyses of dolls and action figures show that they are highly stereotyped, showing hyperfemininity for girls and hypermasculinity for boys (Murnen et al., 2016). Parents may convey indirect stereotyped messages when they read picture books to preschoolers and comment more positively about children engaged in stereotyped activities than about children engaged in counterstereotypical behavior (Mesman & Groeneveld, 2018). And parents may themselves serve as models of gender-stereotyped behavior (Figure 4).

Parents are not the only socializing agents, though. The peer group can have a big impact in socializing for gender roles, particularly in adolescence. Other teenagers can be extremely effective in enforcing gender-role standards; for example, they may ridicule or shun a boy whose behavior is effeminate. Thus peers can exert great pressure for gender-role conformity (Maccoby, 2002).

The media are also important socializing agents. Many people assume that things have changed a lot in the last 30 years and that gender stereotypes are a thing of the past. On the contrary, various media—from television to teen magazines—continue to show females and males in stereotyped roles. An analysis of G-rated films, for example, showed that male characters outnumbered female characters by 2.5 to 1, a pattern that had not changed in 15 years (Smith et al., 2010). Both males and females were shown mainly in gender-stereotyped occupations. And music videos show females as subordinate and males as aggressive (Wallis, 2011).

As children enter adolescence, TV and the movies teach them what to do in romantic and sexual situations

(a)

(b)

Figure 4   Children are very interested in achieving adult gender roles.

(a) ©George Simian/Getty Images; (b) ©Kelly Redinger/Design Pics

(Ward & Aubrey, 2017). The messages are strongly gendered, portraying men as active pursuers, who avoid emotional commitment, and women as sexually passive and the enforcers of sexual limits.

Dozens of studies show that gender stereotypes shown on television affect children's stereotyped ideas (Ward & Harrison, 2005). For example, in one study first- and second-graders were exposed to television commercials in which all boys were playing with a gender-neutral toy (traditional condition), all girls were playing with it (nontraditional condition), or the commercial was not about toys (control) (Pike & Jennings, 2005). After the viewing, children were asked to sort six toys into those that were for boys, those that were for girls, or those that were for both boys and girls. Among the six toys was the toy they had seen in the commercial. Children in the traditional condition were more likely to say that the toy was for boys, whereas children in the nontraditional condition were more likely to say that it was for both boys and girls. These results show not only the power of stereotyped television images, but also that children can respond positively to nonstereotyped messages.

But picture books and TV are old-fashioned media. One might expect the new media to be less stereotyped. To the contrary, however, video games show patterns of extreme gender stereotyping. In Grand Theft Auto, the men are violent and the women are hookers (Chong et al., 2012). Adolescents average more than an hour a day playing video games (Rideout et al., 2010). In short, adolescents' exposure to these games and their gender stereotypes is massive. Even Internet memes show content that is heteronormative and gender-stereotyped (Drakett et al., 2018).

Although gender roles themselves are universal—that is, all societies have gender roles—the exact content of these roles varies from one culture to the next, from one ethnic group to another, and from one social class to another. For example, Margaret Mead (1935) studied several cultures in which gender roles were considerably different from those in the United States. One such group is the Mundugumor of New Guinea. In that culture both females and males were extremely aggressive.

Psychological Gender Differences

Gender differences in personality and behavior have been studied extensively by psychologists (e.g., Hyde, 2014). Here we focus on gender differences in three areas that are particularly relevant to gender and sexuality: aggressiveness, impulsivity, and communication styles.

Males and females differ in *aggressiveness.* Males are generally more aggressive than females. This is true for virtually all indicators of aggression (physical aggression such as fighting, verbal aggression, and fantasy aggression) (Archer, 2004). It is also true at all ages. As soon as children are old enough to perform aggressive behaviors, boys become more aggressive (Alink et al., 2006), and males dominate the statistics on violent crimes.

Stereotypes hold that men are impulsive risk-takers and that women are less so. *Impulsivity* refers to the tendency to act spontaneously and without careful thought (Cross et al., 2011). There are multiple aspects of impulsivity: reward sensitivity (being especially likely to do something because it will feel good right now), sensation-seeking, risk-taking, and impulse control (the opposite of impulsivity, i.e., being able to control one's actions). A meta-analysis found that men did indeed score higher than women on risk-taking ($d = 0.38$) and sensation-seeking ($d = 0.22$) (Cross et al., 2011). Risk-taking and sensation-seeking are highly relevant to sexuality, and especially to risky sexual behavior.

Researchers have found that in the United States, men and women differ in their *style of communicating,* both verbally and nonverbally (Leaper & Ayres, 2007). This research was reviewed in the chapter "Attraction, Love, and Communication"; see A Sexually Diverse World: Gender Differences in Communication. Of particular relevance to sexuality, social psychologists have found gender differences in studies of self-disclosure. For example, adolescent girls self-disclose to friends more than adolescent boys do (Rose & Rudolph, 2006).

Today, of course, males and females do much of their self-disclosure online. In one study of adolescents, girls' online self-disclosure increased greatly between ages 10 and 13; boys displayed a similar increase, but it started about two years later (Valkenburg et al., 2011). Girls engaged in more online self-disclosure than boys did at all ages. Another study examined college students' self-disclosure on their Facebook pages (Special & Li-Barber, 2012). For both males and females, the top motive for using Facebook was maintaining relationships—that is, motives displayed gender similarities. Moreover, there was no gender difference in disclosure of personal information in this particular medium.

Norms about self-disclosure are changing. Traditional gender roles favored emotional expressiveness for females, but emotional repressiveness and avoidance of self-disclosure for males. There is, however, a contemporary ethic of good communication and openness that demands equal self-disclosure from males and females.

There are gender differences in people's ability to understand the nonverbal behaviors of others. The technical phrase for this is *decoding nonverbal cues*—that is, the ability to read others' body language correctly. It might be measured, for example, by one's accuracy in interpreting facial expressions. Research shows that women are better than men at decoding such nonverbal cues and discerning others' emotions (Hall, 1998). Certainly this is consistent with the gender-related expectation that women will show greater interpersonal sensitivity. Girls and women are also somewhat better at reading others' emotions than boys and men are, although the difference is small ($d = 0.19$) (Thompson & Voyer, 2014).

What are the implications for sexuality of these gender differences in communication styles? For example, if men are unwilling to disclose personal information about themselves, consider whether this might hamper their ability to communicate their sexual needs to their partners.

Gender Differences in Sexuality

In this section the discussion focuses on areas of sexuality in which there is some evidence of male–female differences. As we point out, differences do exist, but they are in a rather small number of areas—masturbation, attitudes about casual sex, use of pornography,

What are some major ways in which males and females differ in their sexuality?

consistency of orgasm during sex, and sex drive. There is a danger in focusing on these differences to the point of forgetting about gender similarities. As you consider the evidence on male–female differences that follows, keep in mind that males and females are in many ways quite similar in their sexuality—for example, in the physiology of their sexual responses (see the chapter "Sexual Arousal"). Gender patterns may be similar or different in other cultures.

Masturbation

In a meta-analysis of 730 studies of gender differences in sexuality, the authors found that one of the largest gender differences was the incidence of masturbation (Petersen & Hyde, 2010).

Recall that in the Kinsey data 92 percent of the males had masturbated to orgasm at least once in their lives, as compared with 58 percent of the females. Not only did fewer women masturbate, but, in general, those who did masturbate had begun at a later age than the men. Virtually all men said they had masturbated before age 20 (most began between ages 13 and 15), but substantial numbers of women reported masturbating for the first time at age 25, 30, or 35. This gender difference still appears in recent studies. For example, for adults between 25 and 29 in the NSSHB, 94 percent of the men had masturbated at least once in their lives, compared with 85 percent of the women (Herbenick et al., 2010a). And 20 percent of the men masturbated four or more times per week, compared with 5 percent of the women (Herbenick et al., 2010b; Reece et al., 2010b). In another sample, 61 percent of the men and 36 percent of the women had masturbated in the past 2 weeks (Regnerus et al., 2017). The data suggest, then, that there is a gender difference in the incidence of masturbation, with men more likely to have masturbated than women.

Attitudes about Casual Sex

In the meta-analysis mentioned above, another substantial gender difference noted was in attitudes toward casual sex—that is, intercourse in a situation, such as a "one-night stand," in which there is no emotionally committed relationship between the partners (Petersen & Hyde, 2010; Yost & Zurbriggen, 2006). Men are considerably more approving of such interactions, and women tend to be disapproving. Many women feel that intercourse is ethical or acceptable only in the context of an emotionally committed relationship. For many men, that is a nice context for sex, but it isn't absolutely necessary.

One study has gained legendary status as an illustration of men's greater interest in casual sex. Clark and Hatfield (1989) had female and male research assistants, who were confederates of the experimenters, approach opposite-gender people and invite them to engage in casual sex. No women agreed to such a sexual encounter, whereas 70 percent of men agreed (see also Guéguen, 2011). Evolutionary theorists see these results as evidence of men's selection to have sex with many partners and women's selection to be choosy (see the chapter "Theoretical Perspectives on Sexuality"). However, socialization explanations are equally plausible (Conley, 2011). Girls are socialized to perceive risk in the environment and, in particular, to be sensitive to the possibility of rape. Boys, in contrast, are encouraged to ignore risk. Moreover, it may be more about the proposer than about the person receiving the proposal. Male proposers may be perceived as dangerous and female proposers as harmless. Then there is the issue of sexual pleasure. Doubtless men anticipate sexual pleasure from the encounter, whereas women would be less likely to think that the male proposer would give them pleasure. Several clever laboratory experiments support these socialization explanations (Conley, 2011).

With these different attitudes, no wonder there is some conflict in relationships between women and men.

Use of Pornography

The third substantial gender difference found in the meta-analysis noted above was in the use of pornography (Petersen & Hyde, 2010). Men were considerably more likely to report using porn than women were. Women often report deep ambivalence toward porn, feeling aroused by it, yet repulsed by the way it portrays women (Fahs et al., 2018). And many women report watching porn because their male partners want them to (Fahs et al., 2018).

Arousal to Erotica

Traditionally in our society most erotic material—sexually arousing pictures, movies, or stories—has been produced for a male audience. The corresponding assumption presumably has been that women are not interested in such things. Does the scientific evidence bear out this notion?

Laboratory research shows that men are more aroused by erotic materials, but the gender difference is not large (Murnen & Stockton, 1997). Laboratory experiments provide insight into the responses of men and women to erotic materials. In one typical study, participants were shown a variety of video clips; some portrayed sexual interactions (e.g., partially clothed man and woman kissing; man and woman engaged in oral sex) and others portrayed neutral, nonsexual content (e.g., beach scene of waves lapping the shore) (Suschinsky et al., 2009). The participants were sexually experienced, heterosexual young adults. The researchers took measures as the participants watched the video clips. Not only did the researchers obtain participants' self-reported ratings of their sexual arousal as they viewed the stimuli, but they also obtained objective measures of their physiological levels of arousal. To do this, they used two instruments:

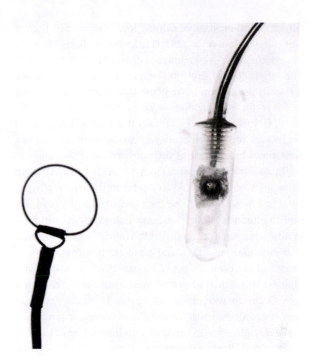

Figure 5   Two devices used to measure physiological sexual response in males and females. The penile strain gauge (*left*) consists of a flexible band that fits around the base of the penis. The photoplethysmograph (*right*) is an acrylic cylinder containing a photocell and a light source, which is placed just inside the vagina.

©J.R. Heiman

a **penile strain gauge** and a vaginal **photoplethysmograph** (Figure 5). The penile strain gauge (which our students have dubbed the "peter meter") is used to get a physiological measure of arousal in a male; it is a flexible loop that fits around the base of the penis and records its expansion. The photoplethysmograph measures physiological arousal in a female; it is an acrylic cylinder, about the size of a tampon, that is placed just inside the entrance to the vagina. Both instruments measure vasocongestion in the genitals, which is the major physiological response during sexual arousal (see the chapter "Sexual Arousal").

As predicted, both women and men showed near-zero subjective ratings of arousal to the neutral content and significantly higher ratings of arousal to the sexual interaction clips. Similarly, the physiological measures of arousal were significantly higher during sexual content than neutral content, and that was true for both women and men. But here's the most interesting finding. For men, the correlation between their subjective ratings of arousal and their

> **Penile strain gauge:** A device used to measure physiological sexual arousal in the male; it is a flexible loop that fits around the base of the penis.
> **Photoplethysmograph (foh-toh-pleth-ISS-moh-graf):** An acrylic cylinder placed inside the vagina to measure physiological sexual arousal in the female. Also called a *photometer.*

physiological arousal was much higher ($r = .66$) than it was for women ($r = .29$). These correlations measure the *concordance* or agreement between subjective arousal and physiological arousal. Numerous studies, from the 1970s to the present, have documented that concordance is lower for women than it is for men (Chivers et al., 2010; Heiman, 1975). Essentially this means that men are well aware of their physiological arousal, but women can sometimes be unaware of their physiological arousal.

In an interesting related study, one experimental group of women was instructed to attend to their genital signs of sexual arousal ("While rating these slides, I would like you to attend to various changes that may occur in your genital area such as vaginal lubrication, pelvic warmth, and muscular tension"), and a second group was told to attend to nongenital signs of arousal ("While rating these slides, I would like you to attend to various changes that may occur in your body. These are heartrate increase, nipple erection, breast swelling, and muscular tension"), while a control group was given no instructions (Korff & Geer, 1983). Both experimental groups showed high correlations between self-reports and physiological measures of arousal, whereas the control group showed the same low correlation that other research has found. This shows that women can be quite accurate in realizing their physical arousal if they are simply told to focus their attention on it. The broader culture, of course, does not give women such instructions but rather tells them to focus on the environment outside themselves—the love, romance, partner—so that many women have not learned to focus on their body. But the experiment described here shows quite clearly that they can.

Other studies have used fMRI brain scans to examine gender differences in response to erotic materials (Rupp & Wallen, 2008). The results show that the brain regions that fire, mostly in the limbic system, are the same in women and men. However, only men show increased activation in the hypothalamus, which, as we have seen in earlier chapters, is important to the release of testosterone.

The Orgasm Gap

Men are more consistent than women at having orgasms during sex. For example, according to the NSSHB, 91 percent of men—but only 64 percent of women—had an orgasm during their most recent sexual encounter (Herbenick et al., 2010c). The gap is narrower for orgasm consistency during masturbation, but even here men seem to be more effective: 80 percent of men, compared with 60 percent of women, report that they usually or always have an orgasm when masturbating (Laumann et al., 1994, p. 84).

An interesting related finding has to do with orgasm consistency in heterosexual compared with same-gender sexual interactions. In one study, men reported having an orgasm, on average, 85 percent of the time during sexual activity, and the percentage was the same whether they were straight or gay, that is, whether they had a female or a male partner (Garcia et al., 2014). Lesbian women, however, had a significantly higher rate of orgasm (75 percent) than heterosexual women (62 percent). These findings indicate that, for women, gender of the partner is important, and having a female partner can mean more orgasms, perhaps because women understand each other's bodies better than men understand women's bodies.

Sex Drive

Evidence from a number of sources indicates that men, on average, have a stronger sex drive than women do (Baumeister et al., 2001; Peplau, 2003). Men think about sex more often and have more frequent and varied fantasies than women do. Compared with women, men desire more sexual partners and a greater frequency of intercourse. In a study across 52 nations, the gender difference in the preferred number of partners was found worldwide (Schmitt, 2003). It is important to remember, of course, that these are average differences. For a particular heterosexual couple, it is quite possible that the woman's level of desire would exceed the man's.

Do men have sex on the brain—that is, do they think about sex constantly? And do women never think about sex? Flashy media reports suggest that this is true. However, a clever study indicates otherwise. Undergraduates were given golf tally counters, to tally their thoughts about sex for one week (Fisher et al., 2012). Men thought about sex on average 19 times a day, compared with 10 times a day for women, so men thought about sex more, but not anything like 100 times per day. Moreover, other students tallied their thoughts about food and about sleep, and men thought about both food and sleep more than women did, so it isn't just sex on their brains. Also, the range was enormous for men—one man thought about sex only once a day and, at the other end of the spectrum, another thought about it 388 times per day. One woman thought about sex 140 times per day. The differences from one man to the next, or from one woman to the next, are far greater than the average difference between women and men.

Why the Differences?

Five differences in male and female sexuality—the lower percentage of females, compared with males, who masturbate; women's more disapproving attitudes toward casual sex; women's lesser orgasm consistency; men's greater use of porn; and men's greater sex drive—are fairly well documented and in need of explanation. A wide variety of scholars have suggested possible explanations.

Are the Differences Bogus?

One possibility is that many of these gender differences, typically documented by self-report, are not true differences. Instead, it could be that people report what is expected of them, shaped by gender norms. Men are expected to want lots of sex, so they exaggerate their desire in self-reports, or women minimize theirs.

A clever study used the *bogus pipeline method* to investigate this possibility (Alexander & Fisher, 2003; see also Jonason & Fisher, 2009; Conley et al., 2011). College students were brought to the lab to fill out questionnaires about their sexual attitudes and behaviors. They were randomly assigned to one of three experimental conditions. In the *bogus pipeline condition,* the student was hooked up to a fake polygraph, or lie detector machine, and told that the machine could detect false answers. People should respond very honestly in this condition. In the *anonymous condition,* the student simply filled out the questionnaire anonymously, as is typical of much sex research, and placed the questionnaire in a locked box when finished. In the *exposure threat condition,* respondents were instructed to hand their completed questionnaires directly to the experimenter, who was an undergraduate peer, and the experimenter sat in full view while the respondents completed their questionnaires, serving as a reminder that this other person would easily be able to see their answers. Figure 6 shows the results for reports of the number of sexual partners the respondents had had.

When people were in the bogus pipeline condition and gave the most honest reporting, men's and women's reports of the number of their sexual partners were nearly identical—in fact, women's were slightly higher than men's. In the standard conditions of anonymity used in most sex research, women reported fewer partners than men did, and under a threat that responses would be made public the largest gap between women and men appeared. In the anonymous condition and the exposure threat condition, differences emerged that were consistent with gender roles. Women confirmed the expectation that they have few partners.

What are the implications of this study? Does it mean that all the differences described in the previous section are bogus? Probably not, but it means that findings of gender differences obtained by self-reports can be exaggerations of the truth. And it is important to note that findings obtained from physiological measures, such as those used in the study with the penile strain gauge and the photoplethysmograph, are not vulnerable to these reporting biases.

> **When men report more different sexual partners than women do, is that accurate? How can it be?**

Let's assume that the gender differences discussed in the previous section are real, although perhaps not as dramatically large as the research suggests. How then can these differences be explained?

Biological Factors

Gender differences in sexuality might be created, in part, by two biological factors: anatomy and hormones.

Anatomy

Men's sexual anatomy is external and visible and has a very obvious response: erection. When a male is nude, he can easily see his sexual organs, either by looking down or by looking in a mirror. The female sexual organs, in contrast, are hidden. A nude female looks down and sees nothing except pubic hair (which really is not very informative); she looks in a full-length mirror and sees the same thing. Only by doing the mirror exercise described in the chapter "Sexual Anatomy" can she get a good view of her own genitals. To make matters worse, the word *clitoris*—but not *penis*—is often missing from books about sexuality, from parents' talk about sex, and from students' knowledge about sexuality (Ogletree & Ginsburg, 2000). Furthermore, the female genitals do not have an obvious arousal response like the male's erection. As a result, she may be less aware of her own arousal, a notion that is supported by concordance research.

The anatomical explanation, then, is that because the woman's genitals are not in plain view and because their arousal response is less obvious than that of the man's genitals, she is less likely to masturbate and less likely

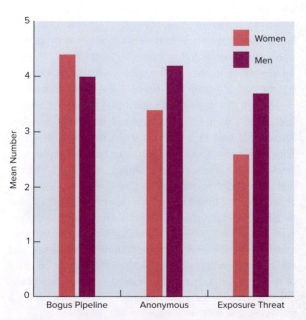

Figure 6   Mean number of sexual partners reported by men and women in the Bogus Pipeline Study (see text for further details).

to develop her full sexual potential (Baldwin & Baldwin, 1997). If this explanation is correct, or is at least part of the answer, could steps be taken to help women develop their sexuality? Perhaps parents could tell their daughters about the mirror exercise at an early age and encourage them to become more aware of their own sexual organs. And parents might want to discuss the idea of masturbation with their daughters.

Hormones

The hormonal explanation rests on the finding that testosterone is related to sexual behavior. This evidence was reviewed in the chapter "Sexual Arousal." Basically, the evidence comes from studies in which male animals are castrated (and thus lose their natural source of testosterone), with the result that their sexual behavior disappears, presumably reflecting a decrease in sex drive. If replacement injections of testosterone are given, the sexual behavior returns.

Women generally have lower levels of testosterone in their tissues than men have. Human females, for example, have about one-quarter the level of testosterone that human males have (Granger et al., 2004).

The hormonal explanation, then, is that if testosterone is important in activating sexual behavior and if females have only one-quarter as much of it as males have, this might result in lower levels of sexual behavior such as masturbation in women, or a lower sex drive.

There are several problems with this logic. First, it may be that cells in the brain or the genitals of women are more sensitive to testosterone than the comparable cells in men; thus a little testosterone might go a long way in women's bodies. Second, we must be cautious about making inferences to humans from studies done on animals. Although some recent studies have demonstrated the effects of testosterone on sexual interest and behavior in humans, the effects are less consistent and more complex than in other species (see the chapter "Sexual Arousal"). Finally, as we saw in the chapter "Sex Hormones, Sexual Differentiation, and the Menstrual Cycle," testosterone levels are not fixed in a given person. Instead, they respond to environment and experience.

Cultural Factors

Our culture has traditionally placed tighter restrictions on women's sexuality than it has on men's, and vestiges of these restrictions linger today. It seems likely that these restrictions have acted as a damper on female sexuality, and thus they may help to explain why some women do not masturbate, why some women have difficulty having orgasms, and why some women are wary about casual sex.

One of the clearest reflections of the differences in restrictions on male and female sexuality is the *double standard*. As we saw in the chapter "Sexuality and the Life

Cycle: Childhood and Adolescence," the double standard says that the same sexual behavior is evaluated differently, depending on whether a male or a female engages in it. The sexual double standard gives men more sexual freedom than women (Crawford & Popp, 2003; Fasula et al., 2014). An example is casual sex, which has been more acceptable for males than for females. Indeed, casual sex might be a status symbol for a man but a sign of being a slut for a woman. The sexual double standard is alive and well in teen girl magazines, where negative consequences of sex are associated more often with girls than with boys (Joshi et al., 2011). Research shows that adolescent girls who more strongly believe in the double standard feel less entitled to sexual pleasure from masturbation (Emmerink et al., 2016).

Generally there seems to be less of a double standard today than there was in the past. The decline of the double standard may help to explain why some of the gender differences found in older studies of sexual behavior have disappeared in more recent studies. When cultural forces do not make such a distinction between male and female, males and females become more similar in their sexual behavior. Yet vestiges of the double standard remain today in regard to casual sex, which is approved more for men than for women (Bogle, 2008; Kettrey, 2016).

Gender roles are another cultural force that may contribute to differences in male and female sexuality, as was discussed earlier in this chapter (Sanchez et al., 2012). Gender roles dictate proper behavior for females and males in sexual interactions—that is, they specify the script. For example, there is a stereotype of the male as the initiator and the female as the passive object of his advances; surely this does not encourage women to take active steps to bring about their own orgasms. One study found that women implicitly associate sex with submission, whereas men do not (Sanchez et al., 2006). For the women, the more they associated sex with submission, the greater their difficulty with becoming sexually aroused.

Marital and family roles may play a part. Children can act as a damper on the parents' sexual relationship. The couple lose their privacy when they gain children. They may worry about their children bursting through an unlocked door and witnessing what Freud called "the primal scene" of their parents making love. Or they may be concerned that their children will hear the sounds of lovemaking. Generally, though, the woman is assigned the primary responsibility for child rearing, so she may be more aware of the presence of the children in the house and more concerned about possible harmful effects on them of witnessing their parents engaging in sex. Once again, her worry and anxiety do not contribute to her having a satisfying sexual experience.

Body image issues also contribute to gender differences in sexuality and, in particular, to women's sexual functioning (Woertman & van den Brink, 2012). Overall,

A Sexually Diverse World

Male Sexuality

Bernie Zilbergeld wrote *The New Male Sexuality* on the basis of his experience as a sex therapist and psychotherapist.

He argues that the media have taught us a Fantasy Model of Sex, which is ultimately detrimental to men, and to women as well. He captures this idea in his chapter title "It's Two Feet Long, Hard as Steel, Always Ready, and Will Knock Your Socks Off," describing the Fantasy Model of the erect penis and its power over women. The Fantasy Model of Sex creates unrealistic expectations and performance pressures on men.

Zilbergeld discusses a number of cultural myths based on the Fantasy Model. Here are four of them.

Myth 1. We're liberated folks who are very comfortable with sex. The media teach us that we have completely shed our Victorian heritage and everyone is totally comfortable with sex. The men and women in the movies and on TV never have any concerns or problems with sex. The women don't worry about their ability to orgasm. The men don't worry about the size or hardness of their penises. But if all this is true, why do we have such poor sex education in the United States? Why do parents have such difficulty talking about sex with their children? The truth is that although public manifestations (like the movies) are very open about sex, in our private lives we have all kinds of discomforts and uncertainties about sex.

Myth 2. A real man isn't into sissy stuff like feelings and communicating. Boys are trained into the male role, which discourages the expression of emotions such as tenderness. Communicating about personal feelings becomes difficult if not impossible. As one man said, "What it really comes down to is that I guess I'm not very comfortable with expressing my emotions—I don't think many men are—but I am pretty comfortable with sex, so I just

sort of let sex speak for me" (Zilbergeld, 1999, p. 21). Men are crippled in forming emotional relationships, as a result, and sexual interactions are less satisfying than they might be if there were more communication.

Myth 3. All touching is sexual or should lead to sex. For men, touching is a means to an end: sex. For women, touch more often is a goal in itself, as when women hug each other. Men need to learn that sometimes they just need to be held or stroked, and that that can provide more emotional satisfaction than sexual intercourse.

Myth 4. Sex is centered on a hard penis and what's done with it. Adolescent boys have a fixation on their penis and its erections, and this fascination persists throughout life. It creates heavy performance pressure for an erection— and not just any old erection, but a really big one. As Zilbergeld puts it, "Penises in fantasyland come in only three sizes: large, extra large, and so big you can't get them through the door." Men need to learn that the penis is not the only sexual part of their bodies, and that many very enjoyable forms of sexual behavior require no erection at all. That relieves a lot of performance pressure.

Zilbergeld's books are not based on a survey or laboratory research, but rather on his experiences as a sex therapist. His work with people having problems and seeking therapy may bias his views. But his observations are tremendously insightful, and many people not seeking therapy have benefited from his books. Moreover, recent scientific studies support many of his observations (Clarke et al., 2015; Farvid & Braun, 2006; Mize & Manago, 2018).

Source: Zilbergeld (1999).

---

there are gender differences in body esteem; compared with men, women feel more dissatisfied with their bodies. And sex is all about bodies. Research shows that women who are dissatisfied with their bodies report lower levels of sexual desire and arousal and more avoidance of sex. In part this is due to a kind of self-conscious monitoring of how one's body looks during sex. These are distracting thoughts and, as we will see in the chapter "Sexual

Disorders and Sex Therapy," distracting thoughts contribute to reduced enjoyment of sexual experiences. Why are women more dissatisfied with their bodies and why do they monitor their appearance more? The major factor appears to be the media, which portray skinny women with airbrushed features that real women can't live up to, making them feel bad about their bodies (Grabe et al., 2008).

Other Factors

A number of other factors, not easily classified as biological or cultural, may also contribute to differences between male and female sexuality.[2]

Women get pregnant and men do not. Particularly in the days before effective contraceptives were available, pregnancy might be a highly undesirable consequence of sexuality for a woman. Thinking that an episode of lovemaking might result in a 9-month pregnancy and another mouth to feed could put a damper on anyone's sexuality. Even today, pregnancy fears can be a force. For example, among sexually active teenage girls, 10 percent used no method of contraception the last time they had sex (Abma & Martinez, 2017). A woman who is worried about whether she will become pregnant—and, if she is an unmarried teenager, about whether her parents will find out that she has been engaging in sexual activity—is not in a state conducive to the enjoyment of sex, much less the experience of orgasm (although this scarcely explains why more women than men do not masturbate).

Ineffective techniques of stimulating the woman may also be a factor. The commonest techniques of intercourse, with the penis moving in and out of the vagina, may provide good stimulation for the male but not for the female, because she may not be getting sufficient clitoral stimulation. Perhaps the problem, then, is that women are expected to orgasm as a result of intercourse, when that technique is not very effective for producing orgasms in women.

A relationship probably exists between the evidence that fewer women masturbate than men and gender differences in orgasm consistency. Childhood and adolescent experiences with masturbation are important early sources of learning about sexuality. Through these experiences we learn how our bodies respond to sexual stimulation and what the most effective techniques are for stimulating our own bodies. This learning is important to our experience of adult, two-person sex.

Not only may women's relative inexperience with masturbation lead to a lack of sexual learning, but it also may create a kind of "erotic dependency" on men. Typically, boys' earliest sexual experiences are with masturbation, which they learn how to do from other boys. More important, they learn that they can produce their own sexual pleasure. Girls typically have their earliest sexual experiences in heterosexual petting. They therefore learn about sex from boys, and learn that their sexual pleasure is produced by the male.

Once again, such ideas might lead to a recommendation that girls be given information about masturbation.

Numerous factors that may contribute to shaping male and female sexuality have been discussed. Our belief is that a combination of several of these factors produces the differences that do exist. The early differences in experiences with masturbation are important. Although these differences may result from differences in anatomy, they could be eliminated by giving girls information on masturbation. Women may enter into adult sexual relationships with a lack of experience in the bodily sensations of arousal and orgasm, and they may be unaware of the best techniques for stimulating their own bodies. Put this lack of experience together with various cultural forces, such as the double standard and ineffective techniques of stimulation, and it is not too surprising that there are some gender differences in sexuality.

Beyond the Young Adults

One of the problems with our understanding of gender differences in sexuality is that so much of the research has concentrated on college students or other groups of young adults (as is true of much behavioral research). For example, the 52-nation study of gender differences in preferred number of partners, discussed earlier, tested college students at nearly all sites (Schmitt, 2003). Using this population may provide a very narrow view of male–female differences; they are considered during only a very small part of the lifespan. In reality, female sexuality and male sexuality change in their nature and focus across the lifespan. For example, it is a common belief in our culture that men reach their sexual "peak" at around age 19, whereas women do not reach theirs until they are 35 or 40 (Barr et al., 2002). There is some scientific evidence supporting this view. Kinsey (1953) found, for example, that women generally had orgasms more consistently at 40 than they did at 25.

Research based on the sexual excitation-inhibition model, discussed in the chapter "Theoretical Perspectives on Sexuality," is helpful in understanding how patterns of gender differences shift at different ages. In one study, a large sample of people between the ages of 14 and 80 was recruited (Pinxten & Lievens, 2016). They completed scales measuring sexual excitation and sexual inhibition. The results showed that sexual excitation scores peaked between 20 and 40 years of age for both women and men, and declined for both after that. The gender gap, with females scoring lower, was about the same at all ages. In contrast, women's level of sexual inhibition was fairly constant from age 20 to age 80; men's inhibition was considerably lower than women's at age 20, but then rose steadily; from about age 55 on, women and men had the same level of inhibition. This study illustrates how the patterns of gender differences that we find with college-student samples of 20-year-olds are not always true later in the lifespan.

[2]Other possible causes of orgasm problems in women are discussed in the chapter "Sexual Disorders and Sex Therapy."

It is important to remember, though, that these patterns may be culturally, rather than biologically, produced. In some other cultures—for example, Mangaia in the South Pacific (see the chapter "Sexuality in Perspective")—females have orgasms 100 percent of the time during coitus, even when they are adolescents.

Transgender Issues and Experience

Many textbooks cover transgender issues and identity in the chapter on sexual variations or deviations. However, we have included it in our chapter on gender because it is fundamentally an issue of gender and, more specifically, gender identity.

The term **transgender** is broad, encompassing people whose gender identity does not match their gender assigned at birth based on the appearance of the genitals (natal gender). Some have an identity that is not male or female, but instead is a third category, *genderqueer*. That is, they see themselves as falling outside the gender binary, and some use the term *nonbinary* (Hegarty et al., 2018; Richards et al., 2016). Others do not wish to be categorized or labeled. And still others are **transsexuals**, whose gender identity does not match their natal gender, e.g., a person born with a male body who has a female identity; typically this term is reserved for those who choose to undergo medical treatments, such as hormone therapy and surgery, so that the gender of their body is consistent with their gender identity. A **male-to-female transsexual (MTF)** or *trans woman* is someone whose natal gender was male and whose gender identity is female, and a **female-to-male transsexual (FTM)** or *trans man* is someone whose natal gender was female but who has a male identity.

The term **trans** is even broader and includes people who identify as transsexual, transgender, cross dressing, gender nonconforming, gender fluid, genderqueer, and other gender-variant people (Devor & Dominic, 2015). Sometimes the term *transgender and gender nonconforming* (TGNC) is used. The terms for various expressions of gender variance have developed rapidly in the last few years and show every sign of continuing to change, so stay tuned for new developments!

What are we to call everyone else, those who are not transgender? It might be tempting to call them "normal," but a more equitable term has been introduced: **cisgender** (named after cis and trans isomers in organic chemistry).

Transgender people are not a new phenomenon. References are found throughout much of recorded history, although that modern term is not used (Devor, 1997). In the early centuries of Christianity, a number of women transformed themselves into men. One example is Pelagia, a woman who refused to marry and fled, dressing as a man and entering a monastery. She became Pelagius, a man, and was later elected prior of a convent. A woman at the convent became pregnant and accused Pelagius of being the father. Nothing, of course, could have been further from the truth, but Pelagius was not in a position to offer the strongest defense. He was expelled from the convent and died in disgrace. When he died, it was discovered that he had a female body.

CDC data estimates the prevalence of transgender individuals in the United States at 0.6 percent, with a range across states from 0.3 percent in North Dakota to 0.8 percent in Hawaii (Flores et al., 2016). The 0.6 percent prevalence translates to 1.4 million adults, which is not a small number. Another U.S. study, using probability sampling, found a prevalence of 0.5 percent (Crissman et al., 2017). The two estimates are quite close to each other. That said, undoubtedly the prevalence will increase in the next decade because transgender is now a much more available label than it was previously, and most Americans have probably heard the term *transgender* because of extensive media attention to some trans individuals.

Diagnosis Issues

Gender dysphoria refers to psychological distress about a mismatch between a person's gender identity and natal gender and is used in the American Psychiatric Association's *Diagnostic and Statistical Manual* (*DSM-5*; American Psychiatric Association, 2013). Other criteria for diagnosis include a strong desire to be treated as a gender different from one's natal gender, and a strong desire for the primary and secondary sex characteristics of another gender (Byne et al., 2018). Gender dysphoria can appear in childhood and is characterized by a strong desire to be the other gender, substantial distress about the situation, a resistance to wearing clothing typical for the natal gender, a preference for toys and games typical of the other gender, and a desire for their genitals to match their gender identity. Gender dysphoria can also appear in adolescence or adulthood and is then called late-onset gender dysphoria. Notice that this diagnosis applies only if the individual is distressed about the mismatch

---

Transgender: A term encompassing a broad range of individuals whose gender identity does not match their gender assigned at birth (natal gender); includes those who identify as genderqueer or genderfluid, gender nonconforming, and transsexuals.

Transsexual: A person who believes they were born with the body of the other gender, e.g., a person born with a male body who has a female identity. These individuals often seek medical gender reassignment procedures.

Male-to-female transsexual (MTF): A transsexual whose natal gender is male and whose identity is female.

Female-to-male transsexual (FTM): A transsexual whose natal gender is female and whose identity is male.

Trans: A broad term encompassing those identifying as transgender, transsexual, agender, and other gender-variant people.

Cisgender: A person whose natal gender and gender identity match, e.g., a person born with female genitals whose identity is female.

Gender dysphoria: Psychological distress about a mismatch between a person's gender identity and natal gender.

between their natal gender and gender identity. People who have the mismatch between identity and body but are not distressed about it would not qualify for the diagnosis.

The gender dysphoria diagnosis is controversial because some people believe that it stigmatizes trans people (Davy, 2015). However, to gain insurance coverage for medical care, such as hormone treatments, one must have a diagnosis, so that is part of the reason for having the gender dysphoria diagnosis.

There is another system of diagnosis used worldwide, the ICD (International Classification of Diseases, by the World Health Organization). The new edition, ICD-11, was released in 2018. It uses somewhat different diagnostic terms: *Gender Incongruence of Childhood* (GIC) and *Gender Incongruence of Adolescence and Adulthood* (GIAA) (Winter et al., 2016). The hope was that these would be less stigmatizing terms.

The Experiences of Trans People

One notable set of experiences for trans people is the experience of prejudice and discrimination. Transphobia and anti-trans prejudice are terms that parallel the terms homophobia and anti-gay prejudice (see the chapter "Sexual Orientation: Gay, Straight, or Bi?"). **Transphobia** refers to a strong, irrational fear of trans people. **Anti-trans prejudice,** which is the more scientific term, refers to negative attitudes and behaviors toward trans individuals (Tebbe, Moradi, & Ege, 2014).

The National Center for Transgender Equality issued a report, *Injustice at Every Turn,* based on a well-conducted national survey (Grant et al., 2011). Rates of discrimination against trans people were high. For example, 53 percent reported being verbally harassed or disrespected in a public place such as a restaurant or hotel; 24 percent reported discrimination in a doctor's office or hospital; and 57 percent experienced significant rejection from their families. Yet respondents also demonstrated remarkable resilience. As one trans person commented,

> My mother disowned me. I was fired from my job after 18 years of loyal employment. I was forced onto public assistance to survive. But still I have pressed forward, started a new career, and rebuilt my immediate family. You are defined not by falling but how well you rise after falling. I'm a licensed practical nurse now and am studying to become an RN. I have walked these streets and been harassed nearly every day, but I will not change. I am back out there the next day with my head up. (Grant et al., 2011)

Focusing on adolescents specifically, a national survey of youth between the ages of 13 and 18 compared the bullying experiences of gender minority (trans, gender-nonconforming) youth to cisgender

Figure 7 Brandon Teena, a female-to-male trans adolescent who was murdered because of the ignorance and prejudice of those around him.

©AP Images

youth (Reisner et al., 2015). Among cisgender youth, 58 percent had experienced bullying in the past 12 months, compared with 83 percent for gender minority youth.

Experiences of prejudice and discrimination can include microaggressions, discrimination in the workplace, discrimination in housing, and discrimination in health care. Microaggressions can occur in numerous situations, including romantic relationships. For example, a romantic partner might minimize the person's transgender identity, such as stating that they don't believe in nonbinary genders (Pulice-Farrow et al., 2017). In the workplace, discrimination might occur at the institutional level, such as an employer not providing insurance coverage for trans-related health care (Ruggs et al., 2015). At the interpersonal level, discrimination might come from unsupportive attitudes expressed by coworkers (Ruggs et al., 2015). Housing discrimination may occur, for example, if a landlord refuses to rent to a trans person (Cutler-Seeber, 2018). In health care, numerous forms of discrimination can occur; one example is when an insurer considers being transgender a "preexisting" condition and therefore not covered by insurance (Cutler-Seeber, 2018).

These experiences of prejudice and sometimes outright violence can take a toll on the mental and physical health of trans people, as discussed in a later section.

Transphobia: A strong, irrational fear of trans people.
Anti-trans prejudice: Negative attitudes and behaviors toward trans individuals.

Milestones in Sex Research

Measuring Anti-Trans Prejudice

E lliot Tebbe, Bonnie Moradi, and Engin Ege (2014) developed a Genderism and Transphobia Scale. Here are some of the items. Each is rated on a scale from 1 (*strongly agree*) to 7 (*strongly disagree*). How would you rate the items?

1. If I found out that my best friend was changing their sex, I would freak out.

2. Women who see themselves as men are abnormal.

3. A man who dresses as a woman is a pervert.

4. Sex change operations are morally wrong.

5. I have behaved violently toward a man because he was too feminine.

On a more mundane level, pronouns can be an issue for trans individuals. One of the problems is *misgendering* by others, that is, being called by pronouns that indicate a gender different from one's identity. Those who identify with one of the two gender binary categories, male or female, prefer to be called by the pronouns that match their gender identity. Those whose identity falls outside those two categories, such as those whose identity is nonbinary, may prefer to be called by gender-neutral pronouns. Table 1 lists traditional pronouns in the first two rows, and then two alternatives for gender-neutral pronouns. The first involves "they," that is, using plural pronouns to refer to an individual. The second alternative, shown in the bottom row, is a new set of pronouns. "Ze," for example, is substituted for "he or she." When interacting with people who have told you they are trans, it is important to ask what pronouns they use.

Beyond these issues, transgender people and the transgender community are diverse in many ways, such as race and social class (Schilt & Lagos, 2017). There is also diversity in norms, such as norms about what the "best" kind of transgender person is. There are two camps within the trans community on this issue (Cutler-Seeber, 2018).

One group believes that the highest goal is to undergo successful medical transition and "pass" as a cisgender person. The other group believes that it is best to challenge the gender binary and remain ambiguous about one's gender, as occurs with identities such as genderqueer and nonbinary.

Reducing Prejudice and Discrimination against Trans People

What can be done to reduce prejudice and discrimination against trans people? Because public attention to transgender issues is relatively new, interventions to reduce prejudice are also very new. Social psychologists have developed techniques for reducing other kinds of prejudice, so it should be possible to apply some of them here. One consideration is that interventions to change attitudes may last only until the end of the experimental session, but we would like them to last for a long time—perhaps months or even years.

Research has shown that even brief interventions can have lasting effects if the individual engages in active, deep processing of the message from the intervention.

Table 1 An Alternate Set of Gender-Neutral Pronouns for Trans People. Some trans individuals do not wish to be called by traditional pronouns based on the gender binary.

	Subject	Object	Possessive	Possessive Pronoun	Reflexive
He	*He* laughed	I called *him*	*His* dog barked	That is *his*	He likes *himself*
She	*She* laughed	I called *her*	*Her* dog barked	That is *hers*	She likes *herself*
They	*They* laughed	I called *them*	*Their* dog barked	That is *theirs*	They like *themselves*
Ze	*Ze* laughed ("zee")	I called *hir* ("heer")	*Hir* dog barked ("heer")	That is *hirs* ("heers")	Ze likes *hirself* ("heerself")

Another element of successful interventions to change attitudes is getting the individual to take the perspective of the group that is the object of prejudice. Applying these principles in one bold experiment, canvassers went door-to-door in Miami, Florida, to discuss a new ordinance protecting transgender people from discrimination (Broockman & Kalla, 2016). The canvassers did several things in their meetings with people (all of whom were registered voters): they informed the person that as a voter they might face a decision on a transgender issue (whether to repeal the ordinance); they asked the person to explain their views on the topic; they showed a video with arguments on both sides of the issue; they defined the term *transgender;* they encouraged perspective-taking by asking the respondent about a time when they themselves had been judged for being different and then encouraged the voter to see how this might apply to transgender people; and, finally, they asked people to describe how the exercise changed their minds. All of this lasted just about 10 minutes and was designed to foster active processing of the information, in comparison to something like a billboard on the highway, which a viewer probably thinks about very little. There was also a control group, but it was complicated and we won't trouble you with it. Participants completed a baseline questionnaire and a series of questionnaires following the intervention going out to 3 months after the intervention, and these questionnaires seemed unconnected to the intervention. The results indicated that the intervention was effective: at 3 days and even 3 months afterward, the intervention group had more positive attitudes toward transgender people than did the control group.

Interventions such as this one show much promise for the future (see also Tompkins et al., 2015).

Transgender Development

When gender dysphoria appears in childhood, it is characterized by a strong desire to be the other gender, substantial distress about the situation, a resistance to wearing clothing typical for the natal gender, a preference for toys and games typical of the other gender, and a desire for their genitals to match their gender identity. This pattern can emerge as early as 3 to 5 years of age (Olson & Gulgoz, 2018).

If parents are supportive, some trans children socially transition (Olson & Gulgoz, 2018). That is, they are called by pronouns that match their identity, trans girls dress as girls, and trans boys dress as boys, but they receive no hormonal or surgical treatments. Socially transitioned transgender children show the same play preferences as cisgender children of the gender that matches their identity (Olson & Gulgoz, 2018). Research also shows that transgender children who are supported and allowed to socially transition score about the same on measures of mental health as cisgender children (Olson et al., 2016). That is, they do well psychologically. When trans children are not supported and not allowed to socially transition, they score poorly on mental health indicators (Ristori & Steensma, 2016).

An interesting study of transgender children aged 5 to 12 used the Implicit Association Test (IAT) to measure their mental gender associations (Olson et al., 2015). The results indicated that the transgender children displayed response patterns consistent with their gender identity, not their natal gender. Their responses differed significantly from the cisgender control group of their natal gender and did not differ significantly from the cisgender group of their gender identity. That is, for example, the children born boys who had a female identity showed responses—even nonconscious, implicit ones—that were the same as cisgender girls. These results indicate that, at some deep level, these natal boys are like girls psychologically.

In another study, adolescents with gender dysphoria were given a whiff of androstadienone, a pheromone that activates the hypothalamus differently in males and females; their hypothalamic response was then monitored using MRI (Burke et al., 2014). Their hypothalamic response resembled that of the control group matching their gender identity, not their natal gender. Thus their brains functioned more like a person of their gender identity than like a person of their natal gender. The researchers suggested that this pattern reflects prenatal brain differentiation in the direction of the gender identity.

Gender dysphoria in childhood does not always persist into adulthood, making it difficult to know how much it should be treated. In studies of children with gender dysphoria, only about 20 percent continue to experience gender dysphoria in adulthood; more often, those who were natal males identify as gay men in adulthood (Coleman et al., 2011). What differentiates the persisters (those who continue to be transgender in adolescence and adulthood) from the desisters (those who return to being cisgender)? One of the best predictors is the intensity of the gender dysphoria (Steensma et al., 2013b). Those who display more intense gender dysphoria are more likely to be the persisters. Gender dysphoria in adolescence is much more likely to persist into adulthood.

In some cases, gender dysphoria first appears in adolescence (Leibowitz & de Vries, 2016). Gender dysphoria after the beginning of puberty indicates a high likelihood of persistence into adulthood (Leibowitz & de Vries, 2016). To use the terminology introduced above, these people are very likely to be persisters, that is, to show a gender identity that does not match their natal gender into adulthood. If the condition is present early in pubertal development, it may be possible to use pubertal suppression drugs, which are discussed in a later section. Gender dysphoria that first appears in later adolescence or adulthood is termed *late onset* (Zucker et al., 2016).

Sexual Orientation and Transgender Identity

Gender identity is a separate issue from sexual orientation, although many people conflate or confuse them (Mizock & Hopwood, 2016). With people undergoing gender transitions, terminology becomes confusing. For example, if a trans individual is straight, does that refer to attractions based on natal gender or gender identity? Therefore, the terms *gynephilic* and *androphilic* are used (Blanchard et al., 1995; Smith et al., 2005). Those who are gynephilic are sexually attracted to women (regardless of their own natal gender or gender identity), and those who are androphilic are sexually attracted to men. For example, if we think of an FTM, he would be classified as androphilic if he is attracted to men and as gynephilic if he is attracted to women. Among FTMs, those who are gynephilic are typically more interested in surgery to construct a penis when compared with those who are androphilic (Chivers & Bailey, 2000). Some trans people, too, are bisexual. In a large sample of MTFs, 23 percent said they were attracted to men, 29 percent to women, and 31 percent to both (Grant et al., 2011). In that same study, among FTMs, 25 percent were attracted to women, 13 percent were attracted to men, 13 percent were attracted to both, and 46 percent identified as queer. Notice that this system of terminology (androphilic/gynephilic) creates new binary categories that rely on the gender binary.

Sexual attraction seems to depend, in part, on the time of onset. Compared with early-onset folks, late-onset trans adults are more likely to be sexually attracted to same-gender partners relative to their gender identity (Zucker et al., 2016). For example, natal females with a male gender identity are more likely to be attracted to men, and these men identify as gay.

In one qualitative study, 25 trans men were interviewed about their sexuality (Williams et al., 2013). The men ranged in age from 20 to 65 and were ethnically diverse. All but one of them were taking testosterone (T). Most had had top surgery (explained later in this chapter). Only two of them had had bottom surgery. For most of the men, the testosterone treatments had a big effect, both physically and psychologically. The clitoris grew considerably for them, so they could consider it more as a penis. And they developed a sense of sexual urgency that is associated with masculinity in our culture. As one man said,

I had a pea-sized clit before I started T (testosterone) and it grew 10-fold, and now I have a dick that's the size of a gherkin. (Williams et al., 2013, p. 726)

Another man said that his sexuality had "gone through the roof. I never had an orgasm before. . . . Now I jack off two to four times a day" (p. 728). Yet some regretted their loss of multiple orgasms. And, for those who had not had bottom surgery, the vagina could seem like an unwelcome reminder of their female body.

The researchers also found generational shifts in patterns of identity development. For the older generation of trans men, many had decided first that they were lesbian. That was an available category and identity at that time. Transgender was not. Only later did they conclude that they were trans. In more recent generations, the trans identity develops earlier and first because it is now better known to the general public.

The same research team also interviewed 25 trans women (Williams et al., 2016). Almost all of the women were on estrogen, and the majority had had cosmetic surgery to appear more feminine. The majority had not had bottom surgery, though. The cosmetic surgery was successful to varying degrees, depending on how masculine the person's body type was to begin with, that is, whether they had very broad shoulders. For most of the women, it was very important to feel sexually attractive and feminine. When they were asked what the most serious problem was for a trans person in a love relationship, the most common response was that it was being truly accepted for who they are.

Trans Health and Mental Health

Trans individuals need health care for a variety of the same conditions and problems that cisgender people have: tobacco use, alcohol abuse, reproductive health, cancer, and mental health issues. Health care provided to trans individuals in the United States needs substantial improvement. For example, all of the medical interventions described in the next section should be covered by health insurance policies, just as they would be for anyone else who needed hormone therapy or surgery, but many insurance programs do not provide such coverage. And, as noted above, many trans people report experiencing discrimination from health care providers, so more education of providers is needed.

Many services should be available for trans individuals short of medical transition treatments (Coleman et al., 2011). These include (1) voice and communication therapy, to help the person speak in the range typical for their gender identity and communicate nonverbally in ways that match their gender identity; (2) supportive therapy and peer support to reduce stress; and (3) for natal males, facial hair removal by electrolysis or other methods. Supportive therapy for the family is important as well.

Experiences of prejudice and sometimes outright violence can take a toll on the mental and physical health of trans people. For example, experiences with people not affirming their gender identity correlate with symptoms of depression for trans individuals (Testa et al., 2015). In one sample, trans individuals who had experienced violence were about 4 times as likely to have attempted suicide (Testa et al., 2012). Overall, among young adults, 52 percent of gender minorities meet symptom levels for depression, compared with 27 percent for cisgender young adults (Reisner et al., 2016).

On a brighter note, research on the mental health of transgender children indicates that their mental health is as good as that of cisgender children if they are supported in their identity, for example, by parents (Olson et al., 2016).

Social, Medical, and Surgical Transition Processes

Social transition refers to the process in which trans youth or adults live openly in a way that matches their gender identity, not their natal gender (Olson et al., 2016). For a natal male who has a female gender identity, for example, it involves dressing as a woman, adopting female pronouns, and so on. Some TGNC individuals socially transition and stop there; that is, they do not undergo medical or surgical treatments. In a Canadian sample, 30 percent of trans individuals were living as their natal gender, 23 percent had socially transitioned but had no medical interventions; 42 percent were using hormones; 15 percent of MTFs had had surgery to create a vagina, and less than 1 percent of FTMs had had surgery to create a penis (Scheim & Bauer, 2015).

Those who wish to transition medically or surgically are often termed *transsexuals*. Typically, transsexuals have a binary gender identity (e.g., their natal gender is male but their gender identity is female) and wish to undergo medical treatments so their body matches their identity. Some refer to this as *gender-confirming therapy* or gender-affirming therapy. A range of medical interventions is possible, and different individuals choose different interventions. The World Professional Association for Transgender Health (WPATH) has set standards of care for trans people, including standards for medical treatment (Coleman et al., 2011; see also Hembree et al., 2017). An assessment by a mental health professional is required before medical treatments can occur.

Medical treatments include the following (Coleman et al., 2011):

- hormone therapy to accomplish *pubertal suppression* in early adolescents with strong gender dysphoria. These

drugs are sometimes called *puberty blockers*. This treatment is helpful in buying some time for the adolescent to mature and make a well-informed decision about whether to go through additional medical interventions. Pubertal suppression treatments are reversible if the adolescent decides not to pursue a transition. If the adolescent does decide to transition, the process will be simpler. For example, for a trans man, it will not be necessary to perform a mastectomy because the breasts did not develop under pubertal suppression. Pubertal suppression is a relatively new technique; the first evaluation of it indicated that, in young adulthood, transgender individuals treated in this manner function as well psychologically as cisgender individuals, in contrast to the distress they had before treatment (de Vries et al., 2014). Nine studies have now investigated the effects of puberty blockers; the studies consistently find improvements from before treatment to after treatment in psychological outcomes such as depression (Chew et al., 2018).

- *hormone therapy* to feminize or masculinize the body. This type of therapy is only partially reversible and is typically applied only with older adolescents and adults who are capable of making a definite decision about wanting to transition. In FTMs, testosterone therapy can lead to a deeper voice, growth in facial hair, growth of the clitoris, and a decrease in percent body fat. In MTFs, anti-androgens are given, along with estrogen, resulting in breast growth, fewer erections, and increased body fat that creates feminine curves.

Surgical treatments are irreversible and should be chosen only by an adult or a mature adolescent over the legal age of consent. The typical requirement is that the individual has to have lived as a member of the gender with which they identify for at least 12 months to ensure that the transition is truly workable and desirable. Surgical treatments include the following:

- *chest surgery* for removal of breasts for FTMs and breast augmentation for MTFs. This is sometimes referred to as "top surgery."
- *genital surgery* for MTF transsexuals can include penectomy (removal of the penis), orchiectomy (removal of the testes), vaginoplasty (creation of a vagina from the skin of the penis), clitoroplasty (creation of a clitoris), and vulvoplasty (surgery to create a female-appearing vulva). The results of this type of genital surgery ("bottom surgery") are shown in Figure 8.
- *genital surgery* for FTM transsexuals can include removal of the uterus (hysterectomy), fallopian tubes, and ovaries; metoidioplasty or phalloplasty (to create a penis); and enlargement of the scrotum with

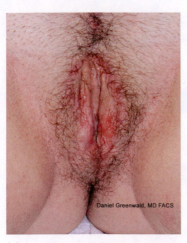

(a)

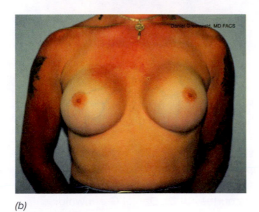

(b)

Figure 8 (a) The appearance of the genitals following male-to-female transsexual surgery. (b) Breast augmentation for an MTF transsexual.

(a) ©Dr. Daniel Greenwald; (b) ©Dr. Daniel Greenwald

insertion of artificial testes (Morrison et al., 2017) (Figure 9). Metoidioplasty involves releasing the clitoris, which enlarges with hormone therapy to create a small penis (Figure 10), whereas phalloplasty involves creation of a penis from tissue such as the forearm. These penis-creating surgeries, especially phalloplasty, are difficult and often not completely successful, so many FTMs decide against them.

According to research, the adjustment of transsexuals who seek surgery is significantly better following surgery. In one study, 86 percent of MTFs were satisfied with their surgery to create a vagina, and 89 percent of FTMs were satisfied with their surgery to create a penis (De Cuypere et al., 2005). In one study of MTFs and FTMs, none expressed regret at having had the surgery (Johansson et al., 2010). In that sense, then, gender transition surgeries are successful.

In many cases, trans people do not seek these medical interventions. Psychotherapy can be very helpful for people with gender dysphoria, and medical interventions may not be necessary. For some, a social transition seems to be all that is needed or wanted. In addition, to the extent that people do not feel forced to fit into one of the two gender binary categories, they may not feel the need for surgery.

Affirmative Psychotherapy with Transgender Individuals

Psychotherapy with TGNC people has shifted from an old model of diagnosing people with a problem to a new model of trans-affirmative practice, and the American Psychological Association has issued guidelines for this new model (APA, 2015; also see Singh & dickey, 2017; dickey & Singh, 2016). The guidelines are clear that the responsibility lies with the clinician to inform themselves and offer affirmative care. Following are some key points in the guidelines:

- Psychologists need to inform themselves with basic knowledge about the transgender experience and transgender research. Examples include understanding that gender identity may not align with natal gender and that gender identity and sexual orientation are two different things.

- Psychologists should understand the prejudice, discrimination, and violence that affect the health and psychological well-being of TGNC people.

- Psychologists should understand transgender development across the lifespan. For example, some TGNC children are persisters and some are desisters. Psychologists need to understand different approaches with TGNC children, including social transition and a wait-and-see approach (Edwards-Leeper et al., 2016).

- In therapy, psychologists should understand that TGNC people have better outcomes if they receive social support and affirmative care.

- Psychologists often are part of interdisciplinary treatment, alongside endocrinologists, surgeons, speech therapists, and social workers.

What Causes Gender Variation?

Most of the research on causes of various kinds of gender variation has been done with transsexuals. There are some inklings of biological factors. One line of thought is that processes in prenatal development are involved, in which the genitals differentiate toward those of one gender and identity differentiates toward the other gender. Two studies have found differences between MTFs and cisgender men in the bed nucleus of the stria terminalis

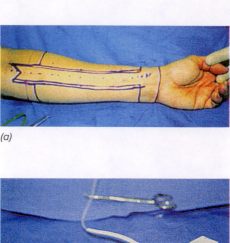

(a)

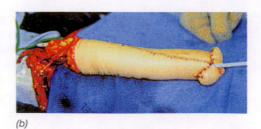

(b)

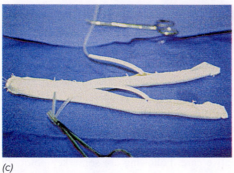

(c)

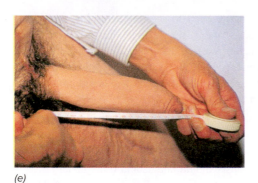

(d)

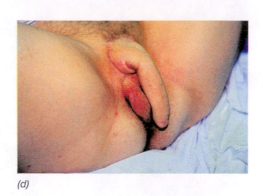

(e)

Figure 9   Female-to-male transsexual surgery.
(*a*) Skin on the forearm marked before transfer to
the groin. (*b*) The penis is constructed (blood vessels
and nerves shown on the left). (*c*) An inflatable prosthesis, wrapped in Goretex and ready for insertion.
(*d*) Penis before insertion of the implant. (*e*) Erect
penis. Photos courtesy of Dr. Daniel Greenwald.

*(a) ©Dr. Daniel Greenwald; (b) ©Dr. Daniel Greenwald;
(c) ©Dr. Daniel Greenwald; (d) ©Dr. Daniel Greenwald;
(e) ©Dr. Daniel Greenwald*

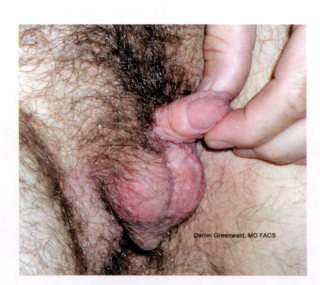

Figure 10   Metoidioplasty, one technique for
female-to-male transsexual surgery.

©Dr. Daniel Greenwald

(BST), which is part of the limbic system (Kruijver et al., 2000; Zhou et al., 1995). As noted in earlier chapters, the limbic system is important in sexuality. In other MRI studies, FTMs displayed brain regions that are intermediate between cis males and cis females (Rametti et al., 2011). This research is complicated by the fact that hormone therapy itself causes brain changes, making it difficult to know what to conclude from research with transsexuals undergoing hormone therapy (Smith et al., 2015).

Other research has identified several genes associated with transsexualism, and the genes are different for MTFs and FTMs (Bentz et al., 2008; Hare et al., 2008; Henningsson et al., 2005). MTFs, for example, are more likely than control males to have a mutation in the androgen receptor gene. However, not all MTFs carry this mutation.

The bottom line is that, right now, we do not know the exact causes of transsexualism or other kinds of gender variation.

Critical THINKing Skill
Understanding stereotyping

Books like John Gray's *Men Are from Mars, Women Are from Venus* have sold millions of copies. In that book, Gray argues that men and women are so different, it's like they are from different planets, and communication between the two is as difficult as communication between an American person and a Japanese person. The scientific data, however, show a very different picture. Men and women are actually quite similar on most, though not all, psychological characteristics, including behaviors such as math performance and leadership (Hyde, 2005). If men and women are so similar, why do people like to believe that they are so different?

The answers lie in *stereotypes* and *motives for stereotyping*. As we noted earlier in the chapter, a stereotype is a generalization about a group of people (e.g., men) that distinguishes those people from another group (e.g, women). Gender stereotypes abound. Women are the talkers while men are strong and silent. Women are emotional and men are unemotional. When we collect rigorous scientific data, it turns out that some stereotypes are fairly accurate and some are not. For example, the difference between boys and girls in talkativeness is tiny (Leaper & Smith, 2004). Girls are stereotyped as being bad at math, but in fact girls perform equally to boys on standardized math tests (Hyde et al., 2008).

If so many stereotypes turn out not to be accurate, why do people continue to stereotype? Social psychologists have uncovered two basic motives for stereotyping (whether gender stereotyping, racial stereotyping, or other kinds of stereotyping): comprehension goals and self-enhancement goals (van den Bos & Stapel, 2009). As for the *comprehension goal,* when we meet a new person, we tend to fill in a lot of assumed information about that person so that we can understand them, until we have more actual information. For example, breadwinner is a key aspect of the male role. When we meet a man, we are likely to invoke that stereotype and ask an opening question such as "What kind of work do you do?" Our first question is not, "Do you stay home full time with the kids?" When people stereotype for comprehension purposes, the stereotypes can be positive or negative.

In contrast, when we stereotype for *self-enhancement* purposes, the stereotypes tend to be negative. We make ourselves feel better by denigrating people from another group. For example, if an adult says or thinks, "Teenagers are so irresponsible," by implication the adult is much more responsible.

Using these principles, why do people engage in gender stereotyping? Answer this question before you proceed to the next paragraph.

When people engage in gender stereotyping, sometimes it is for comprehension goals, as in the example above in which we might assume that a man is employed, so we can ask him about his work. Sometimes, though, people engage in gender stereotyping for self-enhancement purposes. A man might say, "You women are so emotional," which makes him feel emotionally in control and manly. Or a woman might say, "Men are just clueless about how other people feel," which makes her feel good about her skills at reading others' emotions.

Good critical thinking involves understanding why people stereotype and that gender stereotypes are often not accurate. The next time you hear someone (or yourself) making a gender stereotyped comment, ask yourself two questions: (1) What is this person's goal in stereotyping? and (2) Is this an accurate stereotype that is supported by scientific data?

SUMMARY

Gender Roles and Stereotypes

A gender role is a set of norms, or culturally defined expectations, that specify how people of one gender ought to behave. Children are socialized into gender roles first by parents and later by other forces such as peers and the media.

Gender roles are not uniform in the United States. They vary according to ethnic group and other factors, using the concept of intersectionality. African American women, for example, have traditionally played an important economic role in their families. Among Latinx, gender roles tend to be more sharply defined than they are among Anglos. The sexuality of Asian Americans has been stereotyped, with Asian American men seen as sexless and Asian American women viewed as exotic sex toys. Some American Indian tribes traditionally had egalitarian gender roles when compared with White culture.

Psychological Gender Differences

Psychological gender differences have been documented in aggressiveness, communication styles, and impulsivity, all of which have implications for sexuality.

Gender Differences in Sexuality

Three substantial gender differences in sexuality are in the incidence of masturbation (males having the higher incidence), attitudes about casual sex (females being more disapproving), and the use of pornography (males reporting more use). Laboratory research on arousal to erotic materials illustrates how males and females are in some ways similar and in others different in their responses. Males are more consistent at having orgasms, especially during heterosexual intercourse, than females are, and males have a somewhat stronger sex drive.

Why the Differences?

One question is whether some of these gender differences, obtained through self-report, are accurate or whether they are the result of response biases, for example, with men exaggerating and women minimizing. The Bogus Pipeline Study showed that gender differences in number of sexual partners disappeared when the respondents were in a condition in which they thought lying would be detected. Therefore, some of the apparent gender differences in sexuality may be due to biased reporting. Nonetheless, some differences remain.

Three sets of factors have been proposed to explain these gender differences: biological factors (anatomy, hormones); cultural factors (the double standard, gender roles, body image); and other factors (fear of pregnancy, differences in masturbation patterns creating other gender differences).

Beyond the Young Adults

Most research on gender and sexuality has been done with college-age samples. There is reason to believe that patterns of gender differences in sexuality change in middle age and beyond.

Transgender Issues and Experience

The term *transgender* encompasses people whose gender identity does not match their gender assigned at birth (natal gender). Gender dysphoria refers to psychological distress about a discrepancy between a person's gender identity and natal gender. Gender dysphoria may first appear in childhood, but it can also appear in adolescence or adulthood. Trans individuals frequently experience anti-trans prejudice, which can have negative consequences for physical and mental health. Interventions are being developed to reduce anti-trans prejudice. Gender identity is a different issue from sexual orientation. A variety of medical procedures are available for trans people who wish to go through gender-affirming treatments, including hormone therapy and genital surgery. Affirmative psychotherapy for transgender individuals is being developed.

SUGGESTIONS FOR FURTHER READING

Else-Quest, Nicole M., & Hyde, Janet S. (2018). *The psychology of women and gender: Half the human experience +*. Los Angeles: SAGE. A psychology of women textbook that includes much research on transgender folks as well.

Erickson-Schroth, Laura (Ed.). (2014). *Trans bodies, trans selves*. New York: Oxford University Press. This book, modeled on the classic women's health book *Our Bodies, Ourselves,* provides health care information for transgender people.

Howey, Noelle. (2002). *Dress codes: Of three girlhoods— my mother's, my father's, and mine.* New York: St. Martin's Press. This is Howey's extraordinary memoir about growing up with a father who proved to be a male-to-female transsexual.

Nutt, Amy Ellis (2015). *Becoming Nicole: The transformation of an American family.* New York: Random House. This book traces the story of a pair of identical twins, born male. Yet one quickly developed a female identity. In early adolescence, she underwent pubertal suppression, and then transitioned successfully to being a girl.

Shlasko, Davey. (2017). *Trans allyship workbook: Building skills to support trans people in our lives.* Madison, WI: Think Again. This is a very practical book for those who want to support trans folks.

©Hinterhaus Productions/Getty Images

Are YOU Curious?

1. Do children of gay and lesbian couples grow up to be well adjusted, or do they have problems?
2. What percentage of Americans are gay, lesbian, or bisexual?
3. What causes people to be gay?
4. Who is more likely to be bisexual—men or women?

Read this chapter to find out.

CHAPTER

13

Sexual Orientation: Gay, Straight, or Bi?

CHAPTER HIGHLIGHTS

"... for boys, achieving a masculine identity entails the repeated repudiation of the specter of failed masculinity. Boys lay claim to masculine identities by lobbing homophobic epithets at one another."*

*Pascoe, C. J. (2012). *Dude, you're a fag.* Berkeley, CA: University of California Press. Page 5.

One night in June 1969, in response to police harassment, gay men and lesbians rioted in the Stonewall, a gay bar in New York City's Greenwich Village. This may have been the first open group rebellion of homosexual people in history. Gay liberation was born.

Most of us want to know more about sexual orientation. The purpose of this chapter is to try to provide a better understanding of people's sexual orientations, whether gay, straight, or bisexual, as well as an understanding of heterosexism (prejudice against LGB people).

Sexual orientation is defined by whom we are sexually attracted to and also have the potential for loving. Thus a **homosexual** is a person whose sexual orientation is toward members of their own gender; a **heterosexual** is a person whose sexual orientation is toward members of the other gender; and a **bisexual** is a person whose sexual orientation is toward both genders. The word homosexual is derived from the Greek root *homo,* meaning "same" (not the Latin word *homo,* meaning "man"). The term homosexual may be applied in a general way to homosexuals of both genders or specifically to male homosexuals. The term **lesbian,** which is used to refer to female homosexuals, can be traced to the great Greek poet Sappho, who lived on the island of Lesbos (hence "lesbian") around 600 B.C. She is famous for the love poetry she wrote to other women. Sappho was married to a man, apparently happily, and had one daughter, but her lesbian feelings were the focus of her life.

Gay activists prefer the term **gay** to homosexual because the latter emphasizes the sexual aspects of the orientation and can be used as a derogatory label; there are many negative connotations to homosexuality. A heterosexual is then referred to as **straight.** The term gay is generally used for male homosexuals, lesbian for female homosexuals. There are, of course, a number of slang terms for gays and lesbians, such as "queer," "fairy," "dyke," and "faggot" or "fag," which are derogatory when used by straight people to belittle gays. The term **queer** has now been taken back by gay activists and scholars, who use it as a proud term encompassing gays, lesbians, and transgender people. Queer theory, explained in the chapter "Theoretical Perspectives on Sexuality," is prominent in lesbian–gay–bisexual (LGB[1]) studies.

In this chapter, we use the abbreviation LGB for lesbians, gays, and bisexuals, because it is awkward to repeat the phrase gays and lesbians, and even that phrase omits bisexuals. *Sexual minority* is another term that encompasses LGBs.

Attitudes toward Gays and Lesbians

Your sexual orientation has implications for the attitudes people have toward you. First, there is the belief that all people are heterosexual, that heterosexuality is the norm. This belief is termed **heteronormativity.** Furthermore, just as there are stereotypes about other minority groups—for example, the stereotype that Asian American men are asexual—so there are stereotypes about gays and lesbians. These stereotypes and negative attitudes lead to discrimination and hate crimes against gays and lesbians. Here we examine some of the scientific data on these negative attitudes.

Attitudes

Many Americans disapprove of homosexuality. For example, as Table 1 shows, in a well-sampled 2016 survey of adult Americans, 39 percent expressed the opinion that sexual relations between two adults of the same sex are always wrong.

> **Sexual orientation:** A person's erotic and emotional orientation toward members of his or her own gender or members of the other gender.
> **Homosexual:** A person whose sexual orientation is toward members of the same gender.
> **Heterosexual:** A person whose sexual orientation is toward members of the other gender.
> **Bisexual:** A person whose sexual orientation is toward both men and women.
> **Lesbian:** A woman whose sexual orientation is toward other women.
> **Gay:** Homosexual; especially male homosexuals.
> **Straight:** Heterosexual; that is, a person whose sexual orientation is toward members of the opposite gender.
> **Queer:** A self-label used by some LGBs, as well as by some heterosexuals who prefer unusual sexual practices.
> **Heteronormativity:** The belief that heterosexuality is the norm and that all people are heterosexual.

[1]You are probably familiar with the acronym LGBT, which stands for lesbian, gay, bisexual, and transgender. In this chapter we focus on sexual minorities or LGBs. Transgender is covered in the chapter "Gender and Sexuality."

Table 1   Attitudes of Adult Americans toward Homosexuality, 1973, 2012, and 2016

Question and Responses	Percentage of Sample		
	1973	2012	2016
1. Are sexual relations between adults of the same sex:			
Always wrong	74	46	39
Almost always wrong	7	3	4
Wrong only sometimes	8	7	6
Not wrong at all	11	45	52
2. Should an admitted homosexual man be allowed to teach in a college or university?			
Yes	49	85	88
No	51	15	12

Source: General Social Survey, 1973, 2012, 2016 http://icpsr.umich.edu/

Has the gay liberation movement succeeded in changing the negative attitudes of Americans? The answer seems to be yes (Twenge et al., 2016). Table 1 shows that the percentage of people who believe that homosexual behavior is always wrong changed substantially from 1973 to 2012, and even changed in the brief period from 2012 to 2016.

Yet negative attitudes remain among some people; experts believe that some Americans' attitudes toward homosexuals can best be described as homophobic (Moradi et al., 2006). **Homophobia** may be defined as a strong, irrational fear of homosexuals and, more generally, as fixed negative attitudes and reactions to homosexuals. Some scholars dislike the term homophobia because, although certainly some people's feelings are strong enough to be called a phobia, negative attitudes and prejudice are most common. Therefore, some prefer the term **antigay prejudice** or sexual prejudice (Herek, 2000). Another related term is **heterosexism,** which refers to prejudice against and denigration of LGB people (Herek, 2007).

Sometimes the prejudice is subtle. The prevalence of the expression "that's so gay" among high school and college students is hurtful to LGB students who may be listening. Common occurrences such as these qualify as *microaggressions* against LGBs (Nadal et al., 2016; Swann et al., 2016).

The most extreme expressions of antigay prejudice occur in *hate crimes* against LGBs (Cogan & Marcus-Newhall, 2002). One horrifying case occurred in Wyoming (Loffreda, 2000). Matthew Shepard, a University of Wyoming freshman, was found tied to a fence, savagely beaten and comatose, on the outskirts of Laramie. He died five days later. Two men, both 21 and high school dropouts, were charged with the murder. Apparently they had led

Homophobia: A strong, irrational fear of homosexuals; negative attitudes and reactions to homosexuals.
Antigay prejudice: Negative attitudes and behaviors toward gays and lesbians.
Heterosexism: Prejudice against and denigration of LGB persons.

Shepard to believe that they, too, were gay and lured him from a bar to ride in their pickup truck. In the truck, they began beating him with a revolver, then got out and tied him to a fence, beat him more, and left him for dead. The Orlando shootings of 2016 are another example of a hate crime (Healy & Eligon, 2016). The gunman killed 49 people in a gay night club, most of them people of color.

Averaged across more than 100 studies of LGBs, the results indicated that 55 percent reported that they had been verbally harassed, 14 percent had been assaulted with a weapon, 41 percent had experienced discrimination, 19 percent had experienced victimization from the police, 28 percent had been verbally harassed by family members, and 45 percent had been sexually harassed because of their sexual orientation (Katz-Wise & Hyde, 2012). These studies show that hate crimes against and harassment of sexual minority individuals are common—not rare, isolated incidents. Child abuse—whether physical, emotional, or sexual—by family members may have particularly serious consequences for the mental health of sexual minority people (Balsam et al., 2010).

These incidents exact a psychological toll. One high school student said of the verbal harassment, "It's not just name calling. I don't know how schools can isolate it like that. When are they going to see it as a problem? When we're bloody on the ground in front of them?" (Human Rights Watch, 2001).

What role do the media play in antigay attitudes? In previous decades there were almost no portrayals of gays, so they were invisible in the mass media. Gays are now more visible in the media, but are they portrayed positively or negatively? Some argue that even successful programs such as *Ellen* and *Will and Grace* increase stereotypes because they show the LGB character as lacking a stable relationship, being preoccupied with their sexuality, and laughable (Calzo & Ward, 2009). Others argue that programs such as *Glee* and *Modern Family,* although

Milestones in Sex Research

Does Gaydar Exist?

An idea has become part of pop culture, the idea that people have *gaydar,* a kind of sixth sense that allows them to detect who is gay. Some research appears to support the existence of gaydar, but the latest research disputes it.

In one set of studies, researchers found that there are visibly perceptible differences between gay and straight men's faces, and between lesbian and straight women's faces, and that people can accurately identify sexual orientation based on photos of faces (Rule & Ambady, 2008; Rule et al., 2008; Rule, Ambady, & Hallett, 2009). The researchers also argue that gaydar is found in other cultures as well (Rule et al., 2011).

How do scientists go about studying gaydar? In one typical experiment, researchers captured photos posted on dating websites (Rule et al., 2008). The photos were cropped to show just the face and hair and all were gray-scaled, to remove extraneous cues. The researchers assessed sexual orientation by whether the individuals were seeking same-gender or other-gender partners. The photos (81 of them, some of gay men, some of straight men) were then shown to undergraduates, who rated each photo on a scale with labels *very gay, somewhat gay, somewhat straight, straight*. The researchers calculated the correlation between participants' ratings of the photos and whether the photo was actually of a gay or straight person. If participants were completely inaccurate so that their responses were random, the correlation between ratings and actual sexual orientation would be 0. The correlation was $r = 0.31$, which is significantly greater than 0, but it isn't exactly a perfect correlation of 1.0 either. Therefore, participants did better than chance, but they certainly were not perfect in identifying who was gay and who was straight. The researchers also repeated their experiments using stimuli that were photos of lesbian and straight women and obtained similar results (Rule, Ambady, & Hallett, 2009). It is studies like these that people use as evidence for gaydar.

Another research team has challenged the gaydar research (Cox et al., 2015). They argue that gaydar is just a slick-sounding term for the practice of using stereotypes to identify a person's sexual orientation. Many people might reason as follows: A man who is sitting around drinking beer, wearing a dirty t-shirt—well, he must be straight. A man who is carefully groomed and wearing a fashionable shirt—he must be gay. Both of those are stereotypes about gay men and straight men, but it doesn't mean that we are right about either person. But how could plain pictures of faces, without all the extra cues, be judged using stereotypes? When the Cox research team tried to replicate the earlier research by the Rule team, they found that there was a confound in the stimuli. The gay men's pictures were higher quality than the straight men's. The same was true of pictures of lesbian women compared with straight women. The Cox team corrected this problem by choosing pairs of straight and gay men's faces that were matched for rated quality. The results indicated that, when photos were matched for quality, participants judged photos as gay at the same rate for photos of actual gay men and actual straight men—that is, they couldn't tell the difference. Additionally, the researchers created a 2×3 experimental design, in which each face was randomly paired with a stereotypic gay or straight statement such as "He is a hairdresser" or "He drives a pick-up truck" or a neutral statement "He likes spaghetti." So, a respondent might see a gay man's face with a statement that he is a hairdresser or a statement that he drives a pick-up truck or a statement that he likes spaghetti. The results indicated that, whether the photo was of a gay man or a straight man, he was judged as gay 57 percent of the time if the photo had been paired with a gay-stereotyping statement, but he was judged as gay only 20 percent of the time when paired with a straight-stereotypic statement. Stereotypic information about the people, then, guided subjects' judgments, not the photos of faces. This study argues against gaydar.

In another experiment by this same team, participants were randomly assigned to one of three conditions: (1) they were told that gaydar is real; (2) they were told that gaydar is not real and is just another term for stereotyping; or (3) a control group that was told neither (Cox et al., 2015). As in the study described previously, participants made judgments about fictitious men who were described with gay-stereotypic, straight-stereotypic, or neutral statements. The results indicated that those who had been told that gaydar is real relied more on stereotypes in making their judgments, compared to those in the control group. Those who had been told that gaydar is merely another term for stereotyping, however, stereotyped less than the control group. Popular claims about gaydar, then, could be harmful insofar as they lead people to rely on stereotypes more. And yet, by pointing out that gaydar is not real and that it is just a kind of stereotyping, we can actually reduce people's stereotyping.

Overall, then, the evidence for gaydar is not strong. The Cox research shows that gaydar is a folk concept that perpetuates stereotyping.

Figure 1   Portrayals of gays in the media: The CBS drama *Instinct* features Dr. Reinhart (Alan Cumming) as a crime-fighting detective and professor of abnormal behavior. Reinhart is married to Andy (Daniel Ings), and they kiss affectionately on-screen.

©CBS/Getty Images

portraying gays stereotypically, still represent positive portrayals. Research on the actual effects of the media on attitudes is very new and paints a complex picture (Calzo & Ward, 2009). For example, reading popular magazines is associated with more positive attitudes toward LGBs, but reading teen magazines is associated with less positive attitudes, probably because teen magazines tend to be conservative about sexuality.

But we should also recognize the other side of the coin. As we can see from Table 1, some Americans are tolerant of or supportive of homosexuals. For example, 88 percent of Americans approve of an overt homosexual teaching in a college or university. Thus Americans are a strange mixture of bigots and supporters on the issue of homosexuality.

So far we have looked at people's explicit attitudes as determined by self-reports on rating scales. But what about implicit, nonconscious attitudes, as measured by the Implicit Association Test (IAT) described in the chapter "Sex Research"? Research with the IAT shows that people, on average, have an implicit preference for straight people over lesbians and gay men (Westgate et al., 2015). Even though implicit attitudes are more deeply rooted than conscious, explicit attitudes, implicit attitudes toward LGBs have become more favorable over time. Just from 2006 to 2013, the preference for straights declined by 13 percent (Westgate et al., 2015).

Gays and Lesbians as a Minority Group

From the foregoing, it is clear that LGB people are the subject of many negative attitudes, just as other minorities are (Meyer, 2003). Like members of other minority groups, they also suffer from job discrimination. Just as Blacks and women have been denied access to certain jobs, so too have sexual minorities. Wage discrimination occurs as well. According to census data, gay men are more educated than straight men, but gay men earn less (Black et al., 2000).

A clever experiment captured discrimination against gays in the workplace (Hebl et al., 2002). Undergraduates who were confederates of the experimenters applied for jobs at local stores in Houston. Half of them wore a

Figure 2   Homosexuality has been found in many cultures and historical eras. Here we see male–male couples at a banquet in Roman art from the 5th century B.C.E.

©Album/Alamy

baseball cap that said "Gay and Proud" (the experimental group), and the other half wore a cap that said "Texan and Proud" (the control group). A number of measures were collected, including whether the staff person at the store said that a job was available, whether the applicant was given permission to complete a job application, whether they received a callback, and more subtle measures such as the length of the interaction between the applicant and staff. Measures of formal discrimination, such as being allowed to complete an application, showed no differences between the experimental and control groups. However, measures of subtle discrimination did reveal the effects of wearing the Gay and Proud cap. Conversations between the applicant and the staff person were half as long when the applicant wore the gay cap. Those wearing the gay cap also rated their interactions with the staff person as more negative than those wearing the Texan cap, even though they were kept unaware of which cap they were wearing. This study provides tangible evidence about the kind of discrimination that gays and lesbians encounter in the workplace.

Discrimination goes hand in hand with stereotypes. One such stereotype is that gay men are child molesters. As with many stereotypes, this one is false. Research shows that only 2 to 3 percent of those who sexually abuse children are homosexual (Jenny et al., 1994).

In a spirit of reform beginning in the 1980s, a number of states and cities passed laws prohibiting discrimination on the basis of sexual orientation. For example, in the state of Wisconsin it is illegal to discriminate against gays and lesbians in matters such as employment and housing. These legal issues are discussed further in the chapter "Sex and the Law."

There is, however, an important way in which sexual minorities differ from other minorities. In the case of most other minorities, appearance is a fairly good indicator of minority-group status. It is easy to recognize an African American or a woman, for example, but one cannot tell simply by looking at a person what their sexual orientation is. Thus LGBs, unlike other minorities, can hide their status. There are certain advantages to this. It makes it fairly easy to get along in the heterosexual world—to "pass." However, it has the disadvantage of encouraging the person to live a lie and to deny their true identity; not only is this dishonest, but it may also be psychologically stressful (Meyer, 2003). Concealing a stigma—whether it is one's sexual orientation, mental illness, illiteracy, or history of having been raped—exacts a psychological toll (Pachankis, 2007).

We shouldn't leave this discussion of discrimination and prejudice against LGBs without asking a crucial question: What can be done to prevent or end this prejudice? Change must occur at the individual, the interpersonal, and the organizational levels (e.g., corporations, educational institutions), as well as society as a whole and its

(a)

(b)

Figure 3   (a) Harvey Milk (left) and George Moscone (right). Harvey Milk, a gay activist, was an elected member of San Francisco's Board of Supervisors, representing a district including many gays. Milk fought for gay rights throughout California and was supported by Mayor George Moscone. On November 17, 1978, Dan White, a former police officer and a supervisor, entered City Hall and shot and killed Milk and Moscone. White confessed within hours. A jury declined to convict White of first-degree murder, instead finding him guilty of voluntary manslaughter, a lesser offense carrying a reduced jail sentence. The gay community, as well as many sympathetic supporters, were shocked and furious. A protest march and the White Night Riot ensued. The entire incident symbolizes the ambivalent progress achieved by gay liberation: A gay liberationist can be elected to an important public office, but he is then murdered. An observance of these events continues in San Francisco every year. (b) The movie *Milk* with Sean Penn and Victor Garber.

institutions (e.g., the federal government). At the individual level, all of us must examine our own attitudes toward LGBs to see if they are consistent with basic values we hold, such as a commitment to equality and justice. Some people may need to educate themselves or attend workshops to examine their attitudes. These attitudes, though, were formed as we grew up, influenced by our parents, our peers, and the media. Parents must consider the messages they convey to their children about gays. The adolescent peer group can be strongly antigay. What could be done to change it? How can the media change in order not to promote antigay prejudices and stereotypes? At the interpersonal level, people must recognize that LGBs are often a hidden minority. Eric, for example, just told a joke that ridiculed gay men. What he didn't know was that one of his three listeners is gay—just not "out" with him (for obvious reasons). We must examine our interactions with other people, recognizing the extent to which many of us assume that everyone is heterosexual until proven otherwise. At the institutional level, how can education be changed in order to reduce antigay discrimination? A strong program of sexuality education across the grades, with open discussion of sexual orientation, would be a good start (see Looking to the Future: Sexuality Education, at the end of this book).

Scientists have tested a number of interventions designed to reduce antigay prejudice (Bartos et al., 2014). Education designed to reduce prejudice is effective, as is intergroup contact, that is, getting to know gays and lesbians. Intergroup contact has a long history as a social psychological intervention and was initially designed to reduce racial prejudice. Prejudice can also be reduced if tolerance is conveyed to be the norm, either by an expert or by one's peers. There are many possibilities, then, for systematic efforts to reduce antigay prejudice.

Life Experiences of LGBs

In understanding lesbian, gay, and bisexual lifestyles, it is important to recognize that there is a wide variety of experiences. One of the most important aspects of this variability is whether the person is covert (in the closet) or overt (out of the closet) about their homosexuality. A person who is in the closet may be heterosexually married, have children, and be a respected professional in the community, spending only a few hours a month engaging in secret same-gender sexual behavior. Others may live almost entirely within an LGB community, particularly if they live in a large city like New York or San Francisco where there is a large gay subculture. There are also various degrees of being out. Many lesbians and gays are out with trusted

Coming out: The process of acknowledging to oneself, and then to others, that one is gay or lesbian.

friends but not with casual acquaintances. The lifestyle of gay men differs somewhat from that of lesbians, as a result of the different roles assigned to males and females in our society and the different ways that males and females are reared.

The experiences of LGBs are thus far from uniform. They vary according to whether one is male or female and open about one's sexual orientation and also according to social class, occupation, personality, and a variety of other factors.

LGB Development

Some experts believe that sexual orientation is determined by age 5 or 6 or even prenatally, whereas others say that it is determined by age 10 or 12. Scientists don't have exact answers to this question, and without doubt it depends on the individual, in ways that are discussed in the section that follows.

Some evidence indicates that gender variance or nonconformity in childhood predicts later LGB orientation (Steensma et al., 2013b). That is, children who are rated by their parents as having characteristics, at least somewhat, such as "behaves like the opposite sex" and "wishes to be the opposite sex" are more likely, in adulthood, to have same-gender attractions and behaviors. However, this prediction is far from perfect. In one study, the prevalence of homosexuality was 10 to 12 percent in adulthood among those who displayed gender variance in childhood, compared with 1 to 2 percent among those who did not display gender variance in childhood (Steensma et al., 2013b). In fact, then, the majority of gender-variant children did not turn out to be gay.

There are milestones in LGB development: experiencing same-gender attraction, having a same-gender sexual experience, and identifying as LGB—not necessarily in that order (Katz-Wise et al., 2017a). In one study of sexual minority youth, lesbians experienced their first same-gender attraction, on average, at age 14, compared with age 11 for gay men; lesbians had their first same-gender experience on average at age 18, compared with 16 for gay men; and lesbians claimed a sexual-minority identity on average at age 17, compared with age 15 for gay men (Katz-Wise et al., 2017a). There is, of course, plenty of variability around those averages.

As we discussed in the chapter "Sexuality and the Life Cycle: Childhood and Adolescence," a crucial task of adolescence is identity development, and sexual orientation is one important aspect of development that occurs over the adolescent years. Related to identity development is **coming out,** which involves acknowledging to oneself, and then to others, that one is gay or lesbian. Whether the person experiences acceptance or rejection from family, friends, and others to whom they come out can be critical to self-esteem and mental health.

These developmental processes are complicated by the negative climate for sexual minority youth that exists in middle school, high school, and college. Many LGB youth report harassment by peers, especially in middle school (Robinson & Espelage, 2011). The use of homophobic epithets (name-calling) is common in middle school and high school (Pascoe, 2011; Poteat et al., 2012). Boys engage in this name-calling to each other more than girls do, and the frequency for boys actually increases from seventh grade to twelfth grade. Homophobic epithets are, in reality, a form of bullying and, among boys, they enforce the rules of masculinity (Poteat et al., 2011). Ironically, those who dish them out are also the most likely to receive them. And today, cyberbullying also occurs, often allowing perpetrators to remain anonymous and facilitating the "outing" of LGB adolescents to hundreds of peers with the click of a key (Robinson & Espelage, 2011). Harassment can lead sexual minority youth to skip school, which creates another set of problems.

Even at the college level, peer harassment can be intense, and this harassment has been linked to suicidal thoughts and suicide attempts (Robinson & Espelage, 2011). One much publicized example is the case of Tyler Clementi, a Rutgers University student, whose roommate used a webcam to view him kissing another man in the privacy of his room. The roommate then urged many others to view another encounter and Clementi discovered what was happening. The next day, Clementi killed himself by jumping off the George Washington Bridge.

Support from adults, especially parents and adults at school, is crucial as sexual minority youth weather these storms (Darwich et al., 2012; Heatherington & Lavner, 2008). Often schools fail to address individual incidents and lack proactive policies to reduce negative climate. A policy brief from the Williams Institute at UCLA, *Safe at School: Addressing the School Environment and LGBT Safety through Policy and Legislation,* outlines steps that schools and state legislatures can take to improve the climate for sexual minority youth (Biegel & Kuehl, 2010). For example, schools should provide professional development opportunities on LGB issues for all school staff. Schools can also host gay–straight alliances, safe zones, and wellness programs for sexual minority youth.

To this point, we have discussed sexual identity as something that develops during adolescence and then is fixed. That may be true for many people, but psychologist Lisa Diamond has documented what she calls **sexual fluidity,** which refers to changes over time in sexual attractions, identity, or behavior, which can occur with people in their twenties, thirties, or later (Diamond, 2005, 2008a). Her research involved young women, followed longitudinally. Over a period of eight years, women's attractions and identity shifted in all directions, for example, from bisexual to lesbian or from lesbian to heterosexual.

Similar patterns have been documented in men as well (Katz-Wise, 2012). Some of these people report that they are attracted to the person, not the gender. As one man said,

> I find gender matters, but it's definitely not the first priority on the list for me. . . . In terms of attraction, I just like beautiful things, and I don't really classify those in men or women. I find both of them beautiful. (Katz-Wise, 2012, p. 122)

For some people, then, patterns of attraction and behavior can continue to develop and evolve well past adolescence.

Today, American culture has a much wider variety of possible self-labels, and people don't have to fit themselves into just one of two boxes, heterosexual or homosexual. People can be bisexual, queer, questioning, or unlabeled. In one well-sampled national survey, 86 percent of women and 92 percent of men said that their sexual attractions were only to members of the opposite sex, but 10 percent of women and 4 percent of men said that their sexual attractions were "mostly"

> **Sexual fluidity:** Changes that occur over time in sexual attraction, identity, or behavior.

Figure 4 Peer harassment, such as spreading rumors, can be part of school climate for LGB youth.

©*Tetra Images/Getty Images*

(a)

(b)

Figure 5   (*a*) Pop music star Janelle Monae identifies as a queer Black woman and contributes to LGBTQ culture. (*b*) Singer Melissa Etheridge is an icon of lesbian culture.

(a) ©Featureflash Photo Agency/Shutterstock; (b) ©lev radin/Shutterstock

opposite sex (Chandra et al., 2011). They don't fit neatly into the heterosexual box, nor into the gay box.

Lesbian, Gay, and Bisexual Culture and Communities

A loose network of lesbian, gay, and bisexual communities extends around the world. One woman said,

> I have seen lesbian communities all over the world (e.g., South Africa, Brazil, and Israel) where the lesbians of that nation have more in common with me (i.e., they play the same lesbian records, have read the same books, wear the same lesbian jewelry) than the heterosexual women of that nation have in common with heterosexual women in the U.S. (Esther D. Rothblum, 2007, *personal communication*).

These links have been cemented in the last two decades by increases in international travel, globalization, and the international reach of the Internet.

Gay and lesbian communities began flourishing in the United States after World War II (D'Augelli & Garnets, 1995). Ironically, in the gender-segregated military, gay men were able to find each other and lesbians find

each other in a way that had previously not been possible. Activist groups slowly formed in the 1950s and 1960s, energized particularly by the Stonewall rebellion discussed at the beginning of this chapter. The HIV/AIDS crisis of the 1980s cemented together the gay community as it had never been before. Support networks and activist groups formed rapidly in response to the epidemic.

Today many LGB communities exist in neighborhoods in large cities, with bookstores, restaurants, theaters, and social organizations that are an integral part of the community. The lesbian community in particular has been involved in creating a lesbian culture, expressed in music and literature and celebrated at festivals and women's sporting events (Dolance, 2005).

Symbols and rituals are important in defining the LGB community, just as they are with other cultural groups. The pink triangle, which the Nazis used to label gay men, has been adopted as a symbol of pride. The Greek letter lambda is another. Lesbian and gay pride marches held in June each year commemorate the Stonewall uprising. The use of slang is another sign of solidarity among LGBs.

Gay bars are one aspect of the LGB social life. Drinking, perhaps dancing, socializing, and the possibility of finding a sexual partner or a lover are the important elements. Some gay bars look just like any other bar from the outside, whereas others may have names—for example, The Open Closet—that indicate to the alert who the clientele are. Bars are typically gender segregated—that is, they are either for gay men or for lesbians—although a few are mixed. There are far more bars for gay men than for lesbian women. Typically, the atmosphere is different in the two, the male bars being more for finding sexual partners and the female bars more for talking and socializing. Lest the reader be shocked at the none-too-subtle nature of pickup bars, it is well to remember that there are many bars—singles' bars—that serve precisely the same purpose for heterosexuals.

Today, of course, a major way for gays to meet each other is through the Internet (Grov et al., 2014). Cyberspace is also a place where gays can find community when, geographically, they do not live in a place that has a gay community. Gay-related web sites provide chat rooms and other means for gays to form online relationships and perhaps find partners for casual sex or a long-term relationship. Mobile technologies such as smartphones are the newest innovation that can help men find each other, through apps such as Grindr.

Certainly in the last five decades the gay liberation movement has had a tremendous impact on the gay lifestyle and community. In particular, it has encouraged LGBs to be more open and to feel less guilty about their behavior. The National LGBTQ Task Force[2] is the central clearinghouse for activist groups; it can provide information on local organizations.

There are many places for LGBs to socialize besides bars, including the Metropolitan Community Church (a network of gay and lesbian churches), gay athletic organizations, and gay political organizations.

Among their other accomplishments, members of the gay liberation movement have founded numerous gay newspapers, magazines, and Internet sites. These have many of the same features as other media: forums for political opinions, human-interest stories, and fashion news. Probably the best-known LGB magazine is *The Advocate*, www.advocate.com. In 2006, *The Advocate* issued *The Advocate College Guide for LGBT Students,* which lists the 20 most gay-friendly campuses.

Gay and Lesbian Relationships

In many ways, the U.S. Supreme Court decision of 2015 to legalize gay marriage (discussed in the chapter "Sex and the Law") revolutionized gay and lesbian relationships. For the first time, across the nation same-gender couples

[2]The National LGBTQ Task Force, www.thetaskforce.org.

were able to marry legally in the same way that heterosexual couples have taken for granted. In other respects, lesbians and gay men had been forming long-term relationships for decades, and some states had already established marriage equality by 2000. As a result, we have a mixture of research that covers gay and lesbian relationships pre-2015 and post-2015, in the context of different degrees of legalization.

One possibility is to take a positive psychology approach to understanding same-gender couple relationships. Positive psychology focuses not on pathologies but on strengths, whether of individuals or relationships (Fincham & Beach, 2010; Seligman & Csikszentmihalyi, 2000). In positive psychology, one of the pillars of human flourishing and optimal functioning is positive social institutions, and another is positive relationships. For sexual minorities, marriage equality is an example of positive social institutions.

In regard to relationships, research shows that humans benefit from positive relationships, whether parent–child relationships, romantic relationships, or relationships with coworkers (Barnett & Hyde, 2001; Fincham & Beach, 2010). Researchers have applied this approach to understanding the strengths found in same-gender couples (Rostosky & Riggle, 2017). They note several positive aspects of relationships that seem to be more common in same-gender couples than in mixed-gender couples:

- Respecting and appreciating individual differences: in contrast to the emphasis on compatibility and similarities found in mixed-gender couples, same-gender couples tend to value the different strengths that each brings to the relationship.

- Generating positive emotions and interactions: compared with mixed-gender couples, same-gender couples seem to use more positive interaction styles with their partners, even in laboratory studies of conflicts. These positive approaches help them to cope with the stigmatization of sexual minorities in our culture.

- Effectively communicating and negotiating: same-gender couples especially value effective communication and negotiation of conflicts.

- Egalitarian ideals: same-gender couples place an emphasis on equality in their relationships and note that they are freed from traditional gender roles and the male domination found in many heterosexual relationships.

Lesbian and Gay Families

Increasingly, gay couples and lesbian couples are creating families that include children. This is a controversial concept to some heterosexual people in the United States, who view a lesbian family or gay family as a damaging

Milestones in Sex Research

The Ethics of Sex Research: The Tearoom Trade

Sociologist Laud Humphreys's study titled *Tearoom Trade: Impersonal Sex in Public Places* (1970) is a classic in the field of sex research. In light of concerns on the part of both scientists and the general public about ethical standards in research, however, his methods of data collection are questionable from a contemporary perspective. Important issues are raised about the difficulty of doing good sex research within ethical bounds.

As the title of the book implies, the term *tearoom trade* refers to impersonal sexual acts in places like public restrooms. Typically, a man enters the restroom and conveys to another man who is already there an interest in having sex. He may do this by making tapping sounds while in one of the stalls, for example. The men generally perform the sexual act in a stall and may not even exchange a word. The activity is typically fellatio, which can be done rapidly and with a minimum of encumbrance.

In the tearoom situation, a third person generally serves as a lookout who watches for police or other intruders while the other two engage in sex. To obtain his data, Humphreys became a lookout. Not only did he observe the behaviors involved in the tearoom trade, but he also wrote down the license-plate numbers of the participants. He traced the numbers through state records and thus was able to get the addresses of the persons involved. He then went to the homes of the people and administered a questionnaire (which included questions on sexual behavior) to them under the pretense of conducting a general survey.

The research provided some important findings, particularly that a large proportion of the men who engaged in the tearoom trade were respectable, heterosexually married men, and many were leaders in their community. This finding provoked quite a controversy over the book; the notion that "heterosexual" men could engage in homosexual behavior was shocking to many. Indeed, many gays find the tearoom trade to be shocking.

In his report of the research, Humphreys maintained the complete anonymity of the participants. However, his work still entails numerous ethical problems. There was no informed consent procedure (this study was carried out before scientific societies and universities instituted such standards). Participants were deceived—a problem made worse by the fact that they were never debriefed and told the true purpose of the research. But these considerations in turn raise the question, Could Humphreys have obtained good data within the bounds of research ethics? The clearly negative aspects of the study have to be weighed against the benefits that knowing more about this form of sexual behavior offers to society.

Tearoom sex gained publicity again in 2007 when Senator Larry Craig (R, Idaho) was arrested in the Minneapolis airport for behavior in a restroom that seemed to solicit sex. Today, because so many gay men are out of the closet, tearooms are used mainly by older or closeted men.

Source: Humphreys (1970).

---

setting for children to grow up in. The courts have often assumed that lesbians and gay men are unfit parents, and the same-gender sexual orientation of a parent has been grounds for the other, heterosexual parent to gain custody of children following a divorce (Patterson, 2009). What does the research say about these families and the effects on children in them?

It is important to recognize that these families are diverse along dimensions of race, social class, and gender. In some, the children were born to one of the partners in a previous heterosexual relationship. In others, the children were adopted or, in the case of lesbian couples, born by means of artificial insemination. Some have even said that a "lesbian baby boom" is under way.

Gay fathers may have used a surrogate mother. Some are single-parent families, with, for example, a lesbian mother rearing her children from a previous heterosexual marriage.

Three concerns have been raised about how the children fare in these families. First, will they show disturbances in gender identity or sexual identity? Will they become gay or lesbian? Second, will they be less healthy psychologically than children who grow up with two heterosexual parents? Third, will they have difficulties in relationships with their peers, perhaps being stigmatized or teased because of their unusual family situation?

Research on children growing up in lesbian or gay families, compared with those growing up in heterosexual

First Person

A Gay Couple: Lee and Bob

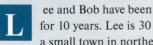

Lee and Bob have been living together as a couple for 10 years. Lee is 30 and Bob is 53; they live in a small town in northern Wisconsin.

Lee feels that he never had a real home while growing up. His father worked in construction, and they moved frequently, living in motel rooms. His parents divorced when he was in kindergarten. His mother remarried soon, but the man turned out to be a wife batterer, so they divorced when Lee was in the fifth grade. His mother, now single, turned to drugs and partying. Home life had no structure and was chaotic, although Lee feels that she loved him. Then his mom was "saved" and joined a repressive, fundamentalist church. She married again, to someone with like beliefs, and is still married to that man.

Lee knew that he liked boys more than girls by the first grade, but he also knew that he shouldn't talk about it. He didn't completely self-label as gay until his first semester in college. At that time he had his first affair, with his boss at Burger King. The affair was tempestuous, and he was heartbroken when it ended badly. His mother sensed that something was up. When he told her that he was gay, she insisted that he go to a psychiatrist to be cured. He agreed to try not to be gay and did try, but of course it didn't work. He and his mother had one more fight about it, and she kicked him out of the house. After two years they reconciled somewhat but not completely, and his stepfather is still rejecting.

Bob, in contrast, had an unremarkable childhood. His parents are still married after 54 years, and he speaks to them every day, although he has never told them that he is gay and they have never asked. Raised as a Catholic in northern Wisconsin, he is nonpracticing today.

Bob began to find boys to be more attractive than girls in high school, but in those days no label of "gay" was available. He first acted on his impulses in college and had dated five or six people before meeting Lee.

They met, improbably, in northern Wisconsin when the first gay bar opened in one small town. They dated briefly and quickly settled down as a couple. They have an agreement to be monogamous, which Bob has never breached and Lee has breached only once.

When asked what they liked best about their relationship, Bob said it was the stability of knowing that there's someone to share life with. The relationship seems to him like an investment built up over time. Lee likes being in a relationship because he loves Bob and knows Bob loves him in return. Lee also appreciates the depth of the relationship, which seems to him to be a major accomplishment. They worry a bit about their age gap. Bob is beginning to think about retirement, whereas Lee is getting ready to launch his career and anticipates a major move in the next few years. They also regret their emotional distance from their families.

Today Lee is working on his PhD in clinical psychology, hoping to become a therapist. Bob is a commercial pilot for a major airline.

Source: Based on an interview conducted by Janet Hyde.

---

families, dismisses these fears. For example, an overwhelming number of children growing up in lesbian or gay households have a heterosexual orientation (Allen & Burrell, 2002; Gartrell et al., 2011).

The adjustment and mental health of children in lesbian and gay families are no different from those of children in heterosexual families (Farr, 2017; Farr et al., 2010; Patterson, 2017). In fact, there is some evidence that children of gay fathers show better adjustment compared with children of heterosexual parents (Miller et al., 2017).

As for the third concern, about peer relationships, research indicates that children in lesbian or gay families fare about as well in terms of social skills and popularity as children in heterosexual families (Patterson, 2009).

In conclusion, although concerns have been raised about children growing up in lesbian and gay families, research consistently shows no difference between these children and those in heterosexual families (Patterson, 2006). Children need at least one loving, supportive parent, and parents who get along pretty well, and that can be found in many family constellations.

Do children of lesbian couples grow up to be well adjusted, or do they have problems?

(a)   (b)

Figure 6   Gay and lesbian political issues: (*a*) The custody issue—lesbian mothers want the right to keep their children after a divorce; (*b*) the right to adoption—a gay couple with their adopted child.

(a) ©Dragon Images/Shutterstock; (b) ©wavebreakmedia/Shutterstock

Recognizing these positive outcomes, in 2002 the American Academy of Pediatrics issued a policy statement supporting adoptions by gay parents (Perrin et al., 2002).

How Many People Are Gay, Straight, or Bi?

Many people believe that homosexuality is rare. What percentages of people in the United States are gay and lesbian? As it turns out, the answer to this question is complex. Basically, it depends on how one defines a homosexual and a heterosexual. First, though, several concepts need to be clarified. A distinction has already been made between sex (sexual behavior) and gender (being male or female) and between gender identity (the psychological sense of maleness or femaleness or something else such as nonbinary) and sexual orientation (gay, straight, or bisexual). To this, the concept of **sexual identity** should be added; it refers to one's self-label or self-identification as heterosexual, lesbian, gay, bisexual, queer, or perhaps something else.

There may be contradictions between people's sexual identity and their choice of sexual partners (their behavior) (Pathela et al., 2006; Weinberg et al., 2001). For example, a woman might identify as lesbian yet occasionally sleep with

> **What percentage of Americans are gay, lesbian, or bisexual?**

Sexual identity: One's self-identity as gay, straight, lesbian, bisexual, queer, or something else.

men. Her behavior is bisexual, but her identity is lesbian. More common are people who think of themselves as heterosexuals but who engage in both heterosexual and same-gender sex.

One source of information we have on the statistical question is Kinsey's research (see the chapter "Sex Research" for an evaluation of the Kinsey data). Kinsey found that about 37 percent of all males had had at least one homosexual experience to orgasm in adulthood. This is a large percentage. Indeed, it was this statistic, combined with some of the findings on premarital sex, that led to the furor over the Kinsey report. The comparable figure for females was 13 percent. However, experts agree that, because of problems with sampling, Kinsey's statistics on homosexuality were almost certainly inflated (Pomeroy, 1972).

Today several well-sampled surveys of the U.S. population have given us improved estimates. One of those is the National Survey of Family Growth (NSFG). Data from that study are shown in Table 2. The statistics are complex because much depends on how *homosexual* is defined. Does the definition require someone to have had exclusively same-gender sexual experiences, or just some same-gender experiences, or perhaps just to have experienced sexual attraction to members of their own gender without ever acting on it? We will return to this point. What we can say here is that, according to the National Survey of Family Growth, about 6 percent of men and 17 percent of women have had at least one same-gender sexual experience in adulthood, and about 4 percent of both men and women experience sexual attraction to members of their own gender. Roughly 2 percent of men and 1 percent of women have a homosexual identity.

These percentages are considerably smaller than Kinsey's. What accounts for the difference? The National

Table 2 The National Survey of Family Growth Statistics on Same-Gender Behavior, Identity, and Attraction, 2013

	Percentage	
	Men	**Women**
Behavior		
Ever had sexual contact with same-gender partner	6.2*	17.4
Sexual Identity		
Homosexual	1.9	1.3
Bisexual	2.0	5.5
Sexual Attraction		
Only or mostly to same gender	2.3	1.6
Equally to both	0.9	3.2
"Mostly" to opposite gender	4.1	12.9

*Different questions were used for males and females, and the male question was narrower, so this percentage is an underestimate.

Source: Copen et al. (2016).

Survey of Family Growth is better sampled; it is generally agreed that Kinsey's unsystematic sampling methods led to overestimates of the incidence of homosexuality. But the NSFG may not be perfectly accurate, either. We can expect underreporting on any kind of sensitive topic like homosexuality, and the NSFG asked nonequivalent questions on behavior to males and females, making gender comparisons inaccurate.

After reading these statistics, though, you may still be left wondering how many people are gay. As Kinsey soon realized in trying to answer this question, it depends on how you count. A prevalent notion is that homosexual and heterosexual are two quite separate and distinct categories. This is what might be called a sexual orientation binary (see Figure 7). Kinsey made an important scientific breakthrough when he decided to conceptualize homosexuality and heterosexuality not as two separate categories but as variations on a continuum (Figure 7, section 2). The black and white extremes of heterosexuality and homosexuality have a lot of shades of gray in between: people who have had both some heterosexual and some same-gender experience, in various mixtures. To accommodate all this variety, Kinsey constructed a scale running from 0 (exclusively heterosexual) to 6 (exclusively homosexual), with the midpoint of 3 indicating equal amounts of heterosexual and homosexual experience. Contemporary research supports Kinsey's idea that sexual orientation exists on a spectrum, not as two separate categories (Savin-Williams, 2014).

The answer to the original question—How many people are gay and how many are heterosexual?—is complex. Probably about 90 percent of men and 90 percent of women are exclusively heterosexual. About 10 percent of men and women have had at least one same-gender sexual experience in adulthood. About 2 percent of men and 1 percent of women have a gay identity. These figures are based on the NSFG, but adjusted somewhat to allow for concealment by some respondents.

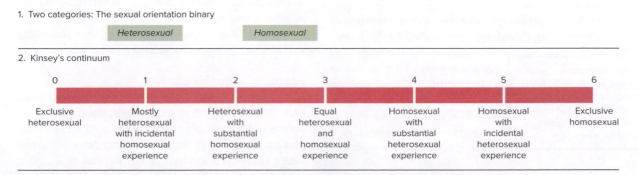

1. Two categories: The sexual orientation binary

2. Kinsey's continuum

Figure 7 Two ways of conceptualizing homosexuality and heterosexuality.

Sexual Orientation and Mental Health

Some Americans believe that homosexuality is a kind of mental illness. Is this really true? Do psychologists and psychiatrists agree that LGBs are poorly adjusted or deviant?

Sin and the Medical Model

The belief that homosexuality is a form of mental illness is actually something of an improvement over previous beliefs about homosexuality. Before the 20th century, the dominant belief in Europe and the United States was that homosexuality was a sin or a heresy. During the Inquisition in Spain, people who were accused of being heretics were also frequently accused of being homosexuals and were burned at the stake. Indeed, in those times, all mental illness was regarded as a sin. In the 20th century, this view was replaced by the **medical model,** in which mental disturbance, and homosexuality in particular, was viewed as a sickness or illness (Bullough & Bullough, 1997).[3]

Psychiatrist Thomas Szasz and others are critical of the medical model. In his writing on "the myth of mental illness," Szasz argues that the medical model is obsolete and that we need to develop a more humane and realistic way of dealing with mental disorders and variations from the norm. He has argued the case particularly for homosexuality (Szasz, 1965). LGB activists have joined in, saying that they do not like being called "sick" and that this is just another form of persecution of gays and lesbians.

Research Evidence

What do the scientific data say? Once again, the answers provided by the data are complex and depend on the assumptions of the particular investigator and on the research design used. Basically, four kinds of research designs have been used, representing progressive sophistication and changing assumptions about the nature of homosexuality.

Clinical Studies

The first, and earliest, approach was clinical; homosexuals who were in psychotherapy were studied by the investigator (usually the therapist). The researcher looked for disturbances in their current adjustment or in past experiences or home life. The data were then reported in the form of a case history of a single individual or a report of

> **Medical model:** A theoretical model in psychology and psychiatry in which mental problems are thought of as sickness or mental illness; the problems in turn are often thought to be due to biological factors.

---

[3]As one gay comedian quipped, "If homosexuality is an illness, hey, I'm going to call in queer to work tomorrow."

common factors that seemed to emerge in studying a group of homosexuals (e.g., Freud, 1920; reviewed by Rosen, 1974). These clinical studies provided evidence that homosexuals were poorly adjusted and neurotic. But the reasoning behind this research was circular. Homosexuals were assumed to be mentally ill, and then evidence was found supporting this view.

Studies with Control Groups

The second group of studies made significant improvements over the previous ones by introducing control or comparison groups. The question under investigation was rephrased. Rather than Do homosexuals have psychological disturbances? (after all, most of us have some problems), it became Do homosexuals have more psychological disturbances than heterosexuals? The research design involved comparing a group of homosexuals in therapy with a group of randomly chosen heterosexuals not in therapy. These studies tended to agree with the earlier ones in finding more problems of adjustment among the homosexual group than among the heterosexual group (Rosen, 1974).

Once again, though, it became apparent that there were problems with this research design. It compared a group of people in therapy with a group of people not in therapy and found, not surprisingly, that the people in therapy had more problems.

Nonpatient Research

A major breakthrough came with the third group of studies, which involved nonpatient research. In these studies, a group of gay people not in therapy (nonpatients) were compared with a group of heterosexuals not in therapy. The nonpatient gay men and lesbians were generally recruited through LGB organizations, advertisements, or word of mouth. Such nonpatient research generally has found no differences between the groups (Ross et al., 1988; Rothblum, 1994). That is, gays and lesbians seem to be as well adjusted as heterosexuals.

This position has received official professional recognition by the American Psychiatric Association. Prior to 1973, the APA had listed homosexuality as a disorder under Section V, "Personality Disorders and Certain Other Nonpsychotic Mental Disorders," in its authoritative *Diagnostic and Statistical Manual of Mental Disorders.* In 1973, the APA voted to remove homosexuality from that listing so that it was no longer considered a psychiatric disorder.

Population Studies

Most recently, a new set of studies has emerged using even better designs that, for example, obtain a random sample of the general population and then compare the gays and straights in the sample on indexes of mental health (Eaton, 2014; Meyer, 2003; Roberts et al., 2010; Wichstrøm & Hegna, 2003). These studies find somewhat higher rates of depression and anxiety among gays and lesbians compared with heterosexuals. And suicide attempts and PTSD are more common among LGBs than among heterosexuals (Hottes et al., 2016; Mustanski et al., 2010; Ploderl et al., 2013).

However, scientists vigorously debate the meaning of the statistics. One controversy concerns how big or meaningful the differences are. For example, in the well-sampled U.S. Youth Risk Behavioral Surveillance Survey, 9.4 percent of LGB adolescents had made a suicide attempt serious enough to be treated by a doctor, compared with 2 percent of heterosexual students (Kann et al., 2016). We could focus on the fact that LGB youth were nearly five times as likely to attempt suicide. Alternatively, we could say that it's a gap of just 7 percentage points and 90.6 percent of the LGBs had not attempted suicide. Should we view the glass as half full or half empty?

Beyond that, scientists agree that higher rates of depression and suicide attempts among LGBs do not mean that homosexuality per se indicates mental illness. Instead, the results are interpreted in the context of Ilan Meyer's (2003) *minority stress model,* which holds that stigma, prejudice, and discrimination create a stressful social environment that causes mental health problems. According to this model, the higher rates reflect the following: (1) the exposure of LGBs to maltreatment, discrimination, and violence (Eaton, 2014; Roberts et al., 2010); (2) the lack of support or downright rejection by family and friends that some LGBs experience (Ryan et al., 2009; Ueno, 2005); and (3) the stress of concealing their true identity (Meyer, 2003).

Resilience in Sexual Minority Individuals

To this point we have focused on negative psychological outcomes such as depression and suicide attempts. A major trend in psychology today is positive psychology, which focuses on people's resilience and factors that contribute to resilience. What is perhaps more striking than the negative outcomes is the resilience that most LGB people display in the face of stigma. Factors that promote resilience in LGBs include social support, especially support for the person's sexual orientation; and personal traits of hope and optimism, which help LGBs maintain their psychological health even when they encounter prejudice (Kwon, 2013). Interventions to promote resilience in LGB adolescents are being developed (Heck, 2015).

Can Sexual Orientation Be Changed by Therapy?

Conversion therapy or reparative therapy—treatments designed to change LGBs into heterosexuals—has been around for more than 100 years (Haldeman, 1994; Shidlo et al., 2002). The latest versions come not from trained psychologists but from far-right religious groups. Many earlier techniques were downright inhumane. They included crude behavior therapy that involved giving gay men electrical shocks while they viewed slides of nude men, as well as surgeries ranging from castration to brain surgery. All these treatments rested on the assumption that homosexuality was an illness that could and should be cured.

Investigations of reparative therapies today reveal the pressures from family and the personal agonies that people experience as they are forced, or perhaps choose, to change their orientation. One man, who is now a psychologist, wrote in his diary,

> I am going to meet with the counselor tomorrow. I don't really know what to think. I feel that I need help but I also feel that I'm trying to do away with a part of myself. I know I should look at it as sinful and ugly, like a wart that needs to be burned off. Is it possible that those emotions are what allow me to be a sensitive caring male? Is it possible that God has allowed this in my life to build certain characteristics? Is it really ugly and sinful that I want to hold and be held by a man and that I want to have a relationship with a man that includes sex? It sure sounds ugly on paper. I don't like admitting these things. I really don't. What is it that causes me to think and feel this way? Is it Satanic? Am I possessed? (Ford, 2001, p. 77)

The consequences of reparative therapy can be ugly, because they do not actually change people's sexual orientation but they do make them feel awfully guilty about it (Dehlin et al., 2014). In fact, some psychotherapists have developed a specialty in helping gay and bisexual men recover from conversion therapies (Haldeman, 2001).

Given the evidence discussed earlier in this section supporting the argument that LGBs are not mentally ill, reparative therapies make no sense. Ethical issues are raised as well: Should a person be changed from gay to straight against their will? By 2000 the scandals associated with conversion therapies had become so great that the American Psychiatric Association issued an official position statement opposing them (American Psychiatric Association, 2000b). And in 2015, the U.S. Department of Health and Human Services called for an end to conversion therapies (SAMHSA, 2015).

In sum, it is probably about as easy to change a homosexual person into a happy heterosexual as it is to change a heterosexual person into a happy homosexual—that is, not very.

Why Do People Become Gay or Heterosexual?

A fascinating psychological question is, Why do people become gay or heterosexual? Several theoretical answers to this question, as

> **Conversion or reparative therapy:** Any one of a number of treatments designed to turn LGBs into heterosexuals.

well as the relevant evidence, are discussed in this section. You will notice that the older theorists and researchers considered it their task to explain homosexuality, reflecting a heteronormative approach. More recent investigators, realizing that heterosexuality needs to be explained as well, are more likely to consider it their task to explain sexual orientation.

Biological Theories

A number of scientists have proposed that homosexuality is caused by biological factors. The likeliest candidates for these biological causes are genetic factors, prenatal factors, differences in brain structure, and an endocrine imbalance.

Genetic Factors

One study recruited gay and bisexual men who had a twin brother or an adopted brother (Bailey & Pillard, 1991). Among the 56 gay men who had an identical twin brother, 52 percent of the cotwins were themselves gay (in the terminology of geneticists, this is a 52 percent concordance rate). Among the 54 gay men who had a nonidentical twin brother, 22 percent of the cotwins were themselves gay. Of the adoptive brothers of gay men, 11 percent were gay. The same research team later repeated the study with lesbians (Bailey et al., 1993). Among the 71 lesbians who had an identical twin, 48 percent of the cotwins were also lesbian. Among the 37 lesbians who had a nonidentical twin sister, 16 percent of the cotwins were lesbian. Of the adoptive sisters of lesbians, 6 percent were lesbian. The statistics for women were therefore quite similar to those for men. Later studies using improved methods found similar results (Kendler et al., 2000b; Kirk et al., 2000).

What causes people to be gay?

The fact that the rate of concordance is substantially higher for identical twins than for nonidentical twins argues in favor of a genetic contribution to sexual orientation. If genetic factors absolutely determined sexual orientation, however, the concordance rate would be 100 percent for the identical twin pairs, and the rates are far from that. The implication is that factors other than genetics also play a role in influencing sexual orientation.

One research group believes that they have discovered a gene, located on the X chromosome, for homosexuality; this research is highly controversial (Hamer et al., 1993; Marshall, 1995). One study has replicated the finding but others have not (Bailey & Pillard, 1995; Rice et al., 1999).

A milestone came in 2005 with the first full genome scan for sexual orientation in men, using modern genotyping methods (Mustanski et al., 2005). The sample consisted of 456 individuals from 146 different families, all of which had two or more gay brothers. The sample included many heterosexual siblings and parents from those families, as well as the gay siblings. This design is ideal for spotting regions of DNA that are the same for two gay brothers but that differ from the heterosexual siblings or parents. The findings indicated possible influence by three genes, found on chromosomes 7, 8, and 10. Another study using similar methods found evidence for linkage between gay orientation in males and genes on chromosome 8 and the X chromosome, supporting both earlier studies (Sanders et al., 2015). It seems likely that multiple genes contribute to sexual orientation. This research is still in its infancy but should yield important findings in the next decade.

Prenatal Factors

Another possible biological cause is that sexual orientation develops as a result of factors during the prenatal period. As we saw in the chapter "Sex Hormones, Sexual Differentiation, and the Menstrual Cycle," exposure to atypical hormones during fetal development can lead a genetic female to have male genitals, or a genetic male to have female genitals. It has been suggested that a similar process might account for homosexuality (and also for transsexualism—see the chapter "Gender and Sexuality").

One line of research that supports this idea has found evidence that severe stress to a mother during pregnancy tends to produce homosexual offspring. For example, exposing pregnant female rats to stress produces male offspring that assume the female mating posture, although their ejaculatory behavior is typical for males (Ward et al., 2002). The stress to the mother reduces the amount of testosterone in the fetus, which is thought to produce homosexual rats. Research with humans designed to test the prenatal stress hypothesis reports mixed results. Some studies find effects like those in the rat studies and others do not (Bailey et al., 1991; Ellis & Cole-Harding, 2001).

Another research group has studied the birth order of gay men. Their research shows that consistently, across many samples, compared with heterosexual men, gay men are more likely to have a late birth order and to have more older brothers but not more older sisters (Blanchard, 1997, 2018). This is termed the *fraternal birth order effect.* The researchers find no birth order or sibling effects for lesbians compared with heterosexual women. They believe that they have uncovered a prenatal effect, hypothesizing that with each successive pregnancy with a male fetus, the mother forms more antibodies against a protein produced by a gene on the Y chromosome (Blanchard, 2001). The hypothesis is that the mother's antibodies to this protein may affect sexual differentiation in the developing fetal brain. In 2018, researchers identified the NLGN4Y protein, which is important in brain development and is coded by the Y chromosome (Bogaert et al., 2018). As hypothesized, mothers of gay sons, and particularly gay sons with older brothers, had higher levels of anti-NLGN4Y than did control samples of women. These researchers estimate that between 15 and 30 percent of gay men had their sexual orientation created in this manner (Blanchard & Bogaert, 2004; Cantor et al., 2002).

Other researchers have documented an odd, but potentially important, pattern concerning the 2D:4D finger-length ratio. This refers to the ratio of the length of the index finger (2D) to the length of the ring finger (4D). In general, men have lower 2D:4D ratios than women; that is, men's index fingers are relatively shorter than their ring fingers, compared with women's. Lesbians have a smaller 2D:4D ratio than heterosexual women; there are no differences between gay men and heterosexual men (Breedlove, 2017). It is thought that the 2D:4D ratio is an indicator of prenatal androgen exposure, so these results suggest possible prenatal effects on women's sexual orientation. Specifically, a lower 2D:4D ratio is thought to reflect more prenatal androgen exposure, implying that lesbians, on average, had more prenatal androgen exposure than other women. Other researchers have found that gays are more likely to be left-handed than are straights; gay men are about 40 percent more likely than straight men to be left-handed, and lesbians are nearly twice as likely as heterosexual women to be left-handed (Lalumière et al., 2000). Both patterns suggest some kind of prenatal hormone effect on the developing brain.

Recall that in the chapter "Sex Hormones, Sexual Differentiation, and the Menstrual Cycle" we introduced the concept of epigenetics and ways in which epigenetic factors may shape prenatal sexual differentiation. Yet another group of researchers has hypothesized that same-gender sexual orientation results from epigenetic factors during prenatal development that make the fetus more or less sensitive to androgens (Rice et al., 2012).

Brain Factors

A related line of theorizing argues that there are anatomical differences between the brains of gays and straights that produce the differences in sexual orientation. A number of studies have pursued this possibility, all looking at somewhat different regions of the brain (Swaab, 2005). A highly publicized study by neuroscientist Simon LeVay (1991) is an example. LeVay found significant differences between gay men and straight men in certain cells in the anterior portion of the hypothalamus. Anatomically, the hypothalamic cells of the gay men were more similar to those of women than to those of straight men, according to LeVay. However, the study had a number of flaws: (1) The sample size was very small: only 19 gay men, 16 straight men, and 6 straight women were included. This small sample size was necessitated by the fact that it was the pre-MRI days and the brains had to be dissected in order to examine the hypothalamus, so brains of living people could not be studied. (2) All of the

gay men in the sample, but only 6 of the straight men and 1 of the straight women, had died of AIDS. The groups are not comparable, then. Perhaps the brain differences were caused by the neurological effects of AIDS. (3) Lesbian women were omitted from the study, making them invisible in the research—as they often have been in psychological and biological research. (4) The gay men were known to have been gay based on records at the time of death; the others, however, were just presumed to be heterosexual—if there was no record of sexual orientation, the assumption was that the person had been heterosexual, scarcely a sophisticated method of measurement. (5) The brains were all from adults, so it is impossible to know whether the different hypothalamic cells caused the sexual orientations, or the different experiences of gay men affected the hypothalamus.

It is difficult to know how much confidence to place in LeVay's findings. Other scientists who looked for this effect found no differences in this region of the hypothalamus as a function of the person's sexual orientation (Byne et al., 2000; Swaab, 2005). Yet animal researchers believe that they have identified a similar region in the hypothalamus of the rat, and it does seem to be involved in sexual behavior (Swaab, 2005). Currently, then, there are no well-documented anatomical brain differences between gays and straights (Gooren, 2006).

Using modern functional brain scanning methods, researchers exposed gay men, heterosexual men, and heterosexual women to human pheromones and recorded their brain responses (Savic et al., 2005). One of the pheromones, AND, is a "male" pheromone and is found in male sweat. The other, EST, is a "female" pheromone and is found in female urine. Gay men and heterosexual women showed activation of a region of the hypothalamus (the medial preoptic area, MPOA, of the anterior hypothalamus) in response to AND, whereas heterosexual men did not show the brain response to AND. As a control, the participants were also exposed to common odors such as lavender oil; these odors did not activate the hypothalamus. In a second experiment, the researchers repeated the study with lesbian women, and found that EST stimulated their hypothalamus, as it does with heterosexual men (Berglund et al., 2006). What do these studies mean? They definitely don't mean that gay men have female brains and lesbians have male brains. What they do show is that both heterosexual men and lesbians are turned on (in their brains) by women's pheromones, and that gay men and heterosexual women are turned on by male pheromones.

Hormonal Imbalance

Investigating the possibility that an endocrine imbalance is the cause of homosexuality, researchers have tried to determine whether the testosterone ("male" hormone) levels of gay men differ from those of straight men. These studies have not found any hormonal differences between the two groups (Gooren, 2006).

Despite these results, in earlier times some clinicians attempted to cure male homosexuality by administering testosterone therapy (Glass & Johnson, 1944). This therapy failed; indeed, it seemed to result in even more homosexual behavior than usual. This is not an unexpected result; as we saw in the chapter "Sexual Arousal," androgen levels seem to be related to sexual desire. A clinician friend of ours replied to an undergraduate male who was seeking testosterone therapy for his homosexual behavior, "It won't make you heterosexual; it will only make you horny."

In conclusion, of the biological theories, the genetic theory and the prenatal theories have the best supporting evidence, but much more research is needed.

Learning Theory

Behaviorists emphasize the importance of learning in the development of sexual orientation. They note the prevalence of bisexual behavior both in other species and in young humans, and they argue that rewards and punishments shape the individual's behavior into predominant homosexuality or predominant heterosexuality. The assumption, then, is that humans have a relatively amorphous, undifferentiated pool of sex drive, which, depending on circumstances (rewards and punishments), may be channeled in any of several directions. In short, people are born sexual, not gay or straight. Only through learning does one of these behaviors become more likely than the other. For example, a person who has early heterosexual experiences that are very unpleasant might develop toward homosexuality. Heterosexuality has essentially been punished and therefore becomes less likely. This might occur, for instance, in the case of a girl who is raped at an early age; her first experience with heterosexual sex was extremely unpleasant, so she avoids it and turns to homosexuality. Parents who become upset about their teenagers' heterosexual activities might do well to remember this notion; punishing a young person for engaging in heterosexual behavior may not eliminate the behavior but rather rechannel it in a homosexual direction.

Another possibility, according to a learning-theory approach, is that if early sexual experiences are same-gender and pleasant, the person may become gay. Same-gender behavior has essentially been rewarded and therefore becomes more likely.

The learning-theory approach treats homosexuality as a normal form of behavior and recognizes that heterosexuality is not necessarily inborn but must also, like homosexuality, be learned.

The evidence on learning theory's explanation of sexual orientation is mixed. A comprehensive study of the

influences on sexual orientation in humans disconfirmed some essential arguments. The idea that homosexuality results from early unpleasant heterosexual experiences was not supported by the data. Lesbian women, for example, were no more likely to have been raped than heterosexual women (Bell et al., 1981). Yet research using an animal model does point to the importance of early learning. Zebra finches are small birds that are monogamous, mate for life, and are almost invariably heterosexual. If the fathers are removed from the cages, though, so that the young birds grow up without adult males or male–female pairs, in adulthood these birds pair with either males or females (Adkins-Regan, 2002). That is, their behavior, which is bisexual, is a result of early experience.

In contrast to the bird research, research with humans indicates that the great majority of children who grow up with a gay or lesbian parent are heterosexual (Allen & Burrell, 2002; Gartrell et al., 2011; Patterson, 2006). In this sense, then, homosexuality is not "learned" from one's parents.

Sociological Theory

Sociologists emphasize the effects of labeling in explaining homosexuality. The label "homosexual" has a big impact in our society. If you are heterosexual, suppose that someone said to you, "I think you are homosexual." How would you react? Your immediate reaction might be negative: anger, anxiety, and embarrassment. The label "homosexual" has derogatory connotations and may even be used as an insult, reflecting our society's predominantly negative attitudes toward homosexuality.

But the label "homosexual" may also act as a self-fulfilling prophecy. Suppose that a young boy—possibly because he is gender nonconforming or poor in sports, or for no reason at all—is called a "fag." He reacts strongly and becomes more and more anxious and worried about his problem. He becomes painfully aware of the slightest homosexual tendency in himself. Finally he convinces himself that he is gay. Later, he begins engaging in same-gender sexual behavior and associates with a gay group. In short, a gay person has been created through labeling.

Reiss's sociological theory of human sexuality is also relevant here (Reiss, 1986). In his theorizing he addressed the issue of sexual orientation, focusing particularly on gay men. Recognizing the need to explain cross-cultural differences in sexual patterns, he contends that it is male-dominant societies with a great rigidity of gender roles that produce the highest incidence of homosexuality. In such societies there is a rigid male role that must be learned and conformed to, but young boys have little opportunity to learn it from adult men precisely because the gender roles are rigid, so that women take care of children and men have little contact with them. It is therefore difficult to learn the heterosexual component of the male role. In addition, because the male role is rigid, there will be a certain number of males who dislike it and reject its heterosexual component. Cross-cultural studies support his observations (Reiss, 1986). Societies that have a great maternal involvement with infants and low paternal involvement with infants and that have rigid gender roles are precisely those that have the highest incidence of same-gender sexual behavior in males.

This pattern describes the negative pathway to homosexuality. Reiss argues that there is also a positive pathway. It exists in less gender-rigid societies with more permissiveness about sexuality. In such societies, individuals feel freer to experiment with same-gender behavior and may find it satisfying.

The Bottom Line

We have examined a number of theories of sexual orientation and the evidence supporting or refuting them. What is the bottom line? Which theory is correct? The answer is, We don't know yet. We do not know what causes sexual orientation. Several theories have strong evidence supporting them, but no one theory accounts for all cases. We believe that a good lesson can be learned from this somewhat frustrating conclusion.

It has generally been assumed that gays form not only a distinct category (which, we have already seen, is not very accurate) but also a homogeneous category, that is, that all gays are fairly similar. Not so. Probably there are many different kinds or "types" of LGBs. If this is the case, then one would not expect a single cause of homosexuality but rather many causes, each corresponding to its type. The next step in research, then, will be to identify the different pathways of development that lead to each.

Differences between Gay Men and Lesbians

Although gay men and lesbians are commonly lumped together in one category and called homosexuals, evidence from a number of sources indicates that there are some important differences between the two groups that go beyond one group being male and the other female (Diamond, 2014).

Who is more likely to be bisexual—men or women?

Women are more likely to be bisexual, and less likely to be exclusively homosexual, than men are. In the NSFG data set, 5 percent of women and 2 percent of men indicated that they identify as bisexual (Table 2).

In related research, among both heterosexuals and LGBs, women show more flexibility or change over time in their sexual orientation (Kinnish et al., 2005). As noted earlier in the chapter, this is what Diamond (2008a) calls *sexual fluidity.* In laboratory research, men are specific in their sexual arousal, whereas women tend not to be (Chivers, 2017). That is, heterosexual men tend to be aroused, physiologically, by female stimuli and not male stimuli, and gay men show the reverse pattern. Women, however, whether lesbian or heterosexual, show arousal to both male and female stimuli.

As noted earlier in the chapter, gay men tend to reach developmental milestones earlier than lesbians (Katz-Wise et al., 2017). For example, in one study, lesbians experienced their first same-gender attraction, on average, at age 14, compared with age 11 for gay men.

Some of the theories discussed earlier in this chapter seem to work for gay men or for lesbians but not for both. For example, the fraternal birth order effect has been found repeatedly; compared with heterosexual men, gays are more likely to have a late birth order and an excess of older brothers. Lesbians, however, are no more or less likely to have a late birth order than heterosexual women (Bogaert, 2003).

We will almost certainly need somewhat different theories to explain the development of sexual orientation in women and in men (Diamond, 2014).

Sexual Orientation in Multicultural Perspective

Just as different cultures around the world hold different views of same-gender sexual behavior (see A Sexually Diverse World: Ritualized Homosexuality in Melanesia), so do various U.S. ethnic minority groups have different cultural definitions for same-gender behaviors.

It is generally thought that there is less tolerance of LGBs in the African American community (Daboin et al., 2015). In one study Whites had the lowest levels of antigay attitudes and Blacks had the highest levels, with Latinx and Asian Americans falling in between (Haslam & Levy, 2006). Ethnic minority LGBs have a double minority status and may experience racism within the gay community and antigay prejudice within their ethnic group (Ibañez et al., 2009). That said, some researchers believe that coping skills can helpfully transfer from one minority status to the other (Kuber et al., 2014). For example, learning coping skills to deal with racial prejudice might also help the person cope with antigay prejudice, and vice versa.

The process of sexual identity development and coming out may differ across U.S. ethnic groups. In a study of African American, Latina, and White lesbians, the African Americans and Latinas began wondering if they were lesbian at younger ages (around age 14) than the Whites (around age 17) (Parks et al., 2004). The African American lesbians were considerably less likely to be "out" with nonfamily than the Latinas and Whites, perhaps because of the stronger antigay attitudes among African Americans noted earlier.

We should not overemphasize ethnic differences, though. In one large study of Asian Americans and Latinx, 88 percent of Asian Americans considered themselves heterosexual, 2 percent LGB, 4 percent something else (and the rest didn't answer) (Chae & Ayala, 2010). The comparable numbers for Latinx were 93, 1, and 1 percent, respectively. This same pattern has been found in numerous studies of mainly White samples.

It is also true that Black and Latino men are more likely than White men to engage extensively in same-gender sexual behavior while still considering themselves to be heterosexual (Muñoz-Laboy, 2008). A sizable number—we don't know the statistics exactly—of African American and Latino men are heterosexually married and present themselves to the world as heterosexual, yet engage in secret sex with other men, a practice called "down low" (Muñoz-Laboy, 2008).

An interesting example of these different cultural definitions comes from a study of Mexican and Mexican American men and their same-gender sexual behavior (Magaña & Carrier, 1991). In Mexico, there is a dichotomizing of same-gender sexual behaviors that parallels traditional gender roles. Anal intercourse, because it most resembles penis-in-vagina intercourse, is the preferred behavior, and fellatio is practiced relatively little. A man adopts the role either of receptive partner or inserting partner and does this exclusively. Those who take the receptive role are considered unmanly, feminine, and homosexual. Those who take the inserting role are considered masculine, are not labeled homosexual, and are not stigmatized. This approach differs substantially from that in Anglo culture, where men commonly switch roles, and both are considered gay.

Such different definitions of homosexuality are not limited to Mexican and Mexican American culture. One researcher described the scene in Egypt:

Figure 8   Ethnicity and sexual orientation. Among Latinas, warmth and physical closeness are very acceptable, but there are strong taboos against female–female sexual relationships.

©Jim West/Alamy

A Sexually Diverse World

Ritualized Homosexuality in Melanesia

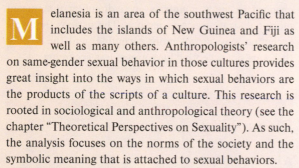

Melanesia is an area of the southwest Pacific that includes the islands of New Guinea and Fiji as well as many others. Anthropologists' research on same-gender sexual behavior in those cultures provides great insight into the ways in which sexual behaviors are the products of the scripts of a culture. This research is rooted in sociological and anthropological theory (see the chapter "Theoretical Perspectives on Sexuality"). As such, the analysis focuses on the norms of the society and the symbolic meaning that is attached to sexual behaviors.

Among Melanesians, same-gender sexual behavior has a very different symbolic meaning from the one it has in Western culture. There it is viewed as natural, normal, and indeed necessary. The Melanesian culture actually prescribes the behavior, in contrast to Western cultures, in which it is forbidden or proscribed.

Sociologists and anthropologists believe that most cultures are organized around the dimensions of social class, race, gender, and age. Among Melanesians, age organizes the homosexual behavior. It is not to occur among two men of the same age. Instead, it occurs between an adolescent and a preadolescent, or between an adult man and a pubertal boy. The older partner is always the inserter for the acts of anal intercourse, the younger partner the insertee.

Ritualized homosexual behavior serves several social purposes in these cultures. It is viewed as a means by which a boy at puberty is incorporated into the adult society of men. It is also thought to encourage a boy's growth, so that it helps to "finish off" his growth in puberty. In these societies, semen is viewed as a scarce and valuable commodity. Therefore, the same-gender sexual behaviors are viewed as helpful and honorable, a means of passing on strength to younger men and boys. One anthropologist observed,

> Semen is also necessary for young boys to attain full growth to manhood. . . . They need a boost, as it were. When a boy is eleven or twelve years old, he is engaged for several months in homosexual intercourse with a healthy older man chosen by his father. (This is always an in-law or unrelated person, since the same notions of incestuous relations apply to little boys as to marriageable women.) Men point to the rapid growth of adolescent youths, the appearance of peach fuzz beards, and so on, as the favorable results of this child-rearing practice. (Schieffelin, 1976, p. 124)

In all cases, these men are expected later to marry and father children. This points up the contrast between sexual identity and sexual behavior. The sexual behaviors are ones that we would surely term homosexual, yet these cultures are so structured that the boys and men who engage in homosexual behaviors do not form a homosexual identity.

Ritualized same-gender sexual behaviors are declining as these cultures are colonized by Westerners. It is fortunate that anthropologists were able to make their observations over the last several decades to document these interesting and meaningful practices before they disappear.

Source: Herdt (1984).

In Egypt, because there was so little sense of homosexuality as an identity, what position you took in bed defined all. Between men, the only sex that counted was anal sex. . . . In the minds of most Egyptians, "gay," if it meant anything at all, signified taking the receptive position in anal sex. On the other hand, a person who took the insertive role—and that seemed to include virtually all Egyptian men, to judge by what my acquaintances told me—was not considered gay. . . . Many of the insults in the Arabic language concern being penetrated anally by another man. (Miller, 1992, p. 76)

As for lesbians, Latinas experience conflicts in the complexities of ethnicity and sexual orientation (Espin, 1987; Gonzalez & Espin, 1996). Although in Latin cultures, emotional and physical closeness among women is considered acceptable and desirable, attitudes toward lesbianism are even more restrictive than in Anglo culture. Familismo, the special emphasis on family—defined as mother, father, children, and grandparents—in Latin cultures makes the lesbian even more of an outsider. As a result, Latina lesbians often become part of an Anglo lesbian community while remaining in the closet with their family and among Latinx, creating difficult choices among identities. One Cuban woman responded to a questionnaire, "I identify myself as a lesbian more intensely than

Table 3	The Global Divide on Homosexuality (a sampling from 141 countries)	
Nation	**LGBT Global Acceptance Index (GAI)* 2004–2008**	**GAI 2009–2013**
Iceland	6.02	7.37
Netherlands	5.84	6.67
Canada	4.91	5.44
United States	4.57	4.90
Japan	4.22	4.50
Uganda	2.46	1.72
Egypt	2.29	1.50
Saudi Arabia	2.16	1.19

*High scores indicate more acceptance.

Source: Flores & Park (2018).

as a Cuban/Latin. But it is a very painful question because I feel that I am both, and I don't want to have to choose" (Espin, 1987, p. 47).

Two features of Asian American culture shape attitudes toward homosexuality and its expression: (1) a strong distinction between what may be expressed publicly and what should be kept private; and (2) a stronger value placed on loyalty to one's family and on the performance of family roles than on the expression of one's own desires (Choi & Israel, 2016; Cochran et al., 2007). Sexuality must be expressed only privately, not publicly. And having an identity, much less a sexual identity or a gay lifestyle, apart from one's family is almost incomprehensible to traditional Asian Americans. As a result, a relatively small proportion of Asian American LGBs seem to be "out" compared with non-Asians. Asian American LGBs who are out tend to be more acculturated, that is, influenced by American culture. They echo the sentiments of the Latina lesbian just mentioned, saying that they would prefer not to have to choose between their ethnic identity and their sexual identity but that when forced to make the choice they are more closely tied to the LGB part of their identities.

In sum, when we consider sexual orientation from a multicultural perspective, two main points emerge: (1) The very definition of homosexuality is set by culture. In the United States, we would say that a man who is the inserting partner in anal intercourse with another man is engaging in homosexual behavior, but other cultures (such as Mexico and Egypt) would not agree. (2) Some ethnic groups are even more disapproving of homosexuality than are U.S. Whites. In those cases, LGBs feel conflicts between their sexual identity and loyalty to their ethnic group.

These variations among ethnic groups in the United States are magnified as we look at attitudes toward homosexuality in nations around the world. As shown in Table 3, acceptance of LGBs varies so much that it has been called a global divide. Some nations, such as Iceland and the Netherlands, have high levels of acceptance. Others, like Canada, the United States, and Japan, are intermediate; and others, such as Uganda, Egypt, and Saudi Arabia, show little acceptance. In addition, Table 3 shows that over a period of just 5 to 6 years, attitudes have changed in many countries, in a direction that means more polarization across nations. The nations that were accepting have grown more accepting, and the nations that were not accepting have grown less accepting.

Bisexuality

A bisexual is a person whose sexual orientation is toward both women and men, that is, toward members of the same gender as well as the other gender. A slang term is "ac–dc" (alternating current–direct current).

Bisexuality is not rare; in fact, it is more common than exclusive homosexuality (if a bisexual is defined as a person who has had at least one sexual experience with a male and at least one with a female). About 2 percent of men and 5 percent of women claim a bisexual identity (see Table 2), although there is probably some underreporting.

Some bisexuals are heterosexually married men who also have sex with men. One researcher recruited a sample of men who fit this description (Malcolm, 2008). In the sample, 65 percent were still married and 35 percent had divorced. Although all the men, behaviorally, were bisexual, 5 percent had a heterosexual identity, 38 percent had a bisexual identity, and 57 percent had a homosexual identity.

Stereotypes and Prejudice

Bisexuals may be viewed with suspicion or downright hostility by the gay community (Matsick & Rubin, 2018; Rust, 2002). Radical lesbians refer to bisexual women as "fence-sitters," saying that they betray the lesbian cause because they can act straight or lesbian whenever convenient. The term LUGs (lesbians until graduation) is used for women who live a lesbian lifestyle when it is easy in college and then shift to convenient heterosexuality afterward. Some gays even argue that there is no such thing as a true bisexual (Rust, 2002). Heterosexuals, too, can be quite biased against bisexuals, especially men (Yost & Thomas, 2012).

Bisexuals tend to be stereotyped as nonmonogamous (Yost & Thomas, 2012). They can also be stereotyped as confused and untrustworthy (Zivony & Lobel, 2014).

First Person

Sexual Fluidity and Questioning

This case is taken from a series of interviews conducted by psychologist Lisa Diamond, author of *Sexual Fluidity* (2008a).

At the first interview, Eleanor described herself as "questioning." She has an outgoing, vivacious demeanor, with a broad, engaging smile and a self-deprecating sense of humor.

Eleanor flatly refused to characterize her same-sex attractions on a 0–100 percent scale. She threw up her hands and exclaimed, "I can't make any sense of that at all! There are too many variables involved when I'm attracted to someone, so there's no way for me to divide it up that way." Eleanor was 20 years old and had first begun to question her sexuality about a year earlier, when her boyfriend told her that he was bisexual. She had been aware of sporadic same-sex attractions since the age of 13, and, in her words, "they scared the hell out of me." Yet the attractions had always confused her. Most of her "gut level" urges were in response to men, but she found women more aesthetically and emotionally desirable. As she put it,

> I prefer to make out with men, but the idea of having sex with a man utterly repulses me. I would, however, like to marry a woman, and that's who I want to make a long-term commitment to. . . . When people ask me if I'm straight and I say yes, I know I'm being dishonest, and I can't tolerate that dishonesty. But if somebody asked me if I was a lesbian, I'd also feel dishonest saying yes. I guess I might be bisexual. I'm annoyed by the uncertainty. I know I'm not straight, it's just a matter of defining my not-straightness. . . .

By the second interview Eleanor had settled on the compromise of a bisexual identification, despite the fact that her feelings for women remained relatively ambiguous. She was eager for more certainty about her sexuality.

I still go through this whole explanation when I tell people I'm bisexual, because the truth is that my attraction to women isn't really all that sexual. It's more aesthetic. Women are just so much better looking than men. I guess I find women magnetic. That's not quite the same as a sexual attraction. . . . I thought that things would resolve themselves. I expected that over time I'd either feel clear sexual attractions and I'd identify as bisexual or I wouldn't feel them at all and I'd identify as heterosexual. But now I realize that won't happen—I still feel the same and I've accepted that.

At the third interview, at age 25, Eleanor had finally reconciled with the fact that her emotional and aesthetic appreciation for women did not really qualify as sexual attraction. Yet contrary to the notion that this might just be a rationalization for not identifying as lesbian or bisexual, Eleanor actually expressed great disappointment that she was not gay.

> I've kind of straightened out! I still call myself bisexual but I'm on the edge of heterosexual, which I'm not pleased about. . . I never really wanted to be heterosexual but I don't have much choice in the matter. . . . I think sexuality definitely changes, because it's not that I'm just more aware of the straight parts of me, I've actually *become* more straight, but I don't have any idea what causes those changes.

Eleanor reported the same basic perspective at the 8-year and 10-year follow-up interviews, when she characterized herself as "reluctantly heterosexual." At the time of the 10-year interview, she described her emotional attraction as 70 percent to women, but her physical attraction as only 5 percent to women.

Source: Sexual Fluidity: Understanding Women's Love and Desire by Lisa M. Diamond, President and Fellows of Harvard College, 2008.

On the question of whether there are true bisexuals, the emerging scientific evidence increasingly indicates that there really are individuals who are attracted to both women and men. For example, in one study the researchers recruited self-identified bisexual women and men, as well as heterosexual women and men (Lippa, 2013). The participants then viewed multiple photos of male and female swimsuit models and rated their sexual attractiveness. Meanwhile, their viewing times for each photo were measured unobtrusively. As might be expected, the heterosexual men rated the female models as very attractive and the male models as not attractive. Similarly, the heterosexual women rated the male models as attractive and the female models as less attractive. The bisexual men found both male and female models to be attractive, as did the bisexual women. That is, the bisexuals really did show a pattern of attractions that was distinct from the heterosexuals. Even more interesting, though, were the findings for the unobtrusive behavioral measure of looking times. The bisexual women and men spent about equal amounts of time looking at the male and the female models, in contrast to heterosexuals, whose looking times were quite skewed toward models of the other gender. Other research, using physiological measures of arousal, shows similar results (Cerny & Janssen, 2011). In short, bisexual people, with bisexual patterns of attraction, really do exist.

Bisexual Development

Some have argued that bisexuality is a developmental stage on the way to discovering that one is truly gay or lesbian. Is that view accurate, or are there some people who are lifelong bisexuals? One longitudinal study over 10 years followed women who initially said they were lesbian, bisexual, or "unlabeled" in their sexual orientation (Diamond, 2008b). At the start of the study, the women ranged in age between 18 and 25. Fully 22 percent of the women maintained their bisexual or unlabeled identity over the 10 years, indicating that it is not just a transitional phase. Many other women changed in their identity over time, often in response to relationship experiences. For example, among women who began the study identifying as lesbian and then switched to bisexual/unlabeled, two-thirds had sexual contact with a man during the two years before the identity change.

Another study followed men and women in New Zealand from age 21 to 26 (Dickson et al., 2003). Women were more likely to change their pattern of attraction than men were, but some men also changed in their attractions. Especially for women, attractions seemed to change in all possible directions.

The timing and flexibility of these sequences argue for the importance of late-occurring experiences in the shaping of one's sexual behavior and identity. As already discussed in this chapter, most of the theory and research rest on the assumption that homosexuality is determined by conditions in childhood, or by prenatal or genetic factors. Yet some people have their first heterosexual and then their first same-gender sexual experience in their twenties. It is difficult to believe that these behaviors were determined by some event that occurred before birth.

Pansexual: People who are sexually or romantically attracted to people regardless of their gender.

Unlike gender identity, which seems to be fixed in the preschool years, sexual identity continues to evolve in adulthood for some people (Diamond, 2003). This contradicts some scientists' assertion that sexual orientation is determined before adolescence (Bell et al., 1981). We think the point at which sexual orientation is determined is still an open question. For some it may be determined by genetic factors or experiences early in life, but for others it may be determined in adulthood or continue to be fluid.

Mostly Heterosexuals

Another group that is being recognized today is the *mostly heterosexuals,* that is, people who are not exclusively heterosexual, but also not quite bisexual (Savin-Williams & Vrangalova, 2013). Kinsey might have called them a 1 on his scale. They have a small amount of same-gender sexual attraction and they engage in same-gender sexual behavior only occasionally. Research on mostly heterosexuals challenges the idea that sexual orientation can be understood as two—or maybe three—distinct categories. Instead, it supports the idea that sexual orientation exists along a continuum.

Pansexuals

The term **pansexual** refers to people who are sexually or romantically attracted to people regardless of their gender (Morandini et al., 2017). As a sexual identity, it seeks to overcome the gender binary assumptions inherent in the label of bisexual.

Concluding Reflections

This consideration of bisexuality raises a question as to whether heterosexuality is really the "natural" state.

The pattern in some theories has been to try to discover the pathological conditions that cause homosexuality (e.g., having a father who is an inadequate role model or a bad dose of prenatal hormones)—all on the basis of the assumption that heterosexuality is the natural state and that homosexuality must be explained as a deviation from it. As discussed earlier, this approach has failed; there appear to be multiple causes of homosexuality, just as there may be multiple causes of heterosexuality. The important alternative to consider is that bisexuality is the natural state, a point acknowledged by the learning theorists and sociological theorists (Weinberg et al., 1994). This chapter closes, then, with some questions. Psychologically, the real question should concern not the conditions that lead to homosexuality but rather the causes of exclusive homosexuality and exclusive heterosexuality. Why do we eliminate some people as potential sex partners simply on the basis of their gender? Why isn't everyone bisexual or pansexual?

Critical *THINK* ing Skill

Interpreting research findings

Earlier in this chapter, we saw that the rate of suicide attempts is higher among sexual minority youth (9.4 percent) than it is among heterosexual youth (2 percent). That is the statistical research result, but how should it be interpreted? What does it mean?

In interpreting research results, it is important to consider two questions: (1) Is the difference big enough to care about? and (2) What factor(s) could cause such an effect?

First, then, is the difference big enough to be important? For example, sometimes we hear a proclamation in the news that the unemployment rate is up, followed by the specifics that it is up from 7.8 percent in January to 7.9 percent in February. True, 7.9 is greater than 7.8, but the difference is tiny and not important. In the case of sexual minority youth, is the difference in suicide attempts big enough to be important? If you have had a statistics course, you will know that one way to evaluate a difference between two groups involves testing whether the difference is statistically significant. Therefore, statistical tests of significance are one way to decide whether a difference is big enough to be important. Another way to think about how big the difference is, especially when the data are given in terms of percentages, is to evaluate the percentages directly. Is it disturbing that the suicide attempt rate is more than twice as high among gay youth as straight youth? Or is a rate under 10 percent for gay youth still low and not cause for concern? We might add to that an evaluation of the cost of the behavior. True, a suicide attempt rate of 9.4 percent represents just a small minority, but some suicide attempts foreshadow actual suicides and the death of a person, so a rate of 9.4 percent might be unacceptably high. Perhaps even the 2 percent rate for straight youth is unacceptably high. Statistical tests of significance cannot answer these questions, which rest much more on personal values.

Assuming that our answer to the first question is yes, there is a big enough difference between sexual minority and straight youth to be important, then we can ask what factor or factors cause the difference? Don't stop with generating just one cause, but think of several, and then ask, might more than one of them be important? It is not always necessary to choose between one cause and another. Think of some possible causes before continuing to the next paragraph.

Some possible causes, not all of them supported by research, include the following: Perhaps there are genetic factors that cause homosexuality, and those same genetic factors also cause depression and suicide attempts. Another possible interpretation might be that homosexuality is a mental illness and therefore more suicide attempts occur among LGB youth. A third possible interpretation involves thinking about what might cause suicide attempts in general, not just among LGB youth. A leading cause is serious stress, so a possible cause of the difference is that sexual minority youth experience more stress—such as bullying—than straight youth do, and that accounts for the higher rate of suicide attempts.

Notice that the way we interpret the research findings in this case could lead to very different conclusions and implications. One person might conclude that the research provides confirmation that homosexuality is a mental illness. Another person might conclude from the same findings that sexual minority youth face intolerable levels of stress and that we should institute social programs in schools and families to reduce the stress. For a person who wanted to pursue this question more, the important next step would be to consider what other research evidence would be needed to decide among these conclusions and then find out what the research says.

SUMMARY

Sexual orientation refers to a person's erotic and emotional orientation toward members of their own gender or members of the other gender.

Attitudes toward Gays and Lesbians

About 39 percent of Americans believe that homosexuality is wrong. This belief is the basis for much antigay prejudice. In some cases this prejudice is so strong that it results in hate crimes and harassment directed at gays and lesbians. Despite popular beliefs in gaydar, there is little scientific evidence that it exists, and better evidence that it is just another kind of stereotyping.

Life Experiences of LGBs

Coming out involves acknowledging to oneself, and then to others, that one is gay or lesbian. LGB communities can be found around the world. These communities are defined by a common culture and social life and by rituals such as pride marches. The legalization of same-gender marriage in the United States in 2015 marked a major shift in LGB couple relationships. Positive psychology approaches stress the strengths found in LGB couples. Although concerns have been voiced about the well-being of children who grow up in lesbian and gay families, these concerns are unfounded, according to the available studies.

How Many People Are Gay, Straight, or Bi?

Well-sampled surveys indicate (when corrected for some underreporting) that about 2 percent of men and 1 percent of women have a gay or lesbian identity and that roughly 6 percent of men and 17 percent of women have had at least one same-gender sexual experience. Kinsey devised a scale ranging from 0 (exclusively heterosexual) to 6 (exclusively homosexual) to measure this diversity of experience. A person's sexual identity may be discordant with their actual behavior.

Sexual Orientation and Mental Health

Well-conducted research indicates that homosexuality per se is not a sign of poor adjustment. Research does show somewhat elevated rates of depression and suicide attempts among LGBs, which is mainly due to exposure to prejudice and maltreatment and the failure of family and friends to support the person. Although some groups claim success in reparative therapy to change the sexual orientation of LGBs, there is no scientific evidence that one's sexual orientation can be changed by any known methods, and many indications that these therapies are psychologically harmful.

Why Do People Become Gay or Heterosexual?

Biological explanations include genetic factors, hormone imbalance, prenatal factors, and brain factors. The genetic and prenatal explanations have some support from the data. Learning theorists stress that the sex drive is undifferentiated at birth and is channeled, through experience, into heterosexuality or homosexuality. Sociologists emphasize the importance of roles and labeling in understanding homosexuality. Available data do not point to any single factor as a cause of sexual orientation but instead suggest that there may be many types of gays and many types of straights, with corresponding different causes.

Differences between Gay Men and Lesbians

Gay men and lesbians differ in some ways. Women are more likely to be bisexual, and some theories that are effective in explaining men's sexual orientation are not supported for women.

Sexual Orientation in Multicultural Perspective

Different ethnic groups in the United States, as well as different cultures around the world, hold diverse views of same-gender sexual behaviors.

Bisexuality

Bisexuals are attracted to both women and men. Bisexuality may be more "natural" than either exclusive heterosexuality or exclusive homosexuality.

SUGGESTIONS FOR FURTHER READING

Diamond, Lisa M. (2008a). *Sexual fluidity: Understanding women's love and desire.* Cambridge, MA: Harvard University Press. Diamond, a noted sex researcher, argues against the principle of lifelong, consistent sexual orientation in women.

LeVay, Simon. (2011). *Gay, straight, and the reason why.* New York: Oxford University Press. LeVay, a neuroscientist, explores the causes of sexual orientation.

Pascoe, C. J. (2011). *Dude, you're a fag: Masculinity and sexuality in high school.* Berkeley: University of California Press. Pascoe conducted an ethnography in a high school in California and describes the way in which masculinity and homophobia feed on each other.

Rostosky, Sharon S., & Riggle, Ellen D. B. (2015). *Happy together: Thriving as a same-sex couple in your family, workplace, and community.* Washington, DC: American Psychological Association. This book represents the new wave of recognizing gays and lesbians who are in same-gender couples and providing helpful advice for them.

©South_agency/Getty Images

CHAPTER

14

Variations in Sexual Behavior

CHAPTER HIGHLIGHTS

Some men love women, some love other men, some love dogs and horses, and occasionally you find one who loves his raincoat.*

*Max Schulman. (1960). *I was a Teen-Age Dwarf.* New York: Bantam.

Most laypeople, as well as most scientists, have a tendency to classify behavior as normal or abnormal. There seems to be a particular tendency to do this with regard to sexual behavior. Many terms are used for abnormal sexual behavior, including *sexual deviance, perversion, sexual variance,* and *paraphilias.* The term *sexual variations* is used in this chapter because it is currently favored in scientific circles. Members of the communities who practice these behaviors refer to them as *kink.*

In the chapter "Sexual Orientation: Gay, Straight, or Bi?" we argued that homosexuality per se is not an abnormal form of sexual behavior. This chapter deals with some behaviors that more people might consider to be abnormal, so it seems advisable at this point to consider exactly when a sexual behavior is abnormal.

When Is Sexual Behavior Abnormal?

Defining *Abnormal*

As we saw in the chapter "Sexuality in Perspective," sexual behavior varies greatly from one culture to the next. There is a corresponding variation across cultures in what is considered to be abnormal sexual behavior. Given this great variability, how can one come up with a reasonable set of criteria for what is abnormal?

One approach is to use a *statistical definition.* According to this approach, an abnormal sexual behavior is one that is rare, or not practiced by many people. Following this definition, then, standing on one's hands while having intercourse would be considered abnormal because it is rarely done, although it does not seem very abnormal in other ways. This definition, unfortunately, does not give us much insight into the psychological or social functioning of the person who engages in the behavior.

In the *sociological approach,* the problem of culture dependence is explicitly acknowledged. A sociologist might define a deviant sexual behavior as a sexual behavior that violates the norms of society. Thus, if a society says that a particular sexual behavior is deviant, it is—at least in that society. This approach recognizes the importance of the individual's interaction with society and of the problems that people face if their behavior is labeled "deviant" in the culture in which they live.

A psychological approach emphasizes the 4Ds of abnormal behavior (Nolen-Hoeksema, 2017): (1) *dysfunctional* behavior impairs the person's functioning in daily life; (2) the behavior causes great emotional *distress* to the person; (3) highly *deviant* behavior (such as hearing voices that no one else can hear, or desiring sex with a corpse); and (4) behavior that is *dangerous* to the self or others (such as committing sexual assault, which clearly harms others). For example, a male clerk in a Minneapolis supermarket was having intercourse with willing shoppers in their cars several times a day. This behavior led to his being fired, which is an example of a dysfunctional impairment.

The American Psychiatric Association (2013), in its *Diagnostic and Statistical Manual of Mental Disorders (DSM-5),* uses the terms *paraphilia* and *paraphilic disorder.* **Paraphilia** refers to sexual activities other than "vanilla sex": sexual intercourse (and oral sex, stroking, and so on) with an adult who consents to the activity. Paraphilias, then, are just atypical sexual interests. *DSM-5* recognizes eight specific paraphilias: fetishism, transvestism, sexual sadism, sexual masochism, voyeurism, frotteurism, exhibitionism, and pedophilia. We consider all of them in this chapter, with the exception of pedophilia, which is covered in the chapter "Sexual Coercion."

A paraphilia rises to the level of **paraphilic disorder** if it causes the person serious distress or impairs their functioning, or causes harm to the self or others. The impairment may be in areas such as relationships with family or job performance. A happy practitioner of BDSM with other adults who consent to the activity does not qualify as having a paraphilic disorder.

The Normal–Abnormal Continuum

Each of the approaches just described provides criteria that attempt to distinguish what is normal from what is abnormal. Although such distinctions may be made in theory, they are often difficult to make in reality. For example, lingerie is often sexually arousing for both men and women. For a woman who is wearing a low-cut bra and silk thong panties, the sensuous feel of the material against her skin may be arousing; for a man it might be the sight of the woman

Paraphilia (par-uh-FILL-ee-uh): Unusual, unconventional sexual behavior.
Paraphilic disorder: Paraphilia that causes the person distress or impairs their functioning, or causes harm to self or others.

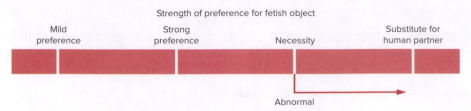

Strength of preference for fetish object

| Mild preference | Strong preference | Necessity | Substitute for human partner |

Abnormal

Figure 1   The continuum from normal to abnormal behavior in the case of fetishes.

wearing the lingerie. At the same time, lingerie is a common sexual fetish object. This is an excellent example of the continuum from normal to abnormal sexual behavior. That is, normal sexual behavior and abnormal sexual behavior—like other normal and abnormal behaviors—are not two separate categories but rather gradations on a continuum. Many people have mild fetishes, finding things such as silk underwear arousing, and that is well within the range of normal behavior; only when the fetish becomes extreme is it abnormal.

This continuum from normal to abnormal behavior might be conceptualized using the scheme shown in Figure 1. A mild preference, or even a strong preference, for the fetish object (say, silk panties) is within the normal range of sexual behavior. When the silk panties become a necessity—when the man cannot become aroused and have intercourse unless they are present—we have crossed the boundary into abnormal behavior. When the man becomes obsessed with white silk panties and shoplifts them at every opportunity, so that he will always have them available, the fetish has become fetishistic disorder. In extreme forms, the silk panties may become a substitute for a human partner, and the man's sexual behavior consists of masturbating with the silk panties present. In these extreme forms, the man may commit burglary or even assault to get the desired fetish object.

The continuum from normal to abnormal behavior holds for many of the sexual variations discussed in this chapter, such as voyeurism, exhibitionism, and sadism.

How can I tell if sexual behavior is normal or abnormal?

Fetishism

Fetishism refers to a sexual fixation on some object other than another human being and attachment of great erotic significance to that object. A common fetish in the United States is for clothing made of leather (Figure 2). Fetishism rises to the level of fetishistic disorder if the person is distressed about it or if the fetish causes significant

Fetishism: A person's sexual fixation on some object other than another human being and attachment of great erotic significance to that object.

impairments in their daily functioning. In extreme cases the person is incapable of becoming aroused and having an orgasm unless the fetish object is present. Typically, the fetish item is something closely associated with the body, such as clothing.

An online survey that recruited women at "kink" community events and online forums assessed whether they had ever participated in 126 specific sexual activities (Rehor, 2015). Seventy-five percent of the women reported being sexually aroused by an object (a fetish behavior). Items of clothing (such as lingerie, shoes, and corsets) and fabrics (such as leather, rubber, and vinyl) were the three most frequently mentioned categories of objects.

Why Do People Develop Fetishes?

Psychologists have proposed different reasons for what causes fetishes to develop. Here we consider two theoretical explanations: learning theory and cognitive theory. These theories can be applied equally well to explaining many of the other sexual variations in this chapter.

According to learning theory (for example, McGuire et al., 1965), fetishes result from classical conditioning, in which a learned association is built between the fetish object and sexual arousal and orgasm. In some cases a

Figure 2   A common fetish is for leather, often in association with sexual sadism and masochism. This store caters to clientele interested or involved in those activities.

©Julian Wasser/Getty Images

First Person

A Case History of a Shoe Fetishist

T he following case history is taken directly from the 1886 book *Psychopathia Sexualis,* by Richard von Krafft-Ebing, the great early investigator of sexual deviance. It should give you the flavor of his work.

Case 114. X., aged twenty-four, from a badly tainted family (mother's brother and grandfather insane, one sister epileptic, another sister subject to migraine, parents of excitable temperament). During dentition [teething] he had convulsions. At the age of seven he was taught to masturbate by a servant girl. X. first experienced pleasure in these manipulations when the girl happened to touch his member [penis] with her shoe-clad foot. Thus, in the predisposed boy, an association was established, as a result of which, from that time on, merely the sight of a woman's shoe, and finally, merely the idea of them, sufficed to induce sexual excitement and erection. He now masturbated while looking at women's shoes or while calling them up in imagination. The shoes of the school mistress excited him intensely, and in general he was affected by shoes that were partly concealed by female garments. One day he could not keep from grasping the teacher's shoes—an act that caused him great sexual excitement. In spite of punishment he could not keep from performing this act repeatedly. Finally, it was recognized that there must be an abnormal motive in play, and he was sent to a male teacher. He then revelled in the memory of the shoe scenes with his former school mistress and thus had erections, orgasms, and, after his fourteenth year, ejaculation. At the same time, he masturbated while thinking of a woman's shoes. One day the thought came to him to increase his pleasure by using such a shoe for masturbation. Thereafter he frequently took shoes secretly and used them for that purpose.

Nothing else in a woman could excite him; the thought of coitus filled him with horror. Men did not interest him in any way. At the age of eighteen he opened a shop and, among other things, dealt in ladies' shoes. He was excited sexually by fitting shoes for his female patrons or by manipulating shoes that came for mending. One day while doing this he had an epileptic attack, and, soon after, another while practicing onanism in his customary way. Then he recognized for the first time the injury to health caused by his sexual practices. He tried to overcome his onanism, sold no more shoes, and strove to free himself from the abnormal association between women's shoes and the sexual function. Then frequent pollutions, with erotic dreams about shoes, occurred, and the epileptic attacks continued. Though devoid of the slightest feeling for the female sex, he determined on marriage, which seemed to him to be the only remedy.

He married a pretty young lady. In spite of lively erections when he thought of his wife's shoes, in attempts at cohabitation he was absolutely impotent because his distaste for coitus and for close intercourse in general was far more powerful than the influence of the shoe-idea, which induced sexual excitement. On account of his impotence the patient applied to Dr. Hammond, who treated his epilepsy with bromides and advised him to hang a shoe up over his bed and look at it fixedly during coitus, at the same time imagining his wife to be a shoe. The patient became free from epileptic attacks and potent so that he could have coitus about once a week. His sexual excitation by women's shoes also grew less and less.

Source: Von Krafft-Ebing (1886), p. 288.

single learning trial might serve to cement the association. For example, one man recalled,

> I was home alone and saw my uncle's new penny loafers. I went over and started smelling the fresh new leather scent and kissing and licking them. It turned me on so much that I actually ejaculated my first load into my pants and have been turned on ever since. (Weinberg et al., 1995, p. 22)

In this case, shoes were associated with sexual arousal as the result of an early learning experience. Another example appears to be the shoe fetishist described in

First Person. This case clearly exemplifies the *DSM-5* criteria. The youth/man experienced sexual fantasies and urges associated with women's shoes for years, experienced arousal and ejaculation only when they were present, and experienced significant impairment in his academic and social life as a result. There was even an experiment that demonstrated that males could, in the laboratory, be conditioned to become sexually aroused when viewing pictures of shoes (Rachman, 1966).

A second possible theoretical explanation comes from cognitive psychology, discussed in the chapter "Theoretical Perspectives on Sexuality" (Walen & Roth,

1987). According to cognitive theorists, fetishists (or other paraphilics) have a serious cognitive distortion in that they perceive a nonconventional stimulus—such as black leather boots—as erotic. Further, their perception of arousal is distorted. They feel driven to the sexual behavior when aroused, but the arousal may actually be caused by feelings of guilt and self-loathing. Thus there is a chain in which there are initial feelings of guilt at thoughts of the unconventional behavior, which produces arousal, which is misinterpreted as sexual arousal (see misattribution of arousal in the chapter "Attraction, Love, and Communication"), which leads to a feeling that the fetish ritual must be carried out; it is, and there are orgasm and temporary feelings of relief, but the evaluation of the event is negative, leading to further feelings of guilt and self-loathing, which perpetuates the chain.

Whatever the cause, fetishism typically develops early in life. In one sample of foot or shoe fetishists, the mean age at which respondents reported first being sexually aroused by feet or shoes was 12 years (Weinberg et al., 1995).

Figure 3 RuPaul's Drag Race All Stars attending the 2016 MTV Video Music Awards, Madison Square Garden, New York.

©Dennis Van Tine/Geisler-Fotopress/picture-alliance/dpa/AP Images

Cross-Dressing

Cross-dressing refers to dressing as a member of the other gender. Cross-dressing may be done by a variety of people for a variety of reasons (see Figure 3). Trans men typically dress as men as part of their transition (transgender experiences are discussed in the chapter "Gender and Sexuality"). Here we discuss three other types of cross-dressing: drag, female impersonation, and transvestism.

Drag

Some gay men—**drag queens**—dress up as women, and some lesbians dress in masculine clothes (drag kings) (Moncrieff & Lienard, 2017). These practices are basically caricatures of traditional gender roles and are usually done in a playful way, as a performance.

Currently, perhaps the most visible example of drag in our culture is the television series RuPaul's Drag Race (see Figure 3).

Female Impersonators

Female impersonators are men who dress as women, often as part of their job as entertainers. For example, Robin Williams as Mrs. Doubtfire and Dustin Hoffman as Tootsie won praise from critics and big box office profits for their impersonations of women.

> **Drag queen:** A man who dresses in women's clothing.
> **Female impersonator:** A man or woman who impersonates a specific woman as part of a job in entertainment.
> **Transvestism:** The practice of dressing as a member of the other gender in order to experience sexual arousal.

Transvestism

In contrast to people who engage in cross-dressing for the reasons discussed above, some men regularly dress in female clothing to produce sexual arousal and experience sexual excitement. This practice is known as **transvestism.** The cross-dressing is often done in private, perhaps by a married man without his wife's knowledge.

Cross-dressing is almost exclusively a male sexual variation; it is essentially unknown among women. There may be a number of reasons for this difference, including our culture's tolerance of women who wear masculine clothing and intolerance of men who wear feminine clothing. Also, traditionally, women's clothing is by design sexual and erotic, whereas men's clothing is functional (Wheeler et al., 2008). The phenomenon illustrates a more general point, namely, that many sexual variations are defined for, or practiced almost exclusively by, members of one gender; the parallel practice by members of the other gender is often not considered deviant. Most sexual variations are practiced mainly by men.

> **Who is more likely to engage in these sexual variations—men or women?**

A survey of a national sample in Sweden asked each participant whether they had ever dressed in clothing of the other gender and experienced sexual arousal (Långström & Zucker, 2005). Almost 3 percent of men and 0.4 percent of women reported at least one such experience.

In one sample of transvestites, 87 percent were heterosexual and 60 percent were married; 66 percent reported that their first cross-dressing experience occurred before age 10 (Docter & Prince, 1997). Sexual excitement and orgasm were reported by 40 percent as frequently occurring with cross-dressing. Almost all preferred dressing completely as women during the activity, but only 14 percent frequently went out in public dressed as women.

How do the wife and children of the cross-dresser react to his unusual behavior? One researcher observed four stages in the process (Lev, 2004). The first is discovery or disclosure, in which the wife discovers her husband's cross-dressing or he discloses it to her. The next stage is marked by turmoil, both in the relationship and for the individual. In the third stage, the couple negotiate: what is acceptable? What are the boundaries? If all of this goes successfully, the couple enter the fourth stage, finding a new balance. One study of wives of cross-dressers—the husbands were either transvestites or trans women—found many ways in which the stories of these relationships unfolded (Erhardt, 2007). For example, in one case, Joe (names are changed to preserve anonymity) told Kate about his cross-dressing by phone while he was out of town. Kate had a strong emotional reaction, even considering suicide, but instead of making a snap decision to leave Joe, she sought both individual and couple counseling. As a result, she set clear limits; for example, he could cross-dress only while he was away on business trips. Their relationship did indeed find a new balance.

Occasional cross-dressing is one of the harmless, victimless sexual variations, particularly when it is done in private. Like other forms of atypical behavior, it is a problem only when it becomes so extreme that it is the person's only source of erotic gratification, or when it becomes a compulsion the person cannot control and it therefore causes distress in other areas of the person's life.

Sadism and Masochism

Definitions

A **sexual sadist** is a person who experiences intense sexual arousal from the physical or psychological suffering of another person. The term *sadism* derives from the name of the Marquis de Sade, who lived around the time of the French Revolution. Not only did he practice sadism—several women apparently died from his attentions (Bullough, 1976)—but he also wrote novels about these practices (the best known is *Justine*), thus ensuring his place in history.

A **sexual masochist** is a person who experiences intense sexual arousal from fantasies or the behavior of being humiliated, beaten, bound, or otherwise made to suffer. This variation is named after Leopold von Sacher-Masoch (1836–1895), who was himself a masochist and who wrote novels expressing masochistic fantasies. Notice that the definitions of sadism and masochism make specific their *sexual* nature; the terms are often loosely used to refer to people who are cruel or to people who seem to bring misfortune on themselves, but these are not the meanings used here. These two are often referred to as a pair because the two behaviors or roles (giving and receiving pain) are complementary.

There are two other styles of interaction that are related to sadism-masochism (S-M). These are bondage and discipline (B-D) and dominance and submission (D-S) (Ernulf & Innala, 1995). **Bondage and discipline** refers to the use of physically restraining devices or psychologically restraining commands as a central aspect of sexual interactions. These devices or commands may enforce obedience and servitude without inducing any physical pain. **Dominance and submission** refers to interaction that involves a consensual exchange of power; the dominant partner uses their power to control and sexually stimulate the submissive partner. In many cases, all of these sexual practices are grouped together under the term BDSM.

Sadomasochistic Behavior

Sadomasochism (S-M) is a rare form of sexual behavior. A review of the literature found, among men evaluated for paraphilic disorders, 3 to 11 percent were diagnosed as sadists, and 2 to 6 percent as masochists (Krueger, 2010). In its milder, nonparaphilic, forms it is probably more common than many people think. A survey of the general population found that 2.2 percent of men and 1.3 percent of women reported involvement in BDSM in the past year (Richters et al., 2008). Sadistic or masochistic fantasies appear to be considerably more common than real-life sadomasochistic behavior.

An online survey of women recruited through the "kink" community included 62 "BDSM-related" behaviors (Rehor, 2015). Many participants (75 to 85 percent) reported behaviors that cause pain, including breast play (slap, clothespins), paddling, flogging, genital play (slap, kick, clothespins), and whipping and caning. The use of bondage toys for sensual or erotic pleasure was reported by 85 percent as well.

A good example of BDSM activity is a Strictly Spanking party in New York City (David, 2011). These bimonthly parties attract men and women who like to be spanked, and spankings are the main activity. People wear colored nametags noting whether they are a top, a bottom, or switch. At one party, most of the participants were over 45, and ordinary-looking people from many walks of life. Most were straight. Spankos talk about being fascinated by spanking from a young age. People do not pair off and have sex during or after the party. For a few participants, spanking becomes a central focus of their lives; they cultivate daddy-daughter relationships, and may

> **Sexual sadist:** A person who experiences intense sexual arousal from the suffering of another person.
> **Sexual masochist:** A person who experiences intense sexual arousal from being beaten, bound, humiliated, or made to suffer.
> **Bondage and discipline:** The use of physical or psychological restraint to enforce servitude, from which both participants derive sensual pleasure.
> **Dominance and submission:** The use of power consensually given to control the sexual stimulation and behavior of the other person.

Milestones in Sex Research

Sexual Addictions?

A divorced mother and self-described "soccer mom," Patricia (not her real name) acknowledges having sex with more than 30 men in 4 years. She described being preoccupied with finding and meeting male partners for sex. "There were men I don't even know their last names." She engaged in behaviors she is now ashamed of. Eventually she "hit rock bottom" and read a pamphlet with questions like "Have you had sex at inappropriate times, in inappropriate places, and/or with inappropriate people?" She answered yes to most of them, and entered a support group for "sex addiction" (Hickey, 2010).

Benoit (real name) drove for three hours to meet a stranger for sex in a deserted grocery store parking lot at 1:00 A.M. "Mike" never showed up, so he called a 19-year-old he had met online who lived nearby, and they hooked up. Benoit realized he "couldn't stop chasing sex, no matter the consequences." "Within three months, I had hooked up with 20 guys from online." Several years later he entered an inpatient treatment program for "sex addicts" (Denizet-Lewis, 2009).

There are tens of thousands of people with stories like these in the United States. Their sexual histories include some characteristics of the paraphilic disorders: frequent sexual activity, intense desire or craving for the activity, and eventually experiencing impairment in work, family, and social functioning in their daily lives. But instead of entering psychiatric care with a diagnosis of a paraphilic disorder, they enter treatment as a "sex addict."

The theory of sexual addiction was popularized by Patrick Carnes (1983) in his book *The Sexual Addiction.* He proposed that some patterns of sexual behavior are the result of an addictive process much like alcoholism. Parallels include the faulty belief systems and denial of reality characteristic of alcoholism; Patricia said of her frequent unprotected (by condoms) hookups, "I thought this was just how dating was done these days." Like alcoholism, the addiction leads to many self-destructive behaviors.

According to Carnes's analysis, each episode of the sexually addictive behavior proceeds through a four-step cycle, which intensifies each time it is repeated.

1. *Preoccupation.* The person can think of nothing other than the sexual act to which they are addicted.
2. *Rituals.* The person enacts certain rituals that have become a prelude to the addictive act.

3. *Compulsive sexual behavior.* The sexual behavior is enacted and the person feels that they have no control over it.
4. *Despair.* Rather than feeling good after the sexual act is completed, the addict falls into a feeling of hopelessness and despair.

Carnes recognizes the distinction between a sexual behavior and a sexual behavior that is out of control and dysfunctional. Thus, for example, the man who masturbates while looking at pornographic magazines two or three times per week is not an addict, and the behavior is well within the normal range. However, the man who buys 20 porn magazines a week, masturbates four or five times a day while looking at them, for a total of perhaps two or three hours, and can think of nothing else but where he can buy the next porn magazine and find the next private place to masturbate—that person is addicted. The key is the compulsiveness, the lack of control, the obsession (constant thoughts of the sexual scenario), and the obliviousness to danger or harmful consequences.

According to Carnes and others, the most effective therapy for the sex addict is the Alcoholics Anonymous program applied to sexual addictions. Several groups have adapted the AA program to sexual addiction, among them Sexaholics Anonymous (SA), Sex Addicts Anonymous (SAA), and Sex and Love Addicts Anonymous (SLAA). These groups can usually be found by searching the Internet; each group has a national website with an app for quickly finding local meetings. The first step in the process of recovery is admitting that one is sexually addicted, that the behavior is out of control, and that one's life has become unmanageable. These are hard admissions to make for someone who has spent years denying the existence of a problem. There are frequent meetings with a support group, an emphasis on recognizing the ways in which the behavior has impaired your life and relationships, and a strong emphasis on dealing with shame and building feelings of self-worth.

The concepts of sexual addiction and therapy as the treatment for addiction have been widely adopted. Media and laypeople casually label persons whose sexual activity seems bizarre (remember our discussion of the subjective nature of this word?) "addicts." The term is frequently used when high-profile celebrities behave badly in the sexual arena. In addition to thousands of support groups, there are dozens of in-patient facilities waiting to welcome the "addict" into "recovery." The support groups are free; the in-patient treatment is really expensive. The concept of addiction has been used in many socio-legal contexts as a defense against charges of sexual misconduct (the anesthesiologist who fondled his female patients while they were sedated) or as a charge in divorce cases to get custody of the children (he frequents prostitutes) (Ley et al., 2015).

Other criticisms have come from therapists and researchers in the field. The term *addiction,* as to alcohol or heroin, has a very specific definition among professionals, and sexual addictions do not meet the definition in some ways. For example, if one is addicted to alcohol and suddenly stops using it, there is a withdrawal phenomenon that involves unmistakable physical symptoms. If a person abstains from an addictive sexual behavior, there are no physiological withdrawal symptoms. A second criticism is that "addiction" may become an excuse for illegal, destructive behavior. For example, a rapist might say, "I'm addicted to violent, nonconsensual sex and therefore can't stop myself."

Critics of the addiction model have suggested several alternatives. One is based on the concept of *compulsive sexual behavior* (e.g., Coleman, 1991). **Compulsive sexual behavior (CSB)**

> is a disorder in which the individual experiences intense sexually arousing fantasies, urges, and associated sexual behaviors that are intrusive, driven, and repetitive. Individuals with this disorder are (*a*) lacking in impulse control, (*b*) often incur social and legal sanctions, (*c*) cause interference in interpersonal and occupational functioning, and (*d*) create health risks. (Coleman et al., 2001, p. 326)

Sexually compulsive individuals experience intrusive sexual thoughts, and they engage in out-of-control sexual behavior to reduce anxiety, depression, and shame

(Rooney et al., 2018). Research shows that, indeed, sexual compulsivity is correlated with depression and anxiety (Rooney et al., 2018).

Across various studies, the prevalence of sexual compulsivity ranges between 1 and 6 percent of the U.S. population (Kraus et al., 2018). About half of those with sexual compulsivity report that it began before age 18 (Reid et al., 2012).

One crucial criterion for a sexual behavior to be considered abnormal is that it creates impairment in the person's daily functioning. People who are sexually compulsive report many kinds of impairment, including negative impacts on mental health, emotionally hurting a loved one, interference with the ability to experience healthy sex, and even loss of their job (Reid et al., 2012).

In regard to status as a diagnosis, neither sexual addiction nor compulsive sexual behavior is a recognized diagnosis in the *DSM-5*. Obsessive-compulsive behavior is. Compulsive sexual behavior has been proposed for inclusion in the ICD-11 (the ICD being the alternative to the DSM for diagnoses); it would be categorized as an impulse-control disorder (Kraus et al., 2018).

Regardless of official status as a diagnosis, some people believe that they have a sexual addiction and seek therapy for it (Wéry et al., 2016). In one sample of people seeking treatment for sexual addiction, 94 percent were men (Wéry et al., 2016). Common patterns involved sex with multiple partners and cybersex.

Sexual compulsivity is in some ways similar to hypersexuality. Some experts say that the two are overlapping yet distinct (Rooney et al., 2018). Other experts use the terms interchangeably.

> **Compulsive sexual behavior (CSB):** A disorder in which the individual experiences intense sexually arousing fantasies, urges, and associated sexual behaviors that are out of control and interfere with daily functioning.

live together. Spanking is also an activity that may be part of disciplinary or bondage scenes, but it has a different meaning in those settings.

Thus there is a spectrum of activities that constitute S-M. People who become involved in it often have tried a variety of these behaviors and find only some of them satisfying. They develop a script of activities (recall the concept of scripts in the chapter "Theoretical Perspectives on Sexuality") that they prefer to enact each time they engage in S-M. One group of researchers identified 29 individual sexual behaviors associated with S-M (Santtila et al., 2002). Four clusters or themes were identified: hypermasculinity (e.g., dildo, enema), administering and receiving pain (e.g., clothespins attached to nipples, caning, hot

wax), physical restriction (e.g., handcuffs, straitjackets), and humiliation (e.g., verbal humiliation, face slapping). Further analyses of the participation in the behaviors within each cluster identified a continuum in frequency from very common to very rare, with the order of the behaviors suggesting that this continuum reflects a dimension from least to most intense. For example, the humiliation continuum ranges from flagellation (reported by 81 percent; least intense) to verbal humiliation (70 percent), gagging (53 percent), and face slapping (37 percent) to using knives to make surface wounds (11 percent; most intense). The results suggest that the S-M activities within each cluster are *scripted,* with the less intense behaviors being much more common.

Some observers note that S-M is about play, as in the theater. S-M sexual activities are organized into "scenes"; one "plays" with one's S-M partners. In addition to the activities such as those discussed above, roles, costumes, and props are important parts of each scene. The roles include slave and master, maid and mistress, and teacher and pupil. The costumes range from simple to elaborate. The props may include tight leather clothing, pins and needles, ropes, whips, and hot wax. In S-M clubs there are often rules governing the social and S-M interaction, particularly the creation and enactment of scenes. Rules may include no touching of another's body without consent, giving players the room they need to enact a scene, and not intruding physically or verbally on a scene in progress; and they may include no sexual penetration.

Interestingly, sexual sadists and masochists do not consistently find experiencing pain and giving pain to be sexually satisfying. For example, the masochist who smashes a finger in a car door will yell and be unhappy just like anyone else. Pain is arousing for such people only when it is part of a carefully scripted ritual. As one woman put it,

> Of course, he doesn't *really* hurt me. I mean quite recently he tied me down ready to receive "punishment," and then by mistake he kicked my heel with his toe as he walked by. I gave a yelp, and he said, "Sorry love—did I hurt you?" (Gosselin & Wilson, 1980, p. 55)

Causes of Sadomasochism

The causes of sadism and masochism are not precisely known. The theories discussed in the section on fetishes can be applied here as well. For example, learning theory points to conditioning as an explanation. A little boy is being spanked over his mother's knee; in the process, his penis rubs against her knee, and he gets an erection. Or a little girl is caught masturbating and is spanked. In both cases, the child has learned to associate pain or spanking with sexual arousal, possibly setting up a lifelong career as a masochist.

Another psychological theory has been proposed to explain masochism specifically, although not sadism (Baumeister, 1988a, b). According to the theory, the masochist is motivated by a desire to escape from self-awareness. That is, the masochistic behavior helps the individual escape from being conscious of the self in the same way that drunkenness and some forms of meditation do. In an era dominated by individualism and self-interest, why would anyone want to escape from the self? Probably because high levels of self-awareness can lead to anxiety as a result of a focus on pressures on the self, added responsibilities, the need to keep up a good image in front of others, and so on. Masochistic activity allows the person to escape from being an autonomous, separate individual. Masochism may be an unusually powerful form of escape because of its link to sexual pleasure. This theory can also explain why patterns of masochism seem to be so gender linked (Baumeister, 1988b). According to the theory, the male role is especially burdensome because of the heavy pressures for autonomy, separateness, and individual achievement. Masochism accomplishes an escape from these aspects of the male role, explaining why masochism is more common among males than among females.

Bondage and Discipline

Sexual bondage, the use for sexual arousal of restraining devices that have sexual significance, has been a staple of erotic fiction and art for centuries. Current mainstream and adult films and videos portray this activity. In some communities, individuals interested in B-D have formed clubs (Figure 4).

We noted earlier the difficulty of gathering data on participation in variant forms of sexual expression. One innovative study downloaded all the messages about bondage mailed to an international computer discussion group (Ernulf & Innala, 1995). Of the messages in which senders indicated their gender, 75 percent were male. Of those indicating a sexual orientation, most were heterosexual; 18 percent said they were gay, 11 percent lesbian. The messages were coded for discussion of what the person found sexually arousing about B-D. Most frequently mentioned (12 percent) was play: "sex is funny, and sex is lovely, and sex is PLAY." Next was the exchange of power (4 percent): "It is a power trip because the active is responsible for the submissive's pleasure." The next most common themes were intensified sexual pleasure, tactile stimulation associated with the use of ropes and cuffs, and the visual enjoyment experienced by the dominant person.

There is a marked imbalance in preferences for the active ("top") and passive ("bottom") roles. Most men and women, regardless of their sexual orientation, prefer to be "bottom." This may be the reason there are an estimated 2,500 professional dominatrices in the United States.

Dominance and Submission

Sociologists emphasize that the key to S-M is not pain but rather dominance and submission (D-S) (Weinberg, 1987). Thus it is not an individual phenomenon but rather a social behavior embedded in a subculture and controlled by elaborate scripts.

Sociologists believe that to understand D-S one must understand the social processes that create and sustain it (Weinberg, 1987). There is a distinct D-S subculture, involving videos, clubs, and bars. It creates culturally defined meanings for D-S acts. Thus a D-S act is not a wild outbreak of violence but instead a carefully controlled performance with a script. One woman reported that

> we got into dominance and submission. Like him giving me orders. Being very rough and pushing me around and

Figure 4 Sexual bondage involves restraining devices and discipline, such as in this scene.

©PBNJ Productions/Getty Images

giving me orders, calling me a slut, calling me a cunt. Making me crawl around . . . on all fours and beg to suck his cock. Dominance-submission is more important than the pain. I've done lots and lots of scenes that involve no pain. Just a lot of taking orders, being humiliated. (Maurer, 1994, pp. 253, 257)

Within the play, people take on roles such as master, slave, or naughty child. Thus American men can play the submissive role in D-S culture, even though it contradicts the U.S. male role, because it is really not they who are the naughty child, just as an actor can play the part of a murderer and know that he is not a murderer.

One interesting phenomenon, from a sociological point of view, is the social control over risk-taking that exists in the D-S subculture (Weinberg, 1987). That is, having allowed oneself to be tied up or restrained and then whipped, one could be seriously injured or even murdered, yet such outcomes are rare. Why? Research shows that complex social arrangements are made in order to reduce the risk and ensure that the play is "safe, sane, and consensual" (Holt, 2016). First, initial contacts are usually made in protected territories such as bars or meetings, which are inhabited by other D-Sers who play by the same rules. Second, the basic scripts are widely shared, so that everyone understands what will and will not occur. When the participants are strangers, the scenario may be negotiated before it is enacted. If an individual violates a boundary, the violation is typically handled within the BDSM community by appointed community members (Holt, 2016).

Voyeurism and Exhibitionism

Voyeurism and exhibitionism are often discussed together because they seem complementary. However, they are rather different, and a voyeur would not find watching an exhibitionist arousing.

Voyeurism

A **voyeur** is a person who experiences intense sexual arousal from watching an unsuspecting person who is naked, in the process of undressing, or engaging in sexual activity. Voyeurism becomes a paraphilia when it is manifested by fantasies, urges, or behaviors (*DSM-5*, 302.82, 2013). Voyeurs are often referred to as "peeping toms."[1] In one national sample from Canada, 50 percent of men and 21 percent of women had engaged in voyeurism at least once in their lifetime (Joyal & Carpenter, 2017).

Voyeurism provides another good illustration of the continuum from normal to abnormal behavior. For example, many men and women find it arousing to watch a man or woman undress and "dance"— otherwise, there would be no strip clubs—and this is certainly well

> **Voyeur:** A person who experiences sexual arousal from viewing unsuspecting person(s) who are nude, undressing, or having sex.

[1]*Voyeur* comes from the French word *voir,* meaning "to see." "Peeping Tom" comes from the story of Lady Godiva; when she rode through town nude to protest the fact that her husband was raising his tenants' taxes, none of the townspeople looked except one, Tom of Coventry.

Figure 5a   Exhibitionism.

©Jutta Klee/Getty Images

Figure 5b   High-rise hotels and apartment buildings provide a new venue for exposing one's body to strangers.

(b1) ©Splash News/Newscom; (b2) ©Splash News/Newscom

within the normal range of behavior. Some women are "crotch watchers," much as men are breast watchers.

The appeal of watching is illustrated by a study of college students that asked whether they would watch an attractive person undress and an attractive couple having sex (Rye & Meaney, 2007). Two-thirds said they would watch someone undress; 45 percent said they would watch the couple.

A study of men who sought treatment for paraphilias included 62 voyeurs (Abel & Rouleau, 1990). One-third reported that their first experience occurred before they were 12 years old. One-half said they recognized their interest in peeping prior to age 15. These men estimated that, on average, they had peeped at 470 people.

This study, however, points out one of the major problems with the research on sexual variations: Much of it has been done only on people who have been arrested for their behavior or sought treatment. One analyst suggests that only a small minority of "peepers" are distressed by their behavior (Lavin, 2008). The "respectable paraphiliac" who

Exhibitionist: A person who derives sexual gratification from exposing his genitals to a nonconsenting person.

has the behavior under somewhat better control or who is skilled enough or can pull enough strings not to get caught is not studied in such research. Thus the picture that research provides for us of these variations may be very biased.

Exhibitionism

The complement to voyeurism is exhibitionism ("flashing"), in which the person derives sexual pleasure from exposing his genitals to a nonconsenting person.[2] The pronoun "his" is used advisedly, because **exhibitionists** are usually men. The woman who wears a dress that reveals most of her bosom is likely to be thought of as attractive rather than abnormal. When a man exposes himself, however, his behavior is considered offensive (Figure 5a).

[2]Here is a classic limerick on exhibitionism:

There was a young lady of Exeter
So pretty, men craned their necks at her.
    One was even so brave
    As to take out and wave
The distinguishing mark of his sex at her.

Here again, whether a sexual behavior is considered abnormal depends greatly on whether the person doing it is a male or a female. (Recall our discussion of the social constructionist view of paraphilias and gender.) A man exposing himself to a man is also quite rare, so the prototype we have for exhibitionism is a man exposing himself to a woman. One study of sex offenders in federal prisons found that about 20 percent of them had engaged in exhibitionism (Drury et al., 2017). A well-sampled study of the Finnish population found that 4 percent of the men and 0.6 percent of the women had engaged in exhibitionism (Baur et al., 2016).

According to the benchmark study of men seeking treatment for paraphilias (Abel & Rouleau, 1990), 15 percent of the exhibitionists had exposed themselves at least once by age 12; one-half had done so by age 15. Research with exhibitionists and other sex offenders who had been arrested for their behavior showed that they were likely to have experienced adverse events in childhood, such as father abandonment and physical or emotional abuse (Drury et al., 2017).

Many women, understandably, are alarmed by exhibitionists. But since the exhibitionist's goal is to produce shock or some other strong emotional response, the woman who becomes extremely upset is gratifying him. Probably the best strategy for a woman to use in this situation is to remain calm and make some remark indicating her coolness, such as suggesting that he should seek professional help for his problem.[3]

Notice that both voyeurism and exhibitionism are considered problematic behavior when the other person involved is an unwilling participant. A man who derives erotic pleasure from watching his partner undress, or a woman who is aroused by exhibiting her body in new lingerie to her husband, is not engaging in criminal or paraphilic behavior.

Hypersexuality and Asexuality

We turn now to several variations that are not explicitly listed in the *DSM-5;* however, each of these may vary from atypical to paraphilic, depending on their frequency, duration, and consequences.

Hypersexuality

Hypersexuality includes nymphomania and satyriasis, conditions in which there is an extraordinarily high level of sexual activity and sex drive; at the extreme, the person is apparently insatiable and sexuality overshadows all

other concerns and interests. When it occurs in women, it is called **nymphomania;** in men it is called **satyriasis** (or *Don Juanism*).[4] Although this definition seems fairly simple, in practice it is difficult to say when a person has an abnormally high sex drive. As was discussed in the two chapters on "Sexuality and the Life Cycle," there is a wide range in the frequencies with which people engage in coitus; therefore, the range we define as "normal" should also be broad. In real life, *nymphomania* or *satyriasis* is often defined by the spouse. Some men, for example, might think that it was unreasonable for a wife to want intercourse once a day or even twice a week, and they would consider such a woman a nymphomaniac.[5] Other men might think it would be wonderful to be married to a woman who wanted to make love every day.

Because these two terms are imprecise, clinicians and researchers prefer the term *hypersexuality.* **Hypersexuality** refers to an excessive, insatiable sex drive in a person. It leads to compulsive sexual behavior in the sense that the person feels driven to it even when there may be very negative consequences. The person is also never satisfied by the activity, and they may not be having orgasms, despite all the sexual activity. Such cases meet the criteria for abnormal behavior discussed at the beginning of this chapter: The out-of-control behavior and the time it consumes leads to the result that it impairs the functioning in other areas of the person's life (Kafka, 2010).

A study of male patients with paraphilia or related disorders focused on creating an operational definition of hypersexuality (Kafka, 1997). The results supported the use of the criterion of seven or more orgasms per week consistently, for a minimum duration of 6 months. The men reported an average of 8 orgasms per week in the preceding 6 months; the modal time per day the men spent in unconventional sexual activity was 1 to 2 hours. The most common unconventional behaviors were compulsive masturbation (67 percent of the sample), protracted promiscuity (56 percent), and dependence on pornography (41 percent). The most common paraphilias were exhibitionism (35 percent of those with a paraphilia), voyeurism (27 percent), and pedophilia (25 percent).

This research provides a useful operational definition for men, but note that the suggested criterion cannot be applied to women. The criterion is stated as the number of orgasms per week. Some women rarely or never experience

> **Nymphomania (nim-foh-MANE-ee-uh):** An excessive, insatiable sex drive in a woman.
> **Satyriasis (sat-ur-EYE-uh-sis):** An excessive, insatiable sex drive in a man; also called *Don Juanism.*
> **Hypersexuality:** An excessive, insatiable sex drive in a person.

---

[3]A joke suggests one such reaction: When the man in the overcoat flashed the gate attendant at the airport, she replied, "I want to see your boarding pass, not your stub."

[4]Satyriasis is named for the satyrs, who were part-human, part-animal beasts in Greek mythology. A part of the entourage of Dionysus, the god of wine and fertility, they were jovial and lusty and have become a symbol of the sexually active male.

[5]Someone once defined a nymphomaniac as a woman whom a man can't keep up with.

Figure 6 Historical painting of a satyr, which gives the name to satyriasis, a sexual variation in which a man has an excessive, insatiable sex drive.

©Christie's Images Ltd./SuperStock

orgasms; in fact, their anorgasmia might cause them to engage in compulsive sexual behavior. Another problem is that women who are orgasmic are capable of multiple orgasms during a single session of activity (see the chapter "Sexual Arousal"). A woman who engages in sexual activity three times a week could experience seven or eight orgasms, which would not be atypical or abnormal. Once again we see that a person's gender is very important in defining sexual variations.

A central debate among experts is whether hypersexuality is truly a disorder, or simply a medically constructed label for someone with high desire (in and of itself, not a disorder). Researchers posted an online survey containing measures of sexual desire, sexual activity, perceived control over one's sexuality, and a variety of potential negative outcomes (Carvalho et al., 2015). Over 4,500 men and women ages 18 to 60 completed the survey. The data were analyzed using cluster analysis, which identifies meaningful clusters based on scores on the various scales. The analyses identified two clusters, one reflecting problematic sexuality—lack of control and experiencing negative outcomes, and the other reflecting high desire and frequent activity. Comparing people in the two clusters on other variables, individuals in the hypersexuality cluster reported more psychopathology. Thus, hypersexuality properly defined/measured appears to be distinct from high desire.

Researchers have developed a scale to assess hypersexuality, the Hypersexuality Behavior Inventory or HBI (Reid et al., 2011). The scale includes 19 items asking respondents to report the relative frequency of

a variety of experiences related to sexuality during the past 90 days. The scale was validated using two samples of male outpatients drawn from several states, including men reporting compulsive masturbation, habitual solicitation of commercial sex workers, extramarital affairs, and multiple anonymous partners. Analyses indicated three characteristics of hypersexuality: lack of control ("My attempts to change my sexual behavior fail"), consequences ("My sexual activities interfere with . . . work or school"), and coping ("I use sex . . . [to] deal with my problems").

A study of hypersexuality in women used data from an online survey that included the HBI and measures of present and past sexual activity (Klein et al., 2014). High-scoring women on the HBI reported significantly more frequent consumption of pornography (more than 30 times per month) and masturbation (more than 6 times per week). The researchers concluded that hypersexuality in women is associated with impersonal sexual activity.

Online surveys give us some idea of the prevalence of behaviors among people in a population. Presumably many of those who attain high scores on a measure like the HBI are not experiencing significant impairments in their daily lives. An alternative approach is to examine the characteristics of those who seek treatment for a condition or disorder. The Sexual Behavior Clinic in Toronto sees a large number of patients every year. Researchers reviewed referrals and consultation requests for "hypersexualty" (Cantor et al., 2013) and identified six types. About one-third of the people exhibited Paraphilic Hypersexuality, extremely high frequencies of behaviors such as pornography consumption or very frequent solicitation of paid partners, and various additional paraphilic interests (fetishes, voyeurism, etc.). A second type was Avoidant Masturbation, men who spend a great deal of time viewing pornography and several hours per day masturbating, often leading to school failure, job loss, or social isolation. A third type, and the one most frequently publicized in the media, is Chronic Adultery, people who chronically cheat on spouses, but have few paraphilic interests and do not spend large amounts of time pursuing sexual gratification. Men in this category often report a desire for daily sex, and that sex with their wives is infrequent or does not occur, due to her dyspareunia, very low libido, or past sexual abuse. The fourth type is Sexual Guilt, men and women whose sexual activity is within the normal range but they feel extremely guilty about it. People in this group are often self-referrals, and more likely to be female. The fifth type is the Designated Patient, someone referred by their romantic partner; the partner has very restrictive beliefs about sex and discovers some activity by the patient that they disapprove of. The patient shows no signs of behavioral extremes/paraphilic disorder. The last type is the person who is diagnosed as exhibiting a nonsexual condition—personality disorders, hypomania, or developmental delays. Sometimes their symptoms are related to medications they are taking. Notice that people in three of these categories are not exhibiting signs of atypical or disordered sexuality, reminding us that we need to be very careful when applying diagnostic labels (such as hypersexuality) to people.

Asexuality

Asexuality is defined as having no sexual attraction to another person. Researchers used data from the National Survey of Family Growth to estimate the prevalence of asexuality in the United States (Poston & Baumle, 2010). Responses to questions were used to construct three indices of asexuality: assessing behavior, identity, and sexual attraction; 0.6 percent of the females and 0.9 percent of the males gave the asexual response to all three. A similar survey in New Zealand found that 0.4 percent of the sample identified as asexual (Greaves et al., 2017). Compared with heterosexuals, the asexuals were more likely to be women, less likely to be cisgender, and less likely to be in a serious romantic relationship.

What is asexuality?

A critical controversy concerns whether asexuality is a sexual orientation, a sexual dysfunction (as described in the chapter "Sexual Disorders and Sex Therapy"), a symptom of a mental disorder, or a paraphilia (Brotto & Yule, 2017). Experts have generally rejected the idea that asexuality is a symptom of a mental disorder; asexuals, for example, have the same rates of depression as the rest of the population. With regard to the possibility that it might be a sexual dysfunction, asexuality might be an arousal disorder or a sexual desire disorder. Research, however, shows that self-identified asexual women show the same genital response to erotic films, assessed by a photoplethysmograph, as heterosexual and lesbian women. Asexuality might be a desire disorder representing extreme lack of desire. However, people with low sexual desire disorder are distressed with their lack of desire, whereas asexuals are fine with their lack of sexual attraction to others. Moreover, asexuals masturbate. They just aren't interested in sex with other people. As for the paraphilia hypothesis, paraphilias are atypical sexual interests; is lack of interest in anyone therefore a paraphilia? Some experts have concluded that asexuality should count as a sexual orientation (Brotto & Yule, 2017). If sexual orientation refers to attraction to members of one's own gender, members of the other gender, or both, shouldn't attraction to neither also be an orientation?

Cybersex Use and Abuse

Researchers have identified a long list of online sexual activities (OSA) that people engage in (Shaughnessy et al., 2017). The activities are grouped into three broad categories:

- Non-arousal OSA: Examples include looking for sex information online; looking for advice online about sexual relationships; joining an online dating service; and joining an online kink community.
- Solitary-arousal OSA: Examples include viewing sexually explicit pictures or videos; watching others engaged in sex on a webcam; and posting a video of yourself engaging in sex.
- Partnered-arousal OSA: Examples include having your avatar engage in sexual activity with another avatar; participating in an online sexual chat for sexual arousal; using an electronic sex toy that is controlled through the Internet by someone else (e.g., with the Sinulator); and engaging in sexual acts by yourself, that someone on IM was telling you to do for a webcam.

The possibilities are endless!

One study surveyed college students in four nations (Canada, Germany, Sweden, and the United States) about their OSA (Döring et al., 2017). Overall, 90 percent had accessed sexual information online, 31 percent had engaged in cybersex, and

Asexuality: A lack of sexual attraction.

1 percent had paid for online sexual services. Patterns looked the same in all four countries, testifying to the global reach of the Internet—at least in more affluent nations.

A major concern in recent years has been whether the use of the Internet to access sexually explicit materials, chat rooms, and bulletin boards can become compulsive or paraphilic. This concern has been raised by therapists and clinicians, who report cases of Internet use leading to job loss, relationship difficulties or divorce, and other adverse consequences (Galbreath et al., 2002).

The Internet is thought to be especially likely to lead to compulsive behavior because it is characterized by the three A's: anonymity, accessibility, and affordability—if you aren't poor. Unlike face-to-face behaviors such as cruising for a partner, Internet users are anonymous. The Internet is available 24/7, and its use is relatively cheap—you can download almost any kind of sexual material, sometimes for free.

Internet "abuse" has been variously characterized as paraphilic, compulsive, or addictive. As noted earlier, intense and persistent use of the Internet in ways that significantly impair daily life or cause distress may constitute hypersexuality. The research reviewing referrals to the Sexual Behavior Center identified extremely high frequencies of pornography consumption as Paraphilic Hypersexuality. Men who spend a great deal of time viewing pornography and several hours per day masturbating were identified as a second group within the hypersexual category. Yet it is likely that only a small number of people access sexually explicit materials in ways that fit the definition of a paraphilic disorder.

What about pornography use as compulsive behavior? Research using a sexual compulsivity scale sought to determine what percentage of users were compulsive users (Cooper et al., 2000). The study found that 83 percent of the participants were not problematic users. Eleven percent attained moderate scores on the scale, 4.6 percent were *sexually compulsive,* and 1 percent were *cybersex compulsives.* People in the cybersex compulsive group reported spending 15 to 25 hours per week in online sexual pursuits. Twenty-one percent of the respondents reported that their online activities had jeopardized at least one area of their life, the most common being personal relationships.

The most common characterization of problematic Internet use involving sexually explicit materials is *porn(ography) addiction.* A search for this term on Google returned 71 million hits, including popular media articles, ads for treatment programs and centers, self-help and professional books, thousands of folk remedies, and too many porn sites to count. We discussed the concept of sexual addiction in the Milestones box earlier in the chapter. The concept

Asphyxiophilia: The practice of inducing in oneself a state of oxygen deficiency in order to create sexual arousal or to enhance excitement and orgasm; also called *erotic asphyxiation.*

of addiction was developed to explain substance abuse. The craving for the substance and the inability to control its use result from neurophysiological changes due to repeated use; such changes have been documented. Advocates of the application of addiction to porn argue that repeated exposure to pornographic images has similar or "parallel" effects. They point to some reported cases where excessive use leads to impairment in occupational or personal functioning or relationships. They also point to cases where men with histories of excessive exposure experience erectile dysfunction as evidence of "addiction." Critics respond that similar neurophysiological changes have not been documented in response to visual stimuli of any kind (Ley et al., 2014). Clearly various responses can become conditioned to viewing online porn (or any visual stimulus for that matter—see the chapter "Theoretical Perspectives on Sexuality"). Conditioning and the desire to experience sexual gratification may account for repeated activity. Whether the user really cannot control the behavior is the key question. As we pointed out earlier, addiction provides a plausible reason (excuse?) for behavior that results in pressure from others to change. Note that the review of referrals for hypersexuality identified one group as "designated patients," people whose partners brought them in for treatment for "addiction."

The research suggests high rates of co-occurrence with other disorders; people whose Internet use is problematic are more likely to be depressed (by standard measures), report sleep disturbances, and report alcohol and drug abuse. The question is which came first: the Internet use, which then led to depression and substance abuse (because the Internet use was causing problems), or the depression and substance abuse, which led to the person finding escape online?

Is my sex-related Internet use compulsive?

Other Sexual Variations

Other sexual variations seem to be rare and have not been the subject of much research. Participation in them, however, may be fatal (asphyxiophilia) or a crime (zoophilia, frotteurism).

Asphyxiophilia, or erotic asphyxiation, is the practice of inducing in oneself a state of oxygen deficiency in order to create sexual arousal or to enhance sexual excitement and orgasm (Zaviačič, 1994). A variety of techniques are used, including temporary strangulation by a rope around the neck, a pillow against the face, or a plastic bag over the head or upper body. Obviously, this is very dangerous behavior; a miscalculation can lead to death.

In fact, it is estimated that it causes between 250 and 1,000 deaths per year in the United States (Innala & Ernulf, 1989). The average age of males who die during this activity is 26, leading investigators to suggest that it may be novices who die, due to their inexperience (Lowery & Wetli, 1982).

Little is known about asphyxiophilia. Most of the deaths attributed to the practice involve men. Such cases are often obvious to the trained investigator. Characteristics that distinguish these deaths from intentional suicides include a male who is nude, cross-dressed, or dressed with genitals exposed, and evidence of sexual activity at the time of death (Hucker & Blanchard, 1992). Pornography or other props such as mirrors are often present (Zaviačič, 1994).

Some cases involving women have been identified (Byard et al., 1993). A review of eight fatal cases among women found that only one involved unusual clothing and none involved pornography or props. Two of the cases were initially ruled homicide, one suicide, and five accidental death. The investigators suggest that death due to asphyxiophilia may be much more common among women than we realize, because these deaths are less often recognized for what they are by investigators.

People engage in asphyxiophilia in the belief that arousal and orgasm are intensified by reduced oxygen. There is no way to determine whether this is true. If the experience is more intense, it may be due to heightened arousal created by the risk rather than by reduced oxygen. Some believe that certain women may experience an orgasm accompanied by urethral ejaculation; this belief has been identified as one reason women engage in asphyxiophilia. Again, there is no evidence.

An online survey collected data from practitioners. Seventy-one percent reported masochistic activities, and 31 percent sadistic ones. Sixty-six percent reported using bondage, and 14 percent reported using electrical stimulation. Forty-one percent engaged in it alone (Hucker, 2008).

Zoophilia is sexual contact with an animal; this behavior is also called *bestiality* or *sodomy,* although the latter term is also used to refer to anal intercourse or even mouth–genital sex between humans. About 8 percent of the males in Kinsey's sample reported having had sexual experiences with animals. Most of this activity was concentrated in adolescence and probably reflected the experimentation and diffuse sexual urges of that period. Not surprisingly, the percentage was considerably higher among boys on farms; 17 percent of boys raised on farms had had animal contacts resulting in orgasm. Kinsey found that only about 3 to 4 percent of all females have had some sexual contact with animals. Contemporary therapists report cases of men and women engaging in sexual activity with household pets. Activities include masturbating the animal, oral–genital contact, and intercourse.

Researchers recruited participants through a network of people with sexual interests in animals (Williams & Weinberg, 2003). Data were obtained from 114 men, all White, with a median age of 27; 64 percent were single, never married. Ninety-three percent defined themselves as "zoophiles" and said this identity involved a concern for the animal's welfare and an emphasis on consensual sexual activity. They viewed themselves as better than "bestialists," who they said were not concerned about an animal's welfare. Given a list of possible reasons for sexual interest in animals, the two most common were a desire for affection and pleasurable sex. The type of sexual contact reported by the men varied by the type of animal. Receiving oral sex and receiving anal intercourse were the most frequent activities with dogs, whereas performing vaginal and anal intercourse were most frequent with horses. Only one man preferred sheep.[6] Many of the men had not had a human partner in the preceding year. The researchers suggest that a preference for sexual activity with animals can be explained by learning theory in that the rewards offered by sex with animals are immediate, easy, and intense, and thus extremely reinforcing. They suggest that the respondents' choice of animal is explained by their earlier conditioning, most men preferring the type of animal they first had sex with.

Frotteurism is a paraphilia identified by the *DSM-5.* It is defined as sexual fantasies or behaviors involving touching or rubbing one's genitals against the body of a nonconsenting person, usually in a crowded public place (Lussier & Piche, 2008). When the behavior is intense, causing clinically significant distress or impairment in functioning, it constitutes *frotteuristic disorder.* Milder forms of this activity are common. A man may approach a woman from the rear and press his penis against her buttocks, or a woman may approach a man from the side and rub her genitals against his leg or hip. The target may be unaware of it if it occurs in a crowded elevator or subway train[7] or in the crush of a crowd at a sports event or concert.

Troilism, or threesomes, refers to a sexual encounter involving three people. Troilism may reflect negotiated nonmonogamy (see the chapter "Sexuality and the Life Cycle: Adulthood"). It is a staple of erotic video and stories. In a sample of young adults, 13 percent had engaged in a threesome

> **Zoophilia:** Sexual contact with an animal; also called *bestiality* or *sodomy.*
> **Frotteurism:** Deriving sexual satisfaction from fantasies, urges, or behaviors involving touching or rubbing one's genitals against the body of a nonconsenting person.
> **Troilism (TROY-uhl-ism):** Three people having sex together.

[6]And there's a relevant joke. What's the difference between Mick Jagger and a Scotsman?
  Mick Jagger sings, "Hey, you, get off of my cloud." The Scotsman says, "Hey, McLeod, get off of my ewe."
[7]Ever ridden the New York subway during rush hour? If you're into frotteurism, it's a dream come true!

and 64 percent expressed at least some interest in doing so, although the level of interest was low (Thompson & Byers, 2017).

Saliromania is a disorder found mainly in men—a desire to damage or soil a woman or her clothes or the image of a woman, such as a painting or statue. The man becomes sexually excited and may ejaculate during the act.

Coprophilia and **urophilia** are both variations having to do with excretion. In coprophilia the feces are important to sexual satisfaction. In urophilia it is the urine that is important. The urophiliac may want to be urinated on as part of the sexual act. Insiders refer to urination as a "golden shower" or "water sports."

Necrophilia is sexual contact with a dead person. Like most sexual variations, it can range from mild to severe. In the mild cases, the person may just fantasize about sexual intercourse with a dead person (Aggrawal, 2009). In the more serious cases, the person actually engages in sexual intercourse with a dead body. In extreme cases, the homicidal necrophiliac kills a person and then has sex with the corpse.

Sexsomnia, or *sleep sex,* refers to automatic, unintentional sexual behaviors during sleep (Williams & Lettieri, 2012); the term was introduced in 2003 (Shapiro et al., 2003). The behavior occurs during nonrapid eye movement sleep, usually in the first hours of sleep, and is related to an abnormal transition between sleep and wake states. It typically arises from slow-wave sleep, which is characterized by reduced cortical control by the brain leading to uninhibited behavior. The person is unaware of the behavior or their surroundings, and if awakened has no memory of what happened.

The range of reported sexual behaviors is broad, from sexual sounds like moaning, to fondling, masturbation, cunnilingus, sexual intercourse with or without orgasm, and sexual assault (Schenck et al., 2007). About 80 percent of the reported cases involve men. Partnered behaviors typically involve another person in the same bed. Partners may experience physical injuries. Both the actor and the partner report various negative psychosocial aftereffects, including guilt, shame, embarrassment, alarm, and low self-esteem. Sexsomnia obviously may cause relationship problems. Sexsomnia has features in common with other sleep somnias (sleepwalking, sleep eating); the distinguishing feature is persistent sexual arousal—erection, lubrication, orgasm—during the episode.

Causes or contributing features include things that can disrupt normal sleep cycles, such as sleep apnea, sleep deprivation, stress, alcohol use or abuse, and some medications. Sexsomnia is considered a sleep disorder rather than a paraphilia, but some reported cases involve paraphilic behavior (e.g., genital fondling of a minor).

Prevention of Sexual Variations

For many of the variations discussed in this chapter, there is a continuum from normal to abnormal. People whose behavior falls at the normal end enjoy these activities at no expense to self or others. People whose behavior falls at the abnormal end are cause for concern.

The misery that many people suffer—for example, the sexually compulsive porn user—not to mention the harm they may do to others (e.g., the child molester), is good reason to want to develop programs for preventing these kinds of sexual variations (Qualls et al., 1978). In preventive medicine, a distinction is made between primary prevention and secondary prevention. Applied to the sexual variations that rise to the abnormal level (let's call these problematic sexual variations), primary prevention would mean intervening in home life or in other factors during childhood to help prevent problems from developing or trying to teach people how to cope with crises or stress so that problems do not develop. In secondary prevention, the idea is to diagnose and treat the problem as early as possible once it has arisen, so that difficulties are minimized.

It would be highly advantageous to do primary prevention of problematic sexual variations—that is, to head them off before they even develop. Unfortunately, this is proving to be difficult, for a number of reasons. One problem is the diagnostic categories. The categories for the diagnosis of sexual variations are not nearly as clear-cut in real life as they may seem in this chapter, and multiple diagnoses for one person are not uncommon. That is, a given person might have engaged in incest, pedophilia, and exhibitionism. If it is unclear how to diagnose sexual variations, it is going to be rather difficult to figure out how to prevent them. Further muddying the waters is the co-occurrence of paraphilias and other psychiatric conditions. A study of men with paraphilic disorders systematically assessed co-occurrence (Kafka & Hennen, 2002). More than two-thirds had mood disorders (39 percent diagnosed with major depression), 38 percent had anxiety disorders, and 34 percent abused psychoactive substances. Men with paraphilias were significantly more likely to abuse cocaine. One-third of the men had retrospectively diagnosed attention-deficit hyperactivity disorder.

An alternative approach that seems promising—rather than figuring out ways to prevent each separate variation—is to analyze the *components of sexual development.* Disturbance in one or more of these components in development might lead to different sexual variations. Two components

---

Saliromania: A desire to damage or soil a woman or her clothes.

Coprophilia (cop-roh-FILL-ee-uh): Deriving sexual satisfaction from contact with feces.

Necrophilia: Sexual contact with a dead person.

Sexsomnia: Refers to automatic, unintentional sexual behaviors during sleep; also called *sleep sex.*

Figure 7 Advertising for partners. Many websites and magazines carry "personal ads."

©Panther Media GmbH/Alamy

are sexual responsiveness (arousal to appropriate or inappropriate stimuli) and formation of relationships with others (Bancroft, 1978).

It seems clear that different developmental components are disturbed in different variations. In the case of the fetishist, it is the second component, sexual responsiveness to appropriate stimuli, that is disturbed. And in the case of the exhibitionist, it may be that the ability to form relationships is disturbed.

The idea would then be to try to ensure that as children grow up their development in each of these components is healthy. Ideally, sexual variations should not occur then.

It is clear that childhood sexual abuse is a risk factor for paraphilic behavior and paraphilic disorders later in life. Because adults are responsible for sexual violence against children, prevention (and treatment) must be targeted at adults. One program whose success has been documented is Stop It Now!, a community-based campaign (Laws, 2008). It involves media campaigns to educate the public and change policy. The project began by collecting survey and focus group research on knowledge and awareness in the community. Then it conducted a social marketing campaign designed to increase public awareness and impact abusive behavior. The campaign used multiple media, including radio, cable and network TV, newspapers, advertising in buses, and an interactive website. It established a toll-free help line to enable offenders to receive information and a referral to a clinician if desired. An evaluation indicated that abusers called for help: 118 people voluntarily sought assistance, and another 25 turned themselves in to the legal system. The program undoubtedly prevented many children from being sexually abused.

Treatment of Sexual Variations

Some of the sexual variations discussed in this chapter, such as the mild fetishes, regular masturbation, or viewing erotic materials, are well within the normal range of sexual expression. There is no need for treatment. Others, however, fall into the abnormal range, causing personal anguish to the individual and possibly harming unwilling victims. Treatments are needed for these problematic variations, particularly those that are paraphilic disorders as defined by the *DSM-5*. Various types of treatments have been tried, each based on a different theory of the causes of sexual variations. We now look at four categories of treatments: medical treatments, cognitive behavioral therapies, skills training, and AA-type 12-step programs. We also review research on the effectiveness of each.

Medical Treatments

Inspired by the notion that sexual variations are caused by biological factors, various medical treatments for sexual variations have been tried over more than a century.

Some of them look today like nothing other than cruel and unusual punishment. Nonetheless, people would love to have a pill that would cure some of these complex and painful or dangerous paraphilic disorders, so the search for such treatments continues.

Surgical castration was used fairly commonly in the United States in the 1800s and early 1900s as a treatment for various kinds of uncontrollable sexual urges (Bullough, 1976). The idea resurfaced in recent years in some court cases in which castration was proposed as a treatment for rapists, as discussed in Sex Offenders—Castration or Incarceration? in the chapter "Sexual Arousal." Such treatments are based on the notion that removing a man's testosterone by removing the testes will lead to a drastic reduction in sex drive, which will in turn erase urges to commit sex offenses. However, as we saw in the chapter "Sexual Arousal," a reduction in testosterone levels in humans does not always lead to a reduction in sexual behavior. Surgical castration cannot be recommended as a treatment for sex offenders either on humanitarian grounds or on grounds of effectiveness.

Hormonal treatment involves the use of drugs to reduce sexual desire, based on the assumption that sexual arousability is dependent on maintaining the level of androgen in the body above a given threshold. Several drugs have been tried in the past 50 years. These drug treatments have typically been used with adult male offenders who are arrested for sexual contacts with children or exhibitionism. The drug medroxyprogesterone acetate (MPA), which binds to androgen receptors, was commonly used in the United States for some years. However, the drug has serious, adverse side effects, and its use has been discontinued in Europe (Thibaut et al., 2010). Moreover, limited evidence suggests it did not reduce the likelihood of reoffending. *Cyproterone acetate* (CPA) is replacing MPA; it acts as both progestin and an antiandrogen. It binds to all androgen receptors, including those in the brain, and blocks testosterone uptake. It is taken daily as a tablet or injected weekly or biweekly.

Clinicians also use *leuprolide acetate* (LA), a synthetic analog of gonadotropin-releasing hormone (GnRH; see the chapter "Sex Hormones, Sexual Differentiation, and the Menstrual Cycle"). These drugs are also called LHRH agonists. A systematic review concluded that these drugs are effective in the treatment of paraphilic disorders and are more effective than other drugs (Turner & Briken, 2018).

The use of an alternative, *psychopharmacological treatment,* is based on the idea that people with problematic paraphilias are often suffering from psychological problems such as depression and that treating the depression will take care of the paraphilic behavior. Here, psychotropic medications, like antidepressants such as Prozac, are administered to offenders. These medications influence patients' psychological functioning and behavior by their action on the central nervous system. Antidepressants are being used with paraphilics who are also diagnosed with obsessive-compulsive disorder or depression. These drugs appear to change the obsessive-compulsive behavior rather than sexual desire (Gijs & Gooren, 1996). There is a great deal of interest in the use of the antidepressants known as selective serotonin reuptake inhibitors (SSRIs). These drugs also have been successfully used to treat compulsive behaviors. Their success with people exhibiting paraphilic disorders is consistent with the idea that these conditions are a type of obsessive-compulsive disorder (Miner & Coleman, 2001). A review of effectiveness research suggests that SSRIs may be most effective with juvenile offenders (Thibaut et al., 2010).

Both hormonal and psychopharmacological treatment should be used as only one element in a complete program of therapy, which should include counseling and treatment for other emotional and social deficits (Saleh & Berlin, 2003). The best results are obtained with people who are highly motivated to change their behavior and therefore comply with the prescribed treatment regimen. If the patient stops taking the drug or participating in other aspects of treatment, the program will fail. Unfortunately, one of the limitations of research on the effectiveness of these treatments is the high dropout rate.

Cognitive Behavioral Therapies

Some treatment programs are based on cognitive behavioral therapies (CBT). Comprehensive programs include elements such as the following (Grubbs et al., 2015; Hallberg et al., 2017):

1. Education on the person's condition and factors that can contribute to the continuation of the behavior, such as classical and operant conditioning.
2. Practice in impulse-control skills and mindfulness (discussed in the chapter "Sexual Disorders and Sex Therapy").
3. Training in problem-solving skills if the person experiences depression, anxiety, or boredom.
4. Cognitive restructuring (modifications of distorted thinking) to help the person deal with negative thoughts.
5. Skills to prevent relapse.

Convicted offenders sent to correctional facilities are likely to be treated with programs of this type, if they receive any treatment. An evaluation of the effectiveness of programs for adult offenders reports that high-quality CBT programs for sex offenders in prison reduced recidivism 15 percent, and for offenders on probation the reduction was 31 percent (Aos et al., 2006). Note that many people do not reoffend following release. If the rate of reoffense for untreated people is 30 percent, a 15 percent reduction would be about 5 people per 100 released offenders. The Regional Treatment Centre is a secure, prison-based treatment facility in Canada; it provides high-risk offenders with an individualized, CBT-based program targeting criminal thinking patterns, criminal associates, deviant arousal, and other elements of the personality. Offenders are typically people diagnosed with paraphilic disorders, including sexual interactions with children, exhibitionism, and sexual sadism. The program typically lasts 7 months. About 250 released offenders were followed for two and one-half years post-release; only 5.5 percent (14 people) reoffended in that period (Wilson et al., 2013).

A meta-analysis found that recidivism rates for women convicted of sexual offenses (only some of which were paraphilic) were much lower than rates for men (Cortoni et al., 2010).

We noted earlier the younger age of some sex offenders in the United States. A therapeutic program targeting young sex offenders using CBT and skills training has been shown to be effective (LeTourneau et al., 2009). The program, Multisystemic Therapy (MST), involves family therapy, behavioral parent (skills) training, and CBT. The intervention is individualized to the specific offender and their caregivers and is presented in home and school. It addresses youth and caregiver denial about the offense, minimizing the youth's access to potential victims, and promoting age-appropriate and normative social experiences with peers. Youth (median age 14, all but 3 male) were randomly assigned to MST or the usual treatment prescribed for juvenile offenders in that jurisdiction, one weekly group treatment session following a standard protocol. At 12-month follow-up, youth in MST showed significant reductions in problematic sexual behavior (77 percent vs. zero decline), delinquency (60 percent vs. 18 percent),

and substance abuse (50 percent vs. 65 percent increase). A review of literature on treatment of sex offenders reports that such programs are more effective with juveniles than adults, and most effective with high-risk juvenile offenders, those with prior arrests (Ward et al., 2008).

Skills Training

According to yet another theoretical understanding, people with paraphilias engage in their behavior because they have great difficulty forming relationships, and so they do not have access to appropriate forms of sexual gratification. This perspective is consistent with data on IQ differences between sex offenders and controls. A meta-analysis of 75 studies found that adult males who committed sex offenses scored significantly lower on IQ tests than nonoffenders, and lower than those who committed nonsexual offenses (Cantor et al., 2005). Among sex offenders, the younger the age of the victims, the lower the IQ score of the offender.

Many of these people do not have the skills to initiate and maintain conversation. They may find it difficult to develop intimacy (see the chapter "Attraction, Love, and Communication") (Keenan & Ward, 2000). Such people may benefit from a treatment program that includes social skills training. The training may include how to carry on a conversation, how to develop intimacy, how to be appropriately assertive, and identifying irrational fears that are inhibiting the person (Abel et al., 1992). These programs may also include basic sexuality education.

Figure 8   Tiger Woods, who was linked in media reports with at least 15 women, several of them claiming long-term affairs with him, entered treatment for sex addiction in 2010.

©Eric Gay-Pool/Getty Images

Figure 9   The centerpiece of 12-step programs such as Sex Addicts Anonymous is group meetings in which participants confront their addiction with the support of other group members.

©David Harry Stewart/Getty Images

AA-Type 12-Step Programs

As we saw in Milestones in Sex Research: Sexual Addictions?, sexual addiction theory argues that many people who engage in uncontrollable, inappropriate sexual patterns are addicted to their particular sexual practice. The appropriate treatment, according to this approach, is one of the 12-step programs modeled on Alcoholics Anonymous.

Treatment programs based on this approach have become very common in the past 30 years. They include Sex Addicts Anonymous (SAA), Sex and Love Addicts Anonymous (SLAA), and Sex Compulsives Anonymous. These programs are run by group members and are generally free to participants. Most of the recovery or "rehab" centers in the United States utilize groups based on AA principles, led by a professional staff member, as the core of their programs. These centers are a multi-billion-dollar industry, and their use has entered everyday language: "going into rehab." Twelve-step programs combine cognitive restructuring, obtaining support from other members who have the same or similar problem behaviors, and enhancing spirituality. This last aspect involves increasing one's awareness of a "higher power" who can be relied on to help one recover.

Given their popularity, the obvious question is whether they are effective. AA-based groups in the community are generally unwilling to cooperate with researchers, believing that to do so would prevent group members from concentrating on recovery. As a result, little research data exist on these programs. One recent study of 12-step treatment for compulsive sexual behavior did find it to be effective (Efrati & Gola, 2018).

What Works?

Meta-analyses of the effectiveness of treatment programs for sex offenders consistently find that some types of programs are more effective than others. Typically the treatment is given to a mixed group of sex offenders, including paraphilics, rapists, and child sexual abusers. A systematic review of controlled outcome evaluations of psychosocial and hormonal treatment programs found that, overall, such programs reduced sexual recidivism by 37 percent, compared to those in control groups (Schmucker & Losel, 2008). A review of all types of treatment programs concluded that only CBT-based programs are consistently shown to be effective (Thibaut et al., 2010). Among programs treating incarcerated offenders, the rate of reoffending 20 years following treatment is estimated at 27 percent. As noted earlier, the intensive multifocal program of the Regional Treatment Centre in Canada reported a reoffending rate of 5.5 percent 2.5 years following treatment. Programs are also more effective with some types of offenders than others. The programs have the largest effect with rapists, the second largest with exhibitionists, and the smallest significant effect with intrafamily child sex offenders.

Critical **THINK** *ing Skill*
Using diagnostic labels accurately

In this chapter, we discuss sexual behaviors that depart from the norm in U.S. society. To bring some clarity and structure to the discussion, we rely on the *Diagnostic and Statistical Manual-5* classification system. It identifies a number of *paraphilias,* which are intense and persistent atypical sexual interests. Paraphilias are distinct from *paraphilic disorders,* which are paraphilias that are recurrent, last at least 6 months, and create distress or impairment to the individual.

A highly publicized paraphilia in North America is pedophilic disorder, in which the objects of the recurrent, intense, sexually arousing fantasies, urges, or sexual behaviors are prepubescent children (generally under 13 years of age). Media frequently report that authorities are looking for or have arrested someone for (attempted) sexual contact with a 9- or 11- or 13-year-old youth. Many people immediately jump to the conclusion that the person is a pedophile, is mentally ill, and should be imprisoned or hospitalized for life. The application of this diagnostic label is more likely if there are reports that the person has engaged in similar activity in the past—that is, "has a history" of such behaviors.

A search of the law enforcement and clinical literature will quickly reveal that many different kinds of people engage in sexual contact with children or adolescents, and many do not fit the *DSM* criteria. For example, there are numerous cases of school teachers engaging in sexual activity with 15- or 16-year-old students, but that does not fit the definition of pedophilia because the students are not prepubescent children. (Note that we are not saying that such behaviors between students and teachers are acceptable—just that it is not correct to call such a teacher a pedophile.)

Critical thinking means that we must think carefully before we apply such labels to people. Often, we don't think critically; we infer from publicity about one incident that the person is a pedophile, "child-molester," or a "monster." The media often contribute by uncritically applying the label, or repeating hearsay about the person's past. Applying the label can lead to tremendous hostility directed at the suspect, and even vigilante groups and death threats, often before a thorough investigation has been conducted. These incidents can ruin lives and devastate communities.

Of course, perpetrators of violence or sexual violence toward children (or anyone else) need to be dealt with appropriately. What should be done needs to be determined by careful investigation of what happened, the perpetrator's circumstances, and the perpetrator's history. Some individuals truly are characterized by pedophilic disorder, with long histories of sexual contact exclusively with children of a particular age and gender, and an inability to control their behavior. They fit the diagnosis and should be treated accordingly. On the other hand, the 23-year-old teacher who has sex with a consenting 16-year-old deserves discipline for inappropriate behavior with a student, but should not be categorized as a pedophile.

SUMMARY

When Is Sexual Behavior Abnormal?

It seems reasonable to define *abnormal sexual behavior* as behavior that creates significant psychological distress for the person, impairs their functioning in other areas of life, or harms others. The American Psychiatric Association defines a *paraphilia* as an intense and persistent atypical sexual interest. Paraphilias are distinct from *paraphilic disorders,* which are paraphilias that are recurrent, last at least 6 months, and create distress or impairment to the individual.

There is a continuum between normal and abnormal sexual behavior.

Fetishism

A fetishist is a person who becomes erotically attached to some object other than another human being. Most likely, fetishism arises from conditioning, and the range of behaviors involved provides a good example of the continuum from normal to abnormal behavior.

Cross-Dressing

There are multiple types of cross-dressing, including trans women, drag, female impersonators, and transvestites.

Sadism and Masochism

Three styles of sexual interaction involve differences in control over sexual interactions. Dominance and submission involve a consensual exchange of power, and the enacting of scripted performances. Bondage and discipline involve the use of physical restraints or verbal commands by one person to control the other. Both D-S and B-D may occur without genital contact or orgasm. Sadism and masochism involve deriving sexual gratification from giving and receiving pain.

Voyeurism and Exhibitionism

The voyeur is sexually aroused by looking at nonconsenting people who are nude, undressing, or engaging in sexual activity. The exhibitionist displays their sex organs to others. Both are generally harmless.

Hypersexuality and Asexuality

Nymphomania and satyriasis are terms used to describe women and men with an extraordinarily high sex drive. Both terms are ambiguous and subject to misuse. The term *hypersexuality* is potentially more precise, particularly if it is defined behaviorally.

Asexuality is defined as having no sexual attractions. In surveys, asexuals report less sexual behavior, but they may be sexually active and in cohabiting or marital relationships. They do not necessarily report suffering from distress.

Cybersex Use and Abuse

Use of the Internet to access sexually oriented materials or people may become compulsive. The Internet may facilitate compulsion because of the three A's—anonymity, accessibility, and affordability. One-fifth of those responding to online surveys report that their online activities have jeopardized at least one area of their lives, most commonly personal relationships.

Other Sexual Variations

Other variations include asphyxiophilia, use of oxygen deprivation in an attempt to enhance sexual sensations, and zoophilia, sexual contact with animals. Others include frotteurism and necrophilia.

Prevention of Sexual Variations

Programs that may prevent sexual variations are being developed and evaluated. One is Stop It Now!, a community-based program that has been shown to be effective in preventing child sexual abuse.

Treatment of Sexual Variations

Available treatment programs include medical and hormonal treatments, cognitive behavioral therapy, skills training, and AA-type 12-step programs. Each form of treatment may help some individuals whose sexual behaviors are problematic, but only CBT-based programs are consistently shown to reduce the frequency of the behavior or reoffending.

SUGGESTIONS FOR FURTHER READING

Carnes, Patrick. (2012). *Out of the shadows.* 3rd ed. Center City, MN: Hazelden. This is the classic statement by Carnes of the theory that various forms of sexual behavior can become addictions, comparable to drug addiction, with the same characteristics and responsive to similar kinds of treatment.

Laws, D. Richard, & O'Donohue, William (Eds.). (2008). *Sexual deviance: Theory, assessment, and treatment.* 2nd ed. New York: Guilford. This book has two well-researched chapters on each of the nine paraphilias, and several other variations. One explores psychopathology and theory, and the other explores assessment and treatment.

Lindemann, Danielle. (2012). *Dominatrix: Gender, eroticism, and control in the dungeon.* Chicago: University of Chicago Press. This book presents a sociological approach to the work of the professional dominatrix in BDSM culture.

Are YOU Curious?

1. How many women are raped at some time in their lives?
2. What factors predispose men to become rapists?
3. When child molesters are released from prison, how likely are they to reoffend?
4. What behaviors in the workplace count as sexual harassment?

Read this chapter to find out.

©Brand X Pictures/Punchstock/Getty Images

CHAPTER

15

Sexual Coercion

CHAPTER HIGHLIGHTS

Rape
The Impact of Rape
Date Rape
Marital Rape
Causes of Rape
The Role of Alcohol in Sexual Assault
Rapists
Men as Victims of Rape
Prison Rape
Ethnicity and Rape
Preventing Rape

Child Sexual Abuse
Patterns of Child Sexual Abuse
Impact on the Victim
The Offenders

Sexual Harassment
Sexual Harassment at Work
Sexual Harassment in Education:
    An A for a Lay
Doctor-Patient Sex

Eboni's basic education about sex came from what she saw and the direct experiences that she had. When she was 5, she and her brother were wrestling with their uncle. Suddenly her uncle locked her brother out of the room and began taking off Eboni's clothes. He held her down on the bed and began to penetrate her but stopped abruptly. Eboni was frightened of him from then on. She didn't really understand what he intended to do or why he wanted to do it, but she knew that his behavior was unexpected and strange.

. . . Eboni's grandmother and father insisted that she not talk to strangers or take money from them. Eboni understood why—she knew that being molested meant being raped. But strangers were not the predators.*

*Gail E. Wyatt, (1997). *Stolen women: Reclaiming our sexuality, taking back our lives*. New York: Wiley.

This chapter is about sexual activity that involves coercion and is not between consenting adults; specifically, we consider rape, child sexual abuse, and sexual harassment at work and in education. All these topics have been highly publicized, and much good scientific research on them has appeared.

Rape

Rape is typically defined, following current laws in many states, as nonconsensual oral, anal, or vaginal penetration, obtained by force, by threat of force, or when the victim is incapable of giving consent (Kilpatrick et al., 2007). Notice that the definition includes not only forced vaginal intercourse but forced oral sex and anal sex as well. The crucial point is that the activity is nonconsensual—that is, the victim did not consent to it. One type of nonconsent occurs when the victim is incapable of giving consent, perhaps because of being drunk, unconscious, or high on drugs.

> **How many women are raped at some time in their lives?**

In 2013, some 80,000 rapes—completed or attempted—were reported to law enforcement in the United States; this means there were 40 reported rapes for every 100,000 women (FBI, 2014). However, also according to the FBI, forcible rape is one of the most underreported crimes. Only about 23 percent of rapes are reported to the police (Morgan & Kena, 2017). According to a well-sampled national survey in the United States, a woman has an 18 percent chance, over her lifetime, of being raped (Kilpatrick et al., 2007). According to a well-sampled survey of Australian women, 21 percent had been sexually coerced (de Visser et al., 2007). Statistics vary somewhat from one study to another, but most find that a woman's lifetime risk of being raped is between 18 and 25 percent (Gavey & Senn, 2014). A good figure to remember is 20 percent, or 1 in 5 (Muehlenhard et al., 2017). More than half of all rapes of women occur before age 18, and 22 percent occur before age 12 (Centers for Disease Control and Prevention, 2004a).

Although there is great concern, as there should be, about rape on college campuses, the data indicate that, among college-age women (ages 18 to 24), the rate of rape is higher for nonstudents than it is for students (Sinozich & Langton, 2014).

The Impact of Rape

Compared with nonvictimized women, women who have experienced rape are more likely to show several types of psychological distress, including anxiety, depression, suicide ideation and attempts, and posttraumatic stress disorder (PTSD) (Martin et al., 2011). **Posttraumatic stress disorder** is defined as the long-term psychological distress suffered by someone who has experienced a terrifying, uncontrollable event. Originally developed to describe the long-term psychological distress suffered by war veterans, most of whom are men, it later became clear that women rape survivors show these same symptoms characteristic of PTSD (Koss & Figueredo, 2004). Typical symptoms can include anxiety, depression, nightmares, and a lack of feeling safe.

According to the cognitive behavioral view of PTSD, people who have experienced a terrifying event form a memory schema that involves information about the situation and their responses to it (Foa et al., 1989). Because the schema is large, many cues can trigger it and thereby

> **Rape:** Nonconsenting oral, anal, or vaginal penetration obtained by force, by threat of force, or when the victim is incapable of giving consent. **Posttraumatic stress disorder (PTSD):** Long-term psychological distress suffered by someone who has experienced a terrifying event.

First Person

A Date-Rape Victim Tells Her Story

During my sophomore year at Northwestern University, I realized I wanted to socialize more. I broke up with my hometown honey, began attending college parties, started drinking, and dated other guys at my school. I was a virgin and didn't want to be anymore. I met my second boyfriend in physics. "G" was a football player and a big, handsome man, the best-looking man I'd ever met. We began to date and at first it was wonderful. He even carried me home once from a party, and I thought, "This is the one." Our first attempt at intercourse was difficult and I began to beg him to stop, but he just kept trying until he was successful and there was blood everywhere. It was awful.

I continued to date G, but he began to act very differently. When he drank, he became extremely violent, and on different occasions I watched him break a vending machine, and pull a toilet out of a wall at a fraternity. He was unhappy with the way he was treated on the football team. He demanded to know where I was at all times and accused me of cheating on him. I wanted to break up with him, especially since sex was rough and not always consensual, but I was scared of him. I tried avoiding him but he always found me.

One night, G arrived very drunk at a party I was attending. I tried to sneak out of the party. He noticed I left and ran out after me. I didn't want trouble so I drove him to his dorm. He claimed he was too drunk to walk to his dorm, so I tried to help him into his room. When I turned around to leave, he sprang up and locked me in. He attacked me. I tried fighting him, but he wouldn't listen or stop. He hit my head into the wall several times and tried to force me to perform oral sex. I bit him, and that made him more angry. He then tried to force anal sex, and I fought as hard as I could. I finally started crying, and he stopped when he lost his erection. The rest of the night, I felt completely trapped in his dorm room. I lay awake all night and tried to leave, but he would wake up and stop me. I've never forgotten how scared I felt that entire night. He got up that morning and showered and acted as if nothing had happened. He was in all my classes for the rest of my college career.

I began to drink very heavily afterward. I told my roommate, J, and another woman on my floor, D. I never thought to report it, since he was my "boyfriend."

A year and a half later, I began to hear voices. It was a male voice calling me a fucking bitch, whore, and other names. I thought I was going crazy and became very depressed. I decided I must be schizophrenic and decided to kill myself. My attempt was unsuccessful.

Soon after, I was shopping in a bookstore. I saw this title staring right at me, "I Never Called It Rape." I started reading it right there in the store, and I began crying and thinking, "This is what happened to me." I spoke with a faculty member, who arranged for immediate counseling.

The first time I went to see the counselor, I couldn't even speak. I sat in her office and cried for the entire hour. She kept saying, "It's not your fault, it's not your fault." I couldn't believe it. Later we discussed how most of the times G and I had sex had actually been rape, including the first and the last. I participated in a "Take Back the Night March." One fraternity threw bottles at us.

I went through medical school and residency. During my first year of residency, I was assaulted again, this time by a man in a stairwell during a New Year's Eve party at a hotel. I started screaming "You're raping me, you're raping me!" He stopped and I got away! But I didn't go to the ER, I just went home and crawled in bed. My old shame came back. I began to drink heavily again. One night I drank all night and never showed up to work that next morning. I finally rolled into my director's office, depressed, hung over, and still smelling of alcohol, and my boss said I had to stop and straighten up right away or he wouldn't let me back for the next year. So I stopped drinking. I also made two very good friends around the same time. Through their support, I really turned my life around.

Three years later, I moved to Madison, Wisconsin. I was living alone for the first time and had a great deal of anxiety. I joined a Sexual Assault Survivors Support Group. Then in the spring, I was invited to speak at my old university for Career Day for high school students, so I went back there 10 years after the incidents. I was finally successful in my career, had strong, loving relationships with my friends and parents, and was happy. I look back at what happened now and think that I really survived a lot. I feel it helps me to be a better physician because I can empathize with how bad life can be for people.

Source: Based on an interview conducted by Janet Hyde.

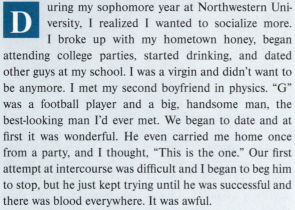

Figure 1   Rape crisis counseling. Many women experience severe emotional distress after a rape, and it is important that crisis counseling be available to them.

©ClarkandCompany/Getty Images

evoke the feelings of terror that occurred at the time; the schema is probably activated at some level all the time. The consequences can be far reaching and long lasting.

Most women who experience a sexual assault have negative psychological reactions immediately afterward. Many, but not all, show significant recovery within a year (Martin et al., 2011). A number of factors are associated with worse psychological outcomes: whether the woman has experienced sexual violence previously (i.e., this is a revictimization), the severity of the violence (more severe violence is associated with worse outcomes), and the reactions of others when the woman discloses the assault (negative reactions from others produce worse psychological outcomes). See First Person: A Date-Rape Victim Tells Her Story, for one woman's account of these effects on her life. The good news is that psychotherapeutic treatments for PTSD are available and they are successful in treating rape survivors (Resick et al., 2012).

Some women experience self-blame. A woman may spend hours agonizing over what she did to cause the rape or what she might have done to prevent it: "If I hadn't worn that tight sweater . . ."; "If I hadn't been dumb enough to walk on that dark street . . ."; "If I hadn't been stupid enough to trust that guy . . ." This is an example of a tendency on the part of both the victim and others to blame the victim. Self-blame is linked to worse long-term psychological outcomes for victims (Koss & Figueredo, 2004).

Researchers are finding increased evidence of the damage to women's physical health that may result from rape (Centers for Disease Control and Prevention, 2004a; de Visser et al., 2007; Paras et al., 2009). Women may suffer physical injuries, such as cuts and bruises, and vaginal pain and bleeding. Women who have been forced to have oral sex may suffer irritation or damage to the throat; rectal bleeding and pain are reported by women forced to have anal intercourse. A raped woman may contract a sexually transmitted infection such as HIV/AIDS or herpes. In about 5 percent of rape cases, pregnancy results (Koss et al., 1991).[1] Women who have been sexually or physically assaulted at some time in the past visit their physician twice as often per year as nonvictimized women (Koss et al., 1991).

Rape affects many people besides the victim. Most women routinely do a number of things that stem from rape fears. For example, many women, when getting into their car at night, almost reflexively check the backseat to make sure no one is hiding there. Most college women avoid walking alone through dark parts of the campus at night. At least once in their lives, most women have been afraid of spending the night alone. If you are a woman, you can probably extend this list from your own experience. The point is that most women experience the fear of rape, if not rape itself, and this fear restricts their activities (Parrot & Cummings, 2006).

Spouses or partners of victims may also be profoundly affected. At the same time, they can provide important support for the woman as she recovers (see First Person: How Can Friends and Family Help a Rape Survivor?).

New research in psychology indicates that not everyone who experiences a serious traumatic event develops PTSD. Some, in fact, display **posttraumatic growth,** that is, positive life changes and psychological development following exposure to trauma (Tedeschi et al., 1998). Research with rape victims—or, more accurately, rape survivors—confirms that some of them do report positive life changes, such as an increased ability to take care of themselves, a greater sense of purpose in life, and greater concern for others in similar situations (Frazier et al., 2004).

Posttraumatic growth: Positive life changes and psychological development following exposure to trauma.

[1]Tests for sexually transmitted infections should routinely be done as part of the hospital treatment of rape victims (Linden, 2011). Pregnancy tests can be done if the woman's period is late. If pregnancy seems likely, emergency contraception can be used (see the chapter "Contraception and Abortion").

First Person

How Can Friends and Family Help a Rape Survivor?

The following is typical of the advice given by numerous universities. This advice comes from University Health Services at the University of Wisconsin–Madison.

Recognize that support from friends and family can make a big difference in how a person heals from trauma. Here are things that friends and family can do to be supportive.

1. **Respect a victim/survivor's decisions.** They need to regain a sense of control over their life. Even though it may be tempting, do not override the person's decisions.

2. **Listen and be available.** Be willing to spend time talking. You don't have to be a trained therapist. You just need to listen supportively.

3. **Believe and accept.** It's easy to fall into the trap of blaming the victim and suggesting what they might have done to bring on the attack. You need to believe the victim/survivor.

4. **Offer a safe place to stay or stay with the survivor.** The survivor may be frightened to be alone, and having a friend or family member there can provide a sense of safety.

5. **Recognize that recovery may take a long time.** Each person recovers on their own time line. Avoid suggesting that the victim/survivor should move on now.

6. **Be sensitive and respectful of the victim/survivor's wishes for closeness and affection.** Some survivors want closeness and others want distance. Ask, for example, before hugging.

7. **Deal with your own feelings.** You may feel anger, guilt, or other emotions about the incident. Don't lay those on the victim. Deal with them elsewhere.

8. **If you are the victim/survivor's intimate partner, understand the impact that sexual assault may have on sexual interactions.** If you are the intimate partner of a victim/survivor, you have an especially important role in helping them heal. You may want to go to counseling yourself, or go to couple counseling.

Source: University of Wisconsin–Madison, University Health Services, https://www.uhs.wisc.edu/prevention/violence-prevention/survivor-support/.

Date Rape

According to national crime victimization statistics, for college students, 78 percent of rapes are committed by someone the victim knows (Sinozich & Langton, 2014). Specifically, 24 percent are committed by a regular dating partner. Date rape is one of the most common forms of rape, especially on college campuses. Younger adolescents are not exempt either; a well-sampled study of U.S. 14- to 21-year-olds found that 3.9 percent of the girls and 1.6 percent of the boys said that their partner had made them have sex (Ybarra et al., 2016). Unfortunately, the gender of the aggressor in these acts was not reported, so we don't know, for example, for the boys, whether the person who forced sex was a girl or another boy.

In some cases, date rape seems to result from male–female miscommunication. Men's traditional view in dating relationships has been that a woman who says no really means yes (Osman, 2003). Men need to learn that no means no. Consider this example of miscommunication and different perceptions in a case of date rape:

Bob: Patty and I were in the same statistics class together. She usually sat near me and was always very friendly. I liked her and thought maybe she liked me, too. Last Thursday I decided to find out. After class I suggested that she come to my place to study for midterms together. She agreed immediately, which was a good sign. That night everything seemed to go perfectly. We studied for a while and then took a break. I could tell that she liked me, and I was attracted to her. I was getting excited. I started kissing her. I could tell that she really liked it. We started touching each other and it felt really good. All of a sudden she pulled away and said "Stop." I figured she didn't want me to think that she was "easy" or "loose." A lot of girls think they have to say no at first. I knew once I showed her what a good time she could have, and that I would respect her in the morning, it would be OK. I just ignored her protests and eventually she stopped struggling. I think she liked it but afterwards she acted bummed out and cold. Who knows what her problem was?

Patty: I knew Bob from my statistics class. He's cute and we are both good at statistics, so when a tough midterm was scheduled, I was glad that he suggested we study together. It never occurred to me that it was anything except a study date. That night everything went fine at first, we got a lot of studying done in a short amount of time, so when he suggested we take a break I thought we deserved it. Well, all of a sudden he started acting really romantic and starting kissing me. I liked the kissing but then he started touching me below the waist. I pulled away and tried to stop him but he didn't listen. After a while I stopped struggling; he was hurting me and I was scared. He was so much bigger and stronger than me. I couldn't believe it was happening to me. I didn't know what to do. He actually forced me to have sex with him. I guess looking back on it I should have screamed or done something besides trying to reason with him but it was so unexpected. I couldn't believe it was happening. I still can't believe it did. (Hughes & Sandler, 1987, p. 1)

Two factors seem to explain why sexually aggressive men misperceive women's communications. First, men in general tend to misperceive women's warmth and friendliness as indicating sexual interest, a pattern that has been found in numerous studies (Farris et al., 2008; Perilloux et al., 2012). Second, sexually aggressive men are likely to have a "suspicious schema," meaning that they generally believe that women do not communicate honestly, particularly when the woman communicates clearly and assertively that she is rejecting an advance (Malamuth & Brown, 1994). The second finding has important implications for prevention and treatment programs for sexual aggressors. Cognitive therapy using cognitive restructuring is probably necessary, the goal being to get the man to change his suspicious schema. Such programs might be used with incarcerated rapists, but they might also be used in prevention programs with high school or college men who have been identified as being rape prone.

One of the most frightening problems today is the emergence of the so-called date-rape drug, rohypnol (row-HIP-nawl, "roofie," drug name flunitrozepam). Numerous cases have been reported of men who slipped the drug into a woman's drink. The drug causes drowsiness or sleep, and the man rapes the woman while she is asleep. The drug also causes the woman not to remember the event the next day. Several strategies for avoiding this situation have been suggested, including, especially, not accepting a drink from a stranger, and never leaving your drink unattended.

Marital Rape

How common is **marital rape,** that is, rape by a current or former spouse? A national probability sample showed that 13 percent of married women had been raped by their current husband (Basile, 2002). The trauma to the woman in marital rape is, of course, no less severe than in other forms of rape (Bennice & Resick, 2003; Brousseau et al., 2011). The terminology

has now been expanded to *intimate partner rape,* which includes not only married couples but also cohabiting couples. Of female rape victims, more than half (51 percent) were raped by an intimate partner (Black et al., 2011).

One phenomenon that emerges from the research is an association between marital violence and marital rape—that is, the man who batters his wife is also likely to rape her (Centers for Disease Control and Prevention, 2004b).

A man might rape his intimate partner for many motives, including anger, power and domination, sadism, or a desire for sex regardless of whether his wife is willing (Russell, 1990). In some cases the husband is extremely angry, perhaps in the middle of a family argument, and he expresses his anger toward his wife by raping her. In other cases, power and domination of the wife seem to be the motive; for example, the wife may be threatening to leave him, and he forces or dominates her into staying by raping her. Finally, some rapes appear to occur because the husband is sadistic—enjoys inflicting pain—and is psychiatrically disturbed.

Causes of Rape

To provide a perspective for the discussion that follows, we can distinguish among four major theoretical views of the nature of rape (Albin, 1977; Baron & Straus, 1989; Zurbriggen, 2010):

1. **Victim-precipitated rape.** This view holds that a rape is always caused by a woman "asking for it." Rape, then, is considered basically the woman's fault. This view represents the tendency to blame the victim.

2. *Psychopathology of rapists.* This theoretical view holds that rape is an act committed by a psychologically disturbed man. His deviance is responsible for the crime occurring.

3. *Feminist.* Feminist theorists view rapists as the product of gender-role socialization in our culture. They have theorized about the complex links between sex and power: In some rapes, men use sex to demonstrate their power over women; in other rapes, men use their power over women to get sex. Feminists also point to the eroticization of violence in our society. Gender inequality is both the cause and the result of rape in this view.

4. *Social disorganization.* Sociologists believe that crime rates, including rape rates, increase when the social organization of a community is disrupted. Under such conditions the community cannot enforce its norms against crime.

You personally may subscribe to one or more of these views. It is also true that researchers in this area have generally based their work on one of these theoretical models, which may influence their research. You should keep these models in mind as you read the rest of this chapter.

What do the data say? Research indicates that a number of factors contribute to rape, ranging from forces at the cultural level to factors at the individual level, including

---

Marital rape: The rape of a person by their current or former spouse.
Victim-precipitated rape: The view that rape is a result of a woman "asking for it."

the following: cultural values; sexual scripts; early family influences; peer-group influences; characteristics of the situation; miscommunication; sex and power motives; and masculinity norms and men's attitudes. The data on each of these factors are considered below.

Cultural values can serve to support rape. In the International Dating Violence Study, researchers collected data from university students at 38 sites around the world, including several states in the United States, and sites in Asia, Europe, Latin America, and the Middle East (Hines, 2007). The results indicated that there was a correlation, across cultures, between hostility toward women and rates of sexual coercion. That is, the more hostility that men from a culture expressed toward women on questionnaires, the higher the rate of women reporting being sexually coerced.

The term **rape culture** has been coined to refer to deeply entrenched cultural attitudes about gender and sexuality that shape people's attitudes about rape (Barnett et al., 2018). Rape culture is supported by *rape myths,* which are false beliefs about rape. Examples include the belief that the victim precipitated the rape, that victims fabricate their story of rape when it was really consensually sex, that the victim wanted to be raped, and that men cannot control themselves in a sexual situation.

Sexual scripts play a role in rape as well (Carroll & Clark, 2006; Krahé et al., 2007). Adolescents quickly learn society's expectations about dating and sex through culturally transmitted sexual scripts. These scripts support rape when they convey the message that the man is supposed to be oversexed and the sexual aggressor. By adolescence, both girls and boys endorse scripts that justify rape. A study of 1,700 middle school students revealed that approximately 25 percent of the boys said that it was acceptable for a man to force sex on a woman if he had spent money on her (Koss et al., 1994). These findings have been replicated in a number of studies of high school and college students (e.g., Goodchilds & Zellman, 1984; Muehlenhard, 1988).

Early family influences may play a role in shaping a man into becoming a sexual aggressor. Specifically, young men who are sexual aggressors are likely to have been sexually abused themselves in childhood (Seto et al., 2010).

The peer group can have a powerful influence, encouraging men to rape. For an example, see Milestones in Sex Research: Fraternity Gang Rape, which describes the ways in which the peer group in a fraternity created a climate that encouraged its members to rape.

Characteristics of the situation play a role. Secluded places foster rape, as do parties in which excessive alcohol use is involved (Koss et al., 1994). Another situational factor is social disorganization, as noted earlier. An extreme example is war, in which rape of women is common (Zurbriggen, 2010).

Miscommunication between women and men is a factor. In the section on date rape we saw a case in which the man and the woman had totally different understandings of what had occurred. Because many people in the United States are reluctant to discuss sex directly, they try to infer sexual interest from subtle nonverbal cues, a process that is highly prone to errors (Abbey, 1991). Specifically, some men have a predisposition to interpret a woman's friendly behavior or sexy clothing as carrying a sexual message that she did not intend (Abbey, 1991; Farris et al., 2006; Lindgren et al., 2008).

Sex and power motives are involved in rape. Feminists have stressed that rape is an expression of power and dominance by men over women (Parrot & Cummings, 2006; Zurbriggen, 2010). Current theory emphasizes that both sexual motives and power motives are involved and interact with each other. For example, rapists may be capable of experiencing sexual arousal and hostile aggression simultaneously, whereas other men find that hostile aggression inhibits sexual arousal.

Finally, masculinity norms and men's attitudes are another factor (Abrams et al., 2003; Zurbriggen, 2010), as we discuss later in the chapter. Supporting the feminist theoretical view, research shows that hypermasculine attitudes are correlated with men's history of sexual aggression (Murnen et al., 2002). The very commonness of rape, especially date rape, argues against the psychopathology of rapists. Hypermasculinity is a far more common cause than psychopathology.

The Role of Alcohol in Sexual Assault

Research has established a link between alcohol consumption and sexual assault (Abbey, 2011; Abbey et al., 2014). Men who are intoxicated are more likely to commit a sexual assault than men who are not intoxicated. That finding is a correlation, though. Does it mean that alcohol actually plays a causal role? Or might it be that a man who wants to commit a sexual assault drinks to get himself ready, or perhaps to give himself an excuse? Or could it be that some third factor, such as impulsivity, accounts for the correlation? A man who is highly impulsive drinks too much and commits sexual assault. Researchers have spent a great deal of effort sorting out these possibilities.

First, let's consider the *effects of alcohol on the perpetrator.* Scientists have documented two categories of effects: pharmacological effects and psychological effects. *Pharmacological effects,* the actual effects of the drug on the body and behavior, have been detected in laboratory experiments. Alcohol impairs higher cognitive functions such as complex decision making, planning, and response inhibition (Abbey et al., 2014). These effects can be found at blood-alcohol concentrations (BAC) as low as .04, which is the equivalent of 2 drinks consumed over 2 hours. At a BAC of .08, the effects are large. For a man who is predisposed to commit rape, alcohol can turn the predisposition into actual behavior.

As for the *psychological effects,* alcohol is glamorized in our culture and is widely believed to improve

> **Rape culture:** Deeply entrenched cultural attitudes about gender and sexuality that shape people's attitudes about rape; rape myths are an integral part of rape culture.

Milestones in Sex Research

Fraternity Gang Rape

Anthropologist Peggy Sanday (1990) investigated a widely publicized case of gang rape in a fraternity at a particular university, as well as many other similar cases documented at other universities.

Men join fraternities for many possible reasons. Some may anticipate establishing networks of friendships that will help them in their future careers. But often freshmen, insecure in a complex new environment, join the fraternity to find security. According to Sanday's analysis, the initiation rituals of many fraternities follow a sequence of creating high levels of anxiety in the new members, followed by a male bonding ritual that makes them "brothers." Essentially the young man's identity as an individual is undermined while loyalty to the group is prized, indeed enforced.

In the case investigated by Sanday, the XYZ fraternity (she used this name to guard the anonymity of the population being studied, as required by the ethical standards for anthropologists) had a practice called the "XYZ express," referring to an express train. It involved a gang rape in which a woman, typically drunk or surreptitiously drugged so that she was barely conscious, was raped successively by a series of brothers who stood in line to take their turn, just as cars in a train are in a line. Often this occurred toward the end of a party, when the brothers themselves were drunk.

Sanday pointed out how this practice has two consequences: It establishes dominance over a woman, and it promotes strong bonds among the fraternity brothers. The practice, of course, fits the definition of rape and is illegal. Yet many of the brothers, when the case was brought to court, said that they had no idea that their activities were wrong or illegal. The culture of the fraternity had dulled their capacity to make a rational judgment. The judge who heard the case was astounded that universities would tolerate, indeed support, institutions that created an environment in which such acts could occur.

Sanday noted anthropologists' findings that, cross-culturally, some societies are free of sexual assault whereas others are rape prone. She concluded, "Social ideologies, not human nature, prepare men to abuse women" (p. 192). The XYZ fraternity and others like it are essentially a subculture that socializes men to have sexist attitudes toward women and creates an environment in which gang rape is likely to occur.

Source: Sanday (1990).

---

men's sexual outcomes (Abbey, 2011). People believe that drinking alcohol will make them more sociable and sexually uninhibited. These beliefs create expectancy effects, and they can be powerful. Moreover, the expectancy effects can amplify the actual pharmacological effects.

Let's consider one particular study to illustrate how researchers go about studying the pharmacological and psychological effects (Abbey et al., 2009). Male college students first completed measures that included past sexual assault perpetration and the trait of general hostility. A month later—so that they wouldn't perceive a connection with the earlier measures—the men were brought to the lab. They were randomly assigned to one of three experimental conditions: intoxicated, sober, or placebo. Those in the intoxicated group drank 4 vodka and tonics to bring their BAC to .08. The sober group was given an equivalent amount of tonic. Those in the placebo group were told they were getting the vodka and tonic, but in fact there was no vodka in their drinks. Each participant then watched an 8-minute video designed to simulate a potential date rape situation. The characters were Lisa and Mark, and participants were asked to imagine themselves as Mark. In a series of scenes, Lisa and Mark talk after a class and then meet at a party and spend time together, after which Mark invites Lisa to his apartment. They proceed to kiss and touch and the film fades out. The men were then asked a series of questions about whether they (Mark) would be justified in forcing sex.

The results indicated that alcohol consumption did not have a simple main effect on ratings of how justified it would be to force sex. However, there was an interaction between alcohol consumption and a man's trait level of hostility; among those in the intoxicated group, the higher the level of hostility, the greater the belief that forcing sex was justified. These findings demonstrate that, among men who are at risk of being a perpetrator (in this case, have high levels of hostility), alcohol consumption makes them feel more justified in raping.

Turning now to the *effects of alcohol on victims,* the basic pharmacological effects are the same as they are for perpetrators. Alcohol consumption leads to a decline in cognitive functioning such as decision making. Alcohol also leads to a reduction in anxiety, so that a woman may miss signs of danger in her environment. And alcohol consumption may lead women to be less effective in resisting an assault if one occurs (Stoner et al., 2007). None of these research findings are meant to blame the victim, of course. Instead, they point to the complex interactions between the perpetrator's drinking and the victim's drinking that contribute to sexual assault.

Although we have focused, in this section, on the role of alcohol in sexual assault, it is also true that other drugs can be contributing factors. For example, in one study men were followed from adolescence through the 4th year of college (Swartout & White, 2010). Increased use of marijuana over time predicted increased sexual aggression over time.

Rapists

What is the profile of the typical rapist? The basic answer is that there is no typical rapist. Rapists vary tremendously in occupation, education, marital status, previous criminal record, and motivation for committing rape.

What factors predispose men to become rapists?

Compared with other men, rapists tend to have the following characteristics (Gannon & Ward, 2008; Seto & Lalumière, 2010; Thakker et al., 2008; Thompson et al., 2015):

1. They believe rape myths and hold a number of social cognitions that support rape. They believe that women are sexual objects; women are dangerous and deceptive; they have a sense of entitlement involving male superiority and control; the world in general is dangerous; and that certain behaviors are uncontrollable in the face of strong urges.

2. They are characterized by poor inhibition and self-regulation. In particular, they are unable to inhibit aggressive impulses.

3. They lack empathy. Specifically, they fail to understand the suffering that a rape victim experiences.

4. They may have experienced environmental triggers, such as being in a war.

5. They tend to be part of a peer group that approves of forced sex and pressures members to have sex with many different women (Swartout, 2013; Thompson et al., 2013, 2015).

Some rapists commit the crime only once, whereas others are repeat or serial rapists. In one study of undetected rapists—men who admitted to rape on a survey but

had never been prosecuted—the majority had committed the crime more than once (Lisak & Miller, 2002). Those who were repeat offenders averaged about six rapes each. A study of serial rapists who were reported to law enforcement found that serial rapists tended to rape strangers and averaged five rapes each (de Heer, 2016).

One clever study was able to analyze rapists' own descriptions of what they had done (Hipp et al., 2017). Someone on Reddit posed the following question: "Reddit's had a few threads about sexual assault victims, but are there any redditors from the other side of the story? What were your motivations? Do you regret it?" People who had committed sexual assault responded with multiple stories, and the researchers—realizing that it was a treasure trove of data—analyzed the posts using content analysis methods. Part of the beauty of the data is that the perpetrators were posting anonymously and therefore presumably telling the truth. One theme that emerged was victim blaming. Respondents, for example, blamed victims who had flirted with them. Hostile sexism was evident in some responses. One man described how he anally raped his wife once a year and how he treated her worse each year. Other perpetrators claimed uncontrollable biological urges. One of them said "an erect dick has no conscience." Others believed that their hormones controlled their behavior. Some responses indicated objectification of women. One man said that his sex partners were just sex toys to him. Notice that these themes that spontaneously emerged from rapists' accounts of their behavior are quite similar to the characteristics of rapists found by researchers, as listed above.

A major goal of treatment for rapists is to reduce the chance of reoffending (Thakker et al., 2008). Their cognitive distortions and denial that they did anything wrong must be challenged, and they need training in empathy.

Men as Victims of Rape

Women are far more likely than men to be the victims of rape. According to a well-sampled national survey, 18 percent of women and 1.4 percent of men have been raped at some time in their lives (Black et al., 2011). In cases of male rape victims, perpetrators are predominantly male (Black et al., 2011).

Research shows that men who have been raped experience symptoms of PTSD, as women do. Men who have been raped by other men also experience very negative psychological consequences (Walker et al., 2005). It is important for counselors and others in the helping professions to recognize this possibility of male rape victims.

Prison Rape

According to a study of 516 men and women prisoners in a state prison system, 22 percent of the men and 7 percent of the women had been the objects of sexual coercion (Struckman-Johnson et al., 1996). Prison staff were the perpetrators in 18 percent of the cases, fellow prisoners in the remainder. Among the male victims, 53 percent had been forced to have receptive anal sex, sometimes with multiple male perpetrators, and 8 percent were forced to have receptive oral sex. The men reported severe emotional consequences. Inmates offered a number of suggestions for ending prison sexual violence. The most frequent was to segregate the most vulnerable: those who are young, nonviolent, new in prison, White. Many also favored allowing conjugal visits.

Prison rape is a particularly clear example of the way in which rape is an expression of power and aggression; prisoners use it as a means of establishing a dominance hierarchy.

Ethnicity and Rape

We have seen how cultural context can promote or inhibit rape and affect the meaning that people attach to rape. The cultural heritages of the various ethnic groups in the United States provide different cultural contexts for people of those groups, so it is important to consider patterns of rape in U.S. ethnic groups.

Rape has a highly charged meaning in the history of African Americans (Feimster, 2009; Sommerville, 2004). In the period following the Civil War, an African American man convicted of rape or attempted rape of a White woman was typically castrated or lynched. In sharp contrast, there was no penalty for a White man who raped a Black woman (Figure 2). Moreover, stereotypes originating at that time and continuing to the present portray both African American men and African American women as being highly sexual. Black women are so highly sexual, the reasoning goes, that they cannot be raped (Abbey et al., 2010). The result is that African American women have a long history of nondisclosure of rape, a pattern that exceeds even that of White women. Many African American women think that no one will believe they can be raped and that they will have no credibility as rape victims.

A study of Black and White female rape survivors found that they were similar in many ways, such as their self-esteem and coping after the rape (Neville et al., 2004). The Black women's responses, though, were linked to the Jezebel stereotype that Black women are sexually "loose," and therefore cannot be raped. Many of the Black women believed that the Jezebel stereotype was one of the reasons they were raped, and women who endorsed this attribution more strongly showed lower self-esteem.

Sometimes ethnic heritage can help. In Asian cultures, saving face is very important. For Asian American men, the potential for loss of face by raping is a deterrent to such activity (Hall et al., 2005).

Figure 2 Ethnicity and rape. Rape has a highly charged meaning in the history of African Americans. In the time of slavery, although there was no penalty for a White man who raped a Black woman, a Black man convicted of raping a White woman was typically castrated or put to death.

Source: New York Public Library

Preventing Rape

Strategies for preventing rape fall into three categories: (1) avoiding situations in which there is a high risk of rape; (2) if the first strategy has failed, knowing self-defense techniques in case a rape attempt is made; and (3) changing attitudes that contribute to rape.

The first strategy, of course, is to be alert to situations in which there is a high risk of rape and to avoid them. Many university websites post practical information. The following is one example of such guidance that is particularly relevant in potential date-rape situations.

1. *Avoid hazardous situations.* Sexual assault can occur in any situation and is never your fault regardless of the circumstances. However, by taking such steps as traveling accompanied and avoiding alcohol and drugs, you can substantially reduce your risks for being victimized.

2. *Communicate your limits clearly.* If someone starts to offend you or cross a line that you have set for yourself, tell them firmly and early. Polite approaches may be misunderstood or ignored. If the person does not respect your wishes, remove yourself from the situation immediately. Miscommunication can be explained later. Do not give someone the chance to violate your wishes or boundaries. This can often contribute to the guilt felt following unwanted sexual advances, but it does not make it your fault.

3. *Be assertive.* Often passivity can be interpreted as permission—it is not. Be direct and firm with someone who is sexually pressuring you. Tell an acquaintance or your partner what you want—or don't want—and stick with your decision. Regardless, there must always be active consent on both sides. Consent to one thing does not imply consent to another.

4. *Trust your instincts. If you feel you are being pressured into unwanted sex, you probably are.* If you feel uncomfortable or threatened around an acquaintance or your partner, get out of the situation immediately. If you misread someone's signals, you can always explain later.

5. *Respond physically. Even clear communication is not always effective.* Some people simply don't listen or don't care. If either person is intoxicated or high, it may also complicate the situation. However, it is not an excuse for someone to commit sexual assault. If someone is assaulting you and not responding to your objections, you have the right to respond physically or to physically defend yourself if you feel you can do so. If possible, push the person away, scream "No!" and say that you consider what the person is doing to be rape. It is understandable that most people instinctively do not respond forcefully to people they know. It is not your fault if you find that you are unable to do so. (University of North Carolina at Charlotte, 2017)

Many universities and other organizations offer self-defense classes for women, and we believe that every woman should take at least one such course (Figure 3). Research

Figure 3 Self-defense classes for women. Many experts believe that all women should take such classes to gain the skills necessary to defend themselves in the case of an attempted rape.

©Dean Mitchell/Getty Images

Figure 4 Child abuse has become a major concern, as exemplified by this educational poster.

©Marjorie Farrell/The Image Works

shows that fighting back—fighting, yelling, fleeing—increases a woman's likelihood of thwarting a rape attempt (Ahrens et al., 2008; Brecklin & Ullman, 2005).

Self-defense, though, is useful to the woman only in defending herself once an attack has been made. It would be better if rape could be rooted out at a far earlier stage so that attacks never occur. To do this, our society would need to make a radical change in the way it socializes males (Ahrens et al., 2008; Zurbriggen, 2010). If little boys were not so pressed to be aggressive and tough, perhaps rapists would never develop. If adolescent boys did not have to demonstrate that they are hypersexual, perhaps there would be no rapists. As we noted earlier, rape is unheard of in some societies where males are socialized to be nurturant rather than aggressive.

A variety of types of rape-prevention programs have been tested, often in academic settings such as with incoming first-year college students. The programs generally are based on one of several strategies (Gidycz et al., 2011):

1. *Awareness-based programs* aim to raise people's awareness of the prevalence of sexual assault and thereby create community change.
2. *Empathy-based programs* seek to increase the audience's understanding of the consequences for victims, thereby increasing empathy for them.
3. *Social norms-based programs* encourage individuals to question the gender-role norms that support violence against women.

4. *Skills-based programs* teach people, especially women, skills that will decrease their risk of being the objects of sexual violence (e.g., avoid excessive drinking).
5. *Bystander intervention programs* encourage people to intervene actively if they see a situation that may become violent or behaviors that reinforce social norms that support violence.

A crucial aspect of effective programs involves having the participants actively practice skills (Gidycz et al., 2011). Passive programs with an expert lecturing to a class are less effective. Peer-led programs that focus on a single gender in a small group (e.g., an athletic team), and for multiple sessions, seem to be most effective. Evaluations of the popular bystander-intervention program Green Dot have found it to be effective in reducing rates of sexual assault on campus (Coker et al., 2015, 2016).

Child Sexual Abuse

In this section we discuss the sexual coercion of children, including the broad category of child sexual abuse and one specific subcategory, incest, when the sexual abuse occurs within the family.

Patterns of Child Sexual Abuse

How common is child sexual abuse? According to a meta-analysis of data across 22 countries, 22 percent of women

Table 1 Categories of People Who Sexually Abuse Children, as Reported by Adults Recalling Incidents of Sexual Abuse in Their Childhood

	Percentage of Reported Abuse by Category*	
Perpetrators	Women	Men
Stranger	7%	4%
Teacher	3	4
Family friend	29	40
Older friend of respondent	1	4
Older brother	9	4
Stepfather or mother's boyfriend	9	2
Father	7	1
Other relative	29	13
Other	19	17

*Percentages do not total 100 because some respondents reported on multiple categories of abuse.

Source: Laumann et al. (1994), adapted from Table 9.14, p. 343.

and 8 percent of men had suffered some form of sexual abuse prior to age 18 (Pereda et al., 2009). The figures for the United States specifically were 25 percent of women and 8 percent of men. Age 18 represents a broad definition of "child," but the statistics do not go down much if the age is set at 15 or even 12 (Freyd et al., 2005; Pereda et al., 2009).

It is common for cases to go unreported. In a sample of adults, among those who had experienced child sexual abuse (CSA), 16 percent never disclosed the abuse and 51 percent did not disclose it until more than 5 years after the events (Hébert et al., 2009). Males are less likely to disclose than females are.

The great majority of perpetrators of child sexual abuse are men. According to the NHSLS, for girls almost all the cases involved sexual contact with men; for boys, some cases involved men and some women, although cases involving men were considerably more common. In another study, 94 percent of all perpetrators were men (Finkelhor, 1984). A number of factors probably account for this great imbalance. Men in our culture are socialized more toward seeing sexuality as focused on sexual acts rather than as part of an emotional relationship. The sexual script for men involves partners who are smaller and younger than themselves, whereas women's sexual script involves partners who are larger and older than they are.

In the majority of cases, both for boys and girls, the activity involves only touching of the genitals (Hébert et al., 2009). About 20 percent of cases of CSA involve forced sexual intercourse.

Sexual abuse may occur at astoundingly young ages. About 10 percent of cases of CSA occur before the child is 6 (Hébert et al., 2009).

Table 1 shows the relationship between adults who committed child sexual abuse and their victims, according to the NHSLS. Notice that sexual abuse by strangers is not common. Most abusers are family friends and relatives.

Child sexual abuse can involve **sexual solicitation on the Internet** (Wolak et al., 2008). In such cases, a sexual predator "meets" a child or adolescent online, gains the youth's confidence, and arranges an in-person meeting of the two. A well-sampled survey of youth between the ages of 10 and 17 found that 18 percent of girls and 8 percent of boys had received a sexual solicitation on the Internet (Mitchell et al., 2007). Only a few of those incidents resulted in an actual meeting, but the sexual solicitation itself can be distressing.

The latest form of online exploitation is termed **sextortion,** which refers to threats to expose sexual images with the goal of coercing victims to provide additional pictures or engage in sex (Wolak et al., 2018). Typically adolescents are the victims. One study recruited a large sample of victims through Facebook (Wolak et al., 2018). Roughly 60 percent of the victims knew the perpetrator in person, and most victims had given the pictures when they were in a relationship with the perp. A majority felt that they had been pressured, tricked, or forced to provide the images in the first place. In other cases, the perp had recorded the images without consent. Perps wanted all kinds of things in return for not publicizing the photos: for the victim to stay in or go back to a relationship with the perp; for the

Sexual solicitation of youth on the Internet: Cases in which a sexual predator "meets" a child or adolescent online, gains the youth's confidence, and arranges an in-person meeting. **Sextortion:** Online threats to expose sexual images with the goal of coercing victims to provide additional pictures or to engage in sex.

victim to give more sexual pictures or videos; or to meet the victim in person. Perps threatened to post the original image online, send the image to friends, and send the image to the victim's family. In some cases, the sextortion continued for 6 months or more. Victims reported impacts on themselves that required seeing a mental health counselor and leaving school or changing schools.

Incest is typically defined as sexual contact between blood relatives, although the definition is often extended to include sex between nonblood relatives—for example, between stepfather and stepdaughter.

The NHSLS data (Table 1) show what a large percentage of child sexual abuse cases are perpetrated by adults within the family. However, because it specified that the sexual contact had to be with an adult or an adolescent aged 14 or older, the NHSLS missed one category of incest, namely, sibling incest. In a general survey of undergraduates, 15 percent of the females and 10 percent of the males said that they had had a sexual experience with a sibling (Finkelhor, 1980). It is likely that sibling incest is the most common form of incest.

Most people, however, feel an aversion to sex with a sibling (Lieberman & Smith, 2012). It is thought that this aversion is an evolutionary adaptation, because offspring of close relatives are likely to suffer from serious genetic diseases.

Impact on the Victim

Many therapists who are experienced with cases of child sexual abuse believe that the effects on the victim can be serious and long lasting (Herman, 1981). Consider the following case:

> A 25-year-old office worker was seen in the emergency room with an acute anxiety attack. She was pacing, agitated, unable to eat or sleep, and had a feeling of impending doom. She related a vivid fantasy of being pursued by a man with a knife. The previous day she had been cornered in the office by her boss, who aggressively propositioned her. She needed the job badly and did not want to lose it, but she dreaded the thought of returning to work. It later emerged in psychotherapy that this episode of sexual harassment had reawakened previously repressed memories of sexual assaults by her father. From the age of 6 until midadolescence, her father had repeatedly exhibited himself to her and insisted that she masturbate him. The experience of being entrapped at work had recalled her childhood feelings of helplessness and fear. (Herman, 1981, p. 8)

If a case is reported and prosecuted, the child may be as traumatized by testifying in court as by the abuse itself. Repeatedly testifying about severe abuse is associated with worse mental health outcomes (Quas et al., 2005). Interestingly, the

Incest: Sexual activity between relatives.

perpetrator receiving a light sentence is also associated with worse mental health outcomes.

Adults who were sexually abused as children display more depression, anxiety, eating disorders, alcohol and drug dependence, negative feelings about sex, and difficulty forming stable, safe romantic relationships, compared with controls (Bulik et al., 2001; Feiring et al., 2009; Kendler et al., 2000a; Rellini & Meston, 2011; Testa et al., 2005). The risk of these difficulties is greater if attempted or completed intercourse occurred, if the abuse was by a relative, and if the victim told someone and received a negative response from that person. Adult survivors of child sexual abuse are also more likely to experience sexual disorders such as fears of sex (sexual aversion), lack of sexual desire, and lack of arousal (Meston et al., 2006; Najman et al., 2005). Women who were sexually abused as children are also more likely to be preoccupied with sex, younger at the time of their first voluntary intercourse, and more likely to be teen mothers (Noll et al., 2003). Their sexuality is ambivalent—they experience both sexual aversion and a preoccupation with sex. Boys who experienced CSA are more likely to engage in risky sexual behaviors (Homma et al., 2012).

Child sexual abuse (CSA) has effects not only on mental health, but on physical health as well. Adults who were victims of CSA are one and a half times as likely as those who weren't abused to have had health problems in the past year (Sachs-Ericsson et al., 2005).

One study, however, reached different conclusions. In a general survey of undergraduates, 17 percent of the students reported having had a sibling sexual encounter in childhood (Greenwald & Leitenberg, 1989; see also Finkelhor, 1980). There were no differences between this group and those who had had no such encounters, on a variety of measures of sexual behavior and adjustment, including incidence of premarital intercourse, age at first intercourse, number of sexual partners, sexual satisfaction, and sexual disorders. The researchers concluded that childhood sexual experiences with a sibling close in age have no effect—positive or negative—on adult sexual adjustment, on average.

What, then, are the psychological consequences of childhood sexual abuse for the victim? Childhood sexual abuse may not be damaging to the victim in some cases, particularly if it is brother–sister incest when the two are close in age and it is consensual. However, in most cases childhood sexual abuse is psychologically damaging and may lead to symptoms such as depression and PTSD. The evidence indicates that the extent of distress is associated with a number of factors, including, especially, the severity of the abuse (Kallstrom-Fuqua et al., 2004). Patterns of sexual abuse can range from 5 minutes of fondling by a distant cousin to repeated forced intercourse by a father or stepfather over a period of several years. The effects of CSA are the most severe when it involved intercourse, occurred repeatedly over years, and was committed by a father or stepfather (Fleming et al., 1999; Kendler et al., 2000a).

Treatments such as cognitive behavioral therapy are available and effective in treating adults with PTSD following child sexual abuse (McDonagh et al., 2005).

The Offenders

What do the data say about child sexual abusers? Are they likely to repeat the offense? Are there effective treatments for them?

Pedophilia involves an adult having fantasies or actual sexual activity with a prepubescent child, generally age 13 or younger (American Psychiatric Association, 2013). To meet the official criteria for diagnosis, the person must have intense sexually arousing fantasies, sexual urges, or behaviors, over a period of at least 6 months, that involve sexual activity with a prepubescent child. Pedophilia is a paraphilia, to use the terminology introduced in the chapter "Variations in Sexual Behavior." Some experts distinguish between pedophilia as a sexual attraction to children versus acting on those urges. At least some people who experience pedophilic urges never act on them (Seto, 2009).

> **When child molesters are released from prison, how likely are they to reoffend?**

Pedophiles fall into a number of categories, depending on the gender of the children they are attracted to and other factors. In one study of 678 pedophiles, all of them men, 27 percent were attracted to boys, 47 percent to girls, and 25 percent to both (Blanchard et al., 1999). Pedophiles tend to be repeat offenders, and their patterns of preference tend to be stable over time. In one sample recruited from websites for adults attracted to children, respondents, on average, found themselves attracted to children when they themselves were 14 (Bailey et al., 2016).

Child molesters score low on measures of heterosocial competence (Dreznick, 2003). That is, they lack the interpersonal skills to function well in adult heterosexual relationships. Pedophiles are more likely than controls to have had accidents involving head injury and unconsciousness before the age of 6 (Blanchard et al., 2002). This suggests that some injury to the developing brain may create this disorder in some cases. Brain scans show that, compared with controls, pedophiles have decreased volume in certain regions of gray matter, including the orbitofrontal cortex and amygdala. The pedophiles also showed atypical patterns of connectivity between certain regions (Cantor et al., 2015).

Researchers are very interested in developing measures that might identify pedophiles who have not been arrested, and perhaps have not even offended yet (Seto, 2004). Sophisticated cognitive tests using reaction times indicate that pedophiles have a strong mental association between children and sex, whereas nonpedophiles have an association between adults and sex (Gray et al., 2005). Phallometric measures, such as those discussed in the chapters "Sex Research" and "Gender and Sexuality," indicate that men who are attracted to child pornography show greater arousal to child photos than to adult photos, and their arousal to child photos is even greater than the arousal of men who have actually sexually offended against children (Seto et al., 2006). Possession of child pornography itself might be an indicator (Seto, 2004). Measures such as these may provide ways to identify men who are likely to offend even before they commit their crime.

One study that attempted to answer the question of recidivism (repeat offending) followed a sample of 206 child molesters and found a recidivism rate of 23 percent (Moulden et al., 2009). Most experts believe that pedophilia itself—the sexual attraction to children—cannot be changed; the best that we can hope for with treatment is to increase the individual's voluntary control over acting on those urges (Seto, 2009).

A number of treatments for pedophilia are in use: surgical castration, antiandrogen drugs, SSRIs (explained below), behavior therapy, and cognitive behavioral therapy (Abracen & Looman, 2004; Camilleri & Quinsey, 2008; Seto, 2009). As discussed in the chapter "Sex Hormones, Sexual Differentiation, and the Menstrual Cycle," the idea behind surgical castration is that removal of a man's testes sharply reduces his levels of testosterone, with the hope that his sexual and aggressive behavior will also be reduced sharply. Leuprolide acetate (LA, trade name Lupron) is an antiandrogen drug—that is, it reduces the action of testosterone in the body—used in the treatment of child sexual abusers. It does seem to be effective in reducing sexual urges (Turner & Briken, 2018). Other antiandrogen drugs seem to be less effective. One class of antidepressants (the SSRIs, which include Prozac and Zoloft) has also been tried in the treatment of sex offenders (Bradford & Greenberg, 1996). Its use is based on the assumption that sex offending can be a particular kind of obsessive–compulsive disorder, and such disorders generally respond well to these antidepressants.

Behavioral treatment generally aims to teach pedophiles to control their sexual arousal to children (Seto, 2009). One method involves aversive classical conditioning, in which an unpleasant stimulus (e.g., the smell of ammonia) is repeatedly paired with sexual pictures of children. This method does seem to increase the individual's voluntary control of his sexual arousal to children. Behavioral treatments to increase pedophiles' positive, appropriate sexual arousal to adults—which would be another important component to the solution—have been less successful. *Cognitive behavioral treatment* targets not only behaviors but also attitudes and beliefs.

> **Pedophilia:** An adult having sexual activity with a prepubescent child.

A major review of both drug and psychotherapy interventions with sex offenders concluded that there is no strong evidence of the success of either kind of treatment (Långström et al., 2013). This conclusion is due, in part, to a shortage of studies, and especially a shortage of high-quality studies. It doesn't necessarily mean the treatments don't work—just that we don't have very good scientific evidence yet. More attention to interventions and evaluating them well is needed. Some experts question whether, at present, there are any successful treatments for pedophiles (Camilleri & Quinsey, 2008).

Sexual Harassment

The issue of sexual harassment exploded into public awareness beginning in 2017 with the #MeToo movement, which encouraged victims to tweet about the issue and give people an idea of the magnitude of the problem. This occurred at about the same time as prominent Hollywood producer Harvey Weinstein fell in the face of extensive allegations of sexual harassment by him (Figure 5). Other well-known figures were also the object of allegations and resigned or were fired from their jobs, including newsmen Matt Lauer and Charlie Rose. Prominent American actresses came forward in support of the movement, including Gwyneth Paltrow and Jennifer Lawrence. The movement has now spread around the globe. The issue is a powerful one—it can force a victim out of a job, but it also might force a perpetrator from a job.

The issue is not just about celebrities, though. It can hit all kinds of workplaces. For example, the scientific community was so concerned about sexual harassment in its ranks that the National Academy of Sciences commissioned a report on sexual harassment within universities in the sciences, engineering, and medicine (Johnson et al., 2018).

The official definition of sexual harassment, given by the U.S. Equal Employment Opportunity Commission (EEOC, 1993), is as follows:

Unwelcome sexual advances, requests for sexual favors, and other verbal or physical conduct of a sexual nature constitute sexual harassment when

A. Submission to such conduct is made either explicitly or implicitly a term or condition of an individual's employment or academic advancement,

B. Submission to or rejection of such conduct by an individual is used as the basis for academic or employment decisions affecting that individual, or

C. Such conduct has the purpose or effect of unreasonably interfering with an individual's work or academic performance or creating an intimidating, hostile, or offensive working or educational environment.

The key ingredients for sexual harassment, then, are that the sexual advances are unwelcome and are coercive in the sense that the victim's job or grade is at stake. This is termed *quid pro quo harassment* (quid pro quo meaning "I'll do something for you if you'll do something for me"). Point C of the definition specifies that a hostile environment also constitutes harassment—that is, a work environment that is so hostile (constant lewd innuendoes, verbal intimidation, and so on) that an employee cannot work effectively fits the definition of harassment, even if no explicit sexual proposition has been directed to the employee.

(a)

(b)

Figure 5   The issue of sexual harassment exploded into public awareness beginning in 2017 with the #MeToo movement. *(a)* Prominent Hollywood producer Harvey Weinstein being arrested. *(b)* Women protesting against sexual harassment.

(a) ©lev radin/Shutterstock; (b) ©Ronen Tivony/NurPhoto/Getty Images

The EEOC definition addresses sexual harassment at work and in education. Sexual harassment may occur in other contexts as well, such as medical settings or on the street (Wesselmann & Kelly, 2010).

Sexual Harassment at Work

Sexual harassment at work may take a number of different forms. A prospective employer may make it clear that sexual activity is a prerequisite to being hired. Stories of such incidents are rampant among actresses, for example, as documented by the #MeToo movement. Once on the job, sexual activity may be made a condition for continued employment, for a promotion, or for other benefits such as a raise. Here is one case:

> I work at a family-owned restaurant. Because I am a bartender, it is often just me behind the bar. On numerous occasions, I have caught one of the owners staring at my backside as I am getting things out of the refrigerator behind the bar. He has also blatantly stared at my legs, if I am wearing a skirt, while I am trying to speak with him. He has also shown me how to clean the nozzle used to foam milk for coffee drinks, but does so in a fashion that looks much like someone manually stimulating a certain piece of the male anatomy, and then looks at me with a grin on his face. There have been times when the dishwasher wasn't working and he made comments to the male bartender, as I was standing right there, such as, "Be gentle with her . . . you have to go slowly so you don't hurt it . . . it needs lubrication." He has walked up behind me and blown on my neck.
>
> All of the comments and actions are very unnerving. (From a student essay)

This situation fits the definition of hostile environment harassment given earlier. It is clear how psychologically damaging such environments are to the victim.

Surveys indicate that sexual harassment at work is far more common than many people realize. In a survey of federal employees, 33 percent had been sexually harassed (Jackson & Newman, 2004). In a well-sampled survey of adult Americans, 47 percent reported that they had experienced sexual harassment at work (Rospenda et al., 2009). Averaged over many studies, between 25 and 50 percent of women have been sexually harassed at work, counting harassment both by supervisors and by coworkers (Ilies et al., 2003).

Sexual harassment and sexual assault in the military have become a serious problem. A nationally representative survey of veterans found that 32 percent of the women and 5 percent of the men had suffered military sexual trauma, which includes both sexual harassment and sexual assault while serving in the military (Klingensmith et al., 2014). Rates were considerably higher among younger veterans (aged 18 to 29) than among older veterans. Women who are in combat have an even higher risk of military sexual trauma (LeardMann et al., 2013).

Both female and male victims report that harassment has negative effects on their emotional and physical health, their ability to work with others on the job, and their feelings about work (Chan et al., 2008; Willness et al., 2007). However, men are more likely to feel that the overtures from women ended up being reciprocal and mutually enjoyable. Women, in contrast, are more likely to report damaging consequences, including being fired or quitting their job. There is evidence linking the experience of sexual harassment to depression, anxiety, and PTSD (Klingensmith et al., 2014; Rederstorff et al., 2007). Even subtle sexual harassment, such as asking, "Do you have a boyfriend?" in a job interview can damage women's performance in the interview (Woodzicka & LaFrance, 2005).

Men who are sexual harassers tend to be repeat offenders (Lucero et al., 2006). Therefore, unless they are disciplined, they will simply move on to another victim.

Why does sexual harassment at work occur? According to one theory, it results from a combination of gender stereotyping and men's ambivalent motives (Fiske & Glick, 1995; Krings & Facchin, 2009). Stereotypes of women in U.S. culture are complex and include three distinct clusters: sexy, nontraditional (e.g., feminist), and traditional (e.g., mother). Many men have ambivalent motives in their interactions with women because they desire both dominance and intimacy. The researchers argue that there are four types of harassment. With the first, *earnest harassment,* the man is truly motivated by a desire for sexual intimacy, but he won't take no for an answer and persists with unwelcome sexual advances. He stereotypes women as sexy. With the second type, *hostile harassment,* the man's motivation is domination of the woman, often because he perceives her as being competitive with him in the workplace. He holds the stereotype of women as nontraditional and therefore competitive with him. His response to rejection by a woman is increased harassment. The third and fourth types of harassment involve ambivalent combinations of the two basic motives, dominance and a desire for intimacy. In the third type, *paternalistic-ambivalent harassment,* the man is motivated by a desire for sexual intimacy but also by a paternalistic desire to be like a father to the woman. This type of harassment may be particularly insidious because the man thinks of himself as acting benevolently toward the woman. Finally, the fourth type, *competitive-ambivalent harassment,* mixes real sexual attraction and a stereotype of women as sexy with the man's hostile desire to dominate the woman, which is based on his belief that she is nontraditional and competitive with him. This theory

What behaviors in the workplace count as sexual harassment?

gives us an excellent view of the complex motives that underlie men's sexual harassment of women.

Social psychologists have developed a clever method for studying sexual harassment experimentally in the laboratory, the Computer Harassment Paradigm (Maass et al., 2003; see also Parrott et al., 2012). In one study, college men were first exposed to a female confederate of the experimenters, who expressed either strong feminist beliefs (intentions to get a high-level career in an area usually reserved for men, and involvement in an organization for women's rights) or traditional beliefs. The men then had the opportunity to harass the woman by sending her pornographic material on a computer (she did not actually receive it). The men exposed to the feminist sent significantly more pornography to her than did men in the control group. However, not all men in the feminist-threat condition responded with harassment; those who did so were mainly men who identified strongly with the male role. The findings of this experiment are consistent with the type of harassment known as hostile environment harassment.

Sexual harassment at work is more than just an annoyance. Particularly for women, because they are more likely to be harassed by supervisors, it can make a critical difference in career advancement. For the working-class woman

Figure 6   Sexual harassment at work: This man is engaging in inappropriate touching, but if he is her supervisor, she may be hesitant to protest.

©Photodisc/Getty Images

who supports her family, being fired for sexual noncompliance is a catastrophe. The power of coercion is enormous.

Sexual Harassment in Education: An A for a Lay

Sexual harassment in education was brought to public attention when, in 1977, women students sued Yale University, complaining of sexual harassment, in the important case *Alexander v. Yale*. The case recognized that sexual harassment of women in education was a violation of Title IX of the Civil Rights Act.

A survey at a Big 10 university found that 33 percent of undergraduates, 43 percent of graduate students, and 50 percent of medical students had experienced harassment by faculty or staff (Johnson et al., 2018).

Sexual harassment is not confined to college or to teachers harassing students. One survey of 14- and 15-year-olds in the Netherlands found that 24 percent of the girls and 11 percent of the boys had been the objects of sexual harassment (Timmerman, 2003). Of those cases, 73 percent reported harassment by peers and 27 percent harassment by teachers (or other school-related adults such as a tutor or principal). Of the teachers who were harassers, 90 percent were men. The psychological consequences were more severe when the harasser was a teacher than when this person was a peer. A U.S. study found that 65 percent of girls and 78 percent of boys reported peer sexual harassment during ninth grade (Petersen & Hyde, 2009).

A National Academy of Sciences report concluded that several institutional factors contribute to sexual harassment in academia (Johnson et al., 2018), and these factors apply to most organizations.

1. *Perceived institutional tolerance for sexual harassment.* The best predictor of sexual harassment occurring within an organization is the perception of tolerance for sexual harassment within the organization. When an institution shows that it is intolerant of sexual harassment, the environment improves. Institutions can signal their intolerance of sexual harassment by supporting and protecting targets of harassment; investigating harassment fairly and in a timely manner; and by appropriately punishing harassers.

2. *Environments where men outnumber women (male-dominated environments).* These environments are found in areas such as engineering and some areas of medical schools.

3. *Hierarchical power structure within the organization.* With such an organizational structure, workers depend heavily on those higher in the organization, so workers are unwilling to report harassment because of fear of retaliation from powerful others.

4. *Compliance with Title IX regulations that is only symbolic.* Federal requirements mandate that universities and

other organizations address sexual harassment with programs such as training, but often the goal becomes avoiding liability rather than actually changing institutional climate.

5. *Uninformed leadership in the organization.* Some individuals, such as university presidents and deans, have been ignorant about sexual harassment issues and have sought to cover up reports to avoid embarrassment to the institution. Much of this is changing with the #MeToo movement and a trend for victims to come forward to report and demand change.

Doctor–Patient Sex

Legal definitions of sexual harassment focus on these problems in the workplace or in education. However, there is another category of coercive and potentially damaging sexual encounters–those between a psychotherapist and client, or between other professionals, such as physicians, and patients (Plaut, 2008). Professional societies such as the American Psychological Association state clearly in their codes that such behaviors are unethical. Nonetheless, they occur and can be damaging.

Experts regard this kind of situation as having the potential for serious emotional damage to the client (Pope, 2001). Like the cases of sexual harassment discussed earlier, it is a situation of unequal power, in which the more powerful person–the doctor–imposes sexual activity on the less powerful person, the patient. The situation is regarded as particularly serious in psychotherapy because people have opened themselves up emotionally to the therapist and therefore are extremely vulnerable emotionally.

Critical THINKing Skill

Analyzing an argument

In the context of critical thinking skills, an argument is a set of statements that has a *conclusion* (perhaps more than one) and at least one *reason* for the conclusion (Halpern, 2002). Consider the following case, which occurred in 2012 (Betz, 2012).

Robb Evans, a police officer, is believed to have done the following. After drinking eight beers, he drove to the Green Room, a Flagstaff supper club that hosts live music events. Evans flashed his badge to get into a concert for free. Once inside, he walked up behind a woman, who was a friend of a friend, put his hand up her skirt, and ran his fingers across her genitals. A jury later convicted him of sexual abuse, which carries a sentence of 6 months to 2½ years in prison. In sentencing, however, Judge Jacqueline Hatch gave him only probation (and time already served). Judge Hatch said that she considered the defendant's lack of a criminal record and strong community support in her sentencing. She also told the victim that she should have been more vigilant, and that if she hadn't been there that night, none of this would have happened.

Answer the following questions before reading the discussion in the paragraph that follows.

1. Did Judge Hatch state an argument?
2. What was her conclusion?
3. What were her reasons for the conclusion?

Judge Hatch's conclusion was that Evans deserved no jail time, only probation–that is, that he deserved little or no punishment. She gave two reasons for her conclusion: (1) Evans had no previous criminal record, and (2) the community supported a light sentence (she had received 25 letters on his behalf). She may have also had a third reason, even though she did not mention it in her list of considerations. That reason was that, according to Judge Hatch, the victim should not have been in the Green Room at all. In saying this, she held the victim partially responsible for the crime (and the perpetrator therefore less responsible), which represents blaming the victim.

In analyzing an argument, another important skill is to evaluate the quality of the reasons. How would you evaluate each of her arguments–how strong is each?

SUMMARY

Rape

Rape is defined as nonconsensual oral, anal, or vaginal penetration obtained by force, by threat of force, or when the victim is incapable of giving consent. A woman's lifetime risk of being raped is approximately 20 percent. Victims may experience posttraumatic stress disorder (PTSD) as a result of the assault. Date rape and intimate partner rape are more common than many people realize. There are four major theoretical views of rape: victim precipitated, psychopathology of rapists, feminist, and social disorganization. Alcohol plays a role in rape, involving both the perpetrator's consumption and the victim's consumption. Compared with other men, rapists tend to hold beliefs that support rape, and to lack empathy. Rape has particularly charged meanings for some ethnic groups within the United States. A variety of approaches are available for rape-prevention programs.

Child Sexual Abuse

Approximately 22 percent of women and 8 percent of men report that they experienced child sexual abuse. Most sexual abuse of children is committed by a relative or a family friend. People who were sexually abused as children are more likely than others to have symptoms such as anxiety, PTSD, depression, and health complaints. More severe psychological consequences are likely to occur when the perpetrator is a close family member who is an adult (sibling incest seems less harmful) and when the sexual contact is extensive and involves penetration. Experts debate whether treatments for pedophiles are effective.

Sexual Harassment

Sexual harassment, whether on the job or in education, involves unwelcome sexual advances when there is some coercion involved, such as making the sexual contact a condition of being hired or receiving an A grade in a course. In another form of sexual harassment, the work or educational environment is made so hostile, on a sexual and gender basis, that the employee cannot work effectively. Surveys show that sexual harassment at work is common. In severe cases it can lead to damaging psychological consequences such as PTSD for the victim. In education, the data indicate that sexual harassment is common and peer sexual harassment is especially common. This abuse can lead to negative consequences for the student, such as being forced to change majors or dropout of school. Several institutional factors can contribute to sexual harassment in an organization, including perceived institutional tolerance for sexual harassment. Sex between doctor and patient is a violation of professional ethics.

SUGGESTIONS FOR FURTHER READING

Feimster, Crystal. (2009). *Southern horrors: Women and the politics of rape and lynching.* Cambridge, MA: Harvard University Press. Feimster, an expert in African American studies, chronicles the deadly combination of race, rape, and lynching in the South after the Civil War.

Levey, Tania. (2018). *Sexual harassment online: Shaming and silencing women in the digital age.* Boulder, CO: Lynne Rienner. The Internet offers a whole new arena for sexual harassment that is unregulated. Sociologist Levey documents the issues.

Raine, Nancy V. (1998). *After silence: Rape and my journey back.* New York: Crown. Raine, a professional writer, provides an intense account of the aftermath of being raped.

Are **YOU** Curious?

1. Why do some people pay for sex?
2. How big of an issue is sex trafficking?
3. What effects does viewing erotica/ pornography have on sexual behavior?

Read this chapter to find out.

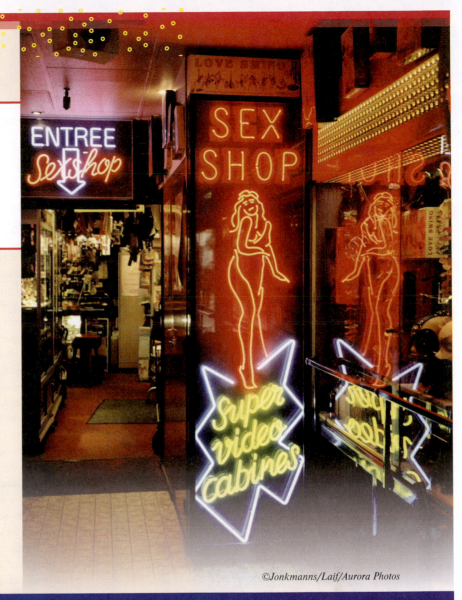

©Jonkmanns/Laif/Aurora Photos

CHAPTER

16

Sex for Sale

CHAPTER HIGHLIGHTS

Pornography is an expression not of human erotic feeling and desire, and not a love of the life of the body, but of a fear of bodily knowledge, and a desire to silence eros.*

*Susan Griffin. (1981). *Pornography and Silence*. New York: Harper & Row. Used by permission of the author.

The exchange of sex for money is a prominent feature of many contemporary societies. The porn industry alone involves at least $13 billion a year in economic activity in the United States (Harris, 2009). In this chapter, we consider two ways in which sex can be bought and sold: prostitution and pornography. Both involve complex legal issues and public controversy, but they also attract a steady stream of eager customers.

Prostitution

Prostitutes or **commercial sex workers** ("hookers") engage in partnered sexual activity or sexualized interactions in return for money, material gifts, or some other form of payment such as drugs (Dewey, 2015). As social critics have pointed out, some dating and living arrangements and long-term relationships, including certain marriages, also fall in this category, so we add to the definition of prostitution that the sex is relatively promiscuous and done in a fairly undiscriminating fashion.

Venues for Sex Work

There are a number of settings or venues in which commercial sexual activity occurs. The nature of the venue or social/sexual context influences the type of sex worker and client found there (e.g., race, social class), the activity that occurs, and its associated risks. Research has focused primarily on female sex workers providing services to male clients. However, keep in mind that there are heterosexual male and female, gay, lesbian, bisexual, and transgender sex workers and clients.

The Urban Institute conducted a large-scale research project to gather information about the "Underground Commercial Sex Trade" (Dank et al., 2014). Researchers interviewed 260 underground economy participants—pimps, traffickers, former sex workers, and child pornographers—and law enforcement personnel. The research focused on eight cities, and the published study provides a detailed description of venues in each of the cities.

The **call girl**—notice the diminutive "girl"—works out of her own residence, making appointments with clients by a landline, cell phone, or online. She is often from a middle-class background and may be a college graduate. She dresses expensively and lives in an upscale neighborhood. A call girl in a medium-size city may charge a minimum of $150 per hour and more if she engages in atypical activities; call girls in major metropolitan areas charge $200 or more per hour. A call girl can earn a great deal of money. But she also has heavy business expenses: an expensive residence, an extensive wardrobe, online marketing, bills for makeup and hairdressers, medical bills for maintaining her health, and tips for doormen and landlords.

A call girl may have a number of regular customers and may accept new clients only on referral. Because she makes dates by telephone or Internet, she can exercise close control over whom she sees and over her schedule. She usually sees clients in her residence, which allows her also to control the setting in which she works. In addition to sexual gratification, she often provides an illusion of intimacy (Lever & Dolnick, 2010). She may provide other services, such as accompanying clients to business and social gatherings. Call girls have considerable autonomy, and their physical and health risks are reduced by the setting in which they work. Many call girls advertise on specialized websites (Bernstein, 2007).

Another venue for commercial sex work is the **brothel.** In the 1800s and early 1900s there were many successful brothels in the United States. They varied from storefront clipjoints, where the customer's money was stolen while he was sexually occupied, to elegant mansions where the customer was treated like a distinguished dinner guest. Brothels declined in number after World War II. Brothels remain in Nevada, where prostitution is legal in five counties. Brothels continued to operate in major cities in 2007; in several cities, the workers were Latinas, and Latinos were the preferred clientele (Dank et al., 2014). The rates were generally $25 to $30 for 15 minutes.

The contemporary equivalent is **in-call services,** which employ women working regular shifts in an apartment or condo, servicing clients who come to the apartment. These services provide sexual gratification; charges are on an hourly basis. In major cities the charge is $150 or $200 per hour; in exchange, the client can participate in standard sexual activity including fellatio, cunnilingus, and vaginal intercourse. Many in-call services require initial contact by telephone, although others advertise their

---

Prostitutes/commercial sex workers: People who engage in sexual acts in return for money or drugs and do so in a promiscuous, fairly nondiscriminating fashion.

Call girl: The most expensive and exclusive category of prostitutes.

Brothel (BRAH-thul): A house of prostitution where prostitutes and customers meet for sexual activity.

In-call service: A residence in which prostitutes work regular shifts, selling sexual services on an hourly basis.

Figure 1 Streetwalkers have little control over the conditions in which they work and are at risk of assault, rape, and arrest.

©Katarzyna Białasiewicz/123RF

location in specialized media or a website. A sex worker in this setting generally has less autonomy than a call girl; there is usually a manager or madam who determines the conditions of work and the fees to be charged and who collects a substantial percentage of each fee. In-call workers have less choice of clients and may be expected to service several per shift.

Another contemporary setting for commercial sex is the **massage parlor.** Some massage parlors provide legitimate massage therapy. In others, male and female employees sell sexual services; these often advertise "sensual massage" or "stripassage," making it pretty clear which type of parlor they are. Some parlors offer a standard list of services and prices; others allow the masseuse or masseur to decide what they will do with a particular client and possibly how much of a "tip" is required for that activity. Massage parlors vary greatly in decor and price. Some are located in "professional" buildings, expensively decorated, and provide food and drinks in addition to sexual gratification. Charges may range from $100 to $300 or more. Such parlors may accept charge cards, with the business listed on the monthly statement as a restaurant. At the other end of the scale, storefront parlors, often located in "commercial sex districts," offer no amenities and charge rates of $40 to $100. Massage parlors offering sexual services in major cities are generally operated by Asian men and women and staffed by women from China, Korea, the Philippines, and Thailand (Dank et al., 2014).

The fact that massage parlors vary from high-end settings with expensive services to storefronts that provide

no amenities and cheap services is not unusual. The sex industry in Vietnam consists of three distinct venues, organized by the social class status of both clients and workers (Hoang, 2011). The "low-end sector" consists of barber shops where local poor, often migrant women serve local working class men. The middle sector consists of bars in which young, attractive women work as bartenders and provide services to clients; the clients are often tourists. The high-end is upscale bars where women of high status "hang out" and meet high-status Vietnamese men, and they may develop continuing relationships with them. The fact that sex workers and their clients are of similar social status is characteristic of sex work in many parts of the world.

Another venue for a sex business is the *escort service.* These services have revealing names such as Alternative Lifestyle Services, First Affair, All Yours, Versatile Entertainment, and Hubbies for Hire. Most escort services employ both men and women who will engage in sexual activity; like massage parlors, the service may have a standard menu, or the escort may have the autonomy to decide what activities they will do with a client. Prostitution in this setting is referred to as an **out-call service** because the escorts go to the clients. This is obviously a more risky business in that the escort cannot control the setting in which the services are provided. Escorts are usually required to telephone the service when they arrive and when they leave the client's location. This not only contributes to their safety but

Massage parlor: A place where massages, as well as sexual services, can generally be purchased.
Out-call service: A service that sends a sex worker to a location specified by the client to provide sexual services.

Figure 2 Denise Richards, known as an actress in films and The Real Housewives of Beverly Hills, was a high-end escort before breaking into Hollywood (therichest.com).

©Noel Vasquez/Getty Images

allows the service to monitor how long the escort spent with the clients, and therefore the amount owed the service.

In major U.S. cities there are upscale (and very expensive) "escort services," such as Brittany's Place in the Atlanta area, and Fantasy Allures in the New York City area. These services provide male and female companions, and websites include disclaimers that sexual services are not being offered. (Compare that with the poses and dress of the companions shown in the online photo galleries!) As a result, charges are flat rate and do not depend on what services the companion provides. Often the companion is providing the GFE (girlfriend experience, and there's also a BFE or boyfriend experience), including personalized attention, conversation, and ego-stroking. Rates often begin at $2,000. The reach of the Internet allows these agencies to develop ties to companions and clients all over the world. Some agencies provide or encourage communication via Skype. Some high-end escorts even break into acting in movies and TV (Figure 2).

Streetwalker: A lower-status sex worker who walks the streets selling sexual services.
Strip club: A bar or business that provides (almost) nude dancers and sexualized interactions, not necessarily physical sexual contact.

In most communities, the most visible sex worker is the **streetwalker.** She sells her wares on the streets of cities. She is generally less attractive and less fashionably dressed than the call girl, and she charges correspondingly less for services, perhaps as little as $20 for a "quickie," usually a hand job or oral sex. She is more likely to impose strict time constraints on the customer. Because her mode of operation is obvious, she is likely to be arrested. Men and women who work on the streets in major cities are often addicted to drugs (Dank et al., 2014). They may have pimps, who often also supply their drugs. In two of the eight cities in the Urban Institute study, some female street workers were not addicts and worked independently.

In some large cities, most women who are arrested and charged with prostitution are streetwalkers and are often members of ethnic minority groups. In part this reflects the limited employment prospects for women of color in U.S. society; in some cases it also reflects a bias on the part of police, who arrest minority women but not White women who work on the streets. Because streetwalkers have relatively little control over the conditions in which they work, they are at greater risk of disease and violence at the hands of their customers, pimps (see below), and even police officers.

The **strip club** provides sexualized interactions, not necessarily physically intimate contact. Like massage parlors, strip clubs exist along a continuum, from very elegant "gentlemen's clubs" employing attractive, articulate young women who provide companionship and female attention in exchange for tips, to "dive" bars where women engage in (almost) nude dance routines and lap dances (Frank & Carnes, 2010). Each club attracts a particular race, class, and gender of workers and clients. Clubs catering to straight men are common; they provide a space for traditionally male behavior, including rowdiness and vulgarity, and consumption—cigars, alcohol. Men seek escape from their daily lives and personal and sexual acceptance from the workers. Thus the interaction is often traditionally gendered and sexualized. Less common are clubs where men dance for heterosexual women (Scull, 2013). Whereas male clients often come to the club alone, women usually come in groups, often to celebrate a special occasion. Male dancers engage in hypermasculine displays of gender and generally dominate the female clients, occasionally mistreating them. There are clubs or events that cater to same-sex desiring women (SSDW). Carnes studied events designed for black SSDWs. Like heterosexual male clients, these women desired sexualized interactions with women in a public space; their experiences were connected to a sense of belonging to a political and erotic community, and feelings of acceptance.

The Internet and cell phones have had a major impact on the delivery of commercial sexual services since 2001 (Delap, 2014). They have made entry into work as an in-call or out-call provider much easier. They also have made access by clients to workers much easier. Potential customers can browse the Internet or specialized apps in complete privacy and arrange a meeting by e-mail, text, or cell phone. In some cities, these technologies have markedly reduced demand for and provision of services by street workers (Venkatesh, 2011). Researchers for *The Economist* analyzed 190,000 female workers' profiles posted on an international website. The majority of the women worked in the United States. From 2006 to 2014, the average price for an hour with one of the women fell from about $340 to $260. The price varied greatly across cities, and also by the characteristics of the woman and services offered. The researcher suggested the decline reflects rapidly increasing numbers of providers due to several factors: increasing ease of entry, migration of young women (especially immigrants) to large cities, and the entry of local women into the market due to the ability to engage in sex work discreetly and anonymously (Delap, 2014).

From the sex worker's point of view, the Internet offers a number of benefits (Cunningham & Kendall, 2011). The sex worker can reach a much larger number of potential clients than would be possible with ads in print media, and they don't have to walk the streets. Sex workers can build their reputations for services with those ubiquitous ratings available on websites—kind of like rating your Uber driver. Imagine receiving a text message asking you to rate the prostitute you just purchased sex from. The main website for reviews is theeroticreview.com.

The Internet has also made possible **camgirls,** who sell erotic services using webcam technology, usually through a public chat room (Jones, 2016). Erotic shows are also available through private Internet rooms at higher prices. In public chat rooms, multiple viewers participate and pay, for example, for a masturbation show. Clients seem to have the sense that they are having an authentic interaction with a "real" woman in real time. An advantage from the sex worker's point of view is that she is physically safe in these interactions because she is not actually involved in an in-person interaction with the client. That said, there are dangers of emotional harm, and camgirls often develop emotional management strategies. For example, they develop ways of dealing with emotionally abusive "trolls." An important point is that the performer can experience real sexual pleasure while performing. As one said, "I get paid to have orgasms" (Jones, 2016).

Studies of commercial sex workers find that the same person may work in several different venues over time (Lewis et al., 2004). For example, in areas with cold winters, people who work on the streets in the summer and fall may work in in-call services or bars during the winter. Women may also move back and forth between an escort service and working as a call girl.

The Role of Third Parties

Many people associate prostitutes with a **pimp** ("The Man"), portrayed as her companion–master. If she has a pimp, she supports him with her earnings, and in return he may provide her with companionship and sex, bail her out of jail, and provide her with food, shelter, clothing, and drugs. If he keeps an eye on her when she is working, he may provide some protection against theft and violence because a prostitute is scarcely in a position to go to the police if she is robbed by a customer. But the pimp may also exercise considerable control over her and engage in verbal, physical, and sexual abuse toward her if she fails to obey him.

Just as many call girls and exotic dancers have day jobs, so do pimps. Many are in the food trades or services (Venkatesh, 2011). Some are students. One pimp worked his way through college connecting male students with women to go on dates, dance at parties, provide sexual services in a variety of places, or deliver the GFE (Adshade, 2010). He knew many of the men and women from school; a man would request a service, and he kept asking women until one agreed. His take depended on the woman's attractiveness and skill, the service, the venue, and the client's willingness to pay—from $20 (for a handjob in a car) to $700 (all night in a luxury hotel). He described his role as helping "women, friends of mine, to find paying customers."

Another third party in commercial sex work is the **madam,** a woman who manages or owns an in-call service, an out-call service, a brothel, or an escort service. A madam is usually experienced and skilled at managing sex workers and businesses. Sometimes she is socially skilled also, with a network of contacts in the community.

In other venues there may be other third parties. Massage parlors employ managers who are on the premises at all times and may exercise close control of their employees. The importance of these third parties is that they reduce the autonomy of the sex workers they supervise and may coerce them to perform activities or work with clients that they object to. There is sharp disagreement among observers over the extent to which a sex worker can exercise choice with regard to their activities. Some argue that workers choose whom they serve and what acts they perform; others argue that they have little choice if they need money. The reality depends, in part, on the involvement of the third parties in the worker's daily life.

Sex Trafficking

Sex trafficking refers to the recruitment and control of people, by threat or use of force or deception, for purposes of sexual exploitation (Hynes & Raymond, 2002; Meshkovska et al., 2015). In one scenario, girls and young

---

Camgirls: Women who sell erotic services using webcam technology, usually through a public chat room.

Pimp: A prostitute's companion, protector, and master.

Madam: A woman who manages a brothel, in-call, out-call, or escort service.

Sex trafficking: The recruitment and control of people for sexual exploitation.

women are recruited in third-world or developing countries, by ads or people who promise them a good job (as a dancer, nanny, secretary), education, or a husband in a developed country. Recruiters may even supply forged travel documents, often for a price. When the women arrive in the destination country, they find themselves captive; often their travel documents are taken away, the money earned by their activity goes to those who control them, and their controllers threaten physical harm to the women or their families if they disobey or run away. The women often work in bars, brothels, and massage parlors and may be moved every few weeks. It is estimated that trafficking produces $7 billion in profit per year (Parrot & Cummings, 2006). An estimated 45,000 to 50,000 girls and women are trafficked into the United States each year, many for the sex industry.

A U.S. study found that women from Latin American countries often work in brothels, women from Asian countries work in massage parlors, and women from Eastern Europe worked in strip clubs (Dank et al., 2014). The researchers reported that some of these women were U.S. citizens, some had entered the country illegally, and some were trafficked.

A different image is the "child sex slave," an image vigorously asserted by some celebrities (e.g., Ashton Kutcher) and numerous media including the *New York Times, Fox News,* and *CNN.* Here the scenario is a girl age 10 or 11 to 17 seduced or kidnapped by an older man and forced into prostitution, in various venues—strip clubs, brothels, massage parlors, private homes. Their exploiters use threats of and actual physical violence, and threats to their families to control them. The usually quoted figure is "100,000 to 300,000 child sex slaves in the United States today" (Cizmar et al., 2011). The problem is that the number is false. It began as a "guestimate" by researchers at University of Pennsylvania in 2001, of the number of children *at risk in all of North America.* Let's look at what actual research finds. Two researchers worked for more than 2 years to recruit a sample of underage sex workers in New York City in order to find out who they are (Hinman, 2011). They interviewed 249 underage prostitutes. Forty-five percent were boys; 90 percent were born in the United States. That is, they had not been trafficked in from other nations. Half said they were recruited by a friend (not a trafficker), and only 10 percent had a pimp. Nearly all said they exchanged sex for money to support themselves.

Research by the Bureau of Justice analyzed 2,515 suspected incidents of human trafficking investigated between 2008 and 2010 (Banks & Kyckelhahn, 2011). About 2,200 (82 percent) were classified as sex trafficking; 1,200 involved allegations of trafficking adults, and 1,000 of prostitution or sexual exploitation of children. Of those incidents investigated for at least 12 months (i.e., cases involving more charges or better evidence), 31 percent were confirmed, 37 percent were not, and 32 percent

were pending. Of the confirmed victims of sex trafficking, 248 (52 percent) were age 17 or younger and 232 (48 percent) were 18 or older.

Thus the results are inconsistent with the assertion that there are even 100,000 "child sex slaves" per year in the United States, and that the number of foreign nationals trafficked for sexual exploitation is equally large. It really shouldn't matter whether the number is large or small, or the victims are children or adults, male or female. Sexual exploitation is wrong, a crime, and very damaging to the victim (see The Role of Early Abuse). We need to increase efforts to eradicate it, based on accurate statistics about the problem.

An additional complication in the prosecution of sex trafficking concerns the treatment of the trafficked individuals when arrests are made (Musto, 2016). Often, well-intentioned efforts to help victims result in the victims themselves being subject to arrest or detention. The goal is to protect victims, but often they are treated as if they are criminals deserving punishment, and they are not given the services that they need.

The Career of a Sex Worker

Given the stigmatized and often risky nature of sex work, many scholars and social service professionals have studied entry into it. There are two general explanations. One emphasizes negative experiences in childhood and adolescence, such as physical and sexual abuse, family instability, poverty, homelessness, and contact with exploitative men such as pimps or drug dealers. The other explanation emphasizes factors in the environment at the point of entry, especially economic need, the lack of job skills (often reflecting poor education), and limited employment opportunity (McCarthy et al., 2014). Past research generally studied small samples of workers in a particular venue or part of the industry, giving a narrow picture of the influences on their entry. New research compared predictors of entry into sex work with predictors of entry into two other service occupations: food and beverage servers, and barbering and hairstyling (McCarthy et al., 2014). The results indicated that family background measures related to becoming a sex worker were family instability (e.g., an additional parent such as a stepfather) and parents receiving public assistance. Childhood experience variables included experiencing physical and sexual abuse and living in a foster home. Influences in emerging adulthood included fewer years of education and indicators of economic need, such as being single or living with an unemployed partner. So, in fact, the data support both of the explanations. Of course, not every sex worker experienced all of these conditions. Some women are motivated by a desire for money, material goods, and an exciting lifestyle. These women are attracted by the image of the call girl, a status some of them attain. For some women—for

First Person

Working Their Way Through College

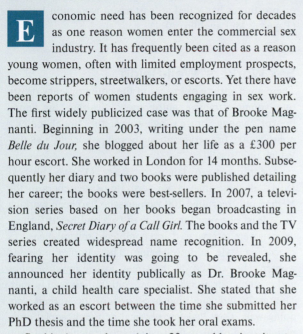

Economic need has been recognized for decades as one reason women enter the commercial sex industry. It has frequently been cited as a reason young women, often with limited employment prospects, become strippers, streetwalkers, or escorts. Yet there have been reports of women students engaging in sex work. The first widely publicized case was that of Brooke Magnanti. Beginning in 2003, writing under the pen name *Belle du Jour,* she blogged about her life as a £300 per hour escort. She worked in London for 14 months. Subsequently her diary and two books were published detailing her career; the books were best-sellers. In 2007, a television series based on her books began broadcasting in England, *Secret Diary of a Call Girl.* The books and the TV series created widespread name recognition. In 2009, fearing her identity was going to be revealed, she announced her identity publically as Dr. Brooke Magnanti, a child health care specialist. She stated that she worked as an escort between the time she submitted her PhD thesis and the time she took her oral exams.

Sophie (a pseudonym) is a 22-year-old university student working as an escort to pay for her education. Her student loans don't cover her living costs, and she is enrolled in an intensive program. She was 19 when she started; she says she had no idea what she was doing, and "suddenly it [sex work] was the better option." She advertises on an adult site and picks her clients based on feedback. She performs both in-call and out-call work. She acknowledges the risk; there is no safety net. She schedules clients around her classes, and sometimes she does not see clients for weeks (Buchanan, 2014). Another student working a few hours per week as an escort said "I made the choice . . . in hopes of having a smaller debt when I am done" (Anonymous, 2012). Both women acknowledge the psychological toll of the work, one stating that she experienced PTSD.

Vaughn Jackson, Amanda Pena, and Maran Gorham all work as strippers at the Show Palace in Queens, New York. Mike Diaz, manager of the all-nude club, is happy to employ students. He sees the jobs he provides as preventing them from accumulating huge debts while they are in school. Plus, he says, they can schedule the work around school. Vaughn, Amanda, and Maran each work, on the average, three nights per week and earn $1,500 to $2,000 per week. All three seem proud of what they do; one finds it "empowering" (Schuster, 2014). Stripping, of course, is less risky because the worker is surrounded by coworkers, customers, and management.

How common are the experiences described by these women? Research in the UK involved recruiting students on 29 university campuses by approaching students in various areas on campus and online. Most participants were full-time undergraduates. About 6 percent of the sample (all but one female) reported currently working in the sex industry as erotic dancers, strippers, or escorts (Roberts, Jones, & Sanders, 2013).

Research in Berlin obtained data from students in major universities in that city (Betzer et al., 2015). Seven percent indicated they were or had been involved in sex work, most reporting they had engaged in sexual intercourse in direct exchange for money or in escort services. Students reporting sex work said they received significantly less financial support from their families and fewer scholarships. The researchers concluded that sex work results from financial hardship, and its appeal is the higher income for fewer hours of work. Sex workers were more likely to report being homosexual or bisexual.

In the United States, students are engaging in sex work due to (a) the steady increase in college and university costs (between 2001–2002 and 2011–2012, 40 percent at public institutions and 28 percent at private nonprofit institutions); (b) the low and unpredictable wages paid by jobs typically available to students (wait staff, student hourly work on campus, door-to-door soliciting); (c) declining availability of student loans and increasing interest rates: and (d) higher rates of unemployment among college graduates since the recession of 2008–2010. Given the risks of commercial sex work, student involvement in it is becoming a serious concern. In England, the Student Sex Work Project (SSWP) (www.thestudentsexworkproject.co.uk) is developing programs to provide information and resources to student sex workers, with a focus on their safety and sexual health. In the United States, the Sex Worker Outreach Project (SWOP) is a national project focusing on sex worker rights and advocacy, staffed by a number of former student sex workers (www.swopusa.org). Improved access to and financial support for higher education for all qualified people should be a national priority.

example, a poor but attractive woman—prostitution can be a means of upward economic mobility. Other women enter out of economic necessity, in order to survive. The importance of the money, which can amount to hundreds of dollars per day, is illustrated by the dramatic increase in applicants for positions in strip and sex clubs, and other establishments, during the recession of 2008–2009 (Associated Press, 2010). A poorly educated single mother may have no alternative means of earning a living.

Force or coercion is another factor. Some women report being coerced physically or psychologically by a husband or lover into selling sex for money. As noted previously, coercion is a major factor in sex trafficking. Some become involved in prostitution through a family member or friend who is already a sex worker and can teach them the ropes.

On entering prostitution, most workers go through an apprenticeship in which they learn the skills of the profession. The apprentice learns sexual techniques, especially fellatio, because many customers want oral sex. She learns how to hustle, to successfully negotiate her services and pricing with potential customers. She learns how to maintain control over the interaction so that she can protect herself from being hurt or robbed by clients. She learns values, like "the customer is always right," and fairness to other "working girls."[1] Women who are recruited into the life by a pimp may be trained by one of his more experienced "wives." Some women are trained by an experienced madam in exchange for a large percentage of their fees.

There has been relatively little research on the "mid-career" sex worker. We have noted that a sex worker may work in several different venues over time. After learning the ropes, a person may work in an in-call or out-call service and try to establish a list of regular clients. If successful, they usually begin to work independently (Bernstein, 2007). A woman might move from the street into work in bars or at truck stops in response to changes in the weather or her health. Sex workers who are addicted to drugs may be forced to work long hours and service many customers in more than one venue to support their habit. Again, some of these changes may result from coercion or exploitation by a pimp, a supplier, or a sex trafficker.

"Squaring up" or "leaving the life" refers to giving up prostitution. Financially it is a difficult thing to do, particularly for the person with no job skills; recognizing this, analysts call for comprehensive programs that provide education and job training, shelters, medical care, and counseling for people who want to leave commercial sex work (Hynes & Raymond, 2002). Several programs are in operation, including the Sex Workers Project (http://sexworkersproject.org/).

Other reasons for leaving include arrest and the threat of a long-term jail sentence, government agencies'

insistence that sex workers give up their children, and the knowledge that a friend was the victim of violence while working as a prostitute. Violence is a major hazard associated with being a prostitute: 81 percent of women who work outdoors, and 48 percent of women who work indoors, reported being kicked, slapped, or punched by a client (Church et al., 2001). The worst risk is being murdered. The latest in a series of serial killers who prey on prostitutes has killed at least seven women in Indiana (Payne & McLaughlin, 2014).

Sex Workers' Well-Being

There are a variety of images of the contemporary prostitute: young, attractive, autonomous, healthy, "the happy hooker"; young, brazen, aggressive, the "tough chick"; not-so-young, bruised emotionally and physically, a victim. Which one is valid?

According to a landmark study (Vanwesenbeeck, 1994), all these images are accurate. Researchers in the Netherlands recruited 100 women who had been working for at least one year for a study of "sex and health"; these women were interviewed and completed several measures of coping style and well-being. The samples included women who worked on the street, in windows, in clubs and brothels, for escort services, and in their own homes. The results indicated that one-fourth of the women were doing well. They had few physical or psychosocial complaints, used problem-focused coping strategies, and were satisfied with their lives. Another quarter were at the opposite end. They complained of headaches, backaches, anxiety, and depression; their coping strategies involved dissociation (seeing problems as unrelated to the self) and denial, and they were dissatisfied with prostitution. The remaining women were in the middle.

The risks to a woman and thus her well-being varied according to the venue in which she worked. In the Netherlands, where sex work has been legalized, women who worked in windows and on the streets were at greater risk. Working the streets was associated with greater risk of arrest and of violence by clients, which obviously influences physical and mental health. Women who worked in windows or on the streets worked faster, had more clients, and earned less per customer than those working in in-call and out-call services. In another study of indoor sex workers in the Netherlands, workers reported having an average 9-hour workday; more than one-third worked in excess of 40 hours per week, and half had taken no holidays in the past year (Venicz & Vanwesenbeeck, 2000). Scores of indoor sex workers on measures of burnout—depersonalization and emotional exhaustion—were compared with scores of female health care workers and people in treatment for work-related problems. Sex workers scored significantly higher on depersonalization, which was mainly explained by

---

[1] A 1986 film titled *Working Girls* provides a realistic look at an in-call service.

contextual factors—working due to coercion, experiences of violence, and lack of control in interaction with clients (Vanwesenbeeck, 2005). An important caveat in interpreting these studies is that they were conducted in the context of legalized prostitution in the Netherlands. Doubtless the health outcomes would be worse in countries in which prostitution is illegal and therefore prostitutes have little recourse if, for example, they are assaulted.

A unique study of the geography of sex worker victimization used reports filed by sex workers in Australia (Prior et al., 2012). An outreach project there encourages workers to voluntarily report instances of victimization they experience. An analysis of 333 reports filed over 8 years identified 528 criminal acts. One-fifth of the acts involved theft, including stealing, defrauding, and nonpayment. One-sixth involved harassment, including stalking, nuisance behavior, and threats. Other actions included disorderly conduct, assault, and abduction. Most incidents occurred indoors, regardless of the venue; victimization occurred in the assailant's car (street work), the premises (brothels), the assailant's home (out-call), or the worker's residence (in-call). The authors concluded that privacy and the worker's lack of control are major situational contributors to victimization.

In an attempt to reduce street prostitution and to reduce risks for sex workers, Zurich, Switzerland, has created "sex drive-ins." Nine garage-style structures have been built; they are equipped with alarm buttons and guarded by security personnel to ensure the safety of the prostitutes. Men enter the area and select from the women who are present. They drive into one of the structures. Customers are not allowed to leave the area with the sex workers. Social and health care services are offered on-site for the workers. Similar sites exist in Utrecht (Netherlands) and Cologne (Germany).

Risks are especially high for women who are being trafficked because they are at risk of suffering abuse and injury by both clients and masters, undergoing illness and infection, and facing medical neglect (Hynes & Raymond, 2002).

There is also the risk of exposure to sexually transmitted diseases, especially HIV/AIDS. Prostitutes infected with HIV are often workers who are also injecting drugs, with research indicating that it is the injecting that is the risk. In the Western world, studies show that the sex worker's risk of HIV infection is greater in their private sex life than in their sex work. In other parts of the world, the risk varies greatly, with high rates of HIV/AIDS in some cities and countries but low rates in others (Vanwesenbeeck, 2001).

It has been suggested that the high levels of violence and of psychological distress found among sex workers are not due to the nature of the sex work per se but instead reflect the stigma associated with the work itself (Bernstein, 2007). Prostitutes are at risk of rape because of attitudes such as the view that you can't rape a prostitute and no harm is done if you do. The risk of arrest and mistreatment by law-enforcement personnel, and the resulting anxiety and distress, reflect the fact that sex work is illegal. Sex workers say that one of the main things that would contribute positively to their mental health would be eliminating the stigma associated with sex work (Benoit et al., 2018; Burnes et al., 2018).

Sex workers use a variety of strategies to cope with the risks of their work. Some use drugs and alcohol to increase their confidence and decrease guilt. Others use a strategy of shutting down their feelings and focusing narrowly on the task. The consequences of this distancing are often referred to as depersonalization (not, of course, an experience unique to sex work). Independent women may view themselves as professionals, providing therapy, "sexual healing," or sex education. They may take courses to enhance their skills—for example, earn massage certification, or use prior training as a therapist or social worker. These women perceive their work as offering opportunities for personal growth (Bernstein, 2007). Some emphasize the rewarding aspects of the work, as perhaps that it supports their children. Many sex workers use as a coping technique the careful management of time and place, locating their sex work in a specific physical and temporal place separated from their private sexual and familial relationships (also not unique to sex work). Sex workers may also use a network of contacts with other sex workers as a source of support; in one such case, workers on one "stroll" worked together to protect a pregnant colleague by giving her all the customers who wanted just a "blow job" and protecting her from clients known to be rough (Anderson, 2004).

Sex workers face risks due to discrimination, criminalization, and exploitation, and perhaps due to violence, disease, and drug use. There are promising approaches available that can reduce harm, including education (especially job training), empowerment, preventive health care, and improved occupational and safety conditions. There are also interventions that have been shown to work, including peer education, training in safe sex negotiating skills, and provision of condoms (Rekart, 2005). Several sex worker rights organizations are working to reduce the risks to sex workers and provide social, medical, and legal services to them, including COYOTE (Cast Off Your Old Tired Ethics) and SWOP (Dewey, 2015).

Childhood experiences can make a difference. The study of women working in the Netherlands found that, in addition to their work venue, having a history of victimization and trauma as children or adolescents, before they entered prostitution, was associated with poorer well-being (Vanwesenbeeck, 1994). Researchers in Ontario conducted semistructured life history interviews with women engaged in sex work (Orchard et al., 2014).

Several themes emerged from the interviews. Most of the women grew up with both their mothers and their fathers, but the women reported difficult relationships with both. One-third reported sexual abuse by their fathers or other men in childhood and adolescence. The women grew up in economically deprived neighborhoods, and sex work was a readily available option. Clearly, any adult who has experienced childhood victimization may have poor well-being. Coercive sexual activity in adolescence or young adulthood is associated with a variety of adverse health and social outcomes (Ganju et al., 2004). Early coercion is associated with subsequent nonconsensual sex (e.g., trafficking), unintended pregnancy, and abortion. Adverse mental health outcomes include low self-esteem as well as substance abuse.

Customers

At the time of the Kinsey research, about 69 percent of all White males had had some experience with prostitutes (Kinsey et al., 1948). According to the NSSHB, in 2009, 4.3 percent of men and 0.8 percent of women reported paying or being paid for sex in the past year (Herbenick et al., 2010c). Thus, the use of prostitutes has declined dramatically in the past 70 years. This reflects in part the increased frequency of nonmarital and casual sexual activity during this same period (see the chapters on "Sexuality and the Life Cycle").

Prostitutes refer to their customers as "johns." About 50 percent of the clients are occasional johns; they may be respectable businessmen who seek only occasional contacts with prostitutes, perhaps while on business trips. Nearly 50 percent are repeat clients who seek a regular relationship with one particular prostitute or a small group of them (Freund et al., 1991). The remainder are compulsive johns, who use prostitutes for their major sexual outlet. They are driven to them and cannot stay away (see the chapter "Variations in Sexual Behavior").

A study of female sex workers in Mexico asked them a series of questions about their current, regular, and non-regular clients (Robertson et al., 2014). *One-time clients* were men the worker did not expect to see again; the transaction was strictly commercial. Some women preferred to avoid such clients but accepted them when other types of clients were scarce. *Regular clients/"friends"* were repeat clients the worker had known for some time. The workers developed friendships with these men and trusted them; the men treated the women with kindness and respect. Several women had clients who had *fallen in love* with them. These men were very difficult to manage because they sought noncommercial relationships and commitments (e.g., living together). Occasionally, a worker would report that her current intimate partner was a former client who had fallen in love with her. The fourth type was *long-term financial providers.* These men provided consistent, substantial financial support, often paying for major expenses on a regular basis. In exchange the client expected special services such as spending the night or traveling together. These were often wealthy older men living in the United States.

A study of Canadian "johns" found that almost one-half were married or cohabiting, and 39 percent were single. On the average, participants had purchased sex 100 times in their lives and had visited indoor sex establishments 4.8 times in the past 12 months. Eighty-six percent preferred female workers, and 10.5 percent preferred male workers. The most recent time they paid for sex, they paid for multiple activities (25 percent), half oral and half vaginal sex (17 percent), the GFE (16 percent), and vaginal intercourse (16 percent). Other research has examined the psychological characteristics of men who buy sex (Farley et al., 2017). Compared to those who don't buy sex, men who buy sex score higher in likelihood to rape and in hostile masculinity. They have less empathy for women prostitutes, viewing them much differently from other women. In short, they have psychological characteristics that are similar to those of men who commit sexual assault.

As for male clients of male escorts (see next section), researchers posted an invitation to complete an online survey on DaddyReviews.com, an escort website (Grov et al., 2014). Three-fourths identified as gay, 18 percent bisexual, and 4 percent heterosexual. Clients paid an average of $250 per hour, and oral and anal sex were the most common sexual activities engaged in.

Men use the services of prostitutes for a variety of reasons. A survey in Australia found that 23 percent of men had paid for sex at least once. These men reported that the main reasons were to satisfy sexual needs, that it was easy, and that it would be entertaining (Pitts et al., 2004). Some married men want sex more frequently than their wives do or want to engage in practices—such as fellatio—that they think their wives would not be willing to do. Some use prostitutes to satisfy their exotic sexual needs, such as being whipped or having sex with a woman who pretends to be a corpse. Others, particularly adolescents, may have sex with prostitutes to prove their manhood or gain sexual experience.

For many clients, a major appeal is the clear and bounded nature of the sexual interaction. Money is paid and services are received. The exchange is limited in time and space and requires no effort to develop or maintain a relationship. The client wants "bounded authenticity"—real sex, a sense that they matter and are desirable, without the effort, expense, and hassles of commitment (Bernstein, 2007).

Why do some people pay for sex?

Commercial sex work is common in locations where there are large numbers of men separated from their usual partners, such as military bases. In the 21st century, the provision of sex workers near bases often involves women who have been trafficked, especially in places like South Korea. In 2004, the U.S. Defense Department proposed making contact with a sex worker a military offense, to aid in the fight against sex trafficking.

Male Sex Workers

Some male sex workers serve a heterosexual clientele, selling their services to women. These men work in a variety of settings. Some of them work for escort services and provide companionship and sexual gratification on an out-call basis. Working in such a setting is much less risky for men than for women. Some men work in massage parlors, under the same conditions as female employees. These male prostitutes virtually never work the street, in contrast to female streetwalkers and male *hustlers* (see below). This reflects gender-role socialization; female clients are unlikely to cruise the streets and pick up a prostitute because they have been taught to let the male take the initiative.

Another category is the **gigolo** (in French, "one who dances"), a man who provides companionship and sexual gratification on a continuing basis to a woman in exchange for money. A gigolo often, though not always, has only one client at a time. There are several types, including the "Golden Boy," the pampered playboy kept by a very wealthy woman; the "Lap Dog," who enters into a series of marriages of convenience; and the "Toy Boy," or stud, who works as a companion on a limited-term basis (Nelson & Robinson, 1994). The demand for gigolos reflects the fact that women, like men, desire sexual gratification on a continuing basis and will pay for it when circumstances require or allow them to do so. On the other hand, women often prefer their sexual activity to be part of an ongoing relationship that involves love.

Many male sex workers sell their services primarily or exclusively to men; some of their clients identify as gay, others identify as heterosexual. Women who engage in sex work are acting in ways that are consistent with their feminine identity, providing emotional and sexual labor for others. Men who engage in sex work with male clients find that their masculine identity is challenged, triggering a stigma not faced by other types of sex workers. Contemporary male sex workers catering to men work in four settings (Minichiello et al., 2013). *Outdoor workers* are often young and identify as heterosexual; they typically solicit pedestrians and motorists and engage in sex in cars, homes, or other locations. Some work in the vicinity of public toilets. Advantages are minimal overhead and the ability to retain their earnings; like women who work the streets, they face the risks of assault and stigma. Male street workers are sometimes referred to as **hustlers.** To emphasize their masculinity, they may wear tight jeans and leather jackets. In some cities there are specific areas known as places where hustlers operate. *Bar workers* are found in gay-identified spaces—gyms,

bars, clubs, and hotels. These are spaces where casual and same-sex activities are common, so these men face less stigma than outdoor workers. These men typically work part-time. A minority of men work in *brothels,* providing sexual services on an in-call basis. Their working conditions and risks are similar to those experienced by women in this setting. Usually a brothel will have only a few male employees. Prices for specific activities are typically fixed, and management retains a significant amount of the fee. The clients may be primarily women. The largest group is *escorts* or *"call boys,"* the male counterpart of the "call girl." They often identify as gay or bisexual. They work in both in-call and out-call services, and their clientele locates them through gay media. Their clients are usually middle- and upper-class men, and these workers can earn large incomes for relatively few hours of work. One study interviewed men working for an escort agency (Smith et al., 2015). The escorts reported that a variety of social and emotional activities were required both to provide good service to clients and to cope with their fear of being stigmatized if they disclosed their sex work to people outside the agency. Sex work in this setting is not just about sex.

In one study of adolescent males in San Francisco, the main reason for engaging in sex work—stated by 87 percent—was money (Weisberg, 1985). Most often they had left home because of conflict in the family, typically leaving when they were 15 or 16 years old, although some had left when they were 11 or 12. The majority (72 percent) reported using drugs while engaging in acts of prostitution. The reason most often cited was the enjoyment of being high. Drugs were also used to reduce feelings of anxiety or fear stemming from the scary nature of the work.

Sex Tourism

An increasingly important type of commercial sex is **sex tourism,** which refers to varieties of leisure travel that have as their purpose the purchase of sexual services (Wonders & Michalowski, 2001). Sex tourism is made possible by three large-scale social forces: the migration of men and women from less developed nations, or from rural to urban areas, in search of jobs; the *commodification* of sexual intimacy, making all types of sex a commodity or service for sale; and increased travel for recreational purposes. All three of these forces are tied to increasing *globalization,* the movement of information and people freely across national boundaries.

The migration of people in search of economic opportunities provides a large group of young people in search of work. In some locales they are aggressively recruited into sex work by pimps or people with ties to

Gigolo (JIG-uh-loh): A man who provides companionship and sexual gratification on a continuing basis to a woman in exchange for money.
Hustler: A male sex worker who sells his services to men.
Sex tourism: Leisure travel with the purpose of purchasing sexual services.

sex trafficking. In other places, they enter into the life more or less voluntarily, often because there are few other opportunities for persons of their ethnic background. In Amsterdam, where the attitude toward sex work can be described as *regulated tolerance,* a few individuals control much of the commercial sex work, recruiting foreign migrants to work in windows and brothels. In Havana, Cuba, commercial sex work is decentralized, with many men and women working independently. They contact potential clients in hotels, bars, and on the street, hoping to connect with someone who will employ them, perhaps for several days.

In some countries, sex tourism is the most rapidly growing economic sector and a major source of hard currency; in such places, governments have little incentive to attempt to reduce or eliminate it. One estimate places the value of the global sex industry at $20 billion per year.

The tourists who can purchase sexual services are obviously wealthy enough to travel, which in turn often means they are citizens of developed countries and members of the middle and upper classes in their home societies. The sex workers are often from a different national and ethnic background. One of the attractions for the tourist is sex with this "dark-skinned other," perhaps someone from a group stereotyped as sexually free and uninhibited. The encounter is appealing because it is a sharp contrast to the tourist's usual sexual experience (Brennan, 2010; Padilla, 2007). Unfortunately, one such appeal for men is sex with a young girl, and in some Asian cities girls as young as 12 and 13 are available in brothels tightly controlled by their managers.

The search for the type of workers—gender, age, and sexual orientation—and experience the tourist seeks is facilitated by the Internet (Padilla, 2007). Websites publish information about sex work, cruising areas and meeting places, and prices; past visitors review their experiences. Sex workers advertise on some of these sites, and some have their own Internet pages.

Pornography

Pornography refers to sexually arousing material (focusing on the consumer) or material intended to produce sexual arousal (focusing on the producer). In either case, we are talking about a very broad range of material/experiences, many of which are discussed in this section. The debate over pornography has been raging for decades. Some political conservatives, religious fundamentalists, and feminists (strange bedfellows, indeed!) agree that some kinds of pornography should be made illegal, and their producers and distributers

Pornography: Sexually arousing art, literature, or films.
Obscenity: That which is offensive to decency or modesty, or calculated to arouse sexual excitement or lust.
Erotica: Sexually arousing material that is not degrading or demeaning to women, men, or children.

jailed. Some liberals, libertarians, civil liberties groups, and some feminists respond that the freedom of expression guaranteed by the Constitution must be preserved, and therefore pornography should not be restricted by law. Meanwhile, Joe Brown sits down at his home computer, clicks on Pornhub.com, and settles down for a pleasurable evening's entertainment.

We can distinguish between pornography, obscenity, and erotica. The term *pornography* comes from the Greek word *porneia,* which means, quite simply, "prostitution," and *graphos,* which means "writing." In general usage today, **pornography** refers to literature, films, and so on that are intended to be sexually arousing (Malamuth, 1998). The term is often used by the person in the street to refer to any image they don't like.

In legal terminology the word used is *obscenity.* **Obscenity** refers to that which is foul, disgusting, or lewd. It is used as a legal term for that which is offensive to the authorities or to society (Wilson, 1973). The U.S. Supreme Court has had a rather hard time defining exactly what is obscene and what can be regulated legally, a point discussed in more detail in the chapter "Sex and the Law."

In the debate over pornography, some make the distinction between pornography (which is unacceptable to them) and erotica (which is acceptable). For example, one sociologist defined pornography as "explicit representations of sexual behavior, verbal or pictorial, that have as a distinguishing characteristic the degrading or demeaning portrayal of human beings, especially women" (Russell, 1980, p. 218). Another term for such material is *hard-core* pornography. In contrast, **erotica** is defined as differing from pornography "by virtue of not degrading or demeaning women, men, or children" (Russell, 1980, p. 218) Such material is also referred to as *soft-core* pornography. According to this distinction, a movie of a woman being raped would be pornography, whereas a movie of two mutually consenting adults who are both enjoying having sexual intercourse together would be considered erotica.

Our discussion of pornography considers several aspects of it. We begin with a brief discussion of the size and scope of the industry. Then we consider in detail the various ways in which sexually arousing material is packaged and delivered in the contemporary world. This leads to a consideration of the people who produce these materials. Next we consider the consumers, who, after all, keep the industry booming (or not). Then we discuss one of the major areas of research for the past several decades, the effects of pornography on users. Finally, we discuss the larger perspective. Throughout, we pay particular attention to social scientists' research. The major legal issues are discussed in the chapter "Sex and the Law."

The Porn Industry

Pornography is big business in the United States. Included in this industry are many different products and services: Internet porn, including "adult" websites,

Figure 3   Internet porn is abundant.

©Wojtek Laski/Getty Images

chat rooms, news groups, and bulletin boards; DVDs, videos, and films; magazines; live entertainment; and kiddie porn. Some of this activity is legal (e.g., publishing *Playboy* online); some of it is illegal (e.g., producing videos of children under 12 engaging in sex); and some is legal depending upon the county you live in (e.g., strip clubs featuring complete nudity and bodily contact). It is impossible to obtain precise data on the economics of pornography. One analysis estimated that in 2006 retail sales of all types totaled almost $13 billion (Mandese, 2007). According to Wikipedia (2012), the global market for Internet pornography alone is worth almost $5 billion.

Internet Porn

In the past 25 years, the Internet has made available a wide variety of sex-related products and services to every computer with an Internet connection. Pornhub.com, arguably the world's largest porn website, celebrated its 10th anniversary in 2017, and celebrated by releasing a data report! Here are some tidbits from it (Pornhub, 2017).

- As of 2017, more than 10 million videos had been uploaded. That includes 2.2 million amateur videos, 1.9 million gay videos, and 1.4 million blow job videos.

- Pornhub has 22 million registered users worldwide.

- Over those 10 years, the top 10 most viewed categories of videos were, in order: lesbian, MILF (mothers I'd like to fuck), amateur, teen, mature, ebony (featuring Black actors), anal, big tits, big dick, and hentai (anime pornography, i.e., cartoon pornography).

- Over those 10 years, Lisa Ann was the most-viewed actress, with over 1 billion views of her videos, followed by Riley Reid, with 771 million views.

A technical analysis of the infrastructure needed to service such sites suggests that porn drives Internet technology. The most visited site has 4.4 billion page views per month, three times the size of CNN. And each viewer spends an average of 15 to 20 minutes (Anthony, 2012). The storage needed for the thousands of videos, and the bandwidth needed to meet the download demand, is something else. Downloads of porn videos at peak times may absorb the equivalent of one-fifteenth of the bandwidth available between New York and London.

The services provided online include access to sexually arousing videos, live performances by cam models who may take requests from viewers: photos, and stories; the availability of an array of goods (sex toys, lingerie, even panties worn by porn stars) and services for sale; online chats with like-minded others; and access to bulletin boards with a variety of specialized materials.

Websites.   Adult websites display and sell a variety of sexual materials and services. According to thechive.com, in 2017 the top most visited sites were Pornhub (8.7 million users per day, value of the site $58 million), Xvideos (2.0 million users/day, $42 million), and Xhamster (1.5 million users/day, $29 million). Different sites offer different menus of options. Xnxx and Youporn are "tube sites," featuring sexually explicit videos that can be viewed online or purchased, explicit photos, profiles of the women, and message forums for communicating about each woman. Livejasmin provides live sex online and the opportunity to chat with the actors. There are hundreds of other sites with names like Amateurs Gone Wild, Asian Pleasures, Lovely Cheerleaders, and Top-sexy-milfs. Each site typically includes thousands of photos organized by content, pornographic videos that can be viewed on your computer or cell phone screen, stories, links to live sex shows, and links to live video cameras in places such as men's and women's locker rooms. Some also sell videos, sex aids such as dildos, and other sexual devices and costumes. Many of these sites specialize, featuring "teenagers" (if the actors are under 18, the material violates the law), Black, Asian, or Hispanic women, gays, lesbians, pregnant women, and on and on. Each site charges a daily, weekly, or monthly "membership fee" for access; the fee can usually be paid by supplying a valid credit card number.

Researchers have analyzed the content of television programs for decades. Recently, similar techniques have been applied to the content posted on tube sites. Most sites organize videos into categories for ease of user access. Research indicates that two of the most popular search terms are *teen* and *MILF.* A team of researchers analyzed five teen and five MILF videos from each of 10 free sites. Across all of the videos, vaginal intercourse and fellatio were most frequently depicted; use of toys, condoms, and coercion were rare. There were no gender differences in who initiated the activity or use of persuasion. MILF videos portrayed the female as more agentic and more in control than teen videos, consistent with the presumed greater experience of a mature woman (Vannier et al., 2014). Another group analyzed the content of 302 videos featuring male performers posted on five sites. Masturbation and anal intercourse were the most common behaviors portrayed, with condoms used in about one-half of the portrayals of intercourse. Longer videos portrayed a larger number of behaviors, including a larger number of high-risk behaviors (Downing et al., 2014).

Chat Rooms.   *Chat rooms* provide a location where individuals can meet and carry on conversations electronically. These rooms are often oriented toward people with particular sexual interests, often captured by their names. The conversations often involve graphic descriptions of sexual activities or fantasies. Some people have left relationships, including marriages, for someone they knew only through electronic conversation. In this context, an interesting feature of these chats is that the other person cannot see you. This allows you to present yourself in any way you desire, to rehearse or try out a broad range of identities (Turkle, 1995).

Virtual Reality.   Technology marches on, and pornography marches right along with it. Virtual reality experiences can be delivered using devices such as Oculus Rift, and now it is able to deliver erotic content (see Figure 4). Pornhub.com offers VR porn videos, and there is a VRporn.com website. This technology is so new that there is little research available on it (Wood et al., 2017).

Videos and Films

Sexually explicit movies were made as early as 1915. The technology remained primitive and distribution was very limited until the 1960s. The *hard-core film* industry began to emerge around 1970. Two films were especially important in this breakthrough. *I Am Curious, Yellow,* appearing in 1970, showed sexual intercourse explicitly. In part because it was a foreign film with an intellectual tone, it became fashionable for people, including married couples, to see it. The other important early film was *Deep Throat,* appearing in 1973. With its humor and creative plot, it was respectable and popular among the middle class. After the success of *Deep Throat,* many more full-length, technically well-done hard-core films soon appeared. *Deep Throat* had made it clear that there were big profits to be

Figure 4   The latest technological innovation in porn is virtual reality (VR) porn.

©Glenn Chapman/AFP/Getty Images

made. It cost $24,000 to make, yet by 1982 it had yielded $25 million in profits.

Loops are short (10-minute) hard-core films. They are set up in coin-operated computers in private booths, usually in adult bookstores. The patron can enter and view the film in privacy and perhaps masturbate while doing so.

In the early 1980s, X-rated *videocassettes* for home viewing began to replace porn theaters. For example, *Deep Throat* became available on videocassette in 1977 and, by 1982, had sold 300,000 copies (Cohn, 1983). Cable television also entered the arena, with porn channels thriving in some areas of the country. This was followed by the DVD. This *privatization* of pornography was furthered by the development of the Internet, and vastly expanded the potential market.

Many hard-core videos are made for a heterosexual audience. According to the General Social Survey (GSS) data, 25 percent of U.S. adults reported seeing an X-rated movie in 2012 (Smith & Son, 2013). Nationally, "adult videos" earn $3.6 billion per year (Mandese, 2007). They portray couples engaging in both male-active and female-active oral sex, and vaginal and anal intercourse in various settings and body positions. Less often, films and videos show sexual activity involving three or more people, or two women (Davis & Bauserman, 1993).

A rapidly expanding part of the porn industry is the "amateur" video. The development of the home-video camera has enabled anybody with a willing partner, friends, or neighbors to produce homemade porn. Such videos cost virtually nothing to make, and distributors are eager to purchase them. These films account for at least 20 percent of all adult videos made in the United States ("The Sex Industry," 1998). Amateur videos are available free on numerous Internet sites. Perhaps as a result, sales and rentals of adult videos fell 30 percent from 2004 to 2006 (Baram, 2007). Sales fell an additional 50 percent from 2006 to 2010 (Johansmeyer, 2010).

In the 1990s, a number of companies began marketing videos designed to educate people about various aspects of human sexuality. With names like the "Better Sex" video series, these include explicit portrayals of a wide variety of consenting heterosexual activities. As such, they are erotica, not pornography. They often include commentary by a psychologist or sex therapist reassuring viewers that the activities portrayed are normal. These series are advertised in national magazines and some daily newspapers.

There is a continuum from the subtle to the explicit in video portrayals of sex. The subtle end is found in *music videos*. (See Figure 5.) The sexual content of many videos is unmistakable. Men are portrayed as dominant and aggressive, with prominent posturing and a clear characterization that they are wanted by and have sex with attractive women (Ward et al., 2005). Women are portrayed in a

Figure 5 The sexual content of many music videos and live performances is unmistakable. Clothing, body language, and physical contact between performers evoke sexual images. Here Lady Gaga performs.

©Kevin Winter/American Idol 2011/Getty Images

condescending manner and are valued almost exclusively for their physical appearance and sex appeal.

Magazines

A declining share of the pornography market consists of magazines, ranging from *soft-core* (genital display such as in *Playboy*) to *hard-core* (penetrative sex, threesomes such as in *Hustler*). The number and sales of slick, color magazines mushroomed in the 1970s and 1980s following the success of *Playboy*. Launched in 1953, *Playboy*'s circulation peaked in 1972 at 7.2 million (Wikipedia). In the 1980s, *Penthouse* and *Hustler* provided stiff competition with more graphic and daring photo and editorial content, and there were dozens of less well-known competitors. Fierce legal and public-relations battles were fought in the 1980s and 1990s over the display and sale of these magazines, forerunners of today's battles over sexual content on the Internet. The development of the high-quality, mass-produced videos available on VHS and later DVD caused the magazine market to go into a long decline.

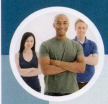

First Person

Behind the Scenes: Making X-Rated Videos

Dave Cummings bounces out of bed. He's working today, so he goes through his routine; he showers, shaves extremely close to get a smooth face, trims his fingernails and his pubic hair, applies lotion to his groin, and finishes with hand lotion. He dresses casually and drives to a large, expensive home in Beverly Hills, rented for the shoot. When he arrives, he greets the other performers, mostly young women and men in their twenties and thirties. In this group, Dave is the odd man out. He is 67 years old, balding, and looks like your doctor, not the typical male performer in an X-rated video. He represents the "graying of porn." It is that appearance that gets him work. Dave provides the realism in the video; he is believable as a doctor, lawyer, judge, or schoolteacher, in roles where a hard-bodied, bronzed guy in his twenties is not credible. It is Dave's appearance that got him into the industry; that and one other characteristic: his sexual stamina. In his own words, he can "get it up, keep it up, not come before [I am] told to, and can climax on cue" (Kikuras, 2004).

Dave points to one of the most important qualifications for a male actor in the world of X-rated videos: the ability to perform sexually. Many videos are budgeted to be shot in three days. The script calls for six to nine episodes of sex, each requiring one or more erect penises; the majority are to end with visible ejaculation. In other words, these videos place a premium on male sexual performance, perhaps not surprising in a performance-oriented culture. It costs money and frustrates everyone involved if a male actor has a long refractory period (see the chapter "Sexual Arousal"). To make it in the industry, a man has to demonstrate that he is up to the demands. Dave is lucky; he has good genes and stamina. In years past, a man without Dave's talents would not last in this line of work. But a pharmaceutical breakthrough—Viagra—has changed all that. Many male porn actors routinely use Viagra, which enables them to get it up and keep it up. (Some actors inject the drug directly into the penis; the resulting needle marks really turn off some of the female performers.) As a result, hundreds of men are competing for the available jobs.

One consequence of this competition is pressure to perform acts and take risks that the actor might prefer to avoid. Even in this era of widespread knowledge of HIV infection and AIDS, condom use is rare in the porn industry; some viewers don't like to see them, some directors and producers don't allow them, and some actors and actresses don't like the resulting hassle or change in sensation. The risk became very real in May 2004 when it was announced that five performers had positive HIV tests. Another consequence of the competition is low pay. Men may be paid as little as $500 for a video. The industry is built primarily around women. It is the women who achieve a kind of stardom, whose names appear in the publicity and on the video boxes, and whose bodies are featured in the videos. Relatively new performers may be paid $350 to $1,000 for a film featuring conventional sex. Engaging in unconventional or rough sex brings a higher fee. Needless to say, no royalties are paid to the performers. Budgets are low, and there is constant pressure to keep costs at a minimum.

The X-rated video industry in the United States reflects our society. Demand for the videos is created by an abstinence-only approach to sexuality education and taboos on portrayals of sexual activities and relationships in other media. The production of them reflects the development of video and Internet technology, enabling both the producer to produce and the purchaser to buy them cheaply. The emphasis on sexual performance reflects the larger culture, and it is often chemically enhanced as are many other performances in the contemporary world. The distribution and sale of the videos reflects the commercialization of sex, turning access to sexual images and sexual gratification into a commodity to be sold for cash or credit.

Penthouse declared bankruptcy in 2003; by 2010, *Playboy*'s circulation had declined to 1.6 million, and in 2014 it became available only online.

Magazines catering to specialized tastes remain on the market. They include material designed for gay men, leather fetishists, swingers, and people interested in interracial sex.

Live Entertainment

Shows providing live, sexualized entertainment are yet another part of the sex industry. Burlesque, which featured women seductively undressing on a stage in a theater, has been transformed into strip clubs. These provide semi-nude (pasties and a g-string) or nude dancing in a lounge setting; often dancers circulate among the patrons when not onstage. These clubs range in style from converted neighborhood bars to upscale gentlemen's clubs. Participant-observation research, supplemented by interviews, indicates that many of the customers are regulars; they come, not for sexual release, but for the opportunity to interact with attractive young women, and the pleasure of a sexualized interaction without the need to "perform" sexually (Frank, 2005).

The *Lion's Den,* a club in a New England town, had a gendered division of labor. Men, in the roles of manager, bartenders, deejays, and bouncers, ran the club and managed the women—the waitresses and strippers. The club employed as many as 51 strippers, mostly White, mostly with a high school education. The strippers worked 7-hour shifts, dividing their time between stage performances lasting 15 to 30 minutes and circulating to solicit private or table dances. A number of the dancers were single mothers; working at night allowed them to spend the days with their children (Price-Glynn, 2010).

The blog lettersfromstripclubs contains posts by men who visit the clubs. One poster, engaged to a "knockout," goes to the club to indulge his fetish for large fake breasts; he frequents clubs where the women allow him to fondle them. A gay man goes with male friends to celebrate events in their lives, and to people watch. A third man considers it therapy; where else can you talk completely openly to someone who won't judge you?

Male strippers catering to a female audience are less common but perform periodically in many communities. In the commercial sex districts of large cities, there are also live sex shows featuring couples or groups engaging in sexual acts onstage. These shows are "second cousins" to the elaborately staged reviews in major casinos and hotels that often feature nudity and simulated sexual activity in a lavish setting.

Kiddie Porn

Kiddie porn refers to any visual depiction—photo, film, video—of sexually explicit conduct involving a person under 18 years of age; it may include images of nude genitalia, or even clothed genitals if the images are "lascivious." It is viewed by many as the most reprehensible part of the porn industry because it produces an obvious victim, the child model. Children, by virtue of their developmental level, cannot truly give informed consent to participation in such activities, and the potential for doing psychological and physical damage to them is great. Every state has enacted laws making it illegal to produce, distribute, or possess such material. From an ethical perspective, ability to consent is a major concern. Although (almost) everyone agrees that children under 12 cannot consent to such activities, some argue that 16- and 17-year-olds are capable of informed consent; in fact, in some states 16-year-olds can legally consent to sexual intercourse.

One offense is producing material involving children (under 18), obtaining still photos or videos of children nude or in sexually provocative poses or engaging in sexual activity. These may or may not involve sexual penetration. Some producers are motivated by pathology, but others may be motivated by profit (Quayle, 2008). Another offense is selling or exchanging these images, including downloading them from the Internet. Again, some offenders may be acting out of addiction or compulsion, but others may not. A third offense is possession, often of hundreds or thousands of images. The United States is among a minority of countries that criminalizes all three. Some of these offenders are referred to as pedophiles, but that term should be reserved for people who engage in sexual contact with children. Of course, pedophilic activity may be involved in the creation of these materials (see First Person: "Nicole"); note that these activities may involve children who are sleeping or otherwise unaware of what is happening to them.

There are commercial websites that distribute sexual images of what appear to be individuals under 18. These sites include words like "nymphet" and variations of "lolita" in their names, and display terms like "little girls/boys." In May 2015, there was a "Lovely Nymphet Network" on tumbler.com with a variety of photos of young women of ambiguous age. It is difficult to regulate such sites because it may be impossible to prove that the subject of a photo or video is under 18.

The most explicit *child pornography* is thought to be distributed on the Internet via "peer-to-peer" (p2p) networks. These networks involve individuals who produce and/or distribute all sorts of materials surreptitiously; they often develop elaborate online distribution systems that are difficult to identify or trace. Most publicized cases of law enforcement arrests involve participants in such networks. In August 2012, as a result of an investigation code-named Holitna, authorities arrested 43 men across seven countries and charged them with sexually abusing children and producing and distributing the resulting images.

Wolak and colleagues (2011a, 2011b) have conducted several studies of law enforcement activities and arrests for child pornography (CP) offenses. They use an elaborate sampling strategy to reach a representative sample of agencies across the United States. They identified 402 arrests in 2000–2001 and 852 in 2006; they believe the increase primarily reflects increased enforcement activity rather than an increase in CP offenses. In 2006, 22 percent of the arrests were for production; the rest were for distribution or possession. Twenty-seven percent involved distribution of sexual images of the self, usually by a teenager (i.e., *sexting* of images).[2] Eighty percent of the

> **Kiddie porn:** Pictures or videos of sexual acts involving children under the age of 18.

[2]Of course, congressmen and star NFL quarterbacks also engage in this activity!

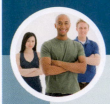

First Person

"Nicole": A Victim of Child Pornography

Nicole's parents divorced when she was young. She lived with her mother and stepfather, and visited her father every other weekend. When she was 9, he began showing her child pornography. He told her it was "normal" for fathers and daughters to play games like those in the pictures. Later he forced her to perform oral sex, and raped her. When she was 12, she told him to stop, but the abuse continued for another year.

Nicole's father had a camera tripod in his bedroom. She asked him if he had shown the pictures to anyone and he said no. Several years later she was using a computer her father gave her. She found a file with a suspicious name that she couldn't open. She showed it to her mother, and they took it to the police. A search detected five deleted pornographic video files, two of them of Nicole and her father. He was charged with producing the videos, and he fled the United States to avoid prosecution.

Some months later, Nicole went on TV to ask viewers for any tips that might help locate her father. A police officer who worked child pornography cases saw the program and recognized Nicole as the child in videos that he had seen. An investigation followed, and ultimately detectives learned that photographs of Nicole have been downloaded to thousands of computers around the world via file-sharing and are widely circulated on the Internet. There are also video clips online that Nicole's father filmed and uploaded. Nicole says the realization that the images had been seen by people all over the world was devastating.

Nicole's experience is, unfortunately, not uncommon. The child pornography featuring her was produced by her father; other cases involve uncles and family friends. Nicole is a victim of child sexual abuse. There is no evidence her father had sexual contact with other children; he is not a pedophile. The anonymity and worldwide availability of the Internet allows images, once uploaded, to be viewed all over the world for years to come, deepening the shame and distress that victims experience.

Source: Details from Bazelon, Emily, "Money is no cure." *The New York Times Magazine*, January 27, 2013, 22–29ff.

arrests for possession involved images displaying sexual penetration, and 20 percent involved violence. Sixty-five percent of the victims appeared to be 13 or older. The majority of cases involved a perpetrator who had intimate access to the victim (i.e., was a family member, relative, neighbor, or babysitter).

There is a continuing debate about the link between CP offenses and child molesting/pedophilic behavior. Clearly, some instances of production involve sexual activity with a child. A study of offenders found that about 17 percent of those arrested had molested the child (Wolak et al., 2011a). Of course, many people involved in CP never get arrested. Seto (2004) assessed 685 men referred to a mental health clinic for various reasons including CP. About 43 percent of those involved in CP had a history of offenses against children. On the other hand, studies of sex offenders find that they are no more likely than male nonoffenders to have been exposed to hard-core pornography (Malamuth & Huppin, 2007).

Some major, well-known films could easily be classified as kiddie porn. *Taxi Driver* featured Jodie Foster as a 12-year-old prostitute. And *Pretty Baby* launched the career of Brooke Shields, playing the role of a 12-year-old brothel prostitute in New Orleans. Shields herself was 12 years old when the film was made. *The Girl Next Door* features abuse and molestation of a 13-year-old by family and friends.

Advertising

As part of our discussion of pornography, we should consider another mating of sex and money that all of us encounter every day—*sex in advertising* (Figure 6). Both subtle and obvious sexual promises are used to sell a wide variety of products. A muscular young man wearing low-slung jeans and no shirt sells Calvin Kleins. Abercrombie & Fitch catalogs feature photos of nude young people in bed or in pools. Perfumes promise that they will make women instantly sexually attractive. One brand of coffee seems to guarantee a warm, romantic, sensuous evening for the couple who drink it.

The saying is that "sex sells." That's precisely why advertisers add sexual content. What do the data say? A meta-analysis looked at studies using experimental designs that examined responses of viewers to sexual content in ads, compared with a control group (Lull & Bushman, 2015;

Figure 6   Sex in advertising. Many advertisers, including Calvin Klein, use sexual images to sell products. Do you consider this image "lascivious"? Some people do.

©John Violet/Alamy

see also Wirtz et al., 2018). Sexual ads did not increase memory for the brand being advertised, nor did they increase intentions to buy the product, which is the whole point of the ad. The researchers coded the intensity of the sexual content in the ads on a scale from 1 (suggestive) to 4 (genitals visible). Buying intentions decreased as intensity of the sexual content increased. The authors theorized that when cues in an ad are emotionally arousing, individuals' attention is focused on those cues (the sexual content), and other content (e.g., the brand, the product) is forced to the periphery of attention, and therefore is not remembered. So much for sex selling.

The Producers

In the 1980s and 1990s, the largest component of the porn industry was the production and distribution of X-rated videos. Some of the major production companies were (are) Adam and Eve, Hustler, Playboy, Vivid, and Wicked. These companies often used a traditional business structure (CEOs, vice-presidents, producers, etc.), and each produced dozens of videos per year. The heads of these firms were generally entrepreneurs interested in making money who saw the X-rated film industry as a business opportunity. Most of these companies had permanent studios resembling those of major filmmakers, which require a substantial investment, high maintenance costs, and numerous employees to manage.

The development of handheld cameras and portable equipment allowed movement away from studio-based production. As noted in First Person: Behind the Scenes, Dave Cummings drives to a large home in Beverly Hills, rented for just three or four days for the filming. Thus, today videos can be made by a small crew that can travel anywhere, allowing much easier access to the production side.

As noted earlier, the Internet has displaced the production and marketing of DVDs with online access to X-rated films, and especially short clips taken from them. Like YouTube, the tube sites accept uploads from almost anyone. Many of the clips on tube sites have the logo of the production company prominently displayed, and they may include links so the viewer can purchase the full version.

The Performers

Many of the performers in hard- and soft-core materials are probably like some of your friends and coworkers. In the discussion of commercial sex, we noted that more than 1 million students may be employed in the industry in the United States, including appearing in videos and stills, performing on sex cam sites, and stripping and working other jobs (servers) in strip clubs. Women who worked in the Lion's Den in upstate New York were young single mothers. We noted that many Internet videos are made by amateurs, ordinary singles and couples who perhaps have some exhibitionist tendencies, like extra money, or just like to imagine other people finding them sexually attractive. The many niche markets for web porn—for videos featuring Black, Asian, or Hispanic women, gays, lesbians, trans people, pregnant women—create a demand for all kinds of people to perform. The videos can be easily uploaded to a tube site.

There are a variety of pathways into performing. Playboy visits major campuses every year and advertises for "models"; they often turn aspiring "Playmates" away because there are too many applicants! Some video producers recruit young women at large parties or popular spring break locations. Dave Cummings (First Person: Behind the Scenes) voluntarily entered the industry at age 54. Once he had demonstrated his prowess, he found himself in continuing demand. In fact, he is now producing his own line of videos. Cummings says he does it because he enjoys sex and for the opportunity to have sex with lots of attractive young women. A 21-year-old starlet, Sienna, drifted into performing in adult videos. She had worked in a fast food outlet and bagel shop; she saw an ad in the newspaper for "nude modeling" and tried it. For the first year she did still photo shoots, $350 to $400 for a few hours. Then she moved to working for an Internet company as a cam model, engaging in masturbation while clients watched her via the Internet. After a few months she thought, "If I'm gonna do this, I might as well do porn and make more money." Sienna says she may leave the industry soon; "I've just been pounded so much in these movies that I'm starting to get tired" (Petkovich, 2004). Some performers report being coerced into performing for stills or movies through the use of alcohol or drugs or through the use of physical force by others on camera.

There are a wide variety of beliefs (stereotypes, myths) about actresses in X-rated films. Researchers recruited 177 female performers in adult films through the Adult Industry Medical Healthcare Foundation. Each completed a survey. Researchers then recruited a comparison sample of women, matched on age, marital status, and ethnicity, in university and community (e.g., airports) settings. Actresses were more likely to identify as bisexual, report an earlier age of first intercourse (15.1 versus 17.3), more sexual partners in the past year, and greater enjoyment of sex. Actresses were not more likely to report sexual abuse in childhood (Griffith et al., 2013a). In a related study, college students were asked to estimate various characteristics of male and female pornography actors. Their estimates were compared with data from surveys of male and female performers. Students underestimated the sexual experience and enjoyment of sex reported by actors, and overestimated their earnings by 300 percent! (Griffith et al., 2013b).

The Consumers

Who is consuming/buying/using all of these sexually explicit materials? It has long been taken as fact that pornography is used primarily by males. The General Social Survey has asked a question about viewing an X-rated movie of representative samples of U.S. adults almost every year since 1973. From 1987 to 2010, the percentage of men reporting that they have has fluctuated between 30 percent and 40 percent (Wright, 2013). Men who are younger are more likely to report viewing. Note that the question does not specify a venue; the viewing could have occurred in a commercial theater, a private party, or on the Internet or a cell phone. The most common venue has probably changed over the years, but viewership is quite stable. Across the same time period, fewer women report viewing an X-rated movie. In recent years, men make up more than two-thirds of those who report viewing

(Smith & Son, 2013). The data show that from 1987 to 2010 the percentage of women has fluctuated between 10 and 15 percent; among women 18 to 30, the percentage reporting viewing is about one-third (Wright et al., 2013).

On college campuses, viewing pornography is also gendered. An online survey of undergraduate and graduate students ages 18 to 26 found that 70 percent of the men but only 10 percent of the women view pornography more than once a month (Carroll et al., 2008). Other research suggests that the main reasons for viewing it are curiosity and to experience sexual arousal. Salmon (2012) suggests that women are not attracted to porn because it emphasizes impersonal sex and sexual variety. Women, she argues, are aroused by an emphasis on relationships and finding Mr. Right, which they find in romance novels. Romance novels account for 13 percent of paperback book sales in the United States and attract 29 million readers (compared to 40 million viewers of Internet porn).

Yet some women do purchase and watch pornographic videos. Research conducted in Australia reported that 65 percent of X-rated videos were purchased by a woman or a heterosexual couple. In data from 280 women, 20 percent said they selected the video, 50 percent said both selected it, 18 percent said the partner selected it with both their preferences in mind, and 9 percent said the partner selected it (Contessini, 2003). Female interest in erotica was recognized 30 years ago by Candida Royale, then a film star, who became a producer and director; her company, *Femme Productions,* has made more than 20 films directed toward women. A growing number of men and women are attempting to market to women, producing what is called *female-empowered* adult entertainment, including films, cable TV programs, sex toy stores, and websites (see Figure 7).

Figure 7   Not all porn directors are men. Jacky St. James is highly successful as both a writer and director and has won numerous awards for her videos from adult video organizations.

©Albert L. Ortega/Getty Images

Table 1 Do You Use Porn? A Survey by the Kinsey Institute (N = 10,453)

Sex			How much time per week in the past month?	
Male		80%	I did not use porn in the past	
Female		17%	month	11%
Age			Less than one hour	18%
18 to 20		11%	1 to 5 hours	37%
21 to 30		31%	6 to 15 hours	16%
31 to 40		29%	16 to 25 hours	6%
41 to 50		15%	26 to 50 hours	3%
51 to 60		7%	More than 50 hours	3%
61 to 70		2%	**Why do you use porn? (Top 5 answers)**	
71 or older		1%	To masturbate / for physical	
Viewed sexual images in the past month?			release	72%
Never have viewed them		3%	To sexually arouse myself and/or	
Not once, but I have in the past		20%	others	69%
One or two times		16%	Out of curiosity	54%
Once a week		10%	To fantasize about things I would not	
A few times a week		27%	necessarily want in real life	43%
Once a day		9%	To distract myself	38%
Several times a day		10%		

Source: An online survey conducted in association with Public Broadcasting System. Results at http://www.pbs.org/wgbh/pages/frontline/shows/porn/etc/surveyres.html.

A study of 617 married or cohabiting heterosexual couples collected data from each partner (Poulsen et al., 2013). Questions included, "During the last 12 months, on how many days did you view or read pornography (i.e., movies, magazines, Internet sites, adult romantic novels)?" Notice that this is a very broad question and includes romance novels. Ninety-four percent of the women reported using these materials once a month or less, compared to only 31 percent of the men. Ten percent of the men reported using three or more days per week, and 16 percent reported using once or twice per week. Obviously most couples were not using the materials together. Users of both genders reported lower religiosity.

We noted earlier that most strip clubs cater to a heterosexual male audience. Most women who enter are with male customers, but increasingly a single woman or groups of two or more women are in the audience. Participant observation research found that even if women actively demonstrated interest, such as by tipping dancers on the stage, dancers often *passed over* (avoided) them as they circulated on the floor (Wosick-Correa & Joseph, 2008). Some dancers acknowledged them as women, by complaining to them about costumes or male customers. Some more experienced dancers treated them as customers and gave them dances; these dances were *tailored* to a woman's body (e.g., involved breast play) and were individualized.

Internet porn attracts a more varied clientele. Chat rooms and news groups attract both men and women of diverse ages (assuming that those who describe themselves online are doing so accurately). Some of these people are married. There have been news reports of a man or woman leaving a spouse or partner in order to live with someone they met via the Internet. Depending on the focus of the room or group, participants may be from diverse racial or ethnic backgrounds and have varied sexual interests. The data on gender of consumers suggest that bulletin boards and adult websites probably attract middle-class White men—although some emphasize materials oriented toward other clienteles. Table 1 presents results from an online survey that assessed the number of times and number of hours per month that users view sexual materials.

The Effects of Exposure

The question of the effects of pornography on the viewer is a contentious one among both laypeople and scientists. One side argues that pornography is not harmful, it's just good clean fun; the other side argues that pornography, and especially violent pornography, can have negative and even dangerous effects on the viewer and may lead to negative attitudes toward women, attitudes condoning rape, or aggressive behavior. What do the data say?

We need a theoretical model to help us think about these issues. There are several relevant models. One is *sexual script theory,* discussed in the chapter "Theoretical Perspectives on Sexuality." Scripts define appropriate

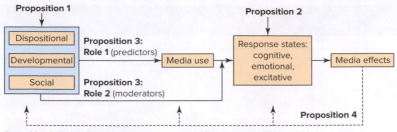

Proposition 1: Media effects depend on three types of differential susceptibility variables.
Proposition 2: Three media response states mediate the relationship between media use and effects.
Proposition 3: The differential susceptibility variables have two roles: they act as predictors and moderators.
Proposition 4: Media effects are transactional.

Figure 8   The four propositions of the differential susceptibility to media effects model (Valkenburg & Peter, 2013).

sexual interactions by identifying the right actors, behaviors, and contexts for sexual activity (Wright, 2013). Media portrayals can be a major socializing influence on people who are exposed to them. For example, how an actor looks tells us what an attractive sexual partner should look like.

Another theoretical perspective is the **differential susceptibility to media effects model,** shown in Figure 8 (Valkenburg & Peter, 2013). We apply it specifically to pornography here, so the label "Media Use" means "Pornography Use" in our discussion. Let's start at the left of the diagram.

The left box shows three factors that contribute to whether a person views pornography—not everyone does. Several factors predict who chooses to view: individual predispositions, developmental factors (age), and social factors (e.g., do peers watch together in a group?). These factors all contribute to media (porn) use, which is shown in the next box.

The next box to the right shows that viewing porn has multiple effects on the viewer at the time of viewing. Some effects are cognitive (e.g., thoughts such as "I'd really like to perform like him"); other effects are emotional, such as making the person feel happy or perhaps sad or angry. Other effects can be to activate physiological arousal, whether it's sexual arousal or a more general sense of excitement. These responses lead to the effects that the media viewing has on the person. These might be changes in the viewer's attitudes about sex or relationships or changes in the person's sexual behavior.

The model is called *differential susceptibility* to media effects for the following reason. Notice that the second arrow, at the bottom, goes from the box at the left and intersects with the arrow from media use to responses. That is the differential susceptibility part. It means that different people show different responses to viewing pornography. Certain people are more

susceptible and others are less susceptible to any negative effects of pornography. You may have heard this idea before in discussions of the effects of violence in the media. Many people watch violence in the media, yet only some of them go on to commit violent crimes. Those are the people who were susceptible, or vulnerable, to the negative effects of violent media. The same principle applies to sexual media; some people are more susceptible to its effects than others.

What do the data say about all the links in the model? Let's proceed, again starting at the left.

Who views pornography? As noted in the section on The Consumers, men are more likely than women to be viewers. Some people view as a couple, demonstrating social influences on viewing. Others do so in a context such as a fraternity party, another example of social influence. As Table 1 shows, viewing is heaviest among people in their twenties and thirties, a developmental pattern. That survey, however, did not include adolescents under age 18, so we don't know about them. In terms of individual predispositions, a history of many sexual partners predicts porn use; liberal sexual attitudes and antisocial personality characteristics also predict use (Kingston et al., 2009).

What effects does porn use have on immediate responses: cognitive, emotional, and physiological arousal? There are gender differences in self-reports of arousal response to sexually explicit materials. Men report higher levels of arousal to such portrayals than do women (Kingston et al., 2009; Malamuth, 1998; Murnen & Stockton, 1997). The differences are larger in response to pornography than to erotica, and the difference is much larger among college students than among older people. This gender difference is often attributed to the fact that most erotica and pornography are male-oriented. The focus is almost exclusively on sexual behavior, with little concern for relationships, and the man typically ejaculates on some part of the woman's body (the "cum shot") rather than inside her. Researchers examined the cognitive effects

Differential susceptibility to media effects model: A theoretical model from communications theory that specifies who chooses to view certain media (e.g., pornography), how the viewing has its effects, and who is especially susceptible to the effects.

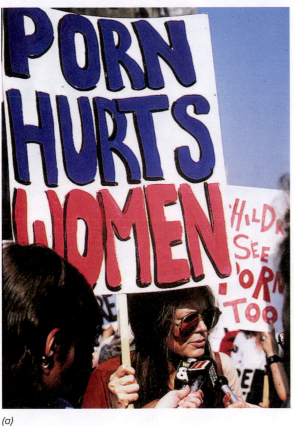

(a)   (b)

Figure 9   Controversies over pornography. (*a*) Feminist Gloria Steinem protests pornography. (*b*) Protests over the British firm Tesco releasing a tablet for children, with no filters to protect children from accidentally viewing pornography.

(a) ©Charles Gatewood/The Image Works; (b) ©Guy Bell/Alamy

of exposure to kiddie porn using a method similar to the Implicit Association Test described in the chapter "Sex Research" (Paul & Linz, 2008). College students were exposed to "barely legal" erotic images of people over 18 but who looked (much) younger. Would exposure create an association relating those images to sex and eroticism? Men and women exposed to "barely legal" images exhibited faster recognition of the words *erotic* and *beautiful* than men and women exposed to similar images of models who were clearly over 21 years of age. Therefore, exposure to porn with apparently underage actors did in fact create a cognitive link to eroticism.

What effects does porn have on viewers (long term)? Researchers have looked primarily at effects on attitudes and on sexual behavior. Using data from national surveys, researchers found that viewing X-rated films is associated with more permissive attitudes toward teen sex, premarital sex, and extramarital sex in both men and women (Wright, 2013; Wright et al., 2013). These results are correlational, though; perhaps people with permissive attitudes are more likely to watch X-rated films. To address this issue, a longitudinal study measured X-rated film viewing and attitudes at Time 1, and then retested the same people 2 years later at Time 2 (Wright, 2015). The results indicated that porn use at Time 1 predicted more permissive attitudes toward premarital sex 2 years later, providing stronger evidence of a cause-and-effect relationship.

Researchers have also examined whether porn use is related to attitudes supporting violence. A meta-analysis found that pornography consumption is correlated with increased attitudes supporting violence against women (Hald et al., 2010). Other studies looked at the correlation between pornography consumption and sexually aggressive behavior. A meta-analysis of studies of this type found a significant positive correlation (Wright et al., 2016); that is, consumption of pornography was associated with an increased likelihood of committing sexual aggression.

Of special concern is whether consumption of pornography is related to high-risk sexual behavior. A survey of men visiting a men-seeking-men website measured the frequency with which men had viewed sexually explicit online videos in the past 3 months, how often the videos portrayed unprotected anal intercourse (UAI, a high-risk sexual behavior), and how often they had engaged in that behavior in the past 3 months (Nelson et al., 2014). There was a highly significant relationship between viewing videos portraying UAI and engaging in that behavior. There was also strong evidence that viewing pornography is associated with a greater number of sexual partners (Harkness et al., 2015). Having multiple partners is a high-risk behavior.

The effects of pornography exposure on aggressive behavior have been studied in experimental research in which the experimental group is exposed to porn and the control group is exposed to a neutral video, and a behavioral measure is taken afterward. Perhaps a woman (a confederate of the experimenter's) accidentally bumps into them in the hallway afterward; does the research participant react aggressively or not? Or perhaps the research participant has the opportunity to administer an electric shock to someone. Do they do it, and what intensity of shock do they use? A meta-analysis found that porn exposure does increase aggressive behavior (Allen et al., 1995).

Another meta-analysis examined the correlation between porn use and satisfaction with one's sexual relationship (Wright et al., 2017). The results indicated that porn use was negatively correlated with relationship satisfaction and with sexual satisfaction. The more often people used porn, the less satisfied they were with their sexual relationship.

Are some people differentially susceptible to the effects of porn? Several studies found evidence of these effects. For example, although most people react negatively to rape and kiddie porn, men who report, before they view pornography, that they would commit rape under some circumstances are aroused by portrayals of rape (Davis & Bauseman, 1993). A major review concluded that pornography is a risk factor for engaging in sexual aggression, specifically for men who are high on susceptibility factors and who use porn frequently (Kingston et al., 2009). The main individual predispositions are antisocial personality characteristics and the personality trait of hostile masculinity, which involves a generally hostile attitude toward life and specifically toward women, combined with feeling satisfaction from dominating women.

It is worth noting that this phenomenon of differential susceptibility helps to explain why some studies find negative effects of porn use and others don't. It may depend on the proportion of highly susceptible individuals in the sample. The inconsistent findings continue to fuel debates about whether porn has negative effects when, in fact, it has negative effects on some people (the highly susceptible ones) and not others.

Issues Related to Pornography

As we stated in the introduction to this section, some groups want to ban most or all "pornography" (though they may disagree about exactly what it is). Political conservatives, religious fundamentalists, and some feminists are very critical of it. Why would feminists (e.g., Griffin, 1981; Lederer, 1980; Morgan, 1978), who prize sexual liberation, be opposed to pornography? There are three basic reasons some feminists and many others object to pornography. First, they argue that pornography debases women. In the milder, soft-core versions it portrays women as sex objects whose breasts, legs, and genitalia can be purchased and then ogled. In the hard-core versions women may be shown being held down, penetrated by several men simultaneously, or urinated upon.

How big of an issue is sex trafficking?

Does mainstream pornography objectify women? The answer depends in part on how one defines the term, and there is controversy over that. Defining objectification as including treating another person as an object, one partner dominating another, and penis worship, one researcher performed a content analysis of the 50 best-selling pornographic videos in Australia (McKee, 2005). Many of the videos were imports from the United States and Europe. Seven measures allowed direct comparison of portrayals of men and portrayals of women. On one measure, not having an orgasm, women were significantly higher than men. On three measures—less time spent looking at the camera, less time spent talking to the camera, and less likely to initiate sex—men were significantly higher than women. On three final measures—having a name, being a central character, and time spent talking—there were no significant differences. One can also argue that porn objectifies men. Most men depicted in porn videos have large penises, are continuously aroused, have buff bodies, and will engage in any type of intercourse with any woman. That is probably as unrealistic as the portrayals of women.

A second reason for objections is that pornography associates sex with violence toward women. As such, it contributes to rape and other forms of violence against women and girls. One feminist writer has put it bluntly: "pornography is the theory and rape is the practice" (Morgan, 1980, p. 139). We have just reviewed the empirical evidence on this point. There is some evidence that exposure of men to aggressive pornography can increase aggression toward women, especially for men who are high on susceptibility. There are some men who are at high risk for whom exposure to aggressive porn does elicit aggressive behavior.

A third reason for objections is that pornography shows—indeed, glamorizes—unequal power relationships between women and men. A common theme in pornography is boss-secretary, doctor-nurse, professor-student sex or men forcing women to have sex, so the power of men and the subordination of women are emphasized. Consistent with this point, feminists and others do not object to sexual materials that portray women and men in equal, humanized relationships—what we have termed *erotica*. Feminists also note the intimate relationship between pornography and traditional gender roles. Pornography is enmeshed as both cause and effect. That is, pornography in part results from traditional gender roles that make it socially acceptable for men to use porn and require hypersexuality and aggressiveness as part of the male role. In turn, pornography may serve to perpetuate traditional gender roles. By seeing or reading about dominant men and submissive, dehumanized women, each new generation of adolescent boys is socialized to accept these roles.

A growing concern over the past decade is *pornography addiction*. The data in Table 1 indicate that about 10 percent of respondents to the survey "viewed sexual images" more than once a day in the preceding month, and that 12 percent spent 16 or more hours per week viewing them. Some commentators and some health professionals believe that exposure to these images at these levels is problematic, that very high levels of viewing reflect behavior that is compulsive and out of control. There is no question that excessive viewing can negatively affect one's life—grades, productivity at work, interpersonal relationships. Also, we reviewed data showing that exposure to pornographic material affects one's sexual scripts and behavior and can lead to poorer quality sexual relationships; these effects are more likely the more time one spends consuming these materials. The issue of sexually compulsive behavior is discussed in detail in the chapter "Variations in Sexual Behavior."

These are disturbing issues. What is the solution? Should pornography be censored or made illegal? Or would this only make it forbidden and therefore more attractive, and still available on the unregulatable Internet? Or should all forms of pornography be legal and readily available, and should we rely on other methods—such as education of parents and students through the school system—to abolish its use? Or should we adopt some in-between strategy, making some forms of pornography—say kiddie porn and violent porn—illegal, but allowing free access to erotica?

Our own opinion is that legal restrictions—known less politely as censorship—are probably not the solution. We agree with the view put forth by a group of researchers that a better solution is education (Donnerstein et al., 1987; Linz et al., 1987). In their experiments, they have debriefed male participants at the conclusion of the procedures. They convey to the participants that media depictions are unreal and that the portrayal of women enjoying forced sex is fictitious. They dispel common rape myths, especially any that were shown in the film used in the experiment. Participants who have been debriefed in this way show less acceptance of rape myths and more sensitivity to rape victims than participants shown a neutral film (Donnerstein et al., 1987).

Subsequently, some researchers introduced *prebriefing* of participants in research involving exposure to sexually explicit materials. The typical briefing—pre or post—consists of a short audiotape or a printed handout pointing out that the material is fictional. It reminds participants that women do not enjoy forced sex and that rape is a serious crime. Researchers identified 10 studies that included prebriefing or debriefing, and measures of the effects of exposure to the material. All 10 found that there were no negative effects of exposure accompanied by an educational briefing. In six of the studies, participants were less accepting of rape myths at the conclusion of the study than at the beginning (Allen et al., 1996). This research provides solid evidence that education can eliminate at least negative effects of pornography on attitudes.

More generally, the research points to the need for education. Programs that involve exposing adolescents in a controlled environment to pornographic material, and then working with them to analyze it, to consider its realism, objectification, gender role portrayals, etc., could go a long way toward reducing the negative effects of sexually explicit media. These programs could be implemented by individual families, churches, boys and girls clubs, and schools. As in so many other areas of sexuality and sexual health, for both individuals and society, the best answer is evidence-based education.

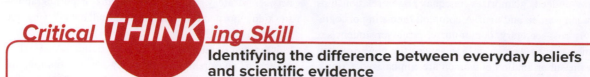

Critical THINKing Skill

Identifying the difference between everyday beliefs and scientific evidence

Each of us has a set of beliefs about ourselves, our behavior, and the influences on us. These everyday beliefs are sometimes referred to as common sense. Often, there is a good deal of research that is relevant to these beliefs. One of the functions of this book is to summarize in an accessible way the research relevant to our sexual beliefs and behavior.

In this chapter, we summarized the research that has been conducted on the effects of exposure to pornography or sexually explicit material. Some of this research is correlational, and some of it is experimental; the experimental results are the basis for making causal claims about the effects of viewing these materials. Let's review the evidence:

- Exposure to pornography is linked to attitudes supporting violence against women.
- Exposure to porn is linked to high-risk sexual behavior.
- Exposure to violent porn increases men's aggressive behavior.
- Exposure to porn is linked to reduced satisfaction with one's sexual relationship.

Now, how much sexually explicit material have you been exposed to in the past month? In films, on TV, on DVDs, online? In video games? What was the content? How much was consensual, how much involved violence directed toward women? Toward men? If you are a typical college student, chances are you have been exposed to porn weekly or more often, perhaps of several types.

Now, apply the scientific evidence summarized above to your exposure. Does porn arouse you? Do you think about sex more often and engage in more sex after you watch porn (not just in the hours after but for 2 or 3 days)? Are you more tolerant of violence against women than you used to be? Chances are you will admit to being aroused, and maybe to thinking more about sex. But you're not sure it affects your behavior, and you are sure you don't tolerate violence against women, right?

We like to think we are different, that things that influence others don't influence us. Time for some critical thinking. If these studies have been done on large samples of students, and they have, and you are a student, why would you not be affected? Porn users, especially those who watch 11 hours per week or more (whom the experts consider compulsive viewers), tell us that it doesn't affect them.

The everyday belief that "I am not affected by mass media" is in direct contradiction to research evidence. Clearly, the effect varies depending upon what content you watch and how much of it. But regular viewers are affected, especially those who are highly susceptible. Critical thinking involves following the scientific evidence, not just everyday beliefs.

SUMMARY

Commercial sex is a major industry in the United States and around the world. Two prominent aspects of it are prostitution and pornography.

Prostitution

Commercial sex workers engage in partnered sexual activity in return for payment, such as money, gifts, or drugs. There are several venues in which they work in the United States, including their own homes, in-call services, out-call services, massage parlors, and through the Internet as camgirls. The working conditions, risks, and income of a sex worker depend on the setting. Third parties who may be involved include a pimp, madam, or manager; the involvement of these people generally limits a worker's autonomy. Sex trafficking involves exploitation and is a serious problem.

Research suggests that a sex worker's well-being depends on the risk level of the setting in which she works, the reasons she entered sex work, and whether she experienced victimization as a child or adolescent.

Data indicate that the use of prostitutes has declined substantially in the United States in the past 50 years.

About one-half of the clients of female workers are occasional johns; the other 50 percent are repeat clients. Some men rely on sex workers for their sexual outlet.

Some male sex workers serve a female clientele. They may work as escorts, employees of massage parlors, or gigolos. Hustlers cater to a male clientele.

Pornography

Distinctions are made among pornography (sexually arousing art, literature, or film), obscenity (material offensive to authorities or society), and erotica (sexual material that shows men and women in equal, humane relationships). Internet porn has mushroomed in the past 25 years; people can discuss explicit sexual activity online, read sexually arousing stories, download sexually explicit images, or purchase a variety of services at websites. Pornographic videos and websites are a multi-billion-dollar business. Children are the star victims in kiddie porn.

The differential susceptibility to media effects model is a framework for understanding the effects of pornography. Research shows that viewing porn is linked to (1) attitudes supporting violence against women; (2) sexually aggressive behavior; and (3) high-risk sexual behavior. Experimental research shows that exposure to porn increases aggressive behavior. Consistent with the differential susceptibility model, research indicates that pornography is most likely to have an effect on sexual aggression if the viewer is a man who is high on susceptibility factors (antisocial personality, hostile masculine personality) and views porn frequently. Education about the effects of pornography is probably the best solution to the problems created by pornography.

SUGGESTIONS FOR FURTHER READING

Bernstein, Elizabeth. (2007). *Temporarily yours: Intimacy, authenticity and the commerce of sex.* Chicago: University of Chicago Press. An insightful analysis of the ways commercial sex work is shaped by contemporary capitalism, cultural changes in sexual beliefs, and the Internet.

Bullough, Vern, and Bullough, Bonnie. (1987). *Women and prostitution: A social history.* Buffalo, NY: Prometheus Books. A fascinating history of the oldest profession, from ancient Greece and Rome through medieval times, India, and China, to the present.

Price-Glynn, Kim. (2010). *Strip club: Gender, power and sex work.* New York: New York University Press. An excellent ethnography of a club in the Northeast. The author explores the role of gender in the organization of the club, the making of masculinities, and the workers' lives in and out of the club.

Weitzer, Ronald (Ed.). (2010). *Sex for sale: Prostitution, pornography and the sex industry.* New York: Taylor and Francis. A balanced, well-documented analysis of the sex industry.

1. What counts as premature ejaculation?
2. What can a woman do if she has trouble having orgasms?
3. How does Viagra work?

Read this chapter to find out.

CHAPTER

17

©Ryan McVay/Getty Images

Sexual Disorders and Sex Therapy

CHAPTER HIGHLIGHTS

The only thing we have to fear is fear itself.*

*Franklin Delano Roosevelt, First Inaugural Address, March 4, 1933.

Sexual disorders—such as premature (early) ejaculation in men and an inability to have orgasms in women—cause a great deal of psychological distress to the individuals troubled by them and to their partners. Until the 1960s, the only available treatment was long-term psychoanalysis, which is costly and inaccessible for most people. Masters and Johnson ushered in a new era in understanding and treatment with the publication, in 1970, of *Human Sexual Inadequacy*. This book reported on the team's research on sexual disorders, as well as on their rapid-treatment program of behavioral therapy. Since then, many additional developments have taken place in the field, including cognitive behavior therapy and medical (drug) treatments. Sex disorders and treatments for them are the topics of this chapter.

A **sexual disorder** is a problem with sexual response that causes a person mental distress. The term *sexual dysfunction* is also used. Examples are an inability to get an erection or an inability to orgasm. This definition seems fairly simple; however, in practice it can be difficult to determine exactly when something is a sexual disorder. In addition, there is a tendency to think in terms of only two categories, people with a sexual disorder and "normal" people. In fact, there is a continuum, much like the Kinsey scale for gradations in sexual orientation that we discussed in the chapter "Sexual Orientation: Gay, Straight, or Bi?" Most of us have had, at one time or another, a sex problem that went away in a day or a few months without treatment. These cases represent the shades of gray that lie between absolutely great sexual functioning and long-term difficulties that require sex therapy.

Sexual disorders can be further classified. A **lifelong sexual disorder** is one that has been present ever since the person became sexual; an **acquired sexual disorder** is a dysfunction that develops after a period of normal functioning.

First we consider the kinds of sexual disorders, then review the causes of these disorders and the treatments for them.

Kinds of Sexual Disorders

In this section we discuss the four categories of sexual disorders: desire disorders, arousal disorders, orgasmic disorders, and sexual pain disorders. Notice that the first three categories correspond to components of the sexual response cycle, discussed in the chapter "Sexual Arousal."

Desire Disorders

Desire disorders include hypoactive sexual desire and discrepancy of sexual desire.

Hypoactive Sexual Desire

Sexual desire, or *libido,* refers to an interest in sexual activity, leading the individual to seek out sexual activity or to be pleasurably receptive to it. When sexual desire is very low, so that the individual is not interested in sexual activity, this is a disorder termed **hypoactive sexual desire** (**HSD;** the prefix *hypo-* means "low") (Basson, 2004; Brotto, 2010). It is also sometimes termed *inhibited sexual desire* or *low sexual desire*. This disorder is found in both women and men. The defining characteristics are lack of interest in sex or sharply reduced interest, or a lack of responsive desire (Basson, 2007). Many people's desire occurs before sexual activity begins and leads them to initiate sex, whereas in other cases they begin to feel desire as sexual activity starts; this latter pattern is called *responsive desire.*

Surveys of the general population indicate that lack of interest in sex is common. Too little sexual desire is the most common sexual issue reported by women (Basson, 2006). Roughly 10 percent of women up to age 49 have problems with lack of desire; rates then increase to about 50 percent in women over 65 (Lewis et al., 2010). About half as many men as women experience desire problems, but men definitely can experience them (Lewis et al., 2010; Meana & Steiner, 2014; Mitchell et al., 2013b).

Like other sexual disorders, HSD poses complex problems of definition. There are many circumstances when it is perfectly normal for a person's desire to be inhibited. For example, one cannot be expected to be turned on by every potential partner.

It is also often true that the problem is not the individual's absolute level of sexual desire but a discrepancy between the partners' levels (Willoughby et al., 2014). That is, if one partner wants sex considerably less frequently than the other does, there is a conflict. This problem is termed **discrepancy of sexual desire.**

In the chapter "Variations in Sexual Behavior," we introduced the American Psychiatric Association's manual of disorders, called the *Diagnostic and Statistical Manual* or *DSM*. In 2013, the APA came out with a new edition of

---

Sexual disorder: A problem with sexual response that causes a person mental distress.

Lifelong sexual disorder: A sexual disorder that has been present ever since the person began sexual functioning.

Acquired sexual disorder: A sexual disorder that develops after a period of normal functioning.

Hypoactive sexual desire (HSD): A sexual disorder in which there is a lack of interest in sexual activity; also termed *inhibited sexual desire* or *low sexual desire.*

Discrepancy of sexual desire: A sexual disorder in which the partners have considerably different levels of sexual desire.

the *DSM, DSM-5.* It is controversial, and not all experts agree with some of the decisions about diagnoses. We don't completely agree with some of them either. In this chapter, we provide *DSM* diagnosis terms but explain why some of them might be challenged.

As a case in point, the *DSM-5* changed the hypoactive sexual desire diagnosis, so now there is male hypoactive sexual desire disorder, and female low sexual desire was merged with female arousal disorder (described below) into **female sexual interest/arousal disorder.** One could debate why hypoactive sexual desire has to be split into male and female versions—and what happens to trans individuals?—and why desire (called interest in *DSM-5*) would be merged with arousal for women (Balon & Clayton, 2014; Basson, 2014). Those favoring the new category say it is appropriate because interest or desire problems so frequently co-occur with arousal problems in women.

Arousal Disorders

The arousal disorders include female sexual arousal disorder and male erectile disorder (ED).

Female Sexual Arousal Disorder

Female sexual arousal disorder refers to a lack of response to sexual stimulation, including a lack of lubrication (Graham, 2010a). The disorder involves both a subjective, psychological component and a physiological element (Basson, 2004). Some cases are defined by the woman's own subjective sense that she does not feel aroused despite adequate stimulation, and others are defined by difficulties with vaginal lubrication.

Difficulties with arousal and lubrication are common, reported by roughly 10 percent of women (Lewis et al., 2010; Mitchell et al., 2013b). These problems become particularly frequent among women during and after menopause (Rosen et al., 2012). As estrogen levels decline, vaginal lubrication decreases. The use of sterile lubricants is an easy way to deal with this problem. The absence of subjective feelings of arousal is more complex to treat.

Erectile Disorder

Erectile disorder is the inability to have an erection or maintain one. Other terms for it are *erectile dysfunction* and *impotence,* the term used by laypersons. One result of erectile disorder is that the man cannot engage in sexual intercourse. Using terminology discussed earlier, a case of erectile disorder may be either lifelong or acquired. In **lifelong erectile disorder,** the man has never been able to have an erection that is satisfactory for intercourse. In **acquired erectile disorder,** the man has difficulty getting or maintaining an erection but has had erections sufficient for intercourse at other times.

According to surveys in North America and Europe, erectile disorder occurs in fewer than 10 percent of men under 40 but then increases to about 30 percent for men in their 60s (Lewis et al., 2010; Mitchell et al., 2013b). Erectile disorder is the most common of the disorders among men who seek sex therapy, particularly since the introduction of Viagra.

Psychological reactions to erectile disorder may be severe. For many men, it is one of the most embarrassing things they can imagine. Depression may follow from repeated episodes. It may also cause embarrassment or worry to the man's partner.

The causes of erectile disorder and its treatment will be discussed later in this chapter.

Orgasmic Disorders

The orgasmic disorders include premature ejaculation, male orgasmic disorder, and female orgasmic disorder.

Premature Ejaculation

Premature ejaculation (PE) occurs when a man has an orgasm and ejaculates too soon. In extreme cases, ejaculation may take place so soon after erection that it occurs before intercourse can even begin. In other cases, the man is able to delay the orgasm to some extent, but not as long as he would like or not long enough to meet his partner's preferences. Some experts prefer the terms *early ejaculation* or *rapid ejaculation* as having fewer negative connotations (Grenier & Byers, 2001; Lewis et al., 2004).

Although the definition given above—having an orgasm and ejaculating too soon—seems simple enough, in practice it is complicated to specify when a man is a premature ejaculator. What should the precise criterion for "too soon" be? Should the man be required to last for at least 30 seconds after erection? For 12 minutes? For 2 minutes after insertion of the penis into the vagina? The definitions used by authorities in the field vary widely (Bettocchi et al., 2008). One source defines "prematurity" as the occurrence of orgasm less than 1 minute after the penis has been inserted into the vagina. Another group's criterion is ejaculation before there have been 10 pelvic thrusts. Psychiatrist and sex therapist Helen Singer Kaplan believed that the key to defining the premature ejaculator is the absence of voluntary control of orgasm; that is, the real problem is that the premature ejaculator has little control over when he orgasms (Grenier &

What counts as premature ejaculation?

Female sexual interest/arousal disorder: A diagnosis in *DSM-5* that encompasses lack of interest in sexual activity and absent or reduced arousal during sexual interactions. The diagnosis is limited to women.
Female sexual arousal disorder (FSAD): A sexual disorder in which there is a lack of response to sexual stimulation.
Erectile (eh-REK-tile) disorder: The inability to have or maintain an erection.
Lifelong erectile disorder: Cases of erectile disorder in which the man has never had an erection sufficient to have intercourse.
Acquired erectile disorder: Cases of erectile disorder in which the man at one time was able to have satisfactory erections but can no longer do so.
Premature (early) ejaculation: A sexual disorder in which the man ejaculates too soon and thinks he cannot control when he ejaculates. Also called *rapid ejaculation.*

Byers, 2001; Kaplan, 1974). Another good definition is self-definition: If a man finds that he has become greatly concerned about his lack of ejaculatory control or that it is interfering with his ability to form intimate relationships, or if a couple agree that it is a problem in their relationship, then it may reasonably be called premature ejaculation.

With all these confusing and contradictory definitions, the International Society for Sexual Medicine stepped in and issued a definition that would create consistency in both research and diagnosis (Althof et al., 2010). The definition involves three parts: (1) ejaculation that always or almost always occurs prior to or within 1 minute of vaginal penetration (note the heteronormativity of the definition); (2) the inability to delay ejaculation; and (3) distress about the problem. This definition therefore includes a time component, a lack of control component, and a distress component.

Premature ejaculation is a common problem in the general male population. Surveys indicate that about 15 percent of men have difficulties with early ejaculation (Lewis et al., 2010; Mitchell et al., 2013b). The great majority of men probably never seek therapy for the problem, either because it goes away by itself or because they are too embarrassed.

Like erectile disorders, premature ejaculation may create a web of related psychological problems. Because the ability to postpone ejaculation and "satisfy" a partner is so important in our concept of a man who is a competent lover, rapid ejaculation can cause a man to become anxious about his sexual competence. Furthermore, the partner may become frustrated because she or he is not having a satisfying sexual experience either. So the condition may create friction in the relationship.

The negative psychological effects of early ejaculation are illustrated by a young man in one of our sexuality classes who handed in an anonymous question. He described himself as a premature ejaculator and said that after several humiliating experiences during intercourse with women, he was now convinced that no woman would want him in that condition. He no longer had the courage to ask women out, so he had stopped dating. He wanted to know how the women in the class would react to a man with such a problem. The question was discussed in class, and most of the women agreed that their reaction to his problem would depend a great deal on the quality of the relationship they had with him. If they cared deeply for him, they would be sympathetic and patient and help him overcome the difficulty. The point is, though, that the early ejaculation had created problems so severe that the young man not only had stopped having sex but also had stopped dating.

Delayed Ejaculation

Delayed ejaculation, sometimes also called *male orgasmic disorder,* is the opposite of premature ejaculation. The man is unable to have an orgasm, or it is greatly delayed, even though he has a solid erection and has had more than adequate stimulation (Perelman, 2014). The severity of the problem may range from only occasional problems with orgasming to a history of never having experienced an orgasm. In the most common version, the man is incapable of orgasm during intercourse but may be able to orgasm as a result of hand or mouth stimulation. Fortunately, these problems are rare.

Male orgasmic disorder is far less common than premature ejaculation. About 10 percent of men experience this problem (Mitchell et al., 2013b).

Male orgasmic disorder is, to say the least, a frustrating experience for the man. One would think that any woman would be delighted to have intercourse with a man who has a long-lasting erection that is not terminated by orgasm. In fact, though, some women react negatively to this condition, seeing their partner's inability to have an orgasm as a personal rejection. Some men, anticipating these negative reactions, have adopted the practice of faking orgasm. In some cases, too, the man's orgasmic disorder can create painful intercourse for the woman because intercourse simply goes on too long.

Female Orgasmic Disorder

Female orgasmic disorder is the inability to have an orgasm (Graham, 2010b). This condition goes by a variety of other terms, including *orgasmic dysfunction, anorgasmia,* and *inhibited female orgasm.* Laypersons may call it *frigidity,* but sex therapists reject this term because it has derogatory connotations and is imprecise. *Frigidity* may refer to a variety of conditions ranging from total lack of sexual arousal to arousal without orgasm. Therefore, the term *female orgasmic disorder* is preferred.

Like the other sexual disorders, cases of female orgasmic disorder may be classified into lifelong and acquired. In addition, a common pattern is **situational orgasmic disorder,** in which the woman has orgasms in some situations but not others. For example, she may be able to have orgasms while masturbating but not while having sexual intercourse. Orgasmic disorders are common among women. Roughly 20 percent of women report difficulties with anorgasmia (Lewis et al., 2010; Mitchell et al., 2013b).

Once again, though, these definitions become more complicated in practice than in theory. Consider the case of the woman who has orgasms as a result of masturbation or hand or mouth stimulation by a partner but who does not orgasm in vaginal intercourse. Is this really a sexual disorder? The notion that it is a disorder can be traced to sexual scripts and beliefs that there is a "right" way to have

---

Delayed ejaculation: A sexual disorder in which the man cannot have an orgasm, even though he is highly aroused and has had a great deal of sexual stimulation; also called *male orgasmic disorder.*

Female orgasmic disorder: A sexual disorder in which the woman is unable to have an orgasm.

Situational orgasmic disorder: A case of orgasmic disorder in which the woman is able to have an orgasm in some situations (e.g., while masturbating) but not in others (e.g., while having sexual intercourse).

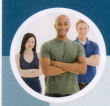

First Person

A Case of Female Orgasmic Disorder

Jane was a self-employed, attractive, divorced woman who came to the clinic at the University of Minnesota at the age of 43, with an acquired inability to reach orgasm, which had then led to a decline in her sexual desire. She had been divorced from her husband, Tom, for 5½ years after a 17-year marriage. Even though she was not in love with him, Jane had married Tom because he was the first man with whom she had sexual intercourse. Jane and Tom had two sons from this marriage, ages 13 (Bruce) and 18 (Dean). Bruce was attending a costly private school paid for by Jane. Dean had a history of emotional and behavioral problems.

At the time she sought help at our clinic, Jane was in a 3-year-long relationship with Frank, a 45-year-old divorced man. Frank directed their sexual relationship. Jane was compliant with Frank's sexual requests, never asking that her needs be met. She reported having an orgasm only once with Frank, although she still reported becoming aroused during their sexual interactions. This lack of orgasm was in contrast to the pattern during her marriage, when she was able to have an orgasm at least half of the time by rubbing her clitoris against her husband's pelvic area when she was on top (her husband did not always have an erection). This difficulty having an orgasm, along with the lack of a supportive response from her partner, affected Jane's sexual desire, which declined precipitously.

Jane came to therapy believing that there was something wrong with her physically—that she was broken sexually.

This belief originated from her boyfriend's assertion that she had a small clitoris, which interfered with her ability to orgasm. She lacked an adequate sexual vocabulary and experienced difficulty talking about sex, often becoming red-faced or tearful. These problems with sexual communication were partially the result of her upbringing in a small rural town in a fundamentalist religious family, where sex was rarely discussed. Jane grew up with her biological parents, two brothers, and two sisters. She described her family as "fundamentally religious," her father as the dominant decision maker, and her mother as "puritanical." In therapy, it emerged that she had been sexually abused by both older brothers, beginning when she was 12 years old.

Jane's treatment proceeded over several years because of the need to help her recover from the child sexual abuse and the PTSD and depression that resulted from it. Treatment used the Sexual Health Model developed at the University of Minnesota and involved multiple treatment methods described in this chapter, including individual, couple, and group therapy and psychiatric care. Jane found a new partner who was more supportive, and treatment ended with Jane feeling sexually confident.

Source: Robinson et al. (2011). Names have been changed to preserve anonymity. Read this article if you want the full details of the therapy.

---

sex—with the penis inside the vagina—and a corresponding "right" way to have orgasms. Because this pattern of situational orgasmic disorder is so common, some experts consider it to be well within the normal range of female sexual response. Perhaps the woman who orgasms as a result of hand or mouth stimulation, but not penile thrusting, is simply having orgasms when she is adequately stimulated and is not having them when she is inadequately stimulated.

Nonetheless, there should be room for self-definition of disorders. If a woman has situational orgasmic disorder, is truly distressed that she is not able to have orgasms during vaginal intercourse, and wants therapy, then it may be appropriate to classify her condition as a disorder and provide

> **Dyspareunia (dis-pah-ROO-nee-uh):**
> Painful intercourse.

therapy. The therapist, however, should be careful to explain to her the problems of definition raised above, in order to be sure that her request for therapy stems from her own dissatisfaction with her sexual responding rather than from an overly idealistic sexual script. Therapy in such cases is probably best viewed as an effort to enrich the client's experience rather than to fix a problem.

Pain Disorders

The pain disorders include painful intercourse and vaginismus.

Painful Intercourse

Painful intercourse, or **dyspareunia,** refers to genital pain experienced during intercourse (Bergeron et al.,

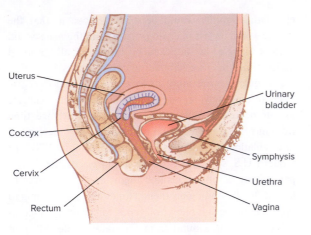

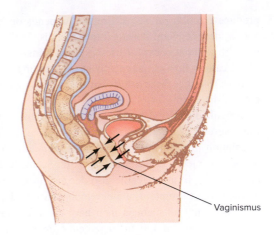

Uterus

Coccyx

Cervix

Rectum

Urinary bladder

Symphysis

Urethra

Vagina

Vaginismus

Figure 1   Vaginismus. (*a*) A normal vagina and other pelvic organs, viewed from the side, and (*b*) vaginismus, or involuntary constriction of the outer third of the vagina.

2014; Binik, 2010b). It is usually thought of as a female sexual disorder, but males occasionally experience it as well. Approximately 8 percent of women and 2 percent of men report pain during sex (Mitchell et al., 2013b). Complaints of occasional pain during intercourse are fairly common among women, but persistent dyspareunia is not very common. In women, the pain may be felt in the vagina, around the vaginal entrance and clitoris, or deep in the pelvis. In men, the pain is felt in the penis or testes. To put it mildly, dyspareunia decreases one's enjoyment of the sexual experience and may even lead one to abstain from sexual activity.

According to another perspective, this disorder is really about pain that happens to occur in the genitals; that is, it is fundamentally about pain, not about sex (Binik et al., 2007). Many people, the reasoning goes, have back pain, some of them because of work-related injuries and others because of sports-related injuries. Yet we don't refer to work-induced back pain and sports-induced back pain but rather focus on the back pain itself. Similarly, with painful intercourse the focus should be on the genital pain suffered by those with this disorder.

Painful intercourse may be related to a variety of physical factors, to be discussed later. Genital pain often triggers other serious problems with sexual functioning, which in turn can create relationship problems (Farmer & Meston, 2007).

In the *DSM-5,* dyspareunia and vaginismus (explained below) were merged into **genito-pelvic pain/penetration disorder** (Reissing et al., 2014). Part of the reason for the merger is that the two tend to occur together.

Vaginismus

Vaginismus (the suffix *ismus* means "spasm") is a spastic contraction of the outer third of the vagina (see Figure 1); in some cases it is so severe that the entrance to the vagina is closed and the woman cannot have intercourse

(Ter Kuile & Reissing, 2014). Vaginismus and dyspareunia are often associated (Binik, 2010a). That is, if intercourse is painful, one result may be spasms that close off the entrance to the vagina.

Vaginismus is not a very common sexual disorder in the general population. Women may be more likely to seek treatment for it than for other disorders because it can make intercourse impossible, creating enormous difficulties in a couple's relationship.

What Causes Sexual Disorders?

There are many causes of sexual disorders, varying from person to person and from one disorder to another. These causes can be grouped into categories: physical factors, drugs, individual psychological factors, combined cognitive and physiological factors, and interpersonal factors. Each of these categories is discussed here.

Physical Causes

Physical factors that cause sexual disorders include **organic factors** (such as diseases or injuries) and drugs.

Erectile Disorder

Diseases associated with the heart and the circulatory system are particularly likely to be associated with erectile disorder because erection itself depends on the circulatory system (Muneer et al., 2014). Any kind of vascular pathology (problems in the blood vessels supplying the penis) can

> **Genito-pelvic pain/penetration disorder:** The term in *DSM-5* for pain during sex (dyspareunia) or vaginismus, which tend to occur together.
> **Vaginismus (vaj-in-IS-mus):** A sexual disorder in which there is a spastic contraction of the muscles surrounding the entrance to the vagina, in some cases so severe that intercourse is impossible.
> **Organic factors of sexual disorders:** Physical factors, such as disease or injury, that cause sexual disorders.

produce erection problems. Erection depends on having a great deal of blood flowing into the penis via the arteries, with simultaneous constricting of the veins so that the blood cannot flow out as rapidly as it is coming in. Thus damage to either these arteries or the veins may produce erectile disorder.

Erectile disorder (ED) is associated with diabetes mellitus. Several aspects of diabetes are involved, including circulation problems, peripheral nerve damage, and low testosterone levels (Algeffari et al., 2018; Sáenz de Tejada et al., 2004). In fact, erectile disorder may in some cases be the earliest symptom of a developing case of diabetes. Of course, not all diabetic men have erectile disorders. Estimates range from 35 to 90 percent of men with diabetes have an erectile disorder (Algeffari et al., 2018). Diabetes is also associated with sexual disorders in women (Giraldi & Kristensen, 2010).

Hypogonadism—an underfunctioning of the testes so that testosterone levels are very low—is associated with ED (Muneer et al., 2014). ED is also associated with a condition called hyperprolactinemia, in which there is excessive production of prolactin (Johri et al., 2001).

Any disease or injury that damages the lower part of the spinal cord may cause erectile disorder because that is the location of the erection reflex center (see the chapter "Sexual Arousal"). Erectile disorder may also result from severe stress or fatigue. Finally, some, though not all, kinds of prostate surgery may cause the condition (Burnett, 2005).

With erectile disorders, as with most sexual disorders, it is important to recognize that the distinction between organic causes and psychological causes is an oversimplification. Many sexual disorders result from a complex interplay of the two causes (Rosen, 2007). For example, a man who has circulatory problems that initially cause him to have erection problems is likely to develop anxieties about erection, which in turn may create further difficulties. This notion of dual causes has important implications for therapy. Many people with such disorders require both medical treatment and psychotherapy.

Premature Ejaculation

Early ejaculation is more often caused by psychological than physical factors. In cases of acquired disorder, though, in which the man at one time had ejaculatory control but later lost it, physical factors may be involved. A local infection such as prostatitis may be the cause, as may degeneration in the related parts of the nervous system, which may occur in neural disorders such as multiple sclerosis.

An intriguing explanation for early ejaculation comes from the sociobiologists (Hong, 1984). Their idea is that rapid ejaculation has been selected for in the process of evolution, what we might call "survival of the fastest." In monkeys and apes, the argument goes, copulating and

ejaculating rapidly would be advantageous in that the female would be less likely to get away and the male would be less likely to be attacked by other sexually aroused males while he was copulating. Thus males who ejaculated quickly were more likely to survive and to reproduce. Interestingly, among chimpanzees, which some see as our nearest evolutionary relatives, the average time from intromission (insertion of the penis into the vagina) to ejaculation is 7 seconds (Tutin & McGinnis, 1981). In modern U.S. society, of course, rapid ejaculation is not particularly advantageous and might even lead a man to have difficulty finding partners. Nonetheless, according to the sociobiologists, plenty of genes for rapid ejaculation are still hanging around from the natural selection that occurred thousands of years ago. (For a critique of this hypothesis, see Bixler, 1986.)

Delayed Ejaculation

Male orgasmic disorder, or delayed ejaculation, may be associated with a variety of medical or surgical conditions, such as multiple sclerosis, spinal cord injury, and prostate surgery (Perelman, 2014). Most commonly, though, it is associated with psychological factors.

Female Orgasmic Disorder

Orgasmic disorder in women may be caused by severe illness, general ill health, or extreme fatigue. Injury to the spinal cord can cause orgasm problems (Sipski et al., 2001). However, most cases are caused by psychological factors.

Painful Intercourse and Vaginismus

Dyspareunia in women is often caused by organic factors, including the following:

1. *Disorders of the vaginal entrance.* Irritated remnants of the hymen; painful scars, perhaps from an episiotomy or sexual assault; or infection of the Bartholin glands.

2. *Disorders of the vagina.* Vaginal infections; allergic reactions to spermicidal creams or the latex in condoms or diaphragms; a thinning of the vaginal walls, which occurs naturally with age; or scarring of the roof of the vagina, which can occur after a hysterectomy.

3. *Pelvic disorders.* Pelvic infection such as pelvic inflammatory disease, endometriosis, tumors, cysts, or a tearing of the ligaments supporting the uterus.

Painful intercourse in men can also be caused by a variety of organic factors. For an uncircumcised man, poor hygiene may be a cause; if the penis is not washed thoroughly with the foreskin retracted, material may collect under the foreskin, causing infection. An allergic reaction to spermicidal creams or to the latex in condoms may also be involved. Finally, various prostate problems may cause pain on ejaculation.

Vaginismus is sometimes caused by painful intercourse, and therefore by organic factors that cause that condition (Binik et al., 2007).

Drugs

Some drugs may have side effects that cause sexual disorders (Ashton, 2007; Segraves & Balon, 2010). For example, some drugs used to treat high blood pressure increase problems with erection in men and with decreased sexual desire in both men and women. Although it would be impossible to list every drug effect on every aspect of sexual functioning, some of the major drugs that may cause sexual disorders are listed in Table 1. Here we consider the effects of alcohol, illicit drugs, and prescription drugs.

Alcohol

The effects of alcohol on sexual responding vary considerably. We can think of these effects as falling into three categories: (1) short-term pharmacological effects, (2) expectancy effects, and (3) long-term effects of chronic alcohol abuse. In regard to the last category, alcoholics, particularly in the later stages of alcoholism, frequently have sexual disorders, typically including erectile disorder, orgasmic disorder, and loss of desire (George et al., 2014; Segraves & Balon, 2003). These sex problems may be the result of any of a number of organic effects of long-term alcoholism. For example, chronic alcoholism in men may cause disturbances in sex hormone production because of atrophy of the testes. Chronic alcohol abuse, too, generally has negative effects on the person's interpersonal relationships, which may contribute to sexual disorders.

What about the person who is not an alcoholic but rather has had one or many drinks on a particular evening and then proceeds to a sexual interaction? As noted earlier, there is an interplay of two effects: expectancy effects and actual pharmacological effects (George et al., 2014). Many people have the expectation that alcohol will loosen them up, making them more sociable and sexually uninhibited. These expectancy effects in themselves produce increased physiological arousal and subjective feelings of arousal. Expectancy effects, though, interact with the pharmacological effects and work mainly at low doses, that is, when only a little alcohol has been consumed. At high dosage levels, alcohol acts as a depressant and sexual arousal is suppressed, in both men and women.[1]

Illicit or Recreational Drugs

There is a widespread belief that *marijuana* (cannabis, "pot") has aphrodisiac properties. Scientific research on its actual effects is limited. Therefore, we can provide only tentative ideas about the effects of marijuana on sexual functioning. In surveys of users, many respondents report

that it increases sexual desire and makes sexual interactions more pleasurable (McKay, 2005). In regard to potential negative effects, there is concern that marijuana use contributes to risky sexual behavior such as unprotected sex (Collins et al., 2005). Chronic users report decreased sexual desire (Segraves & Balon, 2003). In studies of the general population, marijuana use has been associated with orgasmic disorder (Johnson et al., 2004).

To make matters more complicated, the effects of cannabinoids (the active drugs in marijuana) depend on gender (Gorzalka et al., 2010). In women, low doses of cannabis are associated with increased sexual desire and sexual pleasure. It is possible that cannabis boosts the production of androgens in women, leading to the positive sexual effects. At higher doses, though, cannabis creates sexual problems. In men, moderate doses of cannabis appear to increase sexual desire while at the same time creating erection problems.

Among drug users, *cocaine* is reported to be the drug of choice for enhancing sexual experiences. It is said to increase sexual desire, enhance sensuality, and delay orgasm. Chronic use of cocaine, however, is associated with loss of sexual desire, orgasmic disorders, and erectile disorders (George et al., 2014). The effects also depend on the means of administration—whether the cocaine is inhaled, smoked, or injected. The most negative effects on sexual functioning occur among those who regularly inject the drug. Crack cocaine is highly addictive, and the crack epidemic, especially in the inner city, often involves the exchange of sex for drugs (Green et al., 2005).

Stimulant drugs, notably *amphetamines,* are associated with increased sexual desire and arousal in some studies (George et al., 2014).

Crystal methamphetamine ("ice") is a recreational drug that is of particular concern because, while high on it, people have a tendency to engage in risky sexual behaviors (George et al., 2014). One study of heterosexual, HIV-negative adults using meth indicated that, over a 2-month period, they averaged 22 acts of unprotected vaginal sex and nine different sex partners (Semple et al., 2004). Crystal meth can also lead to paranoia, hallucinations, and violent behavior (Brecht et al., 2004). We cannot recommend it.

The *opiates* or narcotics, such as morphine, heroin, and methadone, have strong suppression effects on sexual desire and response (Segraves & Balon, 2003). Long-term use of heroin, in particular, leads to decreased testosterone levels in males.

Prescription Drugs

Table 1 provides a partial list of prescription drugs that can affect sexual responding.

Some *psychiatric drugs*—that is, drugs used in the treatment of psychological disorders—may affect sexual functioning (Clayton et al., 2016). In general, these drugs have their

---

[1]Some refer to the resulting erection problems as "whiskey dick."

Table 1 Drugs That May Impair—or Improve—Sexual Response

Drug	How It Affects Sexual Functioning	Common Medical Uses
1. Psychoactive Drugs		
Antianxiety drugs/tranquilizers		Anxiety, panic disorders
Buspirone	Enhanced desire, orgasm	
Benzodiazepines (Librium, Valium, Ativan)	Decreases desire, improves premature ejaculation	
Antidepressants I: Tricyclics	Desire disorders, erection problems, orgasm problems, ejaculation problems May treat hypersexuality, premature ejaculation	Depression
Antidepressants II: Serotonin reuptake inhibitors (Paxil, Prozac, Zoloft)	Desire disorders, erection problems, orgasm problems	Depression, obsessive-compulsive disorder, panic disorders
Lithium	Desire disorders, erection problems	Bipolar disorder
Antipsychotics Thorazine, Haldol	Desire disorders, erection problems, orgasm problems, ejaculation problems	Schizophrenia
2. Antihypertensives		High blood pressure
Reserpine, Methyldopa	Desire disorders, erection difficulties, orgasm delayed or blocked	
Ace inhibitors (Vasotec)	Erection difficulties	
3. Substance Use and Abuse		
Alcohol	At low doses, increases desire At high doses, decreases erection, arousal, orgasm Alcoholism creates many disorders and atrophied testicles, infertility	
Nicotine	Decreases blood flow to penis, creates erectile disorder	
Opioids Endogenous: Endorphins	Sense of well-being and relaxation	
Heroin	Decrease in desire, orgasm, ejaculation, replaces sex	
Marijuana	Enhances sexual pleasure but not actual performance; chronic use decreases desire	

Sources: Ashton (2007); Clayton et al. (2016); Meston et al. (2004); Segraves & Balon (2003, 2010).

beneficial psychological effects because they alter neurotransmitter levels and the functioning of the central nervous system. But these CNS alterations in turn affect sexual functioning. For example, the drugs used to treat schizophrenia may cause delayed orgasm or "dry orgasm" in men—that is, orgasm with no ejaculation. Tranquilizers and antidepressants often improve sexual responding as a result of improvement of the person's mental state. However, there may also be negative effects. Some of the antidepressants, for example, are associated with problems of both arousal and delayed orgasm in men as well as women. A few antidepressants—most notably, bupropion (Wellbutrin)—have few sexual side effects and are becoming popular for that very reason.

The list of other prescription drugs that can affect sexual functioning is long, so we will mention just two examples. Antihistamines can reduce vaginal lubrication. Some of the antihypertensive drugs (used to treat high blood pressure)

can cause erection problems in men (Segraves & Balon, 2003). Most of the research on antihypertensive drug effects has been done with men, so we know less about these effects on women, although sexual problems have been reported among women using antihypertensive drugs. Some of the drugs used to treat epilepsy appear to cause erection problems and decreased sexual desire, although epilepsy by itself also seems to be associated with sexual disorders. Women who are treated with drugs called aromatase inhibitors following breast cancer and surgery are highly likely to experience problems with sexual desire (Panjari et al., 2011).

Psychological Causes

Psychological causes of sexual disorders can be categorized into immediate causes, prior learning, emotional factors, behavioral or lifestyle factors, and problems with sexual excitation/inhibition.

(a)

(b)

Figure 2 Alcohol and cocaine are popular recreational drugs that many people believe enhance sexual experience. Research shows, though, that high levels of alcohol suppress sexual arousal, and repeated use of cocaine is associated with loss of sexual desire, orgasm disorders, and erection problems.

(a) ©Rehulian Yevhen/Getty Images; (b) ©McGraw-Hill Education/ Gary He

Immediate Psychological Causes

Among the psychological sources of sexual disorders, we can distinguish between immediate causes and prior learning. **Prior learning** refers to the things that people learned earlier—for example, in childhood—that now inhibit their sexual response. **Immediate causes** are various things that happen in the act of lovemaking itself that inhibit the sexual response.

The following four factors have been identified as immediate psychological causes of sexual disorders: (1) anxieties such as fear of failure, (2) cognitive interference, (3) failure of the partners to communicate, and (4) failure to engage in effective, sexually stimulating behavior.

Anxiety during a sexual interaction can be a source of sexual disorders. Anxiety may be caused by fear of failure— that is, fear of being unable to perform, and performance anxiety has especially strong effects for men (McCabe & Connaughton, 2014). But anxiety itself can block sexual response in some people. Often anxiety can create a vicious cycle of self-fulfilling prophecy in which fear of failure produces a failure, which produces more fear, which produces another failure, and so on. For example, a man may have one episode of erectile dysfunction, perhaps after drinking too much at a party. The next time he has sex, he anxiously wonders whether he will "fail" again. His anxiety is so great that he cannot get an erection. At this point he is convinced that the condition is permanent, and all future sexual activity is marked by such intense fear of failure that erectile disorder results. The prophecy is fulfilled. The effects of anxiety, though, are complicated and depend on the individual, as we will see in the research of David Barlow described later in this section.

Cognitive interference is a second immediate cause of sexual disorders. It refers to thoughts that distract the person from focusing on the erotic experience. The problem is basically one of *attention* (de Jong, 2009). Is the person focusing their attention on erotic thoughts or on distracting thoughts (Will my technique be good enough to please her? Will my body be beautiful enough to arouse him?). **Spectatoring,** a term coined by Masters and Johnson, is one kind of cognitive interference. The person behaves like a spectator or judge of their own sexual "performance." People who do this are constantly (mentally) stepping outside the sexual act in which they are engaged to evaluate how they are doing, mentally commenting, "Good job," or "Lousy," or "Could stand improvement." Today, both men and women experience performance-related distractions, but men experience

---

Prior learning: Things that people have learned earlier—for example, in childhood—that now affect their sexual response.

Immediate causes: Various factors that occur in the act of lovemaking that inhibit sexual response.

Cognitive interference: Negative thoughts that distract a person from focusing on the erotic experience.

Spectatoring: Masters and Johnson's term for acting as an observer or judge of one's own sexual performance; thought to contribute to sexual disorders.

more performance-related distractions and women experience more appearance-related distractions (Meana & Nunnink, 2006; Nelson & Purdon, 2011).

Sex researcher David Barlow (1986; Wiegel et al., 2007) ran an elegant series of experiments to test the ways in which anxiety and cognitive interference affect sexual functioning. He studied men who were functioning well sexually and men with sexual disorders, particularly erectile disorder. We will call these two groups the *functionals* and the *dysfunctionals*. He found that functionals and dysfunctionals respond very differently to stimuli in sexual situations. For example, anxiety (induced by the threat of being shocked) *increases* the arousal of functional men but *decreases* the arousal of dysfunctional men while watching erotic films. Demands for performance (e.g., the experimenter says the research participant must have an erection or he will be shocked) increase the arousal of functionals but are distracting to (create cognitive interference in) and decrease the arousal of dysfunctionals. When both self-reports of arousal and physiological measures of arousal (the penile strain gauge) are used, dysfunctional men consistently underestimate their physical arousal, whereas functional men are accurate in their reporting.

From these laboratory findings, Barlow constructed a model that describes how anxiety, positive and negative emotions (affect), and cognitive interference act together to produce sexual disorders such as erectile disorder. When dysfunctionals are in a sexual situation, there is a performance demand. This causes them to feel anxiety and other negative emotions. They then experience cognitive interference and focus their attention on nonerotic thoughts, such as thinking about how awful it will be when they don't have an erection. This increases arousal of their autonomic nervous system. To them, that feels like anxiety and generates more negative affect, whereas a functional person would experience it as sexual arousal. For the dysfunctionals, the anxiety creates further cognitive interference, and eventually the sexual performance is dysfunctional—they don't manage to get an erection. The situation is amplified because the dysfunctionals have various negative cognitive biases. For example, they expect to perform poorly. All of this leads them to avoid future sexual encounters or, when they are in one, to experience negative feelings, and the vicious cycle repeats itself.

This analysis is insightful and is backed by numerous well-controlled experiments. It fails to tell us, however, how the dysfunctionals got into this pattern in the first place. That explanation probably has to do with prior learning, discussed in the next section.

Third, *failure to communicate* is one of the most important immediate causes of sexual disorders. Many people expect their partners to have ESP concerning their own sexual needs. You are the leading expert in the field of what feels good to you, and your partner will never know what turns you on unless you make it known, either verbally or nonverbally. But many people do not communicate their sexual desires. For example, a woman who needs a great deal of clitoral stimulation to have an orgasm may never tell her partner this; as a result, she does not get the stimulation she needs and consequently does not orgasm.

A fourth immediate cause of sexual disorders is a *failure to engage in effective sexually stimulating behavior.* Often this is a result of simple ignorance. For example, some couples may seek sex therapy because of the wife's failure to have orgasms; the therapist soon discovers that neither the husband nor the wife is aware of the location of the clitoris, much less of its fantastic erotic potential. Often such cases can be cleared up by simple educational techniques.

Prior Learning

Another major category of psychological sources of sexual disorders is *prior learning*. This category includes various things that were learned or experienced in childhood, adolescence, or even adulthood.

In some cases of sexual disorders, the person's first sexual act was traumatic. An example would be a young man who could not get an erection the first time he attempted intercourse and was laughed at by his partner. Such an experience sets the stage for future erectile disorder.

Seductive behavior by parents and child sexual abuse by parents or other adults are the more serious of the traumatic early experiences that lead to later sexual disorders (Najman et al., 2005). A history of sexual abuse is frequently reported by women seeking therapy for problems with sexual desire, arousal, or aversion (Leonard & Follette, 2002). The findings are similar for men with desire or arousal problems (Loeb et al., 2002).

In some other cases of sexual disorders, the person grew up in a very strict, religious family and was taught that sex is dirty and sinful. Such a person may have grown up thinking that sex is not pleasurable, that it should be gotten over with as quickly as possible, and that it is for purposes of procreation only. Such learning inhibits the enjoyment of a full sexual response.

Another source of disorders originating in the family occurs when parents punish children severely for sexual activity such as masturbation. An example is the little girl who is caught masturbating, is punished severely, and is told never to "touch herself" again; in adulthood she finds that she cannot orgasm through masturbation or as a result of hand stimulation by her partner.

Parents who teach their children the double standard may contribute to sexual disorders, particularly in their daughters. Many women whose sexual response is inhibited in adulthood were taught as children that no nice lady is interested in sex or enjoys it.

Emotional Factors

Although researchers and therapists have focused mainly on cognitions such as negative or distracting thoughts as psychological sources of sexual disorders, emotions can play a role as well and are now being investigated. Depression, for example, is associated with erectile disorder and other sexual disorders (Frohlich & Meston, 2002; McCabe et al., 2010). Emotions such as anger and sadness can interfere with sexual responding (Araujo et al., 2000). And as we saw earlier, anxiety can be a powerful impediment to sexual functioning in some people.

Disgust is a strong emotion that is the enemy of arousal (de Jong et al., 2013). Disgust—whether it is associated with a particular person, a body part, or an object—makes a person want to avoid sex.

Barlow's model of sexual dysfunction, discussed earlier, is fundamentally a cognitive–affective model (Wiegel et al., 2007). That is, it recognizes the importance of cognitive processes such as attention and cognitive interference. At the same time, it recognizes the importance of affect or emotion, arguing that people with sexual disorders tend to rate high on negative affect and low on positive affect in sexual situations. The negative affect involves anxiety and negative mood, such as feeling sad or in a bad mood. At the same time, those with disorders tend to be low on positive emotions—such as feelings of joy and excitement—in sexual situations.

Behavioral or Lifestyle Factors

Smoking, alcohol consumption, and obesity are all associated with higher rates of sexual disorders, and all involve behavior (Derby et al., 2000; Segraves & Balon, 2003). As such, they are quite modifiable. A study of obese men between the ages of 35 and 55 showed that regular physical exercise reduced their body mass index (BMI) and the incidence of erectile disorder (Esposito et al., 2004).

Sexual Excitation-Inhibition

In the chapter "Sexual Arousal" we discussed the sexual excitation-inhibition model, or dual control model, of sexual response (Bancroft et al., 2009). In brief, the model proposes that two basic processes underlie human sexual response: excitation (responding with arousal to sexual stimuli) and inhibition (inhibiting sexual arousal, not responding to sexual stimuli).

This model can be applied directly to understanding the origins of sexual disorders. In general, the idea is that people who are low on sexual excitation, or high on sexual inhibition, or both, are likely to develop sexual disorders. For example, in research with a community sample of men, scores on the sexual inhibition scale correlated strongly with the men's reports of difficulties in obtaining or maintaining an erection (Bancroft et al., 2009). Similarly, research with a community sample of

women showed that sexual inhibition scores were correlated with their reports of sexual problems (Sanders et al., 2008).

As more evidence accumulates on this model, the next exciting step could be to use the excitation and inhibition scales to maximize the effectiveness of therapies for the disorders. For example, excitation and inhibition scores might be an indicator of which drug would be most effective in treating erectile disorder, or of whether drug therapy or sex therapy would be most effective.

Combined Cognitive and Physiological Factors

In the chapter "Attraction, Love, and Communication," we discussed the two-component theory of love, which holds that we experience love when two conditions are present: physiological arousal and a cognitive label of "love" attached to it (Berscheid & Walster, 1974). An analogous cognitive–physiological model of sexual functioning and dysfunction has also been proposed (Palace, 1995a, 1995b). According to this model, we function well sexually when we are physiologically aroused and interpret that as sexual arousal (rather than something else, like nervousness). As we've seen from Barlow's research, people with sexual disorders tend to interpret that arousal as anxiety. In addition, the physiological processes and cognitive interpretations form a feedback loop. That is, interpreting arousal as sexual arousal increases one's arousal further.

In a clever experiment based on this model, women with sexual disorders were exposed, in a laboratory setting, to a frightening movie, which increased their general autonomic arousal (Palace, 1995b). The women were then shown a brief erotic video and given feedback (actually false) that their genitals had shown a strong arousal response to it. This feedback created a cognitive interpretation for the way they were feeling. The combination of general autonomic arousal and the belief that they were responding with strong sexual arousal led these women, compared with the controls, to greater vaginal arousal responses and subjective reports of arousal in subsequent sessions. This demonstration of the effectiveness of combined physiological and cognitive factors is particularly striking because the women began with problems in sexual responding.

Following from these ideas, many experts today recommend a combination of medical and psychological treatments for sexual disorders, as discussed later in this chapter (Rosen, 2007).

Interpersonal Factors

Problems in a couple's relationship are another leading cause of sexual disorders (Althof et al., 2004; McCabe et al., 2010). Anger or resentment toward one's partner does not create an optimal environment for sexual enjoyment. Sex can also be used as a weapon to hurt a partner; for example, a woman can hurt her husband by refusing to engage in a sexual behavior that he wants. Conflicts over power may contribute to sex problems.

Intimacy problems in a relationship can be a factor in sexual disorders (McCabe et al., 2010). These problems typically represent a combination of individual psychological factors and relationship problems. Some individuals have a fear of intimacy—that is, of deep emotional closeness to another person (Kaplan, 1979). Indeed, some people seem to like sex but fear intimacy. They would prefer to watch TV or talk about the weather or have sex than to engage in a truly intimate, emotionally vulnerable, trusting conversation with another person. They typically progress in a dating relationship to a certain degree of closeness and then lose interest. This pattern is repeated with successive partners. The fear of intimacy may be a result of negative or disappointing intimate relationships, particularly with parents, in early childhood. The fear of intimacy causes a person to draw back from a sexual relationship before it becomes truly fulfilling.

A New View of Women's Sexual Problems and Their Causes

A group of sex therapists specializing in treating women's sex problems worked together to formulate what they call a New View of the nature of women's sexual problems and their causes (Tiefer, 2001). This new view is critical of the categories of disorders formulated by the American Psychiatric Association in the *DSM* and listed earlier in this chapter. It argues that these diagnostic categories have three flaws: (1) they treat male sexuality and female sexuality as totally equivalent, when they differ in some important ways; (2) they ignore the relational context of sexuality and desires for emotional intimacy; and (3) they ignore differences among women and naturally occurring variations in women's sexuality.

These experts proposed new categories of sexual disorders for women, as described below.

Sexual Problems Due to Sociocultural, Political, or Economic Factors

This category includes problems due to (1) ignorance and anxiety due to inadequate sexuality education, lack of access to health services, or other social constraints; (2) sexual avoidance or distress due to perceived inability to meet cultural norms regarding ideal sexuality (e.g., anxiety about one's body or about sexual orientation); (3) inhibitions due to conflict between the norms of one's culture of origin and those of the dominant culture; and (4) lack of interest or fatigue due to family and work obligations.

> **Behavior therapy:** A system of therapy based on learning theory, in which the focus is on the problem behavior and how it can be modified or changed.

Sexual Problems Relating to Partner and Relationship

Problems in this category involve (1) sexual inhibition or distress arising from betrayal or fear of the partner because of abuse; (2) discrepancies in desire or preferences for sexual activities; (3) ignorance or inhibition about sexual communications; (4) loss of sexual interest as a result of conflicts over issues such as money, or resulting from traumatic experiences such as infertility; and (5) loss of arousal due to partner's health or sexual problems.

Sexual Problems Due to Psychological Factors

This category includes the following problems: (1) sexual aversion or inhibition of sexual pleasure due to past experiences of physical, sexual, or emotional abuse; (2) personality problems with attachment or rejection, or depression or anxiety; and (3) sexual inhibition due to fear of sexual acts or their possible consequences, such as pain during intercourse or fear of pregnancy or STIs.

Sexual Problems Due to Medical Factors

When sexual problems arise despite a supportive interpersonal situation, adequate sexual knowledge, and positive attitudes, they may be a result of (1) any number of medical conditions that affect neurological, circulatory, endocrine, or other systems of the body; (2) pregnancy or STIs; (3) side effects of medications.

As you can see, this way of thinking about sexual disorders and their causes in women is considerably different from the dominant ways of thinking and the categories listed in the *DSM*. New research is beginning to support this alternative view (King et al., 2007). For example, official diagnoses of disorders do not correlate well with women's perception that they have a problem or with their psychological distress. This suggests that the traditional diagnostic categories are missing the mark for some women.

Therapies for Sexual Disorders

A variety of therapies for sexual disorders are available, each relying on a different theoretical understanding of what causes sexual disorders. Here we examine five major categories of therapies: behavior therapy, cognitive behavior therapy, mindfulness therapy, couple therapy, and biomedical therapies.

Behavior Therapy

Behavior therapy has its roots in behaviorism and learning theory. The basic assumption is that sex problems are the result of prior learning (as discussed earlier) and that they are maintained by ongoing reinforcements and punishments (immediate causes). It follows that these problem behaviors can be unlearned by new conditioning. One of the key techniques is systematic desensitization, in which the client is gradually led through exercises that reduce anxiety.

In 1970, Masters and Johnson reported on their development of a set of techniques for sex therapy and ushered in a new era of sex therapy. They operated from a behavior therapy model because they saw sexual disorders as learned behaviors rather than as symptoms of psychiatric illness. If sexual disorders are the result of learning, they can be unlearned. Masters and Johnson used a rapid 2-week program of intensive therapy that consisted mainly of education and specific behavioral exercises, or "homework assignments."

One of the basic goals of Masters and Johnson's therapy was to eliminate goal-oriented sexual performance. Many clients believe that in sex they must perform and achieve certain things. If sex is an achievement situation, it can also become the scene of failure, and perceived failures lead people to believe that they have a sexual problem.

In one technique used in behavior therapy to eliminate a goal-oriented attitude toward sex, the couple is forbidden to have sexual intercourse until they are specifically permitted to by the therapists. They are assigned **sensate focus exercises** that reduce the demands on them. As the couple successfully complete each of these exercises, the sexual component of subsequent exercises is gradually increased. The couple chalk up a series of successes until eventually they are having intercourse and the disorder has disappeared.

Sensate focus exercises are based on the notion that touching and being touched are important forms of sexual expression and that touching is also an important form of communication; for example, a touch can express affection, desire, understanding, or a lack of caring. In the exercises, one member of the couple plays the "giving" role (touches and strokes the other), and the other person plays the "getting" role (is touched by the other). The giving partner is instructed to massage or fondle the other, and the getting partner is instructed to communicate to the giver what is most pleasurable. Thus the exercise fosters communication. The partners switch roles after a certain period of time. In the first exercises, the giver is not to stroke the genitals or breasts but may touch any other area. As the couple progress through the exercises, they are instructed to begin touching the genitals and breasts. These exercises also encourage the partners to focus their attention on the sensuous pleasures they are receiving. Many people's sexual response is dulled because they are distracted; they are thinking about how to solve a family financial problem or are spectatoring their own performance. They are victims of cognitive interference. The sensate focus exercises train people to concentrate only on their sexual experience, thereby increasing the pleasure of it.

In addition to these exercises, behavior therapists supply simple education. The couple is given thorough instruction in the anatomy and physiology of the male and female sexual organs. Some couples, for example, have no idea what or where the clitoris is. These instructions may also clear up misunderstandings that either member of the couple may have had since childhood. For example, a man with an erectile disorder may have been told as a child that men can have only a fixed number of orgasms in their lifetime. As he approaches middle age, he starts to worry about whether he may have used up almost all of his orgasms, which creates the erectile disorder. It is important for such men to learn that nature has imposed no quota on them.

In Masters and Johnson's initial development of their therapy techniques, all of the couples were heterosexual. They later used the same techniques in treating sexual disorders in gay and lesbian couples, with a comparable success rate (Masters & Johnson, 1979).

Cognitive Behavior Therapy

Today, many sex therapists use a combination of the behavioral exercises pioneered by Masters and Johnson and cognitive therapy (Heiman, 2007). This is termed **cognitive behavior therapy.**

Cognitive restructuring is an important technique in a cognitive approach to sex therapy (Wincze & Carey, 2001). In cognitive restructuring, the therapist essentially helps the client restructure their thought patterns, helping them to become more positive (for an example, see First Person: A Case of Low Sexual Desire). In one form of cognitive restructuring, the therapist challenges the client's negative attitudes. These attitudes may be as general as a woman's distrusting attitudes toward all men, or as specific as a man's negative attitudes toward masturbation. The client is helped to reshape these attitudes into more positive ones.

Earlier in this chapter we noted that cognitive interference is one of the immediate causes of sexual disorders. That is exactly the kind of issue that a cognitive behavior therapist likes to address. The general idea is to reduce the presence of interfering thoughts during sex. First the therapist must help the client identify the presence of such thoughts. The therapist then suggests techniques for reducing these thoughts, generally by replacing them with erotic thoughts—perhaps focusing attention on a particular part of one's body and how it is responding with arousal, or perhaps having an erotic fantasy. Out go the bad thoughts, in come the good thoughts.

> **Sensate focus exercise:** A part of the sex therapy developed by Masters and Johnson in which one partner caresses the other, the other communicates what is pleasurable, and there are no performance demands.
> **Cognitive behavior therapy:** A form of therapy that combines behavior therapy and restructuring of negative thought patterns.

Mindfulness Therapy

Mindfulness, with its roots in Eastern meditation practices, is a technique of focusing one's attention on experiences in the present moment in a calm, nonjudgmental way (Khoury et al., 2013a). Some also say that mindfulness includes kindness and compassion. **Mindfulness therapy** (also called mindfulness training) is a system of training people in mindfulness practices; one goal is to help people regulate their own negative emotions. Some see it as the most recent extension of cognitive behavior therapy, and research shows that it is effective for a number of psychological disorders, including anxiety and depression (Blanck et al., 2018; Khoury et al., 2013a, 2013b). Will it work for sexual disorders?

Several groups have added mindfulness training to cognitive behavior sex therapy and use it especially for women with sexual desire disorder. Evaluations of the programs show it to be effective, as measured by the clients' self-reports of their sexual problems and their distress about the problems (e.g., Paterson et al., 2017; for a meta-analysis, see Stephenson & Kerth, 2017).

In the chapter "Sexual Arousal," we saw that some women show a lack of agreement or lack of concordance between physiological measures of their arousal (using the photoplethysmograph) and their self-reports of arousal. One study examined whether mindfulness-based sex therapy would increase concordance for women with sexual arousal and desire disorders (Brotto et al., 2016; also Velten et al., 2018). It worked! That is, following the therapy, women showed a closer agreement between their self-ratings and physiological measures of arousal. The hypothesis is that mindfulness training increases women's focus on their own sensations of arousal, amplifying their subjective sense of arousal and improving their sexual functioning.

Other researchers have incorporated mindfulness training into online sex therapy (Hucker & McCabe, 2015). Yes, it's possible to conduct sex therapy online, or at least some experts believe it is possible. The argument is that online sex therapy is available for people who may live in isolated areas with no access to in-person sex therapy. Moreover, the online approach can bring together people who share common problems in chats while maintaining their anonymity. This particular study began with an existing online program based in cognitive behavioral methods for female sexual problems, called Pursuing Pleasure (PP). A mindfulness component was added with a set of homework exercises for practicing it. The results indicated that the therapy group improved significantly compared with the control group, and these improvements were maintained 3 months later. From the design, we can't tell whether it was the cognitive behavior therapy that was effective, the mindfulness training, or a combination of the two. Nonetheless, the combined program was effective.

Couple Therapy

As we noted earlier, a significant cause of sexual disorders is interpersonal difficulties. Accordingly, some sex therapists use couple therapy as part of the treatment. This approach rests on the assumption that there is a reciprocal relationship between interpersonal conflict and sex problems. Sex problems can cause conflicts, and conflicts can cause sex problems. In couple therapy, the relationship itself is treated, with the goal of reducing antagonisms and tensions between the partners. As the relationship improves, the sex problem should be reduced.

For certain disorders and certain couples, therapists may use a combination of cognitive behavior and couple therapy. For example, sex therapists Raymond Rosen, Sandra Leiblum, and Ilana Spector (1994) use a five-part model in treating men with erectile disorder:

1. *Sexual and performance anxiety reduction.* Men with erectile disorder often have a great deal of performance anxiety. This can be treated using such techniques as the sensate focus exercises discussed earlier in this chapter.

2. *Education and cognitive intervention.* Men with erectile disorder often lack sexual information and have unrealistic expectations about sexual performance and satisfaction. For example, older men may not be aware of the natural effects of aging on male sexual response. Cognitive interventions may help the man to overcome "all or nothing" thinking—that is, the belief that if any aspect of his sexual performance is not perfect, the whole interaction is a disaster. An example is the belief "I failed sexually because my erection was not 100 percent rigid."

3. *Script assessment and modification.* The man with erectile disorder and his partner have a sexual script that they enact together. People with sexual disorders typically have a restricted, repetitive, and inflexible script, using a small number of techniques that they never change. Novelty is one of the greatest turn-ons, so therapy is designed to help the couple break out of their restricted script.

4. *Conflict resolution and relationship enhancement.* As we have discussed, conflicts in a couple's relationship can lead to sexual disorders. In therapy, these conflicts are identified and the couple can work to resolve them.

5. *Relapse prevention training.* Sometimes a relapse—a return of the disorder—occurs following therapy. Therapists have developed techniques to help couples avoid

Mindfulness: The technique of focusing one's attention on experiences in the present moment in a calm, nonjudgmental way.

Mindfulness therapy: A system of training people in mindfulness practices; one goal is to help people regulate their own negative emotions.

First Person

A Case of Low Sexual Desire

Sarah, age 27, was referred to a sex therapist by an endocrinologist to be considered for testosterone treatment for her complaints of low sexual desire. Sarah had no ovarian tissue. One ovary that had a large cyst had been removed when she was 13, and her other ovary had undergone torsion (twisting that cut off the blood supply) and had to be removed when she was 16. She had been given estrogen and progesterone replacement immediately so that her menstrual periods never stopped.

When Sara met with the therapist, she explained that sex with her partner Carl was enjoyable. They had been together 4 years and were sexual approximately once a week. Carl would have preferred to be sexual every day, but Sarah resisted. She said that even though sex was enjoyable and satisfying, if she never had sex again, it would be fine with her. She reported that both Carl and her endocrinologist thought that she was very abnormal.

Sarah had very few sexual thoughts about arousal or anticipating sexual activity. Her sexual thoughts were instead troubling and focused on her guilt that their sexual interactions were infrequent and that she was abnormal. During sexual interactions with Carl, she was aroused, she enjoyed the experience, and had orgasms. She found arousing Carl to be pleasurable and arousing for her.

Using the New View of women's sexual problems, the therapist explained to Sarah that her experience was within normal limits. In a meeting with Carl, the therapist described the range of women's sexual experiences. The next question was whether some factors were causing Sarah's behavior to be toward the end of the spectrum. Both biological and psychological factors seemed to be involved. Because of the removal of her ovaries, she was manufacturing no testosterone, although androgens manufactured by the adrenal gland were present. Sarah's life history also gave clues regarding possible psychological factors. Sarah grew up with an alcoholic father who was prone to shouting, arguing, and engaging in emotional abuse; Sarah coped by retreating to her bedroom. She suppressed her feelings of anger and did not rebel even when she was a teenager. This coping style worked well at the time. However, as an adult, she was probably still in the habit of suppressing emotions generally. Sarah agreed about this and understood that her sexual emotions were probably also suppressed.

The therapist decided against testosterone treatment and instead focused on encouraging Sarah to deliberately attempt to feel more nonsexual emotion throughout the day. In addition, she was to deliberately allow more sexual stimuli in her life, such as music, movies, dancing, and erotic conversations.

The therapist met with Carl to explain the situation and assess his own family history. His parents had a bitter divorce when he was just 10. He felt that neither parent had really loved him. For Carl, having sex with his partner was a sign that he was loved. Carl was able to realize that pressuring Sarah did not help the situation, and he ceased doing so, which Sarah appreciated. In addition, when Sarah realized the origins and extent of Carl's need to feel loved, she became strongly motivated to find the triggers that were able to make her feel more sexual. Salsa dancing proved to be one of those triggers, combined with encouraging Carl to flirt with her more often. Sarah's sexual self-image increased markedly, as did her sexual desire.

Source: Basson (2007), pp. 42–43.

or deal with such relapses. For example, they are told to engage in sensate focus sessions at least once a month.

Notice that part 1 represents the behavior therapy techniques pioneered by Masters and Johnson; parts 2 and 3 are cognitive therapy techniques; and part 4 is couple therapy. Most skilled sex therapists today use combined or integrated techniques such as these, tailored to the specific disorder and situation of the couple.

Specific Treatments for Specific Problems

Some very specific techniques have been developed for the treatment of certain sexual disorders.

The Stop-Start Technique

The stop-start technique is used in the treatment of premature ejaculation (see Figure 3) (Althof, 2014). The woman uses her hand to stimulate the man to erection. Then she

Figure 3   The stop-start technique for treating premature ejaculation and the position of the couple while using the stop-start technique.

stops the stimulation. Gradually he loses his erection. She resumes stimulation, he gets another erection, she stops, and so on. The man learns that he can have an erection and be highly aroused without having an orgasm. Using this technique, the couple may extend their sex play to 15 or 20 minutes, and the man gains control over his orgasm. Another version of this method is the squeeze technique, in which the woman adds a squeeze around the coronal ridge, which also stops orgasm.

Masturbation

The most effective form of therapy for women with primary orgasmic disorder is a program of directed masturbation (Graham, 2014; LoPiccolo & Stock, 1986). The data indicate that masturbation is the technique most likely to produce orgasm in women; it is therefore a logical treatment for women who have problems with having orgasms, many of whom have never masturbated. Masturbation is sometimes recommended as therapy for men as well.

What can a woman do if she has trouble having orgasms?

Kegel Exercises

One technique that is used with women is the **Kegel exercises,**

Kegel (KAY-gul) exercises: A part of sex therapy for women with orgasmic disorder, in which the woman exercises the muscles surrounding the vagina; also called *pubococcygeal* or *PC muscle exercises.*

Bibliotherapy: The use of a self-help book to treat a disorder.

named for the physician who devised them (Kegel, 1952). They are designed to exercise and strengthen the *pubococcygeal muscle,* or PC muscle, which runs along the sides of the entrance of the vagina. The exercises are particularly helpful for women who have had this muscle stretched in childbirth and for those who simply have poor tone in the muscle. The woman is instructed first to find her PC muscle by sitting on a toilet with her legs spread apart, beginning to urinate, and stopping the flow of urine voluntarily. The muscle that stops the flow is the PC muscle. After that, the woman is told to contract the muscle 10 times during each of six sessions per day. Gradually she can work up to more.[2] These exercises seem to enhance arousal and facilitate orgasm, perhaps by increasing women's awareness of and comfort with their genitals (Heiman, 2007). They also permit the woman to stimulate her partner more because her vagina can grip his penis more tightly, and they are a cure for women who have problems with involuntarily urinating as they orgasm. Kegel exercises are sometimes also used in treating men.

Bibliotherapy

Bibliotherapy refers simply to the use of a self-help book to treat a disorder. Research shows that bibliotherapy is effective for orgasmic disorders in women (Van Lankveld,

[2]Students should recognize the exciting possibilities for doing these exercises. For example, they are a good way to amuse yourself in the middle of a boring lecture, and no one will ever know you are doing them.

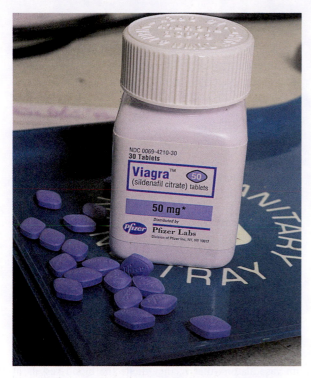

Figure 4 Viagra, one of the prescription drugs available for treating erectile disorder.

©*Larry Mulvehill/The Image Works*

1998). Julia Heiman and colleagues' *Becoming Orgasmic: A Sexual Growth Program for Women* (1976) has been used extensively for this purpose. Bibliotherapy has also been shown to be effective for couples with a mixture of sexual disorders, both in men and in women (Van Lankveld, 2009; Van Lankveld et al., 2001).

Biomedical Therapies

Beginning in the 1990s, there was increased recognition of the biological bases of some sexual disorders. Consistent with this emphasis, many developments in medical and drug treatments and even surgical treatment have occurred.

Drug Treatments

Many promising advances have been made in the identification of drugs that cure sexual disorders or work well when used together with cognitive behavior therapy or other psychological forms of sex therapy (Ashton, 2007; Rosen, 2007).

Certainly the most widely publicized breakthrough among these treatments was the release, in 1998, of **Viagra** (sildenafil) for the treatment of erectile disorder (Figure 4). Earlier biomedical treatments were unsatisfactory for various reasons. For example, intracavernosal injections (discussed in the following section) are not

exactly romantic. Viagra is taken by mouth approximately 1 hour before anticipated sexual activity. It does not, by itself, produce an erection. Rather, when the man is stimulated sexually after taking Viagra, the drug facilitates the physiological processes that produce erection. Specifically, it relaxes the smooth muscles in the corpora cavernosa, allowing blood to flow in and create an erection. Averaged over 27 clinical trials, about 57 percent of men respond successfully to Viagra—compared with 21 percent responding to the placebo (Fink et al., 2002). Men have generally been quite satisfied with Viagra. Side effects are not common; they include headache, flushing, and vision disturbances (Ashton, 2007).

On balance, Viagra seems to be quite safe (Morales et al., 1998; Rosen & McKenna, 2002). It does not seem to cause priapism (an erection that just won't go away). Yet the very ease of its use may lead physicians to overprescribe it and men to demand it in inappropriate circumstances. Today it is easily available on the Internet. If the erection difficulties are due to a relationship problem, Viagra will provide at most a temporary solution. It is not helpful for sexual disorders other than erectile disorder. And there is no evidence that it enhances sexual performance in men who function sexually within the normal range (Mondaini et al., 2003). Its recreational or high-performance use is cause for concern (Harte & Meston, 2011).

Viagra was such a success, financially and otherwise, that drug companies immediately sought successors—drugs that would be more convenient or work in cases that were not effectively treated with Viagra. One of these is Cialis (tadalafil), which is very much like Viagra in that it relaxes the smooth muscle surrounding the arteries to the penis, facilitating engorgement (Montorsi et al., 2004; Padma-Nathan et al., 2001). Whereas Viagra lasts only a few hours, Cialis is effective for as long as 24 to 36 hours. Someone at the drug company apparently decided that planning to have sex, as one does with Viagra, is not a good idea. Drugs such as Cialis have been shown to have no negative effects on sperm production or sex hormone production (Hellstrom et al., 2003).

How does Viagra work?

Levitra (vardenafil) and Zydena (udenafil) are other drugs that work like Viagra, have slightly different formulations, and are as effective as Viagra (Chen et al., 2015). All of these drugs are in the category of *PDE5 inhibitors*. That is, they inhibit or block an enzyme (PDE5), and by doing so, they relax smooth muscles in the arteries to the penis, thereby allowing more blood to flow into it. A particularly important success story is that these drugs are effective in treating erectile dysfunction that results from complete surgical removal of the prostate (Brock et al., 2003).

Viagra: A drug used in the treatment of erectile disorder; sildenafil.

Another issue concerning Viagra involves the wives or partners of men with newfound Viagra-aided erections. Not all women, some of whom had adjusted to a relationship without intercourse, welcome their husbands' new capacity, an issue that has been ignored in the medical "fix" approach (Potts et al., 2003; Rosen & McKenna, 2002). Often it is important to combine couple therapy with drug therapy. Some women, of course, are absolutely delighted with the Viagra results (Montorsi & Althof, 2004).

In cases of *hypogonadism* or testosterone deficiency in men, the gonads (testes) are not producing enough testosterone. The result can be low sexual desire and erection problems. *Testosterone treatments* can be effective in such cases (Brock et al., 2016; Morales et al., 2015). Testosterone treatment should be used only when lab tests confirm that the person's testosterone levels are below the normal range. For a man with testosterone in the typical range, extra T will not be helpful. Critics note that extensive advertising has created a "Low T industry," in yet another case of medicalization.

And how about a Viagra for women? The drug company Pfizer, as well as many scientists, hoped that Viagra would also work for women—that is, that it would cure their orgasm problems. The problem is that Viagra works by increasing vasocongestion, and insufficient vasocongestion is probably not what causes most women's orgasm difficulties. After many failed clinical trials, Pfizer announced in 2004 that it would give up on testing Viagra for women (Harris, 2004).

In another attempt at a female Viagra, the German pharmaceutical company Boehringer developed the drug flibanserin (trade name Addyi). It had originally been developed to be an antidepressant, but it didn't work very well for that purpose. It acts to reduce levels of the neurotransmitter serotonin and to increase levels of dopamine and norepinephrine. To use terms from the Dual Control Model discussed in the chapter "Sexual Arousal," serotonin is thought to have an inhibitory effect on sexual desire, and dopamine and norepinephrine are thought to have excitatory effects. All of that sounds good on paper, but the U.S. Food and Drug Administration investigated it and issued a negative report in 2010, based on clinical trials that showed no actual increase in sexual desire in women taking it, compared with controls. Another problem is that flibanserin has to be taken every day, in contrast to Viagra, which is taken only when needed. Boehringer decided not to pursue further work on the drug.

In 2014 and 2015, the plot thickened for flibanserin (Moynihan, 2014). The drug was acquired by a new company, Sprout Pharmaceuticals. A feminist campaign materialized, pressuring the FDA to approve flibanserin because of the need for a "pink Viagra," and arguing that the FDA was discriminating against women by not approving it. As it turned out, the "feminist" campaign was actually funded by Sprout. And flibanserin still doesn't work (Jaspers et al., 2016). But the FDA approved it in 2015 because of the pink Viagra campaign.

Currently, the most promising approach for women's sexual desire problems is combination drugs that act on two biological systems at the same time. The combinations that have been shown to be effective in clinical trials are either (a) testosterone (T) plus sildenafil (S), or (b) testosterone plus buspirone (B), which is an anti-anxiety drug; the drug is taken just when needed (Tuiten et al., 2018). The choice of which combination drug to use can be personalized to the nature of the woman's desire problem—whether it is low sexual excitation (then use T + S), or high sexual inhibition (then use T + B). These clinical trials are very recent, and it will be interesting to see how these drugs are developed over the next several years.

Intracavernosal Injection

Intracavernosal injection (ICI) is a treatment for erectile disorders (Hsiao et al., 2011; Shabsigh et al., 2000). It involves injecting a drug (such as alprostadil, or Edex) into the corpora cavernosa of the penis. The drugs used are vasodilators—that is, they dilate the blood vessels in the penis so that much more blood can accumulate there, producing an erection.

Since the introduction of Viagra, ICI is now used mainly in cases in which the erection problem is organic and the man does not respond to Viagra or its successors. It can also be used in conjunction with cognitive behavior therapy in cases that have combined organic and psychological causes. Like Viagra, ICI can have positive psychological effects because it restores the man's confidence in his ability to get erections, and it reduces his performance anxiety because he is able to engage in intercourse successfully. There are also potential abuses. Men who have normal erections should not use ICI in an attempt to produce a "super erection."

Alprostadil is also available as a suppository to place inside the urethra or as a cream to rub on, eliminating the need for the needle.

Suction Devices

Suction devices are another treatment for erectile disorders (Rosen, 2007). Essentially, they pump you up! A tube is placed over the penis (see Figure 5). With some devices, the mouth can produce enough suction; with others, a small hand pump is used. Once a reasonably firm erection is present, the tube is removed and a rubber ring is placed around the base of the penis to maintain the engorgement with blood. These devices have been used successfully with, for example, diabetic men. They can also be helpful in combination with cognitive behavior couple therapy for cases of erectile dysfunction that are mainly psychological in origin (Wylie et al., 2003).

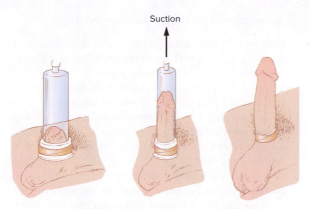

Figure 5 A treatment for erectile disorder. An external tube, with a rubber band around it, is placed over the lubricated penis. Suction applied to the tube produces erection, which is maintained by the constricting action of the rubber band once the plastic tube has been removed.

Surgical Therapy: The Inflatable Penis

For severe cases of erectile disorder, surgical therapy is possible. The surgery involves implanting a **penile prosthesis** (see Figure 6) (Hellstrom, 2003; Lee et al., 2015). A sac or bladder of water is implanted in the lower abdomen, connected to two inflatable tubes running the length of the corpora cavernosa, with a pump in the scrotum. Thus the man can literally pump up or inflate his penis so that he has a full erection.

It should be emphasized that this is a radical treatment that should be reserved only for those cases that have not been cured by sex therapy or drug therapy. The patient must understand that the surgery itself destroys some portions of the penis, so that a natural erection will never again be possible. Research shows that about one-fourth of men who have had this treatment are dissatisfied afterward. Although the treatment is radical and should be used conservatively, it is a godsend for some men who have been incapable of erection because of organic difficulties.

In another version of a surgical approach, a semirigid, silicone-like rod is implanted into the penis (Fathy et al., 2007; Ferguson & Cespedes, 2003). This noninflatable device is less costly than the inflatable version and has a lower rate of complications.

Evaluating Sex Therapy

One of the most basic questions we must ask about sex therapy is, Is it effective?

Since Masters and Johnson created their therapy approach, many additional therapies have been developed, as described in this chapter. Many studies have evaluated

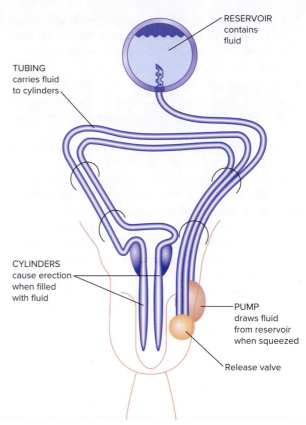

Figure 6 A surgically implanted prosthesis can be used in treating erectile dysfunction, although it should be regarded as a treatment of last resort.

the effectiveness of these therapies. At this point, there is sufficient evidence evaluating certain treatments for certain disorders to reach the following conclusions (Althof, 2007; Fruhauf et al., 2013; Heiman, 2007; McCabe et al., 2010):

- Primary orgasmic dysfunction in women is successfully treated with directed masturbation, and the treatment can be enhanced with sensate focus exercises.

- Treatments for acquired orgasmic dysfunction are somewhat less successful. Therapy that combines some or all of the following components seems to be most effective: sex education, sexual skills training, communication skills training, and body image therapy. The problem here, most likely, is that there are many different patterns of acquired anorgasmia, with a need to match treatment to the pattern of the disorder, something that research has not been able to untangle.

- Vaginismus is successfully treated with progressive vaginal dilators; relaxation, physical therapy, and Kegel exercises may also be helpful, but the evidence is not as strong. Botox injections may be used with the vaginal dilators (Pacik & Geletta, 2017).

> **Penile prosthesis (prahs-THEE-sis):** A surgical treatment for erectile dysfunction, in which inflatable tubes are inserted into the penis.

- For premature ejaculation, drugs, specifically some antidepressants (serotonin reuptake inhibitors), may be combined with CBT to improve effectiveness (Hellstrom, 2011).
- Hypoactive sexual desire disorder in women can be treated successfully with the kind of therapy developed by Masters and Johnson and with cognitive behavior therapy.

One critique points out the *medicalization* of sexual disorders, such as using Viagra to treat male erectile problems (Farrell & Cacchioni, 2012; Tiefer, 1994, 2000, 2012; Wentzell, 2017). Research has increasingly identified organic sources of sexual disorders, with advances that have brought attempts to identify drugs and surgeries, rather than psychotherapies, to treat problems. In part, political and financial issues are involved, as physicians try to seize the treatment of sexual disorders from psychologists. But there is also a cost to the patient, as the disorder may be given a quick fix with drugs while the patient's anxieties and relationship problems are ignored. This medicalization also occurs in a cultural context in Western nations in which there is a new ideal of "successful aging," in which 70-year-olds should perform physically like 40-year-olds (Wentzell, 2017). In this context, erection problems in older men are seen as a threat to masculinity that should be fixed, rather than a natural process of aging. The New View of women's sexual problems, discussed earlier in the chapter, was proposed in part as an alternative to medicalization.

Psychiatrist Thomas Szasz is a critic of sex therapy. In his book *Sex by Prescription* (1980) he criticized the philosophical basis of sex therapy. Szasz has long been an outspoken critic of psychotherapy. He is particularly critical of the medical model in dealing with psychological problems (see, for example, his classic *The Myth of Mental Illness*). His essential argument is that psychologists and psychiatrists take people who have problems in living, or perhaps have freely chosen lifestyles, and classify them as "sick" or "mentally ill" (the medical model) and in need of therapy. Although the professionals may think they are being helpful, they may do more harm than good. For example, once people are classified as "sick," the implication is that they need a psychologist or physician to fix them up; whereas in fact, Szasz maintains, it might be better for them to make active efforts to solve their own problems.

Applying this thinking to the sex therapy field, Szasz argued that sex therapists have essentially created a lot of illnesses by creating the (somewhat arbitrary) diagnostic categories of the sexual disorders. For example, the man who cannot have intercourse because he cannot manage an erection is said to have "erectile dysfunction," yet the man who cannot bring himself to perform cunnilingus is not regarded as having any dysfunction. Why should the first problem be an illness and the second one not? A man who ejaculates rapidly is termed a "premature ejaculator" and considered in need of therapy, but what exactly is wrong with ejaculating rapidly?

Szasz summarized his arguments as follows:

I do not deny that sexual problems exist or are real. . . . I maintain only that such problems—including sexual problems—are integral parts of people's lives. . . .

As some of the examples cited in the book illustrate, one medical epoch's or person's sexual problem may be another epoch's or person's sexual remedy. Today, it is dogmatically asserted—by the medical profession and the official opinion-makers of our society—that it is healthy or normal for people to enjoy sex, that the lack of such enjoyment is the symptom of a sexual disorder, that such disorders can be relieved by appropriate medical (sex-therapeutic) interventions, and that they ought, whenever possible, to be so treated. This view, though it pretends to be scientific, is, in fact, moral or religious: it is an expression of the medical ideology we have substituted for traditional religious creeds. (1980, pp. 164–165)

Some Practical Information

Avoiding Sexual Disorders

The motto "Prevention is better than cure" could well be applied to sexual disorders. That is, people could use some of the principles that emerge from sex therapists' work to avoid having sexual disorders in the first place. In the chapter "Sexuality in Perspective" we introduced the concept of sexual health. The following are some principles of good sexual mental health:

1. *Communicate with your partner.* Don't expect your partner to be a mind reader concerning what is pleasurable to you. One way to do this is to make it a habit to talk to your partner while you are having sex; verbal communication then does not come as a shock. Some people, though, feel uncomfortable talking at such times; nonverbal communication, such as placing your hand on top of your partner's and moving it where you want it, works well too (see the chapter "Attraction, Love, and Communication" for more detail).
2. *Don't be a spectator.* Don't feel like you are putting on a sexual performance that you constantly need to evaluate. Focus your attention on the giving and receiving of sensual pleasures, not on how well you are doing.
3. *Don't set up goals of sexual performance.* If you have a goal, you can fail, and failure can produce disorders. Don't set your heart on having simultaneous orgasms or, if you are a woman, on having five orgasms before your partner has one. Just relax and enjoy yourself.
4. *Be choosy about the situations in which you have sex.* Don't have sex when you are in a terrific hurry or are afraid you will be disturbed. Also be choosy about who your partner is. Trusting your partner is essential to good sexual functioning; similarly, a partner who really

cares for you will be understanding if things don't go well and will not laugh or be sarcastic.

5. *"Failures" will occur.* They do in any sexual relationship. What is important is how you deal with them. Don't let them ruin the relationship. Instead, try to think, How can we make this turn out well anyhow?

Choosing a Sex Therapist

Unfortunately, many states do not have licensing requirements for sex therapists, though most do have requirements for marriage counselors and psychologists. Quite a few quacks have hung out shingles saying "Sex Therapist," and many states have made no attempt to regulate this.

Some of these "therapists" have no more qualifications than having had a few orgasms themselves.

How do you go about finding a good, qualified sex therapist? Your state medical or psychological association can provide a list of psychiatrists or psychologists and may be able to tell you which ones have special training in sex therapy. There are also professional organizations of sex therapists. The American Association of Sex Educators, Counselors, and Therapists certifies sex therapists. Choose a therapist or clinic that offers an *integrated approach* that recognizes the potential biological, cognitive–behavioral, and relationship influences on any sexual disorder and is prepared to address all of these.

Critical THINKing Skill
Using diagnostic labels accurately

In this chapter, we revisit a critical thinking skill introduced in the chapter "Variations in Sexual Behavior," thinking clearly about diagnostic labels and applying them accurately. Consider the following case.

Josh is 22. He has engaged in sexual intercourse on 10 different occasions, with three different women, over a period of the last 2 years. On the first three occasions, he got so excited during foreplay that he had an orgasm and ejaculated before he was able to insert his penis into her vagina. On the next three occasions, when he got excited, he distracted himself by thinking about his grandmother and managed to insert his penis into his partner's vagina, but he still had his orgasm about 30 seconds later. For the most recent four occasions, distracting himself by thinking about his grandmother hasn't worked, and he is back to having his orgasm before he can even insert his penis into his partner's vagina. He is very upset about the problem but doesn't know what to do about it.

Does Josh's case qualify as premature ejaculation? What should he do about it? Answer these questions before you proceed to read the paragraphs that follow.

To decide whether Josh's case qualifies as premature ejaculation, we need to look at the experts' definition, and we will use the one given by the International Society for Sexual Medicine. To meet the criteria for premature ejaculation, the following must occur:

- Ejaculation must always or almost always occur prior to or within 1 minute of vaginal penetration. Every one of Josh's attempts at intercourse meets this criterion.

- In addition, there must be an inability to control or delay when ejaculation occurs. Josh also meets this criterion. Try though he might, he has not been able to delay his orgasms.

- In addition, the man must feel distressed about the problem, and Josh does.

Therefore, Josh meets all three criteria and his case would qualify as premature ejaculation (although only a trained clinician could make this diagnosis, and then only after a thorough interview).

Knowing that he meets the criteria, what should Josh do? First, if he hadn't met the criteria—for example, maybe this had happened to him only once and on all other occasions he functioned fine—we might advise him to ignore the situation because most men have occasional experiences like this and then go on to function well. But Josh does meet the criteria. It is therefore reasonable for him to seek help. A good strategy would be to go to a licensed sex therapist. The American Association of Sex Educators, Counselors, and Therapists (AASECT) licenses sex therapists and can provide a list of qualified providers by location. Going to his primary care physician is probably not the best strategy because primary care physicians receive little or no training in sexuality, much less sex therapy. Another strategy would be to try self-help before seeking professional help. He could ask a willing partner to help him with the start-stop technique described earlier in this chapter.

SUMMARY

Kinds of Sexual Disorders

Sexual disorders fall into four categories: desire disorders (hypoactive sexual desire, discrepancy of sexual desire), arousal disorders (female sexual arousal disorder, erectile disorder), orgasmic disorders (premature ejaculation, delayed ejaculation, female orgasmic disorder), and sexual pain disorders (dyspareunia, vaginismus).

What Causes Sexual Disorders?

Sexual disorders may be caused by physical factors, individual psychological factors, and interpersonal factors. Organic causes include some illnesses, infections, and damage to the spinal cord. Certain drugs may also create problems with sexual functioning. Individual psychological causes are categorized into immediate causes, such as anxiety or cognitive interference; prior learning; emotional factors; behavioral or lifestyle factors; and sexual excitation-inhibition. Interpersonal factors include conflict in the couple's relationship and intimacy problems. The New View of women's sexual problems conceptualizes the issues differently and focuses on different categories of causes, such as inadequate sexuality education, distress about not being able to meet cultural norms regarding ideal sexuality, and sexual inhibition due to fear of abuse by one's partner.

Therapies for Sexual Disorders

Therapies for sexual disorders include behavior therapy (pioneered by Masters and Johnson) based on learning theory, cognitive behavior therapy, mindfulness training, couple therapy, specific treatments for specific problems (e.g., stop-start for premature ejaculation), and a variety of biomedical treatments, which include drug treatments (e.g., Viagra).

Evaluating Sex Therapy

Evaluations of the effectiveness of sex therapy provide evidence that certain disorders can be effectively treated by certain therapies. Criticisms of sex therapy focus on the medicalization of sexual disorders and on the entire enterprise of identifying and labeling particular patterns of behavior as disorders.

Some Practical Information

Steps to prevent the occurrence of sexual disorders include good couple communication and not setting up sexual performance goals. When choosing a sex therapist, it is important that the person is licensed or certified.

SUGGESTIONS FOR FURTHER READING

Barbach, Lonnie G. (1983). *For each other: Sharing sexual intimacy.* Garden City, NY: Anchor Books. Barbach's sequel to *For Yourself;* this volume is designed for couples.

McCarthy, Barry, and McCarthy, Emily. (2009). *Discovering your couple sexual style: The key to sexual satisfaction.* New York: Taylor & Francis. Another good sex therapy book.

Nagoski, Emily. (2015). *Come as you are.* New York: Simon & Schuster. This is a great book to use for bibliotherapy. It is solidly grounded in science.

Tiefer, Leonore. (2004). *Sex is not a natural act, and other essays,* 2nd ed. Boulder, CO: Westview. Tiefer is a brilliant and entertaining writer, and her criticisms of sex therapy are insightful.

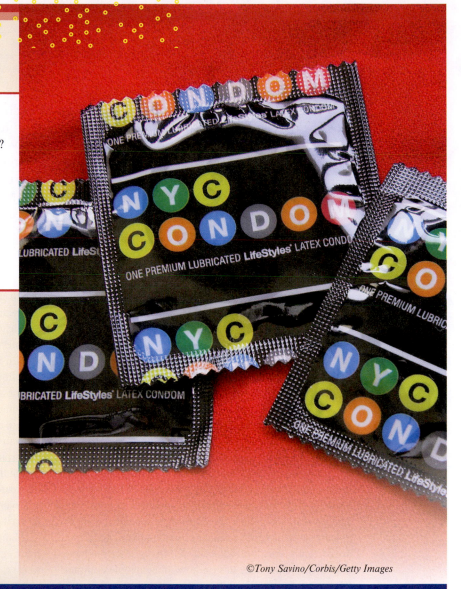

Are **YOU** Curious?

1. I hear there's a lot of chlamydia going around. How can I know whether I have it?
2. Is there a cure for herpes?
3. Why isn't there a vaccine yet against HIV?
4. My partner has no symptoms of any STIs. Should we still practice safer sex?

Read this chapter to find out.

CHAPTER

18

Sexually Transmitted Infections

CHAPTER HIGHLIGHTS

Chlamydia
Symptoms
Treatment
Prevention?

HPV
Diagnosis
Treatment
Vaccine

Genital Herpes
Symptoms
Treatment
Long-Term Consequences
Psychological Aspects:
    Coping with Herpes

HIV Infection and AIDS
An Epidemic?
Transmission
The Virus
The Disease
Diagnosis
Treatment
Women, Children, Ethnic Minorities,
    and AIDS
Psychological Considerations in AIDS
Recent Progress in AIDS Research

Gonorrhea
Symptoms
Diagnosis
Treatment

Syphilis
Symptoms
Diagnosis
Treatment

Hepatitis B

Trichomoniasis

Zika

Pubic Lice

Protecting Yourself

Other Genital Infections
Candida
Prostatitis

Maria and Luis get home after an evening on the town and enter the house hungry for passion. The two embrace, clinging to each other, longing for each other. Luis slowly undresses Maria, hungry for the silky flesh he feels beneath him. As their passion grows, she begins reaching for him, ripping his clothes off as she explores his body with her tongue. As Luis gets more and more excited, Maria rips a condom package open with her teeth and slowly slides the condom over Luis's erect penis. After an hour of incredible lovemaking, Luis, exhausted with pleasure, turns to Maria and says, "You were right, the BEST sex is SAFE sex with LATEX!"*

*From a student essay.

The sexual scene is not the same as it was during the sexual revolution of the 1960s and 1970s. AIDS poses a real threat. We need to do many things to combat such dangers. One is that we must rewrite our sexual scripts, as the quotation above illustrates. We also need to inform ourselves, and the goal of this chapter is to provide you with the important information you need to make decisions about your sexual activity.

Your health is very important, and a good way to ruin it or cause yourself a lot of suffering is to have an untreated case of a *sexually transmitted disease* (STD), also called a *sexually transmitted infection,* or STI. Consequently, it is very important to know the symptoms of the various kinds of STIs so you can seek treatment if you develop any of them. Also, there are some ways to prevent STIs or at least to reduce your chances of getting them, and these are certainly worth knowing about. Finally, after you have read some of the statistics on how many people contract STIs every year and on your chances of getting one, you may want to modify your sexual behavior somewhat. If you love, love wisely.

One of the most disturbing things about the STI epidemic in the United States is that it disproportionately affects teens and young adults. People between the ages of 15 and 24 account for half of all new STDs, and 1 in 4 sexually active adolescent girls have an STD (Centers for Disease Control and Prevention [CDC], 2017b). For people in this age group, three infections—human papillomavirus (HPV), trichomoniasis, and chlamydia—account for the great majority of cases. It is clear that prevention efforts, including sexuality education for youth, must have a higher priority than they have had in the past.

The STIs are presented in this chapter in the following order. First we look at a group of three diseases— chlamydia, HPV (genital warts), and herpes—that are all frequent among college students. After that is a discussion of HIV infection and AIDS, which is less common among college students but is one of the world's major public health problems and is generating an enormous amount of research. Next we discuss gonorrhea, syphilis, hepatitis B, trichomoniasis, and the Zika virus. Then comes not an infection but a bug, the pubic louse. After a practical section for you on preventing STIs, the chapter ends with a section about various other genital infections that, for the most part, are not sexually transmitted.

Some STIs are caused by *bacteria,* some are caused by *viruses,* and a few are caused by other organisms. The distinction between bacterial infections and viral infections is important because bacterial infections can be cured using antibiotics. Viral infections cannot be cured, but they can be treated to reduce symptoms. Chlamydia, gonorrhea, and syphilis are all caused by bacteria. Herpes, AIDS, genital warts, hepatitis B, and Zika are caused by viruses.

Many statistics throughout this chapter are taken from the Centers for Disease Control and Prevention (CDC) website (www.cdc.gov/std). The CDC is in Atlanta, Georgia. It is the federal agency that monitors diseases in the United States and conducts research and prevention programs. Data from the CDC are used so frequently throughout the chapter that we do not provide a citation every time. Information on STIs changes quickly, for the most up-to-date information, check the website.

One final note before we proceed: A lot of illustrations in this chapter show the symptoms of various STIs, and some of the photos may make you say "Nasty!" These illustrations are not meant to scare you but rather to help you recognize the symptoms of STIs. You should know what herpes blisters, for example, look like, in case you spot them on a prospective sexual partner and in case they appear on you.

Chlamydia

Chlamydia trachomatis is a bacterium that is spread by sexual contact and infects the genital organs of all genders.

Statistics indicate that **chlamydia** is one of the major sexually transmitted infections in the United States.

> **Chlamydia (klah-MIH-dee-uh):** An organism causing a sexually transmitted infection; the symptoms in males are a thin, clear discharge and mild pain on urination; females are frequently asymptomatic.

Approximately 1.6 million new cases of chlamydia are reported each year in this country, compared with 470,000 cases of gonorrhea (CDC, 2017a). Adolescent girls have a particularly high rate of infection. When a man consults a physician because of a urethral discharge, his chances of having chlamydia are greater than his chances of having gonorrhea. It is important that the correct diagnosis be made because chlamydia does not respond to the drugs used to cure gonorrhea.

Symptoms

The main symptoms in men are a thin, usually clear discharge from the penis and mild discomfort on urination appearing 7 to 21 days after infection (Stamm, 2008). The symptoms are somewhat similar to the symptoms of gonorrhea in males. However, gonorrhea tends to produce more painful urination and a more profuse, puslike discharge. Diagnosis is made from a urine sample in men and from a sample of cells from the vagina (or urine sample) in women. Tests are then used to detect the bacterium. Unfortunately, 75 percent of the cases of chlamydia infection are **asymptomatic** in women. This means that the woman never goes to a clinic for treatment, and she goes undiagnosed and untreated. The consequences of untreated chlamydia in women are discussed in the next section. Even among men, 50 percent of the cases are asymptomatic.

I hear there's a lot of chlamydia going around. How can I know whether I have it?

Treatment

Chlamydia is quite curable. It is treated with azithromycin or doxycycline (Workowski & Bolan, 2015). It does not respond to penicillin. Poorly treated or undiagnosed cases may lead to a number of complications: urethral damage, epididymitis (infection of the epididymis), Reiter's syndrome,[1] and proctitis in men who have had anal intercourse. Women with untreated or undiagnosed chlamydia may experience serious complications if not treated: **pelvic inflammatory disease (PID),** and possibly infertility due to scarring of the fallopian tubes. A baby born to an infected mother may develop pneumonia or an eye infection.

Prevention?

Scientists doing research on chlamydia have a major goal of developing a vaccine that would prevent infection. Vaccines have been developed that are effective in mice, but technical obstacles prevent their use with humans.

[1] Reiter's syndrome involves the following symptoms: urethritis, eye inflammations, and arthritis.

Until a vaccine is available, one of the most effective tools for prevention is screening. The problem with chlamydia is that so many infected people are asymptomatic and spread the disease unknowingly. In screening programs, asymptomatic carriers are identified, treated, and cured so that they do not continue to spread the disease.

In an innovative program, high school girls attending a school health clinic (not necessarily for STIs) collected vaginal swabs themselves, and the swabs were then subjected to laboratory tests (Wiesenfeld et al., 2001). Overall, 18 percent of the girls were infected with something: 10 percent had trichomoniasis, 8 percent had chlamydia, and 2 percent had gonorrhea. None had symptoms, so these cases would have gone undetected. About half said that they would never have had a gynecological exam to get a test—yet they agreed to self-collection of vaginal swabs. This method is promising for screening teens. Free testing kits are available online at www.iwantthekit.org.

On an individual level, the best method of prevention is the consistent use of a condom.

HPV

HPV stands for human papillomavirus, which increases the risk of certain cancers such as cervical cancer and causes genital warts. **Genital warts** are cauliflower-like warts appearing on the genitals, usually around the urethral opening of the penis, the shaft of the penis, or the scrotum in males, and on the vulva, the walls of the vagina, or the cervix in females (see Figure 1). Warts may also occur on the anus. Typically they appear 3 to 8 months after intercourse with an infected person. The majority of people infected with HPV, however, are asymptomatic.

HPV is the most common sexually transmitted infection in the United States (CDC, 2017b). In the pre-vaccine era, among females aged 14 to 59, 43 percent were infected (CDC, 2014a). Not all of those, though, were the cancer-causing types. Again in the pre-vaccine era (2003–2006), 12 percent of women had one of the cancer-causing types; that number went down to 5 percent in the vaccine era (2007–2010), despite the fact that many people are not getting vaccinated. Just think what we could do if everyone were vaccinated!

HPV infection is the single most important risk factor for cervical cancer (CDC, 2014a). In fact, more than 40 distinct types of HPV are sexually transmitted. Some types (6 and 11) cause genital warts and are

Asymptomatic (ay-simp-toh-MAT-ik): Having no symptoms.
Pelvic inflammatory disease (PID): An infection and inflammation of the pelvic organs, such as the fallopian tubes and the uterus.
HPV: Human papillomavirus, the virus that causes cervical cancer.
Genital warts: A sexually transmitted infection causing warts on the genitals.

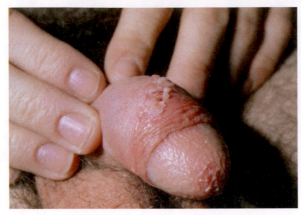

(a)

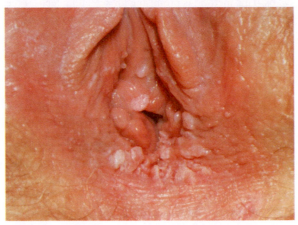

(b)

Figure 1 Genital warts (*a*) on the penis and (*b*) on the vulva.

(a) ©Dr. P. Marazzi/Science Source; (b) ©Bart's Medical Library/Phototake

called "low risk" because they do not cause cancer. Other types sharply increase the risk of cervical cancer and are called high-risk types. HPV 16 and 18 account for 70 percent of the cases of cervical cancer (CDC, 2017b). HPV infection is also associated with cancer of the penis and anus.

Research shows that oral sex can transmit HPV. Individuals infected this way have an increased risk of oral cancers, that is, cancer of the mouth or throat (D'Souza et al., 2007).

It is also true that about 90 percent of HPV infections are asymptomatic and go away by themselves within 2 years (CDC, 2014a). Does that mean there's no need for vaccination or safer sex practices? Of course not, because you don't want to be in the 10 percent who continue to harbor the virus, transmit it to others, or get warts or cervical or other cancers.

Diagnosis

A DNA test can be run on a sample of cells from the cervix to detect the types that are linked to genital cancers. For warts, diagnosis can sometimes be made simply by inspecting the warts, if they are present, because their appearance is distinctive. However, some strains of warts are flat and less obvious. Also, the warts may grow inside the vagina and may not be detected there. And high-risk types do not produce warts.

Treatment

Several treatments for genital warts are available. Chemicals such as podophyllin or bichloroacetic acid (BCA) can be applied directly to the warts. Typically these treatments have to be repeated several times, and the warts then fall off. With cryotherapy (often using liquid nitrogen), the warts are frozen off; again, it is typically necessary to apply more than one treatment. Drugs such as Podofilox cream can be applied by the patient. Many cases of HPV infection go away on their own, but others persist for long periods.

Vaccine

As noted, almost all cases of cervical cancer are linked to HPV infection. Therefore, a vaccine against HPV would prevent most cases of cervical cancer. The vaccine is called Gardasil and must be administered in three shots over a 6-month period. The goal is to administer it to girls around ages 11 to 12, before sexual activity would have started. The "quadrivalent" vaccine protects against four HPV types including 16 and 18, the ones associated with cervical cancer, as well as two other types that cause most cases of genital warts, which would also be good to avoid. Randomized controlled trials show the vaccine to be highly (95 percent) effective (Winer & Koutsky, 2008). We recommend that all girls be given this vaccination against cervical cancer. It is also approved for women up to age 26. The vaccine is also approved for boys, in whom it prevents penile, anal, and mouth cancer from HPV. A newer Gardasil vaccine is "9-valent" and protects against nine types.

There is a race issue here too. Whereas the most common cancer-causing types for European Americans are 16 and 18, the most common ones for African Americans are 33, 35, 45, and 58 (Vidal et al., 2014). The 4-valent vaccination protects against 16 and 18 but not the others. It was developed for the most common U.S. types; because European Americans constitute more than 50 percent of the U.S. population, their pattern dominated the results. The good news is that the newer, 9-valent vaccine protects against additional types that are more common among African Americans.

Genital Herpes

Genital herpes is a disease of the genital organs caused by the herpes simplex virus (HSV). Two strains of HSV are circulating: HSV-1 and HSV-2. In simpler times, HSV-2 caused genital herpes and HSV-1 caused cold sores around the mouth. Today, however, there is more crossing over. Genital herpes, then, can be caused by either HSV-1 or HSV-2. Genital herpes is transmitted by sexual intercourse and by oral–genital sex.

According to well-sampled studies, 16 percent of Americans are infected with HSV-2 and 30 percent are infected with HSV-1 (CDC, 2017b). The great majority are asymptomatic and do not know they are infected. These people transmit the disease to others unknowingly.

Symptoms

The symptoms of genital herpes caused by HSV-2 are small, painful bumps or blisters on the genitals (see Figure 2). Typically they appear within 2 to 3 weeks of infection. In women, they are usually found on the vaginal lips; in men, they usually occur on the penis. They may be found around the anus if the person has had anal intercourse. The blisters burst and can be quite painful. Fever, painful urination, and headaches may occur. The blisters heal on their own in about 3 weeks in the first episode of infection. The virus continues to live in the body, however. It may remain dormant for the rest of the person's life. But the symptoms may recur unpredictably, so that the person repeatedly undergoes 7- to 14-day periods of sores. HSV-1 infections tend to be less severe.

People with herpes are most infectious when they are having an active outbreak. However, people are infectious even when there is no outbreak or if they have never been symptomatic. Therefore, there is no completely safe period.

Treatment

Unfortunately, there is no known drug that kills the virus; that is, there is no cure. Researchers are pursuing two solutions: drugs that treat symptoms in someone who is already infected, and vaccinations that would prevent herpes. The drug acyclovir prevents or reduces the recurring symptoms, although it does not cure the disease.

Is there a cure for herpes?

Valacyclovir and famciclovir are newer drugs that are even more effective at shortening outbreaks and suppressing recurrences (Workowski & Bolan, 2015). They, as

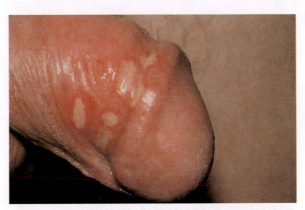

(a)

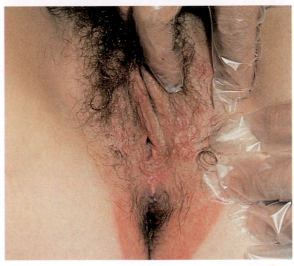

(b)

Figure 2 (*a*) Herpes blisters on the penis. (*b*) Herpes blisters on the vulva.

(a) ©Clinical Photography, Central Manchester University Hospitals NHS Foundation Trust, UK/Science Source; (b) ©Biophoto Associates/ Science Source

well as acyclovir, also reduce rates of transmission from an infected partner to an uninfected one. Scientists are actively working to create a method for immunization against herpes (Corey & Wald, 2008).

Long-Term Consequences

Either men or women with recurrent herpes may develop complications such as meningitis or narrowing of the urethra due to scarring, leading to difficulties with urination. However, such complications do not affect the majority of those with herpes. There are two more serious long-term consequences. One is that having a herpes infection increases one's risk of becoming infected with HIV, probably because the open blisters during an outbreak make

Genital herpes (HER-pees): A sexually transmitted infection, the symptoms of which are small, painful bumps or blisters on the genitals.

it easy for HIV to enter the body. Therefore, people who have herpes should be especially careful to use safer sex practices.

The other serious risk involves the transfer of the virus from mother to infant in childbirth, which in some cases leads to serious illness or death in the baby (Workowski & Bolan, 2015). The risk of transmission to the infant is highest in women who have recently been infected and are having their first outbreak. The risk is less with women who have had the disease longer, and is low if the woman is not having an outbreak. C-sections are therefore usually performed on women with an outbreak, but vaginal delivery is possible if there is not an outbreak.

Psychological Aspects: Coping with Herpes

The psychological consequences of herpes need to be taken as seriously as the medical consequences. The range of psychological responses is enormous. At one end of the spectrum are people with asymptomatic herpes, who are not aware that they have the disease and are happily sexually active—and at the same time unknowingly spreading the disease to others. At the other end of the spectrum are people who experience frequent, severe, painful recurrences, who feel stigmatized because of their disease, and who believe that they should abstain from sex to avoid infecting others (Merin & Pachankis, 2011). These difficulties are aggravated by the fact that outbreaks are often unpredictable, and current scientific evidence indicates that people are somewhat infectious even when they are not having an active outbreak. On the other hand, many people with herpes are able to cope.

HIV Infection and AIDS

In 1981, a physician in Los Angeles reported a mysterious and frightening new disease identified in several gay men. Within two years, the number of cases had escalated sharply and the gay community had become both frightened and outraged; within a few more years, the federal government had funded a major public health effort aimed at understanding and eradicating the disease. The disease was named **AIDS,** an abbreviation for **acquired immune deficiency syndrome.** The virus that causes AIDS is called **HIV,** for human immune deficiency virus.

As the name implies, HIV destroys the body's natural system of immunity to diseases. Once HIV has damaged an individual's

AIDS (acquired immune deficiency syndrome): A sexually transmitted disease that destroys the body's natural immunity to infection so that the person is susceptible to and may die from a disease such as certain pneumonias or cancers.
HIV: Human immune deficiency virus; the virus that causes AIDS.

immune system, opportunistic diseases may take over, and they can kill.

An Epidemic?

By the end of 2016, roughly 1.3 million people in the United States had been diagnosed as having AIDS, and 720,000 of them had died from it (CDC, 2017c). However, public health officials warn that these statistics represent only the tip of the iceberg, for they do not count people who are just infected with HIV but whose symptoms are not severe enough to be classified as AIDS. Experts estimate that 77 million people worldwide have been infected with HIV, although the majority of them show no symptoms yet and are unaware that they are infected (UNAIDS, 2018). In 2017 alone, HIV infection caused approximately 1 million deaths worldwide. Thus the terms *global epidemic* and *pandemic* (a widespread epidemic) have been used, with reason.

Transmission

HIV is transmitted by exchange of body fluids: semen, blood, and possibly secretions of the cervix and vagina. HIV is spread in four ways: (1) by sexual intercourse (either penis-in-vagina intercourse or anal intercourse[2]); (2) by contaminated blood (a risk for people who receive a blood transfusion if the blood has not been screened); (3) by contaminated hypodermic needles (a risk for those who inject drugs or for health care workers who receive accidental sticks); and (4) from an infected woman to her baby during pregnancy or childbirth.

Supporting these assertions, 2016 statistics for adult and adolescent cases of HIV in the United States indicate that infected men are from the following exposure categories: (1) men who have sex with men (83 percent); (2) heterosexual contact (9 percent); (3) injection drug use (4 percent); (4) multiple sources (4 percent); and (5) other, including recipients of contaminated blood transfusions (1 percent) (CDC, 2017c). Among women, the leading categories of exposure are heterosexual contact (87 percent) and injection drug use (12 percent) (CDC, 2017c). Worldwide, the majority of cases result from heterosexual transmission.

How great is your risk of becoming infected with HIV? In essence, it depends on what your sexual practices are (leaving aside the issues of injection drug use, which are beyond the scope of this book). *The sexual behavior most likely to spread AIDS is anal intercourse, and being the receiving partner puts one most at risk.* This is true for heterosexuals as well as gays. Whatever your sexual orientation, *the greater your number of sexual partners, the greater your risk of getting infected with HIV.* You may have

[2]There is also a chance that mouth–genital sex can spread HIV, particularly if there is ejaculation by an infected person into the mouth.

A Sexually Diverse World

AIDS in Thailand

Globally, HIV is pandemic; that is, it is an epidemic that has spread around the world. UNAIDS (2018) estimates that 37 million people are living with HIV today worldwide. Of those, 25.7 million are in sub-Saharan Africa, and an additional 5.2 million are in Asia and the Pacific. In 2017 alone, there were 1.8 million new infections. This pandemic is producing serious social and economic strains on many countries, as well as the suffering of individuals.

Asia initially lagged behind other regions in the spread of HIV. Thailand is a notable exception to the pattern: An epidemic raged there early on. By the early 1990s, depending on the region of the country, 40 to 50 percent of injection drug users were infected, as were 20 to 45 percent of brothel prostitutes. Approximately 1 million of the 60 million people of Thailand are believed to have been infected.

Sociocultural context is the key to understanding why AIDS struck Thailand. Two closely linked factors are Thailand's commercial sex industry and its booming sex tourism (Bishop & Limmer, 2018). A large commercial sex industry flourishes in Thailand. It is estimated that approximately half a million adolescents and young women there work as prostitutes, most of them being in the 16 to 24 age group. A wide variety of forms of prostitution exist, catering to every budget, ranging from call girl agencies, executive clubs, and go-go bars to massage parlors, brothels, streetwalkers, and even mobile operations that go out to rural areas.

Why is there such a large commercial sex industry in Thailand? The major factor is economics. Social and income gaps in Thailand are enormous, ranging from rural areas characterized by great poverty to the conspicuous wealth of Bangkok. A young rural girl may go to the city and enter prostitution to pay off family debts, for example. Prostitution is very lucrative; it has been estimated that commercial sex workers can earn 25 times as much as young women who work as maids and in other jobs available to them. Another factor is a cultural belief that women are of only two types: virtuous women, who are virgins until marriage, and prostitutes. Thailand is also a country that historically practiced polygamy and concubinage. And a man who does not use prostitutes is considered something less than a real man. These cultural factors combine to create great demand for prostitutes. Finally, beginning around the time of the Vietnam War, Thailand became a sex playground for foreign tourists and remains so to the present day.

Tourism provides more clients for prostitutes and therefore provides the incentive for more women to enter prostitution. But sex tourism also plays a major role in the international spread of HIV, bringing it into Thailand and in turn spreading it to the home countries of the tourists.

Yet Thailand is regarded as a major success story. In 1990 AIDS education was introduced into the schools. In 1991 a "100 percent condom program" was instituted with the help of the owners of sex parlors and sex workers, encouraging all clients to use condoms. The government supplied 60 million condoms a year to the effort. Officials estimate that without the condom campaign 10 percent of adult Thais would have been infected by 2000, whereas only 2 percent were.

Despite the success of these efforts, the epidemic is still serious. Thai officials, working with researchers in the United States and other nations, have therefore considered more daring strategies.

Promising vaccines against HIV have been developed in the United States, but conducting clinical trials to test the efficacy of the vaccines in real life is extremely difficult. Think for a moment about what it would require. Thai officials, facing a desperate situation, have taken the lead in conducting trials there. Thus it is possible that Thailand's tragedy will lead to the identification of an effective vaccine that can be used worldwide to halt the pandemic. In fact, in 2009 researchers announced exciting results from a 6-year trial of an HIV vaccine with 8,000 Thais and 8,000 controls (Cohen, 2009; Graham, 2009). The vaccine was about 30 percent effective. The vaccine was far from perfect, but it showed progress and gave researchers hope of creating an improved model (see the section Vaccine for an explanation of all the difficulties in creating a vaccination against this particular virus). Other researchers noted that a partially effective vaccine could lead to vaccine-resistant strains, which would be a terrible outcome (Herbeck et al., 2018). Most recently, results from a trial of a new vaccine, tested in multiple sites in Thailand, Africa, and the United States, found that it stimulated the relevant immune response in humans and, in trials with rhesus monkeys, was 67 percent effective (Barouch et al., 2018; Pavlakis & Felber, 2018). It's not perfect, but it's progress, and Thailand is contributing in major ways to that progress.

Sources: Cohen (2003, 2009); Dhalla et al. (2009); Duerr et al. (2008); Graham (2009); Simon et al. (2006); Stanecki & Marais (2008); Stoneburner et al. (1994).

heard the saying "six degrees of separation." It turns out that it is true for HIV as well. One study found that most people are just a few degrees of sexual separation from someone who is HIV infected (Liljeros et al., 2001). The greater your number of partners, the greater your chances of connecting with that HIV-positive person.

Heterosexual, penis-in-vagina intercourse spreads HIV as well. The risk varies considerably depending on who you have sex with and whether you use a condom. *Sexual intercourse is riskier if it is with a person who is infected with HIV (seropositive), if the person is in a high-risk group (gay, injection drug user), or if condoms are not used.* A study of heterosexual transmission of HIV among 415 Ugandan couples in which one partner was infected at the beginning and one was not indicated that 22 percent of the uninfected became infected over a 2-year period (Quinn et al., 2000). The male-to-female transmission rates and female-to-male rates were about equal. The higher the viral count in the infected person, the greater the rate of transmission. None of the circumcised men became infected.

Most important, condoms are 80 to 95 percent effective in protecting against HIV transmission during heterosexual intercourse if used consistently (Steiner et al., 2008). This isn't perfect protection, but it's darned good and far better than no protection. Far-right religious groups have tried to convince the public—especially schoolchildren—that condoms are totally ineffective, but the scientific studies say otherwise.

The Virus

HIV is one of a group of retroviruses. Retroviruses reproduce only in living cells of the host species, in this case humans. They invade a host cell, and each time the host cell divides, copies of the virus are produced along with more host cells, each containing the genetic code of the virus (see Figure 3 for more detail on the biology of HIV). Current research is aimed at finding drugs that will prevent the virus from infecting new cells. At least two strains of HIV are found in the United States today, HIV-1 and HIV-2, and there are several subgroups of HIV-1 that differ genetically.

HIV invades a specific group of white blood cells (lymphocytes) called CD4+ T-lymphocytes. We'll just call them T cells. These cells are critical to the body's immune response in fighting off infections. When HIV reproduces, it destroys the infected T cell. Eventually the HIV-positive person's number of T cells is so reduced that infections cannot be fought off.

Scientists have pressed hard to understand the functioning of HIV. They have identified two *coreceptors* for HIV, CCR5 and CXCR4, which allow HIV to enter T cells (Harrington & Swanstrom, 2008). CCR5 seems to be the important coreceptor in the early stages of the disease and CXCR4 in the later stages. This discovery may lead to advances in treatment if drugs can be used that block these coreceptors.

The Disease

The Centers for Disease Control established the following categorization for broad classes of HIV infection and progression of the disease (Selik et al., 2014):

1. *Stage 0.* This stage begins with initial infection and development of antibodies to the virus over the next 2 to 8 weeks. The stage is confirmed by a positive test for antibodies to HIV-1 or HIV-2, and lasts as long as the person keeps feeling well and the T cell count stays around 1,000. A normal count is approximately 1,000 T cells per μL of blood. If they haven't been tested, people in Stage 0 can be asymptomatic carriers and can infect others.

2. *Stage 1.* The T cell count drops but is still over 500. The person may still have no outward symptoms. The immune system is silently declining, however. In this stage, people may develop symptoms that are not immediately life-threatening: swollen lymph nodes, night sweats, fever, diarrhea, persistent yeast infections in the throat or vagina, shingles, fatigue, or abnormal cells in the cervix. With systems of early detection and treatment in the United States, though, infected people may have few symptoms. Those in poor nations often are not so fortunate.

3. *Stage 2.* The T cell count falls to between 200 and 499.

4. *Stage 3, AIDS.* The T cell count falls below 200. People in this stage are vulnerable to opportunistic infections that can be life-threatening. Opportunistic infections are ones that occur only in people with severely compromised immune systems. Examples are *Pneumocystis jirovecii* pneumonia (a rare form of pneumonia), Kaposi sarcoma (a rare form of skin cancer), and invasive cervical cancer.

Diagnosis

The blood tests that detect the presence of antibodies to HIV are easy and cheap to perform. They can be used in two important ways: (1) to screen donated blood; all donated blood in the United States is screened, so infections because of transfusions should be rare, although some did occur before the first blood test was developed, and a tiny risk remains even with these tests; and (2) to help people determine whether they are infected (HIV-positive). The latter use is important; if people suspect that they are infected and find through testing that they are, they can begin medical care. In addition, they should either abstain from sexual activity or, at the very least, use a condom consistently, in order not to spread the disease to others.

Multiple tests have been developed. The most common ones use blood, from as little as a finger stick, and they detect antibodies to HIV in the blood (Hurt et al., 2017). Here's the catch. It takes a while after infection for

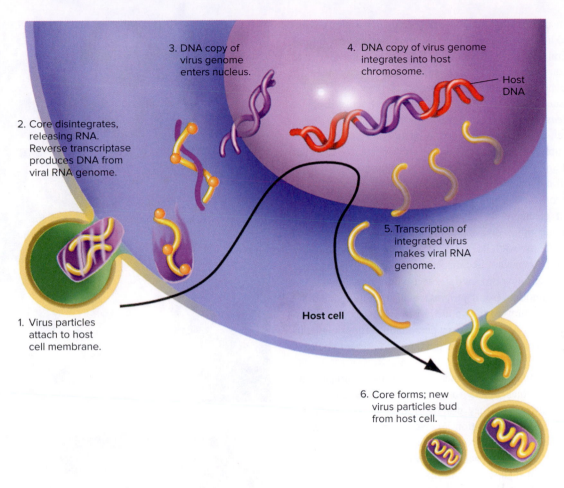

2. Core disintegrates, releasing RNA. Reverse transcriptase produces DNA from viral RNA genome.

3. DNA copy of virus genome enters nucleus.

4. DNA copy of virus genome integrates into host chromosome.

Host DNA

5. Transcription of integrated virus makes viral RNA genome.

1. Virus particles attach to host cell membrane.

Host cell

6. Core forms; new virus particles bud from host cell.

Figure 3   During infection, the AIDS virus binds to and injects its cone-shaped core into cells of the human immune system. It next uses reverse transcriptase to copy its RNA genome into double-stranded DNA molecules in the cytoplasm of the host cell. The double helixes then travel to the nucleus where another enzyme inserts them into a host chromosome. Once integrated into a host-cell chromosome, the viral genome can do one of two things. It can commandeer the host cell's protein synthesis machinery to make hundreds of new viral particles that bud off from the parent cell, taking with them part of the cell membrane and sometimes resulting in the cell host's death. Alternately, it can lie latent inside the host chromosome, which then copies and transmits the viral genome to two new cells with each cell division.

antibodies to form, so these tests are not accurate until enough antibodies have been produced to be detected. The time from initial infection until a test can detect the antibodies is called the "window period." Most tests cannot detect antibodies until about 30 days after infection.

Other blood tests detect antigens and antibodies. These shorten the window period to about 18 days because antigens are produced before antibodies. Notice that none of the currently available tests detect HIV itself. Therefore, they cannot give accurate results until a product of HIV—antigens or antibodies—is produced in the body in sufficient quantities to be detected.

Two additional points are important to keep in mind. Blood tests are more accurate than saliva tests. And

laboratory tests are more accurate than home tests, in part because home tests to detect antigens have not yet been developed. The bottom line: if you want an accurate test—and this is a situation in which accuracy is everything—go to a clinic and have a blood test.

Treatment

There is not yet any cure for AIDS. However, treatments are available that control the disease. One of the first of the effective antiviral drugs is **AZT** (azidothymidine, also called zidovudine or ZDV), and it has been used widely. It can stop the virus

AZT: A drug used to treat HIV-infected persons; also called *ZDV*.

from multiplying, but it cannot repair the person's damaged immune system. Other examples of effective antiretroviral drugs are DDI and D4T. Some people experience serious side effects from these drugs, and sometimes they stop being effective after a period of time, so scientists pursued other drugs. Another class of effective drugs is *protease inhibitors*. They attack the viral enzyme protease, which is necessary for HIV to make copies of itself and multiply. Another drug is darunavir, which acts on viruses that are resistant to the protease inhibitors.

Today, patients take a "drug cocktail" of a combination of these drugs, called ART for antiretroviral treatment (Fauci et al., 2014). Many patients take only a single combination pill per day, with relatively minor side effects. ART has made HIV infection a manageable disease, somewhat like diabetes, with many HIV-infected individuals now expected to survive into their 70s.

On another front, progress is also being made with drugs that prevent the opportunistic infections that strike people with AIDS. The drug pentamidine, for example, in aerosol form, is a standard treatment to prevent *Pneumocystis carinii* pneumonia.

Another major advance is **preexposure prophylaxis (PrEP),** which refers to giving an uninfected person antiretrovirals so they don't become infected. (Prophylaxis means "prevention.") *Science* magazine called it the scientific breakthrough of the year for 2011 (Cohen, 2011b). PrEP is a major prevention strategy for people who are in high-risk situations, such as an HIV-negative person whose sexual partner is HIV-positive, and the CDC has issued guidelines for its use (CDC, 2014b). In a clinical trial, PrEP was highly effective as long as the person took a pill every day or at least 4 times per week (Grant et al., 2014). In another clinical trial, men who had sex with men took PrEP before and after sexual activity, but not at other times. This protocol reduced the risk of infection by 86 percent compared with the untreated control group (Molina et al., 2015).

Women, Children, Ethnic Minorities, and AIDS

In the early days of the AIDS epidemic, men accounted for most cases in the United States, but the picture has since changed considerably. Whereas in 1985 women were only 7 percent of AIDS cases, today they are 24 percent (CDC, 2017c). HIV/AIDS is now the fifth-leading cause of death for U.S. women between the ages of 25 and 44 and is the leading cause of death for African American women between the ages of 25 and 34. The urgency of addressing the needs of women with HIV infection is thus increasing.

New cases of women with HIV infection are most likely to be the result of heterosexual contact (80 percent) and injection drug use (17 percent) (CDC, 2017c).

Preexposure prophylaxis (PrEP): The use of antiretroviral drugs to prevent infection in people who are HIV-negative and are in a high-risk category.

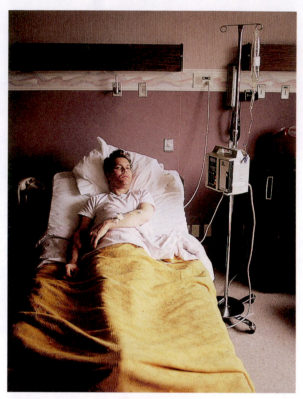

(a)

(b)

Figure 4   AIDS is a multicultural disease. (*a*) An American man with AIDS. (*b*) An African man with AIDS.

(a) ©Thomas Bowman/PhotoEdit; (b) ©Alexander Joe/AFP/Getty Images

Women need far more recognition in AIDS research. For example, intervention programs tailored to the needs of women should be developed. Such programs should include sexual assertiveness training, in which women are empowered to insist that their sex partners use condoms. Women also need to be included in clinical trials of drug treatments.

The other gender group that deserves more attention is transgender individuals, who are at increased risk of HIV

Table 1   Getting Tested: Handy Information about STI Testing

STI	What does the test involve?	How soon is the test accurate?	Who should get tested?
Chlamydia	Men: urine sample or urethral swab Women: urine sample, vaginal swab, or cervical swab	1–2 weeks after infection	Sexually active women under 25 Men who have sex with men People with symptoms, at high risk, or recently exposed
Genital herpes	Blood test or swab of herpes sore	2–6 weeks after infection	People with symptoms
Gonorrhea	Men: urine sample or urethral swab Women: urine sample, vaginal swab, or cervical swab Other sites: swab of throat or rectum	1–2 weeks after infection	Sexually active women under 25 Men who have sex with men People with symptoms, at high risk, or recently exposed
Hepatitis B	Blood test	6–12 weeks	Certain high-risk individuals Pregnant women People with symptoms or exposed
HIV	Blood test or saliva swab	2–12 weeks from infection	Everyone
HPV	Cervical swab	varies	Women over age 30 as part of a routine Pap smear
Syphilis	Blood test	1–6 weeks after infection	Pregnant women Men who have sex with men People who are exposed
Trichomoniasis	Vaginal swab	1–4 weeks after infection	People with symptoms

infection. Transgender women are especially at risk, with estimates as high as 28 percent being infected (CDC, 2016).

Some of the saddest cases are children with AIDS; these cases are known as pediatric AIDS. Children may become HIV-infected at birth from an infected mother. One bright spot is the finding that using antiretrovirals to treat infected women during pregnancy can substantially reduce the rate of infection in their babies. In the United States, AIDS in infants has nearly been eliminated through helping pregnant women know their HIV status and having those who are infected use antiretrovirals.

People of color in the United States—and worldwide—have borne a disproportionate burden of the cases of AIDS. African Americans constitute just 13 percent of the U.S. population, but they account for 44 percent of new infections (CDC, 2017c). The prevalence of AIDS is low among Asian Americans (less than 1 percent of cases).

There is an urgent need to develop education and prevention programs for the Black and Latinx communities (Wyatt et al., 2013). These programs must be culturally sensitive and should focus on the elimination of needle sharing and unsafe sexual practices.

Psychological Considerations in AIDS

Psychological issues for those infected with HIV and for AIDS patients are profound. There are some analogies to people who receive a diagnosis of an incurable cancer,

for AIDS is, at least at present, incurable. Many patients experience the typical reactions for such situations, including a denial of the reality, followed by anger, depression, or both. However, the analogy to cancer patients is

Figure 5   Experts agree that, in the absence of a cure or vaccine for AIDS, the best weapon that we have is education.

©Bill Aron/PhotoEdit

not perfect, for AIDS is a socially stigmatized disease in a way that cancer is not. Thus the revelation that one has AIDS must often be accompanied by the announcement that one is gay or drug addicted.

There is a great need to be sensitive to the psychological needs of AIDS patients. In most cities, support groups for AIDS patients and their families have formed. Social and psychological support from others is essential as people weather this crisis (Gonzalez et al., 2004).

Psychological treatments can be helpful for people living with HIV in several ways (Heckman et al., 2011; Lovejoy & Heckman, 2014). Interventions such as motivational interviewing can improve people's adherence to the drug treatment regimen that is necessary to keep AIDS at bay. Even with ART, HIV-infected people who are depressed have worse medical outcomes than do those who are infected but not depressed (Hartzell et al., 2008). Psychotherapy can reduce depression in infected individuals, improving their quality of life and their medical outcomes, as well as increasing their adherence to ART (Sin & DiMatteo, 2014).

In the chapter "Sexual Coercion" we discussed the phenomenon of *posttraumatic growth* following rape. Between 60 and 80 percent of people with HIV infection report positive psychological growth following diagnosis; people who experience posttraumatic growth and are optimistic tend to have higher T cell counts, helping them to fight disease progression (Milam, 2006).

Recent Progress in AIDS Research

As this discussion makes clear, much more research on HIV and AIDS is needed. We need better treatments to control this disease, we need a cure for it, and we need a vaccine against it. Those are tall orders, and it is unlikely that any of them will appear in the next few years.

Vaccine

Researchers have been working hard to develop a vaccine against HIV, but the job has turned out to be much more difficult than expected (Pavlakis & Felber, 2018; Shattock et al., 2011). The problem is that HIV has many forms, and, even worse, it mutates rapidly and recombines, creating more forms. In effect, the virus doesn't hold still long enough for a vaccine to take effective aim at it. To make matters worse, the strain of HIV that is prevalent in one country (e.g., Thailand) can be different from the strain in another country (the United States), so a vaccine that works in one country might not work in another.

Why isn't there a vaccine yet against HIV?

One strategy in developing a vaccine is to first develop a vaccine that works with monkeys, which can be infected by an analog to HIV called SIV (simian immunodeficiency virus). Progress toward developing vaccines that protect monkeys from infection with SIV has been slow, but steady (Barouch et al., 2018; Hessell & Haigwood, 2015).

Two other strategies involve developing a vaccine that stimulates the body to form resistance (i.e., antibodies) to HIV, or a vaccine that acts at the cellular level by stimulating the production of specialized T cells that are toxic to HIV (Korber & Gnanakaran, 2011; Luzuriaga et al., 2006). Another possibility is a vaccine that combines both. Yet another possibility is a "mosaic" vaccine that contains multiple elements to protect against the multiple strains of HIV (Barouch et al., 2018). Several of these vaccines have moved into clinical trials with humans, and as noted in the section on Thailand, one partially effective vaccine has been identified.

Research on Nonprogressors

Some specific groups of people are being studied for clues to breakthroughs in the war against AIDS. One such group is *nonprogressors* (Duerr et al., 2008; Luque et al., 2014). Approximately 5 percent of HIV-infected people go for 10 years or more without symptoms and with no deterioration of their immune system. Their T cell count remains higher than 500. Nonprogressors turn out to have less HIV in their bodies, even though they have been infected for over a decade. Why? One possibility is that these people have unusually strong immune systems that have essentially managed to contain the virus. Scientists are investigating the mechanisms that might account for the strong immune reactions.

Killer T Cells and Chemokines

Certain lymphocytes (CD8+ T cells) battle against HIV in the body. They do so by secreting chemokines (which are molecules), with names such as RANTES, MIP-1a, and MIP-1b (Chatterjee et al., 2012). The chemokines can bind to the coreceptor CCR5, blocking HIV from entering cells. Scientists hope that these discoveries may lead to improved treatments for HIV-infected people and possibly to vaccines that boost the level of chemokines and therefore boost the body's resistance to HIV infection.

Genetic Resistance

Scientists have discovered a mutation of a gene, and the mutation creates strong resistance to HIV infection (Cohen, 2011a; Novembre et al., 2005). The gene is called CCR5 because it is the gene for the CCR5 receptor that, as discussed earlier, allows HIV to enter cells. The mutation occurred some time in history as humans spread out of Africa. The evidence indicates that the mutation was strongly selected for during the bubonic plague or smallpox plagues that occurred in Europe, and the mutation is much more common there than in other parts of the world.

First Person

Safer Sex in the AIDS Era

I n this age of AIDS, everyone needs to think about positive health practices that will prevent, or at least reduce the chances of, infection. Technically, these practices are called *safer sex,* there being no true safe sex except no sex. What choices are available? Health experts agree that the following practices will make sex safer:

1. If you choose to be sexually active (and abstinence is one alternative to consider), have sex only in a stable, faithful, monogamous relationship with an uninfected partner who you know is uninfected because you both have been tested.

2. If you are sexually active with more than one partner, always use latex condoms. They have a good track record in preventing many sexually transmitted infections. Laboratory tests indicate that latex condoms are effective protection against HIV. Condoms have a failure rate in preventing disease just as they do in preventing pregnancy, but they are still much better than nothing.

3. If there is any risk that you are infected or that your partner is, abstain from sex, always use condoms, or consider alternative forms of sexual expression such as hand–genital stimulation.

4. Do not have sexual intercourse with someone who has had many previous partners.

5. Do not engage in anal intercourse if there is even the slightest risk that your partner is infected.

6. Remember that both vaginal intercourse and anal intercourse transmit HIV. Mouth–genital sex may

Figure 6   Quality control of condoms.

©BEHROUZ MEHR/AFP/Getty Images

also transmit HIV, particularly if semen enters the mouth.

7. If you think that you may be infected, have a blood test to find out. If you learn that you are infected, at the very least use a condom every time you engage in anal or vaginal intercourse, or, preferably, abstain from these behaviors.

8. Consider "outercourse" as an alternative to intercourse. Outercourse involves activities like mutual masturbation and erotic massage, which don't transmit diseases.

People with two copies of the mutation (homozygotes) are resistant to infection, whereas people with one copy (heterozygotes) may become infected but show much slower disease progression.

Microbicides

Microbicides are substances, usually in ointment form, that kill microbes such as HIV. These ointments could be put into the vagina or anus or spread on the penis to battle HIV transmission. The old standby nonoxynol-9 was thought to be effective in killing HIV some years ago, but today we know that it is not only ineffective but actually makes women more vulnerable to infection by irritating the

lining of the vagina. Much effort is now going into developing effective microbicides that will attack HIV as well as other sexually transmitted viruses. Tenofovir gel (tenofovir is an antiretroviral drug) used vaginally by women reduced infection rates by 39 percent (Abdool Karim et al., 2010; Nicol, 2015). That isn't perfect, but it's progress. The same gel is also in trials for those who engage in receptive anal intercourse (Carballo-Dieguez et al., 2017).

Behavioral Prevention

In the last analysis, prevention is better than cure. Until we have a highly effective vaccine, our best hope is interventions that aim to change people's behavior because it is behavior—sexual activity, injection drug use—that spreads HIV. Many successful interventions have been designed that increase condom use, communication with the partner, and other behaviors that help to prevent infection (e.g., Hidalgo et al., 2015). According to meta-analyses, these interventions are most effective if they are tailored to the group (e.g., gay men, college students), if the gender and ethnicity of the communicator of the intervention match those of the group, if arguments are presented to change attitudes, and if training in condom use and interpersonal skills is provided (Covey et al., 2016).

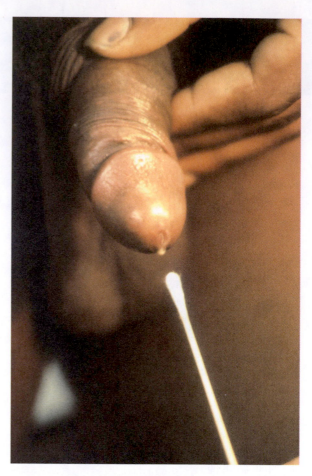

Figure 7 Symptoms of gonorrhea in men include a puslike discharge.

Centers for Disease Control

Gonorrhea

Historical records indicate that **gonorrhea** ("the clap," "the drip") is the oldest of the sexual diseases. Its symptoms are described in the Old Testament, in Leviticus 15 (about 3,500 years ago). The Greek physician Hippocrates, some 2,400 years ago, believed that gonorrhea resulted from "excessive indulgence in the pleasures of Venus," the goddess of love (hence the term *venereal* disease). Albert Neisser identified the bacterium that causes it, the gonococcus *Neisseria gonorrhoeae,* in 1879.

Gonorrhea has always been a particular problem in wartime, when it spreads rapidly among the soldiers and the prostitutes they patronize. In the 20th century, a gonorrhea epidemic occurred during World War I, and gonorrhea was also a serious problem during World War II. Then, with the discovery of penicillin and its use in curing gonorrhea, the disease became much less prevalent in the 1950s; indeed, public health officials thought that it would be virtually eliminated.

Then there was a resurgence of gonorrhea, with about 1 million cases per year reported in the 1970s (CDC, 2003). One of the reasons for the resurgence was the shift in contraceptive practices to the use of the pill, which (unlike the condom) provides no protection from gonorrhea and actually increases a woman's susceptibility. Rates declined to a low point of about 300,000 cases per year in 2009 (due mainly to increased use of condoms) but then steadily climbed to 470,000 cases in 2016 (CDC, 2017b).

Symptoms

Most cases of gonorrhea result from penis-in-vagina intercourse. In males, the gonococcus invades the urethra, producing urethritis (inflammation of the urethra). White blood cells rush to the area and attempt to destroy the bacteria, but the bacteria soon win the battle. In most cases, symptoms appear 2 to

Gonorrhea (gon-uh-REE-uh): A sexually transmitted infection that usually causes symptoms of a puslike discharge and painful, burning urination in males but is frequently asymptomatic in females.

5 days after infection, although they may appear as early as the first day or as late as 2 weeks after infection (Hook & Handsfield, 2008). Initially a thin, clear mucous discharge seeps out of the meatus (the opening at the tip of the penis). Within a day or so it becomes thick and creamy and may be white, yellowish, or yellow-green (Figure 7). This is often referred to as a *purulent* (puslike) discharge. The area around the meatus may become swollen. About half of infected men experience a painful burning sensation when urinating.

Because the early symptoms of gonorrhea in men are obvious and often painful, most men seek treatment immediately and are cured. If the disease is not treated, however, the urethritis spreads up the urethra, causing inflammations in the prostate (prostatitis), seminal vesicles (seminal vesiculitis), urinary bladder (cystitis), and epididymis (epididymitis). Pain on urination becomes worse and is felt in the whole penis. Then these early symptoms may disappear as the disease spreads to the other organs. If the epididymitis is left untreated, it may spread to the testicles and the resulting scar tissue may cause sterility.

Asymptomatic gonorrhea (gonorrhea with no symptoms) does occur in males, but its incidence is low. In contrast, about 50 to 80 percent of women infected with gonorrhea are asymptomatic during the early stages of the disease. Many women are unaware of their infection unless they are told by a male partner. Therefore, it is extremely important for any man who is infected to inform all his female contacts. Because gonorrhea is so frequently asymptomatic in women, it is recommended that all sexually active women under 25 years of age be tested annually (Workowski & Bolan, 2015).

The gonorrheal infection in women invades the cervix. Pus is discharged, but the amount may be so slight that it is not noticed. When present, it is yellow-green and irritating to the vulva, but it is generally not heavy (it is not to be confused with normal cervical mucus, which is clear or white and nonirritating, or with discharges resulting from the various kinds of vaginitis—discussed later in this chapter—that are irritating but white). Although the cervix is the primary site of infection, the inflammation may also spread to the urethra, causing burning pain on urination (not to be confused with cystitis).

If the infection is not treated, the Bartholin glands may become infected. The infection may also be spread to the anus and rectum.

Because so many women are asymptomatic in the early stages of gonorrhea, many receive no treatment, and thus there is a high risk of serious complications. In about 20 percent of women who go untreated, the gonococcus moves up into the uterus. From there it infects the fallopian tubes (Hook & Handsfield, 2008). The tissues become swollen and inflamed, and thus the condition is called pelvic inflammatory disease (PID)—although PID can be caused by diseases other than gonorrhea. The major symptom is pelvic pain and, in some cases, irregular or painful menstruation. If the PID is not treated, scar tissue may form, blocking the tubes and leaving the woman infertile. Indeed, untreated gonorrhea is one of the most common causes of infertility in women. If the tubes are partially blocked, so that sperm can get up them but eggs cannot move down, ectopic pregnancy can result because the fertilized egg is trapped in the tube.

There are three other major sites for nongenital gonorrhea infection: the mouth and throat, the anus and rectum, and the eyes. If fellatio is performed on an infected man, the gonococcus may invade the throat. (Cunnilingus is less likely to spread gonorrhea, and mouth-to-mouth kissing rarely does.) Such an infection is often asymptomatic; the typical symptom, if there is one, is a sore throat. Rectal gonorrhea is contracted through anal intercourse and thus affects both women in heterosexual relations and, more commonly, men who have sex with men. Symptoms include some discharge from the rectum

and itching, but many cases are asymptomatic. Gonorrhea may also invade the eyes. This occurs only rarely in adults, when they touch the genitals and then transfer the bacteria-containing pus to their eyes by touching them. This eye infection is much more common in newborn infants. The infection is transferred from the mother's cervix to the infant's eyes during birth. For this reason, erithromycin is put in every newborn's eyes to prevent any such infection. If left untreated, the eyes become swollen and painful within a few days, and there is a discharge of pus. Blindness was a common result in the pre-antibiotic era.

Diagnosis

A urine test is available for men. If gonorrhea in the throat is suspected, a swab should be taken and cultured. People who suspect that they may have rectal gonorrhea should request that a swab be taken from the rectum, since many physicians will not automatically think to do this.

A urine test is available for women. A pelvic examination should also be performed. Pain during this exam may indicate PID. Women who suspect throat or rectal infection should request that samples be taken from those sites as well.

Treatment

The traditional treatment for gonorrhea was a large dose of penicillin, or tetracycline for those who were allergic to penicillin. However, strains of the gonococcus that are resistant to penicillin and tetracycline became so common that the newer antibiotic Cipro had to be used. In 2007 the CDC announced that cases that were resistant to Cipro had become so common that doctors should stop using it and switch to ceftriaxone. The current treatment is a dual therapy of ceftriaxone plus azithromycin (Workowski & Bolan, 2015). The worry is that if resistance develops to it, there will be no remaining antibiotics for treatment.

Syphilis

There has been considerable debate over the exact origins of **syphilis**. The disease, called "the Great Pox," was present in Europe during the 1400s and became a pandemic by 1500.

The bacterium that causes syphilis is called *Treponema pallidum*. It is spiral shaped and is thus often called a *spirochete*.

The incidence of syphilis is much less than that of gonorrhea or chlamydia. There were 28,000 reported new cases in 2016

> **Syphilis (SIFF-ih-lis):** A sexually transmitted infection that causes a chancre to appear in the primary stage.

(CDC, 2017a). The rate in 2000 was the lowest since reporting began in 1941. Unfortunately, though, rates began to rise after that.

Although syphilis is not nearly as common as chlamydia or gonorrhea, its effects are much more serious if left untreated. In most cases, chlamydia or gonorrhea causes only discomfort and, sometimes, sterility; syphilis, if left untreated, can damage the nervous system and even cause death. There are many cases today of coinfection, in which the person is infected with both syphilis and HIV. Syphilis infection makes one more vulnerable to HIV and vice versa.

Symptoms

The major early symptom of syphilis is the **chancre**—a round, ulcerlike lesion with a hard, raised edge, resembling a crater. One of the distinctive things about the chancre is that although it looks terrible, it is painless. It appears about 3 weeks (as early as 10 days or as late as 3 months) after intercourse with an infected person. The chancre appears at the point where the bacteria entered the body. Typically, the bacteria enter through the mucous membranes of the genitals as a result of intercourse with an infected person. Thus in men the chancre often appears on the penis or scrotum. In women, the chancre often appears on the cervix, and thus the woman does not notice it and is unaware that she is infected (this is one good reason for a woman to do the pelvic self-exam with a speculum as described in the chapter "Sexual Anatomy"). The chancre may also appear on the vaginal walls or, externally, on the vulva (see Figure 8).

If oral sex or anal intercourse with an infected person occurs, the bacteria can also invade the mucous membranes of the mouth or rectum. Thus the chancre may appear on the lips, tongue, or tonsils or around the anus. In addition, the bacteria may enter through a cut in the skin anywhere on the body. Thus it is possible (though rare) to get syphilis by touching the chancre of an infected person. The chancre would then appear on the hand at the point where the bacteria entered through the break in the skin.

Chancre (SHANK-er): A painless, ulcerlike lesion with a hard, raised edge that is a symptom of syphilis.
Primary-stage syphilis: The first few weeks of a syphilis infection during which the chancre is present.
Secondary-stage syphilis: The second stage of syphilis, occurring several months after infection, during which the chancre has disappeared and a generalized body rash appears.
Latent (LAY-tent) syphilis: The third stage of syphilis, which may last for years, during which symptoms disappear although the person is still infected.

The progress of the disease once the person has been infected is generally divided into four stages: primary-stage syphilis, secondary-stage syphilis, latent syphilis, and late syphilis. The phase described earlier, in which the chancre forms, is **primary-stage syphilis.** If left untreated, the chancre goes away by itself within 1 to 5 weeks after it appears. This marks the end of the primary stage. However, the disease has not gone away just because the chancre has healed; it has only gone underground.

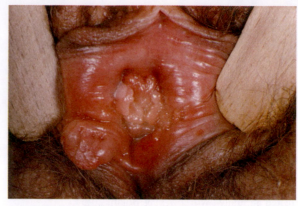

(a)

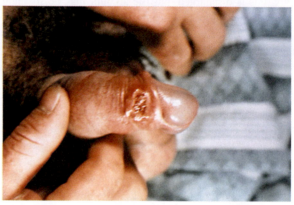

(b)

Figure 8   The chancre characteristic of primary stage syphilis (*a*) on the labia majora and (*b*) on the penis.

(a) ©CNRI/Science Source; (b) Centers for Disease Control

Beginning a few months after the original appearance of the chancre, a generalized body rash develops, marking the beginning of **secondary-stage syphilis.** The rash is variable in its appearance, the most distinctive feature being that it does not itch or hurt. Hair loss may also occur during the secondary stage. Usually the symptoms are troublesome enough to cause the person to seek medical help. With appropriate treatment at this stage, the disease can still be cured and there will be no permanent effects.

Even without treatment, the secondary-stage symptoms go away in a few weeks, leading people to believe mistakenly that the disease has gone away. Instead, it has entered a more dangerous stage.

After the symptoms of the secondary stage have disappeared, the disease is in the latent stage; **latent syphilis** may last for years. Although there are no symptoms in this stage, *Treponema pallidum* is busily burrowing into the tissues of the body, especially the blood vessels, central nervous system (brain and spinal cord), and bones. After the first year or so of the latent stage, the disease is no longer infectious, except that a pregnant woman can still pass it on to the fetus.

About half of the people who enter the latent stage remain in it permanently, living out the rest of their lives without further complications. The other half, however, move into the dangerous **late syphilis.** In *cardiovascular late syphilis* the heart and major blood vessels are attacked; this occurs 10 to 40 years after the initial infection. Cardiovascular syphilis can lead to death. In *neurosyphilis* the brain and spinal cord are attacked, leading to insanity and paralysis, which appear 10 to 20 years after infection. Neurosyphilis may be fatal.

If a pregnant woman has syphilis, the fetus may be infected when the bacteria cross the placental barrier, and the child gets **congenital** (meaning present from birth) **syphilis.** The infection may cause early death of the fetus (spontaneous abortion) or severe illness at or shortly after birth. It may also lead to late complications that show up only at 10 or 20 years of age. Women are most infectious to their baby when they have primary- or secondary-stage syphilis, but they may transmit the infection to the fetus as long as 8 years after the mother's initial infection. If the disease is diagnosed and treated before the fourth month of pregnancy, the fetus will not develop the disease. For this reason, a syphilis test is done as a routine part of the blood analysis in a pregnancy test.

Diagnosis

Syphilis is somewhat difficult to diagnose from symptoms because, as noted earlier, its symptoms are like those of many other diseases.

The physical exam should include inspection not only of the genitals but also of the entire body surface. Women should have a pelvic exam so that the vagina and the cervix can be checked for chancres. If the patient has had anal intercourse, a rectal exam should also be performed.

If a chancre is present, some of its fluid is taken and placed on a slide for inspection under a dark-field microscope. If the person has syphilis, *Treponema pallidum* should be present.

The most common tests for syphilis are blood tests, all of which are based on antibody reactions. The VDRL (named for the Venereal Disease Research Laboratory of the U.S. Public Health Service, where the test was developed) is one of these blood tests. It is fairly accurate, cheap, and easy to perform.

Treatment

The treatment of choice for syphilis is penicillin (Workowski & Bolan, 2015). *Treponema pallidum* is rather fragile, so large doses are not necessary. The recommended dose is two shots of penicillin G, one in each of the buttocks. Latent, late, and congenital syphilis require larger doses. For those allergic to penicillin, the recommended treatment is tetracycline or doxycycline, but it should not be given to pregnant women.

Hepatitis B

Viral hepatitis is a disease of the liver. One symptom is an enlarged liver that is somewhat tender. The disease can vary greatly in severity from asymptomatic cases to ones in which there is fever, fatigue, jaundice (yellowish skin), and vomiting, much as one might experience with a serious case of the flu. There are five types of viral hepatitis: hepatitis A, B, C, D, and E. The one that is of most interest in a discussion of sexually transmitted infections is hepatitis B. Hepatitis C and D (or delta) can also be transmitted sexually, but they are rare compared with B.

The virus for **hepatitis B** (HBV) can be transmitted through blood, saliva, semen, vaginal secretions, and other body fluids. The behaviors that spread it include needle sharing by people who inject drugs, vaginal and anal intercourse, and oral–anal sex. The disease is found among men who have sex with men and among heterosexuals. It has many similarities to AIDS, although hepatitis B is more contagious. People who have had the disease continue to have a positive blood test for it for the rest of their lives.

Many adults infected with HBV are asymptomatic; their bodies fight off the virus and they are left uninfected, with permanent immunity. Others develop an early, acute (short-term) illness and display a variety of symptoms but recover from the illness. A third group develops chronic (long-term) hepatitis B. They continue to be infectious and may develop serious liver disease involving cirrhosis or cancer. Fortunately, antiviral treatments are now available for those with chronic hepatitis B.

The good news is that there is a vaccine against hepatitis B. The current recommendation is that all teenagers and infants be vaccinated. We urge you to be vaccinated if you are a man who has sex with men or a heterosexual man or woman who has had a number of partners. If there is even a hint that you have been exposed, you should be tested.

Trichomoniasis

Trichomoniasis ("trich") is caused by the protozoan *Trichomonas vaginalis*. The organism can survive for a time on toilet seats and other objects, so it is occasionally transmitted nonsexually; but it is transmitted mainly through sexual intercourse.

For women, the symptom is a vaginal discharge that irritates the vulva and has an unpleasant smell.

Late syphilis: The fourth and final stage of syphilis, during which the disease does damage to major organs of the body such as the heart or brain.
Congenital (kun-JEN-ih-tul) syphilis: A syphilis infection in a newborn baby resulting from transmission from an infected mother.
Hepatitis B: A liver disease that can be transmitted sexually or by needle sharing.
Trichomoniasis (trick-oh-moh-NY-us-is): A form of vaginitis causing a frothy white or yellow discharge with an unpleasant odor.

In men, there may be irritation of the urethra and a discharge from the penis, but some men are asymptomatic. It is important that accurate diagnosis be made, because the drugs used to cure trichomoniasis are different from those used to treat other STIs that have similar symptoms, and the long-term effects of untreated trichomoniasis can be serious.

The treatment of choice is metronidazole taken orally. If left untreated, trich can lead to pelvic inflammatory disease and problems with birth (Workowski & Bolan, 2015). It also increases susceptibility to HIV infection.

Zika

The **Zika virus** (ZIKV) causes an infectious disease called Zika fever. ZIKV is transmitted by bites from certain mosquitoes, sexual activity, blood transfusions, and from mother to fetus during pregnancy (Silva et al., 2018). Zika virus has been around for a long time, having been discovered in rhesus monkeys in Uganda in 1947, and in humans in 1953. No one paid much attention to it. Then, in 2015, obstetricians in Brazil noticed that they were delivering an unusual number of babies with microcephaly, or very small brains, and the link to ZIKV was established. These reports attracted worldwide attention and, with the scope of international travel, worries about the spread of the virus. It was found in the United States, particularly in Florida. Major public health efforts aimed to eliminate conditions—such as standing water—that encourage mosquitos. In 2018, no mosquito-borne Zika infections were reported in the continental United States. Because the consequences can be so catastrophic (microcephaly), scientists are energetically pursuing research on Zika. Zika is another good reason to use condoms, especially if you are traveling abroad in tropical regions where Zika is most prevalent.

Pubic Lice

Pubic lice ("crabs" or *pediculosis pubis*) are tiny lice that attach themselves to the base of pubic hairs and there feed on blood from their human host. They are about the size of a pinhead and, under magnification, resemble a crab (see Figure 9). They lay eggs frequently and live for about 30 days, but they die within 24 hours if they are taken off a human host. Crabs are transmitted by sexual contact, but they may also be picked up from sheets, towels, sleeping bags, or toilet seats. (Yes, there are some things you can catch from toilet seats.)

Zika virus: A virus that causes Zika fever and, when transmitted from mother to fetus during pregnancy, causes microcephaly in the baby.
Pubic lice: Tiny lice that attach themselves to the base of pubic hairs and cause itching; also called *crabs*.

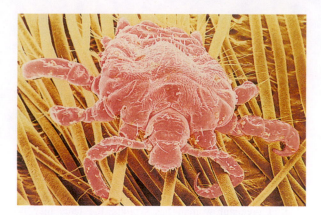

Figure 9   A pubic louse, enlarged. The actual size is about the same as the head of a pin.

©E. Gray/Science Photo Library/Science Source

The major symptom of pubic lice is fierce itching in the region of the pubic hair. Diagnosis is made by finding the lice or the eggs attached to the hairs.

Pubic lice are treated with the drugs Nix and Rid, which are available without prescription. Both kill the lice. After treatment, the person should put on clean clothing. Since the lice die within 24 hours, it is not necessary to disinfect clothing that has not been used for longer than 24 hours. However, the eggs can live for up to 6 days, and in difficult cases it may be necessary to boil or dry-clean one's clothing or use a spray such as R and C.

Protecting Yourself

Most of the literature one reads concentrates on the rapid diagnosis and treatment of STIs, but prevention would be much better than cure, and there are some ways you can avoid getting STIs, or at least reduce your chances of doing so. The most obvious ways, of course, are to limit yourself to a monogamous relationship with an uninfected person or to abstain from sexual activity. If these strategies are unacceptable to you, other techniques are available.

The latex condom, in addition to being a decent contraceptive, gives good (though not perfect) protection against HIV, HPV, gonorrhea, chlamydia, herpes, syphilis, and other STIs (Baldwin et al., 2004; Steiner & Cates, 2006; Wald et al., 2005; Winer et al., 2006). With the rise of the STI epidemic, the condom is again becoming popular. The key is to eroticize condom use. The diaphragm also provides some protection for women, as does the female condom. The First

My partner has no symptoms of any STI. Should we still practice safer sex?

First Person

Cool Lines about Safer Sex

Partner	You
What's that?	A condom, baby.
What for?	To use when we're making love.
I don't like using them.	Why not?
Rubbers are gross.	Being pregnant when I don't want to be is worse. So is getting AIDS.
Don't you trust me?	Trust isn't the point. People carry sexually transmitted infections without knowing it.
I'll pull out in time.	Women can get pregnant from precum. It can also carry sexually transmitted infections.
I thought you said using condoms made you feel cheap.	I decided to face facts. I like having sex, and I want to stay healthy and happy.
Rubbers aren't romantic.	Making love and protecting each other's health sounds romantic enough to me.
Making love with a rubber on is like taking a shower with a raincoat on.	Doing it without a rubber is playing Russian roulette.
It just isn't as sensitive.	With a condom you might last even longer, and that'll make up for it.
I don't stay hard when I put on a condom.	I can do something about that.
Putting it on interrupts everything.	Not if I help put it on.
I'll try, but it might not work.	Practice makes perfect.
But I love you.	Then you'll help me protect myself.
I guess you don't really love me.	I'm not going to prove my love by risking my life.
I'm not using a rubber, no matter what.	Well, then I guess we're not having sex.
Just this once without it.	It only takes once to get pregnant. It only takes once to get AIDS.
It won't fit.	Condoms come in all different sizes.

Source: www.teenwire.com, June 22, 2004.

Person (above) presents possible responses to overcome a partner's objections to condom use.

Some simple health precautions are also helpful. Successful prostitutes, who need to be careful about STIs, take such precautions. Washing the genitals before intercourse helps remove bacteria. This may not sound like a romantic prelude to lovemaking, but prostitutes make a sensuous game out of soaping the man's genitals. You can do this as part of taking a shower or bath with your partner. The other important technique is inspecting your partner's genitals. If you see a chancre, a wart, a herpes blister, or a discharge, put on your clothes and leave or, at the very least, immediately start a conversation about STI status (do not fall for the "it's only a pimple" routine). This technique may sound a little crude or embarrassing, but if you are intimate enough with someone to make love with that person, you ought to be intimate enough to look at their genitals. Once again, if you are cool about it, you can make this an erotic part of foreplay.

However, just because a partner has no obvious symptoms like herpes blisters or warts, don't assume that the person is uninfected. We have seen in this chapter how many of these diseases—for example, chlamydia, herpes, and HPV—can be asymptomatic. The only way to really know is to have a complete battery of tests for STIs, a choice more and more people are making. Not every disease is tested in the standard battery—for example, herpes and HPV usually are not—but it will catch most infections.

Urinating both before and after intercourse helps to keep bacteria out of the urethra.

Finally, each person needs to recognize that it is their ethical responsibility to seek out early diagnosis and treatment. Probably the most important responsibility is that of informing prospective partners if you have an STI and of informing past partners as soon as you discover that you have one. For example, because so many women are asymptomatic for chlamydia, it is particularly important for men to take the responsibility of informing their female partners if they find that they have the disease. It is important to take care of your own health, but it is equally important to take care of your partner's health.

Other Genital Infections

Vaginitis (vaginal inflammation or irritation) is very common among women and is endemic in college populations. Two kinds of vaginitis, as well as prostatitis, are considered here. None of these infections are STIs because they are not transmitted by sexual contact; they are, however, common infections of the sex organs.

A few simple steps can help prevent vaginitis. Every time you shower or take a bath, wash the vulva carefully and dry it thoroughly. Do not use feminine hygiene deodorant sprays; they are unnecessary and can irritate the vagina. Wear cotton underpants; nylon and other synthetics retain moisture, and vaginitis-producing organisms thrive on moisture. Avoid wearing pants that are too tight in the crotch; they increase moisture and may irritate the vulva. Wipe the anus from front to back so that bacteria from the anus do not get into the vagina. For the same reason, never go immediately from anal intercourse to vaginal intercourse.

> **Vaginitis (vaj-in-ITE-is):** An irritation or inflammation of the vagina, usually causing a discharge.
> **Candida:** A form of vaginitis causing a thick, white discharge; also called *moniliasis* or *yeast infection.*
> **Prostatitis (pros-tuh-TY-tis):** An infection or inflammation of the prostate gland.

Candida

Candida (also called *yeast infection* and *moniliasis*) is a form of vaginitis caused by the yeast fungus *Candida*. *Candida* is normally present in the vagina, but if the delicate environmental balance there is disturbed (e.g., if the pH is changed), the growth of *Candida* can get out of hand. Conditions that encourage the growth of *Candida* include long-term use of birth control pills, menstruation, diabetes or a prediabetic condition, pregnancy, and long-term use of antibiotics such as tetracycline. It is not a sexually transmitted infection, but intercourse may aggravate it.

The major symptom is a thick, white, curdlike vaginal discharge, found on the vaginal lips and the walls of the vagina. The discharge can cause extreme itching, to the point where the woman is not interested in having intercourse.

Treatment is by the drugs miconazole or clotrimazole, both available over the counter. Fluconazole, a single-dose treatment, is available by prescription.

If a woman has candida while she is pregnant, she can transmit it to her baby during birth. The baby gets the yeast in its digestive system, a condition known as *thrush*. Thrush can also result from oral–genital sex.

Bacterial vaginosis is another vaginal infection that produces a similar discharge. The distinctive feature is that the discharge has a foul odor.

Prostatitis

Prostatitis is an inflammation of the prostate gland. The infection is often caused by the bacterium *E. coli.* It can also be caused by gonorrhea or chlamydia. The symptoms are fever, chills, pain around the anus and rectum, and a need for frequent urination. It may produce sexual dysfunction, typically painful ejaculation. In some cases, prostatitis may be chronic (long-lasting) and may have no symptoms, or only lower-back pain. Antibiotics are used in treatment.

Critical THINKing Skill

Understanding the concept of probability

In this chapter, we revisit a critical thinking skill introduced in the chapter "Contraception and Abortion." As we saw in that chapter, probability refers to the chance that an event will occur. Probabilities can range between 0 (no chance) and 1.0 (definitely will occur). Often probabilities are stated as percentages ranging between 0 and 100 percent. For example, if we toss a fair coin, the probability that it will come up heads is 0.5, or 50 percent. Consider the following case.

Ryan is planning to go to a party at a senior's house near his college tonight. He thinks that Molly, an attractive woman whom he has noticed in one of his classes, will be there, and he hopes for a hookup with her, including intercourse. Then he starts thinking about how he has heard that chlamydia is widespread on college campuses. Will it be safe to have sex with Molly? Should he use a condom?

Ryan needs to assess some probabilities. The first is the probability that Molly has chlamydia. He doesn't really know that probability. How could he find out? He could ask Molly if she has any of the symptoms, but Molly might not be happy with that line of conversation. Then Ryan remembers that a high percentage of women with chlamydia are asymptomatic and don't even know that they have it. He could ask her if she has been tested for STIs recently. That might not sound romantic, but he needs to protect his health, and he could frame it in terms of his commitment to both her health and his health. He could volunteer that he was tested just a month ago and had nothing. In the end, though, he may not be able to know precisely the probability that she is infected. He could go with a statistic from this chapter, that when high school girls were tested, 8 percent had chlamydia.

Some people make a mistake at this stage and assume that, if Molly looks healthy and attractive, the probability that she is infected is 0. That is a bad assumption. Why?

Another probability that Ryan needs to know, especially if he can't know precisely whether she is infected, is the probability of infection from a single act of intercourse. Even scientists cannot give very precise estimates of these probabilities, and the probabilities depend greatly on factors such as whether the man uses a condom (Garnett, 2008). Gonorrhea, for example, is highly infectious, with a probability of transmission from an infected woman to an uninfected man of 25 percent from one act of unprotected intercourse (but a 50 percent risk of transmission in the reverse direction, from an infected man to an uninfected woman). Ryan probably can't know the exact probability of transmission if Molly is infected.

Overall, then, Ryan faces a great deal of uncertainty. He does know, though, that condoms are highly effective in preventing transmission of STIs like chlamydia. After assessing all of these factors, if Ryan is applying good critical thinking skills, he will use a condom.

SUMMARY

Sexually transmitted infections (STIs) are at epidemic levels in the United States and worldwide. STIs can be caused by bacteria, viruses, or, in some cases, other organisms.

Chlamydia

Chlamydia is often asymptomatic, especially in women. In men, it produces a thin discharge from the penis and mild pain on urination. It is quite curable with antibiotics. If left untreated in women, possible complications include pelvic inflammatory disease and infertility.

HPV

HPV (human papillomavirus) causes genital warts, but many cases are asymptomatic. HPV infection increases women's risk of cervical cancer as well as men's risk of cancer of the penis and anus. A vaccine is now available.

Genital Herpes

Genital herpes, caused by the HSV virus, produces bouts of painful blisters on the genitals, although some infected people experience no or only a few outbreaks. Currently there is no cure, although the drug acyclovir minimizes the symptoms. Herpes infection increases one's risk of HIV infection.

HIV Infection and AIDS

The virus HIV destroys the body's natural immune system and leaves the person vulnerable to certain infections and cancers that lead to death. Most HIV-positive people come from three risk groups: men who have sex with men, injection drug users, and heterosexual partners of infected individuals. A combination of drugs called ART is used to slow the progression of the disease. Several strategies for producing a vaccine are being pursued, but properties of HIV make success difficult. Treatment with ART lowers an infected person's risk of transmitting HIV, and pre-exposure prophylaxis can prevent infection for high-risk individuals.

Gonorrhea

The primary symptoms of gonorrhea in males, appearing 2 to 5 days after infection, are a white or yellow discharge from the penis and a burning pain on urination. Some men and the majority of women with gonorrhea are asymptomatic. Gonorrhea is caused by a bacterium, the gonococcus, and is cured with antibiotics. If left untreated, it may lead to infertility.

Syphilis

Syphilis is caused by the bacterium *Treponema pallidum*. The first symptom is a chancre. Penicillin is effective as a cure. If left untreated, the disease progresses through several stages that may lead to death.

Hepatitis B

Hepatitis B, caused by the virus HBV, is transmitted sexually as well as by needle sharing. Antiviral drugs are available to treat chronic cases. A vaccine is available.

Trichomoniasis

Trichomoniasis produces a discharge that is irritating to the vagina. Drugs are available that cure it.

Zika

The Zika virus (ZIKV) causes Zika fever but, most important, if a pregnant woman is infected, it can cause microcephaly in the fetus. The virus is spread sexually, but it most often is spread by mosquito bites.

Pubic Lice

Pubic lice are tiny lice that attach to the pubic hair. They are spread through sexual and other types of physical contact. Shampoos and creams are available that kill the lice.

Protecting Yourself

Other than abstinence and confining oneself to a single uninfected partner, the best way to prevent infection with an STI is to use a condom consistently.

Other Genital Infections

Other vaginal infections include candida and bacterial vaginosis. Prostatitis is inflammation of the prostate gland.

SUGGESTIONS FOR FURTHER READING

Centers for Disease Control and Prevention. You can find just about anything you need to know about STIs on the website of this federal agency. Different branches are dedicated to HIV and to all other STIs, so there are two relevant web pages: https://www.cdc.gov/std/ and https://www.cdc.gov/hiv/.

Ebel, Charles, and Wald, Anna. (2007). *Managing herpes: Living and loving with HSV.* Research Triangle Park, NC: American Social Health Association. People say this is the best herpes book ever.

Jones, James H. (1981). *Bad blood: The Tuskegee syphilis experiment.* New York: Free Press. The shocking story of the study in which Black men with syphilis were left untreated so that the course of the disease could be observed.

Nack, Adina. (2008). *Damaged goods: Women living with incurable STDs.* Philadelphia: Temple University Press. Nack, a sociologist, recounts her fascinating research with women who have HPV or herpes.

Are **YOU** **Curious?**

1. Why is the Roman Catholic Church opposed to contraception?
2. What does the Bible say about homosexuality?
3. What are some ethical arguments surrounding cloning?

Read this chapter to find out.

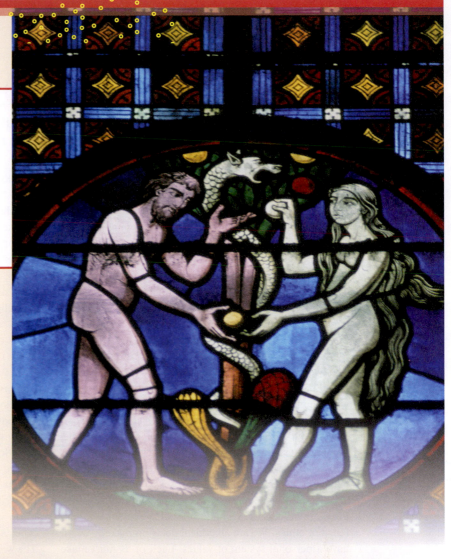

©*Photodisc/Punchstock*

CHAPTER

19

Ethics, Religion, and Sexuality

CHAPTER HIGHLIGHTS

A viable sexual theology for our time will affirm that sexuality is always much more than genital expression. Sexuality expresses the mystery of our creation as those who need to reach out for the physical and spiritual embrace of others. It expresses God's intention that we find our authentic humanness not in isolation but in relationship.*

*James B. Nelson. (1992). *Body theology*. Louisville, KY: Westminster/John Knox Press.

A high school student is in love with her boyfriend and wonders whether they ought to begin sleeping together. A corporation executive hears rumors that one of his employees is gay, and he tries to decide what to do about it. A minister is asked to counsel a husband and wife, one of whom had an affair. A presidential candidate is confronted by a right-to-life group demanding support for a constitutional amendment to ban abortion. All these people, facing the need to make decisions that involve sexuality, find that issues of values make the decisions difficult. The two principal conceptual frameworks for dealing with questions of values are religion and philosophy, both of which consider ethics, the topic of this chapter.

We consider ethical aspects of human sexuality for two reasons. First, the scientific goal of explaining sexual phenomena must take religious beliefs and ethical concerns into account. These are important influences on people's behaviors, especially in matters of sex, so we cannot fully understand why people do what they do without considering these influences. Second, there is the personal importance of ethics. We are all ethical decision makers; we all have a personal system of values. Each of us must make decisions with respect to our own sexuality. Therefore, we would do well to consider how such decisions are made.

Basic Concepts

The term **ethics** is used in various senses. First and most fundamental, it refers to the right or wrong, the good or evil, of behaviors. Sometimes people use *moral* in the same way. Second, the term *ethics* also refers to a system of principles established by some particular group; we might talk about Roman Catholic ethics, for example. We use ethics when there is a conflict between things we prize or desire highly. Sexual pleasure may be an important value for one person but something to be avoided for another. However, regardless of the importance we attach to sex, we need a way of integrating our

sexuality into our patterns of decision making. To do this we use such categories as right or wrong, good or bad, appropriate or inappropriate, and moral or immoral. These are the kinds of distinctions made in the field of ethics; because we use them every day, we are all practical ethicists.

Religion enters the picture as a source of values, attitudes, and ethics. For believers, religion sets forth an ethics code and provides sanctions (rewards and punishments) that motivate them to obey the rules. When a particular religion is practiced by many people in a society, it helps create culture, which then influences even those who do not accept the religion. Therefore, it is important to study the relationship of religion to sexuality for two reasons. First, it is a powerful influence on many individuals. Second, it often shapes a whole society's orientation toward human sexuality.

Let us begin by defining some terms that are useful in discussing sexual ethics. **Hedonism** and **asceticism** have to do with one's approach to the physical and material aspects of life in general and to sexuality in particular. The word *hedonism* comes from the Greek word meaning "pleasure" and refers to the belief that the ultimate goal of human life is the pursuit of pleasure, the avoidance of pain, and the fulfillment of physical needs and desires: "Eat, drink, and be merry, for tomorrow we die." Asceticism, in contrast, holds that there is more to life than its material aspects, which must be transcended to achieve true humanity. Ascetics are likely to view sexuality as neutral at best and evil at worst; they prize self-discipline, the avoidance of physical gratification, and the cultivation of spiritual values. In their affirmations of celibacy, virginity, and poverty, orders of monks and nuns, found in Eastern religions as well as in Christianity, are good examples of institutionalized asceticism.

The terms **legalism** and **situationism** refer to methods of ethical decision making. As an approach to ethics, legalism is concerned with following a moral law, or set of principles, which comes from a source outside the individual, such as religion. Legalistic ethics are focused on the rightness or wrongness of specific acts and set forth a series of rules—"Do this" and "Don't do that"—that people are to follow. The term *situationism* has been used since it was coined by Joseph Fletcher in his 1966 book *Situation Ethics*. The approach is also called *contextual ethics*. Although there may be broad general guidelines for

Ethics: A system of moral principles; a way of determining right and wrong.
Hedonism: A moral system based on maximizing pleasure and avoiding pain.
Asceticism: An approach to life emphasizing self-discipline and impulse control.
Legalism: Ethics based on the assumption that there are rules for human conduct and that morality consists of knowing the rules and obeying them.
Situationism: Ethics based on the assumption that there are no absolute rules, or at least very few, and that each situation must be judged individually.

ethical behavior, this approach suggests that each ethical decision should be made according to the individuals and situations involved. Situationism is based in human experience and, in matters of sexual morality, tends to focus on relationships rather than rules. Whereas legalism deals in universal laws, situationism decides matters on a case-by-case basis, informed by certain guiding principles, such as love. Traditional religious ethical systems (which we might call the *Old Morality*) have tended to be quite legalistic, and many continue to be so today (e.g., Orthodox Judaism, Roman Catholicism, and fundamentalist Protestantism). However, with the advent of the modern scientific worldview, the situationist approach (the *New Morality*) has attracted many adherents (Nelson, 1978). Of course, few ethical systems are purely hedonistic or ascetic or entirely legalistic or situationist; most lie between these extremes.

Sexuality in Great Ethical Traditions

With these ways of looking at sexual ethics as background, let us examine certain great ethical traditions to see how they deal with norms for sexual behavior. Although some attention is given to non-Western sexual ethics, the focus of this section is on ethical traditions of Western culture, primarily because this is a text for U.S. undergraduates, who are part of that culture. This culture can, at the risk of oversimplification, be seen as originating in the confrontation of Greek culture, preserved and developed by the Romans, and Jewish tradition, extended by Christianity. From that point on until rather recently, Western culture was Christian, at least officially. Even self-conscious revolts against Christian culture in the West had roots in this pervasive tradition.

Classical Greek Philosophy

During the Golden Age of Greek culture, covering roughly the 5th and 4th centuries B.C.E.,[1] brilliant philosophers such as Socrates, Plato, and Aristotle pondered most of the great ethics questions (Soble, 2009). They regarded the beautiful and the good as the chief goal of life, and they admired the figure of the warrior–intellectual, who embodied the virtues of wisdom, courage, temperance, justice, and piety.

Although nothing in Greek culture rejected sex as evil—the gods and goddesses of Greek mythology are often pictured enjoying it—the great philosophers did develop a kind of asceticism that assumed an important

[1]Before the Common Era; today it is preferred over the Christian-centered Before Christ (B.C.).

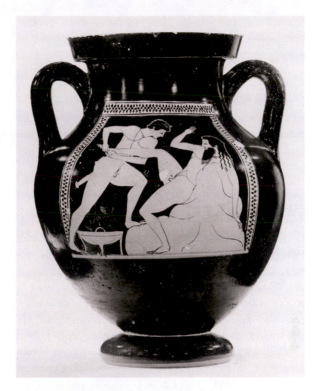

Figure 1 The ancient Greeks not only approved of, but idealized, pederasty.

©*The Metropolitan Museum of Art/Art Resource, NY*

place in Western thought (Soble, 2009). They thought that virtue resulted from wisdom, and they believed that if people could achieve wisdom, they would do what is right, and that people fail to live morally only because of ignorance. To achieve wisdom and cultivate virtue, violent passions must be avoided, and these might well include sex. Plato believed that love led toward immortality and was therefore a good thing. However, because this kind of love was mainly intellectual and more like friendship than sexuality, the term *platonic love* has come to mean sexless affection. There was also, especially among the warrior class, approval of **pederasty** (a sexual relationship between an older man and a younger one) (see Figure 1). The older man was to serve as the younger one's teacher and model of courage and virtue. An army of male couples was thought to be especially fierce because of the desire of each to protect his beloved (Crompton, 2003).

Later, Greek philosophy became even more ascetic than in the Golden Age. Epicurus (341–270 B.C.E.) taught that the goal of life was *ataraxia,* a tranquil state between pleasure and pain in which the mind is unaffected by emotion. He, like other Stoics of the same period, valued detachment from worldly anxieties and pleasures and, indeed, a total indifference to either life or death.

Pederasty: Sex between an older man and a younger man, or a boy; sometimes called *boy love.*

Sex was seen not necessarily as evil but as less important than wisdom and virtue, something to be transcended to achieve the beautiful and good.

Such Stoic thinking was pervasive in the late Roman empire. For example, Emperor Marcus Aurelius was an important Stoic philosopher. Stoicism, the suspicion of pleasure, was "in the air" and influenced St. Augustine powerfully. He became the conduit of asceticism into the Middle Ages. Here, then, is a primary source of the sex negativism in the Western tradition.

Judaism

The basic source of the Judeo-Christian tradition, which is the religious foundation of Western culture, is the Hebrew scriptures or the Old Testament of the Bible, the basis for Judaism and a major source for Christianity as well. Based on ancient traditions and written between approximately 800 and 200 B.C.E., the Hebrew Bible has a great deal to say about the place of sexuality in human life and society, always seen in religious terms.

The view of sexuality in the Hebrew scriptures is fundamentally positive. In the Genesis account of creation we read, "So God created man in his own image, in the image of God he created him; male and female he created them" (Genesis 1:27). Human sexual differentiation is not an afterthought or an aberration; it is an integral part of creation, which God calls "good." Judaism sees sexuality as a gift to be used responsibly and in obedience to God's will, never as something evil in itself. The command to marry and to procreate within marriage is clear (Farley, 1994). Looking at the Hebrew scriptures as a whole, we can find three themes in this view of sexuality.

First, sex is seen not as just another biological function but as a deep and intimate part of a *relationship* between two people. The very ancient story of Adam and Eve states that "a man leaves his father and cleaves to his wife and the two become one flesh" (Genesis 2:24). Biblical Hebrew uses the verb *to know* to mean sexual intercourse (as in "Adam knew Eve and she conceived a child"). It also uses the word *knowledge,* with this suggestion of deep intimacy, to describe the relationship between God and God's people.[2] The use of sexual imagery in describing both marital and divine–human relationships testifies to the positive view of the Hebrew Bible toward sex.

Second, in the Hebrew scriptures, sexuality could never be separated from its *social consequences.* Historically, Israel began as a small group of nomadic tribes fighting to stay alive in

the near-desert of the Arabian peninsula. Sheer survival demanded that there be plenty of children, especially boys, so that there would be enough herdsmen and warriors.[3] Furthermore, because the tribes were small and close-knit, sex had to be regulated to prevent jealousy over sexual partners, which could have divided and destroyed the group. It is not surprising, then, that so much of the Hebrew Bible is concerned with laws regarding people living together in society and that these laws often include the regulation of sexual practices.

Finally, the Hebrew scriptures see sexual behavior as an aspect of *national and religious loyalty.* When the Israelites settled in what is now the state of Israel, about 1200 to 1000 B.C.E., they came into contact with the original inhabitants, whom they called Canaanites. Like many agricultural peoples of the time, the Canaanites sought to encourage the growth of their crops through their religion. In this **fertility cult** Baal, the Sky Father, was encouraged to mate with Asherah (Astarte or Ishtar), the Earth Mother, so that crops would grow. This mating was encouraged by ritual sex, and temple prostitutes (male and female) were a central part of Canaanite religion. Hebrew religious leaders saw in the fertility cult a threat to their religion, and many sexual practices are forbidden in the Hebrew scriptures because they were found among the Canaanites and might lead to infidelity to Israel's God.

The sexual regulations of the Hebrew Bible need to be seen both in the context of the times and against this historical background. From Israel's struggle for survival during the nomadic period came institutions such as polygyny (many wives) and concubinage (slaves kept for childbearing purposes) designed to produce children in the case of a childless marriage. From the confrontation with the fertility cult, Israel derived prohibitions against nakedness, cultic prostitution, and other such typically Canaanite practices. Both themes are present in this passage from Leviticus 20:10–19:

> If a man commits adultery with his neighbor's wife, both adulterer and adulteress shall be put to death. The man who has intercourse with his father's wife has brought shame on his father. They shall both be put to death; their blood shall be on their own heads. . . . A man who has intercourse with any beast shall be put to death, and you shall kill the beast. . . . If a man takes his sister, his father's daughter or his mother's daughter, and they see one another naked, it is a scandalous disgrace. They shall be cut off in the presence of their people. . . . If a man lies with a woman during her monthly period and brings shame upon her, he has exposed her discharge and she has uncovered the source of her discharge; they shall both be cut off from their people.

Fertility cult: A form of nature religion in which the fertility of the soil is encouraged through various forms of ritual magic, often including ritual sexual intercourse.

[2]See, for example, Hosea, the Song of Solomon, and, in the New Testament, Revelation.

[3]Note that the heart of God's promise to the patriarch Abraham was descendants as numberless as the grains of sand or the stars in the sky (Genesis 13:14–17, among many places).

Adultery and incest are threats to the harmony of the group. Bestiality is not only "unnatural" but also nonprocreative and may have been a feature of Canaanite religion. The menstrual taboo is typical of many societies.

It should be noted that all societies have had laws regulating sex and that the Hebrew laws, however exotic they may seem to us, made sense in their historical context and were, for the most part, remarkably humane for the time. The Hebrew scriptures are characterized by a great regard for married love, affection, and sexuality; this is in marked contrast to, for example, the Greek view of marriage as an institution for breeding and housekeeping. The Judaism of the time was legalistic but not particularly ascetic, displaying high regard for responsible sexuality as a good and integral part of human life. In fact, the *Song of Songs,* part of the Hebrew Bible, is an enthusiastic celebration of sexual romance, with no reference to having children.

Christianity

As our discussion turns to Christianity, which grew in three centuries from an obscure Jewish sect to the dominant religion in the West, the complex conditions of the Mediterranean world between 100 B.C.E. and 100 C.E.[4] must be noted. The world in which Christianity developed was one of tremendous ferment in the spheres of philosophy and religion. There were many cults, often characterized by some sort of **dualism.** This was the notion that body and spirit were opposed to each other and that the goal of life was to become purely spiritual by transcending the physical and material side of life. Public morals were notably decadent, and even ethical pagans were shocked by a society in which people—or at least those who could afford it—prized physical pleasure above all things.

Revulsion at the excesses of Roman life affected Judaism, which became markedly more dualistic and antisex by the time of the early Christian Church. That church's ethical tradition, rooted in Judaism, received its direction from the teachings of Jesus, the writings of St. Paul, and the theology of the Fathers of early Christianity. From these beginnings, Christian ethics have evolved and developed over more than 2,000 years in many and various ways. Oversimplification is a real danger, yet it is possible to speak in general terms of a Christian tradition of sexual ethics and morality.

Christianity is distinctive among the major world religions in insisting on monogamy (Parrinder, 1996). Most other religions permit polygyny, or a man's having several wives. The Christian standard of monogamy, which may seem strict by today's standards, may be viewed in another light as a major step toward equality between women and men. Men were no longer permitted to have many wives as "possessions." Similarly, Jesus opposed divorce, which

[4]The Common Era, an alternative to Anno Domini (A.D.).

again may seem strict. However, Jesus's teaching reversed the traditional Hebrew rule—and the practice in many other cultures—that a man could divorce his wife simply at will, yet a wife had no similar power.

The New Testament

At the heart of the Christian scriptures are the Gospels, which describe the life and teachings of Jesus. Because Jesus said almost nothing on the subject of sex, it is difficult to derive a sexual ethic from the Gospels alone. Jesus's ethical teaching was based on the tradition of the Hebrew prophets, and his view of sexuality follows in that tradition. He urged his followers to strive for ethical perfection, and he spoke strongly against pride, hypocrisy, injustice, and the misuse of wealth. Toward penitent sinners, including those whose sins were sexual, the Gospels show Jesus as compassionate and forgiving (see, for example, his dealings with "fallen women" in John 4:1–30, John 8:53–9:11, and Luke 7:36–50). He did not put any particular emphasis on sexual conduct, apparently regarding it as a part of a whole moral life based on the love of God and neighbor.

Contemporary scholarship on the Bible uses the *historical-critical method.* It proposes that the ancient texts mean what their authors originally intended, as best as can be determined, and not what a 21st-century reader would make of the texts translated into English. On this basis, it appears that St. Paul held a surprisingly positive outlook on sex (Countryman, 1994). He was enmeshed in "culture wars" between Jewish and Gentile converts to Christianity. He struggled to reconcile the rampant sexual activities of the Gentiles with the more reverential attitude of the Jews. He had to sort out the beliefs of these two groups from what he believed to be truly right and wrong. As a first example, in a long discussion of sex (1 Corinthians 5–8), Paul compared eating food with having sex, and he anticipated our contemporary psychological understanding that human sexuality has profound interpersonal and spiritual implications; it is not merely a biological function. It is important to understand that Paul had no concern for procreation; he literally believed that the world would end during his lifetime, perhaps at any moment, so he advised against any new enterprises extending into the future, such as marriage and business. In this context, Paul made his notorious comment "better to marry than to burn [with passion]" (1 Corinthians 7:9). Far from demeaning sex and marriage, Paul seemed to be recommending it for people with strong sexual urges, not for the purpose of having children, but for the pleasure, comfort, and mutual bonding that sex provides. Third, Paul seems not even to have insisted that sex belongs only in heterosexual marriage.

> **Dualism:** A religious or philosophical belief that body and spirit are separate and opposed to each other and that the goal of life is to free the spirit from the bondage of the body; thus a depreciation of the material world and the physical aspect of humanity.

Except among the wealthy, marriage was not a regulated institution in his day, and strong arguments have been made that Paul allowed same-gender relationships. When he refers to sexual practices as instances of impurity (Romans 1:24–27), he is placing them in the category of social taboos, not moral evils. The sex negativity of the Christian tradition, therefore, is not rooted in the Bible, but in the philosophies, especially Stoicism and Neo-Platonism, that shaped early Christianity (Boswell, 1980).

The Early Christian Church

The "Fathers of the Church," such as St. Augustine (Figure 2), wrote roughly between 150 and 600 C.E. and determined the basic theology of Christianity. During this time, Christian ethics became increasingly ascetic, for several reasons: the assimilation of often dualistic Greek philosophy (especially Stoicism), the decadence of Roman society, and the conversion of the Roman Emperor Constantine to Christianity in 325. As the Church became the official religion of the Roman Empire, much of its original fervor was lost and it began to grow corrupt and worldly.

Serious Christians revolted against this situation by moving to the desert to become monks and hermits, to fast, to pray, and to practice all sorts of self-denial, including **celibacy.** From this point on, monks and monasticism became a permanent reform movement within the Church, a vanguard of ascetics calling Christians to greater rigor. Their success can be seen in the 12th-century requirement that all clergy in the West be celibate, a departure from early Church practice.[5] The Fathers of the Church, almost all of whom were celibates, allowed that marriage was good and honorable but thought virginity to be a much superior state.

The Middle Ages

During the Middle Ages, these basic principles continued to be elaborated and extended. The most important figure of the period, and even today the basic source of Catholic theology, was St. Thomas Aquinas (1225–1274). His great achievement was the *Summa Theologica,* which answered virtually any question a Christian might have on any topic. Thomas's "natural law" approach to ethics was normative in Western Christianity for many centuries and remains so for Roman Catholicism. His argument was that whatever was natural was good, *natural* being defined by the science of his day. Anything that was not natural was sinful.

Thomas believed that sex was obviously intended for procreation and that, therefore, all nonprocreative sex was sinful,

> **Celibacy:** The practice of remaining celibate. Sometimes used to refer to abstaining from sexual intercourse, the correct term for which is *chastity.* A *celibate* is a person who remains unmarried, usually for religious reasons.

[5]The First Epistle of Timothy, Chapter 3, shows the clear expectation that clergy will be married and father children.

Figure 2   The most notable of the Western Fathers was St. Augustine (354–430 C.E.), who had had a promiscuous youth and overreacted after his conversion to Christianity. For Augustine, sexuality was a consequence of the Fall, and every sexual act was tainted by concupiscence (from the Latin word *concupiscentia,* meaning "lust" or "evil desire of the flesh"). Even sex in marriage was sinful, as he wrote in *The City of God,* "children could not have been begotten in any other way than they know them to be begotten now, i.e., by lust, at which even honorable marriage blushes" (1950 ed., Article 21). The stature of Augustine meant that his negative view of sexuality was perpetuated in subsequent Christian theology.

©Sandro Botticelli/Getty Images

being opposed to human nature and, therefore, to the will of God. In the *Summa,* Thomas devoted a chapter to various sorts of lust and condemned as grave sin such things as fornication (premarital intercourse), nocturnal emissions, seduction, rape, adultery, incest, and "unnatural vice," which included masturbation, bestiality, and homosexuality.

The theology of Aquinas was communicated to the ordinary Christian through the Church's canon law, which determined when intercourse was or was not sinful. All sex outside marriage was, by definition, a sin. Even within

Figure 3   The Virgin Mary. During the Middle Ages, a great devotion to the mother of Jesus developed, emphasizing her perpetual virginity, purity, and freedom from all sin. That devotion lives on in Catholic piety, particularly in most Latin American countries today.

©Hermitage Museum, St. Petersburg, Russia/SuperStock

marriage the Church forbade intercourse during certain times in a woman's reproductive cycle (during menstruation, pregnancy, and up to 40 days postpartum) as well as on certain holy days, fast days (such as Fridays), and even during whole liturgical seasons (such as Advent and Lent). These practices communicated to the ordinary person that the Church regarded sex as basically evil, for procreation only, and probably not something one should enjoy.

The Protestants

The Protestant Reformation in the 16th century destroyed the Christian unity of Europe and shook the theological foundations of the Catholic Church. However, in matters of sexual ethics there were few changes. The Protestant churches abandoned clerical celibacy, regarding it as unnatural and the source of many abuses, and placed a higher value on marriage and family life. Reformers nonetheless feared illegitimacy and approved of sexuality only

in the confines of matrimony. Even then, they were often ambivalent. For example, Martin Luther, the founder of the Reformation, happily married a former nun, and said that sex is as necessary as eating or drinking. Nonetheless, he called marriage "a hospital for the sick" and saw its purpose as being to "aid human infirmity and prevent unchastity" (quoted in Thielicke, 1964, p. 136).

A significant contribution of Reformation Protestantism to Christianity was an emphasis on the individual conscience in matters such as the interpretation of the Bible and ethical decision making. Such an emphasis on freedom and individual responsibility eventually led to the serious questioning of legalistic ethics and, in part, to today's ethical debates.

The Reformation also gave rise to Puritanism. The Puritans followed Augustine in emphasizing the doctrine of "original sin" and the "total depravity" of fallen humanity. This led them to use civil law to try to regulate human behavior in an attempt to suppress immorality. As we discuss in the next chapter, this urge to make people good by law has many sexual applications, although the Puritans were probably no more sexually repressive than other Christians of the time. What we often think of as "Puritan" sexual rigidity is probably more properly referred to as "Victorian." During the 60-year reign of Queen Victoria (1819–1901), English society held sexual expression in exaggerated disgust and probably overemphasized its importance. While strict public standards of decency and purity were enforced, many Victorians indulged in private vices of pornography and prostitution. It is against this typically Victorian combination of repressiveness and hypocrisy that many people of the 20th century revolted, wrongly thinking the Victorian period representative of the whole Christian ethical tradition.

Current Trends

Across Western history there has been a fairly stable consensus on the fundamentals of sexual ethics, which some call the Old Morality. Sex has been understood as a good part of divine creation but also as a source of temptation that needs to be controlled. Although at various times chastity has been exalted, marriage and the family have always been held in esteem and sex outside marriage condemned, in theory if not always in practice. The only approved purpose for sex has been procreation, with nonprocreative sex having been regarded as unnatural and sinful. However, this consensus largely broke down in the 20th century, and sexual ethics is now a topic of heated debate. Several factors, both within the religious community and outside it, have contributed to this ferment.

The rise of historical-critical methods in biblical scholarship led to a questioning of the absoluteness of scriptural norms. Scholars now see them as shaped by the time and culture in which they were written and not necessarily binding today. Traditional understandings of biblical statements about sexuality continue to change as more is learned about the original historical context. The Reformation emphasis on the Bible and individual conscience had already weakened the natural-law approach. The religious community has also been influenced by the behavioral sciences, which suggest that sexuality is much more complex than had been thought and question older assumptions about what is "natural" or "normal." Technology made it possible, for the first time in human history, to prevent conception reliably and to terminate pregnancy safely. These advances blunted the force of arguments against premarital intercourse on the basis of the disapproval of illegitimacy. Indeed, technology itself has raised a host of ethical issues as humans gain more and more control over what had once been a matter of "doing what comes naturally."

It is no wonder, then, that religious groups face serious debate and even conflict. We have learned more about sex in the past century than in all previous human history. Within Judaism, the Orthodox who still live by the rabbinic interpretation of the Bible may be in serious conflict with the Conservative and Reformed groups. Protestants are deeply divided among conservatives who hold to the Old Morality, liberals inclined to the New Morality, and others who come out somewhere in between. Perhaps no single religious community has experienced as much tension over sexual morality as the Roman Catholic Church in the United States (see A Sexually Diverse World: Dissent over Sexual Ethics in the Roman Catholic Church).

Humanism

Not all ethical thinking has been religious in origin. Many ethicists—beginning with Socrates, Aristotle, and Plato—have quite consciously tried to find a framework for moral behavior that does not rely on divine revelation or any direction from a source outside human intellect. Nonreligious ethics covers a wide spectrum; however, we can look at a fairly broad mainstream called **humanism.**

Humanistic ethics insists that values can be found only in human experience in this world, as observed by the philosopher or social scientist. Most humanists would hold that the basic goals of human life are self-awareness, the avoidance of pain and suffering, and the fulfillment of human needs. Of course, the individual pursuit of these ends must be tempered by the fact that no one lives in the world alone and that one important goal is the common good. Another important humanistic principle is that individuals must make their own decisions and accept responsibility for them and their consequences.

In the area of human sexuality, humanism demands a realistic approach to behavior: one that does not create arbitrary or unreasonable standards and expectations.

> **Humanism:** A philosophical system that holds that ethical judgments must be made on the basis of human experience and human reason.

Humanism is very distrustful of the legalistic approach. It seeks real intimacy between people and condemns impersonal and exploitative relationships. Attentive to the complexity of human living, humanism tends to be tolerant, compassionate, and skeptical of claims of absolute right or wrong.

Sexuality in Other Major Religions

The discussion so far has been mostly concerned with Western culture and the Judeo–Christian tradition. It will broaden our outlook if we consider human sexuality in religious traditions outside dominant U.S. culture. Obviously, this could be the topic for a very large book itself; here we provide only a brief look at the three non-Western religions with the largest number of adherents: Islam, Hinduism, and Buddhism.

Islam

Geographically, and in terms of its roots, Islam is the closest faith to the Judeo–Christian heritage. It was founded by the Prophet Muhammad, who lived from 570 to 632 C.E. in what is now Saudi Arabia. Its followers are called *Muslims,* and its sacred scripture is the Koran (Qur'an). Classical Islam values sexuality very positively, and Muhammad saw intercourse in marriage as the highest good of human life. Islam sanctions both polygyny and concubinage, and the Prophet had several wives. Sex outside marriage or concubinage, however, is viewed as a sin. In reality a double standard prevails, in which men's extramarital affairs are tolerated. An adulterous wife, however, may be the object of an *honor killing* in which she is murdered for her transgression (Ilkkaracan, 2001). The Prophet opposed celibacy, and Islam has very little ascetic tradition. A male-dominated faith, Islam has a strong double standard but recognizes a number of rights and prerogatives for women.

Because Islam does not have a single, central source of authority like the Pope, it is not a monolithic faith, and there is great variety in the ways in which Sharia, Islamic law based on the Koran, is applied in societies throughout the Muslim world (Boonstra, 2001; Ilkkaracan, 2001). Some Muslim states (e.g., Iran) are theocracies in which religious law is enacted in civil law. In these nations sexual offenses are likely to be more stringently punished, and women have less freedom. Other Islamic countries (such as Egypt and Syria) are secular states in which Western values have been adopted to some extent. In these, women have more rights, and sexual mores are more pluralistic. Moreover, there is considerable variation in the interpretation of the Koran between the two principal Islamic "denominations," Sunnis and Shi'ites.

Although Islam accepts the Hebrew scriptures as sacred, it does not interpret the Adam and Eve story to mean that humans are tainted by original sin (Ahmadi,

A Sexually Diverse World

Dissent over Sexual Ethics in the Roman Catholic Church

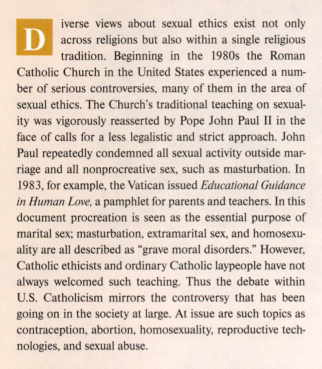

Diverse views about sexual ethics exist not only across religions but also within a single religious tradition. Beginning in the 1980s the Roman Catholic Church in the United States experienced a number of serious controversies, many of them in the area of sexual ethics. The Church's traditional teaching on sexuality was vigorously reasserted by Pope John Paul II in the face of calls for a less legalistic and strict approach. John Paul repeatedly condemned all sexual activity outside marriage and all nonprocreative sex, such as masturbation. In 1983, for example, the Vatican issued *Educational Guidance in Human Love,* a pamphlet for parents and teachers. In this document procreation is seen as the essential purpose of marital sex; masturbation, extramarital sex, and homosexuality are all described as "grave moral disorders." However, Catholic ethicists and ordinary Catholic laypeople have not always welcomed such teaching. Thus the debate within U.S. Catholicism mirrors the controversy that has been going on in the society at large. At issue are such topics as contraception, abortion, homosexuality, reproductive technologies, and sexual abuse.

Contraception

Although the Vatican and the U.S. Roman Catholic hierarchy have not moved from condemning "artificial" birth control as set forth in Pope Paul VI's encyclical *Humanae Vitae* of 1968, there is evidence that many American Catholics ignore the condemnation and use contraceptives, often with the tacit approval of their priests. For example, a 1993 *Newsweek* poll asked U.S. Catholics, "Do you or do other Catholics you know personally use artificial birth control?" and 63 percent responded yes. Moreover, since *Humanae Vitae* was not an infallible teaching, some Catholic ethicists still treat contraception as an open question. In 2015, Pope Francis signaled that he might be a bit more flexible on the issue.

Abortion

There is sharp division among U.S. Catholics on the issue of abortion. A large segment of Catholics actively or passively support the antiabortion, or right-to-life, movement, yet there are many dissenters (Miller, 2014). The *Newsweek* poll asked, "Is the Catholic Church's position on abortion too conservative, too liberal, or about right?" Forty-one percent thought it was too conservative, and 43 percent thought it was about right, showing a nearly even division of opinion. In 2014, Pope Francis reaffirmed the Catholic Church's official opposition to abortion (McKenna, 2014).

Homosexuality

In 1976, Jesuit priest and psychotherapist John J. McNeill published *The Church and the Homosexual,* in which he questioned the Church's traditional teaching on homosexuality and its scriptural and theological bases. At the time, Father McNeill was forbidden by his Jesuit superiors to speak or write further on the subject. He obeyed the order for 10 years, but, feeling compelled to object to a 1986 Vatican pronouncement on homosexuality, he was expelled from the Jesuits. Other Catholic thinkers, such as Daniel Helminiak (2006), are also trying to help the Church rethink its approach to gays and lesbians.

Assisted Reproduction

In 1987, the Congregation for the Doctrine of the Faith issued a document called "Instruction for Human Life in Its Origins and on the Dignity of Procreation." It condemned in vitro fertilization, surrogate motherhood, artificial insemination, and other new reproductive technologies. The document was severely criticized by many U.S. Catholic ethicists, who found it too rigid and ill informed. Similar criticism met the Vatican's 2008 statement that insisted that a zygote must be treated as a human person.

Condoms

Today, condoms pose a dilemma for the Catholic Church. To date it has uniformly prohibited them as a means of birth control. In the AIDS era, however, they represent a method for preventing disease and preserving life, a principle to which the Catholic Church is firmly committed. Essentially the argument is that, between condoms and AIDS, condoms are the lesser of two evils. In 2006 Pope Benedict authorized a study of condoms, a move that would have been unthinkable even 20 years earlier. And in 2010 he issued a statement that the use of condoms could be justified for disease prevention, but not for pregnancy prevention (Donadio, 2010). Pope Francis seems to hold the same view.

Sexual Abuse by Clergy

Perhaps the most difficult sexual issue that faces the Catholic Church today is that of sexual abuse of children by Catholic priests. One of the most publicized cases was that of Father Paul Shanley of the Boston archdiocese. As early as 1961, just a year after his ordination, he had been reported to the police by the father of an 11-year-old boy whom he had

Figure 4   Sexual abuse by clergy has been a major issue in the Catholic Church, across many nations. This protest took place in Dublin.

©Aaron Chown/PA Images/Getty Images

molested. He was finally arrested in 2002 at the age of 71, for raping a 6-year-old boy in 1983. In the process, more than 30 men came forward with allegations of abuse by him spanning more than three decades. He was described as a contradictory combination of protector and predator: a wonderful priest to some, a sexual predator to others. Shanley says that he himself was abused by a priest when he was a child.

As of 2004 approximately 4 percent (4,392) of U.S. priests had been accused of sexually abusing minors (U.S. Conference of Catholic Bishops, reported by Goodstein, 2004). Of the alleged victims, 81 percent are male. Most frequently, they were molested beginning around 12 to 14 years of age.

Reflecting a new attention to the issue of sexual abuse by clergy, the Vatican announced, in 2014, that it had received 3,400 reported cases of abuse since 2004, resulting in 848 priests being defrocked (un-priested) and 2,572 receiving lesser penalties (Associated Press, 2014). And the issue won't go away. In 2018, a Pennsylvania grand jury reported that more than 300 priests in the state, over a period of 70 years, had sexually abused more than 1,000 children (Goodstein & Otterman, 2018).

What is perhaps most distressing to some is that the hierarchy of the Catholic Church covered up these scandals and continued to assign priests like Shanley to other churches and even to youth work. The mother of the boy molested in 1961 wrote to Boston's Cardinal Richard

Cushing, but no investigation resulted. In 1990 Cardinal Bernard F. Law allowed Shanley to go on sick leave to Southern California but never told the local bishop about Shanley's problem, so he continued to serve as a priest. Essentially, bishops allowed priests to continue abusing children. Some even trace the responsibility to Pope John Paul II, who led a conservative backlash against the liberalization of the Catholic Church (which occurred in the 1960s) and insisted on the imperial authority of parish priests (Berry & Renner, 2004).

This scandal has caused an enormous shift in Catholics' views of priests; they were once regarded as holy, because of their renunciation of all sexual activity, but now are revealed to be capable of grave sexual sins. The crisis has led some to question the church's rule of priestly celibacy, the suggestion being that perhaps if priests were allowed to live normal, married lives, these problems would not occur. The scandal has caused a profound shift in authority within the Catholic Church, which once dictated sexual morals for laypeople but now finds itself defending some of its priests on charges of truly serious sexual immorality.

Sources: Berry & Renner (2004); Butterfield (2002); Curran (1988); Donadio (2010); Fisher (2006); Grammick (1986); Helminiak (2006); Investigative Staff of the *Boston Globe* (2002); Jenkins (1996); Maguire (2001); McNeill (1987); Reuther (1985); Sipe (1995).

Figure 5 Contraception is not only permitted but encouraged by Islamic law.

©*Lauren Goodsmith/The Image Works*

2003). Striving for worldly pleasures is therefore acceptable, and sexuality is regarded primarily as a source of pleasure and only secondarily as a means of reproduction.

Contraception is not only permitted but encouraged by Islamic law (Boonstra, 2001; Maguire, 2001). Muhammad himself encouraged the practice of *al'azl* (withdrawal, or *coitus interruptus*). Even the strict state of Iran today has an extensive family planning program, and 73 percent of married women use contraceptives.

Islamic law recognizes intersex conditions (Zainuddin & Mahdy, 2017). Islam uses the term *khunsa* for cases of ambiguous genitals, what today we would call intersex conditions, and the Prophet Muhammad even spoke on the matter. Khunsa is divided into two subcategories: nonproblematic/discernible and problematic/intractable. The first is a person who can be assigned to a gender based on genitals that are dominant in one direction. The second category is for people whose genitals do not lead to an easy classification as male or female. All of this predates our modern understanding of intersex conditions, and some Islamic groups are working to update the concepts.

Islam recognizes four genders: male, female, intersex (khunsa), and effeminate male (*mukhannath*) (Zainuddin & Mahdy, 2017). It therefore goes beyond the dominant idea of the gender binary found in the United States. Fatwa is a formal legal opinion from an expert in Islamic

law. Fatwas have been issued in several Islamic nations (Saudi Arabia, Egypt, Malaysia) on the permissibility of sex change surgery (Zainuddin & Mahdy, 2017). The fatwas do not completely resolve the issue for Islam, though, because the rulings from different nations are not consistent with each other, and they only deal with sex change surgery for intersex individuals.

Hinduism

Hinduism is an inclusive term that refers to a highly varied complex of mythology and religious practice founded on the Indian subcontinent. Here can be found virtually every approach to sexuality that humans have yet invented. However, certain themes can be identified. In Hinduism, four possible approaches to life are acceptable: Kama, the pursuit of pleasure; Artha, the pursuit of success and material wealth; Dharma, the pursuit of the moral life; and Moksha, the pursuit of liberation through the negation of the self in a state of being that is known as nirvana. Kama is notable because it has produced an extensive literature on the achievement of sexual pleasure, notably the *Kama Sutra* of Vatsyayana, a masterpiece of erotic hedonism. This book testifies to the highly positive view of sexuality to be found in Hinduism.

In contrast, the ways of Dharma and Moksha can be as rigorously ascetic as anything in Christianity. By avoiding

Figure 6　Buddhism encourages men to live celibate lives as monks.

©*Victor Paul Borg/Alamy*

all passions, including sex, the follower seeks to pass out of the cycle of continual rebirth to absorption into the godhead. This discipline includes *brahmacharya,* or celibacy, which is to be cultivated at the beginning of life (for the purposes of education and discipline) and at the end of life (for the purpose of finding peace). It is interesting to note that in between it is permissible to marry and raise a family, and thus this form of Hinduism makes active sexuality and asceticism possible in the same lifetime (Noss, 1963).

Buddhism

Buddhism developed out of Hinduism; it originated in the life and thought of Gautama (560–480 B.C.E.), the Buddha, and has been elaborated in many forms since then. There is little discussion of sex in the teachings of the Buddha; his way is generally ascetic and concentrates on the achievement of enlightenment and on escape from the suffering of the world. Two main traditions, Theravada and Mahayana, both found in contemporary Buddhism, differ greatly. The ethics of Theravada include the strict nonindulgence of the desires that bring joy; understanding, morals, and discipline are emphasized. The ethics of Mahayana are more active and directed toward love of others. Both encourage men to live celibate lives as monks (see Figure 6). Originally, Buddha

sought a "middle way" of moderation between extreme asceticism and extreme hedonism (Maguire, 2001). Today, though, the situation is rather like that of medieval Christianity: The masses live ordinary—and usually married—lives while the monks cultivate ascetic wisdom.

Tantric Buddhism, found particularly in Tibet and India, is a form of Buddhism that is of particular interest. It teaches that sexual union epitomizes the essential unity of all things by the joining of female energy (shakti) and male energy (shiva) (Lorius, 1999). In the context of honoring one's partner and the relationship, sexual expression can therefore lead to spiritual enlightenment. This sexual mysticism is not common, but it is one of the various forms that Eastern religion may take (Parrinder, 1980).

Contemporary Issues in Sexual Ethics

Human sexuality is heavily value laden. Thus it is the subject of strongly and emotionally held convictions and becomes the focal point of conflicts in society. There simply is no broad consensus on the norms of sexual behavior. This is clearly the case in contemporary American society. The "sexual revolution" is perceived by some people as a threat to all they hold dear; not surprisingly, they respond with fear and anger. The backlash against the more liberal view of sexuality and the greater freedom of sexual behavior that has come about in the last 50 years has resulted in explosive public debate, organized attempts at legislating the Old Morality back into force, and a reassertion of a highly legalistic view of morality. The debate promises to continue for some time and to generate much heat.

This debate over the limits, if any, of individual sexual freedom can be seen as a clash between the New Morality and the Old Morality. At the end of the chapter, we propose a more helpful model. The Old Morality is, to a great extent, supported by people who believe that there exist clearly and objectively defined standards of right and wrong and that a society has the responsibility to insist that all its members conform to them. This view is termed **moralism;** it can be seen in proponents in the religious community who see the objective standard of morality as deriving from divine law. Opposed to this view are the proponents of **pluralism,** who see the question of public morality as being much more complex. Pluralists deny that standards of morality are objective and unchanging, and they contend that truth is to be discovered in the clash of differing opinions and convictions. According to this view, society is wise to allow many points of view to be advocated and expressed. The conscience and rights of the individual are to be stressed over society's needs for order and uniformity. Pluralists are much less likely than moralists to appeal to either law or religion for the enforcement of their views, and they are more likely to allow freedom to individuals. The debate between moralist and pluralist has been going on for a very long time. It will not be settled any time soon.

Debate about the meaning of "family" offers an illustration. The "pro-family" position is rooted in religious conservatism and makes strong attempts to influence legislation. Pro-family activists are in favor of an absolute constitutional ban on abortion, against any kind of legal tolerance of the cohabitation of unmarried people, and in favor of legal discrimination against gays in such areas as housing, child custody, and employment.

This position is essentially that of the New Religious Right, a coalition of conservative religious and political groups. Members of this movement, largely but not exclusively fundamentalist Protestants, argue that the New Morality has sapped the moral vigor of U.S. society, leaving the country open to inner decay and divine judgment. Their efforts to enforce their religious convictions by legislation have created one of the most intense church–state controversies of the late 20th and early 21st centuries (see the chapter "Sex and the Law"). Their position is odious to pluralists and to those who have

benefited by the liberalization of laws and attitudes concerning sexuality. These people fight to keep what they consider to be gains, whereas pro-family and New Right activists seek to turn the clock back to what they perceive to have been a healthier and more moral time. Middle ground is hard to find.

This conflict is even splintering many religious communities today. Liberal Jewish, Catholic, and Protestant groups, which have tended to accommodate at least some of the New Morality, have been under attack from portions of their own membership on such issues as abortion and homosexuality. Reports in the press of national gatherings of U.S. religious groups reveal a remarkable number of debates related to human sexuality, debates that parallel those in society at large. Here we illustrate this ferment by discussing the ethical issues posed by sex outside marriage, contraception, abortion, homosexuality, AIDS, and reproductive technologies.

Sex Outside Marriage

The religious tradition underlying Western ethics has almost always seen sexual intercourse as legitimate only in marriage. This view is rooted in an understanding of marriage as God's will for most men and women, the way in which sin is avoided and children are cared for. Thus, the tradition has condemned both sex before marriage (**fornication**) and sex by people married to others (**adultery**). Today, this position continues to be held by theological conservatives among Jews, Protestants, and Roman Catholics.[6] A Roman Catholic statement on the subject is typical of this position:

> Today there are many who vindicate the right to sexual union before marriage, at least in those cases where a firm intention to marry and an affection which is already in some way conjugal in the psychology of the subjects require this completion which they judge to be connatural. . . . This option is contrary to Christian doctrine, which states that every genital act must be within the framework of marriage. (Sacred Congregation for the Doctrine of the Faith, 1976, p. 11)

However, trends in society have caused many ethicists to reopen the question and to take less strict positions. Among these are the development of safe and

> **Moralism:** A religious or philosophical attitude that emphasizes moral behavior, usually according to strict standards, as the highest goal of human life. Moralists tend to favor strict regulation of human conduct to help make people good.
> **Pluralism:** A philosophical or political attitude that affirms the value of many competing opinions and believes that the truth is discovered in the clash of diverse perspectives. Pluralists, therefore, believe in the maximum human freedom possible.
> **Fornication:** The term for sex by unmarried people and, more generally, all immoral sexual behavior.
> **Adultery:** Voluntary sexual intercourse by a husband or wife with someone other than one's spouse; thus betrayal of one's marriage vows.

[6]Official statements about sexual topics from Jewish and Christian denominations have been compiled by The Religious Institute, www.religiousinstitute.org.

reliable contraception, later age at first marriage, the fact that many people suffer the loneliness of divorce and widowhood, and scientific evidence indicating widespread sexual activity among adolescents. These ethicists are concerned that people be given more helpful guidance than "thou shalt not" and "just say no." For them, the quality of the relationship is more important ethically than its legal status.

Criteria for judging the morality of nonmarital sexual acts could include the following (Countryman, 1994). First, is there a genuine respect for the personhood of all involved? Virtually all ethicists would agree that sexual exploitation of one person by another (whether married or not)—the use of other human beings merely for one's pleasure—is wrong. Furthermore, most would require genuine affection and commitment from both parties, which would be manifested in responsible behavior such as using precautions against unwanted pregnancies and STIs and being sensitive to each other's needs. Finally, many ethicists would insist that moral sexual behavior must include genuine openness and honesty between the partners. Public and private institutions, in this view, should be involved in helping people to make good ethical choices about sexual behavior in a culture that tends to glorify and exploit sex (Lebacqz, 1987; Moore, 1987).[7]

Yet another approach holds that, particularly with young people, our ethical emphasis should be on sexual violence (Carmody, 2015). This approach holds that the most serious ethical issue is not whether unmarried adolescents engage in sex, it is whether they—or anyone else—coerce sex from another person. An education program using this framework has been developed in Australia and is called the Sex & Ethics Program (Carmody, 2015). It acknowledges young people as active decision makers and seeks to balance ethical consideration of sexual violence with the real pleasures of sex.

Extramarital sex (adultery) has always been regarded as a grave matter. In the Hebrew Bible, the penalty for it was to be stoned to death; in the New Testament, it is the only grounds for divorce allowed by Jesus (Matthew 6:21–22). With increased psychological awareness, adultery has been understood as a serious breach of trust by a spouse, as well as an act of unfaithfulness to God (a violation of religiously significant promises). Few contemporary ethicists seek to modify this position, but many would argue for a less judgmental, more humane approach to those involved. In this view, people in extramarital relationships should be helped to find the root causes of their infidelity and to move toward a reconciliation with their spouses based on forgiveness and love. This approach suggests that counseling is more helpful than condemnation. Above all,

some argue, religious organizations need to assist people in establishing and maintaining good marriages based on mutual respect, communication, and commitment.

Contraception

Roman Catholicism opposes any "artificial" means of contraception; Jews and most Protestants favor responsible family planning by married couples. Moreover, most ethicists would suggest that unmarried people who are sexually active ought to be using birth control.

Those who oppose birth control for religious reasons see it as being contrary to the will of God, against the natural law, or both. Orthodox Judaism cites the biblical command to "be fruitful and multiply" (Genesis 1:26), not to be disobeyed in any way. Furthermore, some members of other Jewish communities warn that limiting family size threatens the future existence of the Jewish people, and they call for a return to the traditionally large Jewish family.

The Roman Catholic position is best articulated in Pope Paul VI's 1968 encyclical, *Humanae Vitae:*

> Marriage and conjugal love are by their nature ordained toward the begetting and educating of children. . . . In the task of transmitting life, therefore, they are not free to proceed completely at will, as if they could determine in a wholly autonomous way the honest path to follow, but they must conform their activity to the creative intention of God, expressed in the very nature of marriage and by its acts, and manifested by the constant teaching of the Church. (p. 20)

Why is the Roman Catholic Church opposed to contraception?

The encyclical continued the Church's approval of "natural family planning," that is, abstinence during fertile periods, popularly known as the "rhythm method" or "Vatican roulette." Not all Catholics enthusiastically accepted *Humanae Vitae,* and the evidence indicates that many Catholic couples, often with the encouragement or tacit approval of their priest, ignore these teachings and use contraceptives anyway.

Those in the religious community who favor the use of contraceptives do so for a variety of reasons. Many express a concern that all children who are born should be "wanted," and they see family planning as a means to this end. Others, emphasizing the dangers that overpopulation poses to the quality and future of human life, the need for a more equitable distribution and conservation of natural resources, and the needs of the emerging nations, call for family planning as a matter of justice. Another point of view regards the use of contraceptives as part of the responsible use of freedom. In this view, any couple who are unwilling or unready to assume the responsibility of children have a duty to use contraceptives. For these

---

[7]A fine discussion of these issues from different perspectives (liberal Protestant and Roman Catholic, respectively) can be found in Nelson (1978) and Genovesi (1987).

(a)

(b)

Figure 7 The abortion controversy. Pro-life and pro-choice advocates are both adamant about their positions. (*a*) Pro-choice protesters demonstrate in front of the U.S. Supreme Court on July 9, 2018, in Washington, D.C. (*b*) Thousands of pro-life supporters take part in the fifth annual March For Life through central London (UK), May 5, 2018.

(a) ©Tasos Katopodis/Getty Images; (b) ©Wiktor Szymanowicz/ Barcroft Media/Getty Images

groups, the decision to use contraceptives is a highly individual one, and the government must allow each individual the free exercise of their conscience (Curran, 1988). Others argue that Thomas Aquinas's natural law, which was based on the science of the Middle Ages, should be updated to a natural law based on current biological and social science, which would lead to very different conclusions about contraception and many other issues, including homosexuality (Helminiak, 2001a, 2001b, 2004).

Abortion

One of the most convulsive debates of our time continues to be waged over the issue of abortion. Pro-life and pro-choice activists are well organized and deeply convinced

of the rightness of their positions. The conflict is a clash of religious belief, political conviction, and worldview in the realm of public policy, one that allows for no easy solutions.

Two distinctions should be made at the outset. First, there is no consensus on the relation between abortion and contraception. For the Roman Catholic Church and others within the pro-life movement, the two are the same in intention; indeed, many pro-life activists wish to ban all contraception except natural family planning (rhythm). In the other camp, there are some pro-choice advocates who also regard abortion as a variety of contraception—less desirable, perhaps, but better than unwanted pregnancy. However, most centrist ethicists do distinguish between abortion and contraception, typically favoring the latter while raising ethical questions about the former. Second, a distinction is frequently made between therapeutic abortion and elective abortion. Therapeutic abortion is a termination of pregnancy when the life or mental health of the woman is threatened or when there is trauma, such as in cases of rape or incest. Many ethical theorists are willing to endorse therapeutic abortion as the lesser of two evils but do not sanction elective abortion—that is, abortion whenever requested by a woman for any reason.

The leadership of the antiabortion movement clearly comes from the Roman Catholic Church, for which putting an end to abortion is a major policy goal. For many Catholics, opposition to abortion is seen as part of an overall commitment to respect for life. The underlying principle of this position is that all life is a gift from God that human beings are not permitted to take. It is the position of the pro-life movement that human life begins at the moment of conception and that the fetus is, from that beginning, entitled to full rights and protections. The Roman Catholic position is shared by Orthodox Jews, Eastern Orthodox Christians, and many conservative, or fundamentalist, Protestants (see A Sexually Diverse World: Religious Position Statements on Abortion). An end to legalized abortion is at the top of the political agenda of many theologically conservative groups and has been a major issue in presidential and congressional elections and Supreme Court appointments for more than 40 years (Table 1).

Nonetheless, there has been some significant dissent from this position even within the Catholic Church. Pro-choice Catholics point out that for most of its history the Church accepted Aristotle's teaching, reaffirmed by St. Thomas Aquinas, that "ensoulment," that is, the entry into the fetus of its distinctively human soul, takes place roughly 3 months after conception (Maguire, 2001; Miller, 2014). Theoretically, this permits at least first-trimester abortion. The distinction between human life and human personhood is crucial here. A first trimester fetus, according to this distinction, is human and alive, but not yet a person. If it is not a person, it cannot be murdered.

Table 1	Gallup Poll Findings on Americans' Attitudes toward Abortion

	Percentage		
	1975	1992	2014
Abortion should be:			
Legal under any circumstances	21%	31%	28%
Legal under only certain circumstances	54	53	50
Illegal under all circumstances	22	14	21
No opinion	3	2	1

Source: www.gallup.com

Though regularly denounced by the Vatican and the U.S. Church's hierarchy, some Catholic ethicists insist that the Church's position is not unchangeable and argue that the concerns and needs of women should be more carefully considered (Kolbenschlag, 1985; Maguire, 2001; Reuther, 1985). As shown in Table 2, reflecting the diversity of Catholic belief, 48 percent of U.S. Catholics believe that

Table 2	Percentage of U.S. Adults in Religious Groups Who Say Abortion Should Be Legal in All or Most Cases

Religious Affiliation	% Saying Abortion Should Be Legal in All or Most Cases
Unitarian Universalist	90
Atheist	87
Jewish	83
Buddhist	82
Episcopal Church	79
United Church of Christ	72
Hindu	68
Presbyterian Church (USA)	65
Evangelical Lutheran Church in America	65
African Methodist Episcopal Church	64
United Methodist Church	58
Muslim	55
Catholic	48
Southern Baptist Convention	30
Mormon	27
Jehovah's Witness	18

Source: Masci (2018).

abortion should be legal in all or most cases; but in that same poll, 47 percent believe it should be illegal in all or most cases.

The pro-choice position takes at least two forms: absolute and modified. The absolute position argues that pregnancy is solely the concern of a woman and that she should have the absolute right to control her own body and determine whether to carry a fetus to term. Ethically, this position is based on the conviction that the individual must be free and autonomous in all personal decisions. It is also inspired by feminism, which regards such autonomy as necessary if women are to be truly equal to men. Feminists also observe that, historically, the rules about abortion were made by men, who do not become pregnant, and thus are deeply suspect. Indeed, for many feminists complete access to abortion is an absolute principle for women's liberation. Concerns for autonomy and individualism have formed a significant part of Western ethics and American social theory for more than two centuries.

For those who hold the modified pro-choice position—which includes most liberal Protestants and Jews—the issue is more complex and means balancing several goods against one another. They affirm that human life is good and ought to be preserved but also argue that the quality of life is important. They argue that a fetus may have a right to life, but ask if the child does not also have the right to be wanted and cared for. In high-risk situations, might not the danger to the well-being of a woman already alive take precedence over the well-being of an unborn fetus? Few in this camp regard abortion as a good thing, but most suggest that there may be many situations in which it is the least bad choice. Moreover, these ethicists tend to observe that there is no real consensus in society over the morality of abortion, so the government ought to keep out and let the individual woman make up her own mind.

The pro-life position is, as is typical with moralism, much more absolute and apparently simple, whereas the pluralist pro-choice position is complex. Both positions agree on the value and dignity of human personhood but are sharply divided on when personhood begins, how various conflicting interests are to be balanced, and how human life is best preserved and enhanced. Several factors ensure that the debate will continue for some time. Advances in neonatal medicine are pushing back the threshold of "viability" (the survival of premature infants), which may affect the ethical acceptability of second-trimester abortions for some people (Callahan, 1986). The politicalization of the issue will keep it in the public consciousness, and legal challenges will undoubtedly continue (see the chapter "Sex and the Law"). Certainly, the intensity is not likely to diminish, as it is a clash about life, law, freedom, and values, and few people are neutral on these issues.

Homosexuality

Mirroring society as a whole, religious communities have been engaged in a vigorous debate on the subject of homosexuality. Until recently, the religious condemnation of homosexual acts, and even homosexual people, was unquestioned. However, many contemporary ethicists, and some religious bodies, have started reexamining their attitudes toward homosexuality (Siker, 1994; White, 2001). This change has occurred in part because some recent scholarship suggests that the traditional interpretation of the Bible passages on this topic is not accurate, and in part because the impact of social science has led many ethicists to question whether homosexuality is truly abnormal and unnatural and therefore against the will of God. There are three positions, broadly speaking, on the issue: rejection, love the sinner but hate the sin, and full acceptance.

What does the Bible say about homosexuality?

Rejectionism

According to the *rejectionist position,* it has generally been presumed that the Judeo–Christian tradition absolutely opposes any sexual acts between people of the same gender and regards those committing such acts as dreadful sinners, utterly condemned by God. Although there are few references in the Bible, all the explicit ones are negative, the most famous being the passage about the destruction of Sodom.[8]

Rejectionists tend to rely on a literal reading of the Bible. They note that the Hebrew Bible calls male–male sex "an abomination" (Leviticus 18:22), and although Jesus made no comment on the subject, they read Paul's statement in Romans (1:26–27) as an unambiguous condemnation of homosexual acts. They allow, however, that Paul did not seem to have found homosexuality any worse than other sexual sins. The rejectionists also note that—in English translation—sodomy is included in lists of sins that include adultery and fornication (1 Corinthians 6:9 and 1 Timothy 1:10). Insisting that the sin of Sodom (Genesis 19) was homosexuality, they also tend to see homosexuality wherever the Bible mentions Sodom.

A thread of condemnation of homosexuality does run through Christian history. Homosexuality was not uncommon in the Mediterranean world of the early Church, and the Church condemned it as part of the immoral world in which it found itself. The Church saw it as a crime against nature that might bring down the wrath of God upon the whole community (Kosnick, 1977). In the Middle Ages, Thomas Aquinas stated that "unnatural vice . . . flouts nature by transgressing its basic

principle of sexuality and is in this matter the gravest of sin" (1968 ed., II-II, q. 154, a. 12).

Many religious people continue to hold the rejectionist position condemning homosexual acts and rejecting homosexual people unless they repent and become heterosexual. An example of this stance is a 2010 resolution of the Southern Baptist Convention, which stated, "[we] affirm the Bible's declaration that homosexual behavior is intrinsically disordered and sinful, and we also affirm the Bible's promise of forgiveness . . . to all sinners who repent of sin."

Love the Sinner but Hate the Sin

Many religious groups would modify the rejectionist position somewhat, through a distinction between homosexual orientation and behavior. In essence this stance regards a person's homosexual orientation—assuming that it cannot be changed—as morally neutral but rejects homosexual behaviors. Thus an ethical homosexual person may be fully obedient to the will of God, as long as they remain abstinent. This is the official position of the Roman Catholic Church, reiterated in a Vatican directive entitled "The Pastoral Care of Homosexual Persons," which states in part,

> Although the particular inclination of the homosexual person is not a sin, it is a more or less strong tendency ordered toward an intrinsic moral evil; and thus the inclination itself must be seen as an objective disorder. Therefore special concern and pastoral attention should be directed toward those who have this condition, lest they be led to believe that the living out of this orientation in homosexual activity is a morally acceptable option. It is not. (Congregation for the Doctrine of the Faith, 1986, p. 379. This position was reiterated in 2003. Documents such as this can be found online at http://www.vatican.va/roman_curia/congregations/cfaith/index.htm)

As a result of this instruction, American bishops denied use of church facilities to most chapters of Dignity, an organization of lesbian and gay Catholics. Various Protestant groups have taken the same stance—that is, being gay per se may not be sinful, but homosexual acts are.

Full Acceptance

At the other end of the spectrum are those in the religious community who favor *full acceptance* of lesbian and gay people, usually basing this stance on a revisionist view of the Bible and church tradition. Some scholars argue that the apparent condemnation in the scriptures is not relevant to homosexuality as we understand it today (Furnish, 1994). Some scholars go further and deny all condemnation. They note that the "abomination" of Leviticus 18:22 implied a ritual taboo, an impurity, not an ethical violation, and the offense was only male–male penetrative sex, not all same-sex acts (Boyarin, 1995; Olyan, 1994). Paul's point

[8]Other relevant biblical passages include Leviticus 18:22 and 20:13; Genesis 19; Romans 1:26; and I Corinthians 6:9.

A Sexually Diverse World

Religious Position Statements on Abortion: Pro-life versus Pro-choice

T he following statements come from a variety of major religious organizations. They reflect the nature of the arguments and the rhetoric of the abortion debate. Consider these statements in relation to the Gallup poll (Table 1) that shows a wide diversity of opinion among the American public.

Pro-Life Statements

Among important issues involving the dignity of human life with which the Church is concerned, abortion necessarily plays a central role. Abortion, the direct killing of an innocent human being, is always gravely immoral (The Gospel of Life, no. 57); its victims are the most vulnerable and defenseless members of the human family. It is imperative that those who are called to serve the least among us give urgent attention and priority to this issue of justice. (United States Conference of Catholic Bishops, 2001)

Our defence of the innocent unborn, for example, needs to be clear, firm and passionate, for at stake is the dignity of a human life, which is always sacred and demands love for each person, regardless of his or her stage of development. Equally sacred, however, are the lives of the poor, those already born, the destitute, the abandoned and the underprivileged, the vulnerable infirm and elderly exposed to covert euthanasia, the victims of human trafficking, new forms of slavery, and every form of rejection. (Pope Francis, 2018)

As Orthodox Christians, we strongly affirm the value and sanctity of all human life, from the moment of conception to the final breath one takes. . . . To artificially terminate life is to transgress on that which is holy; it is unthinkable, a grave sin. (Jonah, Metropolitan of all America and Canada, 2010)

The living but unborn are persons in the sight of God from the time of conception. Since abortion takes a human life, it is not a moral option except to prevent the death of another person, the mother. (Lutheran Church–Missouri Synod, 2009)

Whereas, Biblical revelation clearly and consistently affirms that human life is formed by God in His image and is therefore worthy of honor and dignity (Genesis 1:27; 9:6) and. . . Whereas, an estimated fifty-seven million unborn babies have been aborted since the legalization of abortion in 1973 (Roe v. Wade). . . Be it resolved, that we reaffirm our repudiation of the genocide of legalized abortion in the United States and call on civil authorities to enact laws that defend the lives of the unborn. . . . (Southern Baptist Convention, 2015)

Pro-Choice Statements

The United Church of Christ has affirmed and reaffirmed since 1971 that access to safe and legal abortion is consistent with a woman's right to follow the dictates of her own faith and beliefs in determining when and if she should have children, and has supported comprehensive sexuality education as one measure to prevent unwanted or unplanned pregnancies. (United Church of Christ, 2004)

Abortion is an extremely difficult choice faced by a woman. In all circumstances, it should be her decision whether or not to terminate a pregnancy, backed up by those whom she trusts (physician, therapist, partner, etc.). This decision should not be taken lightly (abortion should never be used for birth control purposes) and can have life-long ramifications. However, any decision should be left up to the woman within whose body the fetus is growing. (Union for Reform Judaism, 2004)

Our belief in the sanctity of unborn human life makes us reluctant to approve abortion. But we are equally bound to respect the sacredness of the life and well-being of the mother, for whom devastating damage may result from an unacceptable pregnancy. In continuity with past Christian teaching, we recognize tragic conflicts of life with life that may justify abortion, and in such cases we support the legal option of abortion under proper medical procedures. We cannot affirm abortion as an acceptable means of birth control, and we unconditionally reject it as a means of gender selection. (United Methodist Church, 2000)

We believe that legislation concerning abortions will not address the root of the problem. We therefore express our deep conviction that any proposed legislation on the part of national or state governments regarding abortions must take special care to see that individual conscience is respected and that the responsibility of individuals to reach informed decisions in this matter is acknowledged and honored. (Episcopal Church, 2009)

Judaism does not believe that personhood and human rights begin with conception. The premise that personhood begins with conception is founded on a religious position which is not identical with Jewish tradition. Therefore, under special circumstances, Judaism chooses and requires abortion as an act which affirms

and protects the life, well being and health of the mother. To deny a Jewish woman and her family the ability to obtain a safe, legal abortion when so mandated by Jewish tradition, is to deprive Jews of their fundamental right of religious freedom. (United Synagogue of Conservative Judaism, 1989)

Sources: www.pewforum.org; www.religiousinstitute.org

in Romans (1:18–32), then, would be to dismiss concern over this male–male impurity, this *atypical* sexual behavior (the term *unnatural* is a mistranslation), for "nothing is unclean in itself" (14:14), and Christians of diverse stripes "who are many, are one" (12:5) (Countryman, 1988). Yale historian John Boswell's detailed research into early and medieval Christianity led him to conclude that up until about the 13th century the Christian Church was relatively neutral toward homosexuality and, when it did see homosexual behavior as sinful, did not regard it as any worse than heterosexual transgressions (Boswell, 1980). Boswell found that a gay subculture flourished throughout this period, that it was known to the Church, that clergy and church officials were often part of it, and that it was not infrequently tolerated by religious and civil authorities alike. This sort of historical research has led some theologians, such as Roman Catholic John McNeill and Anglican Norman Pittenger, to question whether the tradition has been understood properly and to conclude that sexual relationships that are characterized by mutual respect, concern, and commitment—by love in its fullest sense—are to be valued and affirmed, whatever the gender of the partners (McNeill, 1987; Pittenger, 1970). The revisionist view has been gaining adherents over time.

Different religious bodies have moved toward acceptance in varied ways. For example, in 2006 the Episcopal Church's General Convention reaffirmed its "historical support of gay and lesbian persons as children of God and entitled to full civil rights." The Episcopal Church stands, with many other religious groups, for full civil rights and liberties for homosexual people.

In 1963 a group of English Friends challenged traditional thinking about sexuality, including homosexuality, in *Toward a Quaker View of Sex.* Since that time, Quakers and Unitarians have been notable for their acceptance not only of gay people but also of their sexual behavior, as long as it is conscientious.

Within virtually all the mainline churches, gay caucuses and organizations have been formed in an effort to move fellow believers toward greater understanding and tolerance. A considerable number of lesbians and gays have simply left the established religious organizations and founded their own churches, synagogues, temples, and other groups, of which the largest is the Metropolitan Community Church (see Figure 9). On the other hand, many gay people reject all forms of religion as oppressive and invalid, making religion as controversial within the gay community as homosexuality is within religious bodies.

Two issues in particular seem to provoke the most debate: ordination and gay marriage. Beginning in the 1970s, most major American Protestant denominations debated the appropriateness of ordaining lesbians and gays to the ministry. The debates were emotional and explosive, and nearly all resulted in legislation forbidding homosexual ordination. The debate in 2004 at the General Conference of the United Methodist Church was typical. In a highly charged atmosphere including demonstrations, the group voted, by a 2 to 1 margin, that "practicing homosexuals" cannot be ordained and that Methodist ministers may not bless same-sex unions (Bloom, 2004). At present, the Unitarian-Universalist Association, the United Church of Christ (Congregationalists), the Evangelical Lutheran Church in America (ELCA), the Presbyterian Church, and both Reform and Conservative Jews are willing to ordain gay and lesbian people openly. And in 2003, the Episcopal Church, amid much controversy, approved the consecration as bishop of an openly gay priest (Davey, 2003). Otherwise, the lines are pretty clearly drawn in other religious groups.

Many who favor full acceptance of LGBs have argued for formal recognition of same-gender marriages by religious groups. At the same time, beginning around 2010, public opinion in the United States increasingly favored

Figure 8 In this Dürer painting, Lot and his family flee as the city of Sodom burns. In Genesis 19:4–11, God sends two angels to the city of Sodom to investigate its alleged immorality. The angels are granted hospitality by Lot, but his house is surrounded by a crowd of men demanding that he send the angels out, "that we may know them." Lot offers his virgin daughters instead, but the men of Sodom insist, the angels strike them blind, and God destroys the city. This story has been understood to condemn all homosexual acts. However, some modern scholars question this interpretation, noting that at most it condemns homosexual rape. More-over, scholars point out that in other portions of the Bible and in Jewish history, the sin of Sodom is never seen as homosexuality but rather as general immorality and lack of hospitality, a serious offense in the ancient Near East (Helminiak, 2000).

©3LH/SuperStock

Figure 9 The Reverend Troy Perry founded the Universal Fellowship of Metropolitan Community Churches in 1968 as part of his coming out—the story of which is told in his book *The Lord Is My Shepherd and He Knows I'm Gay.* Today there are 166 MCC congregations in 33 different countries (mcchurch.org).

©Rick Gerharter

legalized gay marriage. A landmark occurred in 2015 when the Supreme Court said that same-gender marriage was a legal right based on the Equal Protection Clause of the U.S. Constitution (see the chapter "Sex and the Law"). These enormous shifts in the culture at large were accompanied by corresponding changes in the views of many faith communities, while other groups held their ground in opposition to same-gender marriage. As of 2019, same-gender marriage was performed in the Unitarian Church, the United Church of Christ, the Presbyterian Church, the Episcopal Church, the ELCA Lutheran Church, and Reform and Conservative Jewish congregations.

HIV and AIDS

AIDS has raised a host of complex and difficult ethical issues for individuals, religious communities, and society as a whole. These issues are often debated in an atmosphere of fear, anger, and ignorance, which is focused on the fatality of the disease and the fact that the majority of sufferers in the United States are either gay men or injection drug users, two populations about which the society has profound ambivalence. Religious groups, like the rest of society, have struggled to develop effective ways of ministering to people with HIV infection or AIDS. Responses have ranged from declaring AIDS to be God's punishment on sinners to actively organizing to minister to people with AIDS and seeking to educate members of churches and synagogues about the disease and how they can respond compassionately.

Broadly speaking, the major ethical conflicts center on the dignity and autonomy of the person, on one hand, and the welfare of society on the other. This issue has both personal and public aspects. For the person who is HIV-positive, a primary issue is confidentiality. Given that disclosure can lead to the loss of one's job, housing, friends, and family, these individuals may well wonder if anyone has a right to know about their condition. However, many people argue that the public, or at least certain groups within society, have a right to know who is infected in order to be protected from them.

It has been proposed that infected people be registered for the protection of emergency medical personnel, health care workers, coroners, and morticians. In the United States, HIV testing is mandatory for blood and organ donors, military personnel, federal and state prison inmates, and, in some states, newborn infants (Kaiser Family Foundation, 2015). Many public health officials and AIDS researchers oppose mandatory testing because they fear that people at risk would be driven underground. They argue that the public health is best protected by voluntary testing and the fairly stringent protection of confidentiality. In fact, 54 percent of U.S. adults between the ages of 18 and 64 report having been tested in the last year (Kaiser Family Foundation, 2015).

Ethically, a solid middle position would encourage people in high-risk categories to take responsibility for themselves by undergoing voluntary testing and practicing safer sex. This position would argue that infected people have a right to confidentiality but should voluntarily disclose their status to anyone put at risk by it—notably health care personnel and sexual partners. For health care workers, there is the personal ethical problem of whether to treat people who are HIV-positive. It is probable that there is an ethical obligation to treat, but that there is also an obligation to take appropriate precautions.

Many of the ethical issues of public policy revolve around the very high cost of HIV/AIDS, both for treating its victims and in seeking a medical solution. Who should pay this cost? Insurance companies have sought ways in which to deny health coverage to people in high-risk groups. With the passage of the Affordable Care Act in 2010, HIV-infected people were assured of health insurance coverage.

Most of the choices that must be made in dealing with AIDS are unappealing, expensive, or both. American society is being challenged to maintain its own values and to deal compassionately and effectively with what some have described as the greatest health crisis since the bubonic plague.

Technology and Sexual Ethics

A major challenge to ethicists today is the rapid development of technologies that raise new moral issues before the old ones have been resolved. We have already discussed several issues in which technology has played

a major role. Although sex outside marriage is hardly a problem unique to our time, the availability of reliable birth control techniques has probably increased the incidence of premarital and extramarital sex. The fact that millions of people can enjoy vigorous sex lives without conceiving children unless they choose to has markedly changed the basic moral climate.

The issue of abortion has also been intensified by the technological advances of the past few decades and will only get more complicated in the future. The developing medical science of neonatology means that fetuses are viable outside the uterus earlier and earlier. Some late-pregnancy abortions produce a fetus that could be kept alive, confronting hospital staff with agonizing questions about what should be done in such cases. Traditional ethics suggest that such unwanted children be kept alive, yet this can be incredibly costly and the children often have serious disabilities as a result of not having gestated for a full 9 months. To deal with this issue, hospitals may limit, or even forbid, second-trimester abortions.

Another complex of ethical issues arises out of the host of assisted reproductive technologies that enable people to conceive children without sexual intercourse (Green, 2007). These include artificial insemination, either by husband or by donor (AIH or AID), in vitro fertilization (IVF), embryo transfer, and surrogate motherhood.

For many ethicists these technologies can be tentatively approved, because they enable otherwise infertile people to have children with at least one partner's genes (Strong, 1997). Certainly, having children of one's own has had a very high value for most people throughout history, and "barrenness" has been seen as a curse in most cultures.

These technologies bring with them a number of ethical problems, too, chief among is that they involve "playing God." That is, they give human beings control over things that are, it is argued, best left up to nature and raise serious problems of who will decide how they are to be used. It is also argued that separating conception from marital intercourse may confuse the parenthood of children and have a negative effect on the child and family. Another concern is the possibility of exploiting others, particularly in the case of surrogacy. Some ethicists fear that rich couples will "rent wombs" from low-income women. Many question the morality of conceiving and/or carrying a child one never intends to raise. Others worry that AID and IVF will be used to select the sex of a child or predetermine other characteristics, ushering in a "Brave New World" that is profoundly unethical.

Now that technologies such as in vitro fertilization are commonplace, new issues are emerging. Often more than one embryo is implanted, the goal being to maximize the chances of a successful pregnancy. The result in some cases is multiple births of six or more babies, born long before 9 months of gestation. One study of children born at 25 weeks of gestation or earlier—not necessarily as part of a multiple birth—found that 49 percent had a disability and 23 percent had a severe disability (Wood et al., 2000). Is it ethical to use procedures that pose such serious risks to the baby?

Two religious communities have condemned most or all of these technologies, though on somewhat different grounds. Orthodox Judaism might permit the use of techniques that would allow an otherwise infertile couple to have a child if both egg and sperm come from the couple—for example, in AIH or IVF with implantation in the wife's uterus. Any technique involving a third party is condemned as being de facto adultery and confusing the parentage of the child (Green, 1984; Rosner, 1983). The Roman Catholic position was stated clearly in a 1987 statement issued by the Vatican and continues to be reaffirmed today. The statement admitted as an open moral question fertility techniques that remained within the woman's body using her husband's sperm not collected by masturbation. Otherwise, all techniques such as AID, IVF, and surrogacy were unequivocally condemned as an assault on the dignity of the embryo and on the sanctity of marriage as the only licit means of procreation (Congregation for the Doctrine of the Faith, 1987, 2008).

A centrist position on new reproductive technologies might approve their use in many cases, such as AIH in which a married couple use their own egg and sperm and the woman's uterus and simply accomplish fertilization and implantation by artificial means, perhaps because the wife's fallopian tubes are blocked. At the same time, this centrist position might forbid other practices, such as the use of a stranger for her egg and gestation with only the husband's sperm contributed by the "parental" couple. One question then would be whether technological conception should be regulated according to the mother's age. Rosanna Dalla Corte, a 62-year-old Italian woman, created headlines when she gave birth, having used an ovum donation because she was postmenopausal (Strong, 1997). She would be 80 at the time of her son's high school graduation.

The announcement, in 1997, that Scottish scientists had successfully cloned a sheep, Dolly, confronted the public with the possibility of human cloning and its ethical issues when most had thought that cloning was largely a science-fiction fantasy (see Figure 10). The technique itself, called **somatic cell nuclear transfer,** involves substituting the genetic material from an adult's cell for the nucleus in an egg (Shapiro, 1997). President Clinton swiftly asked the National Bioethics

What are some ethical arguments surrounding cloning?

Somatic cell nuclear transfer: A cloning technique that involves substituting genetic material from an adult's cell for the nucleus of an egg.
Therapeutic cloning: Creating tissues or cells that are genetically identical to those of a patient, to treat a disease.

Figure 10   The successful cloning of Dolly, the sheep, was a technological breakthrough that also raised a series of ethical questions.

©*Paul Clements/AP Images*

Advisory Commission to report on the ethical and legal issues surrounding human cloning. The group considered a number of ethical perspectives (Shapiro, 1997). A child born through cloning might have a diminished sense of individuality and personal autonomy, being genetically identical, for example, to her mother. The practice might open the door to a eugenics movement in which many copies of genetically "desirable" individuals were created while others were not permitted to reproduce. Yet these concerns must be balanced against important principles such as the right to privacy and to personal freedom, as well as the need to pursue scientific research. The commission concluded that, at this time, it would be morally unacceptable for anyone to create a human child using somatic cell nuclear transfer cloning, in part because the evidence indicates that the technique, at this time, is not safe and could introduce serious, unknown risks to a fetus. At the same time, the commission concluded that various religious bodies held divergent views on cloning and that widespread public debate needed to occur in order to refine and reach consensus on these ethical issues.

The newest development is **therapeutic cloning,** which refers to creating tissues or cells that are genetically identical to those of a patient who needs them to treat any of a number of diseases (Pollack, 2004). Therapeutic cloning is therefore distinct from reproductive cloning to create another individual, like Dolly. As the cloned embryo develops, *stem cells* can be extracted from it, which hold great promise for treating various neurological diseases such as Alzheimer's. In 2009 President Obama lifted the ban on stem-cell research in the United States, potentially opening the door to therapeutic cloning (Gilgoff, 2009). Such research is also permitted in the United Kingdom. Meanwhile, ethicists debate the morality of stem-cell research, which may involve the destruction of embryos. In response, scientists are developing methods for creating stem cells from sources other than embryos, such as skin or hair (Baker, 2008; Hayashi et al., 2012).

There is no way to stop the development of technology, or to slow its speed. Nonetheless, it is important to recognize that decisions about human life and reproduction should not be made just on scientific grounds. By definition, they have the deepest moral implications, which must be adequately addressed if essential human values are to be preserved.

Toward an Ethics of *Human* Sexuality

The combined forces of the sexual revolution and the New Morality have attacked traditional sexual ethics as narrow and repressive. This accusation may be true, but it has not yet been proven to everyone's satisfaction that the alternatives proposed are a real improvement over the Old Morality. Whether the debate will be resolved, and how, remains to be seen. Some of the arguments and possibilities follow.

The Old Morality tends to be ascetic and legalistic and, at its worst, reduces ethical behavior to following a series of rules. Its asceticism may downgrade the goodness of human sexuality and negate the very real joys of physical pleasure. A healthy personality needs to integrate human physicality and affirm it, and the Old Morality may make this kind of self-acceptance more difficult. Furthermore, if morality is simply a matter of applying universal rules, there is no real choice and human freedom is undermined. In short, opponents of the Old Morality might argue, this approach diminishes the full nature of humanity and impoverishes human life.

However, the traditional approach deserves a few kind words as well. For one thing, with the traditional morality people almost always know where they stand. Right and wrong and good and bad are clearly spelled out.

Moreover, asceticism bears witness to the fact that the human is more than merely the body.

The New Morality, with its situational approach and tendencies toward hedonism, has its own share of pluses and minuses. It affirms quite positively the physical and sexual side of human nature as an integral part of the individual. This is helpful, but if it is pushed too far, it can leave people undisciplined and irresponsible and thus less than fully human. Situation ethics calls for an evaluation of every ethical decision on the basis of the concrete aspects of the people involved and the context of the decision. Its broad principles of love, respect, and interpersonal responsibility are sound, but it can be argued that situationism does not take sufficiently into account the problem of human selfishness. Dishonesty about our real motives may blind us to the actual effects of our actions, however sincere we profess to be. Furthermore, situationism is a much less certain guide than the older approach because so many situations are ambiguous.

There is a middle ground between these two extremes. This approach would incorporate the need for principles (laws) as guidelines for actions, while insisting that guidelines be grounded in the best of current understanding—medical, psychological, and sociological. The result would be an updated version of the long-standing Western tradition of natural law, but 21st-century, evidence-based research, not armchair philosophy, would specify the nature involved. Both scientific and religious concerns, both research and responsibility, would find a balanced integration and produce the consensus needed in a pluralistic society and a global community. This approach differs from the Old Morality by stating that ethical principles must be evidence based and adjusted as technology and society change. This approach differs from the New Morality in holding that, even in human matters, some laws do apply: Life is not a free-for-all, and actions have their consequences, both for the individual and for others. Overall, ethics or morality would mean that which best serves life and health, and human and planetary well-being.

In the specific case of sexual ethics, such a middle-ground approach would affirm the goodness of human sexuality, while insisting that sexual behavior needs to be responsible. That is, choices must be based on collective experience, reasoned understanding, and well-informed conscience. This approach would accept sexuality as a vital part of human experience, but not the sum total of what we humans are.

Critical THINKing Skill

Understanding the difference between questions that can be decided by religious belief versus those that can be decided by scientific data

"Abortion is a sin and you will get seriously depressed if you have one." This is the text in a brochure that activists hand to women entering an abortion clinic. As someone with excellent critical thinking skills, you want to evaluate the accuracy of each of those statements: (1) abortion is a sin; and (2) you will get seriously depressed if you have an abortion.

In cases such as this, it is important to distinguish between questions that can be answered by science and those that can be answered only by religious belief. The statement, Abortion is a sin, is not something that can be evaluated by scientific data. Scientists cannot measure whether something is sinful. The statement can be evaluated with religious beliefs, though. If you are Jewish or Christian, you can evaluate it against what the Bible says, although the Bible does not say anything directly about abortion, so that answer has to be inferred from other teachings in the Bible. Alternatively, you could look to the teachings of your particular religious group. As we saw earlier in the chapter, not all Christian groups, for example, agree about the morality of abortion.

The statement, You will get seriously depressed if you have an abortion, is another matter. It is a statement that can be evaluated against scientific data. Researchers can conduct long-term studies of women having abortions to see if they actually do get depressed. Researchers could add a control group of comparable women to see if depression rates among those who had abortions are higher than the rates for comparable women. The design could be improved in various ways until it provides a very strong answer to the question. As we saw in an earlier chapter, the scientific data do not support the assertion that having an abortion causes a woman to become depressed.

For good critical thinking, it is important to distinguish between questions that can be answered with scientific data and those that cannot and are matters of religious faith.

SUMMARY

Basic Concepts

It is important to study religion and ethics in conjunction with human sexuality because they frequently provide the framework within which people judge the rightness or wrongness of sexual activity. They influence the way members of a society regard sexuality, and they are therefore powerful influences on behavior. Religion and ethics may be hedonistic (pleasure oriented) or ascetic (emphasizing self-discipline). They may be legalistic (operating by rules) or situational (making decisions in concrete situations, with few absolute rules).

Sexuality in Great Ethical Traditions

In the great ethical traditions, ancient Judaism had a positive, though legalistic, view of sexuality. Christian sources are ambivalent about sexuality, with Jesus saying little on the subject, and with St. Paul, influenced by the immorality of Roman culture and his expectation of the end of the world, being somewhat negative. Later, Christianity became much more ascetic, as reflected in the writings of Augustine and Thomas Aquinas, who grounded Catholic moral theology in natural law. The Protestant Reformation abolished clerical celibacy and opened the door to greater individual freedom in ethics. Today, new biblical scholarship has led to a wide variety of positions on issues of sexual ethics.

Humanistic ethics rejects external authority, replacing it with a person-centered approach to ethics.

Sexuality in Other Major Religions

In terms of its roots, Islam is closely related to Judaism and Christianity and sees the Hebrew Bible and the New Testament as sacred. Classic Islam values sexuality very positively, but there is great variation across contemporary Islamic nations in how these teachings are interpreted. Hinduism, rooted in India, recognizes four possible approaches to life, one of which is Kama, the pursuit of pleasure, including sexual pleasure. Buddhism developed out of Hinduism. One Buddhist tradition is ascetic and encourages some men to live celibate lives as monks, but other Buddhist traditions, such as Tantric Buddhism, are much more sex positive.

Contemporary Issues in Sexual Ethics

Ethical issues involving human sexuality have provoked lively debate. Although the Western ethical tradition opposes sex outside marriage, some liberals are open to sex among the unmarried, under certain conditions. Contraception is opposed by Roman Catholicism on natural-law grounds, but it is valued positively by other groups. Abortion provokes a very emotional argument, with positions ranging from condemnation on the grounds that it is murder to a view that asserts the moral right of women to control their own bodies. Although the traditional view condemns homosexuality absolutely, there is some movement toward either approval of at least civil rights for gay people or a more complete acceptance. The spread of AIDS poses serious ethical problems, which involve a balancing of individual needs with the welfare of society.

Technology and Sexual Ethics

The rapid development of sex-related technologies poses challenges in sexual ethics. Some consider assisted reproductive technologies to be ethical because they enable people to conceive children, whereas others worry about issues such as wealthy people using surrogates and how many fertilized embryos should be implanted.

Toward an Ethics of *Human* Sexuality

A possible resolution of the conflict between the Old Morality and the New Morality involves an ethics of *human* sexuality, neither hedonistic nor rigidly ascetic, that takes seriously the historical tradition of ethical thinking while insisting that decisions take into account the specific situation.

SUGGESTIONS FOR FURTHER READING

Biale, David. (1997). *Eros and the Jews*. Berkeley, CA: University of California Press. A history of sex and the Jewish people.

Helminiak, Daniel A. (2000). *What the Bible* really *says about homosexuality*. Millennium edition. New Mexico: Alamo Square Press. The author, a Roman Catholic priest and professor of psychology, questions traditional interpretations of biblical passages about homosexuality, arguing that they have been misinterpreted and do not in fact condemn it. See also his *Sex and the sacred; gay identity and spiritual growth* (2006).

Jung, Patricia B., Hunt, Mary E., and Balakrishnan, Radhika (Eds.). (2001). *Good sex: Feminist perspectives from the world's religions*. New Brunswick, NJ: Rutgers University Press. This book examines the possibilities for women's sexuality in contemporary Islam, Buddhism, Judaism, and Christianity.

Lorius, Cassandra. (2010). *Tantric secrets: 7 steps to the best sex of your life*. New York: HarperCollins. This book explains Tantra and its connection to better sex.

Maguire, Daniel C. (2003). *Sacred rights: The case for contraception and abortion in world religions*. New York: Oxford University Press. Maguire, a Catholic theologian, finds much authority for contraception and even abortion in the world's religions, including Roman Catholicism.

Miller, Patricia. (2014). *Good Catholics: The battle over abortion in the Catholic Church*. Berkeley, CA: University of California Press. Miller traces the pro-choice movement within Catholicism, while also revealing the Catholic hierarchy's linking of pro-life values and politics.

Myers, David G., and Scanzoni, Letha D. (2005). *What God has joined together: A Christian case for gay marriage*. San Francisco: Harper San Francisco. The authors, a psychologist and a sociologist, examine the evidence for why gay marriage is consistent with Christian teaching.

©wavebreakmedia/Shutterstock

Are YOU Curious?

1. How many people in the United States are breaking the law by living together?
2. What laws protect the rights of transgender people?
3. How many and what kinds of laws restrict a woman's access to abortion?

Read this chapter to find out.

CHAPTER

20

Sex and the Law

CHAPTER HIGHLIGHTS

Why Are There Sex Laws?

What Kinds of Sex Laws Are There?
Crimes of Exploitation and Force
Criminal Consensual Acts
Crimes against Good Taste
Crimes against Reproduction
Criminal Commercial Sex

Discriminatory Laws Related to Sexuality
Sexual Orientation and Gender Identity
Same-Sex Marriage

Sex-Law Enforcement

Trends in Sex-Law Reform
Efforts at Sex-Law Reform
Right to Privacy

Equal Protection
Victimless Crimes
Freedom of Speech
Reproductive Freedom
Ethnicity, Social Class, and Sex Laws

Sex and the Law in the Future
Sex-Law Reform and Backlash
AIDS and the Law
The Legal Challenge of Assisted Reproductive Technologies

Sex, although considered by many in our culture the quintessential private activity, is blanketed by a staggering number and variety of laws. Such a crazy quilt of state laws means that a perfectly legitimate sexual practice in one state may be a felony in another. By crossing a state boundary one may be stepping into a different moral universe.*

*Richard Posner & Katherine Silbaugh. (1996). *A guide to America's sex laws*. Chicago: University of Chicago Press.

Every day, millions of people in the United States engage in sexual behaviors that are illegal. In many states or cities, for example, having sex with a person who is married to someone else, viewing child pornography online, and paying for sex are crimes. In fact, numerous laws in the United States tell people, in effect, what they can do and how, where, and with whom they can do it. This chapter considers why such laws exist, what sorts of behaviors are affected, how these laws are enforced, how they are changing, and what the future prospects for sex-law reform might be.

Why Are There Sex Laws?

Why are there laws regulating sexual conduct? This is a very modern question, for throughout most of Western history the regulation of sexual conduct was taken for granted. Sexual legislation is quite ancient, dating back certainly to the time of the Hebrew Bible (see the chapter "Ethics, Religion, and Sexuality"). Since then, in countries where the Judeo–Christian tradition has been influential, attempts to regulate morals have been the rule. Today many regard sex as a private matter, of concern only to those involved. However, historically it has been seen as a matter that very much affects society and therefore is a fit subject for law. Most societies regulate sexual behavior, both by custom and by law.

Certain kinds of sex laws are legitimate and necessary. It seems obvious that people ought to be free from sexual assault and coercion and that children should not be sexually exploited; individual rights and the interests of society are here in agreement.

However, sex laws have also been designed for other purposes that may be open to debate. Historically, one rationale was to preserve the family as the principal unit of the social order by protecting its integrity from, for example, adultery or desertion of a spouse. Sex laws also seek to ensure that children have a supportive family by prohibiting conduct such as **fornication,** which is likely to result in out-of-wedlock births. Changing social conditions may call for revision of these statutes, but the principles behind them are understandable.

There is yet another realm of motivation behind sex laws that is highly problematic: the protection of society's morals. The concern for public morality results in laws against nonprocreative sex, for reasons outlined in the chapter "Ethics, Religion, and Sexuality." Thus there have been laws against homosexual acts, bestiality, and contraception. Religious beliefs as to what is "unnatural," "immoral," or "sinful" have found expression in law, as it was often held that the state had a duty to uphold religion as a pillar of civilized society, using the law to make people good. The example of England is instructive because U.S. law derives so extensively from English law. Church and state in England have historically been seen as identical, and the state had an obligation to protect the interests of the church. A secular government not tied to the church, such as the United States, was unthinkable, and an individual's morals were a matter of public concern.

In the United States, in contrast, the Constitution separates church and state in order to prevent one religious group from imposing its beliefs on others. To the extent that today's laws are derived from the Judeo–Christian (or any other) religious tradition, they violate this principle. Moreover, we have witnessed increasing heterogeneity of moral beliefs in recent decades. The religious right, for example, remains opposed to premarital sex, whereas most Americans see nothing wrong with it, and others advocate polyamory. Even if we accept the use of law to regulate morality, there is no longer—if there ever was—a consensus about which morals should be codified into law.

It can be argued that another principal source of sex laws is *sexism,* which is deeply rooted in Western culture. One scholar has suggested that the history of the regulation of sexual activity could as well be called the history of the double standard. He went on to note,

> The law of marriage and the law controlling sexual expression are really the same question looked at from different angles. Women have always been looked upon as the property of men—whether fathers or husbands. Marriage has frequently in history been a commercial transaction or a way in which the fabric of society could be maintained. The male insistence on chastity was simply an attempt to regulate social relations, to cement dynasties, to ensure the orderly succession of property (particularly real property) and to perpetuate male domination. (Parker, 1983, p. 190)

Fornication: Sex between two unmarried people.

It is probably not coincidental that the movement for sex-law reform has gone hand in hand with the movement for the liberation of women.

The American tradition of moralism in politics, the prudery of the Victorian period (during which much of the U.S. legal system came into being), and the zealousness of "moral entrepreneurs" have combined to provide the United States with an enormous amount of sexual legislation. This legislation reflects a great deal of conflict in our attitudes toward sex, which is perhaps unsurprising in such a pluralistic society. According to one authority, "The United States criminalizes more sexual conduct than other developed countries do and punishes the sexual conduct that it criminalizes in common with those countries more severely" (Posner, 1992, p. 78).

The conflict in our attitudes toward many kinds of sexual activity resulted in the **Victorian compromise;** typically, the law does not criminalize behavior per se but does criminalize conduct that is visible to the outside world (Silbaugh, 2002). Thus laws in many jurisdictions do not criminalize commercial sexual intercourse but do penalize *soliciting* sexual activity in exchange for goods and services. In another example, state laws may criminalize "open and notorious" adultery but not the act of having sex with someone who is married. To some observers, this may appear to be hypocrisy. The rationale is that some (many?) people are offended by visible sexual misconduct and that it therefore harms the community. Also, people who favor maintaining the status quo, as in for instance preserving marriage, do not want to be presented with public examples of alternative forms of conduct that might lead others to adopt these alternative behaviors or lifestyles. And it is true that many people become more open in expressing nontraditional behavior when they learn that others share their interest or preference. This is one of the effects of widespread access to the Internet.

The U.S. legal tradition assumes both the right of the state to enforce morals and a consensus in society as to which morals are to be enforced. However, some citizens have come to question the legitimacy of government interference in what they regard as their private affairs. This tension has led to a widespread demand for a radical overhaul of laws that regulate sexual conduct. It all makes for a fascinating, if frustrating, field of study, for law has a way of reflecting the ambiguities and conflicts of society.

The study of the interrelationship of sex and the law is in its infancy (Frank & Phillips, 2013). One focus is on *sex* and the law, that is, laws that attempt to regulate who can engage in what sexual acts with who and where. A second focus is on *sexuality* and the law, aspects of law that relate to or infringe upon various sexual identities and orientations. A related question that is only infrequently discussed is what rights regarding sex and sexuality should the individual have? This chapter considers these issues and more.

What Kinds of Sex Laws Are There?

Cataloging the laws pertaining to sexual conduct would be a difficult project. It is possible that no one really knows how many such laws there are, given the large number of jurisdictions in the U.S. legal system. When one considers the range of federal law, state laws, municipal codes, county ordinances, and so on, the magnitude of the problem becomes clear. In addition to *criminal law,* portions of civil law that may penalize certain sexual behaviors—such as licensing for professions, personnel rules for government employees, and immigration regulations—are also relevant. Furthermore, these laws are changing all the time, so any list would become obsolete before it went to press. Therefore, what is offered here is not so much a statistical summary of specific sex laws as a look at the *kinds* of laws that are, or have been, on the statute books. The subheadings, all of which contain the word *crime,* have been chosen with care, as a reminder that we are discussing legal offenses that can carry with them the penalty of going to jail, loss of reputation and family, monetary fines, or all of these. However quaint and amusing some of these laws may seem, they are a serious matter.

Crimes of Exploitation and Force

Recalling our earlier discussion about the kinds of sex laws that seem to make sense in a pluralistic society, let us begin with those seeking to prevent the use of force or exploitation in sexual relations—chiefly laws against rape and sexual relations with children. In the past several decades, there has been a movement toward seeing such crimes not so much as sex crimes but as crimes of violence and victimization, with laws being revised to accommodate this different understanding and to protect the victims (see the chapter "Sexual Coercion").

In 2012, the Federal Bureau of Investigation and the U.S. Justice Department adopted a revised definition of **rape:** "penetration, no matter how slight, of the vagina or anus with any body part or object, or oral penetration by the sex organ of another person, without the consent of the victim." This revision brings the federal standard closer to the definition used in many states and cities, though there is still variation. A victim may be incapable of giving consent because of being unconscious, drunk, drugged, or other condition. Note the definition applies to all people. Many states have adopted laws criminalizing

---

Victorian compromise: The decision not to criminalize behavior per se and instead criminalize conduct that is visible to the outside world.

Rape: Nonconsensual oral, anal, or vaginal penetration, obtained by force, by threat of bodily harm, or when the victim is incapable of giving consent.

Figure 1 Many sex laws in the United States have had the goal of regulating behavior between consenting adult and upholding some people's moral standards. Interracial marriage was illegal in Virginia and some other states until those laws were overturned in the Supreme Court case *Loving v. Virgina* (1967), portrayed in the movie *Loving*.

©Pictorial Press Ltd/Alamy

sexual assault and have defined degrees of assault. Rape is typically considered first- or second-degree assault.

Rape of a spouse is a crime in all 50 states and the District of Columbia (National Center for Victims of Crime, 2004). However, in 30 states additional legal hurdles must be overcome in order to prosecute the case. One is a shorter time limit for reporting the rape to authorities. A second hurdle is that the act must be accomplished by force or threat of force; in nonspousal cases, lack of consent is often sufficient to bring charges. A number of states have extended these provisions to unmarried cohabitants.

Laws that seek to prevent the sexual exploitation of children and young people are complicated by the issues of consent, coercion, and immaturity, all of which are rather difficult to define. All states have laws against *statutory rape,* or carnal knowledge of a juvenile. These laws presume that all intercourse by an adult (normally one over 17 or 18) with a person under a certain age is, by definition, illicit because they cannot give genuine consent. The age of consent varies from state to state, ranging from 16 to 18 (Find the data, 2015). Some states have laws that also include a reference to the difference in ages between the two people,

on the assumption that there is a difference in criminality between a 16-year-old girl having intercourse with her 18-year-old boyfriend or with a man in his thirties or forties.

Child sexual abuse is generally covered under state laws against child abuse. Typically those laws define child abuse as harm or threatened harm of physical abuse, neglect, sexual abuse, sexual exploitation, or emotional injury against a child under the age of 18.

Finally, every state includes laws against **incest** in its penal code. These laws prohibit sexual relations between children and "biological parents, ancestors, or other siblings"; some also prohibit activity involving step- and adoptive parents (Posner & Silbaugh, 1996). Most prosecutions are cases involving children and adult relatives. The nearly universal taboo against incest seems to have as its purpose the guarantee to children that the home will be a place where they can be free from sexual pressure. In many states, the closer the relationship, the more severe the penalties against incest (Mueller, 1980). Incest laws also seek to prevent the alleged genetic problems of inbreeding.

> **Incest:** Sexual activity between relatives.

Criminal Consensual Acts

Although it is not difficult to see the logic of laws against force and exploitation of children and adolescents, many people are amazed to discover the number of sexual acts that are legally forbidden to consenting adults. These laws have been justified on the grounds of the prevention of illegitimacy, the preservation of the family, the promotion of public health, and the enforcement of morality (Bernard et al., 1985). There are a number of laws against fornication, **cohabitation,** and adultery. As of 2015, fornication was illegal in seven states and the District of Columbia. An effort to repeal the law in Virginia in 2014 failed. As of 2015, cohabitation was outlawed in six states (www.unmarriedamerica.org). In these states, an estimated 1.6 million unmarried couples are living together. These laws are rarely enforced, although they have been used in child custody cases.

> **How many people in the United States are breaking the law by living together?**

Adultery, intercourse involving at least one person who is married to someone else, is a crime in 21 states (Rhode, 2016). It is grounds for divorce in almost every state.

Besides specifying with whom one may have sex, laws have attempted to regulate what acts are permissible, even in the case of a legally married couple.

In 1986, 24 states had laws prohibiting **sodomy;** in some states, the law defined *sodomy* very broadly, as "crimes against nature" or "deviate sexual intercourse"; in other states, the law was very specific—for example, "contact between the penis and anus, the mouth and the penis, or the mouth and the vulva." The U.S. Supreme Court, in 2003, ruled 6 to 3 that such laws are an unconstitutional invasion of privacy (*Lawrence et al. v. Texas,* 2003). This decision invalidated sodomy laws. The majority opinion included reference to a decision by the European Court of Human Rights supporting gay rights; this is an outstanding example of the impact of the burgeoning human rights—including sexual rights—movement (see A Sexually Diverse World: Universal Sexual Rights).

Cohabitation: Unmarried people living together (with sexual relations assumed).
Adultery: Voluntary sexual intercourse by a husband or wife with someone other than one's spouse; thus betrayal of one's marriage vows.
Sodomy: Originally "crimes against nature"; in contemporary laws, oral and anal intercourse.
Exhibitionism: Showing one's genitals in a public place, to passersby; indecent exposure.
Voyeurism: Secretly watching people who are nude.
Prostitution: The exchange of sex for money or other payment such as drugs.

Crimes against Good Taste

Another broad category of sex offenses can be viewed as crimes against community standards of good taste and delicacy. In this area we find laws against **exhibitionism, voyeurism,** solicitation, disorderly conduct, being a public nuisance, and "general lewdness." These statutes are by and large vague and punish acts that are offensive, or *likely* to be offensive, to someone. Consider public nudity. Forty states have laws prohibiting exhibitionism, intentional display of sexual parts of the body, especially genitals and female nipples. Most states exempt breast-feeding mothers from prosecution, but even today, women are sometimes arrested for doing so. In some jurisdictions simple nudity (e.g., skinny-dipping) is legal but nudity coupled with evidence of intent to shock or offend is prohibited. And what about NIP, nudity in protest? Many communities host a World Naked Bike Ride each year, but few communities arrest nude riders (unless they do something to shock or offend). Twenty-three states have laws declaring sexual contact or activity in a public place to be a crime (Posner & Silbaugh, 1996). In all but two states these activities are misdemeanors. As discussed later, unequal enforcement of these laws, their vagueness, and the difference between what is offensive and what is actually criminal make these statutes suspect.

Crimes against Reproduction

The Judeo-Christian tradition considered behaviors that interfered with reproduction to be sins. English common law criminalized these behaviors, including homosexuality, sodomy, and birth control. (Conception was impossible with these behaviors.)

For decades, laws included a ban on the giving of information concerning the prevention of conception. Until 1973 abortion was prohibited or severely limited in many jurisdictions, and contraception was prohibited in some. These laws are clear examples of the enshrinement in the statute books of the values of another day. They arise from an understanding of reproduction as the only legitimate purpose of sex and a belief in the necessity of vigorous propagation of the species. Such laws were overturned by Supreme Court action, but continuing agitation, at least in the case of abortion and some forms of contraception, ensures that public debate will endure for some time.

Criminal Commercial Sex

The law has deemed it illegal to make money from sex, at least in certain circumstances. It is not illegal to sell products with subtle promises of sexual fulfillment, but it is illegal to provide such fulfillment, either in direct form (i.e., prostitution) or on paper or electronically, as in pornography. We treat both in greater detail later; first, however, let us examine the kinds of laws on these subjects.

Prostitution is the exchange of sex for money or other payment such as drugs. Except in Nevada, where five counties allow it, prostitution is illegal in every jurisdiction in the United States, though it is legal in many other countries. In most states, prostitution is a misdemeanor, punishable by a fine or jail sentence. The law also forbids

A Sexually Diverse World

Universal Sexual Rights

Another basis for sex-law reform is the concept of universal sexual rights. Adoption of such principles would provide a foundation for revising laws in every country so that they recognize individual freedom and dignity while protecting the rights of others. A statement of these rights was adopted at the 14th World Congress of Sexology, in Hong Kong in 1999, and was subsequently adopted by the World Health Organization.

Sexuality is an integral part of the personality of every human being. Its full development depends upon the satisfaction of basic human needs such as the desire for contact, intimacy, emotional expression, pleasure, tenderness and love.

Sexuality is constructed through the interaction between the individual and social structures. Full development of sexuality is essential for individual, interpersonal, and societal well-being. Sexual rights are universal human rights based on the inherent freedom, dignity, and equality of all human beings. Since health is a fundamental human right, so must sexual health be a basic human right.

The list of specific rights was revised and expanded by the World Association of Sexual Health in 2014. To ensure that human beings and societies develop healthy sexuality, these rights must be recognized, promoted, respected, and defended by all societies through all means.

1. **The right to equality and non-discrimination.** Everyone is entitled to enjoy all sexual rights set forth in this Declaration without distinction of any kind such as race, ethnicity, color, sex, language, religion, political or other opinion, national or social origin, place of residence, property, birth, disability, age, nationality, marital and family status, sexual orientation, gender identity and expression, health status, economic and social situation, and other status.

2. **The right to life, liberty, and security of the person.** Everyone has the right to life, liberty, and security that cannot be arbitrarily threatened, limited, or taken away for reasons related to sexuality. These include: sexual orientation, consensual sexual behavior and practices, gender identity and expression, or because of accessing or providing services related to sexual and reproductive health.

3. **The right to autonomy and bodily integrity.** Everyone has the right to control and decide freely on matters related to their sexuality and their body. This includes the choice of sexual behaviors, practices, partners, and relationships with due regard to the rights of others. Free and informed decision making requires free and informed consent prior to any sexually related testing, interventions, therapies, surgeries, or research.

4. **The right to be free from torture and cruel, inhuman, or degrading treatment or punishment.** Everyone shall be free from torture and cruel, inhuman, or degrading treatment or punishment related to sexuality, including: harmful traditional practices; forced sterilization, contraception, or abortion; and other forms of torture, cruel, inhuman, or degrading treatment perpetrated for reasons related to someone's sex, gender, sexual orientation, gender identity and expression, and bodily diversity.

5. **The right to be free from all forms of violence and coercion.** Everyone shall be free from sexuality-related violence and coercion, including: rape, sexual abuse, sexual harassment, bullying, sexual exploitation and slavery, trafficking for purposes of sexual exploitation, virginity testing, and violence committed because of real or perceived sexual practices, sexual orientation, gender identity and expression, and bodily diversity.

6. **The right to privacy.** Everyone has the right to privacy related to sexuality, sexual life, and choices regarding their own body and consensual sexual relations and practices without arbitrary interference and intrusion. This includes the right to control the disclosure of sexuality-related personal information to others.

7. **The right to the highest attainable standard of health, including sexual health; with the possibility of pleasurable, satisfying, and safe sexual experiences.** Everyone has the right to the highest attainable level of health and well-being in relation to sexuality, including the possibility of pleasurable, satisfying, and safe sexual experiences. This requires the availability, accessibility, acceptability of quality health services, and access to the conditions that influence and determine health including sexual health.

8. **The right to enjoy the benefits of scientific progress and its application.** Everyone has the right to enjoy the benefits of scientific progress and its applications in relation to sexuality and sexual health.

9. **The right to information.** Everyone shall have access to scientifically accurate and understandable information related to sexuality, sexual health, and sexual rights through diverse sources. Such information should not be arbitrarily censored, withheld, or intentionally misrepresented.

10. **The right to education and the right to comprehensive sexuality education.** Everyone has the right to education and comprehensive sexuality education. Comprehensive sexuality education must be age appropriate, scientifically accurate, culturally competent, and grounded in human rights, gender equality, and a positive approach to sexuality and pleasure.

11. **The right to enter, form, and dissolve marriage and other similar types of relationships based on equality and full and free consent.** Everyone has the right to choose whether or not to marry and to enter freely and with full and free consent into marriage, partnership, or other similar relationships. All persons are entitled to equal rights entering into, during, and at dissolution of marriage, partnership and other similar relationships, without discrimination and exclusion of any kind. This right includes equal entitlements to social welfare and other benefits regardless of the form of such relationships.

12. **The right to decide whether to have children, the number and spacing of children, and to have the information and the means to do so.** Everyone has the right to decide whether to have children and the number and spacing of children. To exercise this right requires access to the conditions that influence and determine health and well-being, including sexual and reproductive health services related to pregnancy, contraception, fertility, pregnancy termination, and adoption.

13. **The right to the freedom of thought, opinion, and expression.** Everyone has the right to freedom of thought, opinion, and expression regarding sexuality and has the right to express their own sexuality through, for example, appearance, communication, and behavior, with due respect to the rights of others.

14. **The right to freedom of association and peaceful assembly.** Everyone has the right to peacefully organize, associate, assemble, demonstrate, and advocate including about sexuality, sexual health, and sexual rights.

15. **The right to participation in public and political life.** Everyone is entitled to an environment that enables active, free, and meaningful participation in and contribution to the civil, economic, social, cultural, political, and other aspects of human life at local, national, regional, and international levels. In particular, all persons are entitled to participate in the development and implementation of policies that determine their welfare, including their sexuality and sexual health.

16. **The right to access to justice, remedies, and redress.** Everyone has the right to access to justice, remedies, and redress for violations of their sexual rights. This requires effective, adequate, accessible, and appropriate educative, legislative, judicial, and other measures. Remedies include redress through restitution, compensation, rehabilitation, satisfaction, and guarantee of non-repetition.

Source: World Association of Sexual Health, 2014.

activities related to it, such as solicitation, pandering (pimping, procuring), renting premises for prostitution, and enticing minors into prostitution. These activities are felonies in most states. Laws against vagrancy and loitering are also used against prostitutes. Many state laws provide the same penalty for patronizing a prostitute as for prostitution. However, clients are rarely charged. By one estimate, only 10 percent of the 100,000 prostitution-related arrests per year are of clients (Prostitutes Education Network, 1998).

As we discussed in the chapter "Sex for Sale," prostitution occurs in several venues that vary in their visibility and therefore in the risk of arrest, the role of third parties, and the effects of the activity on the worker's well-being. If we think somewhat more broadly, there are other forms of sexualized contact or interaction that involve money and sex, including strippers and exotic dancers, performers in live sex shows, and camgirls. These activities generally do not fall under the purview of laws regulating prostitution, although they may be considered violations of laws regarding public nudity, public lewdness, or obscenity. Even more broadly, consider the person who is being "kept," that is, in a relationship where another person provides financial resources or support in exchange for continuing emotional

Figure 2   The oldest profession. A street walker solicits a potential customer.

©Sean Murphy/Getty Images

or sexual intimacy (Padawer, 2009). The website Seeking-Arrangement.com provides a page where "SugarDaddies/Mommies" can make connections with "Sugar Babies" (of either gender). Isn't this prostitution? Apparently not; no one has been arrested for participating in it. The broad range of relationships involving the exchange of money and sex, and the narrow range of arrests for prostitution, suggest that some fine distinctions are being drawn here (Zelizer, 2006). One distinction involves the narrowness versus breadth of the relationship: Is the exchange only of money for sexual contact (prostitution), or is it an exchange involving money, sex, intimacy, and companionship (being kept)? The other dimension involves duration: Is it a 20-minute, 1-hour, 1-night event, or does it endure for weeks, months, or years?

Obscenity is discussed in more detail in a later section. Suffice it to say here that in most jurisdictions it is a crime to sell material or to present a play, film, or other live performance that is "obscene." That much is fairly simple. The real problem comes in deciding *what* exactly is obscene and how that will be determined without doing violence to the First Amendment's guarantee of freedom of speech. So far, no satisfactory answer has been found. Obscenity laws seem to have a twofold basis. First, they attempt to prevent the corruption of morals by materials that incite sexual thoughts and desires. Second, they attempt to ensure that no one will profit by the production and distribution of such materials. Whether either can be done, or is worth doing, is a question that we take up later in this chapter.

Discriminatory Laws Related to Sexuality

Sexual Orientation and Gender Identity

Gay, lesbian, bisexual, and transgender people face discrimination based on a range of local, state, and federal laws and regulations, although the discriminatory practices and the regulations they are based on are under attack. In many places, these individuals may be denied private employment. However, the federal civil service regulations forbid such discrimination in federal government employment, and some state governors and mayors have issued executive orders

What laws protect the rights of transgender people?

forbidding discrimination based on sexual orientation. Many professional and occupational licensing requirements nevertheless have "good character" or morality clauses that may be used as a basis for discrimination. For example, a number of public school teachers have been dismissed or reassigned when their sexual minority or transgender status has become known. The U.S. Library of Congress rescinded a job offer to a senior research analyst after he informed his future supervisor that he was transitioning. In response to a lawsuit, a federal judge ruled that the termination constituted a violation of Title VII, which prohibits discrimination based on sex (*Schroer v. Library of Congress,* 2008). At least 16 states prohibit discrimination by any employer on the basis of sexual orientation, and others ban it just in government employment; 21 states prohibit discrimination in housing (Cramer et al., 2017). These laws have withstood court tests but are often unpopular and remain subject to repeal by referendum by voters.

Transgender people, too, have been the object of discriminatory laws and policies. These issues, and their current legal status, are summarized in the feature A Sexually Diverse World: Legal Issues for Transgender Persons.

For years, gays and lesbians had an ambiguous status with regard to service in the military; they could be refused entry and dismissed from service. The U.S. Congress enacted the "Don't Ask, Don't Tell Repeal Act of 2010," allowing gays and lesbians to serve openly in the military. The law required that the president and military leaders certify that the military was ready to implement the law, and in September 2011 they did so. Most analysts agree that the transition has gone smoothly and that much of the discrimination has ended.

Obscenity: That which is offensive to decency or modesty, or calculated to arouse sexual excitement or lust.

A Sexually Diverse World

Legal Issues for Transgender Persons

The American Civil Liberties Union (ACLU) is the nation's foremost organization devoted to protecting people's civil liberties as guaranteed in the U.S. Constitution. Here are some legal issues faced by transgender people, and the current status of these issues as analyzed by the ACLU.

Discrimination in employment, housing, and schools. A number of states have passed laws that prohibit discrimination against transgender people in matters such as housing (e.g., renting an apartment) and employment. These states include California, Colorado, Illinois, Iowa, Oregon, Washington, and the District of Columbia. At the federal level, Congress has been slow to pass laws of this kind. Title VII of the Civil Rights Act of 1964 prohibits discrimination on the basis of sex. Various cases are now testing whether the courts will apply this principle to transgender people.

Name change and identity documents. Legally, the best way to change one's name is to file a petition in court. This is a pretty routine matter, as long as the judge is convinced that the goal of the name change is not something like avoiding debts. Once there is a court-ordered name change, the name and gender on the driver's license can generally be changed. With the new popularity of voter ID laws, this could mean the difference between being able to vote and not. Changing the name and gender on one's birth certificate can be trickier. Some states, for example, require proof of surgical treatment to do so.

Family issues. Is a marriage still valid if one person goes through gender transition? Generally, the marriage is still valid unless there is a divorce. Beyond that, though, things can get complicated in matters such as parenting. An interesting case example is given in the Critical Thinking box at the end of this chapter. Sometimes gender transition can be used against a person in a custody battle.

Health care issues. An important one here is insurance coverage for trans-related health care such as hormones and gender-affirming surgeries. Medicare has been back and forth about whether it will cover these costs, so we won't state its current policy because it may have changed by the time you read this. Medicaid coverage varies by state, and some states have Medicaid rules that provide coverage for hormone therapy and, in some cases, surgery. Some private insurance plans provide such coverage and others don't.

Hate crimes. Since 2009, the federal hate crimes law has covered hate crimes based on a person's gender identity.

Source: ACLU (2015).

Same-Sex Marriage

In the United States, until 2015, one of the clearest areas of legal discrimination against sexual minorities was the denial of the right to marry. The first U.S. state began performing gay marriages in 2004, and, by 2015, 37 states had legalized it, but that left 13 states in which it was illegal, and most of those states did not recognize a legal gay marriage performed in another state.

The right to marry legally is a big deal. It allows a couple to formally recognize their commitment to each other, so it is important psychologically and socially. But beyond that there are many other issues. For example, many employers give insurance benefits to an employee and their spouse. Heterosexual couples had that right, but without same-sex marriage (marriage equality) LGB couples did not. Inheritance rights are another example. If one member of a married couple dies, their estate passes pretty easily to their spouse. If the couple aren't married because they are not allowed to marry, inheritance becomes legally complicated and perhaps is even barred. Legal parenthood is also affected by whether the couple are married, and children faced discrimination because of the lack of legal recognition of their parents' marriage.

Various cases made their ways through the courts, but the U.S. Supreme Court wasn't quite ready to make a definitive ruling. For example, in the 2013 case of *Hollingsworth v. Perry,* the court evaded the issue by ruling on a technicality.

Table 1 Americans' Increasing Support for Gay Marriage

	Percent Who Agree or Agree Strongly					
GSS Cohort	2006	2008	2010	2012	2014	2016
2006	37	37	41			
2010			48	55	55	59

Source: Armenia & Troia (2017), based on General Social Survey data; 2016 data added by JSH.

Note: The question was "Homosexuals should be allowed to marry," rated on a scale from strongly disagree to strongly agree. The design is longitudinal so, for example, the 2006 cohort was a sample of people who responded in 2006, again in 2008, and again in 2010.

Meanwhile, Americans' attitudes toward gay marriage were shifting in major ways. As shown in Table 1, even in the brief span of 8 years, from 2006 to 2014, support for gay marriage went from 37 percent to 55 percent (Armenia & Troia, 2017). At that point, same-sex marriage was supported by a majority of Americans.

The breakthrough came in the 2015 U.S. Supreme Court case *Obergefell et al. v. Hodges*. The case bundled together four cases from states that banned same-sex marriage. The ruling stated that the fundamental right to marry was guaranteed to same-sex couples, and that all 50 states must license gay marriages (Figure 3). The legal basis for the ruling was the Equal Protection Clause in the Fourteenth Amendment of the U.S. Constitution; equal protection is discussed in more detail in the section of this chapter on Trends in Sex-Law Reform.

Proponents of same-sex marriage prefer to call the principle marriage equality. That is, it is not a question of whether gays have a right to marriage, it is a question of whether all people have an equal right to marry, and the U.S. Supreme Court affirmed that right.

Figure 3 The U.S. White House was illuminated in rainbow colors to commemorate the Supreme Court's landmark decision in June 2015 paving the way for legal gay marriage across the country.

©Drew Angerer/Bloomberg/Getty Images

Sex-Law Enforcement

From the foregoing, it is clear that the law has intruded into areas readers may well have thought were their own business. We can now ask, How are sex laws enforced? The answer is simple: with *great* inconsistency. One authority estimated that "the enforcement rate of private consensual sex offenders must show incredibly heavy odds against arrest—perhaps one in ten million" (Packer, 1968, p. 304); little has changed since 1968. The contrast between the number and severity of the laws themselves and the infrequency and capriciousness of their enforcement reflects society's ambivalence toward the whole subject.

This contrast leads to serious abuses and to demands for radical reform of sex laws. A summary of the arguments for reform is presented in the next section. First, however, it should be noted that as long as the laws are on the books, the *threat* of prosecution, or even of arrest, can exact a great penalty from the "offender." Loss of job, reputation, friendship, family, and so on can and does in some cases result from the sporadic enforcement of sex laws. For people engaging in the prohibited acts, the threat of blackmail is ever present. Of course, for those convicted on "morals charges," the situation is even worse. That individuals should be subjected to such punishments for private acts is questionable.

Second, the uneven enforcement of sex laws may have a very bad effect on law enforcement in general. It invites arbitrary and unfair behavior and abuse of authority by police and prosecutors. With regard to commercial sex workers, arrest practices seem highly discriminatory. First, 90 percent of all arrests are of workers (not clients). Of these, 50 to 80 percent are of ethnic minority women, even though most sex workers are White. Finally, a large minority of those sentenced to jail are women of color; White women are more likely to be fined (Prostitutes Education Network, 1998). Another serious abuse is entrapment, in which an undercover police agent, posing, for example, as a potential client, solicits the commission of a crime. Because a sexual act between consenting parties means that there is no one to report the act to the authorities, undercover agents must create the crime in order to achieve an arrest for it. There is great diversity in the practices officers use, but they may involve the officer dressing or being undressed and being fondled or masturbated before making the arrest (Eifling, 2015). Such entrapment hardly leads to respect for the law. Moreover, the knowledge that sex laws are violated with impunity creates a general disrespect for the law, particularly among those who know that they are, strictly speaking, "criminals" under it. If nothing else, the failure of Prohibition ought to demonstrate that outlawing activities of which a substantial proportion of the population approves is bad public policy. It may well be said that more violations of the public good result from the enforcement of sex laws than from the acts they seek to prevent.[1] Keeping this in mind, let us turn to the prospects for the future.

Trends in Sex-Law Reform

Several important legal principles have been used and continue to be used to bring about changes to sex laws: the right to privacy, equal protection, victimless crimes, and freedom of speech.

Efforts at Sex-Law Reform

Following a thorough review of legal practices in the United States, the American Law Institute's Model Penal Code recommended **decriminalization** of many kinds of sexual behavior previously outlawed. Under the section dealing with sexual offenses, it includes as reasonable for the law to regulate only rape, deviate sexual intercourse by force or imposition, corruption and seduction of minors, sexual assault, and indecent exposure (American Law Institute, 1962, Article 213). With the notable exception of commercial sex work, which it still makes illegal, the American Law Institute adheres to the principle that private sexual behavior between consenting adults is not really the law's business. The recommendation of the Model Penal Code has been followed by nearly half the states.

Although there are exceptions, a state is more likely to reform its sex laws as part of a complete overhaul of its criminal code than to make specific repeal of such laws. The reason for this is political and is grounded in the distinction between legalization and decriminalization. If legislators "legalize" unconventional sexual practices,

Decriminalization: Removing an act from those prohibited by law, ceasing to define it as a crime.

that is, remove the laws from the legal codes and substitute regulation of the behavior (and perhaps tax it), people are likely to become upset and accuse the state of "condoning" them. It is therefore important to note that what is advocated is decriminalization; that is, ceasing to define certain acts as criminal or removing the penalties attached to them. Decriminalization is morally neutral; it neither approves nor disapproves. Notice that other laws governing assault, theft, and so on would remain on the books and can be used to protect the public.

Right to Privacy

A legal principle that has been very important in sex-law reform is the right to privacy. This has come into play chiefly in attacks on sex laws through the courts. Interestingly enough, although the right to privacy is invoked in connection with an amazing variety of matters—criminal records, credit bureaus and banks, school records, medical information, government files, wiretapping, and the 1974 amendment to the Freedom of Information Act (known as the Privacy Act), to name a few—the definitive articulation of the constitutional principle came in a sex-related case (Brent, 1976).

Before 1965, contraception was illegal in many states, and it was illegal for physicians to prescribe contraception.

In 1965 the Supreme Court decided the case of *Griswold v. Connecticut,* invalidating a state law under which a physician was prosecuted for providing a married couple with information and medical advice concerning contraception. Justice William Douglas stated flatly that "we deal with a right of privacy older than the Bill of Rights, older than our political parties, older than our school system" (*Griswold v. Connecticut,* 1965, p. 486). The problem the justices faced was finding the specific provisions of the Constitution that guaranteed this right. As it turns out, the right to privacy is not stated explicitly in the Bill of Rights, but the Court concluded that it was strongly implied as a right. In invalidating the Connecticut law, the Court defined a right to privacy that was, in this instance, abridged when a married couple was denied access to information on contraception.

While the decision in the Griswold case declared the marriage bed an area of privacy, in the 1972 case of *Eisenstadt v. Baird,* the Court invalidated a Massachusetts law forbidding the dissemination of contraception information to the unmarried. In doing so the Court stated that "if the right of privacy means anything, it is the right of the individual, married or single, to be free from unwarranted governmental intrusion into matters as fundamentally affecting a person as the decision whether to bear or beget a child" (*Eisenstadt v. Baird,* 1972). Other decisions have established one's home as a protected sphere of privacy that the law cannot invade (Brent, 1976).

The right to privacy was invoked by the Court in 1973 in one of its most powerful and controversial cases,

[3]For a good discussion of these and other arguments, see Packer (1968, pp. 301–306).

Roe v. Wade, which invalidated laws prohibiting abortion. Suing under the assumed name of Jane Roe, a Texas resident argued that her state's law against abortion denied her a constitutional right. The Court agreed that "the right of personal privacy includes the abortion decision" (*Roe v. Wade,* 1973, p. 113). However, it held that such a right is not absolute and that the state has certain legitimate interests that it may preserve through law, such as the protection of a viable fetus. Nonetheless, the Court declared that a fetus is not a person and therefore is not entitled to constitutional protection. The effect of the *Roe* case, and of related litigation, was to invalidate most state laws against abortion. The Court limited second- and third-trimester abortions to reasons of maternal health but made a woman's right to a first-trimester abortion nearly absolute. However, the 1989 decision in *Webster v. Reproductive Health Services* and the 1992 decision in *Planned Parenthood v. Casey* changed the shape of abortion laws, as discussed later in this chapter.

The Supreme Court further extended the right to privacy in *Lawrence v. Texas* (2003). The case involved the arrest, under Texas law, of two men engaged in sex in the privacy of their own bedroom. The court invalidated the Texas law and other similar ones on the ground that they violate individuals' right to privacy. This is the strongest statement yet with regard to the protected nature of consensual sexual conduct in one's home.

What about consensual polygamy? Two television programs, *Big Love* (broadcast from 2006 to 2011), and the reality series *Sister Wives* (broadcast from 2010 to 2013), created widespread awareness of polygamy (marrying more than one spouse) in the United States. There are more than 25 enclaves in the United States, most of them in Utah, where *polygyny* (one man marrying several women) is practiced and accepted despite laws prohibiting the practice. In addition to adherents to the Mormon religion, members of some Muslim groups and other sects practice polygamy in the United States.

The stars of *Sister Wives* (in reality, a polygynous family) challenged the laws in the state of Utah prohibiting polygamy, stating they are unconstitutional. In December 2013, a federal judge ruled that the state law prohibiting cohabitation, which is used to prosecute multi-partner families in Utah, is unconstitutional, that it violates the right to privacy (*Brown et al. v. Buhman,* 2013). The judge cited the Supreme Court decision in *Lawrence v. Texas.* At the same time, he ruled that a law prohibiting the granting of multiple marriage licenses to the same person is constitutional.

Even vibrators and dildos have been part of the legal action. In the case of *Williams v. Pryor* (Alabama) (CV-98-S1938-NE), a U.S. District Court ruled unconstitutional the Alabama law that prohibited distribution of "any device . . . for the stimulation of human genitals." The court stated that the plaintiffs had shown that "the right of sexual privacy" protected the use of such devices. In *Reliable Consultants, Inc. v. Ronnie Earl,* the 5th Circuit U.S. Court of Appeals ruled that a Texas statute prohibiting the promotion or sale of sexual devices violated the Fourteenth Amendment and was unconstitutional (U.S. Ct. App., 5th Circuit, 06-51067, 2008).

Equal Protection

Another important legal principle is the right to equal protection of the law (Figure 4). This right is guaranteed by the U.S. Constitution, in the Fourteenth Amendment (and also the Fifth Amendment). The Fourteenth Amendment was passed shortly after the Civil War, with the goal of guaranteeing citizenship rights to former slaves, but its guarantees of equal legal protection to all has strong ramifications today. If law or government action results in disadvantage to some group, it is most likely a violation of equal protection and can therefore be challenged in court.

Challenges to laws or policies that discriminate against gays, lesbians, commercial sex workers, and other groups distinguished by sexual conduct have been based on this principle. A series of cases have been brought by gays and lesbians against policies of the U.S. military, such as policies that disadvantage lesbians or gays in the armed forces. Some of these cases have been decided in favor of the plaintiffs, others not.

Discrimination against gays and lesbians in employment and other arenas has also been challenged in court. One important case was *Romer v. Evans* (1996). In 1992, Amendment 2 to the constitution of the state of Colorado was put on the ballot, prohibiting the enactment of antidiscrimination laws or policies favoring homosexuals. In November 1992, the amendment was adopted with 54 percent of the votes cast. In 1996, the U.S. Supreme Court declared Amendment 2 unconstitutional; that is, states may not prohibit antidiscrimination laws.

As noted earlier, the equal protection clause was the basis for the Supreme Court legalizing same-sex marriage in the 2015 case of *Obergefell v. Hodges.*

Victimless Crimes

In the past five decades, much legislative change has taken place involving the principle of *victimless crimes*—a concept that has broad applicability beyond sexual behavior. The argument is that when an act does no legal harm to anyone or does not provide a demonstrable victim, it cannot reasonably be defined as a crime. The thrust of the argument has been well articulated by Norval Morris, the former dean of the University of Chicago Law School:

> Most of our legislation concerning drunkenness, narcotics, gambling and sexual behavior is wholly misguided. It is based on an exaggerated conception of the capacity of the criminal law to influence men [sic] and, ironically, on

Figure 4 Demonstrations seeking an end to violence against sex workers and increased legal and civil rights are happening all over the world. This Sex Workers Vigil and Protest March through Soho in London, England, took place on December 17, 2014.

a simultaneous belief in the limited capacity of men to govern themselves. We incur enormous collateral costs for that exaggeration and we overload our criminal justice system to a degree that renders it grossly defective where we really need protection—from violence and depredations on our property. But in attempting to remedy this situation, we should not substitute a mindless "legalization" of what we now proscribe as crime. Instead, regulatory programs, backed up by criminal sanctions, must take the place of our present unenforceable, crime-breeding and corrupting prohibitions. (1973, p. 11)

The victimless-crime argument should appeal to the public's sense of privacy and to its pocketbooks. Crimes in which there is no readily identifiable victim account for over half the cases handled by U.S. courts. If the court dockets could be cleared and law enforcement officers reassigned, protection against violent crimes would be rendered more efficient and less expensive.

The application of this principle to some of the issues discussed earlier should be obvious. A sexual act performed by consenting adults produces no legal harm, and neither of the participants is a victim. The only conceivable end served by criminalizing such an act is the protection of "public morals," which, in a society with diverse values, seems like a questionable goal.

Applying this principle, in 2005 the Supreme Court of Canada overturned the conviction of Jean-Paul Lebaye for keeping a common bawdy house. LeBaye operated a club in Montreal that allowed members and their guests admission for the purpose of meeting others, and in some cases engaging in group sex in two private rooms. Prospective members were screened, and participation was voluntary. The majority ruled that the conduct did not cause harm or present a risk of harm to individuals or society (*R. v. Lebaye,* 2005). In recent years, "sex clubs" have become fixtures in major U.S. cities. They are often upscale, and they prescreen guests. Clubs in Denver, Las Vegas, Phoenix, San Diego, and Washington, D.C. have faced a variety of legal challenges.

An analysis of worldwide trends in sex-law reform found that between 1985 and 2005 many countries repealed or contracted the scope of laws regulating adultery and sodomy (Frank et al., 2010). In contrast, during the same time period, many countries expanded the scope of rape/sexual assault and child sex abuse laws. The researchers suggest that nations are moving away from the institutional view that law should protect the family and encourage procreation, toward an individualistic view that encourages consensual sexual activity but prohibits harm to a person. In this sense, the victimless crime perspective is having a major impact around the world.

The most common reference to the decriminalization of victimless acts is with respect to prostitution. Police efforts at curbing the "oldest profession" seem to be ineffective, open to corruption and questionable practices, and tremendously expensive. Since prosecution is normally of the worker and not her customer, there seems to be a clear pattern of discrimination against women that violates the constitutional principle of equal protection. Finally, as all manner of adult consensual behavior comes to be decriminalized, the legitimacy of distinguishing between commercial and noncommercial consensual sex has been questioned (Parnas, 1981). It has been suggested that much of the demonstrable harm associated with commercial sex work, such as the committing of robbery and other crimes by workers and pimps and the connections with organized crime, has resulted *because* the practice is illegal (Caughey, 1974). Thus it has been argued that if it were no longer defined as a crime, all would benefit—the worker, the client, the police, and society at large (Parnas, 1981; Rosenbleet & Pariente, 1973).

San Francisco has a long tradition of prostitution, dating back to the 1860s. It also has thousands of people employed in commercial sexual activity. In 1994, the board of supervisors created a Task Force on Prostitution. After 18 months of hearings and study, the Task Force concluded that

> not only are the current responses ineffective, they are also harmful. They marginalize and victimize prostitutes, making it more difficult for those who want to get out of the industry and more difficult for those who remain in prostitution to claim their civil and human rights. (San Francisco Task Force on Prostitution, 1996)

The Task Force therefore recommended

> that the City departments stop enforcing and prosecuting prostitution crimes. It further recommends that the departments instead focus on the quality of life infractions about which the neighborhoods complain and redirect funds from prosecution, public defense, court time, legal system overhead, and incarceration towards services and alternatives for needy constituencies.

The argument against the criminalization of prostitution assumes that if it were legal, it could be regulated and the problems of crime, public offense, and the spread of sexually transmitted infections associated with it might be avoided. In this case, then, there would be no victims and no societal need to ban the practice. However, this argument can be countered by suggestions that commercial sex work may indeed have victims, as discussed below.

Researchers were able to take advantage of a natural experiment to test some of the hypotheses about the benefits of decriminalizing prostitution (Cunningham & Shah, 2018). A Rhode Island district court judge decriminalized indoor prostitution in 2003. It was criminalized again in 2009. The intervening 6 years can tell us something about the effects of decriminalization. The decriminalization increased the size of the indoor prostitution market and decreased prices (the authors are economists, so they would think of something like that). Most important,

from a sexual health perspective, the incidence of gonorrhea decreased by more than 40 percent in the state of Rhode Island. This finding supports the argument that the legalization of prostitution would result in decreasing the spread of STIs.

As we noted in the chapter "Sex for Sale," some workers, such as those involved in sex trafficking, are forced to engage in sexual activity and may have no opportunity to escape from it. Some workers are forced by a pimp or madam, or perhaps by physical abuse, to stay "in the life." Some young men and women enter commercial sex work because they have few other marketable skills and are lured by the promise of a big income. These cases suggest that there is a continuum of consent, ranging from coercion through lack of options to more or less voluntary participation. This continuum probably characterizes not only workers who sell sexual gratification but also those employed in the porn industry. At what point does such activity become consensual? As a result, some scholars object to lumping all of these together into one category. Calling them all "sex work" may divert attention from the harm being done to those "workers" who are being exploited and suffer sexual harassment and rape on a daily basis (Farley, 2006). Second, a feminist analysis of prostitution suggests that commercial sex work of all kinds is inherently degrading and contributes to the objectification of women and their bodies, thus harming all women. Finally, we should consider the possibility that some consensual activities may result in moral, religious, or ethical harm (Silbaugh, 2002).

Freedom of Speech

Among the most controversial topics in the area of sexual regulation is obscenity and pornography. A substantial portion of the U.S. populace (33 percent in 2014 according to the General Social Survey) finds pornography offensive and wishes it suppressed. Many others do not share this view and find any form of censorship outrageous and unconstitutional. Antivice crusaders consider "smut" dangerous to the average citizen. Legislators are peppered with demands that something be done, and the courts have labored unsuccessfully for years to balance the First Amendment right of freedom of speech with the desire of some to outlaw, or at least regulate, pornography.

To begin with, we have a problem of definition. Here it is helpful to distinguish between *pornography* as a popular term and *obscenity* as a legal concept. In general usage today, pornography refers to literature, art, films, speech, and so on that are intended to be sexually arousing, or presumed to be arousing. Pornography may be *soft-core* (suggestive) or *hard-core,* which usually means it involves an explicit depiction of some sort of sexual activity and genitalia. Pornography, as such, has never been illegal, but obscenity is. The word *obscene* refers to that which is foul, disgusting, or lewd, and it is used as a legal term for that which is offensive to the authorities or to society (Wilson, 1973).

Obscenity has been a legal issue ever since the Supreme Court decided the *Roth* case in 1957. In it the Court explicitly stated that obscenity was not protected by the First Amendment—which guarantees freedom of speech and the press and which, by long-recognized extensions, includes films, pictures, literature, and other forms of artistic expression. However, it also ruled that not all sexual expression is obscene, defining obscenity as material "which deals with sex in a manner appealing to prurient interest" (*Roth v. United States,* 1957). The *Roth* decision evoked much controversy, both from those who thought the Court had opened the floodgates of pornography and from civil libertarians who found the definition too restrictive. The Court continued to try to refine the test for obscenity. However, none of these tests was persuasive to more than five members of the Court, much less to the public at large.[2]

The current standard definition of obscenity by the Supreme Court came in the 1973 case of *Miller v. California.* Chief Justice Burger and the four justices concurring with him proposed the following definition:

> (a) whether "the average person, applying contemporary community standards," would find that the work, taken as a whole, appeals to the prurient interest, (b) whether the work depicts or describes, in a patently offensive way, sexual conduct specifically defined by the applicable state law, and (c) whether the work, taken as a whole, lacks serious literary, artistic, political or scientific value. (*Miller v. California,* 1973, p. 24)

The goals of this decision seem to be to define as obscenity "hard-core pornography" in the popular sense, to require from state statutes precise descriptions of what is to be outlawed, and to give governments more power to regulate it (Gruntz, 1974). The notable problem with the *Miller* test, at least for civil libertarians, is the "contemporary community standards" provision. This allows the local community to determine what is obscene, rather than using national norms, making it impossible to predict what a given jury in a particular town might find obscene.

One important factor that has affected the law on pornography is the extent to which legislators, law-enforcement officers, and courts believe that it causes harm to the general population. For evidence, they have often turned to social science and found a mixture of data and conclusions. The Commission on Pornography appointed by Attorney General Edwin Meese, in its 1986 *Final Report,*

seemed to approve several strategies for combating pornography (U.S. Department of Justice, 1986).

The least controversial of these strategies is concerned with the problem of child pornography, depictions of sexual activities involving children, even when real children are not used. In the 1982 case of *New York v. Ferber,* the U.S. Supreme Court ruled unanimously that child pornography, whether or not it is obscene under the prevailing legal standards, is not protected by the Constitution. This decision gave states broader latitude in legislation, based on the government's obligation to protect children from abuse (Shewaga, 1983). The Court required states to be precise about whether they were prohibiting the production, processing, or distribution of child pornography, and to develop clear definitions of what was to be outlawed. This has proved difficult, but efforts continue. Another approach to the problem is to make tougher and more precise laws against child sexual abuse, without which "kiddie porn" could not be made. This approach would criminalize the very production of such material and sidestep the more complicated constitutional issue of distribution and sale (Shouvlin, 1981).

In regard to prosecution, a U.S. Department of Justice report found that, from 2003 to 2013, a total of 37,000 suspects were investigated and prosecuted at the federal level under the broad category of commercial sexual exploitation of children (Adams & Flynn, 2017). Among those cases, 10 percent were for the production of child pornography, 72 percent were for the possession or distribution of child porn, and 18 percent were for child sex trafficking. Therefore, the great majority of cases were about possession or distribution. As for pornography with adult actors, in 2017 Jeff Sessions, Attorney General in the Trump administration, said that obscenity cases should be vigorously prosecuted. And, of course, there were various "celebrity" cases, such as former member of Congress Anthony Weiner and his sexting scandals. Eventually he pled guilty to sexting to a 15-year-old girl.

A more fruitful approach for those who oppose pornography has been the attempt to regulate, or eliminate, its sale through zoning (Figure 5). In an effort to keep adult movie theaters out of the community, the city of Renton, Washington, passed an ordinance forbidding adult film theaters within 1,000 feet of any residential zone, single- or multiple-family dwelling, church, park, or school. Citing precedents and a municipality's right to prevent crime and protect property values, the Supreme Court upheld the Renton ordinance in 1986. Such zoning laws are content neutral and thus can avoid First Amendment issues.

In 2001 the city of Spokane, Washington, adopted a zoning ordinance that prohibited locating sex-oriented businesses within 750 feet of a public park, library, school, day care center, church, home, apartment building, or farm. At the same time, the city established zones where

[2]The frustration of defining obscenity was perhaps best expressed by Justice Potter Stewart in *Jacobellis v. Ohio* (1964): "I shall not further attempt to define [hard-core pornography], and perhaps I could not ever succeed in intelligibly doing so. But I know it when I see it" (378 U.S. 197).

Figure 5 Cities around the United States are using zoning laws to force adult businesses such as this one out of main shopping areas. The result is to push these stores into lower-income or marginal neighborhoods. Note that to preserve shoppers' anonymity, Hanky Panky thoughtfully provides "Private car park and entrance at rear."

©*Mark Richardson/Alamy*

such businesses could be located and gave nonconforming businesses 1 year to relocate to those zones. World Wide Video, an owner of adult businesses in Spokane, chose not to relocate its nonconforming stores and filed a lawsuit challenging the ordinance. World Wide alleged that the city had not proven that sex-oriented businesses negatively affect a community and argued that 1 year was not a reasonable period for it to relocate or change its retail operation. In 2004 the 9th U.S. Circuit Court of Appeals upheld the ordinance (*World Wide Video v. City of Spokane,* 2004). The Court ruled that the city did not have to conduct research to prove the existence of negative effects. At the same time, zoning often results in sex-oriented businesses being located near lower-class and minority communities, forcing residents to confront it on a daily basis; furthermore, this prevents middle- and upper-class women from engaging in discussions about pornography and challenging the stereotypes in it.

The use of restrictive zoning as a legal strategy has expanded to other areas of criminal activity involving sex. In the past 25 years, it has increasingly been used in an effort to protect children against sex offenders. More than 20 states and hundreds of cities have laws prohibiting sex offenders from living near (for example, within 1,000 feet) churches, schools, playgrounds, day care centers, or residences with children. There is heated debate on the effectiveness of these laws. In jurisdictions where they have been enacted, there is no evidence that these laws have reduced the number of offenses against children or victims. In some cities, the result has been to render larger numbers of offenders homeless. Parole officers say that

such laws make their job harder. In San Francisco, similar laws were enacted against massage parlors, as part of an effort to "crack down" on prostitution. In 1997, before enactment, most licensed parlors were in the downtown or in business districts; in 2005, parlors were spread all over the city, many in residential neighborhoods (Bernstein, 2007). Such *displacement* of commercial sex activity is a common response to efforts to "crack down" (Weitzer, 2010).

The Supreme Court has not abandoned the *Miller* "community standards" test, but it seems likely that attempts will continue to be made to reduce or eliminate the availability of what some see as harmful pornography. The complexity of the legal issues and the continuing debate over what is appropriate for Americans to read and view will undoubtedly keep the matter of pornography, obscenity, and erotica controversial for some time to come. Although it is difficult to define obscenity, the courts have consistently ruled that states and local communities have the right to regulate public conduct and public artistic expression (Leonard, 1993).

Owners of adult businesses are fighting back. In Ohio, prior to the election in 2006, many adult establishments handed out voter registration forms and encouraged patrons to register and vote. Adult-oriented businesses in Las Vegas have formed their own Chamber of Commerce; like their traditional sibling, the Chamber lobbies against laws that would harm members' businesses. ACE, Association of Club Executives, is the trade association for strip clubs in the United States.

Contemporary controversy about pornography is centered on the Internet. We described in the chapter "Sex for Sale" the various sex-oriented goods and services available online to anyone with a computer and Internet access. In the past, a potential user of X-rated books, photographs, or videos had to purchase them through a retail store or a mail-order firm. These businesses could, at least in theory, control who purchased these items. Specifically, they could require proof of age, thereby preventing minors from gaining access to such material. No one serves as a gatekeeper and controls access to these items on the Internet.

Existing laws governing the production, distribution, sale, and possession of kiddie porn apply to the Internet, and some law-enforcement agencies do in fact seek out and arrest offenders. More problematic are materials featuring people over 18. Adult websites require users to click on a statement certifying that they are 18 or older in order to gain access, but there is no practical way to enforce this restriction. Once the user gains access, many adult websites provide free viewing of X-rated photos, videos, and stories; users may download the photographs and videos and print the stories. In response to this situation, in 1996 the U.S. Congress passed the Communications Decency Act, which made it illegal to distribute via the Internet "indecent material" a child could access. Several groups immediately challenged the constitutionality of the act, claiming that it violated individuals' First Amendment rights. The U.S. Supreme Court declared the law unconstitutional in 1997. In 1998, Congress passed the more narrowly written Child Online Protection Act. After several lawsuits, the Supreme Court ruled this act unconstitutional, in *Ashcroft v. American Civil Liberties Union* in 2004.

At least three states have passed laws banning all state employees—including those who teach and do research in human sexuality—from using government computers to access sexually explicit materials. A number of corporations and many school districts have adopted similar policies.

Reproductive Freedom

An even more convulsive controversy is about abortion. Although the Supreme Court's decision in the *Roe* case was quite clear, it has been under continuous attack since it was handed down in 1973. Opposition comes from a broad coalition of antiabortion groups that call themselves *pro-life* and include the Roman Catholic Church, evangelical Protestants, various "New Right" organizations, and the Republican Party. The controversy has been carried on in elections, in the courts, in state legislatures, and in Congress. The pro-life movement is well organized and well financed and has proved to be an effective lobbying force, instrumental in the defeat of a number of legislators who have not supported the antiabortion cause. Those seeking to preserve the right of women to legal abortions, who call themselves *pro-choice,* have also organized and been effective. Beginning in the 1980s and continuing to the present, the pro-life movement has used six basic strategies to eliminate or reduce abortions: (1) funding restrictions; (2) procedural requirements, including parental consent, third-party notification, "education," and clinical restrictions; (3) the Human Life Amendment; (4) a ban on partial birth abortions (the "federal" abortion ban); (5) disruptive action against abortion providers; and (6) crisis pregnancy centers.

Funding Restrictions

The most notable example of funding restrictions is the Hyde Amendment, originally proposed by (former) U.S. Congressman Henry Hyde (no relation to the coauthor of this text). This is a rider to appropriations bills forbidding the expenditure of any federal money for abortions under most circumstances. Originally passed in 1976, it has been passed again every year and has been expanded from Medicaid to other government insurance programs (Adashi & Occhiogross, 2017). One result is that poor women have been denied this means of paying for abortions. Various states have introduced similar restrictions

on state money that has been used to cover the gap in federal funding for abortions. Another strategy involves regulations in Title X of the Public Health Act denying funds to organizations, such as family planning agencies, that make referrals for abortions and granting funds to organizations that oppose abortions (Paul & Klassel, 1987). In 2013, the House attempted to make the Hyde Amendment permanent legislation when it passed the *No Taxpayer Funding for Abortion Act* by a vote of 227 to 188. The bill did not advance in the Senate.

Procedural Requirements

The second strategy to make abortion more difficult to obtain has been to restrict abortion by enacting various procedural requirements for obtaining or performing an abortion. The earliest such efforts required *parental consent* for a minor to have an abortion or *notification* of the husband of a married woman seeking an abortion. In the 1992 case of *Planned Parenthood v. Casey* (2004), the Supreme Court ruled that states could require parental consent for unmarried girls under 18 seeking abortions. However, it struck down the requirement that married women must notify their husbands. In 2018, 38 states required parental consent or notification. (For a complete listing, see plannedparenthood.org.) These requirements are opposed by the American Medical Association, the American Academy of Pediatrics, the American Academy of Obstetrics and Gynecology, and other groups.

What are the effects of these restrictions? A review of the literature identified 29 studies of the impact of parental notification laws on a variety of outcomes (Dennis et al., 2009). "The clearest documented impact of parental involvement laws is an increase in the number of minors traveling outside their home states to obtain abortion services." A number of studies reported a decline in abortion rates among adolescents under 18 in states that enacted such laws, but most of these studies did not measure the number of minors who left the state to obtain abortions. Several studies reported no impact on pregnancy rates among minors.

Another effort to restrict abortion by making it more difficult or unpleasant is to *require women seeking an abortion be given certain information*—for example, that they be informed about fetal development or the medical or psychological consequences of abortion. Some laws along these lines have specified information that is reasonably accurate scientifically, whereas others specify information that is propaganda with little scientific basis or is just plain false. In 1983 the Supreme Court struck down an Akron, Ohio, ordinance that required information of the propaganda variety (Fox, 1983). However, in the 1992 *Planned Parenthood v. Casey* decision, the Supreme Court upheld Pennsylvania's requirement that women seeking abortion be informed about fetal development during the three trimesters of pregnancy and the possible viability of fetuses during the third trimester. A review of the materials used in 22 states, often written by state health department employees, finds that the information is often outdated, biased, or both. In some cases the information is patently wrong—for example, claims that receiving an abortion is linked to breast cancer, or that it is followed by adverse outcomes such as depression (Richardson & Nash, 2006). We reviewed the evidence in the chapter "Contraception and Abortion" showing no adverse mental health outcomes associated with receiving an abortion.

Another tactic is to require a woman seeking an abortion to have an *ultrasound test* and view the resulting images. The woman may be required to pay for the test. A federal appeals court ruled in 2014 that the North Carolina law requiring an ultrasound and a description by the physician of the image violates the the physician's First Amendment rights (*Stuart v. Kamnitz*, 2014).

Another review examined studies of the impact of *mandatory counseling and waiting period* laws (Joyce et al., 2009). Again, the clearest impact is an increase in the number of women who go out of state to obtain services, and an increase in the proportion of second-trimester abortions, which are not as safe. Laws that allow mandatory counseling to be delivered by the Internet, telephone, or mail appear to impose less cost on patients.

The most recent procedural requirement enacted into law is that *physicians performing abortions must have admitting privileges in a nearby hospital*. Clinic physicians who have requested privileges in some local hospitals have been denied them; this is especially likely in hospitals controlled by health care organizations affiliated with various conservative religious denominations. Closely related is the requirement that the clinic meet standards applied to hospitals, including width of hallways and number of parking spaces. Both are justified by supporters as being in the interest of the health and safety of the mother. Numerous professional organizations dispute the claim; first-trimester abortions are among the safest surgical procedures performed in the United States (Guttmacher Institute, 2014).

A major Supreme Court case, *Whole Woman's Health v. Hellerstedt* (2016), ruled on the constitutionality of these kinds of restrictions. The case concerned a 2013 Texas law mandating that (1) abortion providers must have admitting privileges at a hospital within 30 miles; and (2) abortion clinics had to meet the standards of ambulatory surgical centers, including a lot of equipment that is irrelevant to performing abortions. Meeting the second regulation would be expensive, driving up the cost of abortions. The number of abortion clinics in Texas declined from 42 to 19. Texas is a very big state, so the result was that women might have to travel very long distances to get to a clinic, which, of course, is exactly what the pro-life legislators wanted. A group of plaintiffs including Whole Woman's Health challenged the law in court. That case eventually went to the Supreme Court, which ruled in favor of the plaintiffs. In particular, the Court struck down the admitting privileges rule and the costly upgrades of facilities. The reasoning was that this legislation constituted obstacles to women's right to an abortion and placed an "undue burden" on women seeking abortion. Significantly, the decision reaffirmed women's constitutional right to abortion.

Since 2011, legislatures in 31 states have adopted 267 restrictions aimed at limiting the availability of abortion, that is, reducing reproductive freedom. As of 2015, 13 states have a nearly complete ban on abortions. Researchers analyzed the relationship between restrictions adopted by states and state-level statistics on number of abortions performed and number of providers (Jones & Jerman, 2014). Although declines in the rate of abortions performed by physicians were noted from 2008 to 2011, there was no evidence that these declines were related to the restrictions. States that did not pass restrictions experienced similar declines in rates.

In summary, then, *Roe v. Wade* (1973) decriminalized abortion and said that states could not restrict access to first-trimester abortion. Two decisions have since chipped away at *Roe v. Wade,* without overturning it completely. In *Webster v. Reproductive Health Services* (1989) the Court said that states could restrict abortion in some ways, namely, by forbidding it in state-owned hospitals and by banning abortion of viable fetuses. In *Planned Parenthood v. Casey* (1992) the Court again upheld a state law placing restrictions on abortion, involving parental consent, information, and a waiting period. However, requiring a woman to notify her husband was going too far, according to the decision, which said the laws could not place an undue burden on women seeking an abortion.

Pro-life forces have clearly shifted their emphasis to the passage of state laws placing procedural requirements on the provision of abortion in the hope of preventing abortion. The evidence suggests that so far these restrictions have not had a major impact on abortion rates in the United States, although they may have an adverse impact on certain categories of women, particularly poor women, who cannot afford to travel long distances to a dwindling number of abortion clinics.

Human Life Amendment

A third strategy used by opponents of abortion has been to champion the Human Life Amendment to the Constitution, which would prohibit all abortions. This amendment or similar legislation has been introduced repeatedly in Congress since 1983, but no serious effort has been made to bring it

How many and what kinds of laws restrict a woman's access to abortion?

to a vote (Wilcox et al., 1998). This bill is now referred to as the "Personhood" Amendment. Personhood USA, an advocacy group, is working to introduce the amendment in every state (Pesta, 2012).

Bans on Abortion

A fourth strategy to reduce access to abortion is to ban—legally prohibit—various types of abortion. The earliest effort was to ban so-called partial birth abortions, or other broadly defined procedures. Partial birth abortion is not a recognized medical procedure; some bills banning it have not included a description of what is being banned, and others provide only a vague description. The bills' lack of specificity raises the concern that the backers' intent is to have the law enacted, then use it to challenge a broad range of procedures. Between 1995 and 2004, 31 states enacted laws that prohibit partial birth abortion procedures (American Civil Liberties Union, 2004). In 18 of these states the laws have been challenged and declared unconstitutional; in 8 states the laws have not been challenged (Alan Guttmacher Institute, 2004). In the laws in 4 states the banned procedures are narrowly defined, allow for exceptions, and have been ruled constitutional. The accession of George W. Bush to the presidency in 2001 and the Republican control of Congress enabled the passage of a federal ban on partial birth abortion in 2003. Planned Parenthood of America immediately challenged the Partial Birth Abortion Ban Act in the federal courts, and in June 2004 a federal judge ruled the law unconstitutional (*Planned Parenthood Federation of America v. Ashcroft*, 2004). The judge ruled that the language was so vague it could be used to outlaw all or most abortions. In 2007, the Supreme Court ruled in a 5 to 4 decision that the law was not unconstitutional (*Gonzales v. Carhart et al.,* 2007).

In 2014–2015, there was a major push by pro-life advocates to enact state laws banning abortions after 20 weeks' gestation. As of June 2015, 11 states had enacted such a ban, or the equivalent—banning an abortion after 22 weeks after the woman's last menstrual period (Guttmacher Institute, 2015b). An additional 19 laws have been introduced in 12 states to ban terminations after 20 weeks. A bill was passed by the U.S. House of Representatives in 2015; titled the *Pain-Capable Unborn Child Protection Act 2015,* it would ban such abortions in all 50 states and establish a 5-year prison sentence as the penalty for anyone performing one. Supporters argue this ban is justified because a fetus at 20 weeks of gestation can feel pain. There is no scientific support for this claim (DeFrancesco, 2015; Lee et al., 2005). In fact, the evidence indicates that the earliest a fetus can feel pain is about 30 weeks' gestation, which is consistent with knowledge about prenatal development. The bill was reintroduced in 2017 but has yet to pass the Senate, so it has not gone into effect.

Disruptive Actions

A fifth strategy adopted by members of Operation Rescue and other pro-life activists involves disruption, such as picketing and engaging in acts of civil disobedience outside abortion clinics, Planned Parenthood facilities, or the homes of physicians who perform abortions (Figure 6). Some individuals, including members of Defensive Action and the Army of God, have engaged in arson and bombings of clinics where abortions are performed. The Army of God has published a handbook on how to conduct violent protests. In response to these incidents, in 1994 the U.S. Congress passed the Freedom of Access to Clinic Entrances Act. This law makes it a federal crime to use violence or the threat of violence to interfere with access to a reproductive services provider. In October 1995, the Supreme Court ruled that the act is constitutional.

Incidents of violence against abortion clinics and providers—for example, murder, bombings, arson, invasion, and vandalism—peaked in 2001, at 795 across the United States and in Canada. The number of such incidents in 2005 was 761, and then it declined to 88 in 2012; there was a sharp increase to 299 incidents in 2013 (National Abortion Federation, 2015). The decline was due in part to the vigorous prosecution and long sentences given to perpetrators of such acts. In 2012, Bobby Joe Rogers was sentenced to 10 years in prison for arson and damaging a reproductive health facility in Florida. Much of the fluctuation from year to year is variation in the number of trespassing incidents. On the other hand, incidents of disruption—for example, hate mail, Internet/e-mail harassment, bomb threats, and picketing—reached their highest level in 2006, at 14,102. The vast majority are incidents of picketing. The number remained high through 2009, and then dropped to about 6,000 per year. Though small, groups of picketers are sometimes successful in blocking access to clinics by physically blocking entrances and driveways.

Figure 6   Funeral held for a university police officer killed during a Planned Parenthood shooting.

©Stacie Scott-Pool/Getty Images

Crisis Pregnancy Centers

So-called crisis pregnancy centers have sprung up in most cities around the United States. Typically run by conservative Christian nonprofits, these centers advertise on billboards with phrases such as "Pregnant and scared? Call us at (800) xxx–xxx." They therefore attract women who are pregnant but in a difficult situation, who might be considering abortion. The goal of these centers is to counsel women against having an abortion, using various persuasive techniques. Sometimes they provide medical services such as pregnancy testing. The problem is that they have been known to give false information, asserting, for example, that abortion is dangerous to one's mental health or physical health, or that condoms are ineffective (e.g., Bryant & Levi, 2012). Moreover, they do not give women information about the full range of options available to them. At worst, a woman might easily think she is going to an abortion clinic, when in fact it is quite the opposite.

Concerned about this situation, the California legislature passed the Reproductive FACT Act in 2015. It required any licensed health care facility that provided pregnancy services to post a notice that stated "California has public programs that provide immediate free or low-cost access to comprehensive family planning services (including all FDA-approved methods of contraception), prenatal care, and abortion for eligible women." The California legislature wanted women to know about all of their options. As you can imagine, the crisis pregnancy centers were furious, and their national organization, National Institute of Family and Life Advocates (NIFLA), filed a lawsuit challenging the California law on the grounds that it violated their First Amendment rights to free speech, in the sense that it was "compelled speech." Lower courts sided with the state of California, and NIFLA continued to appeal. The case eventually made its way to the Supreme Court. In *National Institute of Family and Life Advocates v. Becerra* (2018) the court ruled, 5 to 4, in favor of NIFLA. (It was a little more complicated than that, but we won't drag you into the details.) Essentially, the ruling said that crisis pregnancy centers are free to say whatever they want, including false information, and that states may not require them to provide accurate, alternative information.

Summary

In summary, a variety of tactics have been used, each of which has succeeded in placing some additional restrictions on a woman's right to an abortion. Laws have been passed requiring third-party involvement—parents, husbands; major medical associations; and many other groups oppose these provisions. Laws have been enacted requiring tests, which are usually unnecessary and drive up the cost, and the provision of information that is often false and

in one state has been ruled unconstitutional. Numerous laws have been passed banning "partial birth abortion," which is poorly defined and not a recognized medical procedure. Laws are being passed to ban abortions after 20 weeks on the grounds that the fetus can feel pain; medical and developmental research indicates that is not true. A critical thinker has to ask, What is going on here? Why all this effort? One answer is that it reflects *pronatalism,* an ideology that prioritizes parenting as normal and desirable and considers other reproductive choices undesirable (Mollen, 2014). According to this view, women are said to be fulfilling their natural role and to achieve their greatest happiness in childbearing and childrearing. This ideology also fuels the debate over whether women, especially mothers, should work outside the home.

The year 2019 may turn out to be a pivotal year in the history of abortion rights in the United States. Who is on the Supreme Court has a big impact on the direction of decisions about abortion cases (Nash et al., 2018). In 2018, Justice Anthony Kennedy retired. He had been a swing vote and, for example, sided with the majority in *Whole Woman's Health* (2016), overturning abortion restrictions in Texas. The president's latest two additions to the Court are Neil Gorsuch and Brett Kavanaugh, who is openly anti-abortion. The fear is that *Roe v. Wade* could be overturned. If that occurs, state laws restricting or banning abortion would go into effect. The positions of these state laws are summarized in Figure 7, which shows that the majority of states have laws on the books that are hostile to abortion. And many state legislatures are busily passing more restrictions or bans.

Ethnicity, Social Class, and Sex Laws

Although the Constitution promises equal protection to people of all races, in practice people of color and low-income people are often at a disadvantage, and this is no less true in the area of sexuality than elsewhere. Here we consider abortion as an example (Nsiah-Jefferson, 1989; Roberts, 1993).

Little information exists on the abortion or reproduction-related needs of women of color. Until 1990, abortion statistics were published for only two categories of U.S. women: White and Black. Data are now available on Hispanic women, but not on American Indian or Asian American women. Given the different cultural heritages of these ethnic groups, abortion undoubtedly has different meanings for women in these groups, yet we lack data on the specifics.

Although for decades White women have had some control over their reproduction, for many women of color this is a new step. They may be wary because of the history of negative experiences of women of color in this area, such as the experimental work on the introduction

States with Hostile Abortion Laws

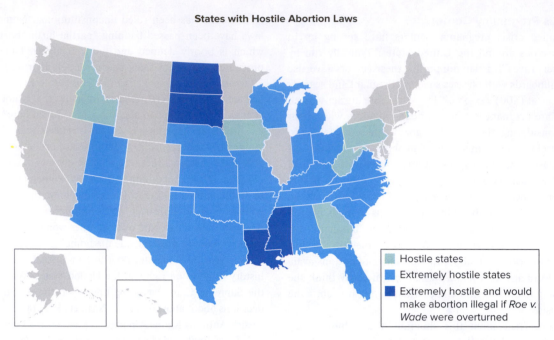

Figure 7   State laws on abortion as of 2018.

Source: Nash et al. (2018), https://www.guttmacher.org/article/2018/07/laws-affecting-reproductive-health-and-rights-state-policy-trends-midyear-2018

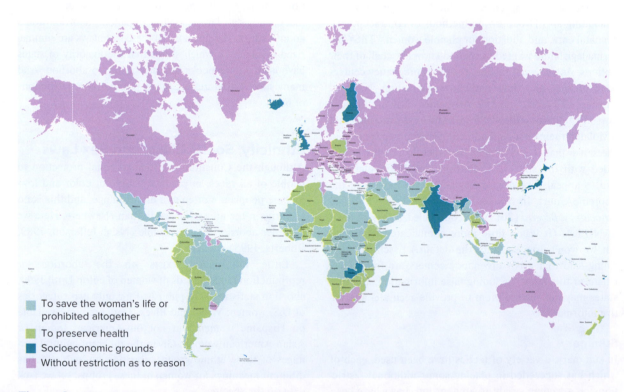

Figure 8   Abortion laws beyond the United States. This map depicts abortion laws worldwide. Several points should be noted. First, abortion is available without restrictions in a large group of countries (although that is a bit of an oversimplification for the United States). Second, abortion is prohibited entirely or allowed only to save the mother's life in numerous countries, especially in Latin America and Africa. Abortion is as controversial around the world as it is within the United States.

Source: https://www.reproductiverights.org/sites/crr.civicactions.net/files/documents/AbortionMap2014.PDF

of the birth control pill, which was done with poor women in Puerto Rico. Therefore, women of color need far more access to information and education, and it is critical that this information be sensitive to their cultural heritage.

Women of color are more likely to have abortions than are White women. Of the reported abortions performed in 2011, 36 percent were for White women (who make up 69 percent of the population of women), 30 percent for Black women (12 percent of the population), and 25 percent for Hispanic women (13 percent of the population; Guttmacher Institute, 2014). A significantly higher percentage of women of color obtain abortions after the first trimester than do White women. Data indicate that 7.5 percent of all abortions obtained by White women were performed after the first trimester (that is, 92.5 percent were done in the first trimester). By comparison, 9.7 percent of all abortions obtained by Black women, and 8.3 percent of all abortions for Hispanic women, were performed after the first trimester (Pazol et al., 2011).

The Hyde Amendment, which prohibits the use of federal Medicaid funds to pay for abortions for low-income women, is a key factor in this difference. Half of all pregnancies in the United States are unintended, and 40 percent of these are terminated by abortion. The rate of unintended pregnancy among women with incomes below the poverty line is 4 times the rate among women with the highest incomes (Wright & Katz, 2006). Women of color, who are disproportionately represented in the low-income group, must often spend a good deal of time raising the funds for an abortion because Medicaid is denied them, and this process of raising funds delays the abortion until the second trimester.

In some cases, women of color may have significantly less access to abortion (Nsiah-Jefferson, 1989). For example, American Indian women living on reservations are denied federal funding for abortions, and, to make matters worse, no Indian Health Service clinics or hospitals may perform abortions even when paid for with private funds. American Indian women can therefore be literally hundreds of miles away from access to an abortion.

The number of abortion providers in the United States has been slowly declining since 1982. Eighty-nine percent of counties in the United States have no known provider, and 38 percent of women of reproductive age live in these counties (Jones & Jerman, 2014). This means that, for millions of women, access to an abortion requires travel to another city, county, or state. Poor women, who are disproportionately women of color, are less likely to be able to afford such travel.

Abortion is only one example of ways in which people of color are disadvantaged under the present system of sex laws. This example illustrates clearly that efforts at sex-law reform need to include a consideration of the laws' impact on people of color (Figure 9).

Figure 9 It is important that women of color have the same access to abortion as middle-class White women.

©2004 Lisa Quinones/Black Star/Newscom

Sex and the Law in the Future

Nothing seems riskier than to try to predict with any degree of confidence how society's views of sex, and the laws that express those views, will develop and change. Thus any look ahead is at best a guess about what might happen, based on what has happened. Unforeseen events have a way of upsetting our calculations and introducing new variables into the mix.

Sex-Law Reform and Backlash

In the 2014 edition of this textbook, we stated that the movement toward more permissive sex laws, rooted in the civil rights movement, the sexual revolution, and feminism, had achieved virtually all the gains they were likely to make for some time. Then, in 2015, in *Obergefell v. Hodges,* the Supreme Court legalized gay marriage, and we had marriage equality, upending our prediction. But in 2017 Donald Trump became president and, as of this writing, has appointed two conservative justices to the Supreme Court, leading to the possibility of a backlash against the liberalization of sex laws. We are not even going to try to predict what might happen over the next 5 to 10 years. Instead, we consider two recent issues that are in need of more careful legal thought: AIDS and assisted reproductive technologies.

AIDS and the Law

The spread of AIDS (see the chapter "Sexually Transmitted Infections") has created some challenging legal issues. Government has two very important responsibilities with respect to HIV infection and those who suffer from it. On one hand, the state is obligated to protect individual rights and defend its citizens from discrimination and injustice. On the other hand, it is equally obligated to protect the health and welfare of the population. AIDS is a tragic case in which these two obligations can be in severe conflict.

Protection of individual rights poses a thorny problem. To have AIDS, or even to be thought to have the disease, has caused many people to be fired from their jobs, divorced parents to lose custody or visitation rights, people to lose health insurance coverage or even to be deprived of medical care, and children to be barred from attending school. People with AIDS (PWA) have also endured all sorts of informal harassment and discrimination. However, federal regulations, laws in some states, and ordinances in some counties and cities prohibit discrimination against PWA or those who are thought to have AIDS.

Individuals who experience discrimination because they are HIV positive or they have AIDS can seek protection under several federal laws. The Vocational Rehabilitation Act of 1973 prohibits discrimination against disabled persons in employment, transportation, and access to public and health services. The Fair Housing Act of 1988 prohibits discrimination in housing practices against disabled individuals and their families. The Americans with Disabilities Act of 1990 prohibits discrimination in employment and places of public accommodation on the basis of disability. In 1998 the U.S. Supreme Court ruled that HIV infection is a disability covered by these statutes, even if the person is asymptomatic.

A major issue concerning HIV and AIDS is the confidentiality of test results and medical records. Most states have laws protecting the confidentiality of antibody test records. Persons with positive tests have a reasonable fear of suffering some or all of the discriminatory actions listed above (Schatz, 1987). Some legal scholars argue that the constitutional right to privacy should protect the records of individuals infected with HIV. Still, positive test results need to be disclosed to medical care providers so they can provide the necessary treatment. In at least half of the states, physicians have the discretion to notify sexual partners of those who test positive for the virus (Burris, 1993). Laws in all 50 states require that names of people with AIDS be reported to local or state health authorities (HIV CLAPP, 2004).

With regard to protecting the population,

An analysis by CDC and Department of Justice researchers found that, by 2011, a total of 67 laws explicitly focused on persons living with HIV had been enacted in 33 states. These laws vary as to what behaviors are criminalized or result in additional penalties. In 24 states, laws require persons who are aware that they have HIV to disclose their status to sexual partners and 14 states require disclosure to needle-sharing partners. Twenty-five states criminalize one or more behaviors that pose a low or negligible risk for HIV transmission. (Lehman et al., 2014)

Researchers examined arrests for HIV-related crimes in Nashville, Tennessee, from 2000 to 2010 (Galletly & Lazzarini, 2013). There were 52 arrests; most involved sexual behavior, and in only three cases were there allegations of transmission of the virus. More than one-half of the arrests involved behavior associated with minimal or no risk of transmission. An effort to collect comprehensive data on HIV-related arrests focused on 19 states (Hernandez, 2013). Researchers were able to obtain complete, non-duplicated records for 1,352 cases since 2003, involving at least 428 people. Of the 751 cases where the outcome was known, 72 percent resulted in a conviction.

The Legal Challenge of Assisted Reproductive Technologies

Very complex legal questions are being raised by the proliferation of techniques enabling previously infertile people, and others, to have children. These include artificial insemination, in vitro fertilization (IVF), surrogate motherhood, and various kinds of embryo fertilization and transfer (see the chapter "Pregnancy and Childbirth").

There are few state laws on the subject. There are, however, in all jurisdictions, laws prohibiting trafficking in children ("baby buying"); some argue that these laws prohibit surrogacy. Twenty-seven states have laws regulating artificial insemination. Fifteen states have laws that prohibit cloning for reproductive purposes; six of these states also prohibit therapeutic cloning, or cloning for research purposes (National Conference of State Legislatures, 2008). There are few federal standards. In March 2004 the President's Council on Bioethics issued a report whose General Conclusion states that "**there is no uniform, comprehensive, and enforceable system of data collection, monitoring, or oversight for the biotechnologies affecting human reproduction** [emphasis in original]. The present system is a patchwork of federal, state, and professional self-regulation." One legal scholar refers to this situation as "a kind of legal 'wild west'" (Kindregan Jr., 2011). One result of the lack of such a system is a number of contentious, highly publicized lawsuits. The fact that these cases are controversial reflects the deep emotions many people feel about reproduction, especially those who have struggled to overcome infertility.

A fundamental difficulty is that these technologies bring a very public quality to what has always been one of the most private of all human activities, the conception of children. Some of them involve a third party—as a donor of sperm, egg, embryo, or uterus—in what had been a matter solely between a man and a woman. Even the nomenclature is complicated. In this section we adopt the convention of designating as *parent(s)* the person(s) who rear the child and accept legal responsibility for them. Those who provide some necessary aspect of the process we call *donors,* or in the special case of women in whose uteruses embryos are implanted, *surrogates.* In the absence of clear legislation or case law, we are mostly able to point to the questions raised.

Perhaps the foremost question is whether there is a fundamental right to reproduce (Panitch, 2015; Quigley, 2010). If there is, it is hard to argue against the use of an appropriate technique to achieve that end, including third-party participation, or what some call *collaborative conception.* On the other hand, if there is no such fundamental right, it may be reasonable to limit or even prohibit the use of such technology. There is a well-established right *not* to conceive under the right to privacy. A Washington State appeals court, in a case involving custody of *pre-embryos,* ruled that there is no right to procreate, but there is a right not to procreate.

Closely related is the question of the legal status of an embryo because in several of these techniques fertilization and conception take place outside the uterus. Is the embryo a *person* (Mohamed, 2018)? Those who assert that life begins at conception would accord full personhood and legal rights to the embryo from the first cell division. Some states have enacted laws aimed at protecting embryos. For example, a Louisiana law specifies that an embryo, even outside anyone's body, is a person and shall not intentionally be destroyed (Andrews, 1989). At the other extreme are those who regard an embryo merely as tissue, to be disposed of at will. This view puts no limits on reproductive technologies. A moderate view sees the embryo as less than a person but more than mere tissue and argues that it should be treated with the respect due potential human life. This view would seem to lead to some regulation of reproductive technology short of prohibition (Robertson, 1986).

The question of *disposition of embryos* that have not been implanted also arises (Kindregan Jr., 2011). Many physicians and clinics providing infertility services require clients to sign in advance an agreement about the disposition of unused embryos under various contingencies. Nevertheless, signers of these agreements have changed their minds, or divorced, and have challenged the agreement in court. Several of these cases have been highly publicized; one is *Roman v. Roman* (2006), a Texas case. The agreement specified that, in case of divorce, unused embryos should be discarded, but the judge in the divorce case 2 years later ruled the embryos were community property and awarded them to Amanda Roman. Randy Roman appealed, and the appellate court ruled, following the lead of courts in several other states, that contract law prevails and the agreement should be enforced. Cases involving disputes over embryos will increase dramatically because there are hundreds of thousands of frozen embryos in storage (Kindregan Jr., 2011).

Another complex of questions is to be found in the matter of *parental rights,* responsibilities, and kinship. When a child is born as a result of these techniques, who exactly are the parents? One commentator notes that there can be five: an egg donor, a sperm donor, the donor of a uterus for all or part of the gestation, and the couple who rear the child (Shapiro, 1986, p. 54) (see Figure 10). Issues of parental rights and responsibilities are especially complex in cases where a couple (regardless of gender) arrange and pay for assisted reproduction, and subsequently separate or divorce. Custody battles, contested visitation rights, and financial responsibility for the child have generated many court cases, involving not only the couple but donors and the

Figure 10   The law has not yet dealt adequately with the consequences of assisted reproductive technologies, as this cartoon indicates.

surrogate as well. It is likely that they will continue to do so (Schwartz, 2003).

Surrogacy and surrogacy contracts raise particularly complex issues, especially if the woman has contributed not only her uterus but an egg as well (Allen, 2018; Feldman, 2018). A man who donates his sperm to a sperm bank renounces any right to further contact with children who may be conceived; however, no equivalent principles have been established for women who donate eggs or a uterus. Some have raised the concern that commercializing reproduction is inherently corrupting and should be prohibited because it turns children into commodities (Almeling, 2011). Surrogacy contracts involve $4 billion in the United States (Allen, 2018). Some are concerned that surrogacy may lead to the exploitation of low-income women, who will "rent" their wombs because they need the money, despite the possible psychological stresses and health risks of surrogate motherhood (Feldman, 2018). As of 2007, 18 states had laws governing surrogacy. Two states ban all such contracts. Two states void any such contract, and provide fines for any party to a contract. Four states void such contracts; two prohibit some contracts but allow others. Eight states allow and regulate contracts. This variation clearly illustrates the lack of uniform laws in this area (Arons, 2007).

Taking a broad perspective, there are a number of alternatives for legal approaches to the issue of surrogacy (Andrews, 1989). The most restrictive one is to outlaw all surrogacy contracts for pay, as four states do. A second alternative is to have courts scrutinize all surrogacy contracts referred to as pre-birth orders, to ensure, for example, that the woman has not been coerced. Four states currently require judicial preauthorization. Some proposed laws require that a mental health professional interview all participants—surrogate, egg donor, sperm donor, potential rearing parents—to be sure that all are truly giving informed consent. Another alternative, to address the concern that the surrogate may be exploited, is to require that surrogates have their own legal counsel when they enter into a contract; two state laws include that requirement. Some suggest that all surrogacy arrangements and contracts should be handled by nonprofit agencies, as adoptions are, to discourage profit making. Another possibility is to declare surrogacy to be a special case of adoption. That is, the surrogate is treated the same as any other birth mother who arranges to give her child up for adoption. This ensures that she has a period of 6 weeks or so after the birth to decide whether she wants to keep the baby, and it clearly establishes whose baby it is.

A final possibility, at the other end of the spectrum, is that the government stay out of this matter entirely, on the grounds that this is a private matter between the people involved. We don't see this as a viable option because contested surrogacy cases have been reaching the courts and the government is already involved. It would be far better to have well-thought-out legislation on this matter to provide guidance and reduce the number of painful contested cases.

Finally, a host of procedural issues will inevitably arise if any of these reproductive techniques become legally permitted and regulated. What will the standards of confidentiality be, especially with regard to the identity of nonparent donors? If something goes wrong during one of these procedures—and they are risky—who is liable? Who will take responsibility for a child with a severe birth defect born through one of these techniques? Who will bear the expense? Must insurance companies pay for artificial insemination, IVF, embryo transfer, or even surrogacy? Should such procedures be covered under Medicaid for the poor? Many more such questions will develop in the future.

Underlying all these issues are the following root questions: What is the government's interest, if any, in human reproduction, and how should it be expressed? What procedures should be used to put into law society's concerns, if this is not deemed to be a strictly private matter? And, above all, who is to decide these issues? The legislatures and courts have shown a marked disinclination to enter this field, but evasion cannot remain a viable strategy much longer.

Our discussion of legal regulation of ART presumes passage and enforcement of state and federal laws and regulations to prevent abuses and harm. An alternative approach was suggested by Goodwin (2010), the use of tort law to redress harms after the fact. ART procedures are risky, and can result in various temporary or permanent physical (and emotional) harms to donors, surrogates, or those commissioning the conception. ART procedures also can result in harm to offspring, through multiple births, premature birth, low birth weight, and disabilities (see the chapter "Pregnancy and Childbirth"). Tort law enables a person harmed, in this case by "intentional and negligent conception," to seek damages. For example, a donor or surrogate who suffers physical damage (e.g., to reproductive organs) can sue the physician, infertility clinic, and others involved in their care. Children who experience harmful outcomes could sue the providers, or their parents. The virtue of this approach is that it focuses on those who are best able to prevent risks, and so it might make them more cautious, reducing the incidence of harm. The downside is, it is after the fact in the cases involved and places the responsibility for and cost of seeking redress on the individual.

Critical THINKing Skill
Using evidence to evaluate legal issues

In this chapter, we have summarized a wide variety of laws that attempt to regulate sexual conduct, and numerous constitutional and legal issues related to these laws. Most laws regulating sexuality are state or local laws, which means that you as a citizen have the opportunity to influence these laws and sometimes vote on them, or on the lawmakers who vote for them. As a citizen, you can make your views known by writing to your legislator or speaking up at a hearing on a law. Millions of dollars are often spent in advertising to influence your views. You need all of your critical thinking skills to evaluate the information and reach a reasoned decision based on evidence rather than emotion.

We can distinguish between legal evidence and scientific evidence, both of which are relevant when evaluating legal issues. Legal evidence includes the U.S. Constitution, state and local laws, and decisions by courts such as the U.S. Supreme Court, federal courts, and state courts. Scientific evidence, in contrast, encompasses data collected by scientists, with findings that can be replicated and maybe even have been meta-analyzed.

Transgender rights are at the forefront of legal work today. The Transgender Law Center is a national organization that works for civil rights for trans people (https://transgenderlawcenter.org/). The following is an interesting case in which they participated.

In *Conover v. Conover,* in the state of Maryland, Michael (a transgender man) and Brittany Conover separated one year after Brittany gave birth to their son, Jaxon. They were married as a same-sex couple a few months after Jaxon was born. When filing for divorce, Brittany said that she was Jaxon's only legal parent because Michael was not legally male and also because Jaxon had not been born during the marriage. The courts ruled in Brittany's favor and held that Michael was not a legal parent of Jaxon. Michael appealed to the Maryland Court of Appeals. The opposition lawyer filed a brief that contained offensive material about transgender parents and argued that trans people are unfit to be parents because their children will suffer from being called names and shunned. The Transgender Law Center filed a brief supporting Michael and rebutting the anti-trans arguments made by Brittany's lawyer. You can read more at https://transgenderlawcenter.org/legal/family-law. The court found in favor of Michael.

What are the legal issues in this case? That is, what kind of legal evidence is relevant? What are the scientific issues in this case? What kind of scientific evidence is relevant? Answer these questions before you proceed.

One fundamental legal issue is whether trans people have the same rights as everyone else. Do they have equal rights, in this case to be a parent? As it happened, Maryland had enacted legislation in 2014, the Fairness for all Marylanders Act, that prohibits discrimination on the basis of gender identity in areas such as employment and housing. Moreover, a number of federal court rulings have established that U.S. civil rights laws prohibit discrimination against transgender people.

Brittany's lawyer also made an argument that should be decided by scientific evidence: Do children with a transgender parent suffer because of teasing and rejection by peers? Research on transgender topics in psychology is so new that we don't have many studies on children with a transgender parent, but the situation is quite similar to the one of children with LGB parents. This research, discussed in the chapter "Sexual Orientation: Gay, Straight, or Bi?," shows that, contrary to many people's intuitions, children with LGB parents fare as well psychologically as children of straight parents. It seems likely that this is true of children of trans parents, but we need the data.

To think critically about legal issues, it is important to distinguish between legal evidence and scientific evidence.

SUMMARY

Why Are There Sex Laws?

Laws to protect adults from coercion, children from sexual exploitation, and the public from offensive behavior are justifiable. However, many laws against sexual conduct originated in a desire to promote public morality and perpetuate sexism, and it is hard to justify them.

What Kinds of Sex Laws Are There?

The laws governing sexual conduct include laws against crimes of exploitation and force (such as rape, carnal knowledge of a juvenile, and child molestation), against various consensual acts (such as fornication and adultery), against offending public taste (exhibitionism, voyeurism, solicitation, disorderly conduct, lewdness, and the like), against behaviors involved in reproduction (contraception and abortion), and against criminal commercial sex (notably prostitution and obscenity). These laws are often capriciously enforced, and this unequal enforcement has high social costs that may require reform.

Discriminatory Laws Related to Sexuality

Gay, lesbian, bisexual, and transgender people have been subjected to discrimination for decades. Some laws and government policies encourage or allow discriminatory practices. To counteract these practices, some states and municipalities have enacted laws prohibiting discrimination in housing and employment. Current court cases are testing whether the ban on sex discrimination (Title VII of the Civil Rights Act) will be applied to transgender people. A related issue is the controversy over same-sex marriage. The U.S. Supreme Court resolved the issue in 2015 in a decision that same-sex couples have a legal right to marry, and that every state must recognize same-sex marriages performed in other states.

Trends in Sex-Law Reform

Certain trends can be discerned in the reform of restrictive sex laws. The American Model Penal Code included proposals to decriminalize consensual sexual behavior. The legal principle that has accounted for much court action to reform laws against contraception and abortion is the right to privacy. The constitutional principle of equal protection has been used to combat discrimination against groups identified by their sexual conduct, including gays and lesbians. Legislators have been influenced by the movement for the decriminalization of victimless crimes; recently, however, critics have challenged the argument that no one is harmed by prostitution or adultery. The issue of pornography and obscenity, which includes such problems as definition, conflicting societal values, and actual demonstration of effects, generally involves First Amendment rights to freedom of speech. The latest controversy is over the availability of X-rated goods and services on the Internet. Abortion remains a volatile and highly controversial matter. Hundreds of state laws have been enacted in the attempt to restrict a woman's right to an abortion; some have succeeded and some have been overturned by the Supreme Court.

Sex and the Law in the Future

Sex-law reform moved more slowly in the 1990s and early 21st century than it did in the previous decades, and there are signs of a conservative backlash, yet in 2015 same-sex marriage was legalized in the United States. In the future, the law will need to balance individual rights and the public interest when it comes to issues such as assisted reproductive technologies.

SUGGESTIONS FOR FURTHER READING

Almeling, Rene. (2011). *Sex cells: The medical market for eggs and sperm.* Berkeley, CA: The University of California Press. A multimethod study (interviews, ethnography) of the commodification of eggs and sperm due to demand for ART. Almeling describes the gendered nature of the market for human reproductive cells.

Messer, Ellen, and May, Kathryn E. (1988). *Backrooms: Voices from the illegal abortion era.* New York: St. Martin's Press. This book is based on interviews with 24 women, all of whom had unwanted pregnancies before *Roe v. Wade.* The women tell the stories of their illegal abortions and the consequences. It is important reading, especially for those who have grown up in the era of legal abortions.

Design Elements: A Sexually Diverse World icon (hands): ©Shutterstock/Dragon Images; First Person icon (people with arms crossed): ©Image Source/Getty Images; Milestones in Sex Research icon (survey): ©Ravi Tahilramani/Getty Images

Are YOU Curious?

1. Why don't all parents provide sex education for their kids?
2. What kinds of sex education programs work?

Read this epilogue to find out.

EPILOGUE

©Creatas/PunchStock

Looking to the Future: Sexuality Education

As we look to the future, a top priority for society has to be comprehensive sexuality education. If you have studied this textbook, you should be prepared to be a good sexuality educator for your own children. You should also be a well-informed citizen who can make thoughtful decisions about sexuality education. Sexuality education, of course, can occur in many settings: home, school, church, mosque, temple, or synagogue, youth programs, relationships, or via information found on the Internet.

In the Home, in the School, or Somewhere Else?

When parents of children and teenagers get together to urge their school system to adopt a sexuality education curriculum, sometimes some citizens of the community raise a protest. They might say that sexuality education promotes promiscuity, teenage pregnancy, or AIDS, and

Table 1   Sources of Information about Sex

How much do children your age find out about sex from:	Percentage Saying "A Lot"	
	Children 10–12	Teens 13–15
Mothers	38%	38%
TV, movies, other entertainment	38	61
Schools and teachers	38	44
Fathers	34	—
Friends	31	64
The Internet	—	40

Source: From Nickelodeon/Talking with Kids: "Talking with Kids about Tough Issues: A National Survey of Parents and Kids," The Kaiser Family Foundation, 2001.

they are sure that it should take place only in the home (or possibly the church), but certainly not in the schools.

What these citizens overlook is the realistic alternative to sexuality education in the schools. Among children aged 10 to 12, at least one-third do get information about sex from their parents (see Table 1). Notice that two frequently mentioned sources in both age groups are TV and magazines; among teens, friends are also an important source. In many cases the information provided about sexuality on TV is sensationalized and unrealistic. Relying on friends for information is a classic case of the blind leading the blind. Teens are increasingly turning to the Internet for information about sex. More than 50 percent of seventh- to twelfth-graders report that they have searched for health information online (Rideout et al., 2010). Asked how they learn about sex, teens say "I Google it." Unfortunately, sexual health websites often contain inaccurate information; one study of 177 sites found that 46 percent of those discussing contraception and 35 percent of those discussing abortion contained inaccurate information (Buhi et al., 2010). One of the best websites is www.mayoclinic.org, and ICYC—In Case You're Curious, a text-chat program run by Rocky Mountain Planned Parenthood. Possibly the worst source? Pornography; some teens say they got their information from watching porn on the Internet. So people who say that sexuality education should be carried out in the home, not the school, are not making a realistic argument. Research does show that parent–child sexual communication can make a difference. According to a meta-analysis of relevant studies, more parent–adolescent sexual communication is linked to adolescents engaging in safer sex behavior, including contraception and use of condoms (Widman et al., 2016).

There are two reasons many parents do not provide more explicit education to their children. First, many people are embarrassed about discussing sexuality. We see few models of how to have an explicit, matter-of-fact discussion; we are much more likely to see people discussing sex indirectly, with euphemisms and innuendo, or telling dirty jokes. Second, there are a number of things about sexuality that many adults do not know. Many did not have good sexuality education themselves, and they may be painfully aware of their ignorance.

Surveys consistently find that a large majority of adults in the United States and Canada favor sexuality education in the schools. For example, a telephone survey of a nationally representative sample in the United States found that 93 percent of the parents of seventh- and eighth-graders and 91 percent of parents of ninth- through twelfth-graders said it is "very important" or "important" that sexuality education be part of the school curriculum (Kaiser Family Foundation, 2004a). A survey of parents of seventh- through twelfth-graders found that the great majority favored teaching children about AIDS and other sexually transmitted infections, premarital sex, birth control, abortion, and homosexuality (Kaiser Family Foundation, 2000). The point is that there is strong support for comprehensive sexuality education in the schools, beginning at least when children are 12 years old or in sixth or seventh grade (Constantine et al., 2007). Despite this high level of public support, a minority continue to try to push sexuality education out of the schools (Fields & Tolman, 2006).

Why don't all parents provide sex education for their kids?

You may be surprised to learn that most adults favor sexuality education. The media regularly publicize controversies, cases in which parents are protesting sexuality education in the schools. There are three things to keep in mind about such cases. First, they are rare. The vast majority of schools with sexuality education programs have not experienced such conflict (Kaiser Family Foundation, 2004b). Second, the protestors are usually in a minority. In a case in Wisconsin, protestors packed a school board meeting and the board voted to delay implementation of a program. A subsequent survey of all the parents in the district found that 71 percent approved and only 18 percent disapproved of the program. Third, the controversy is often not over whether there should be a program but over the use of a particular curriculum, book, or video. A review of 546 controversies between 1993 and 2013 found that in the 1990s, conflicts often involved abstinence-only programs, elementary school programs, and whether programs should be required. Since 2001, controversies have shifted increasingly to comprehensive programs and to issues involving school policies and programs as they relate to LGBTQ students (Rosen & Conklin, 2014).

Sexuality education in the schools is not "instead of" education in the home. In a Kaiser Family Foundation survey, 88 percent of the parents of seventh- and eighth-graders and 80 percent of the parents of ninth- through twelfth-graders agreed that having a program in the school makes it easier to talk to their children about sexual issues (Kaiser Family Foundation, 2004a). Some sexuality education programs actively involve parents by including homework to be done jointly by parent and child. The evaluation of one program of this type found that students receiving classroom instruction plus homework felt more able to refuse high-risk behaviors and more often intended to delay the initiation of intercourse compared to students receiving only classroom instruction (Blake et al., 2001). The homework assignments, which appeared to reinforce the school-based program, resulted in greater parent–child communication about sex.

Standards for Sexuality Education

The Sexuality Information and Education Council of the United States (SIECUS), in partnership with Advocates for Youth and Answer, established the Future of Sex Education (FoSE) Initiative to develop and disseminate standards for comprehensive and responsible sexuality education. The result is *National Sexuality Education Standards: Core Content and Skills,* which is available online (Future of Sex Education Initiative, 2012). The standards were developed in partnership with major national school health and education organizations. Seven topics are identified as the minimum, essential content: anatomy and physiology, puberty and adolescent development, identity, pregnancy and reproduction, sexually transmitted diseases and HIV, healthy relationships, and personal safety.

There are eight National Health Education standards:

1. Students will comprehend concepts related to health promotion and disease prevention.
2. Students will analyze the influence of family, peers, culture, media, technology, and other factors on health behaviors.
3. Students will demonstrate the ability to access valid information and products and services to enhance health.
4. Students will demonstrate the ability to use interpersonal communication skills to enhance health and avoid or reduce health risks.
5. Students will demonstrate the ability to use decision-making skills to enhance health.
6. Students will demonstrate the ability to use goal-setting skills to enhance health.
7. Students will demonstrate the ability to practice health-enhancing behaviors and avoid or reduce health risks.
8. Students will demonstrate the ability to advocate for personal, family, and community health.
(Future of Sex Education Initiative, 2012, p. 11)

Each of these involves learning specific information and developing attitudes, values, and skills.

What to Teach at Different Ages

Sexuality education is not something that can be carried out in one week during fifth grade. Like teaching math, it is a process that must begin when children are young. They should learn simple concepts first, progressing to more difficult ones as they grow older. What is taught at any particular age depends on the child's sexual behavior (see the chapter "Sexuality and the Life Cycle: Childhood and Adolescence"), sexual knowledge, and sexual interests at that age. This section concentrates on theories and research that provide information on the last two points.

Children's Sexual Knowledge

A few researchers have investigated what children know about sex and reproduction at various ages. For example, children begin to develop an understanding of pregnancy and birth at a very early age. Very young children may believe that a baby has always existed: that it existed somewhere else before it got inside the mother. The following dialogue demonstrates this:

(How did the baby happen to be in your Mommy's tummy?) It just grows inside. (How did it get there?) It's there all the time. Mommy doesn't have to do anything. She waits until she feels it. (You said that the baby wasn't in there when you were there.) Yeah, then he was in the other place . . . in America. (In America?) Yeah, in somebody else's tummy. (Bernstein & Cowan, 1975, p. 86)

By age 7 or 8, children have a more sophisticated understanding of reproduction. They may know that three things are involved in making a baby: a social relationship

Table 2   Responses of 9-Year-Olds in Four Cultures in the Goldman Study

	Percentage of Correct Answers Among			
Concept	Australians	British	North Americans	Swedish
Knowing physical sex differences of newborn babies	60	35	23	40
Knowing correct terms for the genitals	50	33	20	—*
Knowing length of gestation is 8 to 10 months	45	32	30	67
Knowing that one purpose of coitus is enjoyment	6	10	4	60
Knowing the meaning of the term "uterus"	0	0	0	23

*Owing to the difficulties of translating from the Swedish language, this percentage is not available.

Source: Goldman & Goldman (1982), pp. 197, 213, 240, 263, 354.

between two people, such as love or marriage; sexual intercourse; and the union of sperm and egg. At age 12, some children can give a good physiological explanation of reproduction that includes the idea that the embryo begins its biological existence at the moment of conception and is the product of genetic material from both parents. As one preteen explained,

> The sperm encounters one ovum, and one sperm breaks into the ovum which produces, the sperm makes like a cell, and the cell separates and divides. And so it's dividing, and the ovum goes through a tube and embeds itself in the wall of the, I think it's the fetus of the woman. (Bernstein & Cowan, 1975, p. 89)

These findings have important implications for sexuality education. Educators need to be aware of the level of children's understanding and should not inundate them with information inappropriate for their age. Instead, the educator should attempt to clarify misunderstandings in the child's beliefs. For example, if a child believes a baby has always existed, the educator might say, "To make a baby, you need two grown-ups: a man and a woman."

Probably the most comprehensive study of children's sexual knowledge was conducted by Ronald and Juliette Goldman (1982), who did a massive cross-cultural study of children's understanding of sexual matters. From their results, they concluded that American children are sexual illiterates! The Goldmans did face-to-face interviews with children aged 5, 7, 9, 11, 13, and 15 in four cultures: Australia, England, North America, and Sweden. The Swedish sample is particularly interesting because there is compulsory sexuality education for all children in Swedish schools, beginning at age 8. The Goldmans questioned children only about sexual concepts, not about their own sexual behavior.

A comparison of the results from the North American children with those from children in the other three cultures led the Goldmans to conclude that American children are strikingly lacking in sexual information. Some of the results are shown in Table 2. Notice, for example, that only 23 percent of North American 9-year-olds, but

60 percent of Australian 9-year-olds, knew the genital differences between newborn baby boys and girls. The Swedish children were consistently more knowledgeable than the American children, indicating the positive effects of sexuality education.

Some of the children's responses can only be classified as amusing. In response to the question "How can anyone know a newborn baby is a boy or a girl?" an 11-year-old English boy said, "If it's got a penis or not. If it has it's a boy. Girls have a virginia." And in all cultures there seems to be a lot of confusion about contraception. Here are some responses:

> The pill goes down the stomach and dissolves the baby and it goes out in the bowels. You should take three pills a day. (American boy, 7 years old)

> If you don't want to start one, you don't get married. There's no other way. (English girl, 7 years old)

> The tubes are tied, the vocal cords. (Australian girl, 15 years old)

If the Goldmans' conclusion is right, that American children are sexual illiterates, the remedy seems to be a massive program of sexuality education in the United States.

In another study, the sexual knowledge of preschool children in the United States was assessed by interviewing 2- to 6-year-olds (Volbert, 2000). The results indicated that sexual knowledge evolves during the preschool years. At age 2, children can identify the sex of others, and use slang to refer to genitals. At age 3, children explain gender differences using cultural characteristics (clothing, earings). At age 5, children explain gender identity based on genital differences; and at age 6, children have some knowledge of vaginal or cesarean birth.

Another, more recent study replicated parts of the Goldmans' research (Caron & Ahlgrim, 2012). Children from the United States still lagged behind in knowledge compared with their peers from other nations. A few children in the sample demonstrated much greater knowledge than others; they were from Sweden and the Netherlands.

An analysis of questions e-mailed to a reproductive health website found that 23 percent involved misconceptions about reproduction (Wynn et al., 2009). The authors suggest that poor sex education and confusing media messages are two causes.

Children's Sexual Interests

Children's knowledge of and interest in sex are reflected in the questions they ask. At age 5, kids may be asking where babies come from. At age 9, a child may ask about sexual behaviors, as for instance, "What's oral sex?" Such questions are often stimulated by hearing the term in conversation or in the media. A 10-year-old may be interested in bodily processes and ask, "What's a period?" By age 11, many children are asking questions related to puberty, such as, "When will I get breasts?" or "When will I grow taller?" Such questions typically reflect an awareness that other youth are experiencing such growth. At age 13 or 14, many youth have specific questions about sexual activity. One boy asked, "Do girls move a lot when they have sex?" (Blake, 2004). It is important that the sexuality education curriculum for a particular age group address the questions of that age group rather than questions members of that age group haven't thought of yet or questions they thought about but answered long ago.

High school students agree that sexuality education should begin in early elementary school and progress from the simple to the complex (Eisenberg et al., 1997). They believe that the ideal class should cover a wide range of topics, including reproduction, pregnancy, abortion, birth control options, disease prevention, sexual violence, relationships and gender roles, and values. They would like all these topics presented by eighth grade. A British survey of people between ages 16 and 24 found that school was the most commonly reported source of information about sexuality (reported by 39 percent of men, 41 percent of women). Respondents said they wanted more information (than they had received) about psychosocial issues (sexual activities, how to say "No," sexual feelings and emotions) and sexually transmitted infections (Wise, 2015).

The Curriculum

The term *sexuality education* has been used to refer to a wide variety of programs. At one end of the continuum are programs that involve showing children one or two videos and distributing some brochures. At the other end are well-developed curricula that include lectures, books, videos, and classroom discussion presented over 4 to 6 weeks. We focus on the more substantial programs. They can be grouped into three categories: abstinence-only programs, HIV/AIDS risk reduction, and comprehensive sexuality education.

Abstinence-Only Programs

Abstinence-only programs developed out of opposition to sexuality education in the schools. The concerns led to passage by the U.S. Congress of the Adolescent Family Life Act in 1981; the AFLA limited the use of federal funds to **abstinence-only programs,** programs that "promoted sexual abstinence as the sole means of preventing pregnancy and exposure to sexually transmitted diseases" (Wilcox & Wyatt, 1997, p. 4). By 2018, more than $2 billion in federal funds had been spent on abstinence-only programs (Boyer, 2018). In 1994 Congress attempted to mandate that all sexuality education in the United States be abstinence-only; this effort failed because at least four federal laws prohibit the federal government from prescribing local curricular standards (Advocates for Youth, 2004a).

There are a number of well-developed abstinence-only curricula. The most widely known is *Sex Respect* which represents a politically conservative approach to sexuality education. Federally funded, it is targeted at middle-school students. The major goal of this curriculum is to teach that abstinence is the only approach that is moral and safe. The curriculum uses cartoons and other attention-grabbing techniques. There are catchy slogans for children to chant in class, such as

Don't be a louse, wait for your spouse!
Do the right thing, wait for the ring!
Pet your dog, not your date!

Students take a "chastity pledge," and the curriculum includes a chart of physical intimacy in which a prolonged kiss is characterized as the "beginning of danger." The curriculum teaches that condoms can be the road to ruin because many fail, resulting in pregnancy.

Sex Respect throws in a lot of gender-role stereotypes as well, characterizing boys as "sexual aggressors" and girls as "virginity protectors." It presents the two-parent, heterosexual couple as "the sole model of a healthy, real family."

In fairness to *Sex Respect,* it may have some good points in that it teaches students skills in resisting peer pressure. On the other hand, it includes a lot of "facts" that are really misinformation (for example, it says that condoms frequently fail, but they actually have a very low failure rate—see Table 2 in the chapter "Contraception and Abortion"), and it seems out of touch with today's teenagers. The widespread adoption of this curriculum points out how important it is for parents to examine the sexuality education materials being presented to their children.

How effective are these curricula? Researchers who assessed the content of *Sex Respect* concluded that it omits a number of important topics, including sexual anatomy (!), sexual physiology, sexual

Abstinence-only programs: Educational programs that promote sexual abstinence as the sole means of preventing pregnancy and exposure to sexually transmitted diseases.

response, contraception, and abortion (Goodson & Edmundson, 1994). As a result of their widespread use, there have been many evaluations of this program's effects on student attitudes and behavior. A review of 52 evaluations that meet minimum methodological standards concluded that "none of the best studies [by methodological criteria] found positive changes . . . in age of onset of sexual activity, rates of sexual activity, pregnancies, or STIs" (Wilcox & Wyatt, 1997, p. 13). A review of published randomized controlled trials (the "gold standard") of programs in high schools identified 16 such projects (Bennett & Assefi, 2005). The conclusion was the same: abstinence-only education was ineffective.

The federal Office of Adolescent Health reviewed the evidence for effectiveness of 36 Teen Pregnancy Prevention Programs (Office of Adolescent Health, n.d.; Goesling et al., 2015). The evaluation considered seven outcomes that such programs should achieve. The best of the abstinence-only programs show evidence of achieving only two of the seven, whereas there is evidence that the best of the comprehensive programs achieve four of them.

In fact, data indicate that an emphasis on abstinence-only curricula is associated with higher teen pregnancy rates (Stanger-Hall & Hall, 2011). The United States has the highest teen pregnancy rate of all the developed nations; abstinence-only sex education may be one reason.

In May 2015, a California judge ruled that the use of an abstinence-only-until-marriage curriculum violated state laws on the grounds of medical inaccuracy and bias. The ruling against the Clovis Unified School district resulted from a 5-year campaign by parents to halt the use of a program that provided misinformation about HIV/AIDS and did not mention condoms and contraceptives. The ruling illustrates the power of parental involvement in sex education in the schools (*American Academy of Pediatrics et al. v. Clovis Unified School District,* 2015).

The Politics of Sexuality Education

Many educators, social scientists, relevant professional organizations, and citizens have concluded that abstinence-only programs do not work and that the hundreds of millions of dollars being spent on them are a gross misuse of federal, state, and local funds. Advocates for Youth, joined by more than 77 national organizations, sent an open letter to President George W. Bush in 2002 asking him to end his support for, and requests to increase, funding for such programs. The American Civil Liberties Union petitioned Congress in March 2004 to oppose new funding for such programs. The American Psychological Association adopted a resolution in 2004 opposing reliance on such programs to

What kinds of sex education programs work?

provide sexuality education to youth. Finally, the results of a national poll of 1,050 adults found that 70 percent oppose the laws that restrict federal funds to abstinence-only programs (Advocates for Youth, 2004b). The Bush administration ignored these requests and the scientific and other evidence on which they are based. One White House insider, when asked how the president could ask for an additional $33 million for abstinence-only sexuality education when it is clear that it doesn't work, replied, "Values trump data" (Wingert, 2002).

The 2008 national elections changed the composition of Congress, resulting in less support for abstinence-only programs. Recognizing that they don't work, President Obama and congressional leaders called for an end to all funding for them. An appropriations bill passed by the House (269–153) in 2009 terminated funding and allocated $114 million for effective, evidence-based Teen Pregnancy Prevention programs (SIECUS, 2009). The TPP initiative, administered by the Office of Adolescent Health, was funded at $105 million in FY 2011 and FY 2012. As part of the health care reform package (Affordable Care Act, also known as Obamacare) passed by Congress in 2010, the Title V Abstinence Only program was reauthorized and provided $50 million per year for these ineffective programs. Title V is administered by the Administration for Children, Youth and Families.

Congress has continued to fund abstinence-only programs by providing funds to states for that purpose, as evidence (reviewed above) has continued to mount that these programs are not effective (Santelli et al., 2017). In 2015, Congress allocated $75 million per year for the Personal Responsibility Education Program (PREP), which funds comprehensive, medically accurate sex education programs. However, it also extended the funding for abstinence-only at the same funding level, $75 million per year (SIECUS, 2015). These actions contrast sharply with public desires for comprehensive sex education in the schools. A poll of 1,000 adults conducted in December 2014–January 2015 found that 66 percent supported providing information about birth control, including 59 percent of Republicans (Klein, 2015).

The latest twist is that the producers of abstinence-only programs, apparently realizing they have gotten a bad reputation, have rebranded them (Boyer, 2018). They are now called *sexual risk avoidance* programs, but they still teach abstinence and don't teach contraception and other crucial information. This new term is now used in federal legislation, which has been funding the programs enthusiastically since 2017, with the Trump presidency and conservatives in control of Congress.

HIV and AIDS Risk Education

In the 1990s the focus of sexuality education shifted from pregnancy prevention to AIDS and other STI prevention.

A Sampling from a Comprehensive Sexuality Education Curriculum

SIECUS, Advocates for Youth, and Answer partnered to form the Future of Sex Education Initiative (FoSE). Following a 2-day forum in 2008, several health education organizations and many individuals worked to develop a comprehensive set of standards (see "Standard for Sexuality Education," earlier in this chapter), Guiding Values and Principles, Theoretical Framework, and list of Topics and Key Indicators. The resulting curricular guidelines were published in 2011 (Future of Sex Education Initiative, 2012).

The guidelines identify seven key topics that should be taught:

1. Anatomy and physiology
2. Puberty and adolescent development
3. Identity (people's understanding of who they are)
4. Pregnancy and reproduction
5. Sexually transmitted diseases and HIV
6. Healthy relationships
7. Personal safety

These topics are considered essential content and skills for K–12 sexuality education.

We noted earlier that education should be geared to the developing child's interests and ability to comprehend. The guidelines define four grade levels and specify the learning outcomes to be achieved by the end of each.

Level 1: By the end of second grade (K–2)
Level 2: By the end of fifth grade (grades 3–5)
Level 3: By the end of eighth grade (grades 6–8)
Level 4: By the end of twelfth grade (grades 9–12)

The following is a sampling of the Core Concepts (Standard 1) identified by the guidelines to be learned at each level.

Key Topic 1: Anatomy and Physiology
Level 1. Use proper names for body parts, including male and female anatomy.

Level 2. Describe male and female reproductive systems, including body parts and their functions.

Level 3. Describe male and female sexual systems, including body parts and their functions.

Level 4. Describe the human sexual response cycle, including the role hormones play.

Key Topic 3: Identity
Level 1. Describe differences and similarities in how boys and girls may be expected to act.

Level 2. Define sexual orientation as the romantic attraction of an individual to someone of the same gender or a different gender.

Level 3. Differentiate between gender identity, gender expression, and sexual orientation.

Level 4. Differentiate between biological sex, sexual orientation, and gender identity and gender expression.

Key Topic 6: Healthy Relationships
Level 1. Identify different kinds of family structures. Describe the characteristics of a friend. Explain that all people, including children, have the right to tell others not to touch their body. Explain what bullying and teasing are, and why they are wrong.

Level 2. Describe the characteristics of healthy relationships.

Level 3. Numerous outcomes, including: Describe a range of ways people express affection in different kinds of relationships. Describe the potential impacts of power differences such as age, status, and position within relationships. Explain why a person who has been raped or sexually assaulted is not at fault.

The guidelines provide equally detailed outcomes for the other four key topics. There are also outcomes identified for each of the seven other standards in relation to each key topic. Obviously the guidelines are very comprehensive. The document includes a list of sources of printed materials, activities, and other aids for teachers to use to achieve these objectives.

A strong case has been made for education about HIV and AIDS in the schools (National Commission on AIDS, 1994). In 2015, 33 states and the District of Columbia required such educational programs (Guttmacher Institute, 2015a). In contrast, only 22 states and the District of Columbia required that sexuality education be taught. A 2003 Kaiser Family Foundation survey found that 99 percent of parents of seventh- and eighth-graders and 97 percent of the parents of high school students believe that such instruction is appropriate in the schools. HIV instruction may be presented alone, or in combination with either abstinence-only or comprehensive sexuality education programs.

Programs of this type are often sharply focused on disease prevention. They have a variety of goals, including challenging myths about AIDS and other STIs, encouraging delay of sexual intercourse, and supporting condom use or abstinence from unprotected intercourse. These programs are usually short, lasting as few as five class periods.

A review of the effectiveness of these programs found that they improved knowledge significantly (Kim et al., 1997). In addition, many studies reported positive changes in respondents' intention to use condoms.

According to the Guttmacher Institute (2012), in 2006–2008, 93 percent of 15- to 19-year-olds had received formal instruction about STIs, 89 percent about HIV, and 84 percent about abstinence. One-fourth of adolescents ages 15 to 19 received abstinence-only education with no instruction about birth control. In 2006, 87 percent of public and private high schools taught abstinence as the most effective method to avoid pregnancy and STIs in required health education courses.

Comprehensive, Theoretically Based Programs

The alternative to abstinence-only education is comprehensive sexuality education, which refers to programs that provide scientifically accurate, comprehensive information about sexuality, including anatomy, contraception, STIs, and the use of condoms. It teaches that sexuality is a normal, healthy part of life, and it teaches interpersonal and communication skills. A number of programs are comprehensive and are explicitly based on social science theories of health promotion, including the Health Belief Model, social inoculation theory, and social learning theory. The curriculum described in the box "A Sampling from a Comprehensive Sexuality Education Curriculum" is of this type. The best known of these curricula are *Postponing Sexual Involvement* and *Reducing the Risk*. These programs include discussion of the social pressures to engage in sex and provide ways to resist these influences (based on inoculation theory). Social learning theory emphasizes the importance of practicing new skills, so these curricula include rehearsal and role-playing activities.

In light of the high levels of teenage pregnancy, and the sharp increases in rates of STIs among people 15 to 24 years of age, it is imperative that we identify sexuality education programs that are effective in reducing risky sexual behavior. At the request of the U.S. Centers for Disease Control and Prevention, a number of researchers undertook a thorough review of the research on the effectiveness of school-based programs (Kirby et al., 1994). They identified six characteristics that, according to the scientific evidence, are associated with delaying the initiation of intercourse, reducing the frequency of intercourse, reducing the number of sexual partners, and increasing the use of condoms and other contraceptives. In general, these are characteristic of the comprehensive programs.

Effective programs focus on reducing risk-taking behavior. Such programs have a small number of specific goals. They do not emphasize general issues such as gender equality and dating.

Effective programs are based on theories of social learning. Programs that utilize theory in designing the curriculum are more effective than nontheoretical programs. The theories suggest that, to be effective, the program must increase knowledge, elicit or increase motivation to protect oneself, demonstrate that specific behaviors will protect the person, and teach the person how to use those behaviors effectively.

Effective programs teach through experiential activities that personalize the messages. Such programs avoid lectures and videos; instead, they use small group discussions, simulation and games, role playing, rehearsal, and similar educational techniques. Some of these programs rely on peer educators.

Effective programs address media and other social influences that encourage sexual risk-taking behaviors. Some programs look at how the media use sex to sell products. All the effective programs analyze the "lines" that young people use to try to get someone else to engage in sex, and teach ways of responding to these approaches.

Effective programs reinforce clear and appropriate values. These programs are not value-free. They emphasize the values of postponing sex and avoiding unprotected sex and high-risk partners. The values and norms must be tailored to the target population. Different programs are needed for middle school students, for White middle-class high school students, and for ethnic minority high school students.

Effective programs enhance communication skills. Such programs provide models of good communication and opportunities for practice and skill rehearsal.

A review of the impact of 55 curriculum-based programs found that two-thirds of the programs that emphasize condoms, contraceptives, and abstinence had positive effects. Many delay sexual initiation, reduce sexual activity, and increase condom or contraceptive use (Kirby & Laris, 2009).

Effective sexuality education is cost effective. A school-based program that prevents HIV infection, STIs, and unintended pregnancy among high school students can save money. Data from sexually active high school students in California and Texas found that the program Safer Choices resulted in a 15 percent increase in condom use and an 11 percent increase in the use of other contraceptives. Using a statistical model, researchers then estimated that the program prevented 0.12 cases of HIV infection, 24 cases of chlamydia, 2.8 cases of gonorrhea, 5.9 cases of pelvic inflammatory disease, and 18 pregnancies. The researchers concluded that the program saved $2.65 in medical and social costs for every dollar spent on the program (Wang et al., 2000). Using these estimates of the prevention accomplished by the $105,000 cost of the program, we can estimate the consequences if federal funds spent on abstinence-only programs were spent on effective, comprehensive sexuality education. If the $899 million spent between 1998 and 2003 to support abstinence-only education had been spent on effective sexuality education, it could have prevented 1,027 cases of HIV infection, 208,000 cases of chlamydia, 23,974 cases of gonorrhea, one-half million cases of PID, and 158,397 cases of unwanted pregnancy among teens (about 18 percent of teen pregnancies). The overall net savings would have been $2.3 billion.

The Teacher

Suppose you have decided to start a program of sexuality education and have found a curriculum that is consistent with your objectives. Wherever the program is to be carried out—in the home, the school, the place of worship, or someplace else—the next resource you need is a teacher. There are two essential qualifications: The person must be educated about sexuality, and they must be comfortable interacting with your learners about sexual topics. High school students in Minneapolis–St. Paul participating in focus groups agreed that these two qualifications are essential (Eisenberg et al., 1997). They also cited as important the ability of the teacher to relate the material to their lives.

A good teacher is also a good listener who can assess what the learner knows from the questions asked and who can understand what a child really wants to know when they ask a question. As one joke had it, little Billy ran into the kitchen one day after kindergarten and asked his mother where he had come from; she gritted her teeth, realized the time had come, and proceeded with a 15-minute discussion of intercourse, conception, and birth, blushing the whole time. Billy listened, but at the end he appeared somewhat confused and walked away shaking his head, saying, "That's funny. Jimmy says he came from Illinois."

In an effort to assess what is being taught, middle and high school instructors of health and sexuality education classes were surveyed (Rhodes et al., 2013). Instructors were given a list of 13 topics and asked to indicate which ones they taught. More than 89,000 responded, 72 percent of them middle school teachers. Professionally prepared educators (those with a health education or public health major or minor) were significantly more likely to teach seven of the topics than teachers without such preparation. Not surprisingly, teaching a class devoted to health education was associated with broader coverage than in classes where health was combined with other topics. Finally, practice-based instruction, which involves the student in various activities and is considered more effective, was more often reported by instructors of classes devoted to health education.

Following the successful development of curricular guidelines, FoSE turned its attention to issues of teacher preparation. Data indicate that at least one-third of the teachers responsible for sexuality education in the United States received no preservice or in-service training in this area. FoSE (SIECUS, 2014) has developed National Teacher Preparation Standards, which address seven areas:

1. Professional Disposition – Teacher candidates demonstrate comfort with, commitment to, and self-efficacy in teaching sexuality education.
2. Diversity and Equity – Teacher candidates show respect for individual, family, and cultural characteristics that may influence student learning.
3. Content Knowledge – Teacher candidates have accurate and current knowledge of the biological, emotional, social, and legal aspects of human sexuality.
4. Legal and Professional Ethics – Teacher candidates make decisions based on applicable federal, state, and local laws, regulations, and policies, as well as professional ethics.
5. Planning – Teacher candidates plan age- and developmentally appropriate sexuality education that is aligned with standards, policies, and laws and reflects the diversity of the community.
6. Implementation – Teacher candidates use a variety of effective strategies to teach sexuality education.
7. Assessment – Teacher candidates implement effective strategies to assess student knowledge, attitudes, and skills in order to implement sexuality education instruction.

Implementation of these standards in the training of health and sexuality educators in colleges and universities and in preservice education programs would result in substantial improvement in the quality of sexuality education in schools and other formal settings.

Condom Availability

One visible conflict has been over whether condoms should be distributed by schools to students. No one knows how many schools in the United States are distributing condoms. A 1997 study identified 418 public schools that made condoms available. Since then, cities large and small—New York, Boston, Springfield, Massachusetts—have initiated condom availability programs. In some schools condoms are available through the school nurse. In others, a teacher, the principal, or other employee may distribute them. In some schools, clinics providing health care services dispense birth control, including condoms.

Data indicate support for the distribution of condoms in the schools. Fifty-five percent of Americans believe it is appropriate for schools to distribute condoms to students (SIECUS, 2004a). The American Academy of Pediatrics supports the use of condoms by adolescents to prevent pregnancy and STIs and endorses their distribution in schools (Committee on Adolescence, 2013).

The most visible opposition to condom distribution programs is by the Roman Catholic Church. Church officials oppose such programs because of their religion's ban on all artificial forms of contraception. Others oppose such programs on the grounds that they will encourage sexual intercourse outside of marriage. As one critic put it,

> Instead of amoral, secular humanistic sex education and condom distribution in the schools, families, churches, schools, social organizations, and the business community must re-emphasize the teaching, learning, and practice of virtues like courtesy, kindness, honesty, decency, moral courage, integrity, justice, fair play, self-respect, respect for others, and the Golden Rule. (Gow, 1994, p. 184)

In January 1996, the U.S. Supreme Court rejected a challenge to a condom distribution program in the Falmouth, Massachusetts, public schools.

Condoms are available in all 15 high schools in Seattle (Brown et al., 1997). Forty-eight percent of the students who reported having intercourse during the two years prior to a survey said they had obtained condoms from school. In focus groups, students said that the availability of condoms had not led to an increase in their rates of sexual activity. Students preferred that condoms be available in private locations (nurse's office) rather than public ones (vending machines). Students also wanted comprehensive sexuality education programs in conjunction with condoms.

Although opponents of condom availability programs argue that they will promote rampant promiscuity among students, research indicates that the programs are associated with either no effect on sexual behavior (in some studies) or reductions in sexual activity (in other studies). A comprehensive review of research evaluating condom availability programs indicated that they increased condom use among sexually active students, and no studies found an increase in sexual activity (Wang et al., 2018).

In a number of schools, condom availability programs are the result of efforts by students. Schools in California, Maine, and Missouri now have such programs, thanks to student initiatives.

Effective Multicultural Sexuality Education

Much of the discussion in this chapter has assumed that the participants in a sexuality education program are homogeneous, that they are all from the same culture. In some situations that assumption is valid, but in other settings the learners may be from diverse cultural backgrounds.

Cultures vary in a number of ways that are directly related to the success or failure of a sexuality education program. Cultural differences exist in sexual practices; some of these were discussed in the chapters "Sexuality in Perspective" and "Sexuality and the Life Cycle: Childhood and Adolescence." The acceptability of explicit sexual language or of particular types of language, such as street slang, varies from one culture to another. Cultures vary in the meaning they attach to sexuality. White, Euro-American cultures have emphasized sex for the purpose of reproduction and thus tend to regard vaginal intercourse as the norm (see the chapter "Ethics, Religion, and Sexuality"). Other cultures place greater emphasis on the pleasure that can be derived from sexual stimulation. Finally, cultures vary in the definition of, and the roles expected within, the family.

Of necessity, sexuality education programs rely on language. Street slang might enhance rapport with Black urban youth but deeply offend Latinx. Curriculum development and teachers base their programs on assumptions about the prevalence of specific sexual practices, such as vaginal and anal intercourse. They implicitly or explicitly identify some practices as desirable, as for example condom use. They reflect assumptions about the purposes of sexual activity; for instance, abstinence-based programs assume that sexual intercourse is meaningful only within marriage.

If sexuality education is to be successful, it must reflect, or at least accept, the cultures of the participants. The educator must assess the audience, the intended messages, and the context, then target the program accordingly (Burnes, 2017). Educators must recognize their own sexual culture, learn about the sexual culture(s) of the students, and be aware of the power differences between groups in our society. In the classroom they should use this knowledge to enhance the effectiveness of the presentation. The use of communication styles and media common to the cultures of the participants—for example, certain rap songs that appeal to young urban African Americans—can be a valuable tool.

It is important that the program not advocate beliefs and practices that are incompatible with participants' culture. In recent years, opposition to school-based programs has expanded from evangelical Christian groups to include people from minority cultures. In Ontario, Canada, one leader of the opposition to proposed changes in the province's curriculum was a Muslim immigrant (Zimmerman, 2015). He opposed the curriculum because it recognizes sexual relationships outside of marriage. The opposition has also attracted support from Chinese Canadian and Filipino Canadians. Thus, global migration patterns may curtail school-based sex education programs unless they can be tailored to a variety of cultures.

One attempt to develop a curriculum for African American adolescents is the *Let the Circle Be Unbroken: Rites of Passage* program (Okwumabua et al., 1998, 2014). This program is based on the premise that a successful transition into adolescence requires preparation and celebration. It is presented to 10- to 14-year-olds, lasts 4 to 6 months, and involves youth, parents, and friends. Staff are specially trained during an "orientation phase." During the "passage phase," there are weekly programs lasting 60 to 90 minutes; these programs focus on preparation for adult roles, including how to make sexual decisions and deciding on appropriate behavior. The last 4 weeks make up the "culminating phase," in which everyone plans for the final celebration, the *rite de passage*. Programs like this one respond to the call for sexuality education that incorporates the family and community context in which our sexuality is grounded.

Another group that needs to have sexuality education tailored to their needs is the developmentally disabled. In a policy statement, the American Academy of Pediatrics (Committee on Children with Disabilities, 1996) addressed the special circumstances of children and adolescents with developmental disabilities. The statement points out that we cannot assume that curricula designed for sixth-graders can be presented to 12-year-olds with these disabilities. Instead, programs need to assess the cognitive and emotional abilities of each child and adolescent, then present developmentally appropriate materials. Information about forms of romantic and sexual expression may have to emphasize social norms about what is appropriate and discourage inappropriate behaviors in public. Also, programs for people with disabilities must recognize their vulnerability to exploitation and make special efforts to teach them self-protection skills.

An institute in Mexico has been involved in a long-term project to develop sexuality education programs appropriate for that culture (Pick et al., 2003). In that cultural context, programs must take into account strong, traditional gender roles. Men who have many sex partners are widely admired; women are to be modest and not display pleasure in sexuality. Decisions regarding sexuality and reproduction are made by the man, with the woman playing a passive role. Ninety-five percent of the population is Roman Catholic, so the traditions of that religion must be considered. Taking into account all these factors, the educational programs that the institute developed emphasize a participatory learning style, concrete knowledge about not only sexuality but gender roles and expectations, and communication skills, especially those for communicating with parents.

As we increasingly recognize diversity within the United States and around the world, the creation of developmentally and culturally effective sexuality education programs should be an important priority.

Bibliography

Abbey, Antonia. (1991). Misperception as an antecedent of acquaintance rape: A consequence of ambiguity in communication between men and women. In A. Parrott & L. Bechhofer (Eds.), *Acquaintance rape: The hidden crime.* New York: Wiley.

Abbey, Antonia. (2011). Alcohol's role in sexual violence perpetration: Theoretical explanations, existing evidence and future directions. *Drug and Alcohol Review, 30,* 481–489.

Abbey, Antonia, Andrews, Frank M., & Halman, L. J. (1992). Infertility and subjective well-being: The mediating roles of self-esteem, internal control, and interpersonal conflict. *Journal of Marriage and the Family, 54,* 408–417.

Abbey, Antonia D., et al. (2010). Sexual assault among diverse populations of women: Common ground, distinctive features, and unanswered questions. In H. Landrine & N. Russo (Eds.), *Handbook of diversity in feminist psychology* (pp. 391–426). New York: Springer.

Abbey, Antonia, et al. (2009). Alcohol's role in men's use of coercion to obtain unprotected sex. *Substance Use & Misuse, 44,* 1329–1348.

Abbey, Antonia, et al. (2014). Review of survey and experimental research that examines the relationship between alcohol consumption and men's sexual aggression perpetration. *Trauma, Violence, and Abuse, 15,* 265–282.

Abbott, A. (2010). Baby boom bags Nobel prize. *Nature, 467,* 641–642.

Abdool Karim, Q., et al. (2010). Effectiveness and safety of tenofovir gel, an antiretroviral microbicide, for the prevention of HIV infection in women. *Science, 329,* 1168–1174.

Abel, Gene, & Rouleau, Joanne-L. (1990). The nature and extent of sexual assault. In W. L. Marshall, D. R. Laws, & H. E. Bartarce (Eds.), *Handbook of sexual assault* (pp. 9–21). New York: Plenum.

Abel, Gene G., et al. (1992). Current treatments of paraphiliacs. *Annual Review of Sex Research, 3,* 255–290.

Abma, Joyce C., & Martinez, Gladys M. (2017). Sexual activity and contraceptive use among teenagers in the United States, 2011–2015. *National Health Statistics Reports,* No. 104.

Abracen, Jeffrey, & Looman, Jan. (2004). Issues in the treatment of sexual offenders: Recent development and directions for future research. *Aggression and Violent Behavior, 9,* 229–246.

Abrams, Dominic, et al. (2003). Perceptions of stranger and acquaintance rape: The role of benevolent and hostile sexism in victim blame and rape proclivity. *Journal of Personality and Social Psychology, 84,* 111–125.

Acker, Michele, & Davis, Mark. (1992). Intimacy, passion and commitment in adult romantic relationships: A test of the triangular theory of love. *Journal of Social and Personal Relationships, 9,* 21–50.

Acoose, Janice. (2015). *Iskwewak Kah' Ki Yaw Ni Wahkomakanak: Neither Indian princesses nor easy squaws.* 2nd ed. Toronto: Women's Press.

Adams, William, & Flynn, Abigail. (2017). Federal prosecution of commercial sexual exploitation of children cases, 2004–2013. Bureau of Justice Statistics, U.S. Department of Justice. NCJ250746.

Adams, M. A., et al. (1997). Vascular control mechanisms in penile erection: Phylogeny and the inevitability of multiple and overlapping systems. *International Journal of Impotence Research, 9,* 85–91.

Adashi, Eli Y., & Occhiogrosso, Rachel H. (2017). The Hyde Amendment at 40 years and reproductive rights in the United States. *JAMA, 317,* 1523–1524.

Addiego, Frank, et al. (1981). Female ejaculation: A case study. *Journal of Sex Research, 17,* 13–21.

Adeoya-Osiguwa, S. A., et al. (2003). 17B-estradiol and environmental estrogens significantly affect mammalian sperm function. *Human Reproduction, 18,* 101–107.

Adimora, Adaora, et al. (2002). Concurrent sexual partnerships among women in the United States. *Epidemiology, 13,* 320–327.

Adkins-Regan, Elizabeth. (2002). Development of sexual partner preference in the zebra finch: A socially monogamous, pair-bonding animal. *Archives of Sexual Behavior, 31,* 27–34.

Adshade, M. (2010). *Confessions of a college pimp.* Retrieved from www.bigthink.com/ideas/24377

Advocates for Youth. (2004a). *Abstinence-only-until-marriage programs: History of government funding.* Retrieved from www.advocatesforyouth.org/rrr/history.htm

Advocates for Youth. (2004b). *Americans support sexuality education.* Retrieved from www.advocatesforyouth.org/rrr/history.htm

Afifi, Mustafa. (2009). Women's empowerment and the intention to continue the practice of female genital cutting in Egypt. *Archives of Iranian Medicine, 12,* 154–160.

Aggrawal, Anil. (2009). A new classification of necrophilia. *Journal of Forensic and Legal Medicine, 16,* 316–320.

Ahlborg, T., et al. (2008). Sensual and sexual marital contentment in parents of small children—A follow-up study when the first child is four years old. *Journal of Sex Research, 45,* 295–304.

Ahmadi, Nader. (2003). Rocking sexualities: Iranian migrants' views on sexuality. *Archives of Sexual Behavior, 32,* 317–326.

Ahrens, Courtney E., et al. (2008). Understanding and preventing rape. In F. L. Denmark & M. Paludi (Eds.), *Psychology of women: A handbook of issues and theories* (pp. 509–554). Westport, CT: Praeger.

Ainsworth, Claire. (2005). The secret life of sperm. *Nature, 436,* 770–771.

Aksglaede, Lise, et al. (2009). Recent decline in age at breast development: The Copenhagen Puberty Study. *Pediatrics, 123,* e932–e939.

Alan Guttmacher Institute. (2004). *State policies in brief: Bans on "partial birth" abortion (as of June 1, 2004).* Retrieved from www.guttmacher.org

Albanesi, Heather P. (2010). *Gender and sexual agency: How young people make choices about sex.* Lanham, MD: Lexington Books.

Albert, Alexa. (2001). *Brothel: Mustang Ranch and its women.* New York: Random House.

Albin, Rochelle S. (1977). Psychological studies of rape. *Signs, 3,* 423–435.

Albright, Julie M. (2008). Sex in America online: An exploration of sex, marital status, and sexual identity in Internet sex seeking and its impacts. *Journal of Sex Research, 45,* 175–186.

Alcid, Sara, & Miller, Ansje. (2014, July–August). Environmental toxins threaten reproductive health & justice. *The Women's Health Activist.* https://nwhn.org/newsletter/node/1689

Alexander, Michele G., & Fisher, Terri D. (2003). Truth and consequences: Using the bogus pipeline to examine sex differences in self-reported sexuality. *Journal of Sex Research, 40,* 27–35.

Alfirevic, Z., Mujezinovic, F., & Sundberg, K. (2009). Amniocentesis and chorionic villus sampling for prenatal diagnosis. *Cochrane Database of Systematic Reviews, 3,* CD003252.

Algeffari, M., et al. (2018). Testosterone therapy for sexual dysfunction in men with Type 2 diabetes: A systematic review and meta-analysis of randomized controlled trials. *Diabetic Medicine, 35,* 195–202.

Alink, Lenneke, et al. (2006). The early child aggression curve: Development of physical aggression in 10- to 50-month-old children. *Child Development, 77,* 954–966.

Aliyu, M., Wilson, R., Zoorob, R., et al. (2008). Alcohol consumption during pregnancy and the risk of stillbirth among singletons. *Alcohol, 42,* 369–374.

Allen, E. S., & Atkins, D. C. (2014). The association of divorce and extramarital sex in a representative U.S. sample. *Journal of Family Issues, 33,* 477–493.

Allen, Adeline. (2018). Surrogacy and limitations to freedom of contract: Toward being more fully human. *Harvard Journal of Law & Public Policy, 41,* 753–787.

Allen, Katherine R., & Goldberg, Abbie E. (2009). Sexual activity during menstruation: A qualitative study. *Journal of Sex Research, 46,* 535–545.

Allen, Mike, & Burrell, Nancy A. (2002). Sexual orientation of the parent: The impact on the child. In M. Allen et al. (Eds.), *Interpersonal communication research: Advances through meta-analysis* (pp. 125–143). Mahwah, NJ: Erlbaum.

Allen, M., et al. (1996). The role of educational briefings in mitigating effects of experimental exposure to violent sexually explicit material. *Journal of Sex Research, 33,* 135–141.

Allen, Mike, et al. (1995). A meta-analysis summarizing the effects of pornography II: Aggression after exposure. *Human Communication Research, 22,* 258–283.

Allgeier, Elizabeth, & Wiederman, Michael W. (1994). How useful is evolutionary psychology for understanding contemporary human sexual behavior? *Annual Review of Sex Research, 5,* 218–256.

Almeling, Rene. (2011). *Sex cells: The medical market for eggs and sperm.* Berkeley, CA: University of California Press.

Almroth, Lars, et al. (2001). Male complications of female genital mutilation. *Social Science and Medicine, 53,* 1455–1460.

Althof, Stanley E. (2007). Treatment of rapid ejaculation: Psychotherapy, pharmacotherapy, and combined therapy. In S. Leiblum (Ed.), *Principles and practice of sex therapy* (4th ed., pp. 212–240). New York: Guilford.

Althof, Stanley E. (2014). Treatment of premature ejaculation: Psychotherapy, pharmacotherapy, and combined therapy. In Y. Binik & K. Hall (Eds.), *Principles and practice of sex therapy* (5th ed., pp. 112–137). New York: Guilford.

Althof, Stanley E., et al. (2004). Psychological and interpersonal dimensions of sexual function and dysfunction. In T. F. Lue et al. (Eds.), *Sexual medicine: Sexual dysfunctions in men and women* (pp. 73–115). Paris: Editions 21.

Althof, Stanley E., et al. (2010). International Society for Sexual Medicine's guidelines for the diagnosis and treatment of premature ejaculation. *Journal of Sexual Medicine, 7,* 2947–2969.

Alvarez-Cubero, Maria J., et al. (2015). Prognostic role of genetic biomarkers in clinical progression of prostate cancer. *Experimental & Molecular Medicine, 47,* e176.

American Academy of Pediatrics. (2010). Policy statement—sexuality, contraception, and the media. *Pediatrics, 126,* 576–582.

American Academy of Pediatrics. (2012). AAP reaffirms breastfeeding guidelines. Retrieved from https://www.aap.org/en-us/about-the-aap/aap-press-room/pages/aap-reaffirms-breastfeeding-guidelines.aspx

American Academy of Pediatrics. (2012). Emergency contraception. *Pediatrics, 130,* 1174–1182.

American Academy of Pediatrics Committee on Genetics. (2000). Evaluation of the newborn with developmental anomalies of the external genitalia. *Pediatrics, 106,* 138–142.

American Academy of Pediatrics et al. v. Clovis Unified School District, 12CECG02608 (2015).

American Cancer Society. (2012). *Some facts about testicular cancer.* www.cancer.org/Cancer/TesticularCancer/.

American Cancer Society. (2014). *Breast cancer facts and figures 2013-2014.* http://www.cancer.org/acs/groups/content/@research/documents/document/acspc-042725.pdf

American Cancer Society. (2015a). *Cancer facts & figures 2015.* http://www.cancer.org/acs/groups/content/@editorial/documents/document/acspc-044552.pdf

American Cancer Society. (2015b). *Testicular cancer.* http://www.cancer.org/acs/groups/cid/documents/webcontent/003142-pdf.pdf

American Civil Liberties Union. (2004). *Abortion bans: In the states.* Retrieved from www.aclu.org

American Civil Liberties Union. (2015). *Transgender people and the law.* Retrieved from www.aclu.org/know-your-rights/transgender-people-and-law

American College of Obstetricians and Gynecologists. (2017). Vaginal birth after cesarean delivery. *Obstetrics & Gynecology, 130,* 1167–1169.

American Law Institute. (1962). *Model penal code: Proposed official draft.* Philadelphia: ALI.

American Psychiatric Association. (2000b). Position statement on therapies focused on attempts to change sexual orientation (reparative or conversion therapies). *American Journal of Psychiatry, 157,* 1719–1721. www.psych.org.

American Psychiatric Association. (2013). *Diagnostic and statistical manual of mental disorders* (5th ed.). Arlington, VA: American Psychiatric Association.

American Psychological Association. (2015). Guidelines for psychological practice with transgender and gender nonconforming people. *American Psychologist, 70,* 832–864.

American Psychological Association, Task Force on the Sexualization of Girls. (2007). *Report of the APA Task Force on the Sexualization of Girls.* Washington, DC: American Psychological

Association. Retrieved from www.apa.org/pi/wpo/sexualization. html

Anderson, E. (1989). Sex codes and family life among poor innercity youths. *Annals of the American Academy of Political and Social Science, 501,* 59–78.

Anderson, Monica, & Jian, Jingjing. (2018). *Teens, social media & technology 2018.* Pew Research Center. Retrieved from www. pewresearch.org

Anderson, Kermyt, Kaplan, Hillard, & Lancaster, Jane. (2001). *Men's financial expenditures on genetic children and stepchildren from current and former relationships.* Ann Arbor, MI: Population Studies Center, Report No. 01–484.

Anderson, M. (2004). *Personal communication.*

Andrews, Lori B. (1989). Alternative modes of reproduction. In S. Cohen & N. Taub (Eds.), *Reproductive laws for the 1990s* (pp. 361–404). Clifton, NJ: Humana Press.

Andro, Armelle, & Lesclingand, Marie. (2017, April). Female genital mutilation around the world. *Population & Societies,* No. 543.

Anonymous. (2012). *Student to sex worker: My life as an escort.* Retrieved from feminspire.com/student-to-sex-worker-my-life-as-an-escort

Anthony, S. (2012). Just how big are porn sites? *ExtremeTech.com.* Retrieved from www.extremetech.com/computing/123929

Antoni, Michael H., et al. (2001). Cognitive-behavioral stress management intervention decreases the prevalence of depression and enhances benefit finding among women under treatment for early-stage breast cancer. *Health Psychology, 20,* 20–32.

Aos, Steve, Miller, Marna, & Drake, Elizabeth. (2006). *Evidence-based adult corrections programs: What works and what does not.* Olympia, WA: Washington State Institute for Public Policy.

Araujo, A., et al. (2000). Relation between psychosocial risk factors and incident erectile dysfunction: Prospective results from the Massachusetts Male Aging Study. *American Journal of Epidemiology, 152,* 533–541.

Archer, John. (2004). Sex differences in aggression in real-world settings: A meta-analytic review. *Review of General Psychology, 8,* 291–322.

Arévalo, Marcos, Jennings, Victoria, & Sinai, Irit. (2002). Efficacy of a new method of family planning: The Standard Days Method. *Contraception, 65,* 333–338.

Aries, Elizabeth. (1996). *Men and women in interaction: Reconsidering the differences.* New York: Oxford University Press.

Armenia, Amy, & Troia, Bailey. (2017). Evolving opinions: Evidence on marriage equality attitudes from panel data. *Social Science Quarterly, 98,* 185–195.

Armstrong, Elizabeth A., England, Paula, & Fogarty, Alison C. K. (2012). Accounting for women's orgasm and sexual enjoyment in college hookups and relationships. *American Sociological Review, 77,* 435–462.

Arnold, Arthur P. (2003). The gender of the voice within: The neural origin of sex differences in the brain. *Current Opinion in Neurobiology, 13,* 759–764.

Arnow, Bruce A., et al. (2002). Brain activation and sexual arousal in healthy, heterosexual males. *Brain, 125,* 1014–1023.

Arons, Jessica. (2007). *Future choices: Assisted reproductive technologies and the law.* Washington, DC: Center for American Progress.

Arum, Richard, Roksa, Josipa, & Buding, Michelle (2008). The romance of college attendance: Higher education stratification and mate selection. *Research in Social Stratification and Mobility, 26,* 107–121.

Ashby, S., Arcari, C., & Edmonson, M. (2006). Television viewing and risk of sexual initiation by young adolescents. *Archives of Pediatric and Adolescent Medicine, 160,* 375–380.

Ashcroft v. ACLU, 542 U.S. 656 (2004).

Ashton, Adam K. (2007). The new sexual pharmacology: A guide for the clinician. In S. Leiblum (Ed.), *Principles and practice of sex therapy* (4th ed., pp. 509–542). New York: Guilford.

Associated Press. (2010). *More women going from jobless to topless.* Retrieved from http://today.msnbc.msn.com/id/29824663/

Associated Press. (2014, May 7). *Vatican reveals how many priests defrocked for sex abuse since 2004.* Retrieved from https://www. cbsnews.com/news/vatican-reveals-how-many-priests-defrocked-for-sex-abuse-since-2004/

Attard-Johnson, Janice, et al. (2017). Heterosexual, homosexual, and bisexual men's pupillary responses to persons at different stages of sexual development. *Journal of Sex Research, 54,* 1085–1096.

Avella, M. A., et al. (2016). ZP2 peptide beads select human sperm in vitro, decoy mouse sperm in vivo, and provide reversible contraception. *Science Translational Medicine, 8,* Article 336ra60.

Avis, Nancy E., & McKinlay, Sonja M. (1995, March–April). The Massachusetts Women's Health Study: An epidemiological investigation of the menopause. *Journal of the American Medical Women's Association, 50,* 45–63.

Ayoub, R., et al. (2017). Comparison of the single dose pharmacokinetics, pharmacodynamics, and safety of two novel oral formulations of dimethandrolone undecanoate (DMAU). *Andrology, 5,* 278–285.

Baber, R. J., et al. (2016). 2016 IMS recommendations on women's midlife health and menopause hormone therapy. *Climacteric, 19,* 109–150.

Bach, G., & Wyden, P. (1969). *The intimate enemy: How to fight fair in love and marriage.* New York: Morrow.

Backstrom, Laura, et al. (2012). Women's negotiation of cunnilingus in college hookups and relationships. *Journal of Sex Research, 49,* 1–12.

Bagemihl, Bruce. (1999). *Biological exuberance: Animal homosexuality and natural diversity.* New York: St. Martin's Press.

Bailey, J. Michael, et al. (2016). Sexual orientation, controversy, and science. *Psychological Science in the Public Interest, 17,* 45–101.

Bailey, J. Michael, & Pillard, Richard C. (1991). A genetic study of male sexual orientation. *Archives of General Psychiatry, 48,* 1089–1096.

Bailey, J. Michael, & Pillard, Richard C. (1995). Genetics of human sexual orientation. *Annual Review of Sex Research, 6,* 126–150.

Bailey, J. Michael, et al. (1993). Heritable factors influence sexual orientation in women. *Archives of General Psychiatry, 50,* 217–223.

Bailey, Robert C., et al. (2007). Male circumcision for HIV prevention in young men in Kisumu, Kenya: A randomised controlled trial. *Lancet, 369,* 643–656.

Baker, F. C., et al. (2002). Acetaminophen does not affect 24-h body temperature or sleep in the luteal phase of the menstrual cycle. *Journal of Applied Physiology, 92,* 1684–1691.

Baker, Monya. (2008). Embryonic-like stem cells from a single human hair. *Nature Reports Stem Cells.* doi: 10.1038/stemcells.2008.142

Baldwin, John D., & Baldwin, Janice I. (1989). The socialization of homosexuality and heterosexuality in a non-Western society. *Archives of Sexual Behavior, 18,* 13–30.

Baldwin, John D., & Baldwin, Janice I. (1997). Gender differences in sexual interest. *Archives of Sexual Behavior, 26,* 181–210.

Baldwin, Susie B., et al. (2004). Condom use and other factors affecting penile human papillomavirus detection in men attending a sexually transmitted disease clinic. *Sexually Transmitted Diseases, 31,* 601–607.

Balon, Richard, & Clayton, Anita H. (2014). Female sexual interest/arousal disorder: A diagnosis out of thin air. *Archives of Sexual Behavior, 43,* 1227–1229.

Balsam, Kimberly F., et al. (2010). Childhood abuse and mental health indicators among ethnically diverse lesbian, gay, and bisexual adults. *Journal of Consulting and Clinical Psychology, 78,* 459–468.

Balzarini, Rhonda N., et al. (2017). Perceptions of primary and secondary relationships in polyamory. *PLoS One, 12(5),* e0177841.

Bancroft, John. (1978). The prevention of sexual offenses. In C. B. Qualls et al. (Eds.), *The prevention of sexual disorders* (pp. 95–116). New York: Plenum.

Bancroft, John. (2004). Alfred C. Kinsey and the politics of sex research. *Annual Review of Sex Research, 15,* 1–39.

Bancroft, John, & Graham, Cynthia A. (2011). The varied nature of women's sexuality: Unresolved issues and a theoretical approach. *Hormones and Behavior, 59,* 717–729.

Bancroft, John, Graham, Cynthia, Janssen, Erick, & Sanders, Stephanie A. (2009). The dual control model: Current status and future directions. *Journal of Sex Research, 46,* 121–142.

Bancroft, John, Herbenick, Debra, & Reynolds, Meredith. (2003). Masturbation as a marker of sexual development. In John Bancroft (Ed.), *Sexual development.* Bloomington: Indiana University Press.

Bandura, Albert. (1977). *Social learning theory.* Englewood Cliffs, NJ: Prentice-Hall.

Bandura, Albert. (1982). Self-efficacy mechanism in human agency. *American Psychologist, 37,* 122–147.

Bandura, Albert. (2009). Social cognitive theory of mass communication. In J. Bryant & M. B. Oliver (Eds.), *Media effects: Advances in theory and research.* 3rd ed. New York: Routledge.

Bandura, Albert, & Walters, Richard H. (1963). *Social learning and personality development.* New York: Holt.

Bang, A. K., et al. (2005). A study of finger lengths, semen quality and sex hormones in 360 young men from the general Danish population. *Human Reproduction, 20,* 3109–3113.

Banks, D., & Kyckelhahn, T. (2011). Characteristics of suspected human trafficking incidents, 2008–2010. Washington, DC: U.S. Department of Justice, Bureau of Justice Statistics, NCJ 233732.

Baram, Marcus. (2007). Free porn threatens adult film industry. *ABC News.* Retrieved from http://abcnews.com

Barash, David P. (1982). *Sociobiology and behavior* (2nd ed.). New York: Elsevier.

Barbach, Lonnie G. (1983). *For each other: Sharing sexual intimacy.* Garden City, NY: Anchor Books.

Barkley-Levenson, Emily, et al. (2018). Prefrontal cortical activity during the Stroop Task: New insights into the why and the who of real-world risky sexual behavior. *Annals of Behavioral Medicine, 52,* 367–379.

Barlow, David H. (1986). Causes of sexual dysfunction: The role of cognitive interference. *Journal of Consulting and Clinical Psychology, 54,* 140–148.

Barnett, Rosalind, & Hyde, Janet S. (2001). Women, men, work, and family: An expansionist theory. *American Psychologist, 56,* 781–796.

Baron, Larry, & Straus, Murray A. (1989). *Four theories of rape in American society.* New Haven, CT: Yale University Press.

Barouch, Dan H., et al. (2018). Evaluation of a mosaic HIV-1 vaccine in a multicenter, randomised, double-blind, placebo-controlled, phase 1/2a clinical trial (APPROACH) and in rhesus monkeys (NHP 13-19). *The Lancet, 392,* 232–243.

Barr, A., Bryan, A., & Kenrick, D. (2002). Sexual peak: Socially shared cognitions about desire, frequency, and satisfaction in men and women. *Personal Relationships, 9,* 287–299.

Bartell, Gilbert D. (1970). Group sex among the mid-Americans. *Journal of Sex Research, 6,* 113–130.

Bartels, A., & Zeki, S. (2004). The neural correlates of maternal and romantic love. *NeuroImage, 21,* 1155–1166.

Bartos, Sebastian, Berger, I., & Hegarty, P. (2014). Interventions to reduce sexual prejudice: A study-space analysis and meta-analytic review. *Journal of Sex Research, 51,* 363–382.

Basile, Kathleen C. (2002). Prevalence of wife rape and other intimate partner sexual coercion in a nationally representative sample of women. *Violence and Victims, 17,* 511–524.

Basson, Rosemary. (2004). Summary of the recommendations on women's sexual dysfunctions. In T. F. Lue et al. (Eds.), *Sexual medicine: Sexual dysfunctions in men and women* (pp. 975–990). Paris: Editions 21.

Basson, Rosemary. (2006). Sexual desire and arousal disorders in women. *New England Journal of Medicine, 354,* 1497–1506.

Basson, Rosemary. (2007). Sexual desire/arousal disorders in women. In S. Leiblum (Ed.), *Principles and practice of sex therapy* (4th ed., pp. 25–53). New York: Guilford.

Basson, Rosemary. (2014). On the definition of female sexual interest/arousal disorder. *Archives of Sexual Behavior, 43,* 1225–1226.

Bauer, Greta R., & Wayne, Linda D. (2005). Cultural sensitivity and research involving sexual minorities. *Perspectives on Sexual and Reproductive Health, 37,* 45–47.

Baulieu, E. E., et al. (2000). Dehydroepiandrosterone (DHEA), DHEA sulfate, and aging: Contributions of the DHEAge Study to a sociobiomedical issue. *Proceedings of the National Academy of Sciences—USA, 97,* 4279–4284.

Baumeister, Roy F. (1988a). Masochism as escape from the self. *Journal of Sex Research, 25,* 28–59.

Baumeister, Roy F. (1988b). Gender differences in masochistic scripts. *Journal of Sex Research, 25,* 478–499.

Baumeister, Roy F., Catanese, K., & Vohs, K. (2001). Is there a gender difference in strength of sex drive? Theoretical views, conceptual distinctions, and a review of relevant evidence. *Personality and Social Psychology Review, 5,* 242–273.

Baur, Elena, et al. (2016). Paraphilic sexual interests and sexually coercive behavior: A population-based twin study. *Archives of Sexual Behavior, 45,* 1163–1172.

Bazelon, Emily. (2007, January 21). Is there a postabortion syndrome? *New York Times Magazine.*

Bazelon, E. (2013, January 27). Money is no cure. *New York Times Magazine.*

Beach, Frank A. (1947). Evolutionary changes in the physiological control of mating behavior in mammals. *Psychological Review, 54,* 297–315.

Becker, Davida, et al. (2014). Cultural measures associated with sexual risk behaviors among Latino youth in southern California: A longitudinal study. *Perspectives on Sexual and Reproductive Health, 46,* 193–201.

Beier, E. G., & Sternberg, D. P. (1977). Marital communication. *Journal of Communication, 27,* 92–103.

Being LGBTI in China. (2016). *Being LGBTI in China: A national survey on social attitudes towards sexual orientation, gender identity and gender expression.* United Nations Development Programme. Retrieved from http://www.asia-pacific.undp.org/content/rbap/en/home/library/democratic_governance/hiv_aids/being-lgbti-in-china–a-national-survey-on-social-attitudes-towa.html

Bell, Alan P., Weinberg, Martin S., & Hammersmith, Sue K. (1981). *Sexual preference.* Bloomington: Indiana University Press.

Belzer, E. G. (1981). Orgasmic expulsions of women: A review and heuristic inquiry. *Journal of Sex Research, 17,* 1–12.

Bem, Sandra L. (1981). Gender schema theory: A cognitive account of sex typing. *Psychological Review, 88,* 354–364.

Bem, Sandra L. (1989). Genital knowledge and gender consistency in preschool children. *Child Development, 60,* 649–662.

Bendas, Johanna, et al. (2018). Olfactory function relates to sexual experience in adults. *Archives of Sexual Behavior, 47,* 1333–1339.

Bender, S. S., et al. (2018). "You stop thinking about yourself as a woman." An interpretive phenomenological study of the meaning of sexuality for Icelandic women during pregnancy and after birth. *Midwifery, 62,* 14–19.

Bennett, Sylvana, & Assefi, Nassim. (2005). School-based teenage pregnancy prevention programs: A systematic review of randomized controlled trials. *Journal of Adolescent Health, 36,* 72–81.

Bennice, Jennifer A., & Resick, Patricia. (2003). Marital rape: History, research, and practice. *Trauma, Violence, & Abuse, 4,* 228–246.

Benoit, Cecilia, et al. (2018). Prostitution stigma and its effect on the working conditions, personal lives, and health of sex workers. *Journal of Sex Research, 55,* 457–471.

Bentz, Eva-Katrin, et al. (2008). A polymorphism of the CYP17 gene related to sex steroid metabolism is associated with female-to-male but not male-to-female transsexualism. *Fertility and Sterility, 90,* 56–59.

Berenbaum, Sheri A. (2006). Psychological outcome in children with disorders of sex development: Implications for understanding typical development. *Annual Review of Sex Research, 17,* 1–38.

Berenbaum, Sheri A. (2018). Beyond pink and blue: The complexity of early androgen effects on gender development. *Child Development Perspectives, 12,* 58–64.

Berg, Bruce L. (2001). *Qualitative research methods for the social sciences.* Boston: Allyn and Bacon.

Berg, J. H., & Derlega, V. J. (1987). Themes in the study of self-disclosure. In V. J. Derlega & J. H. Berg (Eds.), *Self-disclosure: Theory, research and therapy* (pp. 1–8). New York: Plenum.

Bergdall, A. R., Kraft, J. M., Andes, K., Carter, M., Hatfield-Timajchy, K., & Hock-Long, L. (2012). Love and hooking up in the new millennium: Communication technology and relationships among urban African American and Puerto Rican young adults. *Journal of Sex Research, 49,* 570–582.

Bergen, D. J., & Williams, J. E. (1991). Sex stereotypes in the United States revisited: 1972–1988. *Sex Roles, 24,* 413–423.

Bergeron, Sophie, et al. (2014). Genital pain in women and men: It can hurt more than your sex life. In Y. Binik & K. Hall (Eds.), *Principles and practice of sex therapy* (5th ed., pp. 159–176). New York: Guilford.

Berglund, Hans, et al. (2006). Brain response to putative pheromones in lesbian women. *PNAS, 103,* 8269–8274.

Bergman, K. M., Sarkar, P., O'Connor, T. G., Modi, N., & Glover, V. (2007). Prenatal stressful life events predict child cognitive outcomes. *Early Human Development, 83,* 136.

Berman, Jennifer R., Adhikari, S., & Goldstein, I. (2000). Anatomy and physiology of female sexual function and dysfunction. *European Urology, 38,* 20–29.

Berman, Margit, & Frazier, Patricia. (2005). Relationship power and betrayal experience as predictors of reactions to infidelity. *Personality and Social Psychology Bulletin, 31,* 1617–1627.

Bermant, Gordon, & Davidson, Julian M. (1974). *Biological bases of sexual behavior.* New York: Harper & Row.

Bernard, M., et al. (1985). *The rights of single people.* New York: Bantam Books.

Berne, Eric. (1970). *Sex in human loving.* New York: Simon & Schuster.

Bernstein, Anne C., & Cowan, Philip A. (1975). Children's concepts of how people get babies. *Child Development, 46,* 77–92.

Bernstein, Elizabeth. (2007). *Temporarily yours: Intimacy, authenticity, and the commerce of sex.* Chicago: University of Chicago Press.

Berry, Jason, & Renner, Gerald. (2004). *Vows of silence: The abuse of power in the papacy of John Paul II.* New York: Free Press.

Bersamin, Melina M., et al. (2012). Young adults and casual sex: The relevance of college drinking settings. *Journal of Sex Research, 49,* 274–281.

Bersamin, M. M., Zamboanga, B. L., Schwartz, S. J., Donellen, M. B., Hudson, M., Weisskirch, R. S., et al. (2014). Risky business: Is there an association between casual sex and mental health among emerging adults? *Journal of Sex Research, 51,* 43–51.

Berscheid, Ellen, et al. (1971). Physical attractiveness and dating choice: A test of the matching hypothesis. *Journal of Experimental Social Psychology, 7,* 173–189.

Berscheid, Ellen, & Hatfield, Elaine. (1978). *Interpersonal attraction* (2nd ed.). Reading, MA: Addison-Wesley.

Berscheid, Ellen, & Walster, Elaine. (1974). A little bit about love. In T. L. Huston (Ed.), *Foundations of interpersonal attraction.* New York: Academic.

Best, J., & Bogle, K. (2014). *Kids gone wild.* New York: New York University Press.

Bettocchi, Carlo, et al. (2008). Ejaculatory disorders: Pathophysiology and management. *Nature Clinical Practice Urology, 5,* 93–103.

Betz, Eric. (2012, September 6). No jail time for Flagstaff cop in bar groping. *Arizona Daily Sun.*

Betzer, F., Kohler, S., & Schlemm, L. (2015). Sex work among students of higher education: A survey-based, cross-sectional study. *Archives of Sexual Behavior, 44,* 525–528.

Biale, David. (1997). *Eros and the Jews.* Berkeley, CA: University of California Press.

Biegel, Stuart, & Kuehl, Sheila Jamnes. (2010). *Safe at school: Addressing the school environment and LGBT safety through policy and legislation.* National Education Policy Center, University of Colorado. http://nepc.colorado.edu/files/Biegel_LGBT.pdf

Biggs, M. Antonia, et al. (2017). Women's mental health and well-being 5 years after receiving or being denied an abortion: A prospective, longitudinal cohort study. *JAMA Psychiatry, 74,* 169–178.

Billings, Andrew. (1979). Conflict resolution in distressed and nondistressed married couples. *Journal of Consulting and Clinical Psychology, 47,* 368–376.

Binik, Yitzchak M. (2010a). The DSM diagnostic criteria for vaginismus. *Archives of Sexual Behavior, 39,* 278–291.

Binik, Yitzchak M. (2010b). The DSM diagnostic criteria for dyspareunia. *Archives of Sexual Behavior, 39,* 292–303.

Binik, Yitzchak M., et al. (2007). Dyspareunia and vaginismus: So-called sexual pain. In S. Leiblum (Ed.), *Principles and practice of sex therapy* (4th ed., pp. 124–156). New York: Guilford.

Birchler, Gary R., Weiss, R. L., & Vincent, J. P. (1975). Multimethod analysis of social reinforcement exchange between maritally distressed and nondistressed spouse and stranger dyads. *Journal of Personality and Social Psychology, 31,* 349–360.

Bird, S. Elizabeth. (1999, Summer). Gendered construction of the American Indian in popular media. *Journal of Communication, 61*–83.

Biro, Frank, et al. (2013). Onset of breast development in a longitudinal cohort. *Pediatrics, 132,* 1019–1027.

Bishop, Simon, & Limmer, Mark. (2018). Negotiating the edge: The rationalization of sexual risk taking among Western male sex tourists to Thailand. *Journal of Sex Research, 55,* 871–879.

Bivona, Jenny, & Critelli, Joseph. (2009). The nature of women's rape fantasies: An analysis of prevalence, frequency and contents. *Journal of Sex Research, 46,* 33–45.

Bixler, Ray H. (1986). Of apes and men (including females). *Journal of Sex Research, 22,* 255–267.

Black, Michele C., et al. (2011). *The National Intimate Partner and Sexual Violence Survey (NISVS): 2010 Summary Report.* Atlanta, GA: Centers for Disease Control and Prevention. www.cdc.gov/violenceprevention.

Blackless, Melanie, et al. (2000). How sexually dimorphic are we? Review and synthesis. *American Journal of Human Biology, 12,* 151–166.

Blackwell, Courtney K., et al. (2014). Children and the internet: Developmental implications of web site preferences among 8- to 12-year-old children. *Journal of Broadcasting & Electronic Media, 58,* 1–20.

Blair, C. David, & Lanyon, Richard I. (1981). Exhibitionism: Etiology and treatment. *Psychological Bulletin, 89,* 439–463.

Blake, Jeanne. (2004). *Words can work: When talking with kids about sexual health.* Gloucester, MA: Blake Works, Inc.

Blake, S. M., Simkin, L., Ledsky, R., Perkins, C., & Calabrese, J. M. (2001). Effect of a parent-child communications intervention on young adolescents' risk of early onset of sexual intercourse. *Family Planning Perspectives, 33,* 52–61.

Blanchard, Ray. (1997). Birth order and sibling sex ratio in homosexual versus heterosexual males and females. *Annual Review of Sex Research, 8,* 27–67.

Blanchard, Ray. (2001). Fraternal birth order and the maternal immune hypothesis of male homosexuality. *Hormones and Behavior, 40,* 105–114.

Blanchard, Ray. (2018). Fraternal birth order, family size, and male homosexuality: Meta-analysis of studies spanning 25 years. *Archives of Sexual Behavior, 47,* 1–16.

Blanchard, Ray, & Bogaert, A. (2004). Proportion of homosexual men who owe their sexual orientation to fraternal birth order: An estimate based on two national probability samples. *American Journal of Human Biology, 16,* 151–157.

Blanchard, Ray, Dickey, R., & Jones, C. (1995). Comparison of height and weight in homosexual versus nonhomosexual gender dysphorics. *Archives of Sexual Behavior, 24,* 543–554.

Blanchard, Ray, et al. (1999). Pedophiles: Mental retardation, maternal age, and sexual orientation. *Archives of Sexual Behavior, 28,* 111–127.

Blanchard, Ray, et al. (2002). Retrospective self-reports of childhood accidents causing unconsciousness in phallometrically diagnosed pedophiles. *Archives of Sexual Behavior, 31,* 511–526.

Blanchard, Victoria, et al. (2009). Investigating the effects of marriage and relationship education on couples' communication skills: A meta-analytic study. *Journal of Family Psychology, 23,* 203–214.

Blanck, Paul, et al. (2018). Effects of mindfulness exercises as stand-alone intervention on symptoms of anxiety and depression: Systematic review and meta-analysis. *Behavior Research and Therapy, 102,* 25–35.

Bleakley, Amy, et al. (2008). It works both ways: The relationship between exposure to sexual content in the media and adolescent sexual behavior. *Media Psychology, 11,* 443–461.

Bleakley, A., et al. (2009). How sources of sexual information relate to adolescents' beliefs about sex. *American Journal of Health Behavior, 33,* 37–48.

Bleakley, Amy, Hennessy, Michael, & Fishbein, Martin. (2011). A model of adolescents' seeking of sexual content in their media choices. *Journal of Sex Research, 48,* 309–315.

Bleakley, Amy, et al. (2017). Alcohol, sex, and screens: Modeling media influence on adolescent alcohol and sex co-occurrence. *Journal of Sex Research, 54,* 1026–1037.

Bloom, Linda. (2004, May 4). *Delegates retain stance on homosexual issues while demonstrators express beliefs.* Retrieved from www.umc.org/interior?ptid=16&mid=4559

Bodnar, L. M., et al. (2004). Prepregnancy body mass index and the risk of preeclampsia [Abstract]. *Federation of American Societies for Experimental Biology Journal, 18* (5), A928.

Bogaert, Anthony F. (2003). Number of older brothers and sexual orientation: New tests and the attraction/behavior distinction in two national probability samples. *Journal of Personality and Social Psychology, 84,* 644–652.

Bogaert, Anthony F., et al. (2018). Male homosexuality and maternal immune responsivity to the Y-linked protein NLGN4Y. *PNAS, 115,* 302–306.

Bogle, Kathleen. (2008). *Hooking up.* New York: New York University Press.

Bond, Bradley J., & Drogos, Kristin L. (2014). Sex on the Shore: Wishful identification and parasocial relationships as mediators in the relationship between *Jersey Shore* exposure and emerging adults' sexual attitudes and behaviors. *Media Psychology, 17,* 102–126.

Boonstra, Heather. (2001). Islam, women and family planning: A primer. *Guttmacher Report on Public Policy, 4,* 4–7.

Boston Women's Health Book Collective. (2011). *Our bodies, ourselves.* New York: Simon & Schuster, Touchstone Books.

Boswell, John. (1980). *Christianity, social tolerance, and homosexuality.* Chicago: University of Chicago Press.

Bouyer, J., et al. (2003). Risk factors for ectopic pregnancy: A comprehensive analysis based on a large case-control, population-based study in France. *American Journal of Epidemiology, 157,* 185–194.

Bowe, John. (2006, November 19). Gay donor or gay dad? *New York Times Magazine,* pp. 66–73.

Bowen, Anne. (2005). Internet sexuality research with rural men who have sex with men: Can we recruit and retain them? *Journal of Sex Research, 42,* 317–323.

Bowleg, Lisa, et al. (2017). Intersectional epistemologies of ignorance: How behavioral and social science research shapes what we know, think we know, and don't know about U.S. Black men's sexualities. *Journal of Sex Research, 54,* 577–603.

Boyarin, Daniel. (1995). Are there any Jews in "The History of Sexuality"? *Journal of the History of Sexuality, 5,* 333–355.

Boyce, Will, et al. (2006). Sexual health of Canadian youth: Findings from the Canadian Youth, Sexual Health and HIV/AIDS Study. *Canadian Journal of Human Sexuality, 15,* 59–68.

Boyer, Jesseca. (2018). New name, same harm: Rebranding of federal abstinence-only programs. *Guttmacher Policy Review, 21,* 11–16.

Boynton, Petra M. (2003). "I'm just a girl who can't say no"? Women, consent, and sex research. *Journal of Sex & Marital Therapy, 29(s),* 23–32.

Bradford, John M. W., & Greenberg, D. M. (1996). Pharmacological treatment of deviant sexual behaviour. *Annual Review of Sex Research, 7,* 283–306.

Braun, Virginia, & Kitzinger, Celia. (2001). "Snatch," "hole," or "honey-pot"? Semantic categories and the problem of non-specificity in female genital slang. *Journal of Sex Research, 38,* 146–158.

Brecher, Edward M. (1984). *Love, sex, and aging.* Mount Vernon, NY: Consumers Union.

Brecher, Ruth, & Brecher, Edward (Eds.). (1966). *An analysis of human sexual response.* New York: Signet Books, New American Library.

Brecht, M. L., et al. (2004). Methamphetamine use behaviors and gender differences. *Addictive Behaviors, 29,* 89–106.

Brecklin, Leanne R., & Ullman, Sarah E. (2005). Self-defense or assertiveness training and women's responses to sexual attacks. *Journal of Interpersonal Violence, 20,* 738–762.

Breedlove, S. Marc. (2017). Prenatal influences on human sexual orientation: Expectations versus data. *Archives of Sexual Behavior, 46,* 1583–1592.

Brennan, D. (2010). Sex tourism, and sex workers' aspirations. In R. Weitzer (Ed.), *Sex for sale: Prostitution, pornography, and the sex industry* (2nd ed., pp. 307–323). New York: Routledge.

Brent, Jonathan. (1976). A general introduction to privacy. *Massachusetts Law Quarterly, 61,* 10–18.

Brenton, Myron. (1972). *Sex talk.* New York: Stein and Day.

Breslow, N., Evans, I., & Langley, J. (1985). On the prevalence and roles of females in the sadomasochistic subculture: Report of an empirical study. *Archives of Sexual Behavior, 14,* 303–318.

Breton, Sylvie, et al. (1996). Acidification of the male reproductive tract by a proton pumping (H$^+$)-ATPase. *Nature Medicine, 2,* 470–472.

Brewther, Clair T., & Cook, Christian J. (2018). A longitudinal analysis of salivary testosterone concentrations and competitiveness in elite and non-elite women athletes. *Physiology & Behavior, 188,* 157–161.

Brock, G., et al. (2003). Safety and efficacy of vardenafil for the treatment of men with erectile dysfunction after radical retropubic prostatectomy. *Journal of Urology, 170,* 1278–1283.

Brock, Gerald, et al. (2016). 9-month efficacy and safety study of testosterone solution 2% for sex drive and energy in hypogonadal men. *Journal of Urology, 196,* 1509–1515.

Broockman, D., & Kalla, J. (2016). Durably reducing transphobia: A field experiment on door-to-door canvassing. *Science, 352,* 220–224.

Brotto, Lori, et al. (2005). Acculturation and sexual function in Asian women. *Archives of Sexual Behavior, 34,* 595–612.

Brotto, Lori A. (2010). The DSM diagnostic criteria for hypoactive sexual desire disorder in women. *Archives of Sexual Behavior, 39,* 221–239.

Brotto, Lori A., et al. (2016). Mindfulness-based sex therapy improves genital-subjective arousal concordance in women with sexual desire/arousal difficulties. *Archives of Sexual Behavior, 45,* 1907–1921.

Brotto, Lori A., & Yule, M. (2017). Asexuality: Sexual orientation, paraphilia, sexual dysfunction, or none of the above? *Archives of Sexual Behavior, 46,* 619–628.

Brousseau, Mélanie M., et al. (2011). Sexual coercion victimization and perpetration in heterosexual couples: A dyadic investigation. *Archives of Sexual Behavior, 40,* 363–372.

Brown et al. v Buhman, rev'g 947 F. Supp. 2d, 1170 (Utah 2013).

Brown, Jane D., & Bobkowski, Piotr S. (2011). Older and newer media: Patterns of use and effects on adolescents' health and well-being. *Journal of Research on Adolescence, 21,* 95–113.

Brown, Jane, & L'Engle, Kelly. (2009). X-rated: Sexual attitudes and behaviors associated with U.S. early adolescents' exposure to sexually explicit media. *Communication Research, 36,* 129–151.

Brown, Jane, et al. (2006). Sexy media matter: Exposure to sexual content in music, movies, television and magazines predicts Black and White adolescents' sexual behavior. *Pediatrics, 117,* 1018–1027.

Brown, Nancy L., Pennylegion, Michelle, & Hillard, Pamela. (1997). A process evaluation of condom availability in the Seattle, Washington, public schools. *Journal of School Health, 67,* 336–340.

Brown, Susan L., et al. (2017). Relationship quality among cohabiting versus married couples. *Journal of Family Issues, 38,* 1730–1753.

Bruggemann, O., et al. (2007). Support to a woman by a companion of her choice during childbirth: A randomized controlled trial. *Reproductive Health, 4,* 5.

Bryant, Amy G., & Levi, Erika E. (2012). Abortion misinformation from crisis pregnancy centers in North Carolina. *Contraception, 86,* 752–756.

Buchanan, K. M. (1986). *Apache women warriors.* El Paso: Texas Western Press.

Buchanan, R. T. (2014). *The truth about student sex workers: It's far from Belle Du Jour.* Retrieved from http://www.independent.co.uk/life-style/health-and-families/features/the-truth-about-student-sex-workers-its-far-from-belle-du-jour-9757719.html

Buck Louis, G. M., Sundaram, R., Sweeney, A. M., Schisterman, E. F., Maisog, J., & Kannan, K. (2014). Urinary bisphenol A, phthalates, and couple fecundity: The Longitudinal Investigation of Fertility and the Environment (LIFE) Study. *Fertility and Sterility, 101,* 1359–1366.

Buhi, E. R., et al. (2010). Quality and accuracy of sexual health information web sites visited by young people. *Journal of Adolescent Health, 47,* 206–208.

Bulik, C., Prescott, C., & Kendler, K. (2001). Features of childhood sexual abuse and the development of psychiatric and substance use disorders. *British Journal of Psychiatry, 179,* 444–449.

Bullivant, Susan B., et al. (2004). Women's sexual experience during the menstrual cycle: Identification of the sexual phase by non-invasive measurement of luteinizing hormone. *Journal of Sex Research, 41,* 82–93.

Bullough, Bonnie, & Bullough, Vern. (1997). Are transvestites necessarily heterosexual? *Archives of Sexual Behavior, 26,* 1–12.

Bullough, Vern L. (1976). *Sexual variance in society and history.* New York: Wiley.

Bullough, Vern L. (1994). *Science in the bedroom: A history of sex research.* New York: Basic Books.

Bullough, Vern, and Bullough, Bonnie. (1987). *Women and prostitution: A social history.* Buffalo, NY: Prometheus Books.

Bumpass, Larry L., Sweet, James A., & Cherlin, Andrew. (1991). The role of cohabitation in declining rates of marriage. *Journal of Marriage and the Family, 53,* 913–927.

Bureau of Labor Statistics. (2017). *American Time Use Summary.* Retrieved from http://www.bls.gov/news.release/atus.nr0.htm

Burke, Sarah M., et al. (2014). Hypothalamic response to the chemosignal androstadienone in gender dysphoric children and adolescents. *Frontiers in Endocrinology, 5,* Article 60.

Burleson, M. H., et al. (2007). In the mood for love or vice versa? Exploring the relations among sexual activity, physical affection, affect and stress in the daily lives of mid-aged women. *Archives of Sexual Behavior, 36,* 357–368.

Burnes, Theodore. (2017). Flying faster than the birds and the bees: Toward a sex-positive theory and practice in multicultural education. In R.K. Gordon et al. (Eds.), *Challenges associated with cross-cultural and at-risk student engagement* (pp. 170–187). Hershey, PA: ICI Global.

Burnes, Theodore R., et al. (2018). "Wear some thick socks if you walk in my shoes": Agency, resilience, and well-being in communities of North American sex workers. *Archives of Sexual Behavior, 47,* 1541–1550.

Burnett, Arthur L. (2005). Erectile dysfunction following radical prostatectomy. *Journal of the American Medical Association, 293,* 2648–2653.

Burris, Scott. (1993). Testing, disclosure, and the right to privacy. In S. Burris, H. L. Dalton, & J. L. Miller (Eds.), *AIDS law today* (pp. 115–149). New Haven, CT: Yale University Press.

Burton, Frances D. (1970). Sexual climax in Macaca Mulatta. *Proceedings of the Third International Congress on Primatology, 3,* 180–191.

Busko, M. (2014). Practice guideline nixes testosterone therapy for women. *Medscape.* http://www.medscape.com/viewarticle/832898

Buss, David. (2009). The great struggles of life: Darwin and the emergence of evolutionary psychology. *American Psychologist, 64,* 140–148.

Buss, David M. (1988). The evolution of human intra-sexual competition: Tactics of mate attraction. *Journal of Personality and Social Psychology, 54,* 616–628.

Buss, David M. (1991). Evolutionary personality psychology. *Annual Review of Psychology, 42,* 459–491.

Buss, David M. (1994). *The evolution of desire: Strategies of human mating.* New York: Basic Books.

Buss, David M. (2000). *The dangerous passion: Why jealousy is as necessary as love and sex.* New York: Free Press.

Buss, David M. (2016). *The evolution of desire: Strategies of human mating* (Rev. updated ed.). New York: Basic Books.

Buss, David M., & Schmitt, David P. (1993). Sexual strategies theory: An evolutionary perspective on human mating. *Psychological Review, 100,* 204–232.

Buss, David, & Shackelford, Todd. (1997a). From vigilance to violence: Mate retention tactics in married couples. *Journal of Personality and Social Psychology, 72,* 346–361.

Buss, David, & Shackelford, Todd. (1997b). Susceptibility to infidelity in the first year of marriage. *Journal of Research in Personality, 31,* 193–221.

Butler, Judith. (1988). Performative acts and gender constitution: An essay in phenomenology and feminist theory. *Theatre Journal, 4,* 519–531.

Butterfield, Fox. (2002, May 19). A priest's two faces: Protector, predator. *New York Times.*

Buunk, Bram, et al. (1996). Sex differences in jealousy in evolutionary and cultural perspective: Tests from the Netherlands, Germany, and the United States. *Psychological Science, 7,* 359–363.

Byard, Roger, Hucker, Stephen, & Hazelwood, Robert. (1993). Fatal and near-fatal autoerotic asphyxial episodes in women. *American Journal of Forensic Medicine and Pathology, 14,* 70–73.

Byers, E. Sandra, & Demmons, Stephanie. (1999). Sexual satisfaction and sexual self-disclosure within dating relationships. *Journal of Sex Research, 36,* 180–189.

Byne, William, et al. (2000). The interstitial nuclei of the human anterior hypothalamus: Assessment for sexual variation in volume and neuronal size, density, and number. *Brain Research, 856,* 254–258.

Byne, William, et al. (2018). Assessment and treatment of gender dysphoria and gender variant patients: A primer for psychiatrists. *American Journal of Psychiatry, 175,* 1046.

Byrne, Donn. (1971). *The attraction paradigm.* New York: Academic.

Byrne, Donn. (1997). An overview (and underview) of research and theory within the attraction paradigm. *Journal of Social and Personal Relationships, 14,* 417–431.

Cacchioni, T. (2015). The medicalization of sexual deviance, reproduction, and functioning. In J. DeLamater & Rebecca F. Plante (Eds.), *Handbook of the sociology of sexualities* (pp. 435–452). New York: Springer.

Cacioppo, Stephanie, et al. (2012a). The common neural bases between sexual desire and love: A multilevel kernel density fMRI analysis. *Journal of Sexual Medicine, 9,* 1048–1054.

Cacioppo, Stephanie, et al. (2012b). Social neuroscience of love. *Clinical Neuropsychiatry, 9,* 3–13.

Cahill, Larry. (2005). His brain, her brain. *Scientific American, 292* (5), 40–47.

Call, Vaughn, Sprecher, Susan, & Schwartz, Pepper. (1995). The incidence and frequency of marital sex in a national sample. *Journal of Marriage and the Family, 57,* 639–652.

Callahan, Daniel. (1986, February). How technology is reframing the abortion debate. *Hastings Center Report,* 33–42.

Callister, M., Coyne, S. M., Stern, L. A., Stockdale, L., Miller, M. J., & Wells, B. M. (2012). A content analysis of the prevalence and portrayal of sexual activity in adolescent literature. *Journal of Sex Research, 49,* 477–486.

Calzo, Jerel P., & Ward, L. Monique. (2009). Media exposure and viewers' attitudes toward homosexuality: Evidence for mainstreaming or resonance? *Journal of Broadcasting and Electronic Media, 53,* 280–299.

Camilleri, Joseph A., & Quinsey, Vernon L. (2008). Pedophilia: Assessment and treatment. In D. R. Laws & W. T. O'Donohue (Eds.), *Sexual deviance* (pp. 183–212). New York: Guilford.

Campbell, D. A., Lake, M. F., Falk, M., & Backstrand, J. (2006). A randomized control trial of continuous support in labor by a lay doula. *Journal of Obstetric, Gynecologic, & Neonatal Nursing, 35,* 456–464.

Campbell, Rebecca E., & Herbison, Allan E. (2014). Gonadal steroid neuromodulation of developing and mature hypothalamic neuronal networks. *Current Opinion in Neurobiology, 29,* 96–102.

Cantor, James M., Blanchard, R., Robichaud, L., & Christensen, B. (2005). Quantitative reanalysis of aggregate data on IQ in sexual offenders. *Psychological Bulletin, 131,* 555–568.

Cantor, James M., et al. (2002). How many gay men owe their sexual orientation to fraternal birth order? *Archives of Sexual Behavior, 31,* 63–72.

Cantor, J. M., Klein, C., Lykins, A., Rullo, J. E., Thaler, L., & Walling, B. R. (2013). A treatment-oriented typology of self-identified hypersexuality referrals. *Archives of Sexual Behavior, 42,* 883–893.

Cantor, James M., et al. (2015). Diffusion tensor imaging of pedophilia. *Archives of Sexual Behavior, 44,* 2161–2172.

Caplan, Paula. (1995). *How do they decide who is normal?* Reading, MA: Addison-Wesley.

Carballo-Diéguez, Alex, et al. (2017). Preference of oral tenofovir disoproxil fumarate/emtricitabine versus rectal tenofovir reduced-glycerin 1% gel . . . *AIDS and Behavior, 21,* 3336–3345.

Carmody, Moira. (2015). *Sex, ethics, and young people.* New York: Palgrave Macmillan.

Carnes, Patrick. (1983). *The sexual addiction.* Minneapolis, MN: CompCare Publications.

Carnes, Patrick. (2012). *Out of the shadows* (3rd ed.). Center City, MN: Hazelden.

Caron, S. L., & Ahlgrim, C. J. (2012). Children's understanding and knowledge of conception and birth: Comparing children from England, the Netherlands, Sweden, and the United States. *American Journal of Sexuality Education, 7,* 16–36.

Carpenter, Laura M., & DeLamater, John (Eds). (2012). *Sex for life: From virginity to Viagra, how sexuality changes throughout our lives.* New York: New York University Press.

Carpentier, Francesca R. D., et al. (2017). Sex, love, and risk-n-responsibility: A content analysis of entertainment television. *Mass Communication and Society, 20,* 686–709.

Carroll, J. S., et al. (2008). Generation XXX: Pornography acceptance and use among emerging adults. *Journal of Adolescent Research, 32,* 6–30.

Carroll, Marjorie H., & Clark, M. Diane. (2006). Men's acquaintance rape scripts: A comparison between a regional university and a military academy. *Sex Roles, 55,* 469–480.

Carvalho, J., Stulhofer, A., Vieira, A. L., & Jurin, T. (2015). Hypersexuality and sexual desire: Exploring the structure of problematic sexuality. *Journal of Sexual Medicine, 12.* doi: 10.1111/jsm.12865

Carver, K., Joyner, K., & Udry, J. R. (2003). National estimates of adolescent romantic relationships. In P. Florsheim (Ed.), *Adolescent romantic relationships and sexual behavior: Theory, research, and practical implications* (pp. 291–329). New York: Cambridge University Press.

Casey, B. J., et al. (2011). Braking and accelerating of the adolescent brain. *Journal of Research on Adolescence, 21,* 21–33.

Cashdan, Elizabeth. (2008). Waist-to-hip ratio across cultures: Trade-offs between androgen- and estrogen-dependent traits. *Current Anthropology, 49,* 1099–1107.

Castaneda, Donna. (1993). The meaning of romantic love among Mexican-Americans. *Journal of Social Behavior and Personality, 8,* 257–272.

Castellsagué, Xavier, et al. (2002). Male circumcision, penile human papillomavirus infection, and cervical cancer in female partners. *New England Journal of Medicine, 346,* 1105–1112.

Catania, Joseph A., et al. (1990). Response bias in assessing sexual behaviors relevant to HIV transmission. *Evaluation and Program Planning, 13,* 19–29.

Catania, Joseph A., et al. (1995). Methodological research on sexual behavior in the AIDS era. *Annual Review of Sex Research, 6,* 77–125.

Catania, Joseph A., et al. (2015). Nonprobability and probability-based sampling strategies in sexual science. *Journal of Sex Research, 52,* 396–411.

Caughey, Madeline S. (1974). The principle of harm and its application to laws criminalizing prostitution. *Denver Law Journal, 51,* 235–262.

Centers for Disease Control and Prevention. (2002). *Alcohol use and pregnancy: Fact sheet.* www.cdc.gov/ncbddd/factsheets/alcoholuse.pdf

Centers for Disease Control and Prevention. (2003). *STD surveillance 2002.* www.cdc.gov/std

Centers for Disease Control and Prevention. (2004a). *Sexual violence: Fact sheet.* www.cdc.gov/ncipc/factsheets/svfacts.htm

Centers for Disease Control and Prevention. (2004b). *Intimate partner violence: Fact sheet.* www.cdc.gov/ncipc/factsheets/ipvfacts.htm

Centers for Disease Control and Prevention. (2006). Abortion surveillance—United States, 2003. *Morbidity and Mortality Weekly Report, 55,* SS-11.

Centers for Disease Control and Prevention. (2008). Abortion surveillance—United States, 2005. *Surveillance Summaries,* MMWR: 57 (SS13).

Centers for Disease Control and Prevention. (2009). *Key statistics from the National Survey of Family Growth: Teenagers.* www.cdc.gov/nchs/nsfg/abc_list_t.htm/teenagers

Centers for Disease Control and Prevention. (2011a). *Assisted reproductive technology (ART): National Summary Report, 2010.* http//apps.nccd.cde.gov/Apps/NationalSummaryReport.aspx

Centers for Disease Control and Prevention. (2014a). *Other sexually transmitted diseases.* www.cdc.gov/std/stats13/other.htm

Centers for Disease Control and Prevention. (2014b). *Preexposure prophylaxis for the prevention of HIV infection in the United States–2014.* http://www.cdc.gov/hiv/pdf/PrEPguidelines2014.pdf

Centers for Disease Control and Prevention. (2014c). Racial disparities in access to maternal care practices that support breastfeeding-United States, 2011. *Morbidity and Mortality Weekly Report, 63,* 725–728.

Centers for Disease Control and Prevention. (2014d). *Rates of any and exclusive breastfeeding by sociodemographics among children born in 2011.* http://www.cdc.gov/breastfeeding/data/nis_data/rates-any-exclusive-bf-socio-dem-2011.htm

Centers for Disease Control and Prevention. (2015a). *HIV among people aged 50 and older.* http://www.cdc.gov/hiv/risk/age/olderamericans/index.html

Centers for Disease Control and Prevention. (2015b). *Draft CDC recommendations for providers counseling male patients and parents regarding male circumcision and the prevention of HIV infection, STIs, and other health outcomes.* Retrieved from https://www.cdc.gov/nchhstp/newsroom/docs/factsheets/mc-factsheet-508.pdf

Centers for Disease Control and Prevention. (2017a). *Reported STDs in the United States, 2016.* Retrieved from https://www.cdc.gov/nchhstp/newsroom/docs/factsheets/STD-Trends-508.pdf

Centers for Disease Control and Prevention. (2017b). *2016 Sexually Transmitted Diseases Surveillance.* Retrieved from https://www.cdc.gov/std/stats16/toc.htm

Centers for Disease Control and Prevention. (2017c). *HIV surveillance report.* Vol. 28. Retrieved from https://www.cdc.gov/hiv/pdf/library/reports/surveillance/cdc-hiv-surveillance-report-2016-vol-28.pdf

Cerny, Jerome A., & Janssen, Erick. (2011). Patterns of sexual arousal in homosexual, bisexual, and heterosexual men. *Archives of Sexual Behavior, 40,* 687–697.

Chae, David H., & Ayala, George. (2010). Sexual orientation and sexual behavior among Latino and Asian Americans: Implications for unfair treatment and psychological distress. *Journal of Sex Research, 47,* 451–459.

Chan, Connie S. (2003). Psychological issues of Asian Americans. In P. Bronstein & K. Quina (Eds.), *Teaching gender and multicultural awareness* (pp. 179–194). Washington, DC: American Psychological Association.

Chan, Darius K-S., et al. (2008). Examining the job-related, psychological, and physical outcomes of workplace sexual harassment: A meta-analytic review. *Psychology of Women Quarterly, 32,* 362–376.

Chandra, Anjani, et al. (2005). Fertility, family planning and reproductive health of U.S. women: Data from the 2002 National Survey of Family Growth. National Center for Health Statistics. *Vital Health Statistics, 23,* 106–108, 136.

Chandra, Anjani, et al. (2011). Sexual behavior, sexual attraction, and sexual identity in the United States: Data from the 2006–2008 National Survey of Family Growth. *National Health Statistics Reports, 36.* Centers for Disease Control.

Chapman, Audrey. (1997). The Black search for love and devotion: Facing the future against all odds. In H. P. McAdoo (Ed.), *Black families* (3rd ed.). Thousand Oaks, CA: Sage.

Chapman, Heather, et al. (1997). Partners' stress underestimations lead to women's distress: A study of pregnant inner-city women. *Journal of Personality and Social Psychology, 73,* 418–425.

Charon, Joel. (1995). *Symbolic interactionism: An introduction, interpretation, and integration* (5th ed.). Englewood Cliffs, NJ: Prentice-Hall.

Chatterjee, Animesh, et al. (2012). Chemokines and chemokine receptors in susceptibility to HIV-1 infection and progression to AIDS. *Disease Markers, 32,* 143–151.

Chavarro, J., et al. (2007). Diet and lifestyle in the prevention of ovulatory disorder infertility. *Obstetrics & Gynecology, 110,* 1050–1058.

Check, Erika. (2005). Trial aims to measure social effects of choosing babies' sex. *Nature, 437,* 1214–1215.

Chen, Liang, et al. (2015, March). Phosphodiesterase 5 inhibitors for the treatment of erectile dysfunction: A trade-off network meta-analysis. *European Urology, 68,* 674–680.

Cheng, Jeani, et al. (2003, February 21). Pregnancy related mortality surveillance–United States, 1991–1999. *Morbidity and Mortality Weekly Report, 52,* 1–8.

Cheng, Mariah M., & Udry, J. Richard. (2003). How much do mentally disabled adolescents know about sex and birth control? *Adolescent and Family Health, 3,* 28–38.

Cherukuri, R., et al. (1988). A cohort study of alkaloidal cocaine ("crack") in pregnancy. *Obstetrics and Gynecology, 72,* 147–151.

Chesler, Ellen. (1992). *Woman of valor: Margaret Sanger and the birth control movement.* New York: Simon & Schuster.

Chew, Denise, et al. (2019). Hormonal treatment in young people with gender dysphoria: A systematic review. *Pediatrics, 141,* e20173742.

Chiu, Y. H., et al. (2015). Fruit and vegetable intake and their pesticide residues in relation to semen quality among men from a fertility clinic. *Human Reproduction, 30,* 1342–1351. doi: 10.1093/humrep/dev064

Chivers, Meredith L. (2017). The specificity of women's sexual response and its relationship with sexual orientations: A review and ten hypotheses. *Archives of Sexual Behavior, 46,* 1161–1179.

Chivers, Meredith, & Bailey, J. M. (2000). Sexual orientation of female-to-male transsexuals: A comparison of homosexual and nonhomosexual types. *Archives of Sexual Behavior, 29,* 259–278.

Chivers, Meredith, et al. (2014). Experimental, neuroimaging, and psychophysiological methods in sexuality research. In D. Tolman & L. Diamond (Eds.), *APA handbook of sexuality and psychology* (Vol. 1, pp. 99–120). Washington, DC: APA.

Chivers, Meredith L., et al. (2010). Agreement of self-reported and genital measures of sexual arousal in men and women: A meta-analysis. *Archives of Sexual Behavior, 39,* 5–56.

Choi, E. J., et al. (2001). Low-density DNA array coupled to PCR differential display identifies new estrogen-responsive genes during the postnatal differentiation of the rat hypothalamus. *Molecular Brain Research, 97,* 115–128.

Choi, Y., Bishai, D., & Minkovitz, C. (2009). Multiple births are a risk factor for postpartum maternal depression. *Pediatrics, 123,* 1147–1154.

Choi, Andrew Y., & Israel, Tania. (2016). Centralizing the psychology of sexual minority Asian and Pacific islander Americans. *Psychology of Sexual Orientation and Gender Diversity, 3,* 345–356.

Chong, Y. M. G., et al. (2012). Cultivation effects of video games: A longer-term experimental test of first- and second-order effects. *Journal of Social and Clinical Psychology, 31,* 952–971.

Choudhury, Samrat R., et al. (2016). CRISPR-dCas9 mediated TET1 targeting for selective DNA demethylation at BRCA1 promoter. *Oncotarget, 7,* 46545–46556.

Christensen, Cornelia V. (1971). *Kinsey: A biography.* Bloomington: Indiana University Press.

Christopher, F. Scott, & Sprecher, Susan. (2000). Sexuality in marriage, dating, and other relationships: A decade review. *Journal of Marriage and the Family, 62,* 999–1017.

Chu, M., & Lobo, R. (2004). Formulations and use of androgens in women. *Journal of Family Practice, 53,* S3.

Church, Stephanie, et al. (2001). Violence by clients towards female prostitutes in different work settings: Questionnaire survey. *British Medical Journal, 322,* 524–525.

Cizmar, M., Conklin, E., & Hinman, K. (2011). *Real men get their facts straight.* Retrieved from www.villagevoice.com/content/printVersion/2651144/

Clark, Justin T., et al. (2014). Engineering a segmented dual-reservoir polyurethane intravaginal ring for simultaneous prevention of HIV transmission and unwanted pregnancy. *PLOSOne, 9,* e88509.

Clark, R. D., & Hatfield, Elaine. (1989). Gender differences in receptivity to sexual offers. *Journal of Psychology & Human Sexuality, 2,* 39–45.

Clarke, Michael J., et al. (2015). Effect of normative masculinity on males' dysfunctional sexual beliefs, sexual attitudes, and perceptions of sexual functioning. *Journal of Sex Research, 52,* 327–337.

Clayton, Anita H., et al. (2016). Sexual dysfunction due to psychotropic medications. *Psychiatric Clinics of North America, 39,* 427–463.

Cleland, Kelly, et al. (2012). The efficacy of intrauterine devices for emergency contraception. *Human Reproduction, 27,* 1994–2000.

Clemente, Carmine D. (1987). *Anatomy: A regional atlas of the human body* (3rd ed.). Baltimore, MD: Urban & Schwarzenberg.

Clutton-Brock, Tim. (2007). Sexual selection in males and females. *Science, 318,* 1882–1885.

Cochran, Susan D., et al. (2007). Mental health and substance use disorders among Latino and Asian American lesbian, gay, and bisexual adults. *Journal of Consulting and Clinical Psychology, 75,* 785–794.

Cochran, W. G., Mosteller, F., & Tukey, J. W. (1953). Statistical problems of the Kinsey report. *Journal of the American Statistical Association, 48,* 673–716.

Cogan, Jeanine C., & Marcus-Newhall, Amy. (2002). Hate crimes: Research, policy, and action. *American Behavioral Scientist, 45*(12), special issue.

Cohen, Jacob. (1988). *Statistical power analysis for the behavioral sciences.* Hillsdale, NJ: Erlbaum.

Cohen, Jon. (2003). Thailand and Cambodia: Two hard-hit countries offer rare success stories. *Science, 301,* 1658–1663.

Cohen, Jon. (2009). Beyond Thailand: Making sense of a qualified AIDS vaccine "success." *Science, 326,* 652–653.

Cohen, Jon. (2011a). The emerging race to cure HIV infections. *Science, 332,* 784–789.

Cohen, Jon. (2011b). Breakthrough of the year: HIV treatment as prevention. *Science, 334,* 1628.

Cohen, Lior, et al. (2018). Behavior: Oxytocin promotes fearless motherhood. *Current Biology, 28,* R359–R361.

Cohn, Lawrence. (1983, November 16). Pix less able but porn is stable. *Variety, 313*(3), 1–2.

Coker, Ann L., et al. (2015). Evaluation of the Green Dot bystander intervention to reduce interpersonal violence among college students across three campuses. *Violence Against Women, 21,* 1507–1527.

Coker, Ann L., et al. (2016). Multi-college bystander intervention evaluation for violence prevention. *American Journal of Preventive Medicine, 50,* 295–302.

Cole, Elizabeth R. (2009). Intersectionality and research in psychology. *American Psychologist, 64,* 170–180.

Coleman, Eli. (1991). Compulsive sexual behavior: New concepts and treatments. *Journal of Psychology and Human Sexuality, 4*(2), 37–51.

Coleman, Eli, et al. (2001). Compulsive Sexual Behavior Inventory: A preliminary study of reliability and validity. *Journal of Sex and Marital Therapy, 27,* 325–332.

Coleman, Eli, et al. (2011). Standards of care for the health of transsexual, transgender, and gender-nonconforming people, Version 7. *International Journal of Transgenderism, 13,* 165–232.

Collaborative Group on Hormonal Factors in Breast Cancer. (2002). Breast cancer and breast-feeding. *Lancet, 360,* 187–195.

Collins, Nancy L., & Miller, Lynn C. (1994). Self-disclosure and liking: A meta-analytic review. *Psychological Bulletin, 116,* 457–475.

Collins, R. L., et al. (2004). Watching sex on television predicts adolescent initiation of sexual behavior. *Pediatrics, 114,* e280–e289.

Collins, Rebecca L., et al. (2005). Isolating the nexus of substance use, violence and sexual risk for HIV infection among young adults in the United States. *AIDS and Behavior, 9,* 73–87.

Collins, W. Andrew, Welsh, Deborah P., & Furman, Wyndol. (2009). Adolescent romantic relationships. *Annual Review of Psychology, 60,* 631–652.

COMET (Comparative Obstetric Mobile Epidural Trial) Study Group. (2001). Effect of low-dose mobile versus traditional epidural techniques on mode of delivery: A randomised controlled trial. *Lancet, 358,* 19–23.

Committee on Adolescence. (2013). Condom use by adolescents. *Pediatrics, 132,* 873–881.

Committee on Children with Disabilities. (1996). Sexuality education of children and adolescents with developmental disabilities. *Pediatrics, 97,* 275–278.

Compas, Bruce E., & Luecken, Linda. (2002). Psychological adjustment to breast cancer. *Current Directions in Psychological Science, 11,* 111–114.

Congregation for the Doctrine of the Faith. (1986, October 1). The pastoral care of homosexual persons. *Origins, 16,* 198–211.

Congregation for the Doctrine of the Faith. (1987). Instruction on respect for human life in its origin and on the dignity of procreation. *Origins, 16,* 198–211.

Congregation for the Doctrine of the Faith. (2008, September 8). *Regarding the instruction dignitas personae.* www.religiousinstitute.org/statement/regarding-the-instruction-dignitas-personaesummary

Conley, Terri D. (2011). Perceived proposer personality characteristics and gender differences in acceptance of casual sex offers. *Journal of Personality and Social Psychology, 100,* 309–329.

Conley, Terri D., et al. (2011). Women, men, and the bedroom: Methodological and conceptual insights that narrow, reframe, and eliminate gender differences in sexuality. *Current Directions in Psychological Science, 20,* 296–300.

Constantine, Norman, Jerman, Petra, & Huang, Alice. (2007). California parents' preferences and beliefs regarding school-based sex education policy. *Perspectives on Sexual and Reproductive Health, 39,* 167–175.

Contessini, Claudia. (2003). Personal communication.

Cook, K., Chesire, C., Rice, E., & Nakagawa, S. (2013). Social exchange theory. In J. DeLamater & A. Ward (Eds.), *Handbook of social psychology* (2nd ed., pp. 61–88). Dordrecht: Springer.

Cook Jocelynn L., et al. (2015). Fetal alcohol spectrum disorder: A guideline for diagnosis across the lifespan. *Canadian Medical Association Journal, 188,* 191–197.

Cooper, Al, Delmonico, David, & Burg, Ron. (2000). Cybersex users, abusers and compulsives: New findings and implications. *Sexual Addiction and Compulsivity, 7,* 5–29.

Copen, Casey E., et al. (2012a). Prevalence and timing of oral sex with opposite sex partners among females and males aged 15–24 years. *National Health Statistics Report,* No. 56. http://www.cdc.gov/nchs/data/nhsr/nhsr056.pdf

Copen, Casey E., et al. (2012b). First marriages in the United States. *National Health Statistics Reports,* No. 49. http://www.cdc.gov/nchs/data/nhsr/nhsr049.pdf

Copen, Casey E., et al. (2013). First premarital cohabitation in the United States: 2006–2010. National Survey of Family Growth. *National Health Statistics Reports,* No. 64. http://www.cdc.gov/nchs/data/nhsr/nhsr064.pdf

Copen, Casey E., et al. (2016, January 7). Sexual behavior, sexual attraction, and sexual orientation among adults aged 18–44 in the United States: Data from the 2011–2013 National Survey of Family Growth. *National Health Statistics Reports, 88.*

Cordova, Matthew J., et al. (2001). Posttraumatic growth following breast cancer: A controlled comparison study. *Health Psychology, 20,* 176–185.

Corey, Lawrence, & Wald, Anna. (2008). Genital herpes. In K. Holmes et al. (Eds.), *Sexually transmitted diseases* (4th ed., pp. 399–438). New York: McGraw-Hill.

Cortoni, Franca, Hanson, R. Karl, & Coache, Marie-Eve. (2010). The recidivism rates of female sexual offenders are low: A meta-analysis. *Sex Abuse, 22,* 387–401.

Countryman, L. William. (1988). *Dirt, greed, and sex: Sexual ethics in the New Testament and their implications for today.* Philadelphia: Fortress Press.

Countryman, L. William. (1994). New Testament sexual ethics and today's world. In J. B. Nelson & S. P. Longfellow (Eds.), *Sexuality and the sacred* (pp. 28–53). Louisville, KY: Westminster/John Knox Press.

Coussons-Read, M. E. (2012). The psychoneuroimmunology of stress in pregnancy. *Current Directions in Psychological Science, 21,* 323–328.

Coustan, Donald, & Angelini, Diane. (1995). The puerperium. In D. R. Coustan et al. (Eds.), *Human reproduction: Growth and development* (pp. 341–358). Boston: Little, Brown.

Covey, Judith, et al. (2016). A synthesis of meta-analytic evidence of behavioral interventions to reduce HIV/STIs. *Journal of Behavioral Medicine, 39,* 371–385.

Cowley, J. J., & Brooksbank, B. W. L. (1991). Human exposure to putative pheromones and changes in aspects of social behavior. *Journal of Steroid Biochemistry and Molecular Biology, 39,* 647–659.

Cox, William T. L., Devine, P. G., Bischmann, A., & Hyde, J. S. (2015). Inferences about sexual orientation: The role of stereotypes, faces, and the gaydar myth. *Journal of Sex Research, 1–15.*

Cramer, Ryan, et al. (2017). State and local policies related to sexual orientation in the United States. *Journal of Public Health Policy, 38,* 58–79.

Crawford, June, Kippax, Susan, & Waldby, Catherine. (1994). Women's sex talk and men's sex talk: Different worlds. *Feminism and Psychology, 4,* 571–587.

Crawford, Mary, & Popp, Danielle. (2003). Sexual double standards: A review and methodological critique of two decades of research. *Journal of Sex Research, 40,* 13–26.

Creighton, James. (1992). *Don't go away mad.* New York: Doubleday.

Creighton, Sarah, & Minto, Catherine. (2001). Managing intersex: Most vaginal surgery in childhood should be deferred. *British Medical Journal, 323,* 1264–1265.

Creighton, Sarah M., Minto, C., & Steele, S. (2001). Objective cosmetic and anatomical outcomes at adolescence of feminising surgery for ambiguous genitalia done in childhood. *Lancet, 358,* 124–125.

Crissman, Halley P., et al. (2017). Transgender demographics: A household probability sample of US adults, 2014. *American Journal of Public Health, 107,* 213–215.

Crompton, Louis. (2003). *Homosexuality and civilization.* Cambridge, MA: Harvard University Press.

Crone, Eveline A., & Dahl, Ronald E. (2012). Understanding adolescence as a period of social-affective engagement and goal flexibility. *Nature Reviews Neuroscience, 13,* 636–650.

Cross, Catharine P., Copping, L. T., & Campbell, A. (2011). Sex differences in impulsivity: A meta-analysis. *Psychological Bulletin, 137,* 97–130.

Crossman, A. (2015). *Moral panic.* Retrieved from http://sociology.about.com/od/M_Index/g/Moral-Panic.htm

Cuevas, Carlos A., Sabina, C., & Picard, E. H. (2010). Interpersonal victimization patterns and psychopathology among Latino women: Results from the SALAS study. *Psychological Trauma: Theory, Research, Practice, and Policy, 2,* 296–306.

Cunningham, F. Gary, et al. (1993). *Williams obstetrics* (19th ed.). Norwalk, CT: Appleton and Lange.

Cunningham, Scott, & Kendall, Todd D. (2011). Prostitution 2.0: The changing face of sex work. *Journal of Urban Economics, 69,* 273–287.

Cunningham, Scott, & Shah, Manisha. (2018). Decriminalizing indoor prostitution: Implications for sexual violence public health. *Review of Economic Studies, 85,* 1683–1715.

Curran, Charles E. (1988). Roman Catholic sexual ethics: A dissenting view. *Christian Century, 105,* 1139–1142.

Curtis, J. T., & Wang, Z. X. (2003). The neurochemistry of pair bonding. *Current Directions in Psychological Science, 12,* 49–53.

Cutler, Winnifred B. (1999). Human sex-attractant hormones. *Psychiatric Annals, 29,* 54–59.

Cutler-Seeber, Andrew. (2018). *Trans* lives in the United States: Challenges of transition and beyond.* New York: Routledge.

Cuzick, Jack, et al. (2011). Preventive therapy for breast cancer: A consensus statement. *Lancet Oncology, 12,* 496–503.

Czopp, Alexander M., Monteith, Margo, Zimmerman, Rick, & Lynam, Donald R. (2004). Implicit attitudes as potential protection from risky sex: Predicting condom use with the IAT. *Basic and Applied Social Psychology, 26,* 227–236.

D'Augelli, Anthony R., & Garnets, Linda D. (1995). Lesbian, gay, and bisexual communities. In A. D'Augelli & C. Patterson (Eds.), *Lesbian, gay, and bisexual identities over the lifespan* (pp. 293–320). New York: Oxford University Press.

D'Souza, Gypsyamber, et al. (2007). Case-control study of human papillomavirus and oropharyngeal cancer. *New England Journal of Medicine, 356,* 1944–1956.

Daboin, Irene, Peterson, J. L., & Parrott, D. (2015). Racial differences in sexual prejudice and its correlates among heterosexual men. *Cultural Diversity & Ethnic Minority Psychology, 21,* 258–267.

Daniels, Kimberly, et al. (2014). Current contraceptive status among women aged 15–44: United States, 2011–2013. NCHS Data Brief No. 173. http://www.cdc.gov/nchs/data/databriefs/db173.pdf

Dank, M., Khan, B., Downey, P. M., et al. (2014). *Estimating the size and structure of the underground commercial sex economy in eight major US cities.* Washington, DC: The Urban Institute.

Darling, Carol A., Davidson, J. K., & Conway-Welch, C. (1990). Female ejaculation: Perceived origins, the Gräfenberg spot/area, and sexual responsiveness. *Archives of Sexual Behavior, 19,* 29–48.

Darwich, Lina, et al. (2012). School avoidance and substance use among lesbian, gay, bisexual, and questioning youths: The impact of peer victimization and adult support. *Journal of Educational Psychology, 104,* 381–392.

Das, Aniruddha, Waite, Linda, & Laumann, Edward. (2012). Sexual expression over the life course. In Laura Carpenter & John DeLamater (Eds.), *Sex for life: From virginity to Viagra, how sexuality changes throughout our lives* (pp. 236–259). New York: New York University Press.

Davey, Monica. (2003, August 4). Episcopalians give first nod for gay bishop. *New York Times.*

David, A. (2011). The joy of spanking. *Salon.com.* Retrieved from http://www.salon.com/2011/02/11/inside_world_of_spanking/

David, Henry P., Dytrych, Zdenek, & Matejcek, Zdenek. (2003). Born unwanted: Observations from the Prague study. *American Psychologist, 58,* 224–229.

Davies, M. J., et al. (2012). Reproductive technologies and the risk of birth defects. *The New England Journal of Medicine, 366,* 1803–1813.

Davis, Clive M., & Bauserman, R. (1993). Exposure to sexually explicit materials: An attitude change perspective. *Annual Review of Sex Research, 4,* 121–210.

Davy, Zowie. (2015). The DSM-5 and the politics of diagnosing transpeople. *Archives of Sexual Behavior, 44,* 1165–1176.

Dawson, Samantha J., et al. (2012). Sexual fantasies and viewing times across the menstrual cycle: A diary study. *Archives of Sexual Behavior, 41,* 173–183.

De Cuypere, Griet, et al. (2005). Sexual and physical health after sex reassignment surgery. *Archives of Sexual Behavior, 34,* 679–690.

de Graaf, Hanneke, & Rademakers, Jany. (2006). Sexual behavior of prepubertal children. *Journal of Psychology & Human Sexuality, 18,* 1–21.

de Graaf, Hanneke, & Rademakers, Jany. (2011). The psychological measurement of childhood sexual development in western societies: Methodological challenges. *Journal of Sex Research, 48,* 118–129.

de Graaf, Hanneke, et al. (2009). Sexual trajectories during adolescence: Relation to demographic characteristics and sexual risk. *Archives of Sexual Behavior, 38,* 276–282.

de Heer, Brooke. (2016). A snapshot of serial rape: An investigation of criminal sophistication and use of force on victim injury and severity of the assault. *Journal of Interpersonal Violence, 31,* 598–619.

de Jong, David C. (2009). The role of attention in sexual arousal: Implications for treatment of sexual dysfunction. *Journal of Sex Research, 46,* 237–248.

de Jong, Peter J., van Overveld, M., & Borg, C. (2013). Giving in to arousal or staying stuck in disgust? Disgust-based mechanisms in sex and sexual dysfunction. *Journal of Sex Research, 50,* 247–262.

De Vera, Mary A., & Berard, Anick. (2012). Antidepressant use during pregnancy and the risk of pregnancy induced hypertension. *British Journal of Clinical Pharmacology.* doi: 10.1111/1365-2125.2012.04196.x

de Visser, Richard O., et al. (2007). The impact of sexual coercion on psychological, physical, and sexual well-being in a representative sample of Australian women. *Archives of Sexual Behavior, 36,* 676–686.

De Vries, Annelou, et al. (2014). Young adult psychological out-come after puberty suppression and gender reassignment. *Pediatrics, 134,* 696–704.

de Waal, Frans. (2002). Evolutionary psychology: The wheat and the chaff. *Current Directions in Psychological Science, 11,* 187–191.

DeArmond, Sarah, et al. (2006). Age and gender stereotypes: New challenges in a changing workplace and workforce. *Journal of Applied Social Psychology, 36,* 2184–2214.

DeBruine, Lisa M., et al. (2010). The health of a nation predicts their mate preferences: Cross-cultural variation in women's preferences for masculinized male faces. *Proceedings of the Royal Society: Biological Sciences, 277,* 1692–2405.

DeFrancesco, M. (2015, May 27). No evidence to show fetal pain in second trimester. Medscape. Retrieved from https://www.medscape.com/viewarticle/845157

Dehlin, J. P., et al. (2014). Sexual orientation change efforts among current or former LDS church members. *Journal of Counseling Psychology, 62*(2), 95–105.

Del Giudice, Marco, et al. (2009). The juvenile transition: A developmental switch point in human life history. *Developmental Review, 29,* 1–31.

DeLamater, John. (1987). A sociological perspective. In J. H. Geer & W. T. O'Donohue (Eds.), *Theories of human sexuality* (pp. 237–256). New York: Plenum.

DeLamater, John, & Moorman, Sara. (2007). Sexual behavior in later life. *Journal of Aging and Health, 19,* 921–945.

DeLamater, John, Wagstaff, David A., & Havens, Kayt Klein. (2000). The impact of a culturally appropriate STD/AIDS education intervention on Black male adolescents' sexual and condom use behavior. *Health Education and Behavior, 27,* 454–470.

Delap, J. (2014, August 9). The changing business of sex: How the Internet affects prostitution. *The Economist.* Retrieved from https://www.economist.com/newsbook/2014/08/08/how-the-internet-affects-prostitution

Deligeoroglou, E. (2000). Dysmenorrhea. *Annals of the New York Academy of Sciences, 900,* 237–244.

Denizet-Lewis, B. (2009, January 2). Facing my obsession, in the flesh. *New York Times.* Retrieved from https://www.nytimes.com/2009/01/04/fashion/04love.html

Denizet-Lewis, Benoit. (2004, May 30). Friends, friends with benefits, and the benefits of the local mall. *New York Times Magazine,* 30–35ff.

Dennerstein, Lorraine, Alexander, Jeanne L., & Kotz, Krista. (2003). The menopause and sexual functioning: A review of the population-based studies. *Annual Review of Sex Research, 14,* 64–82.

Dennis, Amanda, Henshaw, Stanley, Joyce, Theodore, et al. (2009). *The impact of laws requiring parental involvement for abortion: A literature review.* New York: Guttmacher Institute.

Dennis, Cindy-Lee. (2005). Psychosocial and psychological interventions for prevention of postnatal depression: Systematic review. *British Medical Journal, 331,* 15.

Denzin, Norman K., & Lincoln, Yvonna S. (Eds.). (2011). *The Sage handbook of qualitative research* (4th ed.). Thousand Oaks, CA: Sage.

DePaulo, Bella. (2006). *Singled out: How singles are stereotyped, stigmatized, and ignored, and still live happily ever after.* New York: St. Martin's Press.

Derby, C., et al. (2000). Modifiable risk factors and erectile dysfunction: Can lifestyle changes modify risk? *Urology, 56,* 302–306.

Derlega, Valerian J. (Ed.). (1984). *Communication, intimacy, and close relationships.* New York: Academic.

DeSteno, David, Valdesolo, Piercarlo, & Bartlett, Monica. (2006). Jealousy and the threatened self: Getting to the heart of the green-eyed monster. *Journal of Personality and Social Psychology, 91,* 626–641.

Devor, Aaron, & Dominic, Kim. (2015). Trans* sexualities. In J. DeLamater & R. Plante (Eds), *Handbook of the sociology of sexualities.* Dordrecht: Springer.

Devor, Holly. (1997). *FTM: Female-to-male transsexuals in society.* Bloomington: Indiana University Press.

Dewey, S. (2015). Sex work. In J. DeLamater & R. Plante (Eds.), *Handbook of the sociology of sexualities* (pp. 389–411). Dordrecht, NL: Springer.

Dhalla, S., et al. (2009). HIV vaccine preparedness studies in the non-Organization for Economic Cooperation and Development (non-OECD) countries. *AIDS Care, 21,* 335–348.

Dialani, Vandana, & Levine, Deborah. (2004). Ectopic pregnancy: A review. *Ultrasound Quarterly, 20,* 105–117.

Diamanti-Kandarakis, E., & Gore, A. C. (2009). Endocrine-disrupting chemicals: An Endocrine Society scientific statement. *Endocrine Review, 30,* 293–342.

Diamond, Lisa. (2003). What does sexual orientation orient? A biobehavioral model distinguishing romantic love and sexual desire. *Psychological Review, 110,* 173–192.

Diamond, Lisa M. (2005). A new view of lesbian subtypes: Stable versus fluid identity trajectories over an 8-year period. *Psychology of Women Quarterly, 29,* 119–128.

Diamond, Lisa M. (2008a). *Sexual fluidity: Understanding women's love and desire.* Cambridge, MA: Harvard University Press.

Diamond, Lisa M. (2008b). Female bisexuality from adolescence to adulthood: Results from a 10-year longitudinal study. *Developmental Psychology, 44,* 5–14.

Diamond, Lisa M. (2014). Gender and same-sex sexuality. In D. Tolman & L. Diamond (Eds.), *APA handbook of sexuality and psychology* (Vol. 1, pp. 629–652). Washington, DC: APA.

Diamond, Milton. (1996). Prenatal predisposition and the clinical management of some pediatric conditions. *Journal of Sex and Marital Therapy, 22,* 139–147.

Diamond, Milton. (1999). Pediatric management of ambiguous and traumatized genitalia. *Journal of Urology, 162,* 1021–1028.

Diamond, Milton, & Beh, Hazel. (2008). Changes in the management of children with intersex conditions. *Nature Clinical Practice: Endocrinology & Metabolism, 4,* 4–5.

Diamond, Milton, & Sigmundson, H. Keith. (1997). Sex reassignment at birth: Long-term review and clinical implications. *Archives of Pediatric and Adolescent Medicine, 151,* 298–304.

Diaz, Christina J., & Fiel, Jeremy E. (2016). The effect(s) of teen pregnancy: Reconciling theory, methods, and findings. *Demography, 53,* 85–116.

dickey, lore, & Singh, Anneliese A. (2016). Training tomorrow's affirmative psychologists: Serving transgender and gender non-conforming people. *Psychology of Sexual Orientation and Gender Diversity, 3,* 137–139. (Whole special issue)

Dickson, N., Paul, C., & Herbison, P. (2003). Same-sex attraction in a birth cohort: Prevalence and persistence in early adulthood. *Social Science & Medicine, 56,* 1607–1615.

Dijkstra, P., Barelds, D. P. H., & Groothof, H. A. K. (2013). Jealousy in response to online and offline infidelity: The role of sex and sexual orientation. *Scandinavian Journal of Psychology, 54,* 328–336.

Dindia, Kathryn, & Canary, Daniel. (2006). *Sex differences and similarities in communication.* Mahwah, NJ: Lawrence Erlbaum Associates.

Dion, Karen K. (1973). Young children's stereotyping of facial attractiveness. *Developmental Psychology, 9,* 183–188.

Dion, Kenneth. (1977). The incentive value of physical attractiveness for young children. *Personality and Social Psychology Bulletin, 3,* 67–70.

Dion, Kenneth L., & Dion, Karen K. (1993a). Gender and ethnocultural comparisons in styles of love. *Psychology of Women Quarterly, 17,* 463–474.

Dion, Karen K., & Dion, Kenneth L. (1993b). Individualistic and collectivistic perspectives on gender and the cultural content of love and intimacy. *Journal of Social Issues, 49,* 53–69.

Dixson, Alan F. (1990). The neuroendocrine regulation of sexual behavior in female primates. *Annual Review of Sex Research, 1,* 197–226.

Dixson, Barnaby J., et al. (2011). Eye-tracking of men's preferences for waist-to-hip ratio and breast size of women. *Archives of Sexual Behavior, 40,* 43–50.

Docter, Richard F., & Prince, Virginia. (1997). Transvestism: A survey of 1032 cross-dressers. *Archives of Sexual Behavior, 26,* 589–606.

Dodge, Brian, et al. (2010). Sexual health among U.S. Black and Hispanic men and women: A nationally representative study. *Journal of Sexual Medicine, 7*(SS05), 330–345.

Dolance, Susannah. (2005). "A whole stadium full": Lesbian community at Women's National Basketball Association games. *Journal of Sex Research, 42,* 74–83.

Domchek, S. M., et al. (2010). Association of risk-reducing surgery in BRCA1 and BRCA2 mutation carriers with cancer risk and mortality. *JAMA, 304,* 967–975.

Domingue, B. W., Fletcher, J., Conley, D., & Boardman, J. D. (2014). Genetic and educational assortative mating among US adults. *PNAS.* Advance online publication. doi: 10.1073/pnas.1321426111

Donadio, Rachel. (2010, December 21). Vatican adds nuance to Pope's condom remarks. *The New York Times.* Retrieved from https://www.nytimes.com/2010/12/22/world/europe/22pope.html

Donahue, J. E., et al. (2000). Cells containing immunoreactive estrogen receptor-[alpha] in the human basal forebrain. *Brain Research, 856,* 142–151.

Donnelly, D. A. (1993). Sexually inactive marriages. *Journal of Sex Research, 30,* 171–179.

Donnelly, Denise, et al. (2001). Involuntary celibacy: A life course analysis. *Journal of Sex Research, 38,* 159–169.

Donnerstein, E., Linz, D., & Penrod, S. (1987). *The question of pornography: Research findings and policy implications.* New York: Free Press.

Donohoe, Martin. (2007, February 9). Parental notification and consent laws for teen abortion: Overview and 2006 ballot measures. *Medscape Ob/Gyn and Women's Health.*

Donohue, John J., & Levitt, S. D. (2004). Further evidence that legalized abortion lowered crime. *The Journal of Human Resources, 39,* 1.

Döring, Nicola, et al. (2017). Online sexual activity experiences among college students: A four-country comparison. *Archives of Sexual Behavior, 46,* 1641–1652.

Dorrie, Nora, Focker, Manuel, Freunscht, Inga, & Hebebrand, Johannes. (2014). Fetal alcohol spectrum disorders. *European Child and Adolescent Psychiatry, 23,* 863–875.

Downing, M., Jr., Schrimshaw, E., Antebi, N., & Siegel, K. (2014). Sexually explicit media on the Internet: A content analysis of sexual behaviors, risk, and media characteristics in gay male adult videos. *Archives of Sexual Behavior, 43,* 811–821.

Dragisic, Katherine G., & Milad, M. P. (2004). Sexual functioning and patient expectations of sexual functioning after hysterectomy. *American Journal of Obstetrics and Gynecology, 190,* 1416–1418.

Drakett, Jessica, et al. (2018). Old jokes, new media – Online sexism and construction of gender in Internet memes. *Feminism & Psychology, 28,* 109–127.

Drea, Christine M. (2009). Endocrine mediators of masculinization in female mammals. *Current Directions in Psychological Science, 18,* 221–226.

Dreznick, Michael T. (2003). Heterosocial competence of rapists and child molesters: A meta-analysis. *Journal of Sex Research, 40,* 170–178.

Drucker, Donna J. (2014). *The classification of sex: Alfred Kinsey and the organization of knowledge.* Pittsburgh, PA: University of Pittsburgh Press.

Drury, Alan, et al. (2017). Adverse childhood experiences, paraphilias, ad serious criminal violence among federal sex offenders. *Journal of Criminal Psychology, 7,* 105–119.

Ducharme, Jamie. (2018. February 3). A controversial bill would allow chemical castration of sex offenders in Oklahoma. *Time.* Retrieved from http://time.com/5132314/chemical-castration-sex-offenders/

Duerr, Anne, et al. (2008). HIV vaccines. In K. Holmes et al. (Eds.), *Sexually transmitted diseases* (4th ed., pp. 1937–1954). New York: McGraw-Hill.

Dugger, Celia W. (2011, October 16). Senegal curbs a bloody rite, African-style. *The New York Times,* p. 1.

Duncan, S., Phillips, M., Roseneil, S., Carter, J., & Stoilova, M. (2013). *Living apart together: Uncoupling intimacy and co-residence.* London, UK: Birkbeck, University of London.

Dunn, Marian E., & Trost, Jan E. (1989). Male multiple orgasms: A descriptive study. *Archives of Sexual Behavior, 18,* 377–388.

Dunne, M. P., et al. (1997). Participation bias in a sexuality survey: Psychological and behavioural characteristics of responders and non-responders. *International Journal of Epidemiology, 26,* 844–854.

Durante, Kristina M., et al. (2011). Ovulation, female competition, and product choice. Hormonal influences on consumer behavior. *Journal of Consumer Research, 37,* 921–934.

Dush, Claire M. K., et al. (2003). The relationship between cohabitation and marital quality and stability: Change across cohorts? *Journal of Marriage and Family, 65,* 539–549.

Dutton, Donald G., & Aron, Arthur P. (1974). Some evidence for heightened sexual attraction under conditions of high anxiety. *Journal of Personality and Social Psychology, 30,* 470–517.

Earp, Brian D. (2015). Do the benefits of male circumcision outweigh the risks? A critique of the proposed CDC guidelines. *Frontiers in Pediatrics, 3,* Article 18, 1–6.

Eaton, Danice K., et al. (2012). Youth risk behavior surveillance—United States, 2011. *Morbidity and Mortality Weekly Report, 61*(4), 1–110.

Eaton, Nicholas R. (2014). Transdiagnostic psychopathology factors and sexual minority mental health: Evidence of disparities and associations with minority stressors. *Psychology of Sexual Orientation and Gender Diversity, 1,* 244–254.

Ebel, Charles, & Wald, Anna. (2007). *Managing herpes: Living and loving with HSV.* Research Triangle Park, NC: American Social Health Association.

Edwards, Weston M., & Coleman, Eli. (2004). Defining sexual health: A descriptive overview. *Archives of Sexual Behavior, 33,* 189–196.

Edwards-Leeper, Laura, et al. (2016). Affirmative practice with transgender and gender nonconforming youth. *Psychology of Sexual Orientation and Gender Diversity, 3,* 165–172.

Efrati, Yaniv, & Gola, Mateusz. (2018). Compulsive sexual behavior: A twelve-step therapeutic approach. *Journal of Behavioral Addictions, 7,* 445–453.

Eifling, S. (2015, January 28). Above the law, under the sheets. *The New Republic.* Retrieved from http://www.newrepublic.com/article/120879/can-police-legally-have-sex-prostitutes-only-michigan

Eig, Jonathan. (2014). *The birth of the pill: Four crusaders reinvented sex and launched a revolution.* New York: Norton.

Eisenberg, M. E., Wagenaar, A., & Neumark-Sztainer, D. (1997). Viewpoints of Minnesota students on school-based sexuality education. *Journal of School Health, 67,* 322–326.

Eisenstadt v. Baird, 405 U.S. 438 (1972).

Elder, Glen. (1969). Appearance and education in marriage mobility. *American Sociological Review, 34,* 519–533.

Elias, James, & Gebhard, Paul. (1969). Sexuality and sexual learning in childhood. *Phi Delta Kappan, 50,* 401–405.

Eliot, Lise. (2009). *Pink brain, blue brain: How small differences grow into troublesome gaps—and what we can do about it.* Boston: Houghton Mifflin.

Ellis, Lee. (1996). The role of perinatal factors in determining sexual orientation. In R. C. Savin-Williams & K. M. Cohen (Eds.), *The lives of lesbians, gays, and bisexuals* (pp. 35–70). Fort Worth, TX: Harcourt Brace.

Ellis, Lee, & Cole-Harding, Shirley. (2001). The effects of prenatal stress, and of prenatal alcohol and nicotine exposure, on human sexual orientation. *Physiology and Behavior, 74,* 213–226.

Emmerink, Peggy M. J., et al. (2016). Psychosexual correlates of sexual double standard endorsement in adolescent sexuality. *Journal of Sex Research, 53,* 286–297.

England, P., Allison, P. D., & Sayer, L. C. (2014). When one spouse has an affair, who is more likely to leave? *Demographic Research, 30,* 535–546.

Enns, Carolyn Z. (2004). *Feminist theories and feminist psychotherapies* (2nd ed.). New York: Haworth.

Enzensberger, C., et al. (2012). Fetal loss rate and associated risk factors after amniocentesis, chorionic villus sampling and fetal blood sampling. *Ultraschall Med, 33(7),* e75–e79.

Equal Employment Opportunity Commission. (1993). *Guidelines on discrimination because of sex.* 29 CFR 1604.11. Washington, DC: U.S. Government Printing Office.

Erens, Bob, et al. (2014). Methodology of the third British National Survey of Sexual Attitudes and Lifestyles (Natsal-3). *Sexually Transmitted Infections, 90,* 84–89.

Erhardt, Virginia. (2007). *Head over heels: Wives who stay with cross-dressers and transsexuals.* Binghamton. NY: Haworth Press.

Erikson, Erik H. (1950). *Childhood and society.* New York: Norton.

Erikson, Erik H. (1968). *Identity: Youth and crisis.* New York: Norton.

Erickson-Schroth, Laura (Ed.). (2014). *Trans bodies, trans selves.* New York: Oxford University Press.

Ernulf, Kurt E., & Innala, Sune M. (1995). Sexual bondage: A review and unobtrusive investigation. *Archives of Sexual Behavior, 24,* 631–654.

Eskenazi, B., et al. (2003). The association of age and semen quality in healthy men. *Human Reproduction, 18,* 447–454.

Espin, Oliva. (1987). Issues of identity in the psychology of Latina lesbians. In Boston Lesbian Psychologies Collective, *Lesbian psychologies.* Urbana: University of Illinois Press.

Esposito, Katherine, et al. (2004). Effect of lifestyle changes on erectile dysfunction in obese men: A randomized controlled trial. *Journal of the American Medical Association, 291,* 2978–2984.

Ethics Committee of the American Society of Reproductive Medicine. (2013). Access to fertility treatment by gays, lesbians, and unmarried persons: A committee opinion. *Fertility and Sterility, 100,* 1524–1527.

Evans, Harriet. (1995). Defining differences: The "scientific" construction of sexuality and gender in the People's Republic of China. *Signs, 20,* 357–394.

Ezzell, Carol. (1994, October). Breast cancer genes. *Journal of NIH Research, 6,* 33–35.

Fahs, Breanne. (2011). *Performing sex: The making and unmaking of women's erotic lives.* Albany, NY: State University of New York Press.

Fahs, Breanne, Swank, E., & McClelland, S. (2018). Sexuality, pleasure, power, and danger: Points of tension, contradiction and conflict. In C. Travis and J. White (Eds.), *APA handbook of the psychology of women* (Vol. 1, pp. 229–248). Washington, DC: American Psychological Association.

Fairchild, Halford H., Whitten, Lisa, & Richard, Harriette. (2003). Teaching African American psychology. In P. Bronstein & K. Quina (Eds.), *Teaching gender and multicultural awareness* (pp. 195–200). Washington, DC: American Psychological Association.

Farley, Margaret A. (1994). Sexual ethics. In J. B. Nelson & S. P. Longfellow (Eds.), *Sexuality and the sacred* (pp. 54–67). Louisville, KY: Westminster/John Knox Press.

Farley, Melissa. (2006). Prostitution, trafficking, and cultural amnesia: What we must *not* know to keep the business of sexual exploitation running smoothly. *Yale Journal of Law and Feminism, 109,* 114–115.

Farley, Melissa, et al. (2017). Comparing sex buyers with men who do not buy sex: New data on prostitution and trafficking. *Journal of Interpersonal Violence, 32,* 3601–3625.

Farmer, Melissa A., & Meston, Cindy M. (2007). Predictors of genital pain in young women. *Archives of Sexual Behavior, 36,* 831–843.

Farr, Rachel H. (2017). Does parental sexual orientation matter? A longitudinal follow-up of adoptive families with school-age children. *Developmental Psychology, 53,* 252–264.

Farr, Rachel H., Forssell, Stephen, & Patterson, Charlotte J. (2010). Parenting and child development in adoptive families: Does parental sexual orientation matter? *Applied Developmental Science, 14,* 164–176.

Farrell, Janine, & Cacchioni, Thea. (2012). The medicalization of women's sexual pain. *Journal of Sex Research, 49,* 328–336.

Farris, Coreen, et al. (2006). Heterosocial perceptual organization: Application of the choice model to sexual coercion. *Psychological Science, 17,* 869–875.

Farris, Coreen, et al. (2008). Perceptual mechanisms that characterize gender differences in decoding women's sexual intent. *Psychological Science, 19,* 348–354.

Farvid, Pantea, & Braun, Virginia. (2006). "Most of us guys are raring to go anytime, anyplace, anywhere": Male and female sexuality in *Cleo* and *Cosmo. Sex Roles, 55,* 295–310.

Fast, Anne A., & Olson, Kristina R. (2018). Gender development in transgender preschool children. *Child Development, 89,* 620–637.

Fasula, Amy M., Carry, M., & Miller, K. (2014). A multidimensional framework for the meanings of the sexual double standard and its application for the sexual health of young Black women in the U.S. *Journal of Sex Research, 51,* 170–183.

Fathy, Ahmad, et al. (2007). Experience with Tube® (Promedon) malleable penile implant. *Urologia Internationalis, 79,* 244–247.

Fauci, Anthony S., et al. (2014). Ending the global HIV/AIDS pandemic: The critical role of an HIV vaccine. *Clinical Infectious Diseases, 59*(Suppl. 2), S80–S84.

Faulkner, S. L. (2003). Good girl or flirt girl: Latinas' definitions of sex and sexual relationships. *Hispanic Journal of Behavioral Sciences, 25,* 174–200.

Federal Bureau of Investigation. (2014). *Uniform Crime Reports: Crime in the United States, 2013.* http://www.fbi.gov/about-us/cjis/ucr/crime-in-the-u.s/2013/crime-in-the-u.s.-2013/violent-crime/rape

Federman, Daniel D. (2006). The biology of human sex differences. *New England Journal of Medicine, 354,* 1507–1514.

Feimster, Crystal. (2009). *Southern horrors: Women and the politics of rape and lynching.* Cambridge, MA: Harvard University Press.

Feingold, Alan. (1988). Matching for attractiveness in romantic partners and same-sex friends: A meta-analysis and theoretical critique. *Psychological Bulletin, 104,* 226–235.

Feingold, Alan. (1990). Gender differences in effects of physical attractiveness on romantic attraction. *Journal of Personality and Social Psychology, 59,* 981–993.

Feiring, Candice, et al. (2009). Childhood sexual abuse, stigmatization, internalizing symptoms, and the development of sexual difficulties and dating aggression. *Journal of Consulting and Clinical Psychology, 77,* 127–137.

Feldman, Eric A. (2018). *Baby M* turns 30: The law and policy of surrogate motherhood. *American Journal of Law & Medicine, 44,* 7–22.

Feldman, Ruth, et al. (2007). Evidence for a neuroendocrinological foundation of human affiliation. *Psychological Science, 18,* 965–970.

Ferguson, K. H., & Cespedes, R. D. (2003). Prospective long-term results and quality-of-life assessment after Dura-II penile prosthesis placement. *Urology, 61,* 437–441.

Feuer, A. (2015, February 13). On tinder, taking a swipe at love, or sex, or something, in New York. *New York Times,* MB1.

Fewtrell, M., et al. (2011). Six months of exclusive breastfeeding: How good is the evidence? *BMJ, 342,* c5955.

Fielder, Robyn L., & Carey, Michael P. (2010). Predictors and consequences of sexual "hookups" among college students: A short-term prospective study. *Archives of Sexual Behavior, 39,* 1105–1119.

Fields, Jessica, & Tolman, Deborah. (2006). Risky business: Sexuality education and research in U.S. schools. *Sexuality Research and Social Policy, 3,* 63–76.

Fincham, Frank, & Beach, S. R. H. (2010). Of memes and marriage: Toward a positive relationship science. *Journal of Family Theory & Review, 2,* 4–24.

Find the data. (2015). *Age-of-consent.* Findthedata.org

Findlay, Michael W., et al. (2011). Tissue-engineered breast reconstruction: Bridging the gap toward large-volume tissue engineering in humans. *Plastic and Reconstructive Surgery, 128,* 1206–1215.

Fine, C. (2017). *Testosterone Rex: Myths of sex, science, and society.* New York: Norton.

Finer, Lawrence B., & Zolna, Mia R. (2014). Shifts in intended and unintended pregnancies in the United States, 2001–2008. *American Journal of Public Health, 104,* S43–S48.

Fink, Howard, et al. (2002). Sildenafil for male erectile dysfunction: A systematic review and meta-analysis. *Archives of Internal Medicine, 162,* 1349–1360.

Finkel, Eli J., et al. (2015). When does familiarity promote versus undermine interpersonal attraction? A proposed intergrative model from erstwhile adversaries. *Perspectives on Psychological Science, 10,* 3–19.

Finkelhor, David. (1980). Sex among siblings: A survey on prevalence, variety and effects. *Archives of Sexual Behavior, 9,* 171–194.

Finkelhor, David. (1984). *Child sexual abuse: New theory and research.* New York: Free Press.

Finlay, W. M. L., et al. (2015). "Understanding" as a practical issue in sexual health education for people with intellectual disabilities: A study using two qualitative methods. *Health Psychology, 34,* 328–338.

Fisher, Deborah, et al. (2004, March). *Youth and television: Examining sexual content across program genres.* Paper presented at Society for Research on Adolescence, Baltimore, Maryland.

Fisher, Ian. (2006, January 26). Benedict's first encyclical shuns strictures of orthodoxy. *New York Times,* A6.

Fisher, Terri D., et al. (2012). Sex on the brain? An examination of frequency of sexual cognitions as a function of gender, erotophilia, and social desirability. *Journal of Sex Research, 49,* 69–77.

Fiske, Susan T., & Glick, Peter. (1995). Ambivalence and stereotypes cause sexual harassment: A theory with implications for organizational change. *Journal of Social Issues, 51*(1), 97–115.

Flak, A. L., Su, S., Bertrand, J., Denny, C. H., Kesmodel, U. S., & Cogswell, M. E. (2014). The association of mild, moderate, and binge prenatal alcohol exposure and child neuropsychological outcomes: A meta-analysis. *Alcoholism: Clinical and Experimental Research, 38,* 214–226.

Flak, Vanja, et al. (2007). Forensic assessment of deviant sexual interests: The current position. *Issues in Forensic Psychology, 6,* 70–83.

Flaxman, S. M., & Sherman, P. W. (2000). Morning sickness: A mechanism for protecting mother and embryo. *Quarterly Review of Biology, 75,* 113–148.

Fleming, Douglas T., et al. (1997). Herpes simplex virus type 2 in the United States, 1976 to 1994. *New England Journal of Medicine, 337,* 1105–1111.

Fleming, Jillian, et al. (1999). The long-term impact of child sexual abuse in Australian women. *Child Abuse and Neglect, 23,* 145–159.

Fletcher, J. (1966). *Situation Ethics: The New Morality.* Louisville, KY: Westminster John Knox Press.

Flores, Andrew R., et al. (2016, June). *How many adults identify as transgender in the United States?* Los Angeles, CA: The Williams Institute, UCLA.

Flores, Andrew R., & Park, Andrew. (2018, March). *Polarized progress: Social acceptance of LGBT people in 141 countries, 1981 to 2014.* The Williams Institute, UCLA. Retrieved from https://williamsinstitute.law.ucla.edu/wp-content/uploads/Polarized-Progress-April-2018.pdf

Foa, Edna B., Steketee, G., & Olasov, B. (1989). Behavioral/cognitive conceptualization of posttraumatic stress disorder. *Behavior Therapy, 20,* 155–176.

Foeller, Megan E., & Lyell, Deirder J. (2017). Marijuana use in pregnancy: Concerns in an evolving era. *Journal of Midwifery & Women's Health, 62,* SI 363–367.

Foldès, Pierre, et al. (2012). Reconstructive surgery after female genital mutilation: A prospective cohort study. *The Lancet, 380*(9837), 134–141.

Forbes, Erika E., & Dahl, Ronald E. (2010). Pubertal development and behavior: Hormonal activation of social and motivational tendencies. *Brain and Cognition, 72,* 66–72.

Ford, Clellan S., & Beach, Frank A. (1951). *Patterns of sexual behavior.* New York: Harper & Row.

Ford, Jeffry G. (2001). Healing homosexuals: A psychologist's journey through the ex-gay movement and the pseudoscience of reparative therapy. In A. Shidlo et al. (Eds.), *Sexual conversion therapy: Ethical, clinical, and research perspectives* (pp. 69–86). New York: Haworth.

Fortenberry, J. Dennis, et al. (2005). Daily mood, partner support, sexual interest, and sexual activity among adolescent women. *Health Psychology, 24,* 252–257.

Foster, C. A., Witcher, B. S., Campbell, W. K., & Green, J. D. (1998). Arousal and attraction: Evidence for automatic and controlled processes. *Journal of Personality and Social Psychology, 74,* 86–101.

Foster, Diana G., et al. (2006). Estimates of pregnancies averted through California's family planning waiver program in 2002. *Perspectives on Sexual and Reproductive Health, 38,* 126-131.

Fox, Laura. (1983). The 1983 abortion decisions. *University of Richmond Law Review, 18,* 137-159.

Fox, Nathan, Gelber, Shari, & Chasen, Stephen. (2008). Physical and sexual activity during pregnancy and near delivery. *Journal of Women's Health, 17,* 1431-1435.

Frank, D., & Phillips, N. (2013). Sex laws and sexuality rights in comparative and global perspectives. *Annual Review of Law and Social Science, 9,* 249-267.

Frank, David, J., Camp, Bayliss, J., & Boutcher, Steven. (2010). Worldwide trends in the criminal regulation of sex, 1945 to 2005. *American Sociological Review, 75,* 867-893.

Frank, K., & Carnes, M. (2010). Gender and space in strip clubs. In R. Weitzer (Ed.), *Sex for sale* (2nd ed., pp. 115-137). New York: Routledge.

Frank, Katherine. (2005). Exploring the motivations and fantasies of strip club customers in relation to legal regulations. *Archives of Sexual Behavior, 34,* 487-504.

Frank, Katherine. (2013). *Plays well in groups: A journey through the world of group sex.* Lanham, MD: Rowman and Littlefield.

Frayser, Suzanne G. (1985). *Varieties of sexual experience: An anthropological perspective on human sexuality.* New Haven, CT: Human Relations Area Files Press.

Frayser, Suzanne G. (1994). Defining normal childhood sexuality: An anthropological approach. *Annual Review of Sex Research, 5,* 173-217.

Frazier, Patricia, et al. (2004). Correlates of levels and patterns of positive life changes following sexual assault. *Journal of Consulting and Clinical Psychology, 72,* 19-30.

Frederick, David, Peplau, Anne, & Lever, Janet. (2008). The Barbie mystique: Satisfaction with breast size and shape across the lifespan. *International Journal of Sexual Health, 20,* 200-211.

Freese, Jeremy, & Meland, Sheri. (2002). Seven tenths incorrect: Heterogeneity and change in the waist-to-hip ratios of *Playboy* centerfold models and Miss America pageant winners. *Journal of Sex Research, 39,* 133-138.

Freud, Sigmund. (1948). The psychogenesis of a case of homosexuality in a woman. In *The collected papers* (Vol. II, pp. 202-231). London: Hogarth. (Original work published 1920)

Freud, Sigmund. (1924). *A general introduction to psychoanalysis.* New York: Permabooks, 1953. (Boni & Liveright edition, 1924)

Freud, Sigmund. (1943). *A general introduction to psychoanalysis.* Garden City, NY: Garden City. (Original work published in German 1917)

Freund, M., Lee, N., & Leonard, T. (1991). Sexual behavior of clients with street prostitutes in Camden, NJ. *Journal of Sex Research, 28,* 579-591.

Freyd, Jennifer J., et al. (2005). The science of child sexual abuse. *Science, 308,* 501.

Frisch, Morten, & Earp, Brian D. (2018). Circumcision of male infants and children as a public health measure in developed countries: A critical assessment of recent evidence. *Global Public Health, 13,* 626-641.

Frisch, R. E., & McArthur, J. W. (1974). Menstrual cycles: Fatness as a determinant of minimum weight for height necessary for their maintenance or onset. *Science, 185,* 949-951.

Fritz, Heather A., Dillaway, H., & Lysakc, C. (2015, March/April). "Don't think paralysis takes away your womanhood": Sexual intimacy after spinal cord injury. *The American Journal of Occupational Therapy, 69*(2), 1-10.

Frohlich, Penny, & Meston, Cindy. (2002). Sexual functioning and self-reported depressive symptoms among college women. *Journal of Sex Research, 39,* 321-325.

Frühauf, Sara, et al. (2013). Efficacy of psychological interventions for sexual dysfunction: A systematic review and meta-analysis. *Archives of Sexual Behavior, 42,* 915-933.

Fryar, C., et al. (2007). Drug use and sexual behaviors reported by adults: United States, 1999-2002. *Advance Data from Vital and Health Statistics, 384.* Hyattsville, MD: National Center for Health Statistics.

Fryhofer, Sandra. (2012). Preconception checklist for women planning pregnancy. *Medscape Internal Medicine.* www.medscape.com/viewarticle/762801.

Furman, Wyndol. (2002). The emerging field of adolescent romantic relationships. *Current Directions in Psychological Science, 11,* 177-180.

Furnish, Victor P. (1994). The Bible and homosexuality: Reading the texts in context. In J. S. Siker (Ed.), *Homosexuality in the church* (pp. 18-35). Louisville, KY: Westminster John Knox Press.

Future of Sex Education Initiative. (2012). National sexuality education standards: Core content and skills, K-12. Retrieved from www.futureofsexeducation.org/documents/josh-fose-standards-web.pdf

Gager, Constance, & Yabiku, Scott. (2010). Who has the time? The relationship between household labor time and sexual frequency. *Journal of Family Issues, 31,* 135-163.

Gagnon, John H. (1977). *Human sexualities.* Glenview, IL: Scott, Foresman.

Gagnon, John H. (1990). The explicit and implicit use of the scripting perspective in sex research. *Annual Review of Sex Research, 1,* 1-44.

Gagnon, John H., & Simon, William. (1973). *Sexual conduct: The social origins of human sexuality.* Chicago, IL: Aldine.

Gaither, G. A., et al. (2003). The effect of stimulus content on volunteering for sexual interest research among college students. *Journal of Sex Research, 40,* 240-248.

Galbreath, Nathan, Berlin, Fred, & Sawyer, Denise. (2002). Paraphilias and the Internet. In Al Cooper (Ed.), *Sex and the Internet: A guidebook for clinicians* (pp. 187-205). New York: Brunner-Routledge.

Galletly, C., & Lazzarini, Z. (2013). Charges for criminal exposure to HIV and aggravated prostitution filed in the Nashville, Tennessee prosecutorial region 2000-2010. *AIDS and Behavior 17,* 2624-2636.

Gangestad, Steven W., & Buss, David M. (1993). Pathogen prevalence and human mate preferences. *Ethnology and Sociobiology, 14,* 89-96.

Gangestad, Steven W., & Thornhill, R. (1997). Human sexual selection and developmental stability. In J. A. Simpson & D. T. Kenrick (Eds.), *Evolutionary social psychology* (pp. 169-195). Mahwah, NJ: Erlbaum.

Ganju, D., et al. (2004). *The adverse health and social outcomes of sexual coercion: Experiences of young women in developing countries.* New Delhi: Population Council.

Gannon, Theresa A., & Ward, Tony. (2008). Rape: Psychopathology and theory. In D. R. Laws & W. T. O'Donohue (Eds.), *Sexual deviance* (pp. 336-355). New York: Guilford.

Gao, Fei, et al. (2006). The Wilms tumor gene, Wt1, is required for Sox9 expression and maintenance of tubular architecture in the developing testis. *PNAS, 103,* 11987-11992.

Garcia, Justin R., et al. (2014). Variation in orgasm occurrence by sexual orientation in a sample of U.S. singles. *Journal of Sexual Medicine, 11,* 2645-2652.

Garnett, Geoff P. (2008). The transmission dynamics of sexually transmitted infections. In K. Holmes et al. (Eds.), *Sexually transmitted diseases* (4th ed., pp. 27-40). New York: McGraw-Hill.

Gartrell, Nanette K., et al. (2011). Adolescents of the U.S. National Longitudinal Lesbian Family Study: Sexual orientation, sexual behavior, and sexual risk exposure. *Archives of Sexual Behavior, 40,* 1199–1209.

Gathorne-Hardy, Jonathan. (2000). *Sex the measure of all things: A life of Alfred C. Kinsey.* Bloomington: Indiana University Press.

Gaunt, Ruth. (2006). Couple similarity and marital satisfaction: Are similar spouses happier? *Journal of Personality, 74,* 1401–1420.

Gavey, Nicola, & Senn, C. (2014). Sexuality and sexual violence. In D. Tolman & L. Diamond (Eds.), *APA handbook of sexuality and psychology* (Vol. 1, pp. 339–382). Washington, DC: APA.

Gay, Peter. (1984). *The bourgeois experience: Victoria to Freud.* New York: Oxford University Press.

Gebhard, Paul H. (1976). The Institute. In M. S. Weinberg (Ed.), *Sex research: Studies from the Kinsey Institute.* New York: Oxford University Press.

Genovesi, Vincent J. (1987). *In pursuit of love: Catholic morality and human sexuality.* Wilmington, DE: Michael Glazier.

George, William H., et al. (2014). Sexuality and health. In D. Tolman & L. Diamond (Eds.), *APA handbook of sexuality and psychology* (Vol. 1, pp. 655–696). Washington, DC: APA.

Georges, Eugenia. (1996). Abortion policy and practice in Greece. *Social Science and Medicine, 42,* 509–519.

Georgiadis, J. R., & Kringelbach, M. L. (2012). The human sexual response cycle: Brain imaging evidence linking sex to other pleasures. *Progress in Neurobiology, 98,* 49–81.

Gerbner, George, Gross, L., & Morgan, M. (2002). Growing up with television: Cultivation processes. In J. Bryant & D. Zillman (Eds.), *Media effects: Advances in theory and research* (2nd ed., pp. 43–67). Mahwah, NJ: Erlbaum.

Gerland, Patrick, et al. (2014). World population stabilization unlikely this century. *Science, 346,* 234–237.

Gervais, Sarah J., Vescio, T., & Allen, J. (2011). When what you see is what you get: The consequences of the objectifying gaze for women and men. *Psychology of Women Quarterly, 35,* 5–17.

Ghavami, Negin, & Peplau, L. Anne. (2013). An intersectional analysis of gender and ethnic stereotypes: Testing three hypotheses. *Psychology of Women Quarterly, 37,* 113–127.

Gidycz, Christine A., et al. (2011). Primary prevention of sexual violence. In J. White et al. (Eds.), *Violence against women and children* (Vol. 2, pp. 159–180). Washington, DC: American Psychological Association.

Gijs, Luk, & Gooren, Louis. (1996). Hormonal and psychopharmacological interventions in the treatment of paraphilias. *Journal of Sex Research, 33,* 273–290.

Gilgoff, Dan. (2009, March 24). Did Obama open the door to human cloning with his stem cell order? *U.S. News & World Report.* Retrieved from https://www.usnews.com/news/religion/articles/2009/03/24/did-obama-open-the-door-to-human-cloning-with-his-stem-cell-order

Gill, Michael. (2015). *Already doing it: Intellectual disability and sexual agency.* Minneapolis: University of Minnesota Press.

Gilligan, Carol. (1982). *In a different voice: Psychological theory and women's development.* Cambridge, MA: Harvard University Press.

Gilmartin, Brian G. (1975). The swinging couple down the block. *Psychology Today, 8*(9), 54.

Gilmore, Mary R., et al. (2010). Comparison of daily and retrospective reports of vaginal sex in heterosexual men and women. *Journal of Sex Research, 47,* 279–284.

Ginger, Van Anh T., & Yang, C. C. (2011). Functional anatomy of the female sex organs. In J. P. Mulhall et al. (Eds.), *Cancer and sexual health* (pp. 13–23). New Yorker: Springer.

Ginot, Efrat. (2017). The enacted unconscious: A neuropsychological model of unconscious processes. *Annals of the New York Academy of Sciences, 1406,* 71–76.

Giordano, Peggy, et al. (2010). Affairs of the heart: Qualities of adolescent romantic relationships and sexual behavior. *Journal of Research on Adolescence, 20,* 983–1013.

Giraldi, Annamaria, & Kristensen, Ellids. (2010). Sexual dysfunction in women with diabetes mellitus. *Journal of Sex Research, 47,* 199–211.

Giuliano, François, & Clement, Pierre. (2005). Neuroanatomy and physiology of ejaculation. *Annual Review of Sex Research, 15,* 190–216.

Gjerdingen, Dwenda. (2003). The effectiveness of various postpartum depression treatments and the impact of antidepressant drugs on nursing infants. *Journal of the American Board of Family Practice, 16,* 372–382.

Glass, S. J., & Johnson, R. W. (1944). Limitations and complications of organotherapy in male homosexuality. *Journal of Clinical Endocrinology, 4,* 540–544.

Goesling, B., Lugo-Gil, J., Lee, J., & Novak, T. (2015). *Updated findings from the HHS Teen Pregnancy Prevention Evidence Review: April 2013 through July 2014.* Washington, DC: U.S. Department of Health and Human Services. http://tppevidencereview.aspe.hhs.gov

Goldfoot, D. A., et al. (1980). Behavioral and physiological evidence of sexual climax in the female stump-tailed macaque (*Macaca arctoides*). *Science, 208,* 1477–1478.

Goldman, Ronald J., & Goldman, Juliette D. G. (1982). *Children's sexual thinking.* London: Routledge & Kegan Paul.

Goodstein, Laurie, & Otterman, Sharon. (2018, August 14). Catholic priests abused 1,000 children in Pennsylvania, report says. *New York Times.* Retrieved from https://www.nytimes.com/2018/08/14/us/catholic-church-sex-abuse-pennsylvania.html

Gomez, A. M. (2018). Abortion and subsequent depressive symptoms: An analysis of the National Longitudinal Study of Adolescent Health. *Psychological Medicine, 48,* 294–304.

Gonzales v. Carhart et al., 550 U.S. 124 (2007).

Gonzalez, Francisco, & Espin, Oliva. (1996). Latino men, Latina women, and homosexuality. In R. Cabaj & T. Stein (Eds.), *Textbook of homosexuality and mental health* (pp. 583–601). Washington, DC: American Psychiatric Association.

Gonzalez, Jeffrey S., et al. (2004). Social support, positive states of mind, and HIV treatment adherence in men and women living with HIV/AIDS. *Health Psychology, 23,* 413–418.

Goodchilds, Jacqueline, & Zellman, Gail. (1984). Sexual signaling and sexual aggression in adolescent relationships. In N. Malamuth & E. Donnerstein (Eds.), *Pornography and sexual aggression* (pp. 233–243). New York: Academic.

Goodman, Danya L. (2017). Development and validation of the pretending orgasm reasons measure. *Archives of Sexual Behavior, 46,* 1973–1991.

Goodson, Patricia, & Edmundson, Elizabeth. (1994). The problematic promotion of abstinence: An overview of Sex Respect. *Journal of School Health, 64,* 205–210.

Goodstein, Laurie. (2004, February 28). We swept abusers out, bishops say. *New York Times.*

Goodwin, Michele. (2010). A view from the cradle: Tort law and the private regulation of assisted reproduction. *Emory Law Journal, 59,* 1039–1100.

Goodwin, P. Y., Mosher, W. D., & Chandra, A. (2010). Marriage and cohabitation in the United States. A statistical portrait based on Cycle 6 (2002) of the National Survey of Family Growth. *Vital and Health Statistics, 23*(28). Hyattsville, MD: National Center for Health Statistics.

Gooren, Louis. (2006). The biology of human psychosexual differentiation. *Hormones and Behavior, 50,* 589–601.

Gooren, Louis J. (2011). Ethical and medical considerations of androgen deprivation treatment of sex offenders. *Journal of Clinical Endocrinology and Metabolism, 95,* 3628–3627.

Gordon, R. A., Crosnoe, R., & Wang, X. (2013). Physical attractiveness and the accumulation of social and human capital in adolescence and young adulthood. *Monographs of the Society for Research in Child Development, 78*(6). Hoboken, NJ: Wiley.

Gordts, Sylvie, et al. (2009). Clinical factors determining pregnancy outcome after microsurgical tubal reanastomosis. *Fertility and Sterility, 92,* 1198–1202.

Gore, Andrea C., et al. (2015). EDC-2: The Endocrine Society's second scientific statement on endocrine-disrupting chemicals. *Endocrine Reviews, 36,* E1–E150.

Gorzalka, Boris B., et al. (2010). Male-female differences in the effects of cannabinoids on sexual behavior and gonadal hormone function. *Hormones and Behavior, 58,* 91–99.

Gosling, Samuel D., et al. (2004). Should we trust Web-based studies? A comparative analysis of six preconceptions about Internet questionnaires. *American Psychologist, 59,* 93–104.

Gosselin, Chris, & Wilson, Glenn. (1980). *Sexual variations: Fetishism, sadomasochism, transvestism.* New York: Simon & Schuster.

Gottman, John, et al. (1976). *A couple's guide to communication.* Champaign, IL: Research Press.

Gottman, John, et al. (1998). Predicting marital happiness and stability from newlywed interactions. *Journal of Marriage and the Family, 60,* 5–22.

Gottman, John, Markman, H., & Notarius, C. (1977). The topography of marital conflict: A sequential analysis of verbal and nonverbal behavior. *Journal of Marriage and the Family, 39,* 461–478.

Gottman, John, & Silver, Nan. (2015). *The seven principles for making marriage work: A practical guide from the country's foremost relationship expert.* New York: Harmony Books.

Gottman, John M. (1994). *Why marriages succeed or fail.* New York: Simon & Schuster.

Gould, Stephen J. (1987). *An urchin in the storm.* New York: Norton.

Gould, Terry (1999). *The lifestyle: A look at the erotic rites of swingers.* Buffalo, NY: Firefly.

Gow, Haven Bradford. (1994). Condom distribution in high school. *The Clearing House, 67,* 183–184.

Gowaty, Patricia A. (2018). On being and becoming female and male: A sex-neutral evolutionary perspective. In N. K. Dess et al. (Eds.), *Gender, sex, and sexualities: Psychological perspectives* (pp. 77–102). NY: Oxford University Press.

Gowaty, Patricia A., & Hubbell, S. P. (2009). Reproductive decisions under ecological constraints: It's about time. *PNAS, 106,* 10017–10024.

Gower, D. B., & Ruparelia, B. A. (1993). Olfaction in humans with special reference to odorous 16-androstenes: Their occurrence, perception and possible social, psychological and sexual impact. *Journal of Endocrinology, 137,* 167–187.

Grabe, Shelly, Ward, L. Monique, & Hyde, Janet S. (2008). The role of the media in body image concerns among women: A meta-analysis of experimental and correlational studies. *Psychological Bulletin, 134,* 460–476.

Graham, Barney S. (2009). What does the report of the USMHRP Phase III study in Thailand mean for HIV and for vaccine developers? *Clinical and Experimental Immunology, 158,* 257–259.

Graham, Cynthia A. (2010a). The DSM diagnostic criteria for female sexual arousal disorder. *Archives of Sexual Behavior, 39,* 240–255.

Graham, Cynthia A. (2010b). The DSM diagnostic criteria for female orgasmic disorder. *Archives of Sexual Behavior, 39,* 256–270.

Graham, Cynthia A. (2014). Orgasm disorders in women. In Y. Binik & K. Hall (Eds.), *Principles and practice of sex therapy* (5th ed., pp. 89–111). New York: Guilford.

Grammick, Jeannine. (1986). The Vatican's battered wives. *Christian Century, 103,* 17–20.

Granger, D. A., Shirtcliff, E. A., Booth, A., Kivlighan, K. T., & Schwartz, E. B. (2004). The "trouble" with salivary testosterone. *Psychoneuroendocrinology, 29,* 1229–1240.

Grant, Jaime M., et al. (2011). *Injustice at every turn: A report of the National Transgender Discrimination Survey.* Washington, DC: National Gender for Transgender Equality.

Grant, Robert M., et al. (2014). Uptake of pre-exposure prophylaxis, sexual practices, and HIV incidence in men and transgender women who have sex with men: A cohort study. *Lancet Infectious Diseases, 14,* 820–829.

Grau, Ina, & Kimpf, Martin. (1993). Love, sexuality, and satisfaction: Interventions of men and women. *Zeitschrift fur Sozial Psychologie, 24,* 83–93.

Grauvogl, Andrea, et al. (2015). Disgust and sexual arousal in young adult men and women. *Archives of Sexual Behavior, 44,* 1515–1525.

Gray, Nicola S., et al. (2005). An implicit test of the associations between children and sex in pedophiles. *Journal of Abnormal Psychology, 114,* 304–308.

Gray, P. B., Garcia, J. R., Crosier, B. S., & Fisher, H. E. (2015). Dating and sexual behavior among single parents of young children in the United States. *Journal of Sex Research, 52,* 121–128.

Grazian, D. (2008). *On the make: The hustle of urban nightlife.* Chicago: University of Chicago Press.

Greaves, L. M., et al. (2017) Asexual identity in a New Zealand national sample: Demographics, well-being, and health. *Archives of Sexual Behavior, 46,* 2417–2428.

Greeley, Andrew. (1994). Review of the Janus Report on Sexual Behavior. *Contemporary Sociology, 23,* 221–223.

Greely, Henry. (2011). Get ready for the flood of fetal gene screening. *Nature, 469,* 289–291.

Green, Lesley L., Fullilove, Mindy T., & Fullilove, Robert E. (2005). Remembering the lizard: Reconstructing sexuality in the rooms of Narcotics Anonymous. *Journal of Sex Research, 42,* 28–34.

Green, Ronald M. (1984). Genetic medicine in Jewish legal perspective. *Annual of the Society of Christian Ethics, 4,* 249–271.

Green, Ronald M. (2007). *Babies by design: The ethics of genetic choice.* New Haven, CT: Yale University Press.

Greenwald, Evan, & Leitenberg, Harold. (1989). Long-term effects of sexual experiences with siblings and nonsiblings during childhood. *Archives of Sexual Behavior, 18,* 389–400.

Greer, Arlette E., & Buss, David M. (1994). Tactics for promoting sexual encounters. *Journal of Sex Research, 31,* 185–201.

Gregersen, Edgar. (1996). *The world of human sexuality: Behaviors, customs, and beliefs.* New York: Irvington.

Grenier, Guy, & Byers, E. Sandra. (2001). Operationalizing premature or rapid ejaculation. *Journal of Sex Research, 38,* 369–378.

Griffin, Susan. (1981). *Pornography and silence.* New York: Harper & Row.

Griffith, J., Mitchell, S., Hart, C., Adams, L., & Gu, L. (2013a). Pornography actresses: An assessment of the damaged goods hypothesis. *Journal of Sex Research, 50,* 621–632.

Griffith, J., Hayworth, M., Adams, L., Mitchell, S., & Hart, C. (2013b). Characteristics of pornography film actors: Self-report versus perceptions of college students. *Archives of Sexual Behavior, 42,* 637–647.

Griswold v. Connecticut, 381 U.S. 479 (1965).

Grov, Christian, et al. (2014). Male clients of male escorts: Satisfaction, sexual behavior, and demographic characteristics. *Journal of Sex Research, 51,* 827–837.

Grov, Christian, et al. (2016). Sexual behavior varies between same-race and different-race partnerships: A daily diary study of highly sexually active Black, Latino, and White gay and bisexual men. *Archives of Sexual Behavior, 45,* 1453–1462.

Grubbs, Joshua B., et al. (2015). Evaluating outcome research for hypersexual behavior. *Current Addictions Reports, 2,* 207–213.

Gruntz, Louis, Jr. (1974). Obscenity 1973: Remodeling the house that Roth built. *Loyola Law Review, 20,* 159–174.

Guéguen, Nicolas. (2011). Effects of solicitor sex and attractiveness on receptivity to sexual offers: A field study. *Archives of Sexual Behavior, 40,* 915–919.

Guerrero, Laura, Spitzberg, Brian, & Yoshimura, Stephen. (2004). Sexual and emotional jealousy. In John Harvey, Amy Wenzel, & Susan Sprecher (Eds.), *The handbook of sexuality in close relationships* (pp. 311–345). Mahwah, NJ: Lawrence Erlbaum.

Guffey, M. Bradford, et al. (2014). HPTN 035 phase II/IIb randomized safety and effectiveness study of the vaginal microbicides BufferGel and PRO 2000. *Sexually Transmitted Infections, 90,* 363–369.

Guise, Jeanne-Marie, et al. (2003). The effectiveness of primary care–based interventions to promote breastfeeding: Systematic evidence review and meta-analysis for the U.S. Preventive Services Task Force. *Annals of Family Medicine, 1,* 70–78.

Gummow, Brian M., et al. (2006). Reciprocal regulation of a gluvovorticoid receptor-steroidogenic factor-1 transcription complex on the Dax-1 promoter by glucocorticoids and adrenocorticotropic hormone in the adrenal cortex. *Molecular Endocrinology, 20,* 2711–2723.

Gursoy, Akile. (1996). Abortion in Turkey: A matter of state, family, or individual decision. *Social Science and Medicine, 42,* 531–542.

Guterman, Mark A. (2008). Observance of the laws of family purity in modern-Orthodox Judaism. *Archives of Sexual Behavior, 37,* 340–345.

Guttmacher Institute. (2006). *Facts on American teens' sexual and reproductive health.* Retrieved from www.guttmacher.org

Guttmacher Institute. (2012). *In Brief: Fact Sheet. Facts on American teens' sources of information about sex.* Retrieved from http://www.guttmacher.org/statecenter/spibs/spib_SE.pdf

Guttmacher Institute. (2014). *Fact sheet: Induced abortion in the United States.* Retrieved from http://www.guttmacher.org/pubs/fb_induced_abortion.html

Guttmacher Institute. (2015a). *State policies in brief: Sex and HIV education.* Retrieved from http://www.guttmacher.org/pubs/FB-Teen-Sex-Ed.html

Guttmacher Institute. (2015b). *State policies on later abortions.* Retrieved from http://www.guttmacher.org/statecenter/spibs/spib_PLTA.pdf

Guzzo, Karen. (2015). Twenty-five years of change in repartnering and stepfamily formation. 2015 Working Paper Series, Center for Family and Demographic Research, Bowling Green State University.

Hackney, A. C. (2008). Effects of endurance exercise on the reproductive system of men: The "exercise-hypogonadal male condition." *Journal of Endocrinological Investigation, 31,* 932–938.

Hadden, Benjamin W., et al. (2014). Relationship duration moderates associations between attachment and relationship quality: Meta-analytic support for the temporal adult romantic attachment model. *Personality and Social Psychology Review, 18,* 42–58.

Hald, Gert M., et al. (2010). Pornography and attitudes supporting violence against women. *Aggressive Behavior, 36,* 14–20.

Haldeman, Douglas C. (1994). The practice and ethics of sexual orientation conversion therapy. *Journal of Consulting and Clinical Psychology, 62,* 221–227.

Haldeman, Douglas C. (2001). Therapeutic antidotes: Helping gay and bisexual men recover from conversion therapies. In A. Shidlo et al. (Eds.), *Sexual conversion therapy: Ethical, clinical, and research perspectives* (pp. 117–130). New York: Haworth.

Hall, C. S., & Lindzey, G. (1970). *Theories of personality* (2nd ed.). New York: Wiley.

Hall, Gordon C. Nagayama, et al. (2005). Ethnicity, culture, and sexual aggression: Risk and protective factors. *Journal of Consulting and Clinical Psychology, 73,* 830–840.

Hall, Gordon C. Nagayama, et al. (2016). On becoming multicultural in a monocultural research world: A conceptual approach to studying ethnocultural diversity. *American Psychologist, 71,* 40–51.

Hall, Judith A. (1998). How big are nonverbal sex differences? The case of smiling and sensitivity to nonverbal cues. In D. Canary & K. Dindia (Eds.), *Sex differences and similarities in communication* (pp. 155–178). Mahwah, NJ: Erlbaum.

Hallberg, Jonas, et al. (2017). A cognitive-behavioral therapy group intervention for hypersexual disorder: A feasibility study. *Journal of Sexual Medicine, 14,* 950–958.

Halldorsson, Thorhallur, et al. (2010). Intake of artificially sweetened soft drinks and risk of preterm delivery: A prospective cohort study in 59,334 Danish pregnant women. *American Journal of Clinical Nutrition, 92,* 626–633.

Halpern, Carolyn T. (2010). Reframing research on adolescent sexuality: Healthy sexual development as part of the life course. *Perspectives on Sexual and Reproductive Health, 42,* 6–7.

Halpern, Diane F. (1998). Teaching critical thinking for transfer across domains. *American Psychologist, 53,* 449–455.

Halpern, Diane F. (2002). Teaching for critical thinking: A four-part model to enhance thinking skills. In S. F. Davis & W. Buskist (Eds.), *The teaching of psychology: Essays in honor of Wilbert J. McKeachie and Charles L. Brewer* (pp. 91–105). Mahwah, NJ: Erlbaum.

Hamer, Dean, et al. (1993). A linkage between DNA markers on the X chromosome and male sexual orientation. *Science, 261,* 321–327.

Hamilton, Brady E., & Matthews, T. J. (2016). Continued declines in teen births in the United States, 2015. *NCHS Data Brief,* No. 259. Centers for Disease Control and Prevention, National Center for Health Statistics.

Hammer, G. D., & Ingraham, H. A. (1999). Steroidogenic factor-1: Its role in endocrine organ development and differentiation. *Frontiers in Neuroendocrinology, 20,* 199–223.

Hammoud, A. O., Meikle, A. W., Reis, L. O., Gibson, M., Peterson, M., & Carrell, D. T. (2012). Obesity and male infertility. *Seminars in Reproductive Medicine, 30,* 486–495.

Handler, A., et al. (1991). Cocaine use during pregnancy: Perinatal outcomes. *American Journal of Epidemiology, 133,* 818–825.

Harbison, R. D., & Mantilla-Plata, B. (1972). Prenatal toxicity, maternal distribution and placental transfer of tetrahydrocannabinol. *Journal of Pharmacology and Experimental Therapeutics, 180,* 446–453.

Harden, K. P. (2012). True love waits? A sibling-comparison study of age at first sexual intercourse and romantic relationships in young adulthood. *Psychological Science, 23,* 1324–1336.

Hare, Lauren, et al. (2008). Androgen receptor repeat length polymorphism associated with male-to-female transsexualism. *Biological Psychiatry, 65,* 93–96.

Harkness, E., Mullan, B., & Blaszczynski, A. (2015). Association between pornography use and sexual risk behaviors in adult consumers: A systematic review. *Cyberpsychology, Behavior, and Social Networking, 18,* 59–71.

Harlow, Harry F., Harlow, Margaret K., & Hause, F. W. (1963). The maternal affectional system of rhesus monkeys. In H. L. Rheingold (Ed.), *Maternal behavior in mammals.* New York: Wiley.

Harper, Cynthia C., et al. (2005). The effect of increased access to emergency contraception among young adolescents. *Obstetrics & Gynecology, 106,* 483–491.

Harrington, Patrick R., & Swanstrom, Ronald. (2008). The biology of HIV, SIV, and other lentiviruses. In K. Holmes et al. (Eds.), *Sexually transmitted diseases* (4th ed., pp. 323–339). New York: McGraw-Hill.

Harris, Christine. (2002). Sexual and romantic jealousy in heterosexual and homosexual adults. *Psychological Science, 13,* 7–12.

Harris, Christine. (2003). A review of sex differences in sexual jealousy, including self-report data, psychophysiological responses, interpersonal violence, and morbid jealousy. *Personality and Social Psychology Review, 7,* 102–128.

Harris, Gardiner. (2004, February 28). Pfizer gives up testing Viagra on women. *New York Times.*

Harris, Gardiner. (2009, June 13). H.I.V. found in 22 actors in sex films since 2004. *New York Times.*

Harris, G. W., & Levine, S. (1965). Sexual differentiation of the brain and its experimental control. *Journal of Physiology, 181,* 379–400.

Harris, Laura F., et al. (2014). Perceived stress and emotional social support among women who are denied or receive abortion in the United States: A prospective cohort study. *BMC Women's Health, 14,* 76.

Harrison, Albert. (1977). Mere exposure. In L. Berkowitz (Ed.), *Advances in experimental social psychology* (Vol. 10). New York: Academic.

Harte, Christopher B., & Meston, Cindy M. (2011). Recreational use of erectile dysfunction medications in undergraduate men in the United States: Characteristics and associated risk factors. *Archives of Sexual Behavior, 40,* 597–606.

Hartman, William, & Fithian, Marilyn. (1984). *Any man can: The multiple orgasmic technique for every loving man.* New York: St. Martin's Press.

Hartmann, Katherine, Viswanathan, M., Palmieri, R., Gartlehner, G., Thorp, J., & Lohr, K. (2005). Outcomes of routine episiotomy: A systematic review. *Journal of the American Medical Association, 293,* 2141–2148.

Hartzell, Joshua D., et al. (2008). Impact of depression on HIV outcomes in the HAART era. *Journal of Antimicrobial Chemotherapy, 62,* 246–255.

Haslam, Nick, & Levy, Sheri R. (2006). Essentialist beliefs about homosexuality: Structure and implications for prejudice. *Personality and Social Psychology Bulletin, 32,* 471–485.

Hatcher, Robert A., et al. (1976). *Contraceptive technology, 1976–1977* (8th ed.). New York: Irvington.

Hatcher, Robert A., et al. (2004). *Contraceptive technology* (18th ed.). New York: Ardent Media.

Hatcher, Robert A., et al. (2007). *Contraceptive technology* (19th ed.). New York: Ardent Media.

Hatcher, Robert A., et al. (2011). *Contraceptive technology* (20th ed.). New York: Ardent Media.

Hatfield, Elaine. (1978). Equity and extramarital sexuality. *Archives of Sexual Behavior, 7,* 127–141.

Hatfield, Elaine, & Rapson, Richard. (1993a). Historical and cross-cultural perspectives on passionate love and sexual desire. *Annual Review of Sex Research, 4,* 67–97.

Hatfield, Elaine, & Rapson, Richard. (1993b). *Love, sex, and intimacy.* New York: HarperCollins.

Hatfield, Elaine, & Sprecher, Susan. (1986). Measuring passionate love in intimate relations. *Journal of Adolescence, 9,* 383–410.

Hatfield, Elaine, & Walster, G. William. (1978). *A new look at love.* Reading, MA: Addison-Wesley.

Haupert, M. L., et al. (2017). Prevalence of experiences with consensual Nonmonogamous relationships: Findings from two national samples of single Americans. *Journal of Sex & Marital Therapy, 43,* 424–440.

Hawkins, A. J., & Fackrell, T. A. (2010). Does relationship and marriage education for lower-income couples work? A meta-analytic study of emerging research. *Journal of Couple and Relationship Therapy, 9,* 181–191.

Hawkins, Alan, et al. (2008). Does marriage and relationship education work? A meta-analytic study. *Journal of Consulting and Clinical Psychology, 76,* 723–734.

Hayashi, Katsuhiko, et al. (2012, November 16). Offspring from oocytes derived from in vitro primordial germ cell-like cells in mice. *Science, 338,* 971–975.

Haydon, A. A., Cheng, M. M., Herring, A. H., McRee, A-L., & Halpern, C. T. (2014). Prevalence and predictors of sexual inexperience in adulthood. *Archives of Sexual Behavior, 43,* 221–230.

Hazan, C., & Shaver, P. (1987). Love conceptualized as an attachment process. *Journal of Personality and Social Psychology, 52,* 511–524.

Healy, Jack, & Eligon, John (2016, June 17). Orlando survivors recall night of terror: "then he shoots me again." *New York Times.*

Hearn, Kimberly D., O'Sullivan, Lucia F., & Dudley, Cheryl D. (2003). Assessing reliability of early adolescent girls' reports of romantic and sexual behavior. *Archives of Sexual Behavior, 32,* 513–522.

Heatherington, Laurie, & Lavner, Justin A. (2008). Coming to terms with coming out: Review and recommendations for family systems-focused research. *Journal of Family Psychology, 22,* 329–343.

Heaton, Jeremy P. W. (2000). Central neuropharmacological agents and mechanisms in erectile dysfunction: The role of dopamine. *Neuroscience and Biobehavioral Reviews, 24,* 561–569.

Hébert, Martine, et al. (2009). Prevalence of childhood sexual abuse and timing of disclosure in a representative sample of adults from Quebec. *Canadian Journal of Psychiatry, 54,* 631–636.

Hebl, Michelle R., et al. (2002). Formal and interpersonal discrimination: A field study of bias toward homosexual applicants. *Personality and Social Psychology Bulletin, 28,* 815–825.

Heck, Nicholas C. (2015). The potential to promote resilience: Piloting a minority stress-informed, GSA-based mental health promotion program for LGBTQ youth. *Psychology of Sexual Orientation and Gender Diversity, 2,* 225–231.

Heckman, Timothy G., et al. (2011). A randomized clinical trial of a coping improvement group intervention for HIV-infected older adults. *Journal of Behavioral Medicine, 34,* 102–111.

Heffron, Renee, et al. (2012). Use of hormonal contraceptives and risk of HIV-1 transmission: A prospective cohort study. *Lancet Infectious Diseases, 12,* 19–26.

Hegarty, Peter, et al. (2018). Nonbinary gender identities. In N. K. Dess et al. (Eds.), *Gender, sex, and sexualities: Psychological perspectives* (pp. 53–76). New York: Oxford University Press.

Heiman, Julia R. (1975). The physiology of erotica: Women's sexual arousal. *Psychology Today, 8*(11), 90–94.

Heiman, Julia R. (2007). Orgasmic disorders in women. In S. Leiblum (Ed.), *Principles and practice of sex therapy* (4th ed., pp. 84–123). New York: Guilford.

Heiman, Julia R., LoPiccolo, Leslie, & LoPiccolo, Joseph. (1976). *Becoming orgasmic: A sexual growth program for women.* Englewood Cliffs, NJ: Prentice-Hall.

Heine, Steven J., & Norenzayan, Ara. (2006). Toward a psychological science for a cultural species. *Perspectives in Psychological Science, 1,* 251–269.

Heldman, Caroline, & Wade, Lisa. (2010). Hook-up culture: Setting a new research agenda. *Sexuality Research and Social Policy, 7,* 323–333.

Helgeson, Vicki, et al. (2001). Long-term effects of educational and peer discussion group interventions on adjustment to breast cancer. *Health Psychology, 20,* 387–392.

Hellerstedt, Wendy L., et al. (2006). Environmental, social, and personal correlates of having ever had sexual intercourse among American Indian youths. *American Journal of Public Health, 96,* 2228–2234.

Hellerstein, Herman K., & Friedman, Ernst H. (1969, March). Sexual activity and the post-coronary patient. *Medical Aspects of Human Sexuality, 3,* 70–74.

Hellstrom, W. (2003). Three-piece inflatable penile prosthesis components (surgical pearls on reservoirs, pumps, and rear-tip extenders). *International Journal of Impotence Research, 15,* S136–S138.

Hellstrom, W. J. G. (2011). Update on treatments for premature ejaculation. *International Journal of Clinical Practice, 65,* 16–26.

Hellstrom, W., et al. (2003). Tadalafil has no detrimental effect on human spermatogenesis or reproductive hormones. *Journal of Urology, 170,* 887–891.

Helminiak, Daniel A. (2000). *What the Bible* really *says about homosexuality* (Millennium ed.). New Mexico: Alamo Square Press.

Helminiak, Daniel A. (2001a). Sexual ethics in college textbooks: A survey. *Journal of Sex Education and Therapy, 26,* 106–114.

Helminiak, Daniel A. (2001b). Sexual ethics in college textbooks: A suggestion. *Journal of Sex Education and Therapy, 26,* 320–327.

Helminiak, Daniel A. (2004). The ethics of sex: A call to the gay community. *Pastoral Psychology, 52,* 259–267.

Helminiak, Daniel A. (2006). *Sex and the sacred: Gay identity and spiritual growth.* Binghamton, NY: Harrington Park Press.

Hembree, Wylie C., et al. (2017). Endocrine treatment of gender-dysphoric/gender-incongruent persons: An Endocrine Society Clinical Practice Guideline. *Journal of Clinical Endocrinology and Metabolism, 102*(11), 1–35.

Hendrick, Susan. (1981). Self-disclosure and marital satisfaction. *Journal of Personality and Social Psychology, 40,* 1150–1159.

Hendrick, Susan S., & Hendrick, Clyde. (1992). *Liking, loving, and relating* (2nd ed.). Pacific Grove, CA: Brooks/Cole.

Hendrick, Susan S., Hendrick, Clyde, & Adler, N. L. (1988). Romantic relationships: Love, satisfaction, and staying together. *Journal of Personality and Social Psychology, 54,* 980–988.

Henningsson, Susanne, et al. (2005). Sex steroid–related genes and male-to-female transsexualism. *Psychoneuroendocrinology, 30,* 657–664.

Henrich, Joseph, Heine, Steven J., & Norenzayan, Ara. (2010). The weirdest people in the world? *Behavioral and Brain Sciences, 33,* 61–135.

Herbeck, Joshua T., et al. (2018). HIV population-level adaptation can rapidly diminish the impact of a partially effective vaccine. *Vaccine, 36,* 514–520.

Herbenick, Deborah, et al. (2009). Prevalence and characteristics of vibrator use by women in the United States: Results from a nationally representative study. *Journal of Sexual Medicine, 6,* 1857–1866.

Herbenick, Debby, Reece, M., Sanders, S. A., Schick, V., Dodge, B., & Fortenberry, J. D. (2010a). Sexual behavior in the United States: Results from a national probability sample of males and females ages 14 to 94. *Journal of Sexual Medicine, 7*(SS05), 255–265.

Herbenick, Debby, et al. (2010b). Sexual behaviors, relationships and perceived health status among adult women in the United States. Results from a national probability sample. *Journal of Sexual Medicine, 7*(SS05), 277–290.

Herbenick, D., Reece, M., Schick, V., et al. (2010c). An event-level analysis of the sexual characteristics and composition among adults ages 18 to 59: Results from a national probability sample in the United States. *Journal of Sexual Medicine, 7*(SS05), 346–361.

Herbst, A. (1972). Clear cell adenocarcinoma of the genital tract in young females. *New England Journal of Medicine, 287*(25), 1259–1264.

Herdt, Gilbert H. (1984). *Ritualized homosexuality in Melanesia.* Berkeley: University of California Press.

Herdt, Gilbert. (1990). Mistaken gender: 5-alpha reductase hermaphroditism and biological reductionism in sexual identity reconsidered. *American Anthropologist, 92,* 433–446.

Herek, Gregory M. (2000). The psychology of sexual prejudice. *Current Directions in Psychological Science, 9*(1), 19–22.

Herek, Gregory M. (2007). Confronting sexual stigma and prejudice: Theory and practice. *Journal of Social Issues, 63,* 905–925.

Herman, Judith L. (1981). *Father-daughter incest.* Cambridge, MA: Harvard University Press.

Herman-Giddens, Marcia E., et al. (1997). Secondary sexual characteristics and menses in young girls seen in office practice: A study from the Pediatric Research in Office Setting Network. *Pediatrics, 99,* 505–512.

Herman-Giddens, Marcia E., et al. (2012). Secondary sexual characteristics in boys: Data from the Pediatric Research in Office Setting Network. *Pediatrics, 130,* e1058–e1068.

Hernandez, S. (2013). How we built our HIV crime data set. *Pro Publica: Journalism in the Public Interest.* Retrieved from http://www.propublica.org/article/how-we-built-our-hiv-crime-data-set

Hess, J. S., & Coffelt, T. A. (2012). Verbal communication about sex in marriage: Patterns of language use and its connection with relational outcomes. *Journal of Sex Research, 49,* 603–612.

Hessell, Ann J., & Haigwood, Nancy L. (2015). Animal models in HIV-1 protection and therapy. *Current Opinion in HIV AIDS, 10,* 170–176.

Hewlett, Barry S., & Hewlett, Bonnie L. (2010). Sex and searching for children among Aka foragers and Ngandu farmers of Central Africa. *African Study Monographs, 31*(3), 107–125.

Hickey, B. (2010). The soccer mom sex addict. *Philadelphia Weekly.* Retrieved from http://www.philadelphiaweekly.com/news-and-opinion/The-Soccer-Mom-Sex-Addict.html

Hidalgo, Marco A., et al. (2015). The MyPEEPS randomized controlled trial: A pilot of preliminary efficacy, feasibility, and acceptability of a group-level HIV risk reduction intervention for young men who have sex with men. *Archives of Sexual Behavior, 44,* 475–485.

Hightower, Mindy. (1997). Effects of exercise participation on menstrual pain and symptoms. *Women & Health, 26,* 15–27.

Hill, Mark. (2002). Skin color and the perception of attractiveness among African Americans: Does gender make a difference? *Social Psychology Quarterly, 65,* 77–91.

Hines, Denise A. (2007). Predictors of sexual coercion against women and men: A multilevel, multinational study of university students. *Archives of Sexual Behavior, 36,* 403–422.

Hinman, K. (2011). *Lost boys.* www.laweekly.com/content/printVersion/1535565/

Hipp, Tracy N., et al. (2017). Justifying sexual assault: Anonymous perpetrators speak out online. *Psychology of Violence, 7,* 82–90.

Hirschenhauser, Katharina, et al. (2002). Monthly patterns of testosterone and behavior in prospective fathers. *Hormones and Behavior, 42,* 172–181.

HIV CLAPP. (2004). *HIV reporting.* HIV Criminal Law and Public Policy Project. www.hivcriminallaw.org

Hoang, K. K. (2011). "She's not a low-class dirty girl!": Sex work in Ho Chi Minh City, Vietnam. *Journal of Contemporary Ethnography, 40,* 367–396.

Hobfoll, Stevan, et al. (1995). Depression prevalence and incidence among inner-city pregnant and postpartum women. *Journal of Consulting and Clinical Psychology, 63,* 445–453.

Hoeffel, Elizabeth M., et al. (2012). *The Asian population: 2010.* Washington, DC: U.S. Census Bureau.

Hoffman, Heather (2017). Situating human sexual conditioning. *Archives of Sexual Behavior, 46,* 2213–2229.

Hoffmann, Heather, Janssen, Erick, & Turner, Stefanie L. (2004). Classical conditioning of sexual arousal in women and men: Effects of varying awareness and biological relevance of the conditioned stimulus. *Archives of Sexual Behavior, 33,* 43–54.

Hogben, Matthew, & Byrne, Donn. (1998). Using social learning theory to explain individual differences in human sexuality. *Journal of Sex Research, 35,* 58–71.

Holman, Amanda, & Sillars, Alan. (2012). Talk about "hooking up": The influence of college student social networks on nonrelationship sex. *Health Communication, 27,* 205–216.

Hollingsworth v. Perry, 133 S.Ct. 2652 (2013).

Holt, Karen. (2016). Blacklisted: Boundaries, violations, and retaliatory behavior in the BDSM community. *Deviant Behavior, 37,* 917–930.

Homma, Yuko, et al. (2012). The relationship between sexual abuse and risky sexual behavior among adolescent boys: A meta-analysis. *Journal of Adolescent Health, 51,* 18–24.

Hong, Lawrence K. (1984). Survival of the fastest: On the origin of premature ejaculation. *Journal of Sex Research, 20,* 109–122.

Hook, Edward W., & Handsfield, H. Hunter. (2008). Gonococcal infections in the adult. In K. Holmes et al. (Eds.), *Sexually transmitted diseases* (4th ed., pp. 627–646). New York: McGraw-Hill.

Hopwood, Nancy J., et al. (1990). The onset of human puberty: Biological and environmental factors. In J. Bancroft & J. M. Reinisch (Eds.), *Adolescence and puberty.* New York: Oxford University Press.

Horney, Karen. (1973). The flight from womanhood (1926). In K. Horney, *Feminine psychology.* New York: Norton.

Horowitz, Ava D., & Spicer, L. (2013). "Having sex" as a graded and hierarchical construct: A comparison of sexual definitions among heterosexual and lesbian emerging adults in the U.K. *Journal of Sex Research, 50,* 139–150.

Horrocks, R. (1997). *An introduction to the study of sexuality.* New York: St. Martin's Press.

Hottes, Travis S., et al. (2016). Lifetime prevalence of suicide attempts among sexual minority adults by study sampling strategies: A systematic review and meta-analysis. *American Journal of Public Health, 106*(5), E1–E12.

House, Carrie. (1997). Navajo warrior women: An ancient tradition in a modern world. In S. Jacobs et al. (Eds.), *Two-spirit people* (pp. 223–227). Urbana: University of Illinois Press.

Howey, Noelle. (2002). *Dress codes: Of three girlhoods—my mother's, my father's, and mine.* New York: St. Martin's Press.

Hoyle, C., et al. (2002). Dax1 expression is dependent on steroidogenic factor 1 in the developing gonad. *Molecular Endocrinology, 16,* 747–756.

Hsiao, Wayland, et al. (2011). Satisfaction profiles in men using intracavernosal injection therapy. *Journal of Sexual Medicine, 8,* 512–517.

Hubacher, David. (2002). The checkered history and bright future of intrauterine contraception in the United States. *Perspectives on Sexual and Reproductive Health, 34,* 98–103.

Hucker, Stephen. (2008). Sexual masochism: Psychopathology and theory. In D. R. Laws & W. O'Donohue (Eds.), *Sexual deviance: Theory, assessment, and treatment* (2nd ed., pp. 250–263). New York: Guilford.

Hucker, Stephen, & Blanchard, Ray. (1992). Death scene characteristics in 118 fatal cases of autoerotic asphyxia compared with suicidal asphyxia. *Behavioural Sciences and the Law, 10,* 509–523.

Hucker, Alice, & McCabe, Marita P. (2015). Incorporating mindfulness and chat groups into an online cognitive behavioral therapy for mixed female sexual problems. *Journal of Sex Research, 52,* 627–649.

Hughes, I. A., et al. (2006). Consensus statement on management of intersex disorders. *Archives of Disease in Childhood, 91,* 554–562.

Hughes, Jean O., & Sandler, Bernice R. (1987). *"Friends" raping friends: Could it happen to you?* Washington, DC: Association of American Colleges.

Huh, Joon, et al. (2008). Brain activation areas of sexual arousal with olfactory stimulation in men. A preliminary study using functional MRI. *Journal of Sexual Medicine, 5,* 619–625.

Huizink, A. C. (2014). Prenatal cannabis exposure and infant outcomes: Overview of studies. *Progress in Neuro-Psychopharmacology & Biological Psychiatry, 52,* 45–52.

Human Rights Watch. (2001). *Hatred in the hallways: Violence and discrimination against lesbian, gay, bisexual, and transgender students in U.S. schools.* New York: Human Rights Watch.

Humes, Karen R., et al. (2011). *Overview of race and Hispanic origin: 2010.* Washington, DC: U.S. Census Bureau.

Humphreys, Laud. (1970). *Tearoom trade: Impersonal sex in public places.* Chicago: Aldine.

Hurt, Christopher B., et al. (2017). Selecting an HIV test: A narrative review for clinicians and researchers. *Sexually Transmitted Diseases, 44,* 739–746.

Hust, Stacey J., Brown, Jane, & L'Engle, Kelly. (2008). Boys will be boys and girls better be prepared: An analysis of the rare sexual health messages in young adolescents' media. *Mass Communication and Society, 11,* 3–23.

Huston, T. L., & Levinger, G. (1978). Interpersonal attraction and relationships. In M. R. Rosenzweig & L. W. Porter (Eds.), *Annual Review of Psychology* (Vol. 29). Palo Alto, CA: Annual Reviews.

Hyde, Janet S. (2005). The gender similarities hypothesis. *American Psychologist, 60,* 581–592.

Hyde, Janet S. (2014). Gender similarities and differences. *Annual Review of Psychology, 65,* 373–398.

Hyde, Janet S., & Jaffee, Sara R. (2000). Becoming a heterosexual adult: The experiences of young women. *Journal of Social Issues, 56,* 283–296.

Hyde, Janet S., et al. (1996). Sexuality during pregnancy and the year postpartum. *Journal of Sex Research, 33,* 143–151.

Hyde, Janet S., DeLamater, John, & Hewitt, Erri. (1998). Sexuality and the dual-earner couple: Multiple roles and sexual functioning. *Journal of Family Psychology, 12,* 354–368.

Hyde, Janet S., et al. (2008). Gender similarities characterize math performance. *Science, 321,* 494–495.

Hynes, H. Patricia, & Raymond, Janice G. (2002). Put in harm's way: The neglected health consequences of sex trafficking in the United States. In J. Silliman & A. Bhattacharjee (Eds.), *Policing the national body: Sex, race, and criminalization* (pp. 197–229). Cambridge, MA: South End Press.

Ibañez, Gladys E., et al. (2009). General and gay-related racism experienced by Latino gay men. *Cultural Diversity and Ethnic Minority Psychology, 15,* 215–222.

Ilies, Remus, et al. (2003). Reported incidence rates of work-related sexual harassment in the United States: Using meta-analysis to explain reported rate disparities. *Personnel Psychology, 56,* 607–631.

Ilkkaracan, Pinar. (2001). Islam and women's sexuality. In P. Jung et al. (Eds.), *Good sex: Feminist perspectives from the world's religions* (pp. 61–76). New Brunswick, NJ: Rutgers University Press.

Imperato-McGinley, J., et al. (1974). Steroid 5 reductase deficiency in man: An inherited form of male pseudohermaphroditism. *Science, 186,* 1213–1215.

Innala, Sune M., & Ernulf, Kurt E. (1989). Asphyxiophilia in Scandinavia. *Archives of Sexual Behavior, 18,* 181–190.

Institute of Medicine. (2004). *New frontiers in contraceptive research.* Washington, DC: National Academies Press.

Introcaso, Camille E., et al. (2013). Prevalence of circumcision among men and boys aged 14 to 59 years in the United States, National Health and Nutrition Examination Surveys 2005–2010. *Sexually Transmitted Diseases, 40,* 521–525.

Investigative Staff of the *Boston Globe.* (2002). *Betrayal: The crisis in the Catholic Church.* Boston: Little, Brown.

Israel, Davelen D., et al. (2012). Effects of leptin and melanocortin signaling interactions on pubertal development and reproduction. *Endocrinology, 153,* 2408–2419.

Iversen, L., et al. (2017). Lifetime cancer risk and combined contraceptives. *American Journal of Obstetrics and Gynecology, 216,* 580.

Jaakkola, Jouni, & Gissler, Mika. (2004). Maternal smoking in pregnancy, fetal development and childhood asthma. *American Journal of Public Health, 94,* 136–141.

Jackson, Graham. (2009). Sexual response in cardiovascular disease. *Journal of Sex Research, 46,* 233–236.

Jackson, Robert A., & Newman, Meredith A. (2004). Sexual harassment in the federal workplace revisited: Influences on sexual harassment by gender. *Public Administration Review, 64,* 705–717.

Jacobellis v. Ohio, 387 U.S. 197 (1964).

Jacobs, Sue-Ellen, Thomas, Wesley, & Lang, Sabine (Eds.). (1997). *Two-spirit people.* Urbana: University of Illinois Press.

Jamieson, Denise J., et al. (2002). A comparison of women's regret after vasectomy versus tubal sterilization. *Obstetrics and Gynecology, 99,* 1073–1079.

Janicek, Mike F., & Averette, Hervy E. (2001). Cervical cancer: Prevention, diagnosis, and therapeutics. *CA: Cancer Journal for Clinicians, 51,* 92–114.

Jankowiak, William R., et al. (2015). Is the romantic-sexual kiss a near human universal? *American Anthropologist, 117,* 535–539.

Janssen, E., Vorst, H., Finn, P., & Bancroft, J. (2002). The Sexual Inhibition (SIS) and Sexual Excitation (SES) Scales: I. Measuring sexual inhibition and excitation proneness in men. *Journal of Sex Research, 39*(2), 114–126.

Janus, Samuel S., & Janus, Cynthia L. (1993). *The Janus report on sexual behavior.* New York: Wiley.

Jaspers, Loes, et al. (2016). Efficacy and safety of flibanserin for the treatment of hypoactive sexual desire disorder in women: A systematic review and meta-analysis. *JAMA Internal Medicine, 176,* 453–462.

Jatlaoui, Tara C., et al. (2017). Abortion surveillance – United States, 2014. *MMWR, 66,* No. 24.

Jeffreys, Elaine (Ed.). (2006). *Sex and sexuality in China.* New York: Routledge.

Jemail, Jay Ann, & Geer, James. (1977). Sexual scripts. In R. Gemme & C. C. Wheeler (Eds.), *Progress in sexology.* New York: Plenum.

Jenkins, Philip. (1996). *Pedophiles and priests: Anatomy of a contemporary crisis.* New York: Oxford University Press.

Jenny, Carole, Roesler, Thomas A., & Poyer, Kimberly A. (1994). Are children at risk for sexual abuse by homosexuals? *Pediatrics, 94,* 41–44.

Jensen, T., Gottschau, M., Madsen, J. O. B., Andersson, A., Lassen, T., Skakkebaek, N., et al. (2014). Habitual alcohol consumption associated with reduced semen quality, and changes in reproductive hormones; a cross-sectional study among 1221 young Danish men. *BMJ Open, 4,* e005462. doi: 10.1136/bmjopen-2014-005462

Joel, Daphna. (2011). Male or female? Brains are intersex. *Frontiers in Integrative Neuroscience, 5,* 57.

Johansmeyer, T. (2010). *Even porn stars get the recession blues.* Retrieved from www.dailyfinance.com/2010/01/08/even-porn-stars-get-the-recession-blues/

Johansson, Annika, et al. (2010). A five-year follow-up study of Swedish adults with gender identity disorder. *Archives of Sexual Behavior, 39,* 1429–1437.

John, E. M., Savitz, D. A., & Sandler, D. P. (1991). Prenatal exposure to parents' smoking and childhood cancer. *American Journal of Epidemiology, 133,* 123–132.

Johnsdotter, Sara, & Essén, Birgitta. (2010). Genitals and ethnicity: The politics of genital modifications. *Reproductive Health Matters, 18,* 29–37.

Johnson, Brooke R., Horga, Mihai, & Andronache, Laurentia. (1996). Women's perspectives on abortion in Romania. *Social Science & Medicine, 42,* 521–530.

Johnson, Paula A., et al. (Eds.). (2018). *Sexual harassment of women: Climate, culture, and consequences in academic sciences, engineering, and medicine.* Washington, DC: National Academies Press. Retrieved from www.nap.edu

Johnson, S. (2013). *Love sense: The revolutionary new science of romantic relationships.* New York: Little, Brown.

Johnson, Sarah, et al. (2015). Comparison of analytical sensitivity and women's interpretation of home pregnancy tests. *Clinical Chemistry and Laboratory Medicine, 53,* 391–402.

Johnson, Sharon D., Phelps, D., & Cottler, L. (2004). The association of sexual dysfunction and substance use among a community epidemiological sample. *Archives of Sexual Behavior, 33,* 55–64.

Johnston-Robledo, Ingrid, & Chrisler, Joan C. (2013). The menstrual mark: Menstruation as social stigma. *Sex Roles, 68,* 9–18.

Johri, A., Heaton, J., & Morales, A. (2001). Severe erectile dysfunction is a marker for hyperprolactinemia. *International Journal of Impotence Research, 13,* 176–182.

Joint SOGC-CFAS Guidelines. (2008). Guidelines for the number of embryos to transfer following *in vitro* fertilization. *International Journal of Gynecology and Obstetrics, 102,* 203–216.

Joint SOGC-CFAS Clinical Practice Guidelines. (2010, April). Elective single embryo transfer following in vitro fertilization. *Journal of Obstetrics and Gynecology Canada, 32,* 363–377.

Jonason, Peter K., & Fisher, Terri D. (2009). The power of prestige: Why young men report having more sex partners than young women. *Sex Roles, 60,* 151–159.

Jonason, Peter K., et al. (2009). The "booty call": A compromise between men's and women's ideal mating strategies. *Journal of Sex Research, 46,* 460–470.

Jonason, Peter K., et al. (2011). Positioning the booty-call relationship on the spectrum of relationships: Sexual but more emotional than one-night stands. *Journal of Sex Research, 48,* 486–495.

Jones, Angela. (2016, Autumn). "I get paid to have orgasms": Adult webcam models' negotiation of pleasure and danger. *Signs,* 227–256.

Jones, Rachel K. (2018). Reported contraceptive use in the month of becoming pregnant among U.S. abortion patients in 2000 and 2014. *Contraception, 97,* 309–312.

Jones, Claira, Chan, Crystal, & Farine, Dan. (2011). Sex in pregnancy. *Canadian Medical Association Journal.* doi: 10:1503/cmaj.091580

Jones, Hendree. (2006). Drug addiction during pregnancy: Advances in maternal treatment and understanding child outcomes. *Current Directions in Psychological Science, 15,* 126–130.

Jones, James H. (1981). *Bad blood: The Tuskegee syphilis experiment.* New York: Free Press.

Jones, James H. (1997). *Alfred C. Kinsey: A public/private life.* New York: Norton.

Jones, John, Pelham, Brett, Carvallo, Mauricio, & Mirenberg, Matthew. (2004). How do I love thee? Let me count the Js: Implicit egotism and interpersonal attraction. *Journal of Personality and Social Psychology, 87,* 665–683.

Jones, Lisa M., et al. (2012). Trends in youth Internet victimization: Findings from three youth Internet safety surveys 2000–2010. *Journal of Adolescent Health, 50,* 179–186.

Jones, R., & Jerman, J. (2014). Abortion incidence and service availability in the United States, 2011. *Perspectives in Sexual and Reproductive Health, 46,* 3–14.

Jones, Rachel K., & Jerman, Jenna. (2017). Population group abortion rates and lifetime incidence of abortion: United States, 2008–2014. *American Journal of Public Health, 107,* 1904–1909.

Jones, Rachel, & Kooistra, Kathryn. (2011). Abortion incidence and access to services in the United States, 2008. *Perspectives on Sexual and Reproductive Health, 43,* 41–50.

Joshi, Suchi P., et al. (2011). Scripts of sexual desire and danger in U.S. and Dutch teen girl magazines: A cross-national content analysis. *Sex Roles, 64,* 463–474.

Joyal, Christian C., & Carpenter, Julie. (2017). The prevalence of paraphilic interests and behaviors in the general population: A provincial survey. *Journal of Sex Research, 54,* 161–171.

Joyal, Christian C., Cossette, A., & Lapierre, V. (2015). What exactly is an unusual sexual fantasy? *Journal of Sexual Medicine, 12,* 328–340.

Joyce, Theodore, Henshaw, Stanley, Dennis, Amanda, et al. (2009). *The impact of state mandatory counseling and waiting period laws on abortion: A literature review.* New York: Guttmacher Institute.

Jung, Patricia B., Hunt, Mary E., & Balakrishnan, Radhika (Eds.). (2001). *Good sex: Feminist perspectives from the world's religions.* New Brunswick, NJ: Rutgers University Press.

Kabir, Azad, Pridjian, G., Steinmann, W., Herrera, E., & Khan, M. (2005). Racial differences in cesareans: An analysis of U.S. 2001 national inpatient sample data. *Obstetrics and Gynecology, 195,* 710–718.

Kaestle, Christine E., & Allen, Katherine R. (2011). The role of masturbation in healthy sexual development: Perceptions of young adults. *Archives of Sexual Behavior, 40,* 983–994.

Kafka, Martin P. (1997). Hypersexual desire in males: An operational definition and clinical implications for males with paraphilias and paraphilia-related disorders. *Archives of Sexual Behavior, 26,* 505–526.

Kafka, Martin P. (2010). Hypersexual disorder: A proposed diagnosis for DSM-V. *Archives of Sexual Behavior, 39,* 377–400.

Kafka, Martin, & Hennen, John. (2002). A *DSM-IV* Axis I comorbidity study of males (n = 120) with paraphilias and paraphilia-related disorders. *Sex Abuse, 14,* 349–366.

Kahr, Brett. (2008). *Who's been sleeping in your head? The secret world of sexual fantasies.* New York: Basic Books.

Kaiser Family Foundation. (1998). *Sex in the 90s: 1998 national survey of Americans on sex and sexual health.* Menlo Park, CA: Kaiser Family Foundation, Pub. No. 1430.

Kaiser Family Foundation. (2000). *Sex education in America: A view from inside the nation's classrooms.* Menlo Park, CA: Kaiser Family Foundation.

Kaiser Family Foundation. (2004a). *Sex education in America: General public/parents survey.* Menlo Park, CA: Kaiser Family Foundation.

Kaiser Family Foundation. (2004b). *Sex education in America: Principals survey.* Menlo Park, CA: Kaiser Family Foundation.

Kaiser Family Foundation. (2015). *HIV testing in the United States.* http://kff.org/hivaids/fact-sheet/hiv-testing-in-the-united-states/

Kalick, S. Michael, et al. (1998). Does human facial attractiveness honestly advertise health? Longitudinal data on an evolutionary question. *Psychological Science, 9,* 8–13.

Kalil, Kathleen, et al. (1993). Social and family pressures on anxiety and stress during pregnancy. *Pre- and Perinatal Psychology Journal, 8,* 113–118.

Kallstrom-Fuqua, Amanda C., Weston, R., & Marshall, L. (2004). Childhood and adolescent sexual abuse of community women: Mediated effects on psychological distress and social relationships. *Journal of Consulting and Clinical Psychology, 72,* 980–992.

Kann, Laura, et al. (2016). Youth risk behavior surveillance—United States, 2015. *MMWR,65,* No. 6.

Kapidzic, Sanja, & Herring, S. (2015). Race, gender, and self-presentation in teen profile photographs. *New Media and Society, 17,* 958–976.

Kaplan, Helen S. (1974). *The new sex therapy.* New York: Brunner/Mazel.

Kaplan, Helen S., & Owett, Trude. (1993). The female androgen deficiency syndrome. *Journal of Sex and Marital Therapy, 19,* 3–25.

Kaplan, Helen Singer. (1979). *Disorders of sexual desire.* New York: Simon & Schuster.

Karama, S., et al. (2002). Areas of brain activation in males and females during viewing of erotic film excerpts. *Human Brain Mapping, 16,* 1–13.

Karantzas, Gery C., et al. (2014). Towards an integrative attachment-based model of relationship functioning. *British Journal of Psychology, 105,* 413–434.

Karhus, L. L., Egerup, P., Skovlund, C. W., & Lidegaard, O. (2013). Long-term reproductive outcomes in women whose first pregnancy is ectopic: A national controlled follow-up study. *Human Reproduction, 28,* 241–246.

Karraker, A., DeLamater, J., & Schwartz, C. (2011). Sexual frequency decline from midlife to later life. *Journals of Gerontology Series B: Psychological Sciences & Social Sciences, 66B*(4), 502–512.

Karraker, Amelia, & DeLamater, John. (2013). Past-year sexual inactivity among older married persons and their partners. *Journal of Marriage and Family, 75*(1), 142–163.

Kashdan, Todd B., et al. (2018). Sexuality leads to boosts in mood and meaning in life with no evidence for the reverse direction: A daily diary investigation. *Emotion, 18,* 563–576.

Katz-Wise, Sabra. (2012). *Beyond labels: Sexual fluidity and sexual identity development in sexual minority young adults* (Unpublished doctoral dissertation). University of Wisconsin–Madison.

Katz-Wise, Sabra, & Hyde, Janet S. (2012). Victimization experiences of lesbian, gay, and bisexual individuals: A meta-analysis. *Journal of Sex Research, 49,* 142–167.

Katz-Wise, Sabra L., et al. (2017). Endorsement and timing of sexual orientation developmental milestones among sexual minority young adults. In the Growing Up Today Study. *Journal of Sex Research, 54,* 172–185.

Kaufman, Carol E., et al. (2007). Culture, context, and sexual risk among Northern Plains American Indian youth. *Social Science and Medicine, 64,* 2152–2164.

Keefe, David L. (2002). Sex hormones and neural mechanisms. *Archives of Sexual Behavior, 31,* 401–404.

Keenan, T., & Ward, T. (2000). A theory of mind perspective on cognitive, affective, and intimacy deficits in child sex offenders. *Sex Abuse, 12,* 49–60.

Kegel, A. H. (1952). Sexual functions of the pubococcygeus muscle. *Western Journal of Surgery, 60,* 521–524.

Kelly, Shalonda, & Shelton, J. (2013). African American couples and sex. In K. Hall & C. Graham (Eds.), *The cultural context of sexual pleasure and problems* (pp. 47–83). New York: Routledge.

Kendler, Kenneth S., et al. (2000a). Childhood sexual abuse and adult psychiatric and substance use disorders in women: An epidemiological and cotwin control analysis. *Archives of General Psychiatry, 57,* 953–959.

Kendler, Kenneth S., et al. (2000b). Sexual orientation in a U.S. national sample of twin and nontwin sibling pairs. *American Journal of Psychiatry, 157,* 1843–1846.

Kennedy, Robert, & Suttenfield, Kelley. (2001). Postpartum depression. *Medscape Mental Health 6,* 4.

Kenny, Maureen C., & Wurtele, Sandy K. (2013). Child sexual behavior inventory: A comparison between Latino and normative samples of preschoolers. *Journal of Sex Research, 50,* 449–457.

Kent, A. (2008). Psychiatric disorders in pregnancy. *Obstetrics, Gynaecology, and Reproductive Medicine, 19,* 37–41.

Kerpelman, J. (2014). Healthy adolescent romantic relationships. *Family Focus on Dating and Mate Selection.* National Council on Family Relations, Winter, F1–ff.

Kessler, Suzanne. (1998). *Lessons from the intersexed.* New Brunswick, NJ: Rutgers University Press.

Kettrey, Heather H. (2016). What's gender got to do with it? Sexual double standards and power in heterosexual college hookups. *Journal of Sex Research, 53,* 754–765.

Keverne, Eric B. (1999). The vomeronasal organ. *Science, 286,* 716–720.

Khoury Bassam et al. (2013a). Mindfulness interventions for psychosis: A meta-analysis. *Schizophrenia Research, 150,* 176–184.

Khoury, Bassam, et al. (2013b). Mindfulness-based therapy: A comprehensive meta-analysis. *Clinical Psychology Review, 33,* 763–771.

Kiecolt, K. J., Fossett, M. A., & Smith, W. (1995). Mate availability and marriage among African-Americans: Aggregate- and individual-level analyses. In M. B. Tucker & C. Mitchell-Kerum (Eds.), *The decline in marriage among African-Americans: Causes, consequences, and policy implications* (pp. 103–116). New York: Russell Sage Foundation.

Kiesner, Jeff. (2009). Physical characteristics of the menstrual cycle and premenstrual depressive symptoms. *Psychological Science, 20,* 763–770.

Kikuras, A. (2004). An interview with Dave Cummings, *Unchain the underground.* Retrieved from www.unchain.com

Kilpatrick, D. G., et al. (2007). *Drug facilitated, incapacitated, and forcible rape: A national study.* Washington, DC: U.S. Department of Justice.

Kim, Bryan, Li, Lisa, & Ng, Gladys. (2005). The Asian American values scale. *Cultural Diversity and Ethnic Minority Psychology, 11,* 187-201.

Kim, Janna L., et al. (2007). From sex to sexuality: Exposing the heterosexual script on primetime network television. *Journal of Sex Research, 44,* 145-157.

Kim, N., et al. (1997). Effectiveness of the 40 adolescent AIDS-risk reduction interventions: A quantitative review. *Journal of Adolescent Health, 20,* 204-215.

Kimberly, Claire, & Hans, Jason D. (2017). From fantasy to reality: A grounded theory of experiences in the swinging lifestyle. *Archives of Sexual Behavior, 46,* 789-799.

Kindregan, Charles. (2011). *The current state of assisted reproduction law.* Suffolk University Law School: Legal Studies Research Paper Series 11-47.

King, Mary-Claire, Marks, J., & Mandell, J. (2003). Breast and ovarian cancer risks due to inherited mutations in BRCA1 and BRCA2. *Science, 302,* 643-646.

King, Michael, et al. (2007). Women's views of their sexual difficulties: Agreement and disagreement with clinical diagnoses. *Archives of Sexual Behavior, 36,* 281-288.

Kingston, Drew A., Malamuth, Neil M., Federoff, Paul, & Marshall, William L. (2009). The importance of individual differences in pornography use: Theoretical perspectives and implications for treating sexual offenders. *Journal of Sex Research, 46,* 216-232.

Kinnish, Kelly K., Strassberg, D., & Turner, C. (2005). Sex differences in the flexibility of sexual orientation: A multidimensional retrospective assessment. *Archives of Sexual Behavior, 34,* 173-184.

Kinsey, Alfred C., Pomeroy, Wardell B., & Martin, Clyde E. (1948). *Sexual behavior in the human male.* Philadelphia, PA: Saunders.

Kinsey, Alfred C., et al. (1953). *Sexual behavior in the human female.* Philadelphia, PA: Saunders.

Kirby, Douglas, & Laris, B. A. (2009). Effective curriculum-based sex and STD/HIV education programs for adolescents. *Child Development Perspectives, 3,* 21-29.

Kirby, Douglas, et al. (1994). School-based programs to reduce sexual risk behaviors: A review of effectiveness. *Public Health Reports, 109,* 339-360.

Kirk, K., et al. (2000). Measurement models for sexual orientation in a community twin sample. *Behavior Genetics, 30,* 345-356.

Kirkpatrick, Lee, & Davis, Keith. (1994). Attachment style, gender, and relationship stability: A longitudinal analysis. *Journal of Personality and Social Psychology, 66,* 502-512.

Kiselica, Mark, & Scheckel, Steve. (1995). The couvade syndrome (sympathetic pregnancy) and teenage fathers: A brief primer for counselors. *School Counselor, 43,* 42-51.

Klebanov, Pamela K., & Jemmott, John B. (1992). Effects of expectations and bodily sensations on self-reports of premenstrual symptoms. *Psychology of Women Quarterly, 16,* 289-310.

Klein, R. (2015). Poll: Americans seek better sex education than what states require. *The Huffington Post.* Retrieved from http://www.huffingtonpost.com/2015/01/09/sex-ed-yougov-poll_n_6438080.html

Klein, V., Rettenberger, M., & Briken, P. (2014). Self-report indicators of hypersexuality and its correlates in a female online sample. *Journal of Sexual Medicine, 11,* 1974-1981.

Klingensmith, Katherine, et al. (2014). Military sexual trauma in US veterans: Results from the National Health and Resilience in Veterans Study. *Journal of Clinical Psychiatry, 75,* e1133.

Kniffin, K. M., & Wilson, D. S. (2004). The effect of nonphysical traits on perception of physical attractiveness: Three naturalistic studies. *Evolution and Human Behavior, 25,* 88-101.

Knobloch-Westerwick, S. (2015). *Choice and preference in media use.* New York: Routledge.

Knobloch-Westerwick, Silvia, & Hoplamazian, Gregory J. (2012). Gendering the self: Selective magazine reading and reinforcement of gender conformity. *Communication Research, 39,* 358-384.

Koch, Patricia B., Mansfield, P., Thurau, D., & Carey, M. (2005). "Feeling frumpy": The relationships between body image and sexual response changes in midlife women. *Journal of Sex Research, 42,* 215-223.

Kogan, Paul, & Wald, Moshe. (2014). Male contraception: History and development. *Urological Clinics of North America, 41,* 145-161.

Kolbenschlag, Madonna. (1985). Abortion and moral consensus: Beyond Solomon's choice. *Christian Century, 102,* 179-183.

Koo, Kelly H., et al. (2018). The cultural context of nondisclosure of alcohol-involved acquaintance rape among Asian American college women: A qualitative study. *Journal of Sex Research, 52,* 55-68.

Korber, Bette, & Gnanakaran, S. (2011). Converging on an HIV vaccine. *Science, 333,* 1589-1590.

Korff, Janice, & Geer, James H. (1983). The relationship between sexual arousal experience and genital response. *Psychophysiology, 20,* 121-127.

Kosfeld, Michael, Heinrichs, Markus, Zak, Paul, Fischbacher, Urs, & Fehr, Ernst. (2005, June 2). Oxytocin increases trust in humans. *Nature, 435,* 673-676.

Kosnick, Anthony, et al. (1977). *Human sexuality: New directions in American Catholic thought.* New York: Paulist Press.

Koss, Mary P., & Figueredo, Aurelio. (2004). Change in cognitive mediators of rape's impact on psychosocial health across 2 years of recovery. *Journal of Consulting and Clinical Psychology, 72,* 1063-1072.

Koss, Mary P., et al. (1994). *No safe haven: Male violence against women at home, at work, and in the community.* Washington, DC: American Psychological Association.

Koss, Mary P., Koss, Paul G., & Woodruff, W. Joy. (1991). Deleterious effects of criminal victimization on women's health and medical utilization. *Archives of Internal Medicine, 151,* 342-347.

Kost, Kathryn, et al. (2017). *Pregnancies, births and abortions among adolescents and young women in the United States, 2013.* New York: Guttmacher Institute. Retrieved from https://www.guttmacher.org/sites/default/files/report_pdf/us-adolescent-pregnancy-trends-2013.pdf

Kothari, P. (1984). For discussion: Ejaculatory disorders—a new dimension. *British Journal of Sexual Medicine, 11,* 205-209.

Kovacs, Peter. (2002a). Congenital anomalies and low birth weight associated with assisted reproductive technologies. *Medscape Women's Health, 7*(3). www.medscape.com/viewarticle/435963

Kovacs, Peter. (2002b). Preconception sex selection. *Medscape Ob/Gyn & Women's Health, 7*(2). www.medscape.com/viewarticle/441313

Krahé, Barbara, et al. (2007). The role of sexual scripts in sexual aggression and victimization. *Archives of Sexual Behavior, 36,* 687-701.

Kraus, Shane W., et al. (2018). Compulsive sexual behavior disorder in the ICD-11. *World Psychiatry, 17,* 109-110.

Kraut, Robert, et al. (2004). Psychological research online: Report of Board of Scientific Affairs' Advisory Group on the Conduct of Research on the Internet. *American Psychologist, 59,* 105-117.

Kreider, R. (2006a). Remarriage within the United States. Presented at the American Sociological Association Annual Meeting, Montreal, Canada.

Kreider, Rose. (2006b). Marital status in the 2004 American Community Survey. U.S. Bureau of the Census, Working Paper. U.S. Bureau of the Census, Statistical Abstract of the United States, 2007, Table 62.

Krilis, Matthew et al. (2013). "Popper"-induced vision loss. *Drug and Alcohol Review, 32,* 333–334.

Krings, Franciska, & Facchin, Stephanie. (2009). Organizational justice and men's likelihood to sexually harass: The moderating role of sexism and personality. *Journal of Applied Psychology, 94,* 501–510.

Krippendorff, K. (2004). *Content analysis: An introduction to its methodology.* Thousand Oaks, CA: Sage.

Krueger, R. B. (2010). The DSM diagnostic criteria for sexual masochism. *Archives of Sexual Behavior, 39,* 346–356.

Kruijver, F., et al. (2000). Male-to-female transsexuals have female neuron numbers in a limbic nucleus. *Journal of Clinical Endocrinology and Metabolism, 85,* 2034–2041.

Kuber, Laura E., Coleman, B., & Mustanski, B. (2014). Coping with LGBT and racial-ethnic-related stressors: A mixed-methods study of LGBT youth of color. *Journal of Research on Adolescence, 24,* 689–702.

Kull, Ryan M., et al. (2016). Effectiveness of school district antibullying policies in improving LGBT youths' school climate. *Psychology of Sexual Orientation and Gender Diversity, 3,* 407–415.

Kunkel, Dale, et al. (2005). *Sex on TV 4.* Menlo Park, CA: Kaiser Family Foundation.

Kues, Johanna N., et al. (2018). The effect of manipulated information about premenstrual changes on the report of positive and negative premenstrual changes. *Women & Health, 58,* 16–37.

Kuyper, Lisette, et al. (2012). Doing more good than harm? The effects of participation in sex research on young people in the Netherlands. *Archives of Sexual Behavior, 41,* 497–506.

Kwak-kim, J., Agcaoili, M. S., Aleta, L., Liao, A., Ota, K., Dambaeva, S., et al. (2013). Management of women with recurrent pregnancy losses and antiphospholipid syndrome. *American Journal of Reproductive Immunology, 69,* 596–607.

Kwon, Paul. (2013). Resilience in lesbian, gay, and bisexual individuals. *Personality and Social Psychology Review, 17,* 371–383.

Labrecque, Lindsay T., & Whisman, Mark A. (2017). Attitudes toward and prevalence of extramarital sex and descriptions of extramarital partners in the 21st century. *Journal of Family Psychology, 31,* 952–957.

LaBrie, J. W., Hummer, J. F., Ghaidarov, T. M., Lae, A., & Kenney, S. R. (2014). Hooking up in the college context: The event-level effects of alcohol use and partner familiarity on hookup behaviors and contentment. *Journal of Sex Research, 51,* 62–73.

LaFromboise, Theresa D., Heyle, Anneliese M., & Ozer, Emily J. (1990). Changing and diverse roles of women in American Indian cultures. *Sex Roles,* 455–476.

Lalumière, M. L., & Quinsey, V. L. (1998). Pavlovian conditioning of sexual interests in human males. *Archives of Sexual Behavior, 27,* 241–252.

Lalumière, M., Blanchard, R., & Zucker, K. (2000). Sexual orientation and handedness in men and women: A meta-analysis. *Psychological Bulletin, 126,* 575–592.

Lamb, S., & Plocha, A. (2014). Sexuality in childhood. In D. L. Tolman & L. M. Diamond (Eds.), *APA handbook of sexuality and psychology* (Vol. 1, pp. 415–432). Washington, DC: American Psychological Association.

Lambert, N. M., et al. (2013). A boost of positive affect: The perks of sharing positive experiences. *Journal of Social and Personal Relationships, 30,* 24–43.

Lamberts, Steven W. J., et al. (1997). The endocrinology of aging. *Science, 278,* 419–424.

Lammers, J., Stoker, J. I., Jordan, J., Pollmann, M., & Stapel, D. A. (2011). Power increases infidelity among men and women. *Psychological Science, 22,* 1191–1197.

Langer, Ellen J., & Dweck, Carol S. (1973). *Personal politics: The psychology of making it.* Englewood Cliffs, NJ: Prentice-Hall.

Langfeldt, Thore. (1981). Childhood masturbation. In L. L. Constantine & F. M. Martinson (Eds.), *Children and sex* (pp. 63–74). Boston: Little, Brown.

Långström, Niklas, & Zucker, Kenneth J. (2005). Transvestic fetishism in the general population: Prevalence and correlates. *Journal of Sex and Marital Therapy, 31,* 87–95.

Långström, Niklas, et al. (2013). Preventing sexual abusers of children from reoffending: Systematic review of medical and psychological interventions. *BMJ, 347,* f4630.

Lansford, Jennifer E., et al. (2010). Developmental precursors of number of sexual partners from ages 16 to 22. *Journal of Research on Adolescence, 20,* 651–677.

Lantz, H. R., Keyes, J., & Schultz, H. (1975). The American family in the preindustrial period: From baselines in history to change. *American Sociological Review, 40,* 21–36.

Larsson, IngBeth, & Svedin, Carl-Göran. (2002). Sexual experiences in childhood: Young adults' recollections. *Archives of Sexual Behavior, 31,* 263–274.

Lassek, William D., & Gaulin, Steven. (2007). Menarche is related to fat distribution. *American Journal of Physical Anthropology, 133,* 1147–1151.

Lattimore, Keri, Donn, S., Kaciroti, N., Kemper, A., Neal, C., & Vasquez, D. (2005). Selective serotonin reuptake inhibitor (SSRI) use during pregnancy and effects on the fetus and newborn: A meta-analysis. *Journal of Perinatology, 25,* 595–604.

Lau, J. T. F., et al. (2003). Effects of two telephone survey methods on the level of reported risk behaviours. *Sexually Transmitted Infections, 79,* 325–331.

Laughon, S. Katherine, et al. (2012). Changes in labor patterns over 50 years. *American Journal of Obstetrics and Gynecology, 206*(419), e1–e9.

Laumann, Edward O., & Parish, William. (2004). Chinese Family Health Survey (CFHS). Personal communication.

Laumann, Edward O., et al. (1994). *The social organization of sexuality: Sexual practices in the United States.* Chicago: University of Chicago Press.

Laumann, Edward O., et al. (2004). *The sexual organization of the city.* Chicago: University of Chicago Press.

Laurenceau, J-P., Feldman, Barrett, & Pietromonaco, P. R. (1998). Intimacy as an interpersonal process: The importance of self-disclosure, partner disclosure, and perceived partner responsiveness in interpersonal exchanges. *Journal of Personality and Social Psychology, 74,* 1238–1251.

Lauricella, Alexis R., et al. (2015). Young children's screen time: The complex role of parent and child factors. *Journal of Applied Developmental Psychology, 36,* 11–17.

Lavin, Michael. (2008). Voyeurism: Psychopathology and theory. In D. R. Laws & W. O'Donohue (Eds.), *Sexual deviance: Theory, assessment, and treatment* (2nd ed., pp. 305–319). New York: Guilford.

Lawrence et al. v. Texas, 539 U.S. 102 (2003).

Lawrence, Kelli-An, & Byers, E. Sandra. (1995). Sexual satisfaction in long-term heterosexual relationships: The interpersonal exchange model of sexual satisfaction. *Personal Relationships, 2,* 267–285.

Laws, D. Richard. (2008). The public health approach: A way forward? In D. R. Laws & W. O'Donohue (Eds.), *Sexual deviance: Theory, assessment, and treatment* (2nd ed., pp. 611–628). New York: Guilford.

Laws, D. Richard, & O'Donohue, William (Eds.). (2008). *Sexual deviance: Theory, assessment, and treatment* (2nd ed.). New York: Guilford.

Leander, Else-Marie, et al. (2018). Children's doctor games and nudity at Danish childcare institutions. *Archives of Sexual Behavior, 47,* 863–875.

Leaper, Campbell, & Ayres, Melanie M. (2007). A meta-analytic review of gender variations in adults' language use: Talkativeness, affiliative speech, and assertive speech. *Personality and Social Psychology Review, 11,* 328–363.

Leaper, Campbell, & Friedman, Carly Kay. (2007). The socialization of gender. In J. Grusec & P. Hastings (Eds.), *Handbook of socialization: Theory and research* (pp. 561–587). New York: Guilford.

Leaper, Campbell, & Smith, Tara E. (2004). A meta-analytic review of gender variations in children's language use. *Developmental Psychology, 40,* 993–1027.

LeardMann, Cynthia A., et al. (2013). Combat deployment is associated with sexual harassment or sexual assault in a large, female military cohort. *Women's Health Issues, 23,* e215–e223.

Lever, J., & Dolnick, D. (2010). Call girls and street prostitutes: Selling sex and intimacy. In R. Weitzer (Ed.), *Sex for sale: Prostitution, pornography, and the sex industry* (2nd ed., pp. 187–203). New York: Routledge.

Lebacqz, Karen. (1987). Appropriate vulnerability: A sexual ethic for singles. *Christian Century, 104,* 435–438.

Leca, J. B., Gunst, N., & Vasey, P. (2014). Male homosexual behavior in a free-ranging all-male group of Japanese macaques at Minoo, Japan. *Archives of Sexual Behavior, 43,* 853–862.

Leca, Jean-Baptiste, et al. (2015). Comparative development of heterosexual and homosexual behaviors in free-ranging female Japanese macaques. *Archives of Sexual Behavior, 44,* 1215–1231.

Lederer, Laura (Ed.). (1980). *Take back the night: Women on pornography.* New York: Morrow.

Lee, John Alan. (1977). A typology of styles of loving. *Personality and Social Psychology Bulletin, 3,* 173–182.

Lee, John Alan. (1988). Love-styles. In R. J. Sternberg & M. L. Barnes (Eds.), *The psychology of love* (pp. 38–67). New Haven, CT: Yale University Press.

Lee, Daniel J., et al. (2015). Trends in the utilization of penile prostheses in the treatment of erectile dysfunction in the United States. *Journal of Sexual Medicine, 12,* 1638–1645.

Lee, Peter A., et al. (2006). Consensus statement on management of intersex disorders. *Pediatrics, 118,* e488–e500.

Lee, S., Ralston, J., Drey, E., et al. (2005). Fetal pain: A systematic multidisciplinary review of the evidence. *Journal of the American Medical Association, 294,* 947–954.

Leeman, Lawrence, & Leeman, Rebecca. (2003). A Native American community with a 7% cesarean delivery rate: Does case mix, ethnicity or labor management explain the low rate? *Annals of Family Medicine, 1,* 36–43.

Lehman, J. S., Carr, M. H., Nichol, A. J., et al. (2014). Prevalence and public health implications of state laws that criminalize potential HIV exposure in the United States. *AIDS and Behavior, 18,* 997–1006.

Leibowitz, Scott, & de Vries, Annelou. (2016). Gender dysphoria in adolescence. *International Review of Psychiatry, 28,* 21–35.

Leitenberg, Harold, & Henning, Kris. (1995). Sexual fantasy. *Psychological Bulletin, 117,* 469–496.

Lemieux, Robert, & Hale, Jerold. (2002). Cross-sectional analysis of intimacy, passion, and commitment: Testing the assumptions of the triangular theory of love. *Psychological Reports, 90,* 1009–1014.

Leonard, Arthur S. (1993). *Sexuality and the law: An encyclopedia of major legal cases.* New York: Garland.

Leonard, Leah M., & Follette, Victoria, M. (2002). Sex functioning in women reporting a history of child sexual abuse: Clinical and empirical considerations. *Annual Review of Sex Research, 13,* 346–388.

Lerman, Hannah. (1986). From Freud to feminist personality theory. *Psychology of Women Quarterly, 10,* 1–18.

LeTourneau, Elizabeth, et al. (2009). Multisystemic therapy for juvenile sexual offenders: 1-year results from a randomized effectiveness trial. *Journal of Family Psychology, 23,* 89–102.

Lev, Arlene, I. (2004). *Transgender emergence: Therapeutic guidelines for working with gender-variant people and their families.* Binghamton, NY: Haworth Press.

LeVay, Simon. (1991). A difference in hypothalamic structure between heterosexual and homosexual men. *Science, 253,* 1034–1037.

LeVay, Simon. (1996). *Queer science: The use and abuse of research into homosexuality.* Cambridge, MA: MIT Press.

LeVay, Simon. (2011). *Gay, straight, and the reason why.* New York: Oxford University Press.

Levey, T. (2018). *Sexual harassment online: Shaming and silencing women in the digital age.* Boulder, CO: Lynne Rienner.

Levin, D. (2009). So sexy, so soon: The sexualization of childhood. In S. Olfman (Ed.), *The sexualization of childhood* (pp. 75–88). Westport, CT: Praeger.

Levin, Roy J. (2005). Sexual arousal—Its physiological roles in human reproduction. *Annual Review of Sex Research, 15,* 154–189.

Levine, R., Sato, S., Hashimoto, T., & Verma, J. (1995). Love and marriage in eleven cultures. *Journal of Cross-Cultural Psychology, 26,* 554–571.

Levine, Aaron D., et al. (2017). Contributions of assisted reproductive technology to overall births by maternal age in the United States, 2012–2014. *JAMA, 317,* 1272–1273.

Levine, Ethan C., et al. (2018). Open relationships, nonconsensual nonmonogamy, and monogamy among U.S. adults: Findings from the 2012 National Survey of Sexual Health. *Archives of Sexual Behavior, 47,* 1439–1450.

Levitas, Eliahu, et al. (2003). *Are semen parameters related to abstinence? Analysis of 7,233 semen samples.* Paper presented at European Society for Human Reproduction and Embryology, Madrid, Spain.

Lewis, J. M., & Kreider, R. M. (2015). Remarriage in the United States. *American Community Survey Reports,* ACS-30. Washington, DC: U.S. Census Bureau.

Lewis, Linwood J., & Kertzner, Robert M. (2003). Toward improved interpretation and theory building of African American male sexualities. *Journal of Sex Research, 40,* 383–395.

Lewis, R. W., et al. (2004). Definitions, classification, and epidemiology of sexual dysfunction. In T. Lue et al. (Eds.), *Sexual medicine* (pp. 39–72). Paris: Editions 21.

Lewis, Ronald W., et al. (2010). Definitions/epidemiology/risk factors for sexual dysfunction. *Journal of Sexual Medicine, 7,* 1598–1607.

Ley, D., Brovka, J. M., & Reid, R. C. (2015). Forensic applications of the "sex addiction" in US legal proceedings. *Current Sexual Health Reports.* doi: 10.1007/s11930-015-0049-7

Ley, D., Prause, N., & Finn, P. (2014). The emperor has no clothes: A review of the "pornography addiction" model. *Current Sexual Health Reports, 6,* 94–105.

Li, Kai, & Poirier, D. J. (2001). Using the National Longitudinal Study of Youth in the U.S. to study the birth process: A Bayesian approach. *Research in Official Statistics, 4,* 127–150.

Liao, L-M. Michala, L., & Creighton, Sara. (2010). Labial surgery for well women: A review of the literature. *British Journal of Obstetrics and Gynecology, 117,* 20–25.

Lichtenstein, Bronwen. (2012). Starting over: Dating risks and sexual health among midlife women after relationship dissolution. In Laura Carpenter & John DeLamater (Eds.), *Sex for life: From virginity to Viagra, how sexuality changes throughout our lives* (pp. 180–197). New York: New York University Press.

Lidegaard, O., et al. (2012). Thrombotic stroke and myocardial infarction with hormonal contraception. *New England Journal of Medicine, 366,* 2257–2266.

Lieberman, Debra, & Smith, Adam. (2012). It's all relative: Sexual aversions and moral judgments regarding sex among siblings. *Current Directions in Psychological Science, 21,* 243–247.

Liening, Scott H., et al. (2010). Salivary testosterone, cortisol, and progesterone: Two-week stability, interhormone correlations, and effects of time of day, menstrual cycle, and oral contraceptive use on steroid hormone levels. *Physiology and Behavior, 99,* 8–16.

Liljeros, F., et al. (2001). The web of human sexual contacts. *Nature, 411,* 907–908.

Lin, Ken-Hou, & Lundquist, Jennifer. (2013). Mate selection in cyberspace: The intersection of race, gender, and education. *American Journal of Sociology, 119,* 183–215.

Lindau, S., et al. (2007). A study of sexuality and health among older adults in the United States. *The New England Journal of Medicine, 357,* 762–774.

Lindemann, D. (2012). *Dominatrix: Gender, eroticism, and control in the dungeon.* Chicago: University of Chicago Press.

Linden, Judith A. (2011). Care of the adult patient after sexual assault. *New England Journal of Medicine, 365,* 834–841.

Lindgren, Kristen P., et al. (2008). Gender differences in perceptions of sexual intent: A qualitative review and integration. *Psychology of Women Quarterly, 32,* 423–439.

Linz, Daniel, Donnerstein, E., & Penrod, S. (1987). The findings and recommendations of the Attorney General's Commission on Pornography: Do the psychological "facts" fit the political fury? *American Psychologist, 42,* 946–953.

Lippa, Richard A. (2013). Men and women with bisexual identities show bisexual patterns of sexual attraction to male and female "swimsuit models." *Archives of Sexual Behavior, 42,* 187–196.

Lipsey, M. W., & Wilson, D. B. (2001). *Practical meta-analysis.* Thousand Oaks, CA: Sage.

Lisak, David, & Miller, Paul M. (2002). Repeat rape and multiple offending among undetected rapists. *Violence and Victims, 17,* 73–84.

Liu, Chien. (2003). Does quality of marital sex decline with duration? *Archives of Sexual Behavior, 32,* 55–60.

Ljunger, E., Cnattingius, S., Lundin, C., & Anneren, G. (2005). Chromosomal anomalies in first-trimester miscarriages. *Acta Obstetrica et Gynecologica Scandinavica, 84,* 1103–1107.

Loeb, Tamra B., et al. (2002). Child sexual abuse: Associations with the sexual functioning of adolescents and adults. *Annual Review of Sex Research, 13,* 307–345.

Loffreda, Beth. (2000). *Losing Matt Shepard: Life and politics in the aftermath of anti-gay murder.* New York: Columbia University Press.

Lohiya, N. K., et al. (2014). RISOG: An intravasal injectable male contraceptive. *Indian Journal of Medical Research, 140,* S63–S72.

LoPiccolo, Joseph, & Stock, Wendy E. (1986). Treatment of sexual dysfunction. *Journal of Consulting and Clinical Psychology, 54,* 158–167.

Lorius, Cassandra. (1999). *Tantric sex: Making love last.* London: Thorsons/HarperCollins.

Lorius, Cassandra. (2010). *Tantric secrets: 7 steps to the best sex of your life.* New York: HarperCollins.

Lottes, Ilsa L., & Alkula, Tapani. (2011). An investigation of sexuality-related attitudinal patterns and characteristics related to those patterns for 32 European countries. *Sexuality Research and Social Policy, 8,* 77–92.

Lovejoy, Travis I., & Heckman, T. G. (2014). Depression moderates treatment efficacy of an HIV secondary-prevention intervention for HIV-positive late middle-age and older adults. *Behavioral Medicine, 40,* 124–133.

Lowery, Shearon, & Wetli, Charles. (1982). Sexual asphyxia: A neglected area of study. *Deviant Behavior, 3,* 19–39.

Lucero, Margaret A., et al. (2006). Sexual harassers: Behaviors, motives, and change over time. *Sex Roles, 55,* 331–344.

Luke, Barbara. (1994). Nutritional influences on fetal growth. *Clinical Obstetrics and Gynecology, 37,* 538–549.

Lull, Robert B., & Bushman, Brad J. (2015). Do sex and violence sell? A meta-analytic review of the effects of sexual and violent media and ad content on memory, attitudes, and buying intentions. *Psychological Bulletin, 141,* 1022–1048.

Lundsberg, Lisbet, Pal, Lubria, Gariepy, Aileen, Xu, Xiao, Chu, Micheline, & Illuzi, Jessica. (2014). Knowledge, attitudes, and practices regarding conception and fertility: A population-based survey among reproductive-age United States women. *Fertility and Sterility, 101,* 767–774.

Luo, Minmin, Fee, M., & Katz, L. (2003). Encoding pheromonal signals in the accessory olfactory bulb in behaving mice. *Science, 299,* 1196–1201.

Luque, Maria C., et al. (2014). Gene expression profile in long-term non progressor HIV infected patients: In search of potential resistance factors. *Molecular Immunology, 62,* 63–70.

Lussier, Patrick, & Piche, Lyne. (2008). Frotteurism: Psychopathology and theory. In D. R. Laws & W. O'Donohue (Eds.), *Sexual deviance: Theory, assessment, and treatment.* (2nd ed., pp. 131–149). New York: Guilford.

Lutz, Deborah. (2011). Pleasure *bound: Victorian sex rebels and the new eroticism.* New York: Norton.

Luzuriaga, Katherine, et al. (2006). Vaccines to prevent transmission of HIV-1 via breastmilk: Scientific and logistical priorities. *The Lancet, 368,* 511–521.

Maass, Anne, et al. (2003). Sexual harassment under social identity threat: The computer harassment paradigm. *Journal of Personality and Social Psychology, 85,* 853–870.

Maccoby, Eleanor E. (2002). Gender and group process: A developmental perspective. *Current Directions in Psychological Science, 11,* 54–58.

MacDorman, M. F., Mathews, T. J., & Declerq, E. (2014). Trends in out-of-hospital births in the United States, 1990–2012. NCHS data brief, no. 175. Hyattsville, MD: National Center for Health Statistics.

MacKinnon, Catharine A. (1982). Feminism, Marxism, method, and the state: An agenda for theory. In N. O. Keohane et al. (Eds.), *Feminist theory.* Chicago, IL: University of Chicago Press.

MacLaughlin, David T., & Donahoe, Patricia K. (2004). Sex determination and differentiation. *New England Journal of Medicine, 350,* 367–378.

MacNeil, Sheila, & Byers, E. Sandra. (2009). Role of sexual self-disclosure in the sexual satisfaction of long-term heterosexual couples. *Journal of Sex Research, 46,* 3–14.

Magaña, J. R., & Carrier, J. M. (1991). Mexican and Mexican American male sexual behavior and spread of AIDS in California. *Journal of Sex Research, 28,* 425–441.

Maguire, Daniel C. (2001). *Sacred choices: The right to contraception and abortion in ten world religions.* Minneapolis, MN: Augsburg Fortress.

Maguire, Daniel C. (2003). *Sacred rights: The case for contraception and abortion in world religions.* New York: Oxford University Press.

Maier, Thomas. (2009). *Masters of sex.* New York: Basic Books.

Maines, Rachel P. (1999). *The technology of orgasm: "Hysteria," the vibrator, and women's sexual satisfaction.* Baltimore, MD: Johns Hopkins University Press.

Major, Brenda et al. (2009). Abortion and mental health: Evaluating the evidence. *American Psychologist, 64,* 863–890.

Malamuth, N., & Huppin, M. (2007). Drawing the line on virtual child pornography: Bringing the law in line with the research evidence. *NYU Review of Law and Social Change, 31,* 773–827.

Malamuth, Neil M. (1998). The confluence model as an organizing framework for research on sexually aggressive men: Risk moderators, imagined aggression and pornography consumption. In R. Geen & E. Donnerstein (Eds.), *Aggression: Theoretical and empirical reviews.* New York: Academic Press.

Malamuth, Neil M., & Brown, Lisa M. (1994). Sexually aggressive men's perceptions of women's communications. *Journal of Personality and Social Psychology, 67,* 699–712.

Malcolm, James P. (2008). Heterosexually married men who have sex with men: Marital separation and psychological adjustment. *Journal of Sex Research, 45,* 350–357.

Malm, Heli, et al. (2011). Selective serotonin reuptake inhibitors and risk for major congenital anomalies. *Obstetrics and Gynecology, 118,* 111–120.

Malta, S., & Farquharson, K. (2014). The initiation and progression of late-life romantic relationships. *Journal of Sociology, 50,* 237–251.

Maltz, Wendy, & Boss, Suzie. (1997). *In the garden of desire: The intimate world of women's sexual fantasies.* New York: Broadway Books.

Mandese, Joe. (2007). Feeling blue: Americans consume more adult content. *Media Post.* Retrieved from www.mediapost.com

Manganello, Jennifer, & Blake, Nancy. (2010). A study of quantitative content analysis of health messages in U.S. media from 1985 to 2005. *Health Communication, 25,* 387–396.

Mark, Kristen, Janssen, Erick, & Milhausen, Robin. (2011). Infidelity in heterosexual couples: Demographic, interpersonal, and personality-related predictors of extradyadic sex. *Archives of Sexual Behavior, 40,* 971–982.

Markens, Susan. (2007). *Surrogate motherhood and the politics of reproduction.* Berkeley, CA: University of California Press.

Markman, Howard J., & Floyd, Frank. (1980). Possibilities for the prevention of marital discord: A behavioral perspective. *American Journal of Family Therapy, 8,* 29–48.

Markman, Howard, et al. (2010). The premarital communication roots of marital distress and divorce: The first five years of marriage. *Journal of Family Psychology, 24,* 289–298.

Marshall, B. L. (2012). Medicalization and the refashioning of age-related limits on sexuality. *Journal of Sex Research, 49,* 337–343.

Marshall, Donald C. (1971). Sexual behavior on Mangaia. In D. S. Marshall & R. C. Suggs (Eds.), *Human sexual behavior.* New York: Basic Books.

Marshall, Eliot. (1995). NIH's "Gay Gene" study questioned. *Science, 268,* 1841.

Marsiglio, William, & Diekow, Douglas. (1998). Men and abortion: The gender politics of pregnancy resolution. In L. J. Beckman & S. M. Harvey (Eds.), *The new civil war* (pp. 269–284). Washington, DC: American Psychological Association.

Martin, Carol L., & Halverson, C. F. (1983). The effects of sex-typing schemas on young children's memory. *Child Development, 54,* 563–574.

Martin, Carol, & Ruble, Diane. (2004). Children's search for gender cues: Cognitive perspectives on gender development. *Current Directions in Psychological Science, 13,* 67–70.

Martin, J. A., Hamilton, B. E., & Osterman, M. (2014). Births in the United States, 2013. NCHS data brief, no. 175. Hyattsville, MD: National Center for Health Statistics.

Martin, Sandra L., et al. (2011). Health and economic consequences of sexual violence. In J. White et al. (Eds.), *Violence against women and children: Navigating solutions* (Vol. 1, pp. 173–196). Washington, DC: American Psychological Association.

Martins, Yolanda, et al. (2008). Hair today, gone tomorrow: A comparison of body hair removal practices in gay and heterosexual men. *Body Image, 5,* 312–316.

Martins, Yolanda, Preti, George, et al. (2005). Preference for human body odors is influenced by gender and sexual orientation. *Psychological Science, 16,* 694–701.

Martinson, F. M. (1994). *The sexual life of children.* Westport, CT: Bergin & Garvey.

Marx, Jean. (1995). Sharing the genes that divide the sexes for mammals. *Science, 269,* 1824–1827.

Masci, David. (2018). American religious groups vary widely in their views of abortion. Pew Research Center. Retrieved from http://www.pewresearch.org/fact-tank/2018/01/22/american-religious-groups-vary-widely-in-their-views-of-abortion/

Masters, W. H., Johnson, V. E., & Kolodny, R. C. (1982). *Human sexuality.* Boston: Little, Brown.

Masters, William H., & Johnson, Virginia. (1966). *Human sexual response.* Boston: Little, Brown.

Masters, William H., & Johnson, Virginia. (1970). *Human sexual inadequacy.* Boston: Little, Brown.

Masters, William H., & Johnson, Virginia. (1979). *Homosexuality in perspective.* Boston: Little, Brown.

Masterton, Graham. (1993). *Drive him wild: A hands-on guide to pleasuring your man in bed.* New York: Signet Books.

Matsick, Jes L., & Rubin, Jennifer D. (2018). Bisexual prejudice among lesbian and gay people: Examining the roles of gender and perceived sexual orientation. *Psychology of Sexual Orientation and Gender Diversity, 5,* 143–155.

Matsumoto, David. (2000). *Cultural influences on research methods and statistics.* Pacific Grove, CA: Brooks/Cole.

Matsumoto, David, & Juang, L. (2017). *Culture and psychology* (6th ed.). Boston, MA: Cengage Learning.

Maurer, Harry. (1994). *Sex: Real people talk about what they really do.* New York: Penguin Books.

Mayo Clinic. (2012a). *Male infertility: Lifestyle and home remedies.* www.mayoclinic.com/health/male-infertility/DSO1038/lifestyle-andhome-remedies

Mayo Clinic. (2012b). *Maximizing fertility.* www.mayoclinic.com/health/how-to-get-pregnant/PR00103

Mayo Clinic. (2014). *Labor and delivery: Pain medications.* http://www.mayoclinic.org/healthy-living/labor-and-delivery/in-depth/labor-and-delivery/art-20049326

McAuliffe, Timothy L., et al. (2007). Effects of question format and collection mode on the accuracy of retrospective surveys of health risk behavior: A comparison with daily sexual activity diaries. *Health Psychology, 26,* 60–67.

McCabe, Edward. (1996). Sex and the single DAX1: Too little is bad, but can we have too much? *Journal of Clinical Investigation, 98,* 881–882.

McCabe, Marita, & Connaughton, C. (2014). Psychosocial factors associated with male sexual difficulties. *Journal of Sex Research, 51,* 31–42.

McCabe, Marita, et al. (2010). Psychological and interpersonal dimensions of sexual function and dysfunction. *Journal of Sexual Medicine, 7,* 327–336.

McCallum, Ethan B., & Peterson, Zoë D. (2012). Investigating the impact of inquiry mode on self-reported sexual behavior: Theoretical considerations and review of the literature. *Journal of Sex Research, 49,* 212–226.

McCarthy, B., Benoit, C., & Jansson, M. (2014). Sex work: A comparative study. *Archives of Sexual Behavior, 43,* 1379–1390.

McCarthy, Barry, & McCarthy, Emily. (2009). *Discovering your couple sexual style: The key to sexual satisfaction.* New York: Taylor & Francis.

McClelland, Sara I. (2014). "What do you mean when you say that you are sexually satisfied?" *Feminism & Psychology, 24,* 74–96.

McClintock, Elizabeth A. (2014, August). Beauty and status: The illusion of exchange in partner selection? *American Sociological Review, 79*(4), 575–604.

McClintock, Martha. (1971). Menstrual synchrony and suppression. *Nature, 229,* 244–245.

McClintock, Martha K. (1998). Whither menstrual synchrony? *Annual Review of Sex Research, 9,* 77–95.

McClintock, Martha K. (2000). Human pheromones: Primers, releasers, signalers, or modulators? In K. Wallen & J. Schneider (Eds.), *Reproduction in context* (pp. 355–420). Cambridge, MA: MIT Press.

McClintock, Martha, & Herdt, Gilbert. (1996). Rethinking puberty: The development of sexual attraction. *Current Directions in Psychological Science, 5,* 178–183.

McCoy, Norma L. (1996). Menopause and sexuality. In M. K. Beard (Ed.), *Optimizing hormone replacement therapy: Estrogen-androgen therapy in postmenopausal women* (pp. 32–36). Minneapolis, MN: McGraw-Hill Healthcare.

McCoy, Norma L. (1997). Sexual issues for postmenopausal women. *Topics in Geriatric Rehabilitation, 12,* 28–39.

McCoy, Norma L., & Pitino, Lisa. (2002). Pheromonal influences on sociosexual behavior in young women. *Physiology & Behavior, 75,* 367–375.

McDade-Montez, Elizabeth, et al. (2017). Sexualization in U.S. Latina and White girls' preferred children's television programs. *Sex Roles, 77,* 1–15.

McDaniel, Brandon T., & Drouin, Michelle. (2015). Sexting among married couples: Who is doing it, and are they more satisfied? *Cyberpsychology, Behavior, and Social Networking, 18(11),* 1–7.

McDonagh, Annmarie, et al. (2005). Randomized trial of cognitive-behavioral therapy for chronic posttraumatic stress disorder in adult female survivors of childhood sexual abuse. *Journal of Consulting and Clinical Psychology, 73,* 515–524.

McEwen, B. S. (1997). Meeting report—Is there a neurobiology of love? *Molecular Psychiatry, 2,* 15–16.

McEwen, Bruce S. (2001). Estrogen effects on the brain: Multiple sites and molecular mechanisms. *Journal of Applied Physiology, 91,* 2785–2801.

McFarlane, Jessica M., & Williams, Tannis M. (1994). Placing premenstrual syndrome in perspective. *Psychology of Women Quarterly, 18,* 339–374.

McFarlane, Jessica, Martin, Carol L., & Williams, Tannis M. (1988). Mood fluctuations: Women versus men and menstrual versus other cycles. *Psychology of Women Quarterly, 12,* 201–224.

McGuire, Jenifer K., & Barber, Bonnie L. (2010). A person-centered approach to the multifaceted nature of young adult sexual behavior. *Journal of Sex Research, 47,* 301–313.

McGuire, R. J., Carlisle, J. M., & Young, B. G. (1965). Sexual deviations as conditioned behavior: A hypothesis. *Behavioral Research and Therapy, 2,* 185–190.

McKay, Alexander. (2005). Sexuality and substance use: The impact of tobacco, alcohol, and selected recreational drugs on sexual function. *Canadian Journal of Human Sexuality, 14,* 47–56.

McKee, Alan. (2005). The objectification of women in mainstream pornographic videos in Australia. *Journal of Sex Research, 42,* 277–290.

McKenna, Josephine. (2014, April 26). Pope Francis speaks out on abortion. *Huffington Post.* http://www.huffingtonpost.com/2014/04/26/pope-francis-abortion_n_5215862.html

McKenna, K. E. (2000). Some proposals regarding the organization of the central nervous system control of penile erection. *Neuroscience and Biobehavioral Reviews, 24,* 535–540.

McKinlay, Sonja M., Brambilla, D. J., & Posner, J. G. (1992). The normal menopause transition. *American Journal of Human Biology, 4,* 37–46.

McNeill, John J. (1987). Homosexuality: Challenging the church to grow. *Christian Century, 104,* 242–246.

Mead, Margaret. (1935). *Sex and temperament in three primitive societies.* New York: Morrow.

Meana, Marta, & Nunnink, Sarah E. (2006). Gender differences in the content of cognitive distraction during sex. *Journal of Sex Research, 43,* 59–67.

Meana, Marta, & Steiner, E. (2014). Hidden disorder/hidden desire: Presentations of low sexual desire in men. In Y. Binik & K. Hall (Eds.), *Principles and practice of sex therapy* (5th ed., pp. 42–60). New York: Guilford.

Meeks, Joshua J., et al. (2003). Dax1 is required for testis determination. *Nature Genetics, 34,* 32–33.

Mehta, Aditi, & Sheth, S. (2006). Postpartum depression: How to recognize and treat this common condition. *Medscape Psychiatry and Mental Health, 11,* article 529930.

Meischke, Hendrika. (1995). Implicit sexual portrayals in the movies: Interpretations of young women. *Journal of Sex Research, 32,* 29–36.

Melendez, Rita M., et al. (2013). Understanding Latina women's sexuality in the United States. In K. Hall & C. Graham (Eds.), *The cultural context of sexual pleasure and problems* (pp. 84–110). New York: Routledge.

Melmed, S., et al. (2016). *Williams textbook of endocrinology* (13th ed.). Philadelphia, PA: Elsevier.

Meltzer, Marisa. (2017, February). Match me if you can. *Consumer Reports.*

Mercer, C. H., Tanton, C., Prah, P., Erens, B., Sonnenberg, P., Clifton, S., et al. (2013). Changes in sexual attitudes and lifestyles in Britain through the life course and over time: Findings from the National Surveys of Sexual Attitudes and Lifestyles. *Lancet, 382,* 1781–1794.

Merin, Abigail, & Pachankis, John E. (2011). The psychological impact of genital herpes stigma. *Journal of Health Psychology, 16,* 80–90.

Meshkovska, Biljana, et al. (2015). Female sex trafficking: Conceptual issues, current debates, and future directions. *Journal of Sex Research, 52,* 380–395.

Mesman, Judi, & Groeneveld, Marleen. (2018). Gendered parenting in early childhood: Subtle but unmistakable if you know where to look. *Child Development Perspectives, 12,* 22–27.

Messenger, John C. (1993). Sex and repression in an Irish folk community. In D. N. Suggs & A. W. Miracle (Eds.), *Culture and human sexuality.* Pacific Grove, CA: Brooks/Cole.

Messer, Ellen, and May, Kathryn E. (1988). *Backrooms: Voices from the illegal abortion era.* New York: St. Martin's Press.

Meston, C., & Buss, D. (2007). Why humans have sex. *Archives of Sexual Behavior, 36,* 477–507.

Meston, Cindy M., & Ahrold, Tierney. (2010). Ethnic, gender, and acculturation influences on sexual behaviors. *Archives of Sexual Behavior, 39,* 179–189.

Meston, Cindy M., et al. (2004). Women's orgasm. *Annual Review of Sex Research, 15,* 173–257.

Meston, Cindy M., Rellini, Alessandra H., & Heiman, Julia R. (2006). Women's history of sexual abuse, their sexuality, and sexual self-schemas. *Journal of Consulting and Clinical Psychology, 74,* 229–236.

Meyer, Ilan H. (2003). Prejudice, social stress, and mental health in lesbian, gay, and bisexual populations: Conceptual issues and research evidence. *Psychological Bulletin, 129,* 674–697.

Meyer-Bahlburg, Heino. (2013). Sex steroids and variants of gender identity. *Endocrinology and Metabolism Clinics of North America, 42,* 435–452.

Meyer-Bahlburg, Heino, et al. (2004). Prenatal androgenization affects gender-related behavior but not gender identity in 5–12-year-old girls with congenital adrenal hyperplasia. *Archives of Sexual Behavior, 33,* 97–104.

Meyvis, Inge, et al. (2012). Maternal position and other variables: Effects on perineal outcomes in 557 births. *Birth, 39,* 115–120.

Mezzacappa, Elizabeth, & Katkin, Edward. (2002). Breast-feeding is associated with reduced perceived stress and negative mood in mothers. *Health Psychology, 21,* 187–193.

Michael, Robert T., et al. (1994). *Sex in America: A definitive survey.* Boston, MA: Little, Brown.

Miki, Yoshio, et al. (1994). A strong candidate for the breast and ovarian cancer susceptibility gene BRCA1. *Science, 226,* 66–71.

Miklos, John R., & Moore, Robert D. (2008). Labiaplasty of the labia minora: Patients' indications for pursuing surgery. *Journal of Sexual Medicine, 5,* 1492–1495.

Mikulincer, Mario, & Goodman, Gail (Eds). (2006). *Dynamics of romantic love.* New York: Guilford Press.

Milam, Joel. (2006). Posttraumatic growth and HIV disease progression. *Journal of Consulting and Clinical Psychology, 74,* 817–827.

Miller v. California, 413 U.S. 15 (1973).

Miller, L. C., & Fishkin, S. A. (1997). On the dynamics of human bonding and reproductive success: Seeking windows on the adapted-for-human environmental interface. In J. A. Simpson & D. T. Kenrick (Eds.), *Evolutionary social psychology* (pp. 197–235). Mahwah, NJ: Lawrence Erlbaum.

Miller, Neil. (1992). *Out in the world: Gay and lesbian life from Buenos Aires to Bangkok.* New York: Random House.

Miller, Patricia. (2014). *Good Catholics: The battle over abortion in the Catholic Church.* Berkeley, CA: University of California Press.

Miller, Rickey S., & Lefcourt, Herbert M. (1982). The assessment of social intimacy. *Journal of Personality Assessment, 46,* 514–518.

Miller, S., Corrales, R., & Wachman, D. B. (1975). Recent progress in understanding and facilitating marital communication. *Family Coordinator, 24,* 143–152.

Miller, Saul L., & Maner, Jon. (2010). Scent of a woman: Men's testosterone responses to olfactory ovulation cues. *Psychological Science, 21,* 276–283.

Miller, Benjamin G., et al. (2017). No differences? Meta-analytic comparisons of psychological adjustment in children of gay fathers and heterosexual parents. *Psychology of Sexual Orientation and Gender Diversity, 4,* 14–22.

Miner, Michael, & Coleman, Eli. (2001). Advances in sex offender treatment and challenges for the future. *Journal of Psychology and Human Sexuality, 13,* 5–24.

Minichiello, V., Scott, J., & Callander, D. (2013). New pleasures and old dangers: Reinventing male sex work. *Journal of Sex Research, 50,* 263–275.

Minter, S. P. (2012). Supporting transgender children: New legal, social, and medical approaches. *Journal of Homosexuality, 59,* 422–433.

Minto, Catherine L., et al. (2003). The effect of clitoral surgery on sexual outcome in individuals who have intersex conditions with ambiguous genitalia: A cross-sectional study. *The Lancet, 361,* 1252–1257.

Mitchell, Kimberly J., et al. (2007). Trends in youth reports of sexual solicitations, harassment and unwanted exposure to pornography on the Internet. *Journal of Adolescent Health, 40,* 116–126.

Mitchell, Kimberly J., Jones, L., Finkelhor, D., & Wolak, J. (2013a). Understanding the decline in unwanted online sexual solicitations 2000–2010: Findings from three Internet Youth Safety surveys. *Child Abuse & Neglect, 37,* 1225–1236.

Mitchell, K. R., et al. (2013b). Sexual function in Britain: Findings from the third National Survey of Sexual Attitudes and Lifestyles (Natsal-3). *Lancet, 382,* 1817–1829.

Mize, Trenton, & Manago, Bianca. (2018). Precarious sexuality: How men and woman are differentially categorized for similar sexual behavior. *American Sociological Review, 83,* 305–330.

Mizock, Lauren, & Hopwood, Ruben. (2016). Conflation and interdependence in the intersection of gender and sexuality among transgender individuals. *Psychology of Sexual Orientation and Gender Diversity, 3,* 93–103.

Mohamed, Heather S. (2018). Embryonic politics: Attitudes about abortion, stem cell research, and IVF. *Politics and Religion, 11,* 459–497.

Mollborn, Stefanie. (2017). Teenage mothers today: What we know and how it matters. *Child Development Perspectives, 11,* 63–69.

Molina, J.-M., et al. (2015). On-demand preexposure prophylaxis in men at high risk for HIV-1 infection. *New England Journal of Medicine, 373,* 2237–2246.

Molitch, Mark E. (1995). Neuroendocrinology. In P. Felig et al. (Eds.), *Endocrinology and metabolism.* New York: McGraw-Hill.

Mollen, D. (2014). Reproductive rights and informed consent: Toward a more inclusive discourse. *Analysis of Social Issues and Public Policy, 14,* 162–182.

Mona, Linda R., Syme, M., & Cameron, R. (2014). Sexuality and disability: A disability-affirmative approach to sex therapy. In Y. Binik & K. Hall (Eds.), *Principles and practice of sex therapy* (5th ed., pp. 457–481). New York: Guilford.

Moncrieff, Michael, & Lienard, Pierre. (2017). A natural history of the drag queen phenomenon. *Evolutionary Psychology, 15*(2), 1–14.

Mondaini, N., et al. (2003). Sildenafil does not improve sexual function in men without erectile dysfunction but does reduce the postorgasmic refractory time. *International Journal of Impotence Research, 15,* 225–228.

Money, John. (1987). Sin, sickness, or status: Homosexual gender identity and psychoneuroendocrinology. *American Psychologist, 42,* 384–399.

Money, John, & Ehrhardt, Anke. (1972). *Man and woman, boy and girl.* Baltimore, MD: Johns Hopkins. (Reissued 1996, facsimile edition by Northvale, NJ: Jason Aronson)

Montazeri, Ali. (2008). Health-related quality of life in breast cancer patients: A bibliographic review of the literature from 1974 to 2007. *Journal of Experimental & Clinical Cancer Research, 27,* 32.

Monte, L. M., & Ellis, R. R. (2014). Fertility of women in the United States: June 2012. *Current Population Reports,* P20-575. Washington, DC: U.S. Census Bureau.

Montemurro, Beth. (2014). *Deserving desire: Women's stories of sexual evolution.* New Brunswick, NJ: Rutgers University Press.

Montesi, Jennifer, et al. (2010). The specific importance of communicating about sex to couples' sexual and overall relationship satisfaction. *Journal of Social and Personal Relationships, 28,* 591–609.

Montorsi, F., & Althof, S. (2004). Partner responses to sildenafil citrate (Viagra) treatment of erectile dysfunction. *Urology, 63,* 762–767.

Montorsi, F., et al. (2004). Long-term safety and tolerability of tadalafil in the treatment of erectile dysfunction. *European Urology, 45,* 339–345.

Montoya, R. Matthew. (2008). I'm hot, so I'd say you're not: The influence of objective physical attractiveness on mate selection. *Personality and Social Psychology Bulletin, 34,* 1315–1331.

Moore, Allen J. (1987). Teenage sexuality and public morality. *Christian Century, 104,* 747–750.

Moore, Fhionna, et al. (2006). The effects of female control of resources on sex-differentiated mate preferences. *Evolution and Human Behavior, 27,* 193–205.

Moradi, Bonnie, et al. (2006). Intrapersonal and interpersonal manifestations of antilesbian and gay prejudice: An application of personal construct theory. *Journal of Counseling Psychology, 53,* 57–66.

Morales, A., et al. (1998). Clinical safety of oral sildenafil (Viagra) in the treatment of erectile dysfunction. *International Journal of Impotence Research, 10,* 69–74.

Morales, Alvaro, et al. (2015). Diagnosis and management of testosterone deficiency syndrome in men: Clinical practice guideline. *Canadian Medical Association Journal, 187,* 1369–1377.

Morandini, James S., et al. (2017). Who adopts queer and pansexual sexual identities? *Journal of Sex Research, 54,* 911–922.

Morell, V. (1998). A new look at monogamy. *Science, 281,* 1982–1983.

Morgan, Elizabeth M. (2011). Associations between young adults' use of sexually explicit materials and their sexual preferences, behaviors, and satisfaction. *Journal of Sex Research, 48,* 520–530.

Morgan, Robin. (1978, November). How to run the pornographers out of town (and preserve the First Amendment). *Ms., 55,* 78–80.

Morgan, Robin. (1980). Theory and practice: Pornography and rape. In L. Lederer (Ed.), *Take back the night: Women on pornography.* New York: Morrow.

Morgan, Rachel E., & Kena, Grace. (2017, December). *Criminal victimization, 2016.* U.S. Department of Justice, Bureau of Justice Statistics, NCJ 251150.

Morris-Rush, Jeanine, & Bernstein, Peter. (2002). Postpartum depression. *Medscape Women's Health, 7*(1).

Morris, Norval J. (1973, April 18). The law is a busy-body. *New York Times Magazine,* 58–64.

Morrison, L., et al. (2001). The long-term reproductive health consequences of female genital cutting in rural Gambia: A community-based survey. *Tropical Medicine & International Health, 6,* 643–653.

Morrison, Shane D., et al. (2017). An overview of female-to-male gender-confirming surgery. *Nature Review Urology, 14,* 486–500.

Moser, C. (1998). S/M (Sadomasochistic) interactions in semi-public settings. *Journal of Homosexuality, 36*(2), 19–29.

Mosher, William D., & Jones, Jo. (2010). Use of contraception in the United States: 1982–2008. *Vital Health Statistics, 23*(29). National Center for Health Statistics.

Mosher, William D., Chandra, Anjani, & Jones, Jo. (2005). Sexual behavior and selected health measures: Men and women 15–44 years of age, United States, 2002. *Vital and Health Statistics, 362.* Centers for Disease Control and Prevention.

Moulden, Heather M., et al. (2009). Recidivism in pedophiles: An investigation using different diagnostic methods. *Journal of Forensic Psychiatry & Psychology, 20,* 680–701.

Moynihan, Ray. (2014). Evening the score on sex drugs: Feminist movement or marketing masquerade? *BMJ, 349,* g6246.

Muehlenhard, Charlene L. (1988). Misinterpreted dating behaviors and the risk of date rape. *Journal of Social and Clinical Psychology, 6,* 20–37.

Muehlenhard, Charlene, & Skippee, Sheena. (2010). Men's and women's reports of pretending orgasm. *Journal of Sex Research, 47,* 552–567.

Muehlenhard, Charlene L., et al. (2017). Evaluating the one-in-five statistic: Women's risk of sexual assault while in college. *Journal of Sex Research, 54,* 549–576.

Mueller, G. O. W. (1980). *Sexual conduct and the law* (2nd ed.). Dobbs Ferry, NY: Oceana.

Muller, James, et al. (1996). Triggering myocardial infarction by sexual activity. *Journal of the American Medical Association, 275,* 1405–1409.

Muneer, Asif, et al. (2014). Erectile dysfunction. *BMJ, 348,* g129.

Munk-Olsen, Trine, et al. (2011). Induced first trimester abortion and risk of mental disorder. *New England Journal of Medicine, 364,* 332–339.

Muñoz-Laboy, Miguel. (2008). Familism and sexual regulation among bisexual Latino men. *Archives of Sexual Behavior, 37,* 773–782.

Murnen, Sarah K., & Stockton, Mary. (1997). Gender and self-reported sexual arousal in response to sexual stimuli: A meta-analytic review. *Sex Roles, 37,* 135–154.

Murnen, Sarah K., Wright, Carrie, & Kaluzny, Gretchen. (2002). If "boys will be boys," then girls will be victims? A meta-analytic review of the research that relates masculine ideology to sexual aggression. *Sex Roles, 46,* 359–376.

Murnen, Sarah K., et al. (2016). Boys act and girls appear: A content analysis of gender stereotypes associated with characters in children's popular cultures. *Sex Roles, 74,* 78–91.

Murray, Stephen O. (2000). *Homosexualities.* Chicago, IL: University of Chicago Press.

Mustanski, Brian S., et al. (2005). A genomewide scan of male sexual orientation. *Human Genetics, 116,* 272–278.

Mustanski, Brian S., et al. (2010). Mental health disorders, psychological distress, and suicidality in a diverse sample of lesbian, gay, bisexual, and transgender youths. *American Journal of Public Health, 100,* 2426–2432.

Musto, Jennifer. (2016). *Control and protect: Collaboration, carceral protection, and domestic sex trafficking in the United States.* Oakland, CA: University of California Press.

Myers, David G., & Scanzoni, Letha D. (2005). *What God has joined together: A Christian case for gay marriage.* San Francisco, CA: Harper San Francisco.

Myers, Kristen, & Raymond, Laura. (2010). Elementary school girls and heteronormativity: The girl project. *Gender & Society, 24,* 167–188.

Nack, Adina. (2008). *Damaged goods: Women living with incurable STDs.* Philadelphia, PA: Temple University Press.

Nadal, Kevin L., et al. (2016). Microaggressions toward lesbian, gay, bisexual, transgender, queer, and genderqueer people: A review of the literature. *Journal of Sex Research, 53,* 488–508.

Nagoski, E. (2015). *Come as you are.* New York: Simon & Schuster.

Najman, Jake M., et al. (2005). Sexual abuse in childhood and sexual dysfunction in adulthood: An Australian population-based study. *Archives of Sexual Behavior, 34,* 517–526.

Nakhai-Pour, Hamid, Broy, Perrine, & Berard, Anick. (2010). Use of antidepressants during pregnancy and the risk of spontaneous abortion. *Canadian Medical Association Journal, 182,* 1031–1037. doi: 10.1503/cmaj.091208

Narod, Steven A., et al. (1988). Human mutagens: Evidence from paternal exposure? *Environmental and Molecular Mutagenesis, 11,* 401–415.

Nash, Elizabeth, et al. (2018). *Laws affecting reproductive health and rights: State policy trends at midyear, 2018.* Retrieved from https://www.guttmacher.org/article/2018/07/laws-affecting-reproductive-health-and-rights-state-policy-trends-midyear-2018

National Abortion Federation. (2015). *NAF violence and disruption statistics.* Retrieved from http://prochoice.org/wp-content/uploads/Stats_Table2.pdf

National Campaign to Prevent Teen Pregnancy. (2007). *Why it matters: Teen pregnancy, poverty, and income disparity.* Retrieved from www.teenpregnancy.org/wim/pdf/poverty

National Campaign to Prevent Teen and Unplanned Pregnancy. (2009). *Sex and tech: Results from a survey of teens and young adults.* Retrieved from http://www.thenationalcampaign.org/sextech/PDF/SexTech_Summary.pdf

National Center for Victims of Crime. (2004). *Spousal rape laws: 20 years later.* Retrieved from www.ncvc.org

National Commission on AIDS. (1994). Preventing HIV/AIDS in adolescents. *Journal of School Health, 64,* 39–51.

National Conference of State Legislatures. (2008). *State human cloning laws.* Retrieved from www.ncsl.org/programs/health/genetics/rt-shel.htm

National Institute of Family and Life Advocates v. Becerra, 585 U.S. (2018).

Ndovi, Themba T., et al. (2007). A new method to estimate quantitatively seminal vesicle and prostate gland contributions to ejaculate. *British Journal of Clinical Pharmacology, 63,* 404–420.

Negash, S., Cui, M., Fincham, F. D., & Pasley, K. (2014). Extradyadic involvement and relationship dissolution in heterosexual women university students. *Archives of Sexual Behavior, 43,* 531–539.

Nelson, Teresa. (2018). *Minnesota prosecutor charges sexting teenage girl with child pornography.* American Civil Liberties Union. Retrieved from https://www.aclu.org/blog/juvenile-justice/minnesota-prosecutor-charges-sexting-teenage-girl-child-pornography

Nelson, Adie, & Robinson, Barrie. (1994). *Gigolos and madames bountiful: Illusions of gender, power and intimacy.* Toronto: University of Toronto Press.

Nelson, Andrea L., & Purdon, Christine. (2011). Non-erotic thoughts, attentional focus, and sexual problems in a community sample. *Archives of Sexual Behavior, 40,* 395–406.

Nelson, James B. (1978). *Embodiment: An approach to sexuality and Christian theology.* Minneapolis, MN: Augsburg.

Nelson, James B. (1992). *Body theology.* Louisville, KY: Westminster John Knox Press.

Nelson, K., Simoni, J., Morrison, D., George, W., Leickly, E., Lengua, L., & Hawes, S. (2014). Sexually explicit online media and sexual risk among men who have sex with men in the United States. *Archives of Sexual Behavior, 43,* 833–843.

Neville, Helen A., et al. (2004). General and culturally specific factors influencing Black and White rape survivors' self-esteem. *Psychology of Women Quarterly, 28*, 83–94.

New York v. Ferber, 458 U.S. 747 (1982).

Ngun, Tuck C., Ghahramani, Nega, Sanchez, Francisco, Bocklandt, Sven, & Vilain, Eric. (2011). The genetics of sex differences in brain and behavior. *Frontiers in Neuroendocrinology, 32*, 227–246.

Nicol, Melanie R., et al. (2015). Models for predicting effective HIV chemoprevention in women. *Journal of Acquired Immune Deficiency Syndrome, 68*, 369–376.

Njitray, Alan G., et al. (2010). Test-retest reliability and predictors of unreliable reporting for a sexual behavior questionnaire for U.S. men. *Archives of Sexual Behavior, 39*, 1343–1352.

Nolen-Hoeksema, Susan. (2017). *Abnormal psychology* (7th ed.). New York: McGraw-Hill.

Noll, Jennie, Trickett, Penelope, & Putnam, Frank. (2003). A prospective investigation of the impact of childhood sexual abuse on the development of sexuality. *Journal of Consulting and Clinical Psychology, 71*, 575–586.

Noller, P. (1984). *Nonverbal communication and marital interaction.* New York: Pergamon.

Nosek, Brian A., Banaji, Mahzarin R., & Greenwald, Anthony G. (2002). Math = male, me = female, therefore math ≠ me. *Journal of Personality and Social Psychology, 83*, 44–59.

Noss, John B. (1963). *Man's religions* (3rd ed.). New York: Macmillan.

Nova: The miracle of life. PBS Video: NOVA402 (DVD).

Novak, Emil, & Novak, Edmund R. (1952). *Textbook of gynecology.* Baltimore, MD: Williams & Wilkins.

Novembre, John, et al. (2005). The geographic spread of the CCR5 Delta 32 HIV-resistance allele. *PloS Biology, 3*, e339. www.plosbiology.org

Nsiah-Jefferson, Laurie. (1989). Reproductive laws, women of color, and low-income women. In S. Cohen & N. Taub (Eds.), *Reproductive laws for the 1990s* (pp. 23–68). Clifton, NJ: Humana Press.

Nutt, Amy Ellis (2015). *Becoming Nicole: The transformation of an American family.* New York: Random House.

O'Connell, Helen E., & DeLancey, John. (2005). Clitoral anatomy in nulliparous, healthy, premenopausal volunteers using unenhanced magnetic resonance imaging. *Journal of Urology, 173*, 2060–2063.

O'Hara, Michael W., & Swain, Annette M. (1996). Rates and risk of postpartum depression: A meta-analysis. *International Review of Psychiatry, 8*, 37–54.

O'Hara, R. E., Gibbons, F. X., Gerrard, M., Li, Z., & Sargent, G. D. (2012). Greater exposure to sexual content in popular movies predicts earlier sexual debut and increased sexual risk-taking. *Psychological Science, 23*, 984–993.

O'Shea, P. A. (1995). Congenital defects and their causes. In D. R. Constan, R. V. Haning Jr., & D. B. Singer (Eds.), *Human reproduction: Growth and development.* Boston: Little, Brown.

O'Sullivan, Lucia, & Meyer-Bahlburg, Heino. (2003). African-American and Latina inner-city girls' reports of romantic and sexual development. *Journal of Social and Personal Relationships, 20*, 221–238.

O'Sullivan, Lucia F., & Thompson, A. (2014). Sexuality in adolescence. In D. Tolman & L. Diamond (Eds.), *APA handbook of sexuality and psychology* (Vol. 1, pp. 433–486). Washington, DC: APA.

Obergefell et al. v. Hodges, 576 U.S. (2015).

Obiero, Jael, et al. (2012). Vaginal microbicides for reducing the risk of sexual acquisition of HIV infection in women: Systematic review and meta-analysis. *BMC Infectious Diseases, 12*, 289.

Oeffinger, Kevin C., et al. (2015). Breast cancer screening for women at average risk: 2015 guideline update from the American Cancer Society. *JAMA, 314*, 1599–1614.

Office of Adolescent Health. (n.d.). *Evidence-based teen pregnancy prevention programs at a glance.* Retrieved from http://www.hhs.gov/ash/oah/oah-initiatives/teen_pregnancy/training/Assests/ebp-table.pdf

Ogletree, Shirley M., & Ginsburg, Harvey J. (2000). Kept under the hood: Neglect of the clitoris in common vernacular. *Sex Roles, 43*, 917–926.

Ojeda, Sergio R., & Lomniczi, Alejandro. (2014). Unravelling the mystery of puberty. *Nature Reviews Endocrinology, 10*, 67–69.

Okami, Paul. (1995). Childhood exposure to parental nudity, parent–child co-sleeping, and "primal scenes": A review of clinical opinion and empirical evidence. *Journal of Sex Research, 32*, 51–64.

Okazaki, Sumie. (2002). Influences of culture on Asian Americans' sexuality. *Journal of Sex Research, 39*, 34–41.

Okwumabua, T. M., Okwumabua, J. O., & Elliott, V. (1998). "Let the circle be unbroken" helps African-Americans prevent teen–pregnancy. *SIECUS Report, 26*, 12–17.

Okwumabua, Theresa M., et al. (2014) Promoting health and wellness in African American males through Rites of Passage training. *Journal of Human Behavior in the Social Environment, 24*(6), 702–712.

Olfman, Sharna (Ed.). (2009). *The sexualization of childhood.* Westport, CT: Praeger.

Olson, Kristina R., Key, A. C., & Eaton, N. R. (2015). Gender cognition in transgender children. *Psychological Science, 26*(4), 467–474.

Olson, Kristina, et al. (2016). Mental health of transgender children who are supported in their identities. *Pediatrics, 137*(3), e20153223.

Olson, Kristina R., & Gulgoz, Selin. (2018). Early findings from the TransYouth Project: Gender development in transgender children. *Child Development Perspectives, 12*, 93–97.

Olyan, Saul M. (1994). And with a male you shall not lie the lying down of a woman: On the meaning and significance of Leviticus 18:22 and 20:13. *Journal of the History of Sexuality, 5*, 179–206.

Omarzu, Julia, et al. (2012). Motivations and emotional consequences related to engaging in extramarital relationships. *International Journal of Sexual Health, 24*, 154–162.

Oosterhuis, Harry. (2000). *Step children of nature: Krafft-Ebing, psychiatry, and the making of sexual identity.* Chicago, IL: University of Chicago Press.

Orchard, T., Farr, S., Macphail, S., Wender, C., & Wilson, C. (2014). Expanding the scope of inquiry: Exploring accounts of childhood and family life among sex workers in London, Ontario. *Canadian Journal of Human Sexuality, 23*, 9–18.

Orenstein, P. (2016). *Girls & sex: Navigating the complicated new landscape.* New York: Harper Collins.

Osman, Suzanne L. (2003). Predicting men's rape perceptions based on the belief that "no" really means "yes." *Journal of Applied Social Psychology, 33*, 683–692.

Ostensten, Monika. (1994). Optimisation of antirheumatic drug treatment in pregnancy. *Clinical Pharmacokinetics, 27*, 486–503.

Osterberg, E. Charles, et al. (2017). Correlation between pubic hair grooming and STIs: Results from a nationally representative probability sample. *Sexually Transmitted Infections, 93*, Article No. 162.

Ott, Mary, Millstein, S., Ofner, S., & Halpern-Felsher, B. (2006). Greater expectations: Adolescents' positive motivations for sex. *Perspectives on Sexual and Reproductive Health, 38*, 84–89.

Overgood, Max L. E., et al. (2014). Restoring penis sensation in patients with low spinal cord lesions: The role of the remaining function of the dorsal nerve in a unilateral or bilateral TOMAX procedure. *Neurourology and Urodynamics, 34*, 343–348.

Owen, Jesse J., et al. (2010). "Hooking up" among college students: Demographic and psychosocial correlates. *Archives of Sexual Behavior, 39,* 653-663.

Owen, Jesse, & Fincham, Frank D. (2011a). Effects of gender and psychosocial factors on "friends with benefits" relationships among young adults. *Archives of Sexual Behavior, 40,* 311-320.

Owen, Jesse, & Fincham, Frank D. (2011b). Young adults' emotional reactions after hooking up encounters. *Archives of Sexual Behavior, 40,* 321-330.

Oyserman, Daphna. (2017). Culture three ways: Culture and subcultures within countries. *Annual Review of Psychology, 68,* 435-463.

Özer, Müjde, et al. (2018). Labiaplasty: Motivation, techniques, and ethics. *Nature Reviews Urology, 15,* 175-189.

Pacenza, Nestor et al. (2012). Clinical presentation of Klinefelter's Syndrome: Differences according to age. *International Journal of Endocrinology, 2012,* Article ID 324835. doi: http://dx.doi.org/10.1155/2012/324835

Pachankis, John E. (2007). The psychological implications of concealing a stigma: A cognitive-affective-behavioral model. *Psychological Bulletin, 133,* 328-345.

Pacik, Peter T., & Geletta, Simon. (2017). Vaginismus treatment: Clinical trials follow up 241 patients. *Sexual Medicine, 5,* e114-e123.

Packer, H. L. (1968). *The limits of the criminal sanction.* Stanford, CA: Stanford University Press.

Padawer, Ruth. (2009, April 10). Keeping up with being kept. *New York Times Magazine.*

Padilla, Mark. (2007). *Caribbean pleasure industry: Tourism, sexuality, and AIDS in the Dominican Republic.* Chicago, IL: University of Chicago Press.

Padma-Nathan, H., et al. (2001). On-demand IC351 (Cialis) enhances erectile function in patients with erectile dysfunction. *International Journal of Impotence Research, 13,* 2-9.

Paik, Anthony. (2010a). "Hookups," dating, and relationship quality: Does the type of sexual involvement matter? *Social Science Research, 39,* 739-753.

Palace, Eileen M. (1995a). A cognitive-physiological process model of sexual arousal and response. *Clinical Psychology: Science and Practice, 2,* 370-384.

Palace, Eileen M. (1995b). Modification of dysfunctional patterns of sexual response through autonomic arousal and false physiological feedback. *Journal of Consulting and Clinical Psychology, 63,* 604-615.

Paliwal, P., et al. (2006). Examining accuracy of screening mammography using an event order model. *Statistics in Medicine, 25,* 267-283.

Panitch, Vida. (2015). Assisted reproduction and distributive justice. *Bioethics, 29,* 108-117.

Panjari, Mary, et al. (2011). Sexual function after breast cancer. *Journal of Sexual Medicine, 8,* 294-302.

Paras, Molly L., et al. (2009). Sexual abuse and lifetime diagnosis of somatic disorders: A systematic review and meta-analysis. *Journal of the American Medical Association, 302*(5), 550-561.

Parish, William L., et al. (2007). Sexual practices and sexual satisfaction: A population based study of Chinese urban adults. *Archives of Sexual Behavior, 36,* 5-20.

Parker, Graham. (1983). The legal regulation of sexual activity and the protection of females. *Osgoode Hall Law Journal, 21,* 187-244.

Parker, Richard, et al. (2004). Global transformations and intimate relations in the 21st century: Social science research on sexuality and the emergence of sexual health and sexual rights frameworks. *Annual Review of Sex Research, 15,* 362-398.

Parks, Cheryl A., Hughes, Tonda L., & Matthews, Alicia K. (2004). Race/ethnicity and sexual orientation: Intersecting identities. *Cultural Diversity & Ethnic Minority Psychology, 10,* 241-254.

Parnas, Raymond I. (1981). Legislative reform of prostitution laws: Keeping commercial sex out of sight and out of mind. *Santa Clara Law Review, 21,* 669-696.

Parrinder, Geoffrey. (1980). *Sex in the world's religions.* New York: Oxford University Press.

Parrinder, Geoffrey. (1996). *Sexual morality in the world's religions.* Oxford: Oneworld.

Parrot, Andrea, & Cummings, Nina. (2006). *Forsaken females: The global brutalization of women.* New York: Rowman & Littlefield.

Parrott, Dominic J., et al. (2012). Validity for an integrated laboratory analogue of sexual aggression and bystander intervention. *Aggressive Behavior, 38,* 309-321.

Pascoe, C. J. (2011). *Dude, you're a fag: Masculinity and sexuality in high school.* Berkeley: University of California Press.

Pasqualotto, F., et al. (2008). Effect of cigarette smoking on antioxidant levels and presence of leukocytospermia in infertile men: A prospective study. *Fertility and Sterility, 90,* 278-283.

Paterson, Laurel, Handy, A., & Brotto, L. (2017). A pilot study of eight-session mindfulness-based cognitive therapy adapted for women's sexual interest/arousal disorder. *Journal of Sex Research, 54,* 850-861.

Pathela, Preeti, et al. (2006). Discordance between sexual behavior and self-reported sexual identity: A population-based survey of New York City men. *Annals of Internal Medicine, 145,* 416-425.

Patrick, Megan E., & Lee, Christine M. (2010). Sexual motivations and engagement in sexual behavior during the transition to college. *Archives of Sexual Behavior, 39,* 674-681.

Patterson, Charlotte J. (2006). Children of lesbian and gay parents. *Current Directions in Psychological Science, 15,* 241-244.

Patterson, Charlotte J. (2009). Children of lesbian and gay parents: Psychology, law, and policy. *American Psychologist, 64,* 727-736.

Patterson, Charlotte, J. (2017). Parents' sexual orientation and children's development. *Child Development Perspectives, 11,* 45-49.

Paul, Bryant, & Linz, Dan. (2008). The effects of exposure to virtual child pornography on viewer cognitions and attitudes toward deviant sexual behavior. *Communication Research, 35,* 3-38.

Paul, Catriona, et al. (2008). A single, mild, transient scrotal heat stress causes DNA damage, subfertility and impairs formation of blastocysts in mice. *Reproduction, 136,* 73-84.

Paul, Eva W., & Klassel, Dara. (1987). Minors' rights to confidential contraceptive services. *Women's Rights Law Reporter, 10,* 45-64.

Pavlakis, George N., & Felber, Barbara K. (2018). A new step towards an HIV/AIDS vaccine. *Lancet, 392,* 192-194.

Payne, Ed, & McLaughlin, Eliott. (2014). Police: Indiana man could be serial killer; cases could go back decades. *CNN.com.* Retrieved from http://www.cnn.com/2014/10/21/us/indiana-possible-serial-killer/index.html

Pazol, Karen, et al. (2011). Abortion surveillance—United States, 2008. *Morbidity and Mortality Weekly Report, 60*(15). Atlanta, GA: Centers for Disease Control and Prevention.

Pazol, Karen, et al. (2014). Abortion surveillance—United States, 2011. *Morbidity and Mortality Weekly Reports, 63.* Retrieved from http://www.cdc.gov/mmwr/preview/mmwrhtml/ss6311a1.htm?s_cid=ss6311a1_w#Tab13

Pedersen, William, et al. (2002). Evolved sex differences in the number of partners desired? The long and short of it. *Psychological Science, 13,* 157-159.

Pele, F., Muckle, G., Costet, N., Garlantezec, R., Monfort, C., Multigner, L., Rouget, F., & Cordier, S. (2013). Occupational solvent exposure during pregnancy and child behavior at age 2. *Occupational and Environmental Medicine, 70,* 114-119.

Peplau, L. Anne. (2003). Human sexuality: How do men and women differ? *Current Directions in Psychological Science, 12,* 37-40.

Pereda, Noemi, et al. (2009). The prevalence of child sexual abuse in community and student samples: A meta-analysis. *Clinical Psychology Review, 29,* 328-338.

Perel, Esther. (2006). *Mating in captivity: Unlocking erotic intelligence.* New York: Harper.

Perelman, Michael A. (2014). Delayed ejaculation. In Y. Binik & K. Hall (Eds.), *Principles and practice of sex therapy* (5th ed., pp. 138–158). New York: Guilford.

Perez, Martin A., Skinner, Eila C., & Meyerowitz, Beth E. (2002). Sexuality and intimacy following radical prostatectomy: Patient and partner perspectives. *Health Psychology, 21,* 288–293.

Perilloux, Carin, et al. (2012). The misperception of sexual interest. *Psychological Science, 23,* 146–151.

Perlman, Daniel, & Fehr, B. (1987). The development of intimate relationships. In D. Perlman & S. Duck (Eds.), *Intimate relationships: Development, dynamics, and deterioration.* Newbury Park, CA: Sage.

Perrin, Ellen C., et al. (2002). Technical report: Coparent or second-parent adoption by same-sex parents. *Pediatrics, 109,* 341–344.

Perry, John D., & Whipple, Beverly. (1981). Pelvic muscle strength of female ejaculators: Evidence in support of a new theory of orgasm. *Journal of Sex Research, 17,* 22–39.

Persson, Goran. (1980). Sexuality in a 70-year-old urban population. *Journal of Psychosomatic Research, 24,* 335–342.

Pesta, Abigail. (2012, July 2 & 9). War of the wombs: The battle for "personhood" heats up. *Newsweek,* pp. 21–22.

Peter, Jochen, & Valkenburg, Patti. (2008). Adolescents' exposure to sexually explicit Internet material, sexual uncertainty, and attitudes toward uncommitted sexual exploration. *Communication Research, 35,* 579–601.

Petersen, Jennifer L., & Hyde, Janet S. (2009). A longitudinal investigation of peer sexual harassment victimization in adolescence. *Journal of Adolescence, 32,* 1173–1188.

Petersen, Jennifer L., & Hyde, Janet S. (2010). A meta-analytic review of research on gender differences in sexuality, 1993 to 2007. *Psychological Bulletin, 136*(1), 21–38.

Peterson, B. D., Sejbaek, C. S., Pirritano, M., & Schmidt, L. (2014). Are severe depressive symptoms associated with infertility-related distress in individuals and their partners? *Human Reproduction, 29,* 76–82.

Peterson, Zoë D., & Muehlenhard, Charlene L. (2007). What is sex and why does it matter? A motivational approach to exploring individuals' definitions of sex. *Journal of Sex Research, 44,* 256–268.

Petkovich, A. (2004). From gonzo porn to mainstream? Porn starlet Sienna. *Spectator.* Retrieved from www.spectator.net/1196/1196_sienna.html

Pew Research Center. (2010). *The decline of marriage and the rise of new families.* Pew Research Center Report.

Pew Research Center. (2013, January 16). *Religious groups' official positions on abortion.* Retrieved from http://www.pewforum.org/2013/01/16/religious-groups-official-positions-on-abortion/

Pew Research Center. (2018). *Internet/broadband fact sheet.* Retrieved from http://www.pewinternet.org/fact-sheet/internet-broadband/

Pfaus, James. (2009). Pathways of sexual desire. *Journal of Sexual Medicine, 6,* 1506–1533.

Pfaus, James G., et al. (2014). Biology of the sexual response. In D. Tolman & L. Diamond (Eds.), *APA handbook of sexuality and psychology* (Vol. 1, pp. 145–204). Washington, DC: APA.

Pfeiffer, E., Verwoerdt, A., & Wang, H. S. (1968). Sexual behavior in aged men and women. *Archives of General Psychiatry, 19,* 753–758.

Pfeiffer, Eric. (1975). Sex and aging. In L. Gross (Ed.), *Sexual issues in marriage.* New York: Spectrum.

Phelps, Jerry, et al. (2001). Spinal cord injury and sexuality in married or partnered men: Activities, function, needs, and predictors of sexual adjustment. *Archives of Sexual Behavior, 30,* 591–602.

Phibbs, C. S., Bateman, D. A., & Schwartz, R. M. (1991). The neonatal costs of maternal cocaine use. *Journal of the American Medical Association, 266,* 1521–1526.

Phoenix, C. H., et al. (1959). Organizing action of prenatally administered testosterone propionate on the tissues mediating mating behavior in the female guinea pig. *Endocrinology, 65,* 369–382.

Pick, Susan, Givaudan, Martha, & Poortinga, Ype. (2003). Sexuality and life skills education: A multistrategy intervention in Mexico. *American Psychologist, 58,* 230–234.

Pieterse, Alex L., & Carter, Robert T. (2007). An examination of the relationship between general life stress, racism-related stress, and psychological health among Black men. *Journal of Counseling Psychology, 54,* 101–109.

Pike, Jennifer J., & Jennings, Nancy A. (2005). The effects of commercials on children's perceptions of gender appropriate toy use. *Sex Roles, 52,* 83–92.

Pinxten, Wouter, & Lievens, John (2015). An exploratory study of factors associated with sexual inhibition and excitation: Findings from a representative survey in Flanders. *Journal of Sex Research, 52,* 679–689.

Pinxten, Wouter, & Lievens, John (2016). Gender differences in the development of sexual excitation and inhibition through the life course: Preliminary findings from a representative study in Flanders. *Journal of Sex Research, 53,* 825–835.

Pittenger, W. Norman. (1970). *Making sexuality human.* Philadelphia, PA: Pilgrim Press.

Pitts, Marian K., Smith, Anthony, Grierson, Jeffrey, O'Brien, Mary, & Mission, Sebastian. (2004). Who pays for sex and why? An analysis of social and motivational factors associated with male clients of sex workers. *Archives of Sexual Behavior, 33,* 353–368.

Planned Parenthood Federation of America, Inc. v. Ashcroft, 2004 WL 432222 (N.D. Cal. Mar. 5, 2004).

Planned Parenthood v. Casey, 505 U.S. 833 (1992).

Plaud, J. J., et al. (1999). Volunteer bias in human psychophysiological sexual arousal research: To whom do our research results apply? *Journal of Sex Research, 36,* 171–179.

Plaut, S. Michael. (2008). Sexual and nonsexual boundaries in professional relationships: Principles and teaching guidelines. *Sexual and Relationship Therapy, 23,* 85–94.

Plöderl, M., et al. (2013). Suicide risk and sexual orientation: A critical review. *Archives of Sexual Behavior, 42,* 715–728.

Poeppl, Timm B., et al. (2014). The functional neuroanatomy of male psychosexual and physiosexual arousal: A quantitative meta-analysis. *Human Brain Mapping, 35,* 1404–1421.

Poh, H. L., Koh, S. S., & He, H.-G. (2014). An integrative review of fathers' experiences during pregnancy and childbirth. *International Nursing review, 61,* 543–554.

Pollack, Andrew. (2004, February 13). Medical and ethical issues cloud plans to clone for therapy. *New York Times.*

Pomeroy, Wardell B. (1972). *Dr. Kinsey and the Institute for Sex Research.* New York: Harper & Row.

Pope, Ken. (2001). Sex between therapists and clients. In J. Worell (Ed.), *Encyclopedia of women and gender* (pp. 955–862). New York: Academic Press.

Population Reference Bureau. (2014). *Female genital mutilation/cutting: Data and trends.* Washington, DC: Population Reference Bureau.

Poromaa, Inger S., & Gingnell, Malin. (2014). Menstrual cycle influence on cognitive function and emotion processing – from a reproductive perspective. *Frontiers in Neuroscience, 8,* Article 380.

Posner, Richard. (1992). *Sex and reason.* Cambridge, MA: Harvard University Press.

Posner, Richard, & Silbaugh, Katherine. (1996). *A guide to America's sex laws.* Chicago, IL: University of Chicago Press.

Poston, D. L., Jr., & Baumle, A. K. (2010). Patterns of asexuality in the United States. *Demographic Research, 23,* 509–530.

Poteat, V. Paul, Kimmel, Michael S., & Wilchins, Riki. (2011). The moderating effects of support for violence beliefs on masculine norms, aggression, and homophobic behavior during adolescence. *Journal of Research on Adolescence, 21,* 434-447.

Poteat, V. Paul, O'Dwyer, Laura M., & Mereish, Ethan H. (2012). Changes in how students use and are called homophobic epithets over time: Patterns predicted by gender, bullying, and victimization status. *Journal of Educational Psychology, 104,* 393-406.

Potter, Daniel, & Hanin, Jennifer. (2013). *What to do when you can't get pregnant: The complete guide to all the technologies for couples facing fertility issues.* Boston, MA: Da Capo Press.

Potts, A., et al. (2003). The downside of Viagra: Women's experiences and concerns. *Sociology of Health and Illness, 25,* 697-719.

Powdermaker, Hortense. (1933). *Life in Lesu.* New York: Norton.

Practice Committee of the American Society for Reproductive Medicine. (2008). Obesity and reproduction: An educational bulletin. *Fertility and Sterility, 90*(Suppl. 3), S21-S29.

Pratto, Felicia, & Walker, Angela. (2004). The bases of gendered power. In A. Eagly et al. (Eds.), *The psychology of gender* (2nd ed., pp. 242-268). New York: Guilford.

Prause, Nicole, et al. (2016). Clitorally stimulated orgasms are associated with better control of sexual desire, and not associated with depression or anxiety, compared with vaginally stimulated orgasms. *Journal of Sexual Medicine, 13,* 1676-1685.

Price, James, Allensworth, Diane, & Hillman, Kathleen. (1985). Comparison of sexual fantasies of homosexuals and heterosexuals. *Psychological Reports, 57,* 871-877.

Price, Myeshia, & Hyde, Janet S. (2009). When two isn't better than one: Predictors of early sexual activity in adolescence using a cumulative risk model. *Journal of Youth and Adolescence, 38,* 1059-1071.

Price-Glynn, K. (2010). *Strip club: Gender, power and sex work.* New York: New York University Press.

Prior, J., Hubbard, P., & Birch, P. (2012). Sex worker victimization, modes of working, and location in New South Wales, Australia: A geography of victimization. *Journal of Sex Research.* doi: 10.1080/00224499.2012.668975

Prostitutes Education Network. (1998). *Prostitution in the United States–the statistics.* Retrieved from www.bayswan.org/stats.html

Pulice-Farrow, Lex, et al. (2017). Transgender microaggressions in the context of romantic relationships. *Psychology of Sexual Orientation and Gender Diversity, 4,* 362-373.

Purnine, Daniel, & Carey, Michael. (1997). Interpersonal communication and sexual adjustment: The roles of understanding and agreement. *Journal of Consulting and Clinical Psychology, 65,* 1017-1025.

Quadagno, David, et al. (1998). Ethnic differences in sexual decisions and sexual behavior. *Archives of Sexual Behavior, 27,* 57-75.

Qualls, C. B., Wincze, J. P., & Barlow, D. H. (1978). *The prevention of sexual disorders.* New York: Plenum.

Quas, Jodi A., et al. (2005). Childhood sexual assault victims: Long-term outcomes after testifying in criminal court. *Monographs of the Society for Research in Child Development, 70*(2), 1-127.

Quayle, Ethel. (2008). Online sex offending: Psychopathology and theory. In D. R. Laws & W. O'Donohue (Eds.), *Sexual deviance: Theory, assessment, and treatment* (2nd ed., pp. 439-458). New York: Guilford.

Quigley, Muireann (2010). A right to reproduce? *Bioethics, 24,* 403-411.

Quinn, T. C., et al. (2000). Viral load and heterosexual transmission of human immunodeficiency virus type 1. *New England Journal of Medicine, 342,* 921.

R. v. Lebaye, 3 S.C.R. 728 (2005).

Rachman, S. (1966). Sexual fetishism: An experimental analogue. *Psychological Record, 16,* 293-296.

Raffaelli, Marcela, & Ontai, Lenna L. (2004). Gender socialization in Latino/a families: Results from two retrospective studies. *Sex Roles, 50,* 287-300.

Raine, Nancy V. (1998). *After silence: Rape and my journey back.* New York: Crown.

Rako, Susan, & Friebely, Joan. (2004). Pheromonal influences on sociosexual behavior in postmenopausal women. *Journal of Sex Research, 41,* 372-380.

Ralph, Lauren J., et al. (2017). Measuring decisional certainty among women seeking abortion. *Contraception, 95,* 269-278.

Ramchandani, Paul, Stein, A., Evans, J., O'Connor, T., & ALSPAC Study Team. (2005). Paternal depression in the postnatal period and child development: A prospective population study. *The Lancet, 365,* 2201-2205.

Rametti, Giuseppina, et al. (2011). White matter microstructure in female to male transsexuals before cross-sex hormonal treatment: A diffusion tensor imaging study. *Journal of Psychiatric Research, 45,* 199-204.

Ramsey, Sara, et al. (2009). Pubic hair and sexuality: A review. *Journal of Sexual Medicine, 6,* 2102-2110.

Rastogi, Sonya, et al. (2011). *The Black population: 2010.* Washington, DC: U.S. Census Bureau.

Rawlins, Debbi. (2003). *Anything goes.* New York: Harlequin Blaze.

Ream, Geoffrey, & Savin-Williams, Ritch. (2005). Reciprocal associations between adolescent sexual activity and quality of youth-parent interactions. *Journal of Family Psychology, 19,* 171-179.

Reamy, Kenneth J., & White, Susan E. (1987). Sexuality in the puerperium: A review. *Archives of Sexual Behavior, 16,* 165-186.

Rederstorff, Juliette C., et al. (2007). The moderating roles of race and gender-role attitudes in the relationship between sexual harassment and psychological well-being. *Psychology of Women Quarterly, 31,* 50-61.

Reece, Michael, et al. (2009). Prevalence and characteristics of vibrator use by men in the United States. *Journal of Sexual Medicine, 6,* 1867-1874.

Reece, Michael, Herbenick, D., Schick, B., Sanders, S. A., Dodge, B., & Fortenberry, J. D. (2010a). Background and considerations on the National Survey of Sexual Health and Behavior (NSSHB) from the investigators. *Journal of Sexual Medicine, 7*(SS05), 243-246.

Reece, Michael, et al. (2010b). Sexual behaviors, relationships, and perceived health among adult men in the United States. *Journal of Sexual Medicine, 7*(SS05), 291-304.

Reefhuis, J., et al. (2009). Assisted reproductive technology and major structural birth defects in the United States. *Human Reproduction, 24,* 360-366.

Regan, Pamela. (2004). Sex and the attraction process: Lessons from science (and Shakespeare) on lust, love, chastity, and fidelity. In J. Harvey et al. (Eds.), *The handbook of sexuality in close relationships* (pp. 115-133). Mahwah, NJ: Lawrence Erlbaum.

Regnerus, Mark, et al. (2017). Masturbation and partnered sex: Substitutes or complements. *Archives of Sexual Behavior, 46,* 2111-2121.

Rehor, J. E. (2015). Sensual, erotic, and sexual behaviors of women from the "Kink" community. *Archives of Sexual Behavior, 44,* 825-836.

Reid, Pamela T., & Bing, Vanessa M. (2000). Sexual roles of girls and women: An ethnocultural lifespan perspective. In C. Travis & J. White (Eds.), *Sexuality, society, and feminism* (pp. 141-166). Washington, DC: American Psychological Association.

Reid, Rory, Garos, Sheila, & Carpenter, Bruce. (2011). Reliability, validity, and psychometric development of the Hypersexual Behavior Inventory in an outpatient sample of men. *Sexual Addiction and Compulsivity, 18,* 30-51.

Reid, Rory C., et al. (2012). Report of findings in a DSM-5 field trial for hypersexual disorder. *Journal of Sexual Medicine, 9,* 2868-2877.

Reimers, Stan. (2007). The BBC Internet Study: General methodology. *Archives of Sexual Behavior, 36,* 147-161.

Reis, Elizabeth. (2007). Divergence or disorder? The politics of naming intersex. *Perspectives in Biology and Medicine, 50,* 535–543.

Reis, Harry T., et al. (2011). Familiarity does indeed promote attraction in live interaction. *Journal of Personality and Social Psychology, 101,* 557–570.

Reisenzein, Rainer. (1983). The Schachter theory of emotion: Two decades later. *Psychological Bulletin, 94,* 239–264.

Reisner, Sari L., et al. (2015). Gender minority social stress in adolescence: Disparities in adolescent bullying and substance use by gender identity. *Journal of Sex Research, 52,* 243–256.

Reiss, Ira L. (1986). *Journey into sexuality: An exploratory voyage.* Englewood Cliffs, NJ: Prentice-Hall.

Reissing, E. D., et al. (2014). Throwing the baby out with the bathwater: The demise of vaginismus in favor of genito-pelvic pain/penetration disorder. *Archives of Sexual Behavior, 43,* 1209–1214.

Rekart, Michael. (2005). Sex-work harm-reduction. *The Lancet, 366,* 2123–2134.

Reliable Consultants, Inc. v. Ronnie Earl, U.S. Ct. App., 5th Circuit, 06-51067 (2008).

Rellini, Alessandra H., & Meston, Cindy M. (2011). Sexual self-schemas, sexual dysfunction, and the sexual responses of women with a history of childhood sexual abuse. *Archives of Sexual Behavior, 40,* 351–362.

Renaud, Cheryl, & Byers, E. Sandra. (1997). Sexual and relationship satisfaction in mainland China. *Journal of Sex Research, 34,* 399–410.

Renne, Elisha P. (1996). The pregnancy that doesn't stay: The practice and perception of abortion by Ekiti Yoruba women. *Social Science and Medicine, 42,* 483–494.

Repke, John T. (1994). Calcium and vitamin D. *Clinical Obstetrics and Gynecology, 37,* 550–557.

Resick, Patricia A., et al. (2012). Long-term outcomes of cognitive-behavioral treatments for posttraumatic stress disorder among female rape survivors. *Journal of Consulting and Clinical Psychology, 80,* 201–210.

Reuther, Rosemary Radford. (1985). Catholics and abortion: Authority vs. dissent. *Christian Century, 102,* 859–862.

Rhoades, G., et al. (2009). The pre-engagement cohabitation effect: A replication and extension of previous findings. *Journal of Family Psychology, 23,* 107–111.

Rhode, Deborah L. (2016). *Adultery: Infidelity and the law.* Cambridge, MA: Harvard University Press.

Rhodes, D., Kirchofer, G., Hammig, B., & Ogletree, R. (2013). Influence of professional preparation and class structure on sexuality topics taught in middle and high schools. *Journal of School Health, 83,* 343–349.

Rice, George, et al. (1999). Male homosexuality: Absence of linkage to microsatellite markers at Xq28. *Science, 284,* 665–667.

Rice, William R., et al. (2012). Homosexuality as a consequence of epigenetically canalized sexual development. *Quarterly Review of Biology, 87,* 373–368.

Rice, Eric, et al. (2018). Associations between sexting behaviors and sexual behaviors among mobile phone-owing teens in Los Angeles. *Child Development, 89,* 110–117.

Richard-Davis, G., & Wellons, M. (2013). Racial and ethnic differences in the physiology and clinical symptoms of menopause. *Seminar in Reproductive Medicine, 31,* 380–386.

Richards, Christina, et al. (2016). Non-binary or genderqueer genders. *International Review of Psychiatry, 28*(1), 95–102.

Richardson, Chinue, & Nash, Elizabeth. (2006). Misinformed consent: The medical accuracy of state-developed abortion counseling materials. *Guttmacher Policy Review, 9*(4), 6–11.

Richters, J., de Visser, R. O., Rissel, C. E., Grulich, A. E., & Smith, A. M. A. (2008). Demographic and psychosocial features of participants in bondage and discipline, "sadomasochism" or dominance and submission (BDSM): Data from a national survey. *Journal of Sexual Medicine, 5,* 1660–1668.

Richters, Juliet, et al. (2014). Design and methods of the Second Australian Study of Health and Relationships. *Sexual Health, 11,* 383–396.

Richters, Juliet, de Visser, R., Rissel, C., & Smith, A. (2006). Sexual practices at last heterosexual encounter and occurrence of orgasm in a national survey. *Journal of Sex Research, 43,* 217–226.

Rideout, Victoria J., Foehr, Ulla G., & Roberts, Donald F. (2010). *Generation M²: Media in the lives of 8- to 18-year-olds.* Menlo Park, CA: Kaiser Family Foundation.

Ridgeway, C. L. (2011). *Framed by gender: How gender inequality persists in the modern world.* New York: Oxford University Press.

Ridgeway, Cecilia L., & Bourg, Chris. (2004). Gender as status: An expectation states theory approach. In A. Eagly et al. (Eds.), *The psychology of gender* (pp. 217–241). New York: Guilford.

Ridley, Carl A., et al. (2006). The ebb and flow of marital lust: A relational approach. *Journal of Sex Research, 43,* 144–153.

Ridley, Carl, et al. (2008). Sexual expression: Its emotional context in heterosexual, gay, and lesbian couples. *Journal of Sex Research, 45,* 305–314.

Rigdon, Susan M. (1996). Abortion law and practice in China: An overview with comparisons to the United States. *Social Science and Medicine, 42,* 543–560.

Rinehart, Jenny K., et al. (2017). Do some students need special protection from research on sex and trauma? New evidence for young adult resilience in "sensitive topics" research. *Journal of Sex Research, 54,* 273–283.

Rini, Christine, Dunkel Schetter, C., Hobel, C., Glynn, L., & Sandman, C. (2006). Effective social support: Antecedents and consequences of partner support during pregnancy. *Personal Relationships, 13,* 207–229.

Riportella-Muller, Roberta. (1989). Sexuality in the elderly: A review. In K. McKinney & S. Sprecher (Eds.), *Human sexuality: The societal and interpersonal context* (pp. 210–236). New York: Ablex.

Rissel, Chris E., et al. (2003a). Sex in Australia: Attitudes towards sex in a representative sample of adults. *Australian and New Zealand Journal of Public Health, 27,* 118–123.

Rissel, Chris E., et al. (2003b). Sex in Australia: First experiences of vaginal intercourse and oral sex among a representative sample of adults. *Australian and New Zealand Journal of Public Health, 27,* 131–137.

Rissel, Chris E., et al. (2003c). Sex in Australia: Selected characteristics of regular sexual relationships. *Australian and New Zealand Journal of Public Health, 27,* 124–130.

Rissel, Chris, et al. (2014). First vaginal intercourse and oral sex among a representative sample of Australian adults: The Second Australian Study of Health and Relationships. *Sexual Health, 11,* 406–415.

Ristori, Jiska, & Steensma, Thomas. (2016). Gender dysphoria in childhood. *International Review of Psychiatry, 28,* 13–20.

Robbins, C., Fortenberry, J. D., Reece, M., Herbenick, D., Sanders, S., & Dodge, B. (2010). Masturbation frequency and patterns among U.S. adolescents. *Journal of Adolescent Health, 46*(Suppl. 1), S36–S37.

Roberts, Andrea L., et al. (2010). Pervasive trauma exposure among U.S. sexual orientation minority adults and risk of posttraumatic stress disorder. *American Journal of Public Health, 100,* 2433–2441.

Roberts, Dorothy E. (1993). Crime, race, and reproduction. *Tulane Law Review, 67,* 1945–1977.

Roberts, R., Jones, A., & Sanders, T. (2013). Students and sex work in the UK: Providers and purchasers. *Sex Education, 13,* 349–363.

Roberts, Sarah, Biggs, M., et al. (2014). Risk of violence from the man involved in the pregnancy after receiving or being denied an abortion. *BMC Medicine, 12,* 144.

Robertson, A., Syvertson, J., Amaro, H., Martinez, G., Rangel, M. G., Patterson, T., & Strathdee, S. (2014). Can't buy my love: A typology of female sex workers' commercial relationships on the Mexico-US border. *Journal of Sex Research, 51,* 711–720.

Robertson, John A. (1986). Embryos, families and procreative liberty: The legal structure of the new reproduction. *Southern California Law Review, 59,* 942–1041.

Robertson, Ronald E., et al. (2018). Estimates of non-heterosexual prevalence: The roles of anonymity and privacy in survey methodology. *Archives of Sexual Behavior, 47,* 1069–1084.

Robertson, Sarah, & Sharkey, David. (2001). The role of semen in induction of maternal immune tolerance to pregnancy. *Seminars in Immunology, 13,* 243.

Robinson, B. E., et al. (2011). Application of the sexual health model in the long-term treatment of hypoactive sexual desire and female orgasmic disorder. *Archives of Sexual Behavior, 40,* 469–478.

Robinson, Joseph P., & Espelage, Dorothy L. (2011). Inequities in educational and psychological outcomes between LGBTQ and straight students in middle and high school. *Educational Researcher, 40,* 315–330.

Roe v. Wade, 410 U.S. 113 (1973).

Roehr, Bob. (2007). Dramatic drop in HIV infections halts circumcision trials. *British Medical Journal, 334,* 11.

Rohmann, Elke, et al. (2016). Relationship satisfaction across European cultures: The role of love styles. *Cross-Cultural Research, 50,* 178–211.

Roisman, Glenn, et al. (2004). Salient and emerging developmental tasks in the transition to adulthood. *Child Development, 75,* 123–133.

Roman v. Roman, Tex. Ct. App., 01-04-00541 (Feb. 9, 2006).

Romanelli, Frank, et al. (2004). Poppers: Epidemiology and clinical management of inhaled nitrite abuse. *Pharmacotherapy, 24,* 69–78.

Romans, Sarah E., et al. (2013). Mood and the menstrual cycle. *Psychotherapy and Psychosomatics, 82,* 53–60.

Romer v. Evans, 517 U.S. 620 (1996).

Romer, Daniel, et al. (1997). "Talking computers": A reliable and private method to conduct interviews on sensitive topics with children. *Journal of Sex Research, 34,* 3–9.

Romero, Lisa, et al. (2015). Vital signs: Trends in use of long-acting reversible contraception among teens aged 15-19 years seeking contraceptive services—United States, 2005-2013. *Morbidity and Mortality Weekly Report, 64,* 363–369.

Rondeaux, Candace. (2006, July 5). Can castration be a solution for sex offenders? *Washington Post.*

Rooney, Benjamin M., et al. (2018). Psychosocial syndemic correlates of sexual compulsivity among men who have sex with men: A meta-analysis. *Archives of Sexual Behavior, 47,* 75–93.

Root, Maria P. (1995). The psychology of Asian American women. In H. Landrine (Ed.), *Bringing cultural diversity to feminist psychology: Theory, research, and practice* (pp. 265–302). Washington, DC: American Psychological Association.

Rosario, Margaret, et al. (1996). The psychosexual development of urban lesbian, gay and bisexual youths. *Journal of Sex Research, 33,* 113–126.

Roscoe, B., Cavanaugh, L., & Kennedy, D. (1988). Dating infidelity: Behaviors, reasons, and consequences. *Adolescence, 89,* 36–43.

Roscoe, Bruce, Kennedy, Donna, & Pope, Tony. (1987). Adolescents' views of intimacy: Distinguishing intimate from nonintimate relationships. *Adolescence, 22,* 511–516.

Rose, A. J., & Rudolph, Karen D. (2006). A review of sex differences in peer relationship processes: Potential trade-offs for the emotional and behavioral development of girls and boys. *Psychological Bulletin, 132,* 89–131.

Roselli, Charles E., Resko, J., & Stormshak, F. (2002). Hormonal influences on sexual partner preference in rams. *Archives of Sexual Behavior, 31,* 43–50.

Rosen, David H. (1974). *Lesbianism: A study of female homosexuality.* Springfield, IL: Charles C. Thomas.

Rosen, H., & Conklin, K. (2014). *A cache of controversy: Two decades of data on sexuality education conflicts.* New York: Sexuality Information and Education Council of the U.S.

Rosen, Raymond C. (2007). Erectile dysfunction: Integration of medical and psychological approaches. In S. Leiblum (Ed.), *Principles and practice of sex therapy* (4th ed., pp. 277–312). New York: Guilford.

Rosen, Raymond C., & McKenna, Kevin E. (2002). PDE-5 inhibition and sexual response: Pharmacological mechanisms and clinical outcomes. *Annual Review of Sex Research, 13,* 36–88.

Rosen, Raymond C., et al. (2012). Sexual desire problems in women seeking healthcare. *Journal of Women's Health, 21,* 505–515.

Rosenblatt, Karin A., Wicklund, K., & Stanford, J. (2001). Sexual factors and the risk of prostate cancer. *American Journal of Epidemiology, 153,* 1152–1158.

Rosenbleet, C., & Pariente, B. J. (1973). The prostitution of the criminal law. *American Criminal Law Review, 11,* 373–427.

Rosenfeld, Michael J. (2008). Racial, educational and religious endogamy in the United States: A comparative historical perspective. *Social Forces, 87,* 1–31.

Rosenfeld, Michael J. (2017). Marriage, choice, and couplehood in the age of the Internet. *Sociological Science, 4,* 490–510.

Rosenfeld, M. J., & Thomas, R. J. (2012). Searching for a mate: The rise of the Internet as a social intermediary. *American Sociological Review, 77,* 523–547.

Rosner, Fred. (1983). In vitro fertilization and surrogate motherhood: The Jewish view. *Journal of Religion and Health, 22,* 139–160.

Ross, Michael N., Paulsen, J. A., & Stalstrom, O. W. (1988). Homosexuality and mental health: A cross-cultural review. *Journal of Homosexuality, 15,* 131–152.

Ross, Michael W. (2005). Typing, being, and doing: Sexuality and the Internet. *Journal of Sex Research, 42,* 342–354.

Rostosky, Sharon S., & Riggle, Ellen D. B. (2015). *Happy together: Thriving as a same-sex couple in your family, workplace, and community.* Washington, DC: American Psychological Association.

Rostosky, Sharon S., & Riggle, Ellen D. B. (2017). Same-sex couple relationship strengths: A review and synthesis of the empirical literature (2000–2016). *Psychology of Sexual Orientation and Gender Diversity, 4,* 1–13.

Roth v. United States, 354 U.S. 476 (1957).

Roth, Mara Y., et al. (2014). Acceptability of a transdermal gel-based male hormonal contraceptive in a randomized controlled trial. *Contraception, 90,* 407–412.

Rothblum, Esther D. (1994). "I only read about myself on bathroom walls": The need for research on the mental health of lesbians and gay men. *Journal of Consulting and Clinical Psychology, 62,* 213–220.

Rousseau, S., et al. (1983). The expectancy of pregnancy for "normal" infertile couples. *Fertility and Sterility, 40,* 768–772.

Rowland, David A., & Slob, A. Koos. (1997). Premature ejaculation: Psychophysiological considerations in theory, research, and treatment. *Annual Review of Sex Research, 8,* 224–253.

Ruan, Fang-fu, & Lau, M. P. (1998). China. In R. Francoeur (Ed.), *The international encyclopedia of sexuality* (Vol. 1, pp. 344–399). New York: Continuum.

Ruan, Fang-fu. (1991). *Sex in China.* New York: Plenum.

Rubel, A. N., & Bogaert, A. F. (2014). Consensual nonmonogamy: Psychological well-being and relationship quality correlates. *Journal of Sex Research, 51,* 1–22.

Ruble, Diane N. (1977). Premenstrual symptoms: A reinterpretation. *Science, 197,* 291–292.

Ruble, Diane N., & Stangor, Charles. (1986). Stalking the elusive schema: Insights from developmental and social-psychological analyses of gender schemas. *Social Cognition, 4,* 227–261.

Ruggs, Enrica N., et al. (2015). Workplace "trans"-actions: How organizations, coworkers, and individual openness influence perceived gender identity discrimination. *Psychology of Sexual Orientation and Gender Diversity, 2,* 404–412.

Rule, Nicholas O., & Ambady, Nalini. (2008). Brief exposures: Male sexual orientation is accurately perceived at 50 ms. *Journal of Experimental Social Psychology, 44,* 1100–1105.

Rule, Nicholas O., Ambady, N., & Hallett, K. C. (2009). Female sexual orientation is perceived accurately, rapidly, and automatically from the face and its features. *Journal of Experimental Social Psychology, 45,* 1245–1251.

Rule, Nicholas O., et al. (2008). Accuracy and awareness in the perception and categorization of male sexual orientation. *Journal of Personality and Social Psychology, 95,* 1019–1028.

Rule, Nicholas O., et al. (2011). Found in translation: Cross-cultural consensus in the accurate categorization of male sexual orientation. *Personality and Social Psychology Bulletin, 37,* 1449–1507.

Rupp, Heather A., & Wallen, Kim. (2008). Sex differences in response to visual sexual stimuli: A review. *Archives of Sexual Behavior, 37,* 206–218.

Rusbult, Caryl. (1983). A longitudinal test of the investment model: The development (and deterioration) of satisfaction and commitment in heterosexual involvements. *Journal of Personality and Social Psychology, 45,* 101–117.

Rusbult, Caryl, Johnson, D. J., & Morrow, G. D. (1986). Predicting satisfaction and commitment in adult romantic involvements: An assessment of the generalizability of the investment model. *Social Psychology Quarterly, 49,* 81–89.

Russell, Diana E. H. (1980). Pornography and violence: What does the new research say? In L. Lederer (Ed.), *Take back the night: Women on pornography.* New York: Morrow.

Russell, Diana E. H. (1990). *Rape in marriage* (rev. ed.). Bloomington: Indiana University Press.

Rust, Paula C. Rodriguez. (2002). Bisexuality: The state of the union. *Annual Review of Sex Research, 13,* 180–240.

Ruth, Sheila (Ed.). (1990). *Issues in feminism: An introduction to women's studies* (2nd ed.). Mountain View, CA: Mayfield.

Ryan, Caitlin, et al. (2009). Family rejection as a predictor of negative health outcomes in White and Latino lesbian, gay, and bisexual young adults. *Pediatrics, 123,* 346–352.

Ryan, Suzanne, et al. (2007). Knowledge, perceptions, and motivations for contraception: Influence on teens' contraceptive consistency. *Youth & Society, 39,* 182–208.

Rye, B. J., & Meaney, G. (2007). Voyeurism: It is good as long as we do not get caught. *International Journal of Sexual Health, 1,* 77–93.

Rylko-Bauer, Barbara. (1996). Abortion from a cross-cultural perspective. *Social Science and Medicine, 42,* 479–482.

Sabharwal, Sunil. (2014). Sexual function and reproductive health after SCI. In S. Sabharwal, *Essentials of spinal cord medicine* (pp. 304–312). New York: Demos Medical.

Sachs-Ericsson, Natalie, et al. (2005). Childhood sexual and physical abuse and the 1-year prevalence of medical problems in the National Comorbidity Survey. *Health Psychology, 24,* 32–40.

Sacred Congregation for the Doctrine of the Faith. (1976, January 16). *Declaration on certain questions concerning sexual ethics.* English text in the *New York Times,* p. 2.

Saegert, S., Swap, W., & Zajonc, R. B. (1973). Exposure, context, and interpersonal attraction. *Journal of Personality and Social Psychology, 25,* 234–242.

Sáenz de Tejada, I., et al. (2004). Physiology of erectile dysfunction and pathophysiology of erectile dysfunction. In T. Lue et al. (Eds.), *Sexual medicine* (pp. 287–343). Paris: Editions 21.

Saewyc, Elizabeth M. (2011). Research on adolescent sexual orientation: Development, health disparities, stigma, and resilience. *Journal of Research on Adolescence, 21,* 256–272.

Sakaluk, J., Todd, L., Milhausen, R., Lachowsky, N., & URGIS. (2014). Dominant heterosexual sexual scripts in emerging adulthood: Conceptualization and measurement. *Journal of Sex Research, 51,* 516–531.

Saleh, Fabian M., & Berlin, F. S. (2003). Sex hormones, neurotransmitters, and psychopharmacological treatments in men with paraphilic disorders. *Journal of Child Sexual Abuse, 12,* 233–253.

Saleh, Fabian M., et al. (2010). The management of sex offenders: Perspectives for psychiatry. *Harvard Review of Psychiatry, 18,* 359–368.

Salem, Ruwaida N. (2005). World Health Organization updates guidance on how to use contraceptives. *INFO Reports, 4.* Baltimore, MD: Johns Hopkins University.

Salmon, C. (2012). The pop culture of sex: An evolutionary window on the worlds of pornography and romance. *Review of General Psychology, 16,* 152–160.

San Francisco Task Force on Prostitution. (1996). *Final report.* Retreived from www.bayswan.org

Sanchez, Diana T., Kiefer, Amy K., & Ybarra, Oscar. (2006). Sexual submissiveness in women: Costs for sexual autonomy and arousal. *Personality and Social Psychology Bulletin, 32,* 512–524.

Sanchez, Diana T., et al. (2012). Eroticizing inequality in the United States: The consequences and determinants of traditional gender role adherence in intimate relationships. *Journal of Sex Research, 49,* 168–183.

Sanday, Peggy R. (1990). *Fraternity gang rape.* New York: New York University Press.

Sanders, Alan R., et al. (2015). Genome-wide scan demonstrates significant linkage for male sexual orientation. *Psychological Medicine, 45,* 1379–1388.

Sanders, Stephanie, Graham, Cynthia A., & Milhausen, Robin. (2008). Predicting sexual problems in women: The relevance of sexual excitation and sexual inhibition. *Archives of Sexual Behavior, 37,* 241–251.

Sandfort, Theo, & Ehrhardt, Anke. (2004). Sexual health: A useful public health paradigm or a moral imperative? *Archives of Sexual Behavior, 33,* 181–187.

Sandhu, Ranjit, Wong, Timothy, Kling, Crystal, & Chohan, Kazim. (2014). In vitro effects of coital lubricants and synthetic and natural oils on sperm motility. *Fertility and Sterility, 101,* 941–944.

Sansone, Randy A., & Sansone, Lori A. (2007). Cosmetic surgery and psychological issues. *Psychiatry, 4*(12), 65–68.

Santelli, John S., et al. (2017). Abstinence-only-until-marriage: An updated review of U.S. policies and programs and their impact. *Journal of Adolescent Health, 61,* 273–280.

Santtila, Pekka, et al. (2002). Investigating the underlying structure in sadomasochistically oriented behavior. *Archives of Sexual Behavior, 31,* 185–196.

Sarche, Michelle, et al. (2017). American Indian and Alaska Native boys: Early childhood risk and resilience amidst context and culture. *Infant Mental Health Journal, 38,* 115–127.

Sarrel, Lorna, & Sarrel, Philip. (1984). *Sexual turning points: The seven stages of adult sexuality.* New York: Macmillan.

Sathyanarayana, Sheela, et al. (2016). First trimester phthalate exposure and male newborn genital anomalies. *Environmental Research, 151,* 777–782.

Savic, I., et al. (2005). Brain response to putative pheromones in homosexual men. *Proceedings of the National Academy of Sciences, 102,* 7456–7361.

Savin-Williams, Ritch C. (2014). An exploratory study of the categorical versus spectrum nature of sexual orientation. *Journal of Sex Research, 51,* 446–453.

Savin-Williams, Ritch F., & Vrangalova, Z. (2013). Mostly heterosexual as a distinct sexual orientation group: A systematic review of the empirical evidence. *Developmental Review, 33,* 58–88.

Sayle, A. E., et al. (2001). Sexual activity during late pregnancy and risk of preterm delivery. *Obstetrics and Gynecology, 97,* 283-289.

Schachter, Stanley. (1964). The interaction of cognitive and physiological determinants of emotional state. In L. Berkowitz (Ed.), *Advances in experimental social psychology* (Vol. I). New York: Academic Press.

Schaefer, Mark T., & Olson, David H. (1981). Assessing intimacy: The PAIR Inventory. *Journal of Marital and Family Therapy, 7*(1), 47-60.

Schaffir, Jonathan. (2006). Sexual intercourse at term and onset of labor. *Obstetrics and Gynecology, 107,* 1310-1314.

Schatz, B. (1987). The AIDS insurance crisis: Underwriting or over-reaching? *Harvard Law Review, 100*(7), 1782-1805.

Scheim, Ayden I., & Bauer, Greta. (2015). Sex and gender diversity among transgender persons in Ontario, Canada: Results from a respondent-driven sampling survey. *Journal of Sex Research, 52,* 1-14.

Schenck, Carlos, Arnulf, Isabelle, & Mahowald, Mark. (2007). Sleep and sex: What can go wrong? *Sleep, 30,* 683-702.

Schetter, Christine D. (2011). Psychological science on pregnancy: Stress processes, biopsychosocial models, and emerging research issues. *Annual Review of Psychology, 62,* 531-558.

Scheufele, D. A. (1999). Framing as a theory of media effects. *Journal of Communication, 49,* 103-122.

Schiavi, Raul C., et al. (1994). Sexual satisfaction in healthy aging men. *Journal of Sex and Marital Therapy, 20,* 3-13.

Schick, Vanessa, Calabrese, S., & Herbenick, D. (2014). Survey methods in sexuality research. In D. Tolman & L. Diamond (Eds.), *APA handbook of sexuality and psychology* (Vol. 1, pp. 81-98). Washington, DC: APA.

Schieffelin, E. L. (1976). *The sorrow of the lonely and the burning of the dancers.* New York: St. Martin's Press.

Schiftan, D. (2006). *Sexual behavior in German-speaking Switzerland.* Bern: University of Bern (Dept. of Psychology).

Schilt, Kristen, & Lagos, Danya. (2017). The development of transgender studies in sociology. *Annual Review of Sociology, 43,* 425-443.

Schippers, Mimi. (2016). *Beyond monogamy: Polyamory and the future of polyqueer sexualities.* New York: New York University Press.

Schmitt, David P. (2003). Universal sex differences in the desire for sexual variety: Tests from 52 nations, 6 continents, and 13 islands. *Journal of Personality and Social Psychology, 85,* 85-104.

Schmucker, Martin, & Losel, Friedrich. (2008). Does sexual offender treatment work? A systematic review of outcome evaluations. *Psicothema, 20,* 10-19.

Schoenfeld, Elizabeth A., et al. (2017). Does sex really matter? Examining the connections between spouses' nonsexual behaviors, sexual frequency, sexual satisfaction, and marital satisfaction. *Archives of Sexual Behavior, 46,* 489-501.

Schofield, Alfred T., & Vaughan-Jackson, Percy. (1913). *What a boy should know.* New York: Cassell.

Schooler, Deborah, et al. (2009). Beyond exposure: A person-oriented approach to adolescent media diets. *Journal of Research on Adolescence, 19,* 484-508.

Schubach, Gary. (2002). The G-spot is the female prostate. *American Journal of Obstetrics and Gynecology, 186,* 850.

Schulman, Max. (1960). *I was a teen-age dwarf.* New York: Bantam.

Schultz, W. C. M., et al. (1989). Vaginal sensitivity to electric stimuli: Theoretical and practical implications. *Archives of Sexual Behavior, 18,* 87-96.

Schuster, D. (2014). These NYC coeds are students by day, strippers by night. *New York Post.* Retrieved from http://nypost.com/2014/04/28/these-nyc-coeds-are-students-by-day-strippers-by-night

Schutte, Lisette, et al. (2014). Long Live Love: The implementation of a school-based sex education program in the Netherlands. *Health Education Research, 29,* 583-597.

Schwartz, L. (2003). A nightmare for King Solomon: The new reproductive technologies. *Journal of Family Psychology, 17,* 229-237.

Schwartz, Christine R. (2013). Trends and variation in assortative mating: Causes and consequences. *Annual Review of Sociology, 39,* 451-470.

Scott, John Paul. (1964). The effects of early experience on social behavior and organization. In W. Etkin (Ed.), *Social behavior and organization among vertebrates.* Chicago: University of Chicago Press.

Scull, M. (2013). Reinforcing gender roles at the male strip show: A qualitative analysis of men who dance for women. *Deviant Behavior, 34,* 557-578.

Seabrook, Rita C., et al. (2017). Girl power or powerless girl? Television, sexual scripts, and sexual agency in sexually active young women. *Psychology of Women Quarterly, 41,* 240-253.

Seal, David W., & Ehrhardt, A. E. (2003). Masculinity and urban men: Perceived scripts for courtship, romantic, and sexual interactions with women. *Culture, Health, and Sexuality, 5,* 295-319.

Sedgh, Gilda, et al. (2011). Legal abortion worldwide in 2008: Levels and recent trends. *Perspectives on Sexual and Reproductive Health, 43,* 188-198.

Sedgh, Gilda et al. (2016). Abortion incidence between 1990 and 2014: Global, regional, and subregional levels and trends. *Lancet, 388,* 258-267.

Segraves, R. Taylor, & Balon, Richard. (2010). Recognizing and reversing sexual side effects of medications. In S. Levine (Ed.), *Handbook of clinical sexuality for mental health professionals* (2nd ed., pp. 311-327). London: Routledge.

Segraves, Robert T., & Balon, Richard. (2003). *Sexual pharmacology: Fast facts.* New York: Norton.

Seligman, Martin, & Csikszentmihalyi, M. (2000). Positive psychology: An introduction. *American Psychologist, 55,* 5-14.

Selik, Richard M., et al. (2014). Revised surveillance case definition for HIV infection—United States, 2014. *Morbidity and Mortality Weekly Report, 63*(RR03), 1-10.

Semple, S. J., Patterson, T. L., & Grant, I. (2004). The context of sexual risk behavior among heterosexual methamphetamine users. *Addictive Behaviors, 29,* 807-810.

Seto, Michael C. (2004). Pedophilia and sexual offenses against children. *Annual Review of Sex Research, 15,* 321-361.

Seto, Michael C. (2009). Pedophilia. *Annual Review of Clinical Psychology, 5,* 391-407.

Seto, M. C., & Lalumière, Martin. (2010). What is so special about male adolescent sexual offending? A review and test of explanations through meta-analysis. *Psychological Bulletin, 136,* 526-575.

Seto, Michael C., Cantor, James M., & Blanchard, Ray. (2006). Child pornography offenses are a valid diagnostic indicator of pedophilia. *Journal of Abnormal Psychology, 115,* 610-615.

Setton, Robert, et al. (2016). The accuracy of web sites and cellular phone applications in predicting the fertile window. *Obstetrics & Gynecology, 128,* 58-63.

Setty-Venugopal, Vidya, & Upadhyay, Ushma D. (2002). Three to five saves lives. *Population Reports,* Series L, Number 13. Baltimore, MD: Johns Hopkins University School of Public Health.

Sewell, Kelsey, et al. (2017). Sexual behavior, definitions of sex, and the role of self-partner context among lesbian, gay, and bisexual adults. *Journal of Sex Research, 54,* 825-831.

Sewell, Kelsey K., & Strassberg, Donald S. (2015). How do heterosexual undergraduate students define having sex? A new approach to an old question. *Journal of Sex Research, 52,* 507-516.

"Sex Industry, The." (1998, February 14). *Economist,* 21-23.

Shabsigh, R., et al. (2000). Intracavernous alprostadil alfadex (Edex/viridal) is effective and safe in patients with erectile dysfunction after failing sildenafil (Viagra). *Urology, 55,* 477-480.

Shapiro, Colin, Trajanovic, Nikola, & Federoff, J. Paul. (2003). Sexsomnia—A new parasomnia? *Canadian Journal of Psychiatry, 48,* 311–317.

Shapiro, E. Donald. (1986). New innovations in conception and their effects upon our law and morality. *New York Law Review, 21,* 37–59.

Shapiro, Harold T. (1997). Ethical and policy issues in human cloning. *Science, 277,* 195–196.

Sharma, Bhadra, & Gettleman, Jeffrey. (2018, January 10). In rural Nepal, menstruation taboo claims another victim. *New York Times.* Retrieved from https://www.nytimes.com/2018/01/10/world/asia/nepal-woman-menstruation.html

Sharpstein, Don J., & Kirkpatrick, Lee. (1997). Romantic jealousy and adult romantic attachment. *Journal of Personality and Social Psychology, 72,* 627–640.

Shattock, Robin J., et al. (2011). Turning the tide against HIV. *Science, 333,* 42–43.

Shattuck-Eidens, Donna, et al. (1995). A collaborative survey of 80 mutations in the BRCA1 breast and ovarian cancer susceptibility gene. *Journal of the American Medical Association, 273,* 535–541.

Shaughnessy, Krystelle, et al. (2017). An exploration of prevalence, variety, and frequency data to quantify online sexual activity experience. *The Canadian Journal of Human Sexuality, 26,* 60–75.

Shaw, A. M. M., Rhoades, G. K., Allen, E. S., Stanley, S. M., & Markham, H. J. (2013). Predictors of extradyadic sexual involvement in unmarried opposite-sex relationships. *Journal of Sex Research, 50,* 598–610.

Sheff, Elisabeth. (2005). Polyamorous women, sexual subjectivity, and power. *Journal of Contemporary Ethnographics, 34,* 251–283.

Shell-Duncan, Bettina. (2008). From health to human rights: Female genital cutting and the politics of intervention. *American Anthropologist, 110,* 225–236.

Shewaga, Duane. (1983). Note on *New York v. Ferber. Santa Clara Law Review, 23,* 675–684.

Shidlo, Ariel, Schroeder, M., & Drescher, J. (Eds.). (2002). *Sexual conversion therapy: Ethical, clinical, and research perspectives.* New York: Haworth.

Shifren, Jan L., Nahum, R., & Mazer, N. A. (1998). Incidence of sexual dysfunction in surgically menopausal women. *Menopause, 5,* 189–190.

Shifren, Jan L., et al. (2000). Transdermal testosterone treatment in women with impaired sexual function after oophorectomy. *New England Journal of Medicine, 343,* 682–688.

Shouvlin, David P. (1981). Preventing the sexual exploitation of children: A model act. *Wake Forest Law Review, 17,* 535–560.

SIECUS. (2004). *Is there research that supports condom availability?* New York: Author.

SIECUS. (2009). *House zeros out existing abstinence-only funding.* New York: Author.

SIECUS. (2014). *Leading sexual health organizations release National Teacher Preparation Standards for sexuality education.* Retrieved from http://www.siecus.org/index.cfm?fuseaction=Feature.showFeature&FeatureID=2342

SIECUS. (2015). *Congress extends PREP but increases wasteful spending for AOUM programs.* Retrieved from http://www.siecus.org/index.cfm?fuseaction=Feature.showFeature&FeatureID=2398

Siegel, Rebecca L., et al. (2018). Cancer statistics, 2018. *CA-Cancer Journal for Clinicians, 68,* 7–30.

Sik Ying Ho, P. (2006). The (charmed) circle game: Reflections on sexual hierarchy through multiple sexual relationships. *Sexualities, 9,* 547–564.

Siker, Jeffrey S. (Ed.). (1994). *Homosexuality in the church: Both sides of the debate.* Louisville, KY: Westminster John Knox Press.

Silbaugh, Katharine. (2002). Sex offenses: Consensual. In J. Dressler (Ed.), *Encyclopedia of crime and justice* (pp. 1465–1475). New York: Macmillan Reference USA.

Silva, Gisele Sampaio, et al. (2018). Zika virus: Report from the task force on tropical diseases by the world Federation of Societies of Intensive and Critical Care Medicine. *Journal of Critical Care, 46,* 106–109.

Simon, Viviana, Ho, David, & Karim, Quarraisha. (2006). HIV/AIDS epidemiology, pathogenesis, prevention, and treatment. *The Lancet, 368,* 489–504.

Simpson, J. A. (1990). Influence of attachment styles on romantic relationships. *Journal of Personality and Social Psychology, 59,* 971–980.

Simpson, Jeffry, Collins, W. Andrew, Tran, SiSi, & Haydon, Katherine. (2007). Attachment and the experience and expression of emotions in romantic relationships: A developmental perspective. *Journal of Personality and Social Psychology, 92,* 355–367.

Simpson, David M., et al. (2018). Learning about love: A meta-analytic study of individually-oriented relationship education programs for adolescents and emerging adults. *Journal of Youth and Adolescence, 47,* 477–489.

Sin, Nancy L., & DiMatteo, M. Robin (2014). Depression treatment enhances adherence to antiretroviral therapy: A meta-analysis. *Annals of Behavioral Medicine, 47,* 259–269.

Sinclair, James, et al. (2015). Barriers to sexuality for individuals with intellectual and developmental disabilities: A literature review. *Education and Training in Autism and Developmental Disabilities, 50,* 3–16.

Singer, Lynn, et al. (2002). Cognitive and motor outcomes in cocaine-exposed infants. *Journal of the American Medical Association, 287,* 1952–1960.

Singh, D. (1993). Adaptive significance of female physical attractiveness: Role of waist-to-hip ratio. *Journal of Personality and Social Psychology, 65,* 293–307.

Sinozich, Sofi, & Langton, Lynn. (2014). *Rape and sexual assault victimization among college-age females, 1995–2013.* Washington, DC: Bureau of Justice Statistics, U.S. Department of Justice.

Sipe, A. W. Richard. (1995). *Sex, priests, and power: Anatomy of a crisis.* New York: Brunner/Mazel.

Sipski, Marca L., Alexander, C., & Rosen, R. (2001). Sexual arousal and orgasm in women: Effects of spinal cord injury. *Annals of Neurology, 49,* 35–44.

Sipski, Marca L., Rosen, R., Alexander, C., & Gómez-Marín, O. (2004). Sexual responsiveness in women with spinal cord injuries: Differential effects of anxiety-eliciting stimulation. *Archives of Sexual Behavior, 33,* 295–302.

Skaletsky, Helen, et al. (2003). The male-specific region of the human Y chromosome is a mosaic of discrete sequence classes. *Nature, 423,* 825–837.

Slater, Michael D. (2015). Reinforcing spirals model: Conceptualizing the relationship between media content exposure and the development and maintenance of attitudes. *Media Psychology, 18,* 370–395.

Smahel, D., & Subrahmanyam, K. (2014). Adolescent sexuality on the Internet: A developmental perspective. In F. M. Saleh, A. Grudzinskas Jr., & A. Judge (Eds.), *Adolescent Sexual Behavior in the Digital Age (62–85).* Oxford, UK: Oxford University Press.

Small, Meredith F. (1993). *Female choices: Sexual behavior of female primates.* Ithaca, NY: Cornell University Press.

Smiler, A. P., Ward, L. M., Carruthers, A., & Merriwether, A. (2005). Pleasure, empowerment, and love: Factors associated with a positive first coitus. *Sexuality Research and Social Policy, 3,* 41–55.

Smith, Benjamin J., et al. (2018). Virtually "in the heat of the moment": insula activation in safe sex negotiation among risky men. *Social Cognitive and Affective Neuroscience, 13*(1), 80–91.

Smith, Elke S., et al. (2015). The transsexual brain—A review of findings on the neural basis of transsexualism. *Neuroscience and Biobehavioral Reviews, 59,* 251–266.

Smith, A. M. A., Patrick, K., Heywood, W., Pitts, M. K., Richters, J., Shelley, J. M., et al. (2012). Sexual practices and duration of last heterosexual encounter: Findings from the Australian Longitudinal Study of Health and Relationships. *Journal of Sex Research, 49,* 487–494.

Smith, Anthony, et al. (2003). Sex in Australia. *Australian and New Zealand Journal of Public Health, 27*(2).

Smith, C. V., & Shaffer, M. J. (2013). Gone but not forgotten: Virginity loss and current sexual satisfaction. *Journal of Sex and Marital Therapy, 39,* 96–111.

Smith, George, Frankel, Stephen, & Yarnell, John. (1997). Sex and death: Are they related? Findings from the Caerphilly cohort study. *British Medical Journal, 315,* 1641–1645.

Smith, M., Grov, C., Seal, D., Bernhardt, N., & McCall, P. (2015). Social-emotional aspects of male escorting: Experiences of men working for an agency. *Archives of Sexual Behavior.* doi: 10.1007/s10508-014-0391-2

Smith, S., Pieper, K., Granados, A., & Choueiti, M. (2010). Assessing gender-related portrayals in top-grossing G-rated films. *Sex Roles, 62,* 774–786.

Smith, T., & Son, J. (2013). Trends in public attitudes about sexual morality. Chicago, IL: National Opinion Research Center.

Smith, Tom. (2003). *American sexual behavior: Trends, socio-demographic differences, and risk behavior.* GSS Topical Report No. 25. University of Chicago, National Opinion Research Center.

Smith, Y. L. S., van Goozen, S., Kuiper, A., & Cohen-Ketteris, P. (2005). Transsexual subtypes: Clinical and theoretical significance. *Psychiatry Research, 137,* 151–160.

Snowdon, Charles T., et al. (2006). Social odours, sexual arousal and pairbonding in primates. *Philosophical Transactions of the Royal Society B, 361,* 2079–2089.

Snowdon, Charles T., et al. (2010). Variation in oxytocin is related to variation in affiliative behavior in monogamous, pair bonded tamarins. *Hormones and Behavior, 58,* 614–618.

Soble, Alan. (2009). A history of erotic philosophy. *Journal of Sex Research, 46,* 104–120.

Sokol, R. J., Janisse, J. J., Louis, J. M., Bailey, B. N., Ager, J., Jacobson, S. W., & Jacobson, J. L. (2007). Extreme prematurity: An alcohol-related birth effect. *Alcoholism: Clinical and Experimental Research, 31,* 1031–1037.

Sommerville, Diane M. (2004). *Rape and race in the nineteenth-century South.* Chapel Hill, NC: University of North Carolina Press.

Spark, R. F. (2002). Dehydroepiandrosterone: A springboard hormone for female sexuality. *Fertility and Sterility, 77,* S19–S25.

Special, Whitney P., & Li-Barber, Kirsten T. (2012). Self-disclosure and student satisfaction with Facebook. *Computers in Human Behavior, 28,* 624–630.

Spehr, Marc, et al. (2003). Identification of a testicular odorant receptor mediating human sperm chemotaxis. *Science, 299,* 2054–2058.

Spiers, Helen, et al. (2015). Methylomic trajectories across human fetal brain development. *Genome Research, 25,* 338–352.

Sprecher, Susan. (1987). The effects of self-disclosure given and received on affection for an intimate partner and stability of the relationship. *Journal of Social and Personal Relationships, 4,* 115–127.

Sprecher, Susan. (2014). Evidence of change in men's versus women's emotional reactions to first sexual intercourse: A 23-year study in a human sexuality course at a Midwestern University. *Journal of Sex Research, 51,* 466–472.

Springen, Karen, & Noonan, David. (2002). *Sperm banks go online.* MSNBC News 899016.

Stack, Steven, & Gundlach, James H. (1992). Divorce and sex. *Archives of Sexual Behavior, 21,* 359–368.

Stamm, Walter E. (2008). *Chlamydia trachomatis* infections. In K. Holmes et al. (Eds.), *Sexually transmitted diseases* (4th ed., pp. 575–594). New York: McGraw-Hill.

Stanecki, Karen, & Marais, Hein. (2008). The global epidemiology on HIV and AIDS. In K. Holmes et al. (Eds.), *Sexually transmitted diseases* (4th ed., pp. 41–52). New York: McGraw-Hill.

Stanger-Hall, Kathrin, & Hall, David. (2011). Abstinence-only education and teen pregnancy rates: Why we need comprehensive sex education in the U.S. *PLoS ONE, 6*(10), e24658. doi: 10:1371/journal.pone.0024658

Stanley, S. M., Rhoades, G. K., Loew, B. A., Allen, E. S., Carter, S., Osborne, L. J., et al. (2014). A randomized controlled trial of relationship education in the U.S. Army: 2-year outcomes. *Family Relations, 63,* 482–495.

Stanton, Annette L., et al. (2002). Psychosocial aspects of selected issues in women's reproductive health: Current status and future directions. *Journal of Consulting and Clinical Psychology, 70,* 751–770.

Staples, Robert. (2006). *Exploring Black sexuality.* Lanham, MD: Rowman & Littlefield.

Steensma, T. D., Kreukels, B. P. C., de Vries, A. L. C., & Cohen-Kettnis, P. T. (2013a). Gender identity development in adolescence. *Hormones and Behavior, 64,* 288–297.

Steensma, Thomas D., et al. (2013b). Gender variance in childhood and sexual orientation in adulthood: A prospective study. *Journal of Sexual Medicine, 10*(11), 2723–2733.

Stefanu, Christina, & McCabe, Marita. (2012). Adult attachment and sexual functioning: A review of past research. *Journal of Sexual Medicine, 9,* 2499–2507.

Steinberg, Laurence. (2011). *Adolescence* (9th ed.). New York: McGraw-Hill.

Steinberg, Laurence. (2018). *Adolescence* (11th ed.). New York: McGraw-Hill.

Steiner, Markus J., & Cates, W. (2006). Condoms and sexually-transmitted infections. *New England Journal of Medicine, 354,* 2642–2643.

Steiner, Markus J., et al. (2008). Condoms and other barrier methods for prevention of STD/HIV infection and pregnancy. In K. Holmes et al. (Eds.), *Sexually transmitted diseases* (4th ed., pp. 1821–1829). New York: McGraw-Hill.

Stephens, Dionne P., & Few, April L. (2007). Hip hop honey or video ho: African American preadolescents' understanding of female sexual scripts in hip hop culture. *Sexuality & Culture, 11,* 48–69.

Stephenson, Kyle R., & Kerth, Jonathan. (2017). Effects of mindfulness-based therapies for female sexual dysfunction: A meta-analytic review. *Journal of Sex Research, 54,* 832–849.

Stern, Kathleen, & McClintock, Martha K. (1998). Regulation of ovulation by human pheromones. *Nature, 392,* 177–179.

Sternberg, Robert. (1997). Construct validation of a triangular love scale. *European Journal of Social Psychology, 27,* 313–335.

Sternberg, Robert J. (1986). A triangular theory of love. *Psychological Review, 93,* 119–135.

Sternberg, R. J. (1987). Liking versus loving: A comparative evaluation of theories. *Psychological Bulletin, 102,* 331–345.

Stevenson, Michael R. (1995). Searching for a gay identity in Indonesia. *Journal of Men's Studies, 4,* 93–108.

Stifani, Bianca M., et al. (2018). Factors associated with nonadherence to instructions for using the Nestorone/ethinyl estradiol contraceptive vaginal ring. *Contraception, 97,* 415–421.

Stoneburner, Rand L., et al. (1994). The global HIV pandemic. *Acta Paediatrica,* (Suppl. 400), 1–4.

Stoner, S. A., Norris, J., George, W. H., Davi, K. C., Masters, N. T., & Hessler, D. M. (2007). Effects of alcohol intoxication and victimization history on women's sexual assault resistance intentions: The role of secondary cognitive appraisals. *Psychology of Women Quarterly, 31,* 344–356.

Storey, Anne E., et al. (2000). Hormonal correlates of paternal responsiveness in new and expectant fathers. *Evolution and Human Behavior, 21,* 79–95.

Stothard, K., et al. (2009). Maternal overweight and obesity and the risk of congenital abnormalities: A systematic review and meta-analysis. *Journal of the American Medical Association, 301,* 636–650.

Stranges, Elizabeth, Wier, Lauren, & Elixhauser, Anne. (2011). *Complicating conditions of vaginal deliveries and cesarean sections, 2009. HCUP Statistical Brief #113.* Rockville, MD: Agency for Healthcare Research and Quality. www.hcup-us.ahrq.gov/reports/statbriefs/sb113.pdf

Strassberg, Donald S., & Lowe, Kristi. (1995). Volunteer bias in sex research. *Archives of Sexual Behavior, 24,* 369–382.

Strohm, C. Q., Seltzer, J. A., Cochran, S. D., & Mays, V. M. (2009). Living apart together relationships in the United States. *Demographic Research, 21,* 177–214.

Strong, Carson. (1997). *Ethics in reproductive and perinatal medicine.* New Haven, CT: Yale University Press.

Struckman-Johnson, Cindy, et al. (1996). Sexual coercion reported by men and women in prison. *Journal of Sex Research, 33,* 67–76.

Stryker, Sheldon. (1987). The vitalization of symbolic interactionism. *Social Psychology Quarterly, 50,* 83–94.

Stuart v. Kamnitz, Appeal No. 14-1150 (4th Cir. 2014).

Stubbs, Margaret L. (2008). Cultural perceptions and practices around menarche and adolescent menstruation in the United States. *Annals of the New York Academy of Sciences, 1135,* 58–66.

Styne, Dennis M., & Grumbach, Melvin M. (2008). Puberty: Ontogeny, neuroendocrinology, physiology, and disorders. In H. M. Kronenberg et al. (Eds.), *Williams textbook of endocrinology* (11th ed., pp. 969–1104). Philadelphia, PA: Saunders.

Substance Abuse and Mental Health Services Administration. (2012). *National survey of drug use and health, 2011–2012.* Center for Behavioral Health Statistics and Quality. Retrieved from http://www.samsha.gov/dataNSDUH/2012 SummNatFindDetTables/DetTabs/NSDUH-DetTabsTOC2012.htm

SAMHSA (2015). *Ending conversion therapy: Supporting and affirming LGBTQ youth.* HHS Publication No. (SMA) 15-4928.

Sue, Derald Wing, et al. (2007). Racial microaggressions in everyday life: Implications for clinical practice. *American Psychologist, 62,* 271–286.

Sue, Derald Wing. (2010). *Microaggressions in everyday life: Race, gender, and sexual orientation.* Hoboken, NJ: Wiley.

Sullivan, Nikki. (2003). *A critical introduction to queer theory.* New York: New York University Press.

Sunderam, Saswati, et al. (2018). Assisted reproductive technology surveillance—United States, 2015. *MMWR, 67,* No. 3.

Suschinsky, Kelly D., Lalumière, Martin L., & Chivers, Meredith L. (2009). Sex differences in patterns of genital sexual arousal: Measurement artifacts or true phenomena? *Archives of Sexual Behavior, 38,* 559–573.

Svoboda, J. Steven, & Van Howe, Robert S. (2013). Out of step: Fatal flaws in the latest AAP policy report on neonatal circumcision. *Journal of Medical Ethics, 39,* 323–441.

Swaab, Dick F. (2005). The role of the hypothalamus and endocrine system in sexuality. In J. S. Hyde (Ed.), *Biological substrates of human sexuality* (pp. 21–74). Washington, DC: American Psychological Association.

Swamy, G., Ostbye, T., & Skjaerven, R. (2008). Association of preterm birth with long-term survival, reproduction, and next generation preterm birth. *Journal of the American Medical Association, 299,* 1429–1436.

Swann, Gregory, et al. (2016). Validation of the Sexual Orientation Microaggression Inventory in two diverse samples of LGBTQ youth. *Archives of Sexual Behavior, 45,* 1289–1298.

Swartout, Kevin M. (2013). The company they keep: How peer networks influence male sexual aggression. *Psychology of Violence, 3,* 157–171.

Swartout, Kevin, & White, Jacquelyn. (2010). The relationship between drug use and sexual aggression in men across time. *Journal of Interpersonal Violence, 25,* 1716–1735.

Szasz, Thomas S. (1965). Legal and moral aspects of homosexuality. In J. Marmor (Ed.), *Sexual inversion: The multiple roots of homosexuality.* New York: Basic Books.

Szasz, Thomas S. (1980). *Sex by prescription.* Garden City, NY: Anchor Press/Doubleday.

Taberner, Peter V. (1985). *Aphrodisiacs: The science and the myth.* Philadelphia: University of Pennsylvania Press.

Tafoya, Terry, & Wirth, Douglas A. (1996). Native American two-spirit men. In J. F. Longres (Ed.), *Men of color* (pp. 51–67). New York: Haworth.

Talge, N. M., Neal, C., Glover, V., et al. (2007). Antenatal maternal stress and long-term effects on child neurodevelopment: How and why? *Journal of Child Psychology and Psychiatry, 48,* 245–261.

Tannen, Deborah. (1991). *You just don't understand: Women and men in conversation.* New York: William Morrow.

Tanner, James M. (1967). Puberty. In A. McLaren (Ed.), *Advances in reproductive physiology* (Vol. II). New York: Academic.

Taylor, Diana. (2006). From "It's all in your head" to "Taking back the month": Premenstrual syndrome (PMS) research and the contributions of the Society for Menstrual Cycle Research. *Sex Roles, 54,* 377–392.

Teachman, J. D., Tedrow, L. M., & Crowder, K. D. (2000). The changing demography of America's families. In R. M. Milardo (Ed.), *Understanding families into the new millennium: A decade in review* (pp. 453–465). Minneapolis, MN: National Council on Family Relations.

Tebbe, Elliot A., Moradi, B., & Ege, E. (2014). Revised and abbreviated forms of the genderism and transphobia scale: Tools for assessing anti-trans* prejudice. *Journal of Counseling Psychology, 61,* 581–592.

Tedeschi, R. G., Park, C. L., & Calhoun, L. G. (Eds.). (1998). *Posttraumatic growth: Positive changes in the aftermath of crisis.* Mahwah, NJ: Erlbaum.

Tennant, P. W. G., Rankin, J., & Bell, R. (2011). Maternal body mass index and the risk of fetal and infant death: A cohort study from the North of England. *Human Reproduction, 26,* 1501–1511.

Ter Kuile, Moniek, & Reissing, E. (2014). Lifelong vaginismus. In Y. Binik & K. Hall (Eds.), *Principles and practice of sex therapy* (5th ed., pp. 177–194). New York: Guilford.

Terman, Lewis M. (1948). Kinsey's *Sexual Behavior in the Human Male:* Some comments and criticisms. *Psychological Bulletin, 45,* 443–459.

Terman, Lewis, et al. (1938). *Psychological factors in marital happiness.* New York: McGraw-Hill.

Testa, Maria, VanZile-Tamsen, Carol, & Livingston, Jennifer A. (2005). Childhood sexual abuse, relationship satisfaction, and sexual risk taking in a community sample of women. *Journal of Consulting and Clinical Psychology, 73,* 1116–1124.

Testa, Rylan J., et al. (2012). Effects of violence on transgender people. *Professional Psychology: Research and Practice, 43,* 452–459.

Thakker, Jo, et al. (2008). Rape: Assessment and treatment. In D. R. Laws & W. T. O'Donohue (Eds.), *Sexual deviance* (pp. 356–383). New York: Guilford.

Thibaut, Florence, et al. (2010). The World Federation of Societies for Biological Psychiatry (WFSBP) guidelines for the biological treatment of paraphilias. *The World Journal of Biological Psychiatry, 11,* 604–655.

Thibaut, John, & Kelley, Harold. (1959). *The social psychology of groups.* New York: Wiley.

Thielicke, Helmut. (1964). *The ethics of sex.* New York: Harper & Row.

Thompson, Anthony P. (1983). Extramarital sex: A review of the research literature. *Journal of Sex Research, 19,* 1–22.

Thompson, Ashley E., & Byers, E. Sandra. (2017). Heterosexual young adults' interest, attitudes, and experiences related to mixed-gender, multi-person sex. *Archives of Sexual Behavior, 46,* 813–822.

Thompson, Ashley E., & Voyer, Daniel. (2014). Sex differences in the ability to recognize non-verbal displays of emotion: A meta-analysis. *Cognition & Emotion, 28,* 1164–1195.

Thompson, Martie P., et al. (2013). Trajectories and predictors of sexually aggressive behaviors during emerging adulthood. *Psychology of Violence, 3,* 247–259.

Thompson, Martie P., et al. (2015). Time-varying risk factors and sexual aggression perpetration among male college students. *Journal of Adolescent Health, 57,* 637–642.

Thorne, Natasha, & Amrein, H. (2003). Vomeronasal organ: Pheromone recognition with a twist. *Current Biology, 13,* R220–R222.

Thornton, Leslie-Jean. (2013). "Time of the month" on Twitter: Taboo, stereotype and bonding in a no-holds-barred public arena. *Sex Roles, 68,* 41–54.

Tiefer, Leonore. (1991). Historical, scientific, clinical, and feminist criticisms of "The Human Sexual Response Cycle" model. *Annual Review of Sex Research, 2,* 1–24.

Tiefer, Leonore. (1994). Three crises facing sexology. *Archives of Sexual Behavior, 23,* 361–374.

Tiefer, Leonore. (2000). Sexology and the pharmaceutical industry: The threat of co-optation. *Journal of Sex Research, 37,* 273–283.

Tiefer, Leonore. (2001). A new view of women's sexual problems: Why new? Why now? *Journal of Sex Research, 38,* 89–96.

Tiefer, Leonore. (2004). *Sex is not a natural act and other essays* (2nd ed.). Boulder, CO: Westview Press.

Tiefer, Leonore. (2012). Medicalization and demedicalizations of sexuality therapies. *Journal of Sex Research, 49,* 311–318.

Tiggemann, Marika, & Hodgson, Suzanna. (2008). The hairlessness norm extended: Reasons for and predictors of women's body hair removal at different body sites. *Sex Roles, 59,* 889–897.

Timmerman, Greetje. (2003). Sexual harassment of adolescents perpetrated by teachers and by peers; An exploration of the dynamics of power, culture, and gender in secondary schools. *Sex Roles, 48,* 231–244.

Tolman, Deborah L., & Diamond, Lisa M. (2014). Sexuality theory: A review, a revision, and a recommendation. In D. Tolman & L. Diamond (Eds.), *APA handbook of sexuality and psychology* (Vol. 1, pp. 3–28). Washington, DC: American Psychological Association.

Tolman, Deborah L., & McClelland, Sara I. (2011). Normative sexuality development in adolescence: A decade in review, 2000–2009. *Journal of Research on Adolescence, 21,* 242–255.

Tompkins, Tanya L., et al. (2015). Reducing stigma toward the transgender community: An evaluation of a humanizing and perspective-taking intervention. *Psychology of Sexual Orientation and Gender Diversity, 2,* 34–42.

Toscano, Marco, et al. (2017). Role of the human breast milk-associate microbiota on the newborns' immune system: A mini-review. *Frontiers in Microbiology, 8,* Article 2100.

Tracy, S. K., Hartz, D. L., Tracy, M. B., Allen, J., Forti, A., Hall, B., et al. (2013). Caseload midwifery care versus standard maternity care for women of any risk: M@NGO, a randomised, controlled trial. *The Lancet, 382,* 1723–1732.

Traish, Abdulmaged M., et al. (2002). Biochemical and physiological mechanisms of female genital sexual arousal. *Archives of Sexual Behavior, 31,* 393–400.

Trekels, Jolien, et al. (2018). I "like" the way you look: How appearance-focused and overall Facebook use contribute to adolescents' self-sexualization. *Computers in Human Behavior, 81,* 198–208.

Triandis, H. C., McCusker, C., & Hui, C. H. (1990). Multimethod probes of individualism and collectivism. *Journal of Personality and Social Psychology, 59,* 1006–1020.

Truesdale, Matthew D., et al. (2017). Prevalence of pubic hair grooming-related injuries and identification of high-risk individuals in the United States. *JAMA Dermatology, 153,* 1114–1121.

Truitt, William A., & Coolen, L. (2002). Identification of a potential ejaculation generator in the spinal cord. *Science, 297,* 1566–1569.

Trussell, James. (2007). The cost of unintended pregnancy in the United States. *Contraception, 75,* 168–170.

Tucker, M. E. (2014). Use of unapproved menopausal hormone therapy skyrockets. *Medscape.* Retrieved from http://www.medscape.com/viewarticle/833374

Turkle, S. (1995). *Life on the screen: Identity in the age of the Internet.* New York: Simon & Schuster.

Turner, Daniel, & Briken, Peer. (2018). Treatment of paraphilic disorders in sexual offenders or men with a risk of sexual offending with luteinizing hormone-releasing hormone agonists: An updated systematic review. *Journal of Sexual Medicine, 15,* 77–93.

Tutin, C. E. G., & McGinnis, P. R. (1981). Chimpanzee reproduction in the wild. In C. E. Graham (Ed.), *Reproductive biology of the great apes* (pp. 239–264). New York: Academic Press.

Twenge, Jean M., et al. (2016). Changes in American adults' reported same-sex sexual experiences and attitudes, 1973–2014. *Archives of Sexual Behavior, 45,* 1713–1730.

Twenge, Jean M., et al. (2017a). Sexual inactivity during young adulthood is more common among U.S. millennials and iGen: Age, period, and cohort effects on having no sexual partners after age 18. *Archives of Sexual Behavior, 46,* 433–440.

Twenge, Jean M., et al. (2017b). Declines in sexual frequency among American adults, 1989–2014. *Archives of Sexual Behavior, 46,* 2389–2401.

U.S. Bureau of the Census. (2014). Opposite sex unmarried couples by presence of biological children. *Current Population Survey, 2014 Social and Economic Supplement,* Table UC3.

U.S. Bureau of the Census. (2000a). *The Hispanic population in the United States.* www.census.gov

U.S. Bureau of the Census. (2000b). *Statistical abstract of the United States: 1999* (119th ed.). Washington, DC: Bureau of the Census.

U.S. Bureau of the Census. (2010). *Statistical abstract of the United States, 2012.* Washington, DC: Bureau of the Census.

U.S. Census Bureau. (2010). *American community survey, 2005–2009.* www.census.gov

U.S. Census Bureau. (2015a). Household relationship and living arrangements of children under 18 years, by age and sex: 2014. *Current Population Survey, 2014 Annual Social and Economic Supplement, America's Families and Living Arrangements,* Table C2. http://www.census.gov/hhes/families/data/cps2014C.html

U.S. Census Bureau. (2015b). Households by race and Hispanic origin of household reference person and detailed type: 2014. *Current Population Survey, 2014 Social and Economic Supplement,* Table H3.

U.S. Department of Justice. (1986). *The Attorney General's Commission on Pornography: Final report.* Washington, DC: U.S. Department of Justice.

U.S. National Commission for the Protection of Human Subjects of Biomedical and Behavioral Research. (1978). *The Belmont report: Ethical principles and guidelines for the protection of human subjects of research.* Washington, DC: U.S. Government Printing Office.

Udry, J. Richard. (1988). Biological predispositions and social control in adolescent sexual behavior. *American Sociological Review, 53,* 709–722.

Udry, J. Richard, & Eckland, Bruce K. (1984). Benefits of being attractive: Differential payoffs for men and women. *Psychological Reports, 54,* 47–56.

Udry, J. Richard, et al. (1985). Serum androgenic hormones motivate sexual behavior in adolescent boys. *Fertility and Sterility, 43,* 90–94.

Ueno, Koji. (2005). Sexual orientation and psychological distress in adolescence: Examining interpersonal stressors and social support processes. *Social Psychology Quarterly, 68,* 258–277.

UNAIDS (2018). *Fact Sheet — July 2018.* http://www.unaids.org/sites/default/files/media_asset/UNAIDS_FactSheet_en.pdf

University of California, Berkeley. (2012, April). Better sex in a bottle? *Wellness Letter,* p. 4.

Utley, Ebony A. (2015). Digital indiscretions: Infidelity in the age of technology. In S. Tarrant (Ed.), *Gender, sex, and politics: In the streets and between the sheets in the 21st century*. New York: Routledge.

Vaillancourt, T., & Aanchai, S. (2011). Intolerance of sexy peers: Intrasexual competition among women. *Aggressive Behavior, 37,* 569–577.

Valkenburg, Patti M., & Peter, J. (2013). The differential susceptibility to media effects model. *Journal of Communication, 63,* 221–243.

Valkenburg, P. M., et al. (2011). Gender differences in online and offline self-disclosure in pre-adolescence and adolescence. *British Journal of Developmental Psychology, 29,* 253–269.

Valkenburg, Patti M., et al. (2016). Media effects: Theory and research. *Annual Review of Psychology, 67,* 315–338.

Van Anders, Sari M. (2010). Chewing gum has large effects on salivary testosterone, estradiol, and secretory immunoglobulin A assays in women and men. *Psychoneuroendocrinology, 35,* 305–309.

van Anders, Sari. (2012). Testosterone and sexual desire in healthy women and men. *Archives of Sexual Behavior, 41,* 1471–1484.

Van den Bos, Arne, & Stapel, Diederick. (2009). Why people stereotype affects how they stereotype. *Personality and Social Psychology Bulletin, 35,* 101–113.

Van Dongen, Stefan. (2011). Associations between asymmetry and human attractiveness: Possible direct effects of asymmetry and signatures of publication bias. *Annals of Human Biology, 38,* 317–323.

Van Dongen, Stefan, & Gangestad, Steven. (2011). Human fluctuating asymmetry in relation to health and quality: A meta-analysis. *Evolution and Human Behavior, 32,* 380–396.

Van Goozen, Stephanie H. M., et al. (1997). Psychoendocrinological assessment of the menstrual cycle: The relationship between hormones, sexuality, and mood. *Archives of Sexual Behavior, 26,* 359–382.

Van Lankveld, Jacques. (1998). Bibliotherapy in the treatment of sexual dysfunctions: A meta-analysis. *Journal of Consulting and Clinical Psychology, 66,* 702–708.

Van Lankveld, Jacques. (2009). Self-help therapies for sexual dysfunction. *Journal of Sex Research, 46,* 143–155.

Van Lankveld, Jacques, Everaerd, Walter, & Grotjohann, Yvonne. (2001). Cognitive-behaviorial bibliotherapy for sexual dysfunctions in heterosexual couples: A randomized waiting-list controlled clinical trial in the Netherlands. *Journal of Sex Research, 38,* 51–67.

Van Lent, P. (1996). Her beautiful savage: The current sexual image of the Native American male. In S. E. Bird (Ed.), *Dressing in feathers: The construction of the Indian in American popular culture* (pp. 211–228). Boulder, CO: Westview Press.

Van Preagh, P. (1982). The Hamilton birth control clinic. In response to need. *News/Nouvelles, Journal of Planned Parenthood Federation of Canada, 3*(2).

Vance, Ellen B., & Wagner, Nathaniel N. (1976). Written descriptions of orgasm: A study of sex differences. *Archives of Sexual Behavior, 5,* 87–98.

Vandenbosch, Laura, & van Oosten, Johann. (2018). Explaining the relationship between sexually explicit internet material and casual sex: A two-step mediation model. *Archives of Sexual Behavior, 47,* 1465–1480.

Vannier, S., Currie, A., & O'Sullivan, L. (2014). Schoolgirls and soccer moms: A content analysis of free "Teen" and "MILF" online pornography. *Journal of Sex Research, 51,* 253–264.

Vanwesenbeeck, Ine. (1994). *Prostitutes' well-being and risk.* Amsterdam: VU University Press.

Vanwesenbeeck, Ine. (2001). Another decade of social scientific work on sex work: A review of research 1990–2000. *Annual Review of Sex Research, 12,* 242–289.

Vanwesenbeeck, Ine. (2005). Burnout among female indoor sex workers. *Archives of Sexual Behavior, 34,* 627–640.

Vasey, Paul L. (2002). Same-sex sexual partner preference in hormonally and neurologically unmanipulated animals. *Annual Review of Sex Research, 13,* 141–179.

Vasey, Paul L., & Jiskoot, Hester. (2010). The biogeography and evolution of female homosexual behavior in Japanese macaques. *Archives of Sexual Behavior, 39,* 1439–1441.

Vasilenko, Sara A., et al. (2016). Latent classes of adolescent sexual and romantic relationship experiences: implications for adult sexual health and relationship outcomes. *Journal of Sex Research, 53,* 742–753.

Ve Ard, Cherie, & Veaux, Franklin. (2003). *Polyamory 101.* Retrieved from www.xeromag.com/poly101.pdf

Veale, David, et al. (2015). Am I normal? A systematic review and construction of nomograms for flaccid and erect penis length and circumference in up to 15,521 men. *BJU International, 115*(6), 978–986.

Vedam, Saraswathi, Janssen, Patricia, & Lichtman, Ronnie. (2010). Science and sensibility: Choice of birth place in the United States. *Medscape OB/Gyn & Women's Health.* Retrieved from www.medscape.com/viewarticle/717516

Vedes, Ana, et al. (2016). Love styles, coping, and relationship satisfaction: A dyadic approach. *Personal Relationships, 23,* 84–97.

Velten, Julia, et al. (2018). Effects of a mindfulness task on women's sexual response. *Journal of Sex Research, 55,* 747–757.

Venicz, L., & Vanwesenbeeck, I. (2000). *Something is going to change in prostitution: Social position and psychological well being of indoor prostitutes before the law reform.* Utrecht/The Hague, The Netherlands: NISSO/Ministry of Justice.

Venkatesh, S. (2011). How tech tools transformed New York's sex trade. Retrieved from www.wired.com/magazine/2011/01/ff_sextrade/all

Vespa, Jonathan. (2014). Historical trends in the marital intentions of one-time and serial cohabitors. *Journal of Marriage and Family, 76,* 207–217.

Vidal, Adriana, et al. (2014). HPV genotypes and cervical intraepithelial neoplasia in a multiethnic cohort in the southeastern USA. *Cancer Causes Control, 25,* 1055–1062.

Vilain, Eric. (2000). The genetics of sexual development. *Annual Review of Sex Research, 11,* 1–25.

Vincent, J. P., et al. (1979). Demand characteristics in observations of marital interaction. *Journal of Consulting and Clinical Psychology, 47,* 557–566.

Volbert, Renate. (2000). Sexual knowledge of preschool children. *Journal of Psychology and Human Sexuality, 12,* 5–26.

Von Hertzen, Helena, et al. (2002). Low dose mifepristone and two regimens of levonorgestrel for emergency contraception: A WHO multicenter randomised trial. *The Lancet, 360,* 1803–1810.

Von Krafft-Ebing, Richard. (1965). *Psychopathia sexualis.* New York: Putnam. (Original work published 1886)

Von Kries, Rudifer, et al. (1999). Breast feeding and obesity: Cross sectional study. *British Medical Journal, 319,* 147–150.

Vrangalova, Z. (2015). Does casual sex harm college students' well-being? A longitudinal investigation of the role of motivation. *Archives of Sexual Behavior, 44,* 945–959.

Wade, Lisa. (2017). *American hookup: The new culture of sex on campus.* New York: Norton.

Wade, Lisa, & DeLamater, John. (2002). Relationship dissolution as a life stage transition: Effects on sexual attitudes and behaviors. *Journal of Marriage and the Family, 64,* 898–914.

Wadsworth, M. E., & Markham, H. J. (2012). Where's the action? Understanding what works and why in relationship education. *Behavior Therapy, 43,* 99–112.

Waite, Linda, & Joyner, Kara. (2000). Emotional and physical satisfaction with sex in married, cohabitating, and dating sexual unions: Do men and women differ? In Edward Laumann & Robert Michael (Eds.), *Sex, love, and health in America: Private choices and public policy* (pp. 239–269). Chicago, IL: University of Chicago Press.

Wald, Anna, et al. (2005). The relationship between condom use and herpes simplex virus acquisition. *Annals of Internal Medicine, 143,* 707–713.

Walen, Susan R., & Roth, David. (1987). A cognitive approach. In J. H. Geer & W. T. O'Donohue (Eds.), *Theories of human sexuality.* New York: Plenum.

Walker, Jayne, Archer, J., & Davies, M. (2005). Effects of rape on men: A descriptive analysis. *Archives of Sexual Behavior, 34,* 69–80.

Wallen, Kim, & Parsons, William A. (1997). Sexual behavior in same-sexed nonhuman primates: Is it relevant to understanding human homosexuality? *Annual Review of Sex Research, 8,* 195–223.

Wallen, Kim, & Zehr, Julia L. (2004). Hormones and history: The evolution and development of primate female sexuality. *Journal of Sex Research, 41,* 101–112.

Wallen, Kim. (2001). Sex and context: Hormones and primate sexual motivation. *Hormones and Behavior, 40,* 339–357.

Wallin, Paul. (1949). An appraisal of some methodological aspects of the Kinsey report. *American Sociological Review, 14,* 197–210.

Wallis, Cara. (2011). Performing gender: A content analysis of gender display in music videos. *Sex Roles, 64,* 160–172.

Wallrabenstein, Ivonne, et al. (2015). The smelling of Hedione results in sex-differentiated human brain activity. *NeuroImage, 113,* 365–373.

Walster [Hatfield], Elaine, Walster, William, & Berscheid, Ellen. (1978). *Equity: Theory and research.* Boston, MA: Allyn & Bacon.

Wang, L. Y., et al. (2000). Economic evaluation of *SAFER CHOICES:* A school-based human immunodeficiency virus, other sexually transmitted diseases, and pregnancy prevention program. *Archives of Pediatrics & Adolescent Medicine, 154,* 1017–1024.

Wang, P. Jeremy, et al. (2001). An abundance of X-linked genes expressed in spermatogonia. *Nature Genetics, 27,* 422–426.

Wang, Timothy, et al. (2018). The effects of school-based condom availability programs (CAPs) on condom acquisition, use and sexual behavior: A systematic review. *AIDS and Behavior, 22,* 308–320.

Ward, L. Monique. (2016). Media and sexualization: State of empirical research, 1995–2015. *Journal of Sex Research, 53,* 560–576.

Ward, L. M., & Aubrey, J. S. (2017). *Watching gender: How stereotypes in movies and on TV impact kids' development.* San Francisco, CA: Common Sense. Retrieved from https://www.commonsensemedia.org/research/watching-gender.

Ward, L. M., Reed, L., Trinh, S. L., & Foust, M. (2014). Sexuality and entertainment media. In D. L. Tolman & L. M. Diamond (Eds.), *APA Handbook of Sexuality and Psychology: Contextual Approaches* (Vol. 2, pp. 373–423). Washington, DC: American Psychological Association.

Ward, L. Monique, & Harrison, Kristen. (2005). The impact of media use on girls' beliefs about gender roles, their bodies, and sexual relationships: A research synthesis. In E. Cole & J. H. Daniel (Eds.), *Featuring females: Feminist analyses of media* (pp. 3–24). Washington, DC: American Psychological Association.

Ward, L. Monique, Hansbrough, E., & Walker, E. (2005). Contributions of music video exposure to Black adolescents' gender and sexual schemas. *Journal of Adolescent Research, 20,* 143–166.

Ward, O. Byron, et al. (2002). Hormonal mechanisms underlying aberrant sexual differentiation in male rats prenatally exposed to alcohol, stress, or both. *Archives of Sexual Behavior, 31,* 9–16.

Ward, Tony, Gannon, Theresa, & Yates, Pamela. (2008). The treatment of offenders: Current practice and new developments with an emphasis on sex offenders. *International Review of Victimology, 15,* 179–204.

Warner, T., Roussos-Ross, D., & Behnke, M. (2014). It's not your mother's marijuana. *Clinics in Perinatology, 41,* 877–894.

Waynforth, David, Hurtadoa, A. Magdalena, & Hillary, Kim. (1998). Environmentally contingent reproductive strategies in Mayan and Ache males. *Evolution and Human Behavior, 19,* 369–385.

Weaver, Hilary N. (1999). Through indigenous eyes: Native Americans and the HIV epidemic. *Health and Social Work, 24,* 27–34.

Webster v. Reproductive Health Services, 492 U.S. 490 (1989).

Weinberg, Martin S., Williams, C., & Pryor, D. (2001). Bisexuals at midlife: Commitment, salience, and identity. *Journal of Contemporary Ethnography, 30,* 180–208.

Weinberg, Martin S., Williams, Colin J., & Pryor, Douglas W. (1994). *Dual attraction: Understanding bisexuality.* New York: Oxford University Press.

Weinberg, Martin, Williams, Colin, & Calhan, Cassandra. (1995). "If the shoe fits . . .": Exploring male homosexual foot fetishism. *Journal of Sex Research, 32,* 17–27.

Weinberg, Thomas S. (1987). Sadomasochism in the United States: A review of recent sociological literature. *Journal of Sex Research, 23,* 50–69.

Weinberger, L. E., Sreenivasan, S., Garrick, T., & Osran, H. (2005). The impact of surgical castration on sexual recidivism risk among sexually violent predatory offenders. *Journal of the American Academy of Psychiatry and the Law, 33,* 16–36.

Weisberg, D. Kelly. (1985). *Children of the night: A study of adolescent prostitution.* Lexington, MA: Lexington Books.

Weisman, Alan. (2013). *Countdown: Our last, best hope for a future on earth?* New York: Little, Brown.

Weitzer, Ronald (Ed.). (2010). *Sex for sale: Prostitution, pornography and the sex industry.* New York: Taylor and Francis.

Weller, Leonard, Weller, Aron, & Avinir, Ohala. (1995). Menstrual synchrony: Only in roommates who are close friends? *Physiology and Behavior, 58,* 883–889.

Wellings, K., Collumbien, M., Slaymaker, E., Singh, S., Hodges, Z., Patel, D., & Bajos, N. (2006). Sexual behavior in context: A global perspective. *The Lancet, 368,* 1706–1728.

Wentland, J. J., & Reissing, E. (2014). Casual sexual relationships: Identifying definitions for one night stands, booty call, fuck buddies, and friends with benefits. *The Canadian Journal of Human Sexuality, 23,* 167–177.

Wentzell, Emily (2017). How did erectile dysfunction become "natural"? A review of the critical social scientific literature on medical treatment for male sexual dysfunction. *Journal of Sex Research, 54,* 486–506.

Wenzlaff, Frederike, et al. (2016). Video-based eye tracking in sex research: A systematic literature review. *Journal of Sex Research, 53,* 1008–1019.

Wéry, Aline, et al. (2016). Characteristics of self-identified sexual addicts in a behavioral addiction outpatient clinic. *Journal of Behavioral Addictions, 5,* 623–630.

Wesselmann, Eric D., & Kelly, Janice R. (2010). Cat-calls and culpability: Investigating the frequency and functions of stranger harassment. *Sex Roles, 63,* 451–462.

Westgate, Erin C., Riskind, R., & Nosek, B. (2015). Implicit preferences for straight people over lesbian women and gay men weakened from 2006 to 2013. *Collabra, 1*(1), 1–10.

Wheeler, Garry D., et al. (1984). Reduced serum testosterone and prolactin levels in male distance runners. *Journal of the American Medical Association, 252,* 514–516.

Wheeler, Jennifer, Newring, Kirk, & Draper, Crissa. (2008). Transvestic fetishism: Psychopathology and theory. In D. R. Laws & W. O'Donohue (Eds.), *Sexual deviance: Theory, assessment, and treatment* (2nd ed., pp. 272–284). New York: Guilford.

Whipple, Beverly, Ogden, Gina, & Komisarak, Barry. (1992). Physiological correlates of imagery-induced orgasm in women. *Archives of Sexual Behavior, 21,* 121–133.

Whitam, Frederick L. (1983). Culturally invariable properties of male homosexuality: Tentative conclusions from cross-cultural research. *Archives of Sexual Behavior, 12,* 207–226.

White, Gregory L., Fishbein, S., & Rutstein, J. (1981). Passionate love and the misattribution of arousal. *Journal of Personality and Social Psychology, 41,* 56–62.

White, Leland J. (2001). Romans 1:26–27: The claim that homosexuality is unnatural. In P. Jung & J. Coray (Eds.), *Sexual diversity and Catholicism* (pp. 133–149). Collegeville, MN: The Liturgical Press.

White, Gregory L., & Mullen, Paul E. (1989). Jealousy: Theory, research, and clinical strategies. New York: Guilford.

Whitfield, John. (2010). Brother sperm train together. *Nature.* doi: 10:1038/news.2010.22

Whitley, Bernard, Jr. (1993). Reliability and aspects of the construct validity of Sternberg's Triangular Love Scale. *Journal of Social and Personal Relationships, 10,* 475–480.

Whole Woman's Health v. Hellerstedt (579 U.S., 2016).

Wichstrøm, Lars, & Hegna, Kristinn. (2003). Sexual orientation and suicide attempt: A longitudinal study of the general Norwegian adolescent population. *Journal of Abnormal Psychology, 112,* 144–151.

Wickler, Wolfgang. (1973). *The sexual code.* New York: Anchor Books. (Original work in German published 1969)

Widman, Laura, et al. (2016). Parent-adolescent sexual communication and adolescent safer sex behavior: A meta-analysis. *JAMA Pediatrics, 170,* 52–61.

Wiederman, Michael. (2015). Sexual scripts theory. In J. DeLamater and R. Plante (Eds.), *Handbook of the Sociology of Sexualities* (pp. 7–16). Dordrecht, NL: Springer.

Wiederman, Michael W. (2001). *Understanding sexuality research.* Belmont, CA: Wadsworth.

Wiederman, Michael W., Weis, David L., & Allgeier, Elizabeth R. (1994). The effect of question preface on response rates to a telephone survey of sexual experience. *Archives of Sexual Behavior, 23,* 203–216.

Wiegel, Markus, Scepkowski, L., & Barlow, D. (2007). Cognitive-affective processes in sexual arousal and sexual dysfunction. In E. Janssen (Ed.), *The psychophysiology of sex* (pp. 143–165). Bloomington: Indiana University Press.

Wiesenfeld, H. C., et al. (2001). Self-collection of vaginal swabs for the detection of chlamydia, gonorrhea, and trichomoniasis: Opportunity to encourage sexually transmitted disease testing among adolescents. *Sexually Transmitted Diseases, 28,* 321–325.

Wikipedia. (2012). *Internet pornography statistics.*

Wilcox, A. J., Weinberg, C. R., & Baird, D. D. (1995). Timing of sexual intercourse in relation to ovulation. *New England Journal of Medicine, 333,* 1517–1521.

Wilcox, Brian L., & Wyatt, J. (1997). *Adolescent abstinence education programs: A meta-analysis.* Presented at the annual meeting, Society for the Scientific Study of Sexuality, Arlington, Virginia.

Wilcox, Brian L., Robbenoit, J. K., & O'Keefe, J. E. (1998). Federal abortion policy and politics: 1973 to 1996. In L. J. Beckman & S. M. Harvey (Eds.), *The new civil war: The psychology, culture and politics of abortion* (pp. 3–24). Washington, DC: American Psychological Association.

Wilkinson, Ross. (1995). Changes in psychological health and the marital relationship through child bearing: Transition or process as stressor. *Australian Journal of Psychology, 47,* 86–92.

Willetts, Marion, Sprecher, Susan, & Beck, Frank. (2004). Overview of sexual practices and attitudes within relational contexts. In J. H. Harvey, A. Wenzel, & S. Sprecher (Eds.), *The handbook of sexuality in close relationships* (pp. 57–85). Mahwah, NJ: Lawrence Erlbaum.

Williams v. Pryor, 41 F. Supp. 2d 1257 (N.D. Ala. 1999).

Williams, Colin, & Weinberg, Martin. (2003). Zoophilia in men: A study of sexual interest in animals. *Archives of Sexual Behavior, 32,* 523–535.

Williams, Colin J., Weinberg, M., & Rosenberger, J. (2013). Trans men: Embodiments, identities, and sexualities. *Sociological Forum, 28,* 719.

Williams, Colin J., Weinberg, M., & Rosenberger, J. (2016). Trans women doing sex in San Francisco. *Archives of Sexual Behavior, 45,* 1665–1678.

Williams, Scott, & Lettieri, Christopher. (2012). Sexsomnia: Clinical analysis of an underdiagnosed parasomnia. *Medscape.* Retrieved from www.medscape.com/viewarticle/762976

Willness, Chelsea R., et al. (2007). A meta-analysis of the antecedents and consequences of workplace sexual harassment. *Personnel Psychology, 60,* 127–162.

Willoughby, Brian J., Farero, A., & Busby, D. (2014). Exploring the effects of sexual desire discrepancy among married couples. *Archives of Sexual Behavior, 43,* 551–562.

Wilson, R. J., Looman, J., Abracen, J., & Pake, D. R., Jr. (2013). Comparing sexual offenders at the Regional Treatment Centre (Ontario) and the Florida Civil Commitment Center. *International Journal of Offender Therapy and Comparative Criminology, 57,* 377–395.

Wilson, W. Cody. (1973). Pornography: The emergence of a social issue and the beginning of psychological study. *Journal of Social Issues, 29,* 7–17.

Wimpissinger, Florian, et al. (2009). Magnetic resonance imaging of female prostate pathology. *Journal of Sexual Medicine, 6,* 1704–1711.

Wincze, John P., & Carey, Michael P. (2001). *Sexual dysfunction: A guide for assessment and treatment* (2nd ed.). New York: Guilford.

Winer, Rachel L., & Koutsky, Laura A. (2008). Genital human papillomavirus infection. In K. Holmes et al. (Eds.), *Sexually transmitted diseases* (4th ed., pp. 489–508). New York: McGraw-Hill.

Winer, Rachel L., et al. (2006). Condom use and the risk of genital human papillomavirus infection in young women. *New England Journal of Medicine, 354,* 2645–2654.

Wingert, Pat. (2002, February 11). Sex education: "Values trump data." *Newsweek,* 8.

Winn, Rhonda L., & Newton, Niles. (1982). Sexuality in aging: A study of 106 cultures. *Archives of Sexual Behavior, 11,* 283–298.

Winter, Jeremy S. D., & Couch, Robert M. (1995). Sexual differentiation. In P. Felig, J. D. Baxter, & L. A. Frohman (Eds.), *Endocrinology and metabolism* (3rd ed., pp. 1053–1104). New York: McGraw-Hill.

Winter, Sam, et al. (2016). The proposed ICD-11 gender incongruence of childhood diagnosis: A World Professional Association for Transgender Health membership survey. *Archives of Sexual Behavior, 45,* 1605–1614.

Wirtz, John G., et al. (2018). The effect of exposure to sexual appeals in advertisements on memory, attitude, and purchase intention: A meta-analytic review. *International Journal of Advertising, 37,* 168–198.

Wise, J. (2015). Teenagers want schools to give them more information about sex. *British Medical Journal, 350,* 256.

Wisniewski, A. B., et al. (2000). Complete androgen insensitivity syndrome: Long-term medical, surgical, and psychosexual outcome. *Journal of Clinical Endocrinology & Metabolism, 85,* 2664–2669.

Wisniewski, Amy B., et al. (2001). Congenital micropenis: Long-term medical, surgical, and psychosexual follow-up of individuals raised male or female. *Hormone Research, 56,* 3–11.

Wiswell, Thomas E., et al. (1987). Declining frequency of circumcision: Implications for changes in the absolute incidence and male to female sex ratio of urinary tract infections in early infancy. *Pediatrics, 79,* 338–342.

Woertman, Liesbeth, & van den Brink, Femke. (2012). Body image and female sexual functioning and behavior: A review. *Journal of Sex Research, 49,* 184–211.

Wolak, J., Finkelhor, D., & Mitchell, K. (2011a). Child pornography possessors: Trends in offender and case characteristics. *Sexual Abuse: A Journal of Research and Treatment, 23,* 22-42.

Wolak, J., Finkelhor, D., Mitchell, K. J., & Jones, L. M. (2011b). Arrests for child pornography production: Data at two time points from a national sample of U.S. law enforcement agencies. *Child Maltreatment, 16,* 184-195.

Wolak, Janis, et al. (2008). Online "predators" and their victims. *American Psychologist, 63,* 111-128.

Wolak, Janis, et al. (2012). How often are teens arrested for sexting? Data from a national sample of police cases. *Pediatrics, 129,* 4-12.

Wolak, Janis, et al. (2018). Sextortion of minors: Characteristics and dynamics. *Journal of Adolescent Health, 62,* 72-79.

Wonders, N. A., & Michalowski, R. (2001). Bodies, borders and sex tourism in a globalized world: A tale of two cities—Amsterdam and Havana. *Social Problems, 48,* 545-571.

Wood, Julia T. (1994). *Gendered lives: Communication, gender, and culture.* Belmont, CA: Wadsworth.

Wood, Matthew, et al. (2017). "They're just pixel tits, man": Disputing the 'reality' of virtual reality pornography through the story completion method. *Proceedings of the 2017 ACM Sigchi Conference on Human Factors in Computing Systems,* 5439-5451.

Wood, N. S., et al. (2000). Neurologic and developmental disability after extremely preterm birth. *New England Journal of Medicine, 343,* 378-384.

Woods, Nancy, et al. (2009). Is the menopausal transition stressful? Observations of perceived stress from the Seattle Midlife Women's Health Study. *Menopause, 16,* 90-97.

Woods, Scott, & Raju, Uma. (2001). Maternal smoking and the risk of congenital birth defects: A cohort study. *Journal of the American Board of Family Practice, 14,* 330-334.

Woodzicka, Julie A., & LaFrance, Marianne. (2005). The effects of subtle sexual harassment on women's performance in a job interview. *Sex Roles, 53,* 67-78.

Workowski, Kimberly A., & Bolan, Gail A. (2015). Sexually transmitted diseases treatment guidelines, 2015. *MMWR, 64*(3), 1-135. Retrieved from https://www.cdc.gov/std/tg2015/tg-2015-print.pdf

World Health Organization. (2006). *Sexual health.* Retrieved from http://who.int/mediacentre/factsheets/fs241/en/

World Health Organization. (2012). *Female genital mutilation.* Fact sheet No. 241. Retrieved from www.who.int/mediacentre/factsheets/fs241/en/

World Wide Video v. City of Spokane, CV-02-00074-AAM (May 27, 2004).

Wosick-Correa, Kassia, & Joseph, Lauren. (2008). Sexy ladies sexing ladies: Women as consumers in strip clubs. *Journal of Sex Research, 45,* 201-216.

Wright, Alexi A., & Katz, Ingrid T. (2006). *Roe* versus reality—abortion and women's health. *New England Journal of Medicine, 355,* 1-9.

Wright, Jonathan L., et al. (2012). Circumcision and the risk of prostate cancer. *Cancer, 118,* 4437-4443.

Wright, P. (2013). U.S. males and pornography, 1973-2010: Consumption, predictors, correlates. *Journal of Sex Research, 50,* 60-71.

Wright, P., Bae, S., & Funk, M. (2013). United States women and pornography through four decades: Exposure, attitudes, behavior, individual differences. *Archives of Sexual Behavior, 42,* 1131-1144.

Wright, Paul J. (2009). Sexual socialization messages in mainstream entertainment mass media: A review and synthesis. *Sexuality & Culture, 13,* 181-200.

Wright, Paul J. (2011). Mass media effects on youth sexual behavior: Assessing the claim for causality. *Communication Yearbook, 35,* 343-385.

Wright, Paul J. (2015). Americans' attitudes toward premarital sex and pornography consumption: A national panel analysis. *Archives of Sexual Behavior, 44,* 81-88.

Wright, Paul J., et al. (2016). A meta-analysis of pornography consumption and actual acts of sexual aggression in general population studies. *Journal of Communication, 66,* 183-205.

Wright, Paul S., et al. (2017). Pornography consumption and satisfaction: A meta-analysis. *Human Communication Research, 43,* 315-343.

Wright, V. C., Chang, J., Jeng, G., Chen, M., & Macaluso, M. (2007). Assisted reproductive technology surveillance—United States, 2004. *Morbidity and Mortality Weekly Report, 56* (Surveillance Summary 06).

Wyatt, Gail E. (1997). *Stolen women: Reclaiming our sexuality, taking back our lives.* New York: Wiley.

Wyatt, Gail E., et al. (2013). The intersection of gender and ethnicity in HIV risk, interventions, and prevention. *American Psychologist, 68,* 247-260.

Wyatt, Gail E., Peters, S. D., & Guthrie, D. (1988). Kinsey revisited, Part I: Comparisons of the sexual socialization and sexual behavior of White women over 33 years. *Archives of Sexual Behavior, 17,* 201-240.

Wyatt, Tristram D. (2003). *Pheromones and animal behaviour.* New York: Cambridge University Press.

Wyatt, Tristram D. (2015). The search for human pheromones: The lost decades and the necessity of returning to first principles. *Proceedings of the Royal Society B, 282.*

Wylie, Kevan R., Jones, R., & Walters, S. (2003). The potential benefit of vacuum devices augmenting psychosexual therapy for erectile dysfunction: A randomized controlled trial. *Journal of Sex and Marital Therapy, 29,* 227-236.

Wynn, L. L., Foster, Angel, & Trussell, James. (2009). Can I get pregnant from oral sex? Sexual health misconceptions in emails to a reproductive health website. *Contraception, 71,* 91-97.

Wyrobek, A., Eskenazi, B., Young, W. S., Arnheim, N., Tiemann-Boegr, I., Jabs, E., Glaser, R., Pearson, F., & Evenson, D. (2006). Advancing age has different effects on DNA damage, chromatin integrity, gene mutations, and aneuploidies in sperm. *Proceedings of the National Academy of Sciences, 103,* 9601-9606.

Xue, Feng, et al. (2018). The role of the dorsal anterior insula in sexual risk: Evidence from an erotic Go/NoGo task and real-world risk-taking. *Human Brain Mapping, 39,* 1555-1562.

Yabiku, Scott, & Gager, Constance. (2009). Sexual frequency and the stability of marital and cohabiting unions. *Journal of Marriage and the Family, 71,* 983-1000.

Ybarra, Michele L., et al. (2016). Lifetime prevalence rates and overlap of physical, psychological, and sexual dating abuse perpetration and victimization in a national sample of youth. *Archives of Sexual Behavior, 45,* 1083-1099.

Yeater, Elizabeth, et al. (2012). Trauma and sex surveys meet minimal risk standards: Implications for Institutional Review Boards. *Psychological Science, 23,* 780-787.

Yeh, Hsiu-Chen, Lorenz, F., Wickrama, K. A. S., Conger, R., & Elder, G. H., Jr. (2006). Relationships among sexual satisfaction, marital quality and marital instability at midlife. *Journal of Family Psychology, 20,* 336-343.

Yim, Ilona S., et al. (2015). Biological and psychosocial predictors of postpartum depression: Systematic review and call for integration. *Annual Review of Clinical Psychology, 11,* 99-137.

Yoder, P. Stanley, et al. (2004). *Female genital cutting in the demographic and health surveys: A critical and comparative analysis.* DHS Comparative Reports No. 7. Calverton, MD: ORC Macro.

Yost, Megan R., & Thomas, Genéa. (2012). Gender and binegativity: Men's and women's attitudes toward male and female bisexuals. *Archives of Sexual Behavior, 41,* 691-702.

Yost, Megan R., & Zurbriggen, Eileen L. (2006). Gender differences in the enactment of sociosexuality: An examination of implicit social motives, sexual fantasies, coercive sexual attitudes, and aggressive sexual behavior. *Journal of Sex Research, 43,* 163–173.

Young, Kimberly, et al. (2000). Online infidelity: A new dimension in couple relationships with implications for evaluation and treatment. *Sexual Addiction and Compulsivity, 7,* 59–74.

Zainuddin, Ani A., & Mahdy, Zaleha A. (2017). The Islamic perspectives of gender-related issues in the management of patients with disorders of sex development. *Archives of Sexual Behavior, 46,* 353–360.

Zak, P. J., Kurzban, R. O., & Matzner, W. L. (2003). *The neurobiology of trust.* Society for Neuroscience Annual Meeting. Program No. 195.27.

Zaviačič, M. (1994). Sexual asphyxiophilia (Koczwarism) in women and the biological phenomenon of female ejaculation. *Medical Hypotheses, 42,* 318–322.

Zaviačič, M., et al. (2000a). Immunohistochemical study of prostate-specific antigen in normal and pathological human tissues: Special reference to the male and female prostate and breast. *Journal of Histotechnology, 23,* 105–111.

Zaviačič, M., et al. (2000b). Weight, size, macroanatomy, and histology of the normal prostate in the adult human female: A minireview. *Journal of Histotechnology, 23,* 61–69.

Zelizer, Viviana. (2006). Money, power, and sex. *Yale Journal of Law and Feminism, 18*(109), 303 ff.

Zentner, M., & Mitura, K. (2012). Stepping out of the caveman's shadow: Nations' gender gap predicts degree of sex differentiation in mate preferences. *Psychological Science, 23,* 1176–1185.

Zhang, Na, et al. (2012). Sexual infidelity in China: Prevalence and gender-specific correlates. *Archives of Sexual Behavior, 41,* 861–873.

Zhou, Jiang-Ning, et al. (1995). A sex difference in the human brain and its relation to transsexuality. *Nature, 378,* 68–70.

Zilbergeld, Bernie. (1992). *The new male sexuality.* New York: Bantam Books.

Zilbergeld, Bernie. (1999). *The new male sexuality* (rev. ed.). New York: Bantam.

Zilbergeld, Bernie, & Ellison, Carol Rinklieb. (1980). Desire discrepancies and arousal problems in sex therapy. In S. R. Leiblum & L. A. Pervin (Eds.), *Principles and practice of sex therapy* (pp. 65–104). New York: Guilford.

Zimmer, D. (1983). Interaction patterns and communication skills in sexually distressed and normal couples: Two experimental studies. *Journal of Sex and Marital Therapy, 9,* 251–265.

Zimmer-Gembeck, M., & Helfand, M. (2008). Ten years of longitudinal research on U.S. adolescent sexual behavior: Developmental correlates of sexual intercourse, and the importance of age, gender, and ethnic background. *Developmental Review, 28,* 153–224.

Zimmerman, J. (2015, March 9). The world's problem with sex ed. *The New York Times,* A17.

Zimmerman, Y., et al. (2015). Restoring testosterone levels by adding dehydroepiandrosterone to a drospirenone containing combined oral contraceptive: II. Clinical effects. *Contraception, 91,* 134–142.

Zitzmann, Michael, et al. (2017). Impact of various progestins with or without transdermal testosterone on gonadotropin levels for non-invasive hormonal male contraception: a randomized clinical trial. *Andrology, 5,* 516–526.

Zivony, A., & Lobel, T. (2014). The invisible stereotypes of bisexual men. *Archives of Sexual Behavior, 43,* 1165–1176.

Zlidar, V. M., et al. (2003). The reproductive revolution continues. *Population Reports,* Series M, No. 17. Baltimore, MD: Johns Hopkins University School of Public Health.

Zoldbrod, A. P. (1993). *Men, women, and infertility: Intervention and treatment strategies.* New York: Lexington Books.

Zucker, Kenneth J., et al. (2016). Gender dysphoria in adults. *Annual Review of Clinical Psychology, 12,* 217–247.

Zuk, M. (2002). *Sexual selections: What we can and can't learn about sex from animals.* Berkeley: University of California Press.

Zumpe, D., & Michael, R. P. (1968). The clutching reaction and orgasm in the female rhesus monkey (*Macaca mulatta*). *Journal of Endocrinology, 40,* 117–123.

Zurbriggen, E. L. (2010). Rape, war, and the socialization of masculinity: Why our refusal to give up war ensures that rape cannot be eradicated. *Psychology of Women Quarterly, 34,* 538–549.

Glossary

Abortion The termination of a pregnancy.

Abstinence-only programs Educational programs that promote abstinence as the sole means of preventing pregnancy and exposure to sexually transmitted diseases.

Acculturation The process of incorporating the beliefs and customs of a new culture.

Acquired erectile disorder Cases of erectile disorder in which the man at one time was able to have satisfactory erections but can no longer do so.

Acquired sexual disorder A sexual disorder that develops after a period of normal functioning.

Activating effects of hormones Effects of sex hormones in adulthood, resulting in the activation of behaviors, especially sexual behaviors and aggressive behaviors.

Adrenal glands Endocrine glands located just above the kidneys; in the female they are major producers of androgens.

Adrenarche In childhood, the maturation of the adrenal glands, resulting in increased secretion of androgens.

Adultery Voluntary sexual intercourse by a husband or wife with someone other than one's spouse; thus betrayal of one's marriage vows.

AIDS (acquired immune deficiency syndrome) A sexually transmitted disease that destroys the body's natural immunity to infection so that the person is susceptible to and may die from a disease such as certain pneumonias or cancers.

Amenorrhea The absence of menstruation.

Amniocentesis A test done to determine whether a fetus has birth defects; done by inserting a fine tube into the woman's abdomen in order to obtain a sample of amniotic fluid.

Amniotic fluid The watery fluid surrounding a developing fetus in the uterus.

Anal intercourse Insertion of the penis into the partner's rectum.

Analogous organs Organs in the male and female that have similar functions.

Androgen-insensitivity syndrome (AIS) A genetic condition in which the body is unresponsive to androgens so that a genetic male may be born with a female-appearing body.

Androgens A group of sex hormones, one of which is testosterone.

Anilingus Mouth stimulation of the partner's anus.

Antigay prejudice Negative attitudes and behaviors toward gays and lesbians.

Anti-trans prejudice Negative attitudes and behaviors toward trans individuals.

Aphrodisiac A substance that increases sexual desire.

Artificial insemination A procedure in which sperm are placed into the female reproductive system by means other than sexual intercourse.

Asceticism An approach to life emphasizing self-discipline and impulse control.

Asexuality A lack of sexual attraction.

Asphyxiophilia The practice of inducing in oneself a state of oxygen deficiency in order to create sexual arousal or to enhance excitement and orgasm; also called *erotic asphyxiation.*

Asymptomatic Having no symptoms.

Attachment A psychological bond that forms between an infant and the mother, father, or other caregiver.

Autoeroticism Sexual self-stimulation; for example, masturbation.

AZT A drug used to treat HIV-infected persons; also called *ZDV.*

Bartholin glands Two tiny glands located on either side of the vaginal entrance.

Basal body temperature (BBT) method A type of rhythm method of birth control in which the woman determines when she ovulates by keeping track of her temperature.

Behavior modification A set of operant conditioning techniques used to modify human behavior.

Behavior therapy A system of therapy based on learning theory, in which the focus is on the problem behavior and how it can be modified or changed.

Bibliotherapy The use of a self-help book to treat a disorder.

Bisexual A person whose sexual orientation is toward both men and women.

Bondage and discipline The use of physical or psychological restraint to enforce servitude, from which both participants derive sensual pleasure.

Booty call A communication to a person who is not a relationship partner, conveying an urgent request for sexual activity, perhaps including intercourse.

Braxton-Hicks contractions Contractions of the uterus during pregnancy that are not part of labor.

Brothel A house of prostitution where prostitutes and customers meet for sexual activity.

Calendar method A type of rhythm method of birth control in which the woman determines when she ovulates by keeping a calendar record of the length of her menstrual cycles.

Call girl The most expensive and exclusive category of sex worker.

Camgirls Women who sell erotic services using webcam technology, usually through a public chat room.

Candida A form of vaginitis causing a thick, white discharge; also called *moniliasis* or *yeast infection.*

Causal inference Reaching the conclusion that one factor actually causes or influences an outcome.

Celibacy The practice of remaining celibate. Sometimes used to refer to abstaining from sexual intercourse, the correct term for which is *chastity.* A *celibate* is a person who remains unmarried, usually for religious reasons.

Cervical mucus method A type of rhythm method of birth control in which the woman determines when she ovulates by checking her cervical mucus.

Cervix The lower part of the uterus, which goes to the vagina.

Cesarean section (C-section) A method of delivering a baby surgically by an incision in the abdomen.

Chancre A painless, ulcerlike lesion with a hard, raised edge that is a symptom of syphilis.

Chlamydia An organism causing a sexually transmitted disease. The symptoms in males are a thin, clear discharge and mild pain on urination; females are frequently asymptomatic.

Chorionic villus sampling (CVS) A technique for prenatal diagnosis of birth defects, involving taking a sample of cells from the chorionic villus and analyzing them.

Circumcision Surgical removal of the foreskin of the penis.

Cisgender A person whose natal gender and gender identity match, e.g., a person born with female genitals whose identity is female.

Classical conditioning The learning process in which a previously neutral stimulus (conditioned stimulus) is repeatedly paired with an unconditioned stimulus that reflexively elicits an unconditioned response. Eventually the conditioned stimulus itself will evoke the response.

Clitoral orgasm Freud's term for orgasm in females resulting from stimulation of the clitoris.

Clitoris A highly sensitive sexual organ in the female; the glans is in front of the vaginal entrance, and the rest of the clitoris extends deeper into the body.

Cognitive interference Negative thoughts that distract a person from focusing on the erotic experience.

Cognitive behavior therapy A form of therapy that combines behavior therapy and restructuring of negative thought patterns.

Cohabitation Unmarried people living together (with sexual relations assumed).

Coitus Sexual intercourse; insertion of the penis into the vagina.

Collectivistic cultures Those that emphasize interdependence and connections among people; the group is more important than the individual.

Colostrum A watery substance that is secreted from the breasts at the end of pregnancy and during the first few days after delivery.

Combination birth control pills Birth control pills that contain a combination of estrogen and progestin (progesterone).

Coming out The process of acknowledging to oneself, and then to others, that one is gay or lesbian.

Companionate love A feeling of deep attachment and commitment to a person with whom one has an intimate relationship.

Computer-assisted self-interview (CASI) A method of data collection in which the respondent fills out questionnaires on a computer.

Headphones and a soundtrack reading the questions can be added for young children or poor readers.

Congenital adrenal hyperplasia (CAH) A condition in which a genetic female produces abnormal levels of androgens prenatally and therefore has male-appearing genitals at birth.

Congenital syphilis A syphilis infection in a newborn baby resulting from transmission from an infected mother.

Content analysis A set of procedures used to make valid inferences about text.

Convenience sample A sample chosen in a haphazard manner relative to the population of interest. Not a random or probability sample.

Conversion or reparative therapy Any one of a number of treatments designed to turn LGBs into heterosexuals.

Coprophilia Deriving sexual satisfaction from contact with feces.

Corpora cavernosa Two spongy bodies running the length of the top of the penis.

Corpus luteum The mass of cells of the follicle remaining after ovulation; it secretes progesterone.

Corpus spongiosum A spongy body running the length of the underside of the penis.

Correlation A number that measures the relationship between two variables.

Correlational study A study in which the researcher does not manipulate variables but rather studies naturally occurring relationships (correlations) among variables.

Cost–benefit approach An approach to analyzing the ethics of a research study based on weighing the costs of the research (the participants' time, the stress to participants, and so on) against the benefits of the research (gaining knowledge about human sexuality).

Cowper's glands Glands that secrete a clear alkaline fluid into the male's urethra.

Cryptorchidism Undescended testes; the condition in which the testes do not descend to the scrotum as they should during prenatal development.

Culture The part of the environment created by humans, including the set of meanings that a group adopts; these meanings facilitate social coordination and clarify where boundaries between groups lie.

Cunnilingus Mouth stimulation of the female genitals.

Cyberaffair A romantic or sexual relationship initiated by online contact and maintained primarily via online communication, involving a person who is married or in a committed relationship.

Decriminalization Removing an act from those prohibited by law, ceasing to define it as a crime.

Delayed ejaculation A sexual disorder in which the man cannot have an orgasm, even though he is highly aroused and has had a great deal of sexual stimulation; also called *male orgasmic disorder.*

Diaphragm A cap-shaped rubber contraceptive device that fits inside a woman's vagina over the cervix.

Differential susceptibility to media effects model A theoretical model from communications theory that specifies who chooses to view certain media (e.g., pornography), how the viewing has its effects, and who is especially susceptible to the effects.

Differential susceptibility model Some people are more susceptible than others to certain types of media (e.g., violent media).

Dilation An opening up of the cervix during labor; also called *dilatation.*

Dildo A rubber or plastic cylinder, often shaped like a penis.

Direct observation A behavioral measure in which the scientist directly observes the behavior being studied.

Discrepancy of sexual desire A sexual disorder in which the partners have considerably different levels of sexual desire.

Disorders of sex development (DSD) A newer term for intersex conditions.

Documenting Giving specific examples of the issue being discussed.

Dominance and submission The use of power consensually given to control the sexual stimulation and behavior of the other person.

Drag queen A man who dresses in women's clothing.

Dual control model A model that holds that sexual response is controlled both by sexual excitation and by sexual inhibition.

Dualism A religious or philosophical belief that body and spirit are separate and opposed to each other and that the goal of life is to free the spirit from the bondage of the body; thus a depreciation of the material world and the physical aspect of humanity.

Dysmenorrhea Painful menstruation.

Dyspareunia Painful intercourse.

Ectopic pregnancy A pregnancy in which the fertilized egg implants somewhere other than the uterus.

Edema Excessive fluid retention and swelling.

Editing Censoring or not saying things that would be deliberately hurtful to your partner or that are irrelevant.

Effacement A thinning out of the cervix during labor.

Effective communicator A communicator whose impact matches their intent.

Ego According to Freud, the part of the personality that helps the person have realistic, rational interactions.

Electra complex According to Freud, the sexual attraction of a little girl for her father.

Embryo transfer A procedure in which an embryo is transferred from the uterus of one woman into the uterus of another.

Endocrine disrupters Chemicals in the environment that affect the endocrine system and cause adverse effects on animals, including humans.

Endometriosis A condition in which the endometrium grows abnormally outside the uterus; the symptom is unusually painful periods with excessive bleeding.

Epididymis A highly coiled tube located on the edge of the testes; where sperm mature.

Epigenetics A functional change to DNA that does not alter the genetic code itself but leads to changes in gene expression. Often an epigenetic change involves methylation, that is, a methyl group is attached to the base cytosine in the DNA.

Episiotomy An incision made in the skin just behind the vagina, allowing the baby to be delivered more easily.

Equity theory A theory stating that people mentally calculate the benefits and costs for them in a relationship; their behavior is then affected by whether they feel there is equity or inequity, and they will act to restore equity if there is inequity.

Erectile disorder The inability to have or maintain an erection.

Erogenous zones Areas of the body that are particularly sensitive to sexual stimulation.

Eros According to love styles theory, a powerful physical attraction to the loved person.

Erotica Sexually arousing material that is not degrading or demeaning to women, men, or children.

Estrogens A group of sex hormones, one of which is estradiol.

Ethics A system of moral principles; a way of determining right and wrong.

Ethnocentrism The tendency to regard one's own ethnic group and culture as superior to others and to believe that its customs and way of life are the standards by which other cultures should be judged.

Ethnography A research method used to provide a description of a human group, a social setting, or a society.

Evolution A theory that all living things have acquired their present forms through gradual changes in their genetic endowment over successive generations.

Evolutionary psychology The study of psychological mechanisms that have been shaped by natural selection.

Excitement The first stage of sexual response, during which erection in males and vaginal lubrication in females occur.

Exhibitionism Showing one's genitals in a public place, to passersby; indecent exposure.

Exhibitionist A person who derives sexual gratification from exposing his genitals to a nonconsenting person.

Experiment A type of research study in which one variable (the independent variable) is manipulated by the experimenter while all other factors are held constant; the researcher can then study the effects of the independent variable on some measured variable (the dependent variable); the researcher is permitted to make causal inferences about the effects of the independent variable on the dependent variable.

Extramarital sex Sex between a married person and someone other than the spouse. Adultery.

Eye-tracking A behavioral measure in which a device measures the participant's point of gaze over time.

Failure rate The pregnancy rate occurring using a particular contraceptive method; the percentage of women who will be pregnant after a year of use of the method.

Fallopian tubes The tubes extending from the uterus to the ovary; also called the *oviducts*.

Familismo Among Latinx, a strong cultural valuing of one's nuclear and extended family.

Fellatio Mouth stimulation of the male genitals.

Female genital cutting Cutting or removing parts of the clitoris or inner and outer lips. Also called *female genital mutilation*.

Female impersonator A man or woman who impersonates a specific woman as part of a job in entertainment.

Female orgasmic disorder A sexual disorder in which the woman is unable to have an orgasm.

Female sexual arousal disorder (FSAD) A sexual disorder in which there is a lack of response to sexual stimulation.

Female sexual interest/arousal disorder A diagnosis in *DSM-5* that encompasses lack of interest in sexual activity and absent or reduced arousal during sexual interactions. The diagnosis is limited to women.

Female-to-male transsexual (FTM) A transsexual whose natal gender is female and whose identity is male.

Fertility cult A form of nature religion in which the fertility of the soil is encouraged through various forms of ritual magic, often including ritual sexual intercourse.

Fetal alcohol syndrome (FAS) Serious growth deficiency and malformations in the child of a mother who abuses alcohol during pregnancy.

Fetishism A person's sexual fixation on some object other than another human being and attachment of great erotic significance to that object.

Fighting fair A set of rules designed to make arguments constructive rather than destructive.

First-stage labor The beginning of labor, during which there are regular contractions of the uterus; the stage lasts until the cervix is dilated 8 centimeters (3 inches).

Fluctuating asymmetry Asymmetry of bilateral features, e.g., on the face, that are on average symmetrical in the population.

Follicle-stimulating hormone (FSH) A hormone secreted by the pituitary; it stimulates follicle development in females and sperm production in males.

Follicular phase The first phase of the menstrual cycle, beginning just after menstruation, during which an egg matures in preparation for ovulation.

Foreskin A layer of skin covering the glans or tip of the penis in an uncircumcised male; also called the *prepuce.*

Fornication The term for sex by unmarried people and, more generally, all immoral sexual behavior.

Framing theory The theory that the media draw attention to certain topics and not to others, suggesting how we should think about or frame the issues.

Frequency How often a person does something.

Friends with benefits A situation in which two people who are friends (not romantic partners) occasionally have sex with each other.

Frotteurism Deriving sexual satisfaction from fantasies, urges, or behaviors involving touching or rubbing one's genitals against the body of a nonconsenting person.

Fuck buddy Refers to a partner with whom one regularly engages in sexual activity but not other types of activity and is not a friend.

Gay Homosexual; especially male homosexuals.

Gender Being male, female, or some other gender such as trans.

Gender binary Conceptualizing gender as having only two categories, male and female.

Gender dysphoria Psychological distress about a mismatch between a person's gender identity and natal gender.

Gender-neutral evolutionary theory A theory that human behavior evolved to be flexible and adaptive across different environments; thus behaviors are not predetermined and gender differences in behavior are not predetermined and fixed.

Gender role A set of norms, or culturally defined expectations, that define how people of one gender ought to behave.

Gender-segregated social organization A form of social organization in which boys play and associate with other boys, and girls play and associate with other girls; that is, the genders are separate from each other.

Genital herpes A sexually transmitted disease, the symptoms of which are small, painful bumps or blisters on the genitals.

Genital warts A sexually transmitted infection causing warts on the genitals.

Genito-pelvic pain/penetration disorder The term in *DSM-5* for pain during sex (dyspareunia) or vaginismus, which tend to occur together.

GIFT Gamete intrafallopian transfer, a procedure in which sperm and eggs are collected and then inserted together into the fallopian tube.

Gigolo A man who provides companionship and sexual gratification on a continuing basis to a woman in exchange for money.

GnRH (gonadotropin-releasing hormone) A hormone secreted by the hypothalamus that regulates the pituitary's secretion of gonad-stimulating hormones.

Gonorrhea A sexually transmitted infection that usually causes symptoms of a puslike discharge and painful, burning urination in males but is frequently asymptomatic in females.

Gräfenberg spot (G spot) A small region on the front wall of the vagina, emptying into the urethra, and responsible for female ejaculation.

Hedonism A moral system based on maximizing pleasure and avoiding pain.

Hepatitis B A liver disease that can be transmitted sexually or by needle sharing.

Heteronormativity The belief that heterosexuality is the norm and that all people are heterosexual.

Heterosexism Prejudice against and denigration of LGB persons.

Heterosexual A person whose sexual orientation is toward members of the other gender.

HIV Human immune deficiency virus; the virus that causes AIDS.

Homologous organs Organs in the male and female that develop from the same embryonic tissue.

Homophily The tendency to have contact with people who are equal in social status.

Homophobia A strong, irrational fear of homosexuals; negative attitudes and reactions to homosexuals.

Homosexual A person whose sexual orientation is toward members of the same gender.

Honor cultures Those that stress "face," that is, individuals' reputation and the respect or honor that people show toward others.

Hooking up A sexual encounter that involves people who are strangers or brief acquaintances, without an expectation of forming a committed relationship; the behavior itself may range from making out to oral sex or intercourse.

Hormones Chemical substances secreted by the endocrine glands into the bloodstream.

HPG axis Hypothalamus–pituitary–gonad axis, the negative feedback loop that regulates sex-hormone production.

HPV Human papillomavirus, the virus that causes cervical cancer.

Human chorionic gonadotropin (hCG) A hormone secreted by the placenta; it is the hormone detected in pregnancy tests.

Humanism A philosophical system that holds that ethical judgments must be made on the basis of human experience and human reason.

Hustler A male sex worker who sells his services to men.

Hyaluronidase An enzyme secreted by the sperm that allows one sperm to penetrate the egg.

Hymen A thin membrane that may partially cover the vaginal entrance.

Hypersexuality An excessive, insatiable sex drive in a person.

Hypoactive sexual desire (HSD) A sexual disorder in which there is a lack of interest in sexual activity; also termed *inhibited sexual desire* or *low sexual desire.*

Hypothalamus A small region of the brain that is important in regulating many body functions, including the functioning of the sex hormones.

Hysterectomy Surgical removal of the uterus.

"I" language Speaking for yourself, using the word "I," not mind reading.

ICSI (intra-cytoplasmic sperm injection) A type of assisted reproductive technology in which one sperm is injected directly into the cytoplasm of the egg to accomplish a fertilization outside the body.

Id According to Freud, the part of the personality containing the libido.

Immediate causes Various factors that occur in the act of lovemaking that inhibit sexual response.

Impact What someone else understands the speaker to mean.

In vitro fertilization (IVF) A procedure in which an egg is fertilized by sperm in a laboratory dish.

In-call service A residence in which prostitutes work regular shifts, selling sexual services on an hourly basis.

Incest Sexual activity between relatives.

Incest taboo A societal regulation prohibiting sexual interaction between blood relatives, such as brother and sister or father and daughter.

Incidence The number of new cases within a specified time period.

Individualistic cultures Those that stress independence and autonomy and the individual rights of people.

Infertility A woman's inability to conceive and give birth to a child, or a man's inability to impregnate a woman.

Informed consent An ethical principle in research in which people have a right to be informed, before participating, of what they will be asked to do in the research.

Inhibin A hormone secreted by the testes and ovaries that regulates FSH levels.

Inner lips Thin folds of skin on either side of the vaginal entrance.

Intent What the speaker means.

Intercoder reliability In content analysis, the correlation or percentage of agreement between two coders independently rating the same texts.

Interfemoral intercourse A sexual technique used by gay men in which one man moves his penis between the thighs of the other.

Intersectionality An approach that simultaneously considers the consequences of multiple group memberships, e.g., the intersection of gender and ethnicity.

Intersex A condition in which the individual has a mixture of male and female reproductive structures, so that it is not clear at birth whether the individual is a male or a female. Formerly called a *pseudohermaphrodite.*

Interstitial cells Cells in the testes that manufacture testosterone.

Intimacy A quality of relationships characterized by commitment, feelings of closeness and trust, and self-disclosure.

Intrauterine device (IUD) A plastic device sometimes containing metal or a hormone that is inserted into the uterus for contraceptive purposes; also called *intrauterine contraceptive (IUC).*

Introitus The vaginal entrance.

Justice principle An ethical principle in research that holds that the risks of participation should be distributed fairly across groups in society, as should the benefits.

Kegel exercises A part of sex therapy for women with orgasmic disorder, in which the woman exercises the muscles surrounding the vagina; also called *pubococcygeal* or *PC muscle exercises.*

Kiddie porn Pictures or videos of sexual acts involving children under the age of 18.

Kisspeptin A hormone involved in the initiation of pubertal development.

Lamaze method A method of "prepared" childbirth involving relaxation and controlled breathing.

Laparoscopy A method of female sterilization.

LARC Long-Acting, Reversible Contraceptives; implants and IUDs.

Late syphilis The fourth and final stage of syphilis, during which the disease does damage to major organs of the body such as the heart or brain.

Latent syphilis The third stage of syphilis, which may last for years, during which symptoms disappear although the person is still infected.

Latinx A term for Latinos that gets around the gender designations of Latino and Latina and includes people outside the gender binary.

Legalism Ethics based on the assumption that there are rules for human conduct and that morality consists of knowing the rules and obeying them.

Leptin A hormone related to the onset of puberty.

Lesbian A woman whose sexual orientation is toward other women.

Leveling Telling your partner what you are feeling by stating your thoughts clearly, simply, and honestly.

Libido In psychoanalytic theory, the term for the sex energy or sex drive.

Lifelong erectile disorder Cases of erectile disorder in which the man has never had an erection sufficient to have intercourse.

Lifelong sexual disorder A sexual disorder that has been present ever since the person began sexual functioning.

Lifespan development Development from birth through old age.

Limbic system A set of structures in the interior of the brain, including the amygdala, hippocampus, and fornix; believed to be important for sexual behavior in both animals and humans.

Ludus According to love styles theory, a playful type of love.

Lumpectomy A surgical treatment for breast cancer in which only the lump and a small bit of surrounding tissue are removed.

Luteal phase The third phase of the menstrual cycle, following ovulation.

Luteinizing hormone (LH) A hormone secreted by the pituitary; it regulates estrogen secretion and ovum development in females and testosterone production in males.

Madam A woman who manages a brothel, in-call, out-call, or escort service.

Male condom A contraceptive sheath that is placed over the penis; also called an external condom.

Male-to-female transsexual (MTF) A transsexual whose natal gender is male and whose identity is female.

Marital rape The rape of a person by their current or former spouse.

Massage parlor A place where massages, as well as sexual services, can generally be purchased.

Masturbation Stimulation of one's own genitals with the hand or with some object, such as a pillow or vibrator.

Matching phenomenon The tendency for individuals to choose as partners people who match them, that is, who are similar in attitudes, intelligence, and attractiveness.

Mean The average of respondents' scores.

Median The middle score.

Medical model A theoretical model in psychology and psychiatry in which mental problems are thought of as sickness or mental illness; the problems in turn are often thought to be due to biological factors.

Medicalization of sexuality The process by which certain sexual behavior or conditions are defined in terms of health and illness, and problematic experiences or practices are given medical treatment.

Menarche First menstruation.

Menopause The cessation of menstruation.

Menstrual synchrony The convergence, over several months, of the dates of onset of menstrual periods among women who are in close contact with each other.

Menstruation The fourth phase of the menstrual cycle, during which the endometrium of the uterus is sloughed off in the menstrual discharge.

Mere-exposure effect The tendency to like a person more if we have been exposed to them repeatedly.

Meta-analysis A statistical method that allows the researcher to combine the results of all prior studies on a particular question to see what, taken together, they say.

Mifepristone (RU-486) The "abortion pill."

Mind reading Making assumptions about what your partner thinks or feels.

Mindfulness The technique of focusing one's attention on experiences in the present moment in a calm, nonjudgmental way.

Mindfulness therapy A system of training people in mindfulness practices; one goal is to help people regulate their own negative emotions.

Misattribution of arousal When a person in a state of physiological arousal (e.g., from exercising or being in a frightening situation), attributes these feelings to love or attraction to the person present.

Miscarriage The termination of a pregnancy before the fetus is viable, as a result of natural causes (not medical intervention); also called *spontaneous abortion.*

Mons pubis The fatty pad of tissue under the pubic hair.

Moralism A religious or philosophical attitude that emphasizes moral behavior, usually according to strict standards, as the highest goal of human life. Moralists tend to favor strict regulation of human conduct to help make people good.

Moral panic An extreme social response to the belief that the moral condition of society is deteriorating at a rapid pace.

Müllerian ducts Ducts found in both male and female fetuses; in males they degenerate, and in females they develop into the fallopian tubes, the uterus, and the upper part of the vagina.

Multiple orgasm A series of orgasms occurring within a short period of time.

Myotonia Muscle contraction.

Natural selection A process in nature resulting in greater rates of survival of those plants and animals that are best adapted to their environment.

Necrophilia Sexual contact with a dead person.

Nonverbal communication Communication not through words, but through the body; e.g., eye contact, tone of voice, touching.

Nymphomania An excessive, insatiable sex drive in a woman.

Obscenity That which is offensive to decency or modesty, or calculated to arouse sexual excitement or lust.

Oedipus complex According to Freud, the sexual attraction of a little boy for his mother.

Oophorectomy Surgical removal of the ovaries.

Operant conditioning The process of changing the frequency of a behavior (the operant) by following it with positive reinforcement (which will make the behavior more frequent in the future) or punishment (which should make the behavior less frequent in the future).

Organic factors of sexual disorders Physical factors, such as disease or injury, that cause sexual disorders.

Organizing effects of hormones Effects of sex hormones early in development, resulting in a permanent change in the brain or reproductive system.

Orgasm The second stage of sexual response, an intense sensation that occurs at the peak of sexual arousal and is followed by release of sexual tensions.

Orgasmic platform A tightening of the entrance to the vagina caused by contractions of the bulbospongiosus muscle (which covers the vestibular bulbs) that occur during the excitement stage of sexual response.

Out-call service A service that sends a sex worker to a location specified by the client to provide sexual services.

Outer lips Rounded pads of fatty tissue lying on either side of the vaginal entrance.

Ovaries Two organs on either side of the uterus that produce eggs and sex hormones.

Ovulation Release of an egg from the ovaries; the second phase of the menstrual cycle.

Oxytocin A pituitary hormone that stimulates milk ejections from the nipples and contractions of the uterus during childbirth.

Pansexual A person who is sexually or romantically attracted to people regardless of their gender.

Paraphilia Unusual, unconventional sexual behavior.

Paraphilic disorder Paraphilia that causes the person distress or impairs their functioning, or causes harm to self or others.

Paraphrasing Saying, in your own words, what you thought your partner meant.

Parental investment In evolutionary theories, behaviors or other investments in the offspring by the parent that increase the offspring's chance of survival.

Participant-observer technique A research method in which the scientist becomes part of the community to be studied and makes observations from inside the community.

Passionate love A state of intense longing for union with the other person and of intense physiological arousal.

Pederasty Sex between an older man and a younger man, or a boy; sometimes called *boy love.*

Pedophilia An adult having sexual activity with a prepubescent child.

Pelvic inflammatory disease (PID) An infection and inflammation of the pelvic organs, such as the fallopian tubes and the uterus.

Penile prosthesis A surgical treatment for erectile dysfunction, in which inflatable tubes are inserted into the penis.

Penile strain gauge A device used to measure physiological sexual arousal in the male; it is a flexible loop that fits around the base of the penis.

Penis The male external sexual organ, which functions both in sexual activity and in urination.

Performativity Ways in which we perform gender or sexuality based on society's norms, much as actors perform in a play.

Perineum The skin between the vaginal entrance and the anus.

Pheromones Biochemicals secreted outside the body that are important in communication between animals and that may serve as sex attractants.

Photoplethysmograph An acrylic cylinder placed inside the vagina to measure physiological sexual arousal in the female. Also called a *photometer.*

Pimp A prostitute's companion, protector, and master.

Pituitary gland A small endocrine gland located on the lower side of the brain below the hypothalamus; the pituitary is important in regulating levels of sex hormones.

Placenta An organ formed on the wall of the uterus through which the fetus receives oxygen and nutrients and gets rid of waste products.

Pluralism A philosophical or political attitude that affirms the value of many competing opinions and believes that the truth is discovered in the clash of diverse perspectives. Pluralists, therefore, believe in the maximum human freedom possible.

Polyamory The nonpossessive, honest, responsible, and ethical philosophy and practice of loving multiple people simultaneously.

Population A group of people a researcher wants to study and make inferences about.

Pornography Sexually arousing art, literature, or films.

Postpartum depression Mild to moderate depression in women following the birth of a baby.

Posttraumatic growth Positive life changes and psychological development following exposure to trauma.

Posttraumatic stress disorder (PTSD) Long-term psychological distress suffered by someone who has experienced a terrifying event.

Preeclampsia A serious disease of pregnancy, marked by high blood pressure, severe edema, and proteinuria.

Preexposure prophylaxis (PrEP) The use of antiretroviral drugs to prevent infection in people who are HIV-negative and are in a high-risk category.

Premature (early) ejaculation A sexual disorder in which the man ejaculates too soon and cannot control when he ejaculates. Also called *rapid ejaculation*.

Premenstrual dysphoric disorder (PMDD) A diagnostic category in the *DSM-5,* characterized by symptoms such as sadness, anxiety, and irritability, in the week before menstruation.

Premenstrual syndrome (PMS) A combination of severe physical and psychological symptoms, such as depression and irritability, occurring just before menstruation.

Prenatal period The time from conception to birth.

Prevalence The percentage of people in a population who have engaged in a certain behavior or have a certain condition at a specific point in time.

Primary-stage syphilis The first few weeks of a syphilis infection during which the chancre is present.

Prior learning Things that people have learned earlier—for example, in childhood—that now affect their sexual response.

Probability sampling An excellent method of sampling in research in which each member of the population has a known probability of being included in the sample.

Problem of refusal or nonresponse The problem that some people will refuse to participate in a sex survey, thus making it difficult to study a random sample.

Progesterone A sex hormone secreted by the ovaries as well as the testes.

Prolactin A pituitary hormone that stimulates milk production by the mammary glands.

Prostaglandins Chemicals secreted by the uterus that cause the uterine muscles to contract; they are the cause of painful menstruation.

Prostate The gland in the male, located below the bladder, that secretes some of the fluid in semen.

Prostatectomy Surgical removal of the prostate.

Prostatitis An infection or inflammation of the prostate gland.

Prostitutes/commercial sex workers People who engage in sexual acts in return for money or drugs and do so in a promiscuous, fairly nondiscriminating fashion.

Prostitution The exchange of sex for money or other payment such as drugs.

Pseudocyesis False pregnancy, in which the woman displays the signs of pregnancy but is not pregnant.

Psychoanalytic theory A psychological theory originated by Sigmund Freud; it contains a basic assumption that part of the human personality is unconscious.

Puberty The time during which there is sudden enlargement and maturation of the gonads, other genitalia, and secondary sex characteristics, so that the individual becomes capable of reproduction.

Pubic lice Tiny lice that attach themselves to the base of pubic hairs and cause itching; also called *crabs.*

Pubococcygeus muscle A muscle around the vaginal entrance.

Purposeful distortion Purposely giving false information in a survey.

Qualitative research A collection of naturalistic, holistic methods, including participant observation and in-depth interviewing, in which results are conveyed not in numbers but in words.

Queer A self-label used by some LGBs, as well as by some heterosexuals who prefer unusual sexual practices.

Racial microaggressions Subtle insults directed at people of color and often done nonconsciously.

Radical mastectomy A surgical treatment for breast cancer in which the entire breast, as well as underlying muscles and lymph nodes, is removed.

Random sample An excellent method of sampling in research in which each member of the population has an equal chance of being included in the sample.

Rape Nonconsenting oral, anal, or vaginal penetration obtained by force, by threat of bodily harm, or when the victim is incapable of giving consent.

Rape culture Deeply entrenched cultural attitudes about gender and sexuality that shape people's attitudes about rape; rape myths are an integral part of rape culture.

Refractory period The period following orgasm during which the male cannot be sexually aroused.

Reinforcing spiral theory A theory that one's social identities and ideologies predict one's media use and, in turn, media use affects our identity and beliefs.

Resolution The third phase of sexual response, in which the body returns to the unaroused state.

Retrograde ejaculation A condition in which orgasm in the male is not accompanied by an external ejaculation; instead, the ejaculate goes into the urinary bladder.

Rhythm (fertility awareness) method A method of birth control that involves abstaining from intercourse around the time the woman ovulates.

Saliromania A desire to damage or soil a woman or her clothes.

Sample A part of a population.

Satyriasis An excessive, insatiable sex drive in a man; also called *Don Juanism.*

Schema A general knowledge framework that a person has about a particular topic.

Scrotum The pouch of skin that contains the testes in the male.

Second-stage labor The stage during which the baby moves out through the vagina and is delivered.

Secondary-stage syphilis The second stage of syphilis, occurring several months after infection, during which the chancre has disappeared and a generalized body rash appears.

Selectivity In media theories, the principle that people select and pay attention only to certain media and ignore others.

Self-disclosure Telling personal things about yourself.

Self-efficacy A sense of competence at performing an activity.

Seminal vesicles Saclike structures that lie above the prostate and produce about 60 percent of the seminal fluid.

Seminiferous tubules Tubules in the testes that manufacture sperm.

Sensate focus exercise A part of the sex therapy developed by Masters and Johnson in which one partner caresses the other, the other communicates what is pleasurable, and there are no performance demands.

Sex tourism Leisure travel with the purpose of purchasing sexual services.

Sex trafficking The recruitment and control of people for sexual exploitation.

Sexsomnia Refers to automatic, unintentional sexual behaviors during sleep; also called *sleep sex.*

Sextortion Online threats to expose sexual images with the goal of coercing victims to provide additional pictures or to engage in sex.

Sexual behavior Behavior that produces arousal and increases the chance of orgasm.

Sexual disorder A problem with sexual response that causes a person mental distress.

Sexual fantasy Sexual thoughts or images that alter the person's emotions or physiological state.

Sexual fluidity Changes that occur over time in sexual attraction, identity, or behavior.

Sexual health The state of physical, emotional, mental, and social well-being in relation to sexuality.

Sexual identity One's self-identity as gay, straight, lesbian, bisexual, queer, or something else.

Sexual masochist A person who experiences intense sexual arousal from being beaten, bound, humiliated, or made to suffer.

Sexual orientation A person's erotic and emotional orientation toward members of their own gender or members of the other gender.

Sexual rights Basic, inalienable rights regarding sexuality, both positive and negative, such as rights to reproductive self-determination and sexual self-expression and freedom from sexual abuse and violence.

Sexual sadist A person who experiences intense sexual arousal from the suffering of another person.

Sexual selection A specific type of selection that creates differences between males and females.

Sexual solicitation of youth on the Internet Cases in which a sexual predator "meets" a child or adolescent online, gains the youth's confidence, and arranges an in-person meeting.

Sexualization A process in which a person is valued only for sex appeal or behavior; is held to a standard that equates physical attractiveness with being sexy; is sexually objectified; or sexuality is inappropriately imposed on the person.

Singleism The stigmatizing and stereotyping of people who are not in a socially recognized couple relationship.

Situational orgasmic disorder A case of orgasmic disorder in which the woman is able to have an orgasm in some situations (e.g., while masturbating) but not in others (e.g., while having sexual intercourse).

Situationism Ethics based on the assumption that there are no absolute rules, or at least very few, and that each situation must be judged individually.

Sixty-nining Simultaneous mouth–genital stimulation; also called *soixante-neuf.*

Skene's gland Female prostate gland located on the front wall of the vagina.

Snowball sampling A method for acquiring a sample of people in which existing participants suggest names of future participants to be recruited. Also called *respondent-driven sampling.*

Social cognitive theory In communications theory, the idea that the media provide role models whom we imitate.

Social exchange theory A theory, based on the principle of reinforcement, that assumes that people will choose those actions that maximize rewards and minimize costs.

Socialization The ways in which society conveys to the individual its norms or expectations for their behavior.

Sociobiology The application of evolutionary biology to understanding the social behavior of animals, including humans.

Sodomy Originally "crimes against nature"; in contemporary laws, oral and anal intercourse.

Somatic cell nuclear transfer A cloning technique that involves substituting genetic material from an adult's cell for the nucleus of an egg.

Spectatoring Masters and Johnson's term for acting as an observer or judge of one's own sexual performance; thought to contribute to sexual disorders.

Sperm The mature male reproductive cell, capable of fertilizing an egg.

Spermicide A substance that kills sperm.

SRY Stands for sex-determining region, Y chromosome.

Stereotype A generalization about a group of people (e.g., men) that distinguishes them from others (e.g., women).

Sterilization A surgical procedure by which an individual is made sterile, that is, incapable of reproducing.

Storge In love styles theory, a very stable, reliable type of love.

Straight Heterosexual; that is, a person whose sexual orientation is toward members of the other gender.

Streetwalker A lower-status sex worker who walks the streets selling sexual services.

Strip club A bar or business that provides (almost) nude dancers and sexualized interactions, not necessarily physical sexual contact.

Subincision A form of male genital cutting in which a slit is made on the lower side of the penis along its entire length.

Supercision A form of male genital cutting in which a slit is made the length of the foreskin on top.

Superego According to Freud, the part of the personality containing the conscience.

Swinging A form of extramarital sex in which married couples exchange partners with others.

Symbolic interaction theory A theory based on the premise that human behavior and the social order are products of communication among people. Also called *symbolic interactionism.*

Sympto-thermal method A type of rhythm method of birth control combining the basal body temperature method and the cervical mucus method.

Syphilis A sexually transmitted infection that causes a chancre to appear in the primary stage.

Teratogen A substance that produces defects in a fetus.

Testes The pair of glands in the scrotum that manufacture sperm and sex hormones.

Testosterone A hormone secreted by the testes in males (and also present at lower levels in females).

Test-retest reliability A method for testing whether self-reports are reliable or accurate; participants are interviewed (or given a questionnaire) and then interviewed a second time sometime later to determine whether their answers are the same both times.

Therapeutic cloning Creating cells or tissues that are genetically identical to those of a patient, to treat a disease.

Third-stage labor The stage during which the afterbirth is expelled.

Trans A broad term encompassing those identifying as transgender, transsexual, agender, and other gender-variant people.

Transgender A term encompassing a broad range of individuals whose gender identity does not match their gender assigned at birth (natal gender); includes those who identify as nonbinary or gender-fluid, gender nonconforming, and transsexuals.

Transition The difficult part of labor at the end of the first stage, during which the cervix dilates from 8 to 10 centimeters (3 to 4 inches).

Transphobia A strong, irrational fear of trans people.

Transsexual A person who believes they were born with the body of the other gender, e.g., a person born with a male body who has a female identity. These individuals often seek medical gender confirmation procedures.

Transvestism The practice of dressing as a member of the other gender in order to experience sexual arousal.

Tribadism A sexual technique used by lesbians in which one woman lies on top of another and moves rhythmically in order to produce sexual pleasure, particularly clitoral stimulation.

Trichomoniasis A form of vaginitis causing a frothy white or yellow discharge with an unpleasant odor.

Triphasic model Kaplan's model of sexual response in which there are three components: vasocongestion, muscular contractions, and sexual desire.

Troilism Three people having sex together.

Two-component theory of love The theory that two conditions must exist simultaneously for passionate love to occur: physiological arousal and attaching a cognitive label ("love") to the feeling.

Umbilical cord The tube that connects the fetus to the placenta.

Urethra The tube through which urine passes from the bladder out of the body.

Uterus The organ in which the fetus develops.

Vacuum aspiration A method of abortion that is performed during the first trimester and involves suctioning out the contents of the uterus; also called *suction curettage*.

Vagina The tube-shaped organ into which the penis is inserted during coitus and through which a baby passes during birth.

Vaginal orgasm Freud's term for orgasm in females resulting from stimulation of the vagina in heterosexual intercourse; Freud considered vaginal orgasm to be more mature than clitoral orgasm.

Vaginismus A sexual disorder in which there is a spastic contraction of the muscles surrounding the entrance to the vagina, in some cases so severe that intercourse is impossible.

Vaginitis An irritation or inflammation of the vagina, usually causing a discharge.

Validation Telling your partner that, given their point of view, you can see why they think a certain way.

Vas deferens The tube through which sperm pass on their way from the testes and epididymis, out of the scrotum, and to the urethra.

Vasectomy A surgical procedure for male sterilization involving severing of the vas deferens.

Vasocongestion An accumulation of blood in the blood vessels of a region of the body, especially the genitals; a swelling or erection results.

Vestibular bulbs Erectile tissue running under the inner lips.

Viagra A drug used in the treatment of erectile disorder; sildenafil.

Victim-precipitated rape The view that rape is a result of a woman "asking for it."

Victorian compromise The decision not to criminalize behavior per se and instead criminalize conduct that is visible to the outside world.

Volunteer bias A bias in the results of sex surveys that arises when some people refuse to participate, so that those who are in the sample are volunteers who may in some ways differ from those who refuse to participate.

Voyeur A person who experiences sexual arousal from viewing unsuspecting person(s) who are nude, undressing, or having sex.

Voyeurism Secretly watching people who are nude.

Vulva The collective term for the external genitals of the female.

Withdrawal A method of birth control in which the man withdraws his penis from his partner's vagina before he has an orgasm and ejaculates.

Wolffian ducts Ducts found in both male and female fetuses; in females they degenerate, and in males they develop into the epididymis, the vas deferens, and the ejaculatory duct.

ZIFT Zygote intrafallopian transfer, an assisted reproductive technology in which the egg is fertilized by sperm in the laboratory, and then the developing fertilized egg (zygote) is placed in the fallopian tube.

Zika virus A virus that causes Zika fever and, when transmitted from mother to fetus during pregnancy, causes microcephaly in the baby.

Zoophilia Sexual contact with an animal; also called *bestiality* or *sodomy*.

Zygote A fertilized egg.

Index

Q

R

DIRECTORY OF RESOURCES

Following is a list of resources for additional information on topics covered in *Understanding Human Sexuality*.

I. HEALTH ISSUES: PREGNANCY, CONTRACEPTION, ABORTION, DISEASES

American Cancer Society
1599 Clifton Road, NE
Atlanta, GA 30329-4251
1-800-227-2345
www.cancer.org
Offers up-to-date and accurate information on cancer treatment and support. Funds research on cancer.

CDC National Prevention Information Network
P.O. Box 6003
Rockville, MD 20849-6003
1-800-458-5231
E-mail: info@cdcnpin.org
www.cdcnpin.org
Operated by the U.S. Public Health Service, this clearing house provides information and referrals on a variety of STIs in addition to HIV/AIDS.

La Leche League International
1400 N. Meacham Road
P.O. Box 4079
Schaumberg, IL 60168
847-519-7730
E-mail: lllhq@llli.org
www.llli.org
An organization devoted to helping mothers worldwide to breast-feed by providing mother-to-mother support, encouragement, education, and information.

NARAL Pro-Choice America
1725 Eye Street, NW Suite 900
Washington, D.C. 20006
202-973-3000
www.naral.org
A political action organization working at both state and national levels, dedicated to preserving a woman's right to safe and legal abortion and also to teaching effective use of the political process to ensure abortion rights.

Division of STD Prevention
Centers for Disease Control and Prevention
1600 Clifton Rd.
Atlanta, GA 30333
1-800-CDC-INFO
E-mail: dstd@cdc.gov
www.cdc.gov/std

Offers the most up-to-date information on prevention-related issues and sexually transmitted diseases and HIV; administers federal programs for the prevention of STD and HIV infection.

Lesbian, Gay, Bisexual, and Transgender Health
Centers for Disease Control and Prevention
1600 Clifton Rd.
Atlanta, GA 30333
1-800-CDC-INFO
E-mail: cdcinfo@cdc.gov
www.cdc.gov/lgbthealth
Devoted to the health needs of lesbian, gay, bisexual, and transgender individuals.

National Right to Life Committee, Inc.
512 Tenth Street, NW
Washington, D.C. 20004
202-626-8800
www.nrlc.org
An organization based on the belief that human life begins at conception and that abortions should therefore be opposed.

Healthy Women
157 Broad Street, Suite 106
Red Bank, NJ 07701
1-877-986-9472
www.healthywomen.org
A national clearinghouse on women's health information. Publishes a newsletter, *National Women's Health Report*.

Planned Parenthood Federation of America (PPFA)
434 West 33rd Street
New York, NY 10001
212-541-7800
www.plannedparenthood.org
PPFA is the nation's oldest and largest voluntary family planning agency. Through local clinics (call 1-800-230-PLAN for the clinic nearest you), it offers birth control information and services, pregnancy testing, voluntary sterilization, prenatal care, abortion, pelvic and breast exams, and other reproductive health services, including sexuality education.

Population Information Program (K4Health)
Johns Hopkins Center for Communication Programs
111 Market Place, Suite 310
Baltimore, MD 21202
410-659-6300
www.k4health.org
Publishes *Population Reports*, frequent, up-to-date reports on contraception and family planning with emphasis on developing countries.

II. SEX EDUCATION, SEX RESEARCH, AND SEX THERAPY

The Guttmacher Institute

125 Maiden Lane, 7th Floor
New York, NY 10038
212-248-1111
E-mail: info@guttmacher.org
www.guttmacher.org
A not-for-profit organization for reproductive health research, policy analysis, and public education. It produces many excellent, informative publications.

American Association of Sexuality Educators, Counselors, and Therapists (AASECT)

35 E Wacker Drive, Suite 850
Chicago, IL 60601
E-mail: aasect@aasect.org
www.aasect.org
This organization certifies sex educators, sex counselors, and sex therapists and provides other services associated with sexuality education and sex therapy.

Sexuality Information and Education Council of the United States (SIECUS)

1012 14th Street NW, Suite 1108
Washington, D.C. 20005
202-265-2405
E-mail: info@siecus.org
www.siecus.org
Provides a library and information service on sexuality education, including curricula. Publishes bibliographies and maintains a database of titles of books and journals on human sexuality, currently containing over 8,000 entries.

The Society for Scientific Study of Sexuality

881 Third Street, Suite B5
Whitehall, PA 18052
610-443-3100
www.sexscience.org
An organization devoted to promoting quality sex research; publishes the *Journal of Sex Research*.

III. LGBTQ ISSUES

The World Professional Association for Transgender Health (WPATH)

1300 South Second Street, Suite 180
Minneapolis, MN 55454
www.wpath.org
Society for professionals interested in the study and care of transsexualism and gender dysphoria.

Lambda Legal Defense and Education Fund

120 Wall Street, Suite 1500
New York, NY 10005-3904
212-809-8585
www.lambdalegal.org
Advances the legal rights of lesbians, gay men, and people with AIDS through test case litigation and public education. Publishes many resource manuals, newsletters, bibliographies, and articles on current topics for lesbians, gay men, and people with HIV/AIDS.

National Gay and Lesbian Task Force (NGLTF)

1325 Massachusetts Avenue NW
Washington, D.C. 20500
202-393-5177
www.thetaskforce.org
The oldest gay and lesbian civil rights advocacy organization. Lobbying, grassroots organizing, publications (call or write for listing), and referrals.

Tri-Ess (Society for the Second Self)

P.O. Box 980638
Houston, TX 77098-0638
713-349-9910
E-mail: trichil@aol.com
www.tri-ess.org
An organization for heterosexual men who cross-dress, and their wives.

IV. MEDIA

Sinclair Intimacy Institute

88 Vilcom Center Drive, #150
Chapel Hill, NC 27514
www.sinclairinstitute.com
An organization with a large selection of sexuality education and sex therapy films and videos.

V. SEXUAL VICTIMIZATION

Violence and Traumatic Stress Research Branch National Institute of Mental Health

6001 Executive Boulevard, Room 5197, MSC 9589
Bethesda, MD 20892-9589
301-443-5944
http://www.nimh.nih.gov/about/organization/dtr/traumat-ic-stress-research-and-dimensional-measurement-and-intervention-program/index.shtml
This branch is the focal point at the National Institute of Mental Health for research on violent behavior, including sexual abuse, sexual assault, and trauma (including PTSD).

VI. FEMINISM AND GENDER ISSUES

National Organization for Women (NOW)
1100 H Street NW, 3rd floor
Washington, D.C. 20005
202-628-8669
E-mail: now@now.org
www.now.org
NOW seeks to take action to bring women into full
participation in the mainstream of U.S. society, exercising
all the privileges and responsibilities thereof in truly equal
partnership with men.

VII. JOURNALS

Annual Review of Sex Research
The Society for the Scientific Study of Sexuality
P.O. Box 416
Allentown, PA 18105-0416

Archives of Sexual Behavior
Plenum Publishing Corporation
233 Spring Street
New York, NY 10013-1578

Gender & Society
SAGE Publications
2455 Teller Road
Newbury Park, CA 91320

Journal of Child Sexual Abuse
Routledge
325 Chestnut Street, Suite 800
Philadelphia, PA 18105-0416

Journal of Gay and Lesbian Psychotherapy
Routledge
325 Chestnut Street, Suite 800
Philadelphia, PA 18105-0416

Journal of Homosexuality
Haworth Press
10 Alice Street
Binghamton, NY 13904-1580

Journal of Men's Studies
Men's Studies Press
P.O. Box 32
Harriman, TN 37748-0032

Journal of Sex and Marital Therapy
Routledge
325 Chestnut Street, Suite 800
Philadelphia, PA 19106

Journal of Sex Research
Taylor & Francis
530 Walnut Street, Suite 850
Philadelphia, PA 19106

Journal of the History of Sexuality
University of Texas Press
P.O. Box 7819
Austin, TX 78713

Psychology of Women Quarterly
SAGE Publishing
2455 Teller Road
Thousand Oaks, CA 91320

Sex Roles: A Journal of Research
Springer
11 W. 42nd Street, #15
New York, NY 10036

Sexual Abuse: A Journal of Research and Treatment
Springer
11 W. 42nd Street, #15
New York, NY 10036

Sexual Addiction and Compulsivity
Routledge
325 Chestnut Street, Suite 800
Philadelphia, PA 19106

Sexuality and Disability
Springer
11 W. 42nd Street, #15
New York, NY 10036

COLOR TEXT BOOKS

BIN TRAVELER FORM

Cut By_____ Qty_____ Date_____

Scanned By_Meyveline Mejia_ Qty_____ Date_9/11/24_

Scanned Batch IDs

_____   _____   _____

Notes / Exception

_____

_____

_____

_____